From the Nation's Leading Social Studies Educator

Adventures

ENHANCE YOUR TEACHING AND HAVE MORE FUN HELPING

in

YOUR STUDENTS TO BECOME

GRADE 2

GRADE I

Time

21ST CENTURY CITIZENS &

GRADE 3

GRADE K

GRADE 4
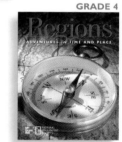

and

GRADE 6/7

GEOGRAPHY-LITERATE EXPLORERS

Place

GRADE 5

& HISTORY-SMART ADVENTURERS

GRADE 6/7

GRADE 6/7
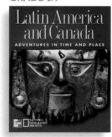

McGRAW-HILL

McGraw-Hill invites you to experience the
Adventures in

COMPONENTS FROM GRADES 1-2
(SAMPLE SHOWN FROM GRADE 1)

COMPONENTS FOR GRADE 3-6
(SAMPLE SHOWN FROM GRADE 5)

Time and Place

Designed for teacher-friendly classroom management

COMPONENTS CHART

	K HERE I AM	1 MY WORLD	2 PEOPLE TOGETHER	3 COMMUNITIES	4 REGIONS	5 UNITED STATES	4/5 A YOUNG NATION	5/6 A NATION GROWS	6/7 WORLD	6/7 LATIN AMERICA AND CANADA	6/7 WORLD REGIONS
PUPIL EDITION		✔	✔	✔	✔	✔	✔	✔	✔	✔	✔
PUPIL EDITION ON CASSETTE		✔	✔	✔	✔	✔	✔	✔	✔	✔	✔
TEACHER'S MULTIMEDIA EDITION	✔	✔	✔	✔	✔	✔	✔	✔	✔	✔	✔
COLOR MAP TRANSPARENCIES		✔	✔	✔	✔	✔	✔	✔	✔	✔	✔
GRAPHIC ORGANIZERS				✔	✔	✔	✔	✔	✔	✔	✔
THEME BIG BOOKS	✔	✔	✔								
STICKERS FOR THEME BIG BOOKS	✔	✔	✔								
LITERATURE BIG BOOKS	✔	✔	✔	✔							
GEO BIG BOOK	✔	✔	✔	✔							
VOCABULARY/WORD CARDS	✔	✔	✔	✔							
PRACTICE BOOK		✔	✔	✔	✔	✔	✔	✔	✔	✔	✔
PROJECT BOOK	✔	✔	✔	✔							
GEOADVENTURES/ DAILY GEOGRAPHY ACTIVITIES		✔	✔	✔	✔	✔	✔	✔	✔	✔	✔
FLOOR MAP	✔	✔	✔	✔							
DESK MAPS	✔	✔	✔	✔	✔	✔	✔	✔	✔	✔	✔
OUTLINE MAPS		✔	✔	✔	✔	✔	✔	✔	✔	✔	✔
INFLATABLE GLOBE	✔	✔	✔	✔	✔	✔	✔	✔	✔	✔	✔
STUDENT ATLAS	✔	✔	✔	✔	✔	✔	✔	✔	✔	✔	✔
SOCIAL STUDIES ANTHOLOGY	✔	✔	✔	✔	✔	✔	✔	✔	✔	✔	✔
ANTHOLOGY CASSETTE	✔	✔	✔	✔	✔	✔	✔	✔	✔	✔	✔
CLASSROOM LIBRARY TRADE BOOKS	✔	✔	✔	✔	✔	✔	✔	✔	✔		
CLASSROOM LIBRARY TEACHER'S GUIDE	✔	✔	✔	✔	✔	✔	✔	✔	✔		
ADVENTURE BOOKS	✔	✔	✔	✔	✔	✔			✔	✔	✔
LANGUAGE SUPPORT HANDBOOK	✔	✔	✔	✔	✔	✔			✔		
POSTERS	✔	✔	✔	✔	✔	✔	✔	✔	✔		✔
UNIT TESTS		✔	✔	✔	✔	✔	✔	✔	✔	✔	✔
CHAPTER TESTS			✔	✔	✔	✔	✔	✔	✔	✔	✔
PERFORMANCE ASSESSMENT	✔	✔	✔	✔	✔	✔					
VIDEODISCS	✔	✔	✔	✔	✔	✔	✔	✔	✔		✔
VIDEOTAPES	✔	✔	✔	✔	✔	✔	✔	✔	✔		✔
CD-ROM			✔	✔	✔	✔	✔	✔	✔	✔	✔
INTERNET PROJECTS		✔	✔	✔	✔	✔	✔	✔	✔	✔	✔

Adventures in Time and Place...

COME ALONG AND BRING YOUR STUDENTS TO JOIN IN ON THE ADVENTURE!

McGraw-Hill School Division

Adventures in Time and Place provides a variety of methods to check both students' recall of factual information and their application of that knowledge. It's your choice:

- **Standardized Test Format**
- **Written Response Format**
- **Performance Assessments with Scoring Rubrics**

There's a way to get an accurate assessment — a real grade — for every child, whichever approach you use for evaluation.

Choices for assessment and accountability

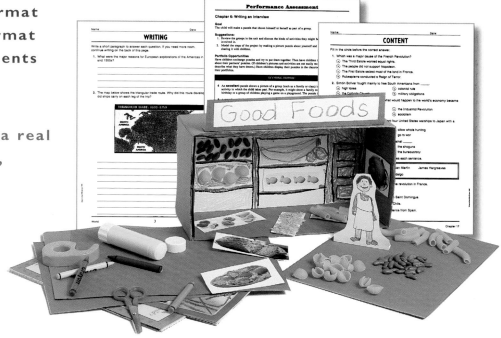

Choices in technology support

Multimedia technology options, correlated directly to the program, are easy extensions at your fingertips. You have the widest variety of choices available to meet your needs.

•Videodiscs   •CD-ROM   •Videotapes

Barcoded lessons on videodisc make enriching your teaching a breeze. These same lessons are also available on videotape to add to your flexibility. And best of all, it's all at point-of-use in your Teacher's Edition.

CD-ROM technology adds sight-and-sound power through an enhanced atlas and searchable database. The correlation to the program's lessons and activities makes this a useful research tool for all students.

National Geographic Technology is now available through McGraw-Hill to support your teaching. Direct correlations of these resources in Adventures in Time and Place ensure that you have the options to support all your students' needs and your teaching style.

Adventures in Rich, Relevant Content

1 **History lessons link past and present in ways that make sense for all students — at all grade levels.**

- More solid content at grades 1 and 2, with a narrative style that puts the "story" back in history, and lets you teach real history at primary grade levels.

- "Many Voices" from meaningful primary sources and literature are integrated in text features to bring history alive in words and pictures.

- Historical figures of many backgrounds, both famous and ordinary, provide reflections on our past from diverse perspectives.

FROM GRADE 3 PUPIL EDITION

2 **Geographic Literacy for all students is assured through the co-authorship of the National Geographic Society.**

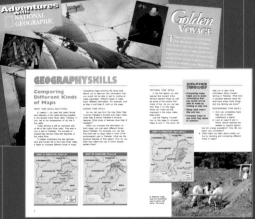

FROM GRADE 6 PUPIL EDITION

- Geography's impact on history is emphasized to teach students the connection between them.

- Geography's five fundamental themes are the focus of skill lessons and features that support the ties among past and present people, places, and events.

- Map skills are developed systematically for use in real life situations and for standardized test-taking.

3 **Active Citizenship is taught through skill lessons, interactive activities and concrete examples.**

- Citizenship and Thinking Skills lessons help form the ideas and thought processes needed by citizens of the 21st century.

- "Making a Difference" introduces everyday people who practice good citizenship in their communities.

FROM GRADE 4 PUPIL EDITION

- "Viewpoints" in grades 3–6 allow students to discover and appreciate many different points of view — and to learn to handle differences.

TABLE OF CONTENTS FOR TEACHER INTRODUCTION

World

ADVENTURES IN TIME AND PLACE

PROGRAM AUTHORS

Dr. James A. Banks
Professor of Education and Director of the Center for Multicultural Education
University of Washington
Seattle, Washington
Related Publications: *An Introduction to Multicultural Education,* Allyn & Bacon, ©1994; *Multiethnic Education: Theory and Practice,* Allyn & Bacon, © 1981
Honors: Teachers of English to Speakers of Other Languages, Inc. 1998 Presidents' Award; National Association of Multicultural Education for the Handbook of Research on Multicultural Education

Dr. Barry K. Beyer
Professor Emeritus,
Graduate School of Education
George Mason University
Fairfax, Virginia
Related Publications: *Hints for Improving the Teaching Thinking in Our Schools: A Baker's Dozen* (Montclair State College: Institute for Critical Thinking) Resource Publication, Series 1#4, 1988; *Using Inquiry in the Social Studies Guidelines for Teaching,* Cooperative Center for Social Science Education, Ohio University, 1968; Guest editor, "Critical Thinking Revisited," Social Education, April 1985; Co-editor, Values of the American Heritage, 46th (Bicentennial) Yearbook of the National Council for the Social Studies, 1976

Dr. Gloria Contreras
Professor of Education
University of North Texas
Denton, Texas
Related Publications: Editor, *Latin American Culture Studies Handbook* Austin, Texas: The University of Texas Institute for Latin American Studies, 1988
Awards: University of North Texas Student Association Honor Professor Award, 1997; "Professing Women" Award, UNT Women's Studies Roundtable, 1996

Jean Craven
District Coordinator of Curriculum Development
Albuquerque Public Schools
Albuquerque, New Mexico
Related Publications: *Teacher's Manual for Government in the United States,* Macmillan Publishing, ©1984
Advisory Boards: Editorial Review Board, The Social Studies, 1994-1997; National Commission on Social Studies in the Schools, 1989-1990

Dr. Gloria Ladson-Billings
Professor of Education
University of Wisconsin
Madison, Wisconsin
Related Publications: *Dictionary of Multicultural Education,* Oryz Press, 1997; *The Dreamkeepers: Successful Teachers of African American Children,* Jossey Bass, 1994
Awards: Mary Ann Raywid Award for Distinguished Scholarship in Education, Society of Professors of Education, American Educational Research Association, 1997; Outstanding Educator Award Research Focus in Black Education, 1996

Dr. Mary A. McFarland
Instructional Coordinator of Social Studies, K-12, and Director of Staff Development
Parkway School District
Chesterfield, Missouri
Grants: Author of Block Grant Project in Social Studies, 1990; Director of Missouri Committee for the Humanities Project, 1985

Dr. Walter C. Parker
Professor and Program Chair for Social Studies Education
University of Washington
Seattle, Washington
Related Publications: *Social Studies in Elementary Education,* 10th ed. Merill/Prentice-Hall, 1997; editor, *Educating the Democratic Mind,* SUNY Press, 1996; *Renewing the Social Studies Curriculum;* Association for Supervision and Curriculum Development, 1991

NATIONAL
GEOGRAPHIC
SOCIETY
Washington, D.C.

HISTORIANS/SCHOLARS

Daniel Berman
Asian Studies Specialist,
Former Coordinator of Social Studies
Bedford Central Schools
Bedford, New York

Dr. John Bodnar
Professor of History
Indiana University
Bloomington, Indiana
Related Publications: *Remaking America: Public Memory, Commemoration, and Patriotism in the Twentieth Century,* (Pulitzer Prize Nominee) Princeton University Press, 1992
Awards: Teaching Excellence Award, Indiana University, 1997; Florence Chair in American History, Florence, Italy (selected by the Fulbright Commission)

Dr. Roberto Calderón
Assistant Professor
Department of Ethnic Studies
University of California at Riverside
Related Publications: *Mexican Coal Mining Labor in Texas and Coahuila, 1830-1930,* Texas A & M University Press, 1999; "All Over the Map: La Onda Tejana and the Making of Selena" in *Chicanos and Chicanas at the Crossroads: Literary and Cultural Change,* Editors: David Maciel, María Herrera-Sobeck and Isidro Ortiz, University of Arizona Press, 1999

Dr. Sheilah Clarke-Ekong
Professor, Department of Anthropology
University of Missouri, St. Louis
St. Louis, Missouri
Related Publications: "Ghana's Festivals: Celebrations of Life and Loyalty" *Journal of African Activist Association, Vol. 23,* 1997; "Traditional Festivals in the Political Economy," *Journal of Social Development in Africa*

Council on Islamic Education
Fountain Valley, California
Related Publications: *Muslim Holidays; Muslim Women Through the Centuries; The Crusades from Medieval European and Muslim Perspectives; Images of the Orient: 19th-century European Travelers to*

Muslim Lands; Beyond A Thousand and One Nights, A Sampler of Literature from Muslim Civilization; The Emergence of the Renaissance: Cultural Interactions Between Europeans and Muslims

Dr. John L. Esposito
Professor of Religion and
International Affairs
Georgetown University
Washington, D.C.
Related Publications: *The Islamic Threat: Myth or Reality,* Oxford University Press, 1992; Editor-in-Chief, *Encyclopedia of the Modern Islamic World,* 4 vols., Oxford University Press, 1995; *Islam: The Straight Path,* Oxford University Press, 1988

Dr. Darlene Clark Hine
John A. Hannah Professor of History
Michigan State University
East Lansing, Michigan
Related Publications: *A Shining Thread of Hope: The History of Black Women in America,* Broadway Books, 1998; *Speak Truth to Power: Black Professional Class in United States History,* Carlson Publishing, Inc. 1995
Awards: Doctor of Humane Letters, University of Massachusetts, 1998; Avery Citizenship Award, Avery Research Center, College of Charleston, 1997

Paulla Dove Jennings
Project Director
The Rhode Island Indian Council, Inc.
Providence, Rhode Island

Henrietta Mann
Professor of Native American Studies
University of Montana, Missoula
Missoula, Montana
Related Publications: *Cheyenne-Arapaho Education 1871-1982,* University Press of Colorado, 1998; "Native American Women of the Southern Plains" in *The Reader's Companion to U.S. Women's History,* Houghton Mifflin Company, 1998

Dr. Gary A. Manson
Department of Geography

Michigan State University
East Lansing, Michigan
Related Publications: *New Perspectives on Geographic Education: Putting Theory Into Practice,* Kendall-Hunt Publishing Company, 1977 (editor)
Grants: National Science Foundation, 1982

Dr. Juan Mora-Torrés
Professor of Latin American History
University of Texas at San Antonio
San Antonio, Texas
Related Publications: *The Making of the Mexican Border: The State, Capitalism and Society, Nuevo Leon, 1848-1970* (in progress)
Honors: Visiting Scholar, University of Chicago, Center for Latin American Studies, 1999

Dr. Valerie Ooka Pang
Professor, School of Teacher Education
San Diego State University
San Diego, California
Related Publications: Editor, *Struggling To Be Heard: The Unmet Needs of Asian Pacific American Children,* 1998, State University of New York
Awards: Senior Fellow, Annenberg Institute for School Reform, Brown University 1998-2000; Distinguished Scholar Award, American Educational Research Association, 1997

Dr. Joseph Rosenbloom
Professor, Classics Department
Washington University
St. Louis, Missouri
Related Publications: *Conversion to Judaism: From the Biblical Period to the Present,* Hebrew Union College Press, 1978; *The Dead Sea Isaiah Scrolls: A Literary Analysis,* William B. Eerdsmans Publishing Company, 1970

Dr. Joseph B. Rubin
Director of Reading/Reading Council Leader, Fort Worth Independent School District
Related Publications: "Language Arts Across the Curriculum," in Language Arts Today, Macmillan Publishing Company,

1989; "What Children Bring to School!" Texas Reading Newsletter, Texas State Council, International Reading Association, 1985
Awards: Graduate School Teaching Award, University of Arizona, 1981

Dr. Robert Seltzer
Professor of Jewish History
Hunter College
City University of New York
Related Publications: *Jewish People, Jewish Thought: The Jewish Experience in History,* Macmillan, 1980; editor, *Judaism: A People and its History,* Macmillan, 1989

Dr. Peter Stearns
Dean, College of Humanities
and Social Studies
Carnegie Mellon University
Pittsburgh, Pennsylvania
Related Publications: *The Industrial Revolution in World History,* Westview, 1998; *World History: Patterns of Change and Continuity,* HarperCollins, 1998
Awards: 1998 finalist History Book of the Year Award; Robert Doherty Educational Leadership Award, Carnegie Mellon, 1995

Ensuring Success For All Learners
Facilitating a Child's Learning and Understanding of English

by Janice Wu
Student Achievement Specialist, Sacramento City Unified School District

Today, nearly one of every five students in the United States entering school (2.5-3.5 million children per year) knows a language other than English. Nearly half of these students are limited in English-language proficiency. According to demographers, in the near future, language-minority students and those acquiring a second language will compose an even larger proportion of our school-age population.

Many English Language Learners (ELL) come into the classroom with a wealth of prior knowledge and a strong oral language base. But some do not experience success in school. Many students who speak a language other than English face barriers that inhibit their learning. As a result, the role of the teacher as facilitator becomes one of nurturing and building upon what a child already knows.

In accessing the curriculum in *Adventures in Time and Place/Aventuras a través del tiempo*, you need to be skillful in utilizing the text to meet the needs of every individual learner. The instruction you provide your students will facilitate the understanding of the curriculum for English Language Learners. As you structure an environment that builds on students' strengths and English language learning, you will make learning a rewarding and meaningful experience for all your students. The information provided below will help you utilize the many resources available in *Adventures in Time and Place/Aventuras a través del tiempo* so that you can effectively meet the needs of every individual learner.

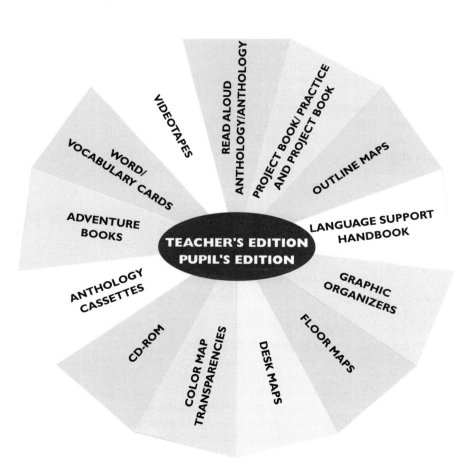

I TEACHER'S EDITION

The **Adventures in Time and Place/Aventuras a través del tiempo** Teacher's Edition provides a variety of features that complement content lessons by offering teacher support and strategies for English Language Learners. These features include:

- **Specially Designed Academic Instruction in English (SDAIE)/Sheltered Instruction** is presented to you to help engage students in active learning. The focus of SDAIE is to provide curriculum content for all students—especially, but not only, those challenged by less than proficient English skills.

- **Second Language Support** offers strategies to help you customize instruction for the English Language Learner. These strategies are designed to help you contextualize the lessons to make them more understandable and meaningful to students who are acquiring English and to help you present lesson content while providing linguistic and conceptual support.

- **Meeting Individual Needs** allows you to re-teach, extend, and enrich the instruction for every child. Scaffolding the instruction for English Language Learners in this manner will foster positive and successful learning experiences in Social Studies.

- **Reading Strategies and Language Development** provides you with teaching suggestions aimed at understanding and clarifying concepts and vocabulary that could be confusing to the English Language Learner.

- **Extending the Lesson Activities** in Grades 1–2 and **Getting Ready for the Chapter** in Grades 3-6 provide activities in a variety of learning styles, such as auditory, kinesthetic, and visual, to satisfy the learning needs of students who are talented in art, language, and physical activity and who may better understand history/social science concepts connected to their own areas of interest.

- **Visual Literacy** is the integration of text with visuals. This integration is especially helpful to the English Language Learner. The Teacher's Edition offers strategies that provide you with opportunities for the teaching of important history/social science concepts by utilizing photographs, artwork, and maps in **Adventures in Time and Place/Aventuras a través del tiempo.**

- **Ongoing Unit Projects** set the stage for all learners by inviting them to participate in a cooperative setting that encourages language development in a natural environment. These projects also engage English Language Learners in high interest, hands-on experiences.

II ADVENTURES IN TIME AND PLACE/AVENTURAS A TRAVÉS DEL TIEMPO COMPONENTS

In addition to the **Adventures in Time and Place/ Aventuras a través del tiempo** Teacher's Edition features mentioned above, there are a variety of supplementary program components that provide teacher support and strategies for English Language Learners. A description of these resources, in addition to suggested ELL classroom activities, is listed below:

• ADVENTURE BOOKS (Grades K-6)

Description: Adventure Books are supplementary "easy readers" that provide additional literacy experiences tailored to specific students' needs and interests. The range and simplicity of the stories allows for independent reading related to the Social Studies content. Students will read about special people, places, and events that reflect many people and cultures around the world.

ELL Strategy: Building Comprehension Skills

To encourage independent reading, set up a student reading center with the Adventure Books. Allow English Language Learners to select from the various stories and report on their favorite readers by making posters or charts with illustrations. Students at different levels of language proficiency in English can label and/or write brief descriptions retelling the story.

• ANTHOLOGY CASSETTES (Grades K-6)

Description: Students will be exposed to a variety of literature selections, songs, and poems that are read in an engaging and entertaining style.

ELL Strategy: Facilitate Listening Comprehension in English

Listening to songs and poetry read by others is a powerful way to provide models of fluent and dramatic reading. Set up a "Listening Post" or "Listening Center" for a small group of students. Model the use of the listening area with your class and assign a student monitor who will be in charge of rotating the cassettes as needed.

• CD-ROM (Grades 3-6)

Description: *The Adventure Time!* CD-ROM enables students to travel the world, meet people, and explore places. Students can experience historical events through photographs, maps, movies, charts, and climographs. The *Adventure Time!* CD-ROM program makes geography fun, puts history in context, and motivates children to learn map and globe skills.

ELL Strategy: Paired Reading

With a click of the computer mouse an English Language Learner can see, hear, and take world tours and experience environments from images on a CD-ROM. Pair an English Language Learner with an English-proficient learner and ask them to read the text in each frame together. Partners should take turns reading. At the end of each frame, the listener should relate back the main ideas of the text. Discussions can also include descriptions of sounds and visuals they are experiencing. Encourage students to work together to discuss these responses.

• COLOR MAP TRANSPARENCIES (Grades 1-6)

Description: Map transparencies support a student-centered map program and encourages active, hands-on geography practice. These maps are from Reviewing Geography Skills lessons, Skills Lessons, and the Atlas in the Pupil's Edition.

ELL Strategy: Using Visuals

The use of visuals like map symbols provides important support in building comprehension and establishing the context-rich environment that fosters language acquisition. Using an overhead projector, have students identify the different map symbols on each Map Transparency. Then have them describe the symbols shown on each map.

• DESK MAPS (GRADES 1-6)

Description: Students will gain a greater understanding of their community and the world around them by using Desk Maps of the United States and the world. These maps are useful in teaching map and globe skills in meaningful and concrete ways.

ELL Strategy: Building Geography Skills

Use of the Desk Maps will encourage students to develop their geography skills. Prompt students to work alone or in groups to use lesson content and other maps to search the text for illustrations and information to help them place details on the map, such as mountain ranges, deserts, oceans, etc. Encourage students to use as many details as possible. Pairing English Language Learners with partners that are fluent English speakers encourages mastery of the English language in a non-threatening environment.

• FLOOR MAPS (Grades K-3)

Description: Students can use a floor map as a base for building three-dimensional models of different types of communities or environments. Floor maps can help English Language Learners move from understanding simple, concrete materials to understanding more difficult and abstract concepts.

ELL Strategy: Using Manipulative Materials

Divide students into groups of four to six students. To encourage rich dialogue include students of different levels of English proficiency in each group. Have each group create simple three-dimensional buildings, cars, people, etc. to place on the floor maps in order to create a community. Students should describe the objects that they have created and discuss where they should be placed on the floor map. Encourage students to use geography and map-related terms and concepts to describe their community.

• GRAPHIC ORGANIZERS (Grades 3-6)

Description: Graphic Organizers provide visual tools to help English Language Learners organize the relationships between and among words, concepts, ideas, and events.

ELL Strategy: Organizing Information Using a Visual Tool

Have students organize information about the natural resources of their community. Encourage them to list on the chart some of the resources they have learned about and whether they are renewable or nonrenewable. Have students display and discuss their completed charts in class.

• LANGUAGE SUPPORT HANDBOOK (Grades K-6)

Description: In working with the English Language Learner it is important to recognize that each child enters the classroom with different levels of oral language proficiency. This means that the production of language may be receptive (absorbing the language but not producing verbally) or productive (verbally producing some English words or phrases). To help you have a better understanding of the various stages of second language acquisition, the Language Support Handbook lists the stages of language production with student behaviors and effective teaching strategies.

ELL Strategy: Shared Reading

It is important for English Language Learners to hear English read by a fluent English speaker. A useful strategy is to read aloud while students are able to read and follow along silently with their own text copies. Ask students to take notes as important concepts are discussed. They can then work with others to write a brief summary of the most important information they have learned.

• OUTLINE MAPS (GRADES 1-6)

Description: Outline Maps offer students the opportunity to improve their basic map skills, such as understanding hemispheres, using cardinal and intermediate directions, and identifying map keys and symbols.

ELL Strategy: Understanding Personal Perspectives

Have students use Outline Maps to locate their community in relation to their state and country. Then have them use the World Map to locate their community in relation to the country that they, or their parents or friends, may have come from. By understanding different geographic perspectives, English Language Learners can gain understanding and confidence in learning about different cultures and places.

• PROJECT BOOK (Grades K-3)
PRACTICE AND PROJECT BOOK (Grades 4-6)

Description: Your students will be actively involved in constructing a variety of projects related to the Social Studies content in their Pupil's Edition. These activities include tracing family ties, connecting their home to their communities, and understanding important dates and events relevant to them.

ELL Strategy: Facilitating Cooperative Learning and Interaction

Set aside an area in the classroom for a work station or center called "Our Projects." This work station should have ample working room for a group of four or five students to design and create projects listed in the Project Book. Projects can then be displayed in this area, as well as in other areas of the classroom. This activity encourages friendly dialogue and discussions among students and encourages positive language learning. Students of all language levels of proficiency will benefit.

• READ ALOUD ANTHOLOGY (Grades K-3)
ANTHOLOGY (Grades 4-6)

Description: Anthologies are rich resources filled with literature, stories, songs, poems, folktales, and more. They are useful in supporting lesson content and themes taught in the Pupil's Edition.

ELL Strategy: Paired Reading

Pair each English Language Learner with a fluent English partner. Tell each pair to choose a character from an Anthology selection in whose voice they will speak or write. Ask them to search the text and illustrations for pertinent information, then have them introduce themselves to their partners and talk about their experiences. Prompt them to expand their stories by suggesting a series of basic questions to which they can respond: *What is your name? Where do you live? What has been happening around you? What do you think will happen next?*

• VIDEOTAPES (Grades K-6)

Description: Videotapes of rich and relevant content covering topics such as communities and geographic location are available at every grade level. These short video presentations provide the teacher and students with another means of "experiencing" events in history.

ELL Strategy: Previewing/Reviewing

A preview/review strategy will facilitate students' understanding of the curriculum. Identify significant concepts and vocabulary that will be used in the video and teach them to students. After watching the video, check student comprehension by asking questions related to the initial concepts and vocabulary presented during the preview lesson. This activity will help reinforce concepts, build vocabulary, and expand students' knowledge.

• WORD/VOCABULARY Cards (Grades K-3)

Description: Word/Vocabulary cards are used to help teach challenging vocabulary words or phrases that appear in the Social Studies Pupil's Edition. Each word or phrase appears on one side of a card. A definition of the word or phrase appears on the other side of the card.

ELL Strategy: Building Vocabulary Skills

Select five important words from the appropriate Pupil's Edition lessons that might be difficult for the English Language Learner to comprehend. Write these words on the chalkboard. Then hand out five blank index cards to each student. Next, use gestures, props, illustrations, etc. to act out the meaning of the word for the students. Students should then write the word you are describing on their index cards. On the backs of the cards they should draw pictures or illustrations to help them remember the meaning of the word. Repeat this process for all five words. Students can learn the definitions of these words by using their index cards as flashcards.

III TIPS FOR CREATING AN EFFECTIVE LEARNING ENVIRONMENT FOR THE ENGLISH LANGUAGE LEARNER

School experiences are long-lasting and set the stage for future performance. By creating a positive, sensitive, and interactive learning environment, you can make a critical difference in preparing English Language Learners for the future. Remember that success for these students means more than acquiring good grades and high test scores. It also means having a positive image of themselves and confidence in their ability to embrace a second language and a new culture. Following is a list of useful tips for helping you create an effective learning environment for the English Language Learner.

• Praise Students' Efforts Regularly

Accept the "half rights" and "yes" and "no" responses from your English Language Learners. A nod of the head in agreement or a simple "yes" response from you will let your students know that they are on the right track.

• Accelerate Students' Learning

Maintaining high expectations for all English Language Learners will accelerate learning. Conveying the belief that all students have the ability and desire to succeed is your responsibility. Provide multiple opportunities for students to "take charge" and be responsible for the work that they produce.

• Encourage Students To Preview Or "Picture Walk"

Students will be eager and excited to learn about the lesson when they are allowed to explore and select information (e.g. picture, caption, word or phrase) that piques their interest. Direct students to share their findings in English or their primary language with a partner or partners. Sampling a lesson in this manner will lower the student's affective filter and make for a more comfortable and positive experience.

• Minimize Structural Error Correction

As students participate in class discussions, modeling appropriate structural responses can be done in a manner that does not directly bring attention to the error. For example, student states, "My country Central America. She country North America." Teacher may respond by modeling, "Yes, your country is in Central America," and "her [for "she"] country is in North America."

• Allow For Appropriate "Wait Time"

English Language Learners need "wait time" to process the information being taught. Give students sufficient time for a response. Keep in mind that responses will vary depending on the students' levels of oral language proficiency. A simple facial expression, physical gesture or short phrase may serve as a response.

• Use A Total Physical Response Approach

Use gestures and facial expressions (as dramatic as you need to be) to assist students in comprehending what is being conveyed. Allow students to respond in the same manner.

• Practice The 3 R's Of Instruction

Revisit, Review, and Repeat the material being taught as much as possible in different ways. Approaching the instruction from a different perspective provides the student with another opportunity to acquire the content being taught. When Social Studies content is familiar it allows students to be freed up to attend to new and challenging content.

• Speak Naturally

Students benefit greatly from having the teacher explain challenging content in clear and simplified speech. Clear enunciation and brief pauses assist the English Language Learner in hearing distinct pronunciation of vocabulary.

• Summarize Content Taught Frequently

For English Language Learners it is important to summarize the content at point of use. Briefly stating in simple sentences the content after one, two, or three paragraphs is a strategy that benefits all students by allowing them to reflect on what they have just read and enables you to check for understanding.

• Sheltered English Strategies

In order to make the content matter meaningful to students, it is important to provide many examples of the concepts being taught. Simplifying the language when presenting a concept is crucial, as is providing visuals (video clip, semantic web, or graphic organizer) to demonstrate the concept. For example, when teaching the concept of "community," rather than just defining the term, you might encourage students to draw, take photographs, or cut clippings from magazines or newspapers to construct a collage or mural of what they perceive as a community.

• Allow Students to Speak Their Native Languages

Encourage students to communicate with their peers who are speakers of the same language. Allow students to write in their primary language and seek others who are literate in that language to translate and provide feedback. Provide primary language resources such as dictionaries, storybooks, videos, audiocassettes, and computer software. Having access to resources that they can read and use independently builds students' confidence in learning.

• Word Walls to Build Vocabulary

A word wall is a designated wall in the classroom that displays a collection of words. Social Studies word walls provide a place to display important vocabulary words with illustrations to clarify definitions and concepts. The word wall can include important words from the curriculum as well as often-used words and/or commonly misspelled words that students can access and use when they write. Students should be encouraged to contribute to the "Social Studies Word Wall" whenever they feel that there are important words that they want clarified.

• Provide Opportunities for Students to Work Together

English Language Learners benefit from working in cooperative learning groups. Working in mixed ability groups, English Language Learners have the opportunity to use language for real communication as they solve problems assigned by the teacher. As English Language Learners work together they learn academic language while investigating new topics or exploring content areas.

• Encourage Classroom Participation

Give students opportunities to talk and interact. Also encourage them to express ideas, feelings, and opinions. Students' self-esteem and motivation are enhanced when teachers elicit their experiences in classroom discussions and validate what they have to say.

• Cross-Age Tutoring and Peer Tutoring

Research indicates that learning is enhanced both for those who are tutored and for the tutors themselves. English Language Learners working one-on-one with tutors develop listening, communication, and problem-solving skills. The tutor develops personal responsibility and self-esteem as he or she works to ensure the success of another child. The tutor becomes a model of success. Pairing intermediate grade students with primary grade students makes for positive and lasting friendships.

By utilizing the resources in the **Adventures in Time and Place/Aventuras a través del tiempo,** the instruction you provide will facilitate learning for English Language Learners. As you structure an environment that builds on students' strengths and English Language Learning, you will make the classroom experience rewarding and meaningful for all your students.

TEACHER'S MULTIMEDIA EDITION

VOLUME 1

World

ADVENTURES IN TIME AND PLACE

James A. Banks

Barry K. Beyer

Gloria Contreras

Jean Craven

Gloria Ladson-Billings

Mary A. McFarland

Walter C. Parker

NATIONAL GEOGRAPHIC SOCIETY

THIS IMAGE WAS CARVED ON THE THRONE OF TUTANKHAMUN, WHO RULED ANCIENT EGYPT MORE THAN 3,000 YEARS AGO. THIS IS ONE OF THE MANY IMAGES THAT HELP TELL THE STORY OF OUR WORLD'S HISTORY.

THE PRINCETON REVIEW

McGraw-Hill School Division

New York   Farmington

PROGRAM AUTHORS

Dr. James A. Banks
Professor of Education and
  Director of the Center for
  Multicultural Education
University of Washington
Seattle, Washington

Dr. Barry K. Beyer
Professor Emeritus, Graduate
  School of Education
George Mason University
Fairfax, Virginia

Dr. Gloria Contreras
Professor of Education
University of North Texas
Denton, Texas

Jean Craven
District Coordinator of
  Curriculum Development
Albuquerque Public Schools
Albuquerque, New Mexico

Dr. Gloria Ladson-Billings
Professor of Education
University of Wisconsin
Madison, Wisconsin

Dr. Mary A. McFarland
Instructional Coordinator of
  Social Studies, K–12, and
  Director of Staff Development
Parkway School District
Chesterfield, Missouri

Dr. Walter C. Parker
Professor and Program Chair for
  Social Studies Education
University of Washington
Seattle, Washington

NATIONAL
GEOGRAPHIC
SOCIETY
Washington, D.C.

PROGRAM CONSULTANTS

Daniel Berman
Asian Studies Specialist
Coordinator of Social Studies
Bedford Central Schools
Bedford, New York

Dr. Khalid Y. Blankinship
Affiliated Scholar, Council on Islamic
  Education
Fountain Valley, California
Assistant Professor of Religion
Temple University
Philadelphia, Pennsylvania

Dr. John Bodnar
Professor of History
Indiana University
Bloomington, Indiana

Dr. Roberto R. Calderón
Department of Ethnic Studies
University of California at Riverside
Riverside, California

Dr. Sheilah Clarke-Ekong
Asst. Professor, Department of
  Anthropology and Research Associate,
  Center for International Studies
University of Missouri, St. Louis
St. Louis, Missouri

Dr. John L. Esposito
Professor of Religion and International
  Affairs
Georgetown University
Washington, D.C.

Dr. Darlene Clark Hine
John A. Hannah Professor of History
Michigan State University
East Lansing, Michigan

Paulla Dove Jennings
Project Director
The Rhode Island Indian Council, Inc.
Providence, Rhode Island

Dr. Henrietta Mann
Professor of Native American Studies
University of Montana, Missoula
Missoula, Montana

Dr. Gary Manson
Professor, Department of Geography
Michigan State University
East Lansing, Michigan

Dr. Juan Mora-Torrés
Professor of Latin American History
University of Texas at San Antonio
San Antonio, Texas

Dr. Valerie Ooka Pang
Professor, School of Teacher Education
San Diego State University
San Diego, California

Dr. Joseph R. Rosenbloom
Professor, Classics Department
Washington University
St. Louis, Missouri

Dr. Joseph B. Rubin
Director of Reading
Fort Worth Independent School District
Fort Worth, Texas

Dr. Robert M. Seltzer
Professor of Jewish History
Hunter College of The City University
  of New York
New York, New York

Dr. Peter N. Stearns
Dean, College of Humanities and
  Social Studies
Carnegie Mellon University
Pittsburgh, Pennsylvania

CONSULTING AUTHORS

Dr. James Flood
Professor of Teacher Education,
  Reading and Language Development
San Diego State University
San Diego, California

Dr. Diane Lapp
Professor of Teacher Education,
  Reading and Language Development
San Diego State University
San Diego, California

GRADE-LEVEL CONSULTANTS

Dianne C. Baker
Sixth Grade Teacher
Ingleside Middle School
Phoenix, Arizona

Maureen F. Barber
Sixth and Seventh Grade
  Social Studies Teacher
Center Based Gifted Program
Manchester Middle School
Chesterfield, Virginia

David H. Delgado
Sixth Grade Social Studies Teacher
Rogers Middle School
San Antonio, Texas

Martha Doster
Sixth Grade Teacher
Northwest Rankin Attendance Center
Brandon, Mississippi

Joyce Garbe Orland
Sixth–Eighth Grade Teacher and Chair-
  person, Social Studies Department
Pershing School
Berwyn, Illinois

CONTRIBUTING WRITERS

Ruth Akamine Wassynger
Winston-Salem, North Carolina

Spencer Finch
Brooklyn, New York

Linda Scher
Raleigh, North Carolina

CONSULTANTS FOR TEST PREPARATION

THE
PRINCETON
REVIEW

The Princeton Review is not affiliated
with Princeton University or ETS.

Acknowledgments

The publisher gratefully acknowledges permission to reprint the following copyrighted material:

From **Lost Civilizations: Sumer: Cities of Eden** by the editors of Time-Life Books. Copyright 1993 Time-Life Books, Inc. Reprinted by permission.
From **Tropical Rainforests** by Arnold Newman. Text copyright 1990 Arnold Newman. Reprinted with permission of Facts On File, Inc., New York.
From **The Iliad of Homer: The Wrath of Achilles,** translated by I.A. Richards, Translation copyright 1950 by W.W. Norton & Company, Inc.,
  renewed 1978 by I.A. Richards. Reprinted with permission of W.W. Norton & Company, Inc.
Excerpts from **Corpus of Early Arabic Sources for West African History.** Copyright University of Ghana, International Academic Union,
  Cambridge University Press 1981. Reprinted with the permission of Cambridge University Press.

(continued on page R79)

McGraw-Hill School Division

A Division of The McGraw·Hill Companies

CONTENTS

UNIT TWO *River Valley Civilizations*

64

UNIT THREE New Ideas and New Empires
186

vi

VOLUME **2**

UNIT SIX   *A Century of Conflict*

520

REFERENCE SECTION

STANDARDIZED TEST SUPPORT

FEATURES

CHARTS, GRAPHS, & DIAGRAMS

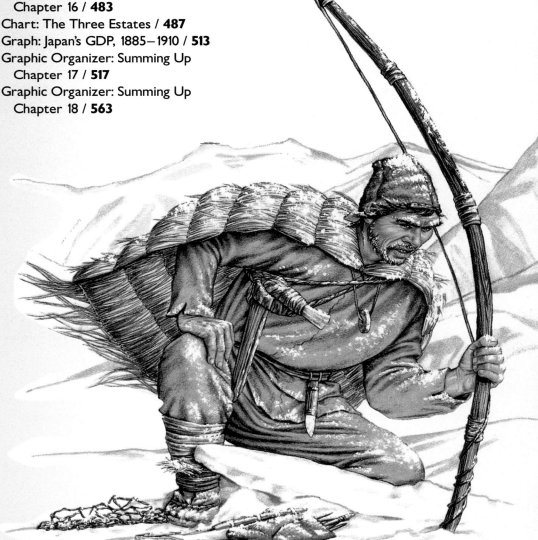

TIME LINES

MAPS

Note that the Table of Contents lists all the different parts of your textbook in page order.

Five Themes of Geography In each unit of *World: Adventures in Time and Place,* students will find a section that describes and illustrates five outdoor adventures for students. *Five Themes of Geography* introduces five key concepts that will help students describe their own adventures as they explore the different parts of *World.*

- **What are the five themes of geography?** *(Region, Human/Environment Interactions, Place, Location, and Movement)*

A Typical Lesson Have students examine the excerpt from Chapter 9, Lesson 2: *The Rise of the Roman Republic.*

- **How does Lesson 2 begin?** *(with a Read Aloud)*

Discussing Features Within Lessons Note that Lesson 2 includes a feature called *Many Voices* (Primary Sources or Literature). Explain that primary sources contain information from persons who were present at what they are describing. Diaries are primary sources.

Other features include *Links* (to different content areas like art or math) and *Did You Know?* (more facts of interest).

- **What is the Many Voices selection in this lesson?** *(an excerpt from Stories of Rome)*

Discussing Infographics Note that *Infographics* combine pictures and words.

- **What is the sample Infographic about?** *(treasures of an ancient tomb)*

Discussing Skills Lessons Note that your text also covers Thinking Skills, Geography Skills, and Study Skills.

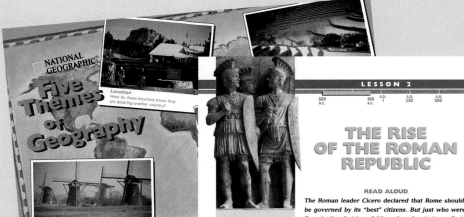

YOUR TEXTBOOK at a glance

Your textbook is called *World: Adventures in Time and Place.* It has 20 chapters, each with two or more lessons. There are also many special features for you to study and enjoy.

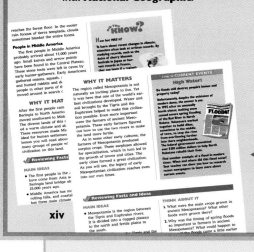

▲ Special pages right after these two pages and before each unit bring you ideas and **Adventures** in geography with **National Geographic.**

◀ Some lessons have features called **Links** or **Did You Know**—activities to try and interesting information to share.

ADDITIONAL FEATURES OF THE TEXTBOOK

UNIT OPENER Have students turn to the Unit Opener on pp. 186–187. Note how the visuals illustrate the Unit's theme.

CHAPTER OPENER Have students examine the Chapter 1 and 9 Openers on pp. 6–7 and 222–223. Ask students to distinguish the information shown in Chapter 1 from the information shown in Chapter 9.

VISUAL AIDS Have students identify visual aids included throughout the text such as: photographs, illustrations, charts, graphs, diagrams, time lines, and maps. (The last five items are also listed in the Table of Contents.)

Look for a variety of lessons and features. **Infographics** bring you information with pictures, charts, graphs, and maps. You will build your **Skills**, learn about **Legacies** that connect us to the past, and meet people who show what **Citizenship** is. ▶

THE CITIZENS OF ROME

As in Greece, society in Rome was divided into two groups: those who were citizens and those who were not. At first, Rome had few slaves. The city did have many women, but none of them were citizens.

The body of citizens included two groups. Most Roman citizens were plebeians (plih BEE unz). Plebeians were men who farmed, traded, and made things for a living. The second group was made up of Rome's handful of patricians (puh TRISH unz). Patricians were members of Rome's noble families. They owned large farms and had plebeians work the land for them.

Plebeians Protest

After Rome's last king was overthrown in 509 B.C., the patricians took power. As they did this they remade the city's government. Only patricians could belong to a ruling assembly or become government leaders.

Rome's many plebeians reacted to the patricians' rules with protest. According to the Roman historian Livy,

A patrician woman had no voice in Rome's government.

A New Government

According to Livy both sides in time agreed to work together to improve Rome's government. The new government was called a republic, which means "public things" in Latin. Latin was the language of ancient Rome. In a republic citizens choose their leaders.

231

▲ Lessons begin with a **Read Aloud** selection and **The Big Picture**. Study the **Read to Learn** question and list of words, people, and places. Enjoy **Many Voices**—writings, songs, and art by various people.

plebeians rebelled in 494 B.C., demanding changes in the government. To calm them down, Livy wrote, the patricians sent a popular leader to speak with the plebeians. He told them this story. How do you suppose the plebeians reacted?

MANY VOICES PRIMARY SOURCE

Excerpt from
Stories of Rome, Livy, 494 B.C.

Once upon a time, the different parts of the human body were not all in agreement. . . . And it seemed very unfair to the other parts of the body that they should worry and sweat away to look after the belly. After all, the belly just sat there . . . doing nothing, enjoying all the nice things that came along. So they hatched a plot. The hands weren't going to take food to the mouth; even if they did, the mouth wasn't going to accept it. . . . They went into a sulk and waited for the belly to cry for help. But while they waited, one by one all the parts of the body got weaker and weaker. The moral of this story? The belly too has its job to do. It has to be fed, but it also does feeding of its own.

sulk: to be in a bad mood and stay silent

Use the Reference Section at the end of your book to look up words, people, and places. This section includes the **World History Time Lines** and a table of **Countries of Our World.** ▼

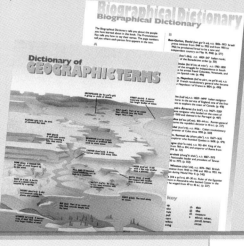

ADDITIONAL FEATURES OF THE TEXTBOOK

ADVENTURES WITH NATIONAL GEOGRAPHIC Have students look at these features, such as on pp. 4–5, which follow the Unit Opener.

CHAPTER SUMMARIES AND REVIEWS Have students examine a typical Chapter Summary and Review, such as on pp. 182–183. Ask students to identify the types of information (for example, vocabulary and facts) and skills (thinking and writing) they are asked to review.

UNIT REVIEWS Have students review a typical Unit Review, such as on pp. 62–63. Explain to students that a Unit Review will help them refresh their memories about information covered in the unit.

REFERENCE SECTION Have students examine the sections not covered above: Atlas (R4–R19), Country Tables (R20–R35), Time Lines (R36–R45), Dictionary of Geographic Terms (R46-R47), Gazetteer (R48-R54), Biographical Dictionary (R55-R59), Glossary (R60–R69), and Index (R70–R77).

● *What kind of sample Skills Lesson is shown?* (a Thinking Skills lesson)

Discussing Citizenship Have students examine the *Citizenship* features in the Table of Contents. Note that *Citizenship* features are of two types: *Viewpoints* and *Making a Difference*.

● *Which type of Citizenship feature is shown on this page?* (Viewpoints)

Exploring the Reference Section Have students examine the reference section that begins on p. R2.

● *What parts are in the reference section?* (Atlas, Country Tables, Time Lines, Dictionary of Geographic Terms, Gazetteer, Biographic Dictionary, Glossary, and Index)

Explain that the *Biographical Dictionary* alphabetically lists the names of the people discussed in the textbook. The Dictionary also provides a brief description and a page reference for each person. The *Dictionary of Geographic Terms* is an illustration of the different types of land and bodies of water, along with a corresponding definition.

Sum up by noting that all these features will help students better understand the history and geography of the world.

● *Where would you look for information of people discussed in your textbook?* (in the Biographical Dictionary)

● *Where would you look for definitions and illustrations of geographic words?* (in the Dictionary of Geographic Terms)

READING INSTRUCTION IN YOUR TEACHER'S EDITION

READING STRATEGIES AND LANGUAGE DEVELOPMENT
A variety of strategies at the start of each lesson helps you develop student vocabulary and language skills. Strategies access prior knowledge and teach clues to understanding the text and improving writing skills.

READING COMPREHENSION
Questions at the end of the lessons in the student book use a variety of reading strategies to assist students in summarizing, interpreting, and analyzing the main ideas of the lessons. Reading strategies are identified after the answers in the teacher's edition.

FIVE THEMES OF GEOGRAPHY

PAGES G2-G3

Lesson Overview

Geographers use five basic themes to study Earth and everything on it.

Lesson Objectives

★ Define *geography*.

★ Describe the five fundamental themes that geographers use to study their subject.

1 PREPARE

MOTIVATE Ask students to tell what they think of when they hear the word *geography*. What clues do the pictures shown here give to what geography is? Write students' thoughts on the board and encourage them to work out a class definition of geography.

SET PURPOSE Have students examine the pictures closely and read the questions posed about them. Point out that although they may not be able to answer these questions now, they will later.

2 TEACH

Discussing Geography Give students a few minutes to do a careful examination of the pictures and their labels. Then discuss with students the five themes of geography:

Region: an area with common features that set it apart from other areas;

Human/Environment Interaction: the relationship between people and the land on which they live;

Place: a description of what an area is like based on various features (natural or built by people);

Location: the exact measurement of where something can be found. Location can be described absolutely (often using numbers, such as longitude and latitude) and relatively (where one place is described in relation to another place).

Movement: the movement of people, goods, and ideas around the world, as well as how patterns of movement affect people and the way in which communities develop.

NATIONAL GEOGRAPHIC

Five Themes of Geography

Location
How do these bicyclists know they are entering another country?

Place
What makes the Netherlands different from other places?

G2

THEMES of GEOGRAPHY

THE FIVE THEMES AND THE NATIONAL GEOGRAPHY STANDARDS

Geography is a vast subject, encompassing all the world. To help educators organize and convey geographic knowledge, the five themes of geography were introduced in 1984. The popularity of the five themes set the stage for the development of a more comprehensive instructional framework—the National Geography Standards, published in 1994.

Guidlines for integrating the Five Themes of Geography with *World: Adventures in Time and Place* are found in each *Adventures with National Geographic* lesson. These guidelines provide teaching suggestions for developing one or two of the five geography themes in each Unit.

For more information about the 1994 National Geography Standards , or to order a copy, contact: National Geographic Society, P.O. Box 98171, Washington, D.C. 20013-8171.

Human/Environment Interactions
How have people changed this landscape in Indonesia?

Region
What are some things that help make the Middle East a special region?

Movement
How do goods travel from place to place?

Ask students to consider how each of the five themes of geography relates to their local area.

- **How would you describe the region in which you live?** *(Answers will vary.)*

- **How would you explain your location using other places as references?** *(Answers will vary. Encourage students to use places from opposing directions.)*

- **What is the most efficient way to transport people in your area?** *(Answers will vary. Possible answers: car, train, bus.)*

⭐3 CLOSE

SUM IT UP

Have students return to the class definition of geography that they worked out in the Motivate section and review it. Encourage them to revise it to incorporate what they learned in their discussion of the five themes of geography.

EVALUATE

Write About It Tell students to list the five themes of geography and after each to write a sentence explaining what each means.

Note that the background map shows the world. Students can turn to pp.R16-R17 in the Atlas to see a map of all 50 states.

Technology CONNECTION
ADVENTURE TIME! CD-ROM
Enrich the National Geographic Adventures Lesson with *Travel* and *Explore* on the *Adventure Time!* CD-ROM.

BACKGROUND INFORMATION

DEVELOPING GEOGRAPHY SKILLS Use this activity to reinforce what students have just learned about aspects of geography

- Have students list three places that they would like to visit anywhere in the world. Encourage them to note down anything they already know about their chosen places.

- Have them locate their choices on their desk maps, with teacher help if necessary.

- Initiate a discussion in which you call for chosen spots and have students locate them on a map of the world. Which are farthest apart? Which are relatively close? What kind of climate is each likely to have? Why? If you were to travel to these places, what route might you be likely to follow? What geographical features might it take you through or over?

These pages are available as a poster.

Resource **REMINDER**

National Geographic Poster
Geo Adventures *Daily Geography Activities*
Technology: *Adventure Time!* CD-ROM
Desk Map

Part I: Using Globes

INTRODUCE

Display a globe or globes so that students can work with it "hands on" as they continue through this lesson.

Refer the class to the *Vocabulary* words and have students supply definitions for each, based on their prior knowledge. As they define each word, have them use the globe to show an example of the term they are defining.

DISCUSS

Have students refer to a map of the world, and invite them to discuss why a globe may be better than a flat map when studying Earth. Help them see that a globe can show land shapes and distances more accurately than a flat map.

If students have access to a globe on a stand, call on them to discuss why it is tilted at an angle. Help them to see that Earth itself rotates at an angle to the sun, and the stand shows the globe at this angle.

Encourage students to follow the flow of water around the globe. Have them identify Earth's four oceans (Atlantic, Arctic, Indian, Pacific) and help them see how the oceans are actually all part of one continuous body of water.

Resource **REMINDER**
Practice and Project Book: *pp. 1-5*
Geo Adventures

Reviewing
GEOGRAPHY SKILLS

PART 1
Using Globes

VOCABULARY

continent	meridian
hemisphere	prime meridian
equator	latitude
longitude	parallel

What do globes show?

- A globe is a model that shows Earth as it looks when seen from outer space.
- A globe shows Earth's seven continents, or large bodies of land. They are Africa, Antarctica, Asia, Australia, Europe, North America, and South America. Which continents are shown on this globe?*
- Much of Earth is covered by four oceans, or large bodies of salt water. They are the Atlantic, Arctic, Indian, and Pacific oceans. Which oceans do you see on the globe? Which continents and oceans are not shown?**

What is a hemisphere?

- A globe, much like Earth, is in the shape of a ball or sphere. Looking at a globe from any direction, you can see only half of it. *Hemi* is a Greek word for "half." Hemisphere means "half a sphere."
- Geographers divide Earth into the four hemispheres shown at the top of the next page.
- An imaginary line dividing the world into the Northern Hemisphere and Southern Hemisphere is called the equator. It lies halfway between the North Pole and South Pole. Which continents are in the Northern Hemisphere? In the Southern Hemisphere?***
- Geographers divide Earth into the Eastern and Western hemispheres. Which hemi-

sphere includes all of Africa? Which hemisphere does not include Antarctica?****

How are longitude and latitude useful?

- You can locate places on a map or globe by using a grid of imaginary lines.
- Running north to south are longitude lines, or meridians. These imaginary lines measure the distance east and west of the prime meridian. The unit of measurement is degrees. Look at the map at the bottom of the next page. What is the longitude of Cape Town? 20°E
- Running east to west are latitude lines, or parallels. These show distance in degrees north and south of the equator. What are the latitude and longitude of Mexico City? 20°N, 100°W

More Practice

You can find longitude and latitude lines on many maps in this book. For examples, see pages 9, 12, and 13.

*Africa, Europe, Asia, Australia **Indian Ocean, Pacific Ocean; continents not shown are North America, South America, Antarctica; oceans not shown are Arctic and Atlantic oceans.

G4

BACKGROUND INFORMATION

SUGGESTIONS FOR USING THE SELECTION

The *Reviewing Geography Skills* section is in three parts:

- Using Globes, pp. G4-G5
- Using Maps, pp. G6-G8
- Different Kinds of Maps, G9-G11

This section reviews and reinforces geography skills learned in prior years. Use the section both to review previously learned geographical concepts and to assess students' skills in understanding and using them. Encourage the class to return to this section from time to time during the year to conduct their own review and reinforcement.

THE HEMISPHERES

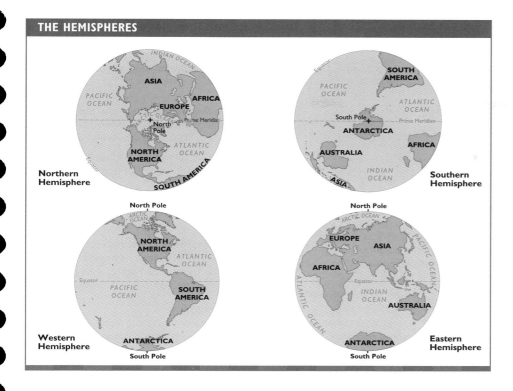

Northern Hemisphere

Southern Hemisphere

Western Hemisphere

Eastern Hemisphere

GLOBAL GRID

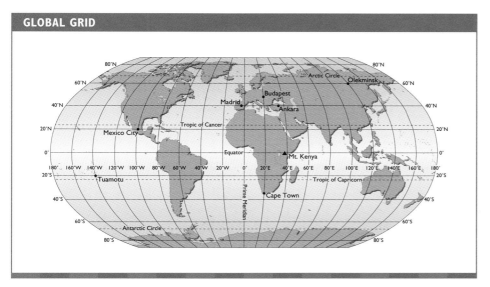

***North America, South America, Europe, Asia, Africa; South America, Africa, Australia, Antarctica, Asia ****Eastern, Northern

G5

Refer the class to the four hemispheres on this page and have them identify each. Help them understand that each shows Earth from a different point of view. Have volunteers identify and contrast those different points (Northern Hemisphere: looking down at the North Pole; Southern Hemisphere: looking down at the South Pole; Western Hemisphere: looking at one side of Earth; Eastern Hemisphere: looking at the other side of Earth.)

Ask volunteers to explain the role that latitude and longitude play in dividing Earth into hemispheres. Is latitude or longitude used to divide Earth into Northern and Southern hemispheres? (latitude; the equator) Which is used to divide Earth into Eastern and Western hemispheres? (longitude; the prime meridian)

As students review the global grid on this page, help them recognize that each measurement has a "twin" on the other hemisphere. Help them find the Tropic of Cancer in the Northern Hemisphere and the Tropic of Capricorn in the Southern Hemisphere.

EXTEND

Have the class work in group, and give each group an outline map of a different area of the world. Have them locate their area on a globe or map and identify it. Then have them draw a global grid over it, showing where in the system of latitude and longitude it belongs.

BACKGROUND INFORMATION

USING THE GLOBES

Give students some time to work with the globes in small groups. Encourage them to make up questions that globe work can answer, such as "What country is on the side of Earth directly opposite of the side we are on?" or "Is Brazil closer to Canada or to France?"

You may also want to ask questions such as these to challenge and reinforce the skills in this section.

- How many continents are there on Earth? What are they? (Africa, Antarctica, Asia, Australia, Europe, North America, South America)

- Which of the continents is farthest south on the globe? (Antarctica)

- Why is the term *hemisphere* used to describe different parts of Earth? (Each hemisphere is one-half of the spherical Earth, and *hemisphere* is the Greek word for "half a sphere.")

- Which of the four oceans is found in the Northern Hemisphere but not in the Southern Hemisphere? (Arctic)

- Which ocean is found in the Eastern Hemisphere but not in the Western Hemisphere? (Indian Ocean)

- What is the "twin" of the Arctic Circle? (the Antarctic Circle)

- Near what latitude and longitude is Madrid found? (40° North and the prime meridian, or 0°)

Part 2: Using Maps

INTRODUCE

Access students' prior knowledge by having them supply definitions for the *Vocabulary* words. If appropriate, have students share times when they have used these terms outside of school.

DISCUSS

It may help students become more comfortable in locating directions if you plot out directions in the classroom.

Help students determine where North is in the room. Then have them identify and locate the other directions. Ask volunteers to tell in which section of the room they are sitting.

Then invite students to choose two or three other cities on the map of Australia and tell in which direction they are from Canberra.

To increase students' facility with directions, have them choose two cities on each of the maps on pp. G7 and G8 and determine in which direction they would travel to get from one to the other.

PART 2
Using Maps

VOCABULARY
cardinal directions
intermediate directions
compass rose
scale
symbol
map key
locator

What are cardinal directions?

● When you face in the direction of the North Pole, you are facing north. Behind you is south. East is to your right and west is to your left. If you turn to face east, what direction is now behind you? What direction is now to your left?*

● There are four cardinal directions–north, south, east, and west.

● The letters **N**, **S**, **E**, and **W** are often used to represent the cardinal directions. What does **W** stand for? west

How can you determine intermediate directions?

● Northeast (**NE**), southeast (**SE**), southwest (**SW**), and northwest (**NW**) are called intermediate directions.

● The intermediate directions are halfway between the cardinal directions. Northeast is the direction halfway between north and east. Where does **SE** lie? between south and east

How can you find directions on maps that do not include the North Pole?

● Most maps are drawn with north toward the top of the map. Many also include a compass rose, a drawing that shows directions.

● In this book, the compass rose usually shows both cardinal and intermediate directions. Look at the map of Australia. Which cities are southwest of Canberra?**

More Practice
You can practice finding directions and using a compass rose on most maps in this book. For examples, see pages 105, 225, and 355.

AUSTRALIA

G6

*west; south **Melbourne, Hobart, Launceston

SECOND-LANGUAGE SUPPORT

TAKING NOTES Second-language learners may confuse some of the *Vocabulary* words with their homographs or homophones, such as *scale, key*, and *symbol/cymbal*. Encourage students to keep a personal list of geography words and definitions for this section. Suggest that they keep the list on hand for ongoing reference.

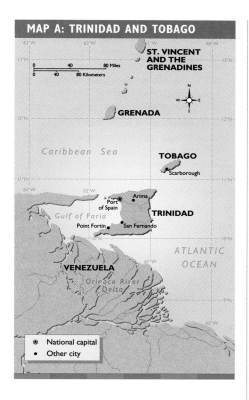

MAP A: TRINIDAD AND TOBAGO

MAP B: TRINIDAD AND TOBAGO

Have students look at the map scales on all the maps in Part 2. Invite volunteers to compare and contrast the information given on each.

Help students understand that the size of the area shown on the map often determines how many miles the map scale covers. Work with them to see the relationship between size and scale, for example, on the two maps of Trinidad and Tobago.

Ask students to use the scale on Map A to measure a specified distance on Map B, and vice versa. Have them talk about any difficulties they encountered, and why one scale or the other might have seemed inappropriate for the map.

What is a map scale?

- Maps are always smaller than the actual places they show. The scale tells you how much smaller the distance on a map is compared with the actual distance.

- Map scales in this book include two lines for measuring distances. Which unit of measurement does each line show?*

How do you use a scale? Why are map scales sometimes different?

- You can use a ruler to measure distances on a map.

- To determine the distance in miles between San Fernando and Scarborough, measure the length on the scale that represents 80 miles on Map A. The length is one inch. Now measure the distance between San Fernando and Scarborough

in inches. Multiply the result by 80 to determine the distance. What is the distance between the two cities? 80 miles

- Different maps often show the same area using different scales. Map A and Map B both show the Caribbean country of Trinidad and Tobago. However, the islands look larger on Map B. They look larger because one inch stands for fewer miles on the Map B scale than on the A scale. The larger scale allows more details to be shown. What kinds of details are shown on Map B that are not on Map A?**

More Practice

Most of the maps in the book show map scales. For example, see pages 76, 135, and 403.

*top line shows miles, bottom kilometers
**Rivers are named, more cities are shown, a peak is shown.

G7

CURRICULUM CONNECTION

LINKS TO MATHEMATICS Have students work with partners to try different measuring tools on the map scales in Part 2. In addition to rulers, they might use paper clips, lengths of yarn, or small squares of paper.

Encourage students to keep a list of how many of each unit of measure they used to find similar distances. Then have them compare their measurements with classmates.

Have students look at the two maps on this page. Invite volunteers to compare and contrast the map keys on the maps.

Then have students look back through Part 2 and identify similarities and differences in the map keys on earlier maps. Ask students to look at other maps that may be posted around the room and compare any map keys they find.

Ask a volunteer to point out the locator map on each of the maps on this page. Help students realize that the use of a locator map is a way to understand where the section of the main map is in a larger area.

EXTEND

You might have some local newspapers on hand for students to browse through. Invite them to find maps of local or regional areas. Have them identify any locator maps that are included, and compare and contrast them to the locator maps on these pages.

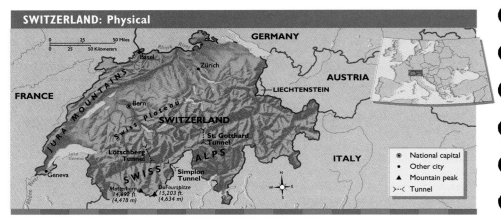

What information does a map key give?

- Maps often use symbols to give information. A symbol is anything that stands for something else. On many maps a black dot stands for a city. Other symbols include triangles, squares, and lines. What are some other symbols found on maps?*

- Symbols do not always stand for the same things on all maps. For this reason it is important to read the map key, which tells you what the symbols stand for. What does the triangle stand for on each map on this page?**

How do locators help in studying maps?

- Maps use locators to show where the subject area of the main map is located.

- In this book the locator is a small map in the shape of a globe or a rectangular portion of Earth's surface. The area of the main map is shown in red. What is the shape of Switzerland's locator?***

- Some locators show a hemisphere. Others may show a continent, a region, or a country. What area does Argentina's locator show?****

More Practice

You will see many keys and locators. For examples of map keys, see pages 172, 280, and 281. For examples of locators, see pages 287, 385, and 601.

G8 *Answers may vary. Example: a tree could stand for a forest. **oil, mountain peak ***flared rectangle ****Western Hemisphere

---

*South Asia **Oman, Iran, Turkmenistan, Tajikistan, China, Myanmar, Laos, Thailand, Cambodia, Malaysia, and Indonesia are the labeled countries not in the subject area.

PART 3
Different Kinds of Maps

VOCABULARY

political map   relief map
physical map   historical map
elevation map   distribution map

Why are there different kinds of maps?

- Maps differ in the kinds of information they give. This section will cover four kinds of maps.

- When studying a map, first look at the map title. It will tell you the subject area and the type of information provided. What subject area does the map below show?*

- A map may include areas that are not part of its subject area. In this book such areas are shown in gray. What countries are not in the subject area of the map below?**

What is a political map?

- A political map shows information such as countries, states, cities, and other important political features. Although many maps include national or state boundaries, a political map may also use colors to highlight countries or states.

- Look at the map below. What color is used to show Nepal? How many different colors are used to show countries? What countries have disputed borders? What are the capital cities of those countries?***

More Practice

You can find other political maps in this book. For examples, see pages 528, 576, and 623.

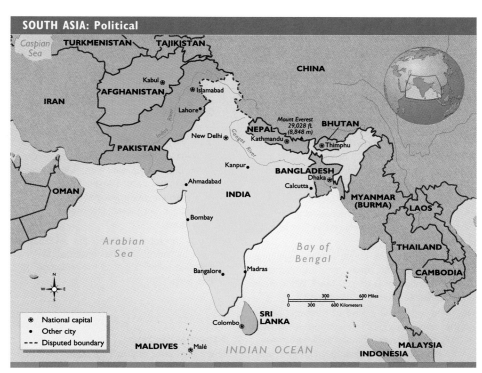

SOUTH ASIA: Political

***pink; five; India, Pakistan, and China; Islamabad and New Delhi are the capitals of Pakistan and India but China is not part of South Asia and its capital isn't shown.

G9

INTRODUCE

Work with students to identify the *Vocabulary* terms and to create a list of definitions. Ask students to share any experience they have had with these different types of maps.

DISCUSS

Have students look at the map of Nepal and Southern Asia and work with a partner to trace the borders. Then have partners work together to write a brief description of what the colors and the special symbol signify.

Then have them turn to the *Atlas* section of this text (pp. R4–R19) and choose another political map. Encourage them to discuss how the map would change if the color and special symbols on the map of southern Asia were applied to it.

SECOND-LANGUAGE SUPPORT

USING PROPS To help second-language learners distinguish between different types of maps, you might post some representative maps around the room and have students create identifying labels to attach to them. Make sure students understand map vocabulary. Explain unfamiliar terms. Have them keep a glossary of geography terms in their notebooks.

Have students look carefully at the two maps of Tanzania. Help them see that while many of the features are the same, they each show very different elements as well.

Have students work with partners to locate two or three areas on the relief map and make a list of the elevations of those places. Then have them write a brief description of each of the places, using the map information to tell about the landforms and elevation.

Encourage students to find other physical maps in the *Atlas* section (pp. R4–R19) and to compare the landforms with these maps.

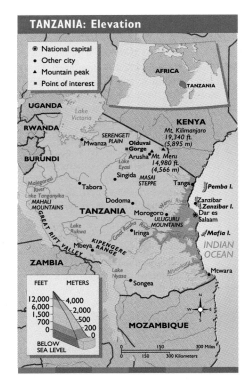

TANZANIA: Elevation

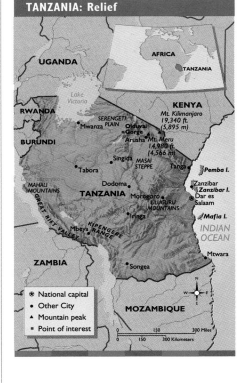

TANZANIA: Relief

What do different kinds of physical maps show?

- **Physical maps** show Earth's natural features. This section will cover two different kinds of physical maps.

- One type of physical map is an **elevation map**. Elevation maps use color to show the height of land above sea level. In this book elevation is measured in feet and in meters.

- Look at the maps above. On the elevation map of Tanzania, what color represents the elevation of 0 to 700 feet? What areas of Tanzania have this elevation?*

- **Relief maps** are a kind of physical map that show changes in elevation. Areas with no shading represent places where there are no changes in elevation. Lightly shaded areas show places where changes are

very gradual. Dark shading represents areas with sharp changes in elevation, such as a steep hill.

- An area can show a lot of relief, or dramatic changes in elevation, without being very high above sea level. An area can be at a high elevation but have very little relief, as a flat plateau high above sea level does.

- Study the relief map and the elevation map of Tanzania. What area has the greatest relief? What is the elevation of this area?**

More Practice

There are other physical maps in this book. For examples, see pages 71, 131, and 317.

G10 *darker green; coastal land by Indian Ocean **Uluguru Mountains, near Morogoro; 1,500–6,000 feet.

CURRICULUM CONNECTION

LINKS TO MATHEMATICS Have students determine the differences in elevation between the areas they chose to compare on the maps of Tanzania. Then have them use other reference sources to locate and identify the elevations of other places in the world and find the differences between those places and the sites in Tanzania.

What is an historical map?

- Maps that show information about the past or where past events took place are called historical maps.

- The map title tells you the subject of the map. Many of the historical maps in this book include dates in the title or in the key. Study the map of the United States' expansion below, in the middle of the page. Between what dates did the expansion shown in this map occur? By what year did the United States own land west of the Mississippi River?*

What is a distribution map?

- Distribution maps show how things such as language, religion, population, and rainfall are distributed throughout an area.

- The map key on the distribution map below shows colors that represent kinds of plants found in Russia. What kind of plants cover the largest area of land?**

More Practice

You can find many different kinds of maps in this book. For historical maps, see pages 280, 281, and 464. For distribution maps, see pages 345, 370, and 371.

Help students understand that maps can provide all types of information. Ask them to look at the historical map of the United States. Invite them to speculate on why a map such as this might be helpful to researchers or historians.

Then have students look at the distribution map of Russia. Help them compare the map keys to reinforce that colors and patterns can show many different things. Ask volunteers to determine where similar patterns might be placed if the map keys were switched.

EXTEND

Have students choose a map from the *Atlas* section. Then have them work with a partner to develop a map key for a distribution or historical map, based on additional research they do for the area shown on the map.

Then have them finish their map keys and present them to the class.

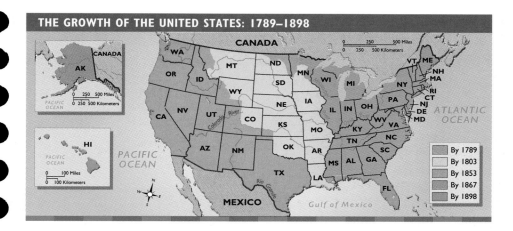

THE GROWTH OF THE UNITED STATES: 1789–1898

By 1789
By 1803
By 1853
By 1867
By 1898

RUSSIA: Vegetation

Deciduous Forest
Evergreen Forest
Grassland
Desert Vegetation
High Mountain Vegetation
Tundra

*1789 and 1898; 1803 **evergreen forest

G11

MEETING INDIVIDUAL NEEDS

RETEACHING (EASY) Have students work in small groups to draw a resource map of resources available in the classroom. Encourage them to create symbols for such items as chalk, class library books, art supplies, and the like and to show them in a legend and on the map.

EXTENSION (AVERAGE) Invite students to identify different kinds of maps in the Atlas, Videodisc, or on the Adventures CD-ROM. In each case, ask students to explain their reason for identifying each map as a particular kind.

ENRICHMENT (CHALLENGING) Ask students to choose a physical, climate, or political geographic feature of their region. Have them research local history to discover how the physical or climate feature affected the development of their area or how the political feature came to develop in their area.

UNIT ORGANIZER

1 Understanding the World

PAGES 2–63

UNIT OVERVIEW

The people of the world vary from one region to another. The people in Mexico City differ culturally from those in Chinese rice terraces. From the discovery of ancient objects, historians know that cultures have changed over time. It is believed humans have lived on Earth for over two million years. People learn about themselves and others from the past.

ADVENTURES WITH NATIONAL GEOGRAPHIC
Stony Silence **pp. 4–5**

UNIT PLANNING GUIDE

CHAPTER	SUGGESTED PACING	RESOURCES	ASSESSMENT
1 Regions Over four billion people live in different parts of the world, and their cultures differ from one region to another. **pp. 6–21**	4–5 days	• **Practice and Project Book, pp. 6–9** • **Anthology, pp. 1–3** • **Desk Map** • **Transparency Maps 10a, 10b** • **Transparency:** Graphic Organizer, Main Idea Table • ⊙ **Technology:** Videodisc/Video Tape • ⊙ **Technology:** *Adventure Time!* CD-ROM	• **Meeting Individual Needs, pp. 11, 13, 19** • **Write About It, 11, 19** • **Chapter Review, pp. 20–21** • **Assessment Book:** *Assessing Think and Write, pp. T45–T47. Chapter 1 Tests: Content, Skills, Writing*
2 A Look into the Past Archaeology helps people learn about themselves and other cultures. **pp. 22–41**	4–5 days	• **Practice and Project Book, pp. 10–13** • **Anthology, pp. 4–7** • **Desk Map** • **Transparency:** Graphic Organizer, Main Idea Map • ⊙ **Technology:** Videodisc/Video Tape • **McGraw-Hill Adventure Book**	• **Meeting Individual Needs, pp. 29, 37** • **Write About It, pp. 29, 37** • **Chapter Review, pp. 40–41** • **Assessment Book:** *Assessing Think and Write, pp. T48–T50. Chapter 2 Tests: Content, Skills, Writing*
3 Early Cultures Objects made by ancient people have been uncovered all over the world. **pp. 42–61**	4–5 days	• **Practice and Project Book, pp. 14–17** • **Anthology, pp. 8–10** • **Desk Map** • ⊙ **Technology:** *Adventure Time!* CD-ROM • **McGraw-Hill Adventure Book**	• **Meeting Individual Needs, pp. 49, 51, 57, 59** • **Write About It, pp. 49, 51, 57** • **Chapter Review, pp. 60–61** • **Assessment Book:** *Assessing Think and Write, pp. T51–T53. Chapter 3 Tests: Content, Skills, Writing*
Unit 1 Review **pp. 62–63**	1–2 days	• **Geo Adventures Daily Geography Activities**	• **Unit 1 Project, p. 63**

The McGraw-Hill School's Home Page at
☞ **http://www.mhschool.com**
on the World Wide Web for projects related to this unit.

FOR FURTHER SUPPORT
• **Language Support Handbook**
• **Standardized Test Support**

UNIT BIBLIOGRAPHY AND RESOURCES

McGraw-Hill Adventure Books

Cassidy, Janet. **History Under Their Feet.** A group of fifth and sixth graders find early Native American artifacts in this informative account of an archaeological dig. **(Easy)**

Ellis, Michael. **Digging in the Sun.** The story of archaeologist Mary Leakey and her pioneering discoveries in East Africa, which changed the way people thought about the development of early humans. **(Easy)**

Classroom Library

■ Dewey, Jennifer Owings. **Stories on Stone.** Boston, MA: Little, Brown and Company, 1996. Some possible theories about the pictures inscribed on rocks found in the southwestern region of the United States.

Student Books

Arnold, Caroline. **The Ancient Cliff Dwellers of Mesa Verde.** New York: Clarion Books, 1992. An exploration of the Anasazi, ancient Americans who lived in the first century A.D. in the southwestern region of the United States. **(Average)**

■ Avi-Yonah, Michael. **Dig This! How Archaeologists Uncover Our Past.** Minneapolis, MN: Lerner Publications, 1993. This is a fascinating discussion of archaeological excavations and the discoveries they led to. **(Average)**

Knowlton, Mary Lee, ed. **Children of the World: India.** Milwaukee, WI: Gareth Stevens, Inc., 1988. This book describes the family, school, customs, and daily life of a young boy living in Rajasthan, India. **(Easy)**

Anderson, Joan. **From Map to Museum: Uncovering the Mysteries of the Past.** New York: Morrow Junior Books, 1988. A description of an archaeological dig, where artifacts come from, and how they end up in a museum. **(Average)**

■ Lauber, Patricia. **Seeing Earth from Space.** New York: Orchard Books, 1990. Text and dramatic photos combine to show Earth from space and discuss its future. **(Challenging)**

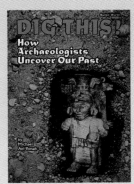

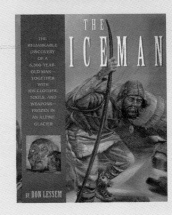

Teacher Books

☐ National Geographic Society. **Exploring Your World: The Adventure of Geography.** Washington, DC: National Geographic Society, 1989. This encyclopedia of geography contains maps, photos, and beautiful illustrations; an excellent reference.

Stiebing, Jr. William H. **Uncovering the Past: A History of Archaeology.** Buffalo, NY: Prometheus Books, 1993. This book traces archaeology from its beginnings to modern methods.

Read-Alouds

Jaspersohn, William. **How People First Lived.** New York: Franklin Watts, 1985. This fascinating account of the development of early man is well-suited for reading aloud.

■ Lessem, Don. **The Iceman.** New York: Crown Publishers, Inc., 1994. This book tells of the discovery—found between Austria and Italy—of the remains of a man estimated to have lived over 5,000 years ago.

Technology Multimedia

Cave Dwellers of the Old Stone Age. Video. No. 1770-106. (18 min.) The life of cave dwellers is recreated from artifacts, cave paintings, and other sources. Britannica Videos. (800) 554-9862.

☐ **Geography: Five Themes for Planet Earth.** Video. No. A51515. (17 min.) Five key themes in geography education are presented for learning about our world. National Geographic. (800) 368-2728.

☐ **ZipZapMap! World.** Software. Students learn geography of the six regions in the world. National Geographic Society. (800) 368-2728.

Free or Inexpensive Materials

For a free video rental called "Of Time, Tombs, and Treasure: The Treasures of Tutankhamun," send to: National Gallery of Art; Department of Education Resources; Washington, DC 20565.

■ Book excerpted in the Anthology

■ Book featured in the student bibliography of the Unit Review

☐ National Geographic technology

Ideas for Active Learning

BULLETIN BOARD

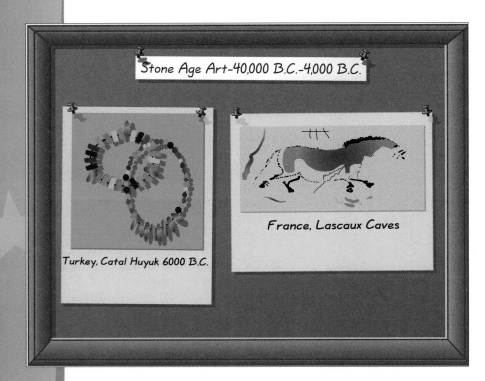

Stone Age Art-40,000 B.C.-4,000 B.C.

Turkey, Catal Huyuk 6000 B.C.

France, Lascaux Caves

Understanding the World

Help students to create a bulletin board titled "Stone Age Art— 40,000 B.C.–4,000 B.C." Have students find photographs of art, artifacts, or tools from the Old Stone Age or the New Stone Age. They can cut pictures out of their own magazines or make photocopies. Ask students to mount each example of art on a piece of oaktag or paper, and label it with the location of the culture that produced the art, the approximate date the art was created, and the materials used to create it. Encourage students to draw conclusions about why the art was made or about why the materials were used. Then have students classify their examples by date or location.

TEACHER EXCHANGE

Thanks to: Mary Helen J. Dixon, Highlands Day School, Birmingham, Alabama

Create a Regions Rainbow

ON YOUR OWN

30 MINUTES OR LONGER

CURRICULUM CONNECTION   Art/Language Arts

Materials: three colors of paint or construction paper, matching colored tape, paper lunch bag, 6" gold-colored circles

1. Use paint or construction paper to create a three-color Regions Rainbow. Use yellow for State, red for Country, and blue for World. The first half of each band is labeled Physical; the second half is labeled Cultural.
2. As they begin each chapter, have students mark off the area and type of region on the appropriate color strip.Then have them write important facts and information about the region.
3. Attach a list of suggested readings to the beginning of the rainbow, and tell students that they will earn a gold coin for each of the suggested readings they complete.
4. Use the paper bag for a "pot of gold" at one end of the rainbow. The "gold coin" circles are rewards for related bonus reading.

Enriching with Multimedia

 RESOURCE: McGraw-Hill School's Home Page

- Have students go to McGraw-Hill School's home page at http://www.mhschool.com on the World Wide Web for projects related to this unit.

 **RESOURCE:** *Videodisc/Video Tape 1*

- Enrich Unit 1 with the *Legacies of the Past* segment on the Videodisc.

Search Frame 45670 Side B

SCHOOL-TO-HOME

Understanding the World

- Throughout the unit, students will have the opportunity to learn about tools that were made and used by peoples in the Old Stone Age and the New Stone Age. Discuss the various tools students have learned about and whether they were used for agriculture or another purpose. With students, generate a chart listing each tool, its purpose, and the material from which the tool was made.

- Ask students to complete the chart at home with their families. For each tool listed on the chart, have students indicate whether the tool is used today, and write the present-day material that is used to make it. In addition, families can expand the chart to list the tools they use at home, their purpose, and the materials of which they are made.

Tool	Material	Today	Material
club	heavy wood	hammer	metal, rubber or wood handle
axe	bone, wood	axe	metal, wood handle

ONGOING UNIT PROJECT

Create an Artifact

CURRICULUM CONNECTION   Art/Language Arts

RESOURCE: Practice and Project Book p. 127.

Throughout the unit, students will work individually and cooperatively to create a collection of artifacts that could have belonged to ancient civilizations.

1. After each chapter is completed, students can work individually to draw, design, or make an artifact that might have been created during the period of time being studied.
2. Provide art materials such as clay and paint for students. Students may want to collect rocks and other materials to help them make their artifacts.
3. At the end of the unit, groups can create a display of artifacts. The display should include an identification card for each artifact that shows its origin and date.
4. Each student can describe the artifacts he or she has created to help the class fill out the artifact exhibition sheets provided.

 Assessment suggestions for this activity appear on page 62.

stone-aged knife
Africa
2 million years ago

Introducing the Unit

Have students read the unit title, *Understanding the World*. Give them a few moments to study the illustration, to get a hint of the infinite variety of things they will meet as they journey into understanding the world. Then have them read *Why Does It Matter?* on p. 3.

Exploring Prior Knowledge Point out to students that they may already know more about the world than they think—from their reading, perhaps from travel, or from television or movies.

- **What have you read or seen about geography features in other parts of the world?** *(Students may describe any features that have impressed them, like a vast sandy desert, or a high waterfall, or towering mountains, or other natural features.)*

- **What have you read or seen about other peoples of the world, especially those who lived in the distant past?** *(Encourage responses, for example, ancient Native American dwellings they may have seen in this country, cave dwellers of prehistoric times, or ancient warriors of Rome.)*

★**THINKING FURTHER:** *Predicting*
How might all this information be part of your journey into understanding the world? *(Help students see that they will learn how to fit all these pieces into a puzzle. All these pieces, and many more, will fit into the big picture, in time and place.)*

Looking Ahead Students will build a foundation of knowledge about physical and cultural regions of the world and will learn how geographers, historians, archaeologists, and other social scientists work to discover the past and help us to understand the past and present.

NEAR LIFE-SIZED CHESS PIECES, INDIA
OLMEC SCULPTURE, MEXICO
PYRAMID AND SPHINX, EGYPT

BACKGROUND INFORMATION

ABOUT THE ARTIFACTS

- **INDIAN CHESS PIECES** These chess pieces were carved in India, where chess is thought to have originated in the 7th century A.D.

- **OLMEC SCULPTURE** This huge human head is one of many such sculptures from the Olmec culture, the earliest known civilization of the Americas (1200–400 B.C.).

- **PYRAMID AND SPHINX** These monuments from the west bank of the Nile in Egypt were built about 4,500 years ago; pyramids were the burial places for Egyptian kings.

UNIT ONE

Understanding the World

"My imagination was caught by the great age of the world."

from *Self Made Man* by Jonathan Kingdon
See page 44.

WHY DOES IT MATTER?

These are the words of scientist Jonathan Kingdon, who was born and grew up in East Africa. They could also be the thoughts of anyone who has imagined what life was like hundreds or even thousands of years ago. How did people live? What did they eat? What was their land like? People have always wanted to know what things were like for those who lived before them.

Thanks to historians and other scholars, answers to many of these questions are being discovered. Objects made by ancient people have been uncovered all over the world. These objects reveal mysteries of the distant past. They also help us to better understand who we are.

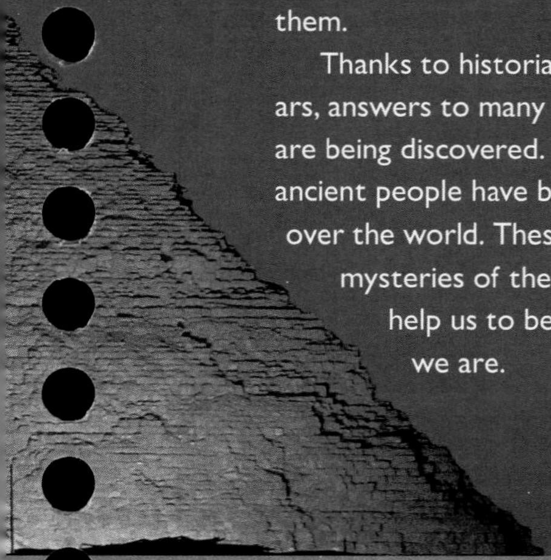

STONEHENGE, ENGLAND
PREHISTORIC BONE NEEDLE, FRANCE

3

BACKGROUND INFORMATION

ABOUT THE ARTIFACTS
- **STONEHENGE** Built from 2800 to 1500 B.C. on the Salisbury Plain in England, Stonehenge was a center for religion and astronomy.
- **BONE NEEDLE** Prehistoric bone needles, such as this one which was found in France, are ancient tools; some date back 35,000 years.

Discussing the Artifacts Use these artifacts to give students an overview of the times and places they are going to investigate and the kinds of clues they will work with.

- *What do all of these pictures have in common?* (They all show objects that human beings have made.)

- *Which show monuments?* (the Olmec head, Stonehenge, the pyramid and sphinx)

> ★THINKING FURTHER: *Making Conclusions* **Based on these examples of human craft, what can you conclude about people's common needs through time?** *(the need to make things; the use of tools; the desire for entertainment; and for monuments)*

Discussing WHY DOES IT MATTER? Have a student read the quotation aloud and have the class review the passage that follows it.

- *Why do you suppose that the past captures the human imagination?* (Help students to recognize the power and universality of human curiosity. "Curiosity," said Dr. Samuel Johnson, "is one of the permanent and certain characteristics of a vigorous mind.")

- *Look around the classroom. What do the objects you see tell about our lives today?* (Students may note that we have advanced technology, care about education, and are capable of producing a great variety of goods.)

> ★THINKING FURTHER: *Making Connections* **How can examining objects from the past help us understand what life was like then?** *(Help students connect the idea that just as modern objects offer clues about our present, ancient objects offer clues about life in the past.)*

Adventures
with
NATIONAL GEOGRAPHIC

Introducing
Stony Silence

Exploring Prior Knowledge Give students a moment to look at the pictures on the spread. Ask them if they have ever seen or read anything about Stonehenge—where it is located, when it was built, by whom, and why. Encourage them to volunteer whatever information they may already have about it.

Links to the Unit As students work through Unit 1, they will learn how archaeologists and historians use artifacts like Stonehenge to uncover and develop information about how people lived and what they believed in times before recorded history.

Stony Silence Have students read the text on Stonehenge and examine the various views of it closely, noting that some are photographs of it as it now appears and others show drawings of how it might have looked when it was first built. Also have the class use their fingers to pinpoint on the pictured globe where in the world it is found (in England in northwestern Europe). Help students to recognize the toll that time has taken on Stonehenge, how thousands of years out in the open, subject to wind and rain, have eroded its pillars and sent many of its stones crashing to the ground.

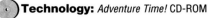

Resource REMINDER

National Geographic Poster
Geo Adventures *Daily Geography Activities*
Technology: *Adventure Time!* CD-ROM
Desk Map

BACKGROUND INFORMATION

MORE ABOUT STONEHENGE
- Stonehenge probably goes back nearly 5,000 years in time to c. 2800 B.C.
- At that time the site was enclosed by a circular ditch. Inside the ditch, a ring of 56 pits were dug in which cremated bodies were buried.
- Placing of the stone uprights probably began about 700 years later and was added to from time to time.
- The stones came from as far away as the mountains of southwestern Wales and as near as about 20 miles. They were chiseled with stone hammers. In about 1500 B.C., the stones were rearranged into the layout that we see today.

Stony Silence

Some of the stones have toppled. But others still stand, tall and mysterious, on this plain in southern England—just as they have for thousands of years. Who built Stonehenge? How were the 50-ton stones transported to this place and raised up by prehistoric people using only simple tools? And, perhaps more mysterious, why? Some archaeologists suggest that Stonehenge may have been a temple that marked the movements of the sun. But we may never know for sure.

GEO JOURNAL

If you could talk to one of the workers who helped build Stonehenge long ago, what questions would you ask?

5

Refer students to the two drawn illustrations showing the building of Stonehenge and its early form. Introduce the term *symmetry* as you point out how the two sides of the circle are mirror images of each other, as are the capped pillars within the circle. You may want to discuss the idea that humans often find symmetry pleasant to the eye, perhaps because they are symmetrical themselves—two arms, two legs, and so on.

Again, refer students to the drawing of the building of Stonehenge and remind them of the text question, "How were the 50-ton stones transported to this place?" Have them identify the answer that this drawing suggests (rolling them on logs across the ground).

Using the Geo Journal As students approach making up questions for their journals, encourage them to think not only in terms of the technical aspects of building Stonehenge, but also about the beliefs that the workers might have held about what they were creating.

 Technology CONNECTION

ADVENTURE TIME! CD-ROM
Have students *Explore* on the *Adventure Time!* CD-ROM.

CURRICULUM CONNECTION

LINKS TO SCIENCE Refer students to the text statement that "Stonehenge may have been a temple that marked the movements of the sun." Explain to them that scientists have determined that Stonehenge's axis is pointed at least roughly in the direction of sunrise on the summer solstice.

Have students work with partners to research what the summer solstice and winter solstice are—what they mark, when they occur, and how they involve Earth's movement. Have each set of partners prepare an illustrated report of their findings.

THEMES of GEOGRAPHY

As you work through Unit 1 with your students, consider the following themes:

Regions Regions are areas with common features that distinguish them from other areas. As you read Lesson 1 of Chapter 1, have students identify regions by characteristics such as landforms, climate, culture, history, and government.

Human/Environmental Interactions The surroundings in which we live influence and are influenced by people. Discuss these interactions as you read about early cultures in Chapter 3. Encourage students to summarize their findings under two headings: "People Affect Their Environment" and "Environment Affects People."

CHAPTER 1 Regions

Pages 6–21

CHAPTER OVERVIEW

There are over four billion people living in different parts of the world and they differ from one region to another. The people in Mexico City have a different culture from the people in a Chinese rice terrace. The variety of the world's regions and cultures is what makes them so interesting.

GEO ADVENTURES DAILY GEOGRAPHY ACTIVITIES

Use **Geo Adventures** Daily Geography activities to assess students' understanding of geography skills.

CHAPTER PLANNING GUIDE

LESSON 1	GEOGRAPHYSKILLS	LESSON 2
SUGGESTED PACING: 2 DAYS	SUGGESTED PACING: 1 DAY	SUGGESTED PACING: 3 DAYS
World Regions pp. 8–11	**Working With Latitude And Longitude** pp. 12–13	**Regions And Culture** pp. 14–19
CURRICULUM CONNECTIONS Links to Science, p. 9	**RESOURCES** Practice and Project Book, p. 7 Transparency Maps 10a, 10b ◉ TECHNOLOGY *Adventure Time!* CD-ROM	**CURRICULUM CONNECTIONS** Links to Language Arts, p. 15
CITIZENSHIP Using Current Events, p. 10		**CITIZENSHIP** Understanding Government, p. 17
RESOURCES Practice and Project Book, p. 6 Anthology, pp. 2–3 Desk Map		**INFOGRAPHIC** Cultures Around the World, pp. 18–19
		RESOURCES Practice and Project Book, p. 8 ◉ TECHNOLOGY *Adventure Time!* CD-ROM

LEARNING STYLE: Visual

ON YOUR OWN

30 MINUTES OR LONGER

Design a Park

Objective: To prepare students to recognize the concept of "regions."

Materials: markers, pencils, drawing paper

1. Ask students to think about different parks they have seen. What special facilities do the parks provide? Point out that a park's recreation area may be a basketball court, playground, swimming pool, etc.
2. Invite students to design their own parks with a variety of areas, and to make a map.
3. Invite students to share their park designs.

CHAPTER REVIEW

SUGGESTED PACING: 1 DAY

pp. 20–21

RESOURCES

Practice and Project Book, p. 9

⬤TECHNOLOGY Videodisc/Video Tape 5

Assessment Book: Chapter 1 Test

Transparency: Graphic Organizer, Main Idea Table

SDAIE SUPPORT SHELTERED INSTRUCTION

READING STRATEGIES & LANGUAGE DEVELOPMENT

Using Visuals/Prefixes, p. 8, Lesson 1
Cause and Effect/Word Origins, p. 12, Geography Skills
Compare and Contrast/Language History and Etymology, p. 14, Lesson 2

SECOND-LANGUAGE SUPPORT

A Glossary of Terms, p. 10
Using Props for Terms, p. 15
Taking Notes, p. 20

MEETING INDIVIDUAL NEEDS

Reteaching, Extension, Enrichment, pp. 11, 13, 19
McGraw-Hill Adventure Book

ASSESSMENT OPPORTUNITIES

Practice and Project Book, pp. 6–9
Write About It, pp. 11, 19
Assessment Book: Assessing Think and Write, pp. T45–T47; Chapter 1 Tests: Content, Skills, Writing

Introducing the Chapter

To give students a sense of the wonder of Earth, invite them to picture themselves aboard a space shuttle looking back at our planet.

THINKING ABOUT GEOGRAPHY AND CULTURE

Have students examine the photograph of Earth and read the text on this page. Then have them examine the other illustrations to get a taste of the variety of geography and people on Earth.

RICE TERRACES OF CHINA

Help students recognize the ways people have changed their environment.

- *On which continent would you find this location in China?* (Asia)

- *How have humans changed geography to assist them in farming?* (by building terraces into the hills to provide more flat surfaces for farming)

HARBOR IN NAMIBIA

Namibia became an independent nation in 1990. Formerly called South-West Africa, it was a German protectorate and later a mandate of South Africa. The German influence has remained strong.

- *On which continent would you find Lüderitz, Namibia?* (Help students locate it in southern Africa.)

- *What tells you that it is a busy place?* (its skyline and busy harbor)

Resource REMINDER

Technology: *Videodisc/Video Tape 5*

Regions of the World

THINKING ABOUT GEOGRAPHY AND CULTURE

What do you think of when you see a photo of Earth from outer space? Try imagining a world of over 6 billion people, living in thousands of places. Some may have lives much like yours. People's lives may be as different as night and day. These differences, as well as the similarities, tell the great story of the world's regions and cultures.

BACKGROUND INFORMATION

SOME THOUGHTS ON GEOGRAPHY

To encourage in students an interest in geography, read them the following quote from American writer Peter Blake describing how he sees U.S. geography:

- "No people has inherited a more naturally beautiful land than we: within an area representing a mere 6 percent of the land surface of the globe we can point to mountain ranges as spectacular as those of the Dolomites and to jungles as colorful as those of the Amazon valley; to lake-studded forests as lovely as those of Finland and to rolling hills as gentle as those around Salzburg; to cliffs that rival those of the French Riviera and to sandy beaches that are unexcelled even by the shores of Jutland; in short, to about as varied and thrilling a geography as was ever presented to man."

China
ASIA
Farmers in China have long used terraces like these in Guangxi to farm in hilly areas. The rice grown on these southern terraces feeds millions of people.

Namibia
AFRICA
Southern Africa has many busy harbors like this one at Lüderitz. People along Africa's coasts have traveled and traded by sea for thousands of years.

Austria
EUROPE
The town of Sankt Gallen lies high in the southern Alps. The people who settled these fertile mountain valleys have long been famous for their herding and dairy farms.

Canada
THE AMERICAS
This icy plain in the Arctic is part of a vast area of awesome beauty. Plants and animals, like this polar bear, have had to adapt to the Arctic's unique environment.

7

SANKT GALLEN, AUSTRIA

Help students recognize how people are influenced by their environment.

● **With which continent is this location connected?** (Help students locate Austria in Europe.)

★**THINKING FURTHER:** *Making Conclusions* **Why might this be a location where farming would be important?** (There are fertile valleys.)

ARCTIC PLAIN, CANADA

Point out that this seemingly desolate plain is home to a variety of plants and animals which have adapted to the unique geography of the place.

● **On which continent is this geography found?** (North America)

★**THINKING FURTHER:** *Making Generalizations* **Based on the contents of all these pictures, what generalizations can you make about the geography and people of Earth?** (Answers should reflect the variety in groups of people, in types of geographic features and resources, and in how people make use of the land.)

Technology CONNECTION

VIDEODISC/VIDEO TAPE 5
Enrich Chapter 1 with the *Legacies of the Past* segment on the videodisc.

BACKGROUND INFORMATION

QUESTIONS GEOGRAPHERS ASK
As geographers go on making their study of places on Earth, they ask themselves these questions:

● Location: Where is this place?

● Place: What is it like?

● Human/Environment Interactions: How have people changed the environment by their interaction with it?

● Movement: How has the place been affected by the movement of people, goods, and ideas?

● Region: How is this place similar to and different from other places?

These are questions students will be asking and answering as they continue through the year.

LESSON 1

PAGES 8–11

Lesson Overview

Dividing Earth into physical and cultural *regions* provides a useful way to study its *geography*.

Lesson Objectives

★ Identify features of geography.

★ Explain how geography shapes people's lives and is shaped by them.

★ Explain physical and cultural regions.

1 PREPARE

MOTIVATE Write *regions* on the board. Then read the *Read Aloud* section to students. Ask them to suggest regions they know and list them on the board.

SET PURPOSE Encourage students to think about Earth's great size. Use the *Read to Learn* question to start a discussion about why we divide Earth into smaller sections to study it. Have students preview the *Vocabulary* words and predict their use in this lesson.

2 TEACH

Understanding THE BIG PICTURE Help students see how geography affects life.

● **How does geography affect what you wear? How did it affect your route to school?** *(Use questions like these to get students to relate* climate *and physical features to their lives.)*

● **How do floods, earthquakes, and snowstorms affect many lives?** *(Encourage students to use news stories to show geography's effects.)*

★**THINKING FURTHER:** *Making Conclusions* **How important is geography to life on Earth?** *(Students should give reasons that geography is important to all living things.)*

Resource REMINDER

Practice and Project Book: *p. 6*

Anthology: *Seeing Earth from Space, pp. 2–3*

Desk Map

WORLD REGIONS

READ ALOUD

How many different living areas do you pass through each day? Bedroom, bathroom, kitchen, classroom, gym, lunchroom . . . all of these areas serve different purposes in your life. When you stop and think about them, these areas, or regions, also reveal a great deal about who you are. The world, too, is divided into many different regions. They can tell us much about what life is like all across planet Earth.

THE BIG PICTURE

Learning about life on planet Earth—that's what geography is all about. Geography is the study of Earth, how it shapes people's lives and is shaped in turn by people's activities. In fact, the word *geography* comes from a Greek word that means "Earth writing," or "writing about Earth."

You don't have to be in a classroom to learn about geography. Geography is a part of almost everything you do. When you coast down a hill on your bike, splash in a pool on a hot summer day, or wipe frost from a window in winter, you are experiencing part of geography. Each time you read a road sign on a highway or listen to the weather report on the radio, you become, for a moment, a geographer. You are using the tools of geography to study planet Earth.

Focus Activity

READ TO LEARN

What does studying regions tell us about the world?

VOCABULARY

geography
region
landform
climate
culture

8

SHELTERED INSTRUCTION

READING STRATEGIES & LANGUAGE DEVELOPMENT

USING VISUALS To help students draw information from visuals as well as text, explain that when we read about world regions, it is important to study pictures as well as words. Invite volunteers to describe times they traveled to a new place. How did they find their way? [landmarks and maps] Point out visuals in this lesson. Ask students how they might use these pictures and maps as they traveled around the world. **[SDAIE STRATEGY:** BRIDGING]

PREFIXES Refer to the photo of Earth on this page and ask students which *hemisphere* it shows. (Northern) Point out that the prefix *hemi* means "half" and have students reason out what *hemisphere* means. (half a sphere) Ask them if they know any other prefixes that mean "half" and, if necessary, help them with *semi* and *demi*. Have a student look up *hemidemisemiquaver* in a dictionary and explain its name.

WHAT IS A REGION?

Geographers divide Earth's surface into different kinds of regions. A region is an area with common features that set it apart from other areas. By studying different regions we can learn more about the world, more about ourselves, and more about people in other parts of the world.

Regions can be huge. Some are as big as half of Earth's surface. You have learned about these kinds of regions, called hemispheres, on pages G4–G5. Regions can also be very small. Your school's playground, for example, is an "exercise region" of your school.

Physical Regions

Regions that are defined by Earth's natural environment are called physical regions. Physical regions often have common landforms, such as mountains or plains.

As you can see from the map on this page, continents are the biggest kind of physical land region. Continents can be divided into many smaller physical regions. In the region of South America, for example, the Andes Mountains make up a physical region.

Climate Regions

Physical regions can also be organized by climate, or the weather pattern that an area has over a long period of time. For example, the climate around Earth's central part, near the equator, is hot and humid. This is the world's tropical region. Around the North Pole, by contrast, the average winter temperature is -30°F. The North Pole is located in one of the two polar regions of the world.

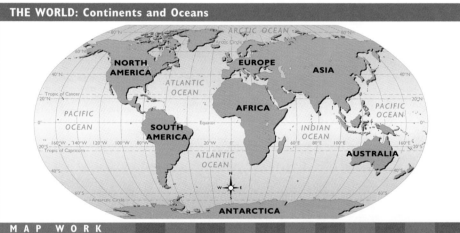

THE WORLD: Continents and Oceans

MAP WORK

Continents are the largest land regions.

1. How many continents are there?
2. What is the largest continent?
3. On which continent do you live?
4. Is most of Earth's land mass north or south of the equator?

MAP WORK: 1. seven 2. Asia 3. North America 4. north of the equator

9

CURRICULUM CONNECTION

LINKS TO SCIENCE Ask students who are interested in astronomy to prepare a class presentation about the constellations Cancer and Capricorn showing where they appear at different times of the year.

USING THE ANTHOLOGY

SEEING EARTH FROM SPACE, PAGES 2-3 After students read the selection, encourage them to discuss how astronauts' ideas about their home planet were affected by seeing Earth from space.

WHAT IS A REGION?
Have students use the map to identify geographic regions. Then have them read the text to define *region*.

Discussing Physical Regions Ask students to name physical features found in their region.

- **What is "physical" about a physical region?** *(natural features that can be seen, such as rivers, mountains, etc.)*

★**THINKING FURTHER:** *Making Conclusions* **Why can a continent be a physical region?** *(Students may suggest that a continent probably has a set of natural physical features.)*

More MAP WORK

Use the map to help students review the obvious geographic features of Earth.

- **Why could most of Earth's water be called one large body of water flowing around the world?** *(The oceans flow in and out of each other.)*

- **What are Earth's seven continents?** *(North America, South America, Asia, Europe, Africa, Australia, Antarctica)*

★**THINKING FURTHER:** *Compare and Contrast* **Which two oceans touch the most continents?** *(the Pacific Ocean and the Atlantic Ocean)*

Learning About Climate Regions Have students discuss the two extremes of climate. Help them locate the Tropics on their Desk Maps.

- **What is a tropical climate?** *(lots of sunshine, warmth or even great heat, possibly a good deal of rain)*

- **What is a polar climate?** *(freezing temperatures, persistent snow or ice)*

★**THINKING FURTHER:** *Compare and Contrast* **How would you compare or contrast our climate with a polar or tropical climate?** *(As students name climate features, reinforce the idea that climate is weather over time, not just that of one season.)*

Have students review the picture of Earth and the map on p. 9. Can they see any cultural regions? Why not? Help students understand that *culture* is something that physical maps cannot show.

Discussing Cultural Regions Help students develop an understanding of *culture* in a social studies sense.

● *How many different elements make up our culture?* (*Answers may include languages, beliefs, art, habits, customs, clothing, entertainment.*)

● *Why is Latin America a cultural region?* (*Most people there share a language, religion, and customs.*)

★THINKING FURTHER: *Classifying* *Why is Chiapas an example of a cultural region?* (*Its people speak a Mayan language and share customs in clothing, food, farming, and other traditions.*)

Discussing Other Regions Have students list their country, state, and city or town. Have them read the text to find out why these are also regions.

● *What do the places you named have in common?* (*All are political regions with their own governments.*)

● *How do these regions overlap?* (*The state is part of the country and the city/town is part of the state.*)

★THINKING FURTHER: *Compare and Contrast* *How are the political regions of Chiapas like those of the United States?* (*There is a country—Mexico, a state—Chiapas, and towns.*)

More MAP WORK

Use the map on p. 11 to help students see that people create regions, as nature does.

★THINKING FURTHER: *Classifying* *Which regions named on the map are created solely by nature? which by people?* (*By nature: the continents, the oceans; By people: the countries, states, and cities.*)

LOOKING AT REGIONS

If you were to fly in an airplane, you would see many landforms that make up the world's physical regions. Another type of region, however, is invisible from an airplane. These regions are based on culture. Culture is the way of life of a group of people, including their daily habits, beliefs, and arts.

Cultural Regions

To learn about cultural regions, you must come down to Earth and meet the people who live in a place. Language, religion, and ethnic heritage are some of the parts of culture that make up cultural regions. For example, South America, Central America, and most of the Caribbean Islands form the cultural region of Latin America. Most people there speak Spanish, Portuguese, or French—all offshoots of an old language called Latin. Religion also ties Latin America together, since many Latin Americans are Roman Catholics.

Within Latin America are many smaller cultural regions, such as the region of Chiapas (chee AH pus) in the southeastern corner of Mexico. In Chiapas, unlike in the rest of Mexico, most people are Indians. Many speak a Mayan Indian language rather than Spanish. They eat traditional foods such as *tamales de frijol* (tuh MAH leez duh FREE hohl), a dish made of corn, black beans, and hot peppers.

Other Regions

Most places are part of more than one type of region. For example, Chiapas is a cultural region, but it is a political region as well. Political regions are

Many people in Chiapas follow traditions of their culture. These include clothing, farming methods, and festivals. In some festivals, people wear masks like the ones shown here.

10

CITIZENSHIP★

USING CURRENT EVENTS Since 1994, Chiapas, one of the poorest states in Mexico, has been in the news often because of an uprising there against the Mexican government. Ask volunteers to use the *Readers' Guide to Periodical Literature* to learn about the uprising, to find the reasons for it, how the government reacted, and the aftermath. Have the researchers report the findings to the class.

SECOND-LANGUAGE SUPPORT

A GLOSSARY OF TERMS By creating a glossary of important terms, second-language learners will have a ready reference to use throughout the chapter. Basic terms to include are *geography, climate, landforms, region, physical region, climate region,* and *cultural region,* along with other terms chosen by individual students.

REGIONS IN THE WESTERN HEMISPHERE

NORTH AMERICA

ATLANTIC OCEAN

See inset map

MEXICO

PACIFIC OCEAN

Central America

SOUTH AMERICA

0   250   500 Miles
0   250 500 Kilometers

Gulf of Mexico

MEXICO

PACIFIC OCEAN

Mexico City

Tuxtla Gutiérrez
CHIAPAS

⊛ National capital
★ State capital
☐ Latin America

0   1,000   2,000 Miles
0   1,000 2,000 Kilometers

MAP WORK

Often, regions are part of other regions. Chiapas is a state in Mexico. It is also part of North America, which in turn is part of the Western Hemisphere.

Is Chiapas a physical or cultural region?

set up by governments. Just as Texas is one state of the 50 United States, Chiapas is one of the 31 states in Mexico.

Many of the people in Chiapas work as farmers. They live in the state's rugged countryside, in rural regions. Their lives are very different from the 20 million Mexicans who live 500 miles away in one of the world's largest urban regions—Mexico City.

By looking at Chiapas you can see that different kinds of regions often overlap. Look at the map on this page. How many different regions is Chiapas a part of?*

* Western Hemisphere (physical), North America (physical), Latin America (cultural), Mexico (political)

WHY IT MATTERS

Throughout this book you will be learning about life in different regions. You will discover how the environment has shaped life in each region. You will explore the physical and cultural features that make regions similar to and different from each other. You will study how these regions have interacted over time. Finally, you will learn how certain cultural forces have, over time, tied all of Earth's regions into one interdependent world.

✔️ Reviewing Facts and Ideas

MAIN IDEAS

● Geographers use regions to help them understand planet Earth.

● Physical regions are often defined by landforms and climate.

● Cultural regions are often defined by language and religion.

● There are many different kinds of regions, and they often overlap.

THINK ABOUT IT

1. What is geography? How is riding downhill on a bike an example of geography in action?

2. Why is it helpful to meet the people in a place when learning about their region?

3. **FOCUS** Why do geographers divide the world into regions?

4. **THINKING SKILL** List different regions of your community and then _classify_ them as physical or cultural regions.

5. **WRITE** Suppose that you are flying around the earth in an airplane. Describe the large bodies of water and landforms you see.

11

Discussing WHY IT MATTERS Help students see how learning about the regions of Earth can broaden our understanding. Introduce the idea of the "global village."

● **In what ways is the world a very large place?** (It is thousands of miles around and has billions of people.)

● **In what ways is it a "small world"?** (Through travel, trade, and electronic telecommunications, Earth's people are closely tied together.)

3 CLOSE

MAIN IDEAS

Have students answer the following questions on the board. Then discuss the answers, refining and expanding on them as appropriate.

● **Why do we divide Earth into regions?** (to make it easier to study)

● **What are major features of a physical region?** (landforms and climate)

● **What makes up a cultural region?** (shared cultural features, such as language, religion, ethnic heritage)

● **How do regions overlap?** (Some examples: A physical region has a climate; a state overlaps a city.)

EVALUATE
✔ **Answers to Think About It**

1. The study of Earth and how it shapes people's lives and is shaped by it; biking downhill involves interacting with a landform—a hill. _Make Conclusions_

2. Meeting people contributes to the understanding of the culture of a region. _Form Generalizations_

3. to break the world down into more manageable units for study _Summarize_

4. Answers should include physical and climate features as well as cultural features, created by people. _Make Judgements and Decisions_

5. Answers should include descriptions of vast oceans, great continents, flowing rivers, major mountain groups, and broad plains. _Main Idea and Supporting Details_

Write About It Ask students to write a paragraph describing differences between a physical and a cultural region.

MEETING INDIVIDUAL NEEDS

RETEACHING (Easy) For a poster-making activity, divide students into two groups. Tell them to create posters to attract visitors to their region. Have one half of the students concentrate on physical and climate features and the other half on cultural features.

EXTENSION (Average) Ask students what it would be like to move into their surrounding region from another part of the world. Have them write a letter to a friend describing the region—its physical, climate, and cultural features.

ENRICHMENT (Challenging) Ask students to choose a physical, climate, or cultural geographic feature of their region. Have them research local history to discover how the physical or climate feature affected the development of their area or how the cultural feature came to develop in their area.

Lesson Overview
Lines of latitude and longitude form a global grid that helps us locate places.

Lesson Objectives
★ Define *latitude* and *longitude*.
★ Explain the term *global grid*.

⭐ 1 PREPARE

MOTIVATE Ask students if people could plan a car trip if each map used a different system to show directions and distances. Preview the *Vocabulary terms.*

SET PURPOSE Help students see the need for a standard system for all maps. Direct students to the *Helping Yourself* box on p. 13. Help them understand how to use this feature to get the most from the lesson.

⭐ 2 TEACH

Why the Skill Matters Ask students to explain how a standard system helps map makers and users. Refer to both maps on this page.

● ***What are lines of latitude? Lines of longitude?*** *(latitude: imaginary lines that run east and west around Earth; longitude: imaginary lines that run north and south around Earth)*

Technology CONNECTION

ADVENTURE TIME! CD-ROM
Enrich the Skills Lesson with grid maps on the *Adventure Time!* CD-ROM.

Resource REMINDER

Practice and Project Book: *p. 7*
Transparency: *Map 10a, Map 10b*
Technology: *Adventure Time!* CD-ROM

GEOGRAPHYSKILLS

Working with Latitude and Longitude

VOCABULARY

latitude	parallel
longitude	meridian
degree	global grid

WHY THE SKILL MATTERS

The people of the world are separated by many differences in language, religion, and customs. One skill that most of us share today, however, is the ability to read maps.

People around the world have long made maps. Yet not all maps were the same. Some people drew their maps so that east, rather than north, was at the top of the map. Others made their own region huge and outlying areas tiny. It was not always easy for people to understand each other's maps.

Over 2,000 years ago, Greek scientists developed a way to divide the world into an imaginary grid so that all places could be exactly pinpointed. The Greeks based their system on two sets of lines called latitude and longitude. Lines of latitude run east and west. Lines of longitude run north and south.

Today mapmakers all over the world use this system. All places have their own unique address and can be located by anyone who knows how to use the system. Refer to the Helping Yourself box on the next page for help in locating places using latitude and longitude.

USING THE SKILL

Although lines of latitude run east and west, they measure distance in degrees north and south of the equator. A degree is a unit of measurement that describes the distance between lines of latitude and longitude. The symbol for degrees is °. As you can see on Map A, the equator is the starting line for measuring latitude.

LINES OF LATITUDE

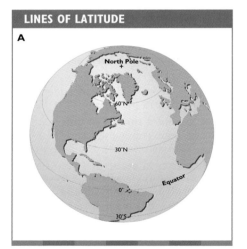

LINES OF LONGITUDE

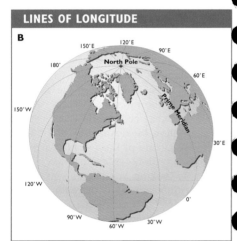

12

READING STRATEGIES & LANGUAGE DEVELOPMENT

CAUSE AND EFFECT Discuss the idea of cause and effect with students. Encourage them to find examples of cause and effect in their own lives. (Cause: I don't study. Effect: I don't do well in class.) Mention that much of their social studies reading concerns cause and effect. Tell students to look for a good example in this Skills Lesson. When they have completed their reading, ask them to identify this example. (Cause: the need for a standard system of mapping. Effect: the development of the global grid.)

WORD ORIGINS Both *latitude* and *longitude* come from Latin words. *Latitude* is derived from the Latin word *latus,* meaning "wide" or "broad." *Longitude* is derived from the Latin word *longus,* meaning "long." Students may find it helpful to think of latitude as lines going around the width of Earth and longitude as lines down its length.

Lines of latitude are also known as parallels. Parallels are lines that run in the same direction and are always the same distance apart.

If you imagine that Earth is an apple, lines of latitude would cut the apple into a stack of rings. Lines of longitude, by contrast, would cut the apple into equal wedges. Lines of longitude run north and south, and measure distance in degrees east and west of the prime meridian.

Look at Map B on page 12. The prime meridian is marked 0°, meaning zero degrees longitude, and it separates east from west. All lines east and west of the prime meridian are called meridians.

HELPING Yourself

- Lines of **latitude** measure the distance north and south of the equator.
- Lines of **longitude** measure the distance east and west of the prime meridian.
- Lines of longitude and latitude cross to form a grid that can be used to locate any place.

TRYING THE SKILL

On Map C the parallels and meridians cross each other to form a global grid. This grid makes it possible to pinpoint exact locations. Which line of latitude is New Delhi, India, closest to? Which line of longitude is it closest to?*

REVIEWING THE SKILL

Now find the correct latitude and longitude of Oslo, Norway, on Map C.

1. Starting from the equator, in which direction do you travel to get to Oslo?
2. Which line of latitude does Oslo lie on?
3. How might latitude and longitude be helpful to travelers?

Using the Skill
Call students' attention to the numbering system on maps A and B.

- *What are degrees?* (units of measurement for lines of latitude, also called parallels, and lines of longitude, also called meridians)
- *What is the symbol for degree?* (˚)
- *What is the number and name of the degree from which latitude is measured?* (0˚, the equator)
- *What is the number and name of the degree from which longitude is measured?* (0˚, the prime meridian)

★THINKING FURTHER: *Making Conclusions* **Could the equator have been set at any other line of latitude? Could the prime meridian have been set at any other line of longitude? Explain.** (Students should recognize that the equator's location is naturally determined; it is an equal distance between the poles and could not be elsewhere. The prime meridian is not at any naturally determined place and could have been set at any line of longitude on which people agreed.)

Trying the Skill Refer students to map C on this page and the *Helping Yourself* tips as you model the lesson.

- *How do latitude and longitude together create a global grid?* (by crossing each other)
- *What do the letters after the degree numbers mean?* (They tell if latitudes are north or south of the equator and if the longitudes are east or west of the prime meridian.)

GLOBAL GRID

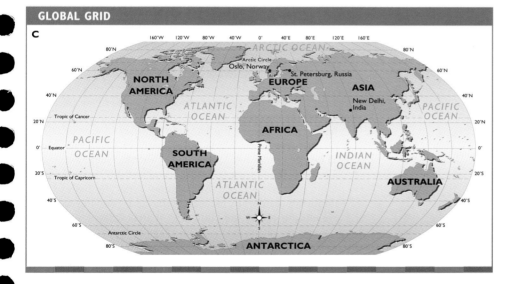

*30°N latitude, 80°E longitude

13

3 CLOSE

SUM IT UP
Refer students to the political maps in the *Atlas*, pp. R4–R19, to help them practice locating cities of the world by latitude and longitude.

EVALUATE
✓ **Answers to Reviewing the Skill**
1. north
2. 60°N
3. Travelers can use them together to find places on a map.

MEETING INDIVIDUAL NEEDS

RETEACHING (Easy) Have students draw a portion of a global grid by tens, from the equator to 40°N and 40°S and from the prime meridian to 40°E and 40°W. Have them label the degree mark of each line and also label the equator and prime meridian.

EXTENSION (Average) Have each student choose a continent shown in the *Atlas* (pp. R4–R19). Then have them prepare a table to name the continent, identify the lines of latitude and longitude that enclose the continent, and identify the latitude and longitude of the major cities.

ENRICHMENT (Challenging) Have each student make a list of ten cities or countries to visit. Have students exchange their lists and use the *Atlas* to locate each place by latitude and longitude.

LESSON 2

PAGES 14–19

Lesson Overview
Culture shapes people's lives and is shaped by people; *interactions* among cultures modifies those cultures.

Lesson Objectives
★ Identify the elements that make up people's culture.

★ Identify clues to understanding a specific culture, that of India.

★ Recognize how cultures interact.

1 PREPARE

MOTIVATE Have a student read the *Read Aloud* to the class. Refer to the photo of Azeez Narain and his family. Ask students what we can learn from the life of one boy in another culture. Tell them to look through the photos to note similarities to and differences from their own culture.

SET PURPOSE Use the *Read to Learn* question and the *Vocabulary* words to encourage students to look for clues about Indian culture.

2 TEACH

Understanding THE BIG PICTURE
Help students recognize the importance of *customs* in everyday life by thinking about their own customs.

● **What are customs?** *(ways of living that people practice regularly)*

● **What examples of customs can you give from American culture?** *(Have students begin with the "dress, play, eat, learn" mentioned.)*

★**THINKING FURTHER:** *Making Conclusions* **What do you think each of these customs tells us about our culture?** *(Examples: dress may show need for protection or modesty, play may show value of recreation.)*

Resource REMINDER

Practice and Project Book: *p. 8*
Technology: *Adventure Time! CD-ROM*

REGIONS AND CULTURE

READ ALOUD

Azeez Narain (uh ZHEEZ nuh RAHN) is an eleven-year old boy who lives in New Delhi, India. Azeez begins each day with prayers in his family's temple room and then heads to the kitchen for breakfast. Sometimes he eats toast and cereal. More often he eats poha, which is puffed rice with nuts and coconut roasted in butter and spices. Then Azeez rides a bus to school, where he studies 11 subjects six days a week. Four of those subjects are different languages.

Focus Activity

READ TO LEARN
What is daily life like for a boy in India?

VOCABULARY
custom
values
interaction

PLACES
New Delhi

THE BIG PICTURE

Do parts of Azeez's life sound familiar to you? Some probably do, like eating cereal for breakfast and riding a bus to school. Many such customs are shared by people around the world. Customs are ways of living that people practice regularly over time. Some of Azeez's customs, however, may not be familiar to you. That is because the cultural region of India is very different from that of the United States.

All cultures are made up of many different customs. Those customs determine how we dress, play, eat, learn, live with other people, and understand the world. Customs can reveal a great deal about what we believe is important in life. In fact, every detail of our life says something about the culture in which we live.

14

SHELTERED INSTRUCTION

READING STRATEGIES & LANGUAGE DEVELOPMENT

COMPARE AND CONTRAST Explain that one way to organize facts is by showing how things are the same (comparing) and how they are different (contrasting). On the board create a comparison/contrast chart for India and America. Have students skim the lesson, identify some similarities and differences, and list these on the chart. Have students complete the chart as they read. **[SDAIE STRATEGY: SCHEMA BUILDING]**

LANGUAGE HISTORY AND ETYMOLOGY In this lesson, the meaning "community-harmony" is given for Azeez's name. Students may want to investigate the meanings of their own names; for example, David means "beloved" in Hebrew, and Felicia means "happy" in Latin. Find a book of names (such as a baby-naming book) with meanings of proper names. Encourage students to look up their own names.

This is a typical street scene in New Delhi, India. How is it similar to an American city?

LIVING IN INDIA

Azeez Narain lives with his parents and six-year-old brother in New Delhi, India. The Narains share many customs with people in other parts of the world. Both parents work, for example. Azeez's mother teaches at a university and his father works as a journalist. Azeez and his friends like to ride their bikes and play computer games.

Many of the Narains' other customs are unique to the culture of India. Before you can understand these customs, however, you need to know a bit about India's past.

Culture and History

Throughout history people have brought new customs and ideas to India. Thousands of years ago the religion of Hinduism began shaping Indian culture. It remains a very important influence on Indian culture.

About 1,000 years ago Muslims began to settle in India. Muslims are people who follow the religion of Islam. Hinduism and Islam call for different ways of thinking and living. These differences in culture have caused conflicts between these groups in India.

About 250 years ago British traders arrived in India and brought their own customs with them. Britain took over

INDIA: Political

0 200 400 Miles
0 200 400 Kilometers

AFGHANISTAN
PAKISTAN
CHINA
HIMALAYAS
New Delhi
NEPAL
BHUTAN
Kanpur
Ganges River
BANGLADESH
Ahmadabad
Vindhya Range
Calcutta
MYANMAR (BURMA)
INDIA
Tropic of Cancer
Bombay
Hyderabad
Arabian Sea
Western Ghats
Eastern Ghats
Bay of Bengal
Madras
Bangalore
SRI LANKA
MALDIVES
INDIAN OCEAN

✷ Capital
• Other city

MAP WORK

The country of India is located in the southern part of Asia.

1. What bodies of water surround India on three sides?
2. Which countries border India?
3. What is the capital of India?

India's government in 1858 and ruled India for nearly 100 years. Today, some Indians still speak English.

The lives of Azeez and his family reflect the different cultures that are part of India's rich past. The Narains speak both Hindi and English. Azeez loves to play cricket, a game invented in Britain that is a bit like baseball. The Narains are Hindu, as are most Indians. However, the name *Azeez* is a combination of Muslim and Hindu words that means "community-harmony."

MAP WORK: **1.** Indian Ocean, Arabian Sea, Bay of Bengal **2.** Pakistan, China, Nepal, Bhutan, Bangladesh, Myanmar **3.** New Delhi

15

LIVING IN INDIA

Have the students locate India and New Delhi on the map on this page. Then have them return to the world map on p. 13 and see if they can locate India on it. (in southern Asia)

More MAP WORK

Use the map on this page both to familiarize the class with India and to review geography concepts.

● *Where does Azeez live?* (in New Delhi, India)

● *Where does New Delhi lie in relation to the Tropic of Cancer? What does that tell you about its climate?* (just north of the Tropic of Cancer; in a subtropical climate)

● *Roughly which line of latitude borders India's southern tip?* (roughly 10°N latitude)

● *The Tropic of Cancer runs through India. What does that tell you about India's climate?* (A good part of India must have a tropical climate.)

★THINKING FURTHER: *Cause and Effect* *Much of India's northern border is formed by the highest mountain range in the world. What effect might this have on reaching India from the northeast by land?* (Mountains act as a barrier to would-be visitors from that direction.)

Discussing Culture and History

Help students see that cultures develop over time. Introduce the concept of cultural borrowing as groups meet each other.

● *Why does India have more than one major religion?* (Muslims settled there after Hindus already lived there.)

● *Why is English a major language in India?* (The English-speaking British ruled India for about 100 years.)

● *What signs can you find that Indians have adopted customs from others?* (Many Indians speak English; many play cricket, a British game.)

★THINKING FURTHER: *Sequencing* *How would you draw a time line to show the sequence of groups living and arriving in India?* (Students should show a sequence from Hindus to Muslims to British.)

CURRICULUM CONNECTION

LINKS TO LANGUAGE ARTS Use the following quotation to launch a discussion of the importance of good use of language to a culture. Ask students whether they agree or disagree with the quotation.

● "Language makes culture, and we make a rotten culture when we abuse words."—Cynthia Ozick, 1972

SECOND-LANGUAGE SUPPORT

USING PROPS FOR TERMS Whenever possible, provide props for items mentioned in the discussion of cultures and daily life. These props often help to reinforce vocabulary for second-language learners. Props may be actual items or photographs of these items. For example, you might show a photograph of the cricket game mentioned on p. 15.

CULTURE
HAS MANY PARTS

Help students recognize how culture touches all aspects of life.

Discussing Values and Beliefs
Help students to appreciate that *values* and beliefs are central to life.

- **What are values?** *(things that people believe are the most important things in life)*

- **From where do people gain their values?** *(often from family members who pass down religious beliefs)*

- **What are Azeez's values?** *(that all living things have souls, the importance of simplicity, not being attracted to money, kindness to all living creatures, a vegetarian diet)*

★**THINKING FURTHER:** *Classifying*
Which of Azeez's customs are like your own? Which are different? *(Students can make two lists and in "customs like their own," they may include "eating breakfast"; in "customs that are different" they may include "foods eaten.")*

Learning About Culture at Home
Encourage students to use both text and pictures to learn about Azeez's culture.

- **What does Azeez's home tell you about his culture's attitudes toward education? toward country? toward religion?** *(Encourage students to point to specific items—books, television, temple, artwork—in the home as evidence for their answers.)*

★**THINKING FURTHER:** *Compare and Contrast* **How alike and how different would you say Azeez's Indian values are from values in the culture you know?** *(Students may note that they are like some of their own values and unlike other values they know.)*

Discussing Cultures Change Remind students of the cultural borrowing that they have already seen in the Indian culture. Also have them discuss the meaning of *interaction* and suggest some modes by which it takes place— trade, war, technology, movies and other internationally distributed media.

CULTURE
HAS MANY PARTS

As you can see, a culture is made up of customs that are passed down through time. Azeez's life shows that the ways we speak, play, and view others can reveal clues about our culture.

Values and Beliefs

One of the most important parts of any culture is its values, or the things people believe are most important in life. Many people's values are shaped by their religious beliefs.

As a Hindu, for example, Azeez believes that all living things have souls and are "a fraction of God." Azeez's parents and grandparents have passed many other Hindu values down to him.

> The most important lessons which my grandparents have taught me are that we should live a simple life and that we should not be attracted by money. We should not hurt anyone, including the animals. That's why we are strict vegetarians and don't even eat eggs.

Think about how the values or religious beliefs that you have been taught affect the way you live from day to day.

Culture at Home

You can get many hints about what a culture is like by seeing how people live at home. The Narains live in a six-room apartment. Their living room is filled with books, sofas, a television with 15 channels, and carvings and pictures of Indian leaders and Hindu gods. Mainly traditional Indian food is cooked in the kitchen, including Azeez's favorite dish—*uttapam* (OOT uh pam). Azeez describes this as "a sort of south Indian pizza made of rice with vegetables, coconut, and dried fruit."

A temple room honors the Hindu god Krishna. Each morning and evening Azeez goes there to offer his prayers. On Sundays the Narains travel to the local temple to worship.

Think about how the way you live at home reflects your family's beliefs and customs.

Cultures Change

Cultures do not stay the same forever. They constantly change through their interaction with other cultures. Interaction is the exchange of ideas and customs.

The Narains, for example, do not cook only Indian food. Sometimes they make Chinese or American food as well. Once in a while Azeez plays chess, a game probably invented in India

---

over 1,000 years ago. The style of chess Azeez plays today, though, was created through interaction between Asian and European cultures.

Another part of Indian culture that has changed is the role of women. Today women in India, especially in cities, have much more freedom and many more rights than in the past. In fact, Indians elected a woman, Indira Gandhi, as head of their government in 1966. Azeez's 11-year-old cousin Kalayani (ka luh YAH nee) says of her future, "I can do anything I want to do."

Azeez at School

Just as home life reveals much about a culture, so does life at school. Azeez attends school six days a week and must wear a uniform. Because so many different languages are spoken in India, Azeez studies four different languages: Hindi, English, Bengali, and Sanskrit, which is an ancient written language. Classes are taught in Hindi and English. Besides languages, Azeez also studies history, geography, math, science, government, and music.

Azeez enjoys playing chess and making music with friends. Here, he is playing the mridanga, a traditional Indian two-headed drum.

* Understanding people in different cultural regions, traveling, and finding information might be difficult.

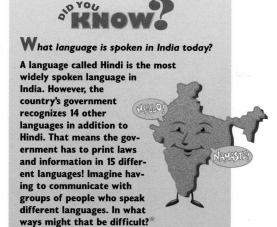

DID YOU KNOW?

What language is spoken in India today?

A language called Hindi is the most widely spoken language in India. However, the country's government recognizes 14 other languages in addition to Hindi. That means the government has to print laws and information in 15 different languages! Imagine having to communicate with groups of people who speak different languages. In what ways might that be difficult?*

HELLO!

NAMASTE!

Other Parts of Culture at School

One instrument Azeez plays in music class at school is the *mridanga* (mri DAHNG guh), a two-headed drum used in Indian music. Every day Azeez eats in the school lunchroom with his friends. No meat or egg dishes are served. Instead, the students have spicy vegetables and lentils with rice, and flat breads fried in butter.

Government

New Delhi, where Azeez lives, is the capital of India. India's government is similar to that of the United States. Indians vote for leaders to represent them in government. This form of government, called a representative democracy, is an important part of India's culture. It gives all Indians a say in how they are ruled. When Azeez turns 18, he, too, will be able to vote for the leaders of his government. How old will you have to be to vote in elections in the United States?**

**18

17

• *What are some examples of changes in Indian culture?* (American and Chinese foods, changing role of women, style of chess Azeez plays)

Discussing Azeez at School Encourage students to use both pictures and text to get to know Azeez's culture.

• *Why does Azeez study so many different languages?* (Many different languages are spoken in his country.)

Extending Did You Know? Have students read *Did You Know?* and discuss the reasons that it is useful to study different languages.

Discussing Other Parts of Culture at School Discuss how your school reveals parts of the students' culture.

• *What evidence can you find that offers clues to the importance of the arts in Indian culture?* (At least one of the arts, music, is important enough to be taught in school.)

> ★**THINKING FURTHER:** *Cause and Effect* **Based on what you learned earlier, what is the cause for no meat or eggs being served at school lunch?** (the religious belief that no animals are to be hurt)

Learning About Government Help students use their knowledge of their own government to discuss the role of governments.

• *What is the role of a capital in a country?* (It's the seat of national government.)

• *What kind of government does India have?* (a representative democracy, in which everyone over the age of 18 can vote for people to represent them in government. Point out to the class that India is the world's largest representative democracy, with nearly four times as many people as the United States.)

> ★**THINKING FURTHER:** *Compare and Contrast* **How would you compare Indian and American beliefs about how people should be governed?** (Students will probably see a great similarity; both systems stress the idea that the people should govern themselves through elected representatives and that everyone over 18 should have the right to vote.)

CITIZENSHIP ★

UNDERSTANDING GOVERNMENT Point out to the class the similarities between the forms of government in India and the United States.

• The British colonized both the area that became the United States and the area that is now India.

• Both countries had the British government as a "parent." After independence, both the United States and India adopted many British ideas of government.

• India drew up its constitution in 1950, after gaining independence in 1947.

• India stayed closer to the British model with a parliamentary form of government, one in which the government leader is chosen by the parliament, not directly by the people. The people of the United States choose its head of government by voting for electors for a candidate.

17

Infographic

Help students see how much they have in common with other children across the world. To start, they all share the institutions of family, school, nation.

Discussing Cultures Around the World Call students' attention to the lineup of home, language, and so on given for each young person in the *Infographic;* list them on the board. Have students fill in each for Azeez's life. Then give students time to read the data about these five people, and look for similarities and differences.

- *What similarities, large or small, do you find among all these young people?* (Students should note that all share the same basic institutions, some school subjects, and hobbies.)

- *What differences, large or small, do you find?* (There are differences in the nations they come from and in details of family makeup and types of homes and in languages and foods.)

- *What two subjects do all these young people study?* (English and math)

★**THINKING FURTHER:** *Making Conclusions* **Would you say that these young people are more like or unlike one another? More like or unlike you?** *(Let students debate this, using data to support conclusions.)*

Technology CONNECTION

ADVENTURE TIME! CD-ROM
Have students pick a country of the world to *Explore* on the *Adventure Time!* CD-ROM.

Infographic

Cultures Around the World

You have met Azeez Narain in this lesson. Now meet five more young people in this Infographic. What do they have in common? What are some differences in their lives?

Rachel Dennis, age 11
Halifax, Nova Scotia, Canada

HOME: Lives in a house on the Atlantic coast with her parents, brother, and dog
LANGUAGE: English
SCHOOL SUBJECTS: Social studies, science, English, math, art, health, music, physical education
HOBBIES: Gymnastics, horseback riding
FAVORITE FOOD: Waffles

Anna Patricia de Martinez, age 12
Lima, Peru

HOME: Lives in a brick house with her mother, brother, and grandparents
LANGUAGE: Spanish
SCHOOL SUBJECTS: Science, math, Spanish, social studies, English, physical education, music, gardening
HOBBIES: Swimming, volleyball, aerobics
FAVORITE FOOD: Pastelle de Manzanas (pie)

Olanike Olakunri, age 10
Lagos, Nigeria

HOME: Lives in a cinder block house with her parents
LANGUAGES: Yoruba, English
SCHOOL SUBJECTS: Math, English, citizenship, music
HOBBIES: Board games, mystery books, school running team
FAVORITE FOOD: Eba (a porridge made of cassava flour and okra)

18

EXPANDING THE INFOGRAPHIC

RESEARCHING AND WRITING Point out to students that so far, they have read about young people from only six other cultures, counting Azeez. What would researching young people in some of the approximately 175 or so countries of the world show? Have each students choose another country to research. Have them write their findings so that the class can assemble a much larger database of cultures.

You may want to suggest some resources to help them:

- Encyclopedia entries under the chosen country names.

- A library subject catalog for country names—"Life in ..."

- Young people's books that are generally in the nonfiction section— "The Land of the People of ..."

Brian Lawlor, age 11
County Tipperary, Ireland

HOME: Lives in a farm cottage with his parents and sister
LANGUAGE: English
SCHOOL SUBJECTS: Math, English, geography, music, science, Gaelic studies, physical education
HOBBIES: Hurling (like field hockey), and playing the accordion
FAVORITE FOOD: Apple tart

Harry Tan, age 10
Singapore

HOME: Lives in an apartment with his parents, brother, sister, and dog
LANGUAGE: Mandarin Chinese
SCHOOL SUBJECTS: English, Chinese, social studies, math, science, art, physical education
HOBBIES: Video games, skateboarding, baseball
FAVORITE FOOD: Rice with chicken in curry gravy

WHY IT MATTERS

Whenever and wherever people have lived, their lives have been shaped by the culture around them. A culture's language, government, values, foods, and entertainment make people who they are. Cultures also change as they interact with others over time.

This process of interaction is a big part of the story you will read in this book. In the chapters to come you will read about the world's many different cultures. Interaction between these cultures over the years has created the fascinating and complex world that we live in today.

✓// Reviewing Facts and Ideas

MAIN IDEAS

- All cultures are made up of similar parts, such as religion, government, and education.
- Values affect not only what people believe, but also how they live.
- Cultures change as people of different cultures interact with one another.

THINK ABOUT IT

1. What are some clues you can study to learn about a culture?
2. How has religion shaped life for people in India?
3. **FOCUS** What has Azeez Narain's life taught you about the many parts of Indian culture?
4. **THINKING SKILL** What are two *generalizations* that you could make about Azeez's family?
5. **WRITE** Write an article for visitors from other countries. Describe how culture in the United States has been shaped by interaction with other cultures.

19

Discussing WHY IT MATTERS
Point out to the class that Adlai Stevenson has compared all the people of the world to "passengers on a little spaceship—Earth." Help students recognize that on Earth, "We're all in it together."

- *Why are we creatures of our cultures?* (Our cultures shape us.)
- *What brings changes in culture?* (interaction with other cultures)

★THINKING FURTHER: *Making Conclusions* **Why is it important for us to learn about other cultures and for other cultures to learn about us?** (Knowledge can lead to understanding and cooperation.)

⭐ 3 CLOSE

MAIN IDEAS

Have students carefully consider each summarizing point.

- *How many different aspects of culture can you name?* (Have students list them on the board: religion, language, government, education.)
- *What examples can you give of a way a value affects how we live?* (To start the class off, remind them of why Azeez doesn't eat meat.)
- *How might the Indian culture have come to adopt Chinese or American foods?* (perhaps by people eating at Chinese or American restaurants)

EVALUATE
✓ **Answers to Think About It**

1. Accept any answers that reflect the items in the *Infographic*. *Recall Details*
2. It has profound affects on their values and behavior, for example, regarding food. *Recall Details*
3. It has given evidence of values, beliefs, customs, food, shelter, education, language, government, play, and family life. *Summarize*
4. Among the possibilities: they are religious, care about education, are middle class, and are patriotic. *Form Generalizations*
5. Hint: the role that immigrants to America have played *Main Idea and Supporting Details*

Write About It Tell students to write "Culture is . . ." on a piece of paper and then complete the statement.

MEETING INDIVIDUAL NEEDS

RETEACHING (Easy) Have students choose six cultural features and write them, spaced out, down the left side of a piece of paper. Opposite each, have them write a sentence saying something about that feature in Azeez's culture.

EXTENSION (Average) Refer students to *Did You Know?* on p. 17. Have them do research on the American national capital, Washington, D.C., and write a *Did You Know?* about it, modeled on the original and giving information about similar topics.

ENRICHMENT (Challenging) Have students do research on the variety of languages spoken in India and the areas of the country in which they are spoken. (India's state boundaries are drawn largely along linguistic lines.) Have them draw maps of India and show in what areas the major languages are spoken.

Answers to
THINKING ABOUT VOCABULARY

1. values
2. longitude
3. region
4. culture
5. latitude
6. geography
7. climate
8. landform
9. degree
10. custom

Answers to
THINKING ABOUT FACTS

1. The study of Earth, how it shapes people's lives and is shaped by people's activities; it can help us learn about Earth and thus help us understand the world.

2. to divide Earth into smaller segments to help us learn about each one

3. physical, climate, cultural

4. its geographic features that can be seen, such as landforms and rivers

5. Each is the starting place for its form of measurement—the equator for latitude and the prime meridian for longitude.

6. A place can be located by where the nearest lines of latitude and longitude cross.

7. the way of life of a people, including their daily habits, beliefs, and arts

8. Accept any reasonable way, including how culture influences language spoken, foods eaten, customs followed, values held, religions practiced, government instituted.

Resource **REMINDER**

Practice and Project Book: *p. 9*
Assessment Book: *Chapter 1 Test*
Technology: *Videodisc/Video Tape 5*
Transparency: *Graphic Organizer,*
Main Idea Table

CHAPTER 1 REVIEW

THINKING ABOUT VOCABULARY

Number a sheet of paper from 1 to 10. Beside each number write the word from the list below that best matches the statement.

climate	landform
culture	latitude
custom	longitude
degree	region
geography	values

1. The things that people believe are most important in life

2. The distance east or west of the prime meridian measured by imaginary lines that run north and south on a map or globe

3. An area with common features that set it apart from other areas

4. The way of life of a group of people at a particular time that includes their daily habits, beliefs, and arts

5. The distance north or south of the equator measured by imaginary lines that run east and west on a map or a globe

6. The study of Earth

7. A weather pattern of an area over a long period of time

8. A physical feature such as a mountain range, plain, or plateau

9. A unit of measurement describing the distance between lines of latitude and longitude

10. A way of living that people practice regularly over time

THINKING ABOUT FACTS

1. What is geography and what can we learn by studying it?

2. Why do geographers use the concept of regions?

3. What are three types of regions?

4. What defines a physical region?

5. What do the equator and the prime meridian have in common?

6. How does a global grid make it possible to find locations?

7. What makes up a culture?

8. Explain one way in which culture influences a country.

9. What is the role that religion plays in a culture?

10. How is India's government an example of cultural interaction?

THINK AND WRITE

WRITING A PARAGRAPH OF DESCRIPTION
Write a paragraph about the region where you live. In it describe the region's major landforms, its climate, and some important features of its culture.

WRITING A LETTER
Write a letter to Azeez Narain in India. Tell him about the culture and values of the community in which you live. Also tell him about some of the ways you think your life is similar to or different from his.

WRITING A TRAVEL PAMPHLET
Write a brief pamphlet about an interesting place you have visited. Suppose you are writing it for people from another country who will be visiting the place you describe.

SECOND-LANGUAGE SUPPORT

TAKING NOTES Introduce second-language learners to the following method of reviewing the information in a chapter. Model for them how to make an outline in their notebooks using the headings in each lesson. For each heading, help them find the most important ideas and list them in phrases from the text. Then work with students to construct summary sentences that express the most important ideas and information under each heading. Teacher modeling and supervision will help students learn how to do this form of review and note-taking on their own. If necessary, demonstrate for students how to use these notes to answer the questions and do the exercises in the Chapter Review. Pay particular attention to second-language learners' acquisition of new vocabulary in these early lessons. Make sure they add new vocabulary to their glossaries and use the vocabulary orally in discussions.

APPLYING GEOGRAPHY SKILLS

LONGITUDE

Use the map on this page to answer the following questions.

1. What are lines of longitude?

2. What is the prime meridian?

3. What is the first line of longitude shown west of the prime meridian? What is the first line of longitude shown east of the prime meridian?

4. How far apart are the lines of longitude shown on the globe?

5. What is useful about having lines of longitude on a map?

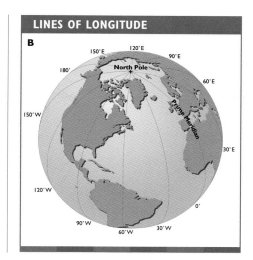

LINES OF LONGITUDE

9. It reflects the values and beliefs of a people and thus influences their behavior.

10. India's government reflects the interaction of various Indian cultures as well as British influence; India's government prints documents in many languages used in the country and borrowed the British idea of representative democracy.

Answers to
APPLYING GEOGRAPHY SKILLS

1. Lines of longitude are imaginary lines that circle Earth running north and south.

2. It is the line of longitude marked 0 that separates east from west.

3. 30 degrees W; 30 degrees E

4. 30 degrees

5. They provide a grid that makes it possible to pinpoint locations of places shown on the map.

Summing Up the Chapter

Copy the main idea table below on a separate sheet of paper. Then place each item in the feature list in the correct category below. Think of other features you might want to add. When you have completed the table, write a paragraph answering the question "How might the land, water, and climate of a region help shape the culture of the people who live there?"

MAIN IDEA	The geographical features of a region—land, water, climate—help shape the culture of the people who live there.
Features	landforms, temperature, religion, education, bodies of water, vegetation, humidity, rainfall, music, natural resources, air currents, government, soil, latitude, values, altitude

PHYSICAL	CLIMATE	CULTURAL
landforms	rainfall	religion
bodies of water	temperature	education
vegetation	latitude	values
natural resources	air currents	government
soil	humidity	music
altitude		

Technology CONNECTION

VIDEODISC/VIDEO TAPE 5
Enrich Chapter 1 with the *Legacies of the Past* segment of the videodisc.

Search Frame 45670 Side B

SUGGESTIONS FOR SUMMING UP THE CHAPTER

After students have copied the Main Idea Table on their papers, have them read the main idea aloud and discuss it. Then have them review the material given in Lesson 1 about the three categories in the table— physical, climate, cultural—and categorize the features listed in the chart in their appropriate columns. (Answers are shown in the reproduced pupil page above.) When students have completed their categorizing, have them study the features in the first two columns and try to think of ways those features affect the ways people live and work. For example, rainfall and temperature affect the kind of crops that can and cannot be grown, the clothing people wear, and the kinds of homes people build. The ways physical and climate features affect people should serve as the basis for students' paragraphs.

ASSESSING, THINK AND WRITE: *For performance assessment, see Assessment Book, Chapter 1, pp. T45-T47.*

CHAPTER 2
A Look into the Past

Pages 22–41

CHAPTER OVERVIEW

People have always wanted to know what life was like before them. There are places that were built by people many centuries ago, such as pyramids and the Parthenon. The ruins remain but the people who built them are gone. People can learn about themselves and others from the past.

GEO ADVENTURES DAILY GEOGRAPHY ACTIVITIES

Use **Geo Adventures** Daily Geography activities to assess students' understanding of geography skills.

CHAPTER PLANNING GUIDE

LESSON 1	**THINKINGSKILLS**	**LESSON 2**
SUGGESTED PACING: 2 DAYS	SUGGESTED PACING: 1 DAY	SUGGESTED PACING: 2 DAYS
Understanding History pp. 24–29	**Decision Making** pp. 30–31	**Iceman Of The Alps** pp. 32–37
CURRICULUM CONNECTIONS Links to Science, p. 25 Links to Math, p. 27 Links to Language Arts, p. 27 **CITIZENSHIP** Linking Past and Present, p. 28 **FIELD TRIP** Visit a Historical Society, p. 25 **RESOURCES** Practice and Project Book, p. 10	**RESOURCES** Practice and Project Book, p. 11 Transparency: Graphic Organizer	**CURRICULUM CONNECTIONS** Links to Science, pp. 34, 35, 36 **CITIZENSHIP** Contributing to the Community, p. 36 **RESOURCES** Practice and Project Book, p. 12 Desk Map Anthology, pp. 4–7

CHAPTER REVIEW
SUGGESTED PACING: 1 DAY

pp. 40–41

RESOURCES
Practice and Project Book, p. 13
TECHNOLOGY Videodisc/Video Tape 1
Assessment Book: Chapter 2 Test
Transparency: Graphic Organizer, Main Idea Map

LEARNING STYLE: Visual

ON YOUR OWN

30 MINUTES OR LONGER

Make a Time Capsule

Objective: To introduce students to artifacts.

Materials: paper

1. Ask the class to make a list of things people use.
2. Discuss how each item would give information to future generations about how people live now.
3. Ask which items to include in a time capsule. Then have each student write and illustrate something about life today, such as music, sports, or TV.
4. Place items in a box and decide with the class where to leave the "time capsule" so that people in the future will find it.

CITIZENSHIP

SUGGESTED PACING: 1 DAY

When Should Cultural Sites Around The World Be Protected? pp. 38–39

CITIZENSHIP
Using Current Events, p. 39

SDAIE SUPPORT

SHELTERED INSTRUCTION

READING STRATEGIES & LANGUAGE DEVELOPMENT

Problem and Solution/Colorful Terms, p. 24, Lesson 1
Fact, Nonfact, or Fantasy/Adjectives, p. 30, Thinking Skills
Predicting/Compound Words, p. 32, Lesson 2

SECOND-LANGUAGE SUPPORT

Sharing Artifacts, p. 26
Pairing Students, p. 34
Retelling/Response Journal, p. 40

MEETING INDIVIDUAL NEEDS

Reteaching, Extension, Enrichment, pp. 29, 37
McGraw-Hill Adventure Book

ASSESSMENT OPPORTUNITIES

Practice and Project Book, pp. 10–13
Write About It, pp. 29, 37
Assessment Book: Assessing Think and Write, pp. T48–T50; Chapter 2 Tests: Content, Skills, Writing

Introducing the Chapter

To give students insights into history, read them this quote from Winston Churchill: "History with its flickering lamp stumbles along the trail of the past, trying to reconstruct its scenes, to revive its echoes, and kindle with pale gleams the passion of former days."

THINKING ABOUT HISTORY AND GEOGRAPHY

Have students read the text on this page and examine the illustrations.

THE TAJ MAHAL, AGRA, INDIA

Let students know that they will investigate this beautiful building—fortunately not in ruins—in Chapter 14, *Empires and Cultures of Asia.*

- *Why would you probably pick this as the newest of the sites shown on these two pages?* (It is surely in the best condition.)

★ **THINKING FURTHER:** *Making Conclusions* **Why do you suppose that many people consider this one of the most romantic buildings ever built?** (perhaps its lush lines and dramatic setting)

MESA VERDE, COLORADO

The people who built their homes here are called *Anasazi,* a Navajo term meaning "the ancient ones." Students will learn more about the Americas in Chapter 15, *Empires and Cultures of the America.*

- *This "Cliff Palace" contained more than 200 rooms. How have people used the natural environment to create homes?* (They built dwellings right into the cliffs.)

Resource **REMINDER**

Technology: *Videodisc/Video Tape 1*

CHAPTER 2

A Look Into the Past

THINKING ABOUT GEOGRAPHY AND CULTURE

These photographs show places built by people many centuries ago. While the places or their ruins remain, the people who built them are gone. Read Chapter 2 to begin your journey into the mystery of the very distant past.

BACKGROUND INFORMATION

MORE ABOUT THE ANASAZI
- Archaeologists use the name *Anasazi* to refer to prehistoric Basket Makers and Pueblo Indians of North America.
- They divide Anasazi culture into eight periods, the first running from 5500 B.C. to 100 B.C. and the final one from 1600 to the present.
- The Cliff Palace shown here is in Mesa Verde National Park in Colorado and was a major center of trade and religion. Anasazi lived here from about 1100 A.D. to 1300 A.D.
- Another 10 national parks or monuments in Colorado, New Mexico, and Arizona are devoted to the Anasazi.

India
ASIA

The Taj Mahal in Agra, India, is among the world's most beautiful buildings. A ruler had it built to honor his wife.

Mesa Verde
THE AMERICAS

In what is now southwestern Colorado, Native Americans began building their homes right into the area's cliffs about 1,400 years ago.

Athens
EUROPE

Ruins at the Acropolis hint at the glory of Ancient Greece. Its people developed a great civilization and formed the first democratic government.

Egypt
AFRICA

Thousands of years ago traders made their way across the dry lands of northern Africa. Their journey was made easier by camels.

23

★**THINKING FURTHER:** *Compare and Contrast* **Though Mesa Verde is an ancient place, to what kind of modern structure might you compare it?** *(an apartment house)*

THE ACROPOLIS, ATHENS, GREECE

Point out to students that they will delve more deeply into the story of these magnificent ruins in Chapter 8, *Ancient Greece.*

● **How would you describe this place?** *(the ruins of what once must have been well-built and well-decorated buildings)*

★**THINKING FURTHER:** *Making Conclusions* **Do you recognize anything about buildings today that you can see in these ruins?** *(certain architectural styles, like the columns)*

DESERT CARAVAN, EGYPT

Explain to students that they will explore the desert environment in Chapter 10, *Ancient Arabia,* and in Chapter 13, *Empires and Cultures of Africa.*

● **What do you already know about deserts?** *(Encourage students to offer any information they have gleaned from television or movies about desert environments.)*

★**THINKING FURTHER:** *Compare and Contrast* **What differences would there be in living in each of the environments shown on this page?** *(Students may note differences in population density, availability of water and other resources, permanence of structures, and the like.)*

BACKGROUND INFORMATION

ABOUT THE LIVING PAST

● **THE TAJ MAHAL** English writer Rudyard Kipling wrote of it: "The splendour seemed to be floating free of the earth . . . the Taj took a hundred new shapes, each perfect and each beyond description." Another poet called it "a sigh made of stone."

● **THE PARTHENON** American writer Ralph Waldo Emerson wrote these poetic lines in praise of Athens' most striking sight: "Earth proudly wears the Parthenon/As the best gem upon her zone."

● **DESERT CARAVANS** Camel caravans have existed for millennia and are still a means of transportation. Camels are also important for milk, meat, wool, hides, and fuel (dried manure).

Technology CONNECTION

VIDEODISC/VIDEO TAPE 1
Enrich Chapter 2 with the *Discovering the Past* segment on the videodisc.

LESSON 1
PAGES 24–29

Lesson Overview
Historians employ a variety of tools to investigate the past and tell its story.

Lesson Objectives
★ Define *history*.

★ Identify tools historians employ to study and record history.

★ Differentiate between oral and written sources and between *primary* and *secondary sources*.

 PREPARE

MOTIVATE Refer students to the picture on this page; have them identify it as an old record player. Ask them to compare it with devices we use today to listen to music. Then have a student read the *Read Aloud* to students. Ask them to think about change over time.

SET PURPOSE Use the *Read to Learn* question to begin a discussion about how historians get information. Encourage students to note the *Vocabulary* words and look for them in the lesson.

2 TEACH

Understanding THE BIG PICTURE
Write *history* on the board and ask students to find a five-letter word within it (*story*).

● **What is history the story of?** *(the past, both the distant and recent past)*

● **Where do historians get the information they need to tell the story of the past?** *(from various sources, including books and bones)*

★**THINKING FURTHER:** *Making Generalizations* **How could you apply the saying, "A worker is only as good as his or her tools," to historians?** *(To write good history, historians need good sources.)*

 **REMINDER**

Practice and Project Book: *p. 10*

UNDERSTANDING HISTORY

Focus Activity

READ TO LEARN
What do historians do to look into the past?

VOCABULARY
history
oral tradition
artifact
primary source
secondary source

READ ALOUD
How has your life changed from the way it was five years ago? You're probably playing different games and have long outgrown your old clothes. Your family may have moved into a new home. Your life will continue to change as you grow older. Look around carefully. Ten years from now, everything around you—every object you use, every song you enjoy listening to—will help tell the story of what your life was like today.

THE BIG PICTURE
As the story of your life unfolds, it becomes part of an even bigger story of human history. History is the story of the past. People who study what has happened in the past are called historians. They may study details of daily life, or they may examine events that have changed the world. Historians have learned, for example, that people in Central America first enjoyed what we now call bubble gum hundreds of years ago. Historians have also learned how terrible wars brought huge changes for these same people in Central America.

Whether they study life-changing events or interesting details, historians use different kinds of sources, from books to bones, to discover what life was like in the past. Sources are an historian's most important tools. Like all tools, they need to be used carefully and skillfully.

24

 SHELTERED INSTRUCTION

READING STRATEGIES & LANGUAGE DEVELOPMENT

PROBLEM AND SOLUTION Explain to students that they can make sense of what they read by identifying problems and solutions. Have them read this page and state the problem and solution. [Historians need to find information about the past to write history.] Have students make collages to show some sources that historians can use. **[SDAIE STRATEGY: TEXT RE-PRESENTATION]**

COLORFUL TERMS In this lesson 1950s cars are referred to as "gas guzzlers," a phrase that calls up an image of a car drinking up gas quickly. Discuss with students how colorful colloquialisms like this enter the language, often enriching it in an amusing way. Point out that back in the 1920s, people called things they admired "the cat's pajamas." Encourage students to try to think of current colorful expressions (such as *channel surfing* and *couch potato*).

HISTORY ALL AROUND

Nina was so excited that she forgot to say hello as she burst through her grandfather's front door.

"Grandpa, guess what? We're getting a new computer tonight!"

"Why, hello Nina," Grandpa Joe replied, putting down his magazine. "What is all this I hear about a new computer?"

An attic or storeroom (above) can be an excellent place to find artifacts from the past. An old camera is an example of an artifact.

"It's a lot more powerful, so my friends and I can play CD-ROMs on it."

"Whoa, Nina," laughed Grandpa Joe. "I still don't understand that much about computers. See, back when I was your age, we didn't even have television. Most people didn't."

"What?" gasped Nina.

"It's true," her grandfather continued. "Back in 1950 our family was the first in our neighborhood to get a TV. That was a big deal! I'll never forget how our neighbors crowded around that TV wanting to see all the new shows. . . ."

Grandpa Joe was describing the past using oral tradition—passing on history by word of mouth. Oral tradition is an important way that people remember the past. This was how history was kept alive before writing was invented.

"You know," mused Grandpa Joe, "I kept that old TV set. It's up in the attic. You should see it! It's nothing like what we have today."

"Hmmm . . . OK," answered Nina, her curiosity getting the better of her.

Learning from Artifacts

The old TV was definitely an artifact (AHR tuh fakt) from another time. An artifact is an object made by someone in the past. The TV's small screen was housed in a big, bulky, wooden cabinet. It was hard to imagine that such a homely machine had once been the center of so much attention. Propped up against the TV was another artifact—a large plastic ring that rattled when Nina picked it up. What did it do? Nina shook it, rolled it, then looped it around her shoulder. She decided to take it with her and figure it out later.

25

HISTORY ALL AROUND

Help students to realize that not only is recent history all around us, but that we are making history. The way we wear our hair today, the cars people drive, forms of entertainment, events we witness will all be tomorrow's history, which later generations will study.

● **When Grandpa Joe tells Nina about the past, what centuries-old history-telling device is he using?** (oral tradition)

● **Why was oral tradition so important to history before writing was invented?** (It was the main way to keep the memories of the past alive.)

★THINKING FURTHER: *Compare and Contrast* **How is an interview with a world leader that you watch on television like a piece of oral tradition?** (It is a passing on of history by word of mouth.)

Discussing Learning from Artifacts Encourage students to look at pictures of artifacts throughout the lesson as they deal with this text.

● **Why is the old television set in the attic an artifact?** (It is an object made by someone in the past.)

● **What other artifacts can you spot in the pictures in this lesson?** (records, record player, old camera, old hats and umbrella, an ad for a car, an old magazine, among other items)

● **What artifacts do you see in our classroom?** (Help students realize that everything they see that was made by human beings is an artifact.)

★THINKING FURTHER: *Making Generalizations* **What might each of the artifacts around us tell future historians about our lives?** (Help students make generalizations. For example, wood, steel, plastics and books, pencils, paper, chalk, television sets, overhead projectors, computers reveal information about our use of materials and tools. The number of desks or size of classrooms suggest the size of a class. A temperature control system tells how we warmed or cooled ourselves.)

FIELD TRIP

If your area has a local historical society, try to arrange to take the class on a field trip there. See if you can find a volunteer to guide you and your students through the displays. Another option is to ask a person who has lived in your area for many years to give a class talk—with old photographs if possible—about earlier times in your area.

CURRICULUM CONNECTION

LINKS TO SCIENCE Have students compare the sizes of old record players and television sets with those of modern equivalents, and point out that the development of the transistor made miniaturization possible. Ask for volunteers to do some research on the development of transistors and their uses and report their findings to the class.

DIFFERENT SOURCES

Help students create a "shopping list" for a historian. As they discuss these pages, have them make two lists on a piece of paper, one headed "primary sources," the other "secondary sources," with examples under each.

Learning About Using Primary Sources Begin by having students define *primary* (first) and *secondary* (second).

- **What is primary about a primary source?** *(It came first in time because it was created or seen at the time of the event.)*

★**THINKING FURTHER:** *Making Decisions* **How would you decide if a source is reliable?** *(Get students to think about the reliability of sources. Students would probably want to know if a source could be trusted or its author had a reason to "bend the truth.")*

Discussing the PRIMARY SOURCE

Encourage students to relate the excerpt to the photos on this page.

- **The primary source describes an event that happened about 35 years earlier. Why would the speaker remember it?** *(The arrival of television was an exceptional event in people's lives.)*

- **How do the photos support what the excerpt says?** *(One photo shows people standing in front of a store window watching television.)*

DIFFERENT SOURCES

On the shelf next to the TV lay other interesting artifacts: a dusty model of an old car, a big scrapbook filled with newspaper clippings, and a yellowing stack of magazines.

Nina scooped up as many items as she could, along with a newer-looking book called *God's Country: America in the Fifties.* Then she headed back downstairs to examine her finds.

Using Primary Sources

Except for the book, all of the items that Nina picked up in the attic were primary sources from the 1950s. Primary sources are materials that were created during the time under study. They can be written things, such as magazine articles or advertisements. They can also be nonwritten things, such as toys or tools or pictures.

Read the following excerpt from one of Nina's written sources. It describes a time in America's past when televisions were a novelty. What clues in the text tell you this is a primary source?

Excerpt from
an interview published in *Television,*
by Michael Winship, 1988.

I first saw television when I was a kid growing up in Brooklyn. . . . We didn't own a television set—most people didn't. But the Texaco Star Theater *with Milton Berle was on Tuesday nights. So we all stood on the street, and the people who had a television set on my block would put it in the window facing the street. Half the block would gather —maybe 50 people would watch the show.*

In the early days of television, not everyone was lucky enough to own their own set (above). Often, people would crowd sidewalks to watch (left).

A Secondary Source

Secondary sources are records of the past that are based on studies of primary sources. Nina's secondary source was the book *God's Country: America in the Fifties.* This is a study of life in the 1950s written by J. Ronald Oakley in 1986. Read the following excerpt from *America in the Fifties.*

In the America of 1950, almost 90 percent of all families did not have a television set. . . . By the early 1960s, 90 percent of all American homes had at least one television set. Never had a new product expanded so rapidly or so quickly become an essential part of American life.

How does the information given in this secondary source differ from the information given in the primary source on the previous page?*

Different Viewpoints

Nina could appreciate the old TV in the attic much more now that she knew how rare TVs were in 1950. But what could she make of the cars from the 1950s?

"They were so *huge,* so different from the cars we have today," Nina marveled as she picked up the old car model. "They couldn't have been very practical—and they must have been real gas guzzlers, too."

"But people didn't *care* that much about being practical back then," Grandpa Joe answered. "We wanted comfort and grandness, and those cars delivered!" To support his opinion, Grandpa Joe turned to an old car advertisement in his scrapbook. Look at the advertisement on this page.

Nina and her grandfather looked at the model car from different viewpoints. Nina noticed how the car contrasted

An advertisement in a scrapbook can show what was important to car buyers in the 1950s.

with today's cars. On the other hand, Grandpa Joe was reminded of people's attitudes about cars during the 1950s. These different viewpoints brought them to different conclusions.

Historians often disagree about how sources should be interpreted, or how life in a past time should be remembered. Since their own viewpoints shape the way they view the past, historians can end up constructing different pictures of the same historical period.

Historians also have trouble reconstructing the past. The further back in time something happened, the harder their job becomes. In addition, many important sources from the past have been destroyed or lost. This makes it impossible to understand certain past cultures and events.

*It is not in the first person.

27

Discussing A Secondary Source
As students read, remind them to fill out their "shopping lists."

● **What is secondary about a secondary source?** *(It was not made at the time under study but is based on primary sources that were.)*

● **How much later did the author of the secondary source quoted here write about the history he reports?** *(25–35 years later; Oakley wrote in 1986 about the 1950s and early 1960s.)*

★ **THINKING FURTHER: Compare and Contrast What advantages do primary sources have over secondary sources? What advantages do secondary sources have over primary sources?** *(Primary: immediacy, being there. Secondary: having many primary sources to draw on, ability to look back at the "big picture.")*

Learning About Different Viewpoints This section provides an opportunity to look at changes of attitudes over time.

● **What does the term "viewpoint" mean? Does everyone have the same viewpoint?** *(Encourage students to see how people can form different opinions about the same thing. Differences may arise from the times people's attitudes were formed.)*

● **What viewpoint did Grandpa Joe have about cars in the 1950s? Why?** *(He thought they should be big, grand, and comfortable.)*

● **What viewpoint does Nina have about cars today?** *(Cars should be smaller and more efficient, reflecting concerns for the environment, for gas economy, and for more maneuverable size.)*

★ **THINKING FURTHER: Making Generalizations How would you support the following statement? Historians must be keenly aware of their own attitudes and must strive to discover as much information as they can about a subject if they are to write reliable history.** *(Students should point out that bias and sketchy facts stand in the way of writing accurate and reliable history.)*

Work through this section so that by the time students have finished it, they can list the steps in the historian's process.

- **How have attitudes toward television changed?** *(In the 1950s it was a novelty; today it is part of life.)*

- **How have attitudes toward the environment changed from the 1950s to today?** *(People today are more aware of threats to the environment than they were in the 1950s.)*

Discussing Looking at an Artifact Help students recognize the role of a primary source in identifying the hula hoop.

- **How did a primary source help Nina discover what the circular artifact was?** *(A magazine article from the time described a hula hoop.)*

★**THINKING FURTHER:** *Sequencing* **How would you list the steps in the process Nina followed to solve her historical problem?** *(1. finding an artifact; 2. questioning its purpose; 3. consulting primary and secondary sources; 4. interpreting from them the use of the artifact)*

Learning About Combining Sources Have students name different sources.

- **What sources did Nina use?** *(a hula hoop, primary and secondary sources, an article, a photo)*

★**THINKING FURTHER:** *Making Conclusions* **Why do multiple sources improve accuracy?** *(They offer different viewpoints.)*

PUTTING IT ALL TOGETHER

Based on the sources she had to work with, Nina was beginning to put together a picture of what life was like in the 1950s. In some ways the 1950s were similar to the 1990s. People worked hard and enjoyed relaxing with their families and friends. There were major differences, too. Television was still a new invention, so it was just starting to become the basic part of American life it is today. Cars were larger and used more gasoline. Conserving natural resources such as oil was not as much of a concern then as it is now.

Looking at an Artifact

But what purpose did the big plastic ring serve? The answer came as Nina flipped through a 1958 issue of *Life* magazine. A photograph in an article caught her eye. It showed teenagers swinging the rings around their waists.

28

A library is a good place to find primary and secondary sources. Your local library probably has sections for books and magazines from the past. Many modern libraries now also have computers and CD-ROMs.

The article called the rings "hula hoops" and said they were "the newest national craze. . . bigger than anything that ever hit the toy business." You can see a page from that article on page 28.

Combining Sources

Nina's article shows why written sources can be so valuable to historians. They can speak for people and things from another time. The article, a written source, helped explain the hula hoop, an artifact.

Without realizing it Nina had done work similar to that of a true historian. She used primary and secondary sources to shed light on her topic, life in the United States in the 1950s. She also examined artifacts to learn their purpose and importance in a culture. Lastly, she used and interpreted written sources to try to understand one of a culture's customs.

WHY IT MATTERS

The work of an historian is like that of a detective. Clues to an historical period or event may be deeply buried. So historians have to rebuild the past as accurately as possible, using the evidence that is available to them. Sometimes key evidence has been lost or destroyed, making the job even harder.

Historians are not alone in their task, however. They have skilled partners—scientists—who help them uncover written and unwritten sources from the past. You will read about these scientists and the work they do in the next lesson.

✓// Reviewing Facts and Ideas

MAIN IDEAS

- History is the study of what happened in the past.
- Before writing was invented, history was passed down through oral tradition, or word of mouth.
- Artifacts, or objects made in the past, can also tell how people lived.
- Historians use primary and secondary sources to interpret what life was like in the past.
- The sources that historians use, the way they use these sources, and their points of view, shape the way the past is remembered.

THINK ABOUT IT

1. How does oral tradition differ from a written source? How can both help to preserve history?

2. What is a secondary source? Give an example of a secondary source you use at school.

3. **FOCUS** How do sources help us to learn about the past?

4. **THINKING SKILL** What _effects_ do the sources available to a historian have on the ways she or he understands the past? How might a historian's point of view affect the way she or he understands history?

5. **WRITE** Use your imagination to write about how the artifacts in your classroom might be viewed by an historian 100 years from now. What are three conclusions the historian could make from these artifacts about life in the 1990s?

29

Understanding WHY IT MATTERS

Quote George Santayana aloud and discuss: "Those who cannot remember the past are condemned to repeat it."

> ★**THINKING FURTHER:** _Making Conclusions Why is it important that historians "get it right"?_ _(History must be accurate if we are to learn from it.)_

★3 CLOSE

MAIN IDEAS

Have students write their answers and then discuss them in pairs.

- **How would you define history?** (the study of the past)

- **How was history kept before writing developed?** (through oral tradition)

- **What are artifacts?** (objects people made)

- **How do primary and secondary sources differ?** (Primary were contemporary; secondary came later.)

- **How does a historian's viewpoint affect our idea of the past?** (Historians interpret data and artifacts.)

EVALUATE
✓ **Answers to Think About It**

1. Oral tradition is transmitted by speech. Both offer historical evidence. _Compare and Contrast_

2. a source recorded after the time under study, for example, a textbook _Main Idea and Supporting Details_

3. They help to tell us what happened. _Make Conclusions_

4. The sources' completeness or incompleteness affects accuracy. Ask students how accurate a story of their life could it be if the writer did not know when they were born, where they went to school, etc. _Form Generalizations_

5. Possibilities: mass production; education in schools; both print and electronic tools. _Make, Confirm, Revise Predictions_

Write About It Have students write a paragraph describing the steps in the historian's process and why each is important.

MEETING INDIVIDUAL NEEDS

RETEACHING (Easy) To encourage students to consult older relatives and friends as historical sources, have them develop in class a few questions to ask about the early days of television or computers. Have students interview their sources and record their answers, for later discussion in class.

EXTENSION (Average) Have students keep a journal of important, amusing, or uncommon events in their lives for one week and then use these primary sources to write a history of their week.

ENRICHMENT (Challenging) Give students a historical problem to solve. Inform them that in the 1970s, Americans were jolted out of their "gas-guzzling" ways by the actions of a group known as OPEC. Have them research OPEC and the action it took that changed drivers' behavior so drastically, and then write a secondary source report.

SKILLS LESSON
PAGES 30–31

Lesson Overview
To make a good *decision*: set a goal, identify alternatives, and choose a way to reach it.

Lesson Objective
★ Identify steps in decision making.

⭐ 1 PREPARE

MOTIVATE Have students read *Why the Skill Matters;* discuss why it is important for historians to make good choices (to present accurate and reliable history).

SET PURPOSE Go on to discuss why it is important for everyone to make well-reasoned decisions. Let students know that they will learn a useful method of making decisions. Have them read *Helping Yourself* for a preview.

⭐ 2 TEACH

Why the Skill Matters Help students understand the nature of historians' choices.

● *Why do historians' choices involve decisions?* (Historians must decide what to study and how to interpret what they find.)

Using the Skill Help students understand the mystery that drove Schliemann and the clues he had.

● *What was Schliemann's goal?* (to find the location of Troy)

● *Which written source did he choose and why?* (Homer's Iliad; it was the earliest known account)

● *What nonwritten source did he use?* (observation of landforms)

Resource REMINDER

Practice and Project Book: *p. 11*
Transparency: *Graphic Organizer*

THINKINGSKILLS

Decision Making

VOCABULARY
decision
evaluate

WHY THE SKILL MATTERS

One of the most important parts of an historian's job is making choices. Every historian chooses which sources to study and how to interpret those sources. When historians make these choices, they are making decisions. To make a decision is to choose from a number of alternatives.

USING THE SKILL

One of the most thrilling historical studies ever made involved the search for the ancient city of Troy by Heinrich Schliemann (HĪN rihk SHLEE mahn) in 1870. Many legends told of a great walled city called Troy, where heroic warriors long ago had fought fierce and bloody battles. You will

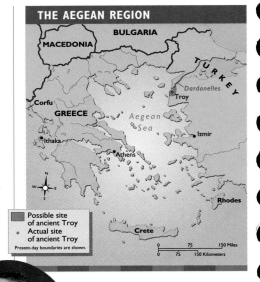

THE AEGEAN REGION

Possible site of ancient Troy
● Actual site of ancient Troy
Present-day boundaries are shown.
0   75   150 Miles
0   75   150 Kilometers

Heinrich Schliemann located the site of ancient Troy (left and above).

READING STRATEGIES & LANGUAGE DEVELOPMENT

FACT, NONFACT, OR FANTASY? Is it truth or is it fiction? Point out to the class that writers often use this tantalizing device to capture the reader's interest in their subject matter. In this lesson Schliemann faced the problem of determining if the stories about Troy were fact or fiction. Encourage students to think about how the question was answered. Also encourage them to evaluate the answer: Was it proved beyond a shadow of a doubt?

ADJECTIVES Call students' attention to the use of adjectives in this lesson, for example, *thrilling, heroic, fierce, bloody, magnificent.* Encourage students to discuss the effects that well-chosen adjectives can have on writing. Help them to see that vivid descriptive adjectives help the reader picture the subject and thus make writing more lively, but also allows a writer a way of inserting opinion, rather than fact.

learn more about these legends when you study ancient Greece in Chapter 8.

No one knew for sure whether Troy had been a real city or whether it had been created in the imaginations of ancient poets. Schliemann was fascinated by the stories of this old city, and he was determined to find its location and learn its secrets.

Now that Schliemann had set his goal, he identified the different alternatives for the possible location of ancient Troy. Some historians thought that Troy could be found on the island of Corfu, northwest of mainland Greece. Others believed that the city was located on the west coast of Turkey. Schliemann himself thought that Troy might be buried under a mound near the Dardanelles Strait in Turkey.

He was then ready to evaluate the different alternatives to choose the most promising location. To evaluate something is to judge its worth. In order to evaluate the possible locations of Troy, Schliemann examined many different sources of information. Among these sources were descriptions of Troy in a book called *The Iliad*, by the Greek poet Homer. Schliemann believed that this book was the most accurate source because it was the oldest one, written about 2,800 years ago. Schliemann also studied the landforms of Greece and Turkey in hopes of finding more clues about Troy.

From his research, Schliemann decided that the mound in Turkey he had seen was the best choice from among the different alternatives. This mound was called Hissarlik (hih sur LIK), and it was there that he began his search. In 1870 Schliemann and his wife Sophia began a large project at Hissarlik to

HELPING Yourself

- **A decision** is a choice between alternatives.
- Identify the **goal** you want to reach.
- Identify the different **alternatives** for reaching the goal.
- **Evaluate** each alternative.
- **Choose** the best alternative.

unearth the long-lost city of Troy. Soon they found the stone walls of an ancient city. As they dug deeper and deeper, they found gold and silver artifacts and other evidence of the magnificent city that had once been Troy. Eventually, the remains of nine cities, newer ones built upon the ruins of older ones, were uncovered. Today historians believe that the sixth city was the one that Homer wrote about in *The Iliad* many years ago.

TRYING THE SKILL

Refer to the Helping Yourself box for help in making a decision. Imagine that you are trying to learn about the history of your hometown. Your goal is to find the best historical source about the first people who lived there. What are three sources that you could choose to find out more about the first people in your hometown? Decide which of these sources is the best one. Why?*

REVIEWING THE SKILL

1. What are the main steps in making a good decision?
2. Why is it important to set a goal when making decisions?
3. Why is it important to identify alternatives for reaching a goal?
4. When might it be useful to be able to make good decisions?

* Books, old newspapers, interviews; each source is from a different point of view, so none should be considered the "best."

31

- ● *What location did Schliemann decide on and why?* (Hissarlik, located on the Aegean Sea, in what is today western Turkey, because it seemed most like Homer's description)

- ● *Where does it lie in relation to the Dardanelles? Judging from the map, what are the Dardanelles?* (just a few miles south; a strait connecting two larger bodies of water)

- ● *What large body of water lies to the west of the Dardanelles?* (the Aegean Sea)

- ● *Where do modern Greece and Turkey lie in relation to each other?* (just across the Aegean from each other)

- ● *What convinced Schliemann that he had indeed found ancient Troy?* (artifacts and other evidence)

★THINKING FURTHER: *Making Decisions* What do historians believe about Schliemann's location for Troy? (Ancient Troy was actually the sixth of nine cities at the site.)

Trying the Skill If students need more help than the *Helping Yourself* tips, add these tips: predict the long- and short-range consequences of each decision; judge the pros and cons of each consequence; determine the probability of each consequence; rank the three best alternatives; re-examine each of the three alternatives.

 3 CLOSE

SUM IT UP

Have students discuss the sources they found for early people in their region, evaluate the sources' reliability, and decide who the people were.

EVALUATE

√ **Answers to Reviewing the Skill**

1. identify the goal; identify and evaluate each alternative; choose the best alternative

2. so the aim of the decision-making process is clear from the start

3. to be sure to consider different possibilities

4. whenever there are choices, especially important choices

BACKGROUND INFORMATION

USING THE GRAPHIC ORGANIZER You may want to have students work with this Graphic Organizer transparency to help them organize their information.

LESSON 2

PAGES 32–37

Lesson Overview
Archaeologists enlarge our knowledge of history by using science to interpret artifacts.

Lesson Objectives
★ Identify methods archaeologists use.
★ Recognize the role of *archaeology* in understanding *prehistory*.
★ Recognize how archaeologists and historians trace ways people adapt to and change the environment over time.

1 PREPARE

MOTIVATE Call students' attention to the lesson title and the photograph of the rugged Alps on this page. Have a student read the *Read Aloud* to the class. Ask the class why the Simons called the police.

SET PURPOSE Read the *Read to Learn* question aloud and encourage students to look for ways that artifacts were used. Have them preview the *Vocabulary.*

2 TEACH

Understanding THE BIG PICTURE
Ask students if they have ever seen any TV shows that show scientists digging for artifacts from the past. Who are these scientists? What do they hope to learn?

● **What is archaeology?** *(the study of the remains of past cultures)*

● **What tools do archaeologists use to do their work?** *(a variety of digging tools, X rays, and tests for age)*

★**THINKING FURTHER:** *Making Conclusions* **Why can archaeologists help historians?** *(They add to evidence historians can use.)*

Resource REMINDER

Practice and Project Book: *p. 12*
Anthology: *Easter Island, pp. 4–7*
Desk Map

ICEMAN OF THE ALPS

READ ALOUD
It was warm and sunny in the Alps on September 19, 1991—a perfect day for hiking. As Erika and Helmut Simon moved along a mountain ridge, they spotted something in the melting ice. At first they thought it was trash, or maybe a doll. When they got closer Erika cried out, "It's a man!" The leathery-brown body was indeed human, lying half-buried in the snow. Shocked, the Simons hurried down the mountain to tell the police. They would not learn until several days later that the body they stumbled upon was over 5,000 years old.

Focus Activity

READ TO LEARN
What can artifacts tell us about the ancient past?

VOCABULARY
archaeology
excavate
prehistory

PEOPLE
Konrad Spindler

PLACES
Alps

THE BIG PICTURE
History is full of mysteries. It is the job of historians to do the detective work needed to solve these mysteries. As you learned in the last lesson, written sources can be a big help to historians trying to interpret past events. Artifacts are helpful clues, too.

The science of archaeology (ahr kee AHL uh jee) is the study of the remains of past cultures. Archaeologists carefully dig up, or excavate, historical sites. They use instruments to discover, identify, and save these remains. They take X rays to see what is inside an object and how it was made. They do tests to determine the age of artifacts. Above all, archaeologists must link different clues to figure out what artifacts and remains might say about how people lived in past cultures.

32

SHELTERED INSTRUCTION

READING STRATEGIES & LANGUAGE DEVELOPMENT

PREDICTING Explain to students that one way to get more from their reading is first to skim the pages, concentrating on headings and illustrations. Based on this preview, they should form predictions about what they will learn and list them on the board; for example, "A mysterious discovery in the Alps will turn into a major archaeological find." As students read the lesson, have them verify or change their predictions. **[SDAIE STRATEGY: MODELING]**

COMPOUND WORDS Point out that this lesson uses many hyphenated compound words such as *knife-blade,* which is made up of two separate words but has a distinct meaning of its own. Encourage students to spot other hyphenated compound words *(belt-pouch)* in the lesson and use the components to explain the compounds.

A DISCOVERY IN THE ALPS

The Alps are Europe's highest mountain range. They contain dozens of snow-covered peaks and massive slabs of ice called glaciers. On some days the Alps are a beautiful and safe place to hike. On other days the Alps can be deadly. In fact, each year more than 100 people die in sudden snowstorms there.

Thus police and local reporters were not too surprised when the Simons found a body in the Alps. Two days after the discovery, a local newspaper reported:

Judging by the dead man's equipment, he was a mountaineer. It seems that the accident occurred some decades ago. The body has not yet been identified.

The article was accurate in many ways, but very wrong in one. Soon it would become clear that this "mountaineer" had been frozen for far more than 40 or 50 years.

A Mystery in the Ice

A few days after the Simons made their discovery, the police set out to recover the body. Look at the map on this page to see where the body was found. The police also saved some items scattered around the area. These included a knife, some bits of rope and leather, and an ax. After a closer look they realized that this ax was no ordinary hiking tool. Its metal blade was lashed to a wooden handle with strips of leather. The ax looked hundreds of years old!

The story of the "Iceman" now became big news, especially to archaeologists. Five days after the Iceman was found, German archaeologist Konrad Spindler came to investigate. When he saw the Iceman's belongings, Spindler's eyes widened. "This [was] something any first-year archaeology student could identify," he later wrote. Spindler estimated the Iceman's age by observing that his ax was made of copper and his knife-blade of chipped stone. Looking up, Spindler announced his conclusion: "Roughly 4,000 years old!"

Later on, detailed testing would prove that the Iceman was actually about 5,300 years old. From these results, archaeologists realized that the Iceman had lived in Europe in the age of prehistory, or the time before writing was developed there. "A fully equipped prehistoric man—nothing like it had ever been seen by an archaeologist," Spindler wrote.

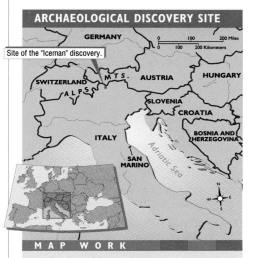

ARCHAEOLOGICAL DISCOVERY SITE

Site of the "Iceman" discovery.

GERMANY

SWITZERLAND · M T S. · AUSTRIA · HUNGARY
A L P S
SLOVENIA
CROATIA
ITALY · BOSNIA AND HERZEGOVINA
SAN MARINO
Adriatic Sea

M A P   W O R K

The site of the Iceman discovery lies high in Europe's Alps mountains.

1. The Iceman was found very near the border of which two countries?

2. In what direction did archaeologist Konrad Spindler travel to get from Germany to the site?

MAP WORK: **1.** Austria and Italy **2.** south

A DISCOVERY IN THE ALPS

Refer students to the rugged environment shown in the picture of the Alps on p. 32 to help them appreciate the conditions the Iceman (nicknamed Otzi, for the nearby Otzal Valley) faced.

Discussing A Mystery in the Ice
Help students capture the surprise and wonder that attended this discovery.

● *What artifacts accompanied the Iceman? (rope, leather, a copper-and-wood ax, a stone knife)*

● *What gave the archaeologist the first clue that this was an ancient man? (the style of the ax)*

★THINKING FURTHER: *Making Conclusions* **Why might the site be dangerous?** *(Rugged mountains and sudden snowstorms pose dangers.)*

More
MAP WORK

Use the map on this page to help students locate the site where the Iceman was found.

● *In what mountain range was the dead man discovered? (the Alps)*

● *What three countries are nearby? On what continent are they? (Austria, Italy, Switzerland; Europe)*

★THINKING FURTHER: *Making Conclusions* **What was the basis for concluding that the body dated back to prehistory?** *(Tests proved the body to be more than 5,000 years old, thus before there was writing in Europe.)*

BACKGROUND INFORMATION

ABOUT KONRAD SPINDLER AND THE RESEARCH
● Konrad Spindler is a prominent archaeologist who is associated with the University of Innsbruck's Institute for Prehistory and Early History.

● This university, located in the Alps, is where the Iceman was brought for study.

● The Iceman was placed in a freezer at the university's Anatomy Institute, where the temperature remains a constant 21°F and the humidity is kept at 98 percent, the exact conditions from which he emerged.

USING THE ANTHOLOGY

EASTER ISLAND, pages 4–7 This selection deals with a mystery that many scientists have tried to solve about artifacts found on Easter Island, an island in the Pacific Ocean, far from other inhabited places. The mystery involves a group of huge stone statues found on Easter Island. Who created them? From where did the people who created these sculptures come? As students read about the work of Thor Heyerdahl, an anthropologist from Norway, ask them to think about additional questions they might want to ask and to begin a list of the many sources of information they would need to begin to answer their questions.

AN AMAZING FIND

Help students see that the discovery was extraordinary. Archaeologists mined each item for information. Have students list on the board each bit of evidence found. Opposite each, have them write the conclusion drawn from it.

Discussing Tools of the Archaeologist Review the archaeologists' tools that the class has studied (X rays, age tests).

- *Why did the archaeologists rush to gather the Iceman's things?* (Snows were expected to cover everything.)

- *What tools did the archaeologists use to record exactly where each item was found?* (maps and photographs)

- *Why do you think it was important to know exactly where each artifact was located?* (Location might offer clues to an artifact's use and importance.)

- *How did archaeologists determine that the Iceman had contact with a certain type of village?* (Flecks of wheat suggested that he had contact with a grain-growing village.)

- *How did they determine that he had died in autumn?* (through microscopic examination of pollen found on him)

★**THINKING FURTHER:** *Compare and Contrast How would you compare the archaeologists' methods with those of a criminologist?* (Students who have seen television shows involving forensic science should recognize the use of a microscope, lab work, photographs of a scene, etc.)

When hikers in the Alps stumbled upon his body, the "Iceman" (left and above) had been frozen for over 5,000 years!

AN AMAZING FIND

Archaeologists have uncovered axes and knives and prehistoric graves before. What made the discovery of the Iceman so interesting? He was found with the tools and clothes he used every day. The Iceman brought a priceless treasure of artifacts into the 1990s.

Tools of the Archaeologist

Several archaeologists rushed to the Alps to recover as many of the Iceman's belongings as possible. They were able to work only a few days, however, before the first winter snows buried the site. The following summer, these archaeologists shoveled away over 600 tons of snow before they could pick up where they had left off.

The archaeologists' first task was to make a detailed map of the location. They also took photographs showing where each artifact was found. Next, they used steam blowers and even hair dryers to melt snow and ice around the artifacts. The melted water was filtered three times. Archaeologists wanted to make sure that even the tiniest specks of evidence were not lost.

The archaeologists found flecks of wheat. This proved that the Iceman must have had contact with a village where grain was grown. Archaeologists also recovered over 2,000 grains of pollen, or plant dust. Study of the pollen with a microscope showed that most of the grains came from alder and pine trees. Scientists reasoned that the

34

BACKGROUND INFORMATION

ABOUT GETTING IN THE ARCHAEOLOGISTS' WAY As students have seen, archaeologists take great care to preserve the site of a find. They arrived too late for the Iceman.

- According to *National Geographic,* "Four days almost undid 5,000 years of preservation" because the Iceman was first thought to be a recent accident victim.

- The first people on the scene trampled the depression in which he lay.

- The police used a jackhammer to free the body; in so doing, they tore into his left hip.

- Workers used ski poles to dig him out and, in the process, scattered his garments about the site.

CURRICULUM CONNECTION

LINKS TO SCIENCE Refer the class to *Did You Know?* on p. 37 to learn about still another archaeologists' tool—carbon dating. Call for volunteers to research how carbon-dating tests are conducted. Have them prepare their findings for an illustrated presentation to the class.

SECOND-LANGUAGE SUPPORT

PAIRING STUDENTS Pair second-language learners with English-proficient students to dramatize the discovery of the Iceman. This will help students become more comfortable with the vocabulary and concepts in the lesson.

Iceman probably died in autumn, the season when pine and alder trees give off the most pollen.

Equipped for Survival

Near the Iceman, archaeologists found all sorts of survival gear, such as knife-blades, rope, and hunting arrows. They also recovered a small net. Was the net used to carry things? Was it a fishing net? The wide spaces in the mesh seemed to rule out both of these possibilities. Then Konrad Spindler compared the net to modern nets used by European farmers to catch birds. They matched exactly. The question of the net's purpose seemed to be answered.

In a leather belt-pouch the Iceman carried needed tools, such as small flint blades and a bone needle probably used to repair equipment. There was also a handful of a black fungus. Chemical study showed that tiny crystals of sulfur and iron were attached to the fungus. These are ingredients in today's matches. Archaeologists concluded that the Iceman used the fungus as a kind of fire-starter.

The Iceman also carried two small beads of a different kind of fungus on a leather strap. Close comparison of samples with those in a huge fungus collection showed that the Iceman's beads were made from birch fungus. Birch fungus contains an ingredient that helps fight disease. Therefore, archaeologists believe that this was the Iceman's "medicine chest."

Artifacts found near the Iceman tell archaeologists much about life in prehistoric Europe. It seems that people then had survival skills possessed by few people today.

Examining the Evidence

The Iceman was moved from the Alps to a special refrigerated room in Innsbruck, Austria. There scientists determined that he was about 5 feet 2 inches tall. From the amount of wear on his teeth, they reasoned that he was 35 to 40 years old when he died. Pieces of his hair showed that he had wavy dark-brown hair and a beard.

X rays indicated that the Iceman had some broken ribs on his right side. Some archaeologists believe that the Iceman was somehow injured before he died, because he was found lying on his left side. Shortly after his death, he was covered by snowfall. Glacier ice gradually encased him. It would imprison—and preserve—him for 5,000 years.

Archaeologists use methods of modern science to discover information from artifacts and other remains. A flint knife (left) tells them about Iceman's survival equipment.

GLOBAL CONNECTION

INTERNATIONAL DISPUTE The Iceman became the center of an intense dispute between two countries, Austria and Italy. Austrian police retrieved the body, but then everyone realized the site lay 303 feet inside the Italian border. Italy demanded that Austria return the Iceman. After lengthy negotiations, however, Italy agreed to allow research on the Iceman to be completed in Austria.

CURRICULUM CONNECTION

LINKS TO SCIENCE The Iceman carried birch fungus to fight disease. Find volunteers to do research on medicinal plants and the uses we make of them today. (For example, penicillin was developed from bread mold.) Have the research team report their findings to the class, then have students ask friends or relatives about medicinal plant uses.

WHO WAS THE ICEMAN?

Help students to see that archaeologists can solve some mysteries, but they cannot solve all mysteries.

More DIAGRAM WORK

Give students time to study the diagram to find clues to how the Iceman used his environment to supply his needs.

- *How did he use animals to supply his needs?* (He used animal skins for clothing and carrying things; he used meat for food, as shown by the bow for hunting and the net for birds.)

- *How did he use grass and trees?* (He wove grass into cloth for a cape and he insulated his shoes with it; he used wood for a bow and ax handle.)

- ★THINKING FURTHER: *Making Conclusions* **What does the copper tell you about his knowledge of metal?** (He knew how to extract copper from ore or how to trade for copper.)

Learning from Living 5,000 Years Ago Point out to the class that this section shows how archaeologists make generalizations about a whole period based on specifics about one person.

- *What have archaeologists decided about how people adapted to their environments 5,000 years ago?* (People used the environment to satisfy their needs.)

- *What have they concluded about metal-working technology?* (People had discovered how to extract metal from ore.)

★THINKING FURTHER: *Making Generalizations* **What generalizations can you make about the work of archaeologists?** (Generalizations will probably center on archaeologists' ability to learn much from a few facts.)

Investigating The Mystery Remains Help students locate the Alps area on their Desk Maps.

★THINKING FURTHER: *Predicting* **What do you think the Iceman was doing in the mountains?** (Accept all reasonable answers.)

WHO WAS THE ICEMAN?

From the body of one man and a few of his belongings, archaeologists have learned much about what life was like in the Alps during prehistoric times. Many mysteries have been solved, but some still remain.

Living 5,000 Years Ago

We now know at least the following about the Iceman's world. The people of the Iceman's time were experts at interacting with their environment. Archaeologists concluded this because as many as 17 different kinds of trees and 8 different kinds of animals were used to make the Iceman's belongings. These prehistoric people were also skilled metalworkers. They were able to shape copper into tools. And the Iceman must have had contact with farmers. We know this because traces of grain were found in his belongings.

The Mystery Remains

What about the Iceman himself? Who was he and what did he do for a living? Why did he hike up into the high mountains of the Alps just before

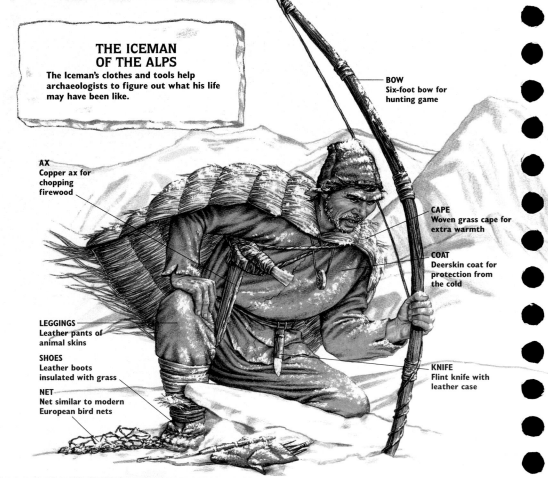

THE ICEMAN OF THE ALPS
The Iceman's clothes and tools help archaeologists to figure out what his life may have been like.

BOW
Six-foot bow for hunting game

AX
Copper ax for chopping firewood

CAPE
Woven grass cape for extra warmth

COAT
Deerskin coat for protection from the cold

LEGGINGS
Leather pants of animal skins

SHOES
Leather boots insulated with grass

NET
Net similar to modern European bird nets

KNIFE
Flint knife with leather case

CURRICULUM CONNECTION

LINKS TO SCIENCE The June 1993 *National Geographic* contains an illustration and explanation of how ancient people extracted metal from copper ore. Call for a few volunteers to study this process and then present a simulation of the process for the class (without using fire).

CITIZENSHIP★

CONTRIBUTING TO THE COMMUNITY Remind students that Spindler believes the Iceman may have been a shepherd who left his village to tend his flock in the mountains. Other scientists suggest he may have been a trader far from his village. Encourage students to discuss how each of these jobs may have contributed to his community. Through the discussion students should recognize that sheep contributed to the food supply, while trading aided the village economy.

winter set in? Spindler believes that the Iceman may have been a shepherd who spent long periods of time in the mountains, away from his village below. We may never know for certain what he was doing high in the mountains that long-ago autumn day. Whatever the reason, the Iceman's misfortune has proven to be history's great gain.

WHY IT MATTERS

We can sometimes learn facts about an entire culture by focusing on one individual, such as the Iceman. Archaeologists looked carefully at artifacts that the Iceman used every day. They discovered much about how people lived in the highlands of prehistoric Europe.

In chapters to come, you can use some of the same methods you learned about in this lesson. You will read about great ideas and events that changed the world. But you will also have the opportunity to think about individuals like the Iceman. These individuals add fullness and detail to the big picture of history.

DID YOU KNOW?

How did archaeologists figure out how old the Iceman was?

Tiny skin samples were sent to four laboratories for carbon-dating tests. All living things contain carbon, and when they die a special type of carbon called carbon-14 slowly begins to break down at a known rate. By measuring the amount of carbon-14 that has broken down in a sample, scientists can then determine its age.

All four test results concluded that the Iceman lived between 5,000 to 5,300 years ago.

✓✓ Reviewing Facts and Ideas

MAIN IDEAS

- Archaeologists use science to study and interpret the remains of past cultures.
- Our understanding of prehistory, or the time before writing was invented, is often based on the work done by archaeologists.
- Archaeologists and historians can sometimes make conclusions about life in past cultures. One of the ways they do this is by looking closely at information about one or two individuals.

THINK ABOUT IT

1. What made Spindler realize that the Iceman was actually very old?
2. What was the Iceman's net probably used for? How did Spindler find out?
3. **FOCUS** How do archaeologists help to uncover secrets of the past?
4. **THINKING SKILL** What are two _facts_ and two _opinions_ presented about the Iceman in this lesson?
5. **GEOGRAPHY** Describe how the Iceman's belongings tell the different ways in which he interacted with his environment.

37

Discussing WHY IT MATTERS Repeat to the class this quote, "All men by nature desire knowledge." (Aristotle) Have students discuss why knowledge of the Iceman is important to us.

- **Do you agree with this statement? Why or why not?** (Encourage students to explore human curiosity and its value in learning.)

Extending Did You Know? Encourage students to find out what carbon is and some of its uses.

⭐ 3 CLOSE

MAIN IDEAS
Discuss each question and answer briefly.

- **How do archaeologists use science to study past cultures?** (They use scientific methods and instruments.)

- **Why must we rely on archaeologists, rather than written sources, to learn about prehistory?** (Because prehistory predates writing, there are no written primary sources; we need scientists to interpret non-written sources.)

- **Using the Iceman as an example, what conclusions can archaeologists and historians make by studying just one individual?** (conclusions about how people used their environment at a particular time and their state of knowledge about the world)

EVALUATE
✓ **Answers to Think About It**
1. the design of the Iceman's copper ax and the chipped-stone knife-blade _Recall Details_

2. Probably for capturing birds; Spindler recognized the net's similarity to bird nets still used in Europe. _Problem and Solution_

3. by first uncovering them and then by using science to interpret them _Sequencing_

4. Opinions may center on what people thought when the Iceman was first discovered and on speculations about why he was in the mountains. Facts will probably relate to items found and scientific test results. _Evaluate Fact and Nonfact_

5. Answers should focus on how he used animals, plants, and minerals. _Five Themes of Geography: Human/Environment Interactions_

Write About It Have students write a paragraph telling how archaeologists use science to do their work.

MEETING INDIVIDUAL NEEDS

RETEACHING (Easy) Tell students to create an archaeologist's "kit." Have them list the tools (from shovels to microscopes and carbon dating) and then illustrate their use.

EXTENSION (Average) Tell students to review and list the artifacts found in connection with the Iceman. Then have students make a parallel list of what a modern-day traveler in the mountains might carry. Have them compare and contrast how each individual has adapted to the same environment.

ENRICHMENT (Challenging) Have students select a photograph from this chapter and write down all the details they can discover in it. If there is any detail that puzzles them, ask them to write a question mark after what it might be. Then have them try to find answers to the puzzling details and put it all together in a descriptive paragraph.

CHAPTER 2

CITIZENSHIP
Viewpoints
PAGES 38-39

Lesson Objective
★ Compare and analyze contrasting points of view on protecting cultural sites.

Identifying the Issue Help students to see that the desire to save precious remnants of the past can come into conflict with economic needs and demands of the present.

● **Why was a serious effort to save archaeological sites begun in 1959?** *(So many precious ancient ruins were being lost forever due to destruction, war, pollution, and making way for other things that world leaders decided ways must be found to protect them.)*

Discussing Three Different Viewpoints Have students read the viewpoints on p. 39.

GUSTAVO ARAOZ

● **What does protecting "our global cultural heritage" mean to Araoz?** *(seeing that they are properly kept up so that they are not drastically changed or destroyed)*

● **Why is the loss of a cultural site so devastating to Araoz?** *(It marks the loss of knowledge that can never be regained.)*

NANCY MARZULLA

● **According to Marzulla, what hardship can the effort to preserve legacies from our history create for people?** *(It can threaten the property rights of owners of property that includes cultural resources by limiting their ability to get full value from it.)*

● **What clash in values does Marzulla's point of view present?** *(legal rights vs. cultural rights)*

CITIZENSHIP
VIEWPOINTS

Rather than let them be flooded, workers took apart and moved the temples at Abu Simbel, in Egypt.

WHEN SHOULD CULTURAL SITES AROUND THE WORLD BE PROTECTED?

Many places have ruins of ancient temples and palaces. These ruins provide clues to ancient cultures. Both in the past and today, people have not always protected such places. Wars and pollution damaged some. Other sites became overgrown. Still others have been destroyed to make room for new buildings.

Serious efforts to protect archaeological sites began in 1959. Archaeologists learned that a huge dam being built at Aswan in Egypt would flood temples thousands of years old. The United Nations Educational, Scientific, and Cultural Organization (UNESCO) worked with the Egyptian government to save these temples.

Along with archaeologists and officials from many nations, UNESCO has drawn up a list of almost 400 "World Heritage sites" to be preserved. The list includes Southeast Asian temples, Mexican pyramids, European cathedrals, and ancient African cities. Sites in the United States are in danger of being destroyed as well. Some people think such sites should be preserved. Nancy Marzulla explains other factors that should be considered, such as the use and value of property. Consider the viewpoints on this issue and answer the questions that follow.

38

BACKGROUND INFORMATION

ABOUT ABU SIMBEL

● The photograph on this page shows the Great Temple of Abu Simbel. It is located about 175 miles south of Aswan, Egypt, on the west bank of the Nile.

● Hewn out of rock 3,300 years ago, it is fronted by four colossal statues of the Egyptian pharaoh Rameses II and contains a pantheon of the Egyptian gods.

● In 1964, construction of the Aswan Dam threatened to flood Abu Simbel and leave it under fathoms of water. UNESCO mounted a $40 million effort to take the temple apart, move it to a site 210 feet higher, and reassemble it. The work was completed in 1968.

Three DIFFERENT Viewpoints

1 GUSTAVO ARAOZ
Architect, Washington, D.C.
Excerpt from Interview, 1995

We need to protect our global cultural heritage, because if such places are not properly kept up, they can be changed beyond recognition or destroyed. Once you lose a cultural site, you can never get it back. It's like losing a book and all the information in it. It's gone forever. When the tombs of ancient Egypt were looted and the artifacts stolen, the world lost a significant source of information about the past.

"It's gone forever."

2 NANCY MARZULLA
Lawyer, Washington, D.C.
Excerpt from Interview, 1995

Historic preservation is fine as long as we also protect the rights of property owners. In the United States the Constitution guarantees these rights. The owner of a house or building has the right to be paid a fair amount for any property to be preserved if it results in the destruction of private property rights. Preservation laws may require the owner to keep a site or building exactly as it is, which could destroy the value of the property.

"... protect the rights of property owners."

3 BREDA PAVLIC
International Relations Specialist, Paris, France
Excerpt from Interview, 1995

Today our global cultural resources are threatened in many ways. Among these threats are industrial pollution, urban growth, war, natural disasters such as earthquakes, floods, hurricanes, and too much tourism. The loss of any one of these unique sites is irreplaceable. These sites are a link between the past and the present, and, if we manage to preserve them, a link with the future. They give us a feeling of belonging to the world as a whole.

"... a link between the past and the present ..."

BUILDING CITIZENSHIP

1. Explain how each person supports her or his view.

2. In what ways are some of the viewpoints alike? In what ways are they different?

3. What other viewpoints might people have on this issue? How could you find out about historical sites in your community?

SHARING VIEWPOINTS
Discuss what you agree with or disagree with about these and other viewpoints. Discuss why you think the speakers might feel as they do. Then, as a class, write two statements that all of you can agree with about preserving historical sites.

39

CITIZENSHIP ★

USING CURRENT EVENTS Conflicts between what is perceived as economic necessity and what is perceived as cultural need come up frequently in modern society: Architecture lovers want a great old mansion retained while developers want to use the land for a multi-apartment building. Lumber companies want to cut down forest areas that campers want left standing. A power company wants to dam a stream that salmon fishing enthusiasts want left free to flow. Check the papers for any disputes like this and bring in clippings for class discussion and debate. Encourage students to find compromises that might solve the problem.

BREDA PAVLIC

- **What does Pavlic mean by "cultural resources"?** (the great physical legacies left to us by the past)

- **What does Pavlic list as the threats to these resources?** (pollution, war, natural disasters, too much tourism)

- **According to Pavlic, what do we lose when any of these resources is destroyed?** (We lose an irreplaceable link to the past, and to the future.)

✓ Answers to Building Citizenship

1. Pavlic and Araoz back up their support of protecting cultural sites by stressing their irreplaceability, while Marzulla uses references to the U.S. Constitution to back up her support of proper compensation for owners of culturally important property.

2. Pavlic and Araoz want to protect cultural resources at all costs while Marzulla does not oppose cultural resource protection but also does not want property owners penalized to protect these resources.

3. Other viewpoints might run the gamut from total hands-off cultural sites, letting the market determine whether they should be retained, to strict protection at any cost, and if that means property owners are not free to use property as they wish or have to take a loss on it, so be it.

Sharing Viewpoints Encourage students to express their own viewpoints and to link the lawyer to her viewpoint and the architect to his. *Three* statements the class can agree on might include: (1) Cultural resources enrich our lives and knowledge. (2) Necessary money should be spent to protect cultural resources. (3) People should find ways to compromise when necessary to preserve the past.

Debating Viewpoints As an extension activity, have students debate cultural values vs. economic values—debating which should take precedence in a conflict that pits them against each other.

Answers to
THINKING ABOUT VOCABULARY

1. oral tradition
2. secondary source
3. artifact
4. primary source
5. archaeology
6. excavate
7. history
8. prehistory
9. archaeology
10. oral tradition

Answers to
THINKING ABOUT FACTS

1. primary sources and secondary sources

2. Primary sources are written records or artifacts from the time under study, while secondary sources are studies based on primary sources.

3. Historians search for clues to help them solve the mystery of the past.

4. They tell us what materials and what tools people used, how people lived and got around, what jewelry they wore, to name just a few examples.

5. History refers only to the story of what happened after writing was developed, while prehistory describes what happened before writing was developed.

6. artifacts from the past to learn about the cultures that produced them

7. that he was thousands of years old, that he was a prehistoric man who carried a kit of tools to help him survive, and that he might have been a shepherd

Resource REMINDER

Practice and Project Book: p. 13
Assessment Book: Chapter 2 Test
Technology: Videodisc/Video Tape 1
Transparency: Graphic Organizer, Main Idea Map

CHAPTER 2 REVIEW

THINKING ABOUT VOCABULARY

Number a sheet of paper from 1 to 10. Beside each number write the word or term from the list below that best completes the sentence. You will need to use some words more than once.

archaeology
artifact
excavate
history
oral tradition
prehistory
primary source
secondary source

1. Before written records were kept, people passed on their history by word of mouth or _____.
2. A written study of the past that is based on a primary source is called a _____.
3. An object made by someone in the past is an _____.
4. The scrapbook that Nina found in her grandfather's attic is an example of a _____.
5. _____ is the study of the remains of past cultures.
6. Archaelogists often dig up, or _____, historical sites.
7. _____ can be identified as the story of the past.
8. The time before the development of writing is called _____.
9. _____ often involves the search for artifacts.
10. Stories and legends were passed on during prehistory through _____.

THINKING ABOUT FACTS

1. What sources do historians use to study the past?
2. What is the difference between primary and secondary sources?
3. How is an historian like a detective?
4. What do artifacts show about the past?
5. How is history different from prehistory?
6. What do archaeologists study?
7. What conclusions did the archaeologist Konrad Spindler make about the frozen man found in the Alps?
8. What belongings of the Iceman were discovered, and what did archaeologists learn from examining them?
9. Name at least one method the archaeologists used to find information about the Iceman.
10. What mysteries still remain to be solved about the Iceman?

THINK AND WRITE

WRITING A SUMMARY
Write a paragraph summarizing what you know about the history of your community.

WRITING AN ARTICLE
Suppose you are writing an article for your school newspaper about "The Iceman of the Alps." Describe the discovery and what archaeologists learned from it.

WRITING AN INTERVIEW
Suppose you were able to interview the Iceman. Write at least three questions you would ask him, and provide the answers you think he might give.

40

SUGGESTIONS FOR SUMMING UP THE CHAPTER

RETELLING Encourage second-language learners to retell sections of the text in order to assess their comprehension and to give them needed oral practice. Assign a paragraph or two to student partners and have them take notes on the most important ideas. Then ask them to retell these ideas aloud in their own words. Ask for explanations and examples of relevant vocabulary. Model using illustrations to gain information.

RESPONSE JOURNAL Invite students to keep a response journal in which they write their thoughts and personal reactions to the information they read in the text. Since archaeology generally captures the interest and imagination of young people, students can begin their journal with their thoughts on this question: Would you enjoy going on an archaeological dig? Why or why not?

APPLYING THINKING SKILLS

DECISION MAKING

Suppose you are Heinrich Schliemann in 1870. You are fascinated by stories of an ancient city called Troy. No one knows for sure if the city is real or imaginary. You decide to find out.

1. What goal do you set for yourself?
2. What alternatives do you consider to reach your goal?
3. What are the possible consequences of each alternative?
4. Will a map like this one help you to set your goal?
5. Do you think you made a good decision?

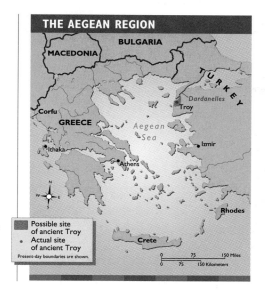

THE AEGEAN REGION

BULGARIA
MACEDONIA
TURKEY
Dardanelles
Troy
Corfu
GREECE
Aegean Sea
Ithaka
Izmir
Athens
Rhodes
Crete

Possible site of ancient Troy
Actual site of ancient Troy
Present-day boundaries are shown.

0   75   150 Miles
0   75   150 Kilometers

8. survival tools, such as an ax, knife-blades, rope, hunting arrows, a net for trapping, a needle, a fire-starter, and a "medicine chest"; that people lived in the Alps over 5,000 years ago and that they interacted well with their environment and were metalworkers

9. any one of the following: studies by microscope, comparison studies, X rays, carbon dating for the age of artifacts

10. Who was he? What did he do for a living? Why was he so high in the mountains when winter set in? How did he die?

Answers to APPLYING THINKING SKILLS

1. to look for evidence that gives clues to whether Troy actually existed and, if so, where it was located
2. to look at written sources that might provide clues to its location; to select the source that would offer the most reliable clues; to look for any landforms that might indicate a long-buried city
3. If the sources did not provide good clues, no city would be found; if the source selected was not reliable, the digging might be in the wrong place; if no landforms indicated the buried city, the existence of Troy could not be proved.
4. Yes, because it shows where Troy was located.
5. Yes, if the decisions led me to the location of Troy.

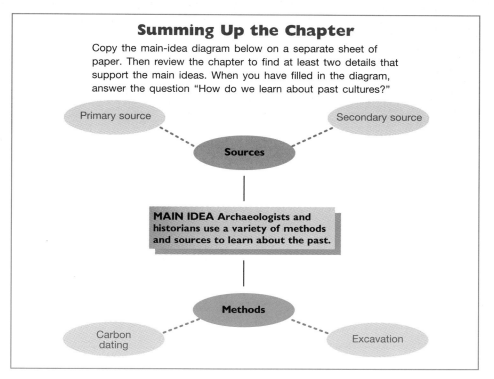

Summing Up the Chapter

Copy the main-idea diagram below on a separate sheet of paper. Then review the chapter to find at least two details that support the main ideas. When you have filled in the diagram, answer the question "How do we learn about past cultures?"

Primary source

Secondary source

Sources

MAIN IDEA Archaeologists and historians use a variety of methods and sources to learn about the past.

Methods

Carbon dating

Excavation

41

Technology CONNECTION

VIDEODISC/VIDEO TAPE 1
Enrich Chapter 2 with the *Discovering the Past* segment on the videodisc.

SUGGESTIONS FOR SUMMING UP THE CHAPTER

After students have copied the main-idea diagram on their papers, have a student read aloud the main idea, and have another student read aloud the two kinds of tools archaeologists and historians use to reconstruct the past—sources and methods. Then have students go through Lesson 1 to review different sources and Lesson 2 to look for methods, scientific and otherwise, used to gather information. Suggested examples of methods are shown in the text page reproduced above. Encourage students to weave together all the sources and methods they identify in the diagram to answer the question.

ASSESSING THINK AND WRITE: *For performance assessment, see Assessment Book, Chapter 2, pp. T48-T50.*

CHAPTER 3 Early Cultures

Pages 42–61

CHAPTER OVERVIEW

Most scientists believe that humans have walked Earth for at least two million years. Objects made by ancient people have been uncovered all over the world. Some of the earliest examples of art were found in cave paintings. One of the first cities was discovered at Catal Huyuk, Turkey.

GEO ADVENTURES DAILY GEOGRAPHY ACTIVITIES

Use **Geo Adventures** Daily Geography activities to assess students' understanding of geography skills.

CHAPTER PLANNING GUIDE

LESSON 1	Legacy	LESSON 2
SUGGESTED PACING: 3 DAYS	SUGGESTED PACING: 1 DAY	SUGGESTED PACING: 3 DAYS
Early People pp. 44–49	**Artists And Their Environments** pp. 50–51	**Agriculture Changes The World** pp. 52–57
CURRICULUM CONNECTIONS Links to Science, p. 45 Links to Language Arts, p. 46 Links to Art, p. 47	**CURRICULUM CONNECTIONS** Links to Art, p. 51 **RESOURCES** Anthology, p. 8	**CURRICULUM CONNECTIONS** Links to Science, p. 53 Links to Math, p. 55
CITIZENSHIP Understanding Environmental Concerns, p. 46		**CITIZENSHIP** Community Cooperation, p. 54
INFOGRAPHIC Old Stone Age Technology Around the World, pp. 48–49		**RESOURCES** Practice and Project Book, p. 15 Anthology, pp. 9–10
RESOURCES Practice & Project Book, p. 14 ⊙ TECHNOLOGY *Adventure Time!* CD-ROM		

CHAPTER REVIEW
SUGGESTED PACING: 1 DAY
pp. 60–61
RESOURCES Practice and Project Book, p. 17 Assessment Book: Chapter 3 Test Transparency: Graphic Organizer, Compare-and-Contrast Chart

LEARNING STYLE: Auditory

 ON YOUR OWN

 30 MINUTES OR LONGER

Make a Before-and-After Chart

Objective: To start students thinking about how technological advances have changed the way people live.

Materials: paper

1. Ask students to think of inventions (the automobile, the washing machine) that changed people's lives.
2. Write the following inventions on the board: refrigerator; train; computer; VCR; airplane; TV. Discuss how life differed before and after each.
3. Later, talk about inventions of the future that might further change human life.

STUDYSKILLS

SUGGESTED PACING: 2 DAYS

Reading Time Lines,
pp. 58–59

RESOURCES
Practice and Project Book, p. 16
⏺ TECHNOLOGY *Adventure Time!* CD-ROM

SDAIE SUPPORT SHELTERED INSTRUCTION

READING STRATEGIES & LANGUAGE DEVELOPMENT

Sequence/Prefixes, p. 44, Lesson 1
Cause and Effect/Root Words, p. 52, Lesson 2
Sequence/Combining Forms, p. 58, Lesson 3

SECOND-LANGUAGE SUPPORT

Semantic Maps, p. 45
About Catal Huyuk, p. 55
Working with Peers/Oral Practice, p. 60

MEETING INDIVIDUAL NEEDS

Reteaching, Extension, Enrichment, pp. 49, 51, 57, 59
McGraw-Hill Adventure Book

ASSESSMENT OPPORTUNITIES

Practice and Project Book, pp. 14–17
Write About It, pp. 49, 51, 57
Assessment Book: Assessing Think and Write, pp. T51–T53; Chapter 3 Tests: Content, Skills, Writing

Introducing the Chapter

To help students see how long people lived on Earth before they made written records, have them examine the time line.

THINKING ABOUT HISTORY AND GEOGRAPHY

Have students read the text and examine the map on this page. To be sure that they properly link the panels with the map, have them trace each map location to its appropriate panel with their fingers.

45,000 YEARS AGO

Focus on the place and the way of life in Olduvai Gorge, Tanzania.

- **On which continent did these early people live?** (Africa)

> ★THINKING FURTHER: *Making Conclusions* **Based on the illustration, in what ways did they use their environment?** (*They hunted its animals for food.*)

40,000 YEARS AGO

Call attention to the development in human skills over time.

- **Where did the people pictured here live?** (in Border Cave, South Africa)

- **How had they progressed in making use of the environment by this time?** (*They had developed ways of making tools from stone.*)

CHAPTER 3

Early Cultures

THINKING ABOUT HISTORY AND GEOGRAPHY

Most scientists believe humans have walked on Earth for many thousands of years. Follow the story of these early people by linking the colored squares on the map to the colored panels of the time line. You will read more of this story as you study Chapter 3.

ATLANTIC OCEAN

45,000 YEARS AGO	40,000 YEARS AGO	30,000 YEARS AGO
OLDUVAI GORGE, TANZANIA	**BORDER CAVE, SOUTH AFRICA**	**AVIGNON, FRANCE**
Early people hunt and gather their food	People make tools from stone	A person creates paintings on the walls of caves

42

BACKGROUND INFORMATION

LINKING THE MAP AND THE TIME LINE
- Olduvai Gorge has four distinct geological levels, with progressively older remains found at each level down. Humanlike fossils, stone tools, and bones of extinct animals have been found at the lowest level, which dates back 2 million years.
- Border Cave in South Africa is a very early site in which humans used fire to warm the homes they made in caves. Tools and medicinal plants have also been found in the cave.

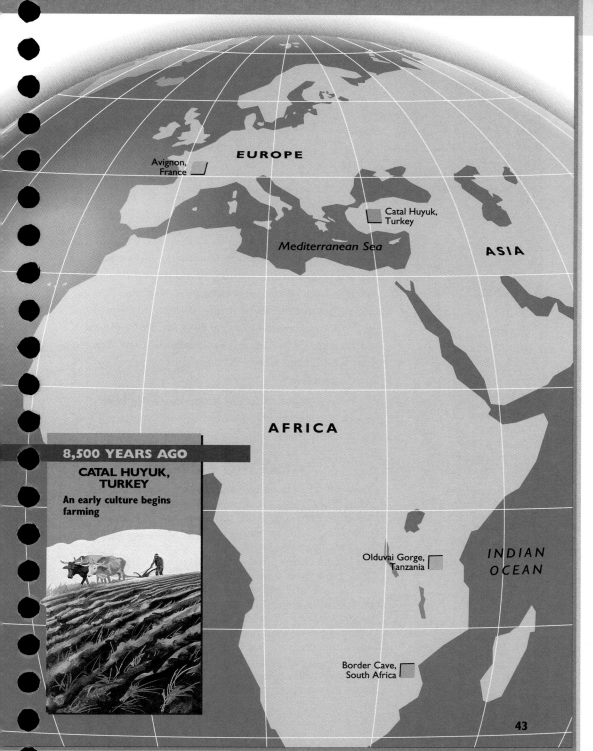

EUROPE

Avignon, France

Catal Huyuk, Turkey

Mediterranean Sea

ASIA

AFRICA

8,500 YEARS AGO

CATAL HUYUK, TURKEY

An early culture begins farming

Olduvai Gorge, Tanzania

INDIAN OCEAN

Border Cave, South Africa

43

30,000 YEARS AGO

Call students' attention to human cultural development at this time, near Avignon, France.

● *What are the people in this panel doing?* (painting pictures on the cave walls)

● *What is the subject matter of their paintings?* (an animal)

★THINKING FURTHER: *Making Conclusions* **Based on these activities, what can you conclude about how humans have developed?** *(They seem to have developed artistic skills.)*

8,500 YEARS AGO

Catal Huyuk, in what is now Turkey, is one of the earliest agricultural sites.

● *To what continent have we moved in this panel?* (Asia)

● *How much time has elapsed since the last panel?* (about 21,500 years)

● *What important human activity are the people here shown performing?* (farming)

● *How might that activity have encouraged living in villages?* (People would have needed to settle down in one place, a village perhaps, to farm.)

★THINKING FURTHER: *Making Conclusions* **How would you say that learning how to farm might have changed human life?** *(Help students recognize that human beings would have greater control over their food supply.)*

BACKGROUND INFORMATION

LINKING THE MAP AND THE TIME LINE
● Prehistoric paintings in caves have been found in southern France (such as at Avignon), in Spain, in North Africa, and many other far-flung parts of the world. Most of these paintings are very accurate pictures of animals; a few show hunters, as well. Of the work in one prehistoric cave, a historian said, "The paintings have both elegance and strength. . . . Their primitive drawing helps to give them a fresh-ness of expression, sometimes rather rugged and naive, suggestive in their own way of the early Renaissance."

● Catal Huyuk is a relatively recent archaeological find. It was discovered in 1958 by James Mellaart, director of the British Institute of Archaeology in Ankara, Turkey, after a seven-year search for the possible remains of early civilizations in remote areas of Turkey.

LESSON 1

PAGES 44–49

Lesson Overview

People of the *Old Stone Age* developed technologies to feed, clothe, and shelter themselves, and art forms and religion to express themselves and find meaning.

Lesson Objectives

★ Define *technology*.

★ Identify the period called the Old Stone Age and place it in time.

★ Describe the characteristics of Old Stone Age culture.

1 PREPARE

MOTIVATE Ask students to close their eyes and listen as you read the *Read Aloud* to them. Encourage them to think about the lives that had come before them in their families and in the place where they live.

SET PURPOSE Refer students to the photo of the cave painting of the person with a spear. As they read the *Read to Learn* question, encourage them to picture themselves with few tools or weapons and little knowledge of local plants and animals. Ask for preliminary definitions of the *Vocabulary* terms.

2 TEACH

Understanding THE BIG PICTURE
Help students to appreciate the idea that early people faced the world with courage.

● **How has your life changed since you were born?** *(Students may suggest that they gained skills, new tools, greater maturity, and the like.)*

★**THINKING FURTHER:** *Making Conclusions* **How might the lives of early people have changed during their lifetimes?** *(Possible answers: They may have gained skills, new tools, greater maturity, and the like.)*

Resource REMINDER

Practice and Project Book: *p. 14*

 Technology: *Adventure Time!* CD-ROM

Desk Map

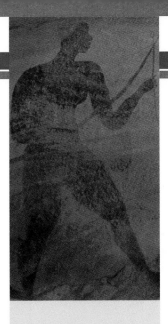

EARLY PEOPLE

Focus Activity

READ TO LEARN
What did early people do to survive?

VOCABULARY
technology
Old Stone Age
hunter-gatherer

PLACES
Border Cave

READ ALOUD

"I was born and grew up in East Africa where, while I was still very young, my imagination was caught by the great age of the world I found myself in. . . . I would visualize the [procession] of lives that had [come before] me there. I would think of those other eyes that had opened on the first flush of sunlight on the hilltops for more than 2 million years, noses that whiffed the smoke of bush fires or scent of acacia blossom."

Archaeologist Jonathan Kingdon wrote these words to describe his fascination with the people of the ancient past.

THE BIG PICTURE

Think about how much your life has changed in ten years. Then think about how much life in the United States has changed from 100 years ago. That was a time when horses far outnumbered cars and most people lived on farms. Now picture in your mind the land of the United States 1,000 years ago. At this time Native Americans lived from coast to coast.

A thousand years is a very long time. When compared to the whole history of the world, however, it is hardly longer than a blink of the eye. Scientists disagree about just how long people have been around. Many think humans have been around for over 40 times 1,000 years, or 40,000 years. Some scientists think that people may have walked on Earth as long as *2,000* times 1,000 years ago—that is, *2 million* years ago!

44

SHELTERED INSTRUCTION

SDAIE SUPPORT

READING STRATEGIES & LANGUAGE DEVELOPMENT

SEQUENCE Explain that it is important to understand the order in which events occur. Point out that chronological order is time sequence. Invite volunteers to model this concept by pantomiming the steps in brushing their teeth, tying their shoelaces, or making a sandwich. Create a flowchart to show the sequence of events. **[SDAIE STRATEGY: MODELING]**

PREFIXES Point out to students the word *microscope,* used in this lesson, as it was in the previous chapter. Write the word on the board and isolate its two parts—*micro* and *scope.* Ask students what they think the prefix *micro* means. If they don't come up with "small," have them consult a dictionary. Explain to them that the opposite, or antonym, of *micro* is the prefix *macro.* Encourage them to make up a word for *The Big Picture*—perhaps *macroview*?

LIFE LONG AGO

When did human life begin, and what was life like for the world's early people? These are big questions for historians and archaeologists. Many different answers have been given over time.

Discoveries in Africa

Scientists do not agree about where or when human life began. Some scientists today think that human life may have begun in Africa over 2 million years ago and then spread throughout the rest of the world. This conclusion is based on remains found by archaeologists in East Africa. Ancient remains uncovered there are the oldest of their kind ever found.

At one site in the country of Tanzania, a long canyon cuts deeply through the surrounding plains. In this canyon are dry beds of big prehistoric lakes. In those ancient lakebeds archaeologists have found remains that some think may be about 2 million years old.

Tools from Long Ago

Along with these remains, archaeologists have found what may have been the world's first tools. Viewed under a microscope, stones like the ones on this page reveal edges that were pounded to create a knife-like sharpness. They may not look like much to us, but the stones could cut through the hides of animals and chop through wood. These simple but useful tools mark the start of technology in culture. Technology is the use of skills and tools to meet practical needs. Stone tools were the most common technology until about 12,000 years ago. That period of time is called the Old Stone Age.

Remains of ancient animal bones found with the stone tools suggest that the early people hunted for survival. During the Old Stone Age, people learned another skill besides hunting and tool-making. This new skill was using fire, and it changed their lives. The technology of fire-building made it possible to cook food for the first time. It also meant people could move into colder climates. Warmth from fires helped people survive through the long winter months.

Early people in Peru made this firestarter (above right). Many stone tools (above) have been found in the Great Rift Valley, Tanzania (right).

CURRICULUM CONNECTION

LINKS TO SCIENCE Have some students investigate how the age of bones is determined. Since bones are organic, carbon dating is certainly a possibility, but have them research any other tests that might be used. They can use encyclopedia articles on archaeology as well as non-fiction books on the subject. Encourage them to consult a librarian for assistance. Have them report their findings to the class.

SECOND-LANGUAGE SUPPORT

SEMANTIC MAPS To help reinforce lesson topics, have second-language learners work in groups of three to create semantic maps using details and terminology from the lesson. Then have the groups explain the information in their maps.

LIFE LONG AGO

Encourage students to examine this lesson's illustrations to discover all the clues they can about life long ago.

Talking About Discoveries in Africa Have students locate East Africa on their Desk Maps. Point out that the archaeologists mentioned here study humans who lived long before the Iceman (Chapter 2).

- *How would you describe the landform shown in the aerial photo on this page?* (a canyon cut into a plain, or a rift, so called because it is a break in the land)

- *Where is this rift located?* (in Tanzania, in East Africa)

- *What clues were found here concerning the beginnings of human life?* (bones from 2 million years ago)

★THINKING FURTHER: *Making Conclusions* **What can you conclude from the existence of a firestarter?** (that early people knew how to use fire)

Examining Tools from Long Ago Help students recognize and appreciate how people build up skills over time.

- *What is the meaning of the term "technology"?* (the use of skills and tools to meet practical needs)

- *What are some examples of technology used by early humanlike beings?* (stone tools that could cut, chop, and be used as spearheads for hunting)

- *How did such technology give one long period of time its name?* (The main technology of that period was the use of stone tools, so the period came to be called the Old Stone Age.)

- *How did the development of the technology of fire-building affect life?* (It made it possible to cook food and move to colder climates.)

★THINKING FURTHER: *Making Generalizations* **What generalizations can you make about how technology affected Old Stone Age life?** (Accept anything that reflects increasing skill, more freedom of movement, or greater comfort.)

LIFE IN THE OLD STONE AGE

Point out to the class that just as one person can tell us much about a long-past time, so can one community.

Discussing Hunting and Gathering Alert students to be on the lookout for advances in technology as they read.

- *What did the people of Border Cave use for shelter? How did they make it more comfortable? (A cave; they lined it with grass and heated it with fire.)*

- *What advantages did its location give them? (nearby water, herds to hunt, a good lookout point)*

- *What technologies other than stone knives and spearheads did they develop? (bow and arrow, medicines)*

★THINKING FURTHER: *Making Conclusions* **Why can the people of Border Cave rightly be called hunter-gatherers?** *(They gained their food by a combination of both methods.)*

More **MAP WORK**

Refer the class to the map on p. 47 and have them locate Border Cave.

- *In what country is Border Cave? on what continent? (South Africa; Africa)*

- *What two oceans border this country? (Atlantic, Indian)*

- *In what part of South Africa does Border Cave lie? (northeast)*

Archaeologists probe the darkness of the Border Cave. History's treasures, in the form of artifacts, await.

LIFE IN THE OLD STONE AGE

Many scientists believe that before 40,000 years ago, stone-age technology gradually became more complex. Smaller, finer blades were crafted, for example. Some blades were tied to wooden handles to make small axes. From about 40,000 years ago, changes came more rapidly. This also marked the time when people began to work more closely together and to develop cultures.

Hunting and Gathering

What was it like to live on Earth about 40,000 years ago? Families that once lived in a cave in South Africa have left behind enough clues to give us an idea.

Border Cave is located in Zululand, the northeastern tip of South Africa. Look at the map on the following page to see where Border Cave is. Back then, much like now, the cave nestled in the side of a cliff. It overlooked a grassy river valley dotted with buffalo-thorn trees and other shrubs. Herds of eland (EE lund), a type of antelope, moved into the valley each year. There they ate grass and drank from the river. Border Cave was an excellent base for people

46

who followed the herds and hunted them for survival.

Remains show that the people of Border Cave made their home as comfortable as possible. They lined its cool dirt floor with grass for bedding. They made campfires to cook on and to light the cave's darkness.

From the opening of the cave high on the cliff, the people of the Border Cave could keep watch over the animals' movement. These people probably traveled many miles to hunt the eland herds. Small, arrowhead-like blades suggest that these people may have used bows and arrows to kill animals for food.

The people of Border Cave were not just hunters, though. They knew a great deal about the plants around them. They knew which ones were tasty, useful as medicine, or filled with dangerous poisons. Ancient remains of seeds and leaves show that they gathered wild plums, oranges, and starchy plants for food. They also may have used seeds from nearby trees to help soothe coughs and upset stomachs. Since these people met their needs by hunting and by gathering plants, they are known as hunter-gatherers.

CURRICULUM CONNECTION

LINKS TO LANGUAGE ARTS Ask students to close their eyes and picture life in Border Cave. What would they see? What would they smell? What might they hear? Have them write short poems to describe the experience.

CITIZENSHIP★

UNDERSTANDING ENVIRONMENTAL CONCERNS Have students review ways that the people of Border Cave used their environment. Then have students discuss environmental concerns the dwellers would have had. (They would probably have wanted a source of clean water to drink and to attract the animals they hunted. They might have hoped no drought would rob them of plant life.)

GLOBAL CONNECTION

CAVE-DWELLING ACROSS THE WORLD Scientists now believe that living in caves began with the discovery of how to control fire for light and warmth. Cave-dwelling sites have been discovered in many parts of the world.

- Hearths that go back 750,000 years have been found in caves in southeastern France.

- Caves near Beijing, China, reveal signs of occupation going back to 500,000 years ago.

- Signs of North American cave-dwelling go back only about 10,000 years ago, for example, in the Ventana Cave in Arizona.

A Changing Culture

At some point many thousands of years ago, a small baby was buried along with a seashell bead towards the back of the cave. This act reveals several important things about life among the people of Border Cave.

It suggests that the baby was deeply cared for. Otherwise people would not have bothered to bury it. It also suggests that the people believed the child would somehow live on after death, or it would not have mattered that the child be buried with the bead. Many archaeologists think that such thoughts about life and death marked the beginning of religious belief in the world.

The seashell bead says other things about the everyday lives of the people of Border Cave. At times they must have traveled to the shores of the Indian Ocean, some 50 miles away. Additionally, the bead shows that these early people valued beauty. Why else would they take the time to make something otherwise "useless" out of the shell?

The earliest signs of art in human culture date back about 40,000 years. Amazing rock paintings in France and Spain date back to about 30,000 years ago. Many other breathtaking rock paintings and carvings dating back

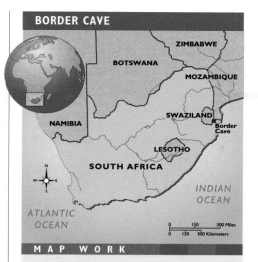

BORDER CAVE

ZIMBABWE

BOTSWANA

MOZAMBIQUE

SWAZILAND

NAMIBIA

Border Cave

LESOTHO

SOUTH AFRICA

INDIAN OCEAN

ATLANTIC OCEAN

150   300 Miles

150   300 Kilometers

MAP WORK

Border Cave is an important archaeological site in South Africa.

1. What bodies of water lie on either side of Africa?

2. Which of them is Border Cave closer to?

10,000 years have been found on every continent inhabited by humans. The exact purpose of these pieces of artwork is not known. It is clear, however, that the makers of each had something they wanted to say. The ancient artists found a way to express themselves through their artwork.

Early hunters made these rock paintings (left) showing great herds of eland in South Africa.

Examining A Changing Culture

Help students see that as life got somewhat easier, people could turn their minds to matters other than simply survival.

- *What precious object did the people of Border Cave bury with the baby? (a seashell bead)*

- *What does such an act tell about their beliefs about life after death? (It seems to indicate that they had developed such a belief—perhaps the beginning of religious belief.)*

- *What does the bead suggest about how far they had traveled? (Since the sea was 50 miles away, they must have traveled at least that far. Another possibility is that a trader could have brought the seashell to them.)*

- *What does the bead say about their ideas of beauty? (that they found it precious and valued it beyond its "usefulness")*

★**THINKING FURTHER:** *Making Conclusions Look at the rock painting on this page. What conclusions can you draw from their content and their style? (Possible answers: Animals were very important to Old Stone Age people because they made animals the major subject of their paintings. People had developed skill both in making the tools needed to create paintings and in painting itself.)*

GLOBAL CONNECTION

WHY SEASHELL BEADS WERE SO PRECIOUS Early Africans living in the Old Stone Age were not the only people who valued beads made from seashells.

- They were revered by the Eastern Woodland Indians in what is today the Eastern United States. The beads were strung together in belts called wampum.
- They were valued because of the intricate workmanship, the delicate hand-crafting it took to make them, and the beauty of the finished product.
- Wampum served different purposes—as a badge of prestige or honor and as a form of currency.
- Once technology created machines that could make seashell beads, they lost their great value.

CURRICULUM CONNECTION

LINKS TO ART Prehistoric animal paintings have been discovered in many parts of the world. Cave paintings about 15,000 years old were found at Lascaux, France, in the early 1940s.

- Two boys were playing with a ball in a field when their dog, chasing the ball, disappeared down a hole.
- Following the sound of his barking, they entered the hole, which was a shaft into the caves. As they lit matches in the darkness, the magnificent cave paintings appeared before their astonished eyes.

Have a group of students use the library to find pictures of these and other prehistoric paintings and bring in the books with the illustrations to present to the class.

Infographic

Help students to recognize how people spread out during the Old Stone Age.

Discussing Old Stone Age Technology Around the World Use the *Infographic* to expand students' understanding of the breadth and depth of Old Stone Age life. Give them a few moments to examine the *Infographic*, identifying each piece of technology and tracing it to its site. Point out that many of these technologies appeared in different sites.

- *Which of these technologies relate to basic physical needs, like food, shelter, and warmth?* (Food: fishing sinkers, arrowheads, spearthrower; Warmth: firestarter)

- *Which of these relate to needs that are not necessarily physical?* (bead necklace, rock art)

- *On what continents were these various technologies found?* (all Earth's continents except Antarctica)

> ★**THINKING FURTHER:** *Making Generalizations* **Based on this Infographic *and anything else you have learned about Stone Age life, what generalizations can you make about that time?*** (Answers might reflect its inventiveness, its harsh—to us—conditions, its practicality, and its need for beauty.)

Technology CONNECTION

ADVENTURE TIME! CD-ROM
Enrich the *Infographic* with the *Time Lines* on the *Adventure Time!* CD-ROM.

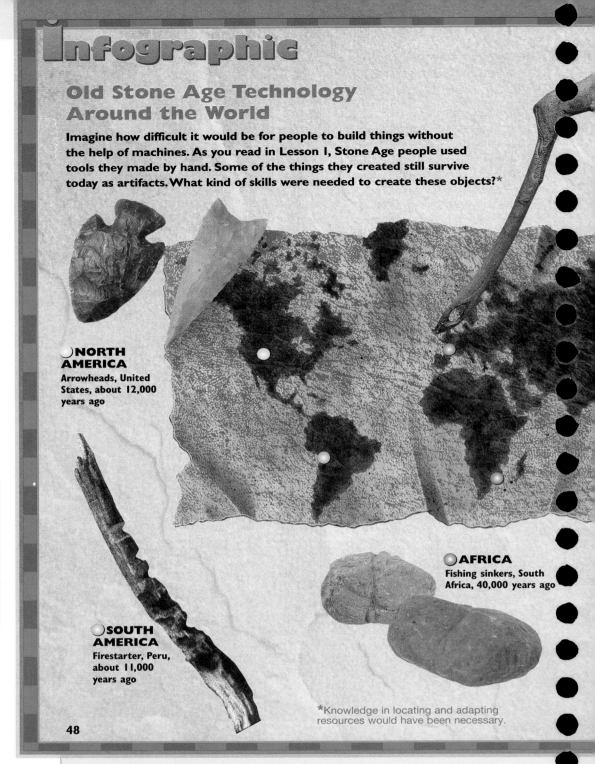

Infographic

Old Stone Age Technology Around the World

Imagine how difficult it would be for people to build things without the help of machines. As you read in Lesson 1, Stone Age people used tools they made by hand. Some of the things they created still survive today as artifacts. What kind of skills were needed to create these objects?*

◗NORTH AMERICA
Arrowheads, United States, about 12,000 years ago

◗SOUTH AMERICA
Firestarter, Peru, about 11,000 years ago

◗AFRICA
Fishing sinkers, South Africa, 40,000 years ago

*Knowledge in locating and adapting resources would have been necessary.

48

EXPANDING THE INFOGRAPHIC

RESEARCHING AND WRITING Use the *Thinking Further* question above to set students off on a project to create "A Profile of Old Stone Age Life." These profiles should be booklets that contain text, drawings, diagrams, and maps. They might follow "a day in the life of" format. You might want to suggest the research sources below to help them on their way. Acquaint the class with the term *Paleolithic* (*paleo*, "old," and *lithic*, "stone") since this is the term used for Old Stone Age in many research sources.

- Encyclopedia sources under such entries as *Stone Age, Old Stone Age, Paleolithic, caves, cave art, cave dwellers*
- A library subject catalog for similar entries
- *National Geographic Index,* 1888–1988 for similar entries
- Data base information on the Adventures CD-ROM

EUROPE
Spearthrower, France, about 14,000 years ago

ASIA
Bead necklace, China, about 30,000 years ago

AUSTRALIA
Rock art, Australia, about 20,000 years ago

WHY IT MATTERS

From about 40,000 years ago until the end of the Old Stone Age roughly 12,000 years ago, human beings spread throughout the world.

During the next 6,000 years, life would change rapidly. For the first time in the long history of the world, some people would live in small cities. Their homes would not be caves, but apartment-like buildings packed side by side. In the next lesson you will read about the changes that made such developments possible.

Reviewing Facts and Ideas

MAIN IDEAS

- Early people survived by hunting animals and gathering plants.
- Technology began with the creation of tools out of stone.
- At the end of the Old Stone Age, art and religious beliefs were a part of human life.

THINK ABOUT IT

1. How did the Old Stone Age get its name?

2. How did life on Earth change during the Old Stone Age, beginning around 40,000 years ago?

3. **FOCUS** What kinds of technology did the people of Border Cave use in order to survive?

4. **THINKING SKILL** Based on what evidence can we make the _conclusion_ that human life became more complex at the close of the Old Stone Age?

5. **WRITE** Write a paragraph that compares your life today with what it might have been like to live in Border Cave in the Old Stone Age.

Discussing WHY IT MATTERS Renew the discussion about why it is important that we learn from the past, both to expand our understanding of the world around us and to enrich our lives.

★**THINKING FURTHER: _Compare and Contrast_ _As you think about people's lives in the Old Stone Age, what do you think they can tell us about ourselves?_** _(Possible answers: We as human beings are innately curious and endlessly inventive. We are problems solvers who seek the skills and technology it takes to assure our survival. We have deep inner needs for meaning, beauty, and self-expression)_

3 CLOSE

MAIN IDEAS
Have students review the sequence in the development of human life.

- **_How did early modern humans get their food?_** _(by hunting and gathering)_

- **_What was the first technology developed?_** _(stone tools)_

- **_What signs do we have that early people had religious beliefs and a need for artistic expression?_** _(burial practices and works of art)_

✓ **EVALUATE**
Answers to Think About It

1. from the stone tools used
Make Inferences

2. Early people spread across the continents and developed new skills and new technologies.
Summarize

3. improving caves for shelter, using stone tools and bow and arrow for hunting, gathering plants for food and medicine
Recall Details

4. People had higher levels of skills, technology, religion, and art.
Make Conclusions

5. Encourage students to think of objects as well as beliefs and values.
Point of View

Write About It Have students write a paragraph describing one event in prehistoric life they would like to have witnessed.

MEETING INDIVIDUAL NEEDS

RETEACHING (Easy) Remind students that they have learned about several of the most important skills and technologies Old Stone Age people developed to survive. Have students make up a list of five skills and technologies they consider to be most important to our survival.

EXTENSION (Average) Remind students of the artifacts archaeologists have found from life in the Old Stone Age. Ask students to think of a personal time capsule to give archaeologists clues to their own lives. What items would they include in their time capsule? Have them list the items and give their reasons for including them.

ENRICHMENT (Challenging) Encourage students to think about future archaeologists and historians finding remains of our society centuries from now. Have them choose three or four artifacts that might be discovered. Then write reports as a historian might interpret them.

Lesson Overview

Artists reflect their environments and give us clues to life and the times when they lived.

Lesson Objective

★ Appreciate the legacy from the past that art provides.

1 PREPARE

MOTIVATE Review with students what they learned in Lesson 1 of this chapter: People's art offers insights into their beliefs and values and their lives.

SET PURPOSE Have students read this page to discover ways in which art can link the past to the present.

2 TEACH

Understanding the Concept of a Legacy Help students see ways in which art reflects the environment by having available a few examples of contemporary art, both representational and abstract. Students should see that in representational pieces, clothing and other furnishings show things that we use in our times. Abstract pieces reflect ideas from our times, for example, that art does not have to be a picture of something, but rather can simply show an artist's feelings.

Examining the Pictures As students study the pictures, help them to recognize the diversity of cultures and times that these pictures reflect. Then go through the pictures one by one.

- **As you look at the cave painting from Avignon, what would you say the artist valued in life?** *(The subject matter of animals hints at recognition of their great importance to survival at the time, or perhaps even at religious feelings about them.)*

Resource REMINDER

Anthology: *Stone Age Cave Paintings, p. 8*

Legacy
LINKING PAST AND PRESENT

ARTISTS
AND THEIR ENVIRONMENTS

Try to picture a world without art—no paintings, no sculpture, no photographs, or music. It would be a less interesting world!

Art has been here from very early times. Although art has changed much since then, there are many similarities between ancient and modern artists.

Artists from ancient times drew their world as they saw it. They painted objects and events that were important to them and their cultures. Modern artists also respond to their environments. They create art that reflects today's concerns.

Art from ancient times becomes especially important when there are no written records. Often historians study this art to discover early people's concerns and beliefs.

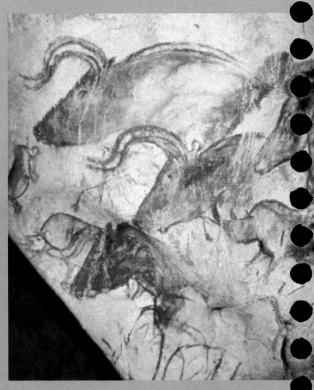

In 1994 hikers discovered cave paintings near Avignon (a vee NYAWN), France. These paintings are believed to be 20,000 years old. The artists used iron dust, sand, and clay to paint these images. Looking at art tells us some of what was important to the people who created it. What do you think was important to the artist who painted the animals here?*

50 *The movement of hunted animal herds may have been important to the artist.

VISUAL LITERACY

ABOUT THE CHINESE PAINTING ON SILK CLOTH This painting is presumably by a painter who created works during the Southern Sung court of China. Southern Sung landscape paintings expressed the artist's ideals of balance and the philosophical beliefs of New-Confucianism about man and nature. Invite students to study the painting. Possible questions include: Which things shown in the painting are man-made? Do these elements blend in with the other elements shown?

USING THE ANTHOLOGY

STONE AGE CAVE PAINTINGS, page 8 Encourage students to read the *Anthology* text and study the illustration of the cave painting from Chauvet, near Avignon. Have students use the painting in their textbooks and the painting in the *Anthology* to create a word picture of one aspect of life in prehistoric times in southern Europe.

This Chinese painting was created around A.D. 1000. The artist painted this scene on silk cloth.

Special Chinese and Japanese Fund 12.889 Courtesy, Museum of Fine Arts, Boston

Dutch painter Pieter Brueghel (BROY gul) painted this agricultural scene in the mid-1500s. What does this painting show about life in Europe in the 1500s?

Similar to artists in ancient France, modern artists use materials available to them to give their impressions of the world. American artist Hima Pamoedjo used a computer to create the image shown here.

51

- **How does the material used in the Chinese piece differ from that in the Avignon piece?** *(The Chinese piece uses silk; the Avignon piece uses the cave wall.)*

- **How does the subject matter differ?** *(The Chinese piece concentrates on nature in general, not just animals in particular.)*

- **Based on the Brueghel painting, what seems to be a major way of life in Europe at that time?** *(Farming must have been very important.)*

- **What does the final picture tell you about life and times in its period?** *(Computers are a major technology of the time and have become, for this artist, the technology to produce art.)*

★**THINKING FURTHER:** *Sequencing*
Using the art pieces shown here, how can you create a flow chart to show art technologies growing more complex over time? *(Help students work out a chart that shows an increasing number of steps, resources, technologies, and skills.)*

⭐ 3 CLOSE

SUM IT UP

To underscore the timelessness of art, help students to see that one type of art does not replace another. Point out that artists working together still create murals (like cave art), silk paintings, and oil paintings on canvas, as well as computer art.

EVALUATE

Write About It Write the following on the board: "Art provides a window to the past." Encourage students to write a paragraph to explain why this is true.

CURRICULUM CONNECTION

LINKS TO ART Have students create their own individual works of art. As they consider what they will create, first have them consider the elements of their environment they want to reflect—a representation of a scene of modern life, a modern landscape, an animal scene, or an expression of an idea, a feeling, or a reaction. Then have them choose a medium available in the classroom—drawing, painting, carving, modeling clay, or computer. When they have created their works, have them present them to the class and allow the class to identify and discuss the ways they reflect their environment.

MEETING INDIVIDUAL NEEDS

RETEACHING (Easy) Have students use art materials to do their own "Stone-Age cave paintings." Have them post their works around the classroom "cave walls."

EXTENSION (Average) Have some art books available. Tell students to select a piece of art that they particularly like. Have them present their choice to the class and tell how they think it reflects the environment it came from.

ENRICHMENT (Challenging) Have students arrange an "Art Through the Ages" exhibit. Divide the class into four groups and assign each an art style pictured in this *Legacy.* Tell them to do library research in their area and bring back picture books that reflect it. Have them arrange a display of open books for the class to view.

LESSON 2

PAGES 52–57

Lesson Overview

In the *New Stone Age*, *agriculture* let people settle in communities, and develop *civilizations*.

Lesson Objectives

★ Identify ways that the development of agriculture changed human life.

★ Understand how *surpluses* led to *specialization* and to *trade*.

★ Explain how trade fosters an exchange of both goods and ideas.

1 PREPARE

MOTIVATE Use the *Read Aloud* to introduce the event that was perhaps the greatest revolution in human history. Have students predict what the revolution was. Then turn to the *Read to Learn* question. Have students identify wheat as the subject of the photo.

SET PURPOSE Tell students they will learn how farming affected people from thousands of years ago right up to today. Use the *Vocabulary* terms to set the stage.

2 TEACH

Understanding THE BIG PICTURE
Help students understand the changes that took place as agriculture developed.

● **How long did the New Stone Age last?** *(about 6,000 years)*

● **What happened to change Earth at about the time the New Stone Age began?** *(Parts of Earth began to warm.)*

★**THINKING FURTHER: Cause and Effect** **On paper, have students organize the events into a chain showing causes and effects.** *(Earth warms → more vegetation → more animals → more people → more food → settling down → agriculture)*

Resource REMINDER

Practice and Project Book: *p. 15*
Anthology: *First Fruits of the Field, pp. 9–10*

50,000 B.C.	40,000 B.C.	30,000 B.C.	20,000 B.C.	10,000 B.C.	4,000 B.C.

AGRICULTURE CHANGES THE WORLD

READ ALOUD

What would you do if there were no markets or restaurants from which to buy food? How would you find something to eat? You learned in the last lesson that early people faced this challenge by hunting and gathering their food from the wild. However, you can probably think of another way people get food from Earth.

Focus Activity

READ TO LEARN
What was life like in an early farming community?

VOCABULARY
agriculture
New Stone Age
domesticate
surplus
specialization
civilization
trade

THE BIG PICTURE

About 12,000 years ago Earth's cool climate began to warm. This change caused the number of plants and animals on Earth to soar. The number of people grew as well, as hunters and gatherers around the world took advantage of Earth's new bounty.

Many archaeologists think that some hunters and gatherers began building permanent homes in places rich with wild grains and animals. In time, these early people started to experiment with agriculture. Agriculture is the raising of crops and animals for human use. These experiments changed life on Earth forever.

The period beginning about 12,000 years ago and ending roughly 6,000 years ago is called the New Stone Age. During this time people all around the world still depended on stone tools, but began experimenting with agriculture. Agriculture continues to shape the ways we live today. It is the reason you can go to a supermarket. It is also the reason you may live on a farm—or in a town or city.

52

SHELTERED INSTRUCTION

READING STRATEGIES & LANGUAGE DEVELOPMENT

CAUSE AND EFFECT Use a bat and ball to demonstrate cause and effect. Then ask students find the causes and effects of the growth of agriculture as they read this lesson. **[SDAIE STRATEGY: MODELING/CONTEXTUALIZATION]**

ROOT WORDS One of the *Vocabulary* terms in this lesson—*civilization*—provides an opportunity to have students investigate the idea of base words or word roots. Have them look this term up in the dictionary to discover that its Latin root is *civis*, which means "citizen." This is also the root for *city, civic,* and *civil.* Help them to recognize that all these belong to the same family of words. Have students look for the relationship between *city* and *civilization* as they read the lesson. Civilization does not develop until people gather together to form communities that often grow into cities.

CATAL HUYUK

On the grassy banks of the Carsamba (chahr SHAHM bah) River in southern Turkey sits a large mound. The mound covers over 32 acres, an area the size of 21 football fields. Underneath this big but ordinary-looking hill rests one of the world's first cities: Catal Huyuk (CHAH tul HOO yook). Parts of this city on the Carsamba River plain existed over 8,500 years ago.

Catal Huyuk is the largest city this old ever uncovered by archaeologists. The city once housed about 5,000 people. How could so many people live close together at a time when most still lived as hunters and gatherers? The answer is agriculture.

Agriculture Brings Change

Agriculture provided a way for people to live in large groups without the need to travel great distances to gather food. To use agriculture, people first had to domesticate (duh MES tih kayt) plants and animals. To domesticate means to train something to be useful to people. For example, people at Catal Huyuk learned to plant seeds and care for edible plants like wheat, barley, peas, and lentils.

The world's first farmers also learned to domesticate animals such as wild goats, cattle, and sheep. Domestica-

CATAL HUYUK

MAP WORK

Catal Huyuk, the site of one of the world's first farming communities, lies in present-day Turkey.

What countries border Turkey?

tion involved more than taming the animals. It meant breeding them to be most useful to humans. Wild sheep, for example, have very little wool. In contrast, domestic sheep have been bred to grow thick layers of the useful material.

The ruins of Catal Huyuk were not discovered until 1958. Today many tourists visit these extensive ruins.

CURRICULUM CONNECTION

LINKS TO SCIENCE Remind students that global warming is sometimes in the news and ask them what they know about it. (Gases in the air are trapping the sun's rays instead of letting them reflect off Earth's surface, thus making the atmosphere surrounding Earth warmer.)

LINKS TO SCIENCE Ask students if they know what caused the global warming 12,000 years ago. Call for a volunteer environmental research team to investigate the warming that took place 12,000 years ago and the scientific reasons for it. Have them prepare a presentation of their findings to the class.

CATAL HUYUK

Help students to pronounce Catal Huyuk so they can discuss it comfortably.

More

MAP WORK

Refer students to the map on this page after they have read the two opening paragraphs on Catal Huyuk.

- *In what modern-day country was the ancient city of Catal Huyuk uncovered?* (Turkey)

- *In what part of Turkey have its remains been found?* (the center, toward the south)

- *How large a population did Catal Huyuk have?* (about 5,000)

★**THINKING FURTHER:** *Making Conclusions* **Describe the geographic features of the area in which this city was located. Why might they have favored the development of a city?** *(The site on a river—the Carsamba—would have furnished water, and the river plain would probably be a good place for farming.)*

Discussing Agriculture Brings Change Help students recognize the development of agriculture as a marvel of human beings adapting their environment to their needs.

- *What does it mean to domesticate something?* (to train it to be useful to human beings)

- *How did human beings domesticate plants and animals?* (They worked out how to plant seeds, tend crops, and tame animals so that they could use them for food and clothing.)

★**THINKING FURTHER:** *Compare and Contrast* **How would you compare and contrast life after agriculture with life before it?** *(Food sources were probably more reliable afterward, and settled community living was probably more comfortable and socially rewarding.)*

LIVING IN CATAL HUYUK

Prepare students to look for clues to the culture of the people of Catal Huyuk. Remind them to use the same tools to interpret them that they used to study Azeez's culture in Chapter 1. Also encourage students to compare life in Catal Huyuk with city life today.

More DIAGRAM WORK

Have students study the diagram and the text. Encourage them to use both to see how one illustrates the other.

- ● *Where did the artisans, or craft-workers, do their work?* (in the courtyard surrounded by houses)

- ● *What activity took place outside the group of houses?* (herding)

Learning About A New Kind of Home Have students point to features in the art that illustrate the text.

- ● *How did roof entrances help people to protect themselves?* (An attacker coming in could be easily hit.)

- ● *How did people in Catal Huyuk get from house to house?* (by climbing to the rooftops and walking across)

★THINKING FURTHER: *Making Generalizations* **How can you support the generalization that housing in Catal Huyuk was sturdy, comfortable, and protective?** (Students may note such features as the roof entrance, fireplaces, and sleeping platforms.)

*Answers should include craftwork, farming, building, herding.

LIVING IN CATAL HUYUK

In some ways living in Catal Huyuk was like living in a city today. In other ways it was very different. The similarities and differences begin with the kinds of houses people lived in.

A New Kind of Home

The homes of Catal Huyuk were built to last. Houses had brick walls coated with white plaster. The large, flat reed roofs were supported by wooden beams. Houses were built right against each other, perhaps to defend the city from attack. There were no streets in Catal Huyuk and no doors on the houses. People entered their homes from the roof, by climbing down ladders!

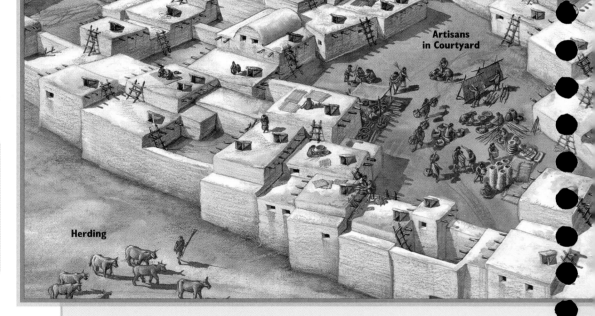

Doorway · **Rooftop Ladder** · **Vessels** · **Sleeping Platforms** · **Artisans in Courtyard** · **Herding**

ROOFTOP LIVING IN CATAL HUYUK

What jobs shown in the diagram required special skills?★

GLOBAL CONNECTION

A CITY OLDER THAN CATAL HUYUK Jericho, an ancient city, was old when Catal Huyuk was just developing.

- Located 10 miles north of the Dead Sea, Jericho is the oldest city yet discovered by archaeologists.

- People began moving into Jericho 12,000 years ago.

- The walls of Jericho were first erected around the city about 10,000 years ago and reached a height of about 17 feet.

- Jericho was periodically destroyed and rebuilt. About 3,500 years ago, the Egyptians destroyed it. The Bible records its destruction a few centuries later when Joshua, successor to Moses, "fit [fought] the battle of Jericho and the walls came tumbling down," in the words of an old gospel song.

CITIZENSHIP★

COMMUNITY COOPERATION Use Catal Huyuk to help students see the need for community cooperation.

- Early people founded and designed their settlements purposefully, often in places high enough so that they could see approaching enemies.

- When early community builders did not have the advantage of height, they often banded together to construct protection from enemies. Often, they built walls around their community to repel attack, as in Jericho.

- Catal Huyuk chose to build houses close together to construct a defense.

About one out of every three buildings in the city was probably a temple. Therefore, archaeologists think that religion played a big role in daily life. And what may have been the world's first wall paintings—of cattle, leopards, and other things—filled these rooms. This fact suggests that religion in Catal Huyuk may have focused on the success of domestic crops and animals. These were important to the survival of people of the city.

Like many apartment buildings today, homes in Catal Huyuk were all about the same size and shape. Coming down from the roof, people entered a home's main living room. Near the base of the ladder were a fireplace and an oven for heating and cooking. Built into the walls were raised platforms covered with reed mats. These platforms served as all-purpose sofas and beds. A tiny doorway led to the family's storage room. There, large clay pots held stores of wheat and barley.

New Ways of Life

People in Catal Huyuk depended on the grain stores kept in these pots. Agriculture created a new food surplus that hunters and gatherers never had. A surplus is an extra supply of something. Enough crops could be harvested to provide food for the whole year. Cattle provided a steady supply of milk and meat.

The people who worked as farmers were able to provide food for all of the people of Catal Huyuk. There was even some left over for winter. But farming for a whole community was a demanding job. It left little time for other tasks.

The demands on farmers' time led to specialization, or people training to do particular kinds of work. Thus, while some people farmed, other people made wheat into bread flour. Others specialized in making things like tools, bricks, and pots. Since farmers could produce more food than their families needed, they could exchange their surplus food with workers who made other products.

Agriculture changed everyday chores in the city as well. Taking out the trash, for example, was not as simple as burying it in a nearby field. People had to carry it up to the roof, across other people's roofs, and over to the nearest empty courtyard. Courtyards, spaces often left by broken-down homes, served as local garbage dumps.

These changes in community life sparked the growth of a complex new civilization (sihv uh luh ZAY shun) at Catal Huyuk. A civilization is a culture that has developed systems of specialization, religion, learning, and government. The busy town grew until it had about 1,000 homes.

Links to MATHEMATICS

That's a Lot of Wheat!

How much more wheat can we produce now than people could during the New Stone Age?

It's impossible to know exactly how much wheat people were able to grow in Catal Huyuk. But one thing is certain. Agriculture has come a long way since the New Stone Age. In the United States today, modern farming methods help to provide wheat for everyone in America—with surplus to sell to other countries.

In the modern United States, each acre of farmland yields about 36 bushels of wheat per year. If each bushel weighs 60 pounds, how many pounds of wheat are produced on each acre of farmland?*

*2,160 pounds

55

- *What tells you that these people held religious beliefs? (the temple rooms)*

Investigating New Ways of Life
Help students see that agriculture had to supply food for everybody in Catal Huyuk.

- *Where did the herders and farmers work? (in the fields away from the dwellings)*

- *What is a surplus and how is it created? (It is something over and above what the people who produce it need for their own immediate use.)*

- *How did the fact that the farmers at Catal Huyuk could produce surplus food lead to specialization? (It freed others from the need to produce food and let them pursue other trades.)*

- *How does specialization both enrich community life and make it more complex? (It gives a community more and probably better goods and it differentiates people by their jobs.)*

★THINKING FURTHER: *Making Conclusions Why must there be differentiation for civilization to develop? (Civilization calls for people with different abilities and specialties to perform the different duties it demands—to produce different goods, to perform the different functions demanded by religion, learning, and government.)*

CURRICULUM CONNECTION

LINKS TO MATHEMATICS: THAT'S A LOT OF WHEAT! Students will have to call upon their multiplication skills to work out this problem. They should multiply 36 (for bushels per year) times 60 pounds (for pounds per bushel) to get an acre yield of 2,160 pounds per year.

LINKS TO MATHEMATICS Students may be encouraged to figure out how much of some farm product (apples, milk, oranges, etc.) they consume in a week. Then have them multiply that amount by 52 weeks and come up with figures about how much a farmer has to produce to provide that farm product for the student.

BACKGROUND INFORMATION

ABOUT CATAL HUYUK Catal Huyuk is the largest New Stone Age mound in Southwest Asia.

- Catal Huyuk is one of the earliest New Stone Age settlements discovered so far by archaeologists.
- The artifacts found at Catal Huyuk are on display at the Archaeological Museum in Ankara, Turkey.

SECOND-LANGUAGE SUPPORT

Have second-language learners create an illustrated chart comparing aspects of life in Catal Huyuk with their own lives. Then have them write and read captions for their illustrations to further aid their language facility and comprehension.

A BUSY CITY

Help students understand how skilled work and trade enrich people's lives.

Learning About Signs of Movement Have a student list the elements of new technology on the board.

- **What technologies did the people of Catal Huyuk develop?** *(pottery, thread making, weaving, metal making and metal working, jewelry making)*

- **What is obsidian and for what was it used?** *(a glassy black rock; used to make mirrors and knives)*

★**THINKING FURTHER:** *Compare and Contrast* **How would you compare the work people at Catal Huyuk did with work in our society today?** *(Students will see there is greater differentiation in our society.)*

Discussing People from Near and Far Develop the understanding that trade adds ideas as well as goods.

- **Why do people trade?** *(to get things they cannot make for themselves and to earn from what they do produce)*

★**THINKING FURTHER:** *Making Conclusions* **Why is trade more than just the exchange of goods?** *(Trade brings people from different places into contact so they learn new ways of doing things.)*

More CHART WORK

Refer students to the chart on p. 57.

- **On which continents had cattle been domesticated?** *(Africa, Asia, Europe)*

- **What evidence can you find that grains were major crops across the world?** *(The chart shows grains on all continents but South America.)*

- **Were horses an Eastern or Western Hemisphere animal?** *(Eastern)*

★**THINKING FURTHER:** *Predicting* **How would you predict that agricultural production will change after the New Stone Age?** *(Possible answer: Agriculture will become more complex and products will be spread around the world.)*

A BUSY CITY

In its time, Catal Huyuk was probably widely known for its arts, crafts, and tools. The city's workers used new kinds of technology to make wonderful assortments of clay pots, woven cloth, and copper jewelry. These were among the first of their kind in the world. By about age 12, girls and boys probably helped to make these products, since they were taught the skills of their mothers and fathers.

Although people in Catal Huyuk depended on stone tools, they began to work with a new material: copper. After gathering pieces of copper, craftworkers made their fires burn hot enough to soften the metal. Once softened, the copper was hammered into the shapes of rings, beads, or pins.

It also took several steps to produce fine wool cloth. First, wool was sheared from domestic sheep. Next, the material was separated and twisted into thread. Finally, the thread was carefully woven into cloth on wooden looms.

Artifacts from Catal Huyuk include necklaces and artwork of a hunt dance.

Signs of Movement

Catal Huyuk's crafts attracted many people to the city. They wanted to own some of the useful and beautiful new products. People in Catal Huyuk wanted to see the things others had to offer. Trade, or the exchange of goods, boomed between city residents and visitors to the city.

One thing that people in Catal Huyuk traded was obsidian (ub SIHD ee un). Obsidian is a glassy, black rock used to make beautiful mirrors and razor-sharp knives. City residents probably traveled to a nearby volcano to gather the black stones. Cattle were used to carry back the heavy loads. Craftworkers then made the obsidian into goods to trade with people from all around the region.

People from Near and Far

The people of Catal Huyuk probably traded obsidian knives and arrowheads with people who lived in forests miles away. In return, they received oak wood needed for house-building, along with such treats as apples and nuts.

Traders from nearby areas probably brought many other popular goods to Catal Huyuk. These goods included red paint used in temples and raw copper to be made into tools and jewelry.

Traders also came to Catal Huyuk from faraway places. Archaeologists have found remains of the city's special obsidian goods in ancient settlements as far away as modern Syria. They have also found pieces of Syrian pottery in Catal Huyuk, along with shells from the Red Sea.

People, as well as goods, were on the move, both to and from Catal Huyuk. Archaeologists have found evidence that people from far and wide

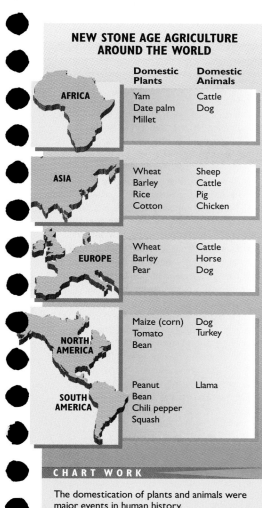

NEW STONE AGE AGRICULTURE AROUND THE WORLD

	Domestic Plants	Domestic Animals
AFRICA	Yam Date palm Millet	Cattle Dog
ASIA	Wheat Barley Rice Cotton	Sheep Cattle Pig Chicken
EUROPE	Wheat Barley Pear	Cattle Horse Dog
NORTH AMERICA	Maize (corn) Tomato Bean	Dog Turkey
SOUTH AMERICA	Peanut Bean Chili pepper Squash	Llama

CHART WORK

The domestication of plants and animals were major events in human history.

1. Which animals were domesticated in Europe?
2. Which plants were grown in South America?

moved to and lived in the city. They brought with them their own skills and traditions. This may be part of the reason for the growth of this rich and complex civilization.

CHART WORK: **1.** cattle, dog, horse **2.** peanut, bean, chili pepper, squash

WHY IT MATTERS

As the chart on this page shows, many groups began to develop agriculture during the New Stone Age. The relatively complex civilization of Catal Huyuk showed just how much agriculture could change life. Even bigger changes were yet to come. In the next chapter you will read about another civilization based on agriculture. It, too, rose up along the banks of a river. Unlike the people of Catal Huyuk, the people there developed ways to tell their secrets to others through the ages.

✓✓ Reviewing Facts and Ideas

MAIN IDEAS

- Agriculture made it possible for a few people to raise food for an entire group. Others could specialize, or concentrate on other tasks.
- People of Catal Huyuk were among the first to make pottery and obsidian and metal products. They also traded.

THINK ABOUT IT

1. What is involved in domesticating plants and animals?
2. How did trade help people, both outside and within Catal Huyuk? How did trade help the city to grow?
3. **FOCUS** How did the development of agriculture change the way people lived?
4. **THINKING SKILL** Suppose that you are a visitor to Catal Huyuk. *Decide* whether you want to become a farmer or craftworker for the city, or to remain a hunter and gatherer in the forests nearby.
5. **GEOGRAPHY** Explain how agriculture changed the way people interacted with their environments.

57

Discussing WHY IT MATTERS Have students refer to cause and effect as they review how civilizations arose.

★**THINKING FURTHER:** *Classifying*
How would you design a chart showing the steps that humans went through to develop civilization? (Students' charts should include some of these elements: hunting and gathering, settling in one spot, developing agriculture, building communities, surpluses, specializing, trading with others, religion, government)

★ 3 CLOSE

MAIN IDEAS

Call on individual students to answer these questions.

- *What revolution occurred during the New Stone Age?* (the agricultural revolution)
- *How did specialization make new and better products available?* (Craftworkers could perfect their skills, improve their technology, and invent new goods.)

EVALUATE
✓ **Answers to Think About It**

1. planting seeds and tending crops; taming, breeding, and tending animals *Summarize*
2. It made more and better goods available to both. *Make Conclusions*
3. People went from the life of hunters and gatherers to the settled life of the established community. *Recall Details*
4. Accept any well-reasoned decision. *Form Generalizations*
5. Students should explain ways that with agriculture and specialization people have both adapted themselves to their environment and adapted the environment to themselves. *Five Themes of Geography: Human/Environment Interactions*

Write About It Tell students to select an occupation that they would've liked to have had during the New Stone Age. Have them write a paragraph in which they tell what made it possible for them to do this job and what their work adds to the community.

MEETING INDIVIDUAL NEEDS

RETEACHING (Easy) Have students create a poster entitled "From Agriculture to Civilization." On their posters they should both spell out the causes and their effects and illustrate them.

EXTENSION (Average) Refer students back to Question 4 of "Think About It." Tell them to elaborate on their original answers by making a chart on which they contrast the benefits and disadvantages of each way of life. Then have them write a complete essay—introduction, body, conclusion—based on it.

ENRICHMENT (Challenging) Ask students what life might be like if agriculture had never been developed. How would life be different today? Have them write a science-fiction story about modern life without agriculture.

SKILLS LESSON
PAGES 58–59

Lesson Overview
Time lines show events in chronological order using B.C. and A.D.

Lesson Objective
★ Explain the meaning and use of B.C. and A.D.

⭐ 1 PREPARE

MOTIVATE After students have read *Why the Skill Matters,* help them to see that time lines are a shorthand way to organize information. Have them discuss the advantages of time lines.

SET PURPOSE Have students read *Helping Yourself* to get an overview of how to read time lines.

⭐ 2 TEACH

Why the Skill Matters Write *B.C.* and *A.D.* and *c.* on the board. Ask the class what these abbreviations stand for. Have them read *Using the Skill.*

- **What system is used to divide the past into two major time periods?** *(We divide time at the birth of Jesus by using* B.C. *and* A.D.*)*

- **What do B.C. and A.D. stand for?** *(*B.C.*—years before the birth of Jesus;* A.D.*—afterward)*

- **What does c. stand for?** *(circa meaning "about" or "around," to indicate a rough date)*

Technology CONNECTION

ADVENTURE TIME! CD-ROM
Enrich the Study Skills lesson with the Unit Activity on the *Adventure Time!* CD-ROM.

Resource REMINDER

Practice and Project Book: *p. 16*
Technology: *Adventure Time!* CD-ROM

STUDYSKILLS

Reading Time Lines

VOCABULARY
time line
circa

WHY THE SKILL MATTERS

During the New Stone Age, agriculture became a worldwide development. People in North Africa began domesticating cattle and barley, while people in Central and South America raised corn, beans, and animals called llamas. Farmers in other regions domesticated other plants and animals.

One of the easiest ways to keep track of when events happened is to use a time line. A time line is a diagram that shows when things took place in a given period of time. Its words tell what happened and when. The spaces between descriptions indicate how much time passed between events.

USING THE SKILL

One of the time lines below shows how agriculture affected human life during the New Stone Age and beyond. Use the hints in the Helping Yourself box on the next page to guide you in reading time lines.

As you study the labels on the time lines, you will notice the letters B.C. and A.D. Today most people in our country use a 1,500-year-old system that divides time into two periods. "B.C." stands for "before Christ," or before Jesus Christ was born (about 2,000 years ago). "A.D." stands for "anno Domini"—Latin for "in the year of our Lord"—and refers to years since Jesus' birth.

To read B.C. dates you need to remember: the *higher* the number, the *earlier* that time is in history. For example, the New Stone Age began about 10,000 B.C. and ended about 4000 B.C. This was 6,000 years after it began. Reading A.D. dates is easier because we do it all the time. The *higher* an A.D. number is, the *later* that time is in history.

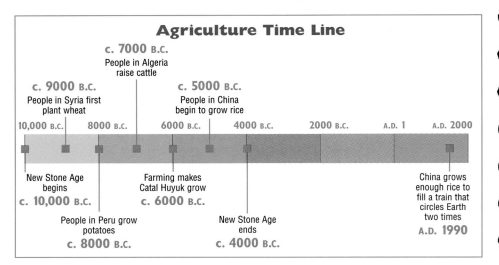

Agriculture Time Line

c. 7000 B.C.
People in Algeria raise cattle

c. 9000 B.C.
People in Syria first plant wheat

c. 5000 B.C.
People in China begin to grow rice

| 10,000 B.C. | 8000 B.C. | 6000 B.C. | 4000 B.C. | 2000 B.C. | A.D. 1 | A.D. 2000 |

New Stone Age begins
c. 10,000 B.C.

Farming makes Catal Huyuk grow
c. 6000 B.C.

China grows enough rice to fill a train that circles Earth two times
A.D. 1990

People in Peru grow potatoes
c. 8000 B.C.

New Stone Age ends
c. 4000 B.C.

58

SEQUENCE Discuss with the class how historians often organize their writings in chronological order. Why would this make sense? (If you're presenting the story of the past, you should tell things in order, so that your reader can follow events.) Point out that making a time line while reading a history lesson—a shorthand way of keeping track of important events—provides a handy study guide for quick review.

COMBINING FORMS Call students' attention to the Latin term *anno Domini* in the lesson and have them translate *anno* from the Latin as "year." Then write *anniversary* and *annual* on the board and have them relate the meaning of these two words to their root word *anno.*

*New Stone Age; B.C.; 1,000 years ** Grass; answers might include plastic, metals, silicon.

CHAPTER 3 • SKILLS LESSON

You will also notice that some dates on the time lines have the letter *c.* before them. The lowercase *c.* stands for *circa,* another Latin word. Circa means "about" or "around." If historians are not sure exactly when something happened, they use the term *circa.*

Study the agriculture time line on the opposite page. On what period of time does it focus? Is most of that time A.D. or B.C.? About how many years passed between the time people in China began to grow rice and the end of the New Stone Age?*

TRYING THE SKILL

After you have practiced reading the agriculture time line, try studying the time line about the growth of technology. Each entry describes how people used materials from

their environments to make useful tools or crafts. With what material did people in Peru make nets and baskets in 8000 B.C.? What sorts of materials are people using in A.D. 1997?**

REVIEWING THE SKILL

Use the technology time line on this page to answer the following questions:

1. What sort of information do time lines show?

2. About how many years does the time line below cover?

3. How many years passed between the time Japanese people first began making clay pots and the time people in Iraq began painting pottery?

4. How does using the time line help you to understand the development of agriculture?

HELPING Yourself

- A time line shows when things happened in the past.
- Look at the first and last dates to see how much time is being covered.
- Read the title and each entry.
- Examine the spaces that separate events.

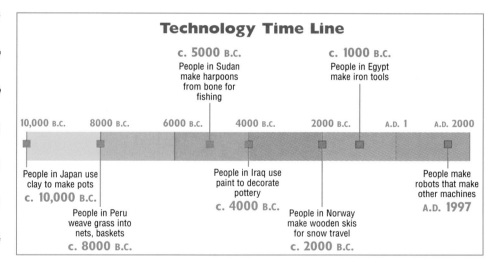

Technology Time Line

c. 5000 B.C. People in Sudan make harpoons from bone for fishing

c. 1000 B.C. People in Egypt make iron tools

10,000 B.C. 8000 B.C. 6000 B.C. 4000 B.C. 2000 B.C. A.D. 1 A.D. 2000

People in Japan use clay to make pots **c. 10,000 B.C.**

People in Peru weave grass into nets, baskets **c. 8000 B.C.**

People in Iraq use paint to decorate pottery **c. 4000 B.C.**

People in Norway make wooden skis for snow travel **c. 2000 B.C.**

People make robots that make other machines **A.D. 1997**

59

- *How do you translate c. 7000 B.C.?* (about 7,000 years before Jesus)

- *How many years separate each of the B.C. years shown here?* (1,000)

- *How many years before the Chinese started growing rice did people first plant wheat in Syria?* (about 4,000)

★THINKING FURTHER: *Making Conclusions* Compare the B.C. dates here, preceded by *c.,* and the A.D. date, which is not. What might account for this difference? *(The more recent an event, the more certain its date.)*

Trying the Skill Refer the class to the Technology Time Line on this page and the *Helping Yourself* tips.

- *Are the intervals between dates on this time line all the same?* (No, the intervals vary: Two intervals are 1,000 years long, two are 2,000 years long, and two are 3,000 years long.)

- *How does this time line show differences in intervals?* (A shorter time span has a shorter space; a longer time span has a longer space.)

★THINKING FURTHER: Compare and Contrast **How would you compare the level of A.D. 2000 technology with that of the B.C. years?** *(The technological leap has been enormous over 2,000 years.)*

 3 CLOSE

SUM IT UP
Have students make a time line of important events in their lives.

EVALUATE
✓ **Answers to Reviewing the Skill**
1. events and when they happened
2. 12,000 years
3. 6,000 years
4. Students may suggest there are more crops as time passes and the crops are more widely spread.

MEETING INDIVIDUAL NEEDS

RETEACHING (Easy) List the following dates on the board. Then have students list them in their proper order and set up a time line to reflect the amounts of time between them. A.D. 1850, 2000 B.C., A.D. 200, 1000 B.C., A.D. 1000, A.D. 2000.

EXTENSION (Average) Have students thumb through the time lines in this unit and choose different events from each of them. Have them make a time line listing the events in their proper order and showing the time between them.

ENRICHMENT (Challenging) Have students do research to find out when the following events happened: the Declaration of Independence, Napoleon's defeat at Waterloo, the birth of Julius Caesar, and Marco Polo's return to Italy. Then have them make a time line giving these dates in order and showing the time between them.

DISCUSSING MAJOR EVENTS Help students use the time line both to sequence the events shown and to get a sense of the length of time covered by the time line.

- **What is the earliest human activity shown and when did it take place?** *(People lived at Border Cave, about 40,000 B.C.)*

- **How long was it from that time until the city of Catal Huyuk developed?** *(40,000 minus 8,500 = 31,500 years, or 315 centuries)*

- **When did the New Stone Age begin, and how long did it last?** *(about 12,000 B.C.; 12,000 minus 6,000 = 6,000 years, or 60 centuries)*

Answers to
THINKING ABOUT VOCABULARY

1. trade
2. Old Stone Age
3. agriculture
4. domesticate
5. surplus
6. specialization
7. New Stone Age
8. circa
9. time line
10. civilization

Answers to
THINKING ABOUT FACTS

1. remains found in Africa that may be 2 million years old

2. In the New Stone Age, people began experimenting with agriculture.

3. Agriculture allowed them to settle down in one place, build permanent homes, and live in large communities.

Resource REMINDER

Practice and Project Book: *p. 17*

Assessment Book: *Chapter 3 Test*

Transparency: *Graphic Organizer, Compare and Contrast Chart*

CHAPTER 3 REVIEW

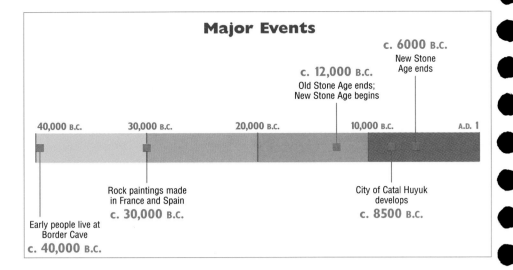

Major Events

- **c. 6000 B.C.** New Stone Age ends
- **c. 12,000 B.C.** Old Stone Age ends; New Stone Age begins

| 40,000 B.C. | 30,000 B.C. | 20,000 B.C. | 10,000 B.C. | A.D. 1 |

- Rock paintings made in France and Spain **c. 30,000 B.C.**
- Early people live at Border Cave **c. 40,000 B.C.**
- City of Catal Huyuk develops **c. 8500 B.C.**

THINKING ABOUT VOCABULARY

Number a sheet of paper from 1 to 10. Beside each number write the word or term from the list below that best matches the definition.

agriculture	Old Stone Age
circa	specialization
civilization	surplus
domesticate	time line
New Stone Age	trade

1. An exchange of goods
2. The period until about 12,000 years ago when the use of stone tools was widespread
3. The raising of crops and animals for human use
4. To train plants or animals to be useful to people
5. An extra supply of something
6. The doing of particular kinds of work
7. The period from 12,000 to 6,000 years ago when people developed agriculture and used stone tools
8. A Latin word that means "about" or "around"
9. A diagram that shows when things took place in a certain period of time
10. A culture with developed systems of religion, learning, and government

THINKING ABOUT FACTS

1. What are the earliest signs of human life that scientists have found?
2. How was the New Stone Age different from the Old Stone Age?
3. What changes in the way people lived did agriculture make possible?
4. What is Catal Huyuk, and where is it located? What did archaeologists learn after they uncovered it?
5. What is obsidian? Why was it important to the people of Catal Huyuk?

60

SECOND-LANGUAGE SUPPORT

WORKING WITH PEERS Assign an English-proficient partner to work with each second-language learner on the Chapter Review. Partners should review notes on the lessons, time lines, and questions together. They can brainstorm ideas to use in their paragraph and writing assignments and create them collaboratively.

ORAL PRACTICE Second-language learners will benefit from reading their written work aloud as oral practice. The English-proficient partner can read the paragraph aloud first as a model. Then the second-language learner can read along with his or her partner on a second reading.

THINK AND WRITE ◄═▷

WRITING A PARAGRAPH OF CONTRAST
Write a paragraph about the differences between the Old Stone Age and the New Stone Age. Discuss methods of obtaining food, types of shelter, and tools.

WRITING A JOURNAL ENTRY
Suppose that you have gone back in time to live in the New Stone Age. Using the diagram of Catal Huyuk on page 54, write a journal entry about your life there. Include details about the way you live, the work you do, and the people you see.

WRITING ABOUT PERSPECTIVES
We are different in many ways from people who lived in the Old Stone Age. However, we also have much in common. Describe three ways you think you are like a person of your age who lived near Border Cave about 40,000 years ago.

APPLYING STUDY SKILLS

READING TIME LINES

1. What is a time line?

2. Look at the time line on page 60. Add the following event in its correct place on the time line: People in Peru weave grass into nets and baskets.

3. Look at the time line on page 60. Add the following event in its correct place: People in China begin to grow rice.

4. On the time line on page 60, add the following event in its correct place: Earth's cool climate began to warm.

5. In what ways are time lines useful?

4. A city settled about 8,500 years ago in southern Turkey; archaeologists learned about its housing, its religion, its pottery, what it grew, animals it raised, its specialized jobs, the products it made, and its trade.

5. A glassy, black rock from which mirrors and razor-sharp knives can be made; products they made from it gave the people of Catal Huyuk valuable goods to trade far and wide.

Answers to
APPLYING STUDY SKILLS

1. a diagram that shows when things took place in a given period of time

2. Students should recognize that the event would be placed at 8000 B.C. on the time line.

3. Students should recognize that the event would be placed at 5000 B.C. on the time line.

4. Students should recognize that the event would be placed at 10,000 B.C. on the time line.

5. Time lines help us to see events in chronological order and thus help us to understand how earlier events can influence or cause later events.

Summing Up the Chapter

Copy the compare-and-contrast chart below on a separate piece of paper. Then review the chapter to find some of the things that changed during the Old and the New Stone Ages. When you have filled in the chart, use the information to write a paragraph that answers the question "How did early people use their environment to improve their lives?"

MAIN IDEA	Early people developed innovative ways of adapting to their environment in order to meet their basic survival needs.

Old Stone Age	New Stone Age
Creation of stone tools	Raising crops
Use of fire	Domestication of plants and animals
Hunting and gathering	Beginning of specialization
Living in a cave	Creation of surplus and exchange of goods

61

SUGGESTIONS FOR SUMMING UP THE CHAPTER

After students have copied the compare-and-contrast chart on their papers, have them read and discuss the main idea aloud and identify the "basic survival needs" (food, clothing, shelter). Then have them review Lesson 1 for examples of ways people used their environments to serve these needs during the Old Stone Age and Lesson 2 for the similar examples during the New Stone Age. Suggested examples for them appear on the reproduced text page above. Before students begin writing their paragraphs, tell them to ponder how each of their examples helped to improve life.

ASSESSING THINK AND WRITE: *For performance assessment, see Assessment Book, Chapter 3, pp. T51-T53.*

UNIT 1 REVIEW

Answers to THINKING ABOUT VOCABULARY

1. civilization
2. geography
3. archaeology
4. values
5. oral tradition
6. climate
7. Old Stone Age
8. time line
9. degree
10. artifact

Suggestions for THINK AND WRITE

1. Students should note seasonal differences in climate and tell why the geographical features they pick are interesting. Also encourage students to consider the level of interest when they choose local customs to describe. Which are most likely to interest a person far away?

2. Invite students to think about the areas of their lives that mean the most to them as they choose their objects. Have them describe what each object means personally and what it might reveal to an historian.

3. Have students recall the difference in the level of technology reached by each period as they make up questions and answers for their two interview subjects. The New Stone Age person will have the benefit of what the Old Stone Age accomplished but the reverse is not true.

THINKING ABOUT VOCABULARY

archaeology
artifact
civilization
climate
degree

geography
Old Stone Age
oral tradition
time line
values

Number a sheet of paper from 1 to 10. Beside each number write the word or term from the list above that best matches the definition.

1. A culture with developed systems of religion, learning, and government
2. The study of Earth, including its land, water, weather, and plants
3. The study of the remains of past cultures
4. The things people believe in and think are important
5. The passing on by word of mouth of stories, history, and information
6. The weather pattern over a long period of time
7. The period from 2 million to about 12,000 years ago when people used mostly stone tools
8. A diagram that shows when things happened during a certain period of time
9. A unit of map measurement that describes distance between lines of latitude and longitude
10. An object made by somebody in the past

THINK AND WRITE

WRITING A LETTER
Write to somebody who lives far away. Describe the climate and two or three interesting geographical features of your area. Also tell about some of the customs of the people who live in your community.

WRITING ABOUT PERSPECTIVES
Suppose that you are asked to bury three things that belong to you. These objects should help some future historian learn about the way you lived. Write a paragraph about what you would choose and why.

WRITING AN INTERVIEW
Suppose you could interview one person from the Old Stone Age and one person from the New Stone Age. Write a set of questions you would ask each person and the answers you think they would give.

BUILDING SKILLS

1. **Latitude and longitude** Look at the map on page 15. What is the approximate latitude and longitude of Sri Lanka?
2. **Latitude and longitude** Look at an atlas of the United States and find a map that shows your area. What is the latitude and longitude of your community? Find a community on the other side of the world that has the same latitude. What is the longitude of that community?
3. **Decision making** What is a good first step in making a decision?
4. **Decision making** How would you go about deciding what book to read for an end-of-unit book report? What are the steps you would take?
5. **Time lines** Using events from Unit 1, make a civilizations time line. Put the events in their correct places. Keep this time line so you can add more events.

62

ONGOING UNIT PROJECT

OPTIONS FOR ASSESSMENT

The ongoing project, begun on page 2D, can be part of your assessment program, along with other forms of evaluation.

PLANNING Explain to students that each artifact should represent the culture and time period they have been learning about in the lesson. Let them know that their oral explanations will be important.

SIGNS OF SUCCESS

- Students' artifacts should reflect the main ideas of the lesson.
- The group should work well together to select and arrange their displays.
- The oral presentations should clarify questions about the artifacts.

 FOR THE PORTFOLIO Individual drawings and identification cards can be included in students' portfolios.

YESTERDAY, TODAY & *TOMORROW*

Historians learn about past civilizations from the artifacts and records that have been left behind. Our civilization will leave large numbers of artifacts and records. Which ones do you think will be most valuable for future historians? Explain your choices.

READING ON YOUR OWN

Here are some books you might find at the library to help you learn more.

THE ICEMAN
by Don Lessem
This book tells of the discovery — found between Austria and Italy — of the remains of a man estimated to have lived over 5,000 years ago.

DIG THIS!
by Michael Avi-Yonah
This discussion highlights archaeological excavations of ancient cities.

STORIES ON STONE
by Jennifer Owings Dewey
Read this story to find out who drew pictures on stone long ago in the southwestern United States.

UNIT PROJECT

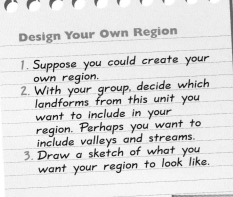

Design Your Own Region

1. Suppose you could create your own region.
2. With your group, decide which landforms from this unit you want to include in your region. Perhaps you want to include valleys and streams.
3. Draw a sketch of what you want your region to look like.

4. Create your region out of clay. You may want to start with a sturdy cardboard base and use different colored clay for the different landforms.
5. Make a label for each landform. Then cut out each label, glue it onto a toothpick and place it by its landform.
6. Give your region a name and write a description of it on an index card.
7. Present your region to the class.

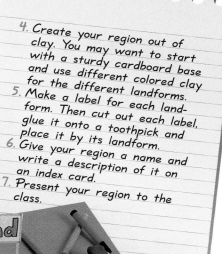

63

Suggestions for BUILDING SKILLS

1. latitude 10° N of equator, longitude of 80° E of Greenwich.
2. After students identify their own latitude and longitude and choose a place on the other side of the world at the same latitude, help them realize that it is about 180° away.
3. Identify the goal you want to reach.
4. Identify what you want to learn, consider books that might serve that goal, choose the best book for the goal.
5. Point out to students that future time lines will cover shorter spans of time than this one.

Suggestions for YESTERDAY, TODAY & TOMORROW

Start students off by asking them what objects and records they think reveal the most about our civilization. Technology, like telecommunications and space travel? Works of art, like books or sculptures? Our beliefs? What else? Ask them to choose artifacts that will best reflect their choices and then to explain them.

Suggestions for READING ON YOUR OWN

The books listed can deepen students' understanding of life in India today or of work archaeologists do and the knowledge gathered from their work. Try to make these books, and those listed in the *Annotated Bibliography* in the Unit Organizer, p. 2B, available. Ask each student to read one of these, or a similar book from the library, and report an interesting anecdote or fact to the class.

UNIT I REVIEW PROJECT

COMPLETING DESIGNING A REGION GROUP — 30 MINUTES OR LONGER

OBJECTIVE: To understand that landforms differ in different regions of the world.

MATERIALS: modeling clay, modeling tools, cardboard

- Divide the class into groups. Suggest that revisiting the text to review the different landforms and natural boundaries they read about may help the groups decide which ones to include in their regions.
- Encourage students to do additional research to find out more about the landforms and natural boundaries they plan to include. Have students sketch what they want their region to look like and confer about how each landform or natural boundary could be represented in clay.

- Give each group a supply of modeling clay, modeling tools, and a sheet of cardboard to use as a base and have them create their region.
- Remind students to write a description of their region on an index card and to make labels for their model.

 FOR THE PORTFOLIO Students' fact sheets and sketches can be included in their portfolios.

OPTIONS FOR ASSESSMENT

The project can be part of your assessment program.

For more performance assessment and portfolio opportunities, see Assessment Book, Unit 1, p. T54.

2 UNIT ORGANIZER

River Valley Civilizations

PAGES 64–185

UNIT OVERVIEW

The first civilizations of the world began in river valleys. The four great river civilizations were in Egypt along the Nile, in ancient Mesopotamia between the Tigris and Euphrates, in India by the Indus, and in China along the Huang. Each of these cultures developed separate systems of writing that tell us about their laws and customs.

☐ **ADVENTURES WITH NATIONAL GEOGRAPHIC**
High and Dry **pp. 66–67**

UNIT PLANNING GUIDE

CHAPTER	SUGGESTED PACING	RESOURCES	ASSESSMENT
4 Ancient Egypt Menes united Egyptian cities along the Nile in 3100 B.C., and Egypt expanded to other regions. pp. 68–101	9–10 days	• **Practice and Project Book, pp. 18–23** • **Anthology, pp. 12–21** • **Outline Map** • **Transparency:** Map 11, Graphic Organizer, Main Idea Pyramid • ⊙ **Technology:** Videodisc/Video Tape • ⊙ **Technology:** *Adventure Time!* CD-ROM • **McGraw-Hill Adventure Book**	• **Meeting Individual Needs,** pp. 73, 81, 83, 91, 93, 99 • **Write About It,** 73, 81, 83, 91, 99 • **Chapter Review,** pp. 100–101 • **Assessment Book:** *Assessing Think and Write,* pp. T55–T57. *Chapter 4 Tests: Content, Skills, Writing*
5 Ancient Mesopotamia Sargon united ancient Mesopotamia into Sumeria, where cuneiform was developed. pp. 102–127	6–7 days	• **Practice and Project Book, pp. 24–28** • **Anthology, pp. 22–25** • **Desk Map** • **Outline Map** • **Transparency:** Graphic Organizer, Main Idea Chart • ⊙ **Technology:** Videodisc/Video Tape • **McGraw-Hill Adventure Book**	• **Meeting Individual Needs,** pp. 107, 115, 117, 125 • **Write About It,** pp. 107, 115, 117, 125 • **Chapter Review,** pp. 126–127 • **Assessment Book:** *Assessing Think and Write,* pp. T58–T60. *Chapter 5 Tests: Content, Skills, Writing*
6 Ancient India Mohenjo-Daro and Harappa were the most powerful cities along the Indus River. pp. 128–157	8–9 days	• **Practice and Project Book, pp. 29–34** • **Anthology, pp. 26–31** • **Desk Map** • **Outline Map** • **Transparency:** Map 12, Graphic Organizer, World Map • ⊙ **Technology:** Videodisc/Video Tape	• **Meeting Individual Needs,** pp. 133, 139, 141, 147, 149, 155 • **Write About It,** pp. 133, 139, 147, 149, 155 • **Chapter Review,** pp. 156–157 • **Assessment Book:** *Assessing Think and Write,* pp. T61–T63. *Chapter 6 Tests: Content, Skills, Writing*
7 Ancient China The Shang Dynasty united Chinese civilizations. The Han Dynasty spread the teachings of Confucius. pp. 158–183	8–9 days	• **Practice and Project Book, pp. 35–40** • **Anthology, pp. 32–34** • **Desk Map** • **Outline Map** • **Transparency:** Graphic Organizer, Main Idea Diagram • ⊙ **Technology:** Videodisc/Video Tape	• **Meeting Individual Needs,** pp. 163, 167, 171, 173, 178, 181 • **Write About It,** pp. 163, 167, 171, 178 • **Chapter Review,** pp. 182–183 • **Assessment Book:** *Assessing Think and Write,* pp. T64–T66. *Chapter 7 Tests: Content, Skills, Writing*
Unit 2 Review pp. 184–185	1–2 days	• **Geo Adventures Daily Geography Activities**	• **Unit 2 Project,** p. 185

The McGraw-Hill School's Home Page at
☞ **http://www.mhschool.com**
on the World Wide Web for projects related to this unit.

FOR FURTHER SUPPORT
• **Language Support Handbook**
• **Standardized Test Support**

McGraw-Hill Adventure Books

Feldman, Eve. **The Dead Sea Scrolls.** A non-fiction account of the discovery and enduring mystery of the ancient scrolls found near the Dead Sea in 1947. **(Easy)**

Stefoff, Rebecca. **The Ancient City of Thebes.** Information of the day-to-day lives and customs of a young brother and sister growing up in the ancient Greek city of Thebes. **(Easy)**

Classroom Library

■ Mann, Elizabeth. **The Great Pyramid.** New York: Mikaya Press, 1996. The story of the Great Pyramid of the pharaoh Khufu and the civilization that produced it.

Student Books

Demi. **Buddha.** New York: Henry Holt and Company, 1996. A very appealing, beautifully illustrated picture book about the Buddha's life, with an introduction on the teachings of Buddha. **(Average)**

■ Giblin, James Cross. **The Riddle of the Rosetta Stone.** New York: Thomas Y. Crowell, 1990. This is a description of the discovery and deciphering of the stone which led to the understanding of hieroglyphics**. (Average)**

■ Lazo, Caroline. **The Terra Cotta Army of Emperor Qin.** New York: Macmillan Publishing Co., 1993. This book tells how a clay army was uncovered during an excavation near the tomb of China's first emperor. **(Average)**

Stanley, Diane, and Peter Vennema. **Cleopatra.** New York: Morrow Junior Books, 1994. This very attractive picture book tells the story of the young woman who became Queen of Egypt at age eighteen. **(Challenging)**

Williams, Brian. **Ancient China.** New York: Viking, 1996. The customs and daily lives of the ancient Chinese civilization are revealed using a technique of see-through cutaways. **(Challenging)**

Teacher Books

Martell, Hazel Mary. **The Kingfisher Book of the Ancient World**. New York: Kingfisher, 1995. A thorough overview of the first civiliza-

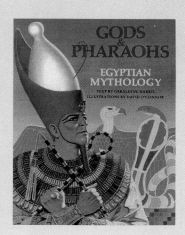

tions from the ice age to the fall of Rome; accompanied by colorful illustrations.

Time-Life Books, ed. **China's Buried Kingdoms**. Alexandria, VA: Time-Life Books, 1993. These archaeological findings examine ancient China's civilization.

Read-Alouds

Demi. **Buddha Stories**. New York: Henry Holt and Company, 1997. Ten of the classic stories from the Buddha's works are gathered; well-suited for reading aloud.

■ Harris, Geraldine. **Gods and Pharaohs from Egyptian Mythology.** New York: Schocken Books, 1982. These imaginative stories tell much about ancient Egypt.

Technology Multimedia

▯ **Ancient Civilizations: China and India**. CD-ROM. Students can learn about the daily life, religious beliefs, and other aspects of these ancient civilizations. National Geographic. (800) 368-2728.

▯ **Ancient Civilizations: Egypt and the Fertile Crescent**. CD-ROM. Students can explore ancient Egypt, Mesopotamia, and the eastern Mediterranean region. National Geographic. (800) 368-2728.

The Five Chinese Brothers. Video. Five identical brothers free the people who are forced to build the Great Wall. **The Tiger and the Brahmin**. Video. An Indian Brahmin learns about the world from a tiger and a jackal. Story Lane Theater, Macmillan/McGraw-Hill. (800) 442-9685.

Mummies, Tombs, and Treasure. By Lila Perl. CD-ROM. (Story 2) Gain insight into ancient Egyptian beliefs. Multimedia Literature. Macmillan/McGraw-Hill. (800) 442-9685.

Free or Inexpensive Materials

For information on "The History of Writing" from ancient to modern times, send to: The Gillette Company; Public Relations; Stationery Products Group; 1400 North Parker Drive; Janesville, WI 53547.

■ *Book excerpted in the Anthology*

■ *Book featured in the student bibliography of the Unit Review*

▯ *National Geographic technology*

Ideas for Active Learning

BULLETIN BOARD

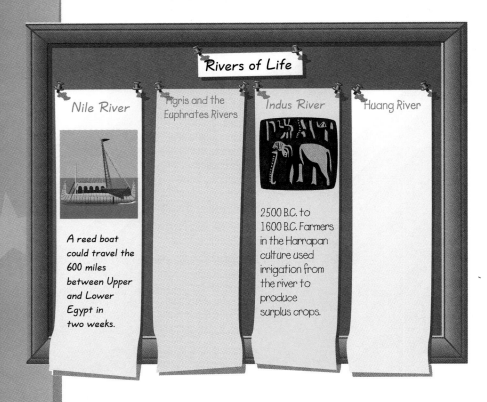

Rivers of Life

Nile River

A reed boat could travel the 600 miles between Upper and Lower Egypt in two weeks.

Tigris and the Euphrates Rivers

Indus River

2500 B.C. to 1600 B.C. Farmers in the Harrapan culture used irrigation from the river to produce surplus crops.

Huang River

River Valley Civilizations

Help students to create a bulletin board titled "Rivers of Life." Divide the bulletin board into four vertical sections and use the following titles: Nile River, Tigris and Euphrates rivers, Indus River, Huang River. Help students create four "rivers" by using four long strips of paper and attaching them to the bulletin board—the paper can extend below the bulletin board. Ask volunteers to contribute visual and written information to create an Infographic about the achievements, lifestyle, and religions of the ancient civilization that developed on each river. Students may make drawings or cut out photographs from magazines and post them on the strips with an accompanying caption. Challenge students to include drawings or photographs that illustrate the kinds of boats or conveyances people used on each river.

TEACHER EXCHANGE

Thanks to: JoAnn Trygestad, Rosemount Middle School, Rosemount, Minnesota

Create a Map ON YOUR OWN 30 MINUTES OR LONGER

CURRICULUM CONNECTION   Art/Language Arts

Materials: tagboard, colored pencils, or markers

1. Tell students that they will create maps of places they have studied in the unit.

2. Tell students that their maps should include at least the following: two countries, two cities, a body of water, a transportation route, signs of economic activity, lines of latitude and longitude, scale of miles, legend, compass rose, place names, colors that show elevation, and a title.

3. When the maps are completed, use them to review map skills.

Enriching with Multimedia

RESOURCE: McGraw-Hill School's Home Page

- Have students go to McGraw-Hill School's home page at http://www.mhschool.com on the World Wide Web for projects related to this unit.

RESOURCE: *Adventure Time! CD-ROM*

- Enrich Unit 2 with the *Key People* and *Key Places* and *Time Lines* sections on the *Adventure Time!* CD-ROM.

SCHOOL-TO-HOME

River Valley Civilizations

- Throughout the unit, students will have the opportunity to learn about the establishment of several religions, such as Judaism, Hinduism, and Buddhism. Discuss with students the cultures in which each religion originated, and work with the class to write a summary of the central beliefs or organizing principles of each religion studied in the chapter.

- Encourage students to share the summaries with family members. Working together, students and their families can write a summary of the main beliefs of their own religion, or another religion that they know about, and discuss how the religion they write about is similar or different from the ones already described.

ONGOING UNIT PROJECT

Album of River Civilizations

CURRICULUM CONNECTION Art/Language Arts

RESOURCE: Practice and Project Book p. 29.

Throughout the unit students will work individually and cooperatively to create pictorials to include in an album of the River Valley Civilizations.

1. After completing each chapter, students will work individually to create an index card-sized pictorial reflecting the civilization being studied, including pictures of objects, statues, monuments, hieroglyphs, or artifacts.
2. Groups can arrange pictorials from each student by civilization or time period.
3. Make available construction paper and paper fasteners. Have students assemble their albums, write titles on the pages, and use tape or glue to display the pictorials. Students should write captions for their pictorials.
4. Individuals should put their contributions in order like a time line and explain their pictorials to the class.

Assessment suggestions for this activity appear on page 184.

Introducing the Unit

Have students read the unit title and ask them to try to picture in their minds what it is like to look down from above on a river valley, a long river winding through a green valley. Give them time to examine the artifacts pictured that came out of such settings and have them read *Why Does It Matter?* on the facing page.

Exploring Prior Knowledge Some students may have seen some of these artifacts in museums or on television.

● **Have you seen any of these artifacts before? Under what circumstances and what do you know about them?** *(Invite students to offer any information they know, for example, relating mummies to ancient Egypt.)*

★**THINKING FURTHER:** *Making Conclusions* **Does each item seem to come from a different place on Earth? How do you know?** *(Clues such as the different styles should tell them they come from different places, evident in the mummy case, the seder plate, the horse man, the panel from Babylon, the statue of Brahma, and the cuneiform tablet.)*

Looking Ahead In this unit students will learn how civilizations developed in four fertile river valleys across the world—Egypt, Mesopotamia, the Indian subcontinent, and China. They will explore each river valley's geography to see why civilization was able to develop there and then trace the steps in each civilization's development. Finally, they will investigate each civilization's major achievements to learn about the legacy it left us.

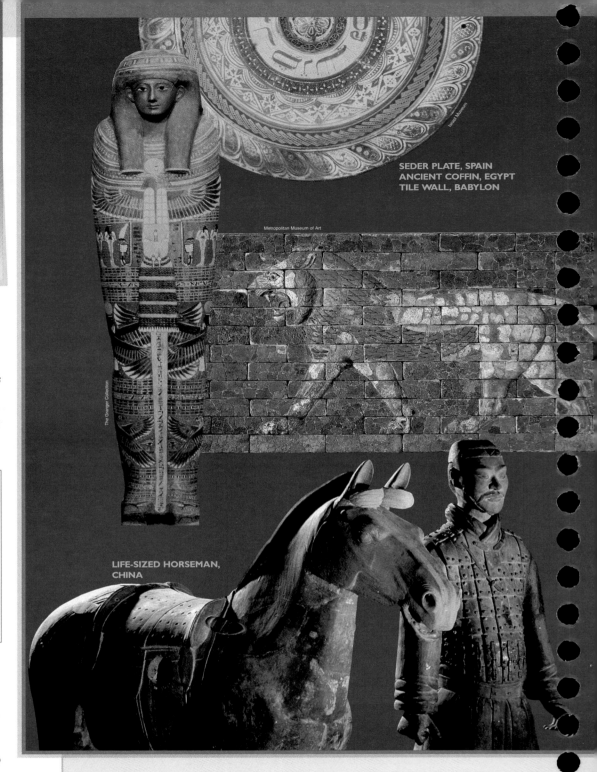

SEDER PLATE, SPAIN
ANCIENT COFFIN, EGYPT
TILE WALL, BABYLON

Metropolitan Museum of Art

LIFE-SIZED HORSEMAN, CHINA

BACKGROUND INFORMATION

ABOUT THE ARTIFACTS

● **THE HEBREW SEDER PLATE** This plate from Spain was used as part of the seder, a feast remembering the Hebrews' escape from Egypt.

● **EGYPTIAN MUMMY CASE** Ancient Egyptians prepared their dead for the afterlife. They preserved the body, wrapped it in linen, and then encased it in a coffin, like this carved mummy case, which was then placed in a tomb.

● **ISHTAR GATE** This brilliantly glazed panel of a walkway of many such panels, shown here after a laborious restoration, marked the grand entrance to a Babylonian temple in Mesopotamia, built *circa* 575 B.C.

UNIT TWO

River Valley Civilizations

"I have inscribed my precious words."

from the Code of Hammurabi
See page 113.

WHY DOES IT MATTER?

Hammurabi, the king of the ancient empire of Babylonia, had these words inscribed in stone about 4,000 years ago. His words introduced the laws he had created for the people of his empire. This is one of the earliest recorded examples of written laws. Even before Hammurabi lived, people in that part of the world had developed systems of writing. They recorded important information about their lives. By studying texts like this, historians have learned about languages, laws, and customs of ancient civilizations.

Babylonia was a powerful civlization that grew in the fertile river valleys of Mesopotamia, in western Asia. Other river valley civilizations developed in Egypt, India, and China. In this unit you will read about legacies left by these ancient peoples that continue to influence the world today.

CUNEIFORM TABLET, IRAQ
STATUE OF BRAHMA, INDIA

65

BACKGROUND INFORMATION

ABOUT THE ARTIFACTS

- **TERRA COTTA FIGURES OF MAN AND HORSE** These are two of 6,000 figures of men and horses discovered in 1974 in Sian, China. They were created in 210 B.C. as an army to guard China's first emperor, Shihuangdi. Each figure is a realistic model of an individual.

- **HINDU GOD** Figures like this of the Hindu god Brahma have been created for centuries in India and nearby lands. Brahma is the Hindu god of creation.

- **CUNEIFORM TABLET** In ancient Mesopotamia, scribes wrote in wedge-shaped characters on wet clay tablets that later hardened. Cuneiform is one of the earliest forms of writing.

Discussing the Artifacts Encourage students to examine these artifacts for clues to the civilization from which they come. List this unit's four civilizations on the board—Egypt, Mesopotamia, India, and China.

★ **THINKING FURTHER:** *Making Connections* **How would you match these artifacts to the civilizations from which they come?** *(Invite students to suggest matches that occur to them and explain why. They should be able to match the Chinese figures to China and the mummy case to Egypt. Possibly they will match the statue of Brahma to India, and the seder plate to ancient Israel. Help them match those artifacts that baffle them.)*

Discussing WHY DOES IT MATTER? Have students read aloud the brief quote from the Code of Hammurabi and then review the passage that follows.

- **What does the word** inscribed **mean?** *(written down)*

- **Why do you suppose he used the word** precious **to describe his words?** *(His words spelled out the laws of his empire for the people living there, and they were supposed to have been given by the sun god.)*

★ **THINKING FURTHER:** *Compare and Contrast* **What is the difference between someone saying a few words to some friends and someone writing something down and publishing it for all to see?** *(Help students to see two important differences that separate written language from spoken language: 1. written language can be seen and read by far more people than the few who could hear something said; and 2. written language can be permanent.)*

Adventures
with
NATIONAL GEOGRAPHIC

Introducing
High and Dry

Exploring Prior Knowledge As students examine the illustrations on this spread, ask them what they already know about ancient Egypt. Have they ever visited a museum that has artifacts from ancient Egypt? Have they seen anything in the movies or on television or in books about the pyramids of Egypt and the Sphinx that guards them? Urge them to share any information they have with the class.

Links to the Unit As students work through Unit 2, they will meet many great leaders from ancient times and will learn how important building great monuments was to these leaders. It will become obvious that a great many of them, from Africa to Asia, had severe "edifice complexes," luckily for us and our study of ancient times.

High and Dry Give students time to read the text and examine the illustrations more closely. Discuss the size of the statues, rightly called "colossal" in the text, and point out that their height of 60 feet makes them as tall as a six-story building. Have students point to the location of the statues on the pictured globe (in Egypt in the northeastern part of Africa). Have students identify the problem that created the need to move the Ramses statues. Ask why many nations may have wanted to cooperate to save them. (The statues would be underwater when a new dam was finished. The statues were universally seen as great treasures from the past.)

BACKGROUND INFORMATION

MORE ABOUT THE TEMPLES OF RAMSES II

● Ramses II came to be called "the Great" in part at least because he did everything on a grand scale, including building some of the biggest and showiest monuments in ancient Egypt.

● The two temples that this Adventure treats were built at Abu Simbel. Actually they were not built as we think of building. Rather, they were carved out of the solid rock that formed a cliff along the Nile, which makes their disassembly all the more amazing.

● The four Ramses shown here were part of a temple he built for himself. The other temple referred to was one he built for his wife Nefertari. It stood a few hundred feet north of his.

HIGH AND DRY

Around 1270 B.C., an Egyptian pharaoh named Ramses II had two temples built along the banks of the Nile. Four colossal statues of Ramses himself—each more than 60 feet high—marked the entrance to the larger temple. For 3,000 years, the statues sat on their enormous stone thrones. Then, in the 1960s, the Egyptians built a dam on the Nile, and water started rising behind the dam. Soon, the water would cover the temples! Many nations got together for a massive rescue effort. Workers cut the temples into more than a thousand pieces, lifted them to a place above the level of the water, and put the pieces together again. Now the statues again sit high and dry.

GEO JOURNAL

You're an Egyptian official in the 1960s. Write a letter to the United Nations, explaining why the world should help save the temples of Ramses II.

Help students to use the inset pictures to identify the steps in the mammoth task of removing and repositioning these colossal statues (cutting the stone temples into pieces, grappling them to get them ready for hoisting, doing the actual hoisting up a steep and rugged incline).

Call students' attention to the small figures that appear beside and between the big statues' legs in the large picture. Explain that these represent other members of his royal family. Their size in relation to his is perhaps a clue to his view of his own "greatness."

Using the Geo Journal Before students begin writing their letters to the UN for their journals, encourage them to list reasons why the temples are worth the expense and effort that will have to go into saving them. Why are they such treasures? Why should the whole world, not just Egypt, want to save them? Then have them base the pleas they make in the letter on these reasons.

 Technology CONNECTION

ADVENTURE TIME! CD-ROM
Enrich this feature with the *High and Dry* activity on the *Adventure Time!* CD–ROM

CURRICULUM CONNECTION

SCIENCE Explain that much of the hoisting and lifting necessary to raise the temple blocks was accomplished with the use of the pulley, one of the basic simple machines. Pulleys are grooved wheels around which a rope or chain is pulled. By changing the direction of the force, a pulley makes it possible to lift heavy objects with less effort.

A block and tackle is an arrangement of a group of pulleys. Have students work in pairs to research how pulleys are set up and how they work. Ask some students to prepare an illustration of a block and tackle.

THEMES of GEOGRAPHY

As you work through Unit 2 with your students, consider the following themes:

Place Place refers to both the natural and human-made features of a particular area. Discuss the natural and human-made characteristics of Egypt, Mesopotamia, India, and China as you read Chapters 4, 5, 6 and 7 of this Unit. Encourage students to make a chart summarizing their findings.

Movement People, goods, and ideas are moved around the world in many ways. Discuss movement as you read Chapter 7. Ask students to identify how factors such as war, trade, religion, and written language contributed to movement within the civilizations discussed.

CHAPTER 4 Ancient Egypt

Pages 68–101

CHAPTER OVERVIEW

Ancient Egypt began with farming communities along the Nile River. Menes united all the Egyptian cities in 3100 B.C. Egypt grew as rulers such as Hatshepsut led trading expeditions to other regions. Great stone monuments, such as the pyramids, were built for Egypt's powerful rulers.

GEO ADVENTURES DAILY GEOGRAPHY ACTIVITIES

Use **Geo Adventures** Daily Geography activities to assess students' understanding of geography skills.

CHAPTER PLANNING GUIDE

LESSON 1	LESSON 2	Legacy
SUGGESTED PACING: 2 DAYS	SUGGESTED PACING: 2 DAYS	SUGGESTED PACING: 1 DAY
Geography Of Ancient Egypt pp. 70–73	**Land Of Pharaohs** pp. 74–81	**Egyptian Boats** pp. 82–83
CURRICULUM CONNECTIONS Links to Science, p. 71 Links to Math, p. 72 **RESOURCES** Practice and Project Book, p. 18 ◉ TECHNOLOGY *Adventure Time!* CD-ROM	**CURRICULUM CONNECTIONS** Links to Spelling, p. 78 Links to Language Arts, p. 78 Links to Science, p. 78 Links to Math, p. 80 **CITIZENSHIP** Preserving Our Heritage, p. 75 Linking Past and Present, p. 78 **FIELD TRIP** Visit a Display of Artifacts, p. 76 **RESOURCES** Practice and Project Book, p. 19 Anthology, pp. 12–13 ◉ TECHNOLOGY *Adventure Time!* CD-ROM	

GEOGRAPHYSKILLS	LESSON 4	CHAPTER REVIEW
SUGGESTED PACING: 1 DAY	SUGGESTED PACING: 2 DAYS	SUGGESTED PACING: 1 DAY
Using Maps At Different Scales pp. 92–93	**Daily Life In Ancient Egypt** pp. 94–99	pp. 100–101
RESOURCES Practice and Project Book, p. 21 Transparency Map 11 ◉ TECHNOLOGY *Adventure Time!* CD-ROM	**CURRICULUM CONNECTIONS** Links to Music, p. 96 **CITIZENSHIP** Linking Past and Present, p. 98 **RESOURCES** Practice and Project Book, p. 22 ◉ TECHNOLOGY *Adventure Time!* CD-ROM	**RESOURCES** Practice and Project Book, p. 23 ◉ TECHNOLOGY Videodisc/Video Tape 1 Assessment Book: Chapter 4 Test Transparency: Graphic Organizer, Main Idea Pyramid

LEARNING STYLE: Visual

 GROUP 30 MINUTES OR LONGER

Write a Help-Wanted Ad

Objective: To introduce students to ancient Egypt.

Materials: paper, construction paper, markers, newspapers

1. Recall with students how Catal Huyuk's success with agriculture made job specialization possible.
2. Have students work in groups to think of specialized jobs in modern as well as ancient communities.
3. Have each student write a help-wanted ad for each community in newspaper style.
4. Let students share their ads with the class. Discuss why specialization is important in modern civilization and how it might have helped an ancient civilization grow.

LESSON 3

SUGGESTED PACING: 3 DAYS

Ancient Egyptian Civilization pp. 84–91

CURRICULUM CONNECTIONS
Links to Art, p. 87
Links to Science, p. 90

CITIZENSHIP
Using Current Events, p. 87

INFOGRAPHIC
Treasures of an Ancient Tomb, pp. 88–89

RESOURCES
Practice and Project Book, p. 20
Anthology, pp. 14, 15–21
Desk Map
⊙TECHNOLOGY *Adventure Time!*
CD-ROM

SHELTERED INSTRUCTION

READING STRATEGIES & LANGUAGE DEVELOPMENT

Context Clues/Word Origins, p. 70, Lesson 1
Main Idea and Details/Suffix, p. 74, Lesson 2
Make and Support Generalizations/Quotation Marks, p. 84, Lesson 3
Classify/Homophones, p. 92, Geography Skills
Making Conclusions/Comparatives and Superlatives, p. 94, Lesson 4

SECOND-LANGUAGE SUPPORT

Retelling, p. 71
Working with a Peer, p. 77
Using Visuals/Oral Practice, p. 85
Summarizing Through Illustrations, p. 100

MEETING INDIVIDUAL NEEDS

Reteaching, Extension, Enrichment, pp. 73, 81, 83, 91, 93, 99
McGraw-Hill Adventure Book

ASSESSMENT OPPORTUNITIES

Practice and Project Book, pp. 18–23
Write About It, pp. 73, 81, 83, 91, 99
Assessment Book: Assessing Think and Write, pp. T55–T57; Chapter 4 Tests: Content, Skills, Writing

Introducing the Chapter

To help students get a sense of the natural progression that the development of civilization follows, give them a few moments to thumb through the chapter to study its illustrations.

THINKING ABOUT HISTORY AND GEOGRAPHY

Have students read the text on this page to follow the time span involved in ancient Egypt's development—from 5000 B.C. to 1200 B.C. Have them use their fingers to trace points on the map to their panels on the time line.

5000 B.C. NILE RIVER DELTA

Tell students that for nearly 4,000 years, Egypt was considered to be the apex of civilization, the one that others tried to copy.

- **On what continent is Egypt located?** *(Africa)*

- **Where in Egypt did farming begin?** *(at the mouth of the Nile River, where it empties into the Mediterranean Sea)*

★ **THINKING FURTHER:** *Making Conclusions* **Why do you suppose farming would be an important factor in the development of a civilization?** *(People must have food to do anything else.)*

3100 B.C. MEMPHIS

Discuss the role of unification of Upper and Lower Egypt in strengthening the civilization.

- **Who was Menes?** *(the leader who united Egypt)*

- **Where was Memphis located?** *(just south of the Nile Delta)*

Resource **REMINDER**

Technology: *Videodisc/Video Tape 1*

CHAPTER 4

Ancient Egypt

THINKING ABOUT HISTORY AND GEOGRAPHY

The story of ancient Egypt begins with farmers along the Nile River. They formed communities that grew into cities. In 3100 B.C. Menes united Egypt. Rulers who came after him ordered the building of large, stone monuments such as the pyramids. They also led trading expeditions south and east and increased their land. By 1200 B.C. goods and ideas spread from Egypt's capital city, Thebes, to three continents.

5000 B.C.	3100 B.C.	2600 B.C.
NILE RIVER DELTA Egyptians begin to farm	**MEMPHIS** Menes unites Egypt	**GIZA** Khufu orders the building of the Great Pyramid

  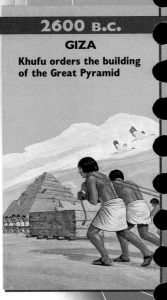

68

BACKGROUND INFORMATION

LINKING THE MAP AND THE TIME LINE
- The Nile River Delta was compared by the ancient Egyptians to the blossom of the lotus flower. The Upper Nile was the long, thin stalk that fed the blossom that burst out in a fan of tributaries flowing toward the Mediterranean Sea.
- Memphis was chosen by Menes to be his capital because it stood at the juncture of the two kingdoms he had united—Upper Egypt and Lower Egypt. Today, what little remains of Memphis lies 16 miles south of the modern capital of Cairo.
- Giza is home to two other pyramids, those built for Khafre and Menkaure, who came after Khufu, as well as to the Sphinx that legend says was built to guard the pyramids of Giza.

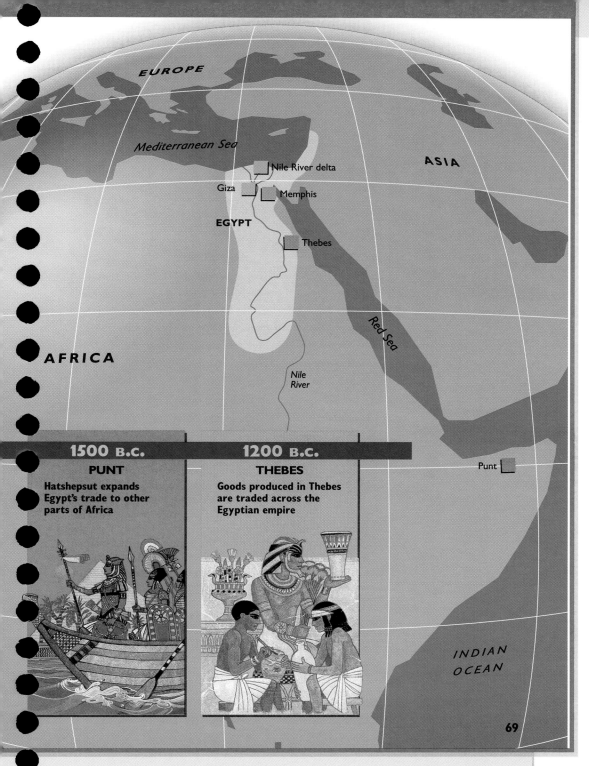

EUROPE

Mediterranean Sea

ASIA

Nile River delta

Giza

Memphis

EGYPT

Thebes

AFRICA

Red Sea

Nile River

Punt

INDIAN OCEAN

1500 B.C.

PUNT

Hatshepsut expands Egypt's trade to other parts of Africa

1200 B.C.

THEBES

Goods produced in Thebes are traded across the Egyptian empire

69

★**THINKING FURTHER:** *Making Conclusions* **Why might unifying a land and people be an important step in development?** *(A greater number of people working together toward a common goal aids development.)*

2600 B.C. GIZA

The Great Pyramid and the sphinx at Giza are two of Egypt's greatest tourist attractions.

● **What world-famous monument was built at Giza?** *(the Great Pyramid)*

● **Who ordered it built?** *(Khufu)*

1500 B.C. PUNT, EAST AFRICA

Discuss the role of Queen Hatshepsut in broadening trade with nearby lands.

● **Who was Hatshepsut?** *(a ruler of Egypt)*

● **What have you learned that she did?** *(She led trading expeditions to the south and east.)*

● **How does the map bear this out?** *(It shows that she had to travel in those directions to reach Punt.)*

★**THINKING FURTHER:** *Making Conclusions* **Why might active trade be important to a people's development?** *(Producing goods and buying and selling them would create jobs.)*

1200 B.C. THEBES

Help students locate Thebes on the map.

★**THINKING FURTHER:** *Making Conclusions* **How might Thebes have contributed to the development of ancient Egypt?** *(Thebes contributed to the increase of trade and contacts across Egypt.)*

BACKGROUND INFORMATION

LINKING THE MAP AND THE TIME LINE

● Punt in East Africa was depicted by Egyptian scribes and artists (who no doubt had never been there) as an earthly paradise where cattle grazed under spreading frankincense trees. As will later be explained, frankincense was indeed a product of the coastal Red Sea.

● Thebes, which had replaced Memphis as the capital of Egypt, was more than just a political and trade center. It was also a religious center. Today, two of its great temple complexes remain and are major tourist attractions. The larger is Karnak, which represents over 2,000 years of building activity, begun about 2000 B.C. The smaller is Luxor, the building of which began in 1417 B.C.

 Technology CONNECTION

VIDEODISC/VIDEO TAPE 1
Enrich Chapter 4 with the *Ancient Egypt* segment on the videodisc.

Search Frame 04892 Side A

LESSON 1

PAGES 70–73

Lesson Overview

The ebb and flow of the Nile River made rich agricultural development possible, which in turn made the development of Egyptian civilization possible.

Lesson Objectives

★ Describe how floods enriched and fertilized Egypt's land.

★ Explain how Egyptians interacted with the Nile to develop a rich agriculture.

⭐1 PREPARE

MOTIVATE Have students do a choral reading of the *Read Aloud*. Help them to appreciate the religious awe that ancient Egyptians felt about their river. Discuss what they believed the river did for them and what they owed it in return.

SET PURPOSE Encourage students to explore this lesson to formulate the answer to the *Read to Learn* question. Call attention to the photo of the sailboats to suggest one possible answer. Then preview the *Vocabulary* terms.

⭐2 TEACH

Understanding THE BIG PICTURE
Help students to appreciate how Egyptians made what is usually considered a natural disaster—a flood—into the core of their way of life.

● *On what continent is the Nile River valley?* (Africa)

● *About when did people begin settling along it?* (about 5,000 B.C.)

● *Why might it have seemed a poor place to settle?* (It was in a desert.)

⭐**THINKING FURTHER:** *Cause and Effect* **What made it a good place for farming?** *(Its flooding turned dry desert land into fertile soil.)*

Resource REMINDER

Practice and Project Book: *p.18*

Technology: *Adventures Time!* CD-ROM

Outline Map

National Geographic Society

GEOGRAPHY OF ANCIENT EGYPT

Focus Activity

READ TO LEARN

In what ways did the ancient Egyptians depend upon the Nile River?

VOCABULARY

silt
delta
irrigation

PLACES

Nile River
Lower Egypt
Upper Egypt

READ ALOUD

"Hail O Nile, who comes to give life to the people of Egypt. Created by the sun-god to give life to all who thirst. Who lets the desert drink with streams descending from heaven. Who makes barley and creates wheat so that temples celebrate. When the Nile overflows, offerings are made to you, cattle are [killed] for you, that your goodness be repaid."

These words are from a 3,000-year-old Egyptian song, "Hymn to the Nile."

THE BIG PICTURE

Around 5000 B.C. people began building farming villages in a river valley in Africa, several hundred miles south of Catal Huyuk. The area around Egypt's Nile River valley probably did not look like a very good place to start farming.

The river wound its way through a vast desert with few signs of life. Yet every year the Nile flooded its banks. The river swamped everything in its path with water and mud for four solid months—from July through October.

This yearly flood made the Nile Valley lush and green. It also allowed people to make use of the land. With the help of water from the Nile River, ancient farmers turned the Nile Valley into a productive agricultural region.

70

SHELTERED INSTRUCTION

READING STRATEGIES & LANGUAGE DEVELOPMENT

CONTEXT CLUES Point out that writers often give readers clues to the meanings of unfamiliar words. Explain that a clue can be the definition in a separate sentence. Have students read the word *delta* and find the definition in a separate sentence. [A delta is very fertile, flat land made of silt left behind as a river drains into a larger body of water.] Have students find the context clues for silt and irrigation. Encourage students to use context clues to define other unfamiliar words as they read the lesson. **[SDAIE STRATEGY: CONTEXTUALIZATION]**

WORD ORIGINS Draw a triangle (Δ) on the board and identify it as the capital letter delta from the Greek alphabet. Have students look at the map on p. 71 to find the delta. Why might such an area have been given that name? (It is shaped somewhat like a triangle, or delta.)

THE GIFT OF THE NILE

In many ways, Egyptian civilization owes its life to the Nile River. The Nile provided water and food in the desert. This seemed like a blessing from the gods of the ancient people. For that reason, Egypt has often been called the "Gift of the Nile."

A Mighty River

The Nile is the world's longest river. It flows over 4,000 miles north from the snowcapped mountains of East Africa. It passes through the present-day countries of Uganda, Ethiopia, Sudan, and Egypt. Then the Nile empties into the warm Mediterranean Sea.

Much of East Africa has a rainy season that lasts from May until September. During that time the Nile swells with rainwater and rushes northward with extra power. The river carries off silt as it goes. Silt is a mixture of tiny bits of soil and rock.

Over time, much of the silt has been deposited where the Nile empties into the Mediterranean. There the river divides into several branches, forming a vast, fan-shaped delta. A delta is very fertile, flat land made of silt left behind as a river drains into a larger body of water. Look at the map on this page. Use the map scale to find the width of the Nile Delta at its widest point.*

The Nile Delta region is in northern Egypt, and appears nearer the top on maps that have north at the top. This makes the delta seem to be "higher." The delta, however, is called Lower Egypt, because it is the lower, or downstream, part of the Nile.

In Upper Egypt, to the south, the Nile cuts through stone cliffs and desert sands. This landscape is very different from the mild, fertile delta.

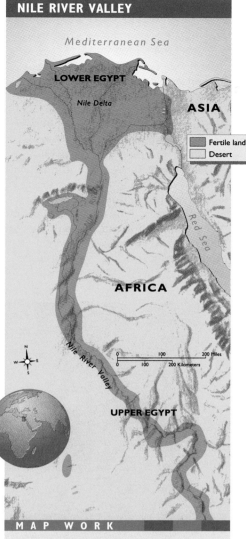

NILE RIVER VALLEY

Mediterranean Sea

LOWER EGYPT

Nile Delta

ASIA

Fertile land
Desert

Red Sea

AFRICA

Nile River Valley

UPPER EGYPT

0   100   200 Miles
0   100   200 Kilometers

MAP WORK

The mighty Nile River winds its way through the northeastern part of Africa.

1. In which direction would you travel to get from the Nile River to the Red Sea?
2. The Nile Delta is near the division between which two continents?
3. Where is the largest fertile region along the Nile?

MAP WORK: **1.** east **2.** Africa and Asia **3.** the Delta, in Lower Egypt

71

THE GIFT OF THE NILE

Encourage students to work back and forth between text and map to understand the role of the Nile River.

Discussing A Mighty River Help students identify the area affected by the Nile.

- *Through which part of Africa does the Nile River flow?* (northeastern Africa)

- *What causes the Nile to flood?* (The May to September rains swell it, causing it to overflow.)

- *What does the swollen river carry with it as it rushes northward?* (silt, which enriches the soil)

- *What has this excess of water created where the Nile empties into the Mediterranean?* (a fan-shaped delta of fertile, flat land)

★**THINKING FURTHER:** *Making Generalizations* **What details support the generalization that Egypt is the "Gift of the Nile"?** (The Nile creates fertile land in Egypt; it supplies two of life's basics needs: water and food.)

More   **MAP WORK**

Refer students to the map on this page and have them trace with their fingers the flow of the Nile from south to north. Mention to them that it resembles the shape of a flower and have them identify the "stem" and the "flower."

- *In which direction does the Nile River flow?* (from south to north)

- *Therefore, which part of the river is upstream? Downstream?* (The southern portion is upstream; the northern portion is downstream.)

- *How does this determine which part of the land is Upper Egypt and which is Lower Egypt?* (Upper Egypt is the area upstream, to the south; Lower Egypt is downstream, to the north.)

★**THINKING FURTHER:** *Making Conclusions* **Where do you think farms would produce more—in Upper Egypt or Lower Egypt? Why?** (Students should conclude that because of the greater area of farmland in the delta, Lower Egypt produced more.)

CURRICULUM CONNECTION

LINKS TO SCIENCE Review with the class the Nile's source and outlet—downhill from East Africa's snow-capped mountains to the Mediterranean. Have a team make a three-dimensional clay model to reflect this "higher in the south, lower in the north" topography. Have them cut a "riverbed" and make a depression for the Mediterranean.

SECOND-LANGUAGE SUPPORT

RETELLING Instruct second-language learners to locate the countries that the Nile River passes through on a modern map. To assess their understanding of the vocabulary words, ask students to explain them in their own words. Having them retell the information about the Nile River on pp. 70 and 71 in their own words would also be a valuable exercise and allow the teacher to assess their comprehension.

A LAND OF DROUGHT AND FLOOD

Explore with students the idea of environmental extremes—drought and floods, too much and too little water. Help them to appreciate how precarious agriculture can be and how people constantly strive to develop skills and technologies to "tame" the extremes and harness them to work to their advantage.

Discussing A System of Agriculture Write the word *irrigation* on the board.

- **To what technology does this term refer?** *(the use of canals or pipes to bring water for crops to the land)*

- **How did the ancient Egyptians use this technology?** *(They dug canals from the Nile to their farms.)*

- **What crops were made possible by irrigation?** *(grains, vegetables, flax)*

- **What is the name for the piece of technology shown in the upper photograph?** *(a shadouf)*

- **How does it act as an aid to irrigation?** *(It helps the farmer move water to exactly where it is needed.)*

★**THINKING FURTHER:** *Making Conclusions* **How would the crops farmers grew help people survive?** *(Grains and vegetables would provide needed food; flax would provide cloth for clothing.)*

Learning About Travel Along the Nile Discuss the importance of the Nile as a travel route.

★**THINKING FURTHER:** *Compare and Contrast* **In what ways was the Nile of ancient Egypt like a modern superhighway?** *(It was the main way that people and goods traveled from place to place. Traffic was heavy all year round.)*

Technology CONNECTION

ADVENTURE TIME! CD-ROM
Enrich the lesson with the *Adventure Time!* CD-ROM *Key Places* segment.

A LAND OF DROUGHT AND FLOOD

Egyptian farmers almost always welcomed the mud left by each summer's Nile flood. This silt-filled mud was rich in minerals needed by plants. The black soil brought by the Nile contrasted sharply with the dry, yellow sand of Egypt's desert. In many places a farmer could stand with one foot on farmland and the other on sand!

Farmers depended on the right amount of flooding each year to grow successful crops. Too little flooding meant farmers' crops failed and people went hungry. Too much meant people and cattle could be swept away and homes destroyed. Life was a delicate balance in the Nile River valley.

Ancient Egyptians found ways to make farming easier and more productive. A shadouf, shown in the picture (above), helped distribute water to the fields. Farmers also built plows, like the one in the model (left), which animals pulled through the fields.

The British Museum

A System of Agriculture

In October the flooded land began to dry. Then farmers planted wheat and barley. They also planted garden vegetables such as cucumbers, lettuce, onions, and beans. Farmers also grew flax, a plant used to make cloth.

To water their newly planted crops, Egypt's farmers used a form of technology called irrigation. Irrigation is the watering of land by means of canals or pipes. At first, farmers simply built dirt walls around their farmland to hold the Nile floodwaters in the fields. Later, they dug small channels, or canals, to bring water from the Nile directly to their farmland. Farmers scooped water from the canals and poured it into the fields, using a bucket-lifter called a shadouf (shah DOOF). The photograph on this page shows how this tool is still used today.

By March the crops were ready for harvesting. In good years the fields were filled with ripe vegetables and grains. Then farm families had more food than they needed. Their surplus, or extra supply of goods, was then gathered up and carried off to storehouses. As in Catal Huyuk, these grain stores made specialization and community life possible.

Travel Along the Nile

Harvest-time ended in late June, before the Nile once again began to flood. During the four-month flood season, farmers could not work in their fields. Instead, many used the time to visit neighboring villages.

Flood season was one of the busiest times for travel on the Nile. Yet river traffic was heavy all year. The Nile was the main way that people and goods moved from place to place. The 600-mile journey between Upper and Lower Egypt would take over a month to walk. In a reed boat it took only about half that time.

WHY IT MATTERS

By 5000 B.C. life in the early farming communities of ancient Egypt centered around the Nile River. The river provided the Egyptian people with fertile soil, water for irrigation, and a means of transportation.

Throughout Egypt's long history, the world's longest river has played a key role. In time, the ancient Egyptians would use the Nile to build the largest civilization the world had ever seen. The following lessons will introduce you to this rich civilization.

Links to MATHEMATICS

The Trusty Nilometer!

How did Egyptians measure the yearly level of the Nile flood?

Ancient Egyptians built special staircases along the river to measure the height of the Nile as it rose. Each step was one "cubit" high—the distance from a person's elbow to the tip of the thumb. One cubit is about 20 inches.

In a good flood year, the Nile rose 16 steps on the Nilometers. How many feet does this equal? In a bad flood year, the Nile rose only 7 steps or less. How many feet is this?*

Reviewing Facts and Ideas

MAIN IDEAS

- The Nile is the world's longest river. It is more than 4,000 miles long.
- Farmers' understanding of the yearly Nile floods made community life in Egypt possible.
- Mineral-rich silt deposits and irrigation technology made farming in ancient Egypt very productive.
- People used boats to get from place to place along the Nile.

THINK ABOUT IT

1. Describe the irrigation methods used by the ancient Egyptians.

2. How did the Nile's yearly floods help ancient Egyptian farmers?

3. **FOCUS** Name three ways the people of ancient Egypt used the Nile River.

4. **THINKING SKILL** As an ancient farmer, _decide_ whether Upper Egypt or Lower Egypt is a better place for farming.

5. **GEOGRAPHY** Look at the map on page 71. Describe three different types of physical regions that the Nile flows through.

73

MEETING INDIVIDUAL NEEDS

RETEACHING (Easy) Have students use the map of the Nile (p. 71) to create their own maps of Egypt's river. Have them label Upper Egypt and Lower Egypt and use arrows to show the direction of flow.

EXTENSION (Average) Tell students to go back through the lesson and take notes on the months for each cycle—flooding, planting, growing, harvesting, and flooding again. Have them create an Egyptian calendar in which they label and illustrate each cycle.

ENRICHMENT (Challenging) Tell students to review "Hymn to the Nile" on p. 70. Now that they have learned the reasons that people of ancient Egypt felt as they did about the Nile, have them try writing a few lines of praise for it. Or they might write a few lines of praise for the ancient Egyptians who developed ways of adapting the Nile to their needs and adapting themselves to the Nile.

Discussing WHY IT MATTERS Help students recognize why the ancient Egypt they just studied was to develop a civilization.

- **What building blocks are necessary for a civilization to begin to develop?** (settled communities, surpluses, specialization, trade, the first signs of religion and government)

★THINKING FURTHER: _Making Conclusions_ **How would you rate Egypt's readiness to develop a civilization?** (Students should recognize that most of these building blocks were in place and Egyptians appear ready to develop cities.)

3 CLOSE

MAIN IDEAS

Help students recognize how much the Egyptians had in their favor.

- **What is the world's longest river?** (Nile)

- **Why were the Egyptians now able to build a rich community life?** (They had learned how to use the flooding of the Nile to develop agriculture and to produce surpluses.)

- **What natural resource and technology have they used to reach this stage?** (Resource: silt. Technology: irrigation.)

- **How did they turn the Nile into a highway?** (They developed boats.)

EVALUATE
√ **Answers To Think About It**

1. watering land by means of canals or pipes; digging canals, using shadoufs _Recall Details_

2. Floods brought water and mineral-rich silt to create good farmland. _Summarize_

3. for drinking water, for irrigating crops, and for use as a travel route _Categories_

4. Students may decide on Lower Egypt because the delta provided richer farmland than Upper Egypt had; accept any reasonable response. _Make Conclusions_

5. mountains, desert, rich delta land _Five Themes Of Geography: Regions_

Write About It Have students choose one way ancient Egyptians adapted the environment for their use and describe it in a paragraph.

LESSON 2

PAGES 74–81

LESSON OVERVIEW

Egyptian civilization grew out of the *unification* of Nile communities and the pharaoh's central role.

Lesson Objectives

★ Explain how Egypt was united.

★ Describe the pharaoh's central role in Egyptian development and life.

★ Describe *hieroglyphics*, the Egyptian system of writing.

★ Analyze the Egyptian *economy*.

1 PREPARE

MOTIVATE Read the *Read Aloud* to the students and discuss with them why a king would want to control "the biggest kingdom in the world." Refer to the photo of the Sphinx, which for many people symbolizes ancient Egypt.

SET PURPOSE Encourage students to predict the answer to the *Read to Learn* question. Then check their predictions. Direct students to the *Vocabulary* terms.

2 TEACH

Understanding THE BIG PICTURE
Briefly review the building blocks of civilization and concentrate here on government.

● **How were the people of those first farming communities along the Nile governed?** *(by village leaders who made rules and enforced them)*

● **How did community government change over time?** *(As communities grew larger, they joined together under kings.)*

★**THINKING FURTHER: Cause and Effect** **Why do you think that government grows more complex as communities grow larger?** *(Perhaps more people bring more problems.)*

Resource REMINDER

Practice and Project Book: *p. 19*
Anthology: *The Rosetta Stone, pp. 12–13*
Technology: *Adventure Time!* CD-ROM

3100 B.C.	2000 B.C.	1500 B.C.	1000 B.C.

LAND OF THE PHARAOHS

READ ALOUD

About 3100 B.C. two mighty kings met in battle. One king wore a white crown and ruled over a long stretch of the Nile River in Upper Egypt. The other king had a red crown and controlled a large area in Lower Egypt. The outcome of the battle was of enormous importance. Whoever won it would control the biggest kingdom in the world.

THE BIG PICTURE

You have already read that farming towns began appearing in different parts of the world during the New Stone Age. Some towns grew into small cities, as people specialized and developed trade with neighboring towns.

These communities created rules to promote peace and fairness among neighbors. Village leaders were usually in charge of creating these rules and making sure that the rules were followed. As the communities grew larger, their governments changed to meet their many new needs.

Along the Nile River in Egypt, groups of villages joined together under the leadership of kings. These larger communities developed complex systems of government. Soon the people of the Nile River valley would see even greater changes in the way their communities were run.

Focus Activity

READ TO LEARN
What role did the pharaohs play in ancient Egypt?

VOCABULARY
unification
pharaoh
economy
hieroglyphics
scribe
papyrus

PEOPLE
Menes
Khufu

PLACES
Memphis
Thebes

74

SHELTERED INSTRUCTION

READING STRATEGIES & LANGUAGE DEVELOPMENT

MAIN IDEA AND DETAILS Tell students that finding a main idea and details can help them understand a passage. Have them read paragraph 1 (p. 75) and state the main idea and details. [Main Idea: Along the Nile, 5,000 years ago, Egypt's villages were thriving. Details: Farmers produced surplus crops, craftworkers made tools, pottery, and jewelry.] Have students chart the main ideas and details as they read.
[SDAIE STRATEGY: TEXT RE-PRESENTATION/SCHEMA BUILDING]

SUFFIX Refer students to the term *information* on p. 79. Call attention to its suffix, *-ation*. Have them look up this suffix in a dictionary and find its meaning ("the act or process of"). Then have them figure out the meaning of *information* ("the act of informing"). Tell them to find other *-ation* words in the lesson (*mummification, communication, civilization, unification*) and do the same.

UNION OF TWO CROWNS

Along the Nile River 5,000 years ago, Egypt's villages were thriving. Farmers were learning how to produce more surplus crops. Craftworkers in villages were using new technology to make tools, pottery, and jewelry. How do you think this affected trade? As you may have guessed, the Nile River became crowded with boats as trade increased between towns.

Egyptians Join Together

In the midst of all this activity, there were also terror and fear. Ruins of walls around early towns and paintings of bloody battle scenes suggest that there were many wars between villages. To better protect themselves and their belongings, the people along the Nile banded together into two separate kingdoms. Towns in Upper Egypt supported a king who wore a white crown. Towns in Lower Egypt followed a king who wore a red crown.

Then, about 3100 B.C., this changed. Forces led by Menes (MEE nees), the king of Upper Egypt, swept north into the Nile Delta. Menes's army overthrew the king of Lower Egypt. To show his victory, Menes wore a double crown. It combined his white crown with the red crown of Lower Egypt. This change stood for the unification of Egypt. Unification is the joining of separate parts into one.

Following this unification of the two kingdoms, Menes became the first pharaoh (FAY roh) of Egypt. The word *pharaoh* actually refers to the "great palace" in which the rulers lived. Later it became the name given to all the rulers of Egypt. The time when Egypt's early pharaohs worked to build unity within the country is called the Old Kingdom. It lasted from about 2686 B.C. until 2181 B.C. Two other major periods in ancient Egypt's history, the Middle Kingdom and the New Kingdom, would follow.

These Egyptian carvings show rulers and the crowns they wore. The middle crown represents a unification of the other two.

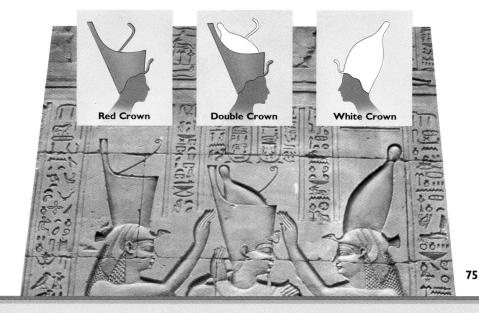

Red Crown   Double Crown   White Crown

75

BACKGROUND INFORMATION

ABOUT THE SPHINX Refer to the illustration on p. 74.

- It is called the Great Sphinx of Giza (the modern village it stands near), and it was built about 4,500 years ago.
- It has the head of a man and the body of a lion and measures 240 feet long and 66 feet high, with a 13-foot wide face.
- In Egypt such mythical creatures were built to guard sacred places.

CITIZENSHIP ★

PRESERVING OUR HERITAGE Call students' attention to the mutilated condition of the Great Sphinx's face. Let them know that this is partly because of vandalism. Invading soldiers used the face for target practice and eventually blew off its nose. Ask students for examples of vandalism in your area and discuss how it harms the community.

UNION OF TWO CROWNS

Help students relate growth to complexity: more surpluses → more specialization → more trade → more contact with other places and more need for organization so all this activity can run smoothly.

Learning How Egyptians Join Together Discuss briefly with the class the need to work out mutually acceptable and peaceable systems when many people are involved. Go on to discuss the structure in ancient Egypt.

- ***What evidence can you find that Egypt 5,000 years ago was not at peace?*** *(wars between villages and between Upper and Lower Egypt)*

- ***What was the outcome of their war?*** *(Menes, king of Upper Egypt, united Upper and Lower Egypt and became* pharaoh, *supreme ruler, of all Egypt.)*

- ***What do we call the first period of Egyptian unity and how long did it last?*** *(the Old Kingdom; about 500 years from around 2686 B.C. to perhaps 2181 B.C. Point out to the class the need to use "about" and "perhaps" when we cannot give precise dates.)*

- ***What does the illustration show?*** *(the combining of two crowns into one)*

- ***Who ordered it and what did it symbolize?*** *(Menes, who meant it to symbolize that Upper and Lower Egypt were united under one pharaoh)*

★THINKING FURTHER: *Making Conclusions* **Why do you think this was an important symbol to ancient Egyptians?** *(It stood for their citizenship in one land and the power of the pharaoh, their supreme leader.)*

Technology CONNECTION

ADVENTURE TIME! CD-ROM
Enrich this lesson with the *Key Places* section on the *Adventure Time!* CD-ROM.

Help students to recognize the firm hand of the pharaoh in government, religion, and the economy.

Discussing Government Under the Pharaohs Call on one student to draw on the board a diagram of Egypt's ruling structure (pharaoh at top; below, many governors reporting to the pharaoh)

- *Who was the undisputed head of Egypt?* (the pharaoh)

- *What was the role of the area governors?* (They carried out the pharaoh's orders in the areas into which the land was divided.)

★THINKING FURTHER: *Compare and Contrast* **How would you contrast Egypt's pharaoh and area-governor system with the U.S. President and 50 state governors system?** (Help students see that U.S. governors are not named by the President and do not take direct orders from nor report to that office.)

More
MAP WORK

Refer students to the map on this page and its scale and legend.

- *What formed the northern border of the Old Kingdom?* (the Mediterranean Sea)

- *Use a ruler to measure the map. Did the Old Kingdom extend farther from north to south or east to west?* (north to south)

- *Was Memphis or Thebes closer to the delta?* (Memphis)

LIFE IN THE OLD KINGDOM

At first, Egypt's pharaohs did not greatly change the civilization that they ruled. They mainly added to the practices of local government, trade, and religion that had existed for hundreds of years along the Nile.

In time, though, the pharaoh became the center of the civilization. His or her actions shaped the fate of all Egypt.

Government Under the Pharaohs

After unification, the most powerful local leaders in Egypt were made area governors for the new government. They performed some of the same services as your local leaders. They were in charge of collecting taxes in their areas and served as local judges. They had different duties as well. Ancient Egyptian governors made sure that precious flood waters were shared fairly among farmers through the use of canals and storage pools.

The area governors reported to the pharaoh's headquarters in Memphis, Egypt's capital city. Memphis was located between Upper and Lower Egypt, near present-day Cairo. From the palace in Memphis, the pharaoh decided how Egypt's affairs should be run, from the highest to the lowest levels.

Religion in Egypt

The pharaoh had great political power in Egypt. He or she had great religious powers as well. In fact, Egyptians believed that the pharaoh was a child of their sun god Ra (RAH). Just as Egyptians believed that Ra gave life to Earth, so they believed that the pharaoh gave life to Egypt and its people. Just as Ra deserved to be worshiped, so, too, did the pharaoh.

EGYPT: Old Kingdom

MAP WORK

Egypt's Old Kingdom pharaohs ruled from Memphis, in Lower Egypt.

1. Why might Lower Egypt, near the Nile Delta, be a good place for a rich capital city?

2. Suppose you lived in Upper Egypt and were invited to Memphis. Would you travel with the flow of the Nile, or against it?

Ra was the most important of the many gods whom ancient Egyptians worshiped. Egyptians believed different gods had different roles. For example, one god caused the flooding of the Nile. Another gave potters and metalworkers their creativity. Other gods took the form of snakes or crocodiles. The god Isis protected people from sickness and harm. Her husband Osiris represented the dead who awaited rebirth.

Osiris was important because belief in the afterlife was central to the religion of Egypt. Egyptians believed that after a person died, he or she would go on to the "Next World." Egyptians believed that the dead could take food and objects into the "Next World." Thus, food and belongings were buried with the dead.

76 MAP WORK: **1.** The Delta is very fertile. **2.** with the flow

---

BACKGROUND INFORMATION

ABOUT MALE AND FEMALE PHARAOHS Although pharaohs were traditionally male, it was possible (generally only after a struggle) for a female to become pharaoh.

- Nitoquerti, or Nitocris, reigned as pharaoh in the Old Kingdom for 12 years around 2170 B.C.

- In about 1789 B.C., Sebeknofru ruled for about three years.

- The most famous female pharaoh was Hatshepsut, who will be discussed in lesson 3 of this chapter.

- Because of the male tradition, females who became pharaohs had to assume the male symbols of authority; for example, they had to wear false beards for ceremonial appearances.

GLOBAL CONNECTION

A WORLDWIDE CRAZE FOR ANCIENT EGYPT A craze for ancient Egyptian artifacts swept the world a century ago. Wealthy patrons financed expeditions to find and bring back artifacts. As a result, many large U.S. cities have Egyptian collections, and a Berlin museum has the priceless sculptured head of Queen Nefertiti.

FIELD TRIP

If your area has an Egypt collection at a museum or college, arrange a field trip to see it. Prepare by having students skim the chapter and list questions to ask. If a trip is not possible, make available books about Egypt and have students prepare a guide for selected objects.

Ancient Egyptians preserved the bodies of dead royalty with a process called *mummification*. The bodies were dried and wrapped in strips of cloth. Sometimes pets such as cats were also mummified to accompany their owners into the afterlife.

Egypt's Economy

Since the pharaoh was considered a god, all things in Egypt belonged to him or her. This put the pharaoh at the center of Egypt's economy. The economy of a country is the way its people manage money and resources for the production of goods and services.

Egypt's economy was based on agriculture. Farmers produced a surplus of food, which fed the whole country. How was that surplus divided? The main way was through taxes. The pharaoh collected a large part of every farmer's crops each year as taxes. The grain, eggs, meat, fruits, and olive oil were then used to feed

the pharaoh's family and servants. The goods were also used to pay for any other items the pharaoh wanted.

The pharaoh also took taxes on everything else made in Egypt, such as leather goods, linen cloth, and baskets. The pharaoh even taxed people's time. During flood season, for example, Egyptians from priests to potters to farmers were called upon to build canals or buildings for the government.

Egypt's craftworkers and artists depended on the pharaohs for their jobs. These people spent most of their time working to keep Egypt's many temples supplied. For example, temples needed golden bowls and stone statues.

Since the pharaoh owned all of Egypt's temples, it was the government's job to pay for all the supplies they used. No money changed hands, since money did not exist in Egypt at that time. Rather, goods of equal value were traded. For their efforts, craftworkers received clothes and food.

Mummies were wrapped in cloth and covered with masks before being put in coffins. Portraits and scenes of daily life were painted on the tomb walls.

The British Museum

The Granger Collection

Exploring Religion in Egypt Remind the class that religious beliefs often reflect what is most important to people.

● *Who was the most important god to the ancient Egyptians? Why?* (The sun god Ra because they believed he was the giver of life.)

● *How was the pharaoh like Ra?* (The pharaoh was considered a powerful god who also gave life to Egypt.)

● *What did the Egyptians believe about life after death?* (It was central to their beliefs. There was a "Next World" to which people must prepare to go.)

● *How did they prepare?* (by preserving the body through mummification and by burying with it food and other necessities of life)

★**THINKING FURTHER:** *Making Generalizations* **Based on the different gods that Egyptians worshiped, what was most important to them?** (the appearance of the sun, the flooding of the Nile, creativity in arts and crafts, health and well-being, the afterlife)

Discussing Egypt's Economy Help students to see that the pharaoh was central to Egypt's *economy* and that the economy was based on agriculture.

● *What is an economy?* (the way a people manages money and resources to produce goods and services)

● *Who was the most important person to Egypt's economy and on what was it based?* (the pharaoh; agriculture and farmers)

● *If it was based on farmers, what part did priests, craftworkers, artists and other specialties play in it?* (They depended on the pharaoh for their jobs and could survive because they were paid with agricultural products.)

● *What was taxed in Egypt?* (The pharaoh taxed all goods produced as well as the time of the citizens.)

★**THINKING FURTHER:** *Compare and Contrast* **In what ways did the pharaoh's government operate like our government?** (It collected taxes, hired workers, and built public works and buildings.)

BACKGROUND INFORMATION

ABOUT BASIC ANCIENT EGYPTIAN RELIGIOUS BELIEFS

• There will be resurrection after death.

• Judgment in the afterlife is based on the lives people lived on Earth.

• Those who lived good lives will be rewarded with eternal happiness.

• Those who lived bad lives will be damned to eternal punishment.

• The divine presence is everywhere.

SECOND-LANGUAGE SUPPORT

WORKING WITH A PEER Second-language students may feel overwhelmed by the amount of text in this lesson. Have groups of students focus on specific sections of the lesson, create three questions, and then share the questions and the corresponding information with the other groups.

A SYSTEM OF WRITING

As students read the introduction, point out to them that written language is a crucial component of civilization. Refer students to the hieroglyphs shown on this page.

- **What are hieroglyphs?** *(individual picture-signs—about 800 in all—that ancient Egyptians developed to stand for objects or for sounds)*

- **Why did they develop hieroglyphics?** *(They needed a written language so that records could be kept and so that the pharaoh's officials could communicate with the governors.)*

★**THINKING FURTHER:** *Compare and Contrast* **How would you compare hieroglyphics to our written language?** *(Our letters stand only for sounds, not for objects.)*

Exploring The Life of a Scribe
Have students begin a list of a scribe's skills.

- **What was a scribe?** *(someone who wrote hieroglyphics and kept records)*

- **How were scribes an example of specialization in Egypt?** *(They worked at a specific skill that only they had.)*

- **How did they learn their skill?** *(by training, beginning in boyhood)*

★**THINKING FURTHER:** *Making Conclusions* **For what reasons do you think it might have been good to be a scribe in ancient Egypt?** *(The job provided security and status; it was useful, necessary, and respected.)*

A SYSTEM OF WRITING

How was it possible for the pharaoh's government to keep track of all of its business details? How could it make sure, for example, that a farmer in Upper Egypt was paying taxes or that a temple in the delta had enough linen?

The pharaoh's local governors helped by communicating with the pharaoh's government in Memphis. What made this communication possible was a system of writing.

Ancient Egyptians developed a system of writing sometime before unification. This system, called hieroglyphics (hi roh GLIF ix), was made up of about 800 picture-signs. These individual picture-signs, or symbols, were called *hieroglyphs*. Hieroglyphs could stand for objects, such as bread, or for sounds, such as *s*. Hieroglyphics are the reason why we now know so much about the lives of ancient Egyptians.

The Life of a Scribe

Pharaohs depended on written records to keep their government in order. A number of writers called scribes traveled throughout Egypt to keep records of details great and small. They went out into the fields with local leaders to record how much grain farmers harvested. Scribes also determined how much farmers owed to the government. Scribes drafted letters and marriage contracts for townspeople. Because writing was taught to only a few, scribes were highly respected in Egyptian culture. It was a great honor to become a scribe.

Only boys could become scribes, and they began training when they were about 10 years old. Each day in school they chanted passages aloud to improve their reading skills. Then they spent hours writing out lessons and

The British Museum

This statue shows Imhotep, a doctor who later was worshiped as the god of medicine. The hieroglyphics are from a king's tomb.

78

---

stories over and over. If their attention wandered, they ran the risk of being beaten. Junior scribes used broken pottery as their "scrap paper."

Writing on Paper

After the boys mastered a simple type of hieroglyphics used for record keeping, they graduated to writing on papyrus (puh PĬ rus). Papyrus is a reed plant that grows along the Nile. Ancient Egyptians used these reeds to make a kind of paper, also called papyrus. Papyrus paper was not very different from the paper we use today. Did you notice how similar the words *papyrus* and *paper* are? Our modern word comes from the ancient one!

Scribes used sharpened reeds as pens. They dipped the reeds into small disks of red or black ink. Then the scribes carefully wrote the information they needed to record on their rolls of papyrus paper.

Scribes had to have good penmanship. They also needed to be good at math. After all, they had to keep correct records of the pharaoh's many goods. Scribes also figured out the number of workers and the amount of materials needed to complete building projects.

The Key to a Lost Language

By about A.D. 400, hieroglyphics fell out of use and their meaning was lost. The ancient symbols found on Egyptian tombs and walls were a mystery to people who came upon them many centuries later.

In 1799 a French soldier was digging in the Nile Delta town of Rosetta. There, he found a large, black stone with writing on it. This stone was later called the Rosetta Stone, after the place where it was found. It contained a passage written three times, in hieroglyphics, Greek, and another type of Egyptian writing called *demotic*. By comparing the three languages, a French scholar named Jean François Champollion (shahm pohl YON) worked to solve the mystery of hieroglyphics. By 1822 he had succeeded. Look at the photograph of the Rosetta Stone. How has its writing helped historians?

MANY VOICES PRIMARY SOURCE

The Rosetta Stone
196 B.C.

Champollion recognized the symbols for Ptolemy (TAH luh mee), a later Egyptian pharaoh. The Rosetta Stone records many of Ptolemy's deeds. For example, the pharaoh lowered taxes, rebuilt certain temples, and freed prisoners!

The stone has the same message in three languages: (from the top) hieroglyphics, late Egyptian (demotic), and Greek.

The British Museum

79

Learning About Writing on Paper
Write *papyrus* and *paper* on the board.

- **How are these two words related?** *(The ancient Egyptians made paper from papyrus, a reed plant, and our word for paper comes from that.)*

- **What did Egyptians scribes use to write on papyrus?** *(pens made from sharpened reeds dipped in ink)*

★**THINKING FURTHER:** *Making Generalizations* **How can you support the generalization that scribes had to be intelligent people?** *(They had to excel at skills like penmanship and math and they had to be able to figure out complex problems, such as how to organize numerous measurements and amounts into clear-cut records.)*

Unlocking The Key to a Lost Language Write the word *extinct* on the board and ask students what it means ("having died out"). Then have students discuss why hieroglyphics became extinct after A.D. 400.

- **Why did hieroglyphics become extinct?** *(They weren't used for centuries, so no one could read them.)*

- **How did the Rosetta Stone help unlock the meaning of hieroglyphics?** *(It contained hieroglyphics and translations into two other languages—Greek and demotic. Because Greek was understood when the Rosetta Stone was found, the hieroglyphics could be translated.)*

MANY VOICES

Discussing the PRIMARY SOURCE

Ask students what other information might be found in hieroglyphics.

- **Did the Rosetta Stone say positive or negative things about Ptolemy?** *(positive: lowering taxes, rebuilding temples, freeing prisoners)*

- **Which languages does the Rosetta Stone show?** *(hieroglyphics, late Egyptian, and Greek)*

BUILDING THE PYRAMIDS

Remind the class that ancient Egyptians were taxed on their goods and also had to give time to the pharaoh's projects.

- **Why were the pyramids built?** *(to serve as tombs for pharaohs)*

- **What were they made of?** *(stone)*

- **How demanding was building the pyramids, in terms of the cost in time and resources?** *(Help students to recognize the monumental demand on the nation—100,000 people's labor, 20 years' time, the huge cost of feeding and clothing so many for so long, the millions of stone blocks hewn from the nation's cliffs.)*

★**THINKING FURTHER:** *Making Conclusions* **How does the building of the pyramids give proof of the importance of the pharaohs to Egypt?** *(Students should conclude that such effort and expense would be directed only toward someone of overwhelming importance.)*

More DIAGRAM WORK

As students study the diagram on this page, note that Egyptians had no heavy machinery.

- **How were the blocks brought higher and higher as the pyramid grew taller?** *(Ramps circled the pyramids, moving higher and higher; the blocks would have to be pushed up or pulled them.)*

- **How heavy was each block?** *(2.5 tons)*

- **What does the inset diagram show?** *(the inside of the pyramid)*

★**THINKING FURTHER:** *Predicting* **How successful would you predict the robbers or others would be in getting into the tombs?** *(probably not too successful)*

BUILDING THE GREAT PYRAMID

GREAT PYRAMID OF KHUFU
Average weight of blocks: 2.5 tons
Total number of blocks: 2,300,000
Number of blocks added each day: 285

Air Shaft   King's chamber   Air Shaft
Queen's chamber
Underground Room

CURRICULUM CONNECTION

LINKS TO MATH Use the labels in the diagram to give the class some math problems. (1) How much weight was added to a pyramid each day? (285 blocks times 2.5 tons = 712.5 tons) (2) How much weight was added to a pyramid each year? (100,000 blocks times 2.5 tons = 250,000 tons) (3) How much would the pyramid weigh upon completion? (2,300,000 blocks times 2.5 tons = 5,750,000 tons)

BACKGROUND INFORMATION

ABOUT THE GREAT PYRAMID
- Khufu, the pharaoh it was built to entomb, is also called Cheops.
- Built near Giza, it was a sacred place the Great Sphinx guarded.
- The Great Pyramid and its neighboring pyramids are among the Seven Wonders of the World.

BUILDING THE PYRAMIDS

No project could have been more challenging to scribes than keeping track of the building of the pyramids. These huge stone structures were built as tombs, or burial places, for pharaohs.

The Great Pyramid is the Old Kingdom's most spectacular monument. It is by far the biggest of all pyramids built in Egypt's history. Pharaoh Khufu (KOO foo) ordered construction to begin about 2600 B.C. This mountain of stone was to be his tomb. It would bring glory not only to himself but to all of Egypt. He would be buried inside with many belongings that he would take into the afterlife.

The 20-year project involved as many as 100,000 people and took a huge amount of Egypt's resources. Few families escaped the call to work at the site. Large amounts of Egyptian taxes went to feed and clothe the project's workers. Even the Nile River landscape changed. Entire cliffs of stone were cut into blocks to make up the pharaoh's great stone monument! Look at the diagram on page 80 to see the construction of the Great Pyramid.

WHY IT MATTERS

Khufu was not the only pharaoh who demanded such massive building projects. Other rulers during the Old Kingdom called for similar, if smaller, monuments. The huge projects took their toll on Egypt's economy and people. Anger against the pharaohs probably began to grow.

Egypt's hard-won unity started breaking down. Local governments began resisting the orders of the pharaohs. In about 2000 B.C. leaders in Upper Egypt revolted and eventually set up a new pharaoh. They based their new capital in the southern town of Thebes. With this division of the country, the Old Kingdom came to an end.

The breakdown of the Old Kingdom, however, led to the rise of an even greater civilization in ancient Egypt. The next lesson tells how the pharaohs learned from their mistakes. They stopped building pyramids. Instead, they built the richest and most powerful civilization the world had ever known.

Reviewing Facts and Ideas

MAIN IDEAS

- Menes united the kingdoms of Upper and Lower Egypt to form the largest government in the world at that time.
- The pharaoh was central to Egypt's government, economy, and religion.
- The writing system of Egypt, called *hieroglyphics,* provided a way for government workers to communicate over long distances.
- Ordinary people worked to build huge, government building projects like the Great Pyramid. This strained both Egypt's economy and its people.

THINK ABOUT IT

1. How did local governors help the pharaoh to rule all of Egypt?
2. Why was Memphis a good place to build Egypt's capital city?
3. **FOCUS** How did the pharaohs' government affect the lives of Egyptians?
4. **THINKING SKILL** What *effects* did hieroglyphic writing have on Egypt? Explain why these were effects.
5. **WRITE** Create your own hieroglyph symbols that represent objects or sounds. See if a partner can read your message.

81

Help students identify the sources of anger in Egypt's Old Kingdom.

- *Why did anger grow in the Old Kingdom?* (Pharaohs demanded too much in property and time.)
- *What happened as a result?* (revolt, overthrow, disunity, a new pharaoh)

★THINKING FURTHER: *Sequencing How would you diagram the stages that the Old Kingdom went through?* (unification, growth and development under powerful pharaohs, discontent, destruction, disunity)

3 CLOSE

MAIN IDEAS

Have students write their answers and then exchange papers with a partner.

- *Why is Menes remembered as a major figure in ancient Egypt?* (He united Upper and Lower Egypt and set the stage for developing a civilization.)
- *How would you describe the role the pharaoh played in Egypt?* (The pharaoh was the major power in government, religion, and the economy.)
- *What role did hieroglyphics play in Egypt?* (It gave government a way to communicate to all parts of Egypt.)
- *How did the government's demand for people's labor affect Egypt?* (It eventually strained the people and economy to the breaking point.)

EVALUATE
✓ Answers to Think About It

1. They carried out the pharaoh's orders. *Problem and Solution*
2. It was right at the base of the rich Nile Delta, the most productive area. *Make Conclusions*
3. It made rules for them, ran their religious temples, controlled how they made a living, and taxed them. *Recall Details*
4. Hieroglyphics allowed record-keeping, and aided economic growth. *Cause and Effect*
5. Encourage students to make their hieroglyphs highly picturesque. *Make Inferences*

Write About It Tell students to choose an identity for themselves in the Old Kingdom and write three journal entries as that person.

MEETING INDIVIDUAL NEEDS

RETEACHING (Easy) Have students copy this list—Menes, hieroglyphics, scribes, Khufu, pyramids—and in a sentence about each, describe its contribution to the Old Kingdom's greatness.

EXTENSION (Average) Ask students to design a tour of the Old Kingdom for a travel agency. Have them go through the lesson and choose five sights to include and write a description of each. For example, "Your first stop is Memphis, the capital . . ." or "You will visit a farm along the Nile to see . . ." Get travel brochures for students to use as models.

ENRICHMENT (Challenging) Tell students that they are going to create "A Gallery of Egyptian Gods" for the classroom. Have them research these gods, how they were pictured, and what their roles were. Have each student choose one, illustrate it, and explain its domain. Then hang the works around the "classroom gallery."

Lesson Overview
Ancient Egyptians developed sailing craft and methods that are still in use today.

Lesson Objectives
★ Compare ancient Egyptian sailing technologies with those used today.

⭐ 1 PREPARE

MOTIVATE Discuss with students what they have already learned about the use of the Nile as superhighway. Why might ancient Egyptians have wanted to travel by water rather than by land?

SET PURPOSE After students realize that travel by water can be easier, cheaper, and quicker than land travel, have them read the column of text on this page to discover the technologies the ancient Egyptians invented to travel by water.

⭐ 2 TEACH

Understanding the Concept of a Legacy Write on the board the proverb: "Necessity is the mother of invention." Discuss its meaning with students and relate it to the ancient Egyptians, their need to move people and goods within their kingdom, and the ways they developed to do it. Help students see that good inventions are improved over time, leading to ever more efficient technology.

Examining the Pictures As students examine each illustration and its caption, tell them to concentrate on the natural materials the ancient Egyptians used for their boats and the natural forces they used to power them.

● **Why do you suppose sails are so prominent in these pictures?** *(Students should note that winds usually blow from the north in Egypt. Sails can catch winds to propel a boat.)*

Legacy
LINKING PAST AND PRESENT
EGYPTIAN BOATS

People have been living along the Nile, the first "superhighway of Egypt," for thousands of years. We may never know when they first tied together bundles of papyrus plant stems to build boats. We do know that boat-building technology was developed very early in ancient Egypt. Egyptians today still sail the Nile, and they see some of the same sights their ancestors saw over 5,000 years ago. As you look at the photos and art on these pages, think about why advances in boat building have played an important part in history.

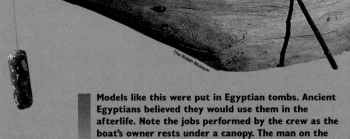

The British Museum

Models like this were put in Egyptian tombs. Ancient Egyptians believed they would use them in the afterlife. Note the jobs performed by the crew as the boat's owner rests under a canopy. The man on the bow is measuring the water's depth with a plumb line.

82

BACKGROUND INFORMATION

ABOUT THE RIDDLE OF THE PYRAMID BOATS
● Khufu was buried with not one, but two, funeral boats.
● The first was unearthed in 1954. The pit in which it had been buried was so well sealed that when opened, one witness described "vapors, perfumes of the . . . sacred wood of the ancient religion."
● The second emerged 33 years later, in 1987. This time scientists studied the buried boat by using a camera lowered into the pit. Then they resealed the pit to prevent pollutants from entering it.
● Why two boats? Perhaps one was a day boat and the other a night boat says one theorist. Perhaps the boats took the dead pharaoh on a pilgrimage, "one ship rowing north with the river current, the other sailing south with the prevailing wind," says another.
● The riddle remains unsolved.

River travel was so important to the ancient Egyptians, even their written language showed it. The hieroglyphic sign for "traveling south" was a boat with sails, because the winds in Egypt usually blow from the north. The sign for "traveling north" was a boat with oars. These signs were used even when the travel was by land!

This boat is made of papyrus stalks tied together. It is similar to boats built by the ancient Egyptians. In 1970 explorer Thor Heyerdahl (HAY air dahl) sailed this papyrus boat from Africa to America. Heyerdahl proved that ancient Egyptians could have made this trip!

This modern Egyptian sailboat, or felucca (fuh LUK uh), is not that different from boats used on the Nile thousands of years ago. Many historians believe that ancient Egyptians invented the sail. Most boats on the Nile today, however, use diesel engines.

83

- **Who invented the sail?** (probably the ancient Egyptians; help students to appreciate this simple, brilliant idea)

- **What other means did the ancient Egyptians develop to power their boats?** (oars, powered by rowers)

- **What determined the method used to power a boat?** (the wind, which blew from the north; usually boats traveling south could use sails, but boats going north required oars)

- **What natural resources did Egyptians use to build boats?** (papyrus stalks lashed together or wood)

- **What powers most boats on the Nile today?** (diesel engines)

★**THINKING FURTHER: Compare and Contrast** **Compare the various technologies on the ancient boats with those on the modern felucca. How are they similar?** (Both have sails, have shallow bottoms, and use steering oars. The felucca uses wood while the ancient boats might have used wood or papyrus stalks.)

⭐ 3 CLOSE

SUM IT UP
Encourage students to list the resources that nature provided (a river, winds, papyrus stalks) and how Egyptians used these resources to create transportation.

EVALUATE
Write About It Have students think about what it would be like to sail south on the Nile in an ancient sailboat. Have them write a paragraph in which they describe the experience.

MEETING INDIVIDUAL NEEDS

RETEACHING (Easy) Have students use art materials to create their own symbols for "traveling north" and "traveling south" along the Nile in ancient Egypt.

EXTENSION (Average) Have students work in teams to create models of an ancient Egyptian sailboat.

ENRICHMENT (Challenging) Have students do further research into Thor Heyerdahl's experiment with papyrus boats, recounted in his 1971 book *The Ra Expeditions*. Have them write reports explaining the theory he wanted to prove and what social scientists now think of it (that Egyptians brought pyramid-building to the Americas; that ancient Americans developed their own technology).

BACKGROUND INFORMATION

ABOUT EGYPTIAN LONG-DISTANCE SAILING
- It is believed that by 3000 B.C., about 400 years before Khufu's reign, Egyptian sailors had ventured beyond the Nile River and into the Mediterranean Sea.
- By that time, they were capable of sailing all the way to Crete, a round trip of about 600 miles.
- It seems reasonable to assume that by that time they could also reach Lebanon, a similar distance.

LESSON 3

PAGES 84–91

Lesson Overview
During the Middle and New King-doms, Egyptian civilization flourished as it met other cultures.

Lesson Objectives
★ Analyze how Egypt's cultural hori-zons were broadened by both trade and war.
★ Describe how the pharaoh Hatshep-sut expanded Egypt's trade.
★ Identify major achievements of the Middle and New Kingdoms.

⭐1 PREPARE

MOTIVATE Have students use their desk maps of the United States as one student reads the *Read Aloud*, while the others estimate the distances on the map. Discuss how long such a trip by boat or donkey might take.

SET PURPOSE Refer to the *Read to Learn* question. Ask students what a "rich civilization" means to them. Help them see that the term means more than economic riches. Point out the photo of King Tutankhamun's throne showing the young pharaoh and his wife. Preview the *Vocabulary* terms.

⭐2 TEACH

Understanding THE BIG PICTURE
Write *trade* and *movement* on the board.

● **Was Egypt the only developing cul-ture at this time?** *(No, neighboring cultures surrounded it.)*

● **What do neighboring cultures offer to one another?** *(a different variety of resources, goods, and ideas)*

⎡★**THINKING FURTHER:** *Predicting*
What influence do you predict Egypt will have on other cul-tures? What influence might they have on Egypt? *(Students may predict possible exchanges.)*⎦

Resource REMINDER

Practice and Project Book: *p. 20*

Anthology: *A Queen's Promise, p. 14; A Visit from an Ancient Pharoh, pp. 15–21*

🔘 **Technology:** *Adventure Time! CD-ROM*

Desk Map

ANCIENT EGYPTIAN CIVILIZATION

READ ALOUD
If you took ancient Egypt's two major trade routes and put them in the United States, one would stretch from Washington, D.C., to Chicago and the other from Washington, D.C., to the northern tip of Maine. These were large distances to travel by boat and caravan. But those distances did not keep Egypt from bringing in a fortune along those roads, as you will see.

Focus Activity

READ TO LEARN
What made Egypt's civilization a rich one?

VOCABULARY
empire
expedition

PEOPLE
Ahmose
Hatshepsut
Tutankhamun

PLACES
Nubia
Kush
Punt
Valley of Kings

THE BIG PICTURE
While Egyptian civilization was spreading along the Nile, neighboring cultures were also growing. To the north, people in Europe were developing the islands and peninsulas across the Mediterranean Sea. To the west, other Africans were finding ways to survive in the harsh desert environment of the Sahara. To the south, the kingdoms of Nubia were thriving, due to gold mines and trade networks. To the east, Asian communi-ties large and small were forming in what are today Israel, Jordan, Lebanon, Syria, and Iraq.

Trade and movement of people and ideas helped to shape development in all of these cultures. Each culture had different resources, products, and ideas to exchange. Egyptian civilization affected neighboring areas. Other cultures had their effects on Egypt as well.

84

SHELTERED INSTRUCTION

READING STRATEGIES & LANGUAGE DEVELOPMENT

MAKE AND SUPPORT GENERALIZATIONS Explain to students that a good way to understand what they read is to identify generalizations (a general conclusion drawn from particular details). Read the second para-graph, find the generalization [Trade and movement of people helped to shape development of all these cultures], and use a Think-Aloud to model the careful reasoning and evidence needed to validate the gen-eralization. **[SDAIE STRATEGY: METACOGNITIVE DEVELOPMENT/MODELING]**

QUOTATION MARKS Ask students to offer examples of uses of quo-tation marks. For example: quotation marks enclose phrases that char-acterize someone or something, for example *"rulers of hill-lands,"* on p. 85. Tell students to look for other such uses as they read the les-son. (See pp. 87, 90, and 91).

NEW RULERS IN EGYPT

Following the collapse of the Old Kingdom, a new era began in Egyptian history. Historians call this period, from about 2100 B.C. until about 1700 B.C., Egypt's Middle Kingdom.

During this time Egypt's contact with other parts of the world increased. For example, the pharaoh's armies conquered kingdoms in Nubia and made use of the area's gold mines. The name *Nubia*, in fact, may come from the Egyptian word *nub*, for gold. Find Nubia on the map on page 86.

Meanwhile Egyptian traders increased their business with cities in western Asia. As trade grew, people also began moving. People from Asia came to live in Egypt's delta region. By 1650 B.C. these new settlers from the hills of western Asia, called Hyksos (HIK sohs), were powerful enough to challenge the pharaoh.

War with the Hyksos

For the next 100 years, the Hyksos—Greek for "rulers of hill-lands"—ruled Lower Egypt. The Hyksos people used horses, chariots, strong bronze weapons, and bows and arrows to defeat Egyptian armies in battle. Egyptian leaders at Thebes, however, continued to control Upper Egypt.

Although they lost Lower Egypt, the Egyptians learned from their war with the Hyksos. In 1550 B.C., about 100 years after the Hyksos gained control of the delta, Egypt rallied behind Pharaoh Ahmose (AH mohs). This time, with the help of weapons and chariots copied from the Hyksos, the Egyptians succeeded in taking back the delta.

The defeat of the Hyksos began the period in Egyptian history called the New Kingdom. Pharaoh Ahmose vowed that outsiders would never again control any part of Egypt. Ahmose and later pharaohs set out to make Egypt the strongest military power in its part of the world.

Tomb walls often had paintings like this scene of the Egyptians fighting the Hyksos. At right is a model Egyptian army.

NEW RULERS IN EGYPT

Briefly review with the class the causes for the collapse of the Old Kingdom.

- **What period succeeded the Old Kingdom?** *(the Middle Kingdom)*

- **What conquest did the Egyptians make during this time and why?** *(Nubia to the south because they wanted the gold found there)*

- **Where did the Egyptians go to expand their business interests?** *(to cities in western Asia)*

- **What evidence can you find that people were moving into Egypt?** *(The Hyksos, from the hills of western Asia, settled in the Nile Delta.)*

★ **THINKING FURTHER:** *Compare and Contrast* **Can you find a parallel between the Egyptians' designs on the Nubians and the Hyksos' designs on the Egyptians?** *(Each wanted what the other had.)*

Discussing War with the Hyksos
Help students to recognize how unequal levels of technology can easily enable one people to prevail over another.

- **How could the Hyksos conquer the Egyptians in Egypt?** *(The Hyksos had better weapons.)*

- **How did the Hyksos victory affect Egypt?** *(Egyptians lost control of Lower Egypt but kept Upper Egypt.)*

★ **THINKING FURTHER:** *Making Conclusions* **How did the Egyptians of the New Kingdom learn from past mistakes?** *(They united, developed a strong army, and set out to avoid threats from outside.)*

BACKGROUND INFORMATION

ABOUT THE HYKSOS
- The Hyksos were probably various non-Egyptians who came to Egypt from Asia, first moving to Egypt's eastern border and then infiltrating the Delta.

- "Hyksos" was not their name at the time. The Egyptians called their kings *hega-khase*. Greeks who later heard this name called all of them *Hyksos*.

- While the best Egyptian military equipment was small axes and ineffective arrows, the Hyksos had armor, powerful bows, sturdy swords and daggers, and, best of all, horses and chariots for cavalry charges.

- The Hyksos allowed Egyptians to keep their religion and language and to serve in the government.

SECOND-LANGUAGE SUPPORT

USING VISUALS Creating illustrations may help clarify information for second-language learners. Have pairs of students illustrate one to two paragraphs of text, then explain their paragraphs in sequence with other pairs of students. This will also reinforce the idea of time order.

ORAL PRACTICE Encourage students to practice reading sections of lessons aloud to gain fluency and to improve their pronunciation. Students can tape-record their practice readings and work on their pronunciation until they can read fluently and clearly.

EXPANSION AND TRADE

Help students recognize the growth and change that Egypt underwent during the New Kingdom—from a nation along the Nile to an *empire* dominant in the southeastern Mediterranean.

Exploring Across Land and Sea
The class should identify Egypt's two routes to becoming an empire—conquest and trade.

● **How did Egypt regain control of Nubia?** *(through military conquest)*

★**THINKING FURTHER: Cause and Effect** *Why would Egypt's expanded trade make it necessary to improve both its navy and army?* (Expanded trade demanded additional ships; threats to trade from bandits demanded additional soldiers and military forts.)

More MAP WORK

Have students sit in pairs with one text open to the map on this page; the other to the map on p. 76.

● **How would you compare the size of the New Kingdom with the Old Kingdom?** *(The New Kingdom was much larger.)*

● **Besides the Nile, what waterways have become important to Egyptian trade?** *(the Mediterranean and Red seas)*

● **How did the conquest of Nubia open new trade for Egypt?** *(It opened trade routes to kingdoms to the south, such as Kush, making available goods such as ebony, animal hides, and ivory.)*

● **With what other regions did Egypt trade?** *(Mediterranean neighbors like Lebanon and Greece)*

★**THINKING FURTHER: Making Generalizations** *How did Egypt change because of trade?* (It became an empire; it had to develop a navy for trade; it had to provide military protection for trade; its craftworkers had many more raw materials with which to work; it was wealthier.)

Learning About Hatshepsut Refer the class to the picture of Hatshepsut on p. 87. If you have not already discussed the *Background Information* concerning male and female pharaohs (p. 76), you may want to do so here.

EXPANSION AND TRADE

During the New Kingdom period, Egypt's leaders worked to win back the lands lost in war. Nubia had gained its independence, but now the armies of the New Kingdom conquered the valuable territory once more.

Egyptian armies also marched northeast, into what is today Israel, and took over that territory. They even pushed as far as the Euphrates River, the edge of another powerful civilization that you will read about in Chapter 5.

During the New Kingdom period, Egypt became an empire. An empire is a group of lands and peoples ruled by one government. Egypt's economy no longer revolved around farming along the Nile. The Egyptian empire now had other valuable resources from conquered lands.

Across Land and Sea

Egypt's New Kingdom traders spread far and wide. Egyptian ships loaded with golden jewelry, linen cloth, and papyrus sailed to what are today Lebanon and Syria. The ships returned carrying silver, timber, and wine—rare treasures in the land of the pharaoh. Remains of oil jars and paintings from what is now Greece have been found in Lower Egypt. These artifacts suggest that Egypt also traded with its neighbors across the Mediterranean Sea.

Egypt's most important trading partner, however, lay to the south. When the pharaoh's armies conquered Nubia, they also gained control of the ancient and wealthy kingdom of Kush (KUSH). Kush controlled rich trade routes to other African kingdoms. Trade goods came from parts of Africa even farther south. The kingdom of Kush traded ebony, leopard skins, and elephant

NEW KINGDOM TRADE

MAP WORK

During the New Kingdom, Egypt drew upon resources from far and wide.

1. What goods did Egypt get from Kush?
2. Which two places were sources of ivory?
3. Which trade route used both the Nile River and land travel?

ivory. Elephant ivory is ivory from elephant tusks. Kush also owned reserves of gold, copper, and precious stones.

Caravans of men and pack animals brought these treasures out of Kush and back to Egypt. On some trading trips, it took 150 men just to carry all of the gold bars that were being sent to Egypt. Soldiers traveled with trading caravans to keep the pharaoh's treasures safe from bandits. Large, castle-

86 **MAP WORK:** **1.** ebony, ivory, animal hides **2.** Kush and Punt **3.** the trade route between Egypt and Kush

---

BACKGROUND INFORMATION

ABOUT THE WORLD'S GREATEST JEWELERS, PAST OR PRESENT
● Egyptian deserts were rich in semiprecious stones like agate, jasper, carnelian, garnet, turquoise, and amethyst. The deserts also yielded gold, but gold came from Nubia and Punt as well.
● Craftworkers fashioned magnificent crowns, bracelets, and necklaces both by embedding jewels in gold and by weaving strands of gold wire around them. They also worked gold, ebony, and ivory together to make delicate boxes to hold jewelry.

USING THE ANTHOLOGY

A QUEEN'S PROMISE page 14 As students read this selection, encourage them to evaluate Hatshepsut's statements about her power and her prediction of enduring fame.

like forts were also built along the Upper Nile to scare away robbers.

Back in Egypt, craftworkers made raw materials into beautiful objects. These included furniture, jewelry, and other fine goods for the pharaoh and Egypt's wealthy families.

Hatshepsut

One pharaoh expanded Egyptian trade well beyond the boundaries of the Egyptian empire. That pharaoh was one of Egypt's few female rulers. Her name was Hatshepsut (hat SHEP soot), "Foremost [first] of the Noble Ladies."

Hatshepsut was a princess and the wife of a pharaoh. She seized the chance to become pharaoh herself when her husband died. Her young stepson was supposed to become the new pharaoh of Egypt. Hatshepsut proclaimed, however, that the ten-year-old boy was too young to rule on his own. In this way she succeeded in being named co-ruler.

Hatshepsut's Trading Journey

In the eighth year of her reign, Hatshepsut organized the biggest trading expedition of her career. An expedition is a group of people who go on a trip for a set reason. The goal of Hatshepsut's expedition was to trade with Egypt's neighbors to the south in Punt. Historians think Punt may have been in what is today Ethiopia or Somalia. Look at the map on page 86. Find the place where the kingdom of Punt is believed to have been located.

The huge caravan of scribes, soldiers, artists, and attendants set off along a dusty road that led east to the Red Sea. There they loaded their cargo onto five sleek ships for the long journey south.

When they finally arrived in Punt, the ships were welcomed by the king and queen. Hatshepsut's scribes then displayed the jewelry, papyrus, and bronze weapons the Egyptians had brought to trade. In exchange the pharaoh received gold, perfume, ivory, leopard skins, and even live apes. Hatshepsut's traders also received rare incense trees. Incense trees produce a perfumelike smell.

After touring the kingdom of Punt, the Egyptians began to prepare for their return home. Scribes carefully recorded the exact numbers of goods loaded aboard the ships. Then the members of the expedition climbed aboard. They also brought with them several leaders from Punt who wanted to visit Egypt, which they knew as Khmet, to meet Pharaoh Hatshepsut. The expedition had lasted two years.

Craftworkers made beautiful jewelry (above) and other items. Hatshepsut (right) organized trade of such objects.

- **Who was Hatshepsut?** *(one of Egypt's few female pharaohs)*

- **How did she get to be pharaoh?** *(by taking over for her stepson)*

> ★**THINKING FURTHER:** *Making Conclusions* **How did Hatshepsut's experience show that women did not become pharaohs easily?** *(She had to seize the office from a minor.)*

Discussing Hatshepsut's Trading Journey Have students find Punt on the map on p. 86. Then have them locate its area on a modern map to see in what modern country the site might be located (probably Ethiopia or Somalia).

- **Why did Hatshepsut send an expedition to Punt?** *(to establish trade)*

- **What route did it follow?** *(east to the Red Sea by land and south by water)*

- **What interaction occurred between the people of Punt and the Egyptian traders?** *(Help students to recognize that besides exchanging goods, they exchanged knowledge. The Egyptians toured Punt to learn about it; the people of Punt wanted to learn about Egypt. Punt leaders returned with the expedition to visit Egypt.)*

> ★**THINKING FURTHER:** *Making Conclusions* **Why might this expedition have been a win-win situation for both countries?** *(Both were enriched by the contact. Each gained goods and knowledge.)*

BACKGROUND INFORMATION

ABOUT HATSHEPSUT

- The coup that accomplished her takeover was carefully planned with her advisers, including priests of the god Amun, whom she claimed had fathered her.

- Traditionally, pharaohs chose their successors. She tried to make the right of succession pass through the pharaoh's wife. She ultimately failed in this ambition.

- When her stepson became an adult, she did not allow him to be pharaoh but did let him command the army.

- When Hatshepsut died after 20 years of rule, her stepson at last became pharaoh. He had her name erased from all wall inscriptions and her statues destroyed and thrown down a quarry.

CURRICULUM CONNECTION

LINKS TO ART Tell students to reread the material on Hatshepsut's expedition and try to picture scenes of it in their minds. Have them make either a drawing or a painting of a scene they can picture. Then have them arrange the artwork in a display called "Hatshepsut's Expedition."

CITIZENSHIP ★

USING CURRENT EVENTS Using current news stories about trade relations—between the United States and other countries or among nations formed into trading blocs—help students relate it to Hatshepsut's expedition. Reinforce for them the importance of trade to nations from ancient times to the present.

Infographic

Briefly review with students the importance of the pharaoh in Egyptian life, to help them understand why so much of the nation's wealth would be dedicated entirely to the glory of the pharaohs.

Discussing Treasures of an Ancient Tomb Have students read the column of type on this page. To impress on them the wonder and excitement of uncovering Tutankhamun's tomb after 3,000 years, tell them the story outlined in the *Background Information* on this page. Then give them time to examine the pictures and their captions.

- **Where is the Valley of the Kings?** *(in the Egyptian desert)*

- **Why is it important?** *(It is the burial ground for 30 New Kingdom pharaohs.)*

- **Who was Tutankhamun?** *(a young pharaoh, who ruled from age 9 until his death at the age of 19)*

- **How do we know that he was a pharaoh?** *(His burial in the Valley of the Kings tells us, as do the lavish trappings of his burial.)*

- **One writer has called Howard Carter "the man who stepped into yesterday." Why is this an apt description?** *(What he found took him back 3,000 years.)*

Technology CONNECTION

ADVENTURE TIME! CD-ROM
Enrich the *Infographic* by having students look at the interactive version on the *Adventure Time!* CD-ROM.

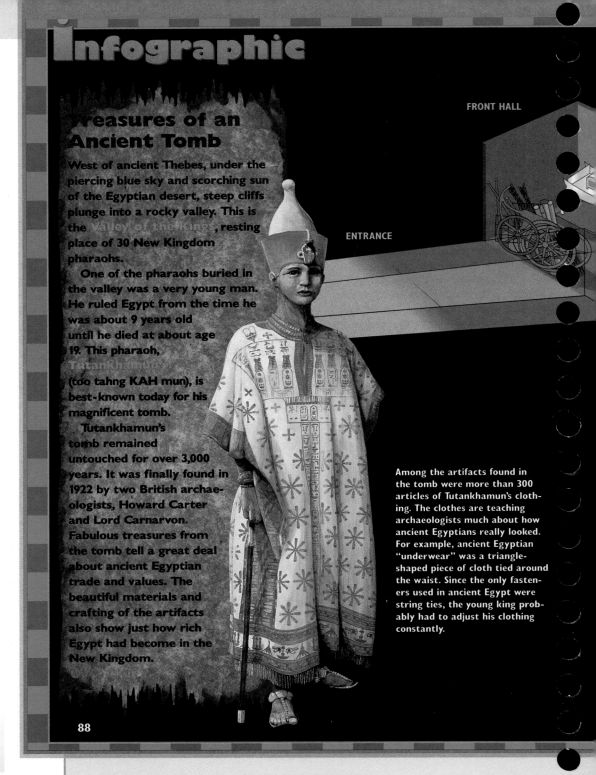

Treasures of an Ancient Tomb

West of ancient Thebes, under the piercing blue sky and scorching sun of the Egyptian desert, steep cliffs plunge into a rocky valley. This is the Valley of the Kings, resting place of 30 New Kingdom pharaohs.

One of the pharaohs buried in the valley was a very young man. He ruled Egypt from the time he was about 9 years old until he died at about age 19. This pharaoh, Tutankhamun (too tahng KAH mun), is best-known today for his magnificent tomb.

Tutankhamun's tomb remained untouched for over 3,000 years. It was finally found in 1922 by two British archaeologists, Howard Carter and Lord Carnarvon. Fabulous treasures from the tomb tell a great deal about ancient Egyptian trade and values. The beautiful materials and crafting of the artifacts also show just how rich Egypt had become in the New Kingdom.

FRONT HALL

ENTRANCE

Among the artifacts found in the tomb were more than 300 articles of Tutankhamun's clothing. The clothes are teaching archaeologists much about how ancient Egyptians really looked. For example, ancient Egyptian "underwear" was a triangle-shaped piece of cloth tied around the waist. Since the only fasteners used in ancient Egypt were string ties, the young king probably had to adjust his clothing constantly.

88

BACKGROUND INFORMATION

ABOUT DISCOVERING TUTANKHAMUN'S TOMB

- Lord Carnarvon was a wealthy British aristocrat with a passion for Egyptology. He financed the expedition.

- Howard Carter began his career in Egyptology as a humble draftsman, but by avidly studying archaeology he became an expert himself and supervised many expeditions into the Valley of the Kings.

- From 1907 on, Carter worked for Lord Carnarvon in search of a tomb Carter believed existed but which had never been found. All he had as evidence for it were a few seals that indicated that a king named Tutankhamun had once been pharaoh. Year after year, Carter dug endless trenches in the floor of the Valley of the Kings but turned up nothing.

- Finally in 1922, Carter's digging unearthed the door of a tomb and he began to open the chamber. Was this at last the tomb he sought? "At first I could see nothing," he later reported. "The hot air escaping from the chamber caused the candle flame to flicker. But presently, as my eyes grew accustomed to the light, details of the room within emerged slowly from the mist, strange figures of animals, statues, and gold—everywhere the glint of gold."

- When Carter flashed a light into the room, "the first light that had pierced the darkness of the chamber for three thousand years," he reported, "the effect was bewildering, overwhelming."

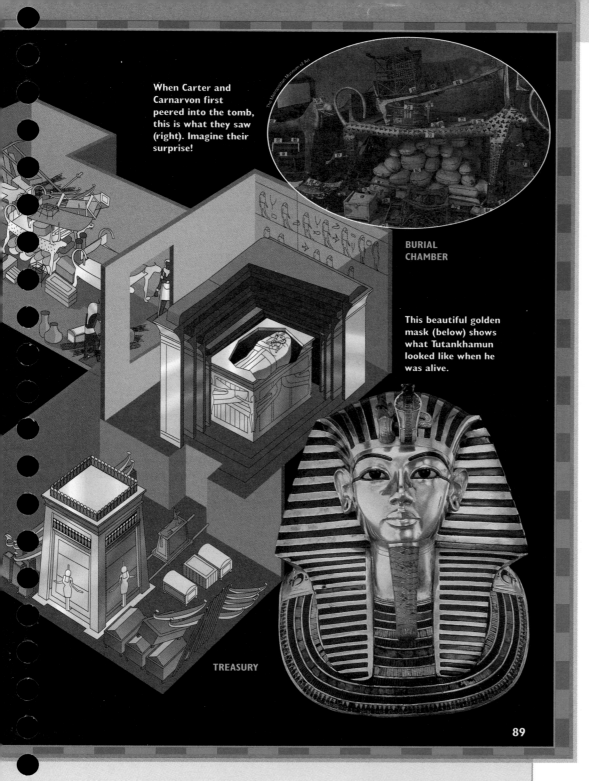

When Carter and Carnarvon first peered into the tomb, this is what they saw (right). Imagine their surprise!

BURIAL CHAMBER

This beautiful golden mask (below) shows what Tutankhamun looked like when he was alive.

TREASURY

89

- *Looking at the diagram of the tomb, why do you suppose it had so many rooms?* (It had to hold not only the body, but also the hundreds of valuable artifacts that were to accompany Tutankhamun on his journey in the other world.)

- *Why do you suppose the artifacts might have been in such a jumble? Do you think Tutankhamun was buried this way?* (Help students to understand that, early on, grave robbers broke into the tomb and got as far as the front hall, where they scattered things about.)

- *What symbolism of ancient Egypt can you find among these artifacts?* (The boats symbolize the Nile. Call students' attention to the double symbol above the forehead on the gold mask. Explain that it shows a vulture and a cobra, the symbols of Upper and Lower Egypt, respectively.)

- *What is a sarcophagus?* (A coffin; explain that Tutankhamun's outermost sarcophagus was carved red granite. Inside it, one inside another, were three coffins carved in human shape, the innermost made of 242 pounds of solid gold. And within this final coffin, the mask shown here covered the head and shoulders of the mummified Tutankhamun.)

★THINKING FURTHER: *Making Conclusions* **Tutankhamun was a minor pharaoh who ruled for a brief time, yet great treasures were buried with him. Might more important pharaohs who ruled for a longer time have had tombs that were even richer and more magnificent?** (Help the students understand that grave robbery through the ages makes this a question that cannot really be answered, since so far only Tutankhamun's tomb has been found relatively undisturbed.)

EXPANDING THE INFOGRAPHIC

RESEARCHING AND WRITING Have students create their own picture books entitled "The Treasures of Tutankhamun's Tomb." In it, they should include pictures that they draw of at least six of the treasures, and each should include a caption that explains the artifact's significance and describes the materials used and the craftwork that went into it. Many books on this subject are available, both lavishly illustrated adult books and well-explained and illustrated juvenile books. Sources might include:

- Encyclopedia treatments of *Ancient Egypt* and of *Tutankhamun*.
- A library card catalog for the same subject entries.
- *National Geographic Index*, 1888–1988 for the same entries.

MOVING IDEAS

Write on the board the following adage: "The pen is mightier than the sword." Discuss its meaning with the class: The communication of ideas can be more powerful than physical force.

Discussing Medicine in Egypt

Briefly review p. 35 with the class to recall what they learned about medicine in Europe 5,000 years ago: Europeans like the Iceman knew about the healing properties of some plants.

- **What level of medical knowledge had the ancient Egyptians reached?** (They knew about plants that heal, could sew up cuts and set bones, had discovered "antibiotic" properties of moldy bread for treating wounds.)

- **Who were the Egyptian doctors and where did they get their training?** (They were priests who learned their skills in temple schools.)

★THINKING FURTHER: *Making Conclusions* **What does this say about the role of priests and temples in Egyptian society?** (Priests were probably scholars and scientists; in addition to being places of worship, temples were schools and libraries.)

Exploring Math and Science Point out to students that the earliest Egyptians could not learn math and science from books. They had to figure it out for themselves. We today benefit from their learning.

- **Why would a sound knowledge of mathematics be essential before the pyramids could be built?** (Pyramids could not have been designed without accurate measurements and an understanding of angles.)

- **What had the Egyptians learned about the science of astronomy?** (They recognized planets as unique objects in the sky and understood eclipses.)

★THINKING FURTHER: *Making Decisions* **What grade would you give the Egyptians in math and science?** (Remind students that the Egyptians had started almost from ground zero.)

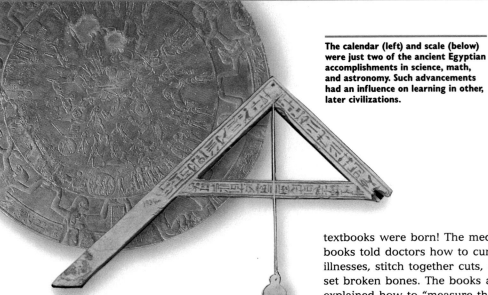

The calendar (left) and scale (below) were just two of the ancient Egyptian accomplishments in science, math, and astronomy. Such advancements had an influence on learning in other, later civilizations.

MOVING IDEAS

In the time of the Egyptian empire, trade goods were not the only things that moved from place to place. Ideas and skills spread too.

You have already read how the Egyptians learned about new weapons from their old enemy, the Hyksos. Other cultures, in turn, learned from Egypt. Egyptian understanding of medicine, mathematics, and astronomy became famous in other countries. Records tell of a king in Lebanon who became sick. He insisted on being treated only by an Egyptian doctor.

Medicine in Egypt

Most Egyptian doctors were actually priests who learned their skills in temple schools. The storehouse of medical knowledge in temple schools was vast and old. For thousands of years priests had noted different kinds of illnesses and injuries and what worked best in treating them. When writing was invented, scribes wrote down this knowledge. The world's first medical

textbooks were born! The medical books told doctors how to cure illnesses, stitch together cuts, and set broken bones. The books also explained how to "measure the heart" to see if it was beating too quickly or slowly. Do you know how to measure your own pulse?

Many ancient Egyptian cures centered around treatments that are no longer used. Many other cures, however, introduced ingredients that we still use today. Chamomile, an herb used to make tea, was used to calm upset stomachs. Moldy bread was often placed on wounds. This sounds terrible until we remember that modern antibiotics, or germ-killing drugs, are often made from certain kinds of molds!

Math and Science

Along with medicine, Egyptian priests knew a great deal about mathematics. They developed the mathematical rules needed in building the pyramids, for example.

The priest-scientists also used their knowledge of math to understand the stars. Without telescopes, Egyptians identified five of the solar system's planets, which they called the "stars that know no rest." The mysterious

90

darkness of eclipses did not scare priests. They had figured out that such events were just "meetings of the Sun and Moon."

WHY IT MATTERS

These ideas and others spread throughout the Egyptian empire. In chapters to come you will learn how Egyptian culture influenced other civilizations.

The creation of an empire made Egypt one of the largest civilizations the world had ever known. With resources gained through new territories and trade, Egypt also became incredibly rich. Pharaoh Tutankhamun's tomb has taught archaeologists much about the empire's riches. In the next lesson you will learn how the growth of the empire affected everyday life.

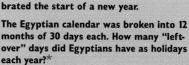

Links to SCIENCE

How Many Days Off Is That?

How did ancient Egyptians invent a 365-day calendar?

They based the calendar on the yearly rising and setting of a star named Sirius. Each year Sirius shines in the sky for about 295 nights. Then the star disappears for 70 days. On the day it reappeared in the sky—just before the Nile began flooding—the Egyptians celebrated the start of a new year.

The Egyptian calendar was broken into 12 months of 30 days each. How many "leftover" days did Egyptians have as holidays each year?*

✓/ Reviewing Facts and Ideas

MAIN IDEAS

- Trade and war helped to link Egypt with its neighbors in the Sahara, Nubia, western Asia, and the Mediterranean.
- Egypt became an empire when it conquered Nubia, Syria, and Lebanon. These new lands gave Egypt a wealth of new resources upon which to draw.
- Pharaoh Hatshepsut expanded trade to a region of eastern Africa called Punt.
- The discovery of Tutankhamun's tomb in 1922 yielded hundreds of New Kingdom artifacts.
- The Egyptians' knowledge of medicine, math, and science became famous among their neighbors. Hyksos skills in metalworking became part of life in Egypt.

THINK ABOUT IT

1. Why were Egypt's leaders interested in conquering Nubia?

2. When was Tutankhamun's tomb discovered? What did archaeologists find there?

3. **FOCUS** In what ways was ancient Egypt a rich civilization?

4. **THINKING SKILL** Think about the different ways Egypt "grew" during the New Kingdom. What *effects* did this growth have on Egypt? How did Egypt affect its neighbors?

5. **GEOGRAPHY** Use the map on page 86 to trace an outline of Egypt and its trading partners during the New Kingdom. Then write in the resources of each territory.

*5 days

91

Discussing WHY IT MATTERS Have students use their notes on information that helps them make and support generalizations about the flowering of the New Kingdom to review this lesson.

> ★**THINKING FURTHER:** *Making Generalizations* **Based on what you have learned, what generalizations can you now make about Egypt during the New Kingdom concerning growth, trade, learning and technology?** (Encourage students to make as many generalizations as they can, with each supported by evidence.)

⭐ 3 CLOSE

MAIN IDEAS

Have students carefully consider each summarizing point.

- *Into what areas did the Egyptian empire expand?* (the Sahara, Nubia, western Asia, the Mediterranean)

- *How did these new areas enrich Egypt?* (It gave Egypt new resources.)

- *Into what area did Hatshepsut expand trade?* (into Punt)

- *Why was the discovery of Tutankhamun's tomb so amazing?* (It revealed the extent of the wealth and power the New Kingdom's pharaohs achieved.)

- *How do cultures learn from one another?* (through interaction)

EVALUATE

✓ Answers to Think About It

1. to gain control of Nubia's gold
   Make Conclusions

2. in 1922; fabulous treasures in gold and other luxuries
   Recall Details

3. It was rich in knowledge, rich in goods.
   Making Analogies

4. It became wealthier and more powerful, its knowledge and technology reached greater heights, and it became respected by neighbors.
   Cause and Effect

5. Remind students to check the map legend to help them list resources.
   Five Themes of Geography: Place

Write About It Tell students to choose anyone in Egypt's New Kingdom and write a paragraph describing that person's contribution to Egypt's civilization.

MEETING INDIVIDUAL NEEDS

RETEACHING (Easy) Tell students to review the map on p. 86 and list the variety of trade goods named. Then have them go back through the illustrations in this lesson and look for uses Egyptians made of these goods. Opposite each trade good item on their list, they should identify the picture that shows it, by page number and brief description.

EXTENSION (Average) Tell students to think about what Punt leaders saw in Egypt after Hatshepsut's expedition to their country. Have students write a letter to Punt describing what Egypt is like.

ENRICHMENT (Challenging) Tell students to thumb back through this lesson to discover one aspect of the New Kingdom civilization that they would like to know more about. Then have them research their topic and prepare a presentation to give to the class.

SKILLS LESSON
PAGES 92–93

Lesson Overview
Large-scale and small-scale maps show more or fewer details about a place.

Lesson Objectives
★ Understand that maps use different scales to serve different purposes.

1 PREPARE

MOTIVATE Have students read *Why the Skill Matters* and discuss the meaning of *scale*—a unit of measure. Help them see that it would be impossible to make maps actual size.

SET PURPOSE Have students thumb through maps in the text and check the scale of each to determine if all maps are drawn to the same scale. Remind them to use the *Helping Yourself* tips on p. 93 for assistance.

2 TEACH

Using the Skill Have students study the text and maps and decide which map is which scale.

● *For what do mapmakers use small-scale maps? (to show large areas)*

● *For what do they use large-scale maps? (to show smaller areas and more details of an area)*

★**THINKING FURTHER:** *Classifying* **When would a large-scale map be needed? a small-scale map? Give examples.** *(Examples: small-scale map to see how far apart two cities are; large-scale map to see the downtown area of a city)*

Resource REMINDER
Practice and Project Book: *p. 21*
Transparency: *Map 11*
Technology: *Adventure Time!* CD-ROM

GEOGRAPHYSKILLS

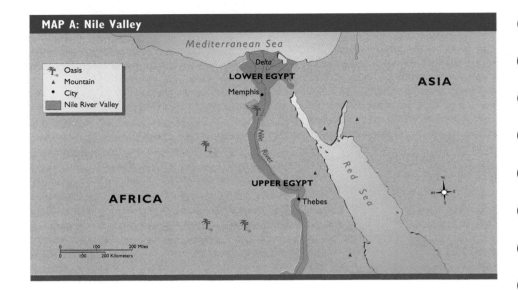

MAP A: Nile Valley

Using Maps at Different Scales

VOCABULARY
scale
small-scale map
large-scale map

WHY THE SKILL MATTERS
As the Egyptian empire grew during the New Kingdom, so did the new capital city at Thebes. Beautiful palaces sprang up along the banks of the Nile. More than a dozen massive temples were built in the surrounding desert to honor gods and pharaohs. Throughout the New Kingdom, Thebes was a symbol of the power of the pharaohs.

92

Mapmakers can show Thebes up close or in relation to the rest of Egypt. Mapmakers can do this with any other place on Earth by using different map scales. A map scale is a unit of measure, such as an inch, used to represent a distance on Earth.

USING THE SKILL
Map scales can be large or small. Mapmakers use small-scale maps to give viewers the "big picture" of a place. Large-scale maps provide more details about smaller areas. Of course, the real distances on Earth stay the same! Both types of maps are useful, however. Depending on the kind of information needed, you might use one or both types.

Look at Map A. On this small-scale map, one inch stands for 200 miles. Compare this map with Map B, on the next page. Map B shows a smaller area and more details than Map A. Because one inch represents differ-

---

READING STRATEGIES & LANGUAGE DEVELOPMENT

CLASSIFY Explain to the class that in this Skills Lesson, they will organize information by classifying it. In this case, they will classify map scales by size—large and small. That is, they are putting map scales into two groups, each having its own—different—purpose. Point out that this organization enables them to identify what each purpose is and to recognize how the size of the scale suits it.

HOMOPHONES This Skills Lesson provides an opportunity to help students differentiate between two homophones that are sometimes confused. Refer to the mention of Thebes as the *capital* of the New Kingdom and discuss what a county, state, or national capital is—the town or city that serves as the seat of the government. Then write *capitol* on the board and help students define it as a building in which government is conducted. Have them use the two words in sentences.

* 1 mile (1.6 kilometers)
** about 1/8 mile (about 1/5 kilometer)
*** map A; about 100 miles (160 kilometers); map A, the small-scale map

ent distances on the two maps, they have different scales. What distance does one inch stand for on Map B?*

Suppose you wanted to figure out how to get from Tutankhamun's tomb to Hatshepsut's temple. First, you need to decide which map to use. Which map shows the detail you need? As you can see, Map B, a large-scale map, better shows the detailed information of a small area. Now measure the distance using the map's scale.**

TRYING THE SKILL

Suppose that you are writing a book about places near Thebes. Use the Helping Yourself box to answer these questions. Which map would

HELPING Yourself

- A map's **scale** is a unit of measure that relates distance on the map to distance on Earth.

- Maps use different scales to show places up close or at great distances from each other.

- Remember that **large-scale maps** measure distance in *smaller* units. **Small-scale maps** measure distance in *larger* units.

you use to find the oasis, or watered area within a desert, nearest to Thebes? Find the Red Sea. How far is ancient Egypt's capital, Thebes, from the Red Sea? Which type of map gives a "big picture" of this place?***

REVIEWING THE SKILL

1. What are the differences between small-scale and large-scale maps?

2. From which map could you find the width of the Nile Delta region?

3. About how wide did the Nile River become near Thebes? Which map gave you the answer to that question?

4. How might using large- and small-scale maps help you in planning a trip?

MAP B: Thebes, c. 1100 B.C.
Valley of the Kings
Tomb of Tutankhamun
Temple of Hatshepsut
Nile River
Artificial Lake (now dried up)
Thebes
Royal Temples
Temple walls
Mountain area
City area
Valley of the Kings
0 1/2 Mile
0 1/2 1 Kilometer

Huge temples, like this one for Hatshepsut, were built to honor Egyptian gods and pharaohs.

- **Which of these maps is the small-scale map?** *(Map A)*

- **How does its scale compare with that of the large-scale map?** *(The small-scale stands for 200 miles to the inch; the large-scale stands for 1 mile to the inch)*

- **Which of these maps would you choose to find your way from Tutankhamun's tomb to Hatshepsut's temple? Why?** *(Map B, the large-scale map, because it gives the detail needed.)*

★**THINKING FURTHER:** *Compare and Contrast* **To differentiate between the uses of the two types of scale, how might you complete the following, in rhyme form: "The larger the scale, ..."** *("... the greater the detail")* **"The smaller the scale, ..."** *("... the lesser the detail. Large-scale maps 'enlarge'.")*

Trying the Skill Students should indicate they would use Map A (small-scale) to find the oasis since it gives the big picture. The large-scale map does not show the oasis.

3 CLOSE

SUM IT UP

Call on students to thumb through the text, locate a map, identify it as large-scale or small-scale, and explain why that scale was used.

EVALUATE
✓ **Answers to Reviewing the Skill**

1. the units of measurement they use and the amount of detail they show

2. Map A, the small-scale map

3. about 1/2 mile, according to Map B, the large-scale map

4. Large-scale maps: directions to and distances between points. Small-scale maps: points of interest, city streets.

Technology CONNECTION

ADVENTURE TIME! CD-ROM
Enrich this Skills Lesson with the . *Compare* feature on the *Adventure Time!* CD-ROM.

MEETING INDIVIDUAL NEEDS

RETEACHING (Easy) Have students make maps of a floor in the school and then, in insets, make large-scale maps showing individual rooms in more detail.

EXTENSION (Average) Tell students to choose a state or a country that they have always wanted to visit and do some research on it. Have them draw a small-scale outline map of it, drawing in and labeling major cities, rivers, lakes, and mountains. As insets, have them draw large-scale maps of at least two places they want to visit.

ENRICHMENT (Challenging) Have students do some research on modern-day tours of Egypt, the stops they make, the modes of travel. Then have them draw a small-scale map of Egypt, labeling important points and features, and showing the route the tour follows. They should prepare at least four large-scale tour stops as inset maps.

LESSON 4
PAGES 94–99

Lesson Overview
Egyptian civilization rested on the labor of stable, well-trained working groups who kept the economy productive.

Lesson Objectives
★ Analyze the makeup of the *social pyramid* that was ancient Egypt.
★ Explain the role of *slavery* there.
★ Describe the work and home life of ordinary ancient Egyptians.

1 PREPARE

MOTIVATE Give students time to think about what might be called ordinary life in the United States. Use the *Read Aloud* paragraph and *Read to Learn* question to begin discussions of how ordinary people lived in ancient Egypt.

SET PURPOSE Explain to the students that the photo shows a water jar from Egypt. Refer students to the *Vocabulary* terms. Encourage them to look for answers to this question: How was ordinary life in ancient Egypt similar to and different from our ordinary life?

2 TEACH

Understanding THE BIG PICTURE
On the board, write *country* and *city*.

● **How did Egyptian workers live in each of these areas in the New Kingdom?** *(Have students work in pairs to write their answers on the board—Country: planting and harvesting crops, working at crafts to supply people's basic needs. City: craftworking in shops, living in small houses in crowded neighborhoods.)*

★**THINKING FURTHER:** *Cause and Effect* **Why would Egyptian civilization have crumbled without these people's work?** *(They produced things needed to survive and develop a civilization.)*

Resource REMINDER
Practice and Project Book: *p. 22*
Technology: *Adventure Time!* CD-ROM

The Granger Collection

| 3000 B.C. | 2500 B.C. | 2000 B.C. | 1550 B.C. | 1100 B.C. |

DAILY LIFE IN ANCIENT EGYPT

Focus Activity

READ TO LEARN
How did people of the New Kingdom live and work?

VOCABULARY
social pyramid
slavery

READ ALOUD
Under the pharaohs of the New Kingdom, Egypt became the largest and most powerful empire in the world. As you have read, the empire spread eastward into western Asia. Egypt also conquered Nubia, to the south. You have also read how Egyptian goods and ideas spread far from the Nile Valley. How did this growing wealth and power affect the ordinary people who lived in the Egyptian empire?

THE BIG PICTURE
While Egypt's armies and traders traveled far and wide, Egyptians at home continued working to make their country strong. Farmers planted and harvested crops between the yearly Nile floods. Weavers made the linen cloth that kept Egyptians clothed. Woodworkers built the plows, benches, and chests that ordinary people used every day.

These hardworking members of Egyptian society rarely had their own farms or shops. Rather, most people worked on huge farms owned by government leaders, army officers, or scribes. Others lived in small houses tucked away in crowded city neighborhoods. There the craftworkers and farmers made simple goods in their homes. As they went about their daily lives, each of these Egyptians was contributing to the great success of the New Kingdom.

94

SHELTERED INSTRUCTION

READING STRATEGIES & LANGUAGE DEVELOPMENT

MAKING CONCLUSIONS Point out that a good way to make sense of a reading is to make conclusions (draw inferences from facts in the text and what you know). Have students read the first two paragraphs of *The Big Picture* and make a conclusion. [Without workday stability, greatness could not develop.] Arrange students in groups to make and share conclusions based on this lesson. **[SDAIE STRATEGY: TEXT REPRESENTATION/METACOGNITIVE DEVELOPMENT]**

COMPARATIVES AND SUPERLATIVES Review with students how the comparative and superlative of adjectives are formed and why they are useful for making comparisons. Review the use of *-er* and *more* for the comparative and *-est* and *most* for the superlative. Encourage students to skim the lesson for examples (On p. 95, some examples are: *earliest, most powerful, largest* part, *lowest* level, *hardest* work.)

A SOCIAL PYRAMID

From the earliest days of Egypt's history, a person's position in society depended on what he or she did for a living. As a result the shape of Egyptian society was similar to that of a pyramid. The most powerful person, the pharaoh, was at the top of this social pyramid. Below the pharaoh ranked government officials, and below them, craftworkers. At the pyramid's base were farmers and captured people who made up the largest part of society.

Egyptians were not the only people who filled the empire's social pyramid. Nubian soldiers made up a large part of the pharaoh's army and police force. Syrian princes joined the ranks of Egypt's government officials. Syrian and Nubian craftworkers worked side by side with Egyptian craftworkers.

Slavery in Egypt

The people at the lowest level of this social pyramid were those who lived under slavery. Slavery is the practice of one person owning another person. When Egypt conquered Nubia and part of western Asia, Egyptians captured prisoners of war and enslaved them. Most of these people were Syrians, though many were Nubians.

Slaves did some of the hardest work that had to be done in Egypt. They worked in the heat of the desert to mine gold in Nubia. They worked alongside free farmers in the floodwaters of the Nile. They dug canals and prepared land for planting. Enslaved people also worked as house servants to wealthy Egyptians.

Egyptians bought enslaved Syrians and Nubians like they did cattle or cloth. One Syrian girl, for example, was sold for the price of four big sacks of grain and a piece of silver. However, enslaved people did have some basic rights in Egypt. They had the right to be treated fairly under the law and even to own property.

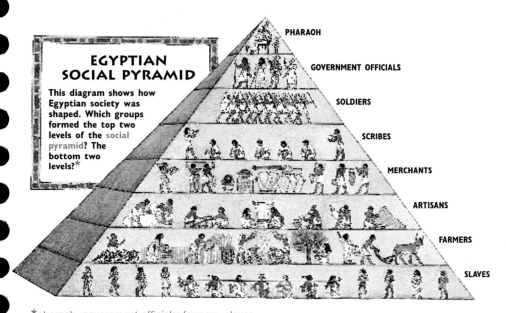

EGYPTIAN SOCIAL PYRAMID

This diagram shows how Egyptian society was shaped. Which groups formed the top two levels of the social pyramid? The bottom two levels?*

PHARAOH
GOVERNMENT OFFICIALS
SOLDIERS
SCRIBES
MERCHANTS
ARTISANS
FARMERS
SLAVES

*pharaoh, government officials; farmers, slaves

A SOCIAL PYRAMID

Encourage students to work back and forth between the text and diagram on this page. Help them to recognize that a social pyramid reflects both the levels of a society—lowest to highest—and the numbers of people in each level. Those at the lowest are most numerous; those nearer the top are fewer in number.

More DIAGRAM WORK

Have the students "read" the diagram as well as the text on this page.

- *What were the two most numerous groups of people in Egyptian society?* (slaves and farmers)

- *Who were least numerous?* (pharaoh, government officials, soldiers)

- *Who might be called the "middle" people?* (scribes, merchants, artisans)

★THINKING FURTHER: *Compare and Contrast* **Which of the people in this social pyramid would not be found in a social pyramid of our society?** (pharaoh, slaves)

Discussing Slavery in Egypt Develop an idea of the nature of slavery in Egypt.

- *What peoples made up the slave population in Egypt?* (mainly Syrians and Nubians captured in battle)

- *Were all non-Egyptians part of the lowest level of Egypt's social pyramid?* (No, some Nubians were soldiers and police; some Syrians were government officials, and many from both groups were craftworkers.)

- *What kinds of work did slaves do?* (much of the hardest, dirtiest work)

- *How was ownership of slavery transferred?* (like any other type of goods, by buying and selling)

- *What rights did ancient Egyptian slaves have?* (They had the right to fair treatment and to own property.)

★THINKING FURTHER: *Making Conclusions* **What does the existence of slavery in Egypt indicate about attitudes toward slavery in the ancient world?** (It hints at the idea that it was an accepted fact of life.)

Encourage students to examine the illustration on this page. Help them to see that the tools and methods the ancient Egyptians used still demanded hard and time-consuming labor.

Discussing Farm Life As students read this section, tell them to think about what they know about plantation life in the United States before the Civil War.

● *What different varieties of workers labored on Egypt's big farms?* *(farmers, herders, bakers, brewers, brickmakers, and a variety of other craftworkers. Point out to the class that slaves probably did mostly farming but could also have worked at other jobs if they were so trained.)*

● *Who ran the farms? Why might they have got this job?* *(Help students review what they learned earlier about scribes and their ability to measure goods and keep records, skills that would be valuable in running farms.)*

● *How was the farm produce divided?* *(The pharaoh got half, another large share went to the farm owner, the workers and slaves got the rest.)*

★**THINKING FURTHER:** *Compare and Contrast* **What parallels can you see between the farms of ancient Egypt and the plantations of the pre-Civil War U.S. South?** *(Both were self-sufficient worlds; both had owners who benefited by what they produced; slaves worked on both.)*

Investigating Planting and Harvesting As students read this section, have them think about being out in the blistering sun, doing the jobs described with only the simplest of tools and no labor-saving mechanized devices.

● *Why was a farmer's work "never done"?* *(Even when the back-breaking work of planting and harvesting was finished, farmers still had to labor for the government on public projects.)*

● *Why were work songs part of the work routine?* *(to try to lighten the load)*

FARMS AND CITIES

During the New Kingdom huge farms and busy cities dotted the shores of the Nile River. Life was very different in the two settings, but some things were similar. In both places ordinary people worked long hours for few rewards. Both in cities and on farms, people also enjoyed simple pleasures, such as celebrating holidays and playing games.

This figure was made from carved limestone over 4,000 years ago. It shows an Egyptian brewer at work.

The Granger Collection

Farm Life

As you have read, most Egyptians lived on big farms owned by powerful people from the top of the social pyramid. These farms were run by loyal scribes. Farmers, craftworkers, and slaves did most of the work. Farms were like small worlds of their own. They produced most of the goods the people living there needed.

Farms bustled with many different kinds of activities. Farmers grew and harvested crops. Herders tended cattle and goats. Bakers ground wheat from the fields and baked bread. Brewers made beer from wheat and barley, and fishers caught fish in the Nile. Brickmakers shaped bricks from river mud for workers' houses.

As many as half of these products went to the pharaoh as taxes. Most of what remained went to the owner of the farm. Workers and slaves divided the little that was left.

Planting and Harvesting

None of the jobs were easy, but farming was perhaps the hardest of all. To prepare the soil for planting, farmers dug up large fields with cattle-drawn wooden plows and hoes. To

bring water to the fields, farmers dug irrigation canals and hauled water using shadoufs. In addition farmers were often called upon by the government to help build canals, temples, or tombs for the pharaoh. It seemed like a farmer's work never ended!

At harvesttime women, men, and children headed out to the fields to cut, stack, and carry grain. As they worked in the blazing sun, a song leader chanted out songs and everyone sang along. Singing helped to make the time pass more quickly.

Farmers loaded the cut stalks into baskets and took them to threshing, or separating, areas. There, oxen or donkeys were walked over the stalks to separate the grain from the straw. Once again people sang songs, like this one, to make the hard work more fun:

> *Strike [sort grain] for yourselves,*
> *Strike for yourselves, oxen!*
> *Straw to eat for yourselves*
> *and barley for your masters.*
> *Don't let your hearts grow weary!*

Once the grain was separated, girls tossed it into the air using wooden

96

CURRICULUM CONNECTION

LINKS TO MUSIC Refer students to the work song quoted in the text and point out that such songs were useful in keeping a rhythm, to help people when they worked a job that required cooperative effort. Play a work song, for example, "Erie Canal," which sets up a cadence for pulling ropes. Point out that the cadences that marching soldiers shout out are also a form of a work song. Break students into groups and have each produce a short work song to present to the class.

SECOND-LANGUAGE SUPPORT

TAKING NOTES Second-language students may better understand life in ancient Egypt if they write information in a familiar format. Have students jot down notes about the jobs and roles described in the lesson. Then encourage them to use their notes to create a job chart or possibly a "want ad" to keep on file for reference.

shovels so the wind would blow the remaining straw away. Scribes measured and took away the shares claimed by the pharaoh and the farm owner. Despite the hard work harvest was a time for celebration. During this time special offerings were made to Ra and Rennunet, the gods of the harvest.

Cities in Egypt

In Egypt's cities craftworkers and artists worked under similar conditions. Most lived in small, mud-brick homes crowded along narrow, winding streets. Archaeologists have uncovered the home of one family that lived in Memphis during Tutankhamun's rule. This house tells us much about life in Egypt's cities during the New Kingdom.

A Busy Neighborhood

The house in which this family lived opened onto a busy, noisy alley. The entrance room served as a workshop where the parents made baskets or leather products. Behind the workshop were a small living room with a fireplace and two tiny rooms that may have been bedrooms. A stairway led up to the flat roof—a cool place to sleep on hot summer nights.

The family also had "everyday" chores to do. Every morning the women of the house went down to the local canal to get water. As the sun rose they chatted with friends who also were getting water. They returned home with clay water pots balanced on their heads. Women also had to bake bread. Bread was an important part of the ancient Egyptians' diet.

Each day the family probably went to market to sell their wares. At local markets the family could buy wheat, grapes, olives, fresh fish, beef, pork, and chicken. They may have bought linen cloth from the woman next door. Archaeologists think she made her living as a weaver. A toolmaker also lived nearby. Imagine the clang of his hammer above the sounds of the city.

Townspeople worked hard at their jobs, but they liked to have fun too. Among the artifacts found in the house in Memphis were board games, for moments of free time.

These statues and walls are the remains of a temple in Luxor, Egypt. Note the size of the statues compared to the people standing nearby.

● **How was harvesting truly a community activity in ancient Egypt?** *(Everyone helped—men, women, and children.)*

● **What evidence can you find that the farmers of Egypt held deep religious beliefs?** *(They made offerings to Ra and Rennunet, gods of the harvest, indicating that the farmers believed these gods were responsible for the harvest and should be thanked.)*

★**THINKING FURTHER:** *Sequencing*
How would you design a flow chart that showed the steps in the planting and harvesting process? *(Have students come to the board to show the steps in order, as described in the text.)*

Learning About Cities in Egypt
Help students to see that ordinary life in ancient Egypt meant hard work.

● **How do we know about city life in ancient Egypt?** *(Archaeologists have uncovered a home in Memphis)*

Discussing A Busy Neighborhood
Encourage students to picture themselves in scenes the text describes.

● **How would you describe housing for ordinary people in the city?** *(It was located along narrow, winding streets, was probably small and made of mud brick, had three tiny rooms and a sleeping roof, and a workshop.)*

● **What kinds of work did people do?** *(made and sold crafts to earn a living; household work like fetching water, shopping, cooking, cleaning)*

● **What opportunities for socializing did cities offer ordinary people?** *(getting water from the local canal and buying and selling at local markets)*

★**THINKING FURTHER:** *Making Generalizations* **Based on what you have read, what generalizations can you make about what it was like to live as an ordinary person in an ancient Egyptian city?** *(Encourage students to see both the harsh and the pleasant—crowded living, long and hard hours of work as well as variety of jobs and opportunity to socialize.)*

CHILDREN IN EGYPT

As students read about childrens' lives in ancient Egypt, tell them to think about how it compares with their own lives.

- **How was Egyptian children's play similar to and different from your play?** *(With the exception of monkeys for pets, Egyptian play was similar, but today we have greater variety of toys.)*

- **How does the time Egyptian children had for play differ from yours?** *(Egyptian children had to stop play and start work much earlier in life. Country children had to help on the farm. City children had to learn their parents' occupations.)*

- **What do you think were disadvantages and advantages of being a child in ancient Egypt?** *(Students may see work at an early age and having to follow in a parent's occupation as disadvantages, but learning skills early as an advantage.)*

★**THINKING FURTHER:** *Making Conclusions* **Why do you suppose that hereditary occupations made ancient Egyptian society very stable?** *(They would have slowed the speed of change, and the people would have known what to expect and what was expected of them throughout life.)*

Technology CONNECTION

ADVENTURE TIME! CD-ROM
Enrich Lesson 4 with the *Ancient Egypt Time Line* on the *Adventure Time!* CD-ROM.

Tomb paintings show many animals living along the Nile River. Tombs also contained mummies of pets, such as dogs and cats.

CHILDREN IN EGYPT

Adults were not the only Egyptians who played games. Children rich and poor loved to spin tops, make cloth dolls, wrestle, run, and play games. Favorite pets included dogs, cats, and monkeys. Young boys and girls often played in the canals that flowed through the farms and villages. The children of pharaohs swam in their own swimming pools!

The amount of time children had to play depended on what their family did for work. Farmers' children had little time to play since they were often needed to help in the fields. Besides working at harvest time, farm children helped

scatter seeds during planting time. Farm children also did daily chores, such as carrying water or feeding the family's many farm animals.

From about age five the children of craftworkers began working alongside their parents. In this way children learned the trade they would work at as adults. At an early age potters' children helped their parents put a smooth finish on their pots. At about age 12 girls studying to become weavers started training. This training could sometimes last up to five years.

98

BACKGROUND INFORMATION

ABOUT CHILDREN IN EGYPT
- Infants were carried in pouches hanging from their mothers' necks.
- Baby food was made of papyrus shoots and boiled roots.
- The young sons of noble families went on hunting trips to the desert with their fathers. There they pursued gazelles and antelopes with bow and arrow.
- Ordinary village boys hunted too, but they used throwing sticks to try to strike their prey.
- Children hunted birds by spreading nets near trees, securing the corners with stakes. When birds landed, children released the corners to catch the birds.

CITIZENSHIP★

LINKING PAST AND PRESENT Tell students that young children used to work in the United States. Beginning at age six or seven, many children worked more than 12-hour days in mills, factories, and mines. In 1938, the U.S. Fair Labor Standards Act banned labor by children under 14 or 15 years of age during school hours. The law also required employers to pay children at least the minimum wage. This law only covered children who worked in industries involved in interstate commerce, but some states passed similar laws. Now, all U.S. states and many other countries regulate child labor, but in some countries, children still work long, hard hours.

Sons of government leaders became assistants to their fathers. They, too, would become leaders one day. Sons of scribes knew that from age ten they would be going to scribe school. That was a skill usually passed down from father to son as well.

WHY IT MATTERS

The Egyptian empire went through great changes around the end of the New Kingdom. New armies from the west and northeast challenged the pharaoh's hold on the empire. The Egyptian army began to lose its firm control over the region. Finally, around 1100 B.C., united Egypt collapsed. The fall of the New Kingdom ended one of the richest civilizations in history.

Still, the "Gift of the Nile" would live on and affect people everywhere for centuries to come. Ancient Egypt's legacy extends even to our own time. Think about this legacy the next time you see a sailor harnessing the wind. You may think of another Egyptian legacy as you answer the Think About It questions on a sheet of *paper!*

The game of "snake" was an early board game. The board looked like a coiled snake with its head in the center. Players moved stones from the tail to the head.

✓/ Reviewing Facts and Ideas

MAIN IDEAS

- While Egypt became a mighty empire, ordinary people continued to work in much the same ways as they had for thousands of years.
- Enslaved Syrians and Nubians became key workers in Egypt's empire. They worked alongside farmers and craftworkers to produce needed crops and goods.
- Most farmers worked on large farms owned by powerful families.
- Most people in Egypt's towns and cities lived in crowded neighborhoods and crafted goods for a living.

THINK ABOUT IT

1. How did Egypt's social pyramid shape life in the New Kingdom?

2. How did the growth of Egypt's empire play a role in the growth of slavery along the Nile? How did enslaved people add to the empire's economy?

3. **FOCUS** What was everyday life like for ancient Egyptians of the New Kingdom?

4. **THINKING SKILL** Make a *conclusion* about the variety of goods available in ancient Egyptian cities. What evidence can you find in the lesson to support your conclusion?

5. **WRITE** Suppose you are a scribe in ancient Thebes. Write a letter to the owner of a large farm. Tell him or her what goods to send to your city.

99

Discussing WHY IT MATTERS Encourage students to offer conclusions about the importance of ordinary people to Egyptian civilization. Then go on to find out why that civilization crumbled.

- *How was Egyptian civilization brought down?* (by attack from outside)

★**THINKING FURTHER: *Making Conclusions* How might learning from the Egyptians have helped others to defeat it?** (*Just as Egyptians learned from the Hyksos, so others learned from them.*)

⭐ 3 CLOSE

MAIN IDEAS
Have students answer on paper.

- *On what steady, dependable action did the Egyptian empire depend?* (on the continuing, productive work of its ordinary people)
- *How were captured Syrians and Nubians key to the Egyptian empire?* (They added to the needed labor pool.)
- *How were Egyptian farms like plantations of the old U.S. South?* (They were owned by powerful families.)
- *How would you describe life and work in Egypt's towns and cities?* (Living was crowded and most people worked at crafts.)

EVALUATE
✓ **Answers to Think About It**

1. pharaoh, government officials, and soldiers were at the top; scribes, merchants, and artisans at center; farmers and slaves at the bottom. *Recall Details*

2. Empire building meant war; war meant capture and enslavement of peoples, whose labor was demanded. *Steps in a Process*

3. busy, work-filled, modestly housed *Summarize*

4. The variety of goods was rich, useful, and luxurious, as shown by the text illustrations. *Make Conclusions*

5. Students letters will perhaps request grain, fish, meat, beer, and linen. *Make Inferences*

Write About It Tell students to write a timetable of the ways an ordinary Egyptian spent a typical day.

MEETING INDIVIDUAL NEEDS

RETEACHING (Easy) Have students choose an ordinary citizen of ancient Egypt by occupation. Tell them to draw a cartoon strip entitled "A Day in the Life of ..." with four scenes from that person's daily life.

EXTENSION (Average) Numerous picture books that treat life in ancient Egypt are available for young people. Divide the class into groups and give each an area of Egyptian life to research—food, fishing and hunting, makeup and dress, religious worship, feasts and merrymaking. Have the groups research their area in books and present their findings, with illustrations, to the class.

ENRICHMENT (Challenging) Explain to students that the chief religious guide to life for Egyptians was called *maat*. Tell students to research *maat* to find out what it was and how it affected the Egyptians' lives. Have them write booklets entitled "Maat and Its Role in Egyptian Life."

DISCUSSING MAJOR EVENTS Help students to use the time line to sense the sweep of ancient Egypt's history and to sequence the major events in that sweep.

- *How does the history of Egypt begin on this time line?* (with the unification of two Egypts in 3100 B.C.)

- *How many different kingdoms succeeded Egypt's unification and what were they?* (three—Old Kingdom, Middle Kingdom, New Kingdom)

- *Which of the three lasted the longest?* (Old Kingdom—505 years)

Answers to
THINKING ABOUT VOCABULARY

1.	I, Unification	**6.**	C
2.	C	**7.**	I, Hieroglyphics
3.	C	**8.**	I, empire
4.	I, delta	**9.**	I, Scale
5.	I, irrigation	**10.**	I, expedition

Answers to
THINKING ABOUT FACTS

1. It provided soil and water for agriculture and served as a water highway through the length of Egypt.

2. He united the two kingdoms of Upper Egypt and Lower Egypt into one kingdom.

3. It made it possible to read hieroglyphics, unlocking Egypt's written records to historians.

4. mainly from Syria in western Asia and from Nubia; everybody was above, but farmers were next above

5. 1,000 years (3100 – 2100 = 1000)

Resource REMINDER

Practice and Project Book: *p. 23*

Assessment Book: *Chapter 4 Test*

Technology: *Videodisc/Video Tape 1*

Transparency: *Graphic Organizer, Main Idea Pyramid*

CHAPTER 4 REVIEW

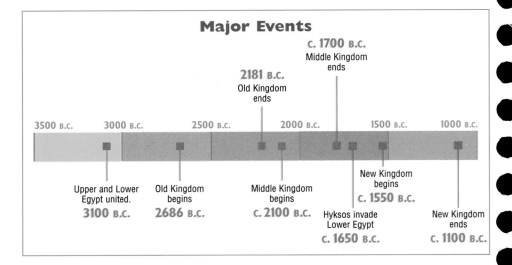

Major Events

c. 1700 B.C.
Middle Kingdom ends

2181 B.C.
Old Kingdom ends

3500 B.C.   3000 B.C.   2500 B.C.   2000 B.C.   1500 B.C.   1000 B.C.

Upper and Lower Egypt united.
3100 B.C.

Old Kingdom begins
2686 B.C.

Middle Kingdom begins
c. 2100 B.C.

New Kingdom begins
c. 1550 B.C.

Hyksos invade Lower Egypt
c. 1650 B.C.

New Kingdom ends
c. 1100 B.C.

THINKING ABOUT VOCABULARY

Number a sheet of paper from 1 to 10. Decide whether the underlined word in each of the following statements correctly completes the sentence. If the word is correct, write **C** beside the number. If the word is incorrect, write **I** and then write the word that completes the sentence.

delta	hieroglyphics	slavery
economy	irrigation	unification
empire	scale	
expedition	scribe	

1. <u>Irrigation</u> is the joining of parts into one.
2. <u>Slavery</u> is the owning of one person by another.
3. A <u>scribe</u> is a writer of records, letters, and contracts.
4. An <u>empire</u> is the flat, fertile land made of silt left behind as a river drains into a larger body of water.
5. The watering of land by means of canals or pipes is called <u>scale</u>.

6. An <u>economy</u> is the way people manage money and resources.
7. <u>Delta</u> is the ancient Egyptian system of writing.
8. A group of lands or peoples ruled by one government is called an <u>expedition</u>.
9. <u>Hieroglyphics</u> is a unit of measure used on a map to represent a distance.
10. A group of people who go on a trip for a set reason is called a <u>unification</u>.

THINKING ABOUT FACTS

1. What was the role of the Nile River in the development of Egyptian civilization?
2. How did its first pharaoh unify Egypt?
3. How has the Rosetta Stone helped historians to understand Egypt's past?
4. Where did Egypt get its slaves? Who were above slaves on the Egyptian social pyramid?
5. Look at the time line above. How many years after Egypt was united did the Middle Kingdom begin?

100

SECOND-LANGUAGE SUPPORT

SUMMARIZING THROUGH ILLUSTRATIONS As a way of summarizing the chapter, have students create a mural of life in ancient Egypt. Second-language learners can work alone or with English-proficient students to make the mural. Interaction between the two groups will provide needed oral practice. The mural can be drawn on butcher paper and be part of a movable display that can be installed in a public space in the school or be part of a traveling exhibit to younger grades. Second-language students will benefit from the oral practice of explaining aspects of Egyptian life to younger students.

THINK AND WRITE

WRITING A LIST
Make a list of three things about ancient Egypt that you think mark it as an important civilization.

WRITING AN EXPLANATION
Explain how the shape of Egyptian society was similar to that of a pyramid. Then describe the groups that made up the Egyptian social pyramid.

WRITING A PARAGRAPH OF ANALYSIS
Write a paragraph about the effect of the Nile River on ancient Egyptian civilization. Tell about the problems the Nile caused and what people did to solve them.

APPLYING GEOGRAPHY SKILLS

USING MAPS AT DIFFERENT SCALES
1. What is meant by the term *scale*?
2. What does a small-scale map show?
3. What does a large-scale map show?
4. Which kind of map can show the most information? How is that possible? Explain.
5. What are the advantages of knowing how to use maps at different scales?

Answers to APPLYING GEOGRAPHY SKILLS
1. the unit of measurement used to represent distance on a map
2. a broad area, the big picture
3. a smaller area, in greater detail
4. A large-scale map can show many more details than a small-scale map because it shows a smaller area. The larger the scale, the more detail can be shown.
5. Knowing how to use maps of different scales makes it possible to gather different kinds of information from maps—from measurement of broad distances to the location of details in a small area.

Technology CONNECTION

VIDEODISC/VIDEO TAPE 1
Enrich Chapter 4 with the *Ancient Egypt* segment on the videodisc.

Search Frame 04892 Side A

Summing Up the Chapter

Copy the main-idea pyramid below on a separate piece of paper. Then review the chapter to find at least two pieces of information that support each part of the main idea. Add these to the bottom of the pyramid. When you have filled in the pyramid, use it to write a paragraph titled "How did the ancient Egyptians create their complex civilization?"

Ancient Egypt

Ancient Egyptians used their environment.

Organization helped the Egyptians to unite.

Overflow of the Nile
Irrigation
Productive farming

Organized government
Hieroglyphics
Social pyramid

101

SUGGESTIONS FOR SUMMING UP THE CHAPTER

After students have copied the main-idea pyramid, have them read its two main ideas aloud and discuss each. For each one, help them to arrive at a question they should keep in mind as they seek answers to it in the chapter, for example, "How did the ancient Egyptians use their environment to serve their needs?" and "What organization systems kept them unified?" Possible answers appear on the reproduced text page above. As they begin writing their paragraphs to answer the question posed, suggest that an organizing main-idea sentence might be: "They used their environment well and were well organized." They can then support this main idea with the details they have identified in their pyramids.

ASSESSING THINK AND WRITE: *For performance assessment, see Assessment Book, Chapter 4, pp. T55-T57.*

CHAPTER 5 Ancient Mesopotamia

Pages 102–127

CHAPTER OVERVIEW

Farmers lived between the Tigris and Euphrates rivers in an area known as ancient Mesopotamia. This area was first called Sumer and then later Babylon under Hammurabi. They built cities and developed cuneiform writing. The Hebrews founded a monotheistic religion and the Kingdom of Israel.

GEO ADVENTURES DAILY GEOGRAPHY ACTIVITIES

Use **Geo Adventures** Daily Geography activities to assess students' understanding of geography skills.

CHAPTER PLANNING GUIDE

LESSON 1	LESSON 2	Legacy
SUGGESTED PACING: 2 DAYS	**SUGGESTED PACING: 2 DAYS**	**SUGGESTED PACING: 1 DAY**
Geography Of The Fertile Crescent pp. 104–107	**Sumer And Babylon pp. 108–115**	**The Wheel pp. 116–117**
CURRICULUM CONNECTIONS Links to Current Events: High Water! p. 106	**CURRICULUM CONNECTIONS** Links to Language Arts: What Did You Call Me? p. 114	
CITIZENSHIP Recognizing Perspectives, p. 105	**CITIZENSHIP** Understanding Government, p. 113 Using Current Events, p. 113	
RESOURCES Practice and Project Book, p. 24 Desk Map	**RESOURCES** Practice and Project Book, p. 25 Anthology, pp. 22, 23	

LESSON 3	CHAPTER REVIEW
SUGGESTED PACING: 2 DAYS	**SUGGESTED PACING: 1 DAY**
The Beginnings Of Judaism pp. 120–125	**pp. 126–127**
CURRICULUM CONNECTIONS Links to Language Arts, p. 124	**RESOURCES** Practice and Project Book, p. 28
CITIZENSHIP Understanding Government, p. 123	●TECHNOLOGY Videodisc/Video Tape 1
RESOURCES Practice and Project Book, p. 27 Anthology, pp. 24–25	Assessment Book: Chapter 5 Test Transparency: Graphic Organizer, Main Idea Chart

LEARNING STYLE: Visual

ON YOUR OWN

30 MINUTES OR LONGER

Make a Word Boat

Objective: To introduce students to the river valley civilization of ancient Mesopotamia.

Materials: drawing paper, scissors, glue

1. Recall how the Nile River affected Egyptian civilization.
2. Ask students to draw six boats on a river, then make and glue on a label for each describing a feature of Egyptian civilization.
3. Have students choose one word-boat idea and write a paragraph on how it depended on the Nile.
4. Briefly discuss how life might be similar along another river in the ancient world.

THINKINGSKILLS

SUGGESTED PACING: 1 DAY

Identifying Cause And Effect p. 118

RESOURCES

Practice and Project Book, p. 26
Transparency: Graphic Organizer

SDAIE SUPPORT SHELTERED INSTRUCTION

READING STRATEGIES & LANGUAGE DEVELOPMENT

Use Visuals/Word Origins, p. 104, Lesson 1
Rereading/Words with Multiple Meanings, p. 108, Lesson 2
Cause and Effect/Words Often Confused, p. 118, Skills Lesson
Sequencing/Synonyms and Antonyms, p. 120, Lesson 3

SECOND-LANGUAGE SUPPORT

Working with a Peer, p. 106
Dialogs, p. 111
Working with Peers, p. 123
Game/Dramatization, p. 126

MEETING INDIVIDUAL NEEDS

Reteaching, Extension, Enrichment, pp. 107, 115, 117, 125

ASSESSMENT OPPORTUNITIES

Practice and Project Book, pp. 24–28
Write About It, pp. 107, 115, 117, 125
Assessment Book: Assessing Think and Write, pp. T58–T60; Chapter 5 Tests: Content, Skills, Writing

Introducing the Chapter

Have students find Mesopotamia on the global map and explain that they will read about many different groups of people, with many different cultures.

THINKING ABOUT HISTORY AND GEOGRAPHY

Have students read the text on this page to get some indications of the variety of cultures in Mesopotamia.

4000 B.C. MESOPOTAMIA

Help students recognize the important aspects of geographic location for Mesopotamia.

- **On what continent is Mesopotamia located?** *(Asia)*

- **What are the people in this panel doing?** *(farming irrigated fields)*

3000 B.C. UR, SUMER

Refer students to the picture of the cuneiform tablet on p. 65.

- **What is shown in this panel?** *(writing on clay tablets)*

★THINKING FURTHER: *Compare and Contrast* **Make a comparison between Mesopotamia and Egypt at the same point in time. How do they compare in the use of written language?** *(Both have developed it, but each uses a different method as well as different writing materials.)*

Resource REMINDER

Technology: *Videodisc/Video Tape 1*

CHAPTER 5

Ancient Mesopotamia

THINKING ABOUT HISTORY AND GEOGRAPHY

Around 4000 B.C. farmers living between the Tigris and Euphrates rivers built canals to try to control flooding. They also built cities and developed a system of writing. Eventually, a strong ruler, Sargon, united the region into a kingdom called Sumer. Much later Hammurabi conquered Sumer and wrote a code of laws. The movement of the Hebrews into Canaan led to the development of Judaism.

AFRICA

4000 B.C.	3000 B.C.	2300 B.C.
MESOPOTAMIA	**UR**	**KISH**
Farmers build irrigation ditches to control river floods	Schools are built in Sumer to teach writing	Sargon unites Sumer

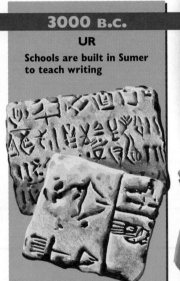 

102

BACKGROUND INFORMATION

LINKING THE MAP AND THE TIME LINE

- Mesopotamia is often referred to as the "Cradle of Civilization." As one writer has put it, "Mesopotamia was the birthplace of civilization, for it was the first place in which man created and sustained, for more than 3,000 years—an urban, literate, technologicially sophisticated society, one whose people shared common values and a common view of the origins and order of the world."

- Ur in Sumer goes back as far as the 5th millenium B.C. Modern studies have produced evidence that settlement there was interrupted by a flood once believed to be what in the Bible is described as the flood that Noah survived.

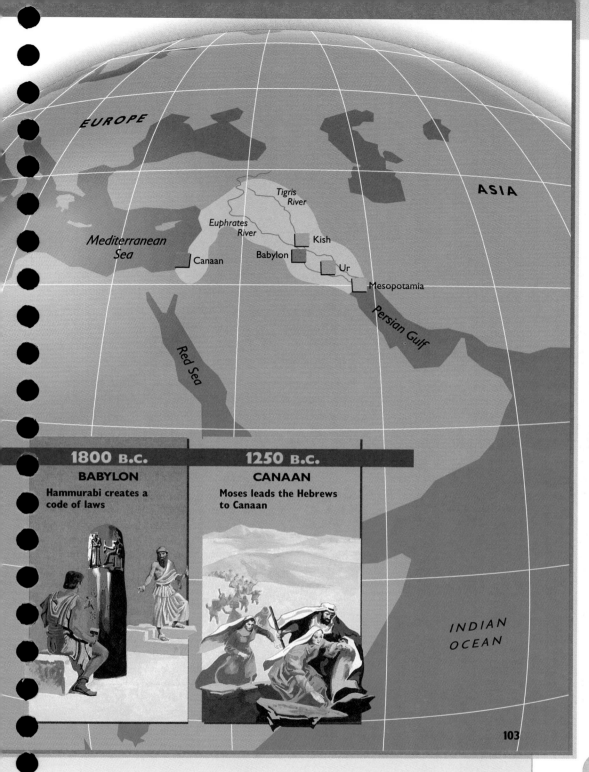

2300 B.C. KISH, SUMER

Discuss with students Sargon's role in uniting Sumerian cities.

- **Who is pictured here?** *(Sargon)*

- **What was he known for, according to what you have just read?** *(for being the strong ruler who united Mesopotamian cities into a kingdom called Sumer)*

1800 B.C. BABYLON

Point out that Hummurabi is considered the author of the world's first code of law.

- **Who is pictured in this panel and what is he doing?** *(Hammurabi, the law giver; directing a scribe in writing out his laws)*

★**THINKING FURTHER:** *Making Conclusions* **Why are laws necessary in the development of a civilization?** *(so people know their rights and duties)*

1250 B.C. CANAAN

The story of Moses leading the Israelites out of Egypt is well known.

- **What is happening in this panel?** *(Moses is leading the Hebrews into Canaan.)*

- **Where is Canaan located?** *(along the southeastern coast of the Mediterranean)*

★**THINKING FURTHER:** *Predicting* **What do you predict this action is going to lead to?** *(the founding of the religion called Judaism)*

Technology CONNECTION

VIDEODISC/VIDEO TAPE 1
Enrich Chapter 5 with the *Ancient Mesopotamia* segment on the videodisc.

Search Frame 16202 Side A

BACKGROUND INFORMATION

LINKING THE MAP AND THE TIME LINE
- Kish, Sumer, was Mesopotamia's most important city-state prior to the time Sargon came to power there. It was continuously occupied from about 3500 B.C. until about A.D. 600.

- Babylon, located at the heart of what would become the Babylonian empire, became important when Hammurabi gained control of Sumer. Invaders sacked it in the 1100s B.C. and stole away the stela on which Hammurabi's Law Code was carved. (Today, it can be found in the Louvre Museum in Paris.)

- Canaan was looked on as the Promised Land by the followers of the Hebrew patriarch Abraham, who set out for Canaan from the city of Ur. Later, Moses and his followers set out across the desert from Egypt, holding the same belief in the Promised Land.

LESSON 1

Lesson Overview

Like Egypt, Mesopotamia was a harsh land that developed into a great civilization because of floods, which could also be destructive.

Lesson Objectives

★ Locate and describe Mesopotamia.

★ Evaluate the effects of the floods of the Tigris and Euphrates rivers.

★ Explain how Mesopotamian farmers controlled these floods.

1 PREPARE

MOTIVATE Have a student do a rehearsed dramatic reading of the *Read Aloud.* Point out the photo showing the continuing use of the Euphrates. Ask volunteers to retell any folktales, stories, or legends they know about floods.

SET PURPOSE Use the *Read to Learn* question to review what students know about the Nile's role in Egypt; encourage them to use this lesson to investigate rivers in another civilization. Alert students to look for *Vocabulary* terms.

2 TEACH

Understanding THE BIG PICTURE
On a map of the world, locate Mesopotamia in relation to Egypt. Reinforce the term *Fertile Crescent.*

● **What helped make the Fertile Crescent fertile?** *(the Tigris and Euphrates rivers)*

● **Was all of the area fertile?** *(No. Much was rocky mountains or desert.)*

★**THINKING FURTHER:** *Predicting*
How do you predict that the Tigris and Euphrates will affect life? *(Using what they have learned about the Nile, students will probably predict that the rivers will be useful for agriculture.)*

Resource REMINDER

Practice and Project Book: *p. 24*
Desk Map
Outline Map

GEOGRAPHY OF THE FERTILE CRESCENT

Focus Activity

READ TO LEARN
In what ways did two great rivers affect life in this region?

VOCABULARY
plateau
drought

PLACES
Fertile Crescent
Tigris River
Euphrates River
Mesopotamia

READ ALOUD

"For six days and seven nights the wind blew, flood and tempest [storm] overwhelmed the land; when the seventh day arrived, the tempest [and] flood . . . blew themselves out. The sea became calm, the . . . wind grew quiet, the flood held back. . . . Silence reigned, for all mankind had returned to clay."

These words come from an ancient western Asian story about a flood that destroyed most of humanity. Ancient stories like this one later influenced people all around the world.

THE BIG PICTURE

Around 4000 B.C. Egyptian farm communities were growing along the Nile River in Africa. Another civilization was also developing in a vast region to the northeast. This region, in western Asia, was later called the Fertile Crescent. A crescent shape looks like a quarter moon. Find the Fertile Crescent on the map on the next page. It covers the present-day countries of Iraq, Syria, Lebanon, and Israel.

Much of this land was either rocky mountains or desert. Parts of the Fertile Crescent, however, were lush and green. Two rivers, the Tigris (TĪ grihs) and the Euphrates (yoo FRAY teez), made life in these areas possible. Like the Nile in Egypt, these rivers affected the people living along the banks. As you can see from the story above, the rivers' effects were not always positive.

104

SHELTERED INSTRUCTION

READING STRATEGIES & LANGUAGE DEVELOPMENT

USE VISUALS To help the class get meaning from visuals as well as text, explain that when we study geography, we can learn from pictures as well as words. Point out the different types of visuals in this lesson [photograph, map, diagram, artwork]. Ask volunteers when they used these visuals to gain information. What did they learn? How was it useful? Ask students what they think they might learn from the visuals here. **[SDAIE STRATEGY: BRIDGING]**

WORD ORIGINS Point out two interesting word origins in this lesson. First, help the class relate *-potamia* (meaning "river") to *hippopotamus* (*hippo-* = "horse" and *-potomus* = "river"), or "river horse." Next, refer the class to the vocabulary term *plateau.* Explain that it too has a Greek origin—*platys* is Greek for "broad, flat." Help them to relate this meaning to *plateau, platter,* and *platypus,* a flat-footed animal.

BETWEEN TWO RIVERS

The region between the Tigris and the Euphrates is known as Mesopotamia (mes uh puh TAY mee uh). In Greek, *Mesopotamia* means "Land Between Two Rivers." This area is now known as Iraq. Mesopotamia included several types of physical regions. Follow the course of the two rivers on the map. Let's see how Mesopotamia's northern and southern regions differ.

From Mountains to the Sea

Both the Tigris and Euphrates rivers begin in the snow-capped Taurus Mountains of what is today Turkey. The rivers rush down narrow canyons to the valleys below. Then the Tigris and Euphrates reach the plateau (pla TOH) of present-day northern Iraq. A plateau is an area of elevated flatland. In southern Iraq the rivers continue to flow to lower land. Here they make their way to the Persian Gulf.

Flood!

As in Egypt, early communities in Mesopotamia depended on river deposits of silt. Silt made the region a good place for farming. Early farmers had to meet several challenges, though.

Mesopotamia's yearly floods did not come as regularly as those in Egypt. In fact, they often came at just the wrong time for farmers. The Tigris and the Euphrates did not flood during planting season, when dry fields needed to be softened and prepared for new growth. Instead, the floods often burst through fields just as crops were about to be harvested. Such deadly floods cost not only crops, but lives and homes as well.

Farmers had to protect their fields from flood damage. They also had to keep their crops watered in the hot, dry climate. Southern Mesopotamia rarely received more than a few sprinkles of rain each year. Droughts, or long periods of dry weather, were a constant threat to farmers and their crops in southern Mesopotamia.

Northern Mesopotamia, in contrast, usually had enough rain to make some farming possible. Yet the rocky earth of the northern plateau had only pockets of fertile soil. The flooding rivers did not leave behind as much silt here in the north as to the south. For this reason southern Mesopotamia became better known for its fertile fields than northern Mesopotamia.

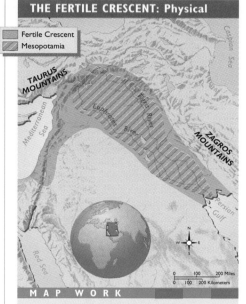

THE FERTILE CRESCENT: Physical

Fertile Crescent
Mesopotamia

TAURUS MOUNTAINS
Caspian Sea
Mediterranean Sea
Euphrates River
Tigris River
ZAGROS MOUNTAINS
Persian Gulf
Red Sea

0   100   200 Miles
0   100   200 Kilometers

MAP WORK

The Fertile Crescent extends from the Persian Gulf to the Mediterranean Sea.

1. Is Mesopotamia larger or smaller than the Fertile Crescent?
2. What mountain range lies east of the Fertile Crescent?

MAP WORK: 1. smaller 2. Zagros Mountains

105

Refer students to the map on this page and develop the reasons for the name.

More

MAP WORK

- **In which part of the Fertile Crescent is Mesopotamia, east or west?** (Students should locate the "Land Between Two Rivers" in the east. Help them note that the Fertile Crescent includes a larger area than just Mesopotamia.)

- **In what direction do the Tigris and Euphrates rivers flow? into what body of water?** (southeast; the Persian Gulf)

- ★**THINKING FURTHER:** *Making Conclusions* **Where along these rivers do you think flooding might be heaviest?** (Possible answer: where the rivers are closest)

Tracing From Mountains to the Sea Reinforce the understanding that water flows from high ground to low.

- **Where do these rivers begin?** (Turkey's snow-capped mountains)

- **Where is the plateau they flow through?** (in northern Iraq)

★**THINKING FURTHER:** *Sequencing* **How would you describe the series of levels that these rivers flow through?** (mountains to plateau to lowland to sea level)

Discussing Flood! Help students apply to Mesopotamia some concepts they developed about Egypt.

- **How did Mesopotamia's floods benefit farmers there?** (The floods brought silt and water for crops.)

- **How did floods bring misfortune too?** (They could come at the wrong time, destroying already planted crops, or they could come on too powerfully, costing lives and homes.)

★**THINKING FURTHER:** *Compare and Contrast* **How would you compare the advantages and disadvantages of farming in northern and southern Mesopotamia?** (Southern: frequent droughts but more and better soil. Northern: enough rain but little soil.)

GLOBAL CONNECTION

FLOODING IN BANGLADESH Some of the most destructive flooding of recent times has occurred in Bangladesh, on the Indian subcontinent. Locate Bangladesh on desk maps; point out the geographic features that resemble Mesopotamia's. Have students trace the course of the Ganges and the Brahmaputra rivers that flow into the Bay of Bengal; compare their flow with the Tigris and Euphrates into the Persian Gulf.

CITIZENSHIP★

RECOGNIZING PERSPECTIVES
- The body of water that English-speaking people call the "Persian Gulf" is the "Arabian Gulf" to Arabic-speaking people. They point out that Arab nations, not Persia, now dominate the region.
- The Arab world also prefers to call Mesopotamia "ancient Iraq."

FROM RIVER TO FIELD

Review with the class the seasons for planting and harvest along the Nile in Egypt (October and March, respectively). Have them compare these with the seasons in Mesopotamia (the same—fall for planting, spring for harvest).

More DIAGRAM WORK

Remind students that "Necessity is the mother of invention" and discuss the role a harsh environment played in forcing Mesopotamian farmers to be innovative in meeting its challenges (finding ways to control floods). Then refer them to the diagram on this page.

- **What technology did Mesopotamians develop to save water for use as needed?** *(They dammed it up in an artificial lake, then let it out through irrigation canals to get it to the crops.)*

- **How did they regulate the amount of water flowing into the canals?** *(through the use of gates)*

- ★**THINKING FURTHER:** *Making Conclusions* **What did the farming technologies the Mesopotamians developed enable them to do?** *(to grow many different crops and to raise a variety of animals)*

Studying Farming in Ancient Mesopotamia Help students appreciate the variety of Mesopotamian crops. If students are unfamiliar with date palms or pomegranates, show them pictures.

- **How was the Mesopotamian diet enriched by what they grew?** *(with many grains, vegetables, and fruits)*

- **How did the animals they raised enrich their diet and their clothing?** *(Animals supplied milk and meat for food, and leather for clothing.)*

★**THINKING FURTHER:** *Making Decisions* **If you had to plan a dinner for a Mesopotamian family, using their farm's products, what dishes might you serve?** *(Encourage students to plan a well-balanced meal using the crops and livestock named in the text.)*

WATER CONTROL IN MESOPOTAMIA
Like the ancient Egyptians, Mesopotamians also adapted rivers for farming.

Tigris River

Artificial Lake

Gate

Irrigation Canal

Gate

FROM RIVER TO FIELD

In the fall farmers in southern Mesopotamia needed water to plant and raise new crops. Unfortunately, fall was the time when the Tigris and the Euphrates were at their lowest. Spring was harvest time in ancient Mesopotamia. However, it was also the time when the rivers flooded their banks. Then farmers often got more water than they wanted.

To solve these difficulties, ancient farmers learned to build water-control and irrigation systems. Look at the diagram shown above to see how these systems worked.

Farming in Ancient Mesopotamia

Early Mesopotamian farmers grew many different crops. If you were able to go back there in time, you would see fields of wheat and barley. These were the region's most important crops. You would also see gardens of beans, onions, lettuce, cucumbers, and spice plants. Ancient farmers also grew date palm, apple, and pomegranate trees. Because crops and trees need plenty of water, Mesopotamian farmers often planted them along canal banks.

In the distance, on the edges of village farmland, you might see shepherds caring for sheep and goats. Shepherds also had to ward off attacks from wild animals such as lions and jackals. Sheep were especially prized in Mesopotamia for their milk and wool. Ancient Mesopotamians also valued cattle. Cattle were good work-animals, besides being used for milk, leather, and meat.

106

CURRICULUM CONNECTION

LINKS TO CURRENT EVENTS: HIGH WATER! After students read *High Water!* on p. 107, have them clip articles about current floods from newspapers or have a resource person in the community describe the effects of a flood. Have students make a list of some of the problems that floods create for people.

SECOND-LANGUAGE SUPPORT

WORKING WITH A PEER To help second-language students learn and remember the place names in this lesson, have them pair with English-proficient students to create their own map like the one on p. 105. Have students share their maps in small groups and compare labels and other information.

WHY IT MATTERS

The region called Mesopotamia is not naturally an inviting place to live. Yet it was here that one of the world's earliest civilizations developed. Water and soil brought by the Tigris and the Euphrates helped to make this civilization possible. Even more important were the farmers of ancient Mesopotamia. These early farmers figured out how to use the two rivers to make the land more fertile.

As in some other early cultures, the farmers of Mesopotamia produced surplus crops. These surpluses allowed for specialization, which in turn led to the growth of towns and cities. The early cities formed a great civilization. As you will see, the legacy of early Mesopotamian civilization reaches even into our own times.

Links to CURRENT EVENTS
High Water!

Do floods still destroy people's homes and property today?

Unfortunately, despite the existence of modern dams, the answer is yes. In 1997, after an unusually harsh winter, melting snow caused severe spring flooding of the Red River in North Dakota. Volunteers worked together to build dikes, sometimes in the middle of town, to stop the river from overflowing further into there neighborhoods. The federal government committed over $150 million dollars to help North Dakotans rebuild their lives.

Find another example of a flood in modern times. When and where did this flood occur? Your teacher can show you how to research recent newspapers to learn more about current events.

✔ Reviewing Facts and Ideas

MAIN IDEAS
- Mesopotamia is the region between the Tigris and Euphrates rivers. It is divided into a rugged plateau to the north and fertile plains to the south.
- Like the Nile River, the Tigris and the Euphrates flooded each year. These floods brought water and silt to Mesopotamia.
- Unlike those in Egypt, floods in Mesopotamia were often destructive and badly timed for farmers.
- Mesopotamian farmers used canal systems to control dangerous flooding, making their land productive.

THINK ABOUT IT
1. What were the main crops grown in ancient Mesopotamia? What other foods were grown there?
2. Why was the timing of spring floods so important to farmers in ancient Mesopotamia? What could happen to crops if the floods came a little earlier than expected?
3. **FOCUS** In what ways did Mesopotamian farmers adapt to and change their environment?
4. **THINKING SKILL** Suppose you lived in ancient Mesopotamia. Write a poem about the Tigris and Euphrates rivers from a farmer's *point of view*.
5. **GEOGRAPHY** Where is the Fertile Crescent located?

107

Discussing WHY IT MATTERS
Have students review Chapter 4, Lesson 1 to recall the early period of ancient Egypt.

★**THINKING FURTHER:** *Compare and Contrast* **What parallels do you see between early Mesopotamia and early Egypt?** *(Both were harsh lands watered by rivers; both developed methods to water the land; both had surpluses and specialization and were based on agriculture; both were ready for civilization.)*

3 CLOSE

MAIN IDEAS
Call on individual students to answer these questions.

- **Why is Mesopotamia called by that name?** *(It is located between two rivers, the Tigris and Euphrates.)*
- **What did the Tigris and Euphrates provide for Mesopotamia?** *(water and silt)*
- **How were the Tigris and Euphrates like and unlike the Nile?** *(They flooded and brought silt to the region, but their floods were often badly timed and highly destructive.)*
- **How did Mesopotamian farmers control flood waters to make them useful for farming?** *(by channeling them into canals and regulating flow)*

EVALUATE
✓ **Answers to Think About It**
1. wheat and barley; a variety of vegetables and fruits *Recall Details*
2. They could provide water for crops or overrun unharvested crops and destroy them. *Summarize*
3. They learned about floods and developed technologies like dammed lakes and irrigation canals to control them and make the land fertile. *Make Conclusions*
4. Students' poems should reflect both gratitude and resentment on the part of farmers toward the rivers. *Point of View*
5. in western Asia, in the area that now includes Iraq, Syria, Lebanon, and Israel. *Five Themes of Geography: Location*

Write About It Have students write a TV news flash describing a Mesopotamian flood and its effects.

MEETING INDIVIDUAL NEEDS

RETEACHING (Easy) Have students make a list of reasons that Mesopotamia is now ready for civilization to develop.

EXTENSION (Average) Have students think of themselves as news reporters who had been sent to cover the annual flooding of the Tigris and Euphrates in both northern and southern Mesopotamia. Tell them to write news stories in which they describe the different effects in each region.

ENRICHMENT (Challenging) Perhaps the closest American counterpart to the Tigris and Euphrates is the Mississippi River. It too has a history of all too often overflowing its banks and causing widespread devastation. Tell students to do research on "Big Muddy" to learn about its flood history and about efforts to control its floods. Have them write up their findings in reports.

LESSON 2

PAGES 108–115

Lesson Overview
Mesopotamian civilization produced a written language and developed the world's first written *code of law*.

Lesson Objectives
★ Explain how *cuneiform* developed and how it affected Mesopotamia.

★ Analyze how Mesopotamian cultural values shaped local life.

★ Explain how Hammurabi's rise helped Babylon gain power.

⭐ 1 PREPARE

MOTIVATE Read the *Read Aloud* riddle to the class, but not the solution. Allow students time to solve it. Then read the final two sentences and ask them to predict how this lesson might "open their eyes" to Mesopotamian civilization.

SET PURPOSE Refer students to the *Read to Learn* question, the lesson title, the illustration of cuneiform writing, and the *Vocabulary* terms on this page. Initiate a discussion of why writing is important to a society.

⭐ 2 TEACH

Understanding THE BIG PICTURE
Have students review the hieroglyph illustration on p. 78 and briefly compare it with the cuneiform here.

● *Where was cuneiform writing developed?* (in Sumer, in southern Mesopotamia)

● *How does it compare with hieroglyphics?* (It is less picture-like.)

● *When in Egypt's history did Sumer emerge as a region?* (in Menes' time)

★THINKING FURTHER: *Making Conclusions How do you know that Sumer has developed a civilization?* (cities, religion, technology, education, government, writing)

Resource REMINDER

Practice and Project Book: *p 25*

Anthology: *The Epic of Gilgamesh, p. 22; A Father's Complaint, p. 23*

The British Museum

| 4000 B.C. | 3500 B.C. | | 689 B.C. | A.D. 1 |

SUMER AND BABYLON

READ ALOUD

This is an ancient Mesopotamian riddle. See if you can solve it.

> "He whose eyes are not open enters it.
> He whose eyes are wide open comes out of it.
> What is it?
> The solution is: It's a school."

How might school "open your eyes"?

THE BIG PICTURE

You have read about southern Mesopotamia's large surpluses. These allowed an increasing number of people to live as skilled workers in cities. By 3000 B.C.—around the time that Menes unified Egypt—about a dozen small cities dotted southern Mesopotamia. This region was also known as Sumer (SOO mur).

The people of Sumer's cities valued their independence highly. They often fought against being ruled by other cities. However, all Sumerians shared a rich cultural heritage. They worked hard to control the Tigris and Euphrates rivers to produce food crops. They worshiped similar gods. The Sumerians made some of the world's first wheeled vehicles and sailboats. They also made simple machines, such as pottery wheels. In addition, early Sumerians explored new ideas in math and science.

The invention of writing helped to bring the ancient cities together. Laws, letters, records, stories, instructions, riddles, and proverbs could all be widely shared, thanks to cuneiform (kyoo NEE uh fawrm). Cuneiform was the system of writing invented in Sumer.

Focus Activity

READ TO LEARN
What changes did the development of writing bring to ancient Mesopotamia?

VOCABULARY
cuneiform
city-state
ziggurat
polytheism
code of law

PEOPLE
Sargon
Hammurabi

PLACES
Sumer
Babylonia

108

SHELTERED INSTRUCTION

READING STRATEGIES & LANGUAGE DEVELOPMENT

REREADING Explain to students that when they read new information, it is often useful to reread the text to be sure of understanding it. Use a Think-Aloud to model the process. Read aloud the first two paragraphs of *The Big Picture*, pausing at the end of each paragraph to ask what information was discovered. Model how to reread confusing passages. Then restate what you read in your own words. **[SDAIE STRATEGY: MODELING/TEXT RE-PRESENTATION]**

WORDS WITH MULTIPLE MEANINGS Write the word *tablet* on the board and ask students what it means. As they offer its different meanings—a pad of writing paper, a pill—refer them to *tablet* on p. 109 and have them define that meaning—a clay slab with writing. Point out that many words have multiple meanings and encourage students to locate and define others on that page (*record, page, school, pen*).

A SYSTEM OF WRITING

Some historians believe that cuneiform was first developed to record farm surpluses. Ancient Sumerians used sharp reeds to scratch the records into wet clay tablets. The dried tablets became permanent records.

In 3500 B.C.—the time of the oldest tablets that have been found—cuneiform symbols looked like the things they described. Over time, however, Sumerian scribes developed faster ways to write. They simplified their figures so they could be formed more quickly. Look at the chart on this page for examples.

About 500 signs were regularly used! These signs could also be combined to form more complex words. Like Egyptian hieroglyphs, cuneiform signs represented sounds and ideas as well as objects. The sign for "arrow," called *ti* (TEE), looked like this: ◄◄. Since *ti* also meant "life," the symbol could stand for this word too.

School in Sumer

As in ancient Egypt few people could write. Even kings usually could not. It was an honor to be able to go to school and learn to be a scribe. Boys and, very rarely, girls spent years studying in local schools. First they learned how to make clay tablets and reed "pens." Then students practiced over and over how to write the basic signs of cuneiform. Scribes in Sumer also had to study mathematics so they would be able to keep accurate records.

Trained scribes could and did write almost anything. They even wrote love letters for people and sealed them in clay "envelopes"! Scribes also recorded stories, laws, and songs.

The sturdy ancient tablets have survived thousands of years. They have helped historians to piece together a detailed picture of early Mesopotamia.

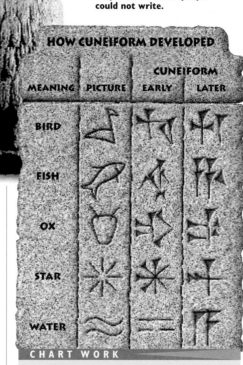

Scribes (left) filled an important role in ancient Sumer. They were record keepers, since most people could not write.

HOW CUNEIFORM DEVELOPED

MEANING	PICTURE	CUNEIFORM EARLY	LATER
BIRD			
FISH			
OX			
STAR			
WATER			

CHART WORK

This chart shows how some Sumerian symbols changed over time.

The photo on page 108 shows a cuneiform symbol found on this chart. What is this symbol? Is it early or later cuneiform?

CHART WORK: a star; early cuneiform

109

A SYSTEM OF WRITING

Encourage students to move back and forth between text and chart.

● *How were the materials used for cuneiform and hieroglyphics similar and different?* (Both used reed pens, but cuneiform was written on wet clay tablets rather than papyrus.)

● *Why did cuneiform symbols grow less picture-like as time passed?* (Scribes simplified the symbols to write faster.)

● *What evidence can you find that, like words in English, words in cuneiform had multiple meanings?* (The same symbol, ti, stood for such different meanings as "arrow" and "life.")

★THINKING FURTHER: *Compare and Contrast* **How would you compare and contrast cuneiform writing with written English?** (It had 500 signs compared to 26 letters in the English alphabet; its symbols stand for sounds, ideas, and objects; letters of the alphabet stand just for sounds.)

More CHART WORK

Help students work with the cuneiform chart on this page.

★THINKING FURTHER: *Compare and Contrast* **Judging from the cuneiform symbols on this chart, how were they simplified over time? how did this make writing faster?** (There are fewer strokes in a symbol; fewer strokes to write means less time to write.)

Discussing School in Sumer Encourage students to recall what they learned about the schooling of scribes in Egypt.

● *How did the rules to become a scribe differ from Egypt to Mesopotamia?* (It was possible, though rare, for girls to study to be scribes in Mesopotamia; in Egypt, it was boys only.)

● *Why did scribes need an education?* (to learn math and writing.)

★THINKING FURTHER: *Making Conclusions* **Why were scribes essential in Sumer?** (They served in many areas—business, law, love, and socializing, to name a few.)

BACKGROUND INFORMATION

ABOUT CUNEIFORM

- The invention of cuneiform probably preceded the development of hieroglyphics in Egypt, though by only a short time. In fact, Egyptians may have gotten the idea for writing from Sumerians. Both started with pictures, but Mesopotamians quickly went on to wedge-shaped strokes while the Egyptians retained pictures.
- Just as Champollion cracked the code of hieroglyphics, so Henry Crewicke Rawlinson cracked the cuneiform code. A young British military officer and classical scholar in 1835, he became intrigued with the "Rock of Behistun" in what is now Iran. It had cuneiform characters no one had yet deciphered. Like the Rosetta Stone, the Rock had writing in three languages. Rawlinson's translation of one, Old Persian, enabled him to decipher the cuneiform.

CITY-STATES OF SUMER

As students read the opening paragraph, they should refer to the map to locate the *city-states* mentioned. Have a student do a dramatic reading of the passage about Gilgamesh.

- **Who was Gilgamesh?** *(a mythical hero of Sumer)*

- **What is "a mythical hero"?** *(Help students understand that it is someone who embodies the beliefs and ideals of a society.)*

- **Do you know that you are able to write in cuneiform one description of Gilgamesh? How is that possible?** *(The Sumerians believed that Gilgamesh was "strong as an ox." The cuneiform symbol for ox appears in the chart on p. 109.)*

- **What other beliefs did the Sumerians hold about Gilgamesh?** *(that he was all-knowing, a great builder, part god and part man, and the strongest and the best fighter)*

> ★**THINKING FURTHER:** *Making Conclusions* **Judging from these beliefs, what attributes do you think the Sumerian culture valued?** *(knowledge, skill, strength, ability to fight)*

More MAP WORK

Refer students to the map on this page and point out that they will be returning to it as the lesson proceeds.

- **Near which river are the city-states of Ur, Uruk, and Eridu located?** *(the Euphrates)*

- **What was the earliest empire of which they were part?** *(the Sumerian empire)*

- **What is a city-state?** *(a self-governing city that also governs surrounding villages)*

- ★**THINKING FURTHER:** *Making Conclusions* **Why do you suppose a city would want to govern surrounding villages?** *(Help students to see that cities need to be fed and that surrounding village farms could supply that food.)*

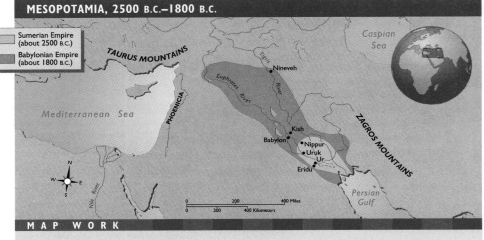

MESOPOTAMIA, 2500 B.C.–1800 B.C.

Sumerian Empire (about 2500 B.C.)
Babylonian Empire (about 1800 B.C.)

MAP WORK

The region of Mesopotamia was home to two important empires, Sumer and Babylonia.

1. Of the two political regions shown, which was larger, Sumer or Babylonia?

2. What is the northernmost **city-state** in Sumer?

3. Why do you think the Babylonian Empire stretched along rivers?

CITY-STATES OF SUMER

Cuneiform writing first appeared in about 3500 B.C. Over the next thousand years, Sumerian life centered around the city-states of southern Mesopotamia. A city-state is a self-governing city that also governs surrounding villages. Find the city-states Ur, Uruk, and Eridu on the map.

Through cuneiform we know about an early Sumerian mythical hero named Gilgamesh (GIHL guh mesh). Read the following passage about Gilgamesh. Think about what made him a hero to the ancient Sumerians.

> *The great Gilgamesh was one who knew everything. He had seen all there was to see and done all there was to do. He had built the walls of the city, Uruk. Look at its brickwork! Nobody could build a better wall. It was made of copper and burnt brick, and was wide enough to walk upon.*
>
> *Gilgamesh was part god and part [man], and as strong as an ox. He was the strongest in the land, and the best fighter.*

Living in a Sumerian City

City-states often went to war to gain control of precious river water. For this reason strong walls were built to protect against attack. Large gateways in city walls allowed people and goods to get into and out of cities. City gates were also where people gathered to buy fresh vegetables and other goods. Goods were brought to the cities by farmers and traders.

The king's palace could be seen from almost everywhere in a city. The palace was where a city-state's planning and

110

USING THE ANTHOLOGY

THE EPIC OF GILGAMESH, page 22 Explain to students that *The Epic of Gilgamesh* is the earliest known epic, or "long narrative poem or prose work, retelling important events in the life of a central hero or heroine, who is usually seen as representative of his or her culture." It was inscribed in about 2000 B.C. on 12 clay tablets found at Nineveh.

- It recounts the story of Gilgamesh, legendary king of Uruk, who is unable to face the idea of death and so goes on a quest to find immortality. After many dangerous confrontations, Gilgamesh returns home and comes to accept death as inevitable for humans.

- It contains a story of a great flood and a character named Utnapishtim that prefigures the Biblical story of the Great Flood and the survivor of it, Noah.

decision making took place. Kings served as generals, judges, and canal overseers. Unlike Egyptian pharaohs, though, Sumerian kings were not considered to be gods.

Religion in Ancient Sumer

In the center of most ancient Sumerian cities stood a towering mud-brick building. That building was a ziggurat (ZIHG oo rat). A ziggurat was a large building with a temple on its peak.

Since these temples were located in the center of cities, historians believe that religion was very important in Sumer. Like the Egyptians, Sumerians' religious beliefs involved polytheism. Polytheism is a belief in many gods and goddesses. Each city-state had a special god or goddess. That god or goddess was worshiped at the city's ziggurat. People also worshiped other gods and goddesses at home. One favorite was Ishtar, the goddess of love and war. Another was Enki, the god of water.

Uniting the City-States

In time the city-states were united under one ruler—Sargon, king of the city-state Kish. Sargon rose to power about 2300 B.C. His rule began a new period in Mesopotamia's history. Sargon expanded his empire to the northern end of the Fertile Crescent, in what is present-day Syria.

Along the Mediterranean Sea, Sumerians traded with the ancient seafaring people called Phoenicians (fih NEE shunz). The Phoenicians also traded with merchants from Egypt. Phoenicians sent wine and timber to Sargon's city-states. In return they received Mesopotamian farm products and other goods.

Cuneiform writing spread through the Fertile Crescent along with trade goods. Other cultures began using cuneiform to write out their own languages. Because cuneiform was used throughout his empire, Sargon could send instructions and govern over great distances.

Sargon, king of Kish, led the world's first empire. Ziggurats (below) dominated most Sumerian cities around 2000 B.C.

Discussing Living in a Sumerian City Help students understand the function of a walled city.

- **Why did the Sumerians build walls around their cities?** *(to protect themselves from one another and from the frequent wars over water)*

- **What other purposes did Sumerian city walls serve?** *(Farmers marketed produce beside the gates.)*

- **What role did the king's palace play in a city-state?** *(It was the center of government.)*

★THINKING FURTHER: *Compare and Contrast* **How would you compare a Sumerian king with an Egyptian pharaoh?** *(Though his palace was imposing, no evidence shows a king was as central to life as a pharaoh; he wasn't considered a god.)*

Exploring Religion in Ancient Sumer Refer the class to the photos of *ziggurats* on this page and on p. 115.

- **What evidence suggests that religion was important to Sumerians?** *(the ziggurat—a towering building with a temple—at the center of their cities for worship of gods and goddesses)*

- **What is the word for belief in many gods and goddesses?** *(polytheism)*

★THINKING FURTHER: *Making Conclusions* **What do the gods named in the text reveal about Sumerian values?** *(Enki: of water; Ishtar: devotion to love and war)*

Discussing Uniting the City-States Remind the class of the frequency with which the Sumerians went to war.

- **Who united the Sumerian city-states?** *(Sargon)*

- **Where was Sargon from?** *(Kish; have students locate Kish on the map on p. 110.)*

- **What trade did the Sumerians carry on with outsiders?** *(They traded their farm products for Phoenician wine and timber.)*

★THINKING FURTHER: *Making Generalizations* **What generalizations can you make about the effect of cuneiform upon life in the Fertile Crescent?** *(It made it possible for Sargon to govern Sumer; it spread writing to other city-states.)*

BACKGROUND INFORMATION

ABOUT ZIGGURATS
- The tall ziggurats, six to seven stories high, rose like mountains above the flat Sumerian plain. They could be seen from afar, and people were comforted by their belief that the gods who dwelled in the ziggurats' temples watched over and protected them.
- Ziggurat steps were stairways for the gods to descend from heaven.
- The Tower of Babel in the Bible may have been a ziggurat.

SECOND-LANGUAGE SUPPORT

DIALOGS Comparing life in Mesopotamia to their own lives will help second-language students understand their reading. Provide a format for students such as: The Sumerians were like us because ... ; They were different because .... Share comparisons aloud in groups.

111

THE RISE OF BABYLON

Tell students that the Standard of Ur, pictured in their texts, gives us a good picture of life in Sumer for many classes of people.

- **What brought on the collapse of the Sumerian Empire?** (rebellion against it by the city-states)

- **How did a new kingdom emerge?** (People from the Syrian desert moved into northern Mesopotamia and created a kingdom around the city-state of Babylon.)

★**THINKING FURTHER:** *Making Conclusions* **Find Babylon on the map on p. 110. What does it suggest about the movement of power through Mesopotamia over the centuries?** (Help students see that power seems to move north, from Ur to Kish and then to Babylon.)

Discussing A Northern Empire
Write *Babylon and Babylonia* on the board.

- **What new ruler marched through Mesopotamia in about 1800 B.C.?** (Hammurabi, king of Babylon)

- **What strategy did he use to weaken the Sumerians?** (He dammed the Euphrates, controlling the water flow.)

- **What is the difference between the two words on the board?** (Babylon was the city-state; Babylonia was the empire it created.)

★**THINKING FURTHER:** *Compare and Contrast* **How did Babylonia affect Sumer and how did Sumer affect Babylonia?** (Sumer joined a wealthy and powerful trading empire; Babylonia adopted Sumer's culture and language.)

THE RISE OF BABYLON

Sargon's rule lasted about 56 years, until about 2279 B.C. Then the city-states rebelled against the empire. Almost 500 years would pass before another empire controlled Mesopotamia.

During those years a group of people from the Syrian desert moved into northern Mesopotamia. They created a small kingdom centered around a city-state called Babylon.

A Northern Empire

About 1800 B.C. Babylon's king, Hammurabi (hah moo RAH bee), began a drive to gain control over the old city-states of Sumer. Hammurabi and the Babylonians dammed key parts of the Euphrates. This gave them the power to cut off the flow of water or cause terrible floods downstream. Next, Hammurabi's armies attacked the weakened Sumerians. Hammurabi also won control of the city-states around Babylon. He created a huge empire. Find Babylon and the Babylonian empire on the map on page 110.

The empire of Babylonia under Hammurabi became rich and powerful. Shipments of silver, copper, timber, and wine poured into Babylonia. These goods came from people in what are today Turkey, Iran, and Syria. In exchange people in Babylonia sent grain and fruits. Servants even floated ice from distant mountains down rivers to refrigerate food and drink.

Under Hammurabi Mesopotamia's center of power shifted north to Babylon. Yet many Sumerian traditions remained. Babylonians used cuneiform to communicate in writing. In fact the world's first dictionaries were created so Babylonians could adopt Sumerian culture and language.

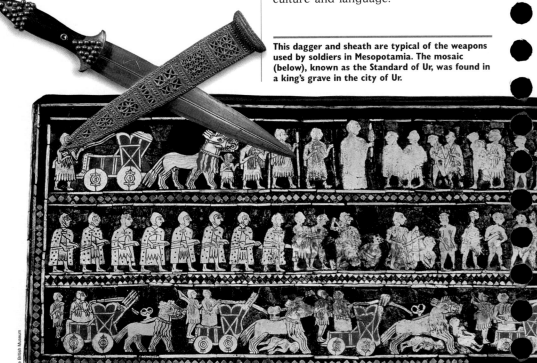

This dagger and sheath are typical of the weapons used by soldiers in Mesopotamia. The mosaic (below), known as the Standard of Ur, was found in a king's grave in the city of Ur.

BACKGROUND INFORMATION

ABOUT SARGON
- Legend has it that Sargon began life in a fashion similar to Moses. His mother floated him down the Euphrates in a pitch-covered basket and he was found by a farmer who raised him as his son.
- As a young man, he served as a cup-bearer to the king of Kish, whom he later overthrew. Adopting the name Sargon, which means "True King," he took the throne.
- His brilliance as a military leader, organizer, and administrator helped him to create and hold together the Sumerian empire, but after his death his sons were not up to the task, and the empire fell apart.

ABOUT HAMMURABI
- Like Sargon, Hammurabi was a strong warrior and a talented administrator.
- At first he was one of many kings in Mesopotamia, all with about equal power. He was driven by a desire to unite all the city-states into one empire so that, like the old Sumerian empire, which he greatly admired, it could be a major power in the ancient world.
- For 25 years Hammurabi worked to strengthen Babylon's position with political and military alliances.
- After three decades of his reign he went on the attack and began crushing his major rivals with force.
- He was also a great patron of scholarly pursuits.

A CODE OF LAW

When Hammurabi gained control of Sumer, he set out to act as the Sumerian kings had done. He oversaw projects to build and repair canals. Hammurabi also acted as a judge. He used some of the laws that Sumerians had written down hundreds of years before him.

In 1901 archaeologists found a large stone pillar from ancient Babylon. The pillar was inscribed with over 200 laws written in cuneiform. Imagine historians' excitement when they realized that the laws had actually been formed by Hammurabi himself. They had been written almost 4,000 years before they were discovered!

The Code of Hammurabi is one of the world's oldest codes of law. A code of law is a written set of laws that apply to everyone under a government.

The pillar shows that slavery existed in Babylonia and that not everyone was treated equally under the law. Copies of the pillar were also found outside of Babylon. This suggests that Hammurabi meant for his laws to be followed throughout the empire. Cuneiform made this possible. How important is writing in our own civilization? What other ways do we have to communicate over long distances?*

Read the following excerpt from the Code of Hammurabi. What does it tell you about what justice meant to Hammurabi and other Babylonians?

MANY VOICES
PRIMARY SOURCE

Excerpt from
The Code of Hammurabi, c. 1800 B.C.

[So] that the strong may not [abuse] the weak, to give justice to the orphan and the widow, I have inscribed my precious words. . . .

If a Freeman has put out the eye of another Freeman, they shall put out his eye.

If he breaks the bone of another Freeman, they shall break his bone.

If he puts out the eye of a Poor Man, or breaks the bone of a Poor Man, he shall pay 1 mina [17.5 ounces] of silver. If he puts out the eye of the Slave of another Freeman . . . , he shall pay half his price.

*Writing is still one of our most important communication tools. Telephones, computer networks, radio, and television are some others.

113

A CODE OF LAW
Discuss with the class the importance of laws and the value of written laws.

- **What evidence can you find that Hammurabi was heavily influenced by Sumerian values?** (He adopted their concern and care for water control. He also adopted some of their ancient laws.)

- **What is the Code of Hammurabi?** (Point out that "code" is another word with multiple meanings; help students define it here not as secret writing, but as a system of laws.)

★**THINKING FURTHER:** *Making Conclusions* **What does a written set of laws tell you about what justice meant to Hammurabi and the Babylonians?** (Use this question from the text to get at the fact that they placed a high value on justice and on applying it throughout their land.)

MANY VOICES

Discussing the PRIMARY SOURCE

As students read the excerpt, write on the board: "An eye for an eye..."

- **According to this excerpt, for what reason was the Code of Hammurabi set down?** (to protect the weak from the strong)

- **Have you ever heard the expression on the board? How does it relate to the Code of Hammurabi?** (It means that if you do something wrong, the same will be done to you; that is what the Code states, at least for crimes against Freemen.)

- **How does the Code show that there were "second-class citizens" in Babylonia?** (Punishment was harsher for wrong done to a Freeman than for wrong done to a Poor Man or a Slave.)

★**THINKING FURTHER:** *Fact and Opinion* **Is it a fact or an opinion that a society must have a code of laws if it is to have justice?** (As the class wrestles with this question, you may want to inject the word "lawless" and have students describe the kind of society it describes.)

CITIZENSHIP★

UNDERSTANDING GOVERNMENT Remind students that in our society we as citizens have the power to create or change the laws under which we live by electing representatives to do it for us. Have the class rewrite the laws quoted from the Code of Hammurabi as they might appear in the American justice system. As students write their laws, ask them to suggest what makes their version appropriate to the United States and therefore different from Hammurabi's laws.

USING CURRENT EVENTS Select a change in a local, state, or federal law that is currently in the news. Use it to help students contrast the American way of making laws with Hammurabi's method. Help students see that, unlike one person's stating what the law should be, in the United States different voices must be heard, compromises must be reached, and many people must agree to enact a law.

THE "NEW" BABYLONIA

Write the following on the board: "A case of history repeating itself."

- **How does this saying tell what happened in Babylonia about 1750 B.C.?** *(This Babylonian empire began to crumble after Hammurabi died just as the Sumerian empire had crumbled after Sargon died, both because city-states rebelled and new powers moved in from the north and west.)*

- **What city-state now gained power and where was it located?** *(Have students refer to the map on p. 110 to locate Nineveh to the north, on the Tigris River.)*

Discussing the "New" Babylon

Tell students that about eleven years after the City of Babylon was destroyed it was rebuilt by Assyrian rulers, who had a capital at Nineveh. After new Babylonian kings replaced the Assyrians, Babylon flourished with even more ambitious construction efforts.

- **What brought about the growth of the New Babylon?** *(It became the capital of a new Mesopotamian empire.)*

- **What made the city magnificent?** *(massive walls, a 100-foot-tall ziggurat, gridded streets, a sewer system, "hanging gardens")*

★**THINKING FURTHER:** *Making Conclusions* **Why might both Babylonian and non-Babylonian kings want to rebuild the city of Babylon?** *(Possible answer: They might want to connect their own reigns to a city with a rich history.)*

Understanding Sorrow in Babylon

Use this quote from the Bible to help students sympathize with the agonies of uprooting and exile.

- **Why does the poet speak of weeping?** *(Captives in Babylon are pining for the home that they have been taken from against their wills.)*

★**THINKING FURTHER:** *Making Conclusions* **What emotions might these people be feeling? What dreams might they have for the future?** *(Encourage students to try to understand the feelings of people in such a predicament.)*

THE "NEW" BABYLONIA

After Hammurabi died, about 1750 B.C., Babylonia began to fall apart. The city-states in the south rebelled again, much as they had against Sargon. Powerful armies from the mountains to the north and east began taking the empire's territory. Throughout western Asia new powers overthrew old ones.

During this time of change, however, Babylon remained one of the most powerful cities in the Fertile Crescent. Just as Hammurabi had used Sumerian ideas, new rulers respected the history of "Old Babylonia." They worshiped its gods and passed down its legends—many of which had begun in Sumer.

In 689 B.C. Babylon was destroyed by powerful rulers from a northern Mesopotamian city called Nineveh. About 60 years later the Babylonians were able to rebuild Babylon and make it the capital of an even stronger empire.

The "New" Babylon

The new Babylon soon became the world's largest city. It grew famous for its great beauty and technology. Two massive walls and a moat now protected Babylon. The city was split in two by the Euphrates River but was connected by a movable bridge and an underwater tunnel! At the center of the city stood a huge ziggurat. It was 200 yards wide and rose 100 yards into the sky. Elsewhere were grid-style streets, sewer and water systems, and three- and four-story homes. Babylon was also known for its marvelous "hanging gardens." Unfortunately, we do not know exactly what they looked like.

Sorrow in Babylon

Not everyone thought of Babylon as a wonderful place. To some who were brought to the great city, Babylon was anything but beautiful and certainly not home. One poet wrote:

> By the rivers of Babylon,
> there we sat,
> sat and wept,
> when we thought of [home].

These newcomers were prisoners. They were brought from what is today Israel.

Links to LANGUAGE ARTS

What Did You Call Me?!

Words are often "borrowed" when different cultures come into contact. Some historians think modern English may have been affected by ancient Mesopotamian languages! On an ancient cuneiform tablet, one student insults another, calling him a "clever fool." Ancient Greeks probably borrowed the phrase for their compound word *sophos-moros*—clever fool. Modern English takes the word from the Greeks. When you reach your second year of high school, you will be known as a *sophomore!*

Most dictionaries show how some English words came from other languages. Look up the English meaning of *sophomore*. What are the meanings and origin of *cuneiform*?*

114   *The word comes from *Cuneus*, which is Latin for "wedge"—formed by a wedge.

BACKGROUND INFORMATION

ABOUT THE HANGING GARDENS OF BABYLON
- They were probably ordered built by the ruler of Babylon, Nebuchadnezzar II, for his Persian wife. Legend says she pined for her more mountainous homeland, and the gardens were built to add interest and some altitude to the Mesopotamian plain.
- They were among the Seven Wonders of the Ancient World.

CURRICULUM CONNECTION

LINKS TO LANGUAGE ARTS: WHAT DID YOU CALL ME? Encourage students to use a dictionary to learn more about origins of words in this lesson. For example, the word *cuneiform* comes from the Latin for "wedge-shaped."

The carving shows a Sumerian husband and wife. The ruins (above) are all that remain of the ziggurat of Ur. It was dedicated to the storm god, Enlil.

Oriental Institute of Chicago

The modern countries of the Fertile Crescent are Iraq, Syria, Lebanon, and Israel. Like the ancient empires, these countries are also covered with farms and cities.

✓// Reviewing Facts and Ideas

MAIN IDEAS

- Cuneiform probably developed as a way to keep track of farm supplies and surplus. The system was later expanded to communicate more complex ideas as well.

- Mesopotamia was not always unified into a single empire. Both government and religion greatly shaped life on a local level.

- Cuneiform writing helped Sargon, king of Kish, to rule over great distances.

- The rise to power of Hammurabi made Babylon one of the world's richest and most powerful cities in ancient times.

WHY IT MATTERS

One cuneiform tablet reads:

The gods alone live forever under the divine sun. But as for [humans], their days are numbered. All their activities will be nothing but wind.

It is hard to believe that the ruins of an ancient Mesopotamian city-state were once home to thousands of people. Yet this land was covered with green fields and bustling cities. The people who lived here shared many of the same concerns that we have today.

The ancient Sumerians and Babylonians left records of their civilizations in cuneiform writing. Ideas formed in ancient times—about schools, literature, science, and law—echo into our own time. Despite the ancient scribe's prediction, the legacy of Mesopotamia has not been lost.

THINK ABOUT IT

1. Why was it an honor to become a scribe in Mesopotamia?

2. How was Egyptian culture similar to the culture of Mesopotamia? How was it different?

3. **FOCUS** How did cuneiform help Sargon to create and rule an empire in Mesopotamia?

4. **THINKING SKILL** Look at the excerpt from the story of Gilgamesh on page 110. *Make conclusions* about what was important in ancient Sumer.

5. **WRITE** Write a one-paragraph response to the laws found in the Code of Hammurabi. How did they protect the people of Babylon?

115

Discussing **WHY IT MATTERS** Review how we know about Mesopotamia.

★THINKING FURTHER: *Cause and Effect How does written language keep human activity from being "nothing but wind"?* (Written language records human activities, thus giving them greater permanence.)

★3 CLOSE

MAIN IDEAS
Have students give their answers aloud.

- *Why did cuneiform first develop and how did it grow?* (It first developed to keep records; later it developed enough to express complex ideas.)

- *How would you describe Mesopotamia in terms of unity and disunity?* (It alternated between them. Sometimes city-states were united and sometimes they were independent.)

- *How did cuneiform aid in governing large areas?* (It allowed laws to reach all corners of an empire.)

- *What did Hammurabi's rise to power do for Babylon?* (It made it one of the ancient world's most powerful cities.)

EVALUATE
✓ **Answers to Think About It**
1. It was a highly important job.
   Make Inferences

2. Similar: both had a written language, polytheism, an agricultural base, trade. Different: Egypt was united, Mesopotamia often was not; unlike Mesopotamian kings, the pharaoh was a god.
   Compare and Contrast

3. Cuneiform allowed him to send instructions and to govern from great distances.
   Steps in a Process

4. knowledge, skill, strength, fighting ability
   Make Conclusions

5. Students may find them harsh but effective deterrents to wrongdoing.
   Make Judgements and Decisions

Write About It Have students write a paragraph comparing their schooling with that of a Mesopotamian scribe.

MEETING INDIVIDUAL NEEDS

RETEACHING (Easy) Have students copy and fill in the following chart:

Achievements Of Mesopotamian Civilization			
Government	Religion	Architecture	Writing

EXTENSION (Average) Tell students to review the lesson and find one place in Mesopotamia that they would like to have visited. Have them write three journal entries describing a visit there.

ENRICHMENT (Challenging) Divide the class into five research teams and assign each team one of the following: Sumerian art, Sumerian toys, the Standard of Ur, the Tower of Babel, the Hanging Gardens of Babylon. Tell them to research their topic, using both encyclopedias and library books on Mesopotamia. Have each team prepare an illustrated presentation for the class.

LEGACY

PAGES 116–117

Lesson Overview

The wheel, the greatest invention ever, probably developed in Mesopotamia.

Lesson Objectives

★ Appreciate the brilliant invention of the wheel and trace its uses.

1 PREPARE

MOTIVATE Use the question in the text to get students thinking about the importance of the wheel: What would life be like if the wheel had never been invented?

SET PURPOSE When students have recognized how much harder life would be without the wheel, have them read the column of type on this page to discover more about the invention of the wheel and its uses around the world.

2 TEACH

Understanding the Concept of a Legacy Encourage students to list both obvious and less obvious uses of the wheel in their lives. Wheeled vehicles—autos, bicycles, strollers—may be obvious. Less obvious may be wheels, rollers, gears in watches, can openers, and a wide variety of both everyday and unusual products.

Examining the Pictures As students study the illustrations of different uses for the wheel, encourage them to note its variations and versatility.

- **Why might the earliest Sumerian wheels have been more useful on farm carts than on war chariots?** (Heavy solid wood wheels made steering difficult; war chariots needed better maneuverability to be useful.)

- **What parallels do you see between the Egyptian development of the sail and the Sumerian invention of the wheel?** (Both were ground-breaking events in the history of transportation.)

Legacy
LINKING PAST AND PRESENT

THE WHEEL

How did you get to school this morning? If you did not walk, you probably used a vehicle with wheels. Can you imagine what life would be like if the wheel had never been invented?

Most archaeologists believe that ancient Mesopotamians invented the wheel. Some of the first wheels were used on farm carts and war chariots. Over time, people found other uses for the wheel.

The wheel still plays an important role in transportation. There are wheels turning in machines in our homes and factories, too. You can find them winding the film on a movie projector or spinning a compact disc. The wheel has proven to be one of the most important inventions in human history!

Some of the earliest wheels found were used on Sumerian war chariots like this one. This 6,000-year-old chariot was pulled by a donkey. The solid wood wheels made it very heavy and difficult to steer.

116

BACKGROUND INFORMATION

ABOUT WHEELS

- Wheels found in Kish show the improvements Sumerian wheelwrights made to produce stronger and more maneuverable wheels. Instead of using solid rounds of wood, they used three separate pieces cut to fit together in a wheel shape. They bound these pieces with wooden battens and leather and later with metal ties and rimmed them with copper studs.

- Later, in an effort to make wheels lighter and easier to steer, spoked wheels were invented. These were what the Hyksos used for the war chariots that they used against the Egyptians and that the Egyptians then adopted to drive out the Hyksos. By the Middle Ages the technology that created a swiveling front axle had been developed, immensely improving the ability to steer carts.

The turning motion of interlocking wheels, or *gears*, is a key part of many machines. The gears in this watch turn at just the right speeds to keep accurate time. What other machines can you think of that use gears?

The wheel can be put to practical use or it can be used for fun. Originally called a *pleasure wheel*, this ride is named after the man who built the largest one ever for the Chicago World's Fair in 1893: George Ferris.

Countries all over the world have built vast networks of roads and highways. Millions of people travel these roads each day. Bicycles and cars share this street in Beijing, China.

- *What in these pictures tells you that the wheel is indispensable to societies all across the world?* (The vast network of roads that crisscross the continents and the sight of cars and bicycles in any city.)

- *What other kinds of transportation use the wheel?* (trains, buses, trucks, airplanes, wagons, tractors, ships)

- *Why are wheels necessary parts of many machines?* (Machines require gears, and gears are an adaptation of the wheel.)

- *What are examples of machines that use gears?* (Students can name many things, from a small watch to a giant turbine.)

- *How many different ways can you think of that the wheel contributes to entertainment?* (In addition to the Ferris wheel, students might name almost any ride at an amusement park—a merry-go-round, a roller coaster, bumper cars, to name a few. Also, there are in-line skates, skate boards, trail bikes, and scooters, motor or otherwise. Recorded music would be impossible without the wheel.)

★THINKING FURTHER: Compare and Contrast First make a list of three areas of life—manufacturing, travel, entertainment. How would each be different if we did not have the wheel? (Help students to grasp the tremendous limitations that lack of the wheel would put on our lives.)

⭐ 3 CLOSE

SUM IT UP
Could the U.S. pattern of cities surrounded by suburbs exist without the wheel? As a final proof of the indispensability of the wheel, have students discuss this question. Help them to see that without the car and commuter buses and trains, our entire pattern of life would be changed.

EVALUATE
Write About It Have students write a thank you note to the Sumerians for their development of the wheel. Tell students to include a passage telling about their favorite use of the wheel.

MEETING INDIVIDUAL NEEDS

RETEACHING (Easy) Tell students to draw a self-portrait entitled "[My Name] with a Wheel." In it, have the students show themselves doing something that involves the wheel.

EXTENSION (Average) Some scholars believe that the development of the potter's wheel may have predated the use of the wheel for transportation. Have students research the potter's wheel and make a simple diagram of how it works.

ENRICHMENT (Challenging) Point out to the class that although there is no solid proof, many experts believe that the wheel was invented only once and that it spread out from Sumer to other societies. Have students do research on this theory of the spread of the wheel to major civilizations and present their findings in a report.

SKILLS LESSON
PAGES 118–119

Lesson Overview
Identifying cause and effect involves looking for connections between events.

Lesson Objectives
★ Explain how to identify cause-and-effect relationships.

1 PREPARE

MOTIVATE Write *Cause → Effect* on the board. Point out to the class that often something happens and we ask, "Why?" We see the effect and want to know its cause. Have students read *Why the Skill Matters* to note the cause it introduces.

SET PURPOSE Explain to students that it is useful to have a strategy to help us relate cause and effect. Refer them to the *Helping Yourself* box on p. 119 to identify the steps in that strategy.

2 TEACH

Using the Skill As students work with this section, have one write on the board the cause: invention of glass-making. Then have another write on the board the effects that they identify, in the order in which they appear.

- *What was the first effect of the invention of glassmaking?* (the making of beautiful glass products)

- *How did that effect turn into a cause that had its own effect?* (Help students recognize how one thing led to another: beautiful glass pieces caused a demand, the demand caused the spread of goods through trade and the spread of glassmaking itself.)

Resource **REMINDER**
Practice and Project Book: *p. 26*
Transparency: *Graphic Organizer*

THINKINGSKILLS

Identifying Cause and Effect

VOCABULARY
cause
effect

WHY THE SKILL MATTERS

By about 3000 B.C. Sumerians had built their first city-states on the plains of southern Mesopotamia. At about the same time, craftworkers in what is today Syria learned how to make a useful and beautiful new material. They mixed together and then heated sand and a certain kind of plant ash. In this way they created the world's first known glass.

The development of glass brought many changes in the ways people lived. These changes interest historians, who analyze cause and effect connections. A cause is something that makes something else happen. What happens as a result of a cause is called an effect. Historians study causes and their effects to understand why events happened the way they did.

USING THE SKILL

Now practice tracing a cause, such as the invention of glassmaking, to its effects.

By Hammurabi's time glassmaking was just being introduced in Mesopotamia. As time passed, craftworkers figured out how to make elegant vases and other containers from glass. These beautiful glass products attracted the eyes of the empire's rich people. Remember, up until now they had seen only clay and metal containers.

People began buying the new glass goods and using them. The glass items also became popular outside the empire. They

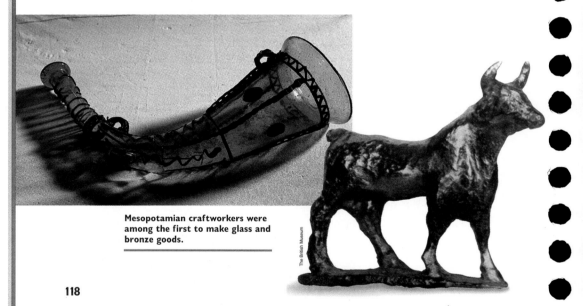

Mesopotamian craftworkers were among the first to make glass and bronze goods.

The British Museum

118

READING STRATEGIES & LANGUAGE DEVELOPMENT

CAUSE AND EFFECT Encourage students to notice the sequence of events, how one thing leads to another. Point out there are at least two ways to relate cause and effect: (1) spot a cause and ask, What were its effects? (2) spot an effect and ask, What caused it? Mastering this skill will help students comprehend their reading.

WORDS OFTEN CONFUSED Two words often confused are *effect* and *affect*. Write them on the board and call on students to tell the difference between them. Then have them look up the two in a dictionary. Can both be nouns? Yes, but *effect* is far more commonly used, meaning a "result." (The noun *affect* is rarely used in everyday speech.) Can both be verbs? Yes again, but *affect* is much more commonly used as a verb, meaning "to have an effect on." The verb *effect* has a specialized meaning. In general, *e* is for noun, *a* for verb.

were traded in such faraway places as what are today Iran and Greece. Some historians also think that glassmakers from the Fertile Crescent may have gone to work in Egyptian workshops. There they introduced their skill to Egyptian craftworkers. It is thought that the art of glassmaking spread from Egypt and Mesopotamia to areas in India, Russia, Spain, and China.

Do you see a cause in the above paragraphs? It is the invention of glass in Mesopotamia. One effect, in this case, was the development of different uses for the new material. Another effect was the spread of glassmaking technology to other parts of the world. As you can see, one cause can have more than one effect. It works the other way around too—an effect can have more than one cause.

Can you trace a cause to all of its effects in this example? Try numbering the events in the order in which they happened. The invention of glass happened first—it is a cause. Related events that happened later are effects of that cause.

TRYING THE SKILL

As you read the following passage, look for cause-and-effect connections. Refer to the Helping Yourself box for help in finding the connections between events.

Glass was not the only material that craftworkers in ancient Mesopotamia experimented with. Around 2000 B.C. Mesopotamians were among the first in the world to blend copper and tin to make bronze.

*It brought different cultures into contact. Information about new technologies was exchanged.

HELPING Yourself

- A **cause** makes something else happen. The result of a cause is an **effect**.
- Arrange events in the order in which they happened.
- Look for long and short term cause-and-effect connections.

Bronze brought many changes to life in Mesopotamia. For one thing, bronze was much harder than the copper products that were used until that time. Because it was harder, bronze made better tools and sharper weapons. This improvement in technology was a help to farmers, craftworkers, and soldiers alike.

Molten [melted] bronze was also easier to pour than the metals used earlier. Craftworkers could pour the hot liquid metal into more varied and detailed molds. As a result, these craftworkers were able to make finer arrows, ax-heads, statues, bowls, and other objects.

More and more tin was needed as the demand for products made from bronze increased. Historians believe that traders brought the tin needed to make bronze from distant regions.

*In what ways did the invention of bronze affect trade between Mesopotamia and its neighbors?**

REVIEWING THE SKILL

1. What are some ways to go about identifying cause-and-effect connections?

2. In the passage on the invention of bronze, what were some different causes and effects?

3. How does finding cause-and-effect connections help you to understand historical events?

119

- *To what areas did glassmaking spread? What caused its spread?* (to Egypt, Europe, and east to China; the demand for beautiful glass pieces)

★**THINKING FURTHER:** *Cause and Effect* **What might have been some effects of the spread of glassmaking on the regions it reached?** (Possible answers: glass might have replaced other materials; trade might have increased for glass objects.)

Trying the Skill Review the *Helping Yourself* steps with students. Call attention to any word or phrase that signals cause and effect. Tell them to look for signals in this passage. If students have difficulty, make sure they identify events before looking for cause or effect. Have them make a cause-and-effect diagram of their reading.

- *What were some effects of bronze-making?* (better tools and weapons)

- *Why could Mesopotamians make finer ax-heads and statues?* (They could pour hot metal into detailed molds.)

★**THINKING FURTHER:** *Making Conclusions* **How is expanded trade both a cause and an effect?** (It is the effect of having surplus goods and it can be the cause of growing wealth and the spread of culture.)

 3 CLOSE

SUM IT UP

Have students discuss the value of being able to identify cause-and-effect relationships in both schoolwork and personal life. Help them see that school subjects have more meaning when we understand the why of a topic. Recognizing cause and effect can help us make good choices and avoid bad ones.

EVALUATE

✓ **Answers to Reviewing the Skill**

1. arranging events in the order in which they happened; looking for long and short term connections

2. The invention of bronze caused the creation of better tools, weapons, and other objects; the need for tin caused an increase in trade.

3. They show how events are related.

BACKGROUND INFORMATION

USING THE GRAPHIC ORGANIZER You may want to have students work with this Graphic Organizer transparency to help them organize their information.

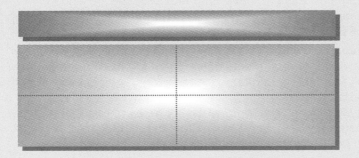

LESSON 3

Lesson Overview

Among polytheistic peoples, the Hebrews founded a monotheistic religion that influenced others.

Lesson Objectives

★ Analyze ways that trade and human movement linked the cities of the Fertile Crescent.

★ Describe the Hebrews' movements.

★ Explain *Judaism,* the religious beliefs of the Hebrews.

1 PREPARE

MOTIVATE Read the *Read Aloud* to the class. Remind students of the leaders they have met so far—pharaohs, lawgivers, empire-builders, conquerors—and refer to the picture on this page of Rembrandt's painting of Moses. What do students know about Moses?

SET PURPOSE Have students try to predict the answer to the *Read to Learn* question. Point out that in this lesson, they will learn about a leader who affected the world by presenting cultural values that had a profound impact on the beliefs, attitudes, and actions of their own and other cultures. Encourage students to look for *Vocabulary* words.

2 TEACH

Discussing THE BIG PICTURE As students read this section, encourage them to try to picture in their minds the scenes the text describes.

● **What is the Hebrew Bible?** *(the Jewish people's record of their history and of Judaism, their religion)*

★**THINKING FURTHER:** *Making Conclusions* **Why is the Hebrew Bible still read today?** *(It is honored by three major world religions—Judaism, Christianity, and Islam.)*

Resource REMINDER

Practice and Project Book: *p. 27*
Anthology: *Praying at the Western Wall, pp. 24–25*
Desk Map

4000 B.C.	3000 B.C.	2000 B.C.	1700 BC.	586 B.C.	A.D. 1

Gemäldegalerie Berlin

THE BEGINNINGS OF JUDAISM

Focus Activity

READ TO LEARN
How did the writings in the Torah shape Judaism?

VOCABULARY
Judaism
Torah
monotheism
Ten Commandments
Sabbath
Diaspora

PEOPLE
Abraham
Moses

PLACES
Jerusalem

READ ALOUD

"Hear, O Israel! The Lord is our God, the Lord is one." This short passage from the Bible expresses the basis of Jewish religious belief. In this lesson you will read about the great meaning it would have for the ancestors of the Jewish people in the changing world of the Fertile Crescent.

THE BIG PICTURE

Hammurabi ruled the Babylonian empire in the late 1700s B.C. Meanwhile people were on the move throughout the Fertile Crescent. Phoenician port cities along the Mediterranean Sea were expanding their trade with Egypt and cities across the sea. Merchants were traveling along the dusty roads that connected Egypt and Mesopotamia.

Some information about this exciting time comes from a source that millions of people continue to read today. That source is the collection of books known as the Hebrew Bible. Its original language was Hebrew. It has been translated into almost every language on Earth. Its writings are sacred to more than 17 million Jews today. Christians and Muslims also read and honor the Hebrew Bible.

The Hebrew Bible is the Jewish people's record of their history and their religion, which is called Judaism. In this lesson you will follow the Bible's account of Judaism's beginnings.

120

SHELTERED INSTRUCTION

READING STRATEGIES & LANGUAGE DEVELOPMENT

SEQUENCING Remind the class that the order in which events occur is their sequence. Explain that chronological order is time sequence. To help students grasp the concept, have them create a time line for the origin of Judaism. Have students skim section headings and subheadings to find key events, adding dates and brief descriptions as they read. **[SDAIE STRATEGY: SCHEMA BUILDING]**

SYNONYMS AND ANTONYMS Write *synonym* and *antonym* on the board and have students define them as "words with the same meaning" and "words with opposite meanings," respectively. Help them find words in the text that have both synonyms and antonyms and give the synonyms and antonyms; for example, on p. 121, *worshiped* (adored/reviled), *linked* (connected/separated), *terrible* (awful/wonderful), *poor* (inadequate/plentiful), *ancient* (old/new).

ABRAHAM OF UR

The first book of the Bible tells of a family that lived in Mesopotamia. This family came from the city-state of Ur. In this city people worshiped the Sumerian moon goddess. However, this family worshiped a different god. The Bible tells about a man named Abraham and his wife Sarah:

> The Lord said to Abraham: "Go forth from your native land and from your father's house to the land that I will show you. I will make of you a great nation, and I will bless you. . . ." [So] Abraham took his wife, Sarah . . . and they set out for the land of Canaan.

The Covenant

To reach the land of Canaan from Mesopotamia, the travelers would have set out on the trade routes that linked major cities of the Fertile Crescent. Look at the map on this page to see their route. The journey would have taken months, and it would have been hard to be a stranger in a new place. When Abraham arrived in Canaan, the Bible says that God made a covenant, or special agreement, with him.

> I am God Almighty. Walk in My ways and be blameless. I will establish My covenant with you, and I will make you exceedingly numerous. . . . I assign the land you sojourn [rest] in to you and your offspring to come . . . I will be their God.

This covenant is considered by the Jewish people to be the beginning of their history. Later, their descendants would become known as people of Israel, or Israelites, after Abraham's grandson Israel. They also came to be known as Jews.

MAP WORK: 1. the Jordan River and the Euphrates River 2. Mt. Sinai

Going to Egypt

As time passed, the Bible says, Abraham's children and grandchildren prospered as shepherds in Canaan. Then came a time of poor crops and terrible hunger. The people of Israel went to Egypt where food could be found.

Here the people of Israel were welcomed. As time passed, things changed. "A new king arose over Egypt," the Bible says. This pharaoh "set taskmasters over [the people of Israel] to oppress them with forced labor." Like others in ancient Egypt, the people of Israel had become slaves.

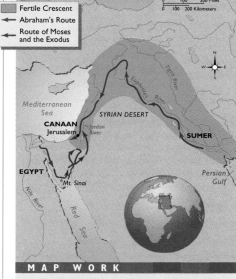

BEGINNINGS OF JUDAISM IN THE FERTILE CRESCENT

Fertile Crescent
← Abraham's Route
← Route of Moses and the Exodus

MAP WORK

Judaism has deep roots in western Asia, in the land along the Mediterranean Sea.

1. Abraham reached which rivers?
2. Moses' route passed a famous mountain. What is it?

121

ABRAHAM OF UR

After students read the command to Abraham, encourage them to discuss what it must have been like for Abraham and Sarah to uproot their family.

More
MAP WORK

Refer students to the map on this page. On their desk maps, have them locate the same area and note its harsh terrain.

● **Where is Canaan? About how many miles was Abraham's journey there?** (at the opposite end of the Fertile Crescent from Sumer; about 1,200–1,300 miles by Abraham's route.)

★THINKING FURTHER: **Making Conclusions Wasn't there a shorter route? Why do you think Abraham did not take it?** (Straight west is shorter, but it crossed a desert.)

Discussing The Covenant Clarify the meaning of *covenant.*

● **What is a covenant?** (an agreement between two parties in which each party makes commitments)

● **What was the covenant between God and Abraham?** (God promised land and an increase of Abraham's people in return for their accepting Him as their God and God's ways.)

★THINKING FURTHER: **Making Comparisons How is a covenant like a contract?** (Both sides promise something for something in return.)

Discussing Going to Egypt Refer students to the map and have them locate Egypt in relation to Canaan.

● **What drove the Hebrews out of their "promised land" of Canaan and into Egypt?** (famine and the hope of food)

● **How did their fortunes change once they were in Egypt?** (They went from being welcomed to being enslaved.)

★THINKING FURTHER: **Cause and Effect What was the cause of their enslavement?** (The decree of a new pharaoh; help students relate this to an idea presented earlier—those made slaves were usually "outsiders.")

BACKGROUND INFORMATION

ABOUT THE BIBLE, GOD, AND ABRAHAM Though the Bible is not a history written by historians, it is a guide to ancient times. Historians and archaeologists search for evidence of events the Bible reports.

● The Hebrew Bible makes up the Old Testament of the Christian Bible. The Quran, the holy book of Islam, has stories similar to Jonah and the whale, Noah and the ark, and Judgment Day.

● Note that *God* is capitalized but *god* and *goddess* are not. God is the proper name of the one supreme deity, as are Yahweh, Jehovah, and Allah. Proper names of gods and goddesses are capitalized.

● According to the Bible, Abraham begot two lineages in the Middle East: Ishmael, born of the Egyptian slave Hagar, is considered to be the ancestor of the Arab lineage; Isaac, born of Sarah, is considered to be the ancestor of the Hebrew lineage.

MOSES IN EGYPT

Tell students the story the Bible tells of how Moses came to be adopted by the pharaoh's daughter. (See *Background Information* at the bottom of this page.)

Discussing Becoming a Prophet
Help students recognize the difficulty of becoming a prophet.

- *Why did Moses have to flee Egypt, although he was a member of the pharaoh's household?* (He had killed a man who was beating a slave and so he was wanted for murder.)

- *What command does the Bible say God gave Moses?* (to return to the pharaoh to free the Israelites)

- *Was Moses eager to obey this command? Explain.* (No, he was very reluctant, but obeyed anyway.)

- *Did Moses succeed in freeing the Hebrews? How?* (The Bible says God helped him lead them out of Egypt.)

★THINKING FURTHER: *Cause and Effect* **To persuade the pharaoh to free the Hebrews, God visited ten plagues on Egypt. How would you describe the cause-and-effect relationship at work here?** *(Cause: God keeps sending plagues. Effect: Pharaoh gives in to Moses to get the plagues to stop.)*

Discussing the Pictures If any students have taken part in a Seder, have them describe the experience. Encourage them to tell about the symbolism of the various dishes in particular and of the Passover celebration in general.

This family celebrates Passover by praying and sharing a traditional meal. The foods on the plate are symbolic of an ancient story.

MOSES IN EGYPT

Fortunately for the Israelites, a man named Moses rose to leadership. According to the Bible, Moses was born to Israelite parents but was adopted as a baby by the pharaoh's daughter. Raised in the royal household, Moses experienced all the wealth and power of Egypt. Yet he would someday become leader and teacher to enslaved Israelites who lived all around him.

Becoming a Prophet

One day, the Bible says, Moses saw an Egyptian beating an Israelite slave. Moses looked around, and seeing no one about, he killed the Egyptian and hid the body in the sand.

Moses was wanted for murder by the pharaoh. He fled to the land of Midian, which was probably in present-day Saudi Arabia. There he remained for years until God called to him,

"Come . . . I will send you to Pharaoh, and you shall free My people, the Israelites, from Egypt."

At first Moses protested, saying, "Please, O Lord, I have never been a man of words. . . . I am slow of speech and slow of tongue." In the end, however, the Bible says, he obeyed God and made the long trek back to Egypt. Moses was now seen as a *prophet*, or a person who speaks for God. Moses walked the halls of the pharaoh's court once again. There he tried to convince

122

BACKGROUND INFORMATION

ABOUT THE STORY OF MOSES IN THE RUSHES
- Fearful of the growing number of Hebrews, the pharaoh ordered all newborn Hebrew boys be killed.
- To save her child, Moses' mother put him in a basket and placed it among the rushes, along the river bank where the pharaoh's daughter bathed each day. She had Moses' sister stay to watch what happened.
- The pharaoh's daughter arrived, heard the baby's cry, and had her handmaiden bring the basket to her.
- Taking pity on little Moses, she realized it was a Hebrew child. Moses' sister appeared and asked if she should get a nurse. When the pharaoh's daughter consented, the sister brought her own mother.

- Not knowing it was the baby's own mother, the pharaoh's daughter said, "Take this child and nurse it for me, and I will repay you."
- So it was that Moses was saved, his mother got to care for him as an infant, and he joined the pharaoh's household.

ABOUT THE PLAGUES The ten plagues: turning the water supply to blood; infestations of frogs, gnats, flies, and locusts; pestilence and boils; hail and darkness; and the killing of all the first-born of Egypt, including the pharaoh's first-born son. The term *Passover* comes from God's "passing over" the houses of the Hebrews when Egyptian first-born sons died.

the pharaoh to free the Israelite slaves. Moses wanted to lead them to safety.

The Bible describes how Moses, with the help of God, led the Israelite captives from Egypt. To this day Jews celebrate the Passover festival each year to remember their freedom from slavery.

The Torah

According to the Bible, Moses led the Israelites into the wilderness of eastern Egypt. There they wandered for 40 difficult years. Early in their journey the Israelites traveled to a mountain called Mount Sinai. There, the Bible says, God gave Moses five books of laws and teachings. These five books are the first books of the Bible. In Hebrew they are known as the Torah, which comes from the word meaning "to teach."

Some of these laws are very similar to laws that were common in Babylonia. Like the Code of Hammurabi, for example, the Torah also had laws that forbade stealing and hurting others. In one very important way, however, the Torah was different. The God of the Hebrews forbade them to worship any other gods. This belief in only one God became known as monotheism. It set the Israelites apart from the other peoples living in the Fertile Crescent.

Among the laws that God gave to Moses at Mount Sinai were the Ten Commandments. These commandments became the core of the Jewish religion and teachings. In what ways do the Ten Commandments differ from Hammurabi's laws?

MANY VOICES PRIMARY SOURCE

The Ten Commandments (Exodus 20:1–14).

I the Lord am your God. . . . You shall have no other gods besides Me.

You shall not make for yourself a sculptured image, or any likeness of what is in the heavens above, or on the earth below. . . . You shall not bow down to them or serve them.

You shall not swear falsely by the name of the Lord your God.

Remember the Sabbath [day of rest] and keep it holy.

Honor your father and your mother.

You shall not murder.

You shall not commit adultery.

You shall not steal.

You shall not bear false witness against your neighbor.

You shall not covet [desire] . . . anything that is your neighbor's.

The Jewish Museum, NYC

Many of the scrolls that hold the Torah are beautifully decorated. The Torah shown here is written in Hebrew.

123

Learning about The Torah Refer students to the map on p. 121 and have them trace Moses' route through the wilderness of eastern Egypt.

- *How long did the Hebrews wander through the desert?* (40 years)

- *What does the Bible say God gave Moses on Mount Sinai?* (the Torah, five books of laws and teachings)

- *What did the Torah demand of the Hebrew people toward God?* (that they worship Him as the one God)

- *How did this make the Hebrews' religion different from those of their Fertile Crescent neighbors?* (It was monotheistic; the others' were polytheistic. Help students contrast the two words, recalling that poly-means "many," mono- means "one.")

- *What part of the laws that Moses received became the core of Jewish teachings?* (the Ten Commandments)

★THINKING FURTHER: *Predicting Which elements of the Torah do you predict will have the greatest influence on beliefs of societies across the ancient world?* (probably monotheism and the Ten Commandments)

MANY VOICES

Discussing the PRIMARY SOURCE

Have students sit in pairs with one text open to this page, the other to Hammurabi's Code, p. 113. Have different students read each Commandment.

- *Which Commandments tell how the people should deal with God? How should they?* (The first four demand that people accept that there is only one God and that He must be honored and never dishonored.)

- *What do the rest concern?* (How people should treat one another.)

★THINKING FURTHER: *Compare and Contrast How would you compare and contrast the Ten Commandments with the Code of Ham-murabi?* (Students should see that the Code concentrates on how people treat each other and offers punishments for crimes rather than simply forbidding them.)

CITIZENSHIP★

UNDERSTANDING GOVERNMENT Explain to the class that the United States is built on a kind of covenant called a social contract. Citizens agree to accept the rules of an organized society so that they can be protected by law from being harmed by others.

SECOND-LANGUAGE SUPPORT

WORKING WITH PEERS Preteaching vocabulary may provide an extra benefit for second-language learners. Give heterogeneous groups of students a list of vocabulary words: *Judaism, Torah, monotheism, Ten Commandments, Sabbath,* and *Diaspora.* Have them discuss "best guess" meanings and share them with the class. As students find the words in context, they may alter definitions for a personal glossary.

THE KINGDOM OF ISRAEL

Read Moses' last words aloud.

★**THINKING FURTHER:** *Making Conclusions* **How does Moses' Instruction pave the way for the Hebrews to return to Canaan?** *(It spells out the covenant made with God: If you will revere and obey, God will see that you triumph.)*

Discussing A Nation of Israel
Connect the laws to the new kingdom.

● *How did "keeping holy the Sabbath" keep the Hebrews' covenant with God?* *(It obeyed a commandment.)*

● *Who were Kings David and Solomon?* *(father and son whose reigns brought Israel to greatness)*

★**THINKING FURTHER:** *Predicting* **Think of what followed the deaths of Sargon and Hammurabi. What do you predict for Israel after Solomon dies?** *(Breaking up is a possibility.)*

Investigating Exile to Babylonia
Note that the Western Wall in the photograph, also called the Wailing Wall, is part of the temple mound.

● *What happened after Solomon's death?* *(Israel split into Israel and Judah.)*

● *What happened to them?* *(Each was conquered; the people of Judah were exiled to Babylon.)*

★**THINKING FURTHER:** *Cause and Effect* **What effect would a Diaspora have on people?** *(perhaps sorrow and anger)*

Jerusalem is the capital of Israel and a religious center. Jews gather at the Western Wall to pray.

THE KINGDOM OF ISRAEL

After 40 years in the wilderness, the Israelites prepared to enter Canaan. The Bible says that Moses spoke to his people one last time before he died.

> This is the Instruction—the laws and the rule—that the Lord your God has commanded me to impart to you . . . so that you, your children, and your children's children may revere [worship] the Lord your God . . . to the end that you may long endure [survive].

The Bible says that after hearing Moses' final words, the Israelites crossed the Jordan River into the land of Canaan. There they defeated several kings and set up a nation of their own, called Israel. Now the Israelites were not only a people defined by their religious beliefs. They were a nation with a land, as well.

124

A Nation of Israel

For the people of Israel, the Torah was the basis of life and faith. It commanded people, for example, to "remember the Sabbath, and keep it holy." The Sabbath is the weekly day of rest, prayer, and study. It falls on Saturday. The instructions of the Torah reminded Israelites of their closeness to God. They continue to do so today.

According to the Bible, Israel became a powerful kingdom under the leadership of King David. He made the city of Jerusalem his capital about 1000 b.c. Jerusalem became even more important to Israel when David's son Solomon built a great temple there. Jerusalem became a center of both religious and political life.

Exile to Babylonia

After Solomon's death, about 928 b.c., the kingdom of Israel split into two kingdoms. The northern kingdom, Israel, was conquered by the Assyrians in 721 B.C. The southern kingdom was called Judah. This is where the name Jews comes from. The kingdom of Judah survived until 586 B.C. When Babylonian armies destroyed Jerusalem and Solomon's temple, many Jews were led away to Babylon. This would not be the last time the Jews were exiled, or forced to leave their homeland. The scattering of the Jews to many parts of the world is called the Diaspora (di AS pur uh).

WHY IT MATTERS

Alas!
Lonely sits the city
Once great with people! . . .
Take us back, O Lord, to Yourself,
And let us come back;
Renew our days as of old!

These words from the Bible record the despair felt by the Jews. However, even in the Diaspora, many Jews would continue to live by the Torah. They would also remember the covenant described in the Bible so many lifetimes earlier.

A Jewish boy studies the Torah in preparation for his bar mitzvah. After this ceremony he will be recognized as an adult.

125

Reviewing Facts and Ideas

MAIN IDEAS

- Trade and movement of people in the 1700s B.C. helped link major cities of the Fertile Crescent and Egypt.
- The Bible says Moses led the Israelites out of slavery in Egypt and passed on laws from God regarding how they should live.
- Monotheism—the belief in one God—set the Hebrews apart from other groups around them.
- Sacred writings, called the Torah, form the heart of Judaism.

THINK ABOUT IT

1. What role did Abraham play in the history of Judaism?
2. Why do Jews still celebrate Passover?
3. **FOCUS** How were Moses and the teachings of the Torah important to the beginnings of Judaism?
4. **THINKING SKILL** According to the Bible, what was the <u>cause</u> of the Israelites' move to Egypt?
5. **WRITE** Briefly compare and contrast polytheism and monotheism.

Discussing WHY IT MATTERS Remind the class of the Biblical quote on p. 114. Have them review it with the quote here.

- ***How are these two quotes related?*** *(Both bemoan the Hebrew exile.)*

★**THINKING FURTHER:** *Making Conclusions* **How does the quote here reflect God's covenant with Abraham?** *(It asks God to give the Jewish people another chance and resume His promise through Abraham.)*

3 CLOSE

MAIN IDEAS

Have students answer these questions.

- ***How did trade and movement link the Fertile Crescent and Egypt and aid cultural exchanges?*** *(Students should see that people on the move take both their goods and their ideas with them, spreading cultural values.)*

- ***How does the Bible say the Hebrews received the Torah and what did it teach them?*** *(God gave it to Moses on Mount Sinai to instruct the Hebrews in the laws to believe in and to live by.)*

- ***What is monotheism and where in the Ten Commandments does the Torah dictate it?*** *(the belief in only one God; in the first two Commandments)*

- ***How does the Torah form the heart of Judaism?*** *(It proclaims Judaism's major teachings and laws.)*

EVALUATE
✓ **Answers to Think About It**

1. He made a covenant with God to found the Hebrew nation and thus Judaism.
   From Generalizations

2. to remember how God helped them to escape enslavement in Egypt
   Make Conclusions

3. Moses was given the Torah, which contained the core of Judaism's teachings and laws.
   Make, Confirm, or Revise Predictions

4. poor crops and hunger in Canaan
   Cause and Effect

5. Paragraphs should make the distinction between many and one God.
   Compare and Contrast

Write About It Have students write a paragraph describing the values of Judaism that they believe have affected other societies the most.

MEETING INDIVIDUAL NEEDS

RETEACHING (Easy) Divide the class into five groups; assign each a subject from this list: Abraham, Moses, monotheism, the Ten Commandments, Solomon. Have each group review its subject and make a poster showing the role it played in Judaism's development.

EXTENSION (Average) Have students use the lesson and the time line on p. 120 to prepare their own illustrated time line of events in the founding of Judaism. Some events are Abraham's journey to Canaan, Egyptian captivity, Moses leading them from Egypt, Moses receiving the Torah on Mount Sinai, the Babylonian captivity, Solomon's reign.

ENRICHMENT (Challenging) Ask each student to do further research on one of the events on the Extension list above to learn more about the subject. Have them prepare an illustrated report of their findings and present it to the class.

DISCUSSING MAJOR EVENTS Help students use the time line to place major powers in Mesopotamia in the sequence in which they held power.

• **Who was the first major group to hold power in Mesopotamia and when did it control Mesopotamia?** (the Sumerians, in 3000 B.C.)

• **How much later did the Babylonian empire emerge there?** (1,200 years later, in 1800 B.C.)

• **How much later than that did the Babylonians capture Jerusalem?** (more than 1,200 years later, in 586 B.C.)

Answers to
THINKING ABOUT VOCABULARY

1. F, *Monotheism* is a belief in one god.

2. F, A *ziggurat* is a large building with a temple on its peak.

3. T

4. F, The *Diaspora* is the scattering of Jews to many parts of the world.

5. F, An area of elevated flatland is called a *plateau*.

Answers to
THINKING ABOUT FACTS

1. a crescent-shaped region in western Asia that stretches from Mesopotamia to the eastern Mediterranean and covers present-day Iraq, Syria, Lebanon, and Israel

2. Ishtar, goddess of love and war, and Enkí, god of water

3. by weakening and then conquering Sumer and by gaining control of the city-states around Babylon

4. in northern Mesopotamia; its rulers destroyed Babylon

Resource **REMINDER**
Practice and Project Book: *p. 28*
Assessment Book: *Chapter 5 Test*
Technology: *Videodisc*
Transparency: *Graphic Organizer, Main Idea Chart*

CHAPTER 5 REVIEW

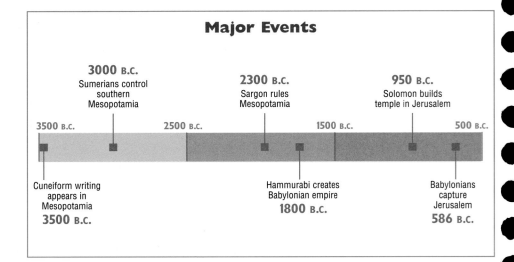

Major Events

- **3000 B.C.** Sumerians control southern Mesopotamia
- **2300 B.C.** Sargon rules Mesopotamia
- **950 B.C.** Solomon builds temple in Jerusalem

3500 B.C.   2500 B.C.   1500 B.C.   500 B.C.

- Cuneiform writing appears in Mesopotamia **3500 B.C.**
- Hammurabi creates Babylonian empire **1800 B.C.**
- Babylonians capture Jerusalem **586 B.C.**

THINKING ABOUT VOCABULARY

Each of the following statements contains an underlined vocabulary word. Number a sheet of paper from 1 to 5. Beside each number write **T** if the statement is true and **F** if the statement is false. If the statement is false, rewrite the sentence using the vocabulary word correctly.

1. <u>Monotheism</u> is a belief in many gods.
2. A <u>ziggurat</u> is a long, pointed weapon used by Sumerian warriors.
3. The system of writing invented in Sumer is <u>cuneiform</u>.
4. The <u>Diaspora</u> is the trip Jews made to live in Israel.
5. An area of fertile land near the coast that is good for farming is called a <u>plateau</u>.

THINKING ABOUT FACTS

1. What is the Fertile Crescent?
2. Who were two of the Sumerian gods?
3. How did Hammurabi create his powerful empire?
4. Where was Nineveh? Why was it famous?
5. According to the Bible, what was the covenant with Abraham? Why is it important in Jewish history?
6. Who invented the wheel? How was it used?
7. What did early Mesopotamian farmers grow?
8. What is the Hebrew Bible? Why is it important?
9. Who was Sargon and what did he accomplish?
10. According to the time line above, about how many centuries before Solomon did Hammurabi live? How many centuries before Hammurabi did Sargon live?

126

SECOND-LANGUAGE SUPPORT

GAME As a way of reviewing the major events, personalities, and concepts in this chapter, students can play a game similar to Twenty Questions. Divide students into two teams. Each team chooses one player at a time to represent a person, place, or vocabulary word from one of the lessons. Each item is written on an index card and pinned to the back of the player who is "It." Then members of the other team ask questions until they guess the word or words.

DRAMATIZATION The events in Lesson 3 lend themselves to Reader's Theater. Students can take turns reading sections of the text aloud while other students act out the events in pantomime and display the emotions through gesture and facial expressions.

THINK AND WRITE

WRITING COMPARISONS

Write a comparison of the governments and rulers of ancient Egypt and Sumer. How were they similar? How were they different?

WRITING AN EXPLANATION

Write two or three paragraphs about the Code of Hammurabi and the Ten Commandments. Explain why they are regarded as important steps forward in civilization.

WRITING BIOGRAPHICAL PARAGRAPHS

Write one paragraph about two of the following people: (1) Sargon, (2) Hammurabi, (3) Abraham, and (4) Moses.

APPLYING THINKING SKILLS

IDENTIFYING CAUSE AND EFFECT

1. What is a cause? What is an effect?

2. Can you think of an example from the chapter of an effect having two or more causes?

3. Name as many causes as you can for the rise of civilization in Mesopotamia.

4. Name two or more effects of the invention of the wheel. Can you think of another example from the chapter of a cause having more than one effect?

5. How do cause-and-effect connections help historians understand the past?

Summing Up the Chapter

Copy the main idea chart below on a separate piece of paper. Then review the chapter to find information for each category on the chart. When you have filled in the chart, use the information to answer the question "What contributions did the peoples of the Fertile Crescent make to civilization?"

MAIN IDEA	People of the Fertile Crescent made many contributions to civilization.		
People	**Writing Systems**	**Government/Law**	**Type of Religion**
Sumerians	cuneiform records	city-states	polytheism
Babylonians	cuneiform	Code of Hammurabi	polytheism
Israelites	Hebrew	Torah Ten Commandments	monotheism

127

SUGGESTIONS FOR SUMMING UP THE CHAPTER

Before students copy the main idea on their papers, have them read the main idea aloud and identify both the peoples and the categories of civilization they will investigate. Also have students identify the "head starts" already given them and encourage them to use these as clues to what to look for as they review the chapter for each category for each group. Possible answers appear on the reproduced text page above. When students have filled in the categories, you may want to discuss with them how they might organize their answer to the question posed—by describing the contributions that each people made? or by summarizing the contributions made by the different peoples taken together?

ASSESSING THINK AND WRITE: *For performance assessment, see Assessment Book, Chapter 5, pp. T58-T60.*

---

5. God promised to assign land to Abraham and his offspring and to be their God, a covenant that began Jewish history.

6. Ancient Mesopotamians probably invented the wheel and used it for transport, from carts to war chariots.

7. grains like wheat and barley and a variety of vegetables and fruits

8. A collection of books of Hebrew writings sacred to Jews and honored by Christians and Muslims; it is the record of the early Jewish religion and history.

9. a king of a Sumerian city state who briefly united Sumer's city-states into the world's first empire

10. 8.5 centuries (1800 B.C.–950 B.C.); 5 centuries (2300 B.C.–1800 B.C.)

Answers to APPLYING THINKING SKILLS

1. A cause makes something else happen; an effect is what happens as a result of a cause.

2. Just about any major development described in the chapter has two or more causes. (An example: Causes: Sumer's independent city-states shared a heritage and cuneiform writing was used throughout Sumer. Effect: Sargon could unify Sumer.) Accept any reasonable examples.

3. any condition that favored agriculture, any quality (such as hard-working, inventive, independent) of the people there

4. improved transportation, advances in weapons, development of factory machines, use in keeping any variety of machines running; again, any major development treated had more than one effect, accept any of them.

5. They help historians figure out why and how events happened.

 Technology CONNECTION

VIDEODISC

Enrich Chapter 5 with the *map of Ancient Mesopotamia* on the videodisc.

 6 Ancient India

Pages 128–157

CHAPTER OVERVIEW

In ancient India at around 2500 B.C., Mohenjo-Daro and Harappa were the most powerful cities along the Indus River. These cities declined with the arrival of Aryans, herders from the north. Both cultures were changed by this encounter and it led to the development of Hinduism.

GEO ADVENTURES DAILY GEOGRAPHY ACTIVITIES

Use **Geo Adventures** Daily Geography activities to assess students' understanding of geography skills.

CHAPTER PLANNING GUIDE

LESSON 1	LESSON 2	GEOGRAPHYSKILLS
SUGGESTED PACING: 2 DAYS	**SUGGESTED PACING: 2 DAYS**	**SUGGESTED PACING: 1 DAY**
Geography Of Ancient India pp. 130–133	**Early Indian Civilization** pp. 134–139	**Comparing Different Kinds Of Maps** pp. 140–141
CURRICULUM CONNECTIONS Links to Science, p. 131 Links to Math, p. 131	**CURRICULUM CONNECTIONS** Links to Math, p. 138	**RESOURCES** Practice and Project Book, p. 31 Transparency Map 12 ⓉTECHNOLOGY *Adventure Time!* CD-ROM
RESOURCES Practice and Project Book, p. 29 Desk Map ⓉTECHNOLOGY *Adventure Time!* CD-ROM	**CITIZENSHIP** Linking Past and Present, p. 136	
	FIELD TRIP Visit a Library, pp. 137	
	RESOURCES Practice and Project Book, p. 30 Desk Map ⓉTECHNOLOGY *Adventure Time!* CD-ROM	

Legacy	LESSON 4	CHAPTER REVIEW
SUGGESTED PACING: 1 DAY	**SUGGESTED PACING: 2 DAYS**	**SUGGESTED PACING: 1 DAY**
Indian Dance, pp. 148–149	**Beginnings Of Buddhism** pp. 150–155	pp. 156–157
FIELD TRIP Visit an Indian Dance Center, p. 149	**RESOURCES** Practice and Project Book, p. 33 Anthology, pp. 30–31 Desk Map Outline Map, p. 12	**RESOURCES** Practice and Project Book, p. 34 ⓉTECHNOLOGY Videodisc/Video Tape 2 Assessment Book: Chapter 6 Test Transparency: Graphic Organizer, Word Map

LEARNING STYLE: Visual GROUP 30 MINUTES OR LONGER

Make a Museum Exhibit

Objective: To start students thinking about ancient India.

Materials: scissors, mural paper, glue

1. Have students divide the mural paper into three sections labeled "Egypt," "Mesopotamia," and "India."
2. Each student should draw an object from Egypt or Mesopotamia and write a brief explanation of the object's significance. Attach the picture and explanation to the mural under the appropriate label.
3. Students can then attach pictures from ancient India with an announcement that the exhibit will open soon and a brief preview of what it may contain.

LESSON 3

SUGGESTED PACING: 2 DAYS

Beginnings Of Hinduism
pp. 142–147

CURRICULUM CONNECTIONS
Links to Language Arts, p. 143

CITIZENSHIP
Understanding Government, p. 145

RESOURCES
Practice and Project Book, p. 32
Anthology, pp. 26–27
Anthology, pp. 28, 29

SHELTERED INSTRUCTION

READING STRATEGIES & LANGUAGE DEVELOPMENT

Predict/Prefix, p. 130, Lesson 1
Making Conclusions/Indo-European Languages, p. 134, Lesson 2
Cause and Effect/Synonym, p. 140, Skills Lesson
Main Idea and Detail/Homophones, p. 142, Lesson 3
Problem Solving/Suffix, p. 150, Lesson 4

SECOND-LANGUAGE SUPPORT

Using Props, p. 132
Language Concepts, p. 136
Graphic Organizers, pp. 144, 153
Mnemonic Devices, p. 156

MEETING INDIVIDUAL NEEDS

Reteaching, Extension, Enrichment, pp. 133, 139, 141, 147, 149, 155
McGraw-Hill Adventure Book

ASSESSMENT OPPORTUNITIES

Practice and Project Book, pp. 29–34
Write About It, pp. 133, 139, 147, 149, 155
Assessment Book: Assessing Think and Write, pp. T61–T63; Chapter 6 Tests: Content, Skills, Writing

Introducing the Chapter

By now students know that people follow a pattern in developing a civilization. Invite them to see if this holds true in the next river valley they will study. Have them locate the Indian subcontinent on the globe map and on a wall map.

THINKING ABOUT HISTORY AND GEOGRAPHY

Have students read the text on this page to introduce themselves to some of the steps in ancient India's march toward civilization. Remind them that as they read each panel, they should follow its trail back to the map to locate it.

6000 B.C. INDUS RIVER VALLEY

Have students locate the Indus River on the map.

- **On what continent is the Indus River Valley located?** (Asia)

- **What step in the development of civilization is apparent here? When did it occur?** (The people have begun farming; 6000 B.C.)

> ★**THINKING FURTHER:** *Making Conclusions* **How have they taken a first step toward civilization?** (They are providing the necessary food supply.)

2500 B.C. MOHENJO-DARO

Have students note development of specialization.

- **How much time has elapsed since the last panel?** (3,500 years)

- **What stage has Indian civilization reached?** (Specialties have developed, creating crafts.)

Resource **REMINDER**

Technology: *Videodisc/Video Tape 1*

CHAPTER 6

Ancient India

THINKING ABOUT HISTORY AND GEOGRAPHY

Indian civilization begins around 6000 **B.C.** in the Indus River valley, in what is today Pakistan. Mohenjo-Daro and Harappa were the most powerful cities in the valley until the arrival of horse-riding herders from the north. Their meeting changed both cultures and led to the development of a religion called Hinduism. India later became the birthplace of Buddhism as well.

6000 B.C.

INDUS RIVER VALLEY

People begin growing rice

2500 B.C.

MOHENJO-DARO

Craftworkers have the time and skill to make beautiful pottery

1900 B.C.

KHYBER PASS

After crossing the Hindu Kush, Aryans win control of the Indus Valley

128

BACKGROUND INFORMATION

LINKING THE MAP AND THE TIME LINE

- The Indus River Valley fostered settlement far back into prehistory, as long ago as 70,000 years. Main routes into it through the mountains included both the Khyber Pass and the Bolan Pass, somewhat south of the Khyber Pass.

- Mohenjo-Daro and other centers of Indus River Valley civilization were completely unknown until this century. It was not until 1922 that the world learned that such a civilization had even existed. It was then that an archaeologist digging in what is today Pakistan came up with a few bricks and seals that began the uncovering of the heretofore unknown civilization.

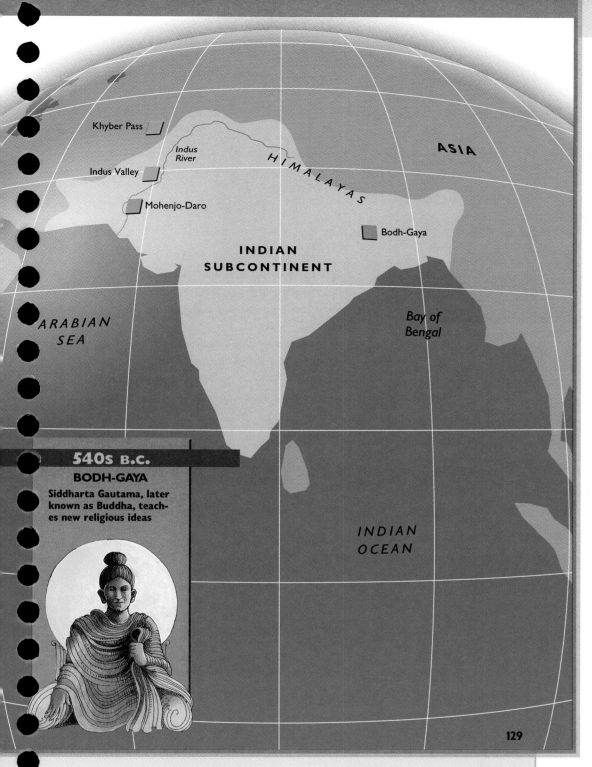

Khyber Pass

Indus
River

HIMALAYAS

ASIA

Indus Valley

Mohenjo-Daro

Bodh-Gaya

INDIAN
SUBCONTINENT

ARABIAN
SEA

Bay of
Bengal

540s B.C.
BODH-GAYA
Siddharta Gautama, later
known as Buddha, teach-
es new religious ideas

INDIAN
OCEAN

129

★**THINKING FURTHER:** *Making
Conclusions* **How does the 2500
B.C. stage show that farming in
the Indus River Valley has been
successful?** *(Farmers are producing enough to create surpluses,
which are necessary for specialties
to develop.)*

1900 B.C. KHYBER PASS

Explain to the class that the Hindu
Kush are rugged mountains that can be
crossed only through breaks between
mountains, like the Khyber Pass.

● *Where is the Khyber Pass located
in relation to Mohenjo-Daro?*
(north, to the west of the Indus River)

★**THINKING FURTHER:** *Making
Connections* **Who do you suppose the Aryans are?** *(They must
be the "horse-riding herders from
the north," mentioned in the text on
this page.)*

540s B.C. BODH-GAYA

Bodh-Gaya remains an important shrine
of Buddhism in this century.

● *How much time has elapsed since
people began farming in the Indus
River Valley?* *(6000 B.C. minus about
540 B.C. = about 5,460 years)*

● *What step in civilization does this
panel reflect?* *(the development of
organized religion)*

★**THINKING FURTHER:** *Making
Conclusions* **What tells you that
ancient Indian civilization has
spread beyond the Indus River
Valley?** *(The map shows that
Bodh-Gaya is far east of the Indus
River.)*

Technology CONNECTION

VIDEODISC/VIDEO TAPE 1
Enrich Chapter 6 with the *Ancient India*
segments on the videodisc.

Search Frame 27953 Side A

BACKGROUND INFORMATION

LINKING THE MAP AND THE TIMELINE
● The Khyber Pass is the most famous pass through the incredibly
rugged Hindu Kush. The Khyber Pass is 33 miles long, 15 feet to 3
miles wide, and 3,500 feet high. It has a long history as a trade route
as well as an invasion route. Today, it links Pakistan and Afghanistan.
● Bodh-Gaya, in northeastern India, is the Buddhist site where, according to tradition, Siddharta Gautama received the enlightenment
that made him Buddha. The remains of a railing there mark the path
he walked after his enlightenment.

LESSON 1
PAGES 130–133

Lesson Overview
As in Egypt and Mesopotamia, river floods helped civilization to develop in the Indus River Valley.

Lesson Objectives
★ Locate the *Indus River* and trace its flow.

★ Describe the terrain through which the Indus flows.

★ Explain ways farmers used the Indus to grow crops.

⭐ 1 PREPARE

MOTIVATE Ask a student to read out loud the *Read Aloud*. Encourage students to close their eyes and try to picture the scenes described. What do these lines describe? (the origin and flow of the Indus River)

SET PURPOSE Have the class read the *Read to Learn* question and preview *Vocabulary* words. Then follow the suggested *Reading Strategy* below.

⭐ 2 TEACH

Understanding THE BIG PICTURE
As students read this section, have them use their fingers to trace the flow of the Indus on the map on p. 131.

● **What section of the Indus is shown in the photo?** *(the section in the mountain peaks)*

● **What words in the poem refer to a "river the color of cocoa"?** *("long, brown line down to the sea")*

★**THINKING FURTHER:** *Compare and Contrast* **In what ways is the Indus River like the Nile, the Tigris, and the Euphrates?** *(All carry silt and water that make farming possible)*

Resource REMINDER
Practice and Project Book: *p. 29*
Desk Map
 Technology: *Adventure Time!* CD-ROM
Outline Map

GEOGRAPHY OF ANCIENT INDIA

Focus Activity

READ TO LEARN
What did the Indus River contribute to a new civilization?

VOCABULARY
subcontinent

PLACES
Indus River
Himalayas
Indus Plain

READ ALOUD
Boulders [ground] to silt by water . . .
deep, round valleys, robed in cloud
against the crag-carving sunlight on
[mountain] peaks . . .
And centuries of cloud have melted, valleys
have sweated froth-white cascades
to draw that long, brown line down to the sea.

This is how Pakistani poet Salman Tarik Kureshi describes the Indus River.

THE BIG PICTURE
As the poem above describes, the Indus River begins in the snow-covered mountains of South Asia. It flows through what are today China, India, and Pakistan. In India and Pakistan other rivers join the Indus as it flows south. The silt it carries makes the river the color of cocoa. During spring floods this silt is spread throughout the Indus Valley.

The silt deposits and river water make farming possible in the otherwise dry environment of western South Asia. For this reason the Indus is similar to the Nile, Tigris, and Euphrates rivers. They have all been great givers of life to people for thousands of years. In fact, the Indus Valley was one of the first places in the world where farming developed. Archaeologists have found evidence of farming communities there that have been dated to around 6000 B.C.

130

🛡 SDAIE SUPPORT
SHELTERED INSTRUCTION
READING STRATEGIES & LANGUAGE DEVELOPMENT

PREDICT Explain to students that making and revising predictions as they read is a good way to make sense of the text. Have volunteers explain what the Read to Learn question asks. [What did the Indus River contribute to a new civilization?] Invite students to brainstorm responses, based on what they have already learned about Egypt and Mesopotamia. Jot their ideas down, and encourage them to revise their predictions as they read this lesson. **[SDAIE STRATEGY:** BRIDGING/SCHEMA BUILDING**]**

PREFIX This lesson describes India as a "subcontinent." Tell students to look up the prefix *sub* in a dictionary. Have them discuss its various meanings and choose the one used in *subcontinent* ("secondary portion of"). Help them see that India is a "secondary portion of" the continent of Asia, a subdivision of it.

MAP WORK: **1.** Arabian Sea, Indian Ocean, Bay of Bengal **2.** east
*The river would affect farming, trade, and transportation.

CHAPTER 6 • LESSON 1

A GREAT RIVER IS BORN

The Indus River begins as an icy stream high in the world's tallest mountains. These mountains are the Himalayas (hihm uh LAY uz). You have probably heard of their highest peak, Mount Everest. It stands 29,028 feet tall. The towering Himalayas separate the Indian subcontinent from much of Asia. A subcontinent is a large landmass that is geographically separated from the rest of a continent. Find the Indian subcontinent, the Himalayas, and the Indus River on the map on this page.

Long Journey of the Indus

In the spring the Indus swells with melting snow. It flows south to the Arabian Sea on an 1,800-mile journey through what is today mainly Pakistan. As the river passes through the Himalayas, it rushes through vast canyons. Some of these canyons are three miles deep! Imagine dropping a coin straight from the top of one canyon. It would take about 90 seconds for it to hit the river below. That same coin would hit the floor of America's Grand Canyon in 30 seconds.

The Indus flows swiftly down the mountains until it is joined by other rivers. Locate these on the map. These rivers join the Indus in the northern part of the dry, desert-like

This palace at Stok, in Northern India, nestles in the Himalayas.

Indus Plain. During the spring flood season, the enlarged river spills across the plain, spreading fertile silt.

The Indus actually carries twice as much silt as the mighty Nile in Egypt. Like the Nile, the Indus branches into a huge delta before it reaches the sea.

Think about what you have learned about other river valleys. How do you think the river might have affected people centuries ago in the Indus Valley?*

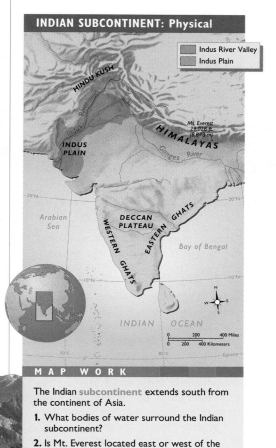

INDIAN SUBCONTINENT: Physical

Indus River Valley
Indus Plain

HINDU KUSH

Mt. Everest
29,028 ft.
(8,848 m)

HIMALAYAS

INDUS PLAIN

Indus

Ganges River

Arabian Sea

DECCAN PLATEAU

WESTERN GHATS

EASTERN GHATS

Bay of Bengal

INDIAN OCEAN

20°N

20°N

10°N

10°N

0° Equator

70°E

80°E

N
W   E
S

0   200   400 Miles
0   200   400 Kilometers

M A P   W O R K

The Indian subcontinent extends south from the continent of Asia.

1. What bodies of water surround the Indian subcontinent?

2. Is Mt. Everest located east or west of the Indus River?

131

A GREAT RIVER IS BORN

On a map, have students locate the Indian *subcontinent* and the *Himalayas*.

Discussing the Long Journey of the Indus Encourage students to use both the text and the map on this page.

● *Where does the Indus River have its source?* (in the Himalayas)

● *How does it become a more powerful river as it reaches the Indus Plain?* (Other rivers empty into it.)

● *How would you describe the Indus Plain?* (dry, desertlike)

● *Why does the Indus flood the plain?* (Spring rains make it flow over its banks.)

★THINKING FURTHER: *Predicting* **How do you think the river might have affected people centuries ago in the Indus Valley?** *(They probably used the river to farm the plain.)*

More **MAP WORK**

Have students refer again to the map.

● *What other mountains separate the Indian subcontinent from the rest of Asia?* (the Hindu Kush)

● *How and where does the Indus form a delta?* (It carries silt south to the Arabian Sea.)

★THINKING FURTHER: *Cause and Effect* **What effect could high mountains have had on relations between people of the Indian subcontinent and other people of Asia?** *(Mountains may have kept them apart.)*

AGRICULTURE AND THE INDUS RIVER

Encourage students to recall the irrigation methods used by other people so that they could fully use their rivers.

- **What irrigation methods did the Indus Valley farmers use?** *(They dug canals and constructed walls.)*

- **What advantage did climate give the Indus farmers that the Egyptians and Mesopotamians did not have?** *(Their climate allowed them to grow two crops a year, not just one.)*

- **What animals did the Indus farmers domesticate and what did they use them for?** *(They domesticated cattle and water buffalo that pulled their plows and wagons, making it possible to farm larger fields.)*

- **Which of the Indus farmer's crops would have helped feed people? clothe them?** *(Food: wheat, barley, beans, sesame, rice, bananas, black pepper, mustard. Clothing: cotton.)*

Technology CONNECTION

ADVENTURE TIME! CD-ROM
Enrich this lesson with the *India* segment on the *Adventure Time!* CD-ROM.

Discussing Working with the Environment Review the difficulties that Indus Valley farmers met.

- **What challenges did the Indus farmers have to face?** *(floods that destroyed fields and villages, wild animals, animals and birds that ate their crops)*

- **How did Indus farmers protect their crops?** *(with slings and clay balls)*

★**THINKING FURTHER:** *Classifying*
How would you classify ways in which animals are the friends of human beings and other ways they are enemies of humans? *(Friends: pets, beasts of burden. Enemies: threats to lives and to crops and livestock.)*

The Indus is still an important source of water for agriculture. These children (left) are washing domestic water buffaloes. A woman in the Indus Valley harvests vegetables (above).

AGRICULTURE AND THE INDUS RIVER

Farmers began planting crops in the rich soil of the Indus Valley around 6000 B.C. This was about 1,000 years before farming began in Egypt. Indus Valley farmers grew wheat, barley, beans, and sesame. Sesame is a seed used for cooking and for making oil. These farmers also grew some of the world's first rice, banana, black pepper, mustard, and cotton crops. In time they domesticated cattle and water buffalo. With animals to pull plows and wagons, farmers could plant larger fields.

Farmers built irrigation canals to bring water from the river to their crops. Thanks to the Indus Valley's hot climate, crops grew quickly. Archaeologists believe that this made it possible for farmers to plant and harvest twice a year.

In the fall, farmers planted wheat and barley. They harvested just before the melting snow caused spring floods. Then farmers quickly planted fields of cotton and sesame. Dirt walls were constructed to protect these crops from the Indus flood. By the next fall, crops were ready for another harvest.

Working with the Environment
Successful harvests did not always come easily in the Indus River valley. Earth and rock walls could not always hold back the floodwaters. Fields and entire villages could sometimes be swept away.

Wildlife in the valley also brought problems. Tigers, jackals, and wild pigs could threaten lives. Deer and such

132

BACKGROUND INFORMATION

ABOUT TIGERS, JACKALS, AND WILD PIGS
- Tigers are night-stalkers, preferring large prey. They bring down their prey after a brief, fast rush at it.
- Jackals are meat-eating members of the dog family. Also night hunters, they seek small mammals and fowl. They also eat carrion.
- Wild pigs will eat anything, and their upward tusks and ability to run fast make them dangerous.

SECOND-LANGUAGE SUPPORT

USING PROPS Indus Valley crops and animals may be unfamiliar. Bring in various kinds of barley, sesame seeds, rice, beans, and bananas. Display pictures of tigers, jackals, wild pigs, deer, and parakeets. Encourage second-language learners to write labels for them.

birds as wild parakeets often ate farmers' crops. Archaeologists think that ancient Indus farmers used slings and clay balls to scare birds from fields and fruit trees. Farm children in India and Pakistan today often have the chore of scaring away birds. Perhaps children in ancient times had this job too.

WHY IT MATTERS

As in ancient Egypt and Mesopotamia, civilization in the Indus River valley developed along a river. The civilization could not have survived without the crops that farmers grew in the fertile valley soil. By about 3000 B.C. villages and small towns had grown throughout the valley. Within 300 years cities would develop along the mighty river. In the next lesson you will read about life in one of those cities.

Chili peppers are an important crop in India. Millions are bought and sold in markets like this one.

✓ Reviewing Facts and Ideas

MAIN IDEAS

- The Indus River brings water and silt that make farming possible.
- The Indus begins in the Himalayas and crosses desert-like plains before reaching the Arabian Sea.
- Ancient Indus Valley farmers irrigated their fields and built dirt walls to protect their crops and homes from terrible floods.

THINK ABOUT IT

1. Compare the Indus and the Nile rivers. How are they similar?
2. What made it possible for Indus Valley farmers to harvest crops two times a year?
3. **FOCUS** In what ways did the Indus River help farmers? In what ways could it hurt them?
4. **THINKING SKILL** You have now learned about three early river-valley civilizations. Based on what you have read, make a _generalization_ about how rivers shaped the lives of early people. On what facts did you base your generalization?
5. **GEOGRAPHY** Draw a map of the Indian subcontinent and the Himalayas. Trace the routes of the Indus and Ganges rivers.

133

Discussing WHY IT MATTERS Help students review the building blocks of civilization.

- _Why did civilization first develop along rivers?_ (Rivers made agriculture possible.)
- _Why was agriculture necessary for civilization to develop?_ (The development of civilization demanded a settled population that could feed itself and produce surpluses.)

3 CLOSE

MAIN IDEAS
Have students write their answers to these questions on a piece of paper and exchange papers with a partner to correct them.

- _How did the Indus River make farming possible?_ (It provided the floods needed to provide water and silt for the Indus Plain.)
- _What kinds of terrain does the Indus River cross from source to mouth?_ (high mountains, deep canyons, desert-like plain, delta)
- _Why did the people of the Indus Valley have to build irrigation canals and walls?_ (to water their crops and to protect their homes from flood waters)

EVALUATE
✓ **Answers to Think About It**
1. Both begin in mountains, carry silt, overflow their banks, and create deltas as they empty into the sea. _Make Analogies_
2. the climate _Make Inferences_
3. It gave them the water and fertile soil they needed; it sometimes destroyed their homes and villages. _Make Inferences_
4. Generalizations should reflect the idea that rivers provided the water and soil for agriculture, the basis of their economies. _Form Generalizations_
5. Maps should show the routes as they appear on the map on p. 131. _Movement_

Write About It Have students picture a visit to the Indus River valley about 6000 B.C. Tell them to write a postcard home describing what they see there.

MEETING INDIVIDUAL NEEDS

RETEACHING (Easy) Tell students to draw a flow chart that shows the flow of the Indus River from the Himalayas, through canyons, across a dry plain, and into the Arabian Sea.

EXTENSION (Average) Tell students to review the lesson to identify when planting and harvesting were done during the two-crop Indus Valley year. Then have them make up a calendar, using our 12 months, to show approximately when each growing season began and ended.

ENRICHMENT (Challenging) Encourage students to choose any aspect of the Himalayas—their height, how they were formed, efforts to climb them, the "abominable snowman," or anything else—and have them do further research about it. Tell them to prepare an oral report and visual materials to present their findings to the class.

LESSON 2
PAGES 134–139

Lesson Overview
The Harappan civilization developed in the Indus Valley 4,500 years ago and was in contact with Egypt and Mesopotamia.

Lesson Objectives
★ Enumerate the achievements of Harappan civilization.

★ Explain how geography helped to destroy Harappan civilization.

★ Describe the migration of the Aryans into the Indus River valley.

1 PREPARE

MOTIVATE After you read the *Read Aloud* to the class, call students' attention to the fact that the civilization they are about to study was totally unknown until very recent times. How many other civilizations might be out there still waiting to be discovered? Would any students want to go looking for them?

SET PURPOSE Encourage students to concentrate on the civilization in this lesson and to look for answers to the *Read to Learn* question. Draw attention to the clay sculpture from Mohenjo-Daro. Preview the *Vocabulary*.

2 TEACH

Understanding THE BIG PICTURE

● *Consider Egypt, Mesopotania, and the Indus Valley. About which one of these civilizations do we know least and why?* (the Indus civilization because we cannot read their writing and have few artifacts)

★ **THINKING FURTHER:** *Making Conclusions Judging from the map on page R11, in what two ways could people have reached Mesopotamia from the Indus Valley?* (either by sea from the Arabian Sea and into the Persian Gulf or by land west across towering mountains)

Resource REMINDER
Practice and Project Book: *p. 30*
 Technology: *Adventure Time!* CD-ROM

	2500 B.C.		1500 B.C.	1000 B.C.	500 B.C.

Karachi Museum, Pakistan

EARLY INDIAN CIVILIZATION

Focus Activity

READ TO LEARN
What was life like in the ancient cities of the Indus River valley?

VOCABULARY
citadel
migrate

PLACES
Harappa
Mohenjo-Daro

READ ALOUD
In 1921 archaeologists gathered around a huge dirt mound on the southern plains of the Indus Valley. They knew remains of the past lay hidden beneath the mound. Earlier visitors had found artifacts there. But how old were the remains? What would they reveal about how Indian people lived long ago?

As the archaeologists dug down, the ruins of a great city began to appear. A new understanding about India's ancient past had begun.

THE BIG PICTURE
Over 1,000 miles separate the Indus River valley from Iraq, the region once known as Mesopotamia. This distance did not keep people from traveling between the two regions over 4,000 years ago, though. Like merchants from Egypt, Indian merchants traded goods in Mesopotamian cities.

Of these three ancient civilizations—Mesopotamia, Egypt, and the Indus River valley—the least is known about the Indus River valley civilization. One reason that historians know less about this culture is that experts have not been able to figure out how to read ancient Indian writing. Another reason is that few Indus artifacts and remains have been found. Despite these limits, historians have pieced together a picture of what ancient life may have been like for the people along the Indus River.

134

SHELTERED INSTRUCTION

READING STRATEGIES & LANGUAGE DEVELOPMENT

MAKING CONCLUSIONS Remind students they make conclusions by using facts in the text and prior knowledge. Have students read paragraph two of *The Big Picture* and find facts to support the conclusion in the last sentence. [Experts cannot read ancient Indian writing; few Indus artifacts have been found.] Arrange students in teams to make conclusions, one team per page. [**SDAIE STRATEGY:** TEXT RE-PRESENTATION/METACOGNITIVE DEVELOPMENT]

INDO-EUROPEAN LANGUAGES Sanskrit, mentioned on p. 135, is an ancient member of the world's largest family of languages, the Indo-European family. Languages in this family have been spoken for more than 5,000 years. Modern Indo-European languages include English and most European languages, as well as Hindi, Bengali, Persian, and Urdu. Like Latin, Sanskrit is no longer a living language.

A CIVILIZATION IN THE INDUS VALLEY

The city described in the Read Aloud is called Harappa (huh RAH puh). The people who lived nearby named the ruins after an Indian god. Archaeologists have no way of knowing what early people living along the Indus called themselves. Therefore, the entire ancient Indus Valley civilization is called Harappan civilization. It lasted from about 2500 B.C. until about 1600 B.C.

One year after the city of Harappa was uncovered, archaeologists found a city almost exactly like it about 400 miles to the south. The local name for it was Mohenjo-Daro (moh HEN joh DAH roh), which means "Mound of the Dead" in Sanskrit. Sanskrit is an ancient Indian language. Locate the ancient cities of Harappa and Mohenjo-Daro on the map on this page.

A City Along the Indus

The city of Mohenjo-Daro was not small. Archaeologists believe that as many as 40,000 people once lived there! Dozens of streets crisscrossed each other. Larger avenues were paved with tan-colored bricks. The streets that crossed them were narrower and were usually left unpaved.

Hundreds of sturdy brick houses lined the streets of Mohenjo-Daro. Most homes were small, one-room buildings. Others were several stories high. Some even had such luxuries as airy courtyards or balconies.

At the west end of the city stood a massive fort, or citadel (SIT uh dul). Surrounding this citadel were thick walls that protected against both floods and enemy attacks. Next to the citadel was an enormous grain warehouse. Judging from its size, farmers around Mohenjo-Daro must have been very successful at growing barley and wheat.

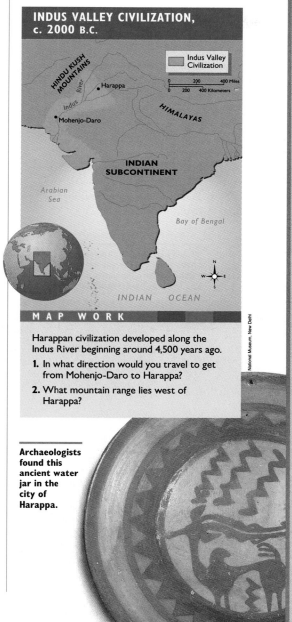

INDUS VALLEY CIVILIZATION, c. 2000 B.C.

Indus Valley Civilization

HINDU KUSH MOUNTAINS
Harappa
Indus River
Mohenjo-Daro
HIMALAYAS
INDIAN SUBCONTINENT
Arabian Sea
Bay of Bengal
INDIAN OCEAN

0 200 400 Miles
0 200 400 Kilometers

National Museum, New Delhi

MAP WORK

Harappan civilization developed along the Indus River beginning around 4,500 years ago.

1. In what direction would you travel to get from Mohenjo-Daro to Harappa?
2. What mountain range lies west of Harappa?

Archaeologists found this ancient water jar in the city of Harappa.

A CIVILIZATION IN THE INDUS VALLEY

Explain to the class that ancient cities are frequently buried and appear as mounds on the horizon. They truly have been covered by "the sands of time." Have students identify the period that Harappan civilization flourished (2500 B.C. to 1600 B.C.) and review events in Egypt and Mesopotamia at that time.

More
MAP WORK

Refer students to the map on this page and have them locate *Harappa* and *Mohenjo-Daro*.

● **Where are these cities in relation to each other?** (Harappa is 400 miles northeast of Mohenjo-Daro.)

★**THINKING FURTHER:** *Making Conclusions* **Why would you say that geography positioned both of them well?** (Both are located along the Indus River system and probably had good farming conditions.)

Discussing A City Along the Indus As students answer each question, ask them what evidence historians must have found to draw the conclusion.

● **How large a population did Mohenjo-Daro have?** (About 40,000; historians must have found signs of housing for that many people.)

● **How was Mohenjo-Daro laid out as a city?** (On a grid of streets and avenues; signs of a grid must remain.)

● **What material did people in Mohenjo-Daro use to pave streets and construct housing?** (Bricks; bricks must have been found, and some brick remains of buildings and streets must still be at the site.)

● **What were probably the largest buildings in the city and what were they used for?** (A thick-walled citadel *to withstand floods and enemy attacks and a warehouse to store grain; enough of the foundations must be left to reveal them.*)

★**THINKING FURTHER:** *Making Conclusions* **What conclusion can you draw from the size of the grain warehouse?** (*Farmers produced very large surpluses.*)

BACKGROUND INFORMATION

ABOUT HARAPPAN GRIDS, CITADELS, AND GRANARIES

● The grids for both Harappa and Mohenjo-Daro were rectangles measuring about three miles around.

● The citadels stood about as high as a modern five-story building.

● The granaries covered nearly 3,000 square yards. They were also called treasuries because the grain they stored served as currency.

● In 1865, before its importance was recognized, the remains of the granary at Harappa were destroyed by British railway builders.

LIFE IN MOHENJO-DARO

Ask students to try to picture their own community 4,000 years from now. What buildings might future archaeologists uncover? What other artifacts? What might they decide about them?

★**THINKING FURTHER:** *Using Visuals* **What can you determine from the pictures on this page?** *(Students may conclude that Mohenjo-Daro was a complex city with sturdy buildings and specialized occupations.)*

Discussing City Planning Encourage students to discuss why city planning is important. Help them appreciate the organization needed for creating wells and a sewer system, paved streets, and public buildings.

● ***What evidence can you find to conclude that Harappan civilization had strong government?*** *(Signs of city planning such as standard-size bricks, a sewer system, and a bath house required strong government.)*

● ***What evidence suggests that religion was important in Mohenjo-Daro?*** *(The great bath may have had religious significance for ritual cleansing.)*

★**THINKING FURTHER:** *Making Generalizations* **What generalizations can you make about how city planning improved life in Mohenjo-Daro?** *(It made it easier to get around and made the city cleaner; it provided public buildings for government, religion, and farm surpluses.)*

LIFE IN MOHENJO-DARO

Suppose that you are an archaeologist living 4,000 years in the future. You have just stumbled upon the ruins of a small North American city dating back to the A.D. 1990s. You uncover buildings and dusty artifacts. You find machines and bits of plastic labels. You cannot read the city's languages, though. How much will you be able to understand about everyday life in this city? How many conclusions will you be able to make about the culture of the North American civilization?

Archaeologists studying ancient Harappan civilization have faced these kinds of challenges since the early 1900s. Yet they have succeeded in making some conclusions about what life was like for ancient Harappans. Many of their conclusions are based on remains found in Mohenjo-Daro.

City Planning

One of the most striking things about Mohenjo-Daro is the exactness of the measurements used in making and building things. Bricklayers used thousands of same-sized bricks to pave streets and build homes. City engineers dug wells throughout the city. They also created a sewer system, complete with "manholes," to keep the city clean.

Projects like this need much planning. Therefore, historians believe

Stone seals (right) and other artifacts have taught archaeologists about Mohenjo-Daro. An artist depicted daily life in the city (below).

Mohenjo-Daro must have had a strong government. Harappa had almost the same layout as Mohenjo-Daro. Therefore, historians conclude that the Indus River valley also must have had a strong central government.

On top of Mohenjo-Daro's citadel are the remains of a large, pillar-supported building. Archaeologists think it may have served as a "city hall," because it overlooked the city. Next door was a building that housed a pool-sized bath. The bath may have had religious importance. Cleansing practices later became a key part of Indian religions. The artwork at left shows what Mohenjo-Daro may have looked like in 2000 B.C.

Working in Mohenjo-Daro

Harappan builders, engineers, and craftworkers were highly skilled. Archaeologists have found remains of their work in the workshops that lined city avenues.

Skilled workers carved beautiful figures into small squares of stone. These stone squares were probably used as seals for marking belongings. Potters made water jars, cooking bowls, and other containers. These were covered with colorful paintings. Metalworkers made everything from copper fish hooks to razors. They also made fine statues of people cast in bronze. Perhaps for the first time anywhere, weavers made cloth from cotton.

As in other ancient cities, such specialization meant that Harappan farmers produced surplus food. Surplus grain was stored in a great warehouse. Perhaps, as in ancient Egypt, government workers collected grain from farmers as taxes. The stored grain could later be measured out again, possibly as payment to city workers.

The once-busy city of Mohenjo-Daro is empty today. These women climb steps that are thousands of years old.

Harappan Trade

Historians are not sure of the exact trade routes used by ancient Harappans. However, historians do know that Harappan merchants traded with neighbors both near and far.

From artifacts, archaeologists know that Harappans sold stone seals in what is today Iran. They brought home blue stones called lapis lazuli from what is today Afghanistan. Beadmakers made necklaces from stones brought from what is today India. These and other goods were then traded in faraway Mesopotamia.

The long journey to Mesopotamia was probably made in small sailboats. From the Indus River delta, the boats headed west along the southern coast of Asia. The sailors may have taken along field birds such as crows and swallows. When set free, the birds would fly toward land.

137

Discussing Working in Mohenjo-Daro Develop an understanding of the skill required for work in Mohenjo-Daro.

● **What specialized jobs had developed to help create Harappan civilization?** (engineers, stone carvers, potters, painters, metalworkers, bronze casters, cotton weavers)

★**THINKING FURTHER: Cause and Effect How might historians have used cause and effect to conclude that there was probably taxation in Harappan civilization?** (Help students see Cause: government workers had to be paid; Effect: means—taxes—needed to pay them.)

Investigating Harappan Trade Have students find Afghanistan and Iran on page R10 and locate trade routes to Mesopotamia on the map on page 138.

● **Why might it have been easier to trade with Mesopotamia than with Afghanistan and Iran?** (There was a water route to the former; there were high mountains to cross to the latter.)

★**THINKING FURTHER: Making Conclusions What evidence must historians have found to tell them where Harappan merchants traded?** (They probably found Harappan goods in other locations or they knew the sources of the stones.)

Technology CONNECTION

ADVENTURE TIME! CD-ROM
Enrich this lesson with the *time lines* activity on the *Adventure Time!* CD-ROM.

BACKGROUND INFORMATION

ABOUT HARAPPAN SEALS AND INDUS WRITING

● The motif of each seal is usually an animal (though occasionally a god) and four to eight pictographs. Not surprisingly, the animals—bulls, elephants, tigers, and antelopes—were found in the Indus Valley and people there had high regard for them.

● The high regard in which the Indus Valley people held bulls, and indeed all cattle, presaged cattle's importance in India to this day. The Hindu religion still forbids killing a cow—the origin of the term "sacred cow."

● In all, about 250 different pictographs have been identified in Indus writing. The longest single inscription contains only 17 pictographs.

FIELD TRIP

Try to plan a class trip to your local library or school library. Arrange with the librarian to acquaint students with standing files, computer files, and the *Readers' Guide to Periodical Literature* to help research recent events. If a field trip is not possible, you may want to make copies of some sample pages and have students practice using them.

NEWCOMERS

Help students to recognize that geography can be a two-edged sword.

● **What causes might have destroyed Harappan civilization?** *(Historians blame geography—an event such as an earthquake may have triggered a change in the Indus River as well as great floods that destroyed the agricultural base for Harappan civilization.)*

★THINKING FURTHER: *Making Conclusions* **Why would it be fair to say that geography can make or break a civilization?** *(Possible answer: Geographical features of the Indus River Valley—flood waters, silt, plain—gave the people the agricultural base to develop a civilization and then geographic events—perhaps an earthquake, a change in river course, or floods—helped destroy it.)*

More MAP WORK

Refer students to the map.

● **Who were the Aryans?** *(cattle and sheep herders from central Asia who migrated into the Indus Valley)*

● **From which direction did they migrate into the Indus Valley?** *(from the northwest over the Hindu Kush)*

● **How did they get through these mountains?** *(through breaks in the mountains, like the Khyber Pass)*

★THINKING FURTHER: *Making Conclusions* **Why might geography have been a cause for their migration?** *(Natural disasters, wars, or population growth might have driven them from home.)*

NEWCOMERS

Sometime around 1600 B.C. the city of Mohenjo-Daro was totally abandoned. So was the city of Harappa. Why?

Unfortunately we may never know for sure why these ancient cities were abandoned. One possible answer, archaeologists say, is that an earthquake caused the Indus to change its course. Without river water, farming would have become very difficult in this area. This earthquake may also have created massive floods. Floods may have destroyed the region's two largest cities. Life went on in the Indus Valley after the disaster. Harappan civilization, however, was never the same again.

Life in the Indus Valley changed even more, beginning around 1500 B.C. At that time newcomers began crossing the icy passes of the Hindu Kush Mountains. The Aryan (AYR ee un) people, originally from central Asia, herded cattle and sheep on horseback. Perhaps due to natural disasters or wars at home, they migrated (MĪ gray tud). To migrate means to move from one place to another to live. The Aryans migrated both to Europe and India. Follow their routes to India on the map.

Aryans means "noble ones" in Sanskrit. The Aryan people brought this language to the Indus Valley and the rest of the subcontinent. They also

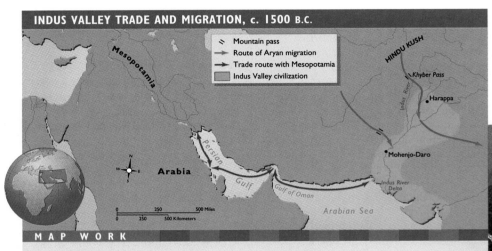

INDUS VALLEY TRADE AND MIGRATION, c. 1500 B.C.

Mountain pass
Route of Aryan migration
Trade route with Mesopotamia
Indus Valley civilization

MAP WORK

Aryan peoples migrated to the Indian subcontinent through mountain passes.

1. What is the name of a mountain pass through which Aryans probably migrated?

2. About how far is Mesopotamia from the city of Mohenjo-Daro?

3. Why would a boat trip from Harappa to Mohenjo-Daro be faster than a return trip by boat?

Narrow passes through the Hindu Kush Mountains continue to be useful in modern transportation of goods.

138

BACKGROUND INFORMATION

ABOUT SANSKRIT
● In the 4th century B.C. an Indian scholar named Panini wrote a grammar of Sanskrit.
● Like Latin in Europe, Sanskrit in India remained the language of the upper class long after it was spoken.
● Similarities of words in Latin, Greek, and Romance languages were first noted by European merchants who traveled to India.
● Examples of related words in several Indo-European languages:

Greek	Latin	Sanskrit	English
mater	mater	mata	mother
pater	pater	pita	father

CURRICULUM CONNECTION

LINKS TO MATHEMATICS Have students do some research to find the average height of the Great, or High, Himalayas (20,000 ft.) and of the Hindu Kush (15,000 ft.). When they have found the figures, have them do the subtraction to find the difference in height and meters.

GLOBAL CONNECTION

"ARYANS" IN THE 20TH CENTURY In the 1920s Adolph Hitler, soon to be the Nazi dictator of Germany, admired stories of the Aryan conquest of India. He adopted the word *Aryan* as a racist term to mean "Germans" and some blond, blue-eyed northern Europeans. Nazi racists glorified these "Aryans" as a "master race."

brought new religious ideas, which you will read about in the next lesson.

WHY IT MATTERS

Harappan civilization existed in the Indus River valley for almost 1,000 years. During that time farmers produced a large surplus of food. This surplus fed the populations of the great cities that developed along the fertile plains. Workers in cities like Mohenjo-Daro created items unknown in other parts of the world at that time. These included cotton cloth, stone seals, and citywide drainage systems.

In the end, Harappan civilization may have been destroyed by the very thing that made it possible—the Indus River. Yet parts of that civilization would continue in new forms. New peoples would come to control the Indian subcontinent. In time their cultures would blend with the culture of the Harappans to create a new, rich culture.

✓// Reviewing Facts and Ideas

MAIN IDEAS

- Little is known about Harappan civilization because its writing system has not yet been figured out.
- The city of Mohenjo-Daro included many brick buildings and a huge citadel. The city also had a sewer system more advanced than any other of its time.
- The orderly layout of the city and its large grain warehouse suggest that Mohenjo-Daro was ruled by a strong local government.
- Harappan merchants traded goods in many places, some of which were as far away as Mesopotamia.
- In about 1500 B.C. people called Aryans migrated to the Indian subcontinent. They brought new ideas to the region.

THINK ABOUT IT

1. Why is ancient Indus Valley civilization called Harappan civilization?

2. What have historians learned about Harappan civilization from written sources? What have they learned from building remains in cities like Mohenjo-Daro?

3. **FOCUS** What do we know about the early culture of Mohenjo-Daro?

4. **THINKING SKILL** Based on the information in this lesson, what _conclusions_ can you make about the people who lived in Mohenjo-Daro? What evidence supports your conclusions?

5. **GEOGRAPHY** Sketch a map of southern and western Asia. Draw the routes of the Aryan migration and the trade route between Harappa and Mesopotamia. Be sure to include physical features like mountains, rivers, and seas in your sketch.

139

Discussing WHY IT MATTERS
Point out that the Indus was creator and destroyer.

★**THINKING FURTHER:** _Sequencing_ **How would you design a flow chart to show the rise and fall of Harappan civilization?** _(Have students create the flow chart as a common effort. Have them take turns coming to the board to add steps in order: farming, surpluses, specialization, city building, trade development, geographic disaster, decline.)_

3 CLOSE

MAIN IDEAS
Call on students individually to answer.

- **Why would we know more about Harappan civilization if another Champollion or Rawlinson came along?** _(Decoding the writing would reveal more of Harappan civilization.)_

- **What kinds of technologies made Mohenjo-Daro a highly livable city?** _(street grids, brick buildings, a citadel, an advanced sewer system)_

- **Why do we believe that Mohenjo-Daro had a strong government?** _(city planning, the grid, the granary)_

- **How far away did Harappan merchants trade?** _(Mesopotamia, Iran, Afghanistan, and the Indus Plain)_

- **Who migrated to the Indus Valley in about 1500 B.C.?** _(the Aryans)_

EVALUATE
✓ **Answers to Think About It**

1. after one of its cities, whose ruins people nearby called Harappa
Summarize

2. Nothing from written sources, but building remains show city planning and advanced technology.
Make Inferences

3. It had about 40,000 people, a sewer system, grid streets, brick houses.
Recall Details

4. They had a strong government—well-run city; farm surpluses—granaries; skilled craftworkers—artifacts show specialties and trade.
Make Conclusions

5. Maps should resemble p. 138.
Five Themes of Geography: Location

Write About It Tell students to write a paragraph explaining why they might like to have lived in Mohenjo-Daro.

SKILLS LESSON

PAGES 140–141

Lesson Overview
Comparing maps can clarify relationships between land and people.

Lesson Objective
★ Compare information about the same area on different maps.

⭐ 1 PREPARE

MOTIVATE Refer students to the maps in this lesson and have them identify the area they show (Pakistan) and the different aspects of it (cities, physical features, where certain crops are grown). Have students read *Why the Skill Matters* to learn why comparing these different maps can provide information that no one of them singly could give.

SET PURPOSE Point out to the class that there is a simple and useful strategy to prepare them to compare maps. Have them read it in the *Helping Yourself* box on p. 141.

⭐ 2 TEACH

Using the Skill Help students to understand that comparing maps is an exercise in looking for and finding relationships between one piece of information and another. Then refer them to Map A and Map B.

- *What does each of these maps tell you that the other doesn't?* (Map A: cities, no physical features. Map B: physical features, no cities.)

- *What kinds of physical features does Map B highlight?* (mountains, deserts, plains, plateaus)

- *What large cities can you locate in southwest Pakistan on Map A?* (none)

- *What does Map B show the main physical feature to be?* (high plateaus)

Resource REMINDER

Practice and Project Book: *p. 31*

Transparency: *Map 12*

Technology: *Adventure Time!* CD-ROM

GEOGRAPHYSKILLS

Comparing Different Kinds of Maps

WHY THE SKILL MATTERS

In Lesson 1 you read that yearly floods and deposits of silt made farming possible in the ancient Indus River valley. Farming, in turn, led to the development of city life in the valley.

Today farming is still an important part of life in the Indus River valley. This area is now a part of Pakistan. The success of present-day farmers there still depends on the Indus River.

To better understand the ties between land and human life in the Indus River valley, it helps to compare different kinds of maps.

Comparing maps showing the same area allows you to discover new information that you would not be able to get by looking at maps separately. Different types of maps show different information. For example, look at Map A and Map B, both on this page.

USING THE SKILL

As you can see from the map titles, Map A shows Pakistan's borders and major cities, while Map B shows Pakistan's physical features. What kinds of features does Map B highlight?*

When you compare the information on both maps, you can learn different things about Pakistan. For example, you can see that there are no large cities in most of the southwestern part of Pakistan. What are the physical features of that region? How do you think they affect the way in which people settled there?**

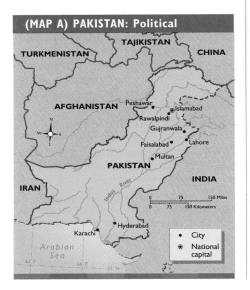

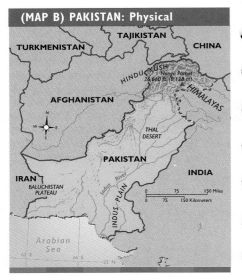

140 *Map B highlights mountains, rivers, plains, and plateaus.
**Mountains and plateaus; the mountains probably made it difficult to settle and grow crops.

READING STRATEGIES & LANGUAGE DEVELOPMENT

CAUSE AND EFFECT Since this Skills Lesson addresses how land and human life are related, it provides an excellent opportunity for students to practice finding cause-and-effect relationships. If necessary, refer students to the Cause and Effect Skill in Chapter 5 (pp. 118–119) for a quick review. Alert them to look for effects—how land is used—and then to seek out the causes—how physical features encourage and discourage particular uses.

SYNONYM You introduced the class to the derivation of *annual* from *Anno Domini* in the Chapter 3 Skills Lesson on p.58. Write the word *annual* on the board and ask students to discover a synonym for it in this Skills Lesson (*yearly* in the opening paragraph).

*It is flat and near water.

TRYING THE SKILL

In the first lesson you also learned that ancient Indus farmers planted wheat as well as some of the world's first crops of rice. As you can see from Map C on this page, those two crops are still important in the Indus Valley area today.

Use the Helping Yourself box on this page to compare Maps B and C. This study will

HELPING Yourself

● **Comparing maps helps you to make conclusions that you would not be able to make by looking at only one.**

● **Study each map's title and key.**

● **Compare maps to see what they share in common.**

help you to gain more information about modern farming in Pakistan. What kind of physical features does the land have where most wheat and rice farming are done?*

REVIEWING THE SKILL

1. How can comparing maps help you to better understand a place?
2. Look at maps B and C. Which natural features are needed to support agriculture for a large population? How did you reach your conclusion?
3. What might you learn about where you live by studying and comparing different kinds of maps?

(MAP C) PAKISTAN: Agriculture

TURKMENISTAN
TAJIKISTAN
CHINA
AFGHANISTAN
Islamabad
PAKISTAN
Indus River
IRAN
INDIA
Karachi
Arabian Sea

0   75   150 Miles
0   75   150 Kilometers

62°E   66°E   22°N

Wheat
Rice
------ Canal

In Pakistan today, oxen are sometimes used to draw well water. The water irrigates crops.

MEETING INDIVIDUAL NEEDS

RETEACHING (Easy) Have students find a political map of the United States, select three major cities, and list them on a piece of paper. Then have them turn to a U.S. physical map, identify physical features where each city is located, and note the features next to the city.

EXTENSION (Average) Have students draw two outline maps of their state. On one they should locate and label the state's major cities. On the other they should draw in the state's major physical features. They should then pick three of the cities and write an explanation of how the physical features of the land might have encouraged it to develop.

ENRICHMENT (Challenging) Have students find political, physical, and population density maps of the United States. Have them compare the three to identify the least heavily populated states and explain what physical features might explain this. Have them write up their findings.

★ **THINKING FURTHER:** *Cause and Effect* **What cause-and-effect relationship can you draw from these maps about the lack of large cities in southwest Pakistan?** *(Cause: mountains and high plateaus. Effect: light settlement.)*

Trying the Skill Have students review *Helping Yourself*.

● **Where does Map C show that wheat and rice are grown in Pakistan?** *(along the Indus River system)*

● **What does Map C show has been done to improve distribution of Indus waters?** *(Canals have been built.)*

● **What kind of physical features does Map B show the farmed land to have?** *(mostly plains, some desert)*

★ **THINKING FURTHER:** *Cause and Effect* **What cause-and effect relationship can you find between the land and the growing of wheat and rice?** *(Cause: water, water control, and plains. Effect: production of crops.)*

⭐ 3 CLOSE

SUM IT UP

Give students additional practice in comparing maps by having them turn to the Atlas on pp.R2-R19, to compare the political and physical maps of continents.

✓ **EVALUATE**

Answers to Reviewing the Skill

1. by presenting different data for the same area

2. Students may suggest a good water supply, good farm land, lack of rocky terrain and should support their answers with data; compare physical areas (map B) with the natural features (map C).

3. Possible answer: how land, water, climate relate to crops and populated areas.

 Technology CONNECTION

ADVENTURE TIME! CD-ROM
Enrich this Skills Lesson with the map *Build-on* feature on the *Adventure Time!* CD-ROM.

LESSON 3
PAGES 142–147

Lesson Overview
Hinduism, one of the world's oldest religions, developed on the Indian subcontinent and has greatly influenced that region's culture.

Lesson Objectives
★ Identify major beliefs of Hinduism.

★ Explain how these beliefs created a unique social structure and identify its chief castes.

⭐ 1 PREPARE

MOTIVATE Have three students present the *Read Aloud* to the class. One will be the narrator, one the father, one the son. Encourage students to recognize the human desire to find truth and meaning in life and to live it well.

SET PURPOSE Point out to students that in this lesson, they will explore another of the world's great religions. Call attention to the relief figure of the Hindu god riding a tiger. Have them read the *Read to Learn* question and be prepared to learn about the Vedas. Preview the *Vocabulary*.

⭐ 2 TEACH

Discussing THE BIG PICTURE Help students make a connection between the *Read Aloud* story and Hinduism.

● *What does the fig seed story teach?* (that the finest element cannot be seen)

● *What major belief of Hinduism does the text mention?* (that a powerful, invisible force links everything)

★**THINKING FURTHER:** *Making Conclusions* **Why might you conclude that Hinduism had a strong influence on a major region of the world?** (It has been a force on the Indian subcontinent since ancient times.)

Resource REMINDER

Practice and Project Book: *p. 32*

Anthology: *Life of a Hindu Priest, pp. 26–27; Mahabharata, p.28; Where the Mind Is Without Fear, p. 29*

| 2500 B.C. | 2000 B.C. | 1500 B.C. | 500 B.C. |

BEGINNINGS OF HINDUISM

Focus Activity

READ TO LEARN
How did the Vedas shape Indian culture?

VOCABULARY
Hinduism
Vedas
caste system
reincarnation
dharma

READ ALOUD

Ancient Hindu writings tell the story of a father who used simple examples to teach his son about the meaning of life. One day he told his son to bring him a fig from a fig tree. The boy did so, and his father told him to split the fruit open.

"What do you see?"

"These fine [tiny] seeds," replied the son.

"Break one open! What do you see?"

"Nothing at all, sir!"

His father said, "This finest element, which you cannot see—out of this finest element comes this big fig tree!" The boy was similar to the tree, he said. The father was teaching his son the Hindu belief that all life is connected by an invisible force.

THE BIG PICTURE

This belief in a link between a powerful, invisible force and everything in the world is a key part of Hinduism (HIHN doo ihz um). Hinduism, one of the world's oldest religions, grew out of the beliefs of the Aryans, whom you read about in the last lesson. Today it has nearly 800 million followers. As is the case with most religions, Hinduism is practiced in many different ways. Yet all Hindus share some basic beliefs. Hindus also share a history that stretches back to the ancient past of the Indian subcontinent.

142

SHELTERED INSTRUCTION

READING STRATEGIES & LANGUAGE DEVELOPMENT

MAIN IDEA AND DETAIL Remind the class that finding main ideas and details can help them understand a passage. Then have students read the first paragraph on p. 143, stating the main idea and details. Record this on a graphic organizer on the board. Have students copy the chart and add to it as they read the rest of the lesson. **[SDAIE STRATEGY:** TEXT RE-PRESENTATION/SCHEMA BUILDING]

HOMOPHONES Help students with the term for a Hindu social level by writing the homophones *cast* and *caste* on the board. Students already know the first, so ask for examples of its different meanings (for example, statements meaning "to throw" or references to "a hard support for a broken bone" or "actors in a play"). When they find *caste* in the lesson, help them observe its different meaning and spelling.

WRITINGS OF A NEW RELIGION

When Aryans migrated to the Indian subcontinent around 1500 B.C., they had little in common with Harappans. The two peoples spoke different languages and had different cultures. Many Harappans lived in great cities like Mohenjo-Daro. As herders, the Aryan people were used to moving around more. They lived in smaller villages and moved often.

As time passed, the two cultural groups began to learn from each other. Aryans began farming and specializing in crafts like their Harappan neighbors.

Harappans, meanwhile, learned ancient Aryan songs about how the world works. These songs, believed to be holy, were passed down by oral tradition. Around 600 B.C. the sacred songs were finally collected. The books containing them were called the Vedas (VAY duz), or "Books of Knowledge."

The Vedas

The Vedas were the first building blocks of Hinduism. They told Hindus how they should live, and explained life. The oldest Veda has more than 1,000 hymns. It says that the world is run by many gods and goddesses. Which Hindu goddess does this hymn praise? What are her "twinkling eyes"?

Song from the *Rig Veda*, first written down in about 1000 B.C.

Goddess Night, with all her twinkling eyes,
To different points in splendor she comes.
Immortal, she **broods over** the high and low;
The Goddess, with her gaze, lightens the dark.

In her trail, her sister Dawn follows,
And with her the darkness vanishes. . . .
The villagers, all that flies and walks
Are closed in their homes. Even vultures ignore their **prey**.

O [Night], fence off the wolf and its mate;
Fence off the thief. Be easy for us to pass.

Bright, she has come near me, the darkness **subdued**
With light's promise. Dawn, cancel darkness.

immortal: never dying
broods over: thinks about
prey: animal hunted for food
subdued: conquered

Many Hindu temples are decorated with statues of gods and goddesses.

143

WRITINGS OF A NEW RELIGION

Help the class to recognize the Aryan-Harappan meeting first as a clash of cultures and then as an exchange of them. Help identify the exchanges.

Discussing The Vedas Write *Vedas* on the board.

● **What are the Vedas?** *("Books of Knowledge" in which sacred Aryan songs were written down)*

● **Why were the Vedas appropriate to become the "first building blocks" of a great world religion?** *(They explained the meaning of life, told people how to live, and said the world was ruled by gods and goddesses.)*

★**THINKING FURTHER: Compare and Contrast How would you compare the Vedas with the Hebrew Bible?** *(Both have teachings on how to live and on who rules the world.)*

Discussing the PRIMARY SOURCE

Have a student rehearse a reading of the song and then present it to the class.

● **Whom does the hymn praise?** *(the goddess Night with twinkling stars)*

● **What does the hymn ask her to do?** *(to protect people and animals from preying animals and sneaking thieves)*

● **What goddess will come to drive Night away?** *(her sister, Dawn)*

★**THINKING FURTHER: Sequencing Hymns often follow a sequence: first praise for the god, then a request for aid. Does this hymn follow that sequence? How?** *(Yes; the opening lines praise Night's splendor; then comes the request for her protection.)*

BACKGROUND INFORMATION

ABOUT THE VEDAS
● The name Vedas means "knowledge" in Sanskrit.
● The oral tradition that preserved the Vedas for centuries before they could be written down was divided up among a number of families. Each family was given one part of the Vedas to memorize and pass down through the generations. Some of these parts are still known by the name of the family that preserved them. For example, the Rig family preserved the hymn quoted in the text.

CURRICULUM CONNECTION

LINKS TO LANGUAGE ARTS Refer students to the words that are defined below the hymn. Invite them to write a short poem in which they make use of all four of the words.

HINDUISM AND CULTURE

Draw a large stick figure person on the board as the class reads the opening paragraph and hymn. When they have finished, call students to the board to draw a line from each named body part and label the class that sprang from it.

★THINKING FURTHER: *Classifying*
How does this classify people? How does the figure reflect social levels from top to bottom?
(Help students relate the prestige of the social classes labeled here with a scale running from top to bottom. They should see the relation of servants to the feet, that is, the bottom of the scale, and so on up.)

Discussing The Caste System Help students understand the permanent lack of mobility throughout one's life in a *caste system*.

● **What is a caste system and what purpose does it serve?** *(a way of organizing people in different levels; to give an order to society and fix people's place in the order)*

● **When a person is born, what determines his or her caste?** *(A person is born into the parents' caste.)*

● **How does one's caste determine what work the person will do through life?** *(Different castes have different jobs.)*

● **How would you illustrate the cycle that the Vedas describe?** *(Have a student come up to the board to picture it: a circle with the labels "life," "death," and "rebirth" running around it.)*

● **How does this circle symbolize reincarnation?** *(It shows that rebirth follows each death, which of course follows each life.)*

★THINKING FURTHER: *Making Conclusions* **Why do you think that such a system might encourage people to live good lives?** *(so that they can rise ever higher in the cycle until they can escape it entirely and become part of truth)*

Bathing in the Ganges is an important Hindu ceremony. Caste is often shown with a mark on the forehead. There are as many as 3,000 castes in India.

HINDUISM AND CULTURE

The Vedas explain how Hindus believe people were created and what is the proper way to live. The following hymn explains the Hindu belief that four different kinds, or classes, of people were created. These first humans were said to be born from the different parts of a god's body.

> The Priest was his mouth;
> The Princes became his arms;
> His [legs] produced the
> Professionals and Merchants;
> His feet gave birth to the [Servant].

The Caste System

These four classes of people developed into India's caste system (KAST SIHS tum). The caste system is a way of organizing people into hundreds of different levels.

In a Hindu caste system a person's place in society is determined by the rank of the family she or he is born into. People born into the priestly caste of India have the highest rank and respect. Their main job is to study and teach people about the Vedas. People of the servant caste are said to be born to serve the other castes.

According to the Vedas, people do have some control over the caste they are born into. The Vedas state that people move in a constant circle of birth, death, and rebirth. This cycle is called reincarnation (ree ihn kahr NAY shun).

Hindus believe that bad deeds done in one lifetime must be paid for in a person's next life. According to this belief, people born as servants, then, are paying for wrongs done in the past. Priests, on the other hand, have done many good things in past lives.

144

GLOBAL CONNECTION

TRANSMISSION OF THE CASTE SYSTEM
● Forms of the caste system appear in Pakistan and Bangladesh.
● It also appears on Sri Lanka, an island nation off the southern coast of India, among the Buddhist Sinhalese people there.
● Remnants of the caste system in a highly simplified form appear in Bali in Indonesia, where emigrants from India brought it with them.

SECOND-LANGUAGE SUPPORT

GRAPHIC ORGANIZERS A Venn diagram may help second-language students create a reference tool to link prior knowledge of religions to information about Hinduism. Work with students to gather data about Hinduism and another religion to complete the diagram. Then encourage them to create diagrams for additional comparisons.

The Importance of Duty

How did Hindus know what was right and good? They followed the dharma (DAHR muh) of their caste, described in the Vedas. Dharma means laws and duties. It includes hundreds of rules that instruct Hindus how to live.

For example, part of the dharma of servants was to do their jobs cheerfully. Professionals and merchants were responsible for producing and selling goods and services. Priests also had to spend some of their time working to support their families. The Vedas told which jobs people in each caste could and could not do.

Following dharma helped to keep Hindu society running in an orderly fashion. When people broke the rules of dharma, the Vedas warned, disorder would be the result. One of the sacred writings said:

> If a person is engaged in doing his proper work, he reaches the highest end.

People who married against the rules of their caste, or who did a job their caste was not allowed to do, were forced to live outside all castes. These "outcastes" were looked down upon by others and said to be "impure." Some Hindu priests performed a "cleansing" ceremony if they were touched by even the shadow of an outcaste.

Outcastes had few rights. Because their children were born outside all castes, they too, had to live their lives as "untouchables."

Many Paths to Truth

Over time, Hinduism developed hundreds of different forms. Some Hindus believed their dharma called them to become priests or to perform special exercises. Others felt it was important to eat no meat, eggs, or fish. Still others explored non-Hindu beliefs in their search to understand the meaning of life and the proper way to live.

These different approaches did not upset Hindu priests. Hinduism allows for the existence of more than one god and more than one way to truth. In a very popular Hindu book—called the *Bhagavad Gita* (BUG uh vud GEE tah)—the god Vishnu says:

> Howsoever people approach me, even so do I accept them; for on all sides, whatever path they may choose is mine.

Today Hindu priests read from the sacred Vedas, just as their ancestors have for hundreds of years.

145

HINDUISM TODAY

Remind students of Azeez Narain, whom they met in Chapter 1. Encourage them to review his story to get a sense of Hinduism today.

- **What does Azeez's story tell you about Hinduism today?** *(Hinduism remains the most important influence on Indian culture; it still teaches that everyone has a soul that is a "fraction of God"; Hindus worship their gods and goddesses at home; their beliefs affect the foods they eat.)*

- **Where else and on what occasions do Hindus worship their gods and goddesses?** *(in temples and at special festivals that honor these deities)*

- **Who are some of the favorite gods and goddesses of the Hindu religion?** *(Vishnu, Shiva, and Devi)*

★**THINKING FURTHER:** *Making Conclusions* **Why do you suppose these would be favorites?** *(They appear to be very powerful, judging from the importance of the areas of life that they are responsible for, like time, destruction, and creation.)*

Discussing A Changing Religion
Ask students about other epics they know. When they recall Gilgamesh in Chapter 5, review the definition of *epic* (a long, eventful story about someone who embodies a society's beliefs and ideals).

- **Why does it make sense, then, that the Hindus would have epics too?** *(They too might want legendary heroes as examples for good living.)*

- **What evidence is there of the popularity of epics among Hindus?** *(Some epics have been turned into popular entertainment.)*

- **What major change has Hinduism had to make so that the rule by the majority would not trample on the rights of the minority?** *(that outcastes no longer be ill-treated and scorned)*

★**THINKING FURTHER:** *Cause and Effect* **What do you think was the cause-and-effect relationship that brought on this change?** *(Cause: it is not humane or just to treat human beings so. Effect: make such treatment illegal.)*

HINDUISM TODAY

As in ancient times, Hindus of today worship many different gods and goddesses. Some gods, however, have become special favorites. The god Vishnu is worshiped as "The One that is the All" by millions of Hindus. Millions more honor Shiva, "The God of Time and Destruction." Still other believers prefer the goddess Devi, "The Mother of All Creation."

Most Hindu families today worship their favorite gods at home, at temples, and at special festivals.

A Changing Religion

Many Hindus still consider the Vedas the most holy books of their religion. Other books of adventure-filled stories, or *epics*, are also considered to be holy guides to living. Some of these stories have even been made into films.

Although Hinduism has roots in the ancient past, it has changed over the years. Some important changes have had to do with the caste system. In 1950, for example, the Indian government made it illegal to mistreat or to show disrespect for Hindu "outcastes."

Karachi Museum, Pakistan

Art of Hindu gods and goddesses shows (clockwise from left) Krishna and his wife Radha, Vishnu, and Ganesh.

146

ABOUT HINDU GODS AND GODDESSES
- Vishnu and Shiva are seen as two sides of the supreme Godhead Brahma. Indeed, each is the idol of a major sect of Hinduism—Vaishnavism (Vishu) and Shaivism (Shiva).
- Vishnu is seen as the preserver and protector of the world. His wife is Lakshmi, goddess of well-being.
- Shiva is seen as the destroyer of the world. His wife Parvati appears in different forms, including that of the goddess Devi.

USING THE ANTHOLOGY

MAHABHARATA, page 28 One great epic of Hindu literature is the Mahabharata, the story of five princes who are robbed of their kingdom and fight to reclaim it. Have students read and discuss the selection from this epic found in the anthology.

Many Hindus observe traditional customs for important occasions, such as weddings. At this wedding ceremony in India, garlands of flowers surround a happy couple.

WHY IT MATTERS

Hinduism, one of the world's oldest religions, is followed by hundreds of millions of people today. Hinduism began in the blending of two cultures and honors many gods and goddesses. Today Hinduism continues to combine beliefs from different cultures. Most modern Hindus live in present-day India and Pakistan.

The legacy of Hinduism has influenced the arts, science, and society for great numbers of Hindus. As you will read in the next lesson, it also affected millions of others. Hinduism became the starting point for another world religion.

✓ Reviewing Facts and Ideas

MAIN IDEAS

- Hinduism is practiced in many different ways. It is one of the world's oldest religions and has nearly 800 million followers today.
- Aryan newcomers to the Indian subcontinent introduced sacred songs written in the Vedas. They became the foundation of Hinduism.
- The Vedas supported a way of dividing Hindu society into four major classes of people. These four classes developed into the caste system.
- An important theme in Hinduism is reincarnation. This is the idea that people live in a constant circle of birth, death, and rebirth.
- By following the dharma, or instruction, of their caste, Hindus believe that people can break free of the cycle of reincarnation.

THINK ABOUT IT

1. What is dharma? Is it the same for all Hindus?

2. Why was it important for Hindus to do the duties expected of their caste?

3. **FOCUS** What are the Vedas? What role did they play in the shaping of Indian culture?

4. **THINKING SKILL** Make three *generalizations* about what can happen when different cultures come into contact. Base your generalizations on what you have learned about each of the ancient river-valley civilizations.

5. **WRITING** Suppose you are interviewing a Hindu for a newspaper article. On a sheet of paper, write a list of questions you would ask.

147

Discussing WHY IT MATTERS
Stress the role of Hinduism in Indian culture.

★**THINKING FURTHER:** *Making Generalizations* **What generalizations can you make about how Hinduism has affected Indian culture through the ages?** *(It gave Hindus their religious beliefs and practices, structured their society into castes, decided the work and behavior of each caste, allowed religious tolerance, and stressed order.)*

★ 3 CLOSE

MAIN IDEAS
Have students work in small groups to answer these questions.

- *Why is Hinduism a major world religion?* (It has 800 million followers.)

- *What is the foundation for Hinduism?* (the Vedas of the Aryan oral tradition)

- *What is the caste system?* (a division of a society into social classes)

- *What is reincarnation?* (the belief that people are continually reborn)

- *How can a person break free of reincarnation?* (by living a life good enough to unite with Brahman)

EVALUATE
✓ **Answers to Think About It**

1. Laws and duties; no, they are different for each caste.
   Recall Details

2. so that they could keep rising to higher castes until they could break free and unite with Brahman
   Steps in a Process

3. sacred songs that taught about gods and goddesses, gave rules for living, and explained life's meaning
   Summarize

4. Students' generalizations should reflect cultural clash, borrowing, and diffusion.
   Form Generalizations

5. Students might ask questions relating to how the Hindu religion affects the person's everyday life.
   Make, Confirm, or Revise Predictions

Write About It Tell students to write a paragraph in which they answer the *Read to Learn* question on p. 142.

MEETING INDIVIDUAL NEEDS

RETEACHING (Easy) Have students use markers or colored pencils to draw the Hindu circle of life, death, and rebirth. They should "illuminate" it with color and add interesting lettering for the words that run around it.

EXTENSION (Average) Refer students to the passage from the Vedas on this text page. Ask them to think about what it would be like to be "untouchables" in traditional India. Have students write new lines from an "untouchable's" point of view.

ENRICHMENT (Challenging) Have students work on the same kind of activity suggested in the chapter on Egypt (p. 81). Tell them to create "A Gallery of Hindu Gods and Goddesses" gallery for the classroom. Have them do some research on the deities, how they were pictured, and what they represented.

Lesson Overview
A tradition of dance in the Hindu culture binds the community.

Lesson Objectives
★ Examine Indian dances for clues to Hindu values and training.

1 PREPARE

MOTIVATE Have you ever watched a small child dance? What seems to be the child's mood as he or she dances? Why do you suppose so many people like to dance? Do you? Use such questions as these to get students thinking about how universal dancing is.

Set Purpose Have you ever seen a professional dance performance? How did the dancing there differ from ordinary social dancing? Help students see that professional dancers are highly trained and perform set pieces.

2 TEACH

Understanding the Concept of a Legacy Have students read the column of type on this page and then help them identify the varieties of Indian dance, dances that tell a story of gods or heroes or dances that are just pure movement for its own beauty. If any students study dance or know people who do, have them describe the endless hours of training and practice that go into becoming a skilled dancer.

Examining the Pictures As students examine the pictures, encourage them to notice who is dancing and what the dance is about.

● **How does the picture on this page tie in with what you have already learned about Shiva?** (Shiva, the destroyer, is dancing to destroy his enemies.)

Legacy
LINKING PAST AND PRESENT

INDIAN DANCE

The ancient Hindus believed that dance was given to them by the gods and goddesses. From the earliest times dance has been an important part of Indian life.

Indian dances vary greatly. Some of them tell a story without words. Other dances were created for their own sakes. In fact the people of ancient India used the same word, *natya* (NAH tyah), for both dance and drama. Both art forms told stories of Hindu gods and heroes.

Many Indian dances require great skill. Today dancers learn rules taught by Bharata (BAH ruh tuh), a teacher who lived some 1500 years ago. He even told dancers how to move their eyelashes!

In Hindu legend the god Shiva created the world by destroying his monster enemies. From then on the gods and goddesses danced. This sculpture shows Shiva performing his dance of destruction.

148

BACKGROUND INFORMATION

ABOUT INDIAN DANCE
● Dance can be traced back to the Indus Valley at least as far as the 2nd Millennium B.C. A figure of a dancing girl cast in bronze has been found from that period.

● One of Shiva's many titles is "Lord of the Cosmic Dance."

● Control is at the heart of Indian dance. Its precise and highly stylized movements require exquisite control, which in turn reflects and expresses the Indian philosophy of control over self.

● In addition to the two mainstream dance forms pictured—Bharata natyam and Kathakali—there are two others. One, Kathak, is strongly rhythmic and stresses fast foot tapping and powerful turns. The other, Manipuri, stresses vigorous movement and great acrobatic skill.

Dance is still an important part of life in India. These dancers are acting out a Hindu story. This ancient sculpture shows that if you had lived in India 1,000 years ago, you might have seen the very same dance performed in a temple.

Museum of Oriental Art, Rome

Bharata natyam is the oldest dance in the world that is still performed today. Hand gestures, or mudras (MOO drus), are an important part of this solo dance. Mudras often stand for animals, plants, or feelings.

149

- **How does the sculpture of Shiva show that Hindus found dance powerful?** *(Shiva's dance is powerful enough to destroy.)*

- **In the Bharata natyam, what are the arms and hands doing and why?** *(They form precise gestures—mudras—with certain meanings, perhaps symbolizing an animal, plant, or feeling.)*

- **Look at the eyes and head position. What strikes you about their role in dance?** *(Students may suggest that these, too, have specific meanings.)*

- **Look at the picture of the dance that is acting out a story. How does it connect people in India to their past?** *(It acts out a Hindu story.)*

- **What does the sculpture reveal about dance?** *(The sculpture shows a dance that has been performed for 1,000 years.)*

- **How do you suppose that this dance was handed down over the last 1,000 years?** *(It would have been handed down by memory from generation to generation. Help students see that only memory could have preserved it.)*

★**THINKING FURTHER:** *Making Generalizations* **What generalizations can you make about Indian dance and its role in Indian life?** *(Answers should center on the Hindu values of religious belief, tradition, order, and mastery and on dance's power to unite people in their tradition.)*

⭐ 3 CLOSE

SUM IT UP
Have students identify the clues to Hindu values found in Indian dance.

EVALUATE
Write About It Ask students to write a paragraph explaining how film can make a difference in the way dance traditions are preserved.

FIELD TRIP

If there is a Indian center in your area, see if it has a dance group that performs. If so, arrange for the class to attend a performance. If not, try to find a video of Indian dance.

MEETING INDIVIDUAL NEEDS

RETEACHING (Easy) Have students prepare posters advertising the dance/drama film shown in the top picture on this page.

EXTENSION (Average) Refer students to the information about the dance teacher Bharata on p.148. Have them prepare advertising brochures to attract new students to his school.

ENRICHMENT (Challenging) Have students do further research into Indian dance, finding pictures showing various movements it uses. Tell them to illustrate these movements and explain their meaning.

LESSON 4

PAGES 150–155

Lesson Overview
Buddhism developed from Hindu roots in India and spread across much of Asia shaping the cultures developing there.

Lesson Objectives
★ Describe the development of *Buddhism*.

★ Identify its major beliefs.

★ Explain its spread across Asia.

1 PREPARE

MOTIVATE Have a student read the *Read Aloud* to the class as though it were from a storybook. Ask, "What world religion are we about to meet?" (Buddhism)

SET PURPOSE Call students' attention to the photo of the statue of the Buddha. Use the *Read to Learn* question to determine whether any students have concepts of Buddhism. Preview the *Vocabulary* terms.

2 TEACH

Discussing THE BIG PICTURE
Have students refer to the map of the Indian subcontinent on p. 138 to trace the paths the Aryans might have taken. Also have them locate the area where the Buddha was born.

● **How did the Buddha begin life?** *(as a wealthy, pampered prince)*

● **How did he radically change his life?** *(He gave up everything to seek the meaning of life.)*

★**THINKING FURTHER:** *Making Conclusions* **How does the Buddha's life so far have the makings of an epic?** *(He could be a cultural hero like Gilgamesh, who goes on a quest and embodies the beliefs of a people.)*

Resource REMINDER
Practice and Project Book: *p. 33*
Anthology: *Becoming a Buddhist Master, pp. 30–31*
Desk Map
Outline Map: *p. 19*

BEGINNINGS OF BUDDHISM

Focus Activity

READ TO LEARN
What did the Buddha teach?

VOCABULARY
Buddhism
monk
karma
Four Noble Truths
Eightfold Path
Middle Way

PEOPLE
Siddhartha Gautama

PLACES
Kosala

READ ALOUD
According to its followers, the founder of one of the world's major religions began his life as a prince in a mountain kingdom of northern India. He enjoyed all the best the world had to offer him—the finest clothes, many servants, and a beautiful palace for each season of the year. As a young man, though, the prince gave up his fame and fortune to seek the true meaning of life. His followers believe he found the answer. The man would become known as "the Buddha."

THE BIG PICTURE
Between about 1500 B.C. and 500 B.C., Aryan settlers spread eastward across the Indian subcontinent. They conquered many towns and cities as they went. By around 500 B.C. Aryan princes were in control of much of the Indian subcontinent.

In the far north, at the base of the Himalayas, some kingdoms held onto their independence. To keep their freedom, however, they had to make yearly payments to Aryan rulers to the south. In spite of this, conflict and struggle remained a part of their lives. Some Indians began to look for answers to life's problems beyond the Vedas. One was the prince described in the Read Aloud. His name was Siddhartha Gautama (sih DAHR tuh GOW tah muh). The answers he found would become Buddhism (BOOD ihz um), a religion that continues to attract followers. Today there are more than 330 million Buddhists.

150

SHELTERED INSTRUCTION

READING STRATEGIES & LANGUAGE DEVELOPMENT

PROBLEM SOLVING Point out that people in the past did not know how events were going to turn out. Historical events can be seen as a series of problems and solutions. Invite volunteers to share times they faced a problem and found a solution. Was the solution effective? What effect might a different solution have had? Explain that in this lesson "Buddha discovers there is suffering in the world—what solutions can he find to end it?" Ask students to propose solutions. **[SDAIE STRATEGY:** BRIDGING]

SUFFIX Students have already encountered several *isms*—Judaism, Hinduism, and now Buddhism. Have students look up this suffix in a dictionary and identify the meaning used in these examples ("a system, practice, belief"). Encourage them to think of other words they know with this suffix and determine which have the same meaning.

LIFE OF THE BUDDHA

Siddhartha Gautama is traditionally said to have been born around 563 B.C. His parents were the king and queen of Kosala, a northern kingdom near the Himalayas. Siddhartha means "He Who Has Reached His Goal" in Sanskrit.

The Young Prince

Ancient Buddhist writings say that Siddhartha's mother dreamed about her son's future. The dreams predicted that if Siddhartha stayed at home, he would rule a great kingdom. If he left home, he would become a wise teacher and monk. A monk is a man who devotes his life to a religious group. Monks often give up all they own and live only a religious way of life.

Siddhartha's father wanted the boy to be a king. From that point on, Buddhist texts state, the king did all he could to keep his son happy at home. He had the best singing groups entertain his son and arranged for the prince to marry the woman of his dreams. He built stunning gardens around the royal palace so Siddhartha would be surrounded by beauty.

Discovery in the Garden

Even in his own garden, though, the king could not shelter Siddhartha from sorrow forever. One day the prince went for a ride in the royal gardens. There he spotted an elderly man hobbling painfully along with a cane. Siddhartha asked his chariot driver what was wrong with the man. He learned that all people grow old someday and said, "Shame on birth, since to everyone that is born, old age must come!"

During another ride through the gardens, Siddhartha saw someone

The young Siddhartha was introduced to sickness, old age, and death in his daily rides through his father's gardens.

who was very ill. It troubled him to find out that sickness was part of life. On yet another day the prince came upon a funeral procession. He learned that death was a part of life.

Finally Siddhartha spotted a man in the park who seemed to be at peace with the world. The man was calm even though he was asking people for help in getting his next meal. Siddhartha asked his driver who the man was and learned that the man was a monk. The prince was amazed that someone could be so at peace in a world filled with sorrow and suffering.

That day, Buddhist texts state, the prince made a difficult decision. He chose to give up all he had and become a monk. After saying good-bye to his wife and newborn son, he left the palace. His journey to find the meaning of life had begun.

151

BACKGROUND INFORMATION

ABOUT THE LEGEND OF THE BUDDHA'S BIRTH
- He was conceived when his mother was visited in a dream by a sacred white elephant who touched her left side with a white lotus.
- He was born from his mother's left side as she stood in a garden
- At that moment, light flooded the world, the blind could see, the deaf could hear, and the lame were cured.

GLOBAL CONNECTION

ANOTHER HOLY MAN: ANOTHER TIME, ANOTHER PLACE About 1,750 years after Prince Siddhartha renounced luxury, another wealthy son did the same. Dissatisfied with his worldly life, he gave all he owned to the poor. He lived as a hermit, then preached the joys of a poor and simple life based on Christian gospels. He was St. Francis of Assisi.

LIFE OF THE BUDDHA

Refer students to the picture on this page. Have them identify its subject and write his name on the board— *Siddhartha Gautama*. Call on students to explain the significance of his first name. Finally, have them identify the Hindu caste above princes (priests).

Discussing The Young Prince
Have students identify the problem in this section and its hoped-for solutions.

- **What problem did Siddhartha's mother's dream create?** (It predicted that if he left his home at Kosala, he would become a monk, *not a king.*)

- **Why was this a problem?** (His father did not want him ever to leave but to stay home and become a great king.)

- **How did his father try to solve this problem?** (by giving Siddhartha everything he could want so he would never be tempted to leave)

★**THINKING FURTHER: *Predicting Why would you predict that Siddhartha will leave?*** (He must if he is to become a monk and found a new religion.)

Exploring the Discovery in the Garden Use the following questions to help students identify another problem and its solution.

- **What troubling discoveries did Siddhartha make in his beautiful garden?** (that sufferings like painful old age, sickness, and death were part of life in this world)

- **What more hopeful discovery did he make there?** (that a monk could find calm and peace, even in a world filled with suffering)

- **What dilemma did these discoveries create for Siddhartha?** (He had to make a choice between staying at home in the comfort of his family or going out in the world to live as a monk in search of the meaning of life.)

★**THINKING FURTHER: *Making Decisions* What steps might he have followed in making his decision?** (He might have identified his goal—to find the meaning of life— weighed his ways of finding it, and chosen the quest as the best alternative.)

THE TRAVELS OF THE BUDDHA

Students should recognize Siddhartha's problem—to find the meaning of life—and solutions he tried to discover it.

- *What did Siddhartha seek?* (the wisdom to know the meaning of life)

- *For how long and where did Siddhartha search?* (for six years as he wandered through northern India)

- *What means did he explore to find his answers?* (questioning Hindu priests, fasting nearly to starvation, and finally pondering beneath a fig tree)

★**THINKING FURTHER:** *Making Conclusions* **How do you know he found the answers he sought?** *(The title he earned, the Buddha, indicates that he was "awakened" to them.)*

Discussing the Teachings of Buddhism Help students compare and contrast Buddhist and Hindu beliefs.

- *How did the Buddha's enlightenment follow Hindu beliefs?* (It kept the belief in reincarnation and in karma.)

- *What is* **karma**? (the belief that our good and bad acts create a force that affects our lives)

★**THINKING FURTHER:** *Compare and Contrast* **Where did Buddha's beliefs differ from Hindu beliefs?** *(His goal of breaking the cycle of reincarnation was less to connect all life than to end suffering.)*

Examining The Way to End Suffering Keep seeking problems and solutions.

- *What are the* **Four Noble Truths**? *(Life is filled with suffering, caused by people wanting too much. Suffering can be ended when people stop wanting too much, which they can do if they follow the Eightfold Path.)*

★**THINKING FURTHER:** *Cause and Effect* **What cause-and-effect relationships can you find in the Four Noble Truths?** *(Cause: people want too much; effect: there is suffering in the world. Cause: follow the Eightfold Path; effect: people will stop wanting too much. Cause: people stop wanting too much; effect: suffering will end.)*

152

THE TRAVELS OF THE BUDDHA

For the next six years, Siddhartha traveled throughout northern India as a monk. In his search for wisdom, he talked at length with Hindu priests, but felt their answers were not enough. To clear his mind, he stopped eating, but began again when he nearly starved himself to death.

At last, Buddhist texts say, an understanding came to the former prince one day as he sat under a fig tree. The wisdom it is said he received that day would later earn him the title *the Buddha,* which means "Awakened One."

The Teachings of Buddhism

Some of the Buddha's ideas were not new to India. He used some Hindu ideas and changed others. Like Hindus, the Buddha believed that all people went through a circle of birth, death, and rebirth, or reincarnation. Also like Hindus, he believed in karma. Karma is described by both Hindus and Buddhists as a force caused by a person's good and bad acts. Karma is said to affect future lives.

152

Buddhist prayer flags (top) float in the breeze near Kanchenjunga, India, the world's third-highest mountain. Buddhist monks (above) in Thailand wear traditional robes.

Unlike Hindus, the Buddha did not search for the one powerful force believed to connect all of life. Instead, the Buddha believed that the most important thing in life was to reach peace by ending suffering. How did he reach his conclusion, and how did he hope to reach this end?

The Way to End Suffering

Buddhist texts say that as he sat under the tree that day, the Buddha concluded that life is ruled by **Four Noble Truths**.

1. Life is filled with suffering.
2. Suffering is caused by people's wants. People may want more pleasure, more power, or a longer life.
3. Suffering can be ended if people stop wanting things.
4. To stop wanting things, people must follow eight basic laws.

The Buddha explained these Four Noble Truths to his followers, but they were not written down until later. He called the way to end suffering the **Eightfold Path**. The Eightfold Path is a set of instructions on the proper way to live. By following the Eightfold Path, the Buddha taught, people could end the suffering in their lives.

The Middle Way

The laws of the Eightfold Path were meant to represent a **Middle Way** of living for Buddhists. This way of life was meant to be neither too strict nor too easy. The Buddha compared the Middle Way to playing a stringed instrument. If the strings are kept too loose, they will not make a sound. On the other hand, if they are too tight, they will break when they are played. Only those strings that are kept at just the right amount of tightness will make beautiful sounds. Life works the same way, the Buddha concluded.

The Buddha's Final Journeys

The Buddha spent the rest of his life traveling around India and sharing his message with people of all castes. One of the first places he went to was his father's palace.

At first the elderly king was shocked. His son looked no different from any other humble monk he had met. But after listening to his son's message, Buddhists believe that the king, too, became a follower of the Buddha. So did the Buddha's wife and son.

By the time the Buddha died at age 80, there were thousands of Buddhists in northern India. They lived according to his Four Noble Truths. Like the Buddha, Buddhist monks gave up all they owned and depended on other Buddhist followers to give them food each day. They worked to live peacefully among all living things and to love others.

Special prayers are written in Sanskrit on "Mani" stones (below). The stones are left along roadsides. Scenes from the Buddha's life are painted in the Ajanta caves in India (right).

Discussing The Middle Way Develop the reasons for calling it "The Middle Way."

● **Why is the Eightfold Path also called the Middle Way?** (It was meant to be neither too hard nor too easy to live by, but to fall in between the two.)

★**THINKING FURTHER: Cause and Effect How might following the Middle Way help end suffering?** (by stopping people from harming each other and helping them solve problems)

Exploring The Buddha's Final Journeys Help students understand that the Buddha's enlightenment was just the beginning of his journey.

● **How did the Buddha spend the rest of his life?** (as a wandering monk spreading his teachings)

★**THINKING FURTHER: Making Conclusions What conclusions can you draw about the Buddha's success?** (He left thousands of followers, including Buddhist monks, to carry on his work and spread his teachings.)

VISUAL LITERACY

ABOUT THE PAINTING OF THE BUDDHA'S LIFE The painting dates from the seventh century and is located in the caves of Ajanta, India. Although painting was a highly developed art in India at this time, few paintings survived to the present day. Those that did, such as this one of Buddha's life, reflect the grace and clarity of Indian art from this period. Invite students to study the painting. Possible questions include: How does the central figure show gracefulness? (He is leaning heavily to one side but doesn't appear to have lost his balance.) Why might more sculptures than paintings have survived from this time period? (Sculptures were probably sturdier than the paint pigments used.)

SECOND-LANGUAGE SUPPORT

GRAPHIC ORGANIZERS Second-language learners will benefit from using extended graphic comparisons of religions. Have students work in heterogeneous groups to prepare a matrix that compares names of religious texts, basic laws and beliefs, and other components of the religions.

BUDDHISM

Founder	Basic Beliefs	Basic Laws
Siddhartha Gautama	Karma Four Noble Truths Middle Way	Eight-fold Path

THE GROWTH OF BUDDHISM

Refer students to their desk maps and have them trace the paths of Buddhism from India to other Asian nations. Help students to conjecture about how it might have interacted with the cultures it touched.

Discussing the PRIMARY SOURCE

Have students read each proverb out loud.

- **What do the proverbs say is the only way to end hatred in the world?** *(by replacing it with love)*

- **The same quality is referred to in the second, third, and fourth proverbs. What is it?** *(control of self)*

- **How is the value of wisdom reflected in the fifth proverb?** *(It says that it is a sign of wisdom when one does not take praise or blame too seriously.)*

- ★**THINKING FURTHER:** *Making Conclusions* **Judging from these proverbs, what qualities does Buddhism value most?** *(love, wisdom, goodness, calm, self-control)*

Investigating Changing Buddhism
Introduce the idea of change over time.

- **How do Buddhists differ from each other in their beliefs?** *(whether the Buddha is a god or a great teacher, how to live by the Middle Way, how to achieve peace and truth)*

- **What Buddhist beliefs are constant?** *(The Buddha and his teachings should be honored, people should try to end suffering, and they should follow the Eightfold Path.)*

★**THINKING FURTHER:** *Making Conclusions* **Why do religions change and their followers' beliefs differ over time?** *(Help students to see that ideas change as times change and new ideas are introduced. It is like our political scene; people's views differ on how government should act. As new situations develop, governments may change, but the foundation for government remains.)*

THE GROWTH OF BUDDHISM

After the Buddha's death in 483 B.C., Buddhism spread throughout southern and eastern Asia. Traveling monks introduced the Buddha's teachings in other places. These included what are today China, Tibet, Sri Lanka, Japan, Korea, Thailand, and Vietnam.

Buddhists everywhere lived by the Buddha's teachings, which were written down as proverbs. According to the proverbs that follow, what qualities do Buddhists value and believe to be the most important in life?

Verses on the Law,
an ancient Buddhist text,
written down around 100 B.C.

*H*atreds never **cease** *by hatred in this world; by love alone they cease. This is an ancient law.*

*The reputation of him who is energetic, mindful, pure in deed, considerate, self-controlled, right-living, and **heedful** steadily increases.*

Calm is his mind, calm is his speech, calm is his action, who, rightly knowing, is wholly freed, perfectly peaceful, and self-controlled.

Irrigators lead the waters; carpenters bend the wood; the wise control themselves.

As a solid rock is not shaken by the wind, even so the wise are not ruffled by praise or blame.

---

cease: stop
heedful: aware

154

Changing Buddhism

As in Hinduism, many different schools of thought developed in Buddhism over the years. Some suggested that the Buddha was a god. Others thought that the Buddha was an ordinary person who discovered a way to end suffering. Buddhists differed with each other on what it meant to live according to the Middle Way. Buddhists also disagreed about how people reached peace and truth and freedom from suffering.

These differences of opinion continue today among Buddhists around the world. Yet some basic teachings continue to be shared by all Buddhists. These include honoring the Buddha and his teachings and helping others to end suffering.

BACKGROUND INFORMATION

ABOUT BUDDHISM TODAY Buddhism is divided into three main branches:

- The Theravada, or "Way of the Elders," is more conservative. It is dominant in Thailand, Sri Lanka, and Myanmar (formerly Burma).

- The Mahayana, or "Great Vehicle," is more liberal. It dominates in China, Japan, Taiwan, and Korea.

- Tibetan Buddhism, or Lamaism, is a branch that arose in Tibet and spread to other Himalayan countries—Nepal, Bhutan, and Sikkim.

- All three branches have followers in the West as well.

- It is difficult to estimate the number of Buddhists in the world. (They may not call themselves Buddhists or may follow another religion as well.) The best estimate is about 330 million.

WHY IT MATTERS

Buddhism developed in ancient India. From the beginning, it centered around the life and thoughts of Siddhartha Gautama. This man had much wealth as a prince, but left it all behind when he chose to become a penniless monk.

The teachings of the Buddha would have a big impact on Indian civilization for a time. However, Buddhism gained even greater influence in other parts of Asia. You will read about more of this story in chapters to come.

In China this giant statue of "sleeping Buddha" (left) is visited by Buddhists and tourists. The smaller statues are other ancient sculptures of the Buddha. A father and son (above, left) share a Buddhist candle ceremony.

✓ Reviewing Facts and Ideas

MAIN IDEAS

- Between about 1500 and 500 B.C., Aryan rulers gained control over much of India and spread Hinduism.
- Siddhartha Gautama founded Buddhism. He gave up all he owned to search for a way to end suffering.
- The Buddha borrowed beliefs from Hinduism. He also taught the Four Noble Truths, the Eightfold Path, and the Middle Way.
- Buddhism spread after the Buddha's death. This religion has 330 million followers today.

THINK ABOUT IT

1. What were the two ways of life that the young prince Siddhartha was said to have to choose between?

2. What might a Buddhist hope to achieve by following the Buddha's Eightfold Path?

3. **FOCUS** How did the Buddha say people should live? What guidelines did he offer?

4. **THINKING SKILL** What _caused_ Siddhartha Gautama to become a monk? What _effects_ did his becoming the Buddha have on life in India?

5. **WRITE** Write a paragraph comparing and contrasting Hindu and Buddhist beliefs. What do they share?

155

Discussing WHY IT MATTERS Encourage students to explain the Buddha's contribution.

> ★**THINKING FURTHER:** _Making Conclusions_ **How does the life of the Buddha show that one person can affect the world?** _(He developed a set of beliefs and teachings that has influenced life in India and other Asian countries, and continues.)_

⭐ 3 CLOSE

MAIN IDEAS

Have students write answers to these questions on a piece of paper.

- **How did Aryan power grow from 1500 B.C. to 500 B.C.?** _(Aryans extended control over much of India and spread Hinduism.)_

- **What major life decision did Siddhartha Gautama make as a young man in his palace?** _(to give up all and seek a way to end suffering)_

- **How would you describe the major beliefs of Buddhism?** _(some Hindu beliefs like reincarnation and karma, together with the Four Noble Truths, the Middle Way, following the Eightfold Path)_

- **How widespread is Buddhism today?** _(It is mainly practiced throughout Asia and today has millions of followers.)_

EVALUATE
✓ Answers to Think About It

1. a life of luxury and kingly power versus a life as a penniless monk
Make Inferences

2. to reach peace by ending suffering
Make Conclusions

3. to believe in the Eightfold Path and resolve to live by it, to do no harm to others, to rid oneself of evil, to take responsibility, to meditate
Recall Details

4. Cause: He wanted to end suffering. Effect: He gave India new beliefs and teachings to reach that goal.
Cause and Effect

5. Paragraphs should reflect the similarities—reincarnation and karma—and contrast the Hindu goal of being united with truth with the Buddhist goal of ending suffering.
Compare and Contrast

Write About It Tell students to write a brief before-and-after profile of Siddhartha Gautama, the Buddha.

MEETING INDIVIDUAL NEEDS

RETEACHING (Easy) Have students use an outline map of Asia to draw in and label India and the other Asian countries listed on p. 154, and add arrows to show Buddhism's spread from India to other places.

EXTENSION (Average) Refer students to the proverbs presented on the text p. 154 and have them rewrite each in their own words.

ENRICHMENT (Challenging) Meditation is an important component of Buddhism and it is widely practiced today, often including yoga practices. Have students do research on meditation—its aims and its practices—and prepare a written report of their findings, with illustrations if appropriate.

DISCUSSING MAJOR EVENTS Help students use this time line to recognize the span of time that ancient Indian civilization covered and how it was fairly evenly divided between two groups.

- **What was ancient India's first civilization? How long did it last?** (Harappan civilization; nearly a thousand years (2500 B.C.–1600 B.C.)

- **What migration followed the end of Harappan civilization?** (the Aryans, in 1500 B.C., just about a century later)

- **What tells you that the Aryans' civilization lasted at least as long as Harappan civilization?** (Aryan sacred songs were written down in 600 B.C., nearly a thousand years after they migrated to India.)

Answers to
THINKING ABOUT VOCABULARY

1. reincarnation
2. subcontinent
3. Vedas
4. karma
5. Middle Way

Answers to
THINKING ABOUT FACTS

1. He was troubled when he discovered people grow old and ill and die.

2. He became the Buddha, the "Awakened One," when he received wisdom sitting under a fig tree.

3. It has to accept legal changes in its caste system in India.

4. according to Buddhism, four principles that rule life

5. princes, priests, professionals and merchants, servants

Resource REMINDER
Practice and Project Book: *p. 34*
Assessment Book: *Chapter 6 Test*
Technology: *Videodisc/Video Tape 2*
Transparency: *Graphic Organizer, Word Map*

CHAPTER 6 REVIEW

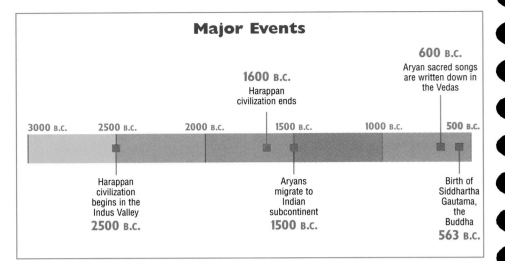

Major Events

600 B.C.
Aryan sacred songs are written down in the Vedas

1600 B.C.
Harappan civilization ends

3000 B.C. | 2500 B.C. | 2000 B.C. | 1500 B.C. | 1000 B.C. | 500 B.C.

Harappan civilization begins in the Indus Valley
2500 B.C.

Aryans migrate to Indian subcontinent
1500 B.C.

Birth of Siddhartha Gautama, the Buddha
563 B.C.

THINKING ABOUT VOCABULARY

Number a sheet of paper from 1 to 5. Beside each number write the word or term from the list below that best completes each sentence.

karma   subcontinent
Middle Way   Vedas
reincarnation

1. The constant cycle of life, death, and rebirth is called _____.

2. A _____ is a large landmass that is geographically separated from the rest of a continent.

3. The sacred songs of the ancient Aryans were written down about 600 B.C. in books called the _____.

4. According to Hindu belief, _____ is the force created by a person's good and bad deeds that affects his or her future life.

5. According to Buddhist belief, the laws of the Eightfold Path lead to the _____.

THINKING ABOUT FACTS

1. What made Siddhartha Gautama give up all he had and become a monk?

2. How did Siddhartha Gautama become the Buddha?

3. How has Hinduism changed recently?

4. What are the Four Noble Truths?

5. What four groups of people make up the Indian caste system?

6. How does the caste system shape the lives of Indians?

7. What was the role of the Indus River in the creation of Indian civilization?

8. Why do historians know less about the Indus River valley civilization than about ancient Egypt and Mesopotamia?

9. What did Harappan workers create that was unknown to other cultures?

10. According to the time line above, how long after the Aryans migrated to the Indian subcontinent were their sacred songs written down?

156

SECOND-LANGUAGE SUPPORT

MNEMONIC DEVICES Ask students to brainstorm ways to remember difficult vocabulary words from this and other chapters. Students might create picture symbols to help them remember what words mean. For example, they might represent the *caste system* with a series of boxes to express the idea that people are born into a caste in India and cannot move out of it. Or students can associate key words with a particular concept to remember its meaning. An example would be linking *dharma* with the words "laws" and "duties," which explain its meaning.

THINK AND WRITE

WRITING A LETTER

Suppose that you are one of the archaeologists who had uncovered the remains of Mohenjo-Daro. In a letter to a friend, describe the most interesting artifacts you found and what they reveal about the lives of the people who lived there.

WRITING A REPORT

Write a class report about the Hindu belief that people live in a constant cycle of birth, death, and rebirth. Explain this cycle and how it affects the way Hindus live.

WRITING AN ESSAY

Write a short essay about India's caste system. Describe what it is and discuss the beliefs that created it. Finally describe how the caste system is changing.

APPLYING GEOGRAPHY SKILLS

COMPARING DIFFERENT KINDS OF MAPS

1. Look back at "Using the Skill" on page 140. What did you learn by comparing Maps A and B?

2. What do you learn about Islamabad by comparing the three maps in the skill?

3. What conclusions can you make by comparing the maps on page 131 and page 135?

4. Look at the map on page 138. Can you learn anything by comparing it with the maps on pages 131 and 135?

5. What kind of information might one map show that another might not?

Summing Up the Chapter

Copy the word map below on a separate piece of paper. Then review the chapter and fill in details that support the main idea. After you have filled in the details, use the word map to write a paragraph that answers the question "How did civilization develop in India?"

Environment
- Indus Valley
- Silt

Way of Life
- Agriculture
- Specialization

MAIN IDEA Ancient India drew on its environment and its variety of people to develop a complex civilization.

- Harappans
- Aryans

People

- Vedas
- Mohenjo-Daro

Achievements

157

SUGGESTIONS FOR SUMMING UP THE CHAPTER

Before the students copy the spider map onto their papers, have them read and discuss the main idea and the categories of facts that support it. Where in the chapter are you likely to find the information to fill in these categories? Students should recognize that Lesson 1 treats the environment but that they will have to dip into the final three lessons for the rest. Possible answers are noted on the reproduced text page above. If you think it is necessary or useful, mention and discuss one possible answer for each category to help students understand the kinds of things they are looking for. Once students have filled in their spider maps, encourage them to weave each entry into the paragraph they write to answer the question.

ASSESSING THINK AND WRITE: *For performance assessment, see Assessment Book, Chapter 6, pp. T61-T63.*

---

6. It gives them their rank in society and tells them the work they will perform and their duties.

7. It gave ancient India the needed base for agriculture on which to develop a civilization.

8. Ancient Indian writing has not yet been deciphered, and few artifacts and remains have been found.

9. cloth made from cotton

10. 900 years (1500 B.C.–600 B.C.)

Answers to
APPLYING GEOGRAPHY SKILLS

1. Most of Pakistan's cities are located in the northeastern part of the country because the mountainous southeastern part discourages heavy settlement; many cities are near rivers.

2. It is the capital of Pakistan, it lies at a fairly high elevation, it does not lie in an agricultural region, it is near other cities.

3. By comparing the two maps you can conclude that the Indus Valley civilization developed around the Indus River Valley and the Indus Plain because they occupied roughly the same area.

4. The map on page 131 shows the relief of the mountains over which the Aryan migrations, shown on page 138, took place as well as the type of land—valleys and plains—to which the Aryans migrated.

5. One map might show physical features, another political borders and cities, and another areas that are suitable or unsuitable for agriculture.

 **Technology CONNECTION**

VIDEODISC/VIDEO TAPE

Enrich Chapter 6 with the *Ancient India* segment on the videodisc.

Search Frame 27953 Side A

CHAPTER OVERVIEW

In ancient China, farmers in the Huang River valley learned to control the river's floods around 3000 B.C. Ruling families, called dynasties, controlled states for hundreds of years at a time. A written language developed around 1100 B.C. From 500 B.C. on, the teachings of Confucius shaped life in China.

GEO ADVENTURES DAILY GEOGRAPHY ACTIVITIES

Use **Geo Adventures** Daily Geography activities to assess students' understanding of geography skills.

CHAPTER PLANNING GUIDE

LESSON 1	LESSON 2	LESSON 3
SUGGESTED PACING: 2 DAYS	SUGGESTED PACING: 2 DAYS	SUGGESTED PACING: 2 DAYS
Geography Of China pp. 160–163	**The First Dynasty** pp. 164–167	**The Emperor's Clay Army** pp. 168–171
CURRICULUM CONNECTIONS Links to Math, p. 161	**CURRICULUM CONNECTIONS** Links to Art, p. 166	**CITIZENSHIP** Linking Past and Present, p. 170
RESOURCES Practice and Project Book, p. 35 Desk Map Outline Map	**CITIZENSHIP** Valuing Orderly Government, p. 165	**FIELD TRIP** Visit an Art Museum, p. 170
	RESOURCES Practice and Project Book, p. 36 Anthology, p. 32	**RESOURCES** Practice and Project Book, p. 37

LESSON 4	CITIZENSHIP	Legacy
SUGGESTED PACING: 2 DAYS	SUGGESTED PACING: 1 DAY	SUGGESTED PACING: 1 DAY
Confucius Changes China pp. 174–178	**Working For Education** p. 179	**Silk Making** pp. 180–181
CURRICULUM CONNECTIONS Links with Art, p. 177 Links with Science, p. 177	**CITIZENSHIP** Understanding Government, p. 179	
CITIZENSHIP Confucius and Citizenship, p. 175		
RESOURCES Practice and Project Book, p. 39 Anthology, pp. 33, 34		

LEARNING STYLE: Visual

ON YOUR OWN

15 TO 30 MINUTES

Make a Keep-the-Peace Cartoon

Objective: To start students thinking about Confucianism and its effect on conflict in China.

Materials: drawing paper, tape, markers

1. Invite students to think about and list the different ways people keep the peace and settle arguments.
2. Encourage students to draw a cartoon about peace. Suggest they use speech balloons to write the dialogue of their characters.
3. Have each student share his or her cartoon with the class.

STUDYSKILLS

SUGGESTED PACING: 1 DAY

Writing A Summary
pp. 172–173

RESOURCES
Practice and Project Book, p. 38
TECHNOLOGY Videodisc

CHAPTER REVIEW

SUGGESTED PACING: 1 DAY

pp. 182–183

RESOURCES
Practice and Project Book, p. 40
TECHNOLOGY Videodisc/Video Tape 2
Assessment Book: Chapter 7 Test
Transparency: Graphic Organizer, Main Idea Diagram

SDAIE SUPPORT · SHELTERED INSTRUCTION

READING STRATEGIES & LANGUAGE DEVELOPMENT

Compare and Contrast/Homographs, p. 160, Lesson 1
Making and Supporting Generalizations/Quotation Marks, p. 164, Lesson 2
Use Visuals/Apostrophes in Possessives, p. 168, Lesson 3
Main Idea and Details/Multiple Meanings, p. 172, Skills Lesson
Context Clues/Possessive Nouns, p. 174, Lesson 4

SECOND-LANGUAGE SUPPORT

Taking Notes, p. 162
Graphic Organizers, pp. 165, 169
Working with a Peer, p. 177
Reviewing Through Illustrating/Response Journal, p. 182

MEETING INDIVIDUAL NEEDS

Reteaching, Extension, Enrichment, pp. 163, 167, 171, 173, 178, 181
McGraw-Hill Adventure Book

ASSESSMENT OPPORTUNITIES

Practice and Project Book, pp. 35–40
Write About It, pp. 163, 167, 171, 178, 181
Assessment Book: Assessing Think and Write, pp. T64–T66; Chapter 7 Tests: Content, Skills, Writing

Introducing the Chapter

Invite students to tell what they know about China today—its size, population, why it is often in the news, what they have seen or read about it. Point out that in this chapter they will have the chance to go back to the roots of China's development. Have them locate China on the map.

THINKING ABOUT HISTORY AND GEOGRAPHY

Have students read the text on this page. Encourage them to draw parallels between the events they read about here and similar events in other river valley civilizations they have studied.

3000 B.C. HUANG RIVER VALLEY

The Huang River is also known as the Yellow River.

● **Where in China is the Huang River?** (It flows west to east through the northern part of China.)

★**THINKING FURTHER:** *Making Conclusions* **What do you think the need for levees says about the Huang River?** (It is given to flooding.)

1100 B.C. ANYANG

Students will probably recall that the development of writing systems is a key part of the development of civilizations.

● **Where is the action in this panel taking place?** (Anyang)

● **Where do you locate it on the globe map?** (about two-thirds of the way along the Huang River's course in China as it flows east)

● **When is it taking place?** (1100 B.C.)

Resource **REMINDER**

Technology: *Videodisc/Video Tape 2*

Ancient China

THINKING ABOUT HISTORY AND GEOGRAPHY

Around 3000 B.C. farmers in the Huang River valley learned to control the river's floods in order to grow food. A group that ruled over a large area of the valley developed a written language around 1100 B.C. This was the beginning of modern Chinese writing. China grew into a large area. Within it, the teachings of a great scholar shaped life from about 500 B.C. to the present.

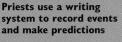

3000 B.C.	1100 B.C.	221 B.C.
HUANG RIVER VALLEY Farmers use levees to control floods	**ANYANG** Priests use a writing system to record events and make predictions	**XIANYANG** A powerful leader creates the first Chinese empire

158

BACKGROUND INFORMATION

LINKING THE MAP AND THE TIME LINE

● The Huang River Valley has been witness to the erratic history of its river. Since the 3rd millennium B.C., the river has changed course a total of 23 times, resulting from buildups in ground level that have come from deposits of loess, and has overrun its levees no fewer than 1,500 times. Because of the loess deposits, the Huang River has the fastest growing delta in the world, growing more than a mile a year.

● Anyang came to prominence as an archaeological center only in this century. Many earlier scholars thought that the tales of the Shang dynasty were mythical. Then, in 1928, archaeologists found the ruins of an ancient city under the current Anyang. Since then, evidence found there has verified Shang life.

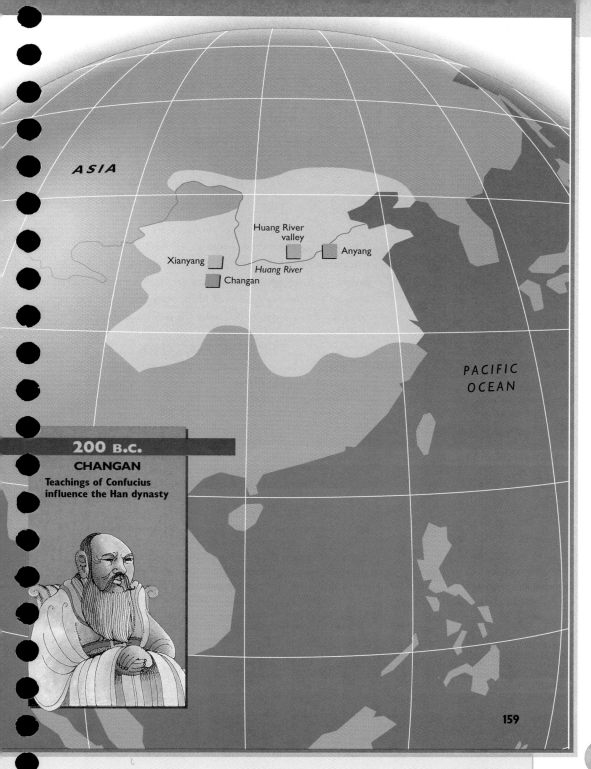

★ **THINKING FURTHER:** *Making Conclusions* **How does the Anyang panel make clear that the development of Chinese civilization is well under way?** *(A writing system has been developed and so have religious beliefs, as reflected by the presence of priests in the picture.)*

221 B.C. XIANYANG

Have students locate Xianyang on the map.

● **When was the first Chinese empire created?** *(221 B.C.)*

● **Where did this take place?** *(in Xianyang)*

★ **THINKING FURTHER:** *Making Conclusions* **How does the map show that Chinese civilization had spread beyond the Huang River?** *(Xianyang is west of the Huang River, not along it.)*

200 B.C. CHANGAN

Point out that the teachings of Confucius have had a lasting influence on China.

● **How much time has elapsed between this panel and the previous one?** *(21 years)*

★ **THINKING FURTHER:** *Making Conclusions* **What can you conclude from this panel about the development of Chinese civilization by this time?** *(An educational system was taking form.)*

Technology CONNECTION

VIDEODISC/VIDEO TAPE 2
Enrich Chapter 7 with the *Ancient China* segment on the videodisc.

Search Frame 39815 Side A

Labels on map: ASIA • Huang River valley • Xianyang • Changan • Huang River • Anyang • PACIFIC OCEAN

200 B.C.
CHANGAN
Teachings of Confucius influence the Han dynasty

159

BACKGROUND INFORMATION

LINKING THE MAP AND THE TIME LINE
● Xianyang is now called Sian and is one of China's greatest tourist attractions because of Shihuangdi's tomb there, about which students will read. Settlement there goes back to 6000 B.C. and the city has served as the capital of 11 of China's dynasties. At one time, it was probably the largest city in the world.

● Nearly 300 years after Confucius's death, his teachings became the basis for much of China's social and political life and remained so for centuries. His teachings influenced Chinese government, education, and personal behavior. Confucius spoke of balance in duties and respect between those in authority and those ruled by authority.

LESSON 1

PAGES 160–163

Lesson Overview

The *Huang River* gave China the great agricultural development it needed to develop a civilization but could also unleash a powerful destructive force.

Lesson Objectives

★ Locate and trace the Huang River.

★ Explain how its flow both enriched the soil and destroyed the fields.

★ Explain methods farmers used to battle its fury and farm its valley.

1 PREPARE

MOTIVATE Tell students that in this chapter they will meet the fourth of the world's earliest civilizations. Ask, *On what geographical feature did the first three depend?* (mighty rivers) Ask, *Do you predict the same for this one?*

SET PURPOSE Read the *Read Aloud* to the class and then the *Read to Learn* question to verify their prediction. Point out the photo of the contemporary Chinese farmer. Then encourage them to use the *Reading Strategy* suggested below. Encourage them to look at the *Vocabulary* terms.

2 TEACH

Understanding THE BIG PICTURE As students read this section, have them use their fingers to trace the flow of the Huang on the map on p. 161 or on their desk maps.

★ **THINKING FURTHER:** *Compare and Contrast* **What similarities can you already see between the Huang and the rivers you have studied in the last three chapters?** *(All carried silt, flooded their banks, created deltas, and gave rise to farming communities.)*

Resource REMINDER

Practice and Project Book: *p. 35*
Desk Map
Outline Map

GEOGRAPHY OF CHINA

Focus Activity

READ TO LEARN
How did the Huang River affect ancient Chinese civilization?

VOCABULARY
loess
levee
erosion
famine
steppe

PLACES
Huang River
North China Plain

READ ALOUD

"Whoever controls the Huang (HWAHNG) River controls China." According to Chinese tradition a powerful ruler spoke these words almost 4,000 years ago. In this lesson you will learn why the river has been so important throughout China's long history.

THE BIG PICTURE

In Chapter 6 you read that the Himalayas separate the Indian subcontinent from the rest of Asia. Within those mountains is "The Roof of the World"—the huge plateau, or raised plain, that forms most of Tibet. This plateau sits higher than most mountaintops in the United States. The Indus and many of Asia's largest rivers begin on this plateau. It is here that the Huang River begins its 3,000-mile trip across northern China.

The Huang has been a major force in China's history. Like the Indus, it starts as a clear stream but grows and picks up silt along its winding journey. During summer floods the Huang spreads enough silt on the North China Plain to create one of the world's largest deltas. The river also creates miles of fertile marshland.

About 4000 B.C. farming communities developed along the lower part of the Huang River. China's oldest civilization grew from these farming communities. This civilization later spread to include many regions and groups of people. Find the Huang River and the North China Plain on the map on the next page.

Loess **washes into the Huang River, giving it a yellow color. The word** Huang **means "yellow" in Chinese.**

160

SHELTERED INSTRUCTION

READING STRATEGIES & LANGUAGE DEVELOPMENT

COMPARE AND CONTRAST Remind students that writers can organize facts by comparing (showing similarities) and contrasting (showing differences). Display two items, such as two books, and have volunteers compare and contrast them. Then create a comparison/contrast chart for the Chinese civilization and another civilization students have studied. Have students complete the chart as they read this lesson. **[SDAIE STRATEGY: CONTEXTUALIZATION/SCHEMA BUILDING]**

HOMOGRAPHS On the board, write: "The *winds* carry loess into the Huang River as it *winds* through a hilly region." Point out that *wind* and *wind* are homographs—words with the same spelling but different meanings, or word origins, or pronunciations. Ask students to look up *wind* and *wind* in a dictionary and explain how they are homographs in all three ways.

MAP WORK: **1.** Ordos Desert **2.** Chang River **3.** because the coastline of the South China Sea has more twists and turns, creating a greater number of protected areas

CHAPTER 7 • LESSON 1

THE HUANG RIVER VALLEY

At one point along its journey, the Huang makes a giant curve around the edge of the Ordos Desert. Find this curve on the map below. As it turns, the Huang cuts through a hilly region. The hills are made almost entirely out of loess (LES). Loess is a dusty, yellow soil that has been deposited in this region by wind.

Working with the Environment

Loess has been a blessing and a curse to Chinese farmers. During summer rains, huge amounts of it are washed into the Huang. In fact, the Huang is the world's muddiest river.

When the Huang floods the North China Plain, the silt deposits create a unique environment. This loess-silt helps farmers because it is fine, rock-free, and very fertile. Because it is so light and fluffy, however, loess is easily carried away by storms. When this happens farmers are left with poor soil.

Like farmers in the Indus Valley, ancient farmers made use of the Huang Valley's fertile soil. They also fought to control river floods. This battle with nature has been going on since China's earliest days. It continues to this day.

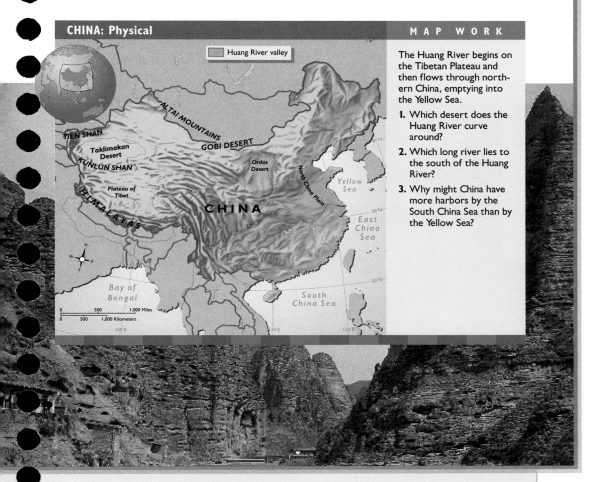

CHINA: Physical

Huang River valley

ALTAI MOUNTAINS
TIEN SHAN
Taklimakan Desert
GOBI DESERT
KUNLUN SHAN
Ordos Desert
Plateau of Tibet
HIMALAYAS
North China Plain
Yellow Sea
CHINA
East China Sea
Bay of Bengal
South China Sea

500   1,000 Miles
500   1,000 Kilometers

MAP WORK

The Huang River begins on the Tibetan Plateau and then flows through northern China, emptying into the Yellow Sea.

1. Which desert does the Huang River curve around?

2. Which long river lies to the south of the Huang River?

3. Why might China have more harbors by the South China Sea than by the Yellow Sea?

CURRICULUM CONNECTION

LINKS TO MATH How does the length of the Huang compare with that of the Nile and Indus? To answer that question, encourage the class to refer to earlier chapters and find the river lengths (p. 71: Nile—4,000 miles; p. 131: Indus—1,800 miles). Have students take the length of the Huang (3,000 miles) and do the arithmetic (4,000 – 3,000 = 1,000; 3,000 – 1,800 = 1,200) The Huang is 1,000 miles shorter than Nile and 1,200 miles longer than the Indus.

GLOBAL CONNECTION

LOESS IN THE UNITED STATES Large loess deposits occur along the Mississippi and its tributaries and on the Columbia Plateau in Oregon, Washington, and Idaho. Most American loess comes from glacial action, not desert origin. The word is from the German for "loose."

THE HUANG RIVER VALLEY

Help students to appreciate the great length of the Huang River (3,000 miles—roughly the width of the 48 United States or the Atlantic Ocean).

More **MAP WORK**

Have students answer the questions by referring to the map on this page. The size and boundaries shown in dark yellow are those of China at the end of the 20th century.

- *Where does the Huang River make a giant curve?* (around the Ordos Desert)

- *What substance does it pick up as it passes through this region?* (loess, *a dusty yellow soil deposited by wind*)

- *What plain does the Huang cross?* (the North China Plain)

- *Into what sea does the river empty?* (Yellow Sea)

★THINKING FURTHER: *Making Conclusions* **How might the production of loess be connected with the Gobi and Ordos deserts?** (*Help students recognize the connection of "dusty, yellow soil" to desert sands.*)

Discussing Working with the Environment Discuss the positive and negative aspects of loess and floods.

- *Why is loess both a blessing and a curse to Chinese farmers?* (*While it provides fertile soil, its lightness makes it easy for storms to carry that kind of soil away.*)

- *Why are river floods both helpful and harmful to Chinese farmers?* (*They bring loess but can also wash it away and destroy everything in their wake.*)

★THINKING FURTHER: *Compare and Contrast* **Which of the rivers you have studied so far is the Huang most like?** (*Students may mention the Tigris and Euphrates for their devastating floods, but they may choose the Indus—it too has destructive floods and also changes color.*)

AGRICULTURE ALONG THE HUANG

Have students contrast the floods of the Nile and the Huang.

Discussing Controlling the River
Use this section to help students see that a solution can be a new problem.

- **What was the first way Chinese farmers tried to control the waters of the Huang River?** (building levees, or walls, to keep the river in its banks)

- **What problem did this solution cause?** (The riverbed silted, causing water to rise above the levees.)

- **What is another solution they tried?** (canals to channel the water)

- **What problem did this create?** (Loess clogged the canals.)

> ★**THINKING FURTHER: Making Conclusions** Why are environmental problems often so difficult to solve? (Solutions can create new problems.)

Investigating Crops Grow in Loess Soil
Stress the richness of the Huang Valley.

- **What crops did the Huang Valley produce?** (grains, vegetables, fruits)

- **What is erosion?** (the wearing away of soil by wind or water)

> ★**THINKING FURTHER: Sequencing** How would you draw a flow chart to show progression from the initial good crop production in the Huang Valley to the famine that could occur? (good crop production→population growth→need to clear land to grow more to feed larger population→erosion→poor crop production→famine)

Finding Other Regions in Ancient China
Compare the steppes to the river valley.

- **How do steppes compare with a river valley?** (A steppe is a dry, treeless plain, not a well-watered valley.)

> ★**THINKING FURTHER: Compare and Contrast** How did life on the steppes of northern China differ from life in the Huang Valley? Why? (People on the steppes were herders, not farmers, because farming conditions are poor on the steppes.)

AGRICULTURE ALONG THE HUANG

Do you remember how Egypt's farmers usually welcomed the Nile's summer floods? China's farmers could not afford to let the Huang overflow freely. Their fields could be washed away. Huang Valley farmers needed to control floods.

Controlling the River

About 3,000 years ago, farmers began building earth levees (LEV eez) to hold back the Huang. A levee is a wall that keeps a river within its banks. Over time, though, a thick layer of mud built up along the riverbed. As the mud deposits grew, the river eventually spilled over the farmers' levees.

Like the Sumerians, ancient Chinese farmers also built canals to bring water to their fields. Yet loess once again caused problems. It constantly clogged the canals and had to be cleared away.

Crops Grow in Loess Soil

In spite of the problems it caused, loess also provided a rich soil. Many kinds of plants could grow in it. Huang farmers grew rice, millet (a type of grain), wheat, green onions, and ginger. They harvested grapes, peaches, plums, and wild chestnuts.

Because Huang Valley farmers were successful, the area's population grew. More farmable land became needed to feed people. Farmers had to clear trees from rich loess-lands to plant crops. One result was erosion. Erosion is the wearing away of soil by wind or water. This loss of soil occurs in areas where trees and shrubs are removed. Erosion of fertile soil sometimes makes it difficult for farmers to grow successful crops. If too much soil washes away and crops fail, a famine can happen. Famine is a time when very little food is available and people starve.

BACKGROUND INFORMATION

ABOUT MILLET
- Millet is a major food grain in Africa and Asia.
- It is eaten in many areas, usually baked into flat bread or made into porridge.
- It grows in long spikes and has a strong flavor.

SECOND-LANGUAGE SUPPORT

TAKING NOTES Simple note-taking formats, such as a +/- list, may help second-language learners better understand the text. For example, in the + column they might write that the Huang River carries dusty yellow soil, and in the - column that the soil makes the river very muddy. Have them continue with additional information and keep the chart handy for reference.

*People of the steppes ate more meat, while people of the valley ate more grain.

Other Regions in Ancient China

Not all of China was as suitable for farming as the Huang River valley. Growing crops is very difficult or impossible in many parts of China. To the north of the Huang Valley are windswept steppes (STEPS). A steppe is a dry, treeless plain. In this region people used another type of agriculture. Here, instead of planting crops, they herded sheep and cattle on horseback.

Lifestyles were very different along the Huang and on the steppes. How might a typical daily meal on the steppes differ from a meal in the river valley?*

WHY IT MATTERS

The hard work of China's ancient farmers paved the way for powerful kingdoms to develop throughout China. Many of those kingdoms grew along the Huang River. You will read about one of the earliest and most powerful of these kingdoms in the next lesson.

DID YOU KNOW?

Why is the Huang River often called "China's Sorrow"?

The flooding of the Huang has cost millions of lives throughout China's history. Famine, as much as drowning, has been a cause of these deaths. When the river washes away crops, it leaves people with little or nothing to eat.

Chinese generals have also used the power of the river as a deadly weapon. In World War II, for example, one general blew up key levees during flood season to stop the Japanese army. His plan worked—but it also took the lives of almost one million farmers. Many more died during the famine that followed.

Reviewing Facts and Ideas

MAIN IDEAS

- Loess has made the Huang River valley extremely fertile, but it causes many problems too.
- Ancient Chinese farmers built dirt levees along the Huang to try to keep the river on its course.
- Like people in other river valleys, farmers along the Huang raised crops. On China's northern steppes, people herded animals.

The farmer (far left) is harvesting rice. China produces about 35 percent of the world's rice each year. Herders who live on China's steppes often live in tents (left). The herders move to new grazing land each season.

THINK ABOUT IT

1. What does the Huang River share in common with the Indus River?

2. How has loess helped China's farmers? How has it caused problems?

3. **FOCUS** Why was it important for ancient farmers to control the Huang River? What made it hard for them to achieve their goal?

4. **THINKING SKILL** What _caused_ ancient farmers to strip loess-lands of their trees and shrubs? What _effects_ did this have on life along the Huang?

5. **GEOGRAPHY** Why is the big curve of the Huang an important part of the river? What happens here?

163

MEETING INDIVIDUAL NEEDS

RETEACHING (Easy) Ask students to use colored markers to create two illustrations showing two things people along the Huang did to try to control floods.

EXTENSION (Average) Tell students to write a description of "A Day in the Life of a Huang Farmer." Have them focus on some element in the battle such a farmer would fight against nature.

ENRICHMENT (Challenging) The Huang River has changed course several times in its history. Have students do research to find out what caused these changes and write an illustrated report on them.

Discussing WHY IT MATTERS Help the class reinforce the lesson of this unit.

- *How does this lesson prove once again that civilization depends on farmers?* (Help students to appreciate ancient farmers' back-breaking toil and endless battle with nature.)

Extending Did You Know? Invite students to do further research on the Huang River to see just how it deserves its reputation as "China's Sorrow." Have them find out about its major floods and about any major projects for overcoming its disastrous tendency to flood.

3 CLOSE

MAIN IDEAS

Call on individual students to answer these questions.

- *How has loess been both good and bad for Chinese farmers?* (It can provide fertile soil but it can also blow away, resulting in floods and clogged canals.)
- *What did ancient Chinese farmers build to try to keep the Huang in its course?* (levees)
- *What were two major ways of life in ancient China?* (farming along the Huang and herding on the steppes)

EVALUATE
✓ **Answers to Think About It**

1. They carry silt down their courses, creating deltas, and threatening major floods.
   Make Analogies

2. It has brought fertile soil but has also contributed to destructive floods.
   Make Inferences

3. The river made farming possible, but the fury of its floods often overcame the farmers' ability to control them.
   Form Generalizations

4. Cause: the need to feed a growing population; Effects: soil erosion, famine.
   Cause and Effect

5. That is where tons of loess wash into the Huang.
   Five Themes of Geography: Place

Write About It Tell students to picture an ancient Huang farmer. Have them write a letter from that farmer to a farmer in another ancient river civilization comparing and contrasting the problems they face.

LESSON 2

PAGES 164–167

Lesson Overview
The Shang civilization shaped China's religion, government, and writing in ways still recognizable in China today.

Lesson Objectives
★ Analyze how *Anyang* developed as the capital of Shang civilization.

★ Identify and describe elements of the cultural legacy that the Shang dynasty shaped for China.

1 PREPARE

MOTIVATE Have a student read the *Read Aloud* to the class, trying to engender a feeling of excitement in making a discovery about ancient secrets. Ask them to examine the details of the Shang bronze ram shown here.

SET PURPOSE Briefly review Champollion's decoding of the Rosetta Stone, which unlocked the secrets of hieroglyphics. Encourage students to read to answer the *Read to Learn* question. Preview the *Vocabulary* terms.

2 TEACH

Understanding THE BIG PICTURE
Use the questions to set the stage.

● *What is a dynasty?* (a family line of rulers that passes control of an area down from generation to generation)

● *Where did the Shang dynasty develop?* (in the Huang River delta)

★ **THINKING FURTHER:** *Making Conclusions* **Why do you think a dynasty could help a civilization develop?** (Help students see that just as the pharaohs' strong leadership in Egypt helped that civilization to develop, so a strong line of rulers in China might have the same effect.)

Resource **REMINDER**

Practice and Project Book: *p. 36*
Anthology: *O Magnificent and Many, p. 32*

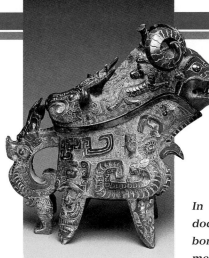

| 2000 B.C. | 1700 B.C. | 1100 B.C. | 500 B.C. | A.D. 1 |

THE FIRST DYNASTY

Focus Activity

READ TO LEARN
What do the remains at Anyang tell us about life in early China?

VOCABULARY
dynasty
nobles
oracle bones

PEOPLE
Fu Hao

PLACES
Anyang

READ ALOUD

In 1899 a Chinese scholar became ill and asked his doctor for help. He was given a packet of animal bones that, when ground up, would make a popular medicine. When the scholar looked closely at the bones, he noticed that they were covered with mysterious ancient writing. He became determined to find out where the bones came from and what they meant. Later the scholar led archaeologists to a site along the Huang River. What they found would change history books about ancient China.

THE BIG PICTURE

By 3000 B.C. Egypt was being united and city-states and towns were expanding in the Fertile Crescent and the Indus Valley. At the same time farms along China's Huang River were growing larger and more productive. Towns grew too, and the largest of these became capitals of states.

By about 1700 B.C. one kingdom had won control over the large Huang River delta. One of its earliest capitals was a city called Shang. That name also became the state's name. Since it was ruled by one family for a long period of time, the government became known as the Shang dynasty. A dynasty is a line of rulers who belong to the same family. Control is passed from one generation to the next. For 600 years the Shang dynasty would shape the lives of people along the Huang River.

164

SHELTERED INSTRUCTION

READING STRATEGIES & LANGUAGE DEVELOPMENT

MAKING AND SUPPORTING GENERALIZATIONS Remind students that a good way to understand what they read is to make generalizations (general conclusions drawn from details.) Arrange students in teams to create word webs with details of this generalization: Dogs make good pets. Then make a chart with these categories: Artifacts, City Development, Government, Written Language, Religion. Have students complete the chart with generalizations and supporting details from this lesson.
[SDAIE STRATEGY: METACOGNITIVE DEVELOPMENT/SCHEMA BUILDING]

QUOTATION MARKS Review with the class the various uses for quotation marks—to cite words someone spoke, to enclose a phrase that characterizes someone, or to enclose a term referring to a name. Refer the class to the various uses of quotation marks on p. 166 and identify each use.

TOWNS ALONG THE HUANG RIVER

The Shang state spread along the Huang River until it ruled hundreds of towns. The Shang kings created new towns by giving land to their relatives, or nobles. These nobles oversaw the construction of the new towns and became their rulers.

Think of what it might have been like to rule a town during the Shang dynasty. You would have been very busy. The towns were important centers of production. They supplied food, clothing, and other products for the king and the nobles. These towns also helped to keep enemy states from invading the vast Shang lands. People from the towns often were part-time soldiers. They were sent to war whenever they were needed.

An Ancient City

Near the end of the Shang dynasty's 600-year rule, the capital was moved. Its new site was near the town that is today Anyang (AHN YAHNG). Find Anyang on the map on this page. The writing on the bones described

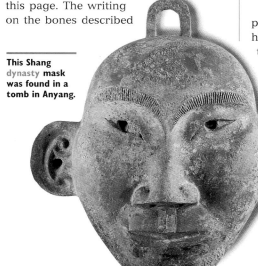

This Shang dynasty mask was found in a tomb in Anyang.

LANDS OF THE SHANG DYNASTY, 1200 B.C.

MAP WORK

The Shang dynasty controlled lands along the Huang River.

1. How far from the Yellow Sea is Anyang?
2. Where was the city of Anyang located—north or south of the Huang River?

in the lesson introduction led archaeologists to the ancient city. Its ruins have taught much about life in Shang China.

Shang society was organized like a pyramid. At the top were the king and his family. Below them were nobles, then craftworkers, then farmers. Prisoners of war were at the bottom.

Archaeologists at Anyang have uncovered many huts. Dug halfway into the ground, these "pit-houses" served as homes and workshops for metal-workers, potters, and servants. Remains of what seem to be palaces lie in the city's center. Bronze cups, stone carvings, and magnificent chariots were found in nearby royal tombs.

165

TOWNS ALONG THE HUANG RIVER

Discuss with students the methods the Shang dynasty used to extend its rule.

● *How did the Shang dynasty encourage the settlement of more lands and towns?* (by granting land and rule to family members)

● *Why were towns necessary to the development of Shang civilization? What roles did they play?* (They served as production and distribution centers, supplied the needs of kings and nobles, and provided soldiers.)

★THINKING FURTHER: *Classifying How would you design an organization chart for Shang government?* (king at the top with lines fanning down to nobles whose power came from him)

Discussing An Ancient City Reinforce the main idea and details of the text.

● *Why is Anyang important?* (It became the capital. Discovery of its ruins provides data on early China.)

● *What do we know about Anyang?* (The wealthy royalty lived in palaces. Ordinary people lived in pit-houses. They knew how to make bronze and to build chariots)

★THINKING FURTHER: *Compare and Contrast How would you compare Shang social structure with that of ancient Egypt?* (Have students refer to the Egyptian social pyramid on p. 95 and match Shang levels to it.)

More MAP WORK

Have students find Anyang on the map.

● *Where was Anyang located in relation to the old capital at Shang?* (to the north)

● *How far has Shang civilization spread out beyond the Huang Valley?* (It has spread south of the next major river.)

★THINKING FURTHER: *Making Decisions What grade would you give the Shang dynasty for extending their control?* (Students will probably rate them high. Point out that the dynasty ruled 4 million people.)

CITIZENSHIP★

VALUING ORDERLY GOVERNMENT Have students tell how governing power was passed on by the Shang dynasty from one generation to the next. Then have them tell how our society passes on governing power (by elections, with the winner continuing in office or replacing the loser). Encourage students to recognize that either system can provide the orderly transfer of power necessary for a stable society.

SECOND-LANGUAGE SUPPORT

GRAPHIC ORGANIZERS Second-language students may need help in following time. Help them create a large time line from 3,000 B.C. to show growth of civilization along the Huang, locate dates such as 1700 B.C. (beginning of the Shang Dynasty), and mark the end of its 600-year rule. Then have students explain events on the time line.

★**THINKING FURTHER:** *Making Generalizations* **What generalizations can you make about Shang craftworkers and rulers? What supports your generalizations?** *(Craftworkers had skill and command of technology, as shown by the quality of the objects they made. Rulers had wealth and power, as shown by the cost of objects found in their tombs and their ability to get such tombs.)*

More **CHART WORK**

Refer students to both chart and text.

● *How did Chinese writing change over time? (Its characters became simpler, thus making it easier to write quickly.)*

● *What other writing system underwent the same change? (cuneiform)*

Discussing a Written Record
Have students consider the artifacts.

● *Why do you suppose no ancient writings on bamboo and silk survive? (Help students see that such products turn to dust over time.)*

● *What was the function of* **oracle bones?** *(Priests "read" the cracks on the bones to reveal the future.)*

★**THINKING FURTHER:** *Cause and Effect* **Why do you think the bones at Anyang were called "dragon bones?"** *(Since dragons are magical beasts, perhaps their bones could reveal the future.)*

BURIED TREASURES

The finds at Anyang are a treasure for archaeologists and historians. One royal tomb found at Anyang contained more artifacts than any other. Hundreds of bronze containers, ivory statues, and other valuable objects were in the grave. Artifacts from this tomb tell how rich Shang rulers were. For whom were all of these riches made?

Archaeologists have determined that this grave belonged to a king's wife. Her name was Fu Hao (FOO HOW), or "Lady Hao." Fu Hao succeeded at many things during her life. She led troops to war. She ruled her own town. Unlike most other Shang leaders, she succeeded at being remembered in history. That is because records about her life have been preserved in her tomb.

A Written Record

A writing system had developed along parts of the Huang River before the Shang dynasty. Like early cuneiform, the earliest Chinese signs looked like pictures of objects. By the time of the Shang dynasty, though, characters were simpler. Symbols could stand for objects or ideas. Look at the diagram on this page to see one way this writing system developed over time.

One ancient Chinese historian mentioned that many records of the Shang were "written on bamboo and silk." Unfortunately, no bamboo tablets or silk cloth have survived from Shang times. However, writing has been found on bronze pots and stone.

More writing has been discovered on the thousands of "dragon bones" found

DEVELOPMENT OF CHINESE WRITING

	TO FISH	TURTLE	HORSE
SHANG DYNASTY ORACLE BONE CHARACTERS (1700–1400 B.C.)			
MODERN CHARACTERS	漁	龜	馬
MODERN SIMPLIFIED CHARACTERS	渔	龟	马

The earliest known Chinese writing is found on oracle bones (above). The chart shows how this early writing developed into modern Chinese characters.

166

This container, found in Fu Hao's tomb, shows the skill of Shang craftworkers.

at Anyang. Most of these bones came from cattle or sheep. They were used by special priests who the Shang believed were oracles (AWR uh kulz), or people who could predict the future. The bones became known as "oracle bones." Priests heated the oracle bones over a fire until they cracked. The pattern of cracks was used to answer questions about the future.

Like most Shang kings, Fu Hao's husband, Wu Ding, depended on priests to read oracle bones and predict the future. Would Fu Hao recover from an illness? Would farmers have a good harvest? Should Wu Ding go to war? It was believed that the pattern of cracks in the oracle bones gave the answers to his questions.

Religion of the Shang

Shang Chinese believed that their ancestors lived in another world and controlled human life. If an oracle's prediction came true, they believed that the king was being helped by his ancestors. This, they believed, proved that he was the right person to be king.

The people of the Shang dynasty worshiped many different gods. They believed these gods controlled nature. The ancient people also believed that when they died, they would join their ancestors and the gods.

WHY IT MATTERS

The Shang dynasty of the Huang River valley created a legacy that would shape life in China for centuries. Shang religious beliefs and style of government would live on for hundreds of years. The writing system developed during this time is similar to the system that is still used in China today. In the next lesson you will read about a man who spread many Shang ideas about religion and government throughout China.

✓ Reviewing Facts and Ideas

MAIN IDEAS

- Around 1700 B.C. the Shang state won control over the Huang Valley region. This area was ruled by the Shang dynasty until about 1100 B.C.
- The Shang used writing to record and predict important events.

THINK ABOUT IT

1. Describe the social pyramid of China during the Shang dynasty.

2. What were oracle bones? How were they used in ancient China?

3. **FOCUS** What were three artifacts found at Anyang? What do they tell us about the people who lived there?

4. **THINKING SKILL** *Compare* the Shang system of government with that of the pharaohs' government in Egypt.

5. **GEOGRAPHY** Imagine you are a noble who is building a town in Shang China. Where would you decide to build? What would you consider in making your decision?

167

Exploring Religion of the Shang

Help students understand the unique Shang religion.

> ★**THINKING FURTHER:** *Compare and Contrast* **How would you compare and contrast Shang and Egyptian religions?** *(Both have gods of nature and an afterlife, but the Shang also included a reverence for ancestors.)*

Discussing WHY IT MATTERS Review with students what the lesson teaches.

> ★**THINKING FURTHER:** *Making Generalizations* **What generalizations can you make about Shang civilization?** *(Encourage students to make many generalizations, but demand evidence to support each.)*

3 CLOSE

MAIN IDEAS

Have students answer in writing.

- **When and for how long did the Shang dynasty rule in China?** *(for about 600 years, from 1700 B.C. to 1100 B.C.)*

- **What do oracle bones tell us about communication in the Shang civilization?** *(Writing on the bones recorded and predicted events.)*

EVALUATE

✓ **Answers to Think About It**

1. from top down, king, nobles, craftworkers, farmers, prisoners of war *Recall Details*

2. They were bones used to answer questions about the future. Cracks that resulted from heating were interpreted by oracles as answers. *Summarize*

3. Tomb artifacts show great wealth and skill; oracle bones show written language; ruins of buildings show palaces and pit-houses. *Make Conclusions*

4. Both were dynastic, but pharaohs were probably more powerful. *Make Analogies*

5. One would probably want to build in the best spot for farming, for a town or city, and for transportation. *Five Themes of Geography: Human/Environment Interaction*

Write About It Have students picture a visit to Anyang in Shang times and write a short letter home describing it.

MEETING INDIVIDUAL NEEDS

RETEACHING (Easy) Tell students to review the social structure of Shang society and then have them illustrate it in the form of a pyramid.

EXTENSION (Average) Try to have available some newspaper travel sections or travel magazine ads that tout the benefits of traveling to various interesting locations. Tell students to write a similar ad encouraging people to visit Shang China. Then help them make a bulletin board display of their ads.

ENRICHMENT (Challenging) Several books about ancient China, or books that include material on it, are available for young people. Tell students to use them to do further research on Shang civilization and prepare their own illustrated booklets presenting aspects of the civilization. The booklets can then become part of a classroom library.

LESSON 3

PAGES 168–171

Lesson Overview
China's first empire, under the harsh rule of its emperor Shihuangdi, centralized China's systems of writing, government, and money.

Lesson Objectives
★ Place in proper sequence the events that helped to build the Chinese empire.
★ Describe the government it developed.

1 PREPARE

MOTIVATE Have four students each read one sentence of the *Read Aloud* to the class. How does this new find give further evidence of ancient Chinese civilization's wealth, power, and accomplishment? Encourage students to examine the clay soldier on this page and to thumb through the lesson's visuals to preview the evidence.

SET PURPOSE Ask a student to read the *Read to Learn* question aloud. Have the class read to find answers to it. Encourage them to view the *Vocabulary*.

2 TEACH

Understanding THE BIG PICTURE
Develop the sense of one dynasty succeeding another.

● *Who was Shihuangdi?* (a general of Qin province who conquered northern China and declared himself emperor)

● *How long did he think his empire would last?* (10,000 generations, 200,000–300,000 years)

★**THINKING FURTHER:** *Sequencing How would you put in order the events from the end of the Shang dynasty to the founding of the empire?* (fall of Shang, conflict and turmoil, build up of Qin strength, Qin control of northern China, Chinese empire)

Practice and Project Book: *p. 37*

2000 B.C.　1500 B.C.　1000 B.C.　500 B.C.　221 B.C.　206 B.C.　A.D. 1

THE EMPEROR'S CLAY ARMY

READ ALOUD

In 1974 farmers living near the southern curve in the Huang River began digging a new well. Imagine their surprise when they began to uncover life-sized clay soldiers! Archaeologists were called to the site. Since that day an entire clay army—more than 8,000 soldiers, horses, and chariots—has been unearthed. No two of the soldiers look alike. Each one once held a real weapon to fight off some unknown enemy. Who built this amazing clay army and why? Following is the story of China's Qin (CHIN) dynasty.

Focus Activity

READ TO LEARN
How did Shihuangdi build an empire in China?

VOCABULARY
emperor
province

PEOPLE
Shihuangdi

PLACES
Qin
Qinling Mountains
Xianyang
Great Wall of China

THE BIG PICTURE

The Shang dynasty came to an end around 1100 B.C. For many years afterward the Huang River valley was a place of conflict and turmoil. Slowly one region, called Qin, built up its strength. Qin's ruler was a general who would one day order the making of the great clay army described above. In 221 B.C. this general led a real army in a bold drive to take control of the Huang River delta. He and his army won battle after battle, eventually conquering all of northern China.

When his victory was complete, the Qin general declared himself China's emperor. An emperor is the supreme ruler of an empire. He celebrated his new role by taking the name Shihuangdi (SHEE hwahng dee), or "First Grand Emperor." Shihuangdi boasted that his Qin dynasty would last for 10,000 generations.

168

SHELTERED INSTRUCTION

READING STRATEGIES & LANGUAGE DEVELOPMENT

USE VISUALS To help students draw greater meaning from visuals, remind them that each type of visual helps describe the text and that one visual can explain another. Point out the different types of visuals in this lesson, including maps, art of the period, and photographs from recent times. Then ask volunteers which books, movies, or TV shows might feature visuals shown in this lesson and why. **[SDAIE STRATEGY: BRIDGING]**

APOSTROPHES IN POSSESSIVES This lesson provides an opportunity to review the formation of the singular possessive—'s—and the plural possessive s'. Call on students to find examples of the possessive in the text and write them on the board (*Qin's, empire's, historian's,* for example). What would happen if *empire* or *historian* were plural rather than singular? They would become *empires'* and *historians'*.

THE RISE OF AN EMPIRE

What made it possible for Shihuangdi and the Qin armies to win control and hold an empire together? Geography played a part in their victory. The original Qin region was protected by the Qinling (CHIN LING) Mountains on one side and by the Huang River on the other. From this central point, soldiers were able to march out and expand the Qin empire.

A New Kind of Government

Shihuangdi had new ideas about how a government should be run. These ideas were even more important than his armies in strengthening Qin's power. Shihuangdi split the empire into 36 provinces (PRAHV in sez), or political divisions of land.

The emperor also let farmers own land. This weakened the power of the nobles. Shihuangdi also forced many nobles to move to the capital city, Xianyang (shee AHN yang). There he took away their bronze weapons.

As in ancient Egypt, new ideas about communication helped to unify China. Shihuangdi set up a single system of writing throughout the empire. Local leaders used this writing system to report to the capital. Written language also helped the government to record and collect taxes.

Shihuangdi also created a single system of money to be used throughout the empire. Craftworkers made coins out of bronze. Holes in the coins allowed people to keep their money on a string. These changes were strictly enforced by the emperor's soldiers.

LANDS OF THE QIN DYNASTY, 221 B.C.

0   500   1,000 Miles
0   500   1,000 Kilometers

Xianyang

QINLING MTS.

Sea of Japan

Yellow Sea

East China Sea

PACIFIC OCEAN

South China Sea

MAP WORK

Shihuangdi's armies marched out of Xianyang to conquer new lands. What sea was located at the southernmost point of the empire?

A bronze chariot and horses were in Shihuangdi's tomb.

THE RISE OF AN EMPIRE

More **MAP WORK**

Have students sit in pairs with one text opened to the map on this page and the other to the map on p. 165.

- **Where was the Qin state located?** (at the southern curve of the Huang)

- **What geographical features gave it a position for conquest?** (The Qinling Mountains on one side and the Huang on another made it like a fortress.)

- ★**THINKING FURTHER:** *Making Comparisons* **How do the lands of the Qin dynasty compare with those of the Shang?** (Qin lands are broader in all directions, bordering on the East China and South China seas.)

Discussing a New Kind of Government Help students to see that "In union, there is strength."

- **How did Shihuangdi organize his empire?** (He divided it into 36 divisions, or provinces.)

- **Think back to how the Shang settled and organized their lands. With whom did Shang kings share power?** (with nobles who had land)

- **How did Shihuangdi change this arrangement and why?** (He granted land ownership to farmers, thus weakening the nobles' ruling power.)

- **Why do you think he wanted to weaken the nobles' power?** (so he could hold all ruling power in a unified government)

- **How did he change communications to strengthen his government?** (by setting up a single system of writing so that officials could carry out his orders across the empire)

- **How did he make money a unifying force?** (He set up a single system of money throughout the empire.)

- **How did he enforce the power of his government?** (with his army)

★**THINKING FURTHER:** *Compare and Contrast* **Why would you say that Shihuangdi's Chinese empire was more highly organized than Shang China?** (It had a strong centralized government and national unity.)

BACKGROUND INFORMATION

ABOUT SHIHUANGDI AND LEGALISM

- Shihuangdi believed in a philosophy called legalism. It emphasized strong government, strict laws, and efficient enforcement of them.
- Legalistic administrative practices have been a continuing force in Chinese governance.
- Today, the term "legalist" is sometimes used to refer to someone who is overly strict in adhering to the letter of the law.

SECOND-LANGUAGE SUPPORT

GRAPHIC ORGANIZERS Second-language learners can create a topic cluster to help them organize and visualize lesson information. Suggest that they create a cluster for each important lesson topic and store them in a folder for later review.

FARMERS BUILD
THE EMPIRE

Refer the class to the italicized paragraph in the Skills Lesson on p. 173 for more information about building the Great Wall of China.

★THINKING FURTHER: *Making Generalizations* **What facts can you find to support this generalization: "There was no rest for the farmers in Shihuangdi's empire"?** *(Have students come to the board and list many jobs demanded of farmers of the time—fighting river floods, growing enough food to feed an empire, paying taxes to support it, building highways, building walls to keep out invaders, serving as soldiers to fight invaders.)*

Discussing Building the Emperor's Tomb Relate the photos to the text on this page and p. 171. Tell students to review what they learned about this tomb in the *Read Aloud.*

● **What was Shihuangdi's grand plan for his tomb?** *(It was to be a mirror world, showing his power in death as in life.)*

● **What was the purpose of the clay army in this plan?** *(to protect the emperor from attack)*

★THINKING FURTHER: *Making Conclusions* **Why will archaeologists have to be even more careful than usual when they open Shihuangdi's tomb?** *(If the ancient Chinese historian is correct, they will have to dodge arrows from crossbows aimed at the entrance.)*

FARMERS BUILD
THE EMPIRE

Under Shihuangdi's leadership, unified China grew bigger and stronger. The empire also became increasingly rich as taxes from China's farmers flowed into the capital. As time went by, the government began making ever greater demands on its people.

Farmers were required to build the highways that linked the cities of the empire. Farmers were also called upon to strengthen and connect walls along the empire's northern border. These walls were built to keep out the people of the northern steppes. Much later, similar walls would be built across these same mountains and valleys. The later walls made up the Great Wall of China that we can see today. The Great Wall of China eventually grew to be more than 1,500 miles long!

Farmers were the backbone of the Qin empire. Their hard work as farmers, soldiers, and builders kept the empire strong. Still, their lives mostly

centered around the seasonal floods of the Huang. As before, they continued to grow the wheat, rice, and other crops needed to feed an empire.

Building the Emperor's Tomb

One of the greatest building projects in the Qin empire was the construction of a tomb for Shihuangdi. The emperor wanted his tomb to be a spectacular mirror of the real world. The clay army, which you read about in the lesson introduction, was just one part of this "mirror world." Its many soldiers and

170

GLOBAL CONNECTION

A CONNECTION WITH SPACE Astronauts report that the only human-built structure on Earth that can be seen from outer space is the Great Wall of China. Point out to students that while they have so far read about two of the Seven Wonders of the Ancient World—the Great Pyramids of Giza and the Hanging Gardens of Babylon—the Great Wall of China has sometimes been called the "Eighth Wonder."

CITIZENSHIP★

LINKING PAST AND PRESENT Explain to the class that building the Great Wall was a great national project directed by the emperor. Point out that the United States effort to reach the moon was also a national project, one approved by elected representatives. Have students research this effort: who proposed it, its time frame, and how well it achieved its aim.

FIELD TRIP

If you have an art museum with an ancient Chinese art collection, try to arrange a field trip with a guide to take the class on a tour of art and artifacts from the period covered in this chapter. If not, see if you can arrange for an in-class audio-visual presentation of such art.

Shihuangdi ordered that these clay soldiers be set up in formation. They stood with their backs to the emperor in order to protect him from attack.

horses stood guard, ready to protect the emperor from attack.

Shihuangdi's burial place lies under a giant mound near the clay army. Archaeologists have not yet uncovered the contents of the tomb. However, an ancient Chinese historian once told what lay inside.

The treasure-filled tomb, the historian wrote, was laid out like a giant map of the empire. Models of the Huang and other rivers, he said, flowed with mercury pumped by machines. On the ceiling sparkled bright stars. To keep out robbers, crossbows were set up that would shoot arrows if the tomb's entrance was disturbed. One day archaeologists may be able to compare the ancient historian's description with the actual remains in the tomb.

WHY IT MATTERS

In 221 B.C. Shihuangdi had boasted that the Qin dynasty would rule China for 10,000 generations. It actually lasted only 15 years. After Shihuangdi's death in 210 B.C., farmers and nobles alike revolted against his dynasty's harsh rule. However, China's first emperor would leave a lasting legacy. The centralized systems of writing, government, and money that he created would live on for centuries.

✔️ Reviewing Facts and Ideas

MAIN IDEAS

● Around 221 B.C. Shihuangdi unified China with his powerful armies and by strengthening government. He created standard writing and money systems across the empire.

● Farmers were the backbone of the Qin economy. They also served as part-time soldiers and builders.

THINK ABOUT IT

1. How did farmers help make Shihuangdi's empire strong?

2. What qualities might have been admired in the first emperor? What qualities were probably feared?

3. **FOCUS** How was Shihuangdi able to gain control over China?

4. **THINKING SKILL** Suppose you are a noble governing your own town in Qin China. Emperor Shihuangdi has just called you to his capital at Xianyang. Write a letter in response to the emperor's request from the noble's *point of view*.

5. **GEOGRAPHY** Look at the map on page 169. How did geographical features help Shihuangdi's army to conquer northern China?

171

Discussing WHY IT MATTERS
Contrast Shihuangdi's prediction with reality.

★**THINKING FURTHER:** *Making Conclusions* **How does the history of Shihuangdi's empire support the idea that great and lasting change can come about in a short span of time?** *(Students should note that although the empire lasted only 15 years, its legacy—government style, written language, and money—profoundly influenced China for centuries.)*

⭐ 3 CLOSE

MAIN IDEAS
Have students work in small groups to answers these questions.

● *What means did Emperor Shihuangdi use to unify and strengthen the empire?* (centralized government, standardized writing and money, military power)

● *In what ways were farmers absolutely crucial to the Qin economy?* (They produced the crops to feed the people, supplied the labor for public projects, and fought as soldiers.)

EVALUATE
✔️ **Answers to Think About It**
1. They kept people fed, built public projects, and fought the enemies. *Make Conclusions*

2. Admired: military leadership, organizational ability. Feared: too demanding of and harsh toward citizens, self-glorification. *Form Generalizations*

3. through military conquest and by weakening the nobles' ruling power *Main Ideas*

4. Letters may reflect outrage at land theft or sound reasons that such a takeover should not occur. *Point of View*

5. Qin's enclave between mountains and a mighty river provided a well-positioned base from which to fight. *Five Themes of Geography: Human/Environment Interaction*

Write About It Tell students to write a paragraph in which they identify the events, in the order they occurred, in the building of China's first empire.

SKILLS LESSON

Lesson Overview
Writing a summary helps a reader to focus on main ideas.

Lesson Objectives
★ Identify main ideas and the details that support them.

1 PREPARE

MOTIVATE Remind students that they have already read about the Great Wall of China. Tell them that in this lesson they will learn to write a *summary* to organize what they learn. Have them read *Why the Skill Matters* and encourage them to think of ways they use summaries in their own lives.

SET PURPOSE Encourage students to read this skills lesson for ways to pick out highlights of what they read. Have them get started by reading *Helping Yourself.*

2 TEACH

Using the Skill Help students identify the aspects of the skill.

- *What do topic sentences do?* (present main ideas)

- *What do sentences around them do?* (give details to support main idea)

- *What are the main ideas in the paragraph about Shihuangdi and the herders?* (Herders threatened; Shihuangdi sought to repel them.)

- *What are some supporting details?* (the skills that made them a threat and Shihuangdi's fears about them)

Technology CONNECTION

VIDEODISC
Enrich this skills lesson with the segment on the Great Wall.

Resource REMINDER

Practice and Project Book: *p. 38*
 Technology: *Videodisc*

STUDYSKILLS

Writing a Summary

VOCABULARY
summary
topic sentence

WHY THE SKILL MATTERS

Soon after Shihuangdi became China's first emperor in 221 B.C., he sent his army to strengthen the northern border of his empire. The story of how and why he did this is complicated, but it is an important part of China's early history. Many stories from history are long and complicated. They usually contain much information. However, people can present the important information in a story by creating a summary. A summary briefly states the main ideas contained in a piece of writing or group of ideas.

USING THE SKILL

Read the following paragraph about Shihuangdi and the herders of northern China.

After Shihuangdi won the battle for control over China in 221 B.C., one challenge remained. Herders who lived on the steppes of northern China had crossed the Huang River and set up their tents on the plains near the river's big curve. This narrowed the distance between these two very different cultures. Because they were expert riders and hunters, the herders were a threat to the empire. Shihuangdi feared that the herders would decide to invade China, taking its land and crops. He ordered his army to push the herders back beyond the Huang.

To prepare for writing a summary, find the topic sentences, or the sentences that contain the main ideas. Often a topic sentence is the first sentence of the paragraph. However, it may also be at the end of the paragraph. The topic sentences in the previous paragraph tell that the people of the steppes became a threat to Shihuangdi. How he responded is also important.

Other sentences give supporting details, such as information about the herders being expert riders and hunters.

After you identify the main ideas and supporting details, you can write a short summary. What main ideas are expressed in the paragraph on Shihuangdi and the herders? What are some supporting details?*

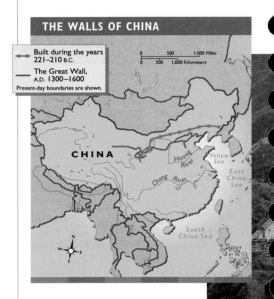

THE WALLS OF CHINA

Built during the years 221–210 B.C.
The Great Wall, A.D. 1300–1600
Present-day boundaries are shown.

500   1,000 Miles
500   1,000 Kilometers

CHINA

Huang River
Yellow Sea
Chang River
East China Sea
South China Sea

Little remains of Shihuangdi's wall (far right). The Great Wall (right) is about 1,500 miles in length.

* Main ideas: Herders moved to the plains near the Huang River; Shihuangdi ordered his army to push the herders away. Supporting details: The herders came from the steppes of northern China; they were expert riders and hunters.

READING STRATEGIES & LANGUAGE DEVELOPMENT

MAIN IDEA AND DETAILS Looking for main ideas and identifying details that support them is a major strategy that students will employ in this skills lesson. Explain to them that identifying cause and effect can help them to identify main ideas. For example, in the italicized paragraph on this page, the main ideas are: the threat that herders from the north posed to China (the cause) and Shihuangdi's efforts to push the herders back (the effect).

MULTIPLE MEANINGS On the board, write two words from this lesson that have multiple meanings—*main* and *plain.* Call on students to define them as used in the lesson and then offer other definitions for them (for example, *main*—"ocean, open sea;" *plain*—"ordinary").

* Main idea: Walls were built to keep invaders out. Supporting details: About 215 B.C. workers strengthened a 100-year-old wall; the Great Wall was made of bricks; despite the walls, invaders made their way into China.

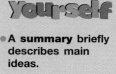

HELPING Yourself

- **A summary** briefly describes main ideas.
- To find main ideas, use **topic sentences**.
- **Combine major details into one or two general statements.**

TRYING THE SKILL

Now read the story below and use the Helping Yourself box to write a summary.

In about 215 B.C. Shihuang-di's army succeeded in driving the herders out. To help keep them out, more than 300,000 workers strengthened a 100-year-old wall along China's northern border. It was just rock-hard mounds of earth. Lookouts posted on the wall would signal an invasion by waving flags or by lighting fires. The army would then come to chase the herders away. China's leaders carried on this idea of wall building. *Most famous of all was the Great Wall. This wall was mostly built between A.D. 1300 and 1600. It was much larger than the previous earthen walls and was made of bricks. Even the Great Wall was not a very effective barrier. Invaders continued to make their way over or around the wall.*

What is the main idea that runs through this entire paragraph? What are the supporting details?*

REVIEWING THE SKILL

1. How does writing a summary differ from simply rewriting an entire piece in your own words?

2. If you had to write a single summary of both paragraphs about Shihuangdi in this lesson, what would that summary include?

3. How did you choose what would go into your summary? Could you use the map?

4. When might writing a summary be a helpful skill?

173

★**THINKING FURTHER:** *Summarizing* **What would you need to put in a summary so that you could understand it later?** *(Have the class work together to write a summary they can agree on.)*

Trying the Skill Review the Helping Yourself steps with students before they start this activity. Also refer them to the map on p. 172 and use its information in the summary.

- *How does the first wall differ in location from the Great Wall? (The first wall is farther north.)*

- *How does the Great Wall differ from the first wall in length? (The Great Wall is longer and extends farther west.)*

★**THINKING FURTHER:** *Main Idea and Details* **What main idea runs through the paragraph? What ideas support it?** *(Main Idea: China needed a wall to keep invaders out. Supporting details: the first wall—its makeup and uses; the Great Wall—when built, makeup, effectiveness.)*

⭐ 3 CLOSE

SUM IT UP

Give students more practice in writing summaries by sending them back to Lesson 3 to write summaries of some of its sections, for example, of "A New Kind of Government" and "Building the Emperor's Tomb." Remind them to review the steps in *Helping Yourself.*

EVALUATE
✓ **Answers to Reviewing the Skill**

1. Writing a summary requires abbreviating a reading by noting only its highlights and telescoping its details.

2. Main idea—China felt threatened with invasion by herders from the north so it built walls to try to keep them out. Supporting details—materials, scope, and effectiveness of the first wall and the Great Wall.

3. by finding main ideas and including the most important details; yes

4. Organizing the main ideas helps a reader identify and remember the most important ideas of a reading.

LESSON 4

PAGES 174–178

Lesson Overview
The teachings of Confucius gave China a framework for orderly government and high civilization.

Lesson Objectives
★ Describe characteristics of Confucius that made him a great teacher.

★ Identify some of his teachings and describe their impact on China.

★ Evaluate the achievements of the Han dynasty.

★ 1 PREPARE

MOTIVATE Write this proverb on the board: "Actions speak louder than words." Then have a student read the statement by Confucius from the *Read Aloud.* Have students discuss the power of good and bad examples.

SET PURPOSE Now that they have had a taste of Confucian wisdom, encourage students to read the lesson to answer the *Read to Learn* question. Point out the painting of a Confucian school. Preview the *Vocabulary* terms.

★ 2 TEACH

Understanding THE BIG PICTURE
As students read this, tell them to look for a striking coincidence. (Confucius and Buddha are contemporaries.)

● **When was Confucius introducing his ideas in China?** *(around 500 B.C.)*

● **Was this before or after the Qin dynasty, Han Gaozu, and Han dynasty?** *(at least three centuries before)*

★**THINKING FURTHER: Compare and Contrast How would you compare the Qin approach to government with the Han approach?** *(Qin—harsh; Han—open to the teachings of Confucius)*

Resource REMINDER

Practice and Project Book: *p. 39*

Anthology: *The Sayings of Confucius, p. 33, A Letter from a Han Emperor, p. 34*

Bibliothèque Nationale

CONFUCIUS CHANGES CHINA

Focus Activity

READ TO LEARN
What effects did the teachings of Confucius have on China?

VOCABULARY
Confucianism
Mandate of Heaven
Grand School
seismograph

PEOPLE
Han Gaozu
Confucius
Wudi

READ ALOUD
"When a prince's personal conduct is correct, his government is effective without the issuing of orders. If his personal conduct is not correct, he may issue orders, but they will not be followed."

These words were spoken by Confucius, an important Chinese philosopher, teacher, and scholar.

THE BIG PICTURE
In 206 B.C. Shihuangdi's Qin dynasty was overthrown by rebel armies. These armies were led by a farmer-turned-general called Han Gaozu (HAHN GOW ZOO). His family began the mighty Han dynasty, which would rule China for over 400 years. During the Han dynasty, China expanded north to what are today North and South Korea and south to the country of Vietnam.

Shihuangdi had lived by the idea that a ruler should be able to do whatever he chooses. Later, Han rulers developed different ideas about government. Their thoughts were based on the teachings of a man named Confucius, who lived between 551 B.C. and 479 B.C.

Like the Buddha, who was teaching in India during this time, Confucius lived through an age of warfare and conflict. In this time of conflict, Confucius suggested a different, more peaceful way of living. Also like the Buddha, he won many followers during and after his lifetime. Unlike the Buddha, Confucius's ideas would not start a new religion. However, Confucius's ideas would reshape entire civilizations.

174

SHELTERED INSTRUCTION

READING STRATEGIES & LANGUAGE DEVELOPMENT

CONTEXT CLUES Review the meaning of the term *context clues* with the class—words found near an unfamiliar word that help define it. Explain that a clue can sometimes be a synonym for the unfamiliar word. Have students read the word *mandate* on p. 175 and find the synonym that defines it [*command*]. Repeat the process with the word *pendulum* on p. 177. Point out the context clues—*long metal* and *swing*—then demonstrate a pendulum to help students understand the word.
[SDAIE STRATEGY: CONTEXTUALIZATION]

POSSESSIVE NOUNS Refer students to the possessive form of Confucius (*Confucius's*) on this page and have them note that it is formed in the normal way the possessive of a singular noun is formed—by adding an *'s*. Explain that it is not a plural, so it gets the full *'s*. (Tradition makes some exceptions to this rule: *Jesus'* and *Moses'*.)

CONFUCIUS

Both of his parents died when he was young, so Confucius had to make his own way in life. He had a passion for learning. He mastered subjects such as writing, mathematics, history, and archery. This helped Confucius to get a job in government. In later years, though, he devoted his life to teaching.

The Followers of Confucius

Confucius's ideas, later called Confucianism, taught that Chinese culture had lost its traditions. According to Confucius, ancient traditions had once made society just and good. Through education, Confucius said, people from rulers to farmers could learn how to become good people once again. Good people would make a good civilization.

A central idea of Confucianism was to have respect within the family. This idea also applied to government. Just as a child must respect a parent, a subject must respect the ruler. However, the ruler had a duty to be wise and good. Some followers of Confucius said that emperors did not have the right to rule just because they came from a certain family. Rather, each emperor received a right to rule from the gods, called the Mandate of Heaven. This mandate, or command, echoed the Shang belief that the gods spoke to kings through oracle bones.

Confucius's thoughts were recorded by his students in a book called *The Analects*. Analects are selected writings. What does a good person do, according to Confucius?

PRIMARY SOURCE

Excerpt from
The Analects of Confucius,
c. 400 B.C.

Do not do unto others what you would not want others to do to you.

If you make a mistake and do not correct it, this is called a mistake.

Be dutiful at home, brotherly in public; be discreet and trustworthy, love all people, and draw near to humanity. If you have extra energy as you do that, then study literature.

If leaders are courteous, their people will not dare to be disrespectful. If leaders are just, people will not dare to be [ungovernable]. If leaders are trustworthy, people will not dare to be dishonest.

A certain pupil asked Confucius about government: "What qualifies one to participate in government?"

Confucius said, "Honor five refinements. . . . Then you can participate in government."

The pupil asked, "What are the five refinements?"

Confucius said, "Good people are generous without being wasteful; they are hard-working without being resentful; they desire without being greedy; they are at ease without being [proud]; they are dignified without being fierce."

refinements: improvements
participate: take part in

175

CONFUCIUS

Have students use the biographical information about Confucius to begin to form an idea of his characteristics. Encourage them to draw conclusions about what his traits were from the facts; for example, from losing his parents when he was young, they might conclude that he was self-reliant.

Discussing The Followers of Confucius Develop in students a sense of why Confucian teachings are important.

- **What did Confucianism say the Chinese had lost?** (traditions that once made society just and good)

- **How could they get them back?** (through education)

★ **THINKING FURTHER: Fact and Opinion** Do you think the statement that good people make a good civilization is a fact or an opinion? (Encourage students to discuss the idea: Is it provable?)

Discussing the PRIMARY SOURCE

Divide the class into five groups; assign each group one Confucian teachings from the Analects. Have students discuss among themselves the questions below. Then have them report their findings to the class and have a class discussion.

- **What specific behaviors does Confucius recommend in this excerpt?** (treating others well, correcting mistakes, being dutiful)

- **According to Confucius, how are relations between children and parents in a family like those between subjects and rulers in a government?** (Help students see that respect goes both ways.)

★ **THINKING FURTHER: Making Conclusions** What individual behaviors make a society good? (As the class discusses this question encourage students to compose class guidelines for society.)

GLOBAL CONNECTION

THE GOLDEN RULE Explain to the class that we call Confucius's first quote here the "Golden Rule." It appears in many versions.

- "We should behave to our friends as we would wish our friends to behave to us."—the Greek Aristotle in the 4th century B.C..
- "If it is hateful to you, do not do it unto your neighbor."—Hillel, Jewish scholar around the time of the birth of Jesus.
- "All things whatsoever ye would that men should do to you, do ye even so to them."—New Testament, Matthew 7:12

CITIZENSHIP ★

CONFUCIUS AND CITIZENSHIP Have the class consider Confucius's teachings as they might relate to our society. What would our society and our government be like if citizens adopted his ideas?

RISE OF
THE HAN DYNASTY

More **MAP WORK**

Point out to the class that the 400-year Han rule lasted from roughly 200 B.C. to A.D. 200. Refer them to the map on this page to see the size of the Han empire.

● **Compare this map to the Qin map on p. 169. How would you describe the growth in empire of the Han dynasty?** *(It has spread in all directions, far to the west and north, and south to the entire coast along the South China Sea. Only an area on the East China Sea is not part of it.)*

● **What did the Han adopt from the Qin? What did they change?** *(They adopted the Qin system of government. They tried to rule fairly and gave jobs to educated people, not just nobles.)*

★**THINKING FURTHER:** *Making Conclusions* **Why do you suppose Han rulers did this?** *(Harsh and unfair treatment of citizens creates unrest and rebellion. Fairer government fosters stability and order.)*

Discussing The Grand School Help the class to appreciate how the Confucian value of education served as the engine of Han success.

● **Why do you think the emperor Wudi established schools throughout China?** *(He must have agreed with Confucius that education was the key to good government.)*

● **How would you describe the education students received? How would the subjects they studied help them as government workers?** *(The emphasis on Chinese culture would deepen their understanding of people they governed; their breadth of knowledge would gain respect for themselves and for the government.)*

★**THINKING FURTHER:** *Classifying* **What advantages from education helped various areas of life in Han China?** *(Examples: government—respect; science—knowledge of new medicines; literature—poetry about China's beauty; language—a rich vocabulary)*

This man is participating in a ceremony to honor Confucius. The ceremony is taking place at a temple in Qufu, located in China's Shandong province.

LANDS OF THE HAN DYNASTY, A.D. 100

MAP WORK

Han rulers expanded their empire into central China.

1. What two cities were located on the Huang River?
2. Which city was farther west?

RISE OF
THE HAN DYNASTY

The powerful Han army expanded the borders of the empire. Look at the Han dynasty lands on the map on this page. Controlling the huge empire was a difficult job. During the Qin dynasty Shihuangdi had many people who disagreed with him killed. Some of them were Confucianists. He did not want anyone to question his right to rule. During the Han dynasty, however, Confucianism became accepted again. Han emperors wanted to find ways to rule more fairly. They also wanted to lessen the power of the nobles.

Han rulers kept the Qin dynasty's system of government. However, they gave government jobs to educated people, rather than just to nobles. Wudi (WOO DEE), was the first strong emperor of the Han dynasty. His rule lasted from 140 B.C. to 87 B.C. Wudi created schools to prepare students for government service. These schools were run by Confucian teachers.

The Grand School

Under Wudi's government, schools were set up in each province, or state. The schools taught Chinese literature to students who would serve in local government. Very good students sometimes were sent to the empire's best school, the Grand School.

176

MAP WORK: 1. Luoyang and Changan **2.** Changan

BACKGROUND INFORMATION

MEDICINE IN ANCIENT CHINA Many of the advancements that ancient China made in medicine grew out of a quest that frequently appears in ancient history—the quest for immortality.

● Acupuncture, the treatment of physical illness by pricking the body with needles at points thought to be connected with the organs causing the illness, was developed in ancient China.

● Chinese herbalists were the first to discover the use of iodine from seaweed for goiter, and a rye fungus for childbirth difficulties.

● As far back as 300 B.C., the Chinese physician Hua T'o pioneered using anesthesia while performing abdominal surgery, including removal of the spleen.

During Wudi's rule only 50 students were allowed to study at the Grand School. By A.D. 200 it had more than 30,000 students. For one year they learned about ancient China's poetry, history, proper behavior, and folk songs. These had all been preserved by Confucius. The teachers were China's most brilliant Confucian scholars. At the end of the year, students at the Grand School took a long test. If they passed, they earned jobs as government workers or as teachers in province schools. They also won great respect in society because they were so well educated.

During the Han dynasty, learning of many different kinds blossomed throughout the empire. Like the ancient Egyptians, Chinese scientists and mathematicians learned to predict eclipses of the sun. Doctors discovered new kinds of medicines, and poets wrote about the beauty of the land. In fact, during the course of the Han dynasty, the Chinese language grew from 3,000 to 9,000 characters. In A.D. 100 scholars wrote the first Chinese dictionary.

The Invention of Paper

Confucian emphasis on education brought increased knowledge and

This is a model of the seismograph invented by Zhang Heng. The original detected an earthquake hundreds of miles away.

discovery in the Han dynasty. This can be seen in the many inventions that appeared during this time. For example, Han craftworkers invented paper. Like Egyptian papyrus, paper provided a way to keep written records. The Chinese made paper by pounding bark of mulberry trees. These are the same trees that feed China's silkworms.

An Amazing Instrument

One of the most remarkable achievements of Han inventors was the seismograph (SĪZ muh graf). This is a machine used to detect earthquakes. Although this ancient seismograph looks like a bronze vase covered with dragons and toads, it is actually a complicated scientific instrument.

Inside the vase swung a long metal pendulum. When the ground shook ever so slightly, the pendulum would swing in the direction in which the earthquake occurred. The pendulum would hit a rod inside the vase. This rod, in turn, would knock a ball out of a dragon's mouth. The ball came out in the direction in which the earthquake had occurred.

In this way Han rulers could learn about an earthquake as soon as it happened. They could immediately send food and supplies to the damaged area.

Understanding the Invention of Paper Help students connect the invention of paper with the emphasis on education.

> ★THINKING FURTHER: *Making Connections* **Why would paper be important to the Han dynasty?** *(Writing on paper would help improve education, which was important to the dynasty.)*

Discussing An Amazing Instrument Refer the class to the illustration of a Chinese seismograph on this page.

- *What function does a seismograph perform?* (registering earthquakes)

- *How does it get its information?* (the trembling of the ground beneath it)

- *How would you diagram the way the seismograph pictured here works?* (Have students come to the board and draw diagrams showing the progression of its actions.)

> ★THINKING FURTHER: *Making Conclusions* **Why do you suppose the ancient Chinese were interested in inventing such a machine?** *(They would want to know when and where a disaster had occurred so that they could send help.)*

177

LINKS WITH ART The emperor Wudi created one of the greatest parks of all time. Surrounded by a wall nearly 100 miles long, it was designed like a small version of the empire, complete with rivulets that symbolized China's rivers and great mounds that symbolized its mountains. The park contained specimens of every plant and animal in the empire and beyond. An Indian rhinoceros was just one of many exotic species that roamed its land. Ornamental gardens stretched as far as the eye could see. Have students draw a possible scene from this immense park.

LINKS WITH SCIENCE Call for a science team to do research on modern seismographs—how seismographs get information, where they are located, what their measurements mean, what their capabilities are and are not. Have them prepare a presentation of their findings for the class.

WORKING WITH A PEER Many of the names and words in Chapter 7 may be especially difficult for second-language learners. Have them work with an English-proficient partner to develop mnemonic devices to help them remember the words and their pronunciations.

LIFE DURING THE HAN DYNASTY

Develop a sense of life at various levels.

> ★**THINKING FURTHER: Compare and Contrast** *How would you contrast the lives of farmers with lives of large landowners?* (endless toil, a diet of rice, rough clothes vs. luxury, comfort, good, varied food)

Discussing WHY IT MATTERS Ask students to review Confucian ideals.

> ★**THINKING FURTHER: Summarizing** *How would you summarize Confucius's philosophy?* (a belief in education, duty, good example, fairness, respectful behavior, and moderation)

⭐ 3 CLOSE

MAIN IDEAS

Have students work in pairs to answer these questions on paper.

- **What Confucian ideas influenced life in the Han dynasty?** *(duty to family and government, education)*
- **In what areas did Han China make great achievements?** *(science, mathematics, the arts, trade)*
- **Which people were the backbone of the Han economy?** *(farmers)*

EVALUATE
✓ **Answers to Think About It**
1. correct personal conduct, fair rule, trustworthiness, respect for citizens
   Recall Details
2. Possible answers: kindness, being loving and courteous, showing respect, being moderate in behavior
   Make Conclusions
3. It tempered government from Qin times. It helped maintain order.
   Summarize
4. Answers may center on good personal conduct, fair laws, and respect for citizens.
   Fact/Opinion
5. It nearly doubles and then more than doubles again.
   Five Themes of Geography: Place

Write About It Have students write a paragraph about why governments today should or should not follow Confucian ideals?

178

LIFE DURING THE HAN DYNASTY

As you have read, the Han empire stretched across thousands of miles and achieved many things. Still, farming continued to be the center of China's economy and society. Most people lived on farms and in small villages. China's farmers grew food for the entire empire. The economy was based on customs handed down over generations. This is an example of a traditional economic system.

The lives of farmers during the Han dynasty centered around their families and the endless work in the fields. This has remained relatively unchanged through much of China's long history.

WHY IT MATTERS

Confucius wanted China to become a civilization of good and dutiful people. He believed it had once been that way. During the Han dynasty China's government adopted some of Confucius's

This model of a house came from a Han dynasty tomb.

ideas. Despite this, however, conflict and hardship remained part of life in ancient China. The Han dynasty ended around A.D. 220. It broke down under the strain of failed military campaigns beyond China and fights among its leaders. In the centuries to come, many Chinese looked to the teachings of Confucius to renew their civilization. The legacy of Confucian ideas of fairness and learning continues in China today.

✓// Reviewing Facts and Ideas

MAIN IDEAS
- Confucian ideas about duty and education influenced life during the Han dynasty.
- The Han emperor Wudi started Confucian schools in order to educate government workers.
- The Han dynasty produced many great achievements in science, mathematics, the arts, and trade.
- As in earlier dynasties, farmers during the Han dynasty produced the food and goods that brought China great wealth.

THINK ABOUT IT
1. What did Confucius believe was the duty of a ruler?
2. What are three ways Confucius defined goodness in people?
3. **FOCUS** How did Confucianism affect life during the Han dynasty?
4. **THINKING SKILL** Imagine that you are Emperor Wudi. *Decide* which aspects of Confucianism you can use to help you govern the empire. Explain how you made your choices.
5. **GEOGRAPHY** Compare the maps on pages 165, 169, and 176. How did China's empire change in the Shang, the Qin, and the Han dynasties?

MEETING INDIVIDUAL NEEDS

RETEACHING (Easy) Divide the class into five groups and assign each group one of the five refinements. Tell them to work together to design a poster that illustrates and encourages their assigned refinement.

EXTENSION (Average) Tell students to think what it would be like to study with Confucius for their teacher. Have them write a letter to a friend describing the kind of man Confucius is.

ENRICHMENT (Challenging) Have students do further research on the life of Confucius and have them write a one-page biography of him. Point out that Confucius is the name that Westerners know him by and tell them to be sure to include his Chinese names.

CITIZENSHIP
MAKING A DIFFERENCE

Working for Education

GUIZHOU (GWEE JOH), CHINA—In this small village in rural China, a group of six women come together once a week. They sit in a circle listening intently to a seventh woman. She reads slowly and clearly from a small magazine. Sometimes she stops and points to pictures on the page.

Except for the woman holding the magazine, none of these women can read. Yet they would like to learn. The magazine, called in English "Rural Women Knowing All," is helping these six women and many thousands more all over China to do just that. The magazine has articles that teach reading and writing. It also has articles about women who have become leaders in their villages and towns.

Ever since the days of the Han dynasty, education has been an important part of Chinese culture. Unfortunately it has not always been easy for girls to receive an education. For much of Chinese history, it was considered more important for boys to go to school. Girls often stayed at home. It is now the law in China that all children, boys and girls, must attend school for at least six years.

Wu Qing (WOO CHING), who teaches at Beijing Foreign Studies University, helped start this magazine in 1993. She is its chief adviser and fundraiser. "The need to educate rural women is great," she says,

"because girls, especially in rural areas, have had fewer chances than boys to go to school. If a poor family could only afford to educate one child, the boy almost always would be chosen."

The magazine, which in American money costs about 12¢ a copy, is growing rapidly. It has over 200,000 subscribers and many thousands more readers. As a fundraiser, Wu convinced several large companies to donate cars, televisions, and other prizes for those women's groups that sell large numbers of subscriptions.

Wu believes in educating rural women because "Once rural women know how to read and write, . . . it will make a lot of difference for China." Helping others comes naturally to Wu. "I feel it is up to me to help change China," she says. "That is why I have the energy to work hard."

"I feel it is up to me to help change China."

Wu Qing

179

CITIZENSHIP ★

UNDERSTANDING GOVERNMENT Explain to students that national governments consider literacy so important that they have made it a matter of national priority. Besides China, examples include countries that were once part of the Soviet Union, as well as Cuba, Mexico, and Argentina. At the start of the twentieth century, these nations had illiteracy rates of 70 percent or more, but since 1945 they substantially decreased these rates. Have students discuss why nations would want to have literate, rather than illiterate, citizens. Help students recognize that our competitive world economy calls for educated workers, and illiteracy is a limitation on a nation's potential competitiveness.

For further information, contact:

*Professor Wu Qing/Unit 34-4,
Professor's Building/Central University
for Nationalities/Beijing, 100081/
China/Telephone: 011-861-842-1841*

Lesson Objective
★ Evaluate how individual initiative can change an old cultural pattern.

Identifying the Focus Help students to see how one person can identify a problem and lead the way to solving it.

● *How have rural women of China been held back for centuries?* (Education was denied them, so they never learned to read or write.)

Point out to the class that people who cannot read and write are limited. They are cut off from sources of information like newspapers and books. Their ability to work is limited to jobs not requiring writing. Their horizons are limited by the boundaries of their communities.

Why It Matters Discuss with the class the benefits of breaking the cycle of illiteracy and reasons that an informed person would encourage literacy.

● *How did the rural women of China get caught in the trap of illiteracy?* (In rural areas, education was often limited to boys.)

● *What decision did Wu Qing make to remedy this situation?* (She started a magazine to teach rural reading and writing in small groups.)

★**THINKING FURTHER: Predicting** *Wu says that rural women learning to read and write "will make a lot of difference for China." What do you predict these changes might be?* (better informed citizens, better parents to children, better job and business opportunities, better equipped work force)

Lesson Overview
The Chinese developed silk-making and kept a monopoly on silk.

Lesson Objective
★ Recognize the economic impact of the silk-making industry on China.

1 PREPARE

MOTIVATE If possible, have some pictures of cocoons in class for students to examine. Also display some silk objects. Encourage students to handle them to feel their luxurious texture and their light weight and to comment on their color and design.

SET PURPOSE Ask students what they know about silk—for example, where it comes from, what role cocoons play in it, and what work goes into making it. Then have them read the column of text on this page to find out.

2 TEACH

Understanding the Concept of a Legacy Encourage students to try to picture the painstaking work of unwinding a cocoon and then twisting the strands into threads. Yet the results seem so well worth it. Have students identify the qualities that make silk a popular and widely-used textile (strength, beauty, smoothness, stretchability, light weight, warmth).

Examining the Pictures Give students a few moments to study the pictures and their captions.

● *According to the painting of ancient silk making, who did most of the work?* (Women and girls. The Chinese say that the discovery of silk making and of the silk reel was the work of a 14-year-old girl.)

● *Once the Chinese discovered how to make silk, how did they corner the market on it?* (They made silk making a secret, under threat of death.)

Legacy
LINKING PAST AND PRESENT

SILK MAKING

Bibliothèque Municipale

Have you ever watched a caterpillar spin a cocoon? One kind of caterpillar, the silkworm, spins a cocoon that can be used to create a special cloth. This cloth is called silk. Ancient Chinese farmers discovered how to make silk around 2700 B.C.

In the spring women cut leaves from mulberry trees to feed the silkworms. After several weeks of noisy eating, the silkworms spun their cocoons. Women unwound the cocoons and twisted the strands into threads. These threads were then woven to make cloth. In China today silk is made the same way, except for the added help of machines.

Silk is a strong, beautiful, smooth fabric. It stretches easily and is light and warm. The legacy of making silk enables people all over the world to enjoy the special qualities of this cloth.

This Chinese painting from the 1800s shows a farm family making silk. Women and girls made most of the silk.

180

GLOBAL CONNECTION

ABOUT SILK AND THE GYPSY MOTH
● Gypsy moths, not silkworms, were brought to the United States from Europe in 1866 to try to start a silk industry in Massachusetts.
● After escaping from a broken jar, they began spreading out, from 10 to 20 miles a year; they are still spreading west.
● Gypsy moths often kill trees from the East Coast to the West Coast.

BACKGROUND INFORMATION

ABOUT SILK'S STRENGTH
● A silk thread is stronger than a comparable filament of steel.
● Benjamin Franklin used a silk kite in his electricity experiments.
● Silk was the only textile strong enough for parachutes until nylon was invented.

Chinese emperors decided to keep silk making a secret from other civilizations. Rulers threatened people with death if they told the secret. This threat worked for over 3,000 years!

Modern factories produce millions of yards of silk cloth. The source of the silk, however, is the same as ever: the cocoon of the silkworm. Today people around the world wear silk to work and to school. It is often used to make suits, shirts, ties, and dresses.

Minneapolis Institute of Arts

181

- **How did the Chinese see that silk could be used only by the elite?** *(Its cost would have priced it out of the market for most people. Explain to the class that Chinese law said that only the nobility could wear silk.)*

- **How would keeping silk manufacturing a secret and limiting its use to the elite make silk a major trade good for the Chinese?** *(A demand was created that only they could fill. Tell students silk became the fabric of choice for nobles as far west as the Mediterranean.)*

- **How have artists made use of silk?** *(Explain that silk takes color very well, thus leading to beautiful silk scrolls, screens, paintings, fans.)*

- **What are some modern uses of silk?** *(suits, shirts, dresses, ties, scarves.)*

★**THINKING FURTHER:** *Making Conclusions* **How would you describe the legacy of silk making for the world?** *(Silk is universally appreciated as a product of high quality and its lower price has made it a product much demanded and enjoyed.)*

⭐ 3 CLOSE

SUM IT UP
Have students compose a class list of the properties of silk and its many uses.

EVALUATE
Write About It Tell students to think of an article made of silk and write an ad to encourage people to buy that article.

MEETING INDIVIDUAL NEEDS

RETEACHING (Easy) On a large piece of paper, have students create color designs for silk scarves or ties. Remind them that silk takes color well.

EXTENSION (Average) Ask students to picture a visit to a silk-making operation in ancient China. Tell them to write a letter home describing the process.

ENRICHMENT (Challenging) Remind students that the Chinese succeeded in keeping the secret of silk making for over 3,000 years. How did the secret finally get out? Tell students to do some detective work to find the answer and write brief reports of their findings to present in class. (There are different versions, so the class should get a cross section of them.)

BACKGROUND INFORMATION

ABOUT SILK PRODUCTION TODAY
- Silk production, or sericulture, is still confined mainly to Asia.
- China remains the largest producer.
- Japan comes in second, with about half of China's production.
- Countries of the former Soviet Union rank third.
- South Korea and India are major producers, but much of India's production is of a lower quality than other Asian silk.
- The only significant producer of silk in the Americas is Brazil. The United States has tried from time to time, but has never succeeded.

DISCUSSING MAJOR EVENTS Use the time line to reinforce for students the idea that dynasties serve as guides to sequence in China's long history.

- ***When was the Shang dynasty founded and what led to its founding?*** *(1700 B.C.; winning control of the Huang River delta.)*

- ***When did the Han dynasty begin, and what major event did its founding follow?*** *(Shihuangdi becoming the first Chinese emperor, 206 B.C.)*

Answers to
THINKING ABOUT VOCABULARY

1. steppe
2. levee
3. seismograph
4. erosion
5. famine
6. dynasty
7. topic sentence
8. emperor
9. province
10. Mandate of Heaven

Answers to
THINKING ABOUT FACTS

1. It brought them the silt that made their soil fertile.

2. The artifacts found there showed that ancient China had reached high levels of metalworking, pottery, and sculpture and had a pyramid-like social structure.

3. Shihuangdi, who with his army gained control of all of northern China and then unified it into the provinces of one empire

Resource REMINDER

Practice and Project Book: *p.40*
Assessment Books: *Chapter 7 Test*
Technology: *Videodisc/Video Tape 2*
Transparency: *Graphic Organizer, Main-Idea Diagram*

CHAPTER 7 REVIEW

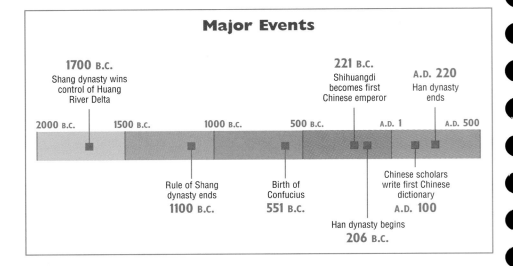

Major Events

1700 B.C.
Shang dynasty wins control of Huang River Delta

221 B.C.
Shihuangdi becomes first Chinese emperor

A.D. 220
Han dynasty ends

2000 B.C.   1500 B.C.   1000 B.C.   500 B.C.   A.D. 1   A.D. 500

Rule of Shang dynasty ends
1100 B.C.

Birth of Confucius
551 B.C.

Chinese scholars write first Chinese dictionary
A.D. 100

Han dynasty begins
206 B.C.

THINKING ABOUT VOCABULARY

Number a sheet of paper from 1 to 10. Beside each number write the word or term from the list below that matches the definition.

dynasty   Mandate of Heaven
emperor   province
erosion   seismograph
famine   steppe
levee   topic sentence

1. A dry, treeless plain
2. A wall that keeps a river within its banks
3. A special machine used to detect earthquakes
4. The wearing away of soil by wind or water
5. A time when food is scarce and people starve
6. A line of rulers who belong to the same family
7. A sentence that contains the main idea
8. The supreme ruler of an empire
9. A division of land
10. A special right to rule that the emperor is thought to receive from the gods

THINKING ABOUT FACTS

1. In what ways did the Huang River help early Chinese farmers?
2. How have discoveries made at Anyang helped historians to understand ancient China?
3. Who was China's first emperor? What did he do to unify China?
4. What is Confucianism?
5. Look at the time line above. How long were the reigns of the Shang and Han dynasties?

182

SECOND-LANGUAGE SUPPORT

REVIEWING THROUGH ILLUSTRATING Invite second-language learners to create illustrations depicting the contributions and achievements of Chinese civilization. Students will then write captions for each illustration. Encourage second-language learners to make a class display of these illustrations and to explain their work to their fellow students.

RESPONSE JOURNAL Ask students to respond to the ideas of Confucius as presented in this chapter in their response journals. Which of these ideas do they think are good guides for people's behavior?

THINK AND WRITE

WRITING A JOURNAL

Suppose you live in the time of the Han Dynasty and are a student in the Grand School. Write an entry in your journal describing your thoughts about your studies and the long test you have to take at the end of the year.

WRITING AN ARTICLE

Write a short article for your school newspaper about ancient Chinese civilization. Describe the contributions it has made to world history.

WRITING ABOUT PERSPECTIVES

Suppose you live in ancient China and your teacher asks you to write about what you learned about the Huang River from books and from your parents' experiences. Write three paragraphs about your impressions.

APPLYING STUDY SKILLS

WRITING A SUMMARY

1. What is a summary?
2. How is writing a summary different from rewriting something entirely?
3. What are topic sentences? How can they be useful in writing a summary?
4. After rereading "Silk Making" on page 180, write a three-sentence summary of what you read.
5. How are summaries useful?

Summing Up the Chapter

Copy the main-idea diagram below on a separate piece of paper. Then review the chapter to find at least two pieces of information that support each part of the main idea. After you have filled in the information, use it to write a paragraph that answers the question "What developments of China's Huang River civilization continue to affect China today?"

developed agriculture along the Huang

built cities

Civilization

MAIN IDEA The people of the Huang Valley created a rich civilization that has continued to this day.

Legacies

silk making

Confucianism

183

---

4. a set of ideas holding that education makes good people and good people make a good civilization and that mutual respect must be shown in both families and in government

5. Shang: 600 years; Han: 426 years

Answers to APPLYING STUDY SKILLS

1. A summary briefly states the main ideas contained in a piece of writing or group of ideas.

2. A summary picks out only the major points, not all the details.

3. Topic sentences are sentences that contain main ideas, often stated at either at the beginning or end of a paragraph; they pinpoint what a summary should include.

4. Summaries should include: silk making was developed in China, silk is woven from threads spun from the cocoons of mulberry leaf-eating silkworms, and silk is a strong, attractive, valuable product.

5. Summaries provide a way of getting a piece of material's major points quickly and memorably.

 **Technology CONNECTION**

VIDEODISC/VIDEO TAPE 2
Enrich Chapter 7 with the *Ancient China* segment on the videodisc.

Search Frame 39815 Side A

SUGGESTIONS FOR SUMMING UP THE CHAPTER

After students copy the main-idea diagram onto a piece of paper, have them read aloud the main idea it states and the two categories of information it tells them to look for—civilization and legacies. On the board, have them list pieces of information that the chapter gives about each. Then have them read aloud the question they are going to answer when they have filled in the diagram. Referring them to the pieces of information on the board, ask: Which of these continue in China today? Suggest that they use this question to choose which items to fill in on their diagrams. Possible answers are noted on the reproduced text page above. Suggest that students use the items they chose as the basis of the paragraphs they write.

ASSESSING THINK AND WRITE: *For performance assessment, see Assessment Book, Chapter 7, pp. T64-T66.*

Answers to
THINKING ABOUT VOCABULARY

1. ziggurat
2. summary
3. empire
4. Vedas
5. polytheism
6. dynasty
7. Torah
8. hieroglyphics
9. reincarnation
10. Sanskrit

Suggestions for
THINK AND WRITE

1. Similar features: all were river valley civilizations, all developed written languages. Dissimilar features: Egypt was unified under the central government of the pharaoh, Sumer was divided into city-states, and China sometimes had a central government and sometimes did not.

2. Travel pamphlets should include a description of the area Han China covered and of the Grand School. It should also describe the amazing inventions to be seen in Han China.

3. When students have chosen their subjects, encourage them to review that person's time and place, experiences, aims, successes, and failures. This will help them tailor appropriate questions for their subject—and write appropriate answers.

Suggestions for
BUILDING SKILLS

1. Summaries should cover children's entertainment, work, and learning.

2. Summaries can serve as reminders of and provide major information about important things studied.

3. Causes: enslavement of Hebrews in Egypt, God's command to Moses to help free them, Moses' plea to the pharaoh. Effects: 40 years in desert, God giving Moses the Ten Commandments, the founding of Israel.

UNIT 2 REVIEW

THINKING ABOUT VOCABULARY

dynasty	Sanskrit
empire	summary
hieroglyphics	Torah
polytheism	Vedas
reincarnation	ziggurat

Number a sheet of paper from 1 to 10. Beside each number write the word from the list above that best completes each sentence.

1. A large religious building with a temple on its peak that stood at the center of most ancient Sumerian cities is called a _____.

2. A brief statement of the main ideas in a piece of writing or group of ideas is a _____.

3. Egypt became an _____ during the New Kingdom period.

4. The books that contain the ancient Aryan sacred songs are called the _____.

5. The belief of the ancient Egyptians and Sumerians in many gods and goddesses is called _____.

6. The Shang _____ of the Huang River valley created a legacy that shaped life in China for centuries.

7. The first five books of the Hebrew Bible are called the _____.

8. Government workers in ancient Egypt could communicate over long distances using a writing system called _____.

9. _____ is what Hindus call a cycle of life, death, and rebirth.

10. In the ancient Indian language of _____, *Mohenjo-Daro* means "Mound of the Dead."

184

THINK AND WRITE ◄▭►

WRITING ABOUT PERSPECTIVES
Write a comparison of the ancient civilizations of Egypt, Sumer, and China. What were their main features? How were they similar? How were they different?

WRITING A TRAVEL PAMPHLET
Suppose you lived in Han China. Write a pamphlet describing some of the things visitors might see there. Describe the geography as well as the people.

WRITING AN INTERVIEW
Interview a person from this unit—for example, Hammurabi, Shihuangdi, or Siddhartha Gautama. Write down your questions and the answers you receive.

BUILDING SKILLS

1. **Summarizing** Reread the section "Children in Egypt" on page 98. Then write four sentences that summarize the section.

2. **Summarizing** Do you think that having summaries of the material you need to know for a test would help you prepare for it or not? Explain.

3. **Cause and effect** Explain the causes and effects of Moses' leading the Hebrews out of Egypt. Tell about the events leading to the departure of the Hebrews from Egypt. What resulted from it?

4. **Different kinds of maps** Look at the map showing the Alps on page 33. Why would knowing only the latitude and longitude of the Alps not be enough to inform you about the temperature and precipitation in the Alps? What other kind of map or information would you need?

5. **Maps at different scales** Explain why it would be helpful to have maps of different scales for a car trip across the country.

ONGOING UNIT PROJECT

OPTIONS FOR ASSESSMENT
The ongoing project, begun on page 64D can be part of your assessment program, along with other forms of evaluation.

PLANNING Explain to students that each pictoral should depict an important feature of each river civilization. Explain that their oral presentations will be important.

SIGNS OF SUCCESS
- Students' pictorals should reflect the main ideas of the lesson.
- The group should work cooperatively to arrange and title their album pages, and to select the pictorals.

 FOR THE PORTFOLIO Individual drawings can be included in students' portfolios.

YESTERDAY, TODAY & TOMORROW

Writing helped in the development of ancient civilizations. Writing is also important to us today. Do you think writing will continue to be as important in the future? Will there be as many books and magazines? Do you think something else will take their place? Explain your answers.

READING ON YOUR OWN

Here are some books you might find at the library to help you learn more.

THE TERRA COTTA ARMY OF EMPEROR QIN
by Caroline Lazo
This book tells how a clay army was uncovered near the tomb of China's first emperor.

THE GREAT PYRAMID
by Elizabeth Mann
This illustrated book describes how the Great Pyramid in ancient Egypt was built.

GODS AND PHARAOHS FROM EGYPTIAN MYTHOLOGY
by Geraldine Harris
These imaginative stories tell much about ancient Egypt.

4. Latitude and longitude do not indicate altitude or precipitation. For those, a physical map showing altitude would be needed as well as information about climate.

5. Maps used to measure distances and find routes between faraway points are different from those to find the way through places to visit.

Suggestions for YESTERDAY, TODAY & TOMORROW

Have students identify reasons we now write: to make lists, leave a note, send a letter, do homework and class work, convey information. Help students see that other media may take over some jobs of conveying information, but even computers rely on written words.

Suggestions for READING ON YOUR OWN

The books listed here will give students more background in the first river valley civilizations. In class, try to have these selections as well as books in the *Annotated Bibliography* in the Unit Organizer on p. 64B. Ask students to share interesting points from the books with the class. You may also have students dramatize scenes from *Gilgamesh*.

UNIT PROJECT

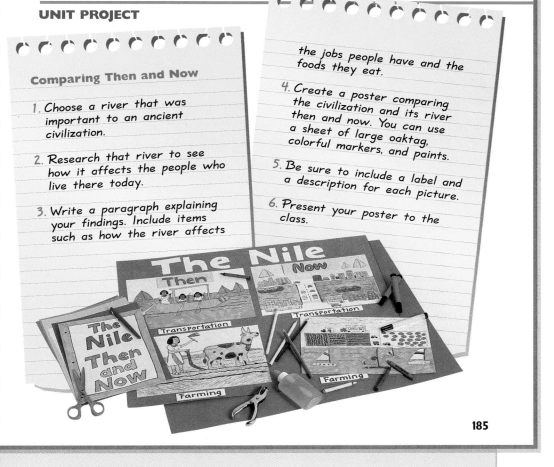

Comparing Then and Now

1. Choose a river that was important to an ancient civilization.

2. Research that river to see how it affects the people who live there today.

3. Write a paragraph explaining your findings. Include items such as how the river affects the jobs people have and the foods they eat.

4. Create a poster comparing the civilization and its river then and now. You can use a sheet of large oaktag, colorful markers, and paints.

5. Be sure to include a label and a description for each picture.

6. Present your poster to the class.

185

UNIT 2 REVIEW PROJECT

COMPLETING THE POSTERS 🎓 GROUP ⏱ 30 MINUTES OR LONGER

OBJECTIVE: Creating a poster will help students compare the effect of rivers on civilization in ancient times and today.

MATERIALS: drawing paper; paints, oaktag, markers

- Divide the class into groups. Suggest that group members revisit the text to choose an ancient river valley civilization on which to base their project.

- Make research tools such as an encyclopedia or other books from the library available to group members. Suggest that, as students do their research, they think about how best they can show a comparison between then and now.

- Suggest groups assign a role to each member before beginning their posters.

- Have groups brainstorm to decide how to organize their posters to show a comparison between ancient and modern times.

- Remind students to include a label and a description for each picture.

 FOR THE PORTFOLIO Students can include their fact sheets in their portfolios.

OPTIONS FOR ASSESSMENT

The comparisons can be part of your assessment program.

For more performance assessment and portfolio opportunities, see Assessment Book, Unit 2, p. T67.

New Ideas and New Empires

PAGES 186–309

UNIT OVERVIEW

Starting with the last few centuries B.C., the world was changed by great empires in ancient Greece, Rome, Arabia, and America. Powerful leaders expanded their territories with strong armies and ruled over many peoples. They all developed new ideas about government, religion, science, and technology that still affect peoples' lives today.

□ **ADVENTURES WITH NATIONAL GEOGRAPHIC**
Lost in Translation **pp. 188–189**

UNIT PLANNING GUIDE

CHAPTER	SUGGESTED PACING	RESOURCES	ASSESSMENT
8 Ancient Greece Democracy was born in Sparta and Athens. Alexander the Great expanded the Greek empire into India. pp. 190–221	9–10 days	• **Practice and Project Book,** pp. 41–46 • **Anthology,** pp. 35–48 • **Outline Map** • **Transparency:** Graphic Organizer, World Map • ⊙ **Technology:** Videodisc/Video Tape • ⊙ **Technology:** *Adventure Time!* CD-ROM • **McGraw-Hill Adventure Book**	• **Meeting Individual Needs,** pp. 195, 201, 203, 209, 217 • **Write About It,** 195, 201, 203, 209, 217 • **Chapter Review,** pp. 220–221 • **Assessment Book:** *Assessing Think and Write,* pp. T68–T70. Chapter 8 Tests: Content, Skills, Writing
9 Ancient Rome Rome grew from a small kingdom to a republic, and finally to a vast empire. Christianity spread with the empire. pp. 222–259	10–11 days	• **Practice and Project Book,** pp. 47–53 • **Anthology,** pp. 49–55 • **Desk Map** • **Outline Map** • **Transparency:** Map 13, Graphic Organizer, Cause and Effect Map • ⊙ **Technology:** Videodisc/Video Tape • ⊙ **Technology:** *Adventure Time!* CD-ROM	• **Meeting Individual Needs,** pp. 227, 229, 235, 243, 245, 251, 257 • **Write About It,** pp. 227, 235, 243, 245, 251, 257 • **Chapter Review,** pp. 258–259 • **Assessment Book:** *Assessing Think and Write,* pp. T71–T73. Chapter 9 Tests: Content, Skills, Writing
10 Ancient Arabia Muhammad founded the new religion of Islam in the city of Mecca. Later, Baghdad became the capital of Islam. pp. 260–283	7–8 days	• **Practice and Project Book,** pp. 54–58 • **Anthology,** pp. 56–62 • **Transparency:** Maps 14, 15, Graphic Organizer, Main Idea Chart • **Desk Map** • ⊙ **Technology:** Videodisc/Video Tape • ⊙ **Technology:** *Adventure Time!* CD-ROM	• **Meeting Individual Needs,** pp. 265, 271, 277, 279, 281 • **Write About It,** pp. 265, 271, 277, 279 • **Chapter Review,** pp. 282–283 • **Assessment Book:** *Assessing Think and Write,* pp. T74–T76. Chapter 10 Tests: Content, Skills, Writing
11 Ancient America The cultivation of corn allowed the Olmec civilization to flower. In A.D. 600, the Maya built stone monuments at Copán. pp. 284–307	7–8 days	• **Practice and Project Book,** pp. 59–63 • **Anthology,** pp. 63–66 • **Transparency:** Graphic Organizer, Main Idea Chart • ⊙ **Technology:** Videodisc/Video Tape • ⊙ **Technology:** *Adventure Time!* CD-ROM • **McGraw-Hill Adventure Book**	• **Meeting Individual Needs,** pp. 289, 291, 296, 303, 305 • **Write About It,** pp. 289, 296, 303, 305 • **Chapter Review,** pp. 306–307 • **Assessment Book:** *Assessing Think and Write,* pp. T77–T79. Chapter 11 Tests: Content, Skills, Writing
Unit 3 Review pp. 308–309	1–2 days	• **Geo Adventures Daily Geography Adventures**	• **Unit 3 Project,** p. 309

The McGraw-Hill School's Home Page at
☞ **http://www.mhschool.com**
on the World Wide Web for projects related to this unit.

FOR FURTHER SUPPORT
• **Language Support Handbook**
• **Standardized Test Support**

UNIT BIBLIOGRAPHY AND RESOURCES

McGraw-Hill Adventure Books

Mattern, Joanne. *The Trojan Horse.* This lively account of the events leading up to the Trojan War tells how the Greeks used a giant wooden horse to win the conflict. **(Easy)**

Rummel, Jack. *A Game to Remember.* The ancient Maya civilization is the setting for this story of a young boy who saves his kingdom when he scores the winning goal in a game of pok-a-tok. **(Easy)**

Classroom Library

■ Garcia, Guy. *Spirit of the Maya: A Boy Explores His People's Mysterious Past.* New York: Walker and Company, 1995. Kin, a twelve-year-old descendant of the ancient Maya, gains pride in his ancestry when he discovers clues to the secrets of his society.

Student Books

Arnold, Caroline. *City of the Gods: Mexico's Ancient City of Teotihuacan*. New York: Clarion Books, 1994. This book explores the ruins of the ancient capital of Teotihuacan and what life was like at the time. **(Average)**

■ Colum, Padraic. *The Children's Homer.* New York: Macmillan Publishing Co., 1982. This book explains the Trojan War, which Greece fought against Troy in the 12th century B.C. **(Average)**

■ Langley, Andrew and Philip De Souza. *The Roman News*. Cambridge, MA: Candlewick Press, 1996. Life in ancient Rome as it would appear in today's newspapers; done with headlines and features on everyday life. **(Average)**

Macaulay, David. *City: A Story of Roman Planning and Construction.* Boston, MA: Houghton Mifflin, 1974. This book describes how one imaginary city in the ancient Roman empire was planned and built. **(Challenging)**

Maestro, Betsy and Giulio Maestro. *The Story of Religion*. New York: Clarion Books, 1996. An attractive picture book on the background of the various religions around the world. **(Average)**

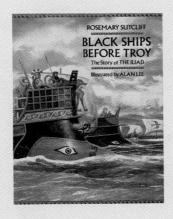

■ Sutcliff, Rosemary. *Black Ships Before Troy: The Story of the Iliad.* New York: Chelsea House, 1986. A thrilling exploration of the Trojan War. **(Challenging)**

Teacher Books

Grant, Michael. *A Social History of Greece and Rome*. New York: Charles Scribner's Sons, 1992. This is a new perspective on the customs and culture of ancient Greek and Roman people.

Sattler, Helen Roney. *The Earliest Americans*. New York: Clarion Books, 1993. Read about who the earliest Americans were, where they came from, when they arrived, and how they lived.

Read-Alouds

Fisher, Leonard Everett. *Pyramid of the Sun, Pyramid of the Moon.* New York: Macmillan Pub. Co., 1988. Explore the story behind the pyramids of Teotihuacan and the Toltec civilization.

Low, Alice. *The Macmillan Book of Greek Gods and Heroes*. New York: Macmillan Publishing Co., 1985. These are well-known myths from ancient Greece.

Technology Multimedia

Aladdin and the Magic Lamp. Video. With the help of the genie in the magic lamp, Aladdin wins his desires. Story Lane Theater, Macmillan/McGraw-Hill. (800) 442-9685.

Ancient Civilizations: Greece and Rome. CD-ROM. Everyday life in Ancient Greece and Rome is presented. National Geographic. (800) 368-2728.

Ancient Maya Indians of Central America. Video. No. 3140-106. Find out how the Mayan civilization reached its peak of power. Britannica Videos. (800) 554-9862.

Free or Inexpensive Materials

For free rental of slides on "The Search for Alexander," send to: National Gallery of Art; Department of Education Resources; 4th and Constitution Avenue, N. W.; Washington, DC 20565.

■ *Book excerpted in the Anthology*

■ *Book featured in the student bibliography of the Unit Review*

☐ *National Geographic technolog*

Ideas for Active Learning

BULLETIN BOARD

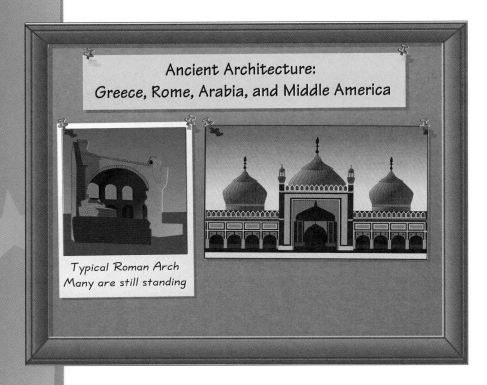

Ancient Architecture:
Greece, Rome, Arabia, and Middle America

Typical Roman Arch
Many are still standing

New Ideas and New Empires

Help students to create a bulletin board titled "Ancient Architecture: Greece, Rome, Arabia, and Middle America." As students learn about monuments and architecture created by ancient civilizations, have them use reference materials such as encyclopedias or magazines, *National Geographic*, to find photographs or drawings of such architectural features as ancient Roman arches, the Greek Parthenon, Mecca, and the ruins of Copán. Students can cut out magazine photographs or make their own drawings. Students should write captions explaining where the building or monument is located and the approximate date it was built. Ask students to include other interesting facts, such as how a structure was engineered, its purpose, and so on. Invite students to make a collage, and to arrange their visuals to highlight similarities or differences.

TEACHER EXCHANGE

Thanks to: Cathy Dunn, St. Paul's the Apostle School, Spartanburg, South Carolina

"Greek and Roman Day"

ON YOUR OWN · **30 MINUTES OR LONGER**

CURRICULUM CONNECTION
Language Arts/Drama
Materials: sheets, dress-up materials and props such as crowns, shields, fake beards

1. Tell students that they will plan a celebration of ancient Greek and Roman culture.
2. Assign one-page, first-person reports on Greek or Roman deities and cultural figures. Tell students that they will act out their presentation as if they were the "person" in the report.
3. Have students look at the manner of dress in the ancient civilizations, and then provide sheets and other props for students to use as their presentation costumes.
4. On "Greek and Roman Day," have students do their presentations at lunchtime, and enjoy grape juice and lunch as they watch the dramatizations.

Enriching with Multimedia

RESOURCE: McGraw-Hill School's Home Page

- Have students go to McGraw-Hill School's home page at http://www.mhschool.com on the World Wide Web for projects related to this unit.

RESOURCE: *Videodisc/Video Tape 3*

- Enrich Unit 3 with the *Ancient Greece* segment.

Search Frame 00304 Side B

SCHOOL-TO-HOME

New Ideas and New Empires

- Throughout the unit, students will have the opportunity to learn about the significant contributions of early civilizations. Discuss with students the various kinds of art, architecture, technology, athletics, agriculture, and urban planning that each culture brought to the "new empires." With the class, make a sample reference book with sections for each civilization in the unit. Tell students to design their own reference books, adding to each section photographs, drawings, and text that show a cultural contribution, such as those mentioned.

- Have students and their families add to the book as they discover information about these early civilizations in newspapers and magazines. Students may wish to share their books with the rest of the class. At the end of the unit, have students add their reference books to their books at home.

ONGOING UNIT PROJECT

Design a Shield of Achievement

CURRICULUM CONNECTION   Art

RESOURCE: Practice and Project Book p. 131.

Throughout this unit, students will be working individually and cooperatively to design shields illustrating ancient people's contributions to civilization.

1. After each chapter is completed, have students make notes about a person, place, or thing that expresses the main idea of a lesson.
2. After the unit is completed, provide students, working in small groups, with a large piece of posterboard or oaktag, scissors, markers, and crayons.
3. Guide students in groups to design their shields with the use of the planning sheets provided and to make a sketch with enough space for name of civilization, dates, and accomplishments.
4. After designing their shields, group members can color and cut out shields and display them in the classroom.

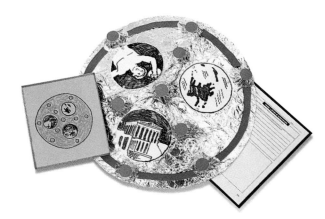

Assessment suggestions for the activity appear on page 308.

Introducing the Unit

Remind students that change over time is a major theme of social studies. Have them read the unit title and ask how it reflects this theme (the use of "New" twice reflects change in ideas and in empires). Give students a few moments to examine the artifacts pictured here and have them read *Why Does It Matter?* on p. 187.

Exploring Prior Knowledge Help students draw on images they may have encountered in reading or the media, or on museum trips or from travel.

- *Are you familiar with any of these artifacts? Where have you seen them and what do you know about them?* (Invite any responses based on students' prior experience.)

★THINKING FURTHER: *Compare and Contrast* **What seems "new" about any of the artifacts, in comparison with what you've seen of earlier civilizations?** (The construction and the helmet may seem advanced, and perhaps the art seems more realistic, but accept any well-reasoned answers.)

Looking Ahead In this unit students will learn how civilization continued to develop on Earth in four new settings— Greece and Rome in Europe, Arabia in Asia, and in the Americas. Students will explore the geography of each setting to see how it assisted or challenged development, and they will trace both difficulties each civilization faced and achievements of each.

ISLAMIC TILE, SPAIN;
STATUE OF GODDESS OF WISDOM, ROME;
STATUE OF MAYA GODDESS, HONDURAS;
THE COLOSSEUM, ROME

186

BACKGROUND INFORMATION

ABOUT THE ARTIFACTS

- **ISLAMIC TILE** The ornate tile from Muslim Spain reveals the emphasis on design that developed in a culture that did not permit representations of humans or animals. From the eighth through the fifteenth centuries, large sections of Spain were ruled by Muslims.

- **MINERVA, THE GODDESS OF WISDOM** The Romans identified their goddess Minerva with Athena, the Greek goddess of wisdom. Like Athena, Minerva is often shown wearing armor and carrying the *aegis*, a shield.

- **MAYAN GODDESS** This statue of a Mayan goddess was found in Honduras. Some of the decorative elements are hieroglyphs that tell something about the subject. Only recently have archaeologists begun to be able to decode Mayan hieroglyphics.

UNIT THREE

New Ideas and New Empires

"The armor upon their bodies flashed in the sun."

from the *Iliad*, by Homer
See page 200.

WHY DOES IT MATTER?

A poet in ancient Greece wrote these words to describe a great battle. Today people around the world are familiar with Homer's words as well as many other achievements of his time. People of the world today owe much to the early peoples of Greece, Rome, Arabia, and the Americas. Their ideas about government, law, beauty, education, science, and religion continue to influence us today. Such accomplishments are only a few of the reasons for calling certain periods "Classic."

VASE WITH BATTLE
SCENE, GREECE

187

Discussing the Artifacts Write on the board the names of the four civilizations—Greece, Rome, Arabia, the Americas—covered in this unit. Divide the class into five groups and assign each group one of the artifacts. Have each group try to decide from which civilization its artifact comes.

★**THINKING FURTHER:** *Making Conclusions* **From which civilization do you think your artifact comes? Why?** *(Call on each group to respond and invite the opinions of any other students. Then have students thumb through the unit to make positive identifications of the origins of their artifacts.)*

Discussing WHY DOES IT MATTER? Have a student read the quotation aloud and then have students review the paragraph.

● **How does Homer create a word picture here?** *(His words, though brief, create a vivid picture in the mind.)*

● **Which of this unit's civilizations does Homer represent?** *(Greece)*

● **What aspects of these civilizations will you investigate?** *(government, law, beauty, education, science, and religion)*

★**THINKING FURTHER:** *Making Conclusions* **How would you define "Classic" based on its use here?** *(Help students recognize that the term refers to periods when civilizations are at their very best and have reached their highest achievement. Point out to the class that in this social studies course they will explore the Classic—or Classical—periods of several civilizations.)*

BACKGROUND INFORMATION

ABOUT THE ARTIFACTS
● **ROMAN COLOSSEUM** The Colosseum in Rome, was constructed in the first century A.D. and dedicated in A.D. 80. Built of brick and concrete, it was the largest outdoor arena in ancient Rome and it features arches and other typical elements of Roman architecture. Its ruins today are a major tourist attraction in modern Rome.

● **GREEK VASE** The battle scene shown on this vase is an example of one visual source we have for knowledge of ancient Greece; other vases show scenes from daily life.

Adventures
with

NATIONAL GEOGRAPHIC

Introducing
Lost in Translation

Exploring Prior Knowledge As students look at the pictures on this spread, ask them what they think is going on in them, based on what they have already studied in this course. Help them to recognize that these illustrations reflect archaeologists' digs, like those they encountered in Egypt and elsewhere. Encourage them to recap what digs are for and the kinds of knowledge they uncover.

Links to the Unit As students continue through Unit 3, they will broaden their knowledge of the ancient world, moving on to Europe, Arabia in Asia, and the Americas. They will learn that in these places, too, archaeological finds have been invaluable in discovering information about ancient civilizations.

Lost in Translation Have students read the text on the Etruscans as "mystery people of the ancient world." Have them identify why the Etruscans are more mysterious than, say, the ancient Egyptians or Mesopotamians, to reinforce how important being able to understand an ancient people's written language is in solving mysteries about them. On the pictured globe, have students point to where the Etruscans developed their civilization (in Italy on the continent of Europe). Help students to identify the kinds of artifacts being uncovered in the digs pictured here and encourage them to tell what different kinds of information each imparts about the people who created them (for example, how they built, the level their arts had reached).

Resource REMINDER

National Geographic Poster
Geo Adventures *Daily Geography Activities*
Technology: *Adventure Time!* CD-ROM

BACKGROUND INFORMATION

MORE ABOUT THE ETRUSCANS AND THEIR LANGUAGE

- The Etruscans flourished in Italy from about the 8th century to the 1st century B.C. in an area called Etruria. Some scholars think that they may have been one of the Sea Peoples who were driven from their homes in the Aegean Sea in the 13th century B.C. and resettled in various parts of the Mediterranean.

- Their language remains a mystery to us because it does not seem to be related to any of the Indo-European languages or to any other languages of the Mediterranean.

- Etruscan writing uses the Greek alphabet, so the words can be read but their meaning cannot be understood. Etruscan inscriptions survive on walls and monuments, but no Etruscan literature has been found.

LOST IN TRANSLATION

You poke your head into the doorway of a ruined tomb, and you wonder about the people who painted the walls more than 2,000 years ago. You're not alone. Archaeologists also wonder about the Etruscans, who lived in Italy about the same time that the ancient Greeks were flourishing nearby. The Etruscans built great cities and elaborate tombs. But unlike the Greeks, they left few written records. And the records they *did* leave— well, no one can read them now, for no one knows the language. So archaeologists hunt through the ruins, looking for other clues about the mystery people of the ancient world.

GEO JOURNAL

List some ways you might find out about a culture even if you couldn't read its language.

189

Refer the class to the picture in the lower lefthand corner and explain that this artwork is a recreation of the Temples of the Dead that lined the cliffs of the Etruscan city of Norchia. Today, all that remains of them are ruins of tombs cut out of rock.

Call students' attention to the center insert on this page and help students note that many young people are shown here at work on an Etruscan dig. Explain that they are volunteers donating their time and effort. Digs are often run primarily on the work of volunteers who are eager to learn both about archaeology and about the people who once lived on the dig's site.

Refer students to the piece of pottery being unearthed in the lower righthand inset. Explain that it was found near the surface of a shallow tomb near a modern Italian town. This particular piece reflects strong Greek influence, common in Etruscan art.

Using the Geo Journal Before students begin listing ways to find out about a culture without knowing its language, urge them to review what they have already learned about artifacts and what they can tell us about a society.

Technology CONNECTION

ADVENTURE TIME! CD-ROM
Enrich this feature with the *Early Cultures* time line on the *Adventure Time!* CD-ROM.

CURRICULUM CONNECTION

ART Explain to the class that the Etruscans reached a very high level of art and their painting, pottery, sculpture, jewelry making, and other metal work is treasured in museums across the world.

Divide the class into research teams and assign each of the teams one of the five above-mentioned areas of Etruscan art. Have each team do library research on its area in both art history books and *National Geographic*, June 1988. Tell them to prepare an illustrated report on it for presentation in class.

THEMES of GEOGRAPHY

As you work through Unit 3 with your students, consider the following theme:

Location Location is the position of a place on the earth's surface. The location of a place can be described with its relative location (its distance to another place) or its absolute location (its longitude and latitude). Identify the relative and absolute locations of the following places as you read Unit 3: Crete, Rhodes (Ch. 8, Lesson 1), Athens, Sparta (Ch. 8, Lesson 2), Alexandria (Ch. 8, Lesson 4), Rome (Ch. 9, Lesson 1), Carthage (Ch. 9, Lesson 2), Pompeii (Ch. 9, Lesson 3), Red Sea (Ch. 10, Lesson 1), Mecca (Ch. 10, Lesson 2), Baghdad (Ch. 10, Lesson 3), and Middle America (Ch. 11, Lesson 1).

CHAPTER 8 Ancient Greece

Pages 190–221

CHAPTER OVERVIEW

People learned to farm and sail in ancient Greece at around 800 B.C. Just after that time the city of Sparta formed a strong military. By 450 B.C., the city of Athens established the first democratic form of government. Alexander the Great expanded a united Greek empire into India in 331 B.C.

GEO ADVENTURES DAILY GEOGRAPHY ACTIVITIES

Use **Geo Adventures** Daily Geography activities to assess students' understanding of geography skills.

CHAPTER PLANNING GUIDE

LESSON 1	**LESSON 2**	**Legacy**
SUGGESTED PACING: 2 DAYS	SUGGESTED PACING: 2 DAYS	SUGGESTED PACING: 1 DAY
Geography Of Ancient Greece pp. 192–195	**The Rise Of Greek Cities** pp. 196–201	**The Olympics** pp. 202–203
CITIZENSHIP Linking Past and Present, p. 193	**CURRICULUM CONNECTIONS** Links to Language Arts, p. 198	
FIELD TRIP Visit a Museum, p. 193	**CITIZENSHIP** Recognizing Perspectives, p. 199	
RESOURCES Practice and Project Book, p. 41	**RESOURCES** Practice and Project Book, p. 42 Anthology, pp. 36–38, 39–44	

THINKINGSKILLS	**LESSON 4**	**CITIZENSHIP**
SUGGESTED PACING: 1 DAY	SUGGESTED PACING: 3 DAYS	SUGGESTED PACING: 1 DAY
Making Conclusions pp. 210–211	**The Greek Empire** pp. 212–217	**How Great Was Alexander The Great?** pp. 218–219
RESOURCES Practice and Project Book, p. 44	**CURRICULUM CONNECTIONS** Links to Language Arts, pp. 213, 215	**CITIZENSHIP** Using Current Events, p. 219
	INFOGRAPHIC Seven Wonders of the World, pp. 216–217	
	RESOURCES Practice and Project Book, p. 45 Desk Map ◉ TECHNOLOGY *Adventure Time!* CD-ROM	

LEARNING STYLE: Visual

 GROUP

 30 MINUTES OR LONGER

Plan an Election

Objective: To introduce the government of ancient Greece.

Materials: paper, oaktag, art supplies

1. Suggest that local schools might form a league for sports. Each school will elect one student to help make decisions about the league. Have small groups plan the election.
2. Have groups write rules: number of candidates, how chosen, how long a campaign, how students will vote.
3. Have each group choose a speaker to share the group's plans with the class. Have the class compare and contrast the rules created by each group.

LESSON 3

SUGGESTED PACING: 2 DAYS

Athens' Age Of Glory
pp. 204–209

CURRICULUM CONNECTIONS
Links to Language Arts, p. 207

CITIZENSHIP
Recognizing Perspectives, p. 206

RESOURCES
Practice and Project Book, p. 43
Anthology, pp. 45–46
📖 Anthology, pp. 47–48
🌐 TECHNOLOGY Videodisc/Video Tape 3

CHAPTER REVIEW

SUGGESTED PACING: I DAY

pp. 220–221

RESOURCES
Practice and Project Book, p. 46
🌐 TECHNOLOGY Videodisc/Video Tape 3
Assessment Book: Chapter 8 Test
Transparency: Graphic Organizer, Word Map

SDAIE SUPPORT — SHELTERED INSTRUCTION

READING STRATEGIES & LANGUAGE DEVELOPMENT

Problem and Solution/Word Roots, p. 192, Lesson 1
Compare and Contrast/Prefixes, p. 196, Lesson 2
Predicting/Word Origins, p. 204, Lesson 3
Making Conclusions/Word Roots, p. 210, Thinking Skills
Rereading/ Synonyms and Antonyms, p. 212, Lesson 4

SECOND-LANGUAGE SUPPORT

Discussion, p. 194
Taking Notes, p. 199
Working with a Peer, p. 206
Making Connections. p. 214
Note Taking/Portrait Gallery, p. 220

MEETING INDIVIDUAL NEEDS

Reteaching, Extension, Enrichment, pp. 195, 201, 203, 209, 217
McGraw-Hill Adventure Book

ASSESSMENT OPPORTUNITIES

Practice and Project Book, pp. 41–46
Write About It, pp. 195, 201, 203, 209, 217
Assessment Book: Assessing Think and Write, pp. T68–T70; Chapter 8 Tests: Content, Skills, Writing

Introducing the Chapter

Point out to students that in this chapter they will shift to a new continent—Europe—to explore a civilization. Have them locate Europe on a map of the world and then find Greece and the Aegean and Mediterranean seas.

THINKING ABOUT HISTORY AND GEOGRAPHY

Have students read the text on this page to pinpoint the civilization they are about to study (Greece) and the time (about 3,000 years ago) it began to develop. Have them trace each panel on the time line to its location on the map.

1400 B.C. AEGEAN SEA

- **As you look at the Aegean Sea on the map, what geographic features are very evident?** *(islands, water, coasts)*

- **Into what larger sea does the Aegean flow?** *(the Mediterranean Sea)*

★THINKING FURTHER: *Making Conclusions* **Why does it make sense that the Greeks would become seafarers?** *(They had a long coastline and many islands.)*

800 B.C. SPARTA

Point out that Sparta lies inland.

- **In what part of Greece is Sparta located?** *(in the southwestern part)*

★THINKING FURTHER: *Making Conclusions* **Why might this location lead it to build up an army instead of a navy?** *(Since it is not on the sea, it might do its fighting by land rather than by sea.)*

Resource REMINDER

Technology: *Videodisc/Video Tape 3*

CHAPTER 8

Ancient Greece

THINKING ABOUT HISTORY AND GEOGRAPHY

In this chapter you will read about a civilization that developed in the rocky landscape by the Aegean Sea more than 3,000 years ago. Following the time line, you see how the ancient Greeks built cities with unique ways of life. In time, interaction and conflict among the cities and peoples of the region led to a period of tremendous creativity. Greek civilization eventually spread to areas around the Mediterranean Sea.

1400 B.C.
AEGEAN SEA
Seagoing people trade among the islands of Greece

800 B.C.
SPARTA
Boys and girls train to build a strong city

450 B.C.
ATHENS
Pericles encourages poor and rich citizens to take part in government

190

BACKGROUND INFORMATION

LINKING THE MAP TO THE TIME LINE
- In about 1100 B.C. Greece's population grew so large that Greeks began emigrating to colonize the islands of the Aegean. The islands they settled became known as Ionia.

- Sparta's inland location helped it to develop and maintain a fierce isolationism. It resisted entering the mainstream of Greek trade and other economic life, preferring instead to remain a self-sufficient agricultural society.

- Pericles on democracy: ". . . power is in the hands not of a minority but of the whole people. When it is a question of settling private disputes, everyone is equal before the law; when it is a question of putting one person before another in positions of public responsibility, what counts . . . is ability."

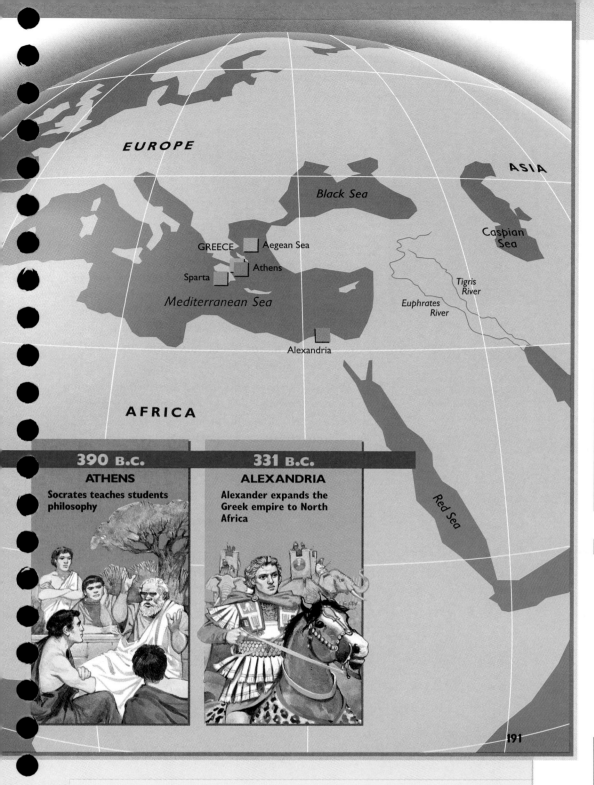

EUROPE

ASIA

Black Sea

Caspian Sea

GREECE

Aegean Sea

Sparta

Athens

Mediterranean Sea

Tigris River

Euphrates River

Alexandria

AFRICA

Red Sea

191

390 B.C.
ATHENS
Socrates teaches students philosophy

331 B.C.
ALEXANDRIA
Alexander expands the Greek empire to North Africa

- **Where in Greece is Athens located?** *(in the southeastern part along the coast)*

- **Where does it lie in relation to Sparta?** *(northeast of it)*

★**THINKING FURTHER:** *Making Conclusions* **What does this panel indicate about government in Athens?** *(All citizens—rich and poor—were allowed to participate.)*

- **What is happening in this panel?** *(Socrates is teaching students philosophy.)*

★**THINKING FURTHER:** *Making Conclusions* **What does this tell you about who Socrates was? What does it tell you about education in Athens?** *(He was a philosopher who taught philosophy; if it is illustrated here, philosophy must have been important to Athens.)*

- **On what continent is Alexandria located?** *(Africa)*

- **In what civilization that you already studied is it found?** *(Egypt; if necessary, refer students to a map to make this identification.)*

- **What is happening in this panel?** *(Alexander the Great is leading a march on North Africa to expand the Greek empire.)*

★**THINKING FURTHER:** *Making Conclusions* **What does this tell you about what Greece must have achieved?** *(It must have spread its power and influence over a broad area.)*

Technology CONNECTION

VIDEODISC/VIDEO TAPE 3
Enrich Chapter 8 with *Ancient Greece* on the Videodisc.

Search Frame 304 Side B

BACKGROUND INFORMATION

LINKING THE MAP AND THE TIME LINE
- The term *philosophy*, literally "love of knowledge," has its origins in Greek. For Greeks, it grew out of their search for general principles for learning more about the nature of things around them through argument and proof of hypotheses. Said the Roman Cicero: "Socrates was the first to call philosophy down from the heavens and to place it in cities, and even to introduce it into homes and compel it to inquire about life and standards and goods and evils."

- Alexandria in Egypt had many distinctions including a great library and one of the Seven Wonders of the World, the Lighthouse of Pharos, which was built on an island in its harbor.

LESSON 1

PAGES 192–195

Lesson Overview
Rocky *peninsulas* and islands as well as excellent *harbors* spurred Greece to master sea travel and to trade afar.

Lesson Objectives
★ Analyze how the rugged terrain challenged people of ancient Greece.

★ Explain why the environment led Greeks to become seafarers.

★ Describe how sea trade served as a lifeline for Greece.

1 PREPARE

MOTIVATE Call on two students for the *Read Aloud*, one to read the quotation from Homer, the other the narration. Have students thumb through the lesson's illustrations for clues to why the sea was so important to Greeks.

SET PURPOSE Refer to the photo of rocky land on this page. Encourage students to figure out the role rugged geography may have played in turning Greeks toward the sea. Then direct them to the *Read to Learn* question and have them read to find answers to it. Preview the *Vocabulary* words.

2 TEACH

Understanding THE BIG PICTURE
Prepare students to compare Greece's geography with other regions studied.

● **Along what major sea did Greece develop?** (the Mediterranean)

● **How long ago did its civilization begin to develop?** (4,500 years ago—1,000 years before the Shang in China and the New Kingdom in Egypt)

★ **THINKING FURTHER: Compare and Contrast How did Greece differ from the four civilizations you have already explored?** (They were all river valley civilizations; Greece was on the sea.)

Resource **REMINDER**

Practice and Project Book: *p. 41*

Outline Map

GEOGRAPHY OF ANCIENT GREECE

Focus Activity

READ TO LEARN
What effects did the sea have on life in ancient Greece?

VOCABULARY
peninsula
harbor

PLACES
Mediterranean Sea
Crete
Rhodes
Attica
Peloponnesus
Phoenicia

READ ALOUD

"The good Odysseus (oh DIHS ee us) gladly spread his sail: seated, he steered. . . . Seventeen days he sailed across the sea; on the eighteenth he saw that he'd drawn close to shadowed peaks: he now was near the coast of [an] island; in the mist that land took on the likeness of a shield."

About 2,700 years ago Greeks first began listening to the exciting tales, like the one above, of a poet named Homer. Homer's stories about Odysseus helped the ancient Greeks imagine a distant age much different from their own. They also expressed the strong connection the people of ancient Greece felt with the sea.

THE BIG PICTURE

In 1500 B.C. the Shang dynasty ruled much of the land along the Huang River. In Egypt the pharaohs of the New Kingdom were building an empire along the southeastern shores of the Mediterranean Sea. Along the Mediterranean's northeastern shores, meanwhile, another civilization was growing. It was that of ancient Greece, a civilization that had been developing for more than 1,000 years.

No great river carrying thick layers of silt flowed through this land. Rather than being located in a fertile river valley, ancient Greek civilization was rooted in a rocky landscape surrounded by the sea.

SHELTERED INSTRUCTION

READING STRATEGIES & LANGUAGE DEVELOPMENT

PROBLEM AND SOLUTION Remind students that they can often make sense of what they read by identifying problems and solutions. Explain that one problem facing the ancient Greeks was rugged geography. Since the land lacked the level, well-watered valley of the river valley civilizations, farming was difficult. Arrange students in small groups to brainstorm solutions they might have used to overcome this problem.
[SDAIE STRATEGY: BRIDGING]

WORD ROOTS Point out to the class that their vocabulary work has already introduced them to many English words that have their roots in Greece. This lesson presents several more, for example, *poet, dynasty, acre, economy, climate, diet,* and *olive.* Split the class into teams and assign each team one of these words. Have each team research and present its word's derivation.

MOUNTAINS AND SEA

The land of ancient Greece was made up of a part of the southern European mainland along with over 400 islands. This is the same area that makes up Greece today. As you can see on the map, the biggest of the islands is Crete. Crete lies about one day's sail south of the Greek mainland. East of Crete lies Rhodes, an island near what is today Turkey. Rhodes provides an ideal rest stop for ships sailing between Greece and western Asia.

Mountains and hills cover about nine out of every ten acres in Greece. The most mountainous region, however, is located in western Greece. There, travel by land is difficult, and little farmable land exists. Herds of sheep and goats live on wild plants that grow on the rugged hillsides.

Land Along the Coast

Larger plains suitable for farming lie in eastern Greece, near the coast. A few of these plains are on Attica, a wedge-shaped peninsula that juts into the Mediterranean Sea. A peninsula is an area of land nearly surrounded by water. Attica also contains excellent natural harbors for ships. A harbor is a sheltered place along a coast.

A large peninsula called the Peloponnesus (pel uh puh NEE sus) lies to the southwest of Attica. Shaped like a giant hand reaching toward Crete, the Peloponnesus is a mountainous region ringed by a thin band of fertile land. Like the rest of Greece, the Peloponnesus contains several rivers. Many of the region's rivers, however, dry up in the summertime, unlike rivers in Egypt or Mesopotamia.

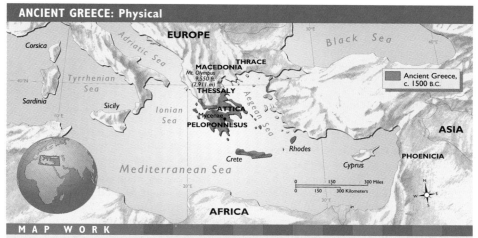

ANCIENT GREECE: Physical

Corsica · EUROPE · Adriatic Sea · Black Sea · THRACE · MACEDONIA · Mt. Olympus 9,550 ft (2,911 m) · THESSALY · Tyrrhenian Sea · Sardinia · Sicily · Ionian Sea · ATTICA · Mycenae · PELOPONNESUS · Aegean Sea · ASIA · Rhodes · Crete · Cyprus · PHOENICIA · Mediterranean Sea · AFRICA

Ancient Greece, c. 1500 B.C.

0 150 300 Miles
0 150 300 Kilometers

MAP WORK

For its size, the land of ancient Greece had a very long coastline. Much of the land is also mountainous. This geography had a great impact on life in the region.

1. What method of transportation do you suppose was quickest in ancient Greece?

2. About how long is the island of Crete? Use the map scale to find this answer.

3. What body of water lies east of Attica?

4. In which direction would you travel to get from Crete to Rhodes?

MAP WORK: **1.** boat **2.** about 150 miles (about 241 kilometers) **3.** Aegean Sea **4.** northeast

193

FIELD TRIP

If you have a nearby museum or university with an ancient Greek division, try to arrange a class field trip there. Prior to taking the trip, preview the chapter with students, especially the illustrations, to give them an idea of what they will be learning. If a field trip is not possible, create a classroom "museum" of postcards, travel posters, and such.

CITIZENSHIP★

LINKING PAST AND PRESENT Explain to the class that the Greeks have never lost their ability to use the seas for economic reasons. Today, although Greece is a small nation with a population of only about 10 million, its merchant fleet ranks fifth in the world in total tonnage. Income from shipping continues to be important to Greece. Have students do research to identify Greece's main trading partners.

MOUNTAINS AND SEA

If possible, have available travel posters or picture books on Greece to dramatize Greece's rugged mountains and well-indented coastlines.

More
MAP WORK

Refer students to the map on this page.

● *What sea does much of ancient Greece surround?* (the Aegean Sea)

● *What are two of Greece's large islands?* (Crete and Rhodes)

● *What do physical features shown on the map as well as information in the text tell you about Greece's land?* (that most of it is covered by mountains or hills)

● *How does such land affect life in an area?* (It makes travel difficult and provides little farmable land.)

★**THINKING FURTHER:** *Cause and Effect* **Why might such geography cause people to turn to the sea?** (The sea can provide the highways the land lacks, and sea trade can bring in farm crops the land is unable to produce.)

Discussing Land Along the Coast
Encourage students to use both the map and text. Call attention to the land shapes shown on the map and to the indentations of the Greek coastline.

● *What are land shapes like Attica and the Peloponnesus called?* (peninsulas—areas nearly surrounded by water)

● *What do the many indentations along Greece's long coastline help to create?* (harbors, or sheltered spots, where boats can pull up to shore. Discuss with students why harbors need the protection of indented land—for shelter from sea winds and places to anchor in calmer water.)

★**THINKING FURTHER:** *Making Conclusions* **Why do you think Greeks became great seafarers?** (rugged terrain and geographical features that encouraged sea travel)

Review with students the agricultural conditions in Greece that they have studied—some farmable plains in eastern Attica, a thin band of fertile land around the Peloponnesus, and rivers likely to dry up in summer.

Discussing Agriculture in Ancient Greece Reinforce the concept that the Greeks coped well with geography.

- *In addition to having little land to farm, how were Greek farmers challenged by climate?* (dryness during the best growing season, wet and windy conditions in winter)

- *What are some ways that Greek farmers adapted to the environment?* (They grew crops well suited to the environment and herded animals that could live off the shrubs)

★**THINKING FURTHER:** *Classifying* **As a result, what were Greece's major agricultural products?** (wheat, barley, olives, grapes, sheep, goats, cattle)

Exploring Crossing the Seas Discuss with students the idea that the sea helped the Greeks survive.

★**THINKING FURTHER:** *Cause and Effect* **How did Greece's agricultural limitations help cause it to become a sea trader?** (Greece produced many olives but needed grain, so Greeks turned to the sea to trade their olive oil for grain from other countries.)

Like their ancestors in ancient times, many farmers in Greece today herd sheep (left) and raise olives (above).

EARLY ECONOMY IN GREECE

Greece is not as fertile as the valleys of the Indus or Huang rivers. However, ancient Greeks figured out how to make a living from the few fertile valleys as well as from the sea.

Agriculture in Ancient Greece

Besides having little fertile land, Greece has a climate that presents special challenges for farmers. Summers are hot and dry. Winters can be wet and fiercely windy. Fields can become parched in the summer but soaked with rain in the winter.

Ancient Greek farmers raised crops and animals that were well suited to this environment. They grew some wheat and barley to make bread, which was important to the Greek diet. Olives and grapes became Greece's other major crops. Both grew well in rocky and hilly areas. Shrubs on Greece's many hills and mountains provided food for herds of sheep, goats, and cattle.

Timing was important to successful farming in Greece. The Greek poet Hesiod (HEE see ud), who wrote during the 700s B.C., urged farmers:

Take careful note of the time when you hear the voice of the crane uttering high in the clouds her yearly trumpeting cry [in the fall]. She announces the signal for plowing and points to the time of winter and rain.

If farmers waited until winter to plow their land, Hesiod warned, they would "gather only a small little handful" of grain in the spring.

Crossing the Seas

Because farmers could not produce huge grain surpluses, and because travel on the hilly land was difficult, sailing became an important part of life in Greece. Sailors traveled as far as

194

GLOBAL CONNECTION

AMERICAN TIES TO GREEK COOKING Greek Americans have traditionally been active in the American restaurant business, and Greek food is popular. Make some Greek cookbooks available to the class. Encourage students to find recipes that use traditional Greek agricultural products: lamb, feta cheese, olives, and grapes.

SECOND-LANGUAGE SUPPORT

DISCUSSION Invite second-language learners to discuss how access to the sea can make a civilization prosper. Have them use the examples of the ancient Greeks and the Phoenicians, retelling information they have read in this lesson. Share the background information on the Phoenicians with students.

BACKGROUND INFORMATION

ABOUT PHOENICIA Phoenicia's borders were roughly those of modern Lebanon.

- The Phoenicians were closely related in culture and language to the people of Canaan, a land students read about in their study of the Hebrews in Chapter 5.

- Phoenician sailors were renowned for their skill and daring. Some historians think that they even sailed beyond the Strait of Gibraltar, into the Atlantic and north to Cornwall in Britain.

- Among Phoenicia's prized exports were pungent cedar wood (cedars of Lebanon) and a cloth with a purple dye only Phoenicians could produce. In many societies, only royalty were permitted to wear purple.

ancient Egypt to trade. Greek merchants competed with traders from Phoenicia (fuh NEE shuh), in what is today Lebanon. Phoenician sailors were as skilled as the Greeks and traveled to ports all across the Mediterranean Sea.

For many years olive oil was one of the most prized of Greek exports. People loved the flavor it gave food as well as its usefulness as lamp fuel and body lotion. The sale of olive oil made it possible for Greeks to buy much-needed grain for their markets at home.

WHY IT MATTERS

In the lessons to come, you will read the story of Greek civilization. Beginning around 800 B.C., great changes would take place on these rocky islands and peninsulas. Some things, however, would never change. Farming and sailing would always be lifelines for the people of ancient Greece.

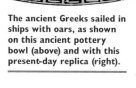

The ancient Greeks sailed in ships with oars, as shown on this ancient pottery bowl (above) and with this present-day replica (right).

Reviewing Facts and Ideas

MAIN IDEAS

- Unlike the Nile or Huang River valleys, Greece has land that is hilly and rocky, making farming difficult in most areas.
- Ancient Greeks used the Mediterranean Sea as a "highway" to trade for goods they could not produce themselves.
- Olive oil—a product of a crop that grows well in Greece's rocky soil—became valuable to trade for grain.

THINK ABOUT IT

1. Why was farming a challenge in Greece? Why was timing important?
2. Contrast the geography of Greece with that of an ancient river valley civilization such as Mesopotamia or the Indus Valley.
3. **FOCUS** How did ancient Greeks use the sea to spread their products and culture to other regions?
4. **THINKING SKILL** What *effects* did geography have on the ways ancient Greeks met their needs?
5. **GEOGRAPHY** Draw a map of the Mediterranean Sea region. Draw in arrows to show where ancient Greeks sailed.

195

LESSON 2

PAGES 196–201

Lesson Overview

Two great city-states emerged in Greece; they showed two sides of Greek culture: the strict discipline of Sparta and the art and learning of Athens.

Lesson Objectives

★ Analyze the *polis* organization of ancient Greece.

★ Compare and contrast the cultures of Sparta and Athens.

★ Describe the spread of Greek culture.

⭐ 1 PREPARE

MOTIVATE Have a student present the *Read Aloud* to the class, and discuss the pride in a shared heritage.

SET PURPOSE Establish the *Read to Learn* question as a guide for understanding the lesson. Ask students to define the *Vocabulary* words that they recognize and look for the meanings and pronunciations of the others. Call attention on both pages to the photos of the Acropolis, which they will study in this lesson.

⭐ 2 TEACH

Understanding THE BIG PICTURE Remind students that they have also encountered city-states in studying Mesopotamia.

● **What is a city-state?** *(a self-governing city that also governs surrounding villages)*

● **What did the Greeks call it?** *(a polis)*

⭐**THINKING FURTHER:** *Making Conclusions* **Why might the Greeks have developed the polis?** *(A polis probably provided a workable, governable unit.)*

Resource REMINDER

Practice and Project Book: *p. 42*

Anthology: *The Iliad, pp. 36–38; How The City of Athens Got Its Name, pp. 39–44*

 Technology: *Adventure Time!* CD-ROM

---

700 B.C.	600 B.C.	500 B.C.	400 B.C.	300 B.C.

THE RISE OF GREEK CITIES

READ ALOUD

"Shared blood, shared language, shared religion, and shared customs." Long ago a Greek historian named Herodotus (hih RAHD uh tus) used these words to describe what it meant to be Greek. Greeks were very proud of what they shared. However, they prized just as highly those things that made them different from one another. Those differences began in the many city-states that dotted the mainland and islands of ancient Greece.

THE BIG PICTURE

By 1100 B.C. both Egypt's New Kingdom empire and China's Shang dynasty had lost their power. Historians know little about how people in Greece lived during this period or during the next 400 years. Very few artifacts from Greece at this time have been found. However, many artifacts dating from about 700 B.C. onward have been found. They show that life had changed greatly since the earliest days of ancient Greece. In many cities, groups of powerful men worked together to make decisions for their communities. Each community usually revolved around one city. The Greek word for this kind of city-state was polis (POH lihs).

Focus Activity

READ TO LEARN

What was life like in the ancient Greek cities of Sparta and Athens?

VOCABULARY

polis
acropolis
agora
citizen
oligarchy
monarchy
democracy
colony

PEOPLE

Homer

PLACES

Athens
Sparta
Mount Olympus

196

SHELTERED INSTRUCTION

READING STRATEGIES & LANGUAGE DEVELOPMENT

COMPARE AND CONTRAST Remind students that writers can organize facts by comparing and contrasting. Explain that students will now read about the Greek polises, Sparta and Athens, and write the names on a chart. In the lefthand column write Location, Education, Government, Entertainment. As students read, have them make notes in each category to compare and contrast Sparta and Athens. **[SDAIE STRATEGY: METACOGNITIVE DEVELOPMENT/SCHEMA BUILDING]**

PREFIXES Refer the class to the word *automatically* on p. 197, and have them identify its prefix (*auto-*). What other words do they know with this prefix? (*automobile, autograph*) Explain that once again, the prefix comes from Greek. Have them look up *auto* in a dictionary to find its derivation (Greek for "same," "self") and explain how and why the prefix fits the words they know.

A GREEK POLIS

Most city-states were laid out according to a similar plan. Most were built around an acropolis (uh KROP uh lihs). An acropolis was a large hill where city residents could seek shelter and safety in times of war. In a nearby clearing farmers would gather to trade with each other and with craftworkers. The clearing, called an agora (AG ur uh), often served both as a marketplace and as a meeting place.

Developing Governments

Although city-states often looked similar, each one had a different type of government. In each type, however, leaders had to be citizens of their polis. Today a citizen is a person who has certain rights and responsibilities in his or her country or community. In ancient Greece, though, only men could be citizens. Women and slaves were not allowed to be citizens and had few rights. Slaves, or helots (HEL uts), in ancient Greece were usually conquered

neighbors. Slavery was common throughout ancient Greece.

Being a citizen did not automatically give men a role in their government. In many city-states a small group of the richest, most powerful citizens controlled decision making. This type of government is called an oligarchy (OL ih gahr kee). By 600 B.C. the Greek city-state of Athens was governed by an oligarchy. One Athenian said:

> Oligarchy is a government resting on the value of property, in which the rich have power and the poor have none.

Before the oligarchy Athens had another form of government. Like other Greek city-states, it was ruled by one ruler, or king. This type of government is called a monarchy. In fact the word monarchy comes from two Greek words meaning "rule by one."

The Acropolis in Athens is the best known of the many acropolises built in Greece.

A GREEK POLIS

After students have read the opening paragraph, have a few come to the board and draw a diagram of a Greek city-state as described in the paragraph. Have them label the *acropolis* and the *agora*.

- **What was an acropolis? What was its role?** (An acropolis is a large hill where city residents could find shelter when the city was attacked, where they could take the high ground)

- **What was the agora and what role did it play?** (It was a clearing set aside as a market and also served as a meeting place.)

★**THINKING FURTHER:** *Making Conclusions* **Where do you suppose the city residents made their homes?** (probably on the hill and around it, as space permitted, so that they had access to the hill and the market. Have students draw residential areas on their diagram.)

Discussing Developing Governments Help students to see that over time governments can change from one form to another; they can broaden ruling power or limit it.

- **How did citizenship in ancient Greece differ from citizenship in modern countries?** (Today, a person who was born in a country is usually a citizen of it; in ancient Greece, only free men could be citizens. Women and slaves could not be.)

- **Did all free men have an equal opportunity to be part of the government? Explain.** (No, in Athens, for example, only a group of the few richest men held power, thus making the polis rulers an oligarchy.)

★**THINKING FURTHER:** *Compare and Contrast* **How does an oligarchy differ from a monarchy?** (In a monarchy, only one ruler holds supreme governmental power; in an oligarchy a few people join to rule.)

BACKGROUND INFORMATION

ABOUT SLAVERY IN ANCIENT GREECE

- Slavery was part of Greek life as far back as 1200 B.C., according to the poems of Homer.
- War, debt, and piracy were the chief means the Greeks used to acquire slaves. In a major battle, as many as 20,000 slaves might have been captured and put on slave markets in Athens, Rhodes, Corinth, or Delos.
- Sparta, where slaves heavily outnumbered citizens, acquired most of its slaves by overpowering its neighbors, the Messenians.
- In Attica, where Athens was located, slaves numbered about 115,000 out of a total population of 315,000, or more than one in three.

TWO GREEK CITIES

This is a good opportunity to have students compare and contrast the characteristics of Athens and Sparta.

More MAP WORK

Have students sit in pairs with one textbook open to the map on p. 193 and one to the map on this page.

- **Using the two maps, locate Sparta and Athens. On what peninsula is each located?** *(Sparta is on the Peloponnesus; Athens on Attica)*

- **Which appears closer to the sea?** *(Athens)*

- **Which lies in more mountainous terrain?** *(Sparta)*

- ★**THINKING FURTHER:** *Making Conclusions* **Which do you suppose might be more open to ideas from other cultures? Why?** *(perhaps Athens because it lies nearer the sea and on more easily reached land)*

Discussing Sparta Develop students' understanding of Sparta's specific characteristics.

> ★**THINKING FURTHER:** *Compare and Contrast* **How was Sparta like any other polis? How was it different?** *(Similar: It had an acropolis and an agora; it had slaves. Different: It was Greece's largest polis; its central "city" was not a city but a cluster of villages; it had more slaves than any other polis.)*

Investigating The Spartan Military Help students understand the reasons that Sparta developed military power.

- **What effect did the slave revolt have on Sparta?** *(Sparta became militaristic.)*

- **How was militarism reflected in the education of boys? in the education of girls?** *(Boys trained to be soldiers from age seven. Girls trained physically in the belief it would help them produce strong soldiers.)*

> ★**THINKING FURTHER:** *Making Generalizations* **What generalizations might you make about life in Sparta?** *(harsh, disciplined, physically active)*

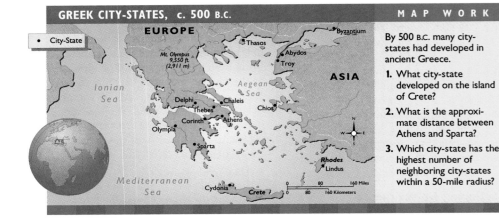

GREEK CITY-STATES, c. 500 B.C.

MAP WORK

By 500 B.C. many city-states had developed in ancient Greece.

1. What city-state developed on the island of Crete?

2. What is the approximate distance between Athens and Sparta?

3. Which city-state has the highest number of neighboring city-states within a 50-mile radius?

TWO GREEK CITIES

Of Greece's many city-states, historians know most about Athens and Sparta. Many documents and artifacts from those cities have been preserved. Like all Greek city-states, they had much in common. The way people lived in the two powerful city-states from day to day, however, differed a great deal.

Sparta

In 700 B.C. Sparta covered much of the southern Peloponnesus and was Greece's largest city-state. Dozens of villages belonged to this polis. Sparta's central "city" was a cluster of villages that lay almost 30 miles from the Mediterranean Sea. A low mountain nearby formed Sparta's acropolis. Near its base lay the polis agora, or meeting place. Here Sparta's leaders made the decisions that shaped life in this polis.

As in other city-states, farmers gathered at Sparta's agora to do business. Most of Sparta's farm workers, however, were slaves. Sparta had many more slaves than other city-states. At some times, there were as many as seven slaves for every one Spartan.

198

The Spartan Military

Around 600 B.C. Sparta's slaves revolted. The Spartans, however, managed to overpower their slaves. Polis leaders then set out to make Sparta the strongest military power in Greece. They wanted to make sure that neither slaves nor another polis could ever gain control of Sparta.

Sparta's people dedicated much of their lives to making their polis strong. Spartan children, too, were expected to do their part for the polis. At about age seven, boys and girls began training. Although they spent some time learning to read and write, boys spent even more time training to be soldiers. Girls practiced running, throwing spears called javelins, and playing ball games. In Sparta, girls trained not to become soldiers, but rather to be strong mothers of strong children.

Athens

Life for girls and boys was very different in the city of Athens. Athens lay on the peninsula of Attica, northeast of Sparta. Athenian girls did not practice sports. Rather, they were told to "see

---

CURRICULUM CONNECTION

LINKS TO LANGUAGE ARTS Briefly review with the students the meaning of the word *Spartan* in the context they have just read—"having to do with the polis of Sparta." Point out that among English-speaking people today, it has another meaning, as in "a Spartan life" or "a Spartan diet." Have students look up the word to find its modern meaning—"marked by self-denial, avoiding comfort." Ask them to explain the background of the modern English usage.

BACKGROUND INFORMATION

ABOUT SPARTAN SELF-DENIAL Part of the Spartans' self-denial was to make no effort to make their food taste good. Legend has it that after finishing a meal in a Spartan mess hall, a visitor said, "Now I understand why the Spartans do not fear death."

little, hear little, and ask no more questions than are absolutely necessary." Girls stayed at home to help their mothers. They carried out such duties as weaving cloth from sheep's wool. Girls who lived on farms helped in the fields at harvesttime.

Many Athenian boys worked each day with their fathers in the fields, or in pottery or stoneworking shops. If their parents could afford to send them to school, boys studied reading and writing. After classes they would practice wrestling or boxing at a local gymnasium before returning home.

Government in Athens

Life in Athens was different from that in Sparta. Athenians did not spend as much time and energy building a strong army. Yet Athens had challenges of its own.

Remember, Athens' government around 600 B.C. was an oligarchy. Most of Athens' early leaders belonged to noble families that were both rich and powerful. In time the poorer citizens of Athens demanded to have more say in how their government was run. The nobles were forced to share some of their power with other citizens.

Power to the People

The developing new government featured large meetings where all the citizens could take part in making decisions for the polis. This form of government is today called a democracy. The word *democracy* combines two Greek words meaning "rule by the people." It means that citizens vote to make government decisions.

The beginnings of democracy marked an important time in world history. Some historians, in fact, trace our own ideas of democracy back to ancient Greece. In the next lesson you will read about further developments in Greece's new democratic system.

Spartan women trained vigorously (right) while women in Athens led more gentle lives (below).

CITIZENSHIP★

RECOGNIZING PERSPECTIVES Through the ages, poets have sung the praises of cities. Here is what the Greek poet Pindar had to say about Athens during the 5th century B.C: "O bright and violet-crowned and famed in song, bulwark of Greece, famous Athens, divine city!"

Read the quotation to the class and ask if students know any words written in praise of U.S. cities. Songs about New York, Chicago, San Francisco, and other cities may come to mind. Have students find out if there is an official song praising your community.

SECOND-LANGUAGE SUPPORT

TAKING NOTES Using a Venn diagram to compare and contrast Athens and Sparta will give second-language learners an information organizer that they can refer to throughout the lesson.

Discussing Athens As students gain an understanding of Athens, encourage them to compare it with Sparta.

- *What would you say was the biggest difference between the training of Athenian girls and boys?* (Though both were trained for work, boys had more opportunity to learn to read and write and to train physically.)

- *What would you say was the biggest difference between Athenian girls and Spartan girls? between Athenian boys and Spartan boys?* (Athenian girls probably led quieter, less physically active lives. Athenian boys were not trained primarily as soldiers.)

★**THINKING FURTHER:** *Making Decisions* **Which would you have rather been—a girl or boy of Sparta or a girl or boy of Athens? Why?** (Accept any well-explained choice.)

Learning about Government in Athens Develop an understanding of changes taking place.

- *Why did Athenians have more time than Spartans for government?* (Athenians placed less stress on military.)

- *From which people did the desire to change the government in Athens spring?* (from the poorer citizens)

★**THINKING FURTHER:** *Making Conclusions* **Why do you suppose these people wanted change?** (They probably grew to resent being controlled by an oligarchy.)

Exploring Power to the People Stress the evolution of democracy.

- *How did government change in Athens?* (Large meetings of citizens rather than a small group of the richest men made ruling decisions.)

- *What was this new form of government called and how did it foreshadow our government today?* (Democracy; it spread ruling power to more people, as our representative democracy does today.)

★**THINKING FURTHER:** *Sequencing* **How would you diagram the progression of forms of government in Athens?** (monarchy to oligarchy to democracy)

Have students locate Mount Olympus on the map on p. 198. Explain that this is Greece's tallest mountain.

Discussing Special Festivals
Reinforce the importance of shared celebrations.

- **What form did Greek festivals take?** (singing, dancing, processions, ceremonial sacrifice, athletic competitions)

- **Whom did they honor?** (goddesses and gods, like Zeus and Athena)

★**THINKING FURTHER: Cause and Effect How do you suppose that such festivals helped to unify Greek culture?** (They celebrated aspects of culture that all Greeks shared—their religious beliefs and love of sports contests.)

Learning about A Greek Poet
Remind students that they have already met Homer on p. 192, in the Lesson 1 *Read Aloud* from the *Odyssey*. The quotation here is from Homer's *Iliad*.

★**THINKING FURTHER: Making Conclusions Why do you think people like hearing stories about their shared past?** (perhaps for adventure and excitement, perhaps to get more in touch with where they came from and what they share with others)

Discussing the PRIMARY SOURCE

Set the stage by having a student describe why the Trojan War began. Then have a student give a dramatic reading of Homer's words here. Encourage students to close their eyes and picture the images Homer creates.

- **What simile does Homer use to show how the Greek lines went into battle?** (a breaking wave)

- **How does he capture the great silence?** (no "voice among them")

★**THINKING FURTHER: Making Generalizations Why would people respond to this excerpt?** (It rates high for excitement, vividness, suspense.)

SHARED CULTURE

The citizens of Athens did not meet to discuss government policies every day. Like the people of the other Greek cities, Athenians reserved a few days of every month for religious celebrations to honor gods and goddesses.

Ancient Greeks believed that many gods and goddesses ruled the world. The most powerful were said to live on **Mount Olympus**. Mount Olympus is a mountain in northern Greece.

Special Festivals

Each polis honored at least one god or goddess as its special protector and provider. In Athens people worshiped *Athena,* the goddess of wisdom. Every summer they held a huge festival in her honor. After singing and dancing all night, Athenians walked to the top of the city's acropolis. There, as the sun rose in the sky, priests killed cattle in honor of Athena.

People from all over Greece also gathered at temples to worship Zeus (ZOOS), the most powerful god in the ancient Greek religion. The city-states also came together to compete in athletic competitions. You will read more about the most well known of these games, the Olympics, in this chapter's Legacy on pages 202–203. At the Olympic Games crowds cheered athletes from many city-states.

A Greek Poet

People in all city-states loved to hear the stories of the poet **Homer**. Many of these stories described Greece's past. Homer is thought to have lived sometime between 800 and 700 B.C. His most famous epic poems, the *Iliad* and the *Odyssey,* tell stories of war and adventure. The *Iliad* describes what happened

when a prince from Troy, an ancient city in what is today Turkey, kidnapped Helen, a Greek queen. The poem also describes how the gods created Greek cities. How does Homer describe the Greek army?

**Excerpt from
the *Iliad*, by Homer,
c. 700 B.C.**

As when, at the edge of the sounding sea, wave after wave comes up under the driving of the West Wind—out on the deep it lifts its crest and is broken on the land with a noise like thunder, and far over the headlands shoots its salt foam—so did the Greek lines then go into battle. Each chief gave his men their orders, but the rest said not a word. You would not have thought that all that great army had a voice among them, in such silence they all went through fear of their chiefs. And as they moved, the armor upon their bodies flashed in the sun.

USING THE ANTHOLOGY

THE ILIAD, Pages 36–38 Remind students that they encountered Homer's *Iliad* earlier in their texts, when they read of Heinrich Schliemann's quest for ancient Troy. Students may be encouraged to illustrate their reading from the *Iliad*.

If students wish to read more of Homer's work, tell them that young people's versions of both the *Iliad* and the *Odyssey* are available in many libraries.

Beyond Greece

Not long after the Greek festivals and Olympics were begun, athletes from faraway Greek colonies came to participate. The colonies were made up of groups of people who lived apart from, but kept ties with, Greece. Colonies were founded by Greeks in the 700s B.C. Many colonies became important trading partners because they grew grains that were much in demand in Greece. Greek ships also traveled south to Egypt's Nile Delta.

By 500 B.C. Greek city-states ringed the Mediterranean "like frogs around a pond," as a teacher named Plato put it. Some of Greece's eastern territories, however, were being taken over by a growing empire that was already vastly larger than Greece. At its height this empire of Persia—based in what is today Iran—was bigger than any that had yet existed in the world. It included all lands from Egypt and the western edge of the Mediterranean Sea to the Indus Valley.

Ancient Greeks worshiped Apollo, their god of the sun.

WHY IT MATTERS

The city-states of ancient Greece had their differences and valued their independence. Many of the Greek cities even had different types of government. One of these cities, Athens, began to develop a new kind of government called democracy. The idea of democracy is important in the United States.

Despite their differences, the cities of ancient Greece shared many cultural ties. In 499 B.C. a Greek colony on the edge of what is today Turkey wanted to break free from Persian control. People of the colony asked the Greek city-states for help. Athens, Sparta, and other city-states joined together to fight Persia. The war that followed would change Greece forever.

Reviewing Facts and Ideas

MAIN IDEAS

- Life in most of the Greek city-states revolved around an agora and an acropolis.

- Spartans spent much of their time working to strengthen their bodies and their army. In Athens free women and girls worked at home. Boys and men worked, went to school, or took part in government.

THINK ABOUT IT

1. What did city-states have in common? What made them different?

2. Who was allowed to vote in the developing democracy of Athens?

3. **FOCUS** Why was life in Sparta so different from life in Athens?

4. **THINKING SKILL** What *effects* did slavery have on life in Sparta?

5. **GEOGRAPHY** What made the agora a center for cultural interaction?

201

MEETING INDIVIDUAL NEEDS

RETEACHING (Easy) Have students refer to the description of Sparta's acropolis and agora on p. 198. Tell them to draw a diagram of what Sparta's center must have looked like.

EXTENSION (Average) Tell students to write a brief article for a travel magazine in which they contrast a visit to Sparta with a visit to Athens.

ENRICHMENT (Challenging) Divide the class into four groups and assign each group one of the following: Spartan girl, Spartan boy, Athenian girl, Athenian boy. Tell the groups to do further research on their subject and then prepare an illustrated presentation for the class entitled "A Day in the Life of … "

Have students prepare a presentation on Ancient Greece using *My Scrapbook* and *Create* on the *Adventure Time* CD-ROM.

Discussing Beyond Greece Help students understand the method by which Greek culture was spread.

- **What is a colony?** (a group of people who live apart from but keep ties with the "mother country")

★**THINKING FURTHER:** *Making Conclusions* **How would Greek seafaring skill help it to establish colonies?** (Seafaring made distant travel and trade possible.)

Discussing WHY IT MATTERS Review the historical impact of ancient Greece.

★**THINKING FURTHER:** *Summarizing* **How would you summarize the cultural ties that united Greece?** (polises, religious beliefs, celebrations)

⭐ 3 CLOSE

MAIN IDEAS
Have students write their answers on a piece of paper.

- **Around what two main features was a Greek polis built?** (acropolis, agora)

- **How would you contrast life for the young people of Sparta and Athens?** (Spartan boys concentrated on military and physical training, Spartan girls on being mothers to soldiers; Athenian boys spent more time on job training and formal education, Athenian girls on domestic skills.)

EVALUATE
✓ **Answers to Think About It**

1. In common: independence, religious beliefs, festivals and competitions. Different: forms of government, degree of militarism.
   Compare and Contrast

2. only free men
   Main Idea

3. The stress in Sparta was on maintaining a military state.
   Make Inferences

4. It made Spartans fearful of a slave rebellion; therefore they built up their army, requiring long military service.
   Cause and Effect

5. meeting place and trading site
   Five Themes of Geography: Place

Write About It Have students write a paragraph comparing and contrasting one aspect of life in Sparta and Athens.

Lesson Overview
The Olympic Games carry on a Greek ideal of cooperation.

Lesson Objective
★ Recognize that modern Olympics are borrowed from ancient Greece.

1 PREPARE

MOTIVATE Encourage students to tell what they already know about the modern Olympic Games—who participates, what sports are involved, what Olympic athletes they admire. If Olympic Games have appeared recently on television, have students recount their most exciting moments.

SET PURPOSE Ask students why we hold Olympic Games. Encourage them to offer their reasons and then have them read the column of text on this page to see what it adds to their reasons.

2 TEACH

Understanding the Concept of a Legacy Have students set up two categories on the board—Ancient Olympics and Modern Olympics. Have them note when each was begun and what its aims were. Encourage students to say how the modern version borrows from and continues the ancient version.

Legacy
LINKING PAST AND PRESENT

THE OLYMPICS

Have you ever dreamed of competing in the Olympic Games? You may have imagined yourself crossing the finish line at the end of a race. Perhaps you simply enjoy watching the events on television.

The Olympic Games were first held nearly 3,000 years ago in ancient Greece. City-states cooperated to make the games an important part of Greek culture.

By about A.D. 400 the ancient Olympics had faded away. The tradition was revived in 1896. Today the international games take place every two years. Most nations of the world send their best athletes to take part in the Summer and the Winter Olympic Games.

Look at the pictures on these pages. Think about how the modern Olympic Games help people to remember an important legacy of the past.

202

BACKGROUND INFORMATION

ABOUT THE OLYMPICS—ANCIENT AND MODERN
- The earliest ancient Olympic Games featured only one race and lasted only one day. It was not until the 14th Olympics that a second race was added.
- By the 23rd Olympics, wrestling, jumping, spear and discus throwing, boxing, and chariot racing had become events, and the games lasted five days.
- Ancient Olympic Games were not limited to sports. Competitions in music, oratory, and theater also became Olympic events.
- As a reminder of the Olympics' beginnings, the modern Olympic flame is kindled by the sun's rays at Olympia and is then carried by relay to the Olympic site.

- The five linked rings or circles that serve as the Olympics' symbol represent five continents—Asia, Europe, Africa, Australia, and both North and South America (counted as one continent). Each ring is a different color—blue, yellow, black, green, and red. At least one of these colors appears in the flag of every nation that competes.
- The modern Olympic creed reads as follows: "The most important thing in the Olympic Games is not to win but to take part, just as the most important thing in life is not the triumph but the struggle. The essential thing is not to have conquered but to have fought well."

Disabled athletes compete in Special Olympic Games. The first Special Olympic Games were held in Chicago in 1968. Today athletes from more than 100 different countries participate in these events.

Unlike ancient Olympic Games, women now compete in most sports. American speed skater Bonnie Blair won two gold medals during the 1994 Winter Olympics. Also new to the Winter Olympics are cold-weather sports, such as skiing, ice hockey, and bobsledding. Those events became part of Olympic competition in 1924.

The modern games begin with a parade of Olympic athletes from every participating nation. Today many of the athletes take part in team competitions. Such team events were not part of ancient Olympic Games.

Examining the Pictures Give students a few moments to study the pictures and their captions.

- *Where did the ancient Olympic Games begin?* (Have students name Mt. Olympus and locate it on the map on p. 198.)

- *In what ways have the Olympic Games changed from ancient to modern times?* (Today, there are team events, not just individual competition; women can compete now, they could not in the past; we have Summer and Winter Games; there are also Olympics for disabled athletes.)

★THINKING FURTHER: *Making Conclusions* **Why might the modern revival of the ancient Greek Olympic Games be a good thing?** *(Encourage students to identify and discuss the ideals that the Olympics try to foster—nations putting aside differences and coming together in cooperation and a spirit of shared interests, individuals meeting people of other nations in a spirit of good will and good sportsmanship.)*

⭐ 3 CLOSE

SUM IT UP
Have students offer opinions on how the ancient Olympics contributed to Greece and how the modern Olympics contribute to our world.

EVALUATE
Write About It Tell students to decide what they like best or admire most about the Olympics. Have them write a thank-you note to the ancient Greeks explaining why they appreciate the heritage of the Olympic Games.

MEETING INDIVIDUAL NEEDS

RETEACHING (Easy) Explain that countries that host Olympic Games commemorate the event by issuing postage stamps naming the city, date, and stamp price as well as an illustration to symbolize the Olympic Games. Have students decide on a location and time for a future Games and design a postage stamp to honor it.

EXTENSION (Average) Pierre de Coubertin's dream in the late 1800s was to revive the Olympic tradition. Have students research the facts about his dream and then combine the information they gather to create a class report, "How the Modern Olympics Began."

ENRICHMENT (Challenging) Explain that the ideal of putting aside political differences to hold the Olympics has not always been met. Have students research Olympics history and write a report describing world events that have interrupted the Olympic Games.

LESSON 3

PAGES 204–209

Lesson Overview

During the 400s B.C., Athens reached the height of its culture and power, and left a rich legacy in the arts, government, and learning.

Lesson Objectives

★ Identify the great achievements and thinkers of Athens' Golden Age.

★ Describe the form of government during Athens' Golden Age.

★ Analyze the effects of war on Athens.

1 PREPARE

MOTIVATE Refer students to *Beyond Greece* on p. 201. On their desk maps of the Mediterranean area, have them identify areas to which Greek influence and trade spread. Then have a student read the *Read Aloud* to underscore Athens' role in this growth.

SET PURPOSE Refer the class to the photo of Athena on this page, the *Read to Learn* question, and *Vocabulary* terms. Encourage students to predict what the lesson will reveal.

2 TEACH

Understanding THE BIG PICTURE
Note the underdog aspect of Greece fighting Persia by explaining that the Persian Empire extended as far east as the Indus River and as far west as the northern and eastern Aegean.

● **Why could Greece defeat Persia?** (*Athens' navy and Sparta's army*)

● **In what other way did Athens benefit from its navy?** (*They were paid to protect other Greek colonies.*)

★**THINKING FURTHER: Cause and Effect** **How might this wealth contribute to a "Golden Age"?** (*perhaps by providing money for arts and learning*)

Resource REMINDER

Practice and Project Book: *p. 43*

Anthology: *The Birds, pp. 45–46; Funeral Speech for Athenian Heroes, pp.47–48*

 Technology: *Videodisc*
Desk Map

| 700 B.C. | 600 B.C. | 500 B.C. | 460 B.C. | 399 B.C. | 300 B.C. |

ATHENS' AGE OF GLORY

READ ALOUD

If Athenians living in 500 B.C. could somehow have traveled 65 years into the future, they would have been amazed by what they saw. In the city's harbor many ships would be tied at a long dock leading straight to a huge trading area. People could buy a wide range of goods, from Egyptian papyrus to Italian cheese, with coins from Athens or Persia. Walking up the road to the city—now surrounded by walls—they would have seen grand stone temples where far simpler ones had once stood. Athens, clearly, was flourishing.

Focus Activity

READ TO LEARN
What did the Athenians achieve during Athens' "Golden Age"?

VOCABULARY
assembly
jury
philosophy
Peloponnesian Wars

PEOPLE
Pericles
Socrates
Plato

PLACES
Acropolis
Parthenon

THE BIG PICTURE

What happened to bring about the success of Athens? As you read in the last lesson, the city-states of Greece went to war against the empire of Persia in 499 B.C. Understanding the importance of sea power, the Athenians built a mighty naval fleet. Over the next 20 years they joined forces with the armies of Sparta and other city-states. Together they defeated the Persians.

Many Greek colonies were still in danger of Persian attack, however. Some of them began paying money for protection by the Athenian navy. Athens became rich from these payments. Some of that money went toward building an even more powerful navy. Much of the rest went to improve life in the city itself.

Around 460 B.C. Athens entered a period of rich culture. Some historians call the next 30 years the "Golden Age" of Athens. It was a time of great achievement.

204

 SHELTERED INSTRUCTION

READING STRATEGIES & LANGUAGE DEVELOPMENT

PREDICT Review with students how making and revising predictions as they read can help them understand text. Then have students brainstorm a list of achievements made by civilizations they have already studied after a stable economic and political system [great literature, learning, and architecture] had been established. Write the Read to Learn question on the board and have students predict what Athenians might achieve. Record their predictions. Have students refer to them as they read. **[SDAIE STRATEGY: BRIDGING]**

WORD ORIGINS Point out that not only did our theater come from the Greeks, but so did our words for two forms of theatrical works— comedy and tragedy. Have students look in a dictionary to discover that *comedy* derives from the Greek for "revel songs" and *tragedy* from "goat songs."

GOLDEN AGE OF ATHENS

In the middle 400s B.C. Athens was the same in many ways as it had been 65 years earlier. Life still revolved around the agora and the acropolis. Citizens still voted on issues that shaped life in the city. Festivals honoring Athena were still held every summer. Much, however, had changed.

A Walk Through Athens

The Acropolis, high above the city, was the religious center of Athens. Many Greek cities had their own acropolises. The one at Athens, however, was larger than others—that is why it is generally spelled with a capital *A*. Here a group of buildings displayed the city's new wealth and power. At their center rose a temple to Athena made of marble cut from a nearby mountain. This stunning temple was the Parthenon (PAHR thuh nahn). It still sits on the highest point of the Acropolis and can be seen from all over the city.

Beautifully made vases (left) and the Parthenon (below) were among the many achievements of the ancient Greeks.

Looking down from the Acropolis, one could see many buildings. About 100,000 people lived in Athens, making it the largest city in Greece.

Activity in the Agora

Following the winding road down from the Acropolis, one might see crowds of people. Many had come to do business at the agora. There were shopkeepers, students, and lawyers heading for the market or government buildings. In one corner of the agora, citizens gathered at a monument that served as the city's "bulletin board." Here people could leave messages or read postings about upcoming matters to be voted on.

Merchants sold perfume, vegetables, and clothing or offered haircuts. In nearby workshops, potters crafted vases and bowls. The diagram on page 207 shows what Athens may have looked like.

BACKGROUND INFORMATION

ABOUT THE ACROPOLIS AND THE PARTHENON
- The Parthenon was the first major monument on the Acropolis. Built 447–432 B.C., it was dedicated to Athena Parthenos (Athena the Warrior Maiden). A giant ivory and gold statue of her was at its center.
- In later times, the Parthenon served a long series of roles—a Byzantine church, a Roman Catholic church, a Turkish harem, and finally a storage space for Turkish gunpowder.
- On September 16, 1687, during a battle between the occupying Turks and the Venetians, the Venetian artillery scored a direct hit on the Parthenon, causing the stored gunpowder to explode and to send marble fragments streaming across the Acropolis. A little more than a century later, magnificent Parthenon sculptures that survived the explosion were removed and sent to England by Lord Elgin.

GOLDEN AGE OF ATHENS

Give students a time to thumb through the lesson's illustrations to preview what made the Golden Age golden.

Exploring A Walk Through Athens Refer students to the photos on these pages of the *Parthenon* and of the entire *Acropolis.* Explain that both have suffered the normal ravages of time, as well as damages from disasters. Have on hand some books showing what they looked like when first built.

★**THINKING FURTHER:** *Making Conclusions* **What does the fact that Athenians lavished wealth and artistry on their Acropolis tell you about their religious beliefs?** *(Their dedication of the most important point in their city to a religious center seems to reflect strong religious belief.)*

Discussing Activity in the Agora If any students have ever been to an outdoor market, encourage them to describe the general hubbub and specific activities that they saw there.

- **How many different activities can you name taking place in the agora on any given day?** *(Students should include examples of buying, selling, studying, passing through, gathering and leaving information, meetings.)*

- **Would you describe what goes on there as local or international? Explain.** *(Both; goods traded might come from a local craftworker or a trader from another continent.)*

★**THINKING FURTHER:** *Making Conclusions* **Why would you say that the activities that went on in Athens' agora were crucial to the city's growth and survival?** *(Help students to recognize the role that providing goods and services plays in making a city livable and in giving people work and a means to earn a living.)*

Technology CONNECTION
VIDEODISC
Enrich Lesson 3 with the *The Greek World* on the Videodisc.

Search 1340, Play To 1810   Side B

ATHENIAN GOVERNMENT

Review what the class already knows about Athenian government and have students discuss how the *assembly* of citizens helped to broaden democracy.

Discussing A Great Statesman
Read Pericles' quotation aloud to the class before discussing his contribution.

- *Who was Pericles?* (an Athenian leader during the mid 400s B.C.)

- *What measures did he take to see that poor men as well as rich men were represented in the government?* (He saw that all were paid for their time in holding office or serving on juries, so the poor could afford to serve.)

★THINKING FURTHER: *Making Conclusions* **How did this help to include both rich and poor?** *(by giving the opportunity to rule to poor as well as rich citizens)*

Learning about Philosophy in Athens Write the word *philosophy* on the board. Point out that the word's literal meaning is "love of wisdom."

- *What is philosophy?* (the search for wisdom and the right way to live)

- *What kinds of questions do philosophers investigate and think about?* (questions about good government, love, good citizenship, in short, "What makes a good life?")

- *What kinds of questions did the philosopher Socrates raise?* (questions about laws, customs, religion)

- *Why did some Athenian citizens object to his questions?* (They feared that if young people found fault with these areas of life in Athens, they might revolt and threaten stability.)

★THINKING FURTHER: *Making Decisions* **If you were on the jury trying Socrates, how would you have judged him? Why?** *(Encourage free discussion of the trial and its decision, with students balancing threats to stability against freedom of speech and thought and commenting on the severity of the sentence.)*

ATHENIAN GOVERNMENT

In the early 400s B.C. a small council of powerful citizens made all of the city's important decisions. Later in the century, though, the council's powers had been taken over by an assembly of citizens. An assembly is a lawmaking body of a government. The assembly voted on issues that helped to shape the future of the city.

Do you remember from the last lesson who were considered citizens in Athens and who were not? No women and no enslaved men had a voice in Athens' government. In fact they did not enjoy any of the rights of citizenship, such as land ownership. However, the people of ancient Athens took a big step toward creating a government that represented the people.

*W*hat did ancient Greeks do for entertainment?

Famous people such as Socrates and Pericles were made fun of by writers such as Aristophanes (ar uh STOHF uh neez). He wrote funny plays called comedies. Comedies, along with serious plays called tragedies, were performed at festivals. Another playwright, Aeschylus (ES kuh lus), wrote tragedies about events in Greek history.

Over 13,000 people crowded into outdoor theaters to watch the popular plays. Actors played their parts with the help of big masks. A group called the "chorus" sang, danced, and acted in the plays.

A Great Statesman

Pericles (PER ih kleez), an Athenian leader around 450 B.C., explained his city's government this way:

Our city is called a democracy because it is governed by the many, not the few. . . . No one, moreover, if he has it in him to do some good for the city, is barred because of poverty or humble origins.

Pericles made sure poor as well as rich citizens could take part in government.

Citizens served on the assembly and sat on juries. A jury is a group of citizens chosen to hear evidence and make decisions in a court of law. Pericles arranged for citizens to be paid when they held office or served on a jury. This meant that farmers and other poor citizens could afford to take the time to become involved in government.

Philosophy in Athens

While citizens debated government issues, famous teachers like Socrates (SAHK ruh teez) led discussions about the right way to live. Socrates lived around the middle 400s B.C. He taught his students philosophy, or the search for wisdom and the right way to live. They discussed what makes the best kind of government or what it means to love or to be a good citizen.

Shortly before 400 B.C. Socrates began questioning Athenian values, such as laws, customs—even religion. It made some Athenians angry that he would doubt anything about the polis. In 399 B.C. Socrates was brought to trial for "urging Athens' young people to revolt." The jury decided he was guilty and sentenced him to death. His teachings, however, were written down by a student, Plato (PLAY toh), who also became a famous philosopher.

CITIZENSHIP★

RECOGNIZING PERSPECTIVES U.S. democracy was once limited, too.

- Until after the Civil War, U.S. citizens could own slaves.
- Until the 1830s only free men who owned property could vote.
- Through much of the 19th century, some states did not let married women own property. Their property belonged to their husbands.
- Until 1920 most women in the United States could not vote.

SECOND-LANGUAGE SUPPORT

WORKING WITH A PEER Have second-language learners work with a partner to create word webs about Athenian achievements. Students should discuss what the Athenians did and add a word or sentence to a web with "Achievements" at its center. Then invite students to summarize and explain their additions.

DORIC   IONIC   CORINTHIAN

Ancient Greeks developed three types of columns.

PARTHENON

ACROPOLIS

AGORA

THE GOLDEN AGE OF ATHENS

In the 400s B.C. Athens was flourishing. Many daily activities took place at the Acropolis. What do you see going on?

Extending Did You Know? Point out the pictures of the masks of comedy and tragedy (symbols of the theater). Help students link the masks to their Greek originals.

More DIAGRAM WORK

Give students a few minutes to examine the diagram and identify various aspects of Athenian life that it portrays—architecture, trading, discussion.

- *How does this diagram show that life was full and well rounded in Athens during its Golden Age?* (It shows a variety of activities and a high level of cultural development, for example, in its architecture.)

- *Where is the agora in relation to the Parthenon and Acropolis?* (Help students to note that the agora is below both, on level land.)

- *Besides its role as a market, what other activities can you see in the agora?* (discussions and simply walking through the area)

- *As you look at the small drawing, how would you compare the three styles of column architecture shown there?* (Have students note the progressively more ornate styles and identify any similar examples in your community.)

★THINKING FURTHER: *Making Decisions* **Would you like to have lived in Athens during its Golden Age? Why or why not?** (Encourage well-reasoned responses.)

BACKGROUND INFORMATION

ABOUT PERICLES
- Though the family into which he was born in about 495 B.C. had both wealth and power, it was firmly for democracy. Pericles' grandfather was responsible for many democratic reforms in Athens.
- Here is how Pericles summed up his vision for Athens' role: "Our city is an education for Greece."

ABOUT SOCRATES
- Socrates himself never wrote down his ideas. All we know of his teachings is what Plato recorded.
- His execution, by being made to drink a cup of deadly hemlock, is one of the most famous in history.

ABOUT PLATO
- Plato was 30 when his teacher Socrates was executed, an event that changed his life.
- Instead of entering public life, as expected, he decided to become a teacher himself, and founded an outdoor school called the Academy.

CURRICULUM CONNECTION

LINKS TO LANGUAGE ARTS Call for a team of volunteers who are interested in plays to do research into the development of theater in ancient Greece. They should investigate the use of music and dance, how theaters were designed, and what a theater festival involved. Have them present their findings to the class.

More MAP WORK

Remind students that they have already learned about the relative strengths of the Athenian navy and the Spartan army and refer them to the map on this page.

- **What large land masses make up the Peloponnesian League, Sparta's allies?** (most of the Peloponnesus, a large area just north of Athens, and Macedonia)

- **How do Athens' allies reflect that Athens was more a naval power than a land power?** (In general, they are more open to the sea than to land.)

- **Who was the victor in the final battle?** (Sparta, over Athens, 404 B.C.)

- ★**THINKING FURTHER:** *Making Conclusions* **Why do you suppose the Peloponnesian War continued for so long?** (perhaps because the sides were evenly matched)

Learning about Battles on Land and Sea Have students discuss the merits of a strong navy versus a strong army.

- **How was Athens' navy able to hold off defeat for so long?** (It could win battles at sea and feed the city.)

- ★**THINKING FURTHER:** *Cause and Effect* **What non-battle event caused a weakening of Athens?** (a disease that killed one third of its people)

Discussing a Final Blow Remind students that the Athenian navy had been able to maintain grain supplies.

- **What finally broke the Athenian defense?** (starvation, when the navy could no longer supply grain)

- ★**THINKING FURTHER:** *Making Conclusions* **What do you think Thucydides meant when he said that war "is a violent teacher"?** (Encourage students to suggest lessons each side might have learned from the war.)

WAR AND CONFLICT

The Golden Age of Athens did not last, however. Sparta and other Greek city-states were jealous of the power and wealth of Athens. They formed what they called the Peloponnesian League. You can see where the allies of Sparta and the allies of Athens were located on the map on this page. In 431 B.C. the two sides began what became known as the Peloponnesian (pel uh puh NEEZH un) Wars.

Battles on Land and Sea

The wars began with an attack by the Spartan army. Pericles knew that his army was no match for Sparta's. He called for Athenians living outside the city to move inside the city walls. The walls protected the city, but Sparta's army destroyed the farmland around Athens. The Athenians did not starve, however, because their navy controlled the Aegean Sea. Ships were able to bring in grain from other areas.

In fact the powerful Athenian navy kept the wars in a deadlock for many years. Athens was able to win most of the battles at sea while Sparta won more often on land. However, the course of the wars worsened for Athens. A terrible disease swept through the crowded city. At least one third of the population died from it. One of its victims was Pericles. Meanwhile the wars continued, taking many more lives.

A Final Blow

In 404 B.C. Sparta was able to cut off the Athenian grain supply from the Black Sea. The starving Athenians had to surrender. All of Greece had suffered great losses from the Peloponnesian

THE PELOPONNESIAN WAR, 431–404 B.C.

MACEDONIA · THESSALY · Ionian Sea · Aegean Sea · 411 B.C. · 429 B.C. · 404 B.C. Athens · 406 B.C. · 418 B.C. · Athens surrenders · Sparta · PERSIAN EMPIRE · Mediterranean Sea · Rhodes

Athens and allies · Sparta and allies · Other Greek areas · Athenian victory · Spartan victory

0 75 150 Miles / 0 75 150 Kilometers

MAP WORK

The Peloponnesian Wars cost many lives.
1. How long did the Peloponnesian Wars last?
2. Which side, Athens or Sparta, controlled more coastal areas? Why do you suppose that might have been?
3. What northern region did Sparta control?
4. How does this map show that Athens and its allies were mainly on the defensive during the Peloponnesian War?

208 MAP WORK: **1.** 27 years **2.** Athens; they had the stronger navy. **3.** Macedonia **4.** by showing that most battles were fought on lands allied to Athens

GLOBAL CONNECTION

LAYING SIEGE TO A CITY Laying siege to a town, or militarily blockading it, as Sparta did to Athens, has been repeated numerous times as a military strategy throughout history.

- The goal of a siege is to capture a town or force it to surrender by either starving or attacking the people within, often both.

- For attack, besiegers used scaling equipment, such as ladders and towers, as well as battering rams and catapults.

- To resist a siege, people in a town might use secret tunnels or food supplies as well as catapults and missiles to attack the besiegers.

- Have students look up "siege" in the index of an encyclopedia to learn how a siege was implemented and how it was resisted.

Ancient Greek soldiers went into battle protected by bronze helmets and chest plates.

WHY IT MATTERS

Between 500 B.C. and 400 B.C. Athens gave the world some of ancient Greece's most enduring legacies. Athenians improved their democracy and built splendid temples. They searched for wisdom through philosophy and created new dramatic forms. After 400 B.C. a young warrior-king from another land would spread those legacies far and wide. His name was Alexander. You will read about him in the following lesson.

Reviewing Facts and Ideas

MAIN IDEA

- In the 400s B.C., during their "Golden Age," Athenians discussed philosophy, wrote plays, and built many grand buildings.

- Though democracy was still limited to male citizens, Pericles worked to give poorer citizens a voice in Athenian government.

- The Peloponnesian Wars ended the "Golden Age" of Athens. Afterward no single polis dominated Greece.

THINK ABOUT IT

1. How did the war against Persia bring new wealth and power to Athens?

2. What changes did Pericles introduce in Athens?

3. **FOCUS** List three things that reflect how the century before 400 B.C. was a "golden age" for Athens.

4. **THINKING SKILL** Make a *generalization* about the changes that occurred in Athenian government between 500 B.C. and 400 B.C.

5. **WRITE** Write a paragraph comparing democracy in Athens with democracy in the United States.

209

Wars. The Greek historian Thucydides (thoo SIHD ih deez), who lived during the time, concluded that war "is a violent teacher."

The End of a Golden Age

Following the Peloponnesian Wars, Sparta was once again the leading polis in Greece. Yet its victory was short-lived. For the next 50 years no city-state was able to maintain control for long before others challenged it. These unsettled times would leave Greece open to threats from a new power to the north.

Exploring The End of a Golden Age Reinforce the understanding that Sparta won the Peloponnesian Wars.

> ★**THINKING FURTHER:** *Cause and Effect* **Why does conflict inside a place invite threats from the outside?** *(Internal disputes weaken the unity and strength of the larger group. The group is then more vulnerable to attack.)*

Discussing WHY IT MATTERS Have students review Athens' achievements.

> ★**THINKING FURTHER:** *Making Generalizations* **What generalizations can you make about the legacy of Golden Age ?** *(Answers should touch on the fields of government, philosophy, the arts, and athletics.)*

⭐ 3 CLOSE

MAIN IDEAS
Call on students to answer orally.

- **What did Athens' Golden Age leave us in philosophy, theater, and architecture?** *(works of Socrates and Plato, theater's comedy and tragedy, architectural styles—Doric, Ionic, Corinthian)*

- **How did the Athenians extend political power to poorer citizens?** *(by paying them to participate in government)*

- **How did the Peloponnesian Wars weaken Greek power in the world?** *(by ending the dominance of one polis)*

EVALUATE
✓ **Answers to Think About It**

1. It helped Athens to develop a navy that brought wealth and power. *Summarize*

2. broader democracy by extending it to the poorer citizens *Main Idea*

3. Answers should reflect achievements in government, arts, philosophy. *Recall Details*

4. Generalizations should reflect broader participation in government. *Form Generalizations*

5. Comparisons should note greater U.S. citizenship and participation. *Make Analogies*

Write About It Have students write a letter home describing a visit to Athens during the Golden Age.

Lesson Overview

Making *conclusions* helps readers to organize and use information.

Lesson Objective

★ Make conclusions based on evidence.

⭐ 1 PREPARE

MOTIVATE Use the Raphael painting to have students think about how philosophers come to conclusions about ideas. In addition to portraits of philosophers, the artist included a portrait of himself and Michelangelo. Ask students to think about the artist's reasons for doing so. Have them read *Why the Skill Matters* and relate reasons that making sound conclusions is as important in studying history as it is in doing well in life.

SET PURPOSE Ask students to think about the phrase, "Don't jump to conclusions." Point out that making sound conclusions is a skill and that there are logical steps to follow in going about it. Have students read the *Helping Yourself* tips to preview these steps.

⭐ 2 TEACH

Using the Skill Remind the class of the *Dragnet* phrase "Just the facts, ma'am." Encourage students to follow this caution first as they begin the process of making conclusions.

● *How many different facts can you find in the paragraph in the first column of p. 211?* (Students should list at least six facts about education in Athens.)

Resource **REMINDER**

Practice and Project Book: *p. 44*

THINKINGSKILLS

The painting *School of Athens* by Raphael shows Socrates with other philosophers. Plato (left), shown in another part of the painting, takes notes.

Making Conclusions

VOCABULARY

conclusion

WHY THE SKILL MATTERS

In the last lesson you read about a type of government that developed in Athens. While you read, you may have made certain conclusions about democracy. A conclusion is a final statement about the meaning of many facts. The skill of making conclusions is especially important to students of history because it helps them to see events within the "big picture."

Making a conclusion also helps you to make sense of specific facts because you can see how they fit into the big picture. Use the Helping Yourself box for some hints on "adding up" facts to make conclusions.

USING THE SKILL

Read the paragraph on the next page. Look for a common idea suggested by all of the facts. Then, make a conclusion based upon this idea.

210

MAKING CONCLUSIONS Point out to students that they often must come to conclusions in school work. They study evidence and judge the reasonable conclusions that can be made from it. *Evidence* is the key word. A conclusion can be no more reliable than the evidence on which it is based. Warn students that as they read they must get enough information and that the evidence should be reliable enough for them to base a conclusion on it.

WORD ROOTS Explain that the word *conclude* comes from two Latin terms. The prefix *con-* means "to bring together" and the second part comes from *claudere*, which means "to close." In other words, bring together facts to close out with an idea.

In the 400s B.C. more schools were created in Athens than ever before—though none were for girls or slaves. Families who could afford the cost began sending their boys to school at age seven. There they learned to read, write, and memorize the poems of Homer. Math and science were rarely taught. Most students left school after learning basic skills. The sons of wealthy families kept studying until they were teenagers. Their teachers worked to make them good thinkers and speakers so they would be respected in the city's assembly.

This sculpture shows Aristotle, a student of Plato, thinking. Aristotle is considered to be one of the greatest Greek philosophers.

HELPING Yourself

- The making of **conclusions** involves finding a meaning by combining facts or information.
- Think about what each piece of information means.
- Think about what all the information means when it is linked together.
- Make a statement that sums up the meaning of all the information.

The paragraph provides information about education in Athens. Because many schools were created and some students attended until they were teenagers, you might conclude that education became more important in Athens during the 400s B.C. You might also conclude that the sons of wealthy families were given more opportunities to learn. You can often make more than one conclusion from the same information.

TRYING THE SKILL

Read the following paragraph. What is the paragraph mostly about?*

Most teachers of wealthy students in Athens charged fees to teach public speaking. A few philosophers like Socrates, though, taught students for free. To those thinkers, understanding the proper way to live was more important than money or the skills that made money. Thanks to Socrates and his fellow philosophers, the search for knowledge and truth would become an important part of life in Athens for years to come.

REVIEWING THE SKILL

1. What conclusion did you make from the paragraph above?
2. What evidence can you give to support your conclusion?
3. How does making a conclusion help you to better understand something that you've just read?

211

- **What grade would you give the paragraph for quantity of facts and reliability?** *(probably a good grade)*

★**THINKING FURTHER: *Making Conclusions*** **What other conclusions can you make from this paragraph—about the role of women in Athens? about how important math and science were? about what people thought of the city's assembly?** *(Ask for at least one fact to support each conclusion.)*

Trying the Skill Tell students to take another look at the steps in *Helping Yourself* before they begin reading the paragraph. Suggest that students need to identify the topic about which they make a conclusion.

- **What information gives you Socrates' thoughts?** *(the third sentence)*

★**THINKING FURTHER: *Classifying*** **What pieces of information tell you that teachers differed on their attitude toward money?** *(Some charged; some did not.)*

3 CLOSE

SUM IT UP

Have students summarize the value of being able to make sound conclusions about academic subjects and in everyday life. Help them to see that having a way to organize and evaluate information and understanding its meaning helps us to process it better, making us better informed students, citizens, and human beings.

EVALUATE
✓ **Answers to Reviewing the Skill**

1. a statement about the meaning of many facts
2. identifying a topic; finding an idea about the topic that is supported by the facts
3. It shows how specific facts fit into the big picture, like pieces of a jigsaw puzzle.

VISUAL LITERACY

ABOUT THE PAINTING *SCHOOL OF ATHENS*

The School of Athens is a fresco painting by Raphael (1483–1520), and was painted 1510–1511. It is located in one of the rooms of the Vatican Palace in Rome. The *School of Athens* depicts a group of famous Greek philosophers gathered around Plato and Aristotle. Have students note the balance of elements within the painting. For example, note the similar shape of the two groups of people immediately surrounding the figures emerging from the open archway. Invite students to study the painting and discuss what they see. Possible questions include: What other examples of visual balance can you see in this painting? How does the painting show that there is a lot of learning taking place?

LESSON 4

PAGES 212–217

Lesson Overview
Through his world conquests, Alexander the Great spread Greek culture from North Africa to the Indus Valley.

Lesson Objectives
★ Analyze how Alexander spread Greek culture with his expanding empire.

★ Identify the wonders of *Alexandria*.

★ Describe the legacies of Greek civilization.

1 PREPARE

MOTIVATE Have a student present the *Read Aloud*. Point out that the adjective "young" well describes Alexander (shown in the photo). He was only 20 years old when he came to power. Ask students what they have already read about him (that he was a warrior-king from another land who would spread Greek legacies—p. 209).

SET PURPOSE Refer students to the *Read to Learn* question and have them look for the *People* and *Places* as they learn about this amazing young man.

2 TEACH

Understanding THE BIG PICTURE
Have students use their desk maps to appreciate the area Alexander conquered.

● **What was the most powerful empire when Alexander began?** *(Persian)*

● **Over what different peoples did it rule?** *(Egyptians, Phoenicians, Jews, Babylonians, Indians, Persians)*

★**THINKING FURTHER:** *Making Conclusions* **How do you suppose the Persian Empire's transportation system aided Alexander the Great in his conquests?** *(A network of good roads would have been an advantage to invading armies, allowing them to penetrate areas more easily.)*

Resource REMINDER

Practice and Project Book: *p. 45*

Technology: *Adventure Time!* CD-ROM

Desk Map

Outline Map

700 B.C.	600 B.C.	500 B.C.	400 B.C.	336 B.C.	300 B.C.

THE GREEK EMPIRE

READ ALOUD
Stadium. Gymnasium. Museum. Democracy. *These words represent things that are important in our lives today. All of them had beginnings in ancient Greece. The story of Greek civilization continues with a young man named Alexander.*

Focus Activity

READ TO LEARN
What did Alexander the Great do to spread legacies of Greek civilization?

PEOPLE
Alexander
Aristotle

PLACES
Macedonia
Alexandria

THE BIG PICTURE

In the late 400s B.C. the Peloponnesian Wars raged in Greece. During this time the Persian empire, which you read about in the last lesson, still controlled a huge part of the world. Egyptians, Phoenicians, Jews, Babylonians, and Indians all lived under the rule of Persian kings. Connecting this empire was a network of roads and messenger services.

The Greek historian Herodotus may have traveled those roads around 450 B.C. He once made a 1,500-mile journey in about 90 days. He was amazed by the relay of royal messengers who traveled the same roads in just nine days! "Neither snow nor rain nor heat nor night holds back [the messenger from] the accomplishment of the course that has been assigned him," he marveled. Today the United States Postal Service uses similar words to describe the task of letter carriers as they transport mail across the country and around the world.

A man named Alexander traveled the roads of the Persian empire between 334 and 323 B.C., a little over 100 years after Herodotus. He conquered many areas and eventually became known as "Alexander the Great." As a result of his victories, Greek language and traditions spread as far as Egypt in Africa and the Indus Valley in Asia.

212

SHELTERED INSTRUCTION

READING STRATEGIES & LANGUAGE DEVELOPMENT

REREADING Remind students of the benefits of rereading a passage that contains a lot of new information. Model the process for the class with a Think-Aloud of your own. Read aloud the first two paragraphs of *The Big Picture.* Stop after each paragraph to restate the main ideas in your own words and clarify any confusing points. Demonstrate when to reread confusing passages. **[SDAIE STRATEGY: MODELING/METACOGNITIVE DEVELOPMENT]**

SYNONYMS AND ANTONYMS Synonyms and antonyms help strengthen comprehension. Ask students to define *synonym* and *antonym*. Then help them to identify words for which they can suggest both a synonym and antonym. For example, in the opening paragraph on p. 213: *conflict* (synonym: war; antonym: agreement), *weaken* (synonym: exhaust; antonym: strengthen), *powerful* (synonym: strong; antonym: weak), *conquered* (synonym: defeated; antonym: lost).

ALEXANDER OF MACEDONIA

Although the Peloponnesian Wars ended in 404 B.C., conflict continued to weaken the Greek city-states. This left them open to attack from Macedonia (mas ih DAHN nee uh), a powerful kingdom to the north. By 336 B.C. Macedonia's army had conquered most of Greece.

Macedonia's king at this time was a 20-year-old man named Alexander. He had already proven that he was a bold commander. He was also well educated. Aristotle (AR uh staht ul), one of the most famous philosophers in Athens, had been his private teacher. Because of Aristotle's teachings, Alexander developed a deep respect for Greek culture and traditions.

Expanding the Empire

In 334 B.C. Alexander and his armies set out to conquer Persia. Find their route on the map on the next page. For three years they fought their way along the eastern coast of the Mediterranean. Everywhere they went, they seized food and whatever else they needed to continue their journey.

The powerful Macedonian army never lost a battle. In 331 B.C. Alexander proclaimed, or publicly declared, himself ruler of Persia's vast empire as well as of Greece. To secure his power, Alexander pushed his army farther east.

In a few more years his troops had entered the Indus River valley. There they defeated an army that used elephants. Many of Alexander's soldiers had never seen such animals before. After his victory, though, the young emperor became sick. Unable to complete the journey, he died in June 323 B.C., in Babylon.

Alexander the Great was a brilliant military leader. These works of art show Alexander in battle.

213

ALEXANDER OF MACEDONIA

As students work with this page, have them sit in pairs with one book open here and the other to the map on p. 214.

- **Where is Macedonia in relation to Greece?** *(Have students locate it on the map, just to Greece's north.)*

- **Why was Macedonia tempted to invade Greece?** *(Greece's weakness after the Peloponnesian War)*

★**THINKING FURTHER:** *Cause and Effect* **What caused Alexander of Macedonia to admire Greece?** *(Aristotle had taught him to respect Greece's culture and traditions.)*

Discussing Expanding the Empire
Help students understand the speed and extent of Alexander's conquests.

- **How long did it take for Alexander to complete his conquests?** *(334-323=11 years)*

- **What major areas became part of his empire?** *(Greece and Persia)*

- **What finally ended the expansion of Alexander's empire?** *(He fell sick and died.)*

★**THINKING FURTHER:** *Making Conclusions* **What conclusions can you make about Alexander's abilities as a general?** *(He must have been a military genius to conquer so much of the world.)*

BACKGROUND INFORMATION

ABOUT ALEXANDER THE GREAT
- Alexander inherited his crown when his father, Philip, who was preparing to invade the Persian Empire, was murdered, possibly by a Persian agent.

- From boyhood on, Alexander had as his favorite book Homer's *Iliad*, probably given to him by his teacher Aristotle. Alexander identified with its hero, Achilles.

- From boyhood on, Alexander was also a great rider. In fact, he was only 12 when he won his favorite horse, Bucephalus, because he was the only one who could ride this unbroken young stallion. Later, when Bucephalus was killed as he carried Alexander into battle, Alexander named a city Bucephala for the horse.

- Though Alexander enjoyed strength and good health for most of his short life, his repeated wounds in battle gradually weakened him. He was in Babylon in 323 B.C., preparing to attack Arabia, when a fever struck him.

- As he lay dying, his captains filed past his bed as he raised his hand in final farewell. He was not yet 33.

CURRICULUM CONNECTION

LINKS TO LANGUAGE ARTS Call on students to think back over the life and times of Alexander the Great and then write a fitting epitaph for his tombstone. If possible, have some epitaphs available for use as inspiration.

A CITY IN THE EMPIRE

Point out to the class that Alexander did not lack a desire for self-glorification. Mention that *Alexandria*, Egypt, was not the only city he named after himself; there were no fewer than 16!

Discussing A Blending of Cultures Note for students the apparent contradiction of Alexander's spreading Greek culture while creating cities with mixtures of peoples.

● *How did Alexander's layout for Alexandria in Egypt reflect his admiration for Greek heritage?* (He laid out Alexandria like a Greek city, with agora, temples, theater, stadium, and gymnasium.)

● *Find Alexandria, Egypt, on the map on this page. How did its location make it a hub of Mediterranean trade?* (It lies on a harbor on the Mediterranean.)

● *What device did the Alexandrians develop for their harbor?* (one of the world's first lighthouses. Point out to the class that this lighthouse is the third of the Seven Wonders of the World they have encountered so far, after the Pyramids and the Hanging Gardens of Babylon.)

★**THINKING FURTHER:** *Making Conclusions* **What evidence can you find to support the conclusion that Alexander allowed different peoples to hold onto their own beliefs?** *(the mixture of Greek, Egyptian, and Jewish traditions and beliefs)*

A CITY IN THE EMPIRE

About nine years before he died, Alexander planned the creation of a city in Egypt, on the western edge of the Nile Delta. Alexandria, named after the emperor, soon became one of the most important cities in the Greek empire. The city of Alexandria was an example of how Greek civilization and ideas were carried far beyond Greece.

A Blending of Cultures

Like the many cities that Alexander had built, Alexandria's basic layout mirrored a Greek polis. It had an agora, a theater, several temples, a stadium, and a gymnasium. Alexandria's harbor became a major hub of Mediterranean trade. At the mouth of the harbor stood a gigantic lighthouse. This was one of the first lighthouses in the world. Its beam was a guide for sailors many miles away at sea.

The mixture of peoples and cultures in Alexandria created an unusual community. Besides building temples to Greek gods, Alexander planned a temple to the Egyptian goddess Isis. The Greek and Macedonian citizens of Alexandria took part in democratic assemblies. Egyptians in Alexandria had courts of their own. So did the city's Jews, who lived in their own section of the city. Craftworkers made Greek-style pottery. Papermakers continued to practice their ancient craft.

A Legacy of Learning

Not far from Alexandria's busy agora stood the city's museum. At the museum, scholars studied the world and how it worked. To help with their research,

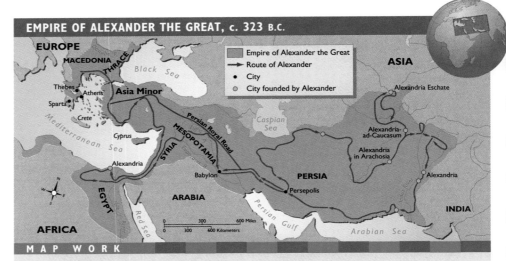

EMPIRE OF ALEXANDER THE GREAT, c. 323 B.C.

Empire of Alexander the Great
→ Route of Alexander
● City
⊙ City founded by Alexander

EUROPE — MACEDONIA — THRACE — Black Sea — ASIA — Thebes — Athens — Asia Minor — Sparta — Crete — Cyprus — Mediterranean Sea — Persian Royal Road — Caspian Sea — Alexandria Eschate — MESOPOTAMIA — Alexandria-ad-Caucasum — Alexandria in Arachosia — SYRIA — Alexandria — Babylon — PERSIA — Alexandria — EGYPT — Persepolis — ARABIA — INDIA — AFRICA — Red Sea — Persian Gulf — Arabian Sea

MAP WORK

Alexander the Great controlled enormous territories with the help of a very powerful army.

1. Alexander's vast empire included land on three continents. What are they?

2. What region south of Mesopotamia did Alexander not gain control of?

3. What is the easternmost river within Alexander's empire?

4. What river marks the northernmost border of Alexander's empire?

5. In which direction did Alexander travel along the coast of the Arabian Sea?

214 MAP WORK: **1.** Africa, Asia, and Europe **2.** Arabia **3.** Indus River **4.** Danube River **5.** west

---

BACKGROUND INFORMATION

ABOUT ALEXANDRIA
● It began as a fishing village about 1500 B.C.
● Alexander chose it because he needed a capital for his newly conquered Egyptian kingdom, and he wanted it to be accessible to Macedonia by sea.
● The site suited all his needs—a magnificent harbor, good climate, fresh water, limestone for building, and easy access to the Nile River.
● Alexander ordered his architect Dinocrates to build a magnificent Greek city on the site and then the conqueror departed.
● Alexander would die before ever seeing a building erected in Alexandria.

GLOBAL CONNECTION

CITIES THEN AND NOW Write *cosmopolitan* on the board and explain that it comes from two Greek words: *kosmos* meaning "universe" and *polis* "of a city." It refers to the great international cities that have emerged in the last centuries. Why can it also describe ancient Alexandria?

SECOND-LANGUAGE SUPPORT

MAKING CONNECTIONS Help second-language learners understand that modern life is linked to life in ancient Greece. Work with them to list elements of their world that were also found in Greece, such as museums, libraries, a written language, and other suggestions.

Alexander (left) founded Alexandria, one of the most important cities in the Greek empire. Today it is the second largest city in Egypt.

they used the books in the library nearby. Alexandria's library had almost 500,000 books written on papyrus rolls, and librarians were always searching for more! Inspectors at the harbor searched newly arrived ships to see if they carried any books. They kept whatever they found until copies could be made for the city's library.

An Alphabet

Scholars from many countries visited the library in Alexandria to study the books there. The skills of reading and writing had become important for preserving information. Unlike Egyptian hieroglyphics, Mesopotamian cuneiform, and Chinese characters, written Greek used a simple alphabet. Each symbol represented a sound. Learning to read required mastering less than 30 letters, rather than hundreds of symbols. The alphabet made it easier for more people to learn to read and write.

Math and Science

The library in Alexandria contained many books on mathematics. Ancient Greece produced brilliant mathematicians. They had learned a great deal from earlier Egyptian scholars, whose achievements in math and science you learned about in Chapter 4. Today many of the things you do in math class are legacies of their work. *Arithmetic, geometry,* and *mathematics* are all words that have Greek origins.

215

BACKGROUND INFORMATION

ABOUT THE LIBRARY OF ALEXANDRIA
- It was the most celebrated library of the ancient world.
- Its main part was damaged by fire when Julius Caesar besieged Alexandria in 47 B.C.
- Fifth-century Christians destroyed its remaining treasures.
- None of its books or buildings has survived to this day.

CURRICULUM CONNECTION

LINKS TO LANGUAGE ARTS Refer students to the term *alphabet*; explain that it comes from both Phoenician and Greek. The first two letters of the Phoenician alphabet are *aleph* and *beth*. The first two letters of the Greek alphabet are *alpha* (α) and *beta* (β). Some dictionaries show Phoenician and Greek alphabets. Have students compare the letters.

More MAP WORK

Have students follow Alexander's route on the map on p. 214.

- *As Alexander fought his way along the eastern and southern Mediterranean, what lands would he have entered?* (Asia Minor, then through Syria, down to Egypt)

- *How far east did his armies march?* (to the Indus River valley)

Analyzing A Legacy of Learning Review with the class the concept of cultural borrowing—one culture borrows from another or two borrow from each other. Ask students to look for examples in this section.

★THINKING FURTHER: *Making Conclusions How were the museum and library at Alexandria examples of cultural borrowing?* (They gathered wisdom and information from any culture they encountered, from anyone who sailed into the harbor.)

Discussing An Alphabet Encourage students to compare the Greek alphabet with other writing in the ancient world.

★THINKING FURTHER: *Problem Solving How did an alphabet simplify the problem of reading and writing?* (People had to learn fewer than 30 letters instead of hundreds of characters.)

Learning About Math and Science Remind the class that in this chapter's Skills Lesson, pp. 210-211, they learned that math and science were rarely studied in Athens' Golden Age.

- *What had changed about Greeks and their knowledge of math and science by the time of Alexandria?* (Greece produced math experts.)

★THINKING FURTHER: *Making Conclusions What seems to have brought this change about?* (cultural borrowing of knowledge about math by the Greeks from the Egyptians)

Infographic

Call on students to identify the three of the Seven Wonders of the World that they have met so far (the Pyramids, the Hanging Gardens, the Lighthouse of Alexandria). Have them locate the wonders in the pictures in this *Infographic*. Explain that the list of seven was gradually compiled by Greek and Roman authors beginning as early as about 130 B.C. These authors believed that the wonders represented the greatest ancient feats of art, technology, and architecture.

Discussing the Seven Wonders of the World Give students a few minutes to read the introduction, study the map, and relate the pictures and captions to their map locations. To help students get a sense of the height of each, tell them that in today's terms, a building story is about 10 feet, so a 450-foot pyramid stands 45 stories tall.

- ***Over what period of time were these wonders constructed?*** *(2,400 years, from 2600 B.C. to about 200 B.C.)*

- ***What were some reasons for which they were they built?*** *(to honor gods or goddesses or a wife, to serve as tombs or as a beacon to shipping)*

- ***Which of the wonders can still be seen today?*** *(Only the pyramids remain. Explain to the class that the only idea we have of what the others looked like comes from written descriptions from ancient times and archaeological evidence.)*

★**THINKING FURTHER:** *Making Decisions* ***Which of the seven do you think is most impressive? Why?*** *(Encourage students to discuss their reactions. Allow statements of taste, but ask them to explain their choices, whether based on beauty, technological achievement, purpose, or other criteria.)*

Technology CONNECTION

ADVENTURE TIME! CD-ROM
Choose your own modern-day wonders of the world on the *Adventure Time!* CD-ROM.

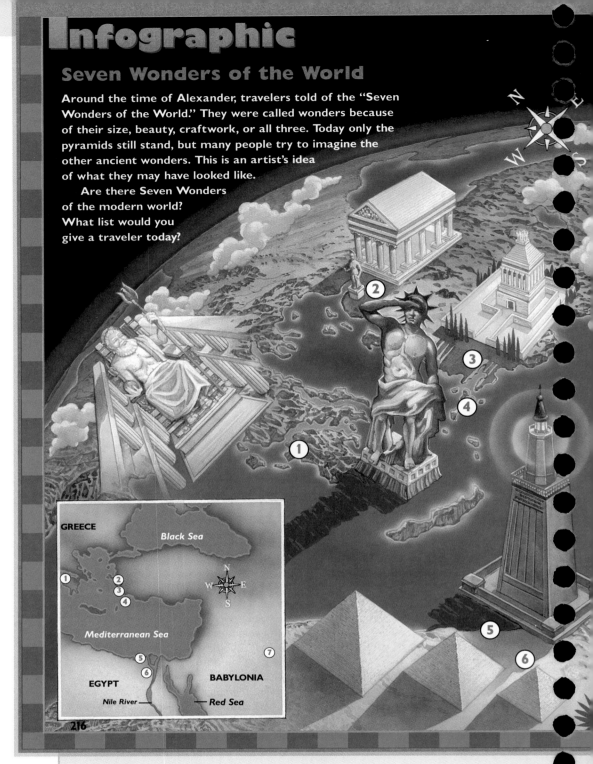

Infographic

Seven Wonders of the World

Around the time of Alexander, travelers told of the "Seven Wonders of the World." They were called wonders because of their size, beauty, craftwork, or all three. Today only the pyramids still stand, but many people try to imagine the other ancient wonders. This is an artist's idea of what they may have looked like.

Are there Seven Wonders of the modern world? What list would you give a traveler today?

216

EXPANDING THE INFOGRAPHIC

RESEARCHING AND CREATING A PRESENTATION Divide the class into seven groups and assign each group one of the Seven Wonders presented here. Tell each group to do further research on their wonder by gathering more information about its building, its uses, and its deterioration or outright destruction. Also, have them gather different artists' renderings of what it looked like. Each team should then work up an illustrated presentation of their findings for the class, with each team member taking part. Suggest they begin their research with the following sources:

- Encyclopedia entries on the *Seven Wonders of the World* and on the specific wonder they are assigned.

- A library subject catalog for similar entries. (*The Seven Wonders of the World*, by Kenneth McLeish is written for this age group.)

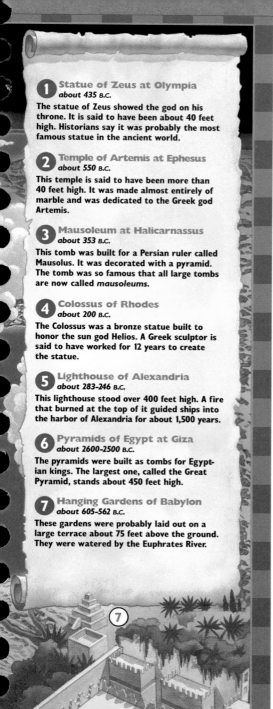

1 Statue of Zeus at Olympia
about 435 B.C.

The statue of Zeus showed the god on his throne. It is said to have been about 40 feet high. Historians say it was probably the most famous statue in the ancient world.

2 Temple of Artemis at Ephesus
about 550 B.C.

This temple is said to have been more than 40 feet high. It was made almost entirely of marble and was dedicated to the Greek god Artemis.

3 Mausoleum at Halicarnassus
about 353 B.C.

This tomb was built for a Persian ruler called Mausolus. It was decorated with a pyramid. The tomb was so famous that all large tombs are now called *mausoleums*.

4 Colossus of Rhodes
about 200 B.C.

The Colossus was a bronze statue built to honor the sun god Helios. A Greek sculptor is said to have worked for 12 years to create the statue.

5 Lighthouse of Alexandria
about 283-246 B.C.

This lighthouse stood over 400 feet high. A fire that burned at the top of it guided ships into the harbor of Alexandria for about 1,500 years.

6 Pyramids of Egypt at Giza
about 2600-2500 B.C.

The pyramids were built as tombs for Egyptian kings. The largest one, called the Great Pyramid, stands about 450 feet high.

7 Hanging Gardens of Babylon
about 605-562 B.C.

These gardens were probably laid out on a large terrace about 75 feet above the ground. They were watered by the Euphrates River.

WHY IT MATTERS

After Alexander died, no one person was able to control the vast empire. By 300 B.C. Alexander's generals had divided it up.

Although Alexander's empire did not last, his short rule had far-reaching effects. One of the most important was the mixing of cultures throughout North Africa and western and central Asia.

Many legacies of ancient Greece continue to influence cultures today. You can see Greek influence in classes on such subjects as math, philosophy, and science. Perhaps most important, Greek ideas live on in the way our government operates—as a democracy.

Reviewing Facts and Ideas

MAIN IDEAS

- When Alexander the Great conquered the Persian empire, he spread Greek culture from Egypt to India.

- Alexandria, one of the empire's most powerful cities, reflected the great mix of cultures within the empire.

- Legacies from ancient Greece influence today's education, government, philosophy, sports, and drama.

THINK ABOUT IT

1. How was Alexander influenced by Greek culture?

2. What did Alexandria have in common with a polis? How was it influenced by a variety of cultures?

3. **FOCUS** How did Alexander change life around the Mediterranean region?

4. **THINKING SKILL** What *conclusions* can you *make* about Greece's importance to history?

5. **WRITE** In one paragraph describe how a Greek legacy affects your life.

217

Discussing WHY IT MATTERS Ask students to review the enormous changes Alexander brought in a short time and the lack of a strong leader after his death.

★**THINKING FURTHER: Compare and Contrast** *How does the breakup of Alexander's empire suggest a repeated theme in history?* (Help students to recall similar cases of rule falling apart after a strong leader's death—Sargon and the Sumerian Empire, Hammurabi and the Babylonian Empire, King Solomon and Israel, Shihuangdi and the Chinese empire)

3 CLOSE

MAIN IDEAS

Have students write their answers to these questions on a piece of paper.

- *Over what area did Alexander spread Greek culture?* (from Egypt to India)

- *In what ways was Alexandria an international city?* (It drew scholars, merchants, and traders from all over and was home to several different ethnic groups.)

- *What areas of modern life are influenced by the legacy of ancient Greece?* (education, government, philosophy, sports, drama)

EVALUATE
✓ **Answers to Think About It**

1. through his teacher, Aristotle
Summarize

2. It was designed around the same elements; it attracted people from many different cultures.
Make Analogies

3. He brought it under his control and spread Greek culture through it.
Make Conclusions

4. that it influenced cultures that followed it in many ways
Make Conclusions

5. Students should mention education, democracy, entertainment, sports.
Make Analogies

Write About It On the board, write this quotation from Edith Hamilton, the scholar of ancient Greece: "...the modern spirit is a Greek discovery." Tell students to write a paragraph that explains why this is true.

MEETING INDIVIDUAL NEEDS

RETEACHING (Easy) Tell students to review what they have learned about Alexander the Great, his character, and his achievements. Have them write five adjectives or other descriptive phrases that they think apply to him.

EXTENSION (Average) Tell students to write a letter to Alexander the Great, telling him how he is remembered in the modern world and what achievements of his they admire.

ENRICHMENT (Challenging) The text mentions that Alexander's generals divided up his empire. Seleucus, Ptolemy, and Antigonus the One-Eyed each founded a dynasty that ruled part of Alexander's world. Divide the class into three groups and have each group research one dynasty. Have the groups write reports identifying the area their general ruled and telling what happened to his dynasty.

CITIZENSHIP
Viewpoints
PAGES 218–219

Lesson Objective
★ Analyze three opinions about the character and achievements of Alexander the Great.

Identifying the Issue Help students understand how historians can disagree about historical events and figures.

- **What time periods are these viewpoints from?** (the first and second centuries A.D.)

Discussing Three Different Viewpoints Give students a few minutes to read the viewpoints on these pages.

PLUTARCH

- **What is Plutarch's opinion of the people Alexander conquered?** (they were barbarians with uncivilized customs)

- **Why does Plutarch believe the barbarian tribes were fortunate to have been conquered by Alexander?** (because by conquering them, Alexander helped suppress their savage and uncivilized customs)

- **What does Plutarch think was the reason that Alexander conquered people?** (to unite all of mankind into a single people under one government)

ARRIAN

- **According to Arrian, how did Alexander dispel fear among his soldiers?** (by showing them that he, himself, was not afraid)

- **What conclusion does Arrian draw about Alexander's birth, based on his personality and fame?** (that he was born with the help of the gods)

- **Arrian talks most about which of Alexander's qualities?** (his fame)

CITIZENSHIP
VIEWPOINTS

Historians often have very different viewpoints on historical figures such as Alexander the Great.

HOW GREAT WAS ALEXANDER THE GREAT?

Over the centuries, historians have had different opinions of Alexander the Great, some good and some not. One historian has called him the "greatest general of all times." Others, however, have labeled him a "ruthless murderer" and a "cruel dictator."

One ancient Greek historian, Plutarch, believed that Alexander was a man of vision who tried to bring people of different areas into a great world state. Plutarch lived around the first century A.D., over 300 years after the death of Alexander. Arrian, a Greek historian from the second century A.D., also praised Alexander. Arrian wrote a biography of Alexander, saying that he was very heroic and inspired great confidence in his men. Arrian based the biography on the accounts of two of Alexander's generals.

A modern historian, Eugene Borza, offers a different view. He feels that Alexander needlessly killed many people and that he was considered ruthless by those he conquered. He also believes that Alexander was more interested in gaining a large empire than in spreading civilization. Consider three viewpoints on this issue and answer the questions that follow.

218

BACKGROUND INFORMATION

ABOUT PLUTARCH Plutarch is remembered as one of the world's most famous historians and biographers.

- Plutarch was born in Boeotia, located in central Greece, circa 46 A.D. He died sometime after 119 A.D. He founded a school in his native land, but also traveled widely and taught in Rome.

- Plutarch is credited with writing more than 227 works. His most famous achievement is *Parallel Lives*, which is also known as *Plutarch's Lives*. It presents short biographies of Greek and Roman figures such as soldiers, writers, and statesmen. Plutarch regarded his subjects as heroes and hoped that they would provide role models for future generations. His writings shaped the image of Greek and Roman historical figures for many centuries. Plutarch's work also contributed to the development of the essay.

Three **DIFFERENT** Viewpoints

1 PLUTARCH
Historian, Ancient Greece
Excerpt from writings, A.D. 90

Alexander, by founding more than seventy cities among the barbarian tribes, . . . suppressed their savage and uncivilized customs. . . . Those whom Alexander conquered were more fortunate than those who escaped. . . . [He] conducted himself . . . out of a desire to [give] all the races in the world . . . one rule and one form of government, making all mankind a single people.

". . . making all mankind a single people."

2 ARRIAN
Historian, Ancient Greece
Excerpt from *The Age of Alexander,* A.D. 171

[Alexander] was . . . very [famous] for rousing the courage of his soldiers, filling them with hopes of success and dispelling their fear in the midst of danger by his own freedom from fear. . . . I think there was at that time no race of men, no city . . . to whom Alexander's name and fame had not [reached]. For this reason it seems to me that a hero [like him] could not have been born without the [help of the gods].

". . . filling them with hopes of success and dispelling their fear . . ."

3 EUGENE N. BORZA
Historian and professor of ancient history, North Dakota
Excerpt from interview, 1997

[Alexander] slaughtered hundreds of thousands of innocent civilians in his conquests. . . . He ended the Persian empire, but he was not a good organizer and his empire fell apart as soon as he died. He was ill-tempered and had a strange personality. . . . In Central Asia he is remembered as a ruthless conqueror. He did not intend to spread the civilization of the Greeks to the East. It happened as a by-product of his wars, but it was not his intent.

"He did not intend to spread the civilization of the Greeks . . ."

★ BUILDING CITIZENSHIP

1. What is the viewpoint of each person?
2. In what ways are some of the viewpoints alike? In what ways are they different? How might the time period in which a person lived affect his or her viewpoint?
3. What resources could you use to form your own opinion of Alexander the Great?

SHARING VIEWPOINTS

Discuss what you agree with or disagree with about these and other viewpoints. Discuss what makes an historical figure truly "great." Then as a class, write three statements that all of you can agree with about Alexander the Great.

219

CITIZENSHIP ★

USING CURRENT EVENTS When leaders are in power, people's opinions of them are sometimes different from the way they are remembered many years later. They will often, for example, be remembered for a few main issues while many others are later forgotten. In today's world, with such a large media network, we receive quite a bit of information about our current leaders and elected officials. It is difficult to say what will be remembered in the future. Ask students to choose an elected official and to collect newspaper and magazine clippings about that person. Would they vote for that official if he or she ran again? What do students think future historians will have to say about that official's character, motives, and achievements? Ask students to write a summary of the official's career as it might appear in a future encyclopedia.

EUGENE N. BORZA

- ***What opinion does Borza give that comes from other people?*** *(the opinion of the people of Central Asia that Alexander was ruthless)*

- ***What is one possible reason why Borza's opinion of Alexander is so different from Plutarch's?*** *(Perhaps Borza has new evidence that was unknown to Plutarch; or perhaps Borza has a different definition of "greatness.")*

✓ Answers to Building Citizenship

1. Plutarch believed that Alexander was a great leader who wanted to unite all people. Arrian believed Alexander inspired courage and had the gods on his side. Borza regards Alexander as a brutal murderer and a disorganized leader who never intended to spread civilization.

2. Plutarch and Arrian agree that Alexander was great. Plutarch and Borza agree that he spread civilization. Plutarch and Arrian differ in the reasons they find Alexander great. Borza's is the only negative opinion of Alexander. A given time period affects both people's values and the information they have available.

3. Possible sources are encyclopedias, biographies, the Internet, and other books and magazines that deal with this period of history.

Sharing Viewpoints Encourage students to look at all the viewpoints that people may have had during Alexander's time, including those of Greeks, of Alexander's soldiers, and of the people he conquered. Three agreed-on statements might include: 1. Alexander was a famous military leader. 2. He conquered many people. 3. He spread the civilization of the Greeks to the East.

Debating Viewpoints Divide the class into two groups. Ask students to imagine they are citizens of Alexandria in the years just after Alexander's death. Have them debate whether or not Alexander deserves to be called a great man from the viewpoints of Alexandrians.

DISCUSSING MAJOR EVENTS Use this time line to reinforce for students how often national ambitions and rivalries brought the world of ancient Greece into war.

- **What different examples of major wars does this time line show?** *(the Persian Wars beginning in 499 B.C., the Peleponnesian Wars beginning in 431 B.C., the Conquests of Alexander beginning in 334 B.C.)*

- **What city-states of Greece were the greatest rivals, based on this time line?** *(Athens and Sparta)*

Answers to
THINKING ABOUT VOCABULARY

1. monarchy
2. assembly
3. democracy
4. jury
5. acropolis
6. peninsula
7. harbor
8. polis
9. philosophy
10. oligarchy

Answers to
THINKING ABOUT FACTS

1. any two of the following—wheat, barley, olives, grapes

2. Sparta; its military, which demanded service until age 60, and its rigorous training of its boys and girls, to be soldiers and mothers of soldiers

3. philosophy; he questioned Athenian values and was convicted of urging the young to revolt against them.

4. He united the world from Egypt to India into an empire and spread Greek culture throughout it.

Resource REMINDER

Practice and Project Book: *p. 46*
Assessment Book: *Chapter 8 Test*
Technology: *Videodisc*
Transparency: *Graphic Organizer, Word Map*

CHAPTER 8 REVIEW

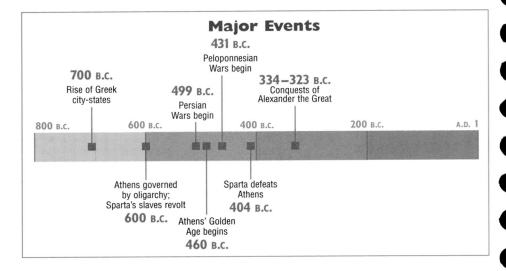

Major Events

- **700 B.C.** Rise of Greek city-states
- **499 B.C.** Persian Wars begin
- **431 B.C.** Peloponnesian Wars begin
- **334–323 B.C.** Conquests of Alexander the Great
- **600 B.C.** Athens governed by oligarchy; Sparta's slaves revolt
- **460 B.C.** Athens' Golden Age begins
- **404 B.C.** Sparta defeats Athens

800 B.C.　600 B.C.　400 B.C.　200 B.C.　A.D. 1

THINKING ABOUT VOCABULARY

Number a sheet of paper from 1 to 10. Beside each number write the word from the list below that matches the statement.

acropolis　monarchy
assembly　oligarchy
democracy　peninsula
harbor　philosophy
jury　polis

1. A government of one ruler
2. A law-making body of government
3. Rule by the people
4. A group of citizens chosen to decide in court cases
5. A large hill where city residents went for safety
6. An area of land nearly surrounded by water
7. A sheltered place along a coast
8. A Greek city-state
9. The search for wisdom and the right way to live
10. Rule by a small, rich group

THINKING ABOUT FACTS

1. What were two main crops of the ancient Greeks?
2. What was the largest city-state in Greece in 700 B.C.? What made this city-state strong?
3. What did Socrates teach? Why was he put to death?
4. How did Alexander the Great affect the history of his time?
5. Look at the time line above. What important events happened between 500 and 400 B.C? Why was the century such an important one for Athens?

SECOND-LANGUAGE SUPPORT

NOTE-TAKING Have students practice summarizing the material in this chapter with a partner. Instruct students to make an outline in their notebooks using the headings in the text. Under each heading, they will write a one- or two-sentence summary of the most important information. Remind students to review the lesson on summarizing on pages 172-173.

PORTRAIT GALLERY Invite students to create a portrait gallery of famous Greeks of antiquity and of the Greek gods and goddesses mentioned in this chapter. Attached to each portrait should be a paragraph describing the person's achievements or identifying the god or goddess. Encourage students to do research to find a myth about one of the Greek gods or goddesses and retell it to the class.

THINK AND WRITE

WRITING ABOUT CONTRASTS

Reread pages 198–199. Then write a paragraph describing the main differences between Athens and Sparta.

WRITING ABOUT PERSPECTIVES

Suppose you live in ancient Athens. Write a paragraph about why you think women should or should not participate fully in Athenian democracy.

WRITING BIOGRAPHIES

Write one paragraph about two of the following people: (1) Homer, (2) Socrates, (3) Pericles, and (4) Alexander the Great.

APPLYING THINKING SKILLS

MAKING CONCLUSIONS

1. What is a conclusion?

2. Reread "Did You Know?" on page 206 and make a conclusion about why the Greeks liked drama. What information did you use to come to your conclusion?

3. If you were asked to make a conclusion about how successful drama is today in America, what facts would you need to know?

4. When in your life have you made a conclusion about something but later made a different conclusion about the same thing?

5. Why is the ability to make conclusions important for studying history?

Summing Up the Chapter

Review the chapter, then copy the word map below on a separate sheet of paper. Next, fill in each box with at least two related details. After you have filled in the details, use the word map to write a paragraph that answers the question "What did the ancient Greeks contribute to world civilization?"

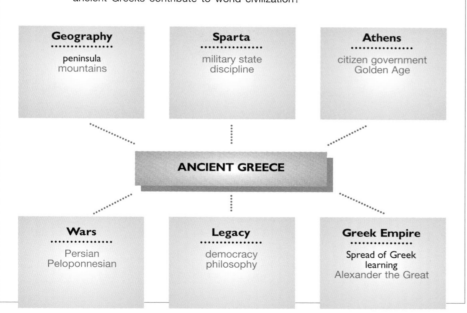

Geography
peninsula
mountains

Sparta
military state
discipline

Athens
citizen government
Golden Age

ANCIENT GREECE

Wars
Persian
Peloponnesian

Legacy
democracy
philosophy

Greek Empire
Spread of Greek learning
Alexander the Great

221

---

5. Persian Wars, Athens' Golden Age, the Peloponnesian Wars, Sparta's victory over Athens; Athens reached its highest level of civilization and was brought down in defeat by Sparta.

Answers to APPLYING THINKING SKILLS

1. A conclusion is a meaning drawn from combining factors or information.

2. Greek drama included comedies that made jokes about those in high places and reenacted events from Greek history. Those are the kinds of things the Greeks must have liked to see. That would account for the popularity of drama among the Greeks.

3. perhaps how many theaters are in operation, how many plays theaters present each year, how many people in the total population attend dramas regularly, how many people can make a living in the theater

4. Encourage students to tell not only what conclusions they later changed but also why they changed it.

5. It helps us to organize information from the past and draw meaning from it, making it possible to understand history and learn lessons from it.

Technology CONNECTION

VIDEODISC
Enrich Chapter 8 with the segment about *Alexander the Great*.

Search Frame 53023 Side B

SUGGESTIONS FOR SUMMING UP THE CHAPTER

As students copy the word map on their papers, point out to them that this is a way to create a graphic review of highlights of the chapter. When they have finished copying, go over the headings for the boxes and call for students "off the top of their heads" to suggest possible details for each. You may want to suggest a few from the possible answers that appear in the reproduced pupil page above. Then have students review the chapter for additional details. When they have filled in their word maps, have them go over the boxes and identify those details that might be called "contributions to world civilization." Encourage them to weave those details into the paragraph they write to answer the question posed.

ASSESSING THINK AND WRITE: *For performance assessment, see Assessment Book, Chapter 8, pp. T68–T70.*

CHAPTER

9 Ancient Rome

Pages 222–259

CHAPTER OVERVIEW

People settled near the Tiber River around 1000 B.C. and eventually founded the city of Rome. The Romans overthrew their king and formed a republic ruled by the citizens in 509 B.C. A general named Julius Caesar took over the government and greatly expanded the empire by 48 B.C.

GEO ADVENTURES DAILY GEOGRAPHY ACTIVITIES

Use **Geo Adventures** Daily Geography activities to assess students' understanding of geography skills.

CHAPTER PLANNING GUIDE

LESSON 1	**GEOGRAPHYSKILLS**	**LESSON 2**
SUGGESTED PACING: 2 DAYS	SUGGESTED PACING: 1 DAY	SUGGESTED PACING: 2 DAYS
Geography Of Ancient Rome pp. 224–227	**Reading Elevation Maps And Profiles** pp. 228–229	**The Rise Of The Roman Republic** pp. 230–235
RESOURCES Practice and Project Book, p. 47 Desk Map Outline Map	**RESOURCES** Practice and Project Book, p. 48 Transparency Map 13 ◉ TECHNOLOGY *Adventure Time!* CD-ROM	**CURRICULUM CONNECTIONS** Links to Language Arts, p. 232 **CITIZENSHIP** Understanding Government, p. 232 **FIELD TRIP** Visit a Museum, p. 231 **RESOURCES** Practice and Project Book, p. 49

Legacy	**LESSON 4**	**LESSON 5**
SUGGESTED PACING: 1 DAY	SUGGESTED PACING: 2 DAYS	SUGGESTED PACING: 2 DAYS
Domes & Arches pp. 244–245	**Beginnings Of Christianity** pp. 246–251	**The Decline Of The Roman Empire** pp. 252–257
FIELD TRIP Visit Buildings Illustrating Roman Architecture, p. 244	**CURRICULUM CONNECTIONS** Links to Art, p. 250 **CITIZENSHIP** Understanding Government, p. 247 **RESOURCES** Practice and Project Book, p. 51 Anthology, pp. 52–53	**CURRICULUM CONNECTIONS** Links to Language Arts, p. 256 **CITIZENSHIP** Understanding Government, p. 253 **RESOURCES** Practice and Project Book, p. 52 Anthology, pp. 54, 55

LEARNING STYLE: Visual ON YOUR OWN 30 MINUTES OR LONGER

Write a Planet Report

Objective: To introduce the legacy of ancient Rome by researching names of planets in our solar system.

Materials: paper, flour, water, newspaper

1. Tell students the word "planet" is from a Greek word for "wanderer." Ask how a planet is like a wanderer.
2. Note that all the names come from Greek and Roman myths. Have each student choose a planet name to research.
3. Ask students to make papier-mâché models of their planets and to tell about the gods and goddesses they were named for.

LESSON 3

SUGGESTED PACING: 3 DAYS

The Roman Empire
pp. 236–243

CURRICULUM CONNECTIONS
Links to Math, p. 238

CITIZENSHIP
Using Current Events, p. 239

INFOGRAPHIC
Daily Life in Pompeii, pp. 242–243

RESOURCES
Practice and Project Book, p. 50
Anthology, pp. 49–50, 51
⊙ TECHNOLOGY *Adventure Time!*
CD-ROM

CHAPTER REVIEW

SUGGESTED PACING: 1 DAY

pp. 258–259

RESOURCES
Practice and Project Book, p. 53
⊙ TECHNOLOGY Videodisc/Video
Tape 3
Assessment Book: Chapter 9 Test
Transparency: Graphic Organizer,
Cause-and-Effect map

SDAIE SUPPORT **SHELTERED INSTRUCTION**

READING STRATEGIES & LANGUAGE DEVELOPMENT

Making and Supporting Generalizations/Compound
 Words, p. 224, Lesson 1
Compare and Contrast/Words with Multiple
 Meanings, p. 228, Geography Skills
Sequence/Word Origins, p. 230, Lesson 2
Context Clues/Word Families, p. 236, Lesson 3
Rereading/Apostrophes, p. 246, Lesson 4
Compare and Contrast/Words with Multiple
 Meanings, p. 252, Lesson 5

SECOND-LANGUAGE SUPPORT

Taking Notes, pp. 225, 254
Dramatization, p. 233
Working with a Peer, pp. 238, 250

MEETING INDIVIDUAL NEEDS

Reteaching, Extension, Enrichment, pp. 227, 229,
 235, 243, 245, 251, 257
McGraw-Hill Adventure Book

ASSESSMENT OPPORTUNITIES

Practice and Project Book, pp. 47–53
Write About It, pp. 227, 235, 243, 245, 251, 257
Assessment Book: Assessing Think and Write,
 pp. T71–T73; Chapter 9 Tests: Content, Skills,
 Writing

Introducing the Chapter

Point out to students that their studies are first moving westward in Europe, to the ancient civilization of Rome. On the map on this page, have them locate Greece and then have them pinpoint the city of Rome in relation to it (west of Greece).

THINKING ABOUT HISTORY AND GEOGRAPHY

Have students read the text on this page and ask them to use it, the time line, and the map to preview the period they will explore (from 700 B.C. to after A.D. 306) and the sweep of territory, by locating on the map each place named on the time line.

509 B.C. ROME

- **Where on the Italian Peninsula is the city of Rome located?** *(about halfway up the west coast)*

- **When did citizens of Rome found a republic?** *(in 509 B.C.)*

- **Who ruled this republican government?** *(the citizens)*

★ **THINKING FURTHER:** *Compare and Contrast* **How does the time of the founding of Rome's republic compare with the period of Greek's Golden Age?** *(about half a century earlier)*

48 B.C. ALEXANDRIA

- **Which people are pictured in this panel and where and when did they meet?** *(Julius Caesar and Cleopatra, in Alexandria in Egypt in 48 B.C.)*

- **What positions did these people hold?** *(Caesar was a Roman ruler; Cleopatra was an Egyptian ruler.)*

Resource **REMINDER**

 **Technology:** *Videodisc/Video Tape 3*

CHAPTER 9

Ancient Rome

THINKING ABOUT HISTORY AND GEOGRAPHY

About 700 B.C. people of the Italian peninsula founded a city called Rome. Within 200 years, Rome would develop a government ruled by its citizens. Under later rulers, Rome grew into a vast empire that stretched across Europe, touching Africa and western Asia. The influence of this great empire, including its laws, language, technology, and religion, spread far and wide and has lasted into modern times.

509 B.C.	48 B.C.	27 B.C.
ROME	**ALEXANDRIA**	**ROME**
Roman citizens start a republic	Julius Caesar and Cleopatra join forces	Augustus becomes the first Roman emperor and continues expansion of the empire

222

BACKGROUND INFORMATION

LINKING THE MAP TO THE TIME LINE

- In pre-republic days, Romans followed the leadership of kings. In 509 B.C., they rebelled against kings but maintained the idea of a supreme authority, which they called the *imperium*. Instead of placing the *imperium* in the hands of a king, Romans gave the authority to two consuls who held it for one year. Their power was absolute, but either consul could veto the other—a very early case of "checks and balances."

- Under Roman rule, Alexandria became a center for world commerce. Since then, it has remained a strategic location, right up to World Wars I and II, when it served as a major British naval base.

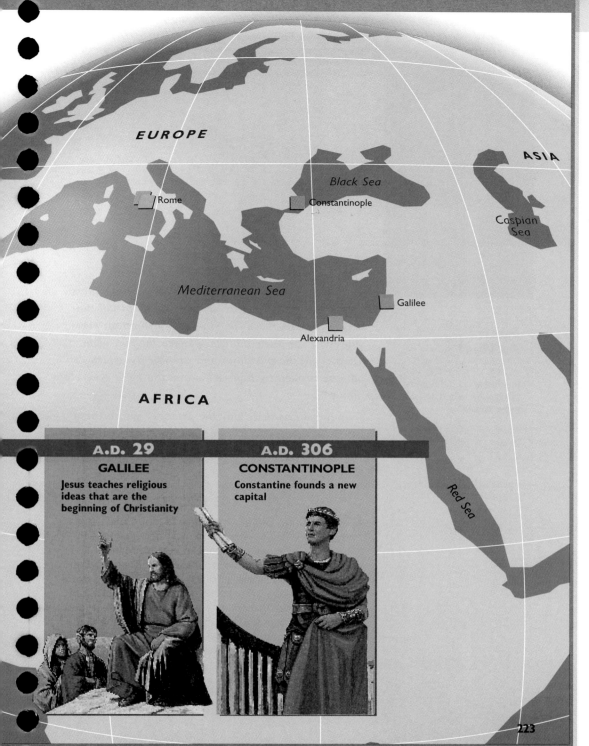

EUROPE

ASIA

Rome

Black Sea

Constantinople

Caspian Sea

Mediterranean Sea

Galilee

Alexandria

AFRICA

Red Sea

A.D. 29
GALILEE

Jesus teaches religious ideas that are the beginning of Christianity

A.D. 306
CONSTANTINOPLE

Constantine founds a new capital

223

★**THINKING FURTHER:** *Making Conclusions What might their meeting have to do with expanding the Roman empire? (The empire probably included Egypt.)*

27 B.C. ROME

● *How much time has passed since the last panel? (21 years)*

● *How has the title of Rome's ruler changed in this time? (Julius Caesar was the ruler of the republic of Rome; Augustus became Rome's first emperor.)*

★**THINKING FURTHER:** *Making Conclusions How do you know that Julius Caesar's work continued under Augustus? (Both set out to expand the empire.)*

A.D. 31 GALILEE

● *Where is Galilee located? (in Asia, near the eastern shore of the Mediterranean Sea)*

● *In what ancient civilization that you have already studied is Galilee? (in the Fertile Crescent—If necessary, refer students to the map on p. 121 to make this identification.)*

★**THINKING FURTHER:** *Predicting How would Jesus affect civilization? (His followers introduced a whole new religion—Christianity.)*

A.D. 306 CONSTANTINOPLE

● *In this panel, how much time has passed after the republic of Rome was founded? (about 800 years)*

★**THINKING FURTHER:** *Making Conclusions What can you assume from this panel has happened to the Roman world? (It appears to be getting a new capital.)*

Technology CONNECTION

VIDEODISC/VIDEO TAPE 3
Enrich Chapter 9 with the *Ancient Rome* segments on the Videodisc.

Search Frame 11660

BACKGROUND INFORMATION

LINKING THE MAP AND THE TIME LINE

● In 27 B.C. in Rome, Octavian, who had been co-consul with Mark Antony after Caesar's death, but who had eliminated this rival, entered the Senate in Rome and declared that the republic had been restored. Modestly, he offered to resign his post, but strong armies were at his command. The Senate, knowing it could not oppose him and his armies, allowed him to choose the title Augustus ("honored one") and take over Rome as emperor.

● Galilee was the northern province of ancient Palestine, and its boundaries roughly matched those of today's northern Israel. It was in the Galilean city of Nazareth that Jesus grew up.

● Constantinople has one of the world's most strategic locations; it is at the crossroads of Europe and Asia and just a short boat trip across the Mediterranean to Africa.

LESSON 1
PAGES 224–227

Lesson Overview

The Italian peninsula's fertile plains helped make it an excellent location for a major civilization to develop.

Lesson Objectives

★ Describe the geography of the Italian peninsula.

★ Explain why such geography would attract human settlement.

★ Describe Rome's legendary founding.

1 PREPARE

MOTIVATE Have the class do a choral reading of the Pliny quote in the *Read Aloud.* Refer to the photo on this page of the terrain around Rome. If possible, have some picture books of Italy available for students to inspect for geographic features.

SET PURPOSE Have students recall ways that Greece's geography affected its development. Refer them to the *Read to Learn* question; encourage them to look for answers and *Places* as they read.

2 TEACH

Understanding THE BIG PICTURE
Help students connect the development of Rome with colonizing by Greece.

● *Why were Greek colonists attracted to Italy? (Its rich and fertile land encouraged farm production, and Greece needed wheat from Italy.)*

● *Were Greeks the only people in Italy? (No, there were many other people and cultures.)*

★**THINKING FURTHER:** *Compare and Contrast* **How would Rome eventually become more powerful than Athens or Sparta?** *(Rome would be dominant, uniting its peninsula; Greece was not united.)*

Resource REMINDER

Practice and Project Book: *p. 47*

Desk Map

Outline Map

GEOGRAPHY OF ANCIENT ROME

READ ALOUD

"The countryside round here is very beautiful. . . . The broad, spreading plain is ringed by mountains, their summits topped by ancient woods of tall timber. . . . Below these the vineyards extend on every side, weaving their uniform pattern far and wide. . . . Then come the meadows and grainfields, which can only be broken by huge oxen and the most powerful plows."

A Roman named Pliny the Younger wrote these words in a letter to a friend almost 2,000 years ago. As you will see, they describe the land around ancient Rome well.

Focus Activity

READ TO LEARN
In what ways did Rome's geography help it to grow strong?

PLACES
Rome
Sicily
Alps
Apennine Mountains
Latium
Tiber River

THE BIG PICTURE

Around 700 B.C. people from Sparta and other city-states began leaving Greece to start new colonies in other parts of the Mediterranean region. Many sailed west to present-day Italy, where the land was rich and fertile. There the Greek colonists settled among several groups of peoples who spoke different languages and followed different customs. The communities shared in common their ways of making a living from the land.

While Sparta and Athens rose to power in Greece, another city was growing strong in Italy. That city was Rome. In time, Rome would unify all of Italy's many communities under its rule and eventually conquer Greece itself.

224

SHELTERED INSTRUCTION

READING STRATEGIES & LANGUAGE DEVELOPMENT

MAKING AND SUPPORTING GENERALIZATIONS Remind students that readers make generalizations to help them understand ideas. Have volunteers make generalizations about their region. Which geographic features draw people to the area? Write the Read to Learn question on the board. As students read, have them note generalizations that answer the question. **[SDAIE STRATEGY: BRIDGING/SCHEMA BUILDING]**

COMPOUND WORDS Point out to students that this lesson contains several compound words that join two nouns without a hyphen to form one noun with its own distinct meaning. Point out *countryside, vineyards,* and *grainfields* in the Pliny quote on this page. Encourage them to find others *(farmland, backbone, mountainsides, seaports, grapevines, marketplace, mealtimes).* Discuss how we understand the meaning of a compound by knowing the meanings of its parts.

A BOOT INTO THE SEA

The Italian peninsula is part of the European continent. It juts out into the Mediterranean Sea like a kicking boot. Find the "toe" of the boot on the map on this page. The island to the west of the toe is called Sicily. It was a popular destination for ancient Greek colonists because of its rich farmland.

Mountains of Italy

At the northern border of present-day Italy stand the craggy Alps. The Alps are Europe's highest mountain range. Do you remember how the Himalayas separate the Indian subcontinent from the rest of Asia? The Alps wall off the Italian peninsula from the rest of Europe in a similar way.

Another mountain range has had an even greater effect on life in Italy. The Apennine (AP uh nin) Mountains form a giant "backbone" through the Italian peninsula. Their towering height makes it difficult to travel across the peninsula. The Apennines also lack rich soil, so there is more sheep herding than farming on the mountainsides.

Fertile Plains

Italy, like Greece, has much mountainous land. Also like Greece, Italy has a number of fertile plains. One important plain, Latium (LAY shee um), is located on the west coast of central Italy. The Tiber River runs through the center of this plain. Archaeologists have found remains of ancient communities on the Latium plain that date back about 3,000 years. Eventually, a great city called Rome would also arise on the plain along the Tiber River.

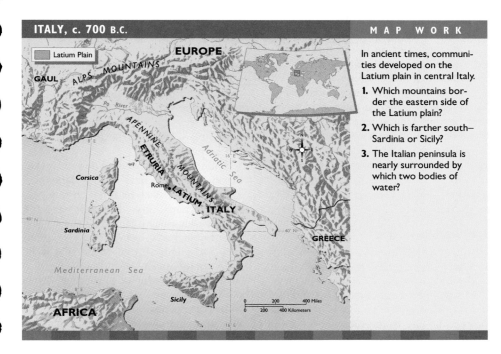

ITALY, c. 700 B.C.

Latium Plain

MAP WORK

In ancient times, communities developed on the Latium plain in central Italy.

1. Which mountains border the eastern side of the Latium plain?
2. Which is farther south—Sardinia or Sicily?
3. The Italian peninsula is nearly surrounded by which two bodies of water?

MAP WORK: **1.** Apennine Mountains **2.** Sicily
3. the Mediterranean Sea and the Adriatic Sea

225

GLOBAL CONNECTION

MOUNTAINS AS "BACKBONES" Explain that many writers have described the Alps as the backbone of Europe. Refer students to the *Atlas* on p.R18 showing North and South America and ask if they can spot a mountainous backbone. Help students locate the mountain ranges that stretch from Alaska to Chile.

SECOND-LANGUAGE SUPPORT

TAKING NOTES Second-language learners may remember more geography if they actively locate places as you point them out. Have students use outline maps to mark the places mentioned in the lesson. Encourage them to use corresponding maps in the *Atlas* for reference.

A BOOT INTO THE SEA
Emphasize Italy's boot shape, which makes it easy to locate on maps.

More

MAP WORK

Refer students to the map on this page and have them trace Italy's boot shape with their fingers.

- **Into what sea does the Italian "boot" extend?** *(the Mediterranean)*

- **Along what smaller sea does its east coast run?** *(the Adriatic)*

- **What rugged geographic feature forms the northern border of the Italian peninsula?** *(mountains—the Alps)*

- **Where along the Italian peninsula is Rome located?** *(halfway down the west coast, at the Tiber's mouth)*

★**THINKING FURTHER:** *Making Conclusions* **Why is it accurate to say that the Italian peninsula is centrally located?** *(Its location in the midst of the Mediterranean makes northern Africa, western Asia, and southern Europe accessible by sea.)*

Discussing Mountains of Italy Have students locate the Alps and Apennines.

★**THINKING FURTHER:** *Making Conclusions* **How might mountains have served as both a help and a hindrance to ancient people of the Italian peninsula?** *(Help students to see that mountains serve as barriers which discouraged attackers, but could hinder travel within the people's own land. Also, while the Apennine Mountains discouraged farming, they encouraged sheep herding.)*

Exploring Fertile Plains Encourage students to work with map and text.

- **Where is the Latium plain?** *(on the west coast of central Italy)*

- **What river runs through it?** *(Tiber)*

★**THINKING FURTHER:** *Making Conclusions* **Why does it make sense that a great city might develop in this location?** *(fertile soil, flat land, fresh water, seacoast site)*

A CITY ALONG THE TIBER

Have the class again pinpoint Rome's location on the map on p. 225.

Discussing The Legend of Romulus and Remus Review with the class what a legend is—a story coming down from the past that, though popular, may not be verifiable. Explain that the legend of Romulus and Remus is one of the best known and most popular legends passed down from ancient times.

● *Why does this legend make a good story?* (Help students identify its dramatic elements—brother against brother, struggle for power, attempted murder, miraculous rescue by an animal.)

● *Why is it a bittersweet tale?* (First evil, then good triumphed; finally through tragedy a great city was created.)

★**THINKING FURTHER:** *Classifying* **What parts of this legend might be fact? Which might be fiction?** (Let students express and support their opinions.)

Exploring City of Seven Hills Have students analyze the advantages of Rome's location.

★**THINKING FURTHER:** *Making Generalizations* **What evidence would you offer to support this generalization: "The city of Rome was well-situated to become a world leader"?** (hills for defense, river "highway," rich farmlands for food, accessible seaport)

Discussing Peoples of the Peninsula Write *Etruscan* on the board and pronounce it—ih TRUS kin—for the class.

● *Who were the Etruscans?* (people of Italy before Rome was founded)

● *How did they unite Italy?* (by conquering other peoples there)

★**THINKING FURTHER:** *Making Conclusions* **How might they have helped Rome to gain dominance?** (The Romans inherited a unified Italy that the Etruscans had created.)

A CITY ALONG THE TIBER

Today Rome is a large, modern city beside the Tiber River, on the northern edge of the Latium plain. Rome was also a great city over 2,000 years ago. How did this city come into being?

The Legend of Romulus and Remus

According to Roman legend, a king ruled a small city near the Tiber River over 2,700 years ago. His younger brother overthrew him and drove away the rest of the royal family. Later the older brother's daughter gave birth to twin boys, Romulus and Remus. The new king was afraid these boys would try to claim the throne. He gave orders to throw the twins into the flooded Tiber River. This was done—but miraculously the boys did not drown. They were both washed up on a hilltop where a wolf happened along and rescued them.

The story goes on to say that a shepherd came upon the wolf's den and took the boys home. Romulus and Remus grew up to be strong and brave. In the end they helped their grandfather become king again. Then Romulus and Remus founded a new city on the hill where they had been rescued. The two brothers fought over the naming of the city, and Romulus killed Remus. The city was named Rome after its first king, Romulus.

City of Seven Hills

The story of Romulus and Remus is a legend. There are, however, many good reasons why Rome grew where it did. First, as Rome developed, it expanded across seven hills. These hills helped to protect the city from attack. Second, the Tiber River made a fine "highway" for

An ancient Roman bridge spans the Tiber River (above). Grapes remain a major crop in Italy (right).

travel between the mountains and the Mediterranean coast. Boats brought goods from faraway seaports as well as news from communities upriver. Last but not least, the Latium plain was surrounded by inactive volcanoes. Ash from earlier eruptions had created a thin but rich soil. As a result, farmers were able to produce large surpluses on the Latium plain.

Latium farmers grew wheat to make bread. They also grew beans, cabbage, and lettuce, as well as figs and other fruits. Perhaps most important were the grapes they raised to make wine. Grapevines grow best in rocky soil, and Italy had plenty of that. Wine sold well in the marketplace. Most people drank watered-down wine at mealtimes. People poured wine into cuts and wounds to help them heal. In time, Italy's fine wines became one of the peninsula's most valued trade goods.

BACKGROUND INFORMATION

ABOUT FERAL CHILDREN Stories of feral children—children adopted by animals and reared in the wild—have recurred in both fiction and in fact from Romulus and Remus on.

● In fiction, Rudyard Kipling created Mowgli in his *Jungle Book.*

● Edgar Rice Burroughs created Tarzan in his *Tarzan of the Apes* and many other adventures.

● Several motion pictures, including 1995's *Nell,* have been based on stories of feral children.

● In the realm of fact, although sometimes questionable, more than 40 cases of children reared by animals have been recorded since the 14th century.

● In general, feral children have not done well when they rejoined society. They never fully adjusted, and most died young.

WHY IT MATTERS

During the period of Etruscan rule, Rome continued to grow and develop. However, the people of the small city on the Tiber River could not have known what the future would hold. As you will soon see, Rome would one day become the center of a mighty empire. Roman laws, language, and achievements would affect not only all of Italy, but in time, much of the world.

✔ Reviewing Facts and Ideas

MAIN IDEAS

- At the base of Italy's two mountain ranges—the Alps and the Apennines—lie fertile regions, such as the Latium plain.

- Italy's fertile plains were well used by local farmers as well as colonists from ancient Greece.

- The city of Rome was founded on seven hills. They helped to protect it from attack. The nearby Latium plain provided fertile farmland.

- Etruscan kings ruled Rome and other regions of Italy before being overthrown by Romans in 509 B.C.

THINK ABOUT IT

1. Why did grapes become an important crop in ancient Italy?

2. How did Rome come to be founded, according to legend? What role does geography play in this story?

3. **FOCUS** Why was the location of Rome a good place for a city?

4. **THINKING SKILL** What were the _causes_ of farmers' success at growing grapevines in Italy?

5. **GEOGRAPHY** How did the mountains of Italy affect communication and transportation?

227

Peoples of the Peninsula

Before the founding of Rome, there were other peoples who developed civilizations in Italy. One group, called the Etruscans, settled on the plain northwest of the Tiber River. Find this plain, called Etruria (ih TRUR ee uh), on the map on page 225.

Around 575 B.C. the Etruscan army conquered much of the Italian peninsula, including Rome. Etruscan kings led the city to victory over many of its neighbors in Latium. However, in about 509 B.C., the leading families of Rome overthrew their Etruscan king.

Discussing WHY IT MATTERS Have students refer to the notes they took as suggested in the *Reading Strategy* for this lesson.

> ★**THINKING FURTHER:** *Making Generalizations* **What generalizations can you make about how geography helped put Rome on the path to becoming "the center of a mighty empire"?** *(Generalizations should touch on fertile farmlands, central location in the Mediterranean, access to river and sea transportation, defensible city location, and ambitious people.)*

⭐ 3 CLOSE

MAIN IDEAS

Call on students to answer these questions.

- **What was Italy's richest area of farmland?** *(the Latium plain)*

- **How did local farmers and Greek colonists use the Italian environment?** *(They grew crops—wheat, vegetables, grapes, other fruits—and herded sheep.)*

- **What geographic advantages did the city of Rome have?** *(defensible hills and surrounding fertile farmland)*

- **Whose rule did the Romans overthrow in 509 B.C.?** *(Etruscans)*

EVALUATE
✔ Answers to Think About It

1. They yielded wine, which had several uses and was a valuable trade item. *Make Conclusions*

2. Romulus and Remus founded it on the hill where they had been rescued; it had hills for defense and a port. *Form Generalizations*

3. Hills provide good defense. *Make Judgements*

4. Italy's bounty of rocky soil *Cause and Effect*

5. The Alps were a barrier to the north and the Apennines created a barrier down the center of the peninsula. *Five Themes of Geography: Location*

Write About It Ask students to picture themselves as advertising copywriters for a real estate developer in ancient Rome. Have them write an ad telling people why they should invest in Rome as an up-and-coming city.

SKILLS LESSON
PAGE 228–229

Lesson Overview
Elevation maps and profiles indicate varying heights in a region.

Lesson Objective
★ Interpret elevation maps and profiles.

1 PREPARE

MOTIVATE Ask students if they have ever climbed a high hill or mountain. Have them read *Why the Skill Matters* and relate the term *elevation* (the height to which they climbed) to their experience. Then have them think of a giant cleaver cutting through the center of the hill or mountain, like a knife cutting through a cake. Have them relate this to a *profile* (a cross-section of the hill they climbed).

SET PURPOSE Give students a few minutes to look at Maps A and B. Encourage them to explore this skills lesson to learn how to interpret these two graphics. Ask them to read *Helping Yourself* as a preview.

2 TEACH

Why the Skill Matters Write *elevation* and *profile* on the board.

● **What does the elevation map show?** *(the varying heights of Rome)*

● **Does the profile—Map B—show as much information as Map A? Why or why not?** *(No, it captures just one cross-section of the area of Map A.)*

Using an Elevation Map Have students analyze Map A.

● **How are different heights shown?** *(different colors keyed to legend)*

● **How many different levels of elevation does this map show?** *(six, from 30 feet above sea level to 200 feet)*

Resource REMINDER
Practice and Project Book: *p. 48*
Technology: *Adventure time! CD-ROM*
Transparency: *Map 13*

GEOGRAPHYSKILLS

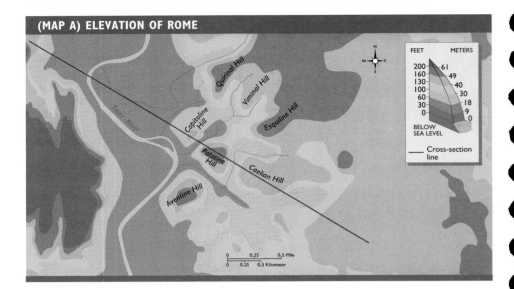

(MAP A) ELEVATION OF ROME

Reading Elevation Maps and Profiles

VOCABULARY
elevation
profile

WHY THE SKILL MATTERS

The geography of the region around Rome includes a variety of landforms, ranging from jutting hills to flat plains. You can see the height of such landforms on maps. Mapmakers show differences in the height of land in several ways. For example, the varying heights of Rome can be shown using an elevation map. Elevation means height above sea level. Elevation can also

be shown in another way. Mapmakers can take an imaginary slice of the land through a place such as Rome and make a profile map of the area. Profile means to view something from the side. Another term for *profile* is "cross section."

USING AN ELEVATION MAP

Study Map A. This is an elevation map of Rome and the region around it. According to the map key, elevation is measured in feet and in meters on the map. What color shows the highest elevation? What color shows the lowest elevation? Look for the part of the city with the lowest elevation. Notice that it is the area around the Tiber River, shown on the left of the map. According to the map key, the elevation here is almost at sea level. Notice that the seven hills of Rome are east of the river. One of the purposes of elevation maps is to show relative location—or, how one place in a region relates to another.*

* brown; purple

228

---

* about 170 feet
** Palatine Hill; about 40 meters

USING A PROFILE MAP

Now study Map B. This is a profile map of the same region. Find the Palatine hill on the map. This hill was where the richest people in ancient Rome lived. Based on the map key, how many feet high is this hill? Look at the height of the Palatine Hill as compared to the height of the Caelian (SEE lee un) Hill. You might find that it is often easier to see differences in elevation using a profile map like Map B. Because profile maps show only a "slice" of land, however, they do not show an area's relative location as well as elevation maps do.*

TRYING THE SKILL

Now try to find other information using the elevation map and the profile map. Refer to the Helping Yourself box if you need help answering questions.

In the last lesson you read that, according to the story about the founding of Rome,

HELPING Yourself

- **Elevation and profile** maps show the varying heights of a region.
- **You can see relative height more easily on a profile map. Elevation maps show relative location better.**

the twins Romulus and Remus were thrown into the flooded Tiber River. They were saved when they washed up on a hill. The story says the twins built the city of Rome on the spot where they were saved. Assuming that the twins washed up on the highest hill in Rome, which hill was it? How many meters higher is it than the land along the Tiber River? You can see this well on the profile map below. Find that same hill on the elevation map of Rome.**

REVIEWING THE SKILL

1. What facts about these maps let you know that they are elevation and profile maps?

2. What is the difference in elevation between the Aventine Hill and the Latium plain? How did you arrive at this answer?

3. When might it be helpful to be able to read elevation and profile maps?

(MAP B) ROME: A PROFILE

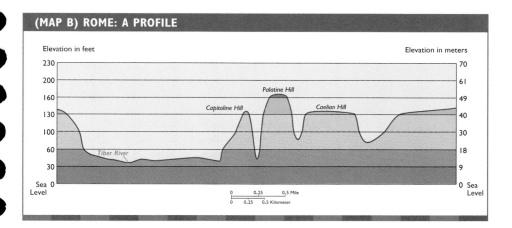

229

MEETING INDIVIDUAL NEEDS

RETEACHING (Easy) Have students write two brief statements, one saying what an elevation map can and cannot show and the other giving the same information about a profile.

EXTENSION (Average) Invite students to make up a terrain of their own that combines landforms of varying elevations, to which they assign names and elevations. Then have them draw a profile of their terrain that shows its varying elevations.

ENRICHMENT (Challenging) In encyclopedias, each entry for one of the U.S. states shows an elevation map for that state. Assign each student a different state and have him or her locate and trace on tracing paper an elevation map of it. Then have the student draw on the tracing paper a line across one part of the state to cross-section it and create a profile showing its varying elevations.

Understanding Using a Profile Map Have students examine Map B.

- **How many feet high is the Caelian Hill? How do you know?** (over 130 ft.; as shown on the axis at the left)

★THINKING FURTHER: *Compare and Contrast* **What advantages does the elevation map have over the profile? the profile over the elevation map?** (Elevation map: shows a broader area and more locations. Profile: makes it easier to measure relative elevations in cross-section.)

Trying the Skill Have students pose questions based on the maps for other students to answer.

★THINKING FURTHER: *Compare and Contrast* **Why does a profile map give a more precise measure of elevation than an elevation map?** (An elevation map gives a range—on it the Palatine Hill is from 160–200 ft. high. A profile shows where the height falls—on it the Palatine Hill is about 170 ft. high.)

 Technology CONNECTION

ADVENTURE TIME! CD-ROM
Enrich this Skills Lesson with the *Shading* map layer in *Build* on the *Adventure Time!* CD-ROM.

3 CLOSE

SUM IT UP

Invite students to make up a statement summarizing the relative strengths of elevation maps and profiles; for example, "Elevation maps for more relative locations; profiles for more precise measurements."

EVALUATE
✓ **Answers to Reviewing the Skill**

1. their titles, the elevation map's legend, the profile map's vertical axes showing heights

2. 130 feet; by subtracting the elevation of the plain (30 ft.) from that of the Aventine Hill (160 ft.)

3. in planning a climb, in determining how to use land, in building

LESSON 2

PAGES 230–235

Lesson Overview

As gifted organizers, the Romans established and strengthened a republic that stood on the brink of world empire.

Lesson Objectives

★ Define *republic* and describe how Rome's republic worked.

★ Analyze the cause-and-effect relationships of the *Punic Wars*.

1 PREPARE

MOTIVATE Have a student do the *Read Aloud*. Give the class time to discuss the questions it raises. Encourage students to arrive at a definition of "best" citizens. Ask who they think should govern.

SET PURPOSE Refer students to the *Read to Learn* question. Preview the *Vocabulary* and note the photo of Roman soldiers. Based on students' definition of who should govern, ask them for their ideal of government. Have them read the lesson to compare their ideal to Rome's government.

2 TEACH

Understanding THE BIG PICTURE
Help students to make a connection between growth and complexity in a community and the need for organized government.

● **What evidence can you find that Rome was growing and becoming more complex?** *(greater area settled, more trade, stone temples, rich/poor)*

★**THINKING FURTHER:** *Cause and Effect* **Why do you think such a community would need a well-organized government?** *(to maintain order and to provide a framework for people to understand their rights and duties in their city)*

Resource REMINDER

Practice and Project Book: *p. 49*

LESSON 2

509 B.C.	100 B.C.	A.D. 1	A.D. 250	A.D. 500

THE RISE OF THE ROMAN REPUBLIC

Focus Activity

READ TO LEARN
What kind of government did the Romans establish?

VOCABULARY
plebeian
patrician
republic
representative
Senate
tribune
consul
Twelve Tables
Punic Wars

PEOPLE
Livy
Hannibal
Scipio

PLACES
Forum
Carthage
Zama

230

READ ALOUD

The Roman leader Cicero declared that Rome should be governed by its "best" citizens. But just who were Rome's "best" citizens? Were they the city's small circle of nobles? Or did they also include the many other citizens, poor and rich, who contributed to life in Rome? The way Romans answered this question would shape their lives and ours.

THE BIG PICTURE

Almost 3,000 years ago, when the city of Anyang in China was losing power, Rome was only a cluster of mud huts on the hills overlooking the Tiber River. From the hilltops, farmers could enjoy a view of two small lakes that rippled in the valley below. The sound of lowing cattle drifted across the marshland at the river's edge.

By 509 B.C. Romans had overthrown their king, Tarquinius. They began setting up a new government in which citizens played a larger part. Their community became a city. A wooden bridge now crossed the Tiber River. The valley's marshland was drained and served as a busy market and meeting place.

High atop one of Rome's hills stood a stone temple as big as any in Greece. On other hilltops, fine brick homes housed Rome's wealthy. Some Romans clearly had become richer than others. The division between rich and poor, powerful and not so powerful, would affect the shape of the new government Romans were creating for themselves.

SHELTERED INSTRUCTION

READING STRATEGIES & LANGUAGE DEVELOPMENT

SEQUENCING Remind the class that the order in which events occur is their sequence. Review chronological order, time sequence. To help students review the lesson concept, have them create a time line that traces the rise of the Roman republic. Have students skim the section headings and subheadings to find key events, then add dates and brief descriptions as they read the chapter. [**SDAIE STRATEGY:** TEXT REPRESENTATION/SCHEMA BUILDING]

WORD ORIGINS By now the class has seen many examples of words with Greek roots. Point out that here, as they might expect, they will meet many words with Latin origins. Divide the class into seven groups and assign each group one of the first seven words in the *Vocabulary* list on this page. Have each group look up its word in the dictionary and report on its Latin origins to the class.

THE CITIZENS OF ROME

As in Greece, society in Rome was divided into two groups: those who were citizens and those who were not. At first, Rome had few slaves. The city did have many women, but none of them were citizens.

The body of citizens included two groups. Most Roman citizens were plebeians (plih BEE unz). Plebeians were men who farmed, traded, and made things for a living. The second group was made up of Rome's handful of patricians (puh TRISH unz). Patricians were members of Rome's noble families. They owned large farms and had plebeians work the land for them.

Plebeians Protest

After Rome's last king was overthrown in 509 B.C., the patricians took power. As they did this they remade the city's government. Only patricians could belong to a ruling assembly or become government leaders.

Rome's many plebeians reacted to the patricians' rules with protest. According to the Roman historian Livy,

A patrician woman had no voice in Rome's government.

plebeians rebelled in 494 B.C., demanding changes in the government. To calm them down, Livy wrote, the patricians sent a popular leader to speak with the plebeians. He told them this story. How do you suppose the plebeians reacted?

MANY VOICES
PRIMARY SOURCE

Excerpt from
Stories of Rome, Livy, 494 B.C.

*Once upon a time, the different parts of the human body were not all in agreement. . . . And it seemed very unfair to the other parts of the body that they should worry and sweat away to look after the belly. After all, the belly just sat there . . . doing nothing, enjoying all the nice things that came along. So they hatched a plot. The hands weren't going to take food to the mouth; even if they did, the mouth wasn't going to accept it. . . . They went into a **sulk** and waited for the belly to cry for help. But while they waited, one by one all the parts of the body got weaker and weaker. The moral of this story? The belly too has its job to do. It has to be fed, but it also does feeding of its own.*

───────────

sulk: to be in a bad mood and stay silent

A New Government

According to Livy both sides in time agreed to work together to improve Rome's government. The new government was called a republic, which means "public things" in Latin. Latin was the language of ancient Rome. In a republic citizens choose their leaders.

231

THE CITIZENS OF ROME

Have students compare Rome with Greece and note that both denied citizenship—thus a role in government—to women. Also help students recognize that *plebeians* far outnumbered *patricians.*

Discussing Plebeians Protest Note the succession of rule from king to patricians—neither offering democracy.

- *After the overthrow of the king, what group took over the power of government in Rome? (the patricians)*

- *Who disputed their right to govern? (the plebeians)*

★THINKING FURTHER: *Making Decisions If you were a Roman patrician, how would you deal with the plebeian protest? (Encourage students to consider the options— repression, strict orders, discussion, compromise—and the probable consequence of each option.)*

MANY VOICES

Discussing the PRIMARY SOURCE

Have a student read aloud the Livy excerpt.

- *Why did parts of the body hatch a conspiracy against the belly? (They believed that they did all the work while the belly just lived off them.)*

- *What lesson did they learn? (that the belly did do necessary work and that they depended on it as it did on them)*

★THINKING FURTHER: *Making Connections What message does this story deliver? (Everyone has something to contribute to society.)*

Understanding The Republic Discuss the meaning of *republic.*

- *What did the Romans create to work out a compromise between patricians and plebeians? (a republic, in which all citizens could take part)*

★THINKING FURTHER: *Predicting How do you think that such a compromise would strengthen Rome? (It would limit rebellion and widen opportunity.)*

FIELD TRIP

If you have a museum or college in your area with a section on ancient Rome, arrange a field trip there. Arrange for a staff member to conduct the class on a tour through it. If a trip is not possible, have students locate and present their own exhibit of pictures of Roman artifacts.

GLOBAL CONNECTION

GROUP DIVISIONS Explain to the class that the idea of divisions between social groups—for example, patricians and plebeians—would live on in Europe for centuries. For example, in England, it was the aristocrats and the common people. In France, society was divided into three groups, or estates. The clergy formed one, but the other two were divided as in Rome—the nobles made up the Second Estate and the much more numerous commoners made up the Third Estate.

GOVERNING THE REPUBLIC

Encourage students to work back and forth between the chart and text.

- **What role do representatives play in government?** *(They are elected by the citizens to act for the citizens.)*

- **How many branches did the Roman republic's government have?** *(three)*

- **What was the oldest and most powerful branch and who controlled it?** *(the Senate; the patricians)*

- **Over what areas of government did the Senate hold power?** *(over action toward other governments and over collecting and spending taxes.)*

★**THINKING FURTHER:** *Making Conclusions* **Why would control of money make the Senate the strongest branch?** *(Help the class recognize that government cannot run without money.)*

Discussing Power for the Plebeians Explore and evaluate the position of the plebeians in Rome's government.

- **What branch of government did the plebeians form?** *(citizen assembly)*

- **Who represented the plebeians?** *(the tribunes that the assembly elected)*

Learning about The Consuls Discuss the third branch of Rome's government.

- **What was the third branch of government?** *(the consuls)*

- **How did they gain power?** *(election by the citizen assembly)*

★**THINKING FURTHER:** *Making Conclusions* **What evidence tells you that consuls were powerful figures?** *(They commanded the army, served as judges, and proposed new laws.)*

More **CHART WORK**

★**THINKING FURTHER:** *Making Conclusions* **Why do you suppose the Romans wanted governing power spread out among three groups?** *(perhaps so that no one group would get too powerful)*

232

GOVERNING THE REPUBLIC

Unlike in the democracy of Athens, not all Roman citizens participated in the assembly that ran their city. Instead, they elected representatives, people who acted for them.

Does this sound familiar? The government of the United States is often called a republic. Citizens elect representatives who serve in Congress or in state legislatures. Unlike in the United States, however, not all the votes of Roman citizens were equal. In Rome the more powerful a man was, the greater influence his vote had.

Rome's republic lasted for nearly 500 years. During that time, three different government branches ran the city's affairs. Each of these branches had decision-making powers that allowed it to have some control over the actions of the other branches. What were the three branches?

The oldest and most powerful branch of the republic was the Senate. The Senate was controlled by Rome's patricians. Like the Senate of the United States, the Roman Senate determined how Rome would act toward other governments. It also had control of all the money collected and spent by the Roman Republic.

Power for the Plebeians

To make their voices heard in Rome, plebeians formed a citizen assembly. Beginning in 494 B.C., the citizen assembly elected tribunes (trih BYOONZ) who worked to gain rights for the plebeians of Rome. The tribunes were the leaders of the large citizen assembly.

The Consuls

Early tribunes worked to make sure plebeians got fair trials. They brought plebeian complaints before the Senate and the consuls. The consuls were the third branch of Rome's republic.

Each year the citizen assembly elected two men to become consuls. Consuls served as Rome's army commanders and the city's most powerful judges. They could order anyone to be arrested. The consuls could also propose new laws for Rome. The citizen assembly, however, could veto, or stop, any of the consuls' actions.

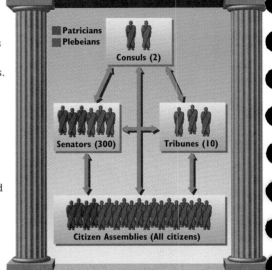

ROMAN GOVERNMENT ABOUT 287 B.C.

- ■ Patricians
- ■ Plebeians

Consuls (2)

Senators (300) Tribunes (10)

Citizen Assemblies (All citizens)

CHART WORK

Both patricians and plebeians had a role in the government of Rome.

1. Which citizens served as Rome's consuls?
2. How many citizens served as Senators?
3. In which parts of government could plebeians participate?

232 CHART WORK: **1.** both patricians and plebeians **2.** 300 **3.** all parts

---

CURRICULUM CONNECTION

LINKS TO LANGUAGE ARTS Point out to the class that American newspapers sometimes have the name "Tribune" in their title. Ask students why newspapers may have chosen this name. Help students evaluate the tensions between a newspaper's roles in acting on behalf of the rights of ordinary people and in being an objective reporter.

CITIZENSHIP★

UNDERSTANDING GOVERNMENT Explain to the class that the founders of our country wanted to guard against any group gaining too much power over government. Following Rome's lead, they divided governing power among three branches and designed a system of "checks and balances" so that each could limit the others. Have students make a chart of the three branches of the U.S. government.

Power in Rome was shared, if very unevenly, among the different branches of the republic. Study the chart to see how power was divided.

Plebeian Influence Grows

The citizens in the assembly often met to vote in a large field along the Tiber River. The field was also the headquarters of Rome's mostly plebeian army. Rome's patricians depended heavily on the army. In its early years Rome was constantly at war.

The plebeian army protected both the city of Rome and its patrician leaders. This role gave plebeians added power to change Rome's government in an important way.

For many years patrician leaders had ruled Rome according to laws that were unwritten. Only the patrician leaders had knowledge of those laws. As a result, plebeians had no way of knowing just what was and was not against the law. If brought to court, plebeians could only hope that the patrician judges would give them a fair trial.

About 450 B.C. the plebeians protested the unfairness of Rome's unwritten laws. Finally the patricians agreed to write a collection of laws on twelve wooden tablets, or tables. These became known as the Twelve Tables.

The Laws of the Republic

Historians today know little about what the Twelve Tables actually said. They do know, though, that the laws governed everything from marriage to slavery. Plebeians could not marry patricians. People who did not pay their debts could be made slaves. Like Hammurabi's Code in Babylon, the Twelve Tables were an important step in the development of written laws.

The Twelve Tables were posted in the city's crowded Forum. In the late 400s B.C. the Forum was a gravel clearing not much bigger than a soccer field. This clearing was the center of life in Rome. Here senators met and citizens pleaded their cases before judges. Women sometimes joined in the debates that took place there, hoping to influence those who could vote.

This painting shows a Roman trial by law. The Twelve Tables developed into a code of laws that influenced the laws of many future governments.

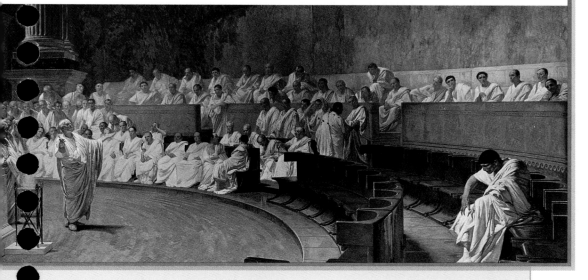

THE REPUBLIC EXPANDS

Use this material to help students see the path of empire-building: conquering neighbors→making enemies→frequent wars→unrest at home.

Discussing A Rival Across the Sea Use modern examples to discuss the rivalry.

- **Look at the map on this page. Why does it seem likely that Carthage and Rome would be enemies?** (Rome wanted land in the Mediterranean that Carthage controlled.)

- **Why are Rome's wars with Carthage called the Punic Wars?** (Carthage was originally a Phoenician colony and Punic came from the Latin word for Phoenicia.)

Following Hannibal's Plan Emphasize and discuss the daring of the plan.

- **Who was Hannibal?** (a general's son who sought to avenge Rome's conquests of Carthaginian lands)

★**THINKING FURTHER:** *Making Conclusions* **Why might he have been so dedicated to this cause?** (a promise to his father)

More MAP WORK

Refer students to the map. Have them trace Hannibal's route with their fingers.

- **Why did Hannibal choose a land route?** (Romans controlled the sea.)

- **What was his "secret weapon"?** (elephants, to scare the Romans)

- **What mountain range did he cross with his elephants?** (Alps)

★**THINKING FURTHER:** *Making Decisions* **How would you grade Hannibal on daring? sense? success or failure?** (Encourage open discussion.)

Discussing The Changing Republic Review the aftermath of Rome's victory.

★**THINKING FURTHER:** *Cause and Effect* **How would you describe cause and effect in the Punic Wars?** (Cause: Rome's thirst for land and power. Effect: a highly militarized, ambitious Rome more bent on conquering an empire abroad than maintaining republican rule at home.)

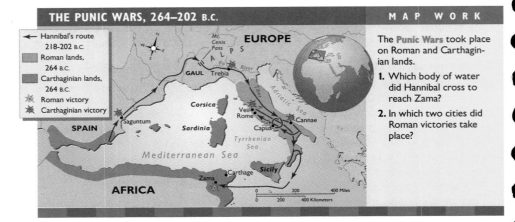

THE PUNIC WARS, 264–202 B.C.

← Hannibal's route 218–202 B.C.
Roman lands, 264 B.C.
Carthaginian lands, 264 B.C.
✶ Roman victory
✶ Carthaginian victory

EUROPE · GAUL · SPAIN · Saguntum · Corsica · Sardinia · Veii · Rome · Capua · Cannae · Tyrrhenian Sea · Adriatic Sea · Trebia · Mt. Cenis Pass · ALPS · Po River · Mediterranean Sea · Sicily · Zama · Carthage · AFRICA

0   200   400 Miles
0   200   400 Kilometers

MAP WORK

The **Punic Wars** took place on Roman and Carthaginian lands.

1. Which body of water did Hannibal cross to reach Zama?

2. In which two cities did Roman victories take place?

THE REPUBLIC EXPANDS

The Roman army moved out across the peninsula to conquer other areas. By 265 B.C. Rome controlled all of the Italian peninsula.

A Rival Across the Sea

In 264 B.C. Roman soldiers landed on the island of Sicily. Their arrival sparked a long conflict with the powerful empire of Carthage. Carthage was a city based in present-day Tunisia, on the northern coast of Africa. This city controlled much of the land around the western Mediterranean, including Sicily. Since Carthage had once been a colony of Phoenicia, Romans named their conflicts with that city the Punic Wars. *Punic* comes from the Latin word for Phoenicia.

In 241 B.C., after more than 20 years of fighting, Carthage surrendered control of Sicily to Rome. Rome then seized even more of the lands controlled by Carthage. The leaders of Carthage were outraged! One general asked his son Hannibal to seek revenge. In 218 B.C., when he was 29 years old, Hannibal led an army against the forces of Rome.

234

Hannibal's Plan

Hannibal came up with a daring plan. Since Rome's navy controlled the waters around Italy, he decided to attack by land. Hannibal marched from Spain to Rome with an army of about 90,000 men. He also brought elephants, which scared the Romans, who had never before seen these huge animals. In front of Hannibal, though, lay 1,000 miles of enemy territory.

More than 15 soldiers could ride atop one of Hannibal's elephants.

The Granger Collection

BACKGROUND INFORMATION

ABOUT HANNIBAL AND CARTHAGE

- Legend has it that Hannibal was only 10 when his father, Hamilcar, made him swear eternal hatred of Rome. Hamilcar had led troops against Rome in the first of the Punic Wars.

- Hannibal's early success against the Romans was phenomenal in the second of the Punic Wars. The sudden appearance of the Carthaginian force over the Alps took the Romans by surprise.

- For the next nearly 15 years, Hannibal outwitted and outfought the Romans on the Italian peninsula. He scored his soundest defeat of them at the battle of Cannae. (The strategy he used there has since become classic and was used in the Persian Gulf War in 1991.)

- Only the Roman attack on Carthage itself impelled Hannibal to leave Italy and return home, where he at last met defeat.

The army from Carthage actually carried out much of this plan, though thousands died along the way. Hannibal won major battles in Italy and caused great destruction there. Hannibal's success, however, did not win victory for Carthage. In Rome a 25-year-old general, Scipio (SIHP ee oh), was elected as consul. Scipio's large army defeated Hannibal outside Carthage in the Battle of Zama in 202 B.C. The defeat of Hannibal gave Rome control over Carthage's vast territory. Rome became the most powerful nation in the Mediterranean region.

The Changing Republic

All of these changes upset the workings of the republic. Patricians and plebeians struggled for government control. Slaves and conquered peoples revolted against their Roman leaders. Roman generals used their troops to take control of the government. By about 100 B.C. the republican government of Rome was fighting for its life.

WHY IT MATTERS

When the Roman republic was first set up, participation was limited to those who lived in and around the city. By 100 B.C., though, the republic was huge. It extended around the Mediterranean Sea and included millions of people.

The republic would not long survive. However, the ideas about how people could govern themselves—using a Senate, a people's assembly, and elected officials—would inspire the creators of the United States government over 2,000 years later.

Reviewing Facts and Ideas

MAIN IDEAS

• After about 509 B.C. Rome's citizens created a republic in which citizens elected leaders to run the government. Wealthy patrician citizens had more power than plebeian citizens.

• The republic of Rome was divided into three main branches—the Senate, the citizen assembly, and the consuls.

• Defeating Carthage in the Punic Wars made Rome the leading power in the Mediterranean region by 202 B.C.

THINK ABOUT IT

1. Describe the differences between patricians and plebeians.

2. Why was it important for Rome's laws to be written down?

3. FOCUS How did the struggle between the plebeians and patricians affect Roman government?

4. THINKING SKILL *Make conclusions* about the importance of the Punic Wars to Rome's history.

5. WRITE In a paragraph, explain the branches of Rome's republic.

235

LESSON 3

PAGES 236–243

Lesson Overview
Through military conquest and brilliant management, Rome built one of the greatest empires the world had ever known.

Lesson Objectives
★ Explain how Julius Caesar changed Roman government.

★ Define the Pax Romana.

★ Analyze how Rome built up and governed its empire.

1 PREPARE

MOTIVATE Have students read the *Read Aloud* and then discuss the quotation's meaning. Help them recognize that "brick" to "marble" is a way of saying from "simple" to "grand." Identify the photo as a statue of Augustus.

SET PURPOSE Write *Pax Romana* on the board and refer students to the *Read to Learn* question. Help them to work out the meaning of the term. (*Pax* means "Peace" and *Romana* means "Roman.") Preview the remaining *Vocabulary.* Encourage students to study the lesson to see how they fit together.

2 TEACH

Understanding THE BIG PICTURE
Help students place Rome in the world of its time.

★ **THINKING FURTHER:** *Making Connections* **Why do you suppose that a period of peace might also be a period of thriving trade among regions of the world?** *(Help students to recognize that when money does not need to be spent on war, it can go for trade goods. Also help them see that peace encourages freer travel because the world is a safer place.)*

Resource REMINDER

Practice and Project Book: *p. 50*

Anthology: The Aeneid, *pp. 49–50;* The Eruption of Mount Vesuvius, *p. 51*

Technology: *Adventure Time! CD-ROM*

Outline Map

500 B.C.	250 B.C.	100 B.C.	A.D. 14	A.D. 250	A.D. 500

THE ROMAN EMPIRE

READ ALOUD
"He found Rome built of brick and left it in marble." About 2,000 years ago, the biographer Suetonius (swih TOH nee us) wrote these words to describe how greatly Rome had changed under the leadership of one man. That leader was Augustus (aw GUS tus), the first Roman emperor.

Focus Activity

READ TO LEARN
What events led to the Pax Romana?

VOCABULARY
Pax Romana
civil war
dictator
aqueduct
census
gladiator

PEOPLE
Julius Caesar
Cleopatra
Augustus

PLACES
Gaul
Colosseum
Pantheon
Pompeii

THE BIG PICTURE
About 100 B.C. the leaders of the Han dynasty were ruling a unified China. Around the Mediterranean, meanwhile, the struggle for power in Rome grew. Patricians and plebeians each tried to win control for themselves. As problems in Rome increased, conquered peoples rebelled against their Roman governors.

By the century's end, though, a period known as the Pax Romana began. *Pax Romana* is Latin for "Roman peace." During the Pax Romana, which lasted about 200 years, goods moved freely within Rome's far-reaching borders. In Rome the people had bread to eat each day, thanks to shipments of North African wheat. They could cook in pots made from Spanish copper. Wealthy Romans ordered clothes made from Greek wool, Egyptian linen, or even Chinese silk! These goods were bought, along with pepper and pearls, by traders at markets in Asia. The Pax Romana benefited other nations, too, as Roman money and goods flowed in.

How did peace replace war in Rome? The story is a complex one. The story of Augustus and the building of a Roman empire actually begins with a leader who ruled before him.

236

SDAIE SUPPORT

SHELTERED INSTRUCTION

READING STRATEGIES & LANGUAGE DEVELOPMENT

CONTEXT CLUES Remind students that it is helpful to use context clues to figure out meanings of unfamiliar words and phrases. Explain that a clue can sometimes be a visual, such as a photograph or chart, as well as a synonym in the text. Then have students read the word *aqueduct* on p. 238 and find the synonym, *waterway.* Point out to students that they would not know the kind of waterway an aqueduct was unless they looked at the picture. **[SDAIE STRATEGY: CONTEXTUALIZATION]**

WORD FAMILIES Ask students what *colossal* means (of great size or degree). Remind them of the Colossus of Rhodes they read about on p. 217, "The Seven Wonders of the Ancient World," and refer them as well to the Colosseum, pictured on p. 241. Point out that all three terms have one "l" and a double "ss" and are related in meaning.

THE RULE OF CAESAR

Julius Caesar (JOOL yus SEE zur) was born into a patrician family in 100 B.C. As a boy, he dreamed of becoming a Senate leader, which he did. He also served as a commander in the army.

By 59 B.C. Caesar was elected consul of Rome. The following year he became the military governor of Gaul—which today is France. There he won fame, riches, and the loyalty of a great army. Caesar could now try for his biggest goal—total control of Rome.

Civil War

In 49 B.C. Caesar and his rebel army marched into Italy. Civil war, or war between groups within one country, began. This war spilled into Egypt. There Caesar joined forces with Cleopatra (klee uh PA truh). She was the 21-year-old ruler of the Egyptian government based in Alexandria. In Chapter 8 you read about this Greek city-state on the Nile Delta.

Caesar helped Cleopatra defeat her brother, the pharaoh of Egypt. She gave Caesar money he needed to continue fighting for control of Rome. In 45 B.C. Caesar returned in triumph to Rome and made himself dictator. A dictator is someone who rules with absolute power. Government under a dictator is called a dictatorship.

A New Government

As dictator, Julius Caesar made important changes to life in Rome. He changed the way people measured time—creating the basis for the calendar we still use today. In Julius's honor the month of his birth was named "July." Caesar also gave land to his soldiers and free grain to poor citizens. He increased the number of people who could serve in the Senate. Also, he granted Roman citizenship to many people not born in Rome.

Some senators hated Caesar for ruling as a dictator. They felt he was destroying the traditions of Rome's republican government. Some began plotting to kill him. According to legend, a friend warned Caesar to "Beware the Ides (ĪDZ) of March," which is March 15. Caesar ignored the warning. On that day in 44 B.C. he arrived at the Senate, as usual without a bodyguard. There he was stabbed to death by enemies. The senators who killed Caesar believed they had saved the republic from dictatorship.

Cleopatra (coin, above) supported Caesar before his murder (right).

237

GLOBAL CONNECTION

CAESAR'S DESCENDANTS? Explain to the class that since ancient times, other leaders have yearned to associate themselves with the memory of Caesar. Until World War I, the monarchs who ruled both Germany and Russia called themselves by names rooted in *Caesar*—the German *kaiser* and the Russian *czar* or *tsar*.

BACKGROUND INFORMATION

ABOUT ROMAN DATES Romans did not number the days of the month as we do. Instead, they had three important days of each month and counted backward and forward from these dates.
- The *calends* were the first day of the month.
- The *ides* were the middle of the month, usually the 13th or 15th.
- The *nones* were the ninth day before the ides.

THE RULE OF CAESAR

Help students define Julius Caesar's route to power.

★**THINKING FURTHER:** *Classifying* **On the basis of these two opening paragraphs, how would you classify the achievements of Julius Caesar?** *(Senate leader, army commander, consul, military governor, great general, amasser of wealth, seeker of greater power)*

Discussing Civil War Remind students of the U.S. Civil War and the grief it caused.

- **Why would Caesar's march on Rome bring on civil war?** *(Many Romans might not have wanted him to take control of Rome and so they fought him.)*

- **What bargain did he strike with Cleopatra?** *(He would help her overthrow her brother, the pharaoh, and she would support him financially in the civil war to control Rome.)*

- **How did Rome's civil war turn out?** *(Caesar won and took absolute power over Rome, becoming dictator.)*

★**THINKING FURTHER:** *Cause and Effect* **How did his action destroy Rome's republican government?** *(He seized for himself the ruling power formerly held by the three branches.)*

Examining A New Government Help students recognize that Julius Caesar did not simply assume power, but also made substantial changes in Rome.

- **What steps did Caesar take to make himself popular in Rome?** *(He gave away land and grain, enlarged the Senate, broadened citizenship.)*

- **How did he make himself unpopular with some Romans?** *(He gained the hatred of those who opposed his destruction of republican government.)*

★**THINKING FURTHER:** *Making Decisions* **If you had lived in Caesar's Rome, do you think you would have been pro-Caesar or anti-Caesar? Why?** *(Encourage any well-reasoned responses and pro-and-con discussion.)*

EMPEROR AUGUSTUS

Note that Julius Caesar's death did not restore Rome's republican government.

- **Why did civil war follow Caesar's death?** *(Different groups wanted to control Rome.)*

- **Who won this civil war?** *(Caesar's relative Octavian, known as Augustus)*

★**THINKING FURTHER:** *Making Conclusions* **Throughout his reign, Augustus tightly controlled the army. How might this have made him powerful?** *(He would have the means to put down wars or other threats.)*

Discussing Pax Romana Help the class to see that an empire must consolidate new lands to spread control over them.

- **How did Augustus take advantage of the Pax Romana to strengthen the Roman empire?** *(He united the empire by building infrastructure and giving it one system of government and money.)*

★**THINKING FURTHER:** *Compare and Contrast* **How would you compare and contrast the city of Rome pre-Augustus and post-Augustus?** *(His extensive public works beautified the city and improved its comforts with water, fire, and police protection, baths and theaters, and grand public buildings. But Rome also grew more cramped.)*

Discussing the PRIMARY SOURCE

Explain that Juvenal was a writer who made fun of his subject matter, often by using exaggeration, or hyperbole.

- **Who and what does he make fun of here?** *(the rich, the crowds, the military, his own situation)*

- **What exaggeration does he use?** *(everything hitting him, huge feet, being trampled to death)*

★**THINKING FURTHER:** *Making Conclusions* **Generally, there is a grain of truth in any amusing writing. What might be the grain of truth here?** *(Rome, with one million people, was crowded.)*

EMPEROR AUGUSTUS

After Caesar's death, civil war broke out once more as different groups fought for control. After 14 long years of fighting, the winner was Julius Caesar's grand-nephew and adopted son Octavian. He was just 18 years old when the fighting began. By 27 B.C. Octavian had defeated some of Rome's most experienced generals. These victories cleared the way for him to become dictator in all but name. As a sign of his new power, Octavian took the name Augustus, or "honored one." The month of August is named after this powerful ruler and general who helped to build Rome into a huge empire.

Pax Romana

Under Augustus, life throughout the Roman empire underwent great changes. Most important, his rule began the Pax Romana. During this period of peace Augustus ordered the building of new roads, buildings, and water systems. Like the emperors of China, Augustus also worked to create a single system of government and money throughout the empire.

Both the empire itself and the city of Rome now were bigger than ever. About one million people lived in the city of Rome. In the city's center the Forum now included large marble temples and government buildings. Nearby stood new theaters and public baths. New waterways called aqueducts (AK wuh duktz) were built to bring streams of fresh water into the city.

Thanks to Augustus, Romans now enjoyed police and fire protection. Even so, daily life had its unexpected dangers. Read this amusing description of Roman life. How did Rome's cramped quarters affect the way people lived?

MANY VOICES PRIMARY SOURCE

Excerpt from
Satires, by Juvenal, c. A.D. 100.

*To get to an urgent business call, the rich man travels by **litter** and the crowd has to give way as the huge contraption is hurried along over their heads—while inside he reads, or writes, or just sleeps. . . . We might get a move on but for the people in front blocking our way. . . . Someone digs me in the ribs with his elbow; someone else hits me with a **sedan-chair** pole. A **beam** catches me full in the face; someone else drops a barrel on my head. My legs are caked with mud and I'm trampled to death by huge feet and my toes are flattened by a soldier's hobnailed boot.*

---

litter: a covered couch used for carrying a single passenger
sedan-chair: a chair carried on poles by two people
beam: a long piece of heavy wood

CURRICULUM CONNECTION

LINKS TO MATHEMATICS Point out to the class that the reign of Augustus spanned B.C. and A.D.—he ruled from 27 B.C. until his death in A.D. 14. Have students work out the arithmetic to determine how long a reign this was. (They must add the 27 years of B.C. time to the 14 years of A.D. time to arrive at 41 years.)

SECOND-LANGUAGE SUPPORT

WORKING WITH A PEER Have second-language learners work with English-proficient partners to create questions about sections in the lesson. Encourage second-language learners to present their questions for the class to answer aloud.

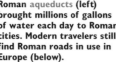

Roman aqueducts (left) brought millions of gallons of water each day to Roman cities. Modern travelers still find Roman roads in use in Europe (below).

Running an Empire

From Spain to Sparta, Alexandria to Jerusalem, people felt the pull of Rome through its laws. Laws were upheld by governors who also acted as judges.

The pull of Rome was even stronger through its taxes. Taxes paid by craft-workers and merchants helped to pay for the upkeep of the empire. Few people escaped paying. Every five years Rome took a census, or count, of people living in the empire.

Army units were posted far and wide to enforce Roman law, as well as to help build the empire's roads. Unlike the soldiers of the old Roman Republic, most soldiers of the Roman empire were not citizens. They were paid to serve in the army full-time. For many poor men, the army offered the best chance to earn a decent living.

"All Roads Lead to Rome"

Amid the crowds of people who filled the Forum each day stood a tall stone marker. Its size reflected its importance. It marked the start of all major roads leading out of Rome.

The Roman empire at its peak was crisscrossed by more than 50,000 miles of roads! Those roads—along with boats—helped to make communication, trade, and travel throughout the empire possible. Not all the roads led to Rome, of course. Many of the people and goods traveling along the stone pathways, however, either began or finished there. Rome acted like a giant magnet. Everyone in the empire felt its pull on their lives in one way or another.

Travel and Trade

One sign of the strength of the Roman government was safe travel. In the empire, the army made sure that bandits could not threaten citizens on land or sea. On the empire's roads, soldiers passed messengers carrying letters written on papyrus sheets. The Roman empire had a mail system similar to America's pony express. Every 8 miles riders would exchange their tired horses for fresh ones.

Merchants clattered along on ox-drawn carts, bringing goods like wine or dried fish to market. If their paths overlooked the sea, travelers probably saw merchant sailboats cutting through the blue waters. The cargoes might have included anything from Spanish silver to Egyptian linen.

239

Understanding "All Roads Lead to Rome" Reinforce the concept that for many people Rome really was the center of the world.

● **What was the purpose of the stone marker in the Forum?** (It marked the point at which many major roads out of Rome began.)

★**THINKING FURTHER:** *Making Conclusions* **Why would Roman rulers have placed the marker in the Forum?** (Students might suggest that the rulers wanted Romans to see the importance of their city as a hub.)

Learning about Running an Empire Help students see the complexity of ruling an empire.

★**THINKING FURTHER:** *Classifying* **If you had to name three things that Rome used to link its empire to itself, what would they be and how were they done?** (Possible answers: Roman law, by uniting people under a single system; Roman taxes, by demanding payment from all subject peoples; the Roman census, by counting its people; the Roman army, by enforcing obedience to the law and payment of taxes)

Discussing Travel and Trade Return to the benefits of good transportation and communication.

● **How did the Roman government make travel safe?** (with soldiers to keep order)

● **How did it improve communication?** (by creating a "pony express")

★**THINKING FURTHER:** *Making Conclusions* **How might safe travel contribute to prosperity?** (It could encourage trade, which enriches merchants and customers alike.)

CITIZENSHIP★

USING CURRENT EVENTS Explain that there has long been a debate over the role the U.S. government should play in the nation's transportation system.

● In the early 1800s, debate raged over whether the government should pay for building roads to connect the sections of the country. Many argued against it, saying that such "internal improvements" should not be made at public expense. Gradually, though, tax money did go into building national roads.

● In the middle 1800s, the government heavily supported the building of a railroad to link the nation from east to west.

● Today, debate rages over whether the government should have any role in maintaining the nation's railroad system. Have students research and discuss the use of public moneys for railroads.

Give students time to look through the lesson to examine the illustrations showing Roman building projects. If possible, have a picture book available to show both ruins of Roman structures and their images when first built.

- **Look at the aqueduct pictured on pp. 238–239. For what purpose was such a structure used?** *(to carry water from distant sources into cities)*

- **What evidence can you find that the Romans were interested in personal hygiene?** *(the public baths they built)*

- **What tells you about Roman tastes in entertainment?** *(Gladiators reflect the Roman taste for personal combat, chariot races for contests of speed.)*

- **Why was the Colosseum truly colossal?** *(It held 50,000 people and fake sea battles were staged there.)*

★**THINKING FURTHER:** *Making Conclusions* **How do the structures the Romans built show that they were brilliant engineers and lovers of beauty?** *(Help students recognize and appreciate the brilliance and beauty of the arch, the basis of much Roman construction. Students will learn more about arches and domes in the Legacy, pp. 244–245.)*

More MAP WORK

Have students identify the time period and the area covered in the map.

- **This map show the Roman empire. What is the date?** *(A.D. 14)*

- **How far east does it extend? south? west?** *(Greece, Judea and Syria; Egypt; Spain and Gaul)*

- **Locate Rome on the map. How is Rome like the hub of a wheel?** *(It is at the center of the lands it controls; roads and sea routes radiate from it.)*

★**THINKING FURTHER:** *Making Connections* **Why is it important for a capital to be well connected to the lands governed?** *(A government needs to know conditions within its borders and to spread directives to its parts. These require good transportation and communications.)*

VAST PROJECTS

The sheer size of the Roman empire united some of the world's most skilled craftworkers and engineers. They built beautiful—as well as useful—structures that reflected the empire's great wealth and power.

Throughout the empire Roman engineers built long aqueducts to bring fresh water to cities. Engineers spanned rivers with stone bridges to speed up the movement of soldiers and merchants. For cleanliness, engineers built public baths complete with heated floors. For entertainment, they created huge stadiums where gladiators fought animals, such as lions or bears, or each other—often

Crowds of Romans often filled the Colosseum seats (right) to watch the popular sport of chariot racing (below).

ROMAN EMPIRE, A.D. 14

ATLANTIC OCEAN
BRITAIN
EUROPE
Brigantium
GAUL
ALPS
ITALY
SPAIN
Rome
Pompeii
Sicily
Zama
Carthage
Black Sea
Adriatic Sea
GREECE
Athens
Sparta
Constantinople
ASIA
SYRIA
JUDEA
Jerusalem
Alexandria
Mediterranean Sea
AFRICA
EGYPT
Nile River

← Sea trade routes
Roman roads
Roman Empire

0   200   400 Miles
0 200 400 Kilometers

MAP WORK

The Roman empire extended through parts of Europe, Asia, and Africa.

1. How did traders from Alexandria reach Rome?

2. What sea did traders northeast of the Roman empire cross to reach Constantinople?

3. How might people north of the Alps have traveled to Rome?

240 MAP WORK: **1.** They sailed across the Mediterranean Sea. **2.** Black Sea **3.** by Roman roads

BACKGROUND INFORMATION

ABOUT AQUEDUCTS
- Water flowed through a concrete channel at the aqueduct's top.
- The arches could be one, two, or even three tiers high.
- Nine aqueducts brought water to Rome, supplying 200 million gallons per day to the one million inhabitants.

ABOUT GLADIATORS
- Most gladiators were either prisoners of war, slaves, or criminals who were forced to go to harsh gladiator schools to learn how to fight animals or one another.
- "Hail Emperor, those who are about to die salute you" were the solemn words gladiators had to recite as they filed past the emperor's box on their way to gladiatorial contests.

A Fabulous Temple

About a mile west of the Colosseum stood another Roman monument—the Pantheon. The Pantheon was just one of many temples in the city. It honored all the gods and goddesses of the Roman world.

By the time of the empire, Romans honored gods and goddesses from many parts of the world. They believed that these gods and goddesses had helped Rome to grow. For example, the Romans worshiped the major gods and goddesses of Greece, although they gave them Latin names. Many Romans also made sacrifices to Isis, the powerful goddess of Egypt, and Mithra, a Persian sun-god.

Large temples were also built to honor emperors like Augustus. Emperors of Rome were thought to become gods when they died.

to the death. Most of the gladiators were slaves. Some, however, were condemned criminals or prisoners of war. All were forced to fight in bloody contests of strength.

Many of these contests were held in the largest and most famous stadium in Rome, the Colosseum (kol uh SEE um), completed in 80 A.D. It held about 50,000 people. The Colosseum was so vast that fake sea battles were staged in it! Among the other contests that ancient Romans held in their stadiums were chariot races.

DID YOU KNOW?

How were Roman architects able to build large, lasting structures?

Roman architects mixed sand, lime, and pieces of stone and brick to make the very first cement. They used this material to bind stones and bricks into walls and foundations. Using its strength, the Romans built temples, bridges, and baths that still stand today.

Modern builders make cement in much the same way. They use it to build sidewalks, swimming pools, apartment buildings, and bridges. Perhaps some of these structures will last 2,000 years too.

241

Discussing A Fabulous Temple
Refer to the Pantheon pictured on p. 244.

- **What does the fact that the Romans built the Pantheon tell you about their religious beliefs?** (Romans believed in many gods and goddesses, and they honored them by building an impressive monument.)

- **What evidence of cultural borrowing can you find in the religious beliefs of the Romans?** (They borrowed gods and goddesses from the religions of Greece, Egypt, Persia, and elsewhere.)

- **How were Roman emperors treated in religious practice?** (They were recognized as gods when they died.)

★THINKING FURTHER: *Classifying*
What were some of the ways that the Romans added to the gods they worshiped? (Some ways include adopting gods and goddesses of lands Rome conquered, adding major gods of other countries, and turning emperors who had died into gods.)

Extending Did You Know Among the many extraordinary buildings that Roman architects created using cement were the Baths of Caracalla, public baths that covered 33 acres on the outskirts of Rome. Invite students to do research to learn more about this "city within a city" that will introduce them to bathing on an amazing scale.

BACKGROUND INFORMATION

ABOUT ROMAN MONUMENTS
- Rome might be called the first city with a mania for building monuments. At Rome's height, it had 10,000 statues, 700 public pools, 500 fountains, and 37 monumental gates.
- To celebrate the opening of the Colosseum in A.D. 80, chariot races were held there for 100 days straight.
- A short distance away was the even larger Circus Maximus, an oval race track 656 yards long and 95 yards wide surrounded by three tiers of seats. Here crowds five times the size of those at the Colosseum—over 250,000—could watch chariot races.

BACKGROUND INFORMATION

ABOUT CULTURAL BORROWING AND ROMAN RELIGION
The Roman writer Horace once summed up how much Roman culture borrowed from Greek culture when he wrote, "Captive Greece took Rome captive." Here are some of the Greek gods and goddesses the Romans borrowed. Greek names appear first and the Roman names for them second.

- Zeus=Jupiter
- Hestia=Vesta
- Hephaestus=Vulcan
- Athena=Minerva
- Artemis=Diana

- Hera=Juno
- Poseidon=Neptune
- Ares=Mars
- Aphrodite=Venus
- Hermes=Mercury

Infographic

Remind students of the "Iceman" found frozen in the Alps (Chapter 2). Though he lived 5,000 years ago, he was "frozen in time" by Alpine ice. Explain to them that volcanic ash had a similar effect on the ancient Roman city of Pompeii after the eruption of Mt. Vesuvius in A.D. 79. Much of the city of Pompeii was "frozen in time" and preserved as it had been in one moment of time centuries ago.

Discussing Daily Life in Pompeii

Have students find Pompeii on the map on p. 240 and have them trace its location in relation to the city of Rome. Point out that many wealthy citizens of Rome used Pompeii as a resort getaway from their crowded city. Give students a few minutes to read the text on this page and to examine the illustrations and their captions.

- **When did a volcanic eruption entomb Pompeii?** *(A.D. 79)*

- **What are examples of mosaics that the volcanic ash preserved?** *(the portrait of a wealthy woman and the "Beware of Dog" sign)*

- **How was the eruption able to preserve food from two millennia ago?** *(by preserving it in volcanic ash, thus keeping it from further decay)*

- **What clues to daily life does such evidence provide?** *(information about the Roman diet)*

- **What other clues to daily life did the volcanic ash provide?** *(The makeup kit gives evidence that then, as now, many women made up their faces.)*

★ **THINKING FURTHER:** *Making Conclusions* **Why is it fair to say that Pompeii is a treasure trove for archaeologists?** *(Students should see that it captures a moment in ancient time and gives archaeologists innumerable clues to how life was lived almost 2,000 years ago in ancient Rome.)*

Technology CONNECTION

ADVENTURE TIME! CD-ROM
Have students experience this *Infographic* on the *Adventure Time!* CD-ROM.

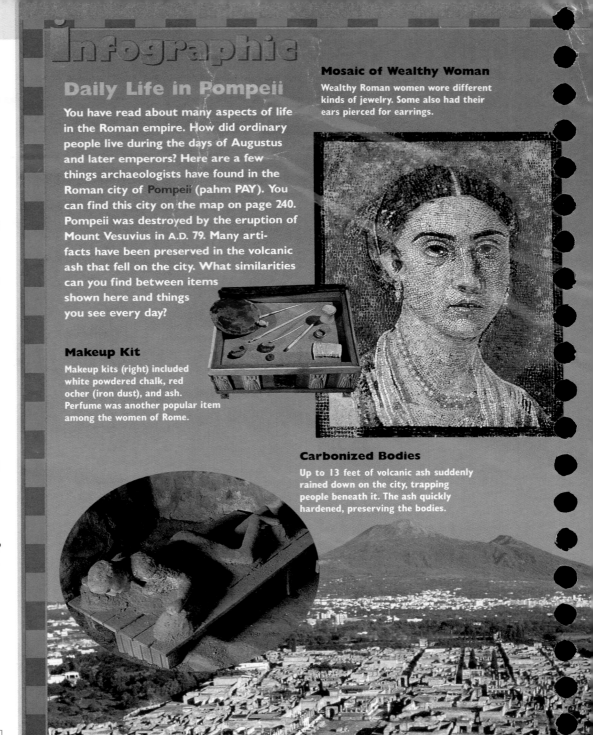

Infographic

Daily Life in Pompeii

You have read about many aspects of life in the Roman empire. How did ordinary people live during the days of Augustus and later emperors? Here are a few things archaeologists have found in the Roman city of Pompeii (pahm PAY). You can find this city on the map on page 240. Pompeii was destroyed by the eruption of Mount Vesuvius in A.D. 79. Many artifacts have been preserved in the volcanic ash that fell on the city. What similarities can you find between items shown here and things you see every day?

Mosaic of Wealthy Woman
Wealthy Roman women wore different kinds of jewelry. Some also had their ears pierced for earrings.

Makeup Kit
Makeup kits (right) included white powdered chalk, red ocher (iron dust), and ash. Perfume was another popular item among the women of Rome.

Carbonized Bodies
Up to 13 feet of volcanic ash suddenly rained down on the city, trapping people beneath it. The ash quickly hardened, preserving the bodies.

EXPANDING THE INFOGRAPHIC

RESEARCHING AND PRESENTING Divide the class into groups to research and report to the class on various aspects of Pompeii, for example, the volcanic history of Mt. Vesuvius before the A.D. 79 eruption, the timetable and spread of the actual eruption, how and when the long-forgotten buried city was rediscovered, and priceless art treasures found there. You might suggest the following sources for research:

- Encyclopedia entries under *Pompeii*.
- Library catalog entries under *Pompeii*. For example, Christopher Fagg's juvenile book *The Ancient Romans* offers good information.
- The *National Geographic* May 1984 article "The Dead Do Tell Tales at Vesuvius" is particularly useful, including the scientific section entitled "Two Days When Vesuvius Went Mad."

Serving Bowls
Partly eaten meals—here eggs and hazelnuts (left and below)—were among the items in Pompeii preserved in volcanic ash.

"Beware of Dog"
Guard dogs were sometimes kept chained to a door. Signs (above) warned would-be thieves not to enter.

WHY IT MATTERS

Under Julius Caesar, and later, Augustus, Roman citizens lost some of the political rights they had once enjoyed. Yet under Augustus, Rome was also more peaceful than it had been for many years. Before his death in A.D. 14, Augustus also had made many improvements in daily life.

Around this time in a dusty town not far from Jerusalem another important development began that would affect the entire world. You will read about it in the next lesson.

✔️ Reviewing Facts and Ideas

MAIN IDEAS

- Julius Caesar became dictator of Rome in 45 B.C. He was killed by senators opposed to his rule on the Ides of March in 44 B.C.

- Under Augustus, around 27 B.C., the Roman empire began a 200-year period of peace and active trade called the Pax Romana.

- Roman religion shared many similarities with that of ancient Greece. Romans also worshiped Egyptian and Persian gods and goddesses.

THINK ABOUT IT

1. What happened to the republican government of Rome when Julius Caesar took control?

2. What did Roman religion have in common with that of ancient Greece?

3. **FOCUS** How did life in Rome change during the Pax Romana?

4. **THINKING SKILL** What *effects* did Augustus's rule have on life throughout the Mediterranean?

5. **GEOGRAPHY** Why were roads a major lifeline for the Roman empire?

243

Discussing WHY IT MATTERS Review this lesson and prepare students for the *Legacy*, which follows.

> ★**THINKING FURTHER:** *Compare and Contrast* **How would you say that Roman citizens were better off under Caesar and, later, Augustus than they had been under the republic? How would you say they were worse off?** *(They had more political rights under the republic, but they had greater wealth and power as a nation under Caesar and Augustus.)*

⭐ 3 CLOSE

MAIN IDEAS
Call on students to answer the questions orally.

- *How did Julius Caesar change Roman government and what happened to him as a result?* (He overthrew the republic and became dictator, which led to his assassination in 44 B.C.)

- *How did the Romans borrow from other religions?* (They borrowed gods and goddesses from Greece, Egypt, and Persia.)

EVALUATE
✔ **Answers to Think About It**

1. It was replaced by Caesar's dictatorship.
Confirm Predictions

2. many gods and goddesses
Make Analogies

3. It became more crowded, but it also had more public services and grander buildings.
Form Generalizations

4. It brought the whole area under Roman rule, meaning Roman law, taxes, army, and trade.
Cause and Effect

5. As the center of government for a vast empire, Rome had to have ready access to lands near and far. Roads gave it this access.
Five Themes of Geography Movement

Write About It Picture yourself as a citizen of Greece. Write a paragraph in which you describe changes that Greece's capture by Rome has made in your life.

MEETING INDIVIDUAL NEEDS

RETEACHING (Easy) Tell students to picture themselves having been sent back in time to the imperial city of Rome. Have them draw a scene that they might have witnessed there.

EXTENSION (Average) Tell the class that one historian has written that "Rome became the most spectacular tourist attraction of the ancient world." Have students write out a descriptive itinerary of at least four places to visit in ancient Rome.

ENRICHMENT (Challenging) There are several books for young people that describe daily life in ancient Rome. Divide the class into groups and assign each group one of the following: home life, education, work, food, entertainment, public services. Have each group research their subject and prepare a presentation of their findings for the class.

Lesson Overview
Roman engineers were among the most brilliant and practical ever.

Lesson Objective
★ Appreciate the legacy that Roman engineering left to the world.

1 PREPARE

MOTIVATE Mention some structures in your area that show the influence of Roman architecture, perhaps some domed government building or a domed church. Help students to note how pleasing to the eye such structures are and also how much engineering know-how went into building such a weighty, sturdy, graceful structure.

SET PURPOSE Explain to the class that much of Roman architecture was based on the arch and the dome, two construction methods that Roman engineering brought to perfection. Tell students to read the column of text on this page to explore these two methods.

2 TEACH

Understanding the Concept of a Legacy Have students draw examples of the arch and the dome on the board. Then have them name familiar places that use these legacies from Rome.

Legacy
LINKING PAST AND PRESENT

DOMES & ARCHES

How would you begin to build something? You might first look at how similar things have been built by others. That is how the ancient Romans began when they built houses, temples, and public buildings. They learned the building techniques used by other civilizations, such as the Egyptian and the Greek. Then they developed some new techniques.

Romans used arches in many of their building projects. An arch is a curved structure used as a building support.

Learning how to use arches helped Roman engineers develop a new structure. This was the dome. A dome is a curved roof that looks like a bowl turned upside down. A dome can cover a huge space without any supports.

Roman engineering is a legacy that can be seen throughout the world. Look around you to see domes and arches.

You have already read that ancient Romans worshiped the gods and goddesses represented at the Pantheon. The Pantheon is a temple with one of the largest domes ever built.

244

The famous Pont du Gard was built by the Romans in France. Arches help support it. The structure was once used as an aqueduct. Water flowed through a channel along the top which gradually sloped downward.

The large area covered by the Houston Astrodome (above) can seat 70,000 people—with no supports other than itself! The United States Capitol (left) has both arches and a dome.

245

Examining the Pictures Give students a few minutes to examine the pictures and their captions.

● *As you look at the picture of the Pantheon in Rome, what reflects a Greek influence on Roman architecture?* (the columns with Corinthian upper sections)

● *How would you compare the dome on the Capitol in Washington, D.C., with the dome on the Pantheon?* (Help students note that while domes are the same basic shape, they can be deeper or shallower. The dome on the Pantheon is more gently curved than that of the Capitol.)

● *How did the Romans use arches for both support and decor on the Pont du Gard?* (Help students note the use of two tiers of large arches to span the gorge. To further reinforce the skill of Roman engineers, explain that each block of stone here weighs up to two tons and that they are put together without the use of cement.)

★**THINKING FURTHER:** *Making Connections* **What might the engineers who built the Houston Astrodome in Texas have had in common with the engineers who built the Colosseum in Rome?** (Each group built a large stadium for entertainment. The engineers in Texas borrowed ideas about building circular structures from the Roman engineers.)

3 CLOSE

SUM IT UP
Encourage students to summarize ways that Roman engineering—its design ideas and technology—has enriched life since Roman times. Students should recognize both the practical and aesthetic contributions.

EVALUATE
Write About It Have students choose one of the structures pictured in this *Legacy* and write a paragraph explaining how Roman engineering made it possible.

MEETING INDIVIDUAL NEEDS

RETEACHING (Easy) Have students use cardboard, scissors, and clear tape to cut out and construct their own aqueducts.

EXTENSION (Average) As a class project, have students organize a bulletin board display entitled "Influences of Roman Engineering in Our Area." Help them to recognize examples of Roman influences in your area—bridges and churches, for example. Then have students photograph and/or draw the structures and arrange their depictions on the bulletin board.

ENRICHMENT (Challenging) Explain to the class that the most modern domed structures, like the Houston Astrodome, owe a debt not just to the Romans but to R. Buckminster Fuller, designer of what is called the geodesic dome. Have them research his work on this development and write a report of their findings.

LESSON 4

PAGES 246–251

Lesson Overview

From its beginnings as a small sect in Judea, *Christianity* gradually spread through the Roman empire and became one of the world's major religions.

Lesson Objectives

★ Explain how Christianity developed.

★ Identify major beliefs of Christianity.

★ Describe the spread of Christianity.

1 PREPARE

MOTIVATE Have two students rehearse the *Read Aloud* and read it to the class. Invite students to identify the "babe wrapped in swaddling clothes" (Jesus, from whose teachings Christianity arose) and the significance of the birth.

SET PURPOSE Refer the class to the *Read to Learn* question to verify their identification of Jesus, shown in the painting on this page. Discuss how these teachings differed from those of other religions they studied. Encourage students to read the lesson to find out. Have them preview the *Vocabulary*.

2 TEACH

Understanding THE BIG PICTURE
Have the class briefly review what they learned about Judaism in Chapter 5.

● **How does the New Testament differ from the Old Testament?** *(The New Testament: the story of Christianity; Old Testament, or Hebrew Bible: the story of Judaism)*

★**THINKING FURTHER:** *Making Connections* **You may have heard of "the Judeo-Christian tradition." Why can it be said that the Bible is a Judeo-Christian book?** *(Books of the Old Testament are shared by Jews and Christians.)*

Resource REMINDER

Practice and Project Book: *p. 51*
Anthology: *A Craftsman in Bethlehem, pp. 52–53*

BEGINNINGS OF CHRISTIANITY

Focus Activity

READ TO LEARN
What did Jesus teach?

VOCABULARY
Christianity
New Testament
Messiah
parable
apostle
bishop
pope

PEOPLE
Jesus
Peter
Paul

PLACES
Judea
Bethlehem
Nazareth

READ ALOUD

"Fear not; for, behold, I bring you good news of great joy . . . for to you is born in the city of David a Savior, who is Christ the Lord. And this will be a sign for you; you will find the babe wrapped in swaddling clothes, lying in a manger."

These words, taken from the writings of an important new religion, announce the birth of a child in the Roman empire. Despite his humble birth, this child grew up to change the world.

THE BIG PICTURE

During the rule of Augustus, Rome increased its control over Judea, the region that once had been known as Canaan. You read in Chapter 5 that many Jews had been exiled from this land and brought to ancient Babylon. Many descendants had by now returned from their exile to rebuild their towns and cities. In Jerusalem they built a new temple that stood on the remains of the one that had been destroyed long ago. Elsewhere, towering aqueducts stood as reminders of the newer, Roman rule.

Into this world a new religion, Christianity, was born. The story of its birth is told in a collection of books called the New Testament. The Hebrew Bible, which you read about in Chapter 5, came to be called the Old Testament by followers of Christianity. Together, the Old and New Testaments formed their Bible. Its words are sacred to nearly 2 billion Christians living in the world today.

246

SHELTERED INSTRUCTION

READING STRATEGIES & LANGUAGE DEVELOPMENT

REREADING Review the importance of rereading passages containing new material. Explain that to clarify confusing passages it helps to form a question based on text subtitles. Use a Think-Aloud to model the process. Read the subtitle "Jesus' Childhood" on p. 247 and form the question, "What were key events in Jesus' childhood?" Then read the passage aloud, answering the question as you go. Reread confusing sentences. **[SDAIE STRATEGY: MODELING/METACOGNITIVE DEVELOPMENT]**

APOSTROPHES IN POSSESSIVES Refer the class again to the *Jesus' Childhood* section. Point out that this is one of the exceptions to using 's to form the possessive of names ending in *s* as explained in *Language Development* on p. 174.

THE LIFE OF JESUS

One book of the New Testament begins with an important order from Emperor Augustus that a census be taken throughout the entire empire. Augustus's order meant that all the people in the empire had to return to the towns where they were born so that they could be counted. So a Jewish carpenter named Joseph and his wife Mary set out for Bethlehem (BETH luh hem), a small town south of Jerusalem. Find Bethlehem on the map on this page. While there, the Bible says, Mary gave birth to a son, Jesus.

Jesus' Childhood

The New Testament says little about Jesus' childhood. Jesus and his family lived in Nazareth (NAZ ur uth), a tiny village in the northern hills of Judea. The New Testament does say, though, that as a boy Jesus learned a great deal about the teachings of Judaism. According to the Bible, that became clear when Jesus was 12 years old and he went to Jerusalem with his parents. They went to celebrate the Passover festival there.

When the festival was ended and they started to return, the boy Jesus stayed behind in Jerusalem, but his parents did not know it. . . . When they did not find him, they returned to Jerusalem to search for him. After three days they found him in the temple, sitting among the teachers, listening to them and asking them questions. And all who heard him were amazed at his understanding and his answers.

This passage would by no means be the last one in which the New Testament describes how Jesus amazed those around him.

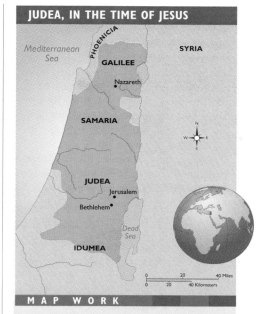

JUDEA, IN THE TIME OF JESUS

Mediterranean Sea
PHOENICIA
SYRIA
GALILEE
Nazareth
SAMARIA
JUDEA
Jerusalem
Bethlehem
Dead Sea
IDUMEA

0   20   40 Miles
0   20   40 Kilometers

MAP WORK

Jesus lived in Nazareth, in northern Judea.

1. Which is farther east—Jerusalem or Bethlehem?

2. About how many miles from Jerusalem is Nazareth?

From the age of 30 on, the Bible says, Jesus spent much of his time teaching crowds of people. Many came to hear him, the Bible says, because he healed sick people and performed many other miracles.

According to Jewish belief, the Messiah is a special leader to be sent by God in order to guide the Jewish people and to set up God's rule on Earth. The word *Messiah* in Greek is *Christos*. In time the followers of Jesus came to believe that he was the Messiah, or Christos. The people who followed Jesus became known as Christians. Their religion soon became known as Christianity.

247

THE LIFE OF JESUS

Refer students to p. 239 and have them find the vocabulary term census.

- *Why do you suppose the Romans demanded a census every five years?* (probably to keep track of people in the empire to tax them)

- *What did Mary and Joseph have to do to obey the order for a census?* (travel to Bethlehem to be counted)

- *What major event took place there?* (the birth of Jesus)

More MAP WORK

Refer students to the map on this page.

- *Where does Bethlehem lie in relation to Jerusalem?* (a short distance to the south)

- *About how long a journey did Mary and Joseph make from Nazareth to Bethlehem?* (about 60 miles)

- ★**THINKING FURTHER:** *Making Conclusions Why might this have been a difficult journey?* (In those days, both the length of the journey and modes of transportation would have made it difficult.)

Discussing Jesus' Childhood Note the Judaic roots of Jesus' training.

- *Where did Jesus grow up?* (Nazareth)

- *What evidence can you find that Jesus was a good student of Judaism?* (the knowledge he displayed in the temple)

- *At what age did he begin teaching?* (30)

- *In Jewish belief, who is the Messiah?* (a special leader sent by God to guide the Jews to God's rule on Earth)

★**THINKING FURTHER:** *Making Conclusions Why, even when Jesus was a child, were people impressed by his abilities? Do you find these abilities impressive?* (He had the ability to listen to people, and he asked questions that amazed people. Answers will vary; encourage students to understand that the questions Jesus asked probably were unusually searching and sophisticated for a boy his age.)

CITIZENSHIP★

UNDERSTANDING GOVERNMENT Ask students whether they know if the U.S. government takes a census of its citizens. Call for volunteers to form a census research team to gather information about the United States Census—how often it is taken, what agency of the government takes it, what kinds of questions it asks of people, and what uses are made of information gathered. Have the team prepare a presentation of their findings for the class. If possible, have them include an actual census form to pass around for the class to examine.

USING THE ANTHOLOGY

A CRAFTSMAN IN BETHLEHEM, pages 52–53 Use the anthology selection to help students see how events that took place 2,000 years ago affect the daily life of one man in 20th-century Bethlehem.

THE TEACHINGS OF JESUS

Remind the class that Judaism was the faith in which Jesus was raised and have them review its major teachings (belief in and honoring of one God, obedience to the Ten Commandments).

● **Why might a parable be a good way to teach a lesson?** *(Stories capture people's interest, so they are likely to learn from them.)*

★**THINKING FURTHER: Compare and Contrast How do these lessons reflect the teachings of the Ten Commandments?** *(They reflect a person's relation to God and how to do right by other people.)*

Discussing the PRIMARY SOURCE

Read the excerpt aloud to the class.

● **What do we call the final teaching given here? Where have you seen it before?** *(Help students to recall that the Golden Rule appears in Confucius's teachings.)*

★**THINKING FURTHER:** *Making Generalizations* **What generalizations can you make about the teachings given here?** *(very loving, giving, meek, and self-denying)*

Discussing the Twelve Apostles
Help students understand the *apostles'* role.

● **Who were the apostles?** *(Jesus' 12 closest followers)*

★**THINKING FURTHER:** *Making Conclusions* **Why were the apostles vital to Christianity?** *(They spread its teachings.)*

THE TEACHINGS OF JESUS

The New Testament states that Jesus often used **parables**, or simple stories that contain a message or truth. Some of these stories taught the value of seeking the right path in life. Others described the greatness of God's love for all people. Still others stressed the importance of loving other people. Many of Jesus' parables are recorded in the New Testament. How does Jesus describe love in this passage?

Excerpt from the Gospel of Luke, New Testament, c. A.D. 90

I say to you that listen, love your enemies, do good to those who hate you, bless those who curse you, pray for those who abuse you. If anyone strikes you on the cheek, offer the other also; and from anyone who takes away your coat do not withhold even your shirt. Give to everyone who begs from you; and if anyone takes away your goods, do not ask for them again. Do to others as you would have them do to you.

In the Sermon on the Mount, Jesus revealed many of his most important teachings.

248

Twelve Apostles

Jesus' closest followers were called **apostles** (uh PAHS ulz). The apostles were 12 men Jesus had chosen to help him in his teaching. The Bible says they came from all walks of life. One of the apostles, **Peter**, had fished for a living before joining Jesus. Another, Levi, had been a tax collector for Rome. The Bible tells us that the apostles had little in common before they met Jesus. It goes on to say, however, that they became united through Jesus' teachings. The apostles helped to spread Jesus' teachings after he died.

A Growing Following

The New Testament says that while he taught, Jesus also cured many people of illnesses. Both Jews and non-Jews benefited from these miracles, the Bible says. As a result, the number of Jesus' followers grew. The New Testament states that a prophet called John the Baptist sent people to ask Jesus if he was the Messiah the Jews were

Christian church services (left) honor Jesus' life and teachings. Leonardo da Vinci's *The Last Supper* (above) shows Jesus' final meal with the twelve apostles.

waiting for. The Bible says Jesus answered:

Go and tell John what you hear and see: the blind receive their sight, the lame walk . . . , the deaf hear, the dead are raised, and the poor have good news brought to them.

Jesus' answer was made up of quotes from the Hebrew Bible.

Trouble with Rome

Jesus' growing popularity troubled many people. Some of them were afraid that he wanted to be a king and was going to set up a new kingdom in Judez. These beliefs added to the fears of the Roman governors that talk of revolt was spreading throughout Judea.

When crowds jammed the streets of Jerusalem to celebrate the Passover festival, soldiers moved in on Jesus to arrest him. After questioning Jesus, a Roman governor sentenced him to die by crucifixion (kroo suh FIK shun). The word *crucifixion* means "putting to death by hanging from a cross." Roman leaders throughout the empire commonly used crucifixion to punish slaves, rebel leaders, and others regarded as criminals.

According to the New Testament, Jesus may have been in his thirties when he died. The Bible also tells us that Jesus rose from the dead three days after he was crucified. Then he rejoined his apostles and told them again about the coming kingdom of God. Afterwards, the Bible says, Jesus rose to heaven. Today Christians try to follow Jesus' teachings and to celebrate his renewed life and message of hope on Easter Sunday.

249

Discussing A Growing Following

Have students look up *miracle* in the dictionary. Help them to see that not only are miracles extraordinary events but they are also thought to come from a divine source—from God.

● **Why would performing miracles draw followers to Jesus?** *(People must have thought he had Godlike powers; perhaps they hoped for their own miracles.)*

> ★THINKING FURTHER: *Making Conclusions* **Why did many people consider Jesus the Messiah?** *(He was believed to have worked miracles that only a Messiah could work.)*

Exploring Trouble with Rome

Identify the reasons for the trouble.

● **Why did Rome come to fear Jesus?** *(Roman governors feared he would become popular enough to lead a rebellion in Judea.)*

● **How did they deal with the threat they thought he posed?** *(They sentenced him to death by crucifixion.)*

● **How did Jesus' death offer hope to his followers?** *(His rising from the dead offered them hope that death was not the end of life. Remind students that the quest for immortality goes back at least to Gilgamesh.)*

> ★THINKING FURTHER: *Making Conclusions* **Why has the cross become a major symbol of Christianity?** *(It symbolizes Jesus' crucifixion.)*

VISUAL LITERACY

ABOUT THE PAINTING THE LAST SUPPER

The Last Supper is a mural painting by Leonardo da Vinci (1452–1519). The painting shows the events of The Last Supper according to the Bible. Christ has just spoken the words, "One of you shall betray me," and the disciples are asking, "Lord, is it I?" In this moment each apostle reveals his own personality and relationship with Christ. Leonardo da Vinci wrote that the highest aim in painting is to show "the intention of man's soul." Invite students to study the painting. Possible questions include: Where does the painting show things that are very far away? (Answer: through the far windows) How has the painter made the central figure stand out?

BACKGROUND INFORMATION

ABOUT UNREST IN JUDEA

● By the 60s B.C., Judea had become a Roman province. The Romans allowed Jewish kings—the Herods—to rule there under Roman direction, but these kings were unpopular with the people.

● During the 1st century B.C., Judea became a hotbed of unrest. The people yearned for someone—a Messiah—to deliver them from Roman rule. They hoped another King David would appear to free them.

● No deliverer appeared, so from A.D. 66–70, the Jews staged a full-scale revolt against the Romans. The bitter conclusion was a Roman sacking of Jerusalem and destruction of the Second Temple there.

THE SPREAD OF CHRISTIANITY

Help students to recognize how astounding the spread of Christianity was, considering the brevity of Jesus' public life and the fact that Jesus had been nothing more than a minor political rebel to the powerful Romans.

Discussing A Christian Church
Explore the beginnings of the Christian Church.

★THINKING FURTHER: *Classifying*
How would you classify (1) the advantages the Christians had in spreading their new religion and (2) the obstacles they faced?
(Advantages: strong faith, strong will to set up churches all over, a message of love and hope, an appeal to all ranks, a sense of equality, having a champion like Paul to defend their beliefs. Obstacles: Roman anger that the Christians refused to worship the emperor; perhaps the opposition of a polytheistic Roman religion to monotheistic Christianity.)

Investigating Christianity in Rome Discuss Paul and Peter.

● ***Why was Paul well equipped to spread Christianity to Rome and elsewhere?*** *(He was well educated, a good debater, and a firm believer.)*

● ***What did Peter and Paul accomplish in Rome?*** *(They laid the foundation for the Christian church there and made Rome's Christian community the largest in the Roman empire.)*

● ***What important church office was Peter the first to fill?*** *(He became bishop of Rome—the first pope.)*

★THINKING FURTHER: *Making Conclusions* ***Why do you suppose Peter and Paul thought it was so important to establish a strong Christian base in Rome if they were to spread the Christian faith?*** *(As capital of the Roman empire, Rome would be a central location and natural headquarters from which to propagate and run the new religion throughout the empire.)*

THE SPREAD OF CHRISTIANITY

The New Testament does not end with the story of Jesus' ascent, or rise, into heaven. It goes on to tell how Christianity spread throughout the Roman world. Leading the growth of Christianity were the apostles of Jesus.

A Christian Church

The New Testament says that after the death of Jesus, Christians scattered to cities throughout the Roman empire. There they set up dozens of Christian churches. Soon these churches drew the attention of Roman leaders. Some Roman rulers were angry at the Christians for refusing to worship the emperor. Still, the new religion continued to grow and attract followers.

According to the New Testament, the new churches included people from all ranks in life. These included the Roman commander Cornelius, the cloth merchant Lydia, and the slave Onesimus.

A church leader named Paul reminded them that

There is no longer Jew or Greek, . . . slave or free, . . . male or female; for all of you are one in Christ Jesus.

Paul was not one of the first 12 apostles. Unlike the earliest followers of Jesus, Paul grew up in a big city, Tarsus, in what is today Turkey. Paul was well educated in both the Hebrew Bible and Greek classics. At first he was against Christianity, but later he became a Christian himself. Paul spoke in many different cities about Christianity. The New Testament says he debated with Jewish teachers in Jerusalem and with philosophers in the streets of Athens. Paul, together with other Christians, spread Christianity throughout the Roman world.

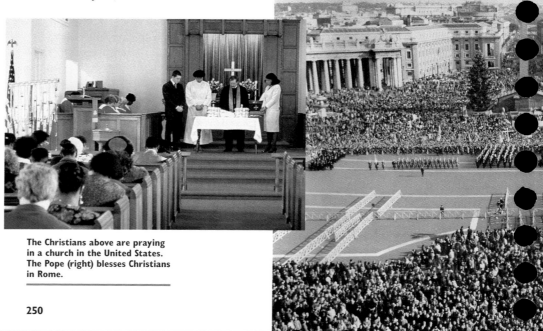

The Christians above are praying in a church in the United States. The Pope (right) blesses Christians in Rome.

250

Christianity in Rome

Early church historians wrote that the apostle Peter helped bring Christianity to Rome's crowded neighborhoods. Before they died, Peter and Paul helped build the framework that would make Rome's Christian community the largest in the empire. Christians call Peter the first bishop, or regional church leader, of Rome. Later, Christians would give the bishop of Rome the title pope—from the Latin word for "father." The pope today is the leader of a branch of Christianity known as Roman Catholicism.

As time passed, Christians were tortured and killed by the Roman government. Despite increasing violence against Christians, Christianity continued to flourish in Rome and elsewhere. Both rich and poor continued to be drawn to Jesus' message of love and hope.

WHY IT MATTERS

One of the most powerful supporters of Christianity was a man who became emperor of Rome. You will read about this man and the effects of his actions in the next lesson.

Since its beginnings in the hills of Judea and its spread throughout the Roman empire, Christianity has become one of the world's major religions. In chapters to come you will read about how Christianity has affected life on every continent on Earth.

✓/// Reviewing Facts and Ideas

MAIN IDEAS

- Christianity developed in Roman-occupied Judea during the Pax Romana.
- The life and teachings of Jesus are recorded in the New Testament of the Christian Bible.
- The New Testament says that the followers of Jesus believed that he was the Messiah.
- Two of Jesus' followers, Peter and Paul, helped to spread Christianity throughout the Roman world.

THINK ABOUT IT

1. Why, according to the New Testament, was Jesus born in Bethlehem?
2. Why were the followers of Jesus called *Christians*?
3. **FOCUS** How were Jesus' teachings rooted in Judaism?
4. **THINKING SKILL** *Make a conclusion* about the importance of the Apostles to the spread of Christianity.
5. **GEOGRAPHY** What role did the Roman empire play in the movement of Christianity throughout the ancient Mediterranean world?

251

Discussing WHY IT MATTERS Relate the lesson to Christianity today.

> ★**THINKING FURTHER: *Predicting***
> ***In what ways do you predict that Christianity will affect life in the years and centuries following the period covered in this lesson?*** *(Predictions will probably deal with the continuing and broad spread of the teachings of Jesus and their becoming a model for living for millions of people on Earth.)*

★ 3 CLOSE

MAIN IDEAS

Have students write their answers on paper and then exchange papers to verify the answers.

- ***Where and during what historic period did Christianity first emerge?*** *(in Judea during the Pax Romana)*
- ***In what collection of books are the life and teachings of Jesus recorded?*** *(the Christian Bible's New Testament)*
- ***When the followers of Jesus accepted him as the Messiah, what did they expect of him?*** *(They believed him to be a leader sent by God to set up God's rule on Earth.)*
- ***What major leaders helped spread Christianity throughout the Roman world?*** *(Peter and Paul)*

EVALUATE
✓ **Answers to Think About It**

1. Mary and Joseph had to go there to be counted in a Roman census. *Recall Details*
2. The Greek word for Messiah is *Christos,* leading to the word *Christians. Sequencing*
3. They are rooted in monotheism and the Ten Commandments. *Make Inferences*
4. Without them, Christianity would perhaps have ended with Jesus' crucifixion. *Make Conclusions*
5. Christians spread their faith along its roads and sea routes and through its organization. *Five Themes of Geography: Movement*

Write About It Write a paragraph in which you explain the democratic nature of early Christianity.

MEETING INDIVIDUAL NEEDS

RETEACHING (Easy) Have students make a time line of the important events in Jesus' life, from his birth to his crucifixion.

EXTENSION (Average) Have students use the lesson and the time line on p. 246 to construct their own illustrated time lines of the major events in the founding and spread of Christianity.

ENRICHMENT (Challenging) What ultimately happened to Peter and to Paul? How do we know? Divide the class into halves and assign each half one of the two to trace. Have students in each group individually research their subject and write a report on what is known or presumed about his final years. Tell students to cite the sources on which their findings are based.

LESSON 5

PAGES 252–257

Lesson Overview
Beset by troubles within and from outside, the Roman empire declined and split in two.

Lesson Objectives
★ Identify cause and effect relationships in the decline of the Roman empire.

★ Describe and compare the two empires into which the Roman empire divided.

★ Identify legacies of the empire.

1 PREPARE

MOTIVATE Refer the class to the lesson's ominous title and have a student do the *Read Aloud.* Help students to recognize how deep the fear of "barbarians" (shown being attacked by Romans in the photo) had to be in Rome in A.D. 400 for there to be laws to ban dressing like them.

SET PURPOSE Encourage students to review their last view of the Roman empire—vibrant and confidant, with an unbeatable army, in control of far-flung territories and great wealth. What could have led to Rome's decline? Have students consider the *Read to Learn* question and preview the *Vocabulary.*

2 TEACH

Understanding THE BIG PICTURE
Ask students to name some other great empires that rose and fell.

● **What threats to the Roman empire began to emerge?** *(a strong Persian empire to the east, groups of people in the north seeking new, fertile land)*

★**THINKING FURTHER:** *Making Connections* **Can you identify a recurring theme in history at work here?** *(Students should recognize the theme of land hunger and the desire of one group to move in and take control of the land of another.)*

Resource REMINDER

Practice and Project Book: *p. 52*

Anthology: *Theodora's Bravery, p. 54; A Description of Constantinople, p. 55*

500 B.C.	250 B.C.	A.D. 1	A.D. 180	A.D. 500

THE DECLINE OF THE ROMAN EMPIRE

Focus Activity

READ TO LEARN
What contributed to the decline of Rome?

VOCABULARY
Eastern Orthodox Christianity
architecture
Roman Catholicism

PEOPLE
Diocletian
Constantine

PLACES
Palestine
Constantinople
Byzantine empire

READ ALOUD
About A.D. 400 Rome's emperor passed a law banning people from wearing pants or certain kinds of boots. People who broke the law faced losing all of their belongings and being thrown out of the city. Why did the emperor pass such laws about fashion? Pants were the everyday clothes of foreign soldiers whom the Romans called "barbarians." By A.D. 400 these peoples had the power to take over the once-mighty city of Rome.

THE BIG PICTURE
During the Pax Romana from 27 B.C. to A.D. 180, the Roman empire was by no means the only power in its area of the world. On Rome's eastern border, a new Persian empire was developing and growing. North of Rome, different groups were beginning to outgrow the heavily forested lands of northern Europe. After a while some of these people began looking toward the fertile lands within Rome's borders. Like the hunters of China's northern steppes, Europe's northern peoples began raiding the wealthy lands to their south.

Invasions from the north would eventually bring many changes to the Roman empire. The Pax Romana came to an end while new groups moved through the lands of the empire. Many Romans tried to protect themselves and their property. As fear spread, a Roman emperor made a decision that would have a tremendous impact on the Roman empire.

252

SHELTERED INSTRUCTION

READING STRATEGIES & LANGUAGE DEVELOPMENT

COMPARE AND CONTRAST Review with the class how writers sometimes arrange information by showing how it is the same (comparing) and how it is different (contrasting). Then invite students to read "The Empire Is Divided" on p. 253. Arrange students in small groups to create posters that compare and contrast the western and eastern empires. Have groups give brief oral reports explaining the categories they chose, such as territory, capital, religion, and ultimate fate. **[SDAIE STRATEGY: TEXT RE-PRESENTATION]**

WORDS WITH MULTIPLE MEANINGS Refer to the term *crafted* on p. 256 and have students identify it as a verb. Point out that as a noun, *craft* has several different meanings. Call for any they can think of; have them use the dictionary to find any they missed.

THE DECLINE OF AN EMPIRE

Despite its name, the Pax Romana was not a completely peaceful time in Rome's history. Revolts and border wars flared up often, but the Roman army had always managed to regain control. The Pax Romana ended when large armies from northern Europe began to invade the empire in the late A.D. 100s.

The Empire Under Attack

The northern invaders were German-speaking peoples. They were attacking a Roman empire that had become too big to control. There were increasing difficulties with communicating and collecting taxes. The army weakened, and the empire became poorer.

The raids from the north destroyed cities and farmlands. They made the empire's roads and coasts unsafe. Thieves held up travelers, and pirates hijacked ships. Trade suffered.

As time passed the raids caused life in the empire to change in almost every way. Many cities in the western empire isolated themselves behind thick new walls. In the countryside, wealthy landowners withdrew into their well-protected villas. In the west, where most invasions took place, the Roman empire was rapidly falling apart.

The Empire Is Divided

In A.D. 284 an emperor who was named Diocletian (di uh KLEE shun) came to power. Like other emperors who ruled during this time of war, Diocletian was a powerful general. He realized that the empire was simply too big to be ruled by one man, so he divided it into two main parts.

Three assistants took charge of affairs in the troubled western empire. Diocletian became head of the eastern empire. This region included the wealthy cities of Egypt, Greece, and Palestine—the Roman name for Judea. By choosing to oversee the eastern empire, Diocletian created a major turning point in Roman history. For the first time, Rome was no longer the most important city in the empire. Power was shifting from west to east.

This painting shows the northern invaders who began to attack the Roman empire in the late A.D. 100s.

CITIZENSHIP★

UNDERSTANDING GOVERNMENT Point out to the class that a major role of any government is to protect the public safety. Police forces are responsible for keeping streets safe; the military is responsible for resisting attack from foreign enemies. To help students recognize how critical this role is, have them identify ways that failure to maintain public safety affected the Roman empire.

GLOBAL CONNECTION

ATTACKERS UNDER ATTACK German-speaking peoples began pushing into the Roman empire because they in turn were under attack from another group, the Huns. In about the fourth century A.D., the Huns had burst out of central Asia and began conquering peoples of Eastern Europe, pushing them relentlessly toward the Roman empire.

THE DECLINE OF AN EMPIRE

As students read the opening paragraph, help them consider that although the Roman army could put down the occasional revolt or border raid, what could it do if unrest became much more frequent and widespread? Wouldn't this stretch even a powerful army too thin?

Discussing The Empire Under Attack This entire section lends itself to tracing cause and effect and recognizing how effect can in turn become cause.

● *What effects did the raids from the north cause?* (destruction, danger, chaos, interruption of trade)

● *What did these effects in turn cause?* (disunity, individuals looking out for themselves, a crumbling empire)

★THINKING FURTHER: *Cause and Effect What effects did the Roman empire's great size cause?* (breakdown of communication and tax collection and weakening of the army. Help students to see that this undermined the three main underpinnings of the empire—law, taxes, and the army.)

Discussing The Empire Is Divided Help students see division as a solution.

● *Who was Diocletian?* (a Roman emperor from A.D. 284)

● *What step did he take to deal with the oversized empire?* (He divided it in two—a western empire and an eastern empire)

● *What areas were among those included in the eastern empire?* (Egypt, Greece, Palestine)

★THINKING FURTHER: *Cause and Effect How did Diocletian's action relocate ruling power in the old Roman world?* (It shifted power from Rome, in the western part, to the eastern part.)

A CAPITAL IN THE EAST

Have students locate Constantinople on the map on this page.

- **Why did Emperor Constantine choose this location for his new imperial capital?** *(It was easy to protect, was on major trade routes, and was far from the old imperial capital, Rome, and its traditions.)*

- **Why did he want to escape the old ways?** *(They no longer worked.)*

- **How did the city of Constantinople at its height compare to Rome at its height?** *(Similarities include meeting places, elegant structures, entertainment.)*

> ★**THINKING FURTHER:** *Cause and Effect* **Why does it make sense that Constantinople would become a grand and busy city?** *(It took over from Rome as imperial capital, so it would take on the trappings of Rome.)*

More **MAP WORK**

Use the map on this page to develop students' understanding of the empire.

- **What major areas made up the western empire?** *(Italy, Gaul, Spain, Britain, part of northern Africa)*

- **What major areas made up the eastern empire?** *(Greece, the western Asia peninsula to the east of it, Syria, Egypt)*

> ★**THINKING FURTHER:** *Compare and Contrast* **Which empire was better situated for trade? Why?** *(Encourage students to examine the trade routes. Accept any reasoned opinions.)*

Discussing Freedom for Christians Help students note the change from being an unwelcome to a welcome religion.

> ★**THINKING FURTHER:** *Sequencing* **What was the sequence of events that took Christians from persecution to power?** *(persecution → Constantine's conversion → his giving Christians freedom of worship → his support for Christian building, government positions for Christians, general protection of the Christian religion)*

A CAPITAL IN THE EAST

In 306 Constantine became emperor. He reunited the Roman empire under his rule. Like Diocletian, Constantine focused on the eastern half of the empire. He based the empire in a new city on the site of an ancient Greek colony named Byzantium (bih ZAN tee um). Renamed Constantinople (kahn stan tuh NOH pul) in his honor, it became the capital of a huge empire. The city still exists today, as Istanbul, Turkey.

The location of the new capital was perfect for many reasons. Surrounded on three sides by water, Constantinople was easy to protect. It was on major trade routes between the eastern empire and Asia. Finally, the city was far away from Rome and all its traditions of government and religion. This distance made changing the government easier.

Constantinople had an elegant marble forum and aqueducts that flowed with clear water. Thousands of fans attended events in the city stadium. Constantinople, however, not only had temples to many gods but numerous Christian churches as well.

Freedom for Christians

Earlier emperors had Christians killed for refusing to honor Rome's gods and goddesses. Constantine, however, became a supporter of Christianity.

In a dream Constantine was said to have had the night before a major battle in 312, he was told to mark the sign of the cross on his soldiers' shields. He had this done and won the battle. The cross is a religious symbol of Christians.

As a result, Constantine granted freedom to Christians. He donated

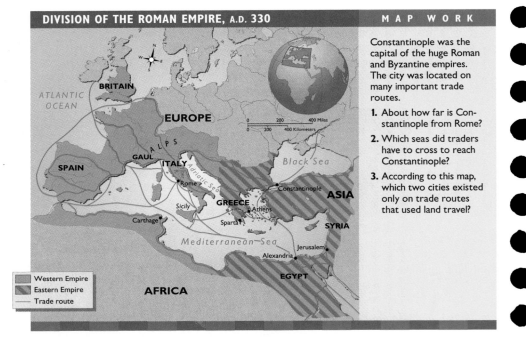

DIVISION OF THE ROMAN EMPIRE, A.D. 330

MAP WORK

Constantinople was the capital of the huge Roman and Byzantine empires. The city was located on many important trade routes.

1. About how far is Constantinople from Rome?

2. Which seas did traders have to cross to reach Constantinople?

3. According to this map, which two cities existed only on trade routes that used land travel?

254 MAP WORK: **1.** about 600 miles (about 965 kilometers) **2.** Mediterranean Sea, Black Sea, Adriatic Sea **3.** Jerusalem and Carthage

BACKGROUND INFORMATION

ABOUT PERSECUTION OF THE CHRISTIANS IN ROMAN TIMES Christians became convenient scapegoats when things went wrong in Rome.

- In A.D. 64 Rome burned, and Emperor Nero accused the Christians of starting the fire and had many of them executed.

- In the 3rd century, emperors instigated new waves of executions. One of the most savage was ordered by Emperor Diocletian.

SECOND-LANGUAGE SUPPORT

TAKING NOTES Second-language learners may better understand the progression of lesson events by creating and maintaining a time line. Have them work on graph paper to plot out the events. Then encourage them to annotate the time line with additional information they discover as they continue through the lesson.

Istanbul, Turkey (above), was founded by Constantine (below) as Constantinople. It lies partly in Europe and partly in Asia.

money to build Christian churches throughout the empire. He also appointed Christians to important government posts. Constantine became the first of many future rulers in Europe who saw themselves as protectors of Christianity.

End of the Roman Empire

Meanwhile the western empire continued to weaken. Northern peoples settled into more parts of the empire. In 410 their soldiers took Rome itself. In 476, Rome's last emperor was removed from the throne. The city of Rome—once all-powerful in the western Mediterranean—no longer had much influence.

The Eastern Empire Lives On

After the fall of the western Roman empire, the eastern half lived on for another 1,000 years. It became known as the Byzantine empire, in honor of its roots in the Greek city of Byzantium.

Greek culture had a large role in Byzantine life. People spoke Greek rather than the Latin of Rome. Greek as well as western Asian cultures also influenced Byzantine art and building styles. Christianity spread through the empire and influenced the life and arts as well.

Christianity in the Byzantine empire was influenced by Greek culture. As a result, Christianity developed differently than in the west. Western Christians regarded the pope as the only leader who could speak for the church. Eastern Christians did not agree. Their religion, Eastern Orthodox Christianity, would also have a deep influence on people's lives in eastern Europe and western Asia.

Even though there were differences, Byzantine civilization preserved the strong traditions of the Roman empire. Many years later, Roman laws would revive in western Europe thanks to their survival in the Byzantine empire.

255

Discussing End of the Roman Empire
Discuss the reasons the empire came to an end.

★THINKING FURTHER: *Making Connections* **"How the mighty have fallen!" How does this saying describe what happened to Rome?** *(Once-mighty Rome was conquered by peoples from the north, and the western empire collapsed in the 400s.)*

Learning how The Empire Lives On Refer to the map on p. 254 to see which part of the empire survived.

- **How did the eastern empire fare better than the western empire?** *(It survived as the Byzantine empire.)*

- **In what ways did the Byzantine empire differ from the old Roman empire?** *(language, art and building styles, stronger Greek and western Asian cultural influences)*

- **How did Christianity fare in the Byzantine empire?** *(It spread, strongly influencing culture there.)*

- **How did the old western empire and the Byzantine empire differ on religion?** *(Because of a dispute over the pope, the Byzantine empire kept its branch of Christianity separate, as Eastern Orthodox Christianity.)*

★THINKING FURTHER: *Making Conclusions* **People often cite A.D. 476 as "the fall of the Roman empire." Do you think this is accurate? Why or why not?** *(Not all of it "fell"—part of it, the Byzantine empire, would go on for another 1,000 years and keep many Roman traditions alive.)*

BACKGROUND INFORMATION

ABOUT THE LAST DAYS OF ROME
- In A.D. 410 the Visigoths, under their leader Alaric, broke through Rome's defenses and for six days sacked and burned the city. In 455, the Vandals appeared and repeated the attack.

- In A.D. 475, Orestes, commander of Roman forces, forced the Senate to elect his young son Romulus Augustulus ("Little Augustus") emperor of the western empire.

- In A.D. 476, the Ostrogoths swept into Italy. Their leader, Odoacer, slew Orestes, deposed his son, ended the imperial line, and made himself king.

- Thus, Rome's first and last emperors were Augustus.

BACKGROUND INFORMATION

ABOUT BYZANTINE ART AND ARCHITECTURE
- Byzantine art and architecture represent a fusion of Roman, Greek, and Persian styles.

- Today, the Byzantine style is most evident in Constantinople, Greece, Russia, and the Italian cities of Venice and Ravenna.

- Among the most famous Byzantine structures still visited today are Hagia Sophia (Santa Sofia) in Constantinople and St. Mark's Basilica in Venice.

- Byzantine art is renowned for its vivid mosaics. Churches were decorated with richly colored mosaics that depicted Bible stories, much as stained glass windows did in Western European churches.

THE LEGACY OF ROME
Discussing Law and Government
Relate Rome's government to ours today.

> ★**THINKING FURTHER:** *Making Connections* **Why should we as citizens be grateful for the Roman republic's legacy?** *(It gave us law and three branches of government.)*

Exploring New Languages Discuss the meaning of *Romance language*.

- **Where does the term Romance language come from?** *(Help students to see that the word "Romance" comes from "Roman.")*

More **CHART WORK**

Use the chart to help students understand language change.

- **Look at the chart on this page. What important element did Latin borrow from Greek?** *(an alphabet)*

- **From whom did the Greeks borrow it?** *(the Phoenicians)*

- **What debt does English owe to the Romans?** *(the Latin alphabet)*

- ★**THINKING FURTHER:** *Making Conclusions* **What other debt does English owe to the Roman language legacy?** *(Many English words come from Latin and Romance languages.)*

Discussing Roman Buildings
Briefly review the *Legacy* lesson with students.

> ★**THINKING FURTHER:** *Making Conclusions* **Why does Roman architecture look different from Greek architecture?** *(Although Rome borrowed ideas from Greece, Romans added ideas, creating their own style.)*

Studying Christianity in the West
Discuss the West's religious heritage.

> ★**THINKING FURTHER:** *Compare and Contrast* **How did western Christianity keep closer ties than eastern Christianity to the Roman legacy?** *(It kept Latin as the church language, Roman building styles for churches, and Rome as the headquarters of Roman Catholicism.)*

THE LEGACY OF ROME

Though the western Roman empire collapsed in the 400s, many important legacies live on. You read about Roman engineering earlier. There were many others too.

Law and Government

Even before the empire was born, Romans crafted the foundations of their laws and government. That was to be their most important legacy. The basic framework of the Roman republic has often been copied. Founders of the United States were inspired by the republic's idea of having leaders serve in three branches of government. They also used the word *senate* and the idea of *veto* power.

New Languages

As the Roman empire spread, the Latin language spread as well. Long after the western empire died, many new languages grew out of Latin. Today these "Romance" languages are still spoken in western Europe and the rest of the world. They include Italian, Spanish, French, Portuguese, and Romanian.

Today even more people use the Roman alphabet. Look carefully at the chart. The Roman alphabet owed much to the Greek alphabet, which in turn grew out of the Phoenician alphabet. The Roman style of letters, though, became the base for the ones we use today. English is just one of many languages that are written with the Roman alphabet.

256

DEVELOPMENT OF MODERN ALPHABET

CHART WORK

The Roman alphabet developed from the Greek and Phoenician alphabets.

1. In what way is the Roman 'A' different from the Phoenician symbol for ox?

2. Which Greek letter is similar to the Roman "E"?

CURRICULUM CONNECTION

LINKS TO LANGUAGE ARTS Another legacy the Romans left us was a wealth of our everyday expressions. Have students create amusing illustrations of some of the sayings.

- "Love conquers all."—Virgil
- "It is quality rather than quantity that matters."—Seneca
- "Not worth his salt."—Petronius
- "No sooner said than done."—Quintus Ennius
- "Better late than never."—Livy
- "A rolling stone gathers no moss."—Publius Syrus
- "Absence makes the heart grow fonder."—Sextus Propertius
- "There is no place more delightful than home."—Cicero
- "More brawn than brain."—Cornelius Nepos

Roman Buildings

As you read earlier, architecture, or the science of planning and constructing buildings, was a major legacy of ancient Rome. Roman architecture borrowed heavily from other cultures. Greek columns and Etruscan arches were parts of many Roman buildings. Yet Roman engineers developed new ideas from these old forms.

Christianity in the West

Roman language and architecture enriched the development of Christianity. Church ceremonies and writings were in Latin. Many huge churches all over Europe were built in the Roman style. Some of the grandest were built in Rome itself. Rome would be the city that would later become the leader of Christianity in western Europe. This western Christianity was later known as Roman Catholicism. Like Eastern Orthodox Christianity, Roman Catholicism has many followers today.

The remains of the Roman Forum (below), mark the site where the senate met in 27 B.C. to name Augustus emperor.

WHY IT MATTERS

The civilization of ancient Rome influenced life in the eastern Mediterranean and western Europe for centuries. As the peoples of western Europe developed a new civilization, they would carry Roman ideas with them. Eventually these ideas influenced peoples throughout the world. The story of this influence will be told in chapters to come.

✓ Reviewing Facts and Ideas

MAIN IDEAS

- Invasions, tax collection problems, and other factors weakened the Roman empire in the A.D. 200s.

- In about 284 Diocletian divided the Roman empire into two parts, making it easier to rule.

- Constantine established the Byzantine empire in the east, where Christianity also became a powerful force.

- While the eastern empire continued to live on, the western empire collapsed in the 400s.

- Rome has left legacies of government, language, and architecture.

THINK ABOUT IT

1. What brought about the end of the Pax Romana?

2. How did Romans use the legacies of other civilizations? What Roman legacies affect our lives today?

3. FOCUS Why did the western empire finally collapse?

4. THINKING SKILL What _conclusions_ can you make about the changes that occurred in the Eastern Roman empire under Constantine?

5. WRITE Why was Constantinople a good location for the new capital?

257

Discussing WHY IT MATTERS
Sum up Rome's legacy to the world.

★THINKING FURTHER: _Making Conclusions_ Why was Roman civilization richer for borrowing from other civilizations? Why are we richer for borrowing from it? _(Help students appreciate how cultural borrowing builds up ideas—later civilizations have some work already done for them and can move on to develop new cultural ideas.)_

⭐ 3 CLOSE

MAIN IDEAS
Call on students for answers.

- **What factors weakened the Roman empire?** (becoming too big to rule, loss of taxes, threats from outside)

- **What step did Diocletian take to make the Roman empire easier to rule?** (dividing it into two parts, a western empire and an eastern empire)

- **What important role did Constantine play in strengthening the empire?** (He established the Byzantine empire in the east and empowered Christianity.)

- **How did the fates of the western and eastern empires differ?** (western—collapse; eastern—1,000-year life)

- **In what areas did Rome leave a powerful legacy?** (government, language, architecture)

EVALUATE
✓ **Answers to Think About It**

1. the invasion of northern armies
   Form Generalizations

2. They adopted religious beliefs, architectural styles, and an alphabet; government, language, architecture.
   Make Analogies

3. conquest by the armies from the north
   Main Idea

4. It grew strong, adopted Christianity, and developed a culture influenced by Greece and western Asia.
   Draw Conclusions

5. could be protected, on major trade routes, and far from Rome
   Make Inferences

Write About It Write a paragraph explaining why the western empire fell while the eastern empire survived.

MEETING INDIVIDUAL NEEDS

RETEACHING (Easy) Tell students to prepare a chart showing the sequence of events leading to Rome's fall in A.D. 476.

EXTENSION (Average) Tell students to picture themselves as foreign correspondents sent to cover the last days of Rome. Have them use outline managers to help them write a report for their paper or news broadcast.

ENRICHMENT (Challenging) Divide the class into seven groups and assign to each group one of the following: to the first group, the Huns, invaders from Asia, and to the next six groups, the six German-speaking invaders—Visigoths, Ostrogoths, Vandals, Lombards, Burgundians, and Franks. Have each group research its invading group—where they came from, who they were, where they invaded. Tell them to use outline managers to help them prepare a report, with a map tracing their invaders' route, for presentation to the class.

DISCUSSING MAJOR EVENTS Use these questions to help students pinpoint highlights in ancient Rome's long history and put them in proper sequence.

● **What was Rome's system of government when the Twelve Tables became the foundation of Roman law?** (republic)

● **How much later did the Pax Romana begin and how long did it last?** (about four and a quarter centuries; 207 years)

● **When was the Roman empire divided in two and how long did the western half survive?** (A.D. 284; 192 years)

Answers to
THINKING ABOUT VOCABULARY

1. elevation
2. civil war
3. patrician
4. republic
5. representative
6. consul
7. Messiah
8. profile
9. dictator
10. architecture

Answers to
THINKING ABOUT FACTS

1. The Alps acted as a barrier to the rest of Europe, and the Appenines made it difficult to cross the Italian peninsula.

2. This general made war on Rome, and his ultimate defeat gave Rome control of his homeland, Carthage.

3. to try to save Rome from dictatorship and preserve it as a republic

Resource REMINDER

Practice and Project Book: *p. 53*
Assessment Book: *Chapter 9 Test*
● **Technology:** *Videodisc/Video Tape 3*
Transparency: *Graphic Organizer, Cause-and-Effect Chart*

CHAPTER 9 REVIEW

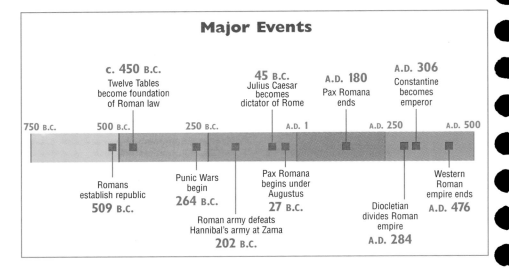

Major Events

c. 450 B.C. Twelve Tables become foundation of Roman law

45 B.C. Julius Caesar becomes dictator of Rome

A.D. 180 Pax Romana ends

A.D. 306 Constantine becomes emperor

750 B.C. — 500 B.C. — 250 B.C. — A.D. 1 — A.D. 250 — A.D. 500

Romans establish republic 509 B.C.

Punic Wars begin 264 B.C.

Pax Romana begins under Augustus 27 B.C.

Roman army defeats Hannibal's army at Zama 202 B.C.

Diocletian divides Roman empire A.D. 284

Western Roman empire ends A.D. 476

THINKING ABOUT VOCABULARY

Number a sheet of paper from 1 to 10. Beside each number write the word or phrase from the list below that best completes the sentence.

architecture   Messiah
civil war   patrician
consul   profile
dictator   representative
elevation   republic

1. Height above sea level is called _____.
2. A _____ is a war between groups inside a country.
3. A _____ is a member of a noble family.
4. In a _____ people get to choose their own government leaders.
5. A person elected to act for others is called a _____.
6. A _____ was one of the Roman leaders elected by the citizen assembly.
7. The _____ is believed by his followers to have been a special leader sent by God to lead the Jewish people.
8. A _____ is a view of something from the side or a cross section.
9. A _____ is somebody who rules with absolute power.
10. _____ is the science of planning and constructing buildings.

THINKING ABOUT FACTS

1. How did the Alps and the Apennine Mountains cause difficulty for travelers in Italy?
2. What role did Hannibal play in Roman history?
3. Why was Julius Caesar assassinated?
4. What is the New Testament? Why is it important to Christianity?
5. According to the time line above, for about how long had Rome been a republic before Julius Caesar became a dictator?

258

SECOND-LANGUAGE SUPPORT

SEQUENCE OF EVENTS To keep track of events in the history of Roman civilization, students should keep a time line in their notebooks. As they read each lesson in the chapter, students will write down important events that occurred in each time period.

DISCUSSION To prepare second-language learners for a discussion of what makes empires powerful and what makes them decline, have students brainstorm words and phrases that they can use in discussing this topic. Then have these students work in small groups to review the chapter material, formulate their ideas, and practice expressing their thoughts. This preparation should help them hold their own in a discussion with English-proficient peers.

THINK AND WRITE

WRITING AN EXPLANATION
Write two paragraphs about Rome's republican government. First explain how it worked. Then compare and contrast it with Athenian democracy.

WRITING A TV REPORT
Suppose you are a television reporter sent back in time to ancient Rome to cover the assassination of Julius Caesar. Write a report that you will give on the evening news.

WRITING A COMPARISON
Write a paragraph about the decline of the Roman empire. Compare the problems of the western empire with the successes of the Byzantine empire in the east.

APPLYING GEOGRAPHY SKILLS

READING ELEVATION PROFILES AND MAPS

1. What is an elevation map? What is a profile map?

2. Look at the elevation map of Rome (Map A) on page 228 to find the elevations of the seven hills. Which hills are the highest? Which is the lowest? List the hills of Rome in order of elevation from highest to lowest.

3. Look at the profile map of Rome (Map B) on page 229. How much higher is the Palatine Hill than the Caelian Hill? How much higher is the Caelian Hill than the Tiber River?

4. Why can an elevation map show the locations of places in an area better than a profile map can? What is the advantage of a profile map?

5. Why are elevation and profile maps useful? When may they be too limiting?

4. the second part of the Christian Bible; a collection of books that describe the life and teachings of Jesus Christ

5. 464 years

Answers to APPLYING GEOGRAPHY SKILLS

1. An elevation map shows an area's heights above sea level; a profile shows the side view, or cross section, of an area.

2. The highest hills of Rome are Aventine, Esquiline, Palatine, and Quirinal. The lowest hills are Capitoline, Viminal, and Caelian.

3. about 35 feet; about 95 feet

4. An elevation map can show a broader area with more relative locations on it. A profile can make it easier to measure relative elevations along the cross section.

5. They give information about an area's terrain, which is useful in planning how land might or might not be used or how roads might be built across it. They may be too limiting if someone needed to know how far apart the hills and valleys were.

Summing Up the Chapter

Copy the cause-and-effect chart below on a separate piece of paper. Then review the chapter to find at least three causes for each effect listed. After you have filled in the causes, use the chart to write a paragraph that answers the question "How did Rome grow into a great empire?"

CAUSE	EFFECT
Rich soil from volcanic ash Natural protection from seven hills Development of an organized republic Growth of a powerful army Strong leadership of Augustus	Rome becomes a powerful empire.
Invasions from the north and west Division of the empire into east and west Destruction of cities and farmland Empire too big to defend from invaders	The Western Roman empire declines.

259

Technology CONNECTION

VIDEODISC/VIDEO TAPE 3
Enrich Chapter 9 with the *Ancient Rome* segment on the Videodisc.

Search Frame 11660 Side B

SUGGESTIONS FOR SUMMING UP THE CHAPTER

After students have copied the cause-and-effect chart on a piece of paper, have them read the two effects aloud and discuss each. Start off by asking them to identify features that make empires powerful (inspired leadership, strong military, people to work toward empire-building goals, for example) and things that lead to decline (trouble within, threats from outside, for example). Then have them go back through the chapter and find the specific causes that led to the two effects stated here. Possible answers appear on the reproduced pupil page above. As they begin to write their paragraphs that answer the question posed, remind them that it will use only the causes for the first effect in the box.

ASSESSING THINK WRITE: *For performance assessment, see Assessment Book, Chapter 9, pp. T71–T73.*

10 Ancient Arabia

Pages 260–283

CHAPTER OVERVIEW

By 300 B.C., the early people of Arabia had built civilizations based on farming, herding, and trade. A leader named Muhammad began to teach the religion of Islam in the city of Mecca in A.D. 630. Later, Baghdad became the capital of Islam and a great center of learning and culture.

GEO ADVENTURES DAILY GEOGRAPHY ACTIVITIES

Use **Geo Adventures** Daily Geography activities to assess students' understanding of geography skills.

CHAPTER PLANNING GUIDE

LESSON 1	LESSON 2	LESSON 3
SUGGESTED PACING: 2 DAYS	SUGGESTED PACING: 2 DAYS	SUGGESTED PACING: 3 DAYS
Geography of Arabia pp. 262–265	**Beginnings Of Islam** pp. 266–271	**A Muslim Caliphate** pp. 272–277
CURRICULUM CONNECTIONS Links to Language Arts, p. 263 Links to Art, p. 264	**CURRICULUM CONNECTIONS** Links to Language Arts, p. 267 Links to Math, p. 270	**CURRICULUM CONNECTIONS** Links to Music, p. 275 Links to Reading, p. 275
RESOURCES Practice and Project Book, p. 54 Outline Map	**CITIZENSHIP** Recognizing Perspectives, p. 268 **RESOURCES** Practice and Project Book, p. 55 Anthology, pp. 56–57	**INFOGRAPHIC** Life in the Caliphate, pp. 276–277 **RESOURCES** Practice and Project Book, p. 56 Desk Map Anthology, pp. 58, 59–61, 62 TECHNOLOGY *Adventure Time!* CD-ROM

GEOGRAPHYSKILLS	CHAPTER REVIEW
SUGGESTED PACING: 1 DAY	SUGGESTED PACING: 1 DAY
Reading Historical Maps pp. 280–281	pp. 282–283
RESOURCES Practice and Project Book, p. 57 Transparency: Maps 14 & 15 TECHNOLOGY *Adventure Time!* CD-ROM	**RESOURCES** Practice and Project Book, p. 58 TECHNOLOGY Videodisc/Video Tape 4

LEARNING STYLE: Visual ON YOUR OWN 30 MINUTES OR LONGER

Write a Book Review

Objective: To prepare students to learn about the influence of literature in ancient Arabia.

Materials: paper

1. Ask students if they have a favorite book. How many times have they read it? Why is it their favorite?
2. Invite each student to write a book review. What is it about and why is it a favorite?
3. Ask students to illustrate their reviews with drawings that show why the book is important to them.
4. Invite students to share their reviews with the class.

Legacy

SUGGESTED PACING: 1 DAY

Map Making pp. 278–279

CURRICULUM CONNECTIONS
Links to Art, p. 278

 SDAIE SUPPORT

SHELTERED INSTRUCTION

READING STRATEGIES & LANGUAGE DEVELOPMENT

Problem and Solution/Words Often Confused, p. 262, Lesson 1
Making Conclusions/Variant Spellings, p. 266, Lesson 2
Main Idea and Details/Word History, p. 272, Lesson 3
Sequence/Prefixes and Suffixes, p. 280, Geography Skills

SECOND-LANGUAGE SUPPORT

Reading Strategies, p. 263
Working with a Peer, p. 270
Graphic Organizers, p. 275

MEETING INDIVIDUAL NEEDS

Reteaching, Extension, Enrichment, pp. 265, 271, 277, 279, 281
McGraw-Hill Adventure Book

ASSESSMENT OPPORTUNITIES

Practice and Project Book, pp. 54–58
Write About It, pp. 265, 271, 277, 279
Assessment Book: Assessing Think and Write, pp. T74–T76; Chapter 10 Tests: Content, Skills, Writing

Introducing the Chapter

Refer students to the chapter title and ask them what Arabia means to them. If they have ever seen movies in this setting, they will perhaps conjure up pictures of deserts, camels, and mosques.

THINKING ABOUT HISTORY AND GEOGRAPHY

Have students read the text on this page to be introduced to an understanding of Arabia they will develop as they study this chapter. Have them trace the panel locations to the map and then identify the region of the world where they are found (southwest Asia).

300 B.C. PETRA

- **What is happening in this panel?** *(Arab traders in a camel caravan are making at stop at Petra.)*

- **Where is Petra located?** *(just east of the isthmus that links Asia to Africa, with the Mediterranean to the northwest and the Red Sea to the south)*

> ★ **THINKING FURTHER:** *Making Conclusions* **Why would this be a good location for a center of trade?** *(It is close to two main bodies of water and is on the route from Egypt to Asia.)*

A.D. 622 MEDINA

- **Where is Medina located?** *(about halfway down the Arabian peninsula, inland from the Red Sea)*

- **What happened in Medina in A.D. 622?** *(Muhammad moved to Medina, and the Islamic calendar began.)*

> ★ **THINKING FURTHER:** *Predicting* **How would Muhammad affect civilization?** *(He will begin spreading the Muslim religion.)*

Resource **REMINDER**

Technology: *Videodisc/Video Tape 4*

CHAPTER 10

Ancient Arabia

THINKING ABOUT HISTORY AND GEOGRAPHY

In this chapter you will read how early peoples lived in the deserts and mountains of Arabia. Farming, herding, and trade developed in this region. The religion of Islam spread rapidly to unite many Arabs in one belief. The civilization that followed built a glorious capital city and created many legacies that still influence people today.

300 B.C.
PETRA
Petra becomes a caravan stop for Arab traders

A.D. 622
MEDINA
Muhammad moves to Medina; Islamic calendar begins

A.D. 762
BAGHDAD
Caliph Al-Mansur founds a capital city

260

BACKGROUND INFORMATION

LINKING THE MAP AND THE TIME LINE

- Petra, located in modern-day Jordan, was the capital of the ancient Arabic kingdom of Nabataea at the time shown in the panel. The town came under strong Hellenistic influence and then fell to Rome in A.D. 106, when it became part of the Roman province of Arabia. Today, it is a major archaeological and tourist site.

- Medina, located in modern-day Saudi-Arabia, was originally settled by Jews expelled from Palestine by the Romans in A.D. 135. After Muhammad arrived there in A.D. 622, he at first treated the Jews well, but then drove them out as he turned Medina into the administrative capital of the Islamic state. It held that position until A.D. 661. Today Medina is a major stop on the Muslim pilgrimage to Mecca.

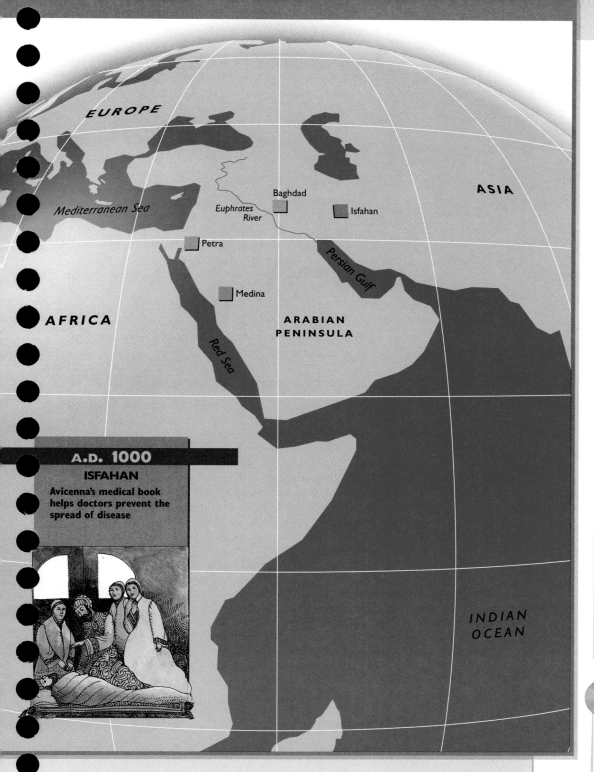

EUROPE

Mediterranean Sea

Euphrates River

Baghdad

Isfahan

ASIA

Petra

Persian Gulf

Medina

Red Sea

AFRICA

ARABIAN PENINSULA

INDIAN OCEAN

A.D. 1000

ISFAHAN

Avicenna's medical book helps doctors prevent the spread of disease

A.D. 762 BAGHDAD

- **On which continent is Baghdad located?** (Asia)

- **In the site of which ancient civilization that you have studied is it located?** (Mesopotamia)

- **What happened to Baghdad in A.D. 762?** (Caliph Al-Mansur established it as a capital city.)

★**THINKING FURTHER: Making Conclusions Of what region do you suppose Baghdad might have been the capital?** (Students might suggest it was capital of a part of the Islamic or the Arab world. They can verify their suggestions later in the chapter.)

A.D. 1000 ISFAHAN

- **Where is Isfahan located in relation to Baghdad? in relation to the Arabian peninsula?** (to the east of Baghdad; north of the Arabian Peninsula)

- **What is happening in this panel?** (A doctor is seeing patients.)

★**THINKING FURTHER: Making Conclusions Who do you think Avicenna was? What do you suppose he had to do with Isfahan?** (He was probably an eminent medical expert; it must have been his home base and perhaps a center of knowledge.)

Technology CONNECTION

VIDEODISC/VIDEO TAPE 4
Enrich Chapter 10 with the *Ancient Arabia* segment on the Videodisc.

‖‖‖‖‖‖‖‖‖‖‖‖‖‖‖

Search Frame 13293, Side B

BACKGROUND INFORMATION

LINKING THE MAP AND THE TIME LINE

- Baghdad, the capital of modern-day Iraq, was the third capital of Islam, following Medina and then Damascus, which is located in modern-day Syria. Though the Arabs called Baghdad "Madinat al-Salaam," or "City of Peace," it has known a long history of war, having suffered sackings by the Mongols and the Persians and conquest by the Turks, who made it part of the Ottoman empire. Most recently, it was a focal point in the Gulf War of 1991.

- Isfahan, today the second largest city in Iran, was conquered by the Arabs in A.D. 642 and made into one of their provincial capitals. Shortly after the time shown in this panel, the Seljuk Turks captured it and made it the capital of their empire. Today many outstanding examples of medieval Islamic art and architecture can be seen there.

LESSON 1

PAGES 262-265

Lesson Overview

The people of the Arabian peninsula developed ways to adapt to the region's often harsh environment to establish several thriving civilizations there.

Lesson Objectives

★ Describe the geography of the Arabian peninsula.

★ Analyze methods the Arabs developed to adapt to this challenging environment.

⭐1 PREPARE

MOTIVATE Tell students to close their eyes and try to picture a desert scene as they listen to the *Read Aloud.* Encourage any students who have experienced a desert to describe it.

SET PURPOSE Refer students to the *Read to Learn* question, *Vocabulary* terms, the photo of a donkey cart on an oasis in Saudi Arabia on this page, and the map on p. 263. Based on what they've seen on movies and TV, have them describe their image of this region's geography. Have them note their ideas on the board, then read the lesson to verify or correct these ideas.

⭐2 TEACH

Understanding THE BIG PICTURE
Help students locate Arabia in its geographical and historical context.

● **Which of Arabia's neighboring lands have we studied?** *(Students may note that Egypt, Mesopotamia, India, and Palestine almost circle Arabia.)*

★**THINKING FURTHER:** *Making Conclusions* **Why might Arabians have had contact with these other civilizations?** *(Other areas were easily reached by sea on three sides or by land to the north.)*

Resource **REMINDER**

Practice and Project Book: *p. 54*

GEOGRAPHY OF ARABIA

READ ALOUD

The summer wind picked up, its passing gusts and fiery blasts.
Back and forth they tugged a flowing train of stirred-up dust
Whose cloud flies up like smoke when the kindling is lit.
This 1,400-year-old Arabic poem describes parts of Arabia in the summertime.

THE BIG PICTURE

Arabia is a huge peninsula in southwestern Asia. It lies south of the Fertile Crescent and east of Egypt. By the time Constantine rose to power in Europe around A.D. 300, Arabia had a number of flourishing civilizations.

Arabian traders had long been traveling to cities in Egypt, Mesopotamia, India, and Palestine. In the busy cities of Palestine, for example, merchants sold luxury items such as frankincense (FRANG kihn sens). This costly, perfume-like ingredient is made from the frankincense tree, which grows in few places outside of southern Arabia.

Today the region of Arabia contains several nations, including Yemen, Kuwait, and Saudi Arabia. In this lesson you will read about the ways in which early people of these areas used their environment to develop thriving civilizations.

Dates are an important crop of the Arabian peninsula.

Focus Activity

READ TO LEARN
How did the people of the Arabian peninsula adapt to the region's geography?

VOCABULARY
oasis
caravan

PLACES
Arabia
Persian Gulf
Arabian Sea
Red Sea
Yemen
Petra

262

SHELTERED INSTRUCTION

READING STRATEGIES & LANGUAGE DEVELOPMENT

PROBLEM AND SOLUTION Review the importance of identifying problems and solutions as students read. Have the class brainstorm problems the environment posed for the Greeks and the solutions they found to adapt to it. Share the Read to Learn question. Have students find problems and solutions as they read. **[SDAIE STRATEGY: BRIDGING]**

WORDS OFTEN CONFUSED Just about everyone knows the difference in meaning between the nouns *desert* (an extremely dry region) and *dessert* (something good to eat at the end of a meal). But the spellings of the two are often confused. Write both words on the board and have students identify their meanings and pronunciations. Then encourage them to think of ways to keep the spellings straight, for example, relating the initials of strawberry shortcake to the *ss* in *dessert*.

THE ARABIAN PENINSULA

The Arabian peninsula is bounded by the Persian Gulf to the east. To the south is the Arabian Sea. To the west, the Red Sea almost completely separates Arabia from Africa. Find these places on the map below.

Arabia can be divided into three environmental areas. Find them on the map. The Jabal al-Hijaz (JAB al al hihj AZ) mountains rise along Arabia's west coast to its southernmost tip. The rainfall here makes agriculture possible.

Arabia's east coast is the second environmental area. It is also fertile enough for farming.

The third area covers the inner part of the Arabian peninsula. It is mostly desert. About one quarter of Arabia gets fewer than 10 inches of rain each year, and there are few rivers.

The Desert Environments

Some of Arabia's deserts contain stone cliffs. Others have huge hills of sand. The world's largest continuous body of sand is on the Arabian peninsula. This region, called the Empty Quarter, is uninhabitable. Some parts have no rain for 10 years or more. Other parts enjoy winter cloudbursts that allow desert plants to grow. All of Arabia's deserts have a lack of water and an oven-like summer heat.

Some parts of a desert are not dry. Such an area is an oasis (oh AY sis). Oases are watered by underground springs. People can grow crops in the soil of these areas. Some oases are even large enough to support towns. However, there are few oases in Arabia, and few people live in any part of the peninsula's deserts.

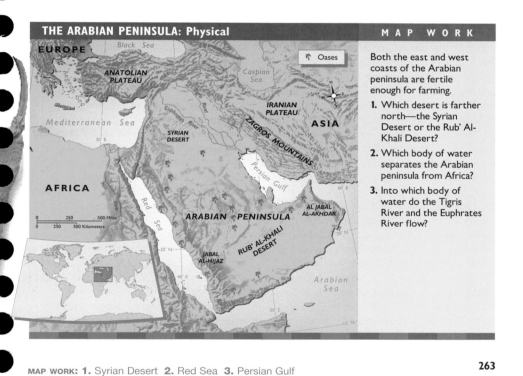

THE ARABIAN PENINSULA: Physical

MAP WORK

Both the east and west coasts of the Arabian peninsula are fertile enough for farming.

1. Which desert is farther north—the Syrian Desert or the Rub' Al-Khali Desert?

2. Which body of water separates the Arabian peninsula from Africa?

3. Into which body of water do the Tigris River and the Euphrates River flow?

MAP WORK: 1. Syrian Desert 2. Red Sea 3. Persian Gulf

263

THE ARABIAN PENINSULA
Have students read the text before turning to the map.

More

MAP WORK

Have students work with text and map.

● **Why is Arabia a peninsula?** (It is bounded on three sides by water— east: Persian Gulf and Arabian Sea, south: Arabian Sea, west: Red Sea)

● **Which are the only main areas where farming is possible?** (along the eastern coast and Persian Gulf)

● **What kind of land covers most of the rest of the peninsula?** (desert)

★ **THINKING FURTHER:** *Making Decisions* **On a scale of 1(low) to 10 (high), how do you rate the wetness of the Arabian peninsula?** (near 1; with few rivers, most of area gets little rain)

Discussing The Desert Environments Call attention to the plural *environments* to help expand students' image of *desert*.

● **How does Arabia's desert environment vary?** (Part is rocky cliffs, part great stretches of sand.)

● **Why are oases important to people in a desert environment?** (Oases offer pockets of water and fertile land that can support life, even towns.)

★ **THINKING FURTHER:** *Predicting* **Where in Arabia would you expect most of the population to live? Why?** (along the coasts and on the oases because these areas can best support life)

BACKGROUND INFORMATION

ABOUT FRANKINCENSE
● The New Testament lists frankincense as one of the three precious gifts that the Wise Men brought to the newborn Jesus, along with myrrh and gold.
● Then frankincense was used to consecrate temples, make cosmetics, and cure a variety of ailments.
● Today it is used as a base for perfume and incense.

CURRICULUM CONNECTION

LINKS TO LANGUAGE ARTS Point out to students that there is a dispute about the name of the gulf to Arabia's east. While Iran, formerly Persia, favors the name "Persian Gulf," Arabs prefer to call it the "Arabian Gulf."

BACKGROUND INFORMATION

ABOUT THE COMBINED DESERTS OF ARABIA
● Covering 1 million square miles, it is the world's third largest desert (after the Sahara and the Australian).
● Its dunes are 700 feet high and are pushed around the desert by the *shamal,* a northwesterly wind.

SECOND-LANGUAGE SUPPORT

READING STRATEGIES Second-language learners may benefit from a preview reading of this lesson. As you flip through, pause to point out on a map of the region each of the geographical locations mentioned. Encourage students to paraphrase challenging passages, and practice pronouncing difficult words together.

PEOPLES OF ARABIA

The terms *Arab* and *Arabian* are sometimes synonyms, but *Arabian* applies particularly to the people of the Arabian peninsula and nearby areas, while *Arab* may refer to a wider group.

Discussing Arabia's Fertile Regions
As each area is mentioned, have students locate it on the map on p. 263.

● **Why did many Arabians settle in the southwestern area?** *(Farming was possible there, so was herding, and its seacoast location allowed trade with the Egyptians.)*

● **Why did other Arabs favor settlement to the north around Petra?** *(Water could be supplied there by aqueduct.)*

★**THINKING FURTHER:** *Making Generalizations* **What generalizations can you make about settlement patterns many Arabians followed?** *(Statements should reflect water availability, fertile land, and trade-friendly sites.)*

Exploring Trade Across Desert and Sea Help students see Petra as a regional hub.

● **For what reasons did Petra grow into a major city?** *(its water supply, its location as a gateway to Egypt and the Fertile Crescent)*

★**THINKING FURTHER:** *Compare and Contrast* **How would you compare camel caravans to the wagon trains that traveled west in our country?** *(Help students see that both groups traveled together to get through a long, hard trip safely and successfully.)*

Discussing Peoples on the Move
Point out that moving regularly was part of a way of life for some of Arabia's people.

★**THINKING FURTHER:** *Compare and Contrast* **How would you compare the lifestyles that the Bedouins and the mountain herders developed?** *(Both lived life on the move, but the Bedouins lived as traders and sometimes raiders, while herders moved for grazing land for their animals.)*

PEOPLES OF ARABIA

The Arabian peninsula is named for the Arabs, the people who have lived there for over 3,000 years. The word "Arab" was first recorded around 800 B.C. It referred to the people living in northern Arabia who had domesticated the camel. Early Arabs used these animals to travel around the peninsula.

Trade caravans like the one above stopped in Petra (right), the capital of the Nabataean civilization. This temple was carved out of rock there.

Arabia's Fertile Regions

Most of the early people of Arabia lived in fertile regions. Some Arabians lived in the mountainous southwestern area that is now the country of Yemen (YE mun). These people became known as the Sabaean (suh BEE un) civilization. Find Yemen on the Atlas map on page R10 in the back of this book.

This area receives enough rainfall to support agriculture. Think about what you read in earlier chapters. What type of agriculture is most successful in mountainous regions?*

Like the people in Italy and Greece, Sabaeans herded sheep and goats and grew grapes and wheat. By building irrigation canals, farmers improved their harvests. As Sabaean coastal towns developed, they began trading with the Egyptians, across the Red Sea.

Another early Arab people lived to the north, in what is today Jordan, around 300 B.C. Their kingdom was

called Nabataea (nab uh TEE uh). They built their capital, Petra (PEH truh), in a place that had a large supply of water brought by aqueducts. Find Petra on the map on page 267.

Trade Across Desert and Sea

It is easy to see why Petra became an important stop on a trade route. There are no other well-watered places for hundreds of miles south of the city. Through trade with Asia and the Mediterranean, the Nabataean (nah buh TEE un) civilization grew rich. It flourished for about 400 years.

Ancient Arabs domesticated camels because they are very useful for desert travel. Camels can carry heavy loads, and go for days without water. They also provide milk to drink. Arab traders often traveled in camel caravans. A caravan is a group of people and animals traveling together. Caravans traveled along routes well known to desert

264   *herding

BACKGROUND INFORMATION

ABOUT SABAEAN CIVILIZATION

● Saba, the home of Sabaean civilization, is the Biblical Sheba. It was there that the legendary Queen of Sheba, who brought "spices and very much gold, and precious stones" to King Solomon of Israel (I Kings 10:2), may have ruled.

● According to one ancient Greek historian, "The Sabaean race . . . is the greatest throughout Arabia."

CURRICULUM CONNECTION

LINKS TO ART Explain to students that the Arabs created art by carving temples, like those at Petra, out of rugged stone cliffs. Ask a team of volunteers to research the works, such as those in and on the way to Petra. Have students prepare an illustrated presentation for the class, using outline maps, if possible, to locate the carvings.

WHY IT MATTERS

The geography of Arabia presented unique challenges to the people who built civilizations in this region. The rugged mountains and water-rich oases of the Arabian peninsula received enough moisture to make farming, herding, and some city-building possible. The people who lived in Arabia's vast stretches of desert had to adapt to very harsh conditions.

Ancient Arabia was divided by geography. However, in the A.D. 600s its people would become unified under a new religion. You will read about this religion in the next lesson.

✓✓ Reviewing Facts and Ideas

MAIN IDEAS

- While some of Arabia is desert, the coastal areas receive enough rain to support agriculture.
- Towns and trade developed in fertile regions, at desert edges, and at oases.
- Trade linked ancient Arabia with Egypt and the Fertile Crescent.

THINK ABOUT IT

1. In what ways do environments differ in various parts of Arabia?

2. How did people live in the mountainous environment of Yemen?

3. **FOCUS** How did varied geography influence the development of different cultures in Arabia?

4. **THINKING SKILL** Explain why the following statement is a _fact_ or why it is an _opinion_: "The best Arabian trade routes were found in the western part of the peninsula."

5. **GEOGRAPHY** Study the map of Arabia. Which coast has more areas of high elevation?

265

experts. Arab traders journeyed throughout the Arabian peninsula. They traded in cities of the Fertile Crescent and across the Red Sea in Egypt.

Peoples on the Move

One of the groups of people who traded in Arabia were called Bedouins (BED uh wunz). The word _Bedouins_ means "people of the desert." They were family groups who lived mostly in the desert, traveling in caravans and sleeping in tents. Many Bedouin traders became wealthy and powerful, sometimes because they raided towns and other caravans.

Other peoples who often moved about were mountain herders. Like the herders of northern China, they moved to new grazing lands at different times of the year. Some went as far as the Fertile Crescent. As in China, the differences in lifestyle between herders and farmers sometimes caused conflict.

Discussing WHY IT MATTERS Reinforce the idea of creative use of environment.

> ★**THINKING FURTHER: _Summarizing_ How would you summarize ways that Arabs adapted their environment to their needs?** _(The majority located where the terrain and water supply could best support life; others learned to make the desert serve their needs.)_

⭐ 3 CLOSE

MAIN IDEAS

Have students write their answers and then discuss them.

- **_Why were coastal areas of Arabia more heavily populated than the interior?_** _(Coastal areas could support farming while the interior could not.)_

- **_Where did towns and trade develop in Arabia?_** _(in fertile areas along the coasts and on oases)_

- **_With what other areas did Arabia trade?_** _(Egypt, the Fertile Crescent)_

EVALUATE

✓ **Answers to Think About It**

1. Coastal areas provide land suitable for farming whereas the interior is mostly desert.
   Make Inferences

2. as farmers, herders, and traders
   Recall Details

3. Coastal areas and oases favored settled life and the development of towns and cities while the desert interior favored life on the move.
   Form Generalizations

4. opinion because it says "the best," but based on factual information
   Evaluate Fact and Opinion

5. the southwestern coast
   Five Themes of Geography: Place

Write About It Tell students to choose a coastal, oasis, or desert interior location and write a postcard message describing a visit there.

LESSON 2

PAGES 266–271

Lesson Overview
The religion of *Islam,* based on the teachings of Muhammad, spread across the Arabian peninsula and far beyond to become a major world religion.

Lesson Objectives
★ Explain how Islam developed.

★ Identify major beliefs of Islam.

★ Describe the spread of Islam.

1 PREPARE

MOTIVATE Read the *Read Aloud* to students. Tell them the opening phrase is shown in Arabic on p. 269. List other religions studied.

SET PURPOSE Have a student present the *Read to Learn* question and write it on the board. Write on the board questions students asked about other religions. (Where were they founded? How did they spread? Whom did they influence?) Tell students to look for similar answers about Islam. Read the *Vocabulary* terms aloud. The photo shows an Islamic frieze with calligraphy.

2 TEACH

Understanding THE BIG PICTURE
Begin to develop a concept of this world religion.

● **What does the word Islam mean?** *("submit to the will of God")*

● **What do you think this means?** *(to follow God's laws)*

● **What is a Muslim?** *(one who submits to God's will as taught by Islam)*

● **What is the Quran?** *(the sacred book containing the teachings of Islam)*

★**THINKING FURTHER: Making Conclusions In Islam who is Allah and who is Muhammad?** *(Allah— God; Muhammad—Allah's prophet)*

Resource REMINDER

Practice and Project Book: *p. 55*

Anthology: *Pilgrimage to Mecca, pp. 56–57*

| 400 | 500 | 750 | 800 | 1000 | 1200 |

BEGINNINGS OF ISLAM

Focus Activity

READ TO LEARN
What are some of the major teachings of Islam?

VOCABULARY
Islam
Quran
Kaaba
hijra
Five Pillars
pilgrimage

PEOPLE
Muhammad
Khadija

PLACES
Mecca
Medina

READ ALOUD

"Allah—there is no god but He . . . Muhammad is the Messenger of Allah." These words are from the Quran (kur AHN), the most holy book of the religion called Islam. It contains the most basic teachings of Islam. In this lesson you will read about how this religion came to hold great influence on the Arabian peninsula. In time Islam would spread throughout many areas of the world.

THE BIG PICTURE

By A.D. 500 Hinduism had deep roots in the Indian subcontinent. Buddhism had spread to Southeast Asia and China. In China, Buddhism mixed with Confucian ideas. Christianity had grown around the Roman empire and spread into North Africa and Mesopotamia. Judaism, which had also grown in the eastern Mediterranean, reached as far as the oasis towns of western Arabia.

In the same region of Arabia, a new religion called Islam (is LAHM) was born. *Islam* means "submit to the will of God" in Arabic, the Arab language. Followers of Islam are called Muslims—which translates "ones who submit to God." The story and teachings of Islam have been written down in the Quran, the most important book of Islam. Its words are sacred to the more than 1 billion Muslims in the world today.

 SDAIE SUPPORT

SHELTERED INSTRUCTION

READING STRATEGIES & LANGUAGE DEVELOPMENT

MAKING CONCLUSIONS Review with students how to make conclusions by using facts in the text and prior knowledge of the subject. Read the second paragraph of *The Big Picture* and model making conclusions about the spread of Islam. Arrange students in a think-pair-share to find the information in the paragraph and the prior knowledge that you used to make the conclusion. **[SDAIE STRATEGY: MODELING/METACOGNITIVE DEVELOPMENT]**

VARIANT SPELLINGS Explain to the class that English spellings can vary for words taken from languages that do not use the Latin alphabet. Alert students to examples that occur in this lesson: *Quran* is used here for what is sometimes spelled *Koran,* and *hijra* is sometimes spelled *hegira. Muslim* is sometimes spelled *Moslem,* and *Muhammad* is sometimes spelled *Mohammed.*

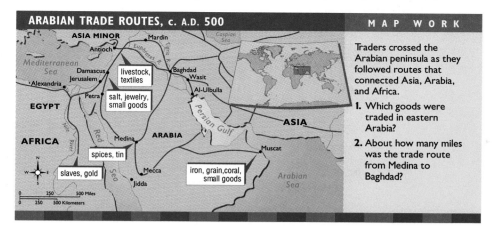

ARABIAN TRADE ROUTES, c. A.D. 500

MAP WORK

Traders crossed the Arabian peninsula as they followed routes that connected Asia, Arabia, and Africa.

1. Which goods were traded in eastern Arabia?

2. About how many miles was the trade route from Medina to Baghdad?

THE BIRTH OF MUHAMMAD

In the last lesson you read that traders had been crisscrossing the Arabian peninsula for hundreds of years. Find some of the caravan trade routes on the map on this page. By A.D. 500 traders carried goods and ideas to and from many different communities. In some towns Arab traders could buy iron tools from a Jewish craftworker or have a tooth pulled by a Christian dentist. Religious beliefs differed from place to place, as did languages and writing systems. The people in western Arabia had developed a written language, Arabic, sometime before 800 B.C. An example of Arabic writing is shown below.

According to Muslim tradition, a boy named Muhammad (mu HAM ud) was born in the oasis city of Mecca about A.D. 570. His father died before he was born. Because Muhammad's mother died not long after his birth, he was raised by an uncle who was a trader. In time Muhammad mastered the skill of leading caravans.

The writings that trace Muhammad's life say that his skills caught the eye of a wealthy widow and merchant, Khadija (ka DEE jah). On her behalf Muhammad traveled to the Fertile Crescent to trade goods. When he returned from his journey, they were married.

The City of Mecca

Muhammad's marriage to Khadija is said to have given him wealth and respect in busy Mecca, where they lived. Mecca lay on the main trading route through western Arabia. Therefore, many merchants came to do business there.

The city also attracted other visitors because of the Kaaba (KAH buh), Mecca's temple. At this time the Kaaba was like the Pantheon of Rome. It honored gods and goddesses worshiped by the people of Mecca.

THE BIRTH OF MUHAMMAD

Develop an understanding of Muhammad's early years.

● **Where and when was Muhammad born?** (Mecca in about A.D. 570)

● **How did he learn his work as a trader?** (by working for his uncle)

★ **THINKING FURTHER: Making Conclusions Why do you suppose Muhammad captured the interest of Khadija?** (She wanted to employ his skill as a trader.)

More **MAP WORK**

Refer the class to the map on this page.

● **Find Mecca on the map. Where is it located on the Arabian peninsula?** (about 250 miles inland from the west coast)

● **What tells you that it was an important trading center?** (Trade routes branch out from it to the east, west, and north.)

● **To what destinations do these roads lead?** (Egypt, Asia Minor, Jerusalem, Damascus, western Asia)

★ **THINKING FURTHER: Making Conclusions What evidence can you find that the Arabians had a thriving trade?** (variety of goods exchanged and many trade partners)

Exploring The City of Mecca Refer to the map when discussing Mecca.

● **Why was Mecca such a busy city?** (It was a center of trade—as a crossroads of trading routes—and of religion, as home of the Kaaba, a temple to gods and goddesses.)

★ **THINKING FURTHER: Making Conclusions Why would Muhammad's occupation and his home city put him in a position to learn about other cultures?** (His travels introduced him to other cultures, as did visitors from other cultures who came to Mecca.)

CURRICULUM CONNECTION

LINKS TO LANGUAGE ARTS Again refer students to the word *Islam* and explain to them that it is related to *salaam,* the word for "peace" in Arabic. Arabs greet one another on meeting by saying "Salaam," just as Jews greet one another with the Hebrew word *shalom.* (Remind students of the Biblical tradition that half-brothers began the two lines—Ishmael, the Arabs, and Isaac, the Jews.)

BACKGROUND INFORMATION

ABOUT THE KAABA
● After Islam took hold in Mecca, the Kaaba ceased to be the temple of Arabic gods and goddesses and was rededicated to Allah.
● Today, it is Islam's most sacred shrine and the goal of the Muslim pilgrimage to Mecca.

TEACHINGS OF ISLAM

Explain to the class that, according to Islamic belief, Allah made revelations to Muhammad through the angel Gabriel, the same angel that Christians believe told Mary that she was to become the mother of Jesus.

Discussing The Prophet Muhammad Discuss Muhammad's role as teacher.

- *What did Muhammad do with the revelations he received?* (He began teaching them in Mecca.)

- *How did city leaders react to these teachings?* (They opposed Muhammad because he preached monotheism and a different way of life.)

> ★**THINKING FURTHER:** *Cause and Effect* *What did the city leaders' opposition cause Muhammad to do?* (flee Mecca in 622)

Exploring Muhammad's Migration Have students locate Medina on the map on p. 267.

- *What does hijra mean?* ("migration")

- *What was Muhammad's hijra?* (his migration from Mecca to Medina)

> ★**THINKING FURTHER:** *Making Conclusions* *Why do you suppose the hijra marked a turning point in Islamic history?* (perhaps because it gave Muhammad a base of support from which to spread Islam)

Discussing Return to Mecca Remind the class of the siege technique used by the Spartans against Athens (pp. 208–209).

- *How did Muhammad use a kind of siege technique to gain control of Mecca?* (He cut off Mecca's lifeline to its source of wealth—trade.)

> ★**THINKING FURTHER:** *Compare and Contrast* *How would you contrast Mecca before and after its surrender to Muhammad?* (Before: center of polytheism. After: center of monotheistic Islam and a holy Muslim city)

A young Bedouin reads from the Quran (left). Thousands of Muslims face the Kaaba as they pray (below).

TEACHINGS OF ISLAM

According to Muslim belief Muhammad often went to a mountain cave near Mecca to pray. The writings say that one night, when Muhammad was about 40 years old, something happened that would change the history of Arabia.

Muslims believe that Muhammad received a message from Allah (ahl LAH). *Allah* is the Arabic word for God. Muhammad was told, "O Muhammad, you are the Prophet of Allah." As you learned in Chapter 5, a prophet is believed by followers to speak for God. Over many years, Allah is said to have given other messages to Muhammad.

The Prophet Muhammad

Muslim writings say that Muhammad's wife Khadija helped him greatly. With her encouragement and support, he set out to teach people in Mecca about Allah. Over the next three years, his group of followers slowly grew.

According to tradition Muhammad aroused the anger of city leaders. They were upset because he criticized the Meccans' way of life and their belief in many gods. His disagreement with city leaders is said to have caused him and his followers to leave Mecca in 622.

Muhammad's Migration

The writings about Muhammad say that he moved over 200 miles from Mecca to another oasis town, Medina (muh DEE nuh). He gained many supporters there. Muhammad's hijra (HIHJ ruh)—Arabic for "migration"— marked a major turning point in Islamic history. The year of the hijra, 622, marks the starting point of the Islamic calendar.

268

CITIZENSHIP ★

RECOGNIZING PERSPECTIVES In Europe and America until rather recently, some people referred to Islam as Muhammadanism and its followers as Muhammadans. But the followers of Islam objected because those names seemed to indicate that they worship Muhammad, as Christians worship Jesus. Since the Quran says that only Allah may be worshiped, Muslims prefer the words *Islam* and *Muslims.*

GLOBAL CONNECTION

HOLY CITIES Major religions often have certain cities that they consider holy, just as Islam has Mecca.

- Roman Catholicism calls Rome the Holy City.

- Hindus consider seven different cities in India to be sacred.

- Jews, Christians, and Muslims all consider the same city holy. Can students guess it? (Jerusalem)

Return to Mecca

Muslim scholars say that in 624 Muhammad led attacks on Meccan caravans, cutting off Mecca's source of riches. Later, with peace agreements, he is said to have won Mecca's surrender. After his victory in 630, Muhammad destroyed the statues of the gods and goddesses in the Kaaba and proclaimed Mecca a Muslim city. It is holy to Muslims to this day.

Writings state that Muhammad won the support of many Arabian communities. In 632 he is said to have spoken to his followers at Mecca. His words, taken from the Quran, were "[Muslim] believers are brothers one of another." Later that year Muhammad died.

The Sacred Book of Islam

In Islamic belief the Quran contains Allah's teachings to Muhammad. Muslims believe these words were written down soon after Muhammad's death. The most important teaching was that there was only one God in the universe—Allah. The Quran says that Allah is the God worshiped both by Christians and Jews.

> We believe in God, and in that which has been sent down on Abraham . . . and that which was given to Moses and Jesus.

The Quran serves as a guide for living for Muslims, as the Bible does for Jews and Christians. Through its words, Muslims learn about Allah's teachings.

The Five Pillars of Islam

The Quran outlines five basic duties of all Muslims. The purpose of these duties—the Five Pillars of Islam—is to strengthen Muslims' ties to Allah and to other people. The first pillar is the belief in one God, Allah, and that Muhammad

is Allah's prophet. The second describes the prayers Muslims offer Allah five times each day. Wherever they are in the world, as they pray, Muslims look toward Mecca, their holy city. The third pillar speaks of giving to those in need, especially the poor. The fourth instructs Muslims to fast during the holy month of Ramadan (rahm uh DAHN). From sunrise to sunset Muslims neither eat nor drink. They spend time in worship. The final pillar instructs Muslims who can afford it to visit Mecca at least once in their lives. A journey for religious purposes is called a pilgrimage.

The Quran's first chapter has important instructions. What do these words say about Islam?

**Excerpt from
The Quran, about A.D. 650
Chapter One, Verses 2–7.**

Praise be to [Allah], The Cherisher and
   Sustainer of the worlds;

Most Gracious, Most Merciful

Master of the Day of Judgment.

Thee do we worship and Thine aid we
   seek.

Show us the straight way,

The way of those on whom Thou hast
   bestowed Thy Grace.

269

Discussing The Sacred Book of Islam As students identify the Quran, ask them to name other sacred writings—the Torah, the Vedas, the Bible.

- *What does the Quran contain?* (the teachings Allah gave to Muhammad)

- *Who does the Quran say that Allah is?* (the one universal God, that is the same God the Jews and Christians worship)

★THINKING FURTHER: *Compare and Contrast* **How are the Quran and the Bible similar?** (Both say there is one God and both offer guides for living.)

Exploring The Five Pillars of Islam Have students tell what a pillar is (a support to hold something up). As they identify the *Five Pillars*, have them draw and label five pillars on the board.

- *What are the Five Pillars of Islam?* (belief in one God, prayer five times daily, giving to the poor, fasting during Ramadan, pilgrimage to Mecca)

★THINKING FURTHER: *Making Conclusions* **What is it that all these pillars hold up?** (the religion of Islam)

Discussing the PRIMARY SOURCE

Help students with any unfamiliar words, like *thee, thou,* or *compassionate.* Call attention to the beautiful writing, or calligraphy, which is the quotation translated in the *Read Aloud.* Explain that the Quran forbids the representation of humans (including Muhammad) and animals, so Arabic script was developed to provide decoration.

- *How does this excerpt praise Allah?* (It refers to Allah's power, kindness, mercy, and worthiness of worship.)

- *What does it ask of Allah?* (guidance and favor)

★THINKING FURTHER: *Making Conclusions* **What does Islam seem to say is the proper relation between Allah and human beings?** (People should honor and obey their powerful and good God.)

MUSLIMS AROUND THE WORLD

Note that the influence of Islam is both religious and secular.

- ***When did Muhammad die?*** *(A.D. 632)*

- ***What legacy did he leave to the next 100 years?*** *(the spread of Islamic faith from Spain to the Indus valley)*

★**THINKING FURTHER:** *Making Conclusions* **How did Islam spread Arab influence and unite people under it?** *(It gave its followers a common language—Arabic—and a common book of teachings and laws to guide them—the Quran.)*

Discussing Islam Today Underline the concept that Islam today is a major, thriving religion.

- ***How many Muslims live around the world today?*** *(more than one billion, mentioned on p. 266)*

- ***About how many Muslims live in the United States?*** *(about 5 million)*

- ***What do they all have in common?*** *(belief in the Five Pillars)*

★**THINKING FURTHER:** *Making Generalizations* **What evidence can you give to support the generalization that, to practicing Muslims, religion is a very important part of life?** *(their adherence to the Five Pillars—fasting at Ramadan, making a pilgrimage to Mecca and the way they encourage their children to learn the Quran and study their faith.)*

MUSLIMS AROUND THE WORLD

Muhammad's death must have caused his followers great sorrow. One said, "O men, if you worship Muhammad, Muhammad is dead; if you worship Allah, Allah is alive." Muslims then joined together to spread the message of Islam.

During the 100 years after the death of Muhammad, the Islamic community grew steadily. It spread and flourished, and by A.D. 750, followers of Islam could be found from Spain all the way to the Indus valley.

Gradually, over a period of time, nonreligious legacies spread throughout this vast region, as well. Just as the Latin language spread through the Roman empire, for example, Arabic became the common language in many Islamic lands. The different peoples who came under Islamic rule also made many important contributions to the heritage of Islam. You will read about some of these contributions in the next lesson.

Islam Today

Of the great number of Muslims in the world today, around 5 million live in the United States. The customs of Muslims often vary from one country to another. However, nearly all Muslims honor the end of Ramadan with a joyful feast. People wear new clothes to celebrate the beginning of the month following the long fast.

Millions of Muslims from all around the world still make the pilgrimage to the holy city of Mecca every year. Muslims everywhere view the pilgrimage as one of the most important events in their lives.

Muslims gather for worship in Cordoba, Spain (top). The end of Ramadan is celebrated by many with music and dance (right).

270

BACKGROUND INFORMATION

ABOUT THE PILGRIMAGE TO MECCA
- Islam adopted the pilgrimage to Mecca from an earlier Arabic religion, which encouraged pilgrimage to the pre-Islamic Kaaba to worship Arab gods and goddesses.
- The pilgrimage to Mecca is known as a *hajj* or *hadj*, and *hajji* is the title given to a person who completes it.
- The pilgrimage can be made at any time of year, but the most popular time is two months after Ramadan.
- When they reach Mecca, all pilgrims, rich and poor, dress in the same simple white clothing and perform the same devotions, to remind themselves that they are all equal before Allah.

CURRICULUM CONNECTION

LINKS TO MATHEMATICS Have students figure out both the fraction and percentage Muslims comprise of (1) the world population and (2) of the U.S. population. First, have students use a current almanac to find recent world and U.S. populations. Then have them divide one billion and 5 million, respectively, into each of those figures.

SECOND-LANGUAGE SUPPORT

WORKING WITH A PEER Second-language learners may benefit by focusing on lesson segments. Have them work with English-proficient partners to study assigned lesson sections. Then have each pair create a summary of their section, and have them present it to the class.

At home Muslim women take time to teach their children about the Quran. Muslim families have celebrations when sons or daughters memorize large parts of the Quran. Some young people go on to study Islam and other subjects at Muslim schools and colleges.

WHY IT MATTERS

The modern city of Mecca, in Saudi Arabia, is the center of a world-wide Muslim community. No matter where they may be in the world, when they pray, Muslims always position themselves to face this holy city.

For almost 1,400 years Islam has been anchored in both the life of Muhammad and the teachings of the Quran. Throughout that long stretch of time, the religion of Islam has shaped civilizations and human achievements. You will read about some of those achievements in the next lesson.

✔// Reviewing Facts and Ideas

MAIN IDEAS

● According to Muslim belief Muhammad, the founder of Islam, lived from A.D. 570 to 632. Muhammad preached that there was only one God—Allah.

● Muhammad journeyed from Mecca to Medina in 622. This event is called the hijra. Muhammad went on to become a powerful leader in Medina. Later he returned and proclaimed Mecca a holy city.

● Muslims believe that the sacred book of Islam, the Quran, contains holy teachings that Muhammad received from Allah.

● The Five Pillars of Islam from the Quran instruct Muslims about how they should honor Allah in their lives.

THINK ABOUT IT

1. Why was Mecca an important religious center even before Islam was founded? Why was it an important trading city?

2. What is the most important teaching of Islam?

3. FOCUS How do the teachings of Islam affect the daily lives of Muslims?

4. THINKING SKILL According to Islamic writings, what was the main *cause* of Muhammad's *hijra*, or migration? What were some of its *effects*?

5. GEOGRAPHY Find the holy city of Mecca on the map on page 267. In what direction would a Muslim living in Mardin face during prayer? Estimate the distance that he or she would need to journey in making a pilgrimage to Mecca.

271

Discussing WHY IT MATTERS Note that Islam has a powerful influence today.

★**THINKING FURTHER:** *Making Conclusions How would you say that Mecca serves as a unifying force for all of the Islamic world?* (Students should recognize Mecca as a focal point that ties all Muslims together—they face it each day to pray and try to make a pilgrimage there at least once.)

⭐ 3 CLOSE

MAIN IDEAS

Call on students to answer these questions.

● *When did Muhammad live and what did he preach regarding God?* (From A.D. 570 to 632; there is one God—Allah.)

● *What caused Muhammad's hijra and what was its outcome?* (He had to flee Mecca because of opposition to him from city leaders. He found a base of support in Medina from which he could go back and take control of Mecca.)

● *What is the Quran?* (the holy teachings of Allah)

● *What do the Five Pillars of Islam set out for Muslims?* (ways they should honor Allah)

EVALUATE

✔ **Answers to Think About It**

1. It had the Kaaba, a temple for the worship of Arab gods and goddesses; it was on important trade routes. *Recall Details*

2. that there is but one God—Allah—and Muhammad is his prophet *Main Idea*

3. The teachings spell out how Muslims should honor Allah every day. *Make Inferences*

4. Cause: opposition to Muhammad's teachings from city leaders. Effects: finding support in Medina, returning to take control of Mecca. *Cause and Effect*

5. A Muslim in Mardin would face south; approximately 1,125 miles. *Five Themes of Geography: Human/Environment Interactions*

Write About It Have students write a paragraph contrasting the Kaaba before and after Islam.

MEETING INDIVIDUAL NEEDS

RETEACHING (Easy) Have students review the events in Muhammad's life and choose one to illustrate. When the illustrations are completed, have students create a bulletin board display showing the events in chronological order.

EXTENSION (Average) Divide the class into several groups and assign each group an event in Muhammad's life. Tell each group to write a dramatization of the event. Have students present their dramatizations in chronological order to the class.

ENRICHMENT (Challenging) Divide the class into four groups and assign each a different area of Muslim life to research: eating and dietary rules, marriage customs, social division of men and women, and rules of etiquette. Have each group research its area and prepare a presentation of its findings to the class.

LESSON 3
PAGES 272–277

Lesson Overview
As the Islamic empire spread, Islamic civilization flourished, enriching and being enriched by other civilizations.

Lesson Objectives
★ Describe the caliphate established and headquartered at Baghdad.

★ Identify contributions of Islamic civilization to the world.

⭐ 1 PREPARE

MOTIVATE Ask a student to do the *Read Aloud*. Have students locate Baghdad on the map on p. 273 as they study its location and the picture of the Islamic pilgrimage from Baghdad on this page.

SET PURPOSE Refer students to the *Read to Learn* question. Encourage them to predict achievements, based on what they have learned about Islam and on the *Read Aloud*. List predictions on the board and have students read the lesson to verify them. Preview the *Vocabulary* terms.

⭐ 2 TEACH

Understanding THE BIG PICTURE
Briefly have students recall earlier civilizations (such as Mesopotamia and Persia) they studied in the region.

- **On what river did the Muslims locate Baghdad?** *(the Tigris)*

- **In what modern-day country is it?** *(Iraq)*

★**THINKING FURTHER:** *Making Conclusions* **Why was Baghdad a good site on which to build an imperial capital?** *(It has access to good river transportation, rich agriculture fed by irrigation canals; both can support a population and an army.)*

Resource REMINDER

Practice and Project Book: *p. 56*

Anthology: *An Islamic Hospital, p. 58; The Ringdove, pp. 59–61; An Honest Counsellor, p. 62*

🔘 **Technology:** *Adventure Time! CD-ROM*
Desk Map

400   600   750   1200

A MUSLIM CALIPHATE

Focus Activity

READ TO LEARN
What did Muslims achieve in the city of Baghdad?

VOCABULARY
caliph
mosque
algebra
astrolabe

PEOPLE
Avicenna

PLACES
Baghdad

READ ALOUD
Lining the docks, ships filled with Egyptian rice, Chinese dishware, Syrian glass, and Arabian pearls could be seen bobbing on the river. The roads leading to the city were crowded with farmers bringing oranges and cucumbers, and with traders carrying elegant carpets. Occasionally the government's "air-mail" service flew overhead. The service was actually pigeons that had been trained to carry letters! Even more wonders lay within the incredible city of Baghdad (BAG dad).

THE BIG PICTURE
Centuries before the founding of Baghdad, Persian rulers controlled lands north of the Arabian peninsula, from Egypt to India. By the A.D. 600s the Persian empire was in decline. As Islam developed in Mecca, Muhammad gained power on the Arabian peninsula. Leaders who ruled after Muhammad extended Islam to Persian lands and other areas. By 700 Muslim rulers controlled the Mediterranean region.

In 762 the Muslim ruler al-Mansur (al man SUR) decided to build a capital city along the Tigris River in present-day Iraq. He reportedly declared, "This is the site on which I shall build. Goods can arrive here by way of the Euphrates, Tigris, and a network of canals. Only a place like this will support the army and the general population." Not long afterwards the city of Baghdad began to take shape. The city along the Tigris quickly became the center of the Muslim civilization's greatest achievements in science, art, and architecture.

272

SHELTERED INSTRUCTION

READING STRATEGIES & LANGUAGE DEVELOPMENT

MAIN IDEA AND DETAILS Review with students how finding main ideas and details can help them understand a passage. Have them read the first two paragraphs in *The Big Picture* and find the main idea and details. [The main idea is in the first sentence; the details follow.] Arrange students in collaborative groups to make a chart showing the main ideas and details in the lesson. **[SDAIE STRATEGY:** TEXT RE-PRESENTATION/ SCHEMA BUILDING]

WORD HISTORY Remind students that many English words come from either Greek or Latin. Point out that Arabic is yet another source for English words. Write *al* on the board and explain that it is Arabic for "the." Our words *alcohol, alcove, alfalfa, algebra, alkali,* and *almanac* all come from Arabic terms.

MUSLIM RULE

In the 760s Islam was just over 100 years old. Much had changed in this time. Caliphs (KAY lihfs) had been chosen to govern the land and religion of Islam. *Caliph* means "successor [to the Prophet]." The lands ruled by the caliph were called the caliphate (KAY luh fayt). As the map below shows, the caliphate expanded to western Asia and North Africa. In many places people welcomed the Muslims, who overthrew hated rulers of old. Many people became Muslims. Others did not, but they learned Arabic. An Islamic civilization united by Muslim leadership developed.

Baghdad

From the late 700s until the 1200s, Baghdad was the capital of the Muslim caliphate. One of the world's largest cities, it had about 1 million residents.

Baghdad's layout reflected the grandness of the Muslim caliphate. At the center of the city stood the caliph's huge, domed palace. Next to it rose a great mosque (MAHSK). A mosque is a place of worship where Muslims go for daily prayers.

From the center of Baghdad, four main roads went to all parts of the caliphate. Traders used these roads to bring riches from all over the caliphate and beyond.

Baghdad had an international flavor. Shoppers packed the streets where Arabian perfume, Indian pepper, African ivory, and Russian furs were among the items sold. Some shops sold only Chinese dishware, while others sold only books. Merchants had learned papermaking from the Chinese, and Baghdad's new paper mill made it possible to create many books.

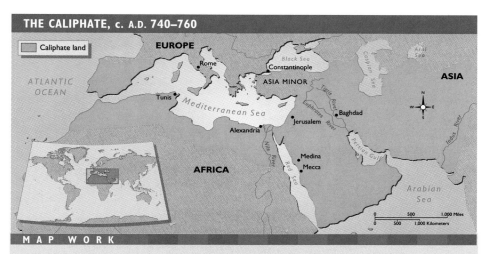

THE CALIPHATE, c. A.D. 740–760

Caliphate land

EUROPE
ATLANTIC OCEAN
Rome
Black Sea
Constantinople
ASIA MINOR
Caspian Sea
Aral Sea
ASIA
Tunis
Mediterranean Sea
Tigris River
Euphrates River
Baghdad
Jerusalem
Alexandria
Nile River
Red Sea
Medina
Mecca
AFRICA
Persian Gulf
Indus River
Arabian Sea

0   500   1,000 Miles
0   500   1,000 Kilometers

MAP WORK

Under the rule of the caliphs, an Islamic civilization spread throughout Arabia, North Africa, and western Asia.

1. Which rivers flowed near Baghdad?

2. Which city is closest to the Persian Gulf—Constantinople, Baghdad, or Mecca?

3. About how far is Baghdad from Mecca?

MAP WORK: **1.** Tigris River, Euphrates River **2.** Baghdad
3. about 950 miles (about 1,520 kilometers)

273

BACKGROUND INFORMATION

ABOUT THE SPREAD OF ISLAM
- In the years following Muhammad's death, Arabian armies burst forth from the Arabian peninsula and spread their religion and influence. Within just 20 years, they had conquered Palestine, Syria, Egypt, Iraq, and most of Persia. Over the next century, they moved on to conquer the areas shown on the map here.
- Because Jews and Christians followed the teachings of the Bible, a book that Muhammad accepted as God's word, he looked on them as "People of the Book." So Muslims did not force Jews and Christians in the areas they conquered to accept Islam as their religion. Yet those Jews and Christians who did not embrace Islam were charged an annual fee for the right to retain and practice their own religions.

MUSLIM RULE

- *What is a caliph?* (a successor to Muhammad, chosen to rule lands under Muslim control)

- *What is a caliphate?* (the lands that a caliph rules)

- *What tied the Muslim caliphate together?* (the rule of Muslim law and leadership, the Arabic language, a developing Islamic civilization)

★THINKING FURTHER: *Making Conclusions* **Have students note that the text says, "In many places people welcomed the Muslims . . ." What might this imply about the other places?** (that there were peoples in the Muslim caliphate who did not want Muslim rule)

More **MAP WORK**

Refer students to the map on this page. They can also use markers to indicate these areas on their desk maps.

- *Into what parts of Africa did the Muslim caliphate spread?* (Egypt and the coastal areas of North Africa to the Atlantic Ocean)

- *What part of Europe did the caliphate control?* (Spain)

- *What parts of Asia were in the caliphate?* (eastern Mediterranean, Arabia, Persia, part of India)

★THINKING FURTHER: *Making Conclusions* **What do you suppose the Christian world thought about the spreading Muslim caliphate?** (They might have been fearful of being swallowed up by it.)

Discussing Baghdad Remind students that Rome had fallen in the A.D. 400s.

- *What was the capital of the caliphate?* (the city of Baghdad)

- *How large did Baghdad grow?* (to about one million people)

★THINKING FURTHER: *Compare and Contrast* **How would you compare the imperial capital of Rome at its height and Baghdad?** (Students should see the striking similarities in population, crowding, magnificent buildings, destination of roads, trade goods available, status as world cities.)

ACHIEVEMENTS OF THE CALIPHATE

Write Muhammad's declaration on the board and have the class discuss its meaning.

★**THINKING FURTHER:** *Making Conclusions* **How did Muhammad's declaration send the Muslims on a worldwide quest for knowledge?** *(It set them off to gather knowledge from other parts of the world and to build on it.)*

Discussing Advances in Medicine
Use the material on these pages to reinforce the advantages of cultural borrowing.

● **Who was Ibn Sina, or Avicenna?** *(a renowned Muslim doctor)*

● **On what did Avicenna and other Arab doctors build their medical knowledge?** *(Greek medical texts)*

★**THINKING FURTHER:** *Making Conclusions* **How did they enlarge on what they learned from the Greeks?** *(They expanded on it, making their own findings about how disease spread and how it could be treated.)*

Exploring Math and Science Explain to the class that Arabic numbers are based on the Hindu numbering system.

● **In what ways did Arab scholars borrow from Hindu scholars?** *(They adopted the Hindu numbering system and learned and then expanded on Hindu algebra.)*

● **What is astronomy and why were Muslims interested in it?** *(Astronomy is the study of stars and planets; they based their calendar on the moon, and the stars helped them find the direction of Mecca from wherever on Earth they were.)*

★**THINKING FURTHER:** *Predicting* **What was the** **astrolabe? How might its development help later explorers, like Columbus?** *(Help the class to see how the ability to use star positions to find one's location would give future explorers a means to strike out over ever greater distances across Earth.)*

ACHIEVEMENTS OF THE CALIPHATE

Baghdad's caliphs valued education and learning. Muhammad was said to have declared, "He who travels in search of knowledge, travels along Allah's path of Paradise." As a result, the caliphs preserved works from all over the caliphate in a huge library, the House of Wisdom. There, Greek, Roman, and Indian works were translated into Arabic. Over time these works spread throughout the caliphate and the world. Arab scholars read these books on history, science, law, and mathematics. Many later developed and improved these fields of study.

Advances in Medicine

Muslim doctors studied translations of Greek medical texts and a work by a famous Muslim doctor who lived in

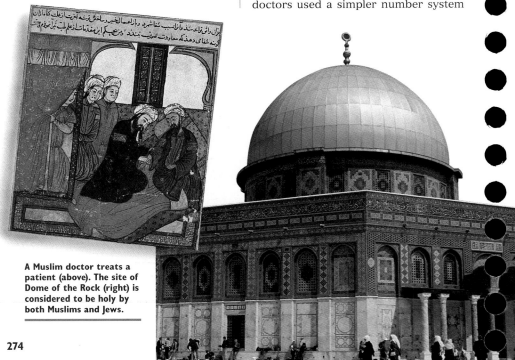

A Muslim doctor treats a patient (above). The site of Dome of the Rock (right) is considered to be holy by both Muslims and Jews.

274

Persia in the early 1000s. His name was Ibn Sina (IHB un SEE nuh), or Avicenna (av ih SEN uh) in Latin. Avicenna described how some diseases spread through air and water. He wrote that stress could cause stomach problems and that cancer could be fought with surgery. In time Avicenna's book became a standard medical text in many parts of North Africa, western Asia, and Europe.

The caliphate had many doctors. Some of them treated patients in Baghdad's large hospitals. Others oversaw the government's "moving hospitals." These doctors and their assistants gave free treatment to patients who lived far from Baghdad. Such traveling medical teams carried beds, medicines, and other supplies by camel.

Math and Science

When calculating doses of medicine, doctors used a simpler number system

GLOBAL CONNECTION

AVICENNA—A LINK BETWEEN CULTURES Avicenna's most famous work, the *Canon of Medicine*, was based largely on medical tracts from ancient Greece and Rome. In the 1100s, European universities made it the foundation of medical training, which it remained until the 1600s. Avicenna also wrote widely on philosophy, building on the work of Plato. Medieval Christian philosophers in turn built on Avicenna's work.

USING THE ANTHOLOGY

AN ISLAMIC HOSPITAL, page 58 The description of the hospital can be used to extend the concepts of advances in medicine and to relate the practices to Islamic principles of concern for the poor.

than that of the Romans. In the Roman system, "XVIII" was "18"—its equal in Arabic numbers. You know the Arabic number system because we use it today.

Muslim mathematicians built on the work of Hindu scholars in India. For example, they helped improve earlier mathematics methods and notation. Muslims also added greatly to the field of *al-jabr* (al JAHB ur). In English, it's algebra, a type of mathematics.

In its vast collections, the House of Wisdom had many Arabic volumes on astronomy. Astronomy, the study of the stars and planets, was of great interest to Muslims. The Islamic calendar was based on the moon's movement. Stars also helped people determine directions. Muslims used a Greek instrument, the astrolabe (AS truh layb), which they improved, to figure out position from the stars.

Places of Worship

Throughout the caliphate, mosque builders took care to follow certain standards. They had to make sure the mosque faced Mecca. Special nooks in the walls showed people the direction of Mecca. From tall towers, religious leaders could call Muslims to prayer. Walled-in courtyards held hundreds of worshipers. Beyond these basic features, builders used their imaginations to make each mosque as beautiful as possible. Many remain standing today.

The oldest Muslim monument still standing is the Dome of the Rock in Jerusalem. Built in 691, this building is not a mosque. Instead it honors the place where Muslims believe Muhammad ascended into heaven. Its Roman-style dome and Greek columns show how Muslims combined old and new ideas to create a unique style of architecture.

Links to MUSIC
Where did you get that guitar?

Before A.D. 700, Arab musicians made and performed on stringed instruments. One of these was the *oud* (OOD) which has a pear-shaped body. Another favorite of Arab musicians was a similar instrument with a flat back, called the guitar. Many historians believe Arabs invented the instrument.

As the caliphate spread, Muslim musicians introduced their stringed instruments in Spain. The oud eventually developed into the lute, a popular instrument in Europe from the 14th to the 16th centuries. The Arabian guitar is the ancestor of the modern guitar that is still popular today. Can you think of any other instruments related to the guitar? Listen to a recording of a guitar.

Literature and Music

Long before Islam was born in Arabia, literature and music had been popular there. You read an excerpt from a pre-Islamic poem in the introduction to Lesson 1. Poetry remained well loved among the people of Baghdad, and its appreciation spread throughout the region at this time.

Folktales were also very popular among the citizens of Baghdad and the rest of the caliphate. Over time, favorites from Persia, India, Arabia, and other places were collected into a book called *The Arabian Nights*. The book's main story is of a wise princess named Scheherazade (she HAIR ah zahd). She is married to a cruel king who threatens to kill her after their wedding. She saves herself by distracting him with tales of Aladdin, Ali Baba and the 40 thieves, and other exciting stories.

275

Discussing Places of Worship If you have a *mosque* in your area, call students' attention to it and discuss its architecture. If possible, have picture books available that show mosques.

- **Why does each mosque have a tall tower?** (It is a place from which Muslims can be called to prayer five times a day.)

- **What architectural feature did the Muslims borrow from Roman engineering?** (the dome)

★THINKING FURTHER: *Making Conclusions* **Why do you think that architects strive for beauty when they build places of worship?** (perhaps because they want to show great honor for the deity worshiped and to elevate worshipers' minds and hearts)

Exploring Literature and Music Tell students that Islam has a rich literature, perhaps unfamiliar to us because little has been translated into English.

- **How did Islamic civilization borrow from other civilizations in developing its literature?** (In addition to incorporating Arabian tales, it took stories from Persia and India.)

- **What musical instruments do many historians say come to us from the Arab culture?** (the lute and guitar)

★THINKING FURTHER: *Making Conclusions* **Why do you suppose that collections like The Arabian Nights became long-lived favorites of Islamic literature?** (Help students see how basic a love of stories is to human nature, perhaps a remnant of prewritten language days when tales were handed down orally.)

CURRICULUM CONNECTION

LINKS TO MUSIC: WHERE DID YOU GET THAT GUITAR? The earliest music of Arabia was mainly vocal, arising from "caravan songs," sung to pass the time as long caravans made their way across vast deserts. The oud and the guitar were developed to accompany this singing. Ask students to find out about other "music on the move," such as that of medieval minstrels, cowboys, and shepherds.

LINKS TO READING The cruel king of *The Arabian Nights* (also called *The Thousand and One Nights*) began his evil ways after his first wife was unfaithful to him. To be sure that no wife would ever be unfaithful to him again, he married a different woman every day and then killed her the next morning—until Scheherazade.

SECOND-LANGUAGE SUPPORT

GRAPHIC ORGANIZERS Have students create a semantic map of terms and information from Lesson 2, and then incorporate related information from this lesson. Invite students to explain their entries.

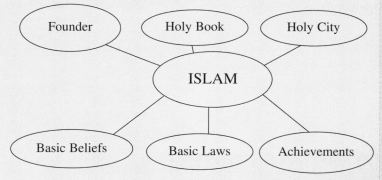

Infographic

Have students review the story of the founding and richness of Baghdad (p. 272). Read to the class these words by Baghdad's founder, al-Mansur, who planned his city to be a "marketplace for the world": "By God I shall build it. Then I shall dwell in it as long as I live and my descendants shall dwell in it after me. It will surely be the most flourishing city in the world." Explain that it was in the lavish Abbasid Palace that he and his descendants lived.

Discussing the Pictures Give students time to read the introduction and examine the people, activities, arts, artifacts, and captions.

● *What is the major design element in the walls of the palace? What is distinctive about them?* (arches; unlike the rounded Roman arch, they come to a sort of point at the top.)

● *What clues can you find that the Caliphate had access to goods from all over the world?* (Students may recall that the oud probably originated in Arabia. The silk the women wore came from China.)

● *Which of the things shown probably reflect the most wealth and highest degree of craft work?* (Possible answers: clothing, musical instruments, stone carving)

★THINKING FURTHER: *Cause and Effect* **Why do you think caliphs wanted to build such spectacular palaces and fill them with luxurious goods?** *(Perhaps it reflects a personal desire to live in comfort surrounded by things of great beauty, but perhaps it also reflects a desire to show their wealth and power to maintain an exalted position in the world for their caliphates.)*

Technology CONNECTION

ADVENTURE TIME! CD-ROM
Have students use the Unit Activity and experience this *Infographic* on the *Adventure Time!* CD-ROM.

Infographic

Life in the Caliphate

During the time of the Baghdad Caliphate, Muslim control spread to parts of Europe, North Africa, and western Asia. Important cultural and scientific achievements spread as well. The stunning architecture of the Alhambra (left), a palace in Spain, is an example. What were some other achievements found in the Caliphate?

Learning
Around 1200, a Muslim teacher (below) who lived in what is today Turkey taught his students about the proper way to form sentences.

Court Life
This painting of court life (above) in what is today Iran shows the wealth of the empire. Notice the oud player on the left.

EXPANDING THE INFOGRAPHIC

RESEARCHING AND WRITING Islamic art, with its distinctive architectural features and decor, rugs and carpets, manuscript illuminations, and decorated pottery, vessels, and weapons, is a continuing source of beauty and fancy. Have students do research to find an object of Islamic art that particularly interests them. On a piece of construction paper, have them draw a copy of it and write a paragraph telling about it. Then have them assemble the pages into "Our Class Book of Islamic Art." You might suggest the following sources:

● Encyclopedia entries for *Islamic art.*

● A library catalog for entries like *Islamic art* and *Early Islam.*

● *Gardner's Art Through the Ages,* Vol. 1, and Time-Life's *Early Islam* are both good sources.

Weaving
Muslim weavers became famous for their beautiful rugs. Rugs from this region are still treasured for their excellent quality.

Design
This jar (left) may have been used to pour water or wine. Notice the expert working of the design and spout.

WHY IT MATTERS

Baghdad's caliphs ruled lands that stretched from Morocco to India. Islam established deep roots in that area. So did a rich heritage that included major achievements in the arts and sciences.

As you have read, the Arabic language developed on the Arabian peninsula. It is now the common language of most of northern Africa and of parts of western Asia. Today Muslims in many different nations are united by the legacy of Islam. People around the world share other Arabian legacies.

✓ Reviewing Facts and Ideas

MAIN IDEAS

- Under the caliphs who came after Muhammad, Islam spread into Asia, Africa, and Europe. For centuries the caliphs ruled from Baghdad.
- The caliphate furthered learning in medicine, math, and astronomy.
- Mosques were centers of Muslim worship throughout the caliphate and remain religious centers today.

THINK ABOUT IT

1. Which of Baghdad's trade goods came from other regions?

2. What were some of the achievements of the Muslim caliphate in medicine?

3. **FOCUS** In what ways did Islam influence life in the city of Baghdad?

4. **THINKING SKILL** Based on your study of the geography of Mesopotamia, _make a conclusion_ about the dangers of building Baghdad on the Tigris.

5. **WRITE** Write an article for a science journal describing Baghdad's House of Wisdom. How might it have helped scientists and mathematicians develop new ideas?

277

Discussing WHY IT MATTERS Review some of the legacies of Islam.

> ★**THINKING FURTHER: Compare and Contrast** _What similarities can you find between the spread of Islamic influence and of Roman influence a few centuries earlier?_ (Both extended over a vast territory, both introduced new ideas and borrowed older ones as they spread, leaving rich legacies.)

★ 3 CLOSE

MAIN IDEAS

Have students write their answers and then exchange papers with a partner to verify and correct answers.

- _**Following the death of Muhammad, what was the capital of the Islamic caliphate and over what territory did it stretch?**_ (Baghdad; to western Asia, North Africa, Spain)

- _**What areas of learning did the Islamic caliphate further?**_ (medicine, math, astronomy)

- _**What are Islamic religious centers called?**_ (mosques)

EVALUATE

✓ **Answers to Think About It**

1. Indian pepper, African ivory, Russian furs, Chinese silk
Recall Details

2. discovering that disease can spread through air and water, that stress can cause stomach problems, that surgery can be used to fight cancer
Summarize

3. It made Baghdad a city of magnificent mosques and it focused the citizenry on living by the Five Pillars.
Make Inferences

4. Students should recall that the Tigris River was subject to destructive flooding.
Make Conclusions

5. Articles should reflect how far-reaching the knowledge held by the House of Wisdom was and how it was open for the use of all scholars.
Make Judgements and Decisions

Write About It Write a paragraph to describe one way Islamic civilization influenced another culture and one way another culture influenced it.

MEETING INDIVIDUAL NEEDS

RETEACHING (Easy) Have students review what they learned about Baghdad as the cultural center of Islam. Encourage them to picture a palace, mosque, street, or market scene and draw it.

EXTENSION (Average) Divide the class into several groups and have books of Arabian tales available for them to examine. Have each group write and illustrate its own Arabian tale. Have the groups present their tales to the class and then bind them together in a class book.

ENRICHMENT (Challenging) Choose a tale from _The Arabian Nights_ to dramatize and perform. Divide the class into groups and assign each group a part of the production: writing the dramatization, doing the costumes, making the set, casting and rehearsing the actors. Present the production to other classes.

Lesson Overview
Cartography has evolved new techniques for map making.

Lesson Objective
★ Trace the development of map making techniques over time.

1 PREPARE

MOTIVATE Ask students if they would have recognized Al-Idrisi's illustration on this page as a map. Ask them to look for clues that suggest it is a map. ("latitude" lines) Have them turn the map upside down and encourage them to realize that south is at the top of the map. Point out that various cultures developed different systems of drawing maps.

SET PURPOSE Ask students to suggest reasons that an expanding empire would need maps. List them on the board.

2 TEACH

Understanding the Concept of a Legacy Give students a few minutes to thumb through their texts to identify the varieties of maps they find—those showing latitude and longitude, maps of different scales, physical maps, political maps, climate maps, and so on. Help students see that, over time, all these different kinds of maps had to be developed if people were to be able to picture Earth for their own knowledge and for practical uses.

Legacy
LINKING PAST AND PRESENT

map making

As the Muslim caliphate expanded, the mapping of new lands became important to the caliphs. The science of making maps is called cartography (cahr TOG ruh fee). To improve their skills, Muslim cartographers, or mapmakers, learned techniques used in earlier civilizations, such as ancient Greece. They also used their mathematical skills to develop new methods that helped make maps more accurate than earlier versions.

One technique that Muslim cartographers used was to draw lines dividing the world into different climate zones. These lines, shown on the map at right, were similar to today's lines of latitude.

Cartography is an important legacy that helps us to understand the world around us. Today, different mapping techniques can be used to show us every part of the world, from the ocean floor to the skies above us.

Muslim cartographer al-Idrisi (al IHD rih see) made this circular map of the world around 1150. The Arabian Peninsula looks different from the way you usually see it, because on this map, north points *down*!

278

BACKGROUND INFORMATION

ABOUT MAP MAKING
- The first known map was drawn on a small clay tablet in Sumer in the 2000s B.C. and shows the borders and physical features of a Sumerian estate.
- Egyptians were avid map makers because they had to reestablish property boundaries after the annual flooding of the Nile.
- The Greco-Egyptian Ptolemy produced *Geographia,* one of the earliest geography textbooks, which mapped the world as known to scholars like him during the A.D. 100s.
- Roman surveyors were inveterate cartographers, measuring and mapping each new acquisition to their empire, locating its cities, towns, and roads.

- The Age of Exploration, 15th–18th centuries—made possible in part by the astrolabe—was a boon to cartography, making it possible to map the world.

CURRICULUM CONNECTION

LINKS TO ART Many old maps may be short on accuracy but are illustrated in ways that make them genuine works of art. Ask a committee of volunteers to research the history of cartography and bring books to class that show some of these old maps. Have them prepare a presentation of them for the class.

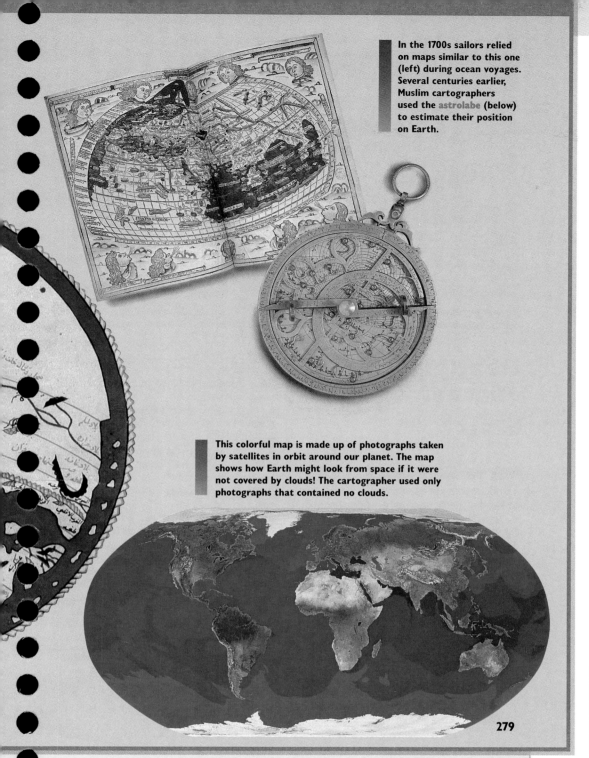

In the 1700s sailors relied on maps similar to this one (left) during ocean voyages. Several centuries earlier, Muslim cartographers used the astrolabe (below) to estimate their position on Earth.

This colorful map is made up of photographs taken by satellites in orbit around our planet. The map shows how Earth might look from space if it were not covered by clouds! The cartographer used only photographs that contained no clouds.

279

Examining the Illustrations Give students a few minutes to examine the pictures and their captions.

● *What is cartography?* (map making)

● *Why do you suppose that there has been a continuing drive over time to improve map making?* (Possible answers: to make maps more accurate, perhaps to know to whom land belonged for taxation, to know more about the extent of land a nation conquered or planned to conquer)

● *As you look at the Al-Idrisi map, why do you think it looks so different from a modern map of the world?* (The cartographer's knowledge of the world was limited to just a portion of it, and his culture used a different style for drawing maps.)

● *How had maps changed by the 18th century?* (They became more complete because explorers had seen and mapped more of the world. Devices such as latitude and longitude added to the usefulness of maps.)

● *What contribution did the astrolabe make to cartography?* (It helped explorers get to more distant places and to map them accurately.)

● *Why would it have been impossible to construct the map at the bottom of this page any earlier than the end of the 20th century?* (The technology it requires was simply not available—photography and satellites are relatively new technologies.)

★THINKING FURTHER: *Predicting*
Do you expect cartography to keep changing in the future? (probably, as new technologies develop)

3 CLOSE

SUM IT UP
Encourage students to summarize ways that cartography has enriched life both in terms of knowledge of the world and practical applications.

EVALUATE
Write About It Have students think about a practical use that they have made of a map in their lives and have them write a paragraph explaining it.

MEETING INDIVIDUAL NEEDS

RETEACHING (Easy) Have students draw a map of the route they follow to school each day.

EXTENSION (Average) Have students picture themselves as 18th-century sailors on a long sea voyage. Tell them to write a letter home in which they explain how the use of maps has made their ship more likely to reach its destination safely.

ENRICHMENT (Challenging) One of the most common kinds of maps Americans see each day are the meteorological maps shown on television news. Have students research meteorological maps to learn how the information for them is gathered and how they are interpreted to forecast weather. Tell students to write their findings and include them in an illustrated report.

SKILLS LESSON
PAGES 280–281

Lesson Overview
A historical map displays information about a part of the world in the past.

Lesson Objective
★ Interpret a historical map.

1 PREPARE

MOTIVATE Ask students if a map of the United States today would be identical to a U.S. map of 200 years ago. Help them see that political boundaries, land ownership, and land use can change. Historical maps show change and other facts of history. Have students read *Why the Skill Matters* and then identify the kinds of historical events that each map here depicts. Have them compare this map with the map on p. 273.

SET PURPOSE Point out that like all other maps, historical maps demand that we know how to interpret them. Refer students to *Helping Yourself* to preview steps in interpreting historical maps.

2 TEACH

Using the Skill Refer the class to the map on this page.

- **What are the dates given in the title?** *(A.D. 711–732)*

- **Why are dates important to interpreting this map?** *(Dates show when events took place, while the body of the map shows where. Together, they place events in order.)*

- **What symbols tell us how some of this spread occurred?** *(Routes show the direction of advances, and battle symbols pinpoint wins and losses.)*

Resource REMINDER
Practice and Project Book: *p. 57*
Transparency: *Maps 14 & 15*
Technology: *Adventure Time! CD-ROM*
Outline Map

GEOGRAPHYSKILLS

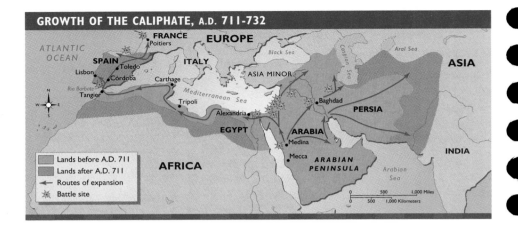

GROWTH OF THE CALIPHATE, A.D. 711-732

- Lands before A.D. 711
- Lands after A.D. 711
- ← Routes of expansion
- ✺ Battle site

Reading Historical Maps

VOCABULARY
historical map

WHY THE SKILL MATTERS

In A.D. 711, while the caliph extended his power throughout western Asia, he also sent an army into Europe. Before very long the caliphate controlled all the land in present-day Spain and Portugal.

One way to get a quick overview of such events is to study historical maps. Historical maps show information about the past. Use the Helping Yourself box on the next page to guide you in reading historical maps.

USING THE SKILL

Study the map of the caliphate's expansion into Europe on this page. Read the map title. It is an historical map because it shows places and events from the past. Notice that the map shows the names of several countries. These are included to help you locate areas and events.

In 711 the caliph's forces crossed from North Africa to Spain and defeated the army of Roderick, a Spanish king. Now read the map key. It explains a symbol that stands for caliphate battles. As you can see, the Muslim army passed Toledo (tuh LEE doh). Actually, the people of Toledo surrendered without a battle. The next year, more Muslim armies arrived. Find Poitiers (pwah TYAY) in France. Did the caliphate army fight a battle in this city?*

Although the caliphate did not conquer France, Muslims ruled parts of Spain for 700 years. In that time Spanish caliphs had magnificent mosques and libraries built. The most stunning mosque, in Córdoba, still stands.

TRYING THE SKILL

The map on page 281 shows events that happened over 600 years after the caliphate victories in Spain. Refer to the Helping Yourself box as you answer questions.

280   *yes

READING STRATEGIES & LANGUAGE DEVELOPMENT

SEQUENCE Point out to the class that historical maps, such as these, often show sequence of events. First, help students identify the sequence in the *Growth of the Caliphate* map (711 crossing from North Africa to Spain, victory at Toledo, march on France: 732 defeat at Poitiers, control of Spain for 700 years). Later, have students list the sequence of events in Ibn Battuta's travels.

PREFIXES AND SUFFIXES Write the word *over* on the board and point out that it is often used as a prefix. Have students locate the instance in this *Skills Lesson* in which *over* occurs as a prefix *(overview)*. Encourage students to think of other *over-* words, and then help them differentiate between those that have a "from above" meaning, as this does, and those that mean either "surpassing" or "excessive," like *overpower* or *overambitious.*

*from 1325 to 1344
**between 1332 and 1344
***Karsh; 1325–1332

HELPING Yourself

- An **historical map** shows places or events from the past.
- Study the map title and map key.
- Find the symbols on the map, and examine any other information given on it.

At the time shown here, a Muslim, Ibn Battuta (IHB un bat TOO tuh), set out on a pilgrimage to Mecca from Tangier in present-day Morocco. Little did he know that he would travel 75,000 miles, exploring Africa, Asia, and Europe before returning home. When did Ibn Battuta travel?*

Ibn Battuta saw the lighthouse at Alexandria and Jerusalem's Dome of the Rock before visiting Mecca. Baghdad followed. When did he visit Jerusalem?**

After he returned to Mecca, Ibn Battuta heard tales about India. Instead of taking the shorter but riskier sea route, he went by land. Constantinople was one stop on this long journey. What city did he visit north of Constantinople? Between what years did

Ibn Battuta visit the Maldive Islands?***

Later Ibn Battuta explored Muslim Spain and went by caravan far into Africa. Before Battuta died in about 1377, he recounted his travels to a scribe. As far as we know, he was the only person who had explored the world so thoroughly up to that time.

REVIEWING THE SKILL

Use the map on this page to answer the following questions.

1. What makes this is a historical map?
2. Between what years did Ibn Battuta visit the east coast of Africa?
3. Did he visit Delhi before or after Mecca? How do you know?
4. When is a historical map helpful?

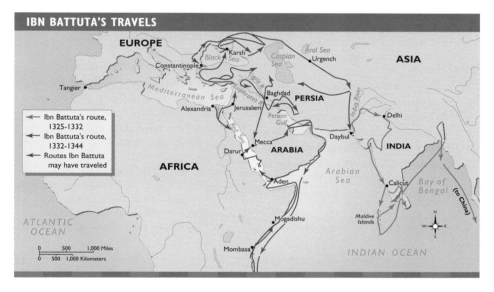

IBN BATTUTA'S TRAVELS

- ← Ibn Battuta's route, 1325-1332
- ← Ibn Battuta's route, 1332-1344
- ← Routes Ibn Battuta may have traveled

281

3 CLOSE

SUM IT UP

Give students additional practice in interpreting historical maps by having them find other examples in the text, both in units already studied and in those to come, and by having them apply the *Helping Yourself* steps to these maps in class.

EVALUATE

✓ **Answers to Reviewing the Skill**

1. It shows information about past events that occurred in the 14th century.

2. between 1332 and 1344

3. Before; the route (shown in green) that went to Delhi is dated 1325–1332; the blue route that included Mecca is dated 1332–1344.

4. when you need a great deal of historical information in a visual and concentrated format

 Technology CONNECTION

ADVENTURE TIME! CD-ROM
Have students look at some historical maps in *Charts* on the *Adventure Time!* CD-ROM.

MEETING INDIVIDUAL NEEDS

RETEACHING (Easy) Have students draw a historical map that shows the place and date of their birth, of their starting school, and of what they are doing today.

EXTENSION (Average) Again refer students to the Ibn Battuta map and tell them to make up two or more additional questions that can be answered by information in the map.

ENRICHMENT (Challenging) Tell students to picture themselves as world travelers in the future. Have them think of and list places in the world that they would like to visit and future dates when they might be able to make these journeys. Have them also make up a map key showing a symbol for each route with its year/s. On an outline map of the world, have them show map title, map key, and the different routes.

DISCUSSING MAJOR EVENTS These questions will help students understand the development of Islam.

- *How old was Muhammed when he fled to Medina from Mecca?* (52)

- *How soon after this had Muslims gained control of Spain?* (less than a century, 89 years)

- *By what time can it be said that there was a full-blown, widespread Muslim empire?* (by A.D. 762, when Baghdad became its capital, just 140 years after Muhammed fled to Medina)

Answers to
THINKING ABOUT VOCABULARY

1. T

2. F, An oasis is an area in a desert that is watered by underground springs.

3. T

4. F, The Five Pillars are the five basic duties of all Muslims.

5. T

6. F, The Quran is the most important book of Islam and contains the teachings Allah gave to Muhammed.

7. F, A caravan is a group of people and animals traveling together, often across a desert.

8. T

9. F, Muslims used an astrolabe to read the position of the stars and thus calculate the exact direction to Mecca and other places.

10. T

Answers to
THINKING ABOUT FACTS

1. Arabian "people of the desert," who are often on the move and live in tents; by trading and raiding.

2. It is their sacred book of teachings that serves as a guide for living.

Resource **REMINDER**

Practice and Project Book: *p. 58*
Assessment Book: *Chapter 10 Test*
Technology: *Videodisc/Video Tape 4*
Transparency: *Graphic Organizer, Main Idea Chart*

CHAPTER 10 REVIEW

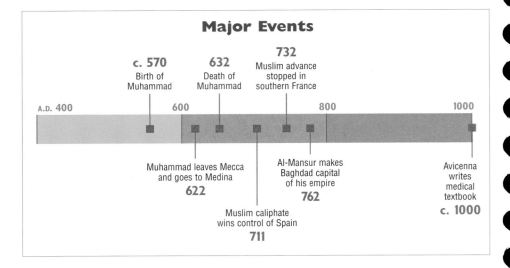

Major Events

732
Muslim advance stopped in southern France

c. 570
Birth of Muhammad

632
Death of Muhammad

A.D. 400   600   800   1000

Muhammad leaves Mecca and goes to Medina
622

Al-Mansur makes Baghdad capital of his empire
762

Avicenna writes medical textbook
c. 1000

Muslim caliphate wins control of Spain
711

THINKING ABOUT VOCABULARY

Each of the following statements contains an underlined vocabulary word. Number a sheet of paper from 1 to 10. Beside each number write **T** if the statement is true and **F** if the statement is false. If the statement is false, rewrite the sentence using the vocabulary word correctly.

1. A <u>caliph</u> is a Muslim ruler.
2. An <u>oasis</u> is a Muslim place of worship.
3. The <u>Kaaba</u> is a temple in Mecca that was used to honor gods and goddesses.
4. The <u>Five Pillars</u> are part of the Kaaba.
5. A journey made for religious reasons is called a <u>pilgrimage</u>.
6. The <u>Quran</u> is a famous mosque in Cairo.
7. A <u>caravan</u> is a desert tent.
8. <u>Algebra</u> is a type of mathematics.

9. Muslims used an <u>astrolabe</u> to help them illustrate books.
10. Muhammad's migration from Mecca to Medina, which marks the beginning of the Islamic calendar, is called the <u>hijra</u>.

THINKING ABOUT FACTS

1. Who are the Bedouins? How did some of them become wealthy and powerful?
2. Why is the Quran important to Muslims?
3. What are the Five Pillars of Islam? What is their purpose?
4. What have been some of the important contributions that Muslims have made to world civilization?
5. Look at the time line above. What information do you find there that would make you conclude that Islam spread very rapidly? In what year did the Muslim caliphate gain control of Spain?

282

WORKING WITH PEERS To review the chapter, have second-language learners work with a partner to retell the most important events and information in each lesson. Students can review each lesson by reading their notes, rereading text where necessary, and answering the questions under **THINK ABOUT IT.**

DRAMATIZATION The events that accompany the founding of the religion of Islam lend themselves to dramatization through Reader's Theater. Students may take turns reading sections of this lesson while their classmates interpret the actions and quotations in pantomime.

THINK AND WRITE

WRITING A DESCRIPTION

Write a paragraph about the geography and climate of the Arabian peninsula. Describe both the fertile and desert parts of the peninsula. Provide information about the climate of the Empty Quarter.

WRITING AN ARTICLE

Write a short article for your school newspaper about Islam. Describe its main beliefs and practices.

WRITING A LETTER

Suppose you are on a pilgrimage to Mecca. Write a letter home describing what you are doing and what you see. Describe the things that impress you the most. Provide descriptions of the art and architecture you see in Mecca.

APPLYING GEOGRAPHY SKILLS

READING HISTORICAL MAPS

1. What is an historical map?

2. Look at the historical map on page 280. What historical information does it provide?

3. What does the map on page 280 tell you about the speed and direction of Muslim expansion?

4. Look at the historical map on page 281. What type of information does it provide? How does the map show different routes of travel?

5. How are historical maps helpful?

Summing Up the Chapter

Review the chapter. Then copy the main-idea chart below on a separate piece of paper. Fill in details in each column that are connected to the main idea. After completing the chart, use it to help you write a paragraph that answers the question "What are the greatest contributions of Muslims to world civilization?"

MAIN IDEA: Islam Spread Throughout Muslim Caliphate

Geographic Setting	Teachings	Achievements
Arabian Peninsula desert fertile area	Allah is God Quran contains words of Allah Five Pillars	Medicine Mathematics Astronomy Literature

283

---

3. The Pillars of Islam are belief in one God, Allah; prayer five times a day; giving to the poor; fasting during holy month; and pilgrimage to Mecca. Their purpose is to show Muslims how to practice their religion and what their basic duties are according to the teachings of Muhammed and Islam.

4. beautiful art and architecture, literature and music, and advances in medicine, math, and science

5. Within two centuries after Muhammed's birth, there was a widespread Muslim empire; in 711.

Answers to APPLYING GEOGRAPHY SKILLS

1. a map that shows places or events from the past

2. the areas held by the caliphate, the period of time they were acquired, battle sites, and routes of expansion

3. It shows what lands the Muslims controlled before 711 and their rapid expansion of control across Asia, Africa, and Europe following 711.

4. The map shows the travels of Ibn Battuta with color-coded arrows for the two routes he is known to have traveled and dotted lines to indicate the possible routes he may have taken also.

5. They help us see boundaries as they were in the past and to follow movements and pinpoint other events as they occurred in another time.

Technology CONNECTION

VIDEODISC
Enrich Chapter 10 with the *Avicenna* segment on the Videodisc.

Search Frame 53264 Side B

SUGGESTIONS FOR SUMMING UP THE CHAPTER

After students copy the main-idea table onto another piece of paper, have them read the main idea aloud and then identify and discuss the three categories in the table. Point out that the three headings in the table correspond to the three lessons in the chapter. Call on them for examples of the Arabian geographic setting from which Islam sprang. Then call for an example or two for each of the other two categories, to see that they understand the kinds of things they are to fill in. Possible answers appear on the reproduced pupil page above. Then have students finish filling in the table on their own. When they begin deciding what to include in their answer to the question posed, suggest that they think about both teachings and achievements.

ASSESSING THINK AND WRITE: *For performance assessment, see Assessment Book, Chapter 10, pp. T74–T76.*

CHAPTER 11 Ancient America

Pages 284–307

CHAPTER OVERVIEW

Hunters and gatherers crossed Beringia in search of game 30,000 years ago. The early people of Mexico cultivated corn around 5000 B.C., and by 1000 B.C. the Olmec people used waterways to transport goods. In A.D. 600, the Maya people built the great city of stone monuments at Copán.

GEO ADVENTURES DAILY GEOGRAPHY ACTIVITIES

Use **Geo Adventures** Daily Geography activities to assess students' understanding of geography skills.

CHAPTER PLANNING GUIDE

LESSON 1	STUDYSKILLS	LESSON 2
SUGGESTED PACING: 2 DAYS	**SUGGESTED PACING: 1 DAY**	**SUGGESTED PACING: 2 DAYS**

LESSON 1

Geography Of Middle America pp. 286–289

CURRICULUM CONNECTIONS
Links to Language Arts, p. 287
Links to Math, p. 287

FIELD TRIP
Visit a Museum, p. 288

RESOURCES
Practice and Project Book, p. 59
Desk Map
Anthology, p. 63

STUDYSKILLS

Reading Climographs pp. 290–291

RESOURCES
Practice and Project Book, p. 60
◉ TECHNOLOGY *Adventure Time!* CD-ROM

LESSON 2

The Olmec Civilization pp. 292–296

CURRICULUM CONNECTIONS
Links to Art, p. 294

CITIZENSHIP
Using Current Events, p. 293

RESOURCES
Practice and Project Book, p. 61
Desk Map
◉ TECHNOLOGY *Adventure Time!* CD-ROM

LESSON 3	Legacy	CHAPTER REVIEW
SUGGESTED PACING: 2 DAYS	**SUGGESTED PACING: 1 DAY**	**SUGGESTED PACING: 1 DAY**

LESSON 3

Maya Civilization pp. 298–303

CITIZENSHIP
Understanding Government, p. 301

RESOURCES
Practice and Project Book, p. 62
Desk Map
Anthology, pp. 64–65, 66

Legacy

Astronomy pp. 304–305

CHAPTER REVIEW

pp. 306–307

RESOURCES
Practice and Project Book, p. 63
◉ TECHNOLOGY Videodisc/Video Tape
Assessment Book: Chapter 11 Test
Transparency: Graphic Organizer, Main Idea Chart

LEARNING STYLE: Visual GROUP **30 MINUTES OR LONGER**

Make an Ancient Building Mural

Objective: To start students thinking about the architecture of ancient Middle American civilizations.

Materials: paper, oaktag, paints, brushes

1. Ask students to write about an ancient structure—its appearance, purpose, location.
2. Working in small groups, students may then paint a picture of their structure on the group's posterboard.
3. Ask groups to share their murals with the class, identifying the structures and the people who built them.

CITIZENSHIP

SUGGESTED PACING: 1 DAY

The Rain Forest Treasures Trail p. 297

CITIZENSHIP
Understanding Environmental Concerns, p. 297

SHELTERED INSTRUCTION

READING STRATEGIES & LANGUAGE DEVELOPMENT

Classifying/Word Families, p. 286, Lesson 1
Classifying/Combining Forms, p. 290, Skills Lesson
Using Visuals/Words with Multiple Meanings, p. 292, Lesson 2
Compare and Contrast/Synonyms, p. 298, Lesson 3

SECOND-LANGUAGE SUPPORT

Using Props, p. 288
Retelling with an Illustration, p. 294
Taking Notes, p. 300
Self-Assessment/Visualization, p. 306

MEETING INDIVIDUAL NEEDS

Reteaching, Extension, Enrichment, pp. 289, 291, 296, 303, 305
McGraw-Hill Adventure Book

ASSESSMENT OPPORTUNITIES

Practice and Project Book, pp. 60–63
Write About It, pp. 289, 296, 303, 305
Assessment Book: Assessing Think and Write, pp. T77–T79; Chapter 11 Tests: Content, Skills, Writing

Introducing the Chapter

Have students read the chapter title to recognize that they have come to their own hemisphere, the region of the two American continents. Invite students to offer any prior knowledge they have of ancient America: What are the most ancient things you know about in the Americas?

THINKING ABOUT HISTORY AND GEOGRAPHY

Have students read the text on this page and then pinpoint on the map the areas of the Americas it mentions. Ask them which large area they would have to cross to go from the land bridge to the areas named? (the area that is now Canada and the United States)

30,000 YEARS AGO BERINGIA

- **What is happening in this panel? When did it happen?** *(Hunters and gatherers are following a herd across a land bridge, about 30,000 years ago.)*

- **What do we call the land bridge and where is it located?** *(Beringia, from Asia to extreme northwestern North America)*

★ **THINKING FURTHER:** *Cause and Effect* **Why are they crossing this bridge?** *(They seek food, meat from the animals crossing Beringia.)*

5000 B.C. VALLEY OF MEXICO

- **Where is the Valley of Mexico located?** *(north of Central America, in the center of Mexico)*

- **How long has passed since the crossing of Beringia?** *(30,000 –5,000 = 25,000 years)*

★ **THINKING FURTHER:** *Compare and Contrast* **How has life changed for the hunters and gatherers?** *(They can cultivate corn. Hunters and gatherers have become farmers.)*

Resource REMINDER

Technology: *Videodisc/Video Tape 5*

Ancient America

THINKING ABOUT HISTORY AND GEOGRAPHY

Some scientists believe that early peoples crossed a land bridge from Asia to North America about 30,000 years ago. From there they moved through North and South America. Some settled on the rich lands of Mexico and Central America. The time line shows that these early peoples developed agriculture and built civilizations there. One group, the powerful Maya, built many large cities, which they suddenly and mysteriously abandoned.

30,000 YEARS AGO	5000 B.C.	1000 B.C.
BERINGIA Hunters and gatherers cross a land bridge in search of food	**VALLEY OF MEXICO** Early people in Mexico cultivate corn	**LA VENTA** The Olmec use waterways to transport goods

284

BACKGROUND INFORMATION

LINKING THE MAP AND THE TIME LINE

- Because Beringia was not covered with glaciers, it was able to support Arctic vegetation—dry grasslands, marshes, and some trees—which provided food for grazing animals such as reindeer, mammoth, and mastodon.

- The Valley of Mexico, the Central Plateau, was the seat of Mexican settlement thousands of years ago and is today the site of Mexico's most populous area. It is the valley between the Sierra Madre Oriental (Eastern Sierra Madre) and the Sierra Madre Occidental (Western Sierra Madre) and is actually a highland region with an elevation range of 6,000–8,000 feet.

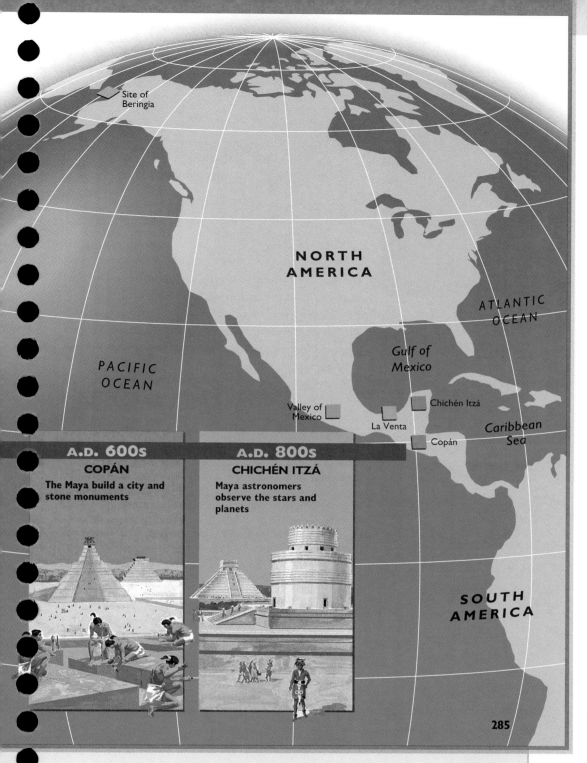

Site of Beringia

NORTH AMERICA

ATLANTIC OCEAN

PACIFIC OCEAN

Gulf of Mexico

Valley of Mexico

La Venta

Chichén Itzá

Copán

Caribbean Sea

SOUTH AMERICA

A.D. 600s
COPÁN
The Maya build a city and stone monuments

A.D. 800s
CHICHÉN ITZÁ
Maya astronomers observe the stars and planets

285

- *What are the people in this panel called?* (the Olmec)

- *When and where did they live?* (1000 B.C. in La Venta, in southern Mexico)

- *How do they relate in time and place to the people in the panel before?* (They lived 4,000 years later, southeast of the Valley of Mexico.)

★**THINKING FURTHER:** *Making Conclusions* **What technology have they developed and why?** (They have developed rafts so that they can use rivers as highways.)

A.D. 600s COPÁN

- *What are the people in this panel called?* (the Maya)

- *How long ago did they live?* (about 1,300 to 1,400 years ago)

- *Where was the settlement shown here located?* (Copán in Central America)

★**THINKING FURTHER:** *Making Conclusions* **Why can you conclude that the Maya had a civilization?** (They have architecture, which usually is found in a city.)

A.D. 800s CHICHÉN ITZÁ

- *Where and how long ago is the action in this panel taking place?* (in Chichén Itzá, in eastern Mexico, 1,100 or 1,200 years ago)

★**THINKING FURTHER:** *Making Conclusions* **How does this panel show that the Maya have a high level of civilization?** (They have developed astronomy.)

 Technology CONNECTION

VIDEODISC/VIDEO TAPE 5
Enrich Chapter 11 with the *Ancient America* segment on the Videodisc.

Search Frame 34295

BACKGROUND INFORMATION

LINKING THE MAP AND THE TIME LINE
- From 900 B.C. to 400 B.C., La Venta was the most powerful center in all of Middle America. It is located in what is today the Mexican state of Tabasco.
- Copán was the southernmost of the Maya cities. It is noted for many architectural features, including a hieroglyphic stairway that has been helpful to archaeologists' attempts to decode Mayan glyphs.
- Chichén Itzá, located in what is today the Mexican state of Yucatan, was, from A.D. 900 to 1100, one of the largest cities in Middle America. Today, people come to visit its many grand buildings, including the Castillo, which has 365 steps, suggesting that it was a giant chronographic marker for the equinox.

LESSON 1
PAGES 286–289

Lesson Overview
The diverse lands and climates of Middle America gave rise to the first American civilizations.

Lesson Objectives
★ Explain how people probably first reached the Americas.
★ Describe the major physical features and climates of Middle America.

1 PREPARE

MOTIVATE Have a student do the *Read Aloud* as the class examines the photo on this page of a temple at Tikal. Ask where Middle America is. Help students to use the name, illustration, and text to identify Mexico and Central America.

SET PURPOSE Ask students the *Read to Learn* question. Encourage them to offer any personal knowledge about the region and about the *Vocabulary* terms. Then tell students to read the lesson to expand their knowledge.

2 TEACH

Understanding THE BIG PICTURE
Begin a discussion of how humans populated the American continents.

● **What was the Ice Age and when did it occur?** *(a time about 40,000 years ago when Earth's climate was so cold that it froze sea water, covered nearly half Earth's land mass with glaciers, and lowered ocean levels)*

● **How did Beringia arise?** *(As ocean levels sank, a bridge of land between Asia and North America emerged.)*

★**THINKING FURTHER:** *Making Conclusions* **Does the process of people spreading across the Americas seem fast or slow?** *(Have students subtract 15,000 years from 40,000.)*

Resource **REMINDER**

Practice and Project Book: *p. 59*
Anthology: *Saving the Rain Forest, p. 63*
Desk Map

GEOGRAPHY OF MIDDLE AMERICA

Focus Activity

READ TO LEARN
What is unique about the geography of Middle America?

VOCABULARY
Ice Age
glacier
tropical
rain forest

PLACES
Beringia
Middle America
Central Plateau

READ ALOUD

The land of Middle America is one of great variety— from the lush green forests, dripping with rain, to the dry brown plateaus, scorched by the sun. Within this diverse region, with its icy mountain peaks and wandering river valleys, early people forged a series of remarkable civilizations.

THE BIG PICTURE

About 40,000 years ago, Earth's climate was much colder than it is today. This period of time is called the Ice Age, because ice covered nearly half of Earth's land mass. Ice formed in great sheets called glaciers that slowly spread south from the North Pole. As more water turned to ice, the level of the oceans began to drop. When the oceans sank, more land became visible. A "land bridge" we call Beringia (buh RIN jee uh) formed between Asia and North America.

Beringia was located where the Bering Strait is today. Find this area on the map on page R11. Many scientists believe that it was across Beringia that people first came to the Americas. Asian hunters probably followed herds of reindeer across the land bridge and onto the unknown continent. By 15,000 years ago, hunters and gatherers had spread throughout the Americas. In this chapter you will read about the region where the first American civilizations developed. It is called Mesoamerica, or Middle America. *Meso* is from the Latin word meaning "middle."

286

 SHELTERED INSTRUCTION

READING STRATEGIES & LANGUAGE DEVELOPMENT

CLASSIFYING Explain that a good way to make sense of information is to classify it into common groups. Invite volunteers to classify the classroom books. Guide them to decide on a system of classification (size, subject, condition) and then to classify the books. Ask students which categories they could use to classify Middle America's climate.
[SDAIE STRATEGY: BRIDGING]

WORD FAMILIES Write on the board the word *temperate,* which appears on p. 287, and ask students if they know any words that look as though they might be related to *temperate (temperature, temper, temperance).* Help students to see that all these words suggest moderation, or lack of an extreme. All can be traced to the Latin word *temperare,* "to moderate, to be moderate."

ENVIRONMENTS OF MIDDLE AMERICA

The early people who traveled south from what is now the United States found warmer lands of great variety. There were towering mountains, lush coastal plains, and dry plateaus. These lands also had large animal populations to hunt and ideal climates for growing food. Many early people settled in Middle America. Look at the map on this page to find this region. It included parts of what are now Mexico and Central America. Here, thousands of years ago, people developed unique cultures that included traditions of farming, religion, government, and art.

The Land of Middle America

Much of Middle America is covered by steep mountains. A large area of rolling hills, called the Central Plateau, is located in the northern part of the region. Ancient volcanoes are found in the valleys of the Central Plateau. As Earth warmed after the Ice Age, this region became home to many different kinds of animals and plants. Not surprisingly, archaeologists have also found bones of early people here. Today the Central Plateau is the location of one of the world's most populous cities, Mexico City.

The Climate of Middle America

Most of Middle America is in the tropical zone. *Tropical* refers to the area of Earth that is near the equator, between the Tropic of Cancer and the Tropic of Capricorn. Middle America has many mountains, so the climate changes with elevation.

The hottest regions, from sea level to 3,000 feet, are called *tierra caliente* (tee AIR ruh cahl YEN tay), which in

English means "hot land." These regions are found mostly in the low coastal plains. Here the temperature is over 80°F most of the time. The next level of elevation in Middle America, which includes the Central Plateau, is called *tierra templada* (tee AIR ruh tem PLAH dah), or "temperate land." At this elevation the climate is generally mild. The highest mountain elevations, above 6,000 feet, are known as *tierra fría* (tee AIR ruh FREE ah), or "cold land." The weather there is usually cooler than that of the other two regions.

These varying climate regions all have one thing in common—the rainy season. Almost all the rain that falls in Middle America comes between the months of May and October. Between the months of November and April, the skies are usually clear.

MIDDLE AMERICA: Physical

MAP WORK

Middle America has a variety of landforms.

1. Where are the highest lands found?
2. The Yucatán Peninsula is bordered by which two bodies of water?

MAP WORK: **1.** along the west coast **2.** Gulf of Mexico and Caribbean Sea

287

ENVIRONMENTS OF MIDDLE AMERICA
Write *Middle America* on the board.

More   **MAP WORK**

Encourage students to work back and forth between text and map.

- **About how far does Middle America extend from the northwest to the southeast?** (*about 1,500 miles along the west coast*)

- **Why did people want to migrate to this region?** (*to find warmer climates, large animal groups to hunt, and good land for farming*)

- ★**THINKING FURTHER:** *Compare and Contrast* **How would you compare Middle America with the lands the migrants first reached after crossing Beringia?** (*warmer climate, more people-friendly physical features*)

Discussing The Land of Middle America Continue to refer to the map.

- **How important are mountains as a physical feature of Middle America?** (*Steep mountains cover much of it.*)

- ★**THINKING FURTHER:** *Making Conclusions* **Why, then, do you suppose the Central Plateau became a center of population?** (*Its rolling hills were better for settlement than steep mountains.*)

Exploring The Climate of Middle America On the board, have students fill in the climate classification chart suggested in the *Reading Strategies.*

- **What do all three climate regions have in common?** (*a rainy season from May to October*)

- **What additional reason can you find for the Central Plateau to be a major population center?** (*its mild climate because it lies in tierra templada*)

- **How does the tierra caliente's climate differ from tierra fría?** (*Tierra caliente: the hottest. Tierra fría: the coldest.*)

- ★**THINKING FURTHER:** *Making Conclusions* **What general rule can you formulate about the relation of elevation to climate?** (*The higher the elevation, the colder the climate; the lower, the warmer.*)

CURRICULUM CONNECTION

LINKS TO LANGUAGE ARTS The area we call *tropical* falls between the Tropic of Cancer and the Tropic of Capricorn. The sun's rays strike most directly all year round in a band that circles Earth in the areas between these two "tropic" lines. Hence the climate is said to be "tropical."

LINKS TO MATH Scientists estimate that for every 1,000 feet increase in altitude, the temperature goes down about 3.5 degrees F. Tell students that the mountains of the Sierra Madre average close to 9,000 feet. Have them figure out how much cooler it would be at the top of an average mountain in that range than it would be along the coast at sea level. (Students should first divide 9,000 by 1,000. Then they should multiply the quotient by 3.5 to get the answer.)

9,000 ÷ 1,000 = 9 x 3.5 = 31.5°F cooler than at sea level

THE RAIN FOREST

If any students have ever visited a rain forest, encourage them to describe what they saw, smelled, and heard there.

Discussing A Unique Environment Try to have picture books showing rain forests on hand for students to examine.

- *What is the kind of a climate in which a rain forest can flourish?* (hot, or at least mild, and very wet)

- *What are some of the striking features of a rain forest?* (the variety of plants and animals that grow there—three quarters of all living things on Earth; the size to which the plants and animals grow; the canopy that stretches like a roof across the trees)

★THINKING FURTHER: *Making Connections* **Where might you have seen rain forests in motion pictures or on TV?** (Help students make a connection between jungles and rain forests.)

Learning about People in Middle America Have students recall ways early people in other places lived.

- *How did the early people of Middle America make their livings?* (as hunter-gatherers on the move)

★THINKING FURTHER: *Predicting* **What do you predict the next step in the development of Middle American culture will be?** (developing agriculture and settling down)

Monkeys like these (below) are found in Middle America's rain forests. Abundant plant and animal life have provided food for the Olmec and modern peoples.

THE RAIN FOREST

One environment of Middle America gets more rain than any other. This region is the rain forest. A rain forest is a forest that receives more than 80 inches of rain per year. That's more rain than the city of San Francisco gets in four years! Most rain forests are in tropical regions. The world's tropical regions lie between the Tropics of Cancer and Capricorn.

A Unique Environment

Rain forests are home to a huge variety of plants and animals. Three-quarters of Earth's living things are found in rain forests. Writer Arnold Newman describes this unique environment:

The forest interior is a magical and mercurial [changing] place—an enchanted realm where anything is possible. . . . There are "roses" with 145-foot trunks; daisies and violets as big as apple trees . . . 18 foot cobras . . . [and] frogs so big they eat rats. . . . The forest's climate is the key to all this.

The rain forests of Middle America are in the tierra caliente and in the tierra templada. The trees in the tropical rain forests near the Gulf of Mexico can grow 200 feet tall—about as high as a stack of 20 school buses. Here thousands of kinds of plants and animals live under the canopy, or roof, of trees.

The canopy is so thick that little sun

288

---

reaches the forest floor. In the cooler rain forests of tierra templada, clouds sometimes blanket the entire forest.

People in Middle America

The first people in Middle America probably arrived about 11,000 years ago. Small knives and arrow points have been found in the Central Plateau. These stone tools were left in caves by early hunter-gatherers. Early Americans gathered onions, squash, and avocados, and hunted rabbits and deer. Like early people in other parts of the world, they moved around in search of food.

WHY IT MATTERS

After the first people came across Beringia to North America, some moved southward to Middle America. The diverse lands of this region provided a warm climate and abundant food. These resources made Middle America ideal for human settlement. In the next lesson you will read about one of the many groups of people who created a civilization on this land.

✓// Reviewing Facts and Ideas

MAIN IDEAS

- The first people in the Americas may have come from Asia across the Beringia land bridge about 40,000 to 25,000 years ago.
- Middle America has mountains, rolling hills, and coastal plains. It also has three main climate regions defined by elevation.
- The rain forests of Middle America are unique environments with a huge variety of plant and animal life.
- The first settlers of Middle America were hunters and gatherers who lived in the Central Plateau region.

THINK ABOUT IT

1. How did a land bridge form between Asia and the Americas thousands of years ago?

2. What are the three major climate regions found in Middle America?

3. **FOCUS** What are three kinds of land areas found in Middle America?

4. **THINKING SKILL** What are three _conclusions_ that you can make about the rain forest environment?

5. **GEOGRAPHY** How might a rainy season affect the pattern of agriculture in an area?

How hot WAS it?

To learn about recent changes in climate, scientists often look at written records. By studying records, such as the dates of cherry blossom festivals in Japan or harvest records in France, they can learn if a region's climate has become hotter or colder, wetter or drier, over time. The study of climate is called climatology.

The study of climates in past ages is called paleoclimatology (pay lee oh kli muh TAHL uh jee). To learn about ice ages and other big changes in climate, scientists study clues such as pollen, seeds, or soil found in rocks, fossils, and glaciers.

289

Extending Did You Know? Encourage students to do some climatological research about their own area and write a paragraph describing that climate.

Discussing WHY IT MATTERS Ask students to predict what they expect next.

> ★**THINKING FURTHER:** _Cause and Effect_ **What caused people to want to settle in Middle America?** _(warm climate, abundant plants and animals)_

⭐ 3 CLOSE

MAIN IDEAS
Call on students for answers.

- **How did people probably first reach the Americas?** _(over the land bridge of Beringia from Asia to North America)_

- **How would you describe the major physical features and climates of Middle America?** _(mountains, rolling hills, coastal plains; hot, mild, and cool, depending on elevation)_

- **What are the major features of rain forests?** _(heavy rain during rainy season, great variety and size of plants and animals, canopy)_

- **Who were the first settlers of Middle America and where did they settle?** _(hunter-gatherers; Central Plateau region)_

EVALUATE
✓ **Answers to Think About It**

1. The Ice Age created glaciers that froze sea water, thus lowering sea level and exposing land. _Make Inferences_

2. tierra caliente, tierra templada, tierra fría—hot, mild, cool _Recall Details_

3. mountains, rolling hills, coastal plains _Recall Details_

4. Answers should reflect how much rain forests encourage variety and size. _Make Conclusions_

5. Major growing might occur during rainy season, but farmers might also save water from the rainy season to use for irrigation during the dry season. _Five Themes of Geography: Place_

Write About It Have students write a paragraph telling why Middle America is a likely place for civilizations to develop.

MEETING INDIVIDUAL NEEDS

RETEACHING (Easy) Have students try to picture a scene from a rain forest in their mind's eye. Then have them use crayons or markers to illustrate that scene. Have them assemble their scenes in a bulletin board display.

EXTENSION (Average) Refer students to p. 287 and have them draw a diagram showing the three major climate regions, as determined by their elevation. Suggest that they might use a pyramid and tell them to be sure to label each level as to elevation, Spanish name, and brief description.

ENRICHMENT (Challenging) Have students construct the same kind of diagram as suggested above, but have them also do research into the kinds of crops that grow well in each climate region. Tell them to include this information in each level of their diagrams.

Lesson Overview
Climographs show the temperature and precipitation of a place over months.

Lesson Objective
★ Interpret climographs.

1 PREPARE

MOTIVATE Review with students how visuals like maps and diagrams present information at a glance. Point out that graphs are another visual device. Have students identify the kind of graphs shown—*climographs*—and briefly discuss why we seek to learn about a place's climate.

SET PURPOSE Have students read *Why the Skill Matters* and identify the two kinds of climate information climographs supply (temperature and precipitation of a place over a period of months). Then have them read *Helping Yourself* to preview the steps that show how to interpret climographs.

2 TEACH

Using the Skill Refer students to Climograph A and have them differentiate between bar graphs and line graphs by having them tell which climate feature it represents. (bar graph: precipitation; line graph: temperature)

● **What does the title say that Climograph A will tell us?** *(the average monthly temperature and precipitation in Acapulco over a period of months)*

Technology CONNECTION

ADVENTURE TIME! CD-ROM
Enrich the skills lesson with the *Climographs* on the *Adventure Time!* CD-ROM.

Resource REMINDER
Practice and Project Book: *p. 60*
Technology: *Adventures CD-ROM*

STUDYSKILLS

Reading Climographs

VOCABULARY
climograph

WHY THE SKILL MATTERS

In the last lesson you read about the three different climate zones that are found in Middle America. They are tierra caliente, tierra templada, and tierra fría. Climate in these zones is largely determined by elevation, or the height of the land above sea level. Other factors that can affect the climate of a place are its distance from the equator and its distance from oceans or mountains.

Since there are many things that influence climate, the climate within a large region can vary greatly. Remember that the two most important parts of climate are temperature and precipitation. In Middle America, for example, temperatures of 90°F are common in some low-lying areas. In high mountain areas, however, the temperature is usually lower, around 40°F. Also, some areas in the region receive more than 80 inches of rain each year while other areas receive less than 15 inches.

The rain does not fall evenly throughout the year in this region. As you have read, Middle America has a rainy season. This means that for part of the year the climate here is very wet and for part of the year it is very dry.

One way to learn about the climate of a place is to study a climograph of that place. A climograph is a graph that shows the temperature and precipitation in a place over a period of months.

USING THE SKILL

Look at Climograph A. Notice that it includes two graphs—a bar graph and a line graph. The bar graph shows the average monthly precipitation. The line graph shows the average monthly temperature.

Read a climograph the same way you would read other kinds of graphs. First read the title. Then read the other information below the title. This useful information will help you to compare the climates of three cities in Mexico. Next read the labels on the sides and bottom of the climograph. The left side lists precipitation and is the key for reading the bar graph. The right side lists the temperature and is the key for reading the line graph. The labels along the bottom show that time is measured in months.

Having temperature and precipitation together on the same graph can be useful. Suppose you wanted to find out in which

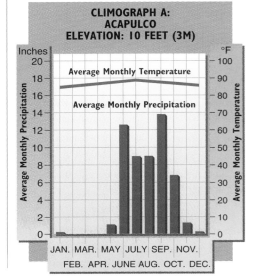

CLIMOGRAPH A: ACAPULCO ELEVATION: 10 FEET (3M)

Average Monthly Temperature
Average Monthly Precipitation

JAN. MAR. MAY JULY SEP. NOV.
FEB. APR. JUNE AUG. OCT. DEC.

READING STRATEGIES & LANGUAGE DEVELOPMENT

CLASSIFYING Point out to the class that graphs like those in this *Skills Lesson* represent a way of organizing information by classifying it. Help students to appreciate the convenience and conciseness that these classifications make possible. First have students identify the various classes into which the information falls—months, number of inches, number of degrees. Then have them analyze why graphs are good devices for presenting such classes of information. (Units of measure lend themselves well to presentation in graphs.)

COMBINING FORMS Write *graph* on the board and point out to the class that graph can be both a word in itself or a combining form—a part of a word. Have students look through this *Skills Lesson* to find *graph* used both ways (*bar graph, line graph,* and *climograph*).

*Veracruz; it's in tierra caliente.
**September; July; Veracruz; by comparing the climographs

month the rainy season begins in Acapulco. By looking for a sharp increase in precipitation on the bar graph, you can tell that the rainy season begins in June. You can also see on the line graph that the average temperature in Acapulco during April, May, and June rises to about 87°F.

TRYING THE SKILL

Climographs are useful for comparing the climate of two different places. Study Climographs B and C on this page. Notice that the elevation of Mexico City and Veracruz are very different. Mexico City is in tierra templada and Veracruz is in tierra caliente. Which city would you expect to have a warmer climate? Why?*

HELPING Yourself

- A **climograph** gives information about temperature and precipitation of a place over time.
- To find the precipitation, read the bar graph with the numbers on the left side.
- To find the temperature, read the line graph with the numbers on the right side.

In which month does Veracruz receive the most rain? In which month does Mexico City receive the most rain? Which city receives the most rain during the month of October? How did you find this answer? **

REVIEWING THE SKILL

1. What is a climograph? How can climographs be useful?

2. Which of the three Mexican cities shown has the most rainfall in August? The least rainfall during June?

3. Which city has hotter temperatures in June, Veracruz or Mexico City?

4. Suppose you were planning a vacation to Acapulco. How would using a climograph help you to plan your trip?

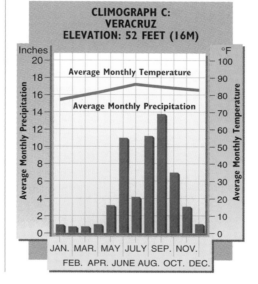

291

- **What does the information under the title tell us?** (Acapulco's elevation—how high it lies above sea level)

- **What information is given at the bottom of the climograph?** (the 12 months of the year)

★**THINKING FURTHER: Compare and Contrast** *How would you compare and contrast the information given down the left side with that down the right side?* (Both signal average monthly figures; left shows inches of precipitation while the right shows degrees Fahrenheit of temperature.)

Trying the Skill Tell students to review the *Helping Yourself* steps before beginning this activity.

- **What do Climographs B and C show and compare?** (average monthly temperature and precipitation in Mexico City and Veracruz)

- **If you wanted to find out how much precipitation Mexico City got in its driest month, how would you proceed?** (Look at Climograph B, look across the bars to find the shortest, read the month below it, look at the left side to find number of inches.)

- **How would you proceed to find the temperature during the warmest month in Veracruz?** (Look at Climograph C, find the highest point in the line graph, look below for its month, look to the right to find the number.)

★ 3 CLOSE

SUM IT UP
Encourage students to make up questions based on the climographs and pose them for the class to answer.

EVALUATE
✓ **Answers to Reviewing the Skill**

1. a graph that shows temperature and precipitation in a place over a period of months; by giving information about climate at a glance and facilitating climate comparisons

2. Veracruz; Mexico City

3. Veracruz

4. It would help you choose the month best suited to your desires—for warmth or coolness, for rain or dryness; it would help you decide what clothing you need.

MEETING INDIVIDUAL NEEDS

RETEACHING (Easy) Tell students to write a brief statement in which they identify and explain the kinds of information that climographs show.

EXTENSION (Average) Tell students to think up a climate that a location on Earth might possibly have—making up figures for average temperature and precipitation for each of the 12 months. Tell them to design a climograph using these figures. Then have them make up five questions the climograph can answer. Have students exchange papers and answer the questions.

ENRICHMENT (Challenging) In their coverage of countries, some encyclopedias (Compton's, Grolier's are two) show climographs for major cities. Have students find two such cities and make climographs for them following the model in this skills lesson.

LESSON 2

Lesson Overview

Rain forests along the Gulf of Mexico gave rise to the Olmec civilization, one of the earliest in the Americas.

Lesson Objectives

★ Explain how the Olmec used the land to develop their agriculture.

★ Identify and describe the achievements of Olmec civilization.

1 PREPARE

MOTIVATE Remind students of how often an everyday task of digging has turned up amazing treasures from the past. Have someone do the *Read Aloud* so they can see that a similar event took place closer to home, in Middle America.

SET PURPOSE Refer the class to the *Read to Learn* question and the Olmec stone head on this page. Encourage students to predict kinds of things they will learn about the Olmec (their farming, their religion, their art, for example). Preview the *Vocabulary*. Then have students read the lesson to test their predictions.

2 TEACH

Understanding THE BIG PICTURE
Direct students to the map on p. 293 and have them locate the Olmec region.

● *Where did the Olmec civilization develop?* (in rain forests along the Gulf of Mexico)

★THINKING FURTHER: *Making Conclusions* **What kind of land and climate would this be?** (coastal plain, hot—tierra caliente—and wet)

Resource **REMINDER**

Practice and Project Book: *p.61*

Desk Map

Technology: *Adventure Time!* CD-ROM

| 1400 B.C. | 1200 B.C. | 400 B.C. | 200 B.C. | A.D. 400 | A.D. 1000 |

THE OLMEC CIVILIZATION

READ ALOUD

In the 1860s a farmer in the Mexican state of Veracruz was clearing dense forest to build a new field for sugarcane. He came upon a large dome-shaped object which he thought was a big, upside-down pot. He called for help to uncover the mysterious object. When the "pot" was finally unearthed, it turned out to be a giant stone head nearly 5 feet high! The uncovering of this sculpture led to more excavations in the area. Slowly the story of an ancient people of Middle America began to unfold. We call these people the Olmec (OHL mek).

THE BIG PICTURE

In the lush rain forest along the Gulf of Mexico arose one of the earliest civilizations of the Americas. In about 1200 B.C. people here settled in communities and built remarkable buildings. Historians call these people the Olmec. In the Aztec language, Olmec means "people of the rubber country," for there were many rubber trees in the area. What the Olmec called themselves remains a mystery. They left behind no written records as far as we know. Fortunately, they did leave a rich assortment of artifacts.

This stone carving was found at La Venta.

Focus Activity

READ TO LEARN
Who were the Olmec?

VOCABULARY
slash and burn

PLACES
La Venta

292

SHELTERED INSTRUCTION

READING STRATEGIES & LANGUAGE DEVELOPMENT

USING VISUALS Review with students the different types of visuals and the information they can draw from each. Arrange students in groups to skim the text and find the different types of visuals in this lesson: maps, photographs, paintings, and art from the period. Then have groups make charts describing the information they glean from each visual. **[SDAIE STRATEGY: SCHEMA BUILDING]**

WORDS WITH MULTIPLE MEANINGS Write the word *squash* on the board and have students find it on p. 293. Have them define *squash* as it is used here ("a food related to a gourd, used as a vegetable"). Do they know another meaning for *squash*? Students should know the verb meaning "to crush." Explain that the plant name comes from a Native American (Algonkian) word; the verb, from French.

Beneath a blanket of forest and greenery at Laguna de los Cerros (right), the remains of an ancient city may hold answers to mysteries of the Olmec.

MIDDLE AMERICA, 500 B.C.

SIERRA MADRE OCCIDENTAL

CENTRAL PLATEAU

SIERRA MADRE ORIENTAL

Gulf of Mexico

Tropic of Cancer

20° N

0   150   300 Miles
0   150   300 Kilometers

MEXICO

Yucatán Peninsula

La Venta

20° N

PACIFIC OCEAN

10° N

10° N

☐ Olmec lands

100° W   90° W

THE OLMEC

Archaeologists believe the Olmec flourished along the Gulf of Mexico from about 1200 B.C. to 400 B.C. The area is still made up almost entirely of rain forest. Rivers cut through the forest on their way to the Gulf of Mexico. This lush environment was rich in food. Fish, turtles, ducks, wild turkeys, boars, and deer were plentiful. The forest also provided fruits, such as guava. The Olmec probably hunted and gathered, as earlier people in the region had done.

It was their success in agriculture, however, that allowed the Olmec to build a stable culture. They used a farming method known as slash and burn. In this method, farmers first cleared, or slashed, the dense jungle growth with stone axes. Then during the dry season, they burned what remained. The left-over ashes helped enrich the soil.

MAP WORK

The Olmec built their civilization on the coastal plain of what is today southern Mexico.

1. To what degree of latitude is La Venta closest?
2. What landform lies to the northeast of the Olmec lands?

Like early farmers in Egypt and China, the Olmec made use of the flooding rivers to grow crops. After the summer floods deposited new soil, the Olmec planted the fertile river banks with crops. Three main crops were corn, beans, and squash.

MAP WORK: 1. 20° N 2. Yucatán Peninsula

293

THE OLMEC

Encourage the class to start to form ideas about the Olmec based on their sculpture and the ancient site.

- **When did the Olmec flourish?** *(about 1200 B.C. to 400 B.C.)*

- **How well watered would you say their land was?** *(Very; it was rain forest, and many rivers cut through it.)*

- **What method did the Olmec use to clear land for farming?** *(slash and burn)*

★**THINKING FURTHER:** *Sequencing* **How would you sequence the steps in slash and burn agriculture?** *(Cut down the jungle growth with axes, set fire to felled growth, leave ashes to enrich soil.)*

More **MAP WORK**

Have students analyze the map features and mark them on their desk maps.

- **What large peninsula lies to the east of Olmec territory?** *(Yucatán)*

- **What are the mountains of Middle America called?** *(the Sierra Madre)*

- **Where is the Central Plateau in relation to Olmec territory?** *(to the northwest)*

★**THINKING FURTHER:** *Compare and Contrast* **How would you compare geographic features of Olmec territory with those of the Central Plateau?** *(Olmec: coastal plain, tierra caliente; Central Plateau: rolling hills, tierra templada)*

GLOBAL CONNECTION

SLASH AND BURN ACROSS EARTH
- Slash and burn agriculture is one of the most ancient forms of farming.
- It has traditionally been practiced around the world, mainly in central Africa, northeastern South America, parts of the Indian subcontinent, Southeast Asia, and Oceania.
- Unfortunately, the fertility of the cleared land's soil sharply decreases within a few years, and the soil can no longer grow anything.
- The farmer must move on to slash and burn another wooded area. That is why slash and burn is also called "shifting agriculture."

BACKGROUND INFORMATION

ABOUT THE OLMEC FOOD SUPPLY By analyzing charred remains of ancient garbage, scientists discovered that people grew corn in Olmec territory as early as 2250 B.C.

CITIZENSHIP★

USING CURRENT EVENTS Explain to students that early in this century, oil was discovered at La Venta, and refineries and housing were built, which threatened the ancient site. Refer students to pp. 38–39, *Citizenship Viewpoints,* dealing with protecting cultural sites. Ask which they think is more important—protecting the past or meeting economic demands? Find a similar dispute in the news, and have students debate the pros and cons.

LIFE IN AN OLMEC TOWN

Have students locate La Venta on the map on p. 293 and also have them examine the artwork on that page and this for visual evidence of what life was like in an Olmec town.

Discussing The People of La Venta As students discuss this section, have them use the board to draw a diagram of the town layout of La Venta following the description in the text.

- *How does the layout of La Venta tell you that the Olmec were a well-organized society?* (Town planning suggests an organized government.)

- *How do we know that stone carving was a major specialization among the Olmec?* (large stone heads, statues and monuments, grinding tools, carved jade and obsidian objects)

- *What do we know about the military in Olmec times?* (Since monuments show successful warriors, the Olmec must have had an army.)

★THINKING FURTHER: *Compare and Contrast* **How was the basis of the Olmec economy like that of the Egyptians and other early civilizations we have studied?** *(The economy was based on agriculture, which was the work of the majority of the people.)*

LIFE IN AN OLMEC TOWN

Archaeologists have uncovered four important Olmec settlements. By about 1000 B.C. the town of La Venta had become the major center of Olmec culture. La Venta is located on a large island, surrounded by swamps and rivers, near the northern coast of what is now southern Mexico. Look at the map on page 293 to find La Venta.

The People of La Venta

In the center of what was La Venta sits a huge earthen mound, 82 feet high. This was probably the base of an Olmec pyramid. Beyond this mound are smaller mounds and a large plaza surrounded by stone pillars. In the plaza are four enormous stone heads. The largest weighs 24 tons! These heads are probably statues of Olmec rulers. Each stone head wears a hat that looks like a football helmet. Each helmet has its own symbol, which may stand for the name of a ruler.

The stone heads and other artifacts reveal interesting clues about the Olmec people. We know, for example, that the people who lived in La Venta did specialized work. Some people worked as stone carvers. They carved the gray basalt, a hard volcanic rock, into statues or into tools for grinding corn. Others carved more delicate items out of jade and obsidian, another kind of volcanic rock. These small objects probably had religious uses. Most of the Olmec, however, were farmers, and growing food was the central activity at La Venta.

The Olmec made this rubber ball (left) over 3,000 years ago. Similar balls were used in games by later cultures in Middle America.

The leaders of La Venta controlled most of the land that was used for farming. They also built stone monuments with carvings. The monuments also reminded the people of the authority of their leaders.

Olmec Religion

Artifacts and ruins in La Venta also provide us with some hints about the religious beliefs of the Olmec. Like the other people of Middle America, the Olmec practiced polytheism. They

294

Crafts of the Olmec

Since they lived in a warm climate, the Olmec probably wore simple, light articles of clothing. The many beads and small carvings that have been found indicate that the Olmec liked to wear jewelry. Both men and women wore bracelets, necklaces, and earrings made of jade and other beautiful stones. Some people, perhaps town leaders, wore headdresses decorated with colorful feathers and beads. These creations may have been worn for special religious ceremonies.

The Olmec collected sap from rubber trees to make rubber balls. They used these balls to play special games in open fields. For musical entertainment, the Olmec made flutes and other musical instruments out of clay and wood.

believed in more than one god, such as gods of fire, rain, and sun. Throughout La Venta archaeologists have found special altars that were used to make sacrifices to the gods. To sacrifice means to give up or destroy something for the sake of something else.

The Olmec also believed that certain animals had special powers. No animal, they believed, was as powerful as the jaguar. This rain forest cat played a central role in Olmec beliefs that remains a mystery to us. Perhaps the Olmec believed that the jaguar helped bring fertile crops. Many carvings and statues of jaguars have been found in Olmec settlements. Near the plaza at La Venta, archaeologists have discovered a large mosaic, or pattern of stones, in the image of a jaguar.

Beautiful jade carvings, like this jaguar-headed figure, have been found at La Venta and other Olmec sites.

295

Discussing Olmec Religion Remind students how we know of religion in other ancient cultures.

- *Why is it accurate to say that the Olmec were polytheistic?* (Archaeologists have found altars to many different gods.)

- *Who were some of these gods? What do they tell us about what was important to the Olmec?* (gods of natural forces such as fire, rain, the sun, all of which would have been crucial to slash and burn farming)

- *What religious meaning did animals have for the Olmec?* (Certain animals had special powers, the most powerful was the jaguar, which played a central role in Olmec religion.)

★**THINKING FURTHER:** *Making Conclusions How do we know that the jaguar was so important to the Olmec?* (It was often the subject of carvings—like the one on this page—and mosaics.)

Exploring Crafts of the Olmec Help students recall crafts in other cultures.

- *How did Olmec crafts satisfy people's taste for adornment?* (by providing jewelry for men and women)

- *How did crafts serve religious purposes?* (with feather headdresses that may have been used for religious ceremonies and with sacred carvings)

- *How did crafts serve entertainment needs?* (with rubber balls and musical instruments)

★**THINKING FURTHER:** *Compare and Contrast How do Olmec crafts tell us that the Olmec tastes and interests had some similarity to ours?* (Students should see that adornment, religion, sports, and music are common to both Olmec and American civilization.)

BACKGROUND INFORMATION

ABOUT THE JAGUAR IN MIDDLE AMERICA

- To the Olmec people of the rain forests, the jaguar symbolized strength and power. They came to worship jaguars as beings with magical powers.

- Anthropologist Peter Furst wrote, "In tropical America, jaguars were the shamans [priests who used magic] of the animal world, the alter ego of the shaman. They were the most powerful predators. That's why in Olmec art you get these combinations of jaguars and humans."

- This same anthropologist said, "You could almost call the Olmec people of the jaguar." Other scholars have called the Olmec worshipers of the jaguar "Middle America's first formal religion."

Learning about Olmec Traders
Emphasize the work of archaeologists.

Suggested Questions

- **How do we know that Olmec traders operated far and wide?** *(Artifacts have been found hundreds of miles from their home.)*

★ **THINKING FURTHER:** *Making Connections* **How are successful crafts work and successful trading connected?** *(Good products create a strong demand for themselves, which traders exploit.)*

Discussing WHY IT MATTERS Have students sum up the Olmec culture.

★ **THINKING FURTHER:** *Making Conclusions* **The Olmec have been called the "mother culture" of Middle America. Why might that be true?** *(They had a well-developed civilization, worthy of cultural borrowing by others.)*

★ 3 CLOSE

MAIN IDEAS
Call on students for answers.

- **When did the Olmec begin to develop their civilization?** *(1200 B.C.)*
- **How did the Olmec turn a dense rain forest environment into farmland?** *(with slash and burn clearing)*
- **How do we know that the Olmec were good craftworkers and traders?** *(Their artifacts were much in demand, and their traders met this demand.)*

EVALUATE
✓ **Answers to Think About It**
1. along the coast of the Gulf of Mexico, west of Yucatán
   Recall Details
2. by slashing down the jungle growth and burning it
   Recall Details
3. Answers should center on clues left by Olmec artifacts.
   Make Inferences
4. The environment led the Olmec to slash and burn, which in turn destroyed parts of the rain forest.
   Cause and Effect
5. Have students use visuals and text to help them to describe trade goods.
   Point of View

Write About It Have students write a diary entry describing an experience they would have had in La Venta.

The figure (above) is typical of the stone monuments carved by the Olmec.

Olmec Traders

Archaeologists believe that the Olmec traded with other groups of people in Middle America. Clay goods and figures made in the Olmec style have been found in places as distant from Olmec lands as central Mexico, more than 300 miles to the north. Perhaps the Olmec traded these objects for food, feathers, and animal skins. Traders would have traveled to distant settlements by foot on narrow forest paths.

WHY IT MATTERS

Around 400 B.C. Olmec civilization was gradually beginning to disappear. Historians are not certain why the culture faded. Some think that the system of

296

agriculture began to break down from overuse of the land. La Venta and the other Olmec settlements were abandoned. Eventually thick rain forest grew up around the Olmec towns. The achievements of this early Middle American civilization lived on, however, in artifacts left behind. You are about to read of a huge civilization that developed in Middle America and built on the achievements of the Olmec.

✓ Reviewing Facts and Ideas

MAIN IDEAS

- The Olmec built one of the earliest civilizations in the Americas, starting around 1200 B.C.
- The Olmec developed a system of slash and burn agriculture in the dense rain forest environment.
- The Olmec were craftworkers who designed objects such as earrings, beads, and necklaces. They probably traded these objects with people in other parts of Middle America.

THINK ABOUT IT

1. In which part of Middle America did the centers of Olmec culture grow?
2. How did the Olmec create fields for growing crops?
3. **FOCUS** What clues have helped archaeologists to gain knowledge about Olmec culture?
4. **THINKING SKILL** What *effects* did the environment of the Olmec have on their system of farming? How in turn might the Olmec have affected their environment?
5. **WRITE** Suppose you were a trader who lived in Olmec times. Write a description of some of the Olmec objects that you would like to trade with other people.

MEETING INDIVIDUAL NEEDS

RETEACHING (Easy) Have students use pieces of colored construction paper to design a mosaic showing subject matter that Olmec craftsworkers might have selected.

EXTENSION (Average) Have students write a "will" left by the Olmecs for succeeding Middle American civilizations. Their "wills" should name the legacies that the Olmec are leaving and tell why each is important.

ENRICHMENT (Challenging) Divide the class into four groups and assign each group one of the following aspects of Olmec life—military exploits, religious missionaries, Olmec writing, and ball playing. Have each group research its topic and then report its findings to the class.

CITIZENSHIP
MAKING A DIFFERENCE

The Rain Forest Treasures Trail

SYLVESTER VILLAGE, BELIZE— The Gallon Jug Community School is located in the middle of a vast rain forest in Belize.

Near the Gallon Jug school, a trail extends into the forest. The school's 75 students helped create the trail. They call it the Rain Forest Treasures Trail, and they use it to teach visitors about the special plants and animals found in the tropical rain forest.

Tropical rain forests cover only about 7 percent of Earth's land. Yet they are home to fully half of Earth's plant species. Many rain forest plants provide medicines that have been used for centuries to treat everything from colds to deadly diseases.

Teacher Nancy Zuniga directs the school along with her husband, Julio. She explains that the trail came about because "the kids were always teaching me about this plant or that plant. They knew from their parents which plants helped soothe a burn or bring down a fever."

Dr. Rosita Arvigo, from Belize's Ix Chel tropical research center, taught students to recognize medicinal plants. Older villagers also helped the students learn the uses of many plants.

After the children and their parents cleared the trail, they located and labeled plants along the path. "Now," says student Adolio Bolaños, "we are tour guides. We take visitors on a half-hour walk on the trail. Along the way we teach them about the different plants and their uses."

Tourists and school groups from other parts of Belize come to walk the Rain Forest Treasures Trail. Adolio tells visitors that rain forests around the world are disappearing. Loggers cut down trees and ranchers clear land for cattle grazing. Now the children of the Gallon Jug school are working to protect rain forest plants and to replace trees. Adolio worries that "if people clear away the rain forest, we will not have medicinal plants. If we keep the forests, someday doctors may find new ways to use these plants to cure sicknesses. I read that somewhere in the forest there is a plant for every sickness. I hope it's true."

"The kids were always teaching me about this plant or that plant."

Nancy L. Winchler-Zuñiga

297

CITIZENSHIP ★

UNDERSTANDING ENVIRONMENTAL CONCERNS Encourage students to identify environmental problems that face your community. Have students select one problem and discuss how they could help solve it. (Possible avenues might include letter writing, poll taking, and lobbying.) Discuss the pros and cons of each avenue and create a plan of action. If possible, have students implement the plan. One avenue that the Gallon Jug Community School has taken to address the problem of deforestation is to plant mahogany seedlings. For further information, contact: *Nancy and Julio Zuñiga/ Gallon Jug Community School/ P.O. Box 37/ Belize City, Belize/ Central America/ Telephone: 011-501-234419/ email: address the Gallon Jug Community School at cocacola@ns.btl.net*

Lesson Objective
★ Evaluate how community involvement and effort can enrich life and knowledge.

Identifying the Focus Help students to see what a community, including young people, can accomplish together.

● *What different kinds of people in the Sylvester community joined to create the Rain Forest Treasures Trail?* (Students, teacher, parents, scientist. Help students see that neither education level nor age stopped anyone. Explain that across the world rain forests are lost at a rate of 55,000 square miles a year.)

Why It Matters Discuss with students the importance of efforts like the Treasures Trail for saving the benefits of the rain forests and how average citizens can contribute to it.

● *Why did the Sylvester community decide to create the Treasures Trail?* (to teach people about rain forest plants and their value)

● *Why did they think this was such an important project?* (The continued cutting down of the rain forests threatens to make these plants extinct.)

● *What is Gallon Jug School doing to protect rain forest plants?* (educating tourists about them, working to protect them and to replace rain forest trees as they are cut down)

★THINKING FURTHER: *Making Conclusions What does the Rain Forest Treasure Trails project prove about community action?* (A variety of concerned people can unite to achieve a worthy goal.)

LESSON 3

PAGES 298–303

Lesson Overview

Maya civilization, which developed in present-day Yucatán and Guatemala, dominated Middle America for centuries.

Lesson Objectives

★ Identify and describe the achievements of Maya civilization.

★ Compare ways the Maya forged their civilization with ways the Greeks forged theirs during each people's classical period.

⭐ 1 PREPARE

MOTIVATE Remind students of the proud city-states of Greek civilization, like Athens and Sparta. Explain that such city-states developed in Middle America too, and have a student do the *Read Aloud* to introduce them.

SET PURPOSE On a wall map or desk map, have students locate Greece and Middle America, to see the distance between them. Refer students to the carving of the Maya ruler, the *Vocabulary*, and the *Read to Learn* question. Then follow the suggestions given in the *Reading Strategies* below.

⭐ 2 TEACH

Understanding THE BIG PICTURE
Begin a class list of Maya achievements.

● **What clues have the Maya left us that reveal their civilization?** *(stone remains of pyramids, other structures, written language, written records)*

★**THINKING FURTHER:** *Predicting*
What kinds of things do you predict these clues will tell us about Maya civilization? *(perhaps things about their religion, government, housing, day-to-day life, history)*

Resource **REMINDER**

Practice and Project Book: *p. 62*
Anthology: *From Mouse to Bat, pp. 64–65; Incidents of Travel, p. 66*
Desk Map

Focus Activity

READ TO LEARN
What were some of the achievements of the Maya civilization?

VOCABULARY
Classic Period
maize
glyph
stela

PLACES
Copán

298

1400 B.C	800 B.C	200 B.C	A.D. 250	A.D. 900	A.D. 1000

MAYA CIVILIZATION

READ ALOUD

Throughout Middle America archaeologists have uncovered ruins of huge stone cities. They were built by a civilization of great builders, astronomers, and craftworkers. By studying the spectacular ruins of the ancient Maya (MAH yuh), archaeologists have developed a picture of a culture that dominated Middle America for almost 1,000 years.

THE BIG PICTURE

The Maya developed their civilization about 600 years after Olmec culture declined. Because most Maya books were lost or destroyed, many details of their lives remain a mystery. Stone pyramids and plazas, however, hint at the complex culture that thrived on the plains and in the valleys of Middle America. The Maya created a written language and achieved a remarkable understanding of the stars and planets. They also kept records of their work in stone carvings. This civilization developed in a region close to where the Olmec had lived.

SHELTERED INSTRUCTION

READING STRATEGIES & LANGUAGE DEVELOPMENT

COMPARE AND CONTRAST Remind students that they can compare and contrast two different civilizations to shed light on each. Invite volunteers to recall the highlights of the Greeks. Jot down responses on chart paper. Have students copy the chart and complete it as they read by noting accomplishments of the Maya. **[SDAIE STRATEGY:** BRIDGING/TEXT RE-PRESENTATION**]**

SYNONYMS Write the word *maize* on the board and have the class locate it on p. 300. Point out that its synonym here is given as "corn." Yet in other places where English is spoken, corn would not be a synonym for maize. Originally, the term *corn* referred to a region's main cereal crop. In England, *corn* still refers to wheat; in Scotland and Ireland, it refers to oats. Ask students to explain why *corn* would have meant *maize* in Middle America.

THE RISE OF THE MAYA

The Maya had lived in the southern part of Middle America as early as 1000 B.C. From the lowlands of the Yucatán (yoo kuh TAN) peninsula to the highlands of present-day Guatemala, they developed a culture based on agriculture and hunting. They had contact, no doubt, with the Olmec and other nearby groups.

Between about A.D. 250 and A.D. 900, the Maya built the richest civilization yet seen in the Americas. Historians call this period of Maya history the Classic Period. A classic period is an important time of cultural achievement for a civilization. Other classic periods often discussed by historians include those of Greece and Rome.

A Maya City

One of the great centers of classic Maya culture was Copán (ko PAHN), a city in present-day Honduras. Even today the ruins at Copán are impressive.

Among the impressive structures at Copán is the ball court. Here a fierce Maya ball game, called *pokta-pok* (POHK tuh POHK), was played. Players wore helmets and padding on their arms and legs, for the game was rough. They were not allowed to touch the five-pound rubber ball with their hands. The two teams rushed up and down the court trying to get the ball through a stone hoop. If they succeeded, they won the game. Excited spectators filled the stands and gave clothing to the winning team.

This game was part of Maya religion. You can see an illustration of a game on page 294. Those who lost were sometimes killed as a sacrifice to Maya gods. The Maya believed their gods would help them if they sacrificed something as important as a human life.

Other buildings in Copán included the tall temple-pyramids and palaces around the main plaza. These structures were built out of huge stone blocks. Since the Maya did not have wheels or work animals, all the moving and lifting was done by humans. Sometimes this work was done by enslaved people who had been captured during wars.

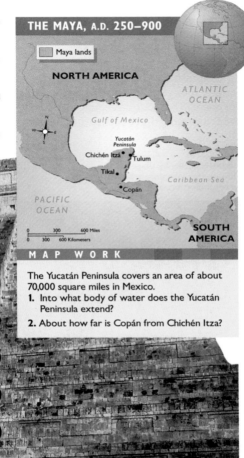

THE MAYA, A.D. 250–900

Maya lands

NORTH AMERICA

ATLANTIC OCEAN

Gulf of Mexico

Yucatán Peninsula

Chichén Itzá • Tulum

Tikal •

• Copán

Caribbean Sea

PACIFIC OCEAN

SOUTH AMERICA

0   300   600 Miles
0   300   600 Kilometers

MAP WORK

The Yucatán Peninsula covers an area of about 70,000 square miles in Mexico.
1. Into what body of water does the Yucatán Peninsula extend?
2. About how far is Copán from Chichén Itza?

This building at Chichén Itza is the Temple of the Feathered Serpent.

THE RISE OF THE MAYA

Use the map and text to identify Maya territory.

More

MAP WORK

Have students sit together in pairs with one textbook opened to this page and the other to the Olmec map on p. 293. Encourage students to work back and forth between maps and text.

- **How far back do the Maya go in Middle America?** *(about 1000 B.C.)*

- **Where did they create their culture?** *(Yucatán to the highlands of Guatemala)*

- **Where was this in relation to Olmec territory?** *(Have students compare maps to see that Maya land was east and southeast of Olmec land.)*

- **What were major Maya cities?** *(Copán, Tikal, Tulum, Chichén Itzá)*

- **What is a civilization's "Classic Period"?** *(a time of great cultural achievement)*

- **When was the Maya Classic Period?** *(from about A.D. 250 to A.D. 900)*

★**THINKING FURTHER: Compare and Contrast How does this compare in time to Greece's classic period?** *(Help students to see that Greece's great cultural achievement occurred from about the 700s B.C. through the Golden Age of Athens in the 400s B.C.— ending about 650 years before the Maya's began.)*

Discussing A Maya City Have students find Copán on the map.

- **What kinds of structures did Copán contain?** *(stadium, pyramids, palaces)*

- **Why was a ball game there more than just a sporting event?** *(It could have religious significance, making the losers possible victims of sacrifice.)*

★**THINKING FURTHER: Compare and Contrast What similarity can you find in the work forces of the Greeks and the Maya?** *(Both used slaves, who might have been captured in war.)*

GLOBAL CONNECTION

REFLECTIONS OF OTHER CIVILIZATIONS Early European travelers who came upon Maya civilization were so struck by it that they compared it to ancient civilizations they knew more about. They compared the Maya to the Greeks because of their science, the Romans because of their engineering, the Egyptians because of their pyramids.

BACKGROUND INFORMATION

ABOUT COPÁN'S ACROPOLIS
- Like Athens, Copán has an Acropolis, known today as the Main Group. It soars 100 feet high—ten stories—above an old riverbed.
- Nearby stands "a forest of kings"—stone figures, larger than life and crowded together, honoring Copán's greatest rulers.

LIFE IN COPÁN

Help students develop an idea of Copán in its time and place.

- **Was Copán a large city?** *(at 20,000 and considering the distance it covered, not by modern standards)*

- **What tells you that it was a busy place?** *(its hundreds of buildings, being a center of trade for outlying villages and other Maya cities)*

> ★**THINKING FURTHER:** *Making Conclusions* **Why would a city like Copán be an "engine" driving Maya cultural development?** *(Reinforce the idea of cities as centers where ideas and goods are exchanged and showcased, thus stimulating cultural growth.)*

Learning About The Most Important Crop Help students recognize our debt to the Maya for foods we eat.

- **What was the most important crop for the Maya?** *(maize, or corn)*

- **Why?** *(It was the most important part of the Maya diet.)*

- **How did Maya dependence on maize affect their beliefs?** *(Maize was so important to them that the maize god was an important part of their religion; they performed ceremonies in connection with planting and harvesting maize, and believed they had been created from it.)*

- **What other foods were part of their diet?** *(beans, squash, peppers, avocado, papaya, meat, and cacao, especially for the rulers)*

> ★**THINKING FURTHER:** *Making Conclusions* **How well rounded a diet would you say the Maya had?** *(It seems a good mix of cereal, vegetables, fruits, and meat.)*

Exploring Growing Up in Copán Have students briefly review growing up in Athens and in Sparta.

> ★**THINKING FURTHER:** *Compare and Contrast* **Was growing up in Copán more like growing up in Sparta or in Athens?** *(Noting the separation of the boys out into group homes and the strict household training for girls, students will probably choose Sparta, although perhaps see less harshness.)*

LIFE IN COPÁN

At its peak between about A.D. 600 to 800, Copán was home to about 20,000 people. The region of Copán was crowded with hundreds of buildings, yet a person could have walked from one side of the city center to the other in less than ten minutes. The buildings ranged from small plaster-and-thatch houses to the huge stone pyramids that still stand today.

Copán had many visitors from nearby villages. Traders came from other Maya cities many miles away. In some ways, however, life in Copán was not so different from life for earlier Middle Americans. For example, most of the people in Copán worked as farmers.

The Most Important Crop

Agriculture was the heart of the Maya economy. Maize (MAYZ), or corn, was the heart of Maya agriculture. Maize was first grown in Middle America in about 5000 B.C. The cob of this early maize was tiny, about the size of a shelled peanut. When it was heated, maize exploded like modern popcorn.

Over the years Middle American farmers improved their crops of maize. It was the most important part of the Maya diet. Yum Kax, the maize god, became a significant part of the Maya religion. According to one belief, the gods created the Maya people from maize dough. The Maya performed special ceremonies for the planting and harvesting of maize.

The farmers of Copán planted other crops, too, such as beans, squash, and peppers. They also grew cacao trees, which provided chocolate—the favorite

In this painting by Diego Rivera, Maya women sort their most important crop, maize.

drink of Maya rulers. Most Maya grew avocado and papaya trees near home. They hunted for animals such as deer. Farmers and hunters sold many of their crops and products in city marketplaces.

Growing Up in Copán

Boys and girls lived very differently in Copán. When boys were in their teens, they moved out of their family homes into large group homes. There they learned to play the ball game. Boys also learned to become soldiers. Girls stayed at home, where they were strictly raised by their mothers. They learned how to cook maize and other food and how to run a household.

Maya Society

At the top of society in Copán was the king. Below the king were warriors, wealthy farmers, and merchants. As in the societies of Egypt and Mesopotamia, farmers made up the largest group. Below the farmers were slaves, who were usually prisoners taken during wars with neighboring cities.

The Religion of the Maya

Religion was very important to the Maya. They believed that the universe was made up of three levels—the upperworld of the heavens, the middleworld of humans, and the underworld of the dead. The Maya believed that their king could communicate with the upperworld. He also could bring spirits into the middleworld.

The Maya worshiped hundreds of gods. In addition to important gods such as Yum Kax, god of maize, they also believed in lesser gods. For example, hunters, poets, and beekeepers each worshiped different gods. The king and other nobles led many of the ceremonies for worshiping these gods. The Maya believed that their ancestors lived on in the upperworld.

As part of their religion, the Maya closely studied the stars and planets. The planet Venus was considered especially important. Its movement was used to make decisions about when to attack other cities. By studying the night sky, the Maya also developed an accurate calendar. This allowed them to record the exact dates of events.

The Maya, like the Olmec, carved stone figures of their gods and leaders.

Discussing Maya Society Have students develop a Maya social pyramid.

★**THINKING FURTHER: Classifying**
How would you construct a social pyramid to show the organization of Maya society? (Refer the class to the Egyptian social pyramid on p. 95. Then have them use it as a model to construct a Maya social pyramid on the board.)

Exploring The Religion of the Maya Remind students of other polytheistic cultures they studied.

● *Was Maya religion monotheistic or polytheistic? Explain. (Polytheistic— Maya worshiped hundreds of gods.)*

● *How would you categorize their gods? (gods of natural things, such as maize, as well as "patron saints" of various occupations)*

● *How was a Maya king like a priest in Maya religion? (Maya kings were thought to have the power to communicate with the heavens, and led ceremonies worshiping gods.)*

★**THINKING FURTHER: Cause and Effect** *How did their religion lead Maya people to develop a calendar? (They studied the heavens for religion, and the knowledge of the movement of the moon and stars they gained told them what they needed to know to create an accurate calendar.)*

301

CITIZENSHIP★

UNDERSTANDING GOVERNMENT
● The city-states of the Maya world were like those of the Greek world in that not one of them ever gained complete dominance over the others.
● Kingship of a city-state was generally passed down through a family. A brother or a son succeeded upon a king's death. In Tikal, kingship was passed down through a single family for over 500 years.

USING THE ANTHOLOGY

FROM MOUSE TO BAT, pages 64–65 Mayan fables, were handed down orally before they were written. After students read this fable, have them find the tale's moral.

BACKGROUND INFORMATION

ABOUT THE MAYA CALENDAR
The Maya actually developed two calendars. One was called the Sacred Round, which had 260 days. Each day was given one of 20 names, each name associated with a different god or goddess, and was given a number from 1 to 13. Based on the combination of gods or goddesses and numbers, astronomer-priests determined which days were lucky and unlucky. The other was the called the Vague Year, which had 365 days. It was divided into 18 20-day months, with five days left over at the end. This five-day period was considered an unlucky time, and during it, Maya fasted and made sacrifices.

MAYA WRITING

Explain to the class that Maya books were destroyed when the Spanish came to the Americas because, as Bishop Diego de Landa explained, "as they contained nothing in which there were not to be seen superstition and lies of the devil, we burned them all."

Discussing Unlocking Written Mysteries Ask students to recall other "lost languages."

- *What are glyphs?* (symbols that can be written or carved on stone)

- *How are they like the hieroglyphs you studied in connection with ancient Egypt?* (Both are written languages, some of the symbols stand for things, some for sounds.)

- *In what other ways did the Maya honor and record historic events?* (by carving descriptions of them on stelae, or tall flat stones)

★ **THINKING FURTHER:** *Making Generalizations* **What generalizations can you make about the Maya based on the stelae that they left?** (They must have valued heroic deeds; their leaders must have been powerful to have such work done.)

Discussing the PRIMARY SOURCE

Point out that the glyphs look like art.

★ **THINKING FURTHER:** *Using Visuals* **Where would you expect to find a number in the stela on this page?** (in the carving at the left)

Exploring Maya Math Explain to the class that the Maya developed a mathematical system based on 20, rather than 10. Point out that they also developed the concept of 0, which may predate its use in India and its adoption by Arabs.

★ **THINKING FURTHER:** *Using Visuals* **Why wouldn't people today easily recognize Maya number glyphs?** (They look much like other glyphs on carvings.)

MAYA WRITING

The Maya were the first people of Middle America to use a written language widely. Although almost all of their books were lost or burned by the Spanish in the 1500s, the Maya left behind a written record in stone. It is from these records as well as from other artifacts that archaeologists have been able to form a picture of what life was like for the Maya.

Unlocking Written Mysteries

Only in the last 50 years have archaeologists begun to understand the writing of the Maya. These symbols, called glyphs (GLIFS), are carved into the stones of Maya cities and towns. Some glyphs are like the pictures of Chinese writing and stand for objects. Others stand for sounds, as in the Roman alphabet.

At Copán the Maya built a magnificent 72-step "hieroglyphic stairway," with over 2,200 glyphs. These symbols tell the story of Copán from its beginnings until A.D. 755, when the stairway was built. Not unlike the epics of Homer in ancient Greece, this stairway recounts the heroic deeds and deaths of Maya leaders.

Maya leaders also had tall, flat stones, called stelae (STEE lee), carved with glyphs. These stones were put on display in the city. A stela was often used to mark an important historical event in the life of the leader. On this page you can see a stela from Copán that told about the life of the king Yax-Pac (YAKS PAK). How are these glyphs similar to Egyptian hieroglyphics?

302

Maya Math

The Maya also created a mathematical system that helped merchants keep track of goods and scribes keep track of history. This system used glyphs that the Maya developed to represent numbers. It helped the Maya to make very exact calculations.

BACKGROUND INFORMATION

ABOUT DECIPHERING MAYA GLYPHS

- The Maya were not the first Middle Americans to develop written language, but theirs was most elaborate, with 800 signs.

- Learning how to decipher the Maya glyphs has been a painstaking process that started more than a century ago. Little by little, scholars began to make out the phonetic system used. Once they figured out the Maya calendar, they had greater insight into the language.

- Learning about various historical events helped scholars match events to written accounts. Then specialists called linguists brought their knowledge of how language works to the effort, speeding up the deciphering process.

- Today about half of the Maya glyphs can be read, but that figure is rising as work on deciphering continues.

WHY IT MATTERS

Many of the great Maya cities were abandoned in the A.D. 900s. No one knows why for sure. Some scientists believe that, like the Olmec, the Maya may have suffered crop failures. Others think that the many wars the Maya waged contributed to the decline of the civilization. Although they abandoned the cities, however, Maya people continued to live in the area.

Today the descendants of the Maya live in the highlands and lowlands of central and southern Middle America. There 4 million Maya continue many of the traditions that began hundreds of years ago. Many speak a version of the Maya language and follow ancient ceremonies of agriculture, marriage, and healing. They also grow maize and other traditional crops. Some Maya raise crops, such as coffee, that are sold around the world. Such products link the rich Maya past with the realities of today's economy.

Descendants of the Maya, like these women in Central America, continue to follow many traditional ways.

✔️ Reviewing Facts and Ideas

MAIN IDEAS

- The Maya built a complex civilization in Middle America from about A.D. 250 until A.D. 900.
- The Maya created large cities throughout Middle America. The cities contained temples, ball courts, and other buildings.
- Religion was an important part of life for the Maya. The Maya practiced polytheism.
- The Maya developed systems of writing and mathematics that allowed them to record important events in their history.

THINK ABOUT IT

1. What was the most important crop to the Maya?

2. What was one kind of god that the Maya worshiped?

3. **FOCUS** What are three achievements that set the Maya apart from earlier Middle American civilizations? What made Maya civilization "classic"?

4. **THINKING SKILL** _Compare_ the systems of learning of the Maya with those of ancient Greece.

5. **WRITE** Suppose you are an archaeologist exploring Maya ruins. Write a description of Copán for a magazine for sixth graders.

303

MEETING INDIVIDUAL NEEDS

RETEACHING (Easy) Tell students to reread the two paragraphs under _Life in Copán_ on p. 300. Then have them draw an illustration based on the description they contain.

EXTENSION (Average) Have students suppose that they have been called on to direct a tour of Copán. Tell them to write an itinerary identifying and describing the sites the tour will visit.

ENRICHMENT (Challenging) Divide the class into four groups and assign each one of these Maya city-states: Tikal, Chichén Itzá, Palenque, Bonampak. Have each group do research on its city—its buildings, its trade, its ceremonies, daily life there—and prepare their findings for presentation to the class. Afterward, have students discuss the cities' similarities and differences.

Discussing WHY IT MATTERS Leave students with a sense of the mystery of the Maya abandonment of cities.

> ★**THINKING FURTHER:** _Compare and Contrast_ **How does what happened to the Maya civilization compare with what happened to the Greek?** (Greek civilization flourished in a crowded part of the world and was transported to many other areas; much of Maya civilization disappeared. Yet both left cultural legacies.)

⭐ 3 CLOSE

MAIN IDEAS

Have students write their answers and then exchange papers.

- **Why is the time from A.D. 250 to A.D. 900 called the Classic Period of the Maya?** (During that time, the Maya developed a complex civilization.)

- **What kinds of structures did Maya cities contain?** (temple pyramids, ball courts, palaces, dwellings)

- **How would you describe the religion of the Maya?** (polytheistic and very important to everyday life)

- **In what areas of learning did the Maya particularly excel?** (writing, astronomy, mathematics)

EVALUATE

✔️ **Answers to Think About It**

1. maize, or corn
Recall Details

2. gods of natural things like corn, gods special to occupations
Summarize

3. developing a calendar based on astronomy, using a written language widely, developing mathematics
Make Inferences

4. Both developed written language, both used it to record history, both probed deeply into mathematics. The Greeks' study of philosophy was matched by the Maya's study of astronomy.
Make Analogies

5. Articles should describe the stately buildings and ball court, the crowds and bustle, the trade and markets.
Make Judgements and Decisions

Write About It Have students write a paragraph in which they describe what they think was the greatest achievement of Maya civilization.

LEGACY

Lesson Overview

Astronomy has fascinated and challenged people through time.

Lesson Objective

★ Appreciate the science of astronomy.

1 PREPARE

MOTIVATE Remind students that in ancient times, people looked up at the changing night sky and worked to figure out the monthly and yearly patterns of stars and planets. Invite them to discuss their own reactions to looking up into the night sky.

SET PURPOSE Encourage students to explore this *Legacy* to trace the development of astronomy and of the technology that continues to open up more knowledge about it.

2 TEACH

Understanding the Concept of a Legacy Have students read the text on this page.

● *What is astronomy?* (the study of stars and planets)

● *Why do you think that studying the heavens has held such fascination for people through the ages?* (Encourage students to recognize and appreciate how mysterious the ever-changing night sky must have been to ancient peoples and how they might have tried to solve its mystery by tracking the movements and changes they saw and trying to find a pattern to them.)

● *What practical use did the Maya make of their studies of astronomy?* (Their studies helped them to create a highly accurate calendar.)

● *What discovery that the Maya made through astronomy echoed an earlier discovery by the Egyptians?* (They discovered how to predict eclipses of the sun and moon)

ASTRONOMY

Have you ever looked up into the sky on a clear night and wondered about the stars and planets? The ancient Maya must have wondered too.

Scientists have discovered that the Maya had a great interest in astronomy, or the study of stars and planets. The Maya spent much time observing the sun, moon, and the planet Venus. Using these observations the Maya were able to design a complex and accurate calendar. Like ancient Egyptians, they also predicted eclipses of the sun and moon.

People have always wanted to know what is in the sky. Astronomy continues to be an important part of scientific life. Through modern high-powered telescopes, satellites, and space shuttle missions, we continue to learn about the universe.

304

BACKGROUND INFORMATION

A GLOSSARY OF ASTRONOMY TERMS

● **galaxy**—A collection of from 100 million to 100 billion stars and planets held in their place by gravity. There are many galaxies spread like islands through space. Earth is part of the galaxy called the Milky Way. Nearest to the Milky Way is the Andromeda galaxy, from 750,000 to 1,500,000,000 light years away.

● **light-year**—The distance that light travels in one year, which is about 5,878,000,000,000 miles, or 5.88 trillion miles.

● **observatory**—A building or institution for the observation and recording of astronomical phenomena.

● **universe**—The entire system of galaxies and all the rest of space, also called the *cosmos.*

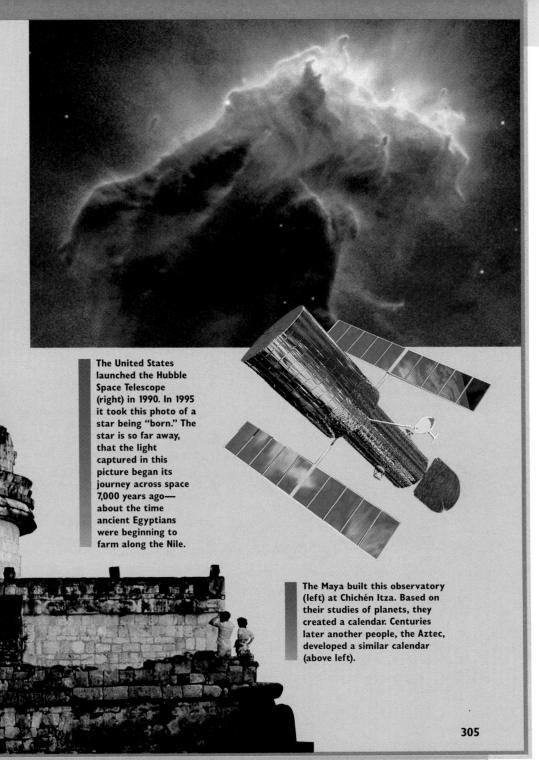

The United States launched the Hubble Space Telescope (right) in 1990. In 1995 it took this photo of a star being "born." The star is so far away, that the light captured in this picture began its journey across space 7,000 years ago—about the time ancient Egyptians were beginning to farm along the Nile.

The Maya built this observatory (left) at Chichén Itza. Based on their studies of planets, they created a calendar. Centuries later another people, the Aztec, developed a similar calendar (above left).

305

★THINKING FURTHER: *Making Conclusions* **Why are we who live in modern times better equipped to solve mysteries of the universe than the ancients?** *(Improved technology like high-powered telescopes, satellites, and space shuttle missions help us to see farther into the universe than anyone before us.)*

Examining the Illustrations Give the class a few minutes to examine the illustrations and read the captions.

● **What are the building remains shown here? For what was the building used?** *(It was an observatory the Maya built at Chichén Itzá to study astronomy.)*

● **What more modern technology for studying astronomy is pictured here? How does it improve on the Maya observatory?** *(When students identify the Hubble space telescope, discuss its capabilities with them, how not only is it a telescope, a technology the Maya did not have, but that it has left Earth to travel far out into space, beyond Earth's often cloudy atmosphere, for a closer look at stars and planets.)*

● **What does the illustration at the upper right show about the universe that no ancients could have known?** *(that there are stars still being "born")*

★THINKING FURTHER: *Compare and Contrast* **How would you compare the calendar devised by the Aztec, a Middle America people you will meet in Chapter 15, with one of our typical wall calendars?** *(Students should note that the Aztec calendar represents time in a circular fashion while we render it in a linear way, with day following day in a straight line.)*

MEETING INDIVIDUAL NEEDS

RETEACHING (Easy) Divide the class into nine groups and assign each one of the nine planets in our solar system. Have each group look its planet up in the encyclopedia or another source and produce a picture of it. Then have students assemble a bulletin board display of the planets in their order from the sun.

EXTENSION (Average) Tell students to pick out something in the universe that interests them—a specific planet, a comet, a meteor, a supernova—and do some research on it. Then have them write a letter to a friend telling about it.

ENRICHMENT (Challenging) Many books on astronomy have been written for young people covering a wide variety of topics. Divide the class into groups and have each group choose a different book and prepare a presentation to make to the class about it.

 3 CLOSE

SUM IT UP
Encourage students to discuss reasons that astronomy is important to us today.

EVALUATE
Write About It Ask students to write short poems about the birth of a star.

DISCUSSING MAJOR EVENTS Use these questions to help students focus on some broad facts about ancient American civilizations.

- *What two American civilizations does this time line trace?* (Olmec, Maya)

- *What similiarity can you find in how long these civilizations lasted?* (There is only about half a century difference in how long they lasted, with the Olmec civilization lasting the longer time.)

- *What is the significance of La Venta and Copan?* (Each was a center of its civilization—La Venta of the Olmec, Copán of the Maya.)

Answers to
THINKING ABOUT VOCABULARY

1. stela
2. Classic Period
3. glacier
4. climograph
5. maize
6. rain forest
7. slash and burn
8. tropical
9. Ice Age
10. glyph

Answers to
THINKING ABOUT FACTS

1. It caused a land bridge to appear that invited people to cross from Asia to the Americas and thus to populate the Americas.

2. They receive more than 80 inches of rain annually and are generally found in tropical parts of the world.

3. through both hunting/gathering and slash and burn agriculture; fish and wild game, corn, beans, and squash

---

Resource **REMINDER**

Practice and Project Book: *p. 63*
Assessment Book: *Chapter 11 Test*
Technology: *Videodisc/Video Tape*
Transparency: *Graphic Organizer, Main Idea-Chart*

CHAPTER 11 REVIEW

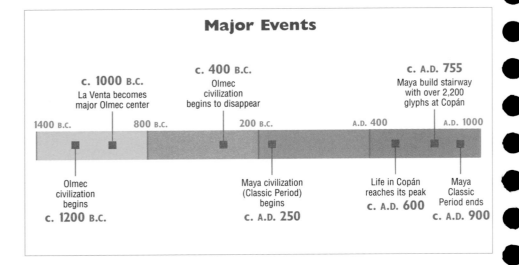

Major Events

c. **1000** B.C.
La Venta becomes major Olmec center

c. **400** B.C.
Olmec civilization begins to disappear

c. A.D. **755**
Maya build stairway with over 2,200 glyphs at Copán

1400 B.C.   800 B.C.   200 B.C.   A.D. 400   A.D. 1000

Olmec civilization begins
c. **1200** B.C.

Maya civilization (Classic Period) begins
c. A.D. **250**

Life in Copán reaches its peak
c. A.D. **600**

Maya Classic Period ends
c. A.D. **900**

THINKING ABOUT VOCABULARY

Number a sheet of paper from 1 to 10. Beside each number write the word or term from the list below that best completes each sentence.

Classic Period   maize
climograph   rain forest
glacier   slash and burn
glyph   stela
Ice Age   tropical

1. A tall, flat stone carved with glyphs is a _____.

2. The Maya civilization was at the height of achievement during its _____.

3. A body of ice that inches along the land is a _____.

4. A _____ measures temperature and precipitation over a period of months.

5. The main food of the Maya was _____.

6. A _____ receives more than 80 inches of rain per year.

7. One way to clear jungle areas for farming is to _____.

8. _____ refers to the climate area near the equator where it is very warm.

9. The _____ was a period when nearly half of Earth's land surface was covered by ice.

10. A symbol called the _____ is the basis of Maya writing.

THINKING ABOUT FACTS

1. How did the Ice Age affect the history of the Americas?

2. What makes rain forests unique?

3. How did the Olmec get food? What types of food did they eat?

4. What was pokta-pok?

5. Look at the time line above. How long did the Olmec and Maya civilizations last? What may have brought them to an end?

306

SECOND-LANGUAGE SUPPORT

SELF-ASSESSMENT Encourage students to assess what they have learned about ancient America by comparing what they knew before they read the chapter with what they know now. Ask students to describe at least three important and new facts they learned about these civilizations. Then have these students discuss the most important achievements of Mayan civilization.

VISUALIZATION Second-language learners might create posters about Olmec and Mayan civilizations to summarize the ways of life and achievements of both groups.

THINK AND WRITE

WRITING ABOUT PERSPECTIVES
Write about the people who traveled between Asia and North America during the Ice Age. Describe why there was a land bridge and the reasons why people may have crossed it.

WRITING A JOURNAL ENTRY
Suppose that you have gone back about 3,000 years to live in the Olmec center of La Venta. Write a journal entry about your life there. Include details about the way you live, the work you do, and some of the interesting features of the town.

WRITING A REPORT
Write a report about the civilization the Maya built in Middle America. Describe their main achievements and the way people lived in the city of Copán.

APPLYING STUDY SKILLS

READING CLIMOGRAPHS
1. What does a climograph measure?
2. Look at the climographs on pages 290–291. Which of the three Mexican cities shown has the highest average annual precipitation? Which has the highest average annual temperature?
3. Is the rainy season the same for all three cities? If not, how is it different?
4. What can you tell about the climate of the three cities by reading the climographs?
5. How are climographs helpful?

4. a fierce Maya ball game that was perhaps more religious than sporting
5. Olmec—800 years, Maya—750 years; possibly breakdowns in agriculture like crop failures and possibly the toll of wars waged

Answers to APPLYING STUDY SKILLS
1. the temperature and precipitation in a place over a period of months
2. Veracruz; Acapulco
3. Yes, it seems to run from May through October in all three, but precipitation is significantly lighter during this period in Mexico City.
4. each climate's range of temperatures, when its rainy and dry seasons are, and how rainy or dry a climate it is
5. Climographs are useful for making comparisons among climates and, practically, for a traveler to know what kind of weather to expect in any given month.

Technology CONNECTION
VIDEODISC/VIDEO TAPE 5
Enrich Chapter 11 with the *Ancient America* segment.

Search Frame 34295 Side B

Summing Up the Chapter

Review the chapter and copy the main idea table below on a separate piece of paper. Then place each feature listed in the correct column. Add any additional features you find when you review the chapter. After filling in the table, use it to help write a paragraph that answers the question "What were some achievements of the early peoples in Middle America?"

MAIN IDEA: Civilizations developed in Middle America.

Features: Central Plateau; Classic Period; Copán; crafts; glyphs; La Venta; worship for Jaguar; rain forests; slash and burn; tropical climate; Yum Kax, god of maize

Geography	Olmec	Maya
Central Plateau	La Venta	Copán
Tropical climate Rain forests	Crafts Slash and burn Worship for Jaguar	Glyphs Growing maize Yum Kax–god of maize Classic period

307

SUGGESTIONS FOR SUMMING UP THE CHAPTER

When students have copied the classification chart, read the main idea to them and have them identify the two civilizations they have studied and locate them on the chart (Olmec and Maya, second and third columns). What features are already filled in for them? (the names of centers of each—La Venta and Copán) Have them also identify the first category (geography) and the feature already filled in for it (Central Plateau). Point out that these three categories correspond to the three lessons in the chapter. Have them fill in the features, reviewing the appropriate lesson if necessary. Possible answers appear on the reproduced pupil page above. Remind them that developing ways to make the environment serve human needs ranks high among achievements.

ASSESSING THINK AND WRITE: *For performance assessment, see Assessment Book, Chapter 11, pp. T77–T79.*

Answers to
THINKING ABOUT VOCABULARY

1. peninsula
2. republic
3. maize
4. New Testament
5. algebra
6. dictator
7. philosophy
8. pilgrimage
9. monarchy
10. glyph

Suggestions for
THINK AND WRITE

1. As students try to identify and compare Spartan and Athenian women's perspectives, urge them to keep in mind basic cultural differences—military state/democracy and physical training/mental training—as well as the secondary role of women in both societies.

2. Essays should present Islam's belief in one God, Allah, and the belief that the Quran contains the teachings Allah gave to Muhammed, as well as enumerate the Five Pillars of Islam.

3. Paragraphs should describe the deserts of the Arabian Peninsula and the rain forests of Middle America, mention how arid and tropical climates differ from one another. They should contrast the herding and caravans of the Bedouin with the hunting and gathering and the waterways of the Olmec.

Suggestions for
BUILDING SKILLS

1. A good conclusion is one that is based on sound evidence. The more evidence there is on which to base a conclusion, the stronger the conclusion is bound to be.

2. Conclusions would necessarily be based on limited evidence but might focus on people met or observed, sites visited, transportation used, or living conditions seen.

3. An elevation map can show all the Alps and how they range in altitude in relation to one another. A profile can show more precise altitudes but only for those Alps that lie along the same cross section.

UNIT 3 REVIEW

THINKING ABOUT VOCABULARY

Number a sheet of paper from 1 to 10. Beside each number write the word or term from the list below that best matches the statement.

algebra	New Testament
dictator	peninsula
glyph	philosophy
maize	pilgrimage
monarchy	republic

1. Area of land mostly surrounded by water
2. Government in which people choose their own leaders
3. Corn
4. Collection of books that describes the beginnings of Christianity
5. Branch of mathematics developed by the Arabs
6. Someone who rules with absolute power
7. Search for wisdom and the right way to live
8. Journey made for religious reasons
9. Government ruled by one person, often a king or queen
10. Mayan symbol carved into stones

THINK AND WRITE ◀▬▬▶

WRITING ABOUT PERSPECTIVES
Write a paragraph comparing the perspectives of a woman from ancient Sparta and a woman from ancient Athens. How would they have viewed city laws and government? What might they have wanted to change? How were their perspectives alike? How were they different? Explain your answers.

WRITING AN ESSAY
Write a short essay about Islam as one of the world's major religions. What are its main beliefs and practices?

308

WRITING ABOUT CONTRASTS
Write a paragraph describing the differences between the environments of the Arabian Peninsula and Middle America. Include information about landforms and climate. Explain the challenges faced by people who have lived in these two regions. Describe how they have adapted to the environments around them.

BUILDING SKILLS

1. **Making conclusions** What is a good conclusion? Why is a conclusion stronger with more evidence to back it up?

2. **Making conclusions** Suppose you visit a distant city for a weekend. Based on what you see during the short time, give an example of a conclusion you might make about the city.

3. **Elevation maps and profiles** What are ways you could use both an elevation map and a profile map of the Alps? Explain your answer.

4. **Historical maps** Look at the historical map on page 280. Explain the information the map provides and how you found the information by using the map.

5. **Climographs** Construct a climograph that shows the monthly temperature and precipitation in your area. Compare it with the climographs of the Mexican cities on pages 290–291. Make a conclusion about how the climate where you live differs from that of Mexico.

ONGOING UNIT PROJECT

OPTIONS FOR ASSESSMENT

This ongoing project, begun on page 186D, can be part of your assessment program, along with other forms of evaluation.

PLANNING Explain to children that each group is responsible for creating the shield of a different ancient civilization. All civilizations discussed in this unit are to be represented.

SIGNS OF SUCCESS

• Children's choice of drawings, symbols, and print should reflect something special about the ancient civilization, that is, the age of Athens' glory, and the expanding Greek empire.

• Children should display shields in the room. Group members should clearly describe their shields of achivement.

 FOR THE PORTFOLIO Individual notes about ancient civilizations can be included in children's portfolios.

YESTERDAY, TODAY &
TOMORROW

You have read about the achievements of great civilizations of the past. Someday future students will read about us. What do you think future historians will say our greatest achievements were? Explain your choices. How are our achievements different from those of the past?

READING ON YOUR OWN

Here are some books you might find at the library to help you learn more.

SPIRIT OF THE MAYA: A BOY EXPLORES HIS PEOPLE'S MYSTERIOUS PAST
by Guy Garcia
Kin, a twelve-year-old descendant of the ancient Maya, gains pride in his ancestry when he discovers clues to the secrets of his society.

THE ROMAN NEWS
by Andrew Langley and Philip De Souza
Life in ancient Rome as it would appear in today's newspapers; done with headlines and features on everyday life.

BLACK SHIPS BEFORE TROY: THE STORY OF THE ILLIAD
by Rosemary Sutcliff
This thrilling story tells the tale of the Trojan War.

UNIT 3 REVIEW PROJECT

Perform a Scene About Life in Ancient Times

1. With your group, choose an ancient civilization from this unit.
2. Research some additional information about the civilization. Your school or local library can provide the information you will need.
3. Then write a scene that includes a character for each group member. You might tell what daily life was like in the civilization or about an event that affected the civilization.
4. Make sure each group member has several lines.
5. Next make costumes out of paper or material. Create scenery using paints and oaktag.
6. Finally, perform the scene for your class.

309

4. Students should describe the growth of the caliphate into Europe and note that they used the map title and map key to find the symbols on the map and to determine the time, place, and events involved such as lands occupied before and after A.D. 711, routes of expansion, and battle sites.

5. Conclusions will depend on climate conditions of your area and how they compare with Mexico City's.

Suggestions for
YESTERDAY, TODAY & TOMORROW

If you followed the suggestions on TE page 63 for the Yesterday, Today & Tomorrow, remind students of the achievements they identified as they discuss what future historians will say our civilization's greatest achievements were. Do students want to add or subtract any? How achievements differ from those of the past may center on ever-higher levels of technology.

Suggestions for
READING ON YOUR OWN

The books listed here are intended to give students a broader and deeper knowledge of life in ancient times in different parts of the world. Try to make them available in class along with the titles listed in the *Annotated Bibliography and Resources* in the Unit Organizer on page 186B. You may want to have students work in teams of two or three who read the same book, prepare a brief report on it to present in class, and then discuss it before the class, telling what they liked about it and what interesting information it gave them and inviting students' questions to them as resource people.

UNIT 3 REVIEW PROJECT: *Perform a Scene About Life in Ancient Times*

COMPLETING THE SCENE

GROUP 30 MINUTES OR LONGER

OBJECTIVE: Performing scenes about ancient times will reinforce students' understanding of how people lived in ancient Greece, Rome, Arabia, and America.

MATERIALS: paper, oaktag, paints, art materials

- Ask each student to write the names of the four ancient civilizations from the unit in order of interest. Divide the class into groups, based on students' interests, so that each group is assigned to one civilization.

- Tell students that the characters in their scenes should represent people who played different roles in the civilizations they chose—one role for each group member.

- Students should avoid including elements in their scenes that would be inconsistent with what they learned about the civilizations they chose.

- Encourage students to make costumes and create scenery to go with their scenes.

- Allow time for students to rehearse their scenes before presenting them to the class.

FOR THE PORTFOLIO Students' scenes can be part of their portfolios.

OPTIONS FOR ASSESSMENT

This project may be part of your assessment program.

For more performance assessment and portfolio opportunities, see Assessment Book, Unit 3, p. T80.

REFERENCE SECTION

The Reference Section has many parts,
each with a different type of information.
Use this section to look up people,
places, and events as you study.

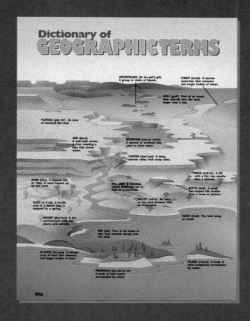

R3

Atlas

An atlas is a collection of maps. An atlas

can be a book or a separate section

within a book. This Atlas is a separate

section with maps to help you study

the history and geography

presented in this book.

MAP BUILDER
The World: Climate and Population

The map on the facing page is a special kind of map. Each transparent overlay shows a different aspect of the world's climate and population. You can see where in the world similar climates exist and how climates relate to latitude. You can also compare population density around the world and see in which climates people live. Start by lifting all of the transparent overlays and observe the base map of the continents and oceans of the world. Then cover the base map with the first overlay and study the climates shown. In which climate do you live?

Allow the second overlay to cover the first and consider how climates are related to latitude. What latitude lines divide the zones shown? What kinds of climates are generally found nearest the equator? Finally, let down the third overlay and compare population densities around the world. Which areas of North America are the most densely populated? In which climates do the fewest people live?

R4

The World: Climates

HOW ARE THEY DIFFERENT? HOW ARE THEY ALIKE?
Objective: To practice reading climate maps.

1. Refer the class to the climate key and give them time to match the map colors to it. Point out how climate regions fall in bands around the world.

2. Ask questions calling for differences and similarities in climate regions—for example, "How are climate regions near a pole different from those near the equator?" "How are climate regions of much of Europe like those of the eastern United States?" Ask students to make up and offer such questions too.

GROUP

15 TO 30 MINUTES

HAVE A NICE VACATION
Objective: To recognize traits of climate regions.

Materials: paper, pens, crayons or colored pencils, travel pictures, glue

1. Divide the class into six groups and assign each group one of the regions in the climate key.

2. Tell each group to prepare a travel brochure for a vacation in that region. Invite groups to draw or gather pictures showing scenes from their region and to brainstorm things that would be fun to do there.

3. Have the groups write and illustrate their vacation brochures and present them to the class.

GROUP

30 MINUTES OR LONGER

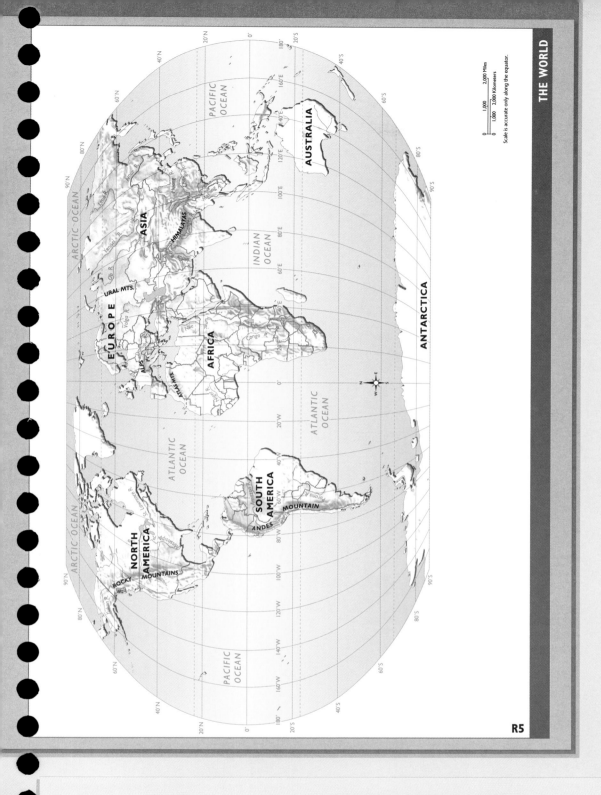

2,000 Miles

2,000 Kilometers

Scale is accurate only along the equator.

R5

The World: Population

MOST POPULOUS, LEAST POPULOUS

ON YOUR OWN

Objective: To practice reading population maps.

Materials: paper, pencil

15 TO 30 MINUTES

1. Refer the class to the population map key and have them identify examples of each symbol on the map.

2. Have students write two headings on a piece of paper—MOST POPULOUS, LEAST POPULOUS. Under the appropriate heading have them list the three most populous areas of the world, by area of continent—for example, Eastern Asia—and three of the least populous.

3. Call on students to compare and discuss their lists.

RELATE DENSITY TO CLIMATE

Objective: To relate population and climate.

Materials: paper, pencil

ON YOUR OWN

30 MINUTES OR LONGER

1. Tell students to choose a most or least populous area of the world and then identify the climate region/regions it occupies.

2. Have them write a paragraph in which they identify their chosen area, describe its climate or climates, and then explain the role that climate probably plays in helping to make it heavily or lightly populated.

3. Call on students to read their paragraphs in class and invite other students' comments on their reasoning.

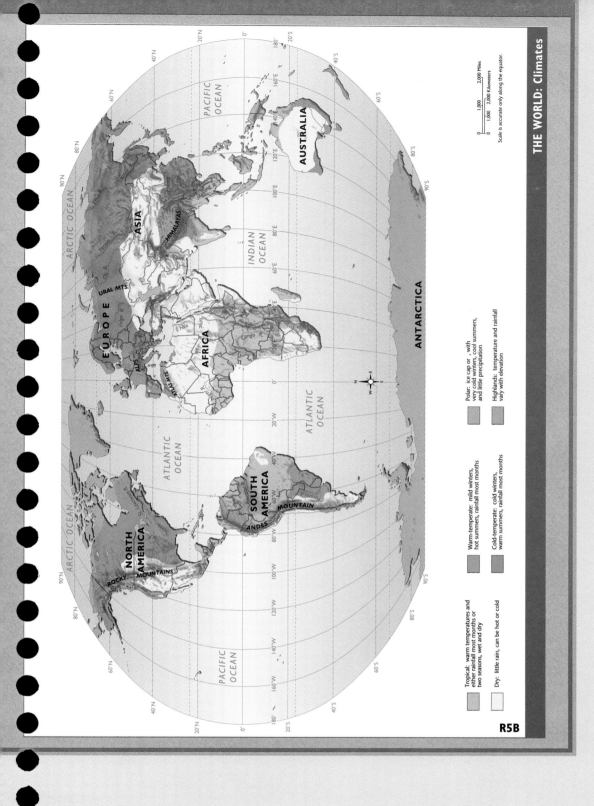

THE WORLD: Climates

Tropical: warm temperatures and either rainfall most months or two seasons, wet and dry

Dry: little rain, can be hot or cold

Warm-temperate: mild winters, hot summers, rainfall most months

Cold-temperate: cold winters, warm summers, rainfall most months

Polar: ice cap or , with very cold winters, cool summers, and little precipitation

Highlands: temperature and rainfall vary with elevation

Scale is accurate only along the equator.

0   1,000   2,000 Miles
0 1,000 2,000 Kilometers

R5B

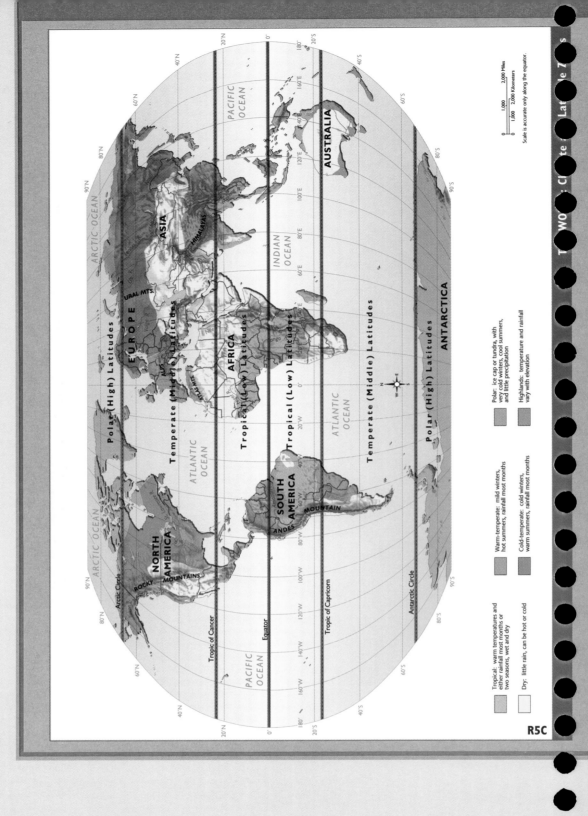

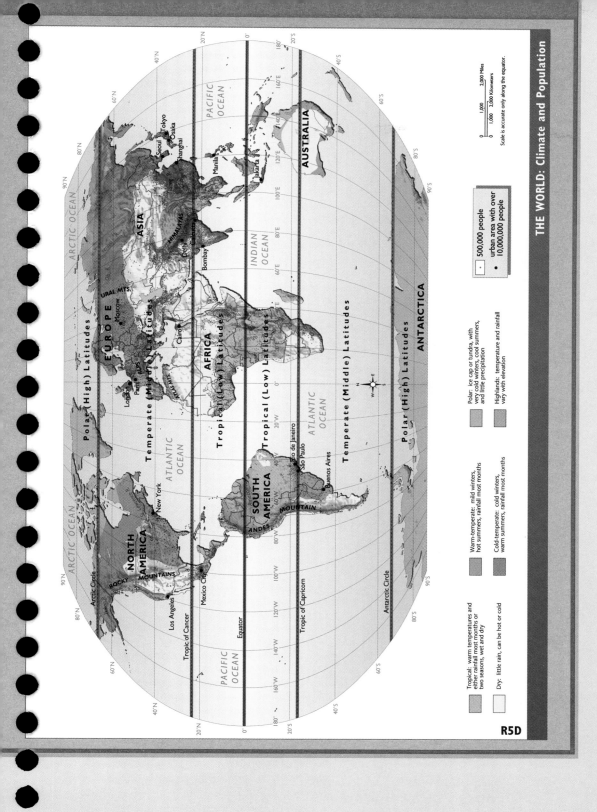

THE WORLD: Climate and Population

Climate legend:

- Tropical: warm temperatures and either rainfall most months or two seasons, wet and dry
- Dry: little rain, can be hot or cold
- Warm-temperate: mild winters, hot summers, rainfall most months
- Cold-temperate: cold winters, warm summers, rainfall most months
- Polar: ice cap or tundra, with very cold winters, cool summers, and little precipitation
- Highlands: temperature and rainfall vary with elevation

Population legend:

- · 500,000 people
- · urban area with over 10,000,000 people

Scale is accurate only along the equator.

0 — 1,000 — 2,000 Miles
0 — 1,000 — 2,000 Kilometers

R5D

EUROPE: Political

R6

Europe: Political Map

FIND THE CAPITAL

Objective: To locate and identify national capitals.

Students can use the European political map to play a guessing game based on geographic clues.

15 TO 30 MINUTES

1. The game begins when one students says, "I am thinking of a national capital in [southwestern Europe]."

2. To narrow the choices, students might ask, "Does it lie near a major body of water or does it lie far inland?" "Is it south of the Bay of Biscay?"

3. The student who guesses correctly gives a clue to a new mystery capital and answers questions about it.

USE THE GRID

Objective: To locate political boundaries by latitude and longitude.

Materials: pencils, paper

15 TO 30 MINUTES

1. Have each group choose three countries in Europe and use the map grid to estimate roughly each country's political borders by latitude and longitude.

2. Have them list the three grid locations on a piece of paper with a blank space following each. Then have them exchange their lists with another group.

3. Challenge the groups to use the map here to fill in the countries that fit the locations they received.

EUROPE: Physical

R7

Europe: Physical Map

PARTNER

30 MINUTES OR LONGER

NATURAL BOUNDARIES/POLITICAL BORDERS
Objective: To compare physical and political maps.

Students can use the two European maps to identify cases in which natural boundaries—like water or mountains—create political borders.

1. Have each pair of students compare the two maps to locate one case where a natural boundary also serves as the political border between two or more countries or forms most or all of one country's political borders.

2. Have each pair write a paragraph describing the case they have found, naming the natural boundary and the borders it creates.

3. Invite the partners to present their cases in class.

MAKE A JIGSAW PUZZLE
Objective: To map and locate major landforms of Europe.

GROUP

30 MINUTES OR LONGER

Materials: construction paper, pencils, scissors

1. Have each group draw an outline of this physical map of Europe and label the following by name: peninsulas, major islands, mountain ranges, major plains areas.

2. Have them cut their maps apart, jigsaw fashion, around the named geographic features. The groups should then exchange sets of puzzle pieces.

3. At the call of "Go," have each group work against the clock to reassemble Europe. The group that completes the task correctly in the best time wins.

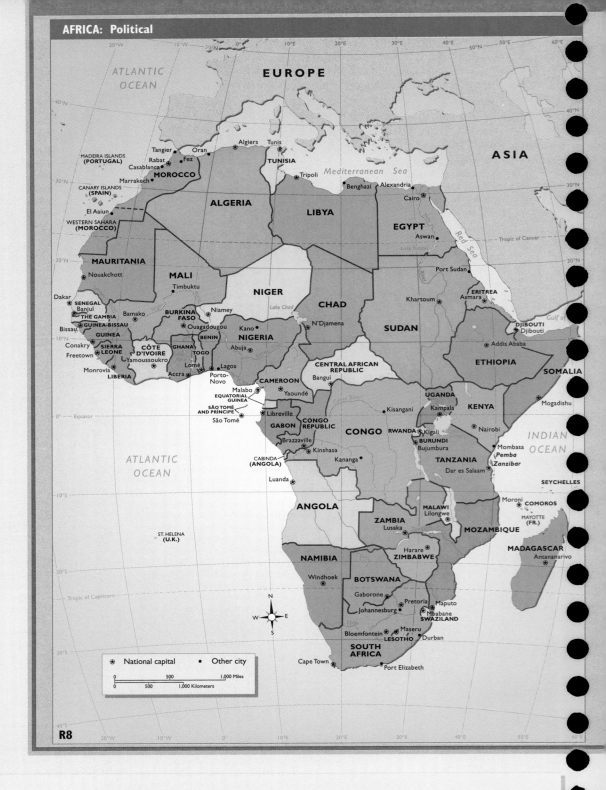

AFRICA: Political

EUROPE

ATLANTIC OCEAN

ASIA

MADEIRA ISLANDS (PORTUGAL)

Tangier • Oran • Algiers Tunis

Rabat • Fez

Casablanca •

TUNISIA

Tripoli •

Mediterranean Sea

MOROCCO

Marrakech •

CANARY ISLANDS (SPAIN)

Benghazi • Alexandria •

Cairo •

El Aaiun •

ALGERIA

LIBYA

EGYPT

WESTERN SAHARA (MOROCCO)

Aswan •

Red Sea

Tropic of Cancer

MAURITANIA

Nouakchott •

MALI

Timbuktu •

NIGER

Lake Chad

CHAD

Khartoum •

Port Sudan •

ERITREA

Asmara •

Dakar •

SENEGAL

Banjul •

THE GAMBIA

Bamako •

Niamey •

BURKINA FASO

N'Djamena •

SUDAN

DJIBOUTI

Djibouti •

GUINEA-BISSAU

Bissau •

GUINEA

Ouagadougou •

Kano •

Addis Ababa •

Conakry •

SIERRA LEONE

Freetown •

CÔTE D'IVOIRE

GHANA

Yamoussoukro •

TOGO

BENIN

NIGERIA

Abuja •

CENTRAL AFRICAN REPUBLIC

ETHIOPIA

SOMALIA

Monrovia •

LIBERIA

Accra •

Lagos •

Porto-Novo

Lomé •

CAMEROON

Bangui •

UGANDA

Kisangani •

Kampala •

KENYA

Mogadishu •

Malabo •

EQUATORIAL GUINEA

Yaoundé •

SÃO TOMÉ AND PRÍNCIPE

Libreville •

GABON

CONGO REPUBLIC

CONGO

RWANDA

Kigali •

Nairobi •

INDIAN OCEAN

São Tomé •

Equator

Brazzaville •

BURUNDI

Bujumbura •

Mombasa •

Pemba

Zanzibar

ATLANTIC OCEAN

CABINDA (ANGOLA)

Kinshasa •

Kananga •

TANZANIA

Dar es Salaam •

SEYCHELLES

Luanda •

ST. HELENA (U.K.)

ANGOLA

MALAWI

Lilongwe •

Moroni •

COMOROS

MAYOTTE (FR.)

ZAMBIA

Lusaka •

MOZAMBIQUE

MADAGASCAR

Antananarivo •

NAMIBIA

Harare •

ZIMBABWE

Tropic of Capricorn

Windhoek •

BOTSWANA

Gaborone •

Pretoria • Maputo •

Johannesburg •

Mbabane

SWAZILAND

Bloemfontein •

Maseru

LESOTHO

Durban •

Cape Town •

SOUTH AFRICA

Port Elizabeth •

⊛ National capital   • Other city

0   500   1,000 Miles

0   500   1,000 Kilometers

N W E S

R8

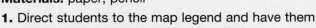

Africa: Political Map

 GROUP

LOCATE PORT CAPITALS

Objective: To link city importance to port location.

Materials: paper, pencil

15 TO 30 MINUTES

1. Direct students to the map legend and have them identify the symbol for national capitals.

2. Have students examine the map to locate national capitals that are ports on major bodies of water.

3. Call on students to identify national capitals and their countries. As they identify each, have students list the capitals and their countries on a piece of paper. When they complete their lists, have them discuss why they suppose so many national capitals in Africa are port cities.

SET UP AN ITINERARY

Objective: To trace routes and measure distance.

Materials: outline map of Africa, pencil, paper

1. Invite students to choose three cities/countries in Africa that they would like to visit.

2. Have them list their cities/countries on a piece of paper and exchange papers with a partner.

3. Invite students to locate and label their partners' choices on the outline map of Africa, draw the land or sea route they would use to get from one place to the next, and use the map scale to list the distance covered on each leg of the trip.

 PARTNER

15 TO 30 MINUTES

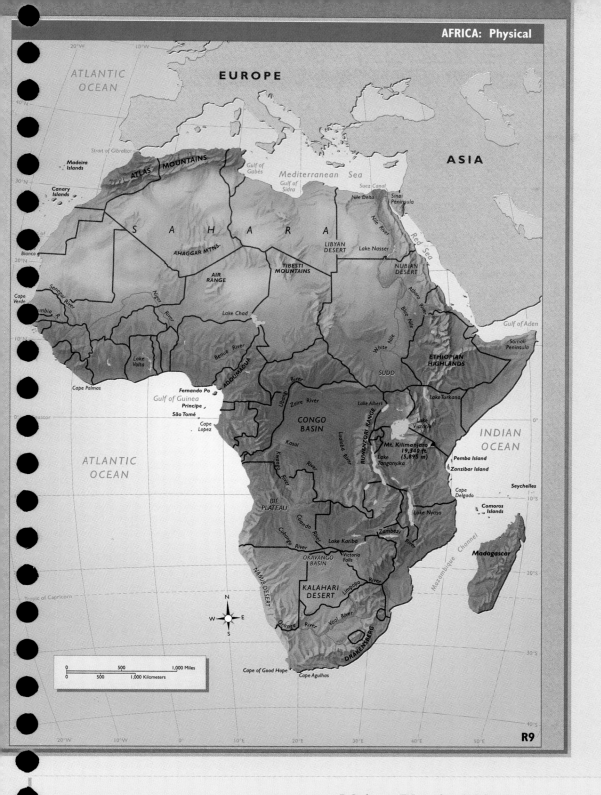

AFRICA: Physical

ATLANTIC OCEAN

EUROPE

ASIA

Strait of Gibraltar

Madeira Islands

Canary Islands

ATLAS MOUNTAINS

Gulf of Gabès

Mediterranean Sea

Gulf of Sidra

Suez Canal

Nile Delta

Sinai Peninsula

Red Sea

S A H A R A

AHAGGAR MTNS.

LIBYAN DESERT

Lake Nasser

Blanco

AIR RANGE

TIBESTI MOUNTAINS

NUBIAN DESERT

Cape Verde

Senegal River

Niger River

Gambia R.

Lake Chad

Benue River

Atbara River

Blue Nile

Gulf of Aden

Somali Peninsula

Lake Volta

ADOUMA

White Nile

SUDD

ETHIOPIAN HIGHLANDS

Cape Palmas

Fernando Po

Gulf of Guinea

Principe

São Tomé

Cape Lopez

Ubangi River

Zaire River

CONGO BASIN

Kasai

Lualaba River

Kwango River

RUWENZORI RANGE

Lake Albert

Lake Turkana

Lake Victoria

Mt. Kilimanjaro 19,340 ft. (5,895 m)

Lake Tanganyika

INDIAN OCEAN

Pemba Island

Zanzibar Island

ATLANTIC OCEAN

BIÉ PLATEAU

Cuando River

Cubango River

Lake Kariba

Zambezi River

Cape Delgado

Lake Nyasa

Seychelles

Comoros Islands

OKAVANGO BASIN

Victoria Falls

NAMIB DESERT

KALAHARI DESERT

Limpopo River

Orange River

Vaol River

Mozambique Channel

Madagascar

DRAKENSBERG

Cape of Good Hope

Cape Agulhas

0   500   1,000 Miles
0   500   1,000 Kilometers

Tropic of Capricorn

Equator

R9

Africa: Physical Map

PLEASE SEND HELP!

GROUP

Objective: To identify places based on geographic clues.

Materials: paper, pencil

15 TO 30 MINUTES

1. Have students examine the physical map of Africa and picture themselves in a downed plane somewhere on it.

2. Have them write a description of their location based on clues on the map: for example, "I'm on a peninsula facing the Indian Ocean, near the equator."

3. Students should look for the location on the physical map and then find the country at that location on the political map. The student who identifies the country correctly reads the description of his or her location.

WHERE AM I GOING?

PARTNER

Objective: To trace a route based on geographic clues.

Materials: paper, pencil

15 TO 30 MINUTES

1. Have each student choose one geographic feature in Africa as a starting point for an overland expedition and another as the ending point.

2. Have students write the names of these locations—for example, "Atlas Mountains/Cape of Good Hope"—on a piece of paper and exchange it with a partner.

3. Invite students to trace a route connecting the two places on the map and then write a list of the geographic features the expedition will travel through.

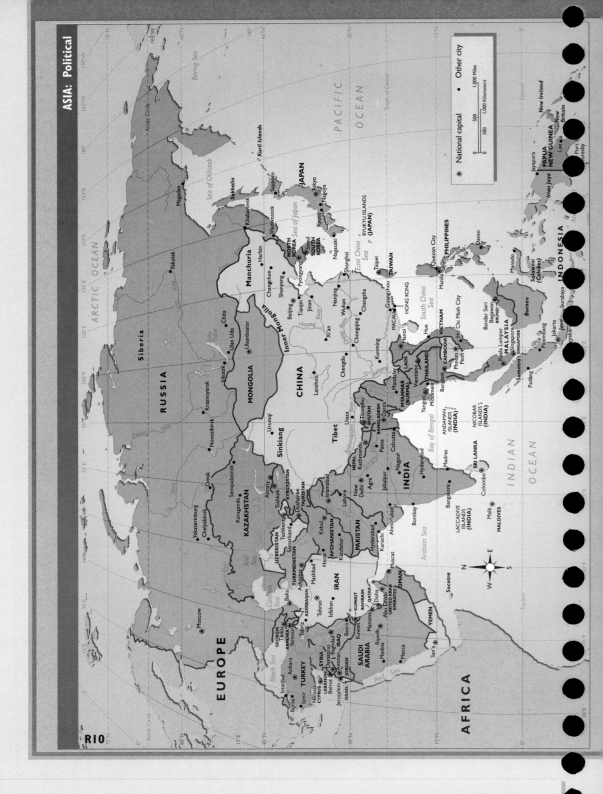

ASIA: Political

R10

Asia: Political Map

GROUP

🕐 15 TO 30 MINUTES

HOW FAR IS IT?

Objective: To use a map scale to measure distances.

Materials: poster board, pencil, scissors

1. Refer the class to the map scale. Have them cut a strip of posterboard and draw on it a sort of "ruler" based on the map scale.

2. Invite a student to pose a question about the distance between two cities on the map—for example, "How far is it from India's capital to China's?"

3. Have students use their "rulers" to measure each distance called for. The student who gives the answer correctly gets to pose the next distance question.

HOWDY, NEIGHBOR

Objective: To identify where Asian countries are located in relation to one another.

Materials: paper, pencil

1. Have each group choose three countries on the map and list them on a piece of paper.

2. For each country, have them write a statement telling with which countries it shares political borders—for example, "My neighbors are China, Laos, and Cambodia."

3. Have groups read their statements and invite the rest of the class to identify the correct countries.

PARTNER

🕐 15 TO 30 MINUTES

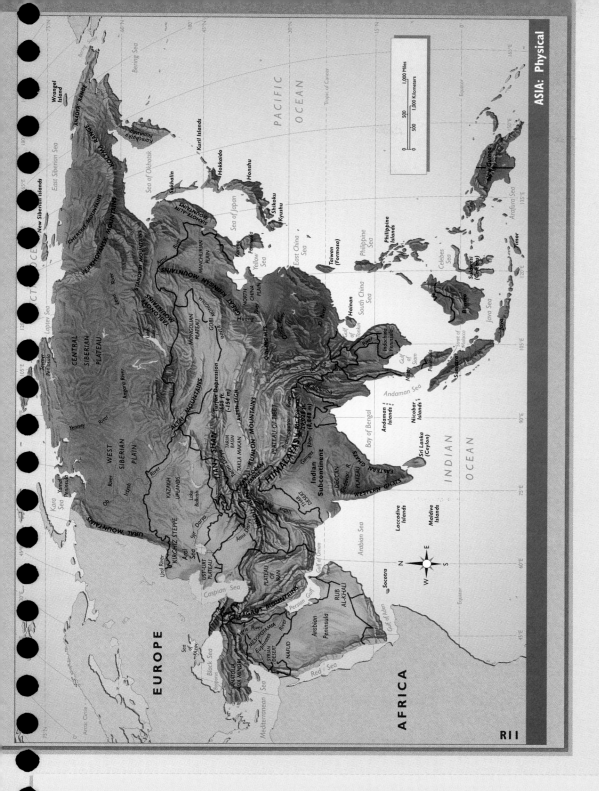

ASIA: Physical

R11

Asia: Physical Map

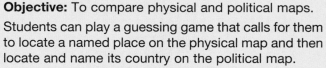

FIND THE COUNTRY

Objective: To compare physical and political maps.

Students can play a guessing game that calls for them to locate a named place on the physical map and then locate and name its country on the political map.

15 TO 30 MINUTES

1. Tell students to find a place on the physical map—for example, "The Deccan Plateau in southern Asia."

2. When a student identifies the country for the place, he or she makes up a similar clue to another place, giving the place name and general area. The game continues as each student answering correctly gives the next clue.

WHAT AM I?

Objective: To locate various geographic features.

Materials: index cards, pencils

15 TO 30 MINUTES

1. Assign each group one form or feature—peninsulas, islands, plateaus, plains, mountain ranges, deserts.

2. Have each group choose three examples of their type from the map. Have them write clues to the location of each example on a separate card—for example, "I am a peninsula bordered by the Red Sea and the Persian Gulf." Have them include the answers.

3. Collect and shuffle the cards. Read each "I am ..." statement and call on students to identify each place.

THE AMERICAS: Political

R12

The Americas: Political Map

CATALOG THE AMERICAS

Objective: To recognize the countries of the Americas and their capitals.

Materials: paper, pencil

1. Have students create a chart with the following heads—North America, Central America, the Caribbean, South America.

2. Under each heading, have them list its countries, with the capital shown next to each one. (Include only the larger Caribbean countries.)

3. Invite students to decorate each list with a symbol for that part of the Americas.

CAPITALS OF THE AMERICAS

Objective: To identify capitals and countries.

Materials: index cards, pen

Create a game of *Jeopardy* using student panels.

1. For each country in the Americas (only the larger ones in the Caribbean), prepare an index card with a country name on one side and its capital on the other.

2. Call up a series of panels to play. As you name a country or a capital, the panelists should try to answer with the correct match. Offer 10 points for a correct answer and an additional 5 points for the correct part of the Americas—North, South, and so on.

THE AMERICAS: Physical

ARCTIC OCEAN

Queen Elizabeth Islands

Greenland

Baffin Bay

Point Barrow

Beaufort Sea

Banks Island

Victoria Island

Baffin Island

Davis Strait

Cape Farewell

BROOKS RANGE

Mt. McKinley 20,320 ft. (6,194 m)

ALASKA

Yukon River

Gulf of Alaska

Mackenzie River

Great Bear Lake

Great Slave Lake

NORTH AMERICA

Hudson Bay

Arctic Circle

Labrador Sea

60°N

Vancouver Island

Saskatchewan River

Lake Winnipeg

CANADIAN SHIELD

LABRADOR

Newfoundland

Cape Mendocino

GREAT PLAINS

Missouri River

Great Salt Lake

GREAT BASIN

ROCKY MOUNTAINS

Ohio River

APPALACHIAN MOUNTAINS

Nova Scotia

Gulf of St. Lawrence

St. Lawrence River

Great Lakes

Columbia River

Cape Cod

Long Island

ATLANTIC OCEAN

30°N

Baja California

Gulf of California

SIERRA MADRE OCCIDENTAL

SIERRA MADRE ORIENTAL

Gulf of Mexico

Florida Peninsula

Straits of Florida

Cuba

WEST INDIES

Greater Antilles

Hispaniola

Lesser Antilles

Tropic of Cancer

Hawaiian Islands

PACIFIC OCEAN

Yucatán Peninsula

Gulf of Honduras

CENTRAL

Lake Nicaragua

AMERICA

Isthmus of Panama

Gulf of Panama

Caribbean Sea

Lake Maracaibo

Orinoco River

GUIANA HIGHLANDS

LLANOS

Galápagos Islands

AMAZON

BASIN

Rio Negro

Amazon River

Madeira River

SOUTH AMERICA

Cape São Roque

São Francisco River

Tocantins River

MATO GROSSO PLATEAU

BRAZILIAN HIGHLANDS

Equator 0°

Lake Titicaca

ANDES MOUNTAINS

GRAN CHACO

Paraguay River

Paraná River

Uruguay River

Tropic of Capricorn

30°S

Mt. Aconcagua 22,834 ft. (6,960 m)

PAMPAS

PATAGONIA

Strait of Magellan

Falkland Islands

South Georgia

Tierra del Fuego

Cape Horn

N
W   E
S

0   1,000   2,000 Miles
0   1,000   2,000 Kilometers

R13

The Americas: Physical Map

GROUP

GROUP

WHERE IS IT FROM HERE?

Objective: To practice using directions.

Materials: paper, pencil

15 TO 30 MINUTES

Students can create directional questions and challenge one another to work out the correct answers.

1. Refer the class to the *N* compass direction on the map and have them deduce the other directions from it.

2. Tell each student to choose two places shown on the map and write a question about what direction the places are from each other.

3. Invite a student to read aloud his or her question. The student who answers it correctly asks the next question.

PLAN A VACATION

Objective: To relate geography to real life.

Materials: paper, pens, crayons, periodicals

30 MINUTES OR LONGER

1. Divide the class into groups and assign each group one of the following—skiing, lake fishing, jungle river travel, mountain climbing, tropical swimming.

2. Have each group locate a place in the Americas where such a vacation could be taken. Have them clip or draw pictures of the area and create an illustrated travel brochure showing vacation possibilities there.

3. Have the groups exchange brochures for examination and then create a bulletin board display of them.

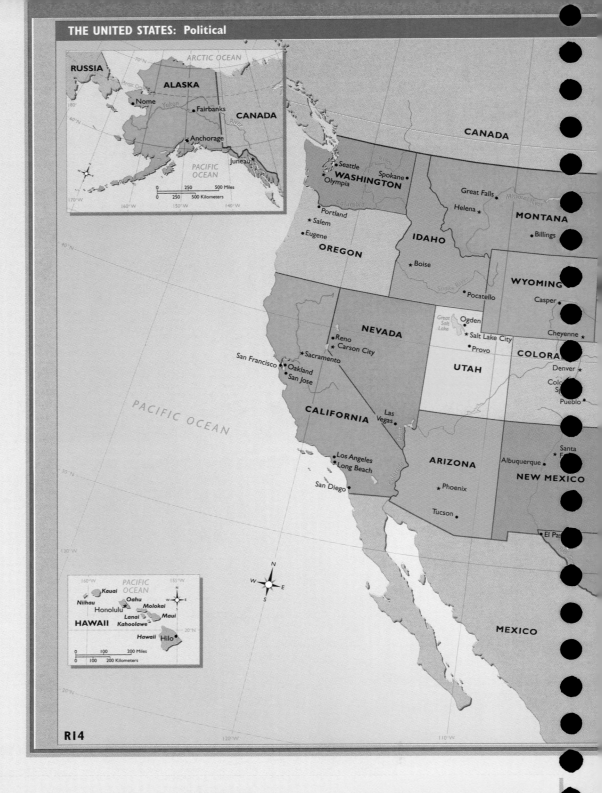

THE UNITED STATES: Political

R14

The United States: Political

ESTABLISH U.S. BORDERS

Objective: To locate the borders of the U.S.

Materials: paper, pencil

15 TO 30 MINUTES

1. Have students create worksheets by listing the following on a piece of paper—Alaska, Hawaii, Contiguous 48 States. Opposite each they should label and leave a space for the four borders of each—North, East, South, West.

2. Tell students to work with the map to fill in each space, using natural barriers like oceans, lakes, gulfs, or rivers where they apply and longitude or latitude where it applies.

MAKE A JIGSAW PUZZLE

Objective: To practice locating states in the U.S.

Materials: blowup of map, posterboard, scissors, outline map of U.S. borders in same size as blowup

30 MINUTES OR LONGER

1. Blow up this map of the U.S. to twice its size here. Cut it in quarters and give one quarter to each group.

2. Have groups mount their quarters on posterboard and then cut the states apart. You may want them to treat smaller states as one unit, for example: Mass., Conn., R.I.

3. Invite students to take turns as individuals or in small groups to reassemble the states where they belong on the outline map.

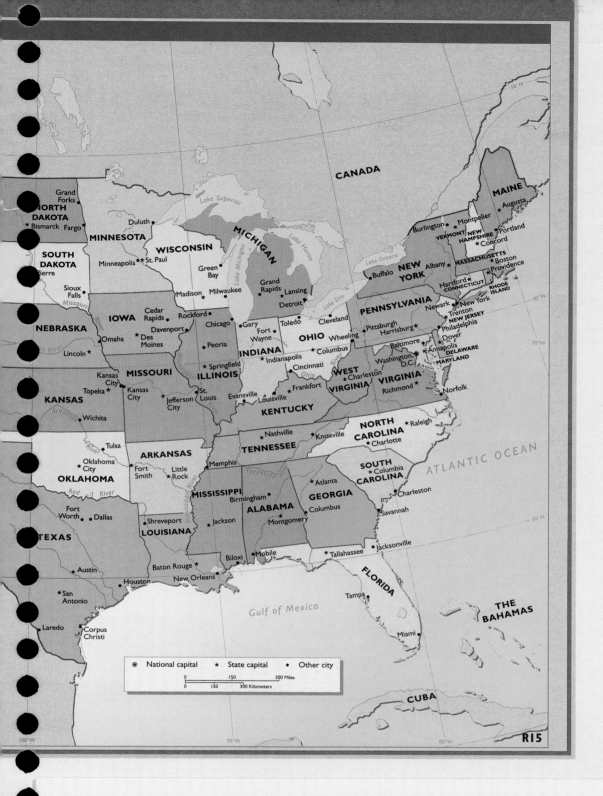

R15

The United States: Political

GROUP

15 TO 30 MINUTES

KNOW YOUR NEIGHBORS

Objective: To practice using map key and scale.

Materials: posterboard, scissors, pencil

1. Have students identify the symbols in the map key and have them cut out and make posterboard "rulers" based on the map scale.

2. Call on students to locate your state and to identify your neighboring states. Have them also identify these states' capitals and other cities.

3. Invite them to make up questions about distances between these cities. Have them use their "rulers" to measure distances. Each correct answerer asks the next question.

WHAT'S THE STATE CAPITAL?

Objective: To identify state capitals.

Materials: index cards, pen

Point out that the category State Capitals often comes up on *Jeopardy*. Here students can play it themselves.

GROUP

30 MINUTES OR LONGER

1. Make up, or have students make up, 50 cards with a state on one side and its capital on the other.

2. Call up a series of panels to play. You may name either the state and or the capital and have the panel vie to identify its capital or state.

3. Score 10 points for each correct answer. The highest individual scorer or scorers is/are *Jeopardy* Champion.

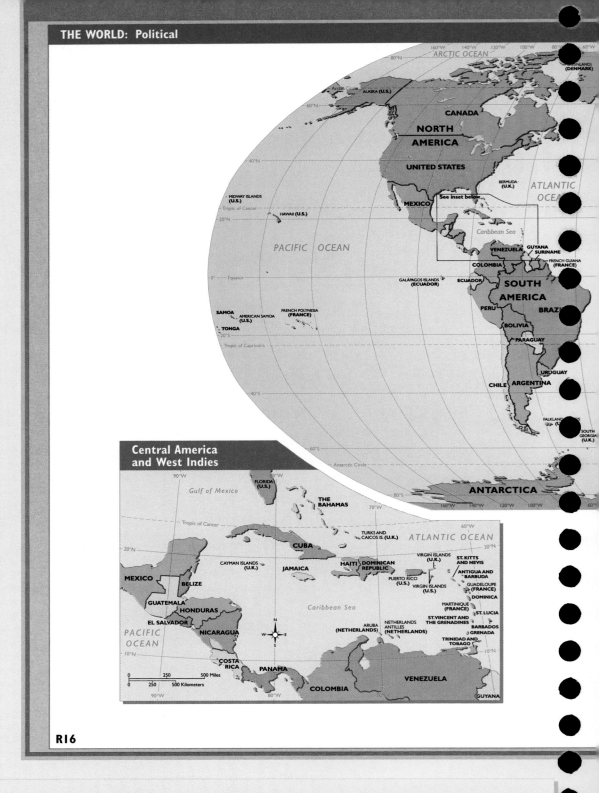

THE WORLD: Political

Central America and West Indies

R16

The World: Political Map

DIFFERENTIATE BETWEEN MAP SCALES

Objective: To understand the purpose of map insets.

Materials: posterboard, pencil, scissors

1. Refer the class to the two inset areas on the large map and have them relate the enlarged inset maps to these areas of the map. Discuss why this inset method is used—to be able to show and label place names in "crowded" areas.

2. To reinforce the idea that insets enlarge an area, have students cut out two strips of posterboard and draw "rulers" based on the two different scales shown.

3. Have students compare the two scales and work out the small-scale to large-scale ratio (about 4:1).

USE MAP SCALES

Objective: To measure distances using map scales.

Materials: posterboard "rulers"

1. Refer the class to the Abbreviation Key and to the Caribbean map inset. Explain that some countries hold political control over areas far from their shores.

2. Have students find examples of such areas in the Caribbean map inset—for example, Martinique (FR.). Invite a student to name such a territory and ask the class how far it is located from its mainland country.

3. The first student to measure the distance correctly gets to name the next area.

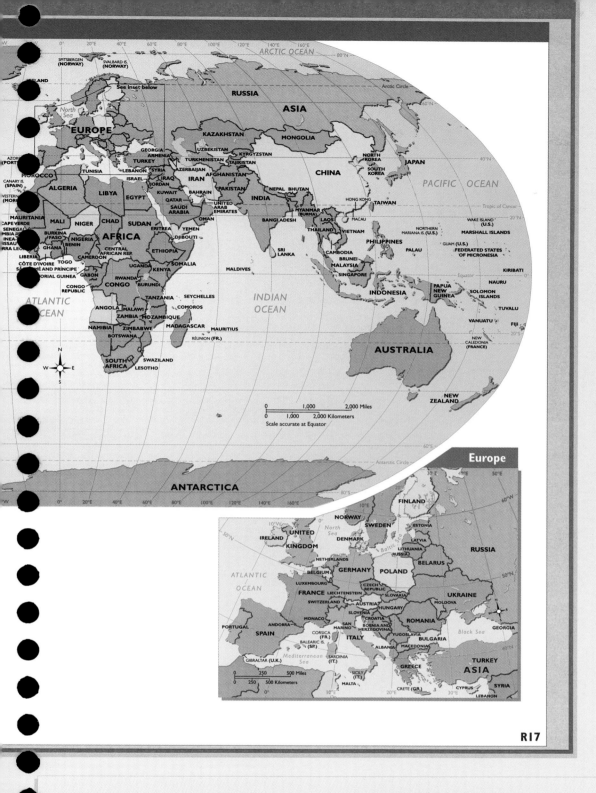

Europe

R17

The World: Political Map

WHAT'S BECOME OF THE FORMER SOVIET UNION?

Objective: To identify countries based on map clues.

15 TO 30 MINUTES

1. Explain to the class that much of easternmost Europe and all of Northern Asia were once part of the Soviet Union.

2. Describe the old Soviet Union borders—all the land east of the Poland-Slovakia-Romania eastern border and the land east of the Black Sea about as far south as latitude 40°N to the China-Mongolia border and east to the Pacific.

3. Call on students to name the countries that this area now includes—Russia, Estonia, Tajikistan, and so on.

COUNTRIES OF THE WORLD

Objective: To identify countries by continent.

Materials: index cards, pencils

30 MINUTES OR LONGER

1. Divide the class into five groups and assign each one of the following—North America and the Caribbean, Central and South America, Europe, Asia, Africa.

2. Have the groups write the name of each of the countries in their area on one side of an index card and its continent (or the Caribbean) on the other.

3. Make a pack of the cards and shuffle them. Line the class up for a kind of "spell-down," calling out country names and having students identify their continent.

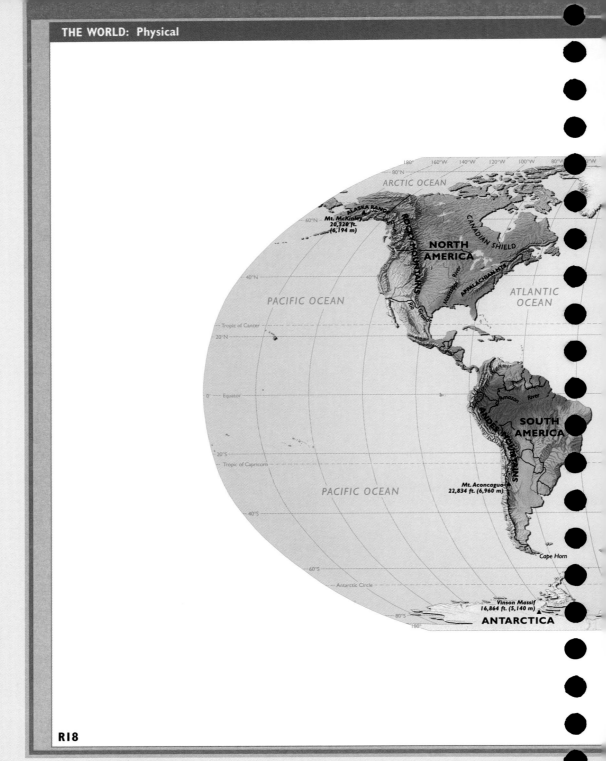

R18

The World: Physical Map

CHART THE WORLD

ON YOUR OWN

Objective: To identify major geographic features.

Materials: paper, pencil, crayons or colored pencils

15 TO 30 MINUTES

1. Explain that this map labels the major geographic features of the world that everyone should know.

2. Invite students to chart the information on this map by making headings of its major categories—mountain ranges, major rivers, deserts, plateaus—and listing the appropriate names and their continents under each.

3. Encourage students to illustrate their charts.

PLOT A TRIP AROUND THE WORLD

PARTNER

Objective: To map a route and measure distances.

Materials: outline maps of the world, pencils

30 MINUTES OR LONGER

1. Invite pairs of students to picture themselves having the opportunity to take a trip around the world.

2. Have partners agree where they would want to stop along the way and have them trace their route on the outline map. Have them label the continents on which they would stop and the oceans they would cross.

3. Finally, they should measure and note on the map the distance covered in each leg of the trip. Encourage them to make a bulletin board display of their work.

R19

The World: Physical Map

WHERE IS IT IN RELATION TO...?

Objective: To practice using directions.

Materials: none

15 TO 30 MINUTES

1. Refer the class to the *N* compass direction and have them deduce the other directions based on it. Remind them that this map is a flat version of a round Earth.

2. Pose directional questions—for example, "If you were on the Canadian Shield, in which direction would you travel to get to Cape Horn?" "What direction would take you from the Cape of Good Hope to Australia?"

3. Encourage students to make up such questions themselves and pose them to the class.

WHERE IN THE WORLD AM I?

Objective: To identify location based on a variety of geographic clues.

Material List: paper, pencil

ON YOUR OWN

15 TO 30 MINUTES

1. Have students pick two locations anywhere on this map and write them on a piece of paper.

2. For each, students should write down three geographic clues. Clues can be anything—relation to another place, latitude and longitude, ocean nearby, type of landform or other geographic feature.

3. Call on a student for one set of clues. The student who names the location correctly gives the next set.

COUNTRIES of the WORLD

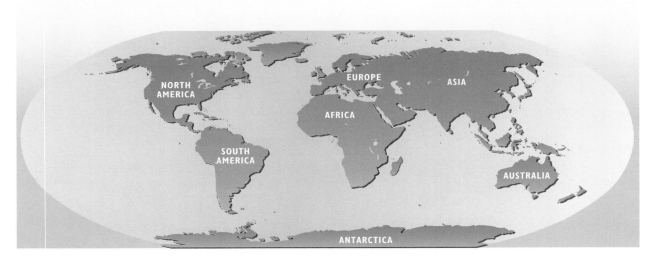

AFGHANISTAN

CAPITAL ★ Kabul

POPULATION: 22.7 million

MAJOR LANGUAGES: Pashtu and Afghan Persian

AREA: 250,000 sq mi; 647,500 sq km

LEADING EXPORTS: fruit, natural gas, and carpets

CONTINENT: Asia

ALBANIA

CAPITAL ★ Tiranë

POPULATION: 3.2 million

MAJOR LANGUAGES: Albanian and Greek

AREA: 11,100 sq mi; 28,748 sq km

LEADING EXPORTS: asphalt, petroleum products, and minerals

CONTINENT: Europe

ALGERIA

CAPITAL ★ Algiers

POPULATION: 29.2 million

MAJOR LANGUAGES: Arabic, Berber, and French

AREA: 919,595 sq mi; 2,381,751 sq km

LEADING EXPORTS: oil and natural gas

CONTINENT: Africa

ANDORRA

CAPITAL ★ Andorra la Vella

POPULATION: 68,000

MAJOR LANGUAGES: Catalan, French, and Castilian Spanish

AREA: 175 sq mi; 453 sq km

LEADING EXPORTS: electricity, tobacco products, and furniture

CONTINENT: Europe

ANGOLA

CAPITAL ★ Luanda

POPULATION: 10.3 million

MAJOR LANGUAGES: Portuguese and Bantu

AREA: 481,350 sq mi; 1,246,700 sq km

LEADING EXPORTS: oil, coffee, diamonds, and fish

CONTINENT: Africa

ANTIGUA AND BARBUDA

CAPITAL ★ St. John's

POPULATION: 66,000

MAJOR LANGUAGE: English

AREA: 171 sq mi; 442 sq km

LEADING EXPORTS: petroleum products and machinery

CONTINENT: North America

ARGENTINA

CAPITAL ★ Buenos Aires

POPULATION: 34.7 million

MAJOR LANGUAGES: Spanish, English, and Italian

AREA: 1,072,067 sq mi; 2,766,654 sq km

LEADING EXPORTS: meat, grain, hides, and wool

CONTINENT: South America

ARMENIA

CAPITAL ★ Yerevan

POPULATION: 3.5 million

MAJOR LANGUAGE: Armenian

AREA: 11,500 sq mi; 29,800 sq km

LEADING EXPORTS: machinery and processed food items

CONTINENT: Asia

AUSTRALIA

CAPITAL ★ Canberra

POPULATION: 18.2 million

MAJOR LANGUAGES: English and aboriginal languages

AREA: 2,966,150 sq mi; 7,682,300 sq km

LEADING EXPORTS: coal, gold, wool, and alumina

CONTINENT: Australia

AUSTRIA

CAPITAL ★ Vienna

POPULATION: 8.0 million

MAJOR LANGUAGE: German

AREA: 32,375 sq mi; 83,851 sq km

LEADING EXPORTS: iron and steel products, and timber

CONTINENT: Europe

AZERBAIJAN

CAPITAL ★ Baku

POPULATION: 7.7 million

MAJOR LANGUAGES: Azeri, Russian, and Armenian

AREA: 33,430 sq mi; 86,600 sq km

LEADING EXPORTS: oil and chemicals

CONTINENT: Asia

THE BAHAMAS

CAPITAL ★ Nassau

POPULATION: 0.3 million

MAJOR LANGUAGES: English and Creole

AREA: 5,380 sq mi; 13,939 sq km

LEADING EXPORTS: crawfish, medicine, and cement

CONTINENT: North America

BAHRAIN

CAPITAL ★ Manama

POPULATION: 0.6 million

MAJOR LANGUAGES: Arabic, English, Farsi, and Urdu

AREA: 240 sq mi; 620 sq km

LEADING EXPORTS: oil, petroleum products, and aluminum

CONTINENT: Asia

BANGLADESH

CAPITAL ★ Dhaka

POPULATION: 123.1 million

MAJOR LANGUAGES: Bangla and English

AREA: 55,598 sq mi; 143,998 sq km

LEADING EXPORTS: textiles, jute, leather, and seafood

CONTINENT: Asia

BARBADOS

CAPITAL ★ Bridgetown

POPULATION: 0.3 million

MAJOR LANGUAGE: English

AREA: 166 sq mi; 431 sq km

LEADING EXPORTS: sugar, molasses, and electrical components

CONTINENT: North America

BELARUS

CAPITAL ★ Minsk

POPULATION: 10.4 million

MAJOR LANGUAGES: Byelorussian and Russian

AREA: 80,200 sq mi; 207,600 sq km

LEADING EXPORTS: machinery and chemicals

CONTINENT: Europe

BELGIUM

CAPITAL ★ Brussels

POPULATION: 10.1 million

MAJOR LANGUAGES: Flemish and French

AREA: 11,781 sq mi; 30,518 sq km

LEADING EXPORTS: machinery, iron, steel, and diamonds

CONTINENT: Europe

BELIZE

CAPITAL ★ Belmopan

POPULATION: 0.2 million

MAJOR LANGUAGES: English and Spanish

AREA: 8,867 sq mi; 22,965 sq km

LEADING EXPORTS: sugar, molasses, clothing, and lumber

CONTINENT: North America

BENIN

CAPITAL ★ Porto-Novo

POPULATION: 5.7 million

MAJOR LANGUAGES: French and Fon

AREA: 43,483 sq mi; 12,622 sq km

LEADING EXPORTS: crude oil, cotton, palm products, and cocoa

CONTINENT: Africa

BHUTAN

CAPITAL ★ Thimphu

POPULATION: 1.8 million

MAJOR LANGUAGES: Dzongkha and Nepali

AREA: 18,000 sq mi; 46,620 sq km

LEADING EXPORTS: cardamom, gypsum, timber, and handicrafts

CONTINENT: Asia

BOLIVIA

CAPITALS ★ Sucre (judicial) and La Paz (administrative)

POPULATION: 7.2 million

MAJOR LANGUAGES: Spanish, Quechua, and Aymará

AREA: 424,162 sq mi; 1,098,581 sq km

LEADING EXPORTS: metals, natural gas, soybeans, and timber

CONTINENT: South America

COUNTRIES of the WORLD

BOSNIA AND HERZEGOVINA

CAPITAL ★ Sarajevo
POPULATION: 2.7 million
MAJOR LANGUAGE: Serbo-Croatian
AREA: 19,741 sq mi; 51,129 sq km
LEADING EXPORTS: (not available)
CONTINENT: Europe

BOTSWANA

CAPITAL ★ Gaborone
POPULATION: 1.5 million
MAJOR LANGUAGES: English and Setswana
AREA: 231,800 sq mi; 600,360 sq km
LEADING EXPORTS: diamonds, copper, and nickel
CONTINENT: Africa

BRAZIL

CAPITAL ★ Brasília
POPULATION: 162.7 million
MAJOR LANGUAGES: Portuguese, Spanish, French, and English
AREA: 3,286,470 sq mi; 8,511,957 sq km
LEADING EXPORTS: coffee, iron ore, and soybeans
CONTINENT: South America

BRUNEI

CAPITAL ★ Bandar Seri Begawan
POPULATION: 0.3 million
MAJOR LANGUAGES: Malay, English, and Chinese
AREA: 2,226 sq mi; 5,765 sq km
LEADING EXPORT: oil
CONTINENT: Asia

BULGARIA

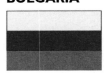

CAPITAL ★ Sofia
POPULATION: 8.6 million
MAJOR LANGUAGE: Bulgarian
AREA: 42,823 sq mi; 110,912 sq km
LEADING EXPORTS: machinery, minerals, and agricultural products
CONTINENT: Europe

BURKINA FASO

CAPITAL ★ Ouagadougou
POPULATION: 10.6 million
MAJOR LANGUAGES: French and Sudanic languages
AREA: 105,870 sq mi; 274,200 sq km
LEADING EXPORTS: oilseeds and cotton
CONTINENT: Africa

BURUNDI

CAPITAL ★ Bujumbura
POPULATION: 5.9 million
MAJOR LANGUAGES: Kirundi, French, and Swahili
AREA: 10,747 sq mi; 27,834 sq km
LEADING EXPORTS: coffee, tea, cotton, and hides
CONTINENT: Africa

CAMBODIA

CAPITAL ★ Phnom Penh
POPULATION: 10.6 million
MAJOR LANGUAGES: Khmer and French
AREA: 69,884 sq mi; 181,035 sq km
LEADING EXPORTS: rubber, rice, pepper, and raw timber
CONTINENT: Asia

CAMEROON

CAPITAL ★ Yaoundé
POPULATION: 14.3 million
MAJOR LANGUAGES: English and French
AREA: 183,569 sq mi; 475,442 sq km
LEADING EXPORTS: coffee, cocoa, timber, and petroleum products
CONTINENT: Africa

CANADA

CAPITAL ★ Ottawa
POPULATION: 29.9 million
MAJOR LANGUAGES: English and French
AREA: 3,851,809 sq mi; 9,976,186 sq km
LEADING EXPORTS: newsprint, wood pulp, and timber
CONTINENT: North America

CAPE VERDE

CAPITAL ★ Praia
POPULATION: 0.4 million
MAJOR LANGUAGES: Portuguese and Crioulo
AREA: 1,557 sq mi; 4,033 sq km
LEADING EXPORTS: fish, bananas, and salt
CONTINENT: Africa

CENTRAL AFRICAN REPUBLIC

CAPITAL ★ Bangui
POPULATION: 3.3 million
MAJOR LANGUAGES: French and Sango
AREA: 241,313 sq mi; 625,000 sq km
LEADING EXPORTS: diamonds, cotton, timber, coffee, and tobacco
CONTINENT: Africa

CHAD

CAPITAL ★ N'Djamena

POPULATION: 7.0 million

MAJOR LANGUAGES: French and Arabic

AREA: 495,752 sq mi; 1,284,000 sq km

LEADING EXPORTS: cotton, cattle, fish, and textiles

CONTINENT: Africa

CHILE

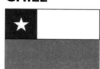

CAPITAL ★ Santiago

POPULATION: 14.3 million

MAJOR LANGUAGE: Spanish

AREA: 292,132 sq mi; 756,622 sq km

LEADING EXPORTS: copper, fish, metals, and minerals

CONTINENT: South America

CHINA

CAPITAL ★ Beijing

POPULATION: 1,210 million

MAJOR LANGUAGES: Mandarin and local Chinese dialects

AREA: 3,691,521 sq mi; 9,561,000 sq km

LEADING EXPORTS: manufactured goods, footwear, and toys

CONTINENT: Asia

COLOMBIA

CAPITAL ★ Bogotá

POPULATION: 36.8 million

MAJOR LANGUAGE: Spanish

AREA: 439,735 sq mi; 1,138,910 sq km

LEADING EXPORTS: coffee, petroleum, coal, and bananas

CONTINENT: South America

COMOROS

CAPITAL ★ Moroni

POPULATION: 0.6 million

MAJOR LANGUAGES: French, Arabic, and Comoran

AREA: 690 sq mi; 1,787 sq km

LEADING EXPORTS: vanilla, cloves, perfume oil, and copra

CONTINENT: Africa

CONGO REPUBLIC

CAPITAL ★ Brazzaville

POPULATION: 2.5 million

MAJOR LANGUAGES: French, Kikongo, Lingala, and other African languages

AREA: 132,046 sq mi; 342,000 sq km

LEADING EXPORTS: crude oil, lumber, coffee, and cocoa

CONTINENT: Africa

COSTA RICA

CAPITAL ★ San José

POPULATION: 3.5 million

MAJOR LANGUAGES: Spanish and English

AREA: 19,652 sq mi; 50,898 sq km

LEADING EXPORTS: coffee, bananas, textiles, and sugar

CONTINENT: North America

CÔTE D'IVOIRE (Ivory Coast)

CAPITAL ★ Yamoussoukro

POPULATION: 14.8 million

MAJOR LANGUAGES: French and many African languages

AREA: 124,502 sq mi; 322,462 sq km

LEADING EXPORTS: cocoa, coffee, tropical woods, and petroleum

CONTINENT: Africa

CROATIA

CAPITAL ★ Zagreb

POPULATION: 5 million

MAJOR LANGUAGE: Serbo-Croatian

AREA: 21,829 sq mi; 56,537 sq km

LEADING EXPORTS: machinery, transport equipment, and other manufactures

CONTINENT: Europe

CUBA

CAPITAL ★ Havana

POPULATION: 11 million

MAJOR LANGUAGE: Spanish

AREA: 44,218 sq mi; 114,524 sq km

LEADING EXPORTS: coffee, sugar, nickel, shellfish, and tobacco

CONTINENT: North America

CYPRUS

CAPITAL ★ Nicosia

POPULATION: 0.7 million

MAJOR LANGUAGES: Greek, Turkish, and English

AREA: 3,572 sq mi; 9,251 sq km

LEADING EXPORTS: fruit, cement, and clothing

CONTINENT: Asia

CZECH REPUBLIC

CAPITAL ★ Prague

POPULATION: 10.3 million

MAJOR LANGUAGES: Czech and Slovak

AREA: 30,464 sq mi; 78,902 sq km

LEADING EXPORTS: manufactured goods and machinery

CONTINENT: Europe

COUNTRIES of the WORLD

DEMOCRATIC REPUBLIC OF CONGO

CAPITAL ★ Kinshasa

POPULATION: 46.5 million

MAJOR LANGUAGES: French, English, Swahili, Lingala and other Bantu dialects

AREA: 905,365 sq mi; 2,344,885 sq km

LEADING EXPORTS: copper, cobalt, diamonds, oil, and coffee

CONTINENT: Africa

DENMARK

CAPITAL ★ Copenhagen

POPULATION: 5.2 million

MAJOR LANGUAGES: Danish and Faroese

AREA: 16,631 sq mi; 43,075 sq mi

LEADING EXPORTS: food, machinery, and chemicals

CONTINENT: Europe

DJIBOUTI

CAPITAL ★ Djibouti

POPULATION: 0.4 million

MAJOR LANGUAGES: Arabic and French

AREA: 8,490 sq mi; 22,000 sq km

LEADING EXPORTS: hides and skins

CONTINENT: Africa

DOMINICA

CAPITAL ★ Roseau

POPULATION: 0.1 million

MAJOR LANGUAGES: English and Creole

AREA: 290 sq mi; 751 sq km

LEADING EXPORTS: bananas, coconuts, soap, and vegetables

CONTINENT: North America

DOMINICAN REPUBLIC

CAPITAL ★ Santo Domingo

POPULATION: 8.1 million

MAJOR LANGUAGES: Spanish

AREA: 18,704 sq mi; 48,442 sq km

LEADING EXPORTS: sugar, coffee, cocoa, gold, and ferronickel

CONTINENT: North America

ECUADOR

CAPITAL ★ Quito

POPULATION: 10.7 million

MAJOR LANGUAGES: Spanish and Quechua

AREA: 106,822 sq mi; 276,670 sq km

LEADING EXPORTS: oil, coffee, bananas, and cocoa

CONTINENT: South America

EGYPT

CAPITAL ★ Cairo

POPULATION: 63.6 million

MAJOR LANGUAGES: Arabic, English, and French

AREA: 386,900 sq mi; 1,002,000 sq km

LEADING EXPORTS: cotton, oil, and textiles

CONTINENT: Africa

EL SALVADOR

CAPITAL ★ San Salvador

POPULATION: 5.8 million

MAJOR LANGUAGES: Spanish and Nahua

AREA: 8,260 sq mi; 21,393 sq km

LEADING EXPORTS: coffee, cotton, sugarcane, and shrimp

CONTINENT: North America

EQUATORIAL GUINEA

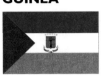

CAPITAL ★ Malabo

POPULATION: 0.4 million

MAJOR LANGUAGES: Spanish, Fang, and Bubi

AREA: 10,830 sq mi; 28,051 sq km

LEADING EXPORTS: cocoa, timber, and coffee

CONTINENT: Africa

ERITREA

CAPITAL ★ Asmara

POPULATION: 3.9 million

MAJOR LANGUAGES: Tigrinya and Arabic

AREA: 45,754 sq mi; 121,300 sq km

LEADING EXPORTS: (not available)

CONTINENT: Africa

ESTONIA

CAPITAL ★ Tallinn

POPULATION: 1.5 million

MAJOR LANGUAGES: Estonian, Latvian, Lithuanian, and Russian

AREA: 18,370 sq mi; 47,549 sq km

LEADING EXPORTS: food products, textiles, vehicles, and metals

CONTINENT: Europe

ETHIOPIA

CAPITAL ★ Addis Ababa

POPULATION: 57.2 million

MAJOR LANGUAGES: Amharic, English, and local languages

AREA: 446,952 sq mi; 1,157,585 sq km

LEADING EXPORTS: coffee, leather products, gold, and petroleum products

CONTINENT: Africa

FIJI

CAPITAL ★ Suva

POPULATION: 0.8 million

MAJOR LANGUAGES: Fijian, Hindi, and English

AREA: 7,078 sq mi; 18,333 sq km

LEADING EXPORTS: sugar, copra, fish, lumber, and gold

CONTINENT: Islands in the Pacific Ocean

FINLAND

CAPITAL ★ Helsinki

POPULATION: 5.1 million

MAJOR LANGUAGES: Finnish and Swedish

AREA: 130,558 sq mi; 338,145 sq km

LEADING EXPORTS: paper and wood

CONTINENT: Europe

FRANCE

CAPITAL ★ Paris

POPULATION: 58.3 million

MAJOR LANGUAGE: French

AREA: 211,208 sq mi; 547,030 sq km

LEADING EXPORTS: manufactured goods and machinery

CONTINENT: Europe

GABON

CAPITAL ★ Libreville

POPULATION: 1.2 million

MAJOR LANGUAGES: French, Fang, and Bantu dialects

AREA: 103,346 sq mi; 267,667 sq km

LEADING EXPORTS: crude oil, manganese, and timber

CONTINENT: Africa

THE GAMBIA

CAPITAL ★ Banjul

POPULATION: 1.0 million

MAJOR LANGUAGES: English and Mandinka

AREA: 4,093 sq mi; 10,600 sq km

LEADING EXPORTS: peanut products, fish, and cotton lint

CONTINENT: Africa

GEORGIA

CAPITAL ★ Tbilisi

POPULATION: 5.2 million

MAJOR LANGUAGES: Georgian and Russian

AREA: 26,900 sq mi; 69,700 sq km

LEADING EXPORTS: agricultural products and machinery

CONTINENT: Asia

GERMANY

CAPITAL ★ Berlin

POPULATION: 83.5 million

MAJOR LANGUAGE: German

AREA: 137,826 sq mi; 356,970 sq km

LEADING EXPORTS: machinery and manufactured goods

CONTINENT: Europe

GHANA

CAPITAL ★ Accra

POPULATION: 17.7 million

MAJOR LANGUAGES: English and African languages

AREA: 92,100 sq mi; 238,537 sq km

LEADING EXPORTS: cocoa, gold, timber, and tuna

CONTINENT: Africa

GREECE

CAPITAL ★ Athens

POPULATION: 10.7 million

MAJOR LANGUAGES: Greek, English, and French

AREA: 50,961 sq mi; 131,990 sq km

LEADING EXPORTS: manufactured goods and food products

CONTINENT: Europe

GRENADA

CAPITAL ★ St. George's

POPULATION: 0.1 million

MAJOR LANGUAGES: English and French patois

AREA: 133 sq mi; 344 sq km

LEADING EXPORTS: nutmeg, cocoa, bananas, and mace

CONTINENT: North America

GUATEMALA

CAPITAL ★ Guatemala City

POPULATION: 11.3 million

MAJOR LANGUAGES: Spanish and Mayan dialects

AREA: 42,042 sq mi; 108,889 sq km

LEADING EXPORTS: coffee, sugar, and bananas

CONTINENT: North America

GUINEA

CAPITAL ★ Conakry

POPULATION: 7.4 million

MAJOR LANGUAGES: French, Soussou, and Manika

AREA: 94,925 sq mi; 245,857 sq km

LEADING EXPORTS: bauxite, alumina, diamonds, and food products

CONTINENT: Africa

GUINEA-BISSAU

CAPITAL ★ Bissau

POPULATION: 1.2 million

MAJOR LANGUAGES: Portuguese and Crioulo

AREA: 13,948 sq mi; 36,125 sq km

LEADING EXPORTS: peanut products, fish, and palm kernels

CONTINENT: Africa

GUYANA

CAPITAL ★ Georgetown

POPULATION: 0.7 million

MAJOR LANGUAGES: English, Hindi, and Urdu

AREA: 83,000 sq mi; 214,969 sq km

LEADING EXPORTS: sugar, bauxite, rice, timber, and shrimp

CONTINENT: South America

COUNTRIES of the WORLD

HAITI

CAPITAL ★ Port-au-Prince
POPULATION: 6.7 million
MAJOR LANGUAGES: French and French Creole
AREA: 10,714 sq mi; 27,750 sq km
LEADING EXPORTS: coffee and assembled lighting products
CONTINENT: North America

HONDURAS

CAPITAL ★ Tegucigalpa
POPULATION: 5.6 million
MAJOR LANGUAGE: Spanish
AREA: 43,872 sq mi; 112,492 sq km
LEADING EXPORTS: coffee, lumber, bananas, shrimp, and lobster
CONTINENT: North America

HUNGARY

CAPITAL ★ Budapest
POPULATION: 10.0 million
MAJOR LANGUAGE: Hungarian
AREA: 35,919 sq mi; 93,030 sq km
LEADING EXPORTS: raw materials, chemicals, and consumer goods
CONTINENT: Europe

ICELAND

CAPITAL ★ Reykjavik
POPULATION: 0.3 million
MAJOR LANGUAGE: Icelandic
AREA: 39,709 sq mi; 102,846 sq km
LEADING EXPORTS: fish, animal products, and aluminum
CONTINENT: Europe

INDIA

CAPITAL ★ New Delhi
POPULATION: 952.1 million
MAJOR LANGUAGES: Hindi, English, and 14 other official languages
AREA: 1,229,737 sq mi; 3,185,019 sq km
LEADING EXPORTS: gems and jewelry, clothing, engineering goods, and fabric
CONTINENT: Asia

INDONESIA

CAPITAL ★ Jakarta
POPULATION: 206.6 million
MAJOR LANGUAGES: Bahasa Indonesian, English, Dutch, and Javanese
AREA: 735,268 sq mi; 1,904,344 sq km
LEADING EXPORTS: oil, gas, timber, rubber, and coffee
CONTINENT: Asia

IRAN

CAPITAL ★ Tehran
POPULATION: 66.1 million
MAJOR LANGUAGES: Farsi, Turkic, and Kurdish
AREA: 636,293 sq mi; 1,648,000 sq km
LEADING EXPORTS: oil, carpets, and fruits
CONTINENT: Asia

IRAQ

CAPITAL ★ Baghdad
POPULATION: 21.4 million
MAJOR LANGUAGES: Arabic and Kurdish
AREA: 168,920 sq mi; 434,913 sq km
LEADING EXPORT: oil and chemicals
CONTINENT: Asia

IRELAND

CAPITAL ★ Dublin
POPULATION: 3.6 million
MAJOR LANGUAGES: English and Irish
AREA: 27,136 sq mi; 70,282 sq km
LEADING EXPORTS: live animals, dairy products, and machinery
CONTINENT: Europe

ISRAEL

CAPITAL ★ Jerusalem
POPULATION: 5.2 million
MAJOR LANGUAGES: Hebrew and Arabic
AREA: 8,020 sq mi; 20,772 sq km*
LEADING EXPORTS: diamonds, fruits, and textiles
CONTINENT: Asia
*does not include the 2,402 sq mi of the Gaza Strip and the West Bank

ITALY

CAPITAL ★ Rome
POPULATION: 57.5 million
MAJOR LANGUAGE: Italian
AREA: 116,500 sq mi; 301,278 sq km
LEADING EXPORTS: clothing, metals, machinery, and chemicals
CONTINENT: Europe

JAMAICA

CAPITAL ★ Kingston
POPULATION: 2.6 million
MAJOR LANGUAGES: English and Jamaican Creole
AREA: 4,411 sq mi; 11,424 sq km
LEADING EXPORTS: alumina, bauxite, sugar, and bananas
CONTINENT: North America

JAPAN

CAPITAL ★ Tokyo
POPULATION: 125.6 million
MAJOR LANGUAGE: Japanese
AREA: 145,874 sq mi; 377,815 sq km
LEADING EXPORT: machinery
CONTINENT: Asia

JORDAN

CAPITAL ★ Amman
POPULATION: 4.2 million
MAJOR LANGUAGE: Arabic
AREA: 34,573 sq mi; 89,544 sq km
LEADING EXPORTS: phosphates
and agricultural products
CONTINENT: Asia

KAZAKHSTAN

CAPITAL ★ Almaty
POPULATION: 16.9 million
MAJOR LANGUAGES: Kazakh and
Russian
AREA: 1,049,000 sq mi; 2,717,300 sq
km
LEADING EXPORTS: oil, metals,
chemicals, wool, and grain
CONTINENT: Asia

KENYA

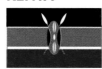

CAPITAL ★ Nairobi
POPULATION: 28.2 million
MAJOR LANGUAGES: English and
Swahili
AREA: 224,960 sq mi; 582,646 sq km
LEADING EXPORTS: tea, coffee, and
petroleum products
CONTINENT: Africa

KIRIBATI

CAPITAL ★ Tarawa
POPULATION: 80,900
MAJOR LANGUAGES: Gilbertese
and English
AREA: 280 sq mi; 726 sq km
LEADING EXPORTS: fish and copra
CONTINENT: Islands in the Pacific
Ocean

KOREA, NORTH

CAPITAL ★ Pyongyang
POPULATION: 23.9 million
MAJOR LANGUAGE: Korean
AREA: 46,768 sq mi; 121,129 sq km
LEADING EXPORTS: minerals and
agricultural products
CONTINENT: Asia

KOREA, SOUTH

CAPITAL ★ Seoul
POPULATION: 45.5 million
MAJOR LANGUAGE: Korean
AREA: 38,031 sq mi; 98,392 sq km
LEADING EXPORTS: agricultural
products, electronics, machinery, and
clothing
CONTINENT: Asia

KUWAIT

CAPITAL ★ Kuwait
POPULATION: 2.0 million
MAJOR LANGUAGE: Arabic
AREA: 6,880 sq mi; 17,820 sq km
LEADING EXPORT: oil
CONTINENT: Asia

KYRGYZSTAN

CAPITAL ★ Bishkek
POPULATION: 4.5 million
MAJOR LANGUAGES: Kyrgyz and
Russian
AREA: 76,000 sq mi; 198,500 sq km
LEADING EXPORTS: wool,
chemicals, cotton, metals, and shoes
CONTINENT: Asia

LAOS

CAPITAL ★ Vientiane
POPULATION: 4.9 million
MAJOR LANGUAGES: Lao, French,
and English
AREA: 91,429 sq mi; 236,800 sq km
LEADING EXPORTS: electricity,
timber, tin, and coffee
CONTINENT: Asia

LATVIA

CAPITAL ★ Riga
POPULATION: 2.5 million
MAJOR LANGUAGES: Latvian and
Russian
AREA: 25,400 sq mi; 65,786 sq km
LEADING EXPORTS: timber, metals,
machinery, and fish
CONTINENT: Europe

LEBANON

CAPITAL ★ Beirut
POPULATION: 3.8 million
MAJOR LANGUAGES: Arabic and
French
AREA: 4,015 sq mi; 10,400 sq km
LEADING EXPORTS: fruits, textiles,
and chemicals
CONTINENT: Asia

LESOTHO

CAPITAL ★ Maseru
POPULATION: 2.0 million
MAJOR LANGUAGES: Sesotho and
English
AREA: 11,720 sq mi; 30,355 sq km
LEADING EXPORTS: wool, mohair,
wheat, cattle, peas, and beans
CONTINENT: Africa

COUNTRIES of the WORLD

LIBERIA

CAPITAL ★ Monrovia
POPULATION: 2.1 million
MAJOR LANGUAGES: English and Niger-Congo languages
AREA: 43,000 sq mi; 111,370 sq km
LEADING EXPORTS: iron ore, rubber, timber, and coffee
CONTINENT: Africa

LIBYA

CAPITAL ★ Tripoli
POPULATION: 5.4 million
MAJOR LANGUAGES: Arabic, Italian, and English
AREA: 679,536 sq mi; 1,759,998 sq km
LEADING EXPORTS: oil, peanuts, and natural gas
CONTINENT: Africa

LIECHTENSTEIN

CAPITAL ★ Vaduz
POPULATION: 31,000
MAJOR LANGUAGE: German
AREA: 61 sq mi; 157 sq km
LEADING EXPORTS: machinery, dental products, stamps, and hardware
CONTINENT: Europe

LITHUANIA

CAPITAL ★ Vilnius
POPULATION: 3.7 million
MAJOR LANGUAGES: Lithuanian, Russian, and Polish
AREA: 25,212 sq mi; 65,300 sq km
LEADING EXPORTS: textiles, chemicals, and mineral products
CONTINENT: Europe

LUXEMBOURG
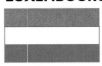
CAPITAL ★ Luxembourg
POPULATION: 0.4 million
MAJOR LANGUAGES: Luxembourgisch, German, French, and English
AREA: 999 sq mi; 2,586 sq km
LEADING EXPORTS: steel products, chemicals, rubber products, and glass
CONTINENT: Europe

MACEDONIA

CAPITAL ★ Skopje
POPULATION: 2.1 million
MAJOR LANGUAGES: Macedonian and Albanian
AREA: 9,928 sq mi; 25,713 sq km
LEADING EXPORTS: manufactured goods, machinery, and transport equipment
CONTINENT: Europe

MADAGASCAR

CAPITAL ★ Antananarivo
POPULATION: 13.7 million
MAJOR LANGUAGES: French and Malagasy
AREA: 226,660 sq mi; 587,050 sq km
LEADING EXPORTS: coffee, cloves, vanilla, and sugar
CONTINENT: Africa

MALAWI

CAPITAL ★ Lilongwe
POPULATION: 9.5 million
MAJOR LANGUAGES: English and Chichewa
AREA: 45,747 sq mi; 118,484 sq km
LEADING EXPORTS: tobacco, sugar, tea, coffee, and peanuts
CONTINENT: Africa

MALAYSIA

CAPITAL ★ Kuala Lumpur
POPULATION: 20.0 million
MAJOR LANGUAGES: Malay, English, and Chinese dialects
AREA: 128,328 sq mi; 332,370 sq km
LEADING EXPORTS: rubber, palm oil, tin, and timber
CONTINENT: Asia

MALDIVES

CAPITAL ★ Malé
POPULATION: 0.3 million
MAJOR LANGUAGE: Divehi
AREA: 115 sq mi; 298 sq km
LEADING EXPORTS: fish and clothing
CONTINENT: Asia

MALI

CAPITAL ★ Bamako
POPULATION: 9.7 million
MAJOR LANGUAGES: Bambara and French
AREA: 478,819 sq mi; 1,240,142 sq km
LEADING EXPORTS: cotton, livestock, and gold
CONTINENT: Africa

MALTA

CAPITAL ★ Valletta
POPULATION: 0.4 million
MAJOR LANGUAGES: Maltese and English
AREA: 122 sq mi; 316 sq km
LEADING EXPORTS: clothing, textiles, and footwear
CONTINENT: Europe

MARSHALL ISLANDS

CAPITAL ★ Majuro

POPULATION: 58,000

MAJOR LANGUAGES: English, Marshallese dialects, and Japanese

AREA: 70 sq mi; 181 sq km

LEADING EXPORTS: coconut oil, fish, live animals, and trichus shells

CONTINENT: Islands in the Pacific Ocean

MAURITANIA

CAPITAL ★ Nouakchott

POPULATION: 2.3 million

MAJOR LANGUAGES: Arabic and Wolof

AREA: 397,953 sq mi; 1,030,700 sq km

LEADING EXPORTS: iron ore and fish

CONTINENT: Africa

MAURITIUS

CAPITAL ★ Port Louis

POPULATION: 1.1 million

MAJOR LANGUAGES: English, Creole, and French

AREA: 787 sq mi; 2,040 sq km

LEADING EXPORTS: sugar, light manufactures, and textiles

CONTINENT: Africa

MEXICO

CAPITAL ★ Mexico City

POPULATION: 95.8 million

MAJOR LANGUAGE: Spanish

AREA: 761,600 sq mi; 1,972,547 sq km

LEADING EXPORTS: motor vehicles, consumer electronics, cotton, and shrimp

CONTINENT: North America

MICRONESIA

CAPITAL ★ Palikir

POPULATION: 125,000

MAJOR LANGUAGES: English, Trukese, Yapese, and Kosrean

AREA: 271 sq mi; 703 sq km

LEADING EXPORT: copra

CONTINENT: Islands in the Pacific Ocean

MOLDOVA

CAPITAL ★ Kishinev

POPULATION: 4.5 million

MAJOR LANGUAGES: Moldovan, Russian, and Gagauz

AREA: 13,000 sq mi; 33,700 sq km

LEADING EXPORTS: food, wine, tobacco, and textiles

CONTINENT: Europe

MONACO

CAPITAL ★ Monaco

POPULATION: 31,000

MAJOR LANGUAGES: French, Monégasque, and English

AREA: 0.7 sq mi; 1.9 sq km

LEADING EXPORTS: (not available)

CONTINENT: Europe

MONGOLIA

CAPITAL ★ Ulaanbaatar

POPULATION: 2.5 million

MAJOR LANGUAGES: Khalkha Mongolian, Turkic, Russian, and Chinese

AREA: 604,250 sq mi; 1,565,000 sq km

LEADING EXPORTS: copper, cashmere, and livestock

CONTINENT: Asia

MOROCCO

CAPITAL ★ Rabat

POPULATION: 29.8 million

MAJOR LANGUAGES: Arabic, Berber, and French

AREA: 172,413 sq mi; 446,550 sq km

LEADING EXPORTS: food, beverages, consumer goods, and phosphates

CONTINENT: Africa

MOZAMBIQUE

CAPITAL ★ Maputo

POPULATION: 17.9 million

MAJOR LANGUAGES: Portuguese and African languages

AREA: 303,073 sq mi; 799,380 sq km

LEADING EXPORTS: cashew nuts, sugar, and shrimp

CONTINENT: Africa

MYANMAR (Burma)

CAPITAL ★ Yangon

POPULATION: 50.0 million

MAJOR LANGUAGE: Burmese

AREA: 261,220 sq mi; 678,560 sq km

LEADING EXPORTS: rice, teak, oilseeds, and metals

CONTINENT: Asia

NAMIBIA

CAPITAL ★ Windhoek

POPULATION: 1.7 million

MAJOR LANGUAGES: English, Afrikaans, and German

AREA: 318,261 sq mi; 824,296 sq km

LEADING EXPORTS: diamonds, metals, and livestock

CONTINENT: Africa

COUNTRIES of the WORLD

NAURU

CAPITAL ★ Yaren
POPULATION: 10,000
MAJOR LANGUAGES: Nauruan and English
AREA: 8 sq mi; 21 sq km
LEADING EXPORT: phosphates
CONTINENT: Islands in the Pacific Ocean

NEPAL

CAPITAL ★ Kathmandu
POPULATION: 22.1 million
MAJOR LANGUAGE: Nepali
AREA: 54,463 sq mi; 141,059 sq km
LEADING EXPORTS: clothing, carpets, leather goods, and grain
CONTINENT: Asia

NETHERLANDS

CAPITAL ★ Amsterdam
POPULATION: 15.5 million
MAJOR LANGUAGE: Dutch
AREA: 16,033 sq mi; 41,526 sq km
LEADING EXPORTS: foodstuffs, natural gas, and chemicals
CONTINENT: Europe

NEW ZEALAND

CAPITAL ★ Wellington
POPULATION: 3.5 million
MAJOR LANGUAGES: English and Maori
AREA: 103,884 sq mi; 270,534 sq km
LEADING EXPORTS: meat, dairy products, and wool
CONTINENT: Islands in the Pacific Ocean

NICARAGUA

CAPITAL ★ Managua
POPULATION: 4.3 million
MAJOR LANGUAGE: Spanish
AREA: 50,180 sq mi; 130,000 sq km
LEADING EXPORTS: coffee, cotton, and foodstuffs
CONTINENT: North America

NIGER

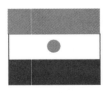

CAPITAL ★ Niamey
POPULATION: 9.1 million
MAJOR LANGUAGES: French, Hausa, and Djerma
AREA: 489,206 sq mi; 1,267,044 sq km
LEADING EXPORTS: uranium ore, cowpeas, and livestock products
CONTINENT: Africa

NIGERIA

CAPITAL ★ Abuja
POPULATION: 103.9 million
MAJOR LANGUAGES: English, Hausa, Yoruba, Ibo, and Fulani
AREA: 356,700 sq mi; 923,853 sq km
LEADING EXPORTS: oil and cocoa
CONTINENT: Africa

NORWAY

CAPITAL ★ Oslo
POPULATION: 4.3 million
MAJOR LANGUAGE: Norwegian
AREA: 125,049 sq mi; 323,877 sq km
LEADING EXPORTS: oil, natural gas, fish, and ships
CONTINENT: Europe

OMAN

CAPITAL ★ Muscat
POPULATION: 2.2 million
MAJOR LANGUAGE: Arabic
AREA: 82,030 sq mi; 212,458 sq km
LEADING EXPORTS: oil and fish
CONTINENT: Asia

PAKISTAN

CAPITAL ★ Islamabad
POPULATION: 129.3 million
MAJOR LANGUAGES: Urdu, Punjabi, and English
AREA: 310,400 sq mi; 803,936 sq km
LEADING EXPORTS: cotton, rice, and textiles
CONTINENT: Asia

PALAU

CAPITAL ★ Koror
POPULATION: 16,952
MAJOR LANGUAGES: Palauan and English
AREA: 196 sq mi; 508 sq km
LEADING EXPORTS: trochus, tuna, and copra
CONTINENT: Islands in the Pacific Ocean

PANAMA

CAPITAL ★ Panama City
POPULATION: 2.7 million
MAJOR LANGUAGES: Spanish and English
AREA: 29,761 sq mi; 77,082 sq km
LEADING EXPORTS: bananas, sugar, shrimp, and coffee
CONTINENT: North America

PAPUA NEW GUINEA

CAPITAL ★ Port Moresby
POPULATION: 4.2 million
MAJOR LANGUAGES: Pidgin English, English, and Motu
AREA: 178,704 sq mi; 462,840 sq km
LEADING EXPORTS: gold, copper, coffee, palm oil, and copra
CONTINENT: Islands in the Pacific Ocean

PARAGUAY

CAPITAL ★ Asunción

POPULATION: 5.5 million

MAJOR LANGUAGES: Spanish and Guarani

AREA: 157,047 sq mi; 406,752 sq km

LEADING EXPORTS: cotton, soybeans, and meat products

CONTINENT: South America

PERU

CAPITAL ★ Lima

POPULATION: 24.5 million

MAJOR LANGUAGES: Spanish, Quechua, and Aymará

AREA: 496,222 sq mi; 1,285,216 sq km

LEADING EXPORTS: copper, fish products, and cotton

CONTINENT: South America

PHILIPPINES

CAPITAL ★ Manila

POPULATION: 74.5 million

MAJOR LANGUAGES: Filipino, Tagalog, and English

AREA: 115,830 sq mi; 300,000 sq km

LEADING EXPORTS: electronics, coconut products, and chemicals

CONTINENT: Asia

POLAND

CAPITAL ★ Warsaw

POPULATION: 38.6 million

MAJOR LANGUAGE: Polish

AREA: 120,727 sq mi; 312,683 sq km

LEADING EXPORTS: coal, machinery, chemicals, and metals

CONTINENT: Europe

PORTUGAL

CAPITAL ★ Lisbon

POPULATION: 9.9 million

MAJOR LANGUAGE: Portuguese

AREA: 35,550 sq mi; 92,075 sq km

LEADING EXPORTS: cotton, textiles, and cork

CONTINENT: Europe

QATAR

CAPITAL ★ Doha

POPULATION: 0.5 million

MAJOR LANGUAGES: Arabic and English

AREA: 4,000 sq mi; 11,437 sq km

LEADING EXPORTS: oil, steel, and fertilizers

CONTINENT: Asia

ROMANIA

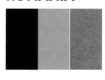

CAPITAL ★ Bucharest

POPULATION: 21.7 million

MAJOR LANGUAGES: Romanian, Hungarian, and German

AREA: 91,700 sq mi; 237,500 sq km

LEADING EXPORTS: machinery, metals, chemicals, and timber

CONTINENT: Europe

RUSSIA

CAPITAL ★ Moscow

POPULATION: 148.2 million

MAJOR LANGUAGE: Russian

AREA: 6,592,800 sq mi; 17,075,400 sq km

LEADING EXPORTS: petroleum, natural gas, wood, and coal

CONTINENTS: Europe and Asia

RWANDA

CAPITAL ★ Kigali

POPULATION: 6.9 million

MAJOR LANGUAGES: Kinyarwanda, French, and Kiswahili

AREA: 10,169 sq mi; 26,338 sq km

LEADING EXPORTS: coffee and tea

CONTINENT: Africa

ST. KITTS AND NEVIS

CAPITAL ★ Basseterre

POPULATION: 41,000

MAJOR LANGUAGE: English

AREA: 65 sq mi; 169 sq km

LEADING EXPORTS: sugar, electronics, and stamps

CONTINENT: North America

ST. LUCIA

CAPITAL ★ Castries

POPULATION: 158,000

MAJOR LANGUAGES: English and French patois

AREA: 238 sq mi; 616 sq km

LEADING EXPORTS: bananas, cocoa, clothing, and vegetables

CONTINENT: North America

ST. VINCENT AND THE GRENADINES

CAPITAL ★ Kingstown

POPULATION: 118,000

MAJOR LANGUAGE: English

AREA: 150 sq mi; 389 sq km

LEADING EXPORTS: bananas, arrowroot starch, taro, and tennis racquets

CONTINENT: North America

COUNTRIES of the WORLD

SAMOA

CAPITAL ★ Apia
POPULATION: 214,000
MAJOR LANGUAGES: Samoan and English
AREA: 1,093 sq mi; 2,831 sq km
LEADING EXPORTS: copra, cocoa, coconut oil, and cream
CONTINENT: Islands in the Pacific Ocean

SAN MARINO

CAPITAL ★ San Marino
POPULATION: 25,000
MAJOR LANGUAGE: Italian
AREA: 23 sq mi; 62 sq km
LEADING EXPORTS: lime, chestnuts, and wheat
CONTINENT: Europe

SÃO TOMÉ AND PRÍNCIPE

CAPITAL ★ São Tomé
POPULATION: 144,000
MAJOR LANGUAGE: Portuguese
AREA: 370 sq mi; 958 sq km
LEADING EXPORTS: cocoa, coffee, copra, and palm oil
CONTINENT: Africa

SAUDI ARABIA

CAPITAL ★ Riyadh
POPULATION: 19.4 million
MAJOR LANGUAGE: Arabic
AREA: 865,000 sq mi; 2,250,070 sq km
LEADING EXPORT: oil
CONTINENT: Asia

SENEGAL

CAPITAL ★ Dakar
POPULATION: 9.1 million
MAJOR LANGUAGES: French and Wolof
AREA: 75,954 sq mi; 196,722 sq km
LEADING EXPORTS: peanuts, phosphates, and canned fish
CONTINENT: Africa

SEYCHELLES

CAPITAL ★ Victoria
POPULATION: 78,000
MAJOR LANGUAGES: Creole, English, and French
AREA: 175 sq mi; 453 sq km
LEADING EXPORTS: fish, canned tuna, copra, and cinnamon bark
CONTINENT: Africa

SIERRA LEONE
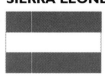
CAPITAL ★ Freetown
POPULATION: 4.8 million
MAJOR LANGUAGES: English, Mende, Temne, and Krio
AREA: 27,925 sq mi; 73,326 sq km
LEADING EXPORTS: diamonds, rutile, bauxite, and cocoa
CONTINENT: Africa

SINGAPORE

CAPITAL ★ Singapore
POPULATION: 3.4 million
MAJOR LANGUAGES: Chinese, English, Malay, and Tamil
AREA: 247 sq mi; 639 sq km
LEADING EXPORTS: petroleum products, rubber, and computer equipment
CONTINENT: Asia

SLOVAKIA

CAPITAL ★ Bratislava
POPULATION: 5.4 million
MAJOR LANGUAGES: Slovak and Hungarian
AREA: 18,917 sq mi; 48,995 sq km
LEADING EXPORTS: machinery, chemicals, fuels, and minerals
CONTINENT: Europe

SLOVENIA

CAPITAL ★ Ljubljana
POPULATION: 2.0 million
MAJOR LANGUAGE: Slovenian
AREA: 7,819 sq mi; 20,251 sq km
LEADING EXPORTS: manufactured goods and chemicals
CONTINENT: Europe

SOLOMON ISLANDS

CAPITAL ★ Honiara
POPULATION: 0.4 million
MAJOR LANGUAGES: English, Pidgin English, and Melanesian
AREA: 11,500 sq mi; 29,785 sq km
LEADING EXPORTS: fish, timber, copra, and palm oil
CONTINENT: Islands in the Pacific Ocean

SOMALIA

CAPITAL ★ Mogadishu
POPULATION: 9.6 million
MAJOR LANGUAGES: Somali and Arabic
AREA: 246,199 sq mi; 637,655 sq km
LEADING EXPORTS: live animals, hides, and bananas
CONTINENT: Africa

SOUTH AFRICA

CAPITALS ★ Pretoria, Cape Town, and Bloemfontein
POPULATION: 41.7 million
MAJOR LANGUAGES: Afrikaans, English, Zulu and other African languages
AREA: 471,440 sq mi; 1,221,030 sq km
LEADING EXPORTS: gold, other minerals, and metals
CONTINENT: Africa

SPAIN

CAPITAL ★ Madrid

POPULATION: 38.8 million

MAJOR LANGUAGES: Spanish and Catalan

AREA: 199,365 sq mi; 505,992 sq km

LEADING EXPORTS: cars and trucks, machinery

CONTINENT: Europe

SRI LANKA

CAPITAL ★ Colombo

POPULATION: 18.5 million

MAJOR LANGUAGES: Sinhala, Tamil, and English

AREA: 25,332 sq mi; 65,610 sq km

LEADING EXPORTS: textiles, tea, rubber, and petroleum products

CONTINENT: Asia

SUDAN

CAPITAL ★ Khartoum

POPULATION: 31.1 million

MAJOR LANGUAGES: Arabic, Nubian and Sudanic languages

AREA: 967,491 sq mi; 2,505,802 sq km

LEADING EXPORTS: cotton, peanuts, gum arabic, and sesame

CONTINENT: Africa

SURINAME

CAPITAL ★ Paramaribo

POPULATION: 0.4 million

MAJOR LANGUAGES: Dutch, English, and Hindi

AREA: 63,251 sq mi; 163,820 sq km

LEADING EXPORTS: bauxite, alumina, rice, and shrimp

CONTINENT: South America

SWAZILAND

CAPITAL ★ Mbabane

POPULATION: 1.0 million

MAJOR LANGUAGES: Siswati and English

AREA: 6,704 sq mi; 17,363 sq km

LEADING EXPORTS: sugar, wood products, asbestos, and citrus

CONTINENT: Africa

SWEDEN

CAPITAL ★ Stockholm

POPULATION: 8.9 million

MAJOR LANGUAGE: Swedish

AREA: 173,800 sq mi; 449,964 sq km

LEADING EXPORTS: machinery, motor vehicles, and wood products

CONTINENT: Europe

SWITZERLAND

CAPITAL ★ Bern

POPULATION: 7.0 million

MAJOR LANGUAGES: German, French, Italian, and Romansch

AREA: 15,941 sq mi; 41,288 sq km

LEADING EXPORTS: machinery, metal products, and textiles

CONTINENT: Europe

SYRIA

CAPITAL ★ Damascus

POPULATION: 15.6 million

MAJOR LANGUAGES: Arabic and Kurdish

AREA: 71,498 sq mi; 185,180 sq km

LEADING EXPORTS: oil, textiles, cotton, fruits, and vegetables

CONTINENT: Asia

TAIWAN

CAPITAL ★ Taipei

POPULATION: 21.3 million

MAJOR LANGUAGES: Mandarin, Taiwanese, and Hakka dialects

AREA: 13,895 sq mi; 35,988 sq km

LEADING EXPORTS: textiles, electronic products, and information products

CONTINENT: Asia

TAJIKISTAN

CAPITAL ★ Dushanbe

POPULATION: 5.9 million

MAJOR LANGUAGES: Tajik and Russian

AREA: 55,300 sq mi; 143,100 sq km

LEADING EXPORTS: aluminum, cotton, and fruit

CONTINENT: Asia

TANZANIA

CAPITAL ★ Dar es Salaam

POPULATION: 29.1 million

MAJOR LANGUAGES: Swahili and English

AREA: 364,879 sq mi; 945,037 sq km

LEADING EXPORTS: coffee, cotton, sisal, and cloves

CONTINENT: Africa

THAILAND

CAPITAL ★ Bangkok

POPULATION: 58.9 million

MAJOR LANGUAGES: Thai and English

AREA: 198,455 sq mi; 514,000 sq km

LEADING EXPORTS: machinery and food

CONTINENT: Asia

COUNTRIES of the WORLD

TOGO

CAPITAL ★ Lomé

POPULATION: 4.6 million

MAJOR LANGUAGES: French, Kabye, Ewe, Mina, and Dagomba

AREA: 21,925 sq mi; 56,785 sq km

LEADING EXPORTS: phosphates, cocoa, coffee, and cotton

CONTINENT: Africa

TONGA

CAPITAL ★ Nuku'alofa

POPULATION: 106,000

MAJOR LANGUAGES: Tongan and English

AREA: 290 sq mi; 751 sq km

LEADING EXPORTS: copra, coconut oil, bananas, and fruits

CONTINENT: Islands in the Pacific Ocean

TRINIDAD AND TOBAGO

CAPITAL ★ Port-of-Spain

POPULATION: 1.3 million

MAJOR LANGUAGES: English, Hindi, and French

AREA: 1,980 sq mi; 5,128 sq km

LEADING EXPORTS: oil and steel products

CONTINENT: North America

TUNISIA

CAPITAL ★ Tunis

POPULATION: 9.0 million

MAJOR LANGUAGES: Arabic and French

AREA: 63,170 sq mi; 163,610 sq km

LEADING EXPORTS: textiles, agricultural products, and chemicals

CONTINENT: Africa

TURKEY

CAPITAL ★ Ankara

POPULATION: 62.5 million

MAJOR LANGUAGES: Turkish, Kurdish, and Arabic

AREA: 300,947 sq mi; 779,452 sq km

LEADING EXPORTS: agricultural products and textiles

CONTINENTS: Asia and Europe

TURKMENISTAN

CAPITAL ★ Ashgabat

POPULATION: 4.1 million

MAJOR LANGUAGES: Turkmen, Russian, and Uzbek

AREA: 188,500 sq mi; 488,100 sq km

LEADING EXPORTS: gas, oil, chemicals, and cotton

CONTINENT: Asia

TUVALU

CAPITAL ★ Funafuti

POPULATION: 10,000

MAJOR LANGUAGES: Tuvaluan and English

AREA: 10 sq mi; 26 sq km

LEADING EXPORT: copra

CONTINENT: Islands in the Pacific Ocean

UGANDA

CAPITAL ★ Kampala

POPULATION: 20.2 million

MAJOR LANGUAGES: English, Luganda, Swahili, and Bantu languages

AREA: 91,459 sq mi; 236,880 sq km

LEADING EXPORTS: coffee, cotton, and tea

CONTINENT: Africa

UKRAINE

CAPITAL ★ Kiev

POPULATION: 50.9 million

MAJOR LANGUAGES: Ukrainian, Russian, Romanian, and Polish

AREA: 233,000 sq mi; 603,700 sq km

LEADING EXPORTS: coal, electric power, and metals

CONTINENT: Europe

UNITED ARAB EMIRATES

CAPITAL ★ Abu Dhabi

POPULATION: 3.1 million

MAJOR LANGUAGES: Arabic, Persian, English, Hindi, and Urdu

AREA: 32,000 sq mi; 82,880 sq km

LEADING EXPORTS: oil and natural gas

CONTINENT: Asia

UNITED KINGDOM

CAPITAL ★ London

POPULATION: 58.5 million

MAJOR LANGUAGES: English, Welsh, and Scottish Gaelic

AREA: 94, 247 sq mi; 244, 100 sq km

LEADING EXPORTS: machinery and chemicals

CONTINENT: Europe

UNITED STATES

CAPITAL ★ Washington, D.C.

POPULATION: 265.1 million

MAJOR LANGUAGES: English and Spanish

AREA: 3,536,341 sq mi; 9,159,123 sq km

LEADING EXPORTS: machinery, chemicals, aircraft, and military equipment

CONTINENT: North America

URUGUAY

CAPITAL ★ Montevideo

POPULATION: 3.2 million

MAJOR LANGUAGES: Spanish and Brazilero

AREA: 68,040 sq mi; 176,224 sq km

LEADING EXPORTS: meat and wool

CONTINENT: South America

UZBEKISTAN

CAPITAL ★ Tashkent

POPULATION: 23.4 million

MAJOR LANGUAGES: Uzbek, Russian, and Tajik

AREA: 172,700 sq mi; 447,400 sq km

LEADING EXPORTS: cotton, gold, textiles, and chemicals

CONTINENT: Asia

VANUATU

CAPITAL ★ Port-Vila

POPULATION: 178,000

MAJOR LANGUAGES: Bislama, English, and French

AREA: 5,700 sq mi; 14,763 sq km

LEADING EXPORTS: copra, cocoa, coffee, and fish

CONTINENT: Islands in the Pacific Ocean

VATICAN CITY (The Holy See)

CAPITAL ★ Vatican City

POPULATION: 830

MAJOR LANGUAGES: Italian and Latin

AREA: 0.17 sq mi; 0.44 sq km

LEADING EXPORTS: (not available)

CONTINENT: Europe

VENEZUELA

CAPITAL ★ Caracas

POPULATION: 22.0 million

MAJOR LANGUAGES: Spanish and Indian dialects

AREA: 352,143 sq mi; 912,050 sq km

LEADING EXPORTS: oil, iron ore, and bauxite

CONTINENT: South America

VIETNAM

CAPITAL ★ Hanoi

POPULATION: 74.0 million

MAJOR LANGUAGES: Vietnamese, French, Chinese, English, and Khmer

AREA: 127,246 sq mi; 329,566 sq km

LEADING EXPORTS: agricultural products, minerals, and marine products

CONTINENT: Asia

YEMEN

CAPITAL ★ San'a

POPULATION: 13.5 million

MAJOR LANGUAGE: Arabic

AREA: 203, 850 sq mi; 527,970 sq km

LEADING EXPORTS: cotton, coffee, hides, and vegetables

CONTINENT: Asia

YUGOSLAVIA

CAPITAL ★ Belgrade

POPULATION: 10.6 million

MAJOR LANGUAGES: Serbo-Croatian and Albanian

AREA: 39,449 sq mi; 102,169 sq km

LEADING EXPORTS: machinery and transport equipment

CONTINENT: Europe

ZAMBIA

CAPITAL ★ Lusaka

POPULATION: 9.2 million

MAJOR LANGUAGES: English and about 70 Bantu dialects

AREA: 290,586 sq mi; 752,618 sq km

LEADING EXPORTS: copper, zinc, lead, cobalt, and tobacco

CONTINENT: Africa

ZIMBABWE

CAPITAL ★ Harare

POPULATION: 11.3 million

MAJOR LANGUAGES: English, Shona, and Sindebele

AREA: 150,698 sq mi; 390,308 sq km

LEADING EXPORTS: gold, tobacco, and asbestos

CONTINENT: Africa

SOURCE: population, languages, area, exports—*Information Please Almanac*, 1997; additional information on languages—*The World Almanac and Book of Facts*, 1997

WORLD HISTORY TIME LINE

	BEFORE 6000 B.C.		6000–5000 B.C.		5000–4000 B.C.	
EUROPE	20,000 years ago	Hunter-gatherers paint the walls of caves near Avignon, France	6000 B.C.	Farming spreads to other parts of the continent	5000 B.C.	Farming villages appear in southern France
	10,000 B.C.	Early Europeans make tiny blades, called *microliths*, out of flint	5500 B.C.	Early pottery decorated with patterned lines is made through much of the continent	4500 B.C.	Stone axes are traded and used to clear forest land for farming
	7000 B.C.	Farming begins in southern Europe, as Greek farmers raise wheat and herd sheep and goats				
AFRICA	10,000 B.C.	People begin to build villages along the Nile River	6000 B.C.	Farmers build irrigation ditches along the Nile River	5000 B.C.	Farmers grow wheat and barley in Egypt
	8000 B.C.	People along the Nile use reed nets to catch fish	6000 B.C.	People use barbed harpoons to catch fish in Africa's rivers and lakes	4500 B.C.	Nubian artisans make pottery in what is now Sudan
	6500 B.C.	Rock paintings in the Sahara Desert show animals long gone from the region, such as buffalo, giraffes and elephants				
ASIA AND AUSTRALIA	40,000 years ago	Aborigines settle in Australia after arriving from Indonesia and Asia	6000 B.C.	Early agriculture begins at Catal Huyuk, in what is today Turkey	5000 B.C.	First towns settled in Sumer
	8000 B.C.	Hunter-gatherers use wild rice in East and Southeast Asia			5000 B.C.	Early settlements emerge in China
	7000 B.C.	Before the development of pottery, early people in western Asia make "white ware" from lime and ash			5000 B.C.	Copper used in Mesopotamia
THE AMERICAS	40,000 years ago	Asian hunters begin to cross the Beringia land bridge	5000 B.C.	Cochise and Chumash cultures develop in southwestern North America	5000 B.C.	Early maize farming begins in what is today Mexico
	15,000 years ago	People have spread throughout the Americas	5000 B.C.	Chinchorros people build settlements in what is today northern Chile	4500 B.C.	Indians use weighted nets to fish the waters of the American northwest
	7000 B.C.	Native American craftworkers use stone tools for woodworking				

4000–3000 B.C.		3000–2000 B.C.		2000–1000 B.C.	
4000 B.C.	Farmers cultivate crops in the British Isles	**3000 B.C.**	Artisans on Crete use bronze and gold	**2000 B.C.**	Minoan palace civilization begins to flourish in Crete
3500 B.C.	New Stone Age period begins in western Europe	**3000 B.C.**	Loom weaving begins in Europe	**1600 B.C.**	Mycenaeans gain power in Aegean region
3300 B.C.	"Iceman" takes his last hike into the Alps	**3000 B.C.**	Huge stone structures built at Stonehenge, England	**1500 B.C.**	Minoan culture ends in Crete
		2200 B.C.	Bronze Age begins in Ireland	**1400 B.C.**	Mycenaean culture spreads to Greece
4000 B.C.	The sail is first used on boats on the Nile River	**2772 B.C.**	Egyptians create a calendar of 365 days	**2000 B.C.**	Kushite culture develops along the Upper Nile
4000 B.C.	Artisans make pottery in Ghana, West Africa	**2600 B.C.**	Pharaoh Khufu orders construction of the Great Pyramid	**1550 B.C.**	Egyptians defeat the Hyksos and begin the New Kingdom period
3200 B.C.	Egyptians begin to develop hieroglyphic writing	**2500 B.C.**	Egyptians build the Great Sphinx at Giza	**1500 B.C.**	Queen Hatshepsut is pharaoh
3100 B.C.	Menes unites Upper and Lower Egypt	**2500 B.C.**	First libraries are built in Egypt	**1362–1352 B.C.**	Tutankhamun is pharaoh
				1250 B.C.	Possible date of Moses' Exodus
4000 B.C.	Sumerians begin to settle in the Fertile Crescent	**3000 B.C.**	City-states begin in Sumer	**1800 B.C.**	Code of Hammurabi recorded
3500 B.C.	City of Ur founded in Mesopotamia	**3000 B.C.**	Plow first used in China	**1700 B.C.**	Babylonians conquer Sumer and more of Mesopotamia
3500 B.C.	Cuneiform writing appears in Sumer	**2500 B.C.**	Writing and trade begin in Indus Valley	**1700 B.C.**	Possible date of Abraham's journey to Canaan
3100 B.C.	Bronzework begins in Mesopotamia	**2300 B.C.**	Mohenjo-Daro and Harappa flourish in Indus River Valley	**1700 B.C.**	The Shang gain control of the Huang Valley
		2250 B.C.	Ziggurat built at Ur	**1500 B.C.**	Aryans migrate into Indus River Valley
3500 B.C.	Villagers in what is now Peru use the llama as a pack animal	**2000 B.C.**	Inuit people hunt caribou and seals in the Arctic	**2000 B.C.**	Andean settlements thrive in Peru
3500 B.C.	Cotton becomes an important crop in what is now Peru			**1400 B.C.**	Farming villages develop in Central America and southwestern North America
3500 B.C.	Haida culture begins on northwest coast of what is now Canada			**1200 B.C.**	Olmec civilization begins in Mexico

WORLD HISTORY TIME LINE

	1000–750 B.C.	750–500 B.C.	500–250 B.C.
EUROPE	**900 B.C.** Etruscans settle north of the Tiber River, in what is now Italy **900 B.C.** Greek city-state of Sparta is founded **776 B.C.** First Olympic Games are held in Greece	**700 B.C.** According to Roman legend, Romulus and Remus found the city on seven hills **700 B.C.** Homer creates the first Greek epics **600–560 B.C.** Aesop tells fables in ancient Greece **509 B.C.** Patricians take power in Rome **500 B.C.** Greeks build the Parthenon to house statues of gods and goddesses	**499 B.C.** Persian Wars begin **450 B.C.** Twelve Tables become basis of Roman Law **431 B.C.** Peloponnesian Wars begin **399 B.C.** Socrates is on trial **336 B.C.** Alexander the Great spreads Greek culture
AFRICA	**900 B.C.** Nok people of Nigeria use terra cotta **900 B.C.** Kushite kingdom in Sudan thrives **814 B.C.** Phoenician traders found colony at Carthage	**700 B.C.** Iron tools made in Egypt **671 B.C.** Assyrians overrun Egypt **600 B.C.** Nok people of Nigeria mine iron **600 B.C.** Carthaginian explorers sail southward from North Africa	**305 B.C.** Ptolemy II founds library in Alexandria **300 B.C.** Kushite kingdom expands and develops extensive trade networks
ASIA AND AUSTRALIA	**950(?)–928 B.C.** King Solomon rules Israel **911 B.C.** Rise of Assyrian power in Mesopotamia	**689 B.C.** Assyrians invade Babylonia and sack Babylon **586 B.C.** Armies of New Babylonia conquer Judah and exile Jews **539 B.C.** Persia's Cyrus the Great conquers Babylon and frees exiled Jews **528 B.C.** Possible date that Siddhartha Gautama, founder of Buddhism, begins teaching in India	**500 B.C.** Indian traders bring Hindu ideas to Southeast Asia **400 B.C.** Buddhism spreads through Asia **400 B.C.** Confucius teaches about duty in China **322 B.C.** Chandragupta founds Mauryan empire in India **273 B.C.** Asoka spreads Buddhist teaching and religious tolerance in India
THE AMERICAS	**1000 B.C.** La Venta becomes center of Olmec culture in Mexico **850 B.C.** Peruvians build temple at Chavín de Huantar in Andes	**600 B.C.** Oaxaca culture begins to dominate Olmec civilization in Mexico	**500 B.C.** Farmers in Ohio Valley construct burial mounds **300–100 B.C.** City of Teotihuacán develops in Mexico

250 B.C.–A.D. 1		A.D. 1–250		A.D. 250–500	
73–71 B.C.	Spartacus leads slave revolt in Rome	A.D. 29	Jesus' religious teachings become the foundation for Christianity	A.D. 306	Constantine rules Roman empire
45 B.C.	Julius Caesar becomes dictator of Rome	A.D. 80	Roman Colosseum is completed	A.D. 312	Christianity tolerated in Roman empire
27 B.C.	Augustus Caesar begins Pax Romana in Roman empire	A.D. 100	Network of Roman roads increases trade and travel through the empire	A.D. 445	Attila the Hun attacks western Europe
				A.D. 476	Rome falls to Germanic invaders
250 B.C.	Kush begins Golden Age, which lasts for about 300 years	A.D. 238	North Africans revolt against Roman empire	A.D. 300	Ptolemy describes Earth-centered universe
202 B.C.	Roman army defeats Hannibal's army at Zama			A.D. 300	Gold-salt trade develops in Ghana
30 B.C.	Egypt becomes Roman province			A.D. 324	King Ezana of Ethiopia becomes a Christian
				A.D. 350	Defeated by Aksum, Kushite civilization at Meroe ends
				A.D. 400	St. Augustine spreads Christianity in North Africa
250 B.C.	Kingdom of Parthia emerges in eastern Persia	A.D. 50	St. Paul spreads Christianity	A.D. 320	Gupta empire emerges in Ganges Valley, India
215 B.C.	Shihuangdi's Qin dynasty begins construction of the Great Wall of China	A.D. 70	Romans destroy Jerusalem, beginning Jewish diaspora	A.D. 330	Constantinople becomes new capital of Roman empire
206 B.C.	Han Dynasty begins in China, adopting many Confucian ideas	A.D. 101	Chinese invent paper	A.D. 400	Chinese manufacture steel
		A.D. 120	Chinese invent seismograph		
		A.D. 220	Fall of Han Dynasty in China		
200 B.C.	Maya culture begins to develop in Central America	A.D. 100	Hopewell culture flourishes on upper Mississippi	A.D. 250	Classic period of Maya civilization in Guatemala, Honduras, and eastern Mexico
200 B.C.	Nazca culture begins in southern Peru	A.D. 100–200	Oaxaca culture reaches height	A.D. 500	Hopewell culture builds burial mounds and makes pottery and iron weapons
100 B.C.	Anasazi culture emerges in southwestern United States				

WORLD HISTORY TIME LINE

	A.D. 500–750		A.D. 750–1000

EUROPE

	A.D. 500–750		A.D. 750–1000
A.D. 500	Middle Ages usually said to begin around this time	A.D. 800	Charlemagne becomes emperor
A.D. 529–534	Byzantine Emperor Justinian issues Codes of Law	A.D. 800	First castles built in western Europe
A.D. 670	Bulgars from Russia settle near Danube River	A.D. 843	Charlemagne's Frankish empire breaks up
A.D. 715	Muslims conquer most of Spain	A.D. 885–886	Vikings raid Paris, France
A.D. 732	Charles Martel, king of Franks, stops Muslim advance into France	A.D. 900	Feudalism is widespread social and economic system
		A.D. 986	Viking explorer Eric the Red founds colony in Greenland

AFRICA

	A.D. 500–750		A.D. 750–1000
A.D. 500	Kingdom of Ghana rises to power in West Africa	A.D. 800	Arabs and Persians explore East African coast and set up trading stations
A.D. 640–641	Islamic leader Caliph Omar conquers Egypt	A.D. 800–950	Christianity continues in Ethiopia after decline of Aksum
A.D. 642	Arabs build first mosque in al-Fustat, new capital of Muslim Egypt	A.D. 950–1050	Igbo-Ukwu culture thrives in eastern Nigeria
A.D. 711	Arab empire conquers North Africa	A.D. 969	Fatimid dynasty conquers Egypt and builds Cairo
		A.D. 970	Fatimids build one of the world's first universities in Cairo
		A.D. 970	Ghana empire flourishes in West Africa

ASIA AND AUSTRALIA

	A.D. 500–750		A.D. 750–1000
A.D. 552	Buddhism spreads to Japan from China and Korea	A.D. 700–1100	Baghdad is capital of Arab empire
A.D. 595	Indian mathematicians use decimal system	A.D. 794–1184	Heian period in Japan
A.D. 605–610	Sui emperors build Grand Canal in China	A.D. 802	Jayavarman II rules the Khmer throne
A.D. 610	According to Muslim sources, the date that Muhammad founds Islam in Arabia	A.D. 868	Chinese use wood blocks to print books
A.D. 622	According to Muslim sources, Muhammad makes the migration, or hijra, from Mecca to Medina	A.D. 889	Khmers build capital at Angkor, in what is today Cambodia
		A.D. 907–26	Mongols conquer inner Mongolia and northern China
		A.D. 970	Chinese introduce paper money

THE AMERICAS

	A.D. 500–750		A.D. 750–1000
A.D. 500	Polynesians from Southeast Asia settle in Hawaiian Islands	A.D. 900	Maya civilization in southern Mexico mysteriously collapses
A.D. 600	Height of Maya civilization	A.D. 900–1000	Pueblo settlements thrive in North America
A.D. 650	Teotihuacán thrives as trade center in Mexico	A.D. 990	Toltec people take over Maya city of Chichén Itzá in Mexico

World Regions in Transition

A.D. 1000–1250		A.D. 1250–1500	
A.D. 1054	Church in Constantinople breaks with Church of Rome	A.D. 1348–1352	Bubonic plague (Black Death) devastates Europe
A.D. 1066	Normans defeat English at Battle of Hastings	A.D. 1350	Renaissance begins in Italy
A.D. 1095	Pope Urban calls for the First Crusade	A.D. 1429	Joan of Arc leads French against the English at Orléans
A.D. 1150	Chartres cathedral built	A.D. 1448	John Gutenberg develops the printing press
A.D. 1209	St. Francis of Assisi founds Franciscan religious order	A.D. 1453	Ottomans capture Constantinople; end of Byzantine empire
A.D. 1215	King John of England signs Magna Carta	A.D. 1478–1492	Renaissance art patron Lorenzo de Medici rules Italy
		A.D. 1492	Columbus sails from Spain to America
		A.D. 1497–1499	Portuguese explorer Vasco da Gama sails around Africa to India
A.D. 1000	Bantu-speaking kingdoms emerge in southern Africa	A.D. 1300	Timbuktu is a major trading center
A.D. 1000	Kingdoms in West Africa flourish from gold trade	A.D. 1324	Mansa Musa, emperor of Mali, goes on pilgrimage to Mecca, Arabia
A.D. 1100	Swahili city-states develop trade with Arabia and India	A.D. 1350	Kingdom of Great Zimbabwe thrives on gold trade
A.D. 1200	City-state of Kilwa prospers	A.D. 1352–1353	Ibn Batuta writes an account of his travels across Africa
A.D. 1235	Sunjata founds Mali empire in West Africa	A.D. 1420	Portuguese sailors begin to explore west coast of Africa
		A.D. 1488	Bartholomeu Dias sails around tip of Africa
		A.D. 1490	Songhai empire begins in West Africa
A.D. 1000	Chinese perfect gunpowder	A.D. 1271	Marco Polo sets out for China
A.D. 1000	Murasaki Shikibu writes *Tale of Genji*	A.D. 1279	Kublai Khan founds Yuan Dynasty
A.D. 1076	Muslim Seljuk Turks capture Jerusalem	A.D. 1301	Osman I founds Ottoman dynasty in Turkey
A.D. 1099	Crusaders from Europe recapture Jerusalem	A.D. 1368	Mongols are driven from China; Ming dynasty begins
A.D. 1100	Samurai dominate Japan	A.D. 1453	Ottoman Turks conquer Constantinople, renaming the city *Istanbul*
A.D. 1100	Angkor Wat is built in what is now Cambodia		
A.D. 1192	Yoritomo becomes first shogun in Japan		
A.D. 1209	Genghis Khan leads Mongols to conquer China		
A.D. 1000	Viking explorer Leif Erickson reaches America	A.D. 1300	Incas expand their empire throughout the central Andes
A.D. 1100	Anasazi people in North America build cliff dwellings at Mesa Verde	A.D. 1325	Aztecs found city of Tenochtitlán in what is today Mexico City
A.D. 1200	Incas in Peru settle at Cuzco	A.D. 1450	Inca city of Machu Picchu built in Peru
		A.D. 1486–1521	Aztec empire at its height
		A.D. 1497	John Cabot claims land in North America for England

WORLD HISTORY TIME LINE

	A.D. 1500–1600	A.D. 1600–1700

EUROPE

A.D. 1503	Leonardo da Vinci paints the *Mona Lisa*
A.D. 1517	Martin Luther nails the 95 Theses on a church door in Germany
A.D. 1519–1522	Ferdinand Magellan's crew completes sailing voyage around the world
A.D. 1534	Henry VIII of England makes himself head of English church
A.D. 1541–1564	John Calvin leads church reforms in Switzerland
A.D. 1550	Reformation spreads throughout Europe
A.D. 1558–1603	Elizabeth I reigns in England
A.D. 1588	English warships fight the Spanish Armada
A.D. 1595	William Shakespeare writes *Romeo and Juliet*

A.D. 1609	Galileo proves the heliocentric theory
A.D. 1643–1715	Louis XIV rules France
A.D. 1653–1658	Oliver Cromwell is Lord Protector of Britain, replacing monarchy with parliamentary rule
A.D. 1682–1725	Peter the Great rules Russia
A.D. 1687	Isaac Newton publishes his "laws of gravity"
A.D. 1689	England's Parliament drafts a Bill of Rights, limiting the power of the monarchy

AFRICA

A.D. 1500	Songhai empire reaches height
A.D. 1575	Portugese begin colonization of Angola
A.D. 1590–591	Moroccan army overthrows Songhai empire
A.D. 1598	Dutch set up trading posts in western Africa

A.D. 1652	Dutch found Cape Town
A.D. 1680	Asante kingdom begins in West Africa

ASIA AND AUSTRALIA

A.D. 1520–1566	Ottoman empire reaches height under Süleyman
A.D. 1556–1605	Mogul emperor Akbar reforms government in India

A.D. 1600–1614	English, Dutch, Danish, and French East India Companies founded
A.D. 1603	Tokugawa period begins in Japan
A.D. 1603	Japan begins to restrict foreign contacts
A.D. 1616	Dutch explorer Dirk Hartog lands on the West Coast of Australia
A.D. 1627	Manchus conquer Korea
A.D. 1632–1648	Shah Jahan builds the Taj Mahal
A.D. 1644	Manchus conquer Beijing and found the Qing dynasty
A.D. 1683	Chinese control Formosa, what is today called Taiwan

THE AMERICAS

A.D. 1500	Pedro Cabral claims Brazil for Portugal
A.D. 1521	Hernando Cortés conquers Aztecs
A.D. 1531–1535	Francisco Pizarro conquers Inca empire
A.D. 1534	Jacques Cartier claims what is now Canada for France
A.D. 1549	Coronado conquers Zuñi pueblos
A.D. 1580	Iroquois League unites Five Nations
A.D. late 1500s	Powhatan confederacy organized

A.D. 1607	The English establish the Jamestown settlement in Virginia
A.D. 1608	French settlers found Quebec
A.D. 1610	Henry Hudson explores Hudson Bay
A.D. 1620	Pilgrims sail to Plymouth in the *Mayflower*
A.D. 1636	Puritans found Harvard University
A.D. 1664	English capture Dutch colony of New Amsterdam and rename it New York
A.D. 1681	Quaker William Penn founds Pennsylvania

A.D. 1700–1800		A.D. 1800–1900	
A.D. 1700	Industrial Revolution begins	A.D. 1804	Napoleon crowns himself emperor
A.D. 1769	James Watt perfects the steam engine	A.D. 1815	Napoleon defeated at Waterloo
A.D. 1776	Adam Smith writes *The Wealth of Nations*	A.D. 1825	The Industrial Revolution spreads to Germany, Belgium, and France
A.D. 1789	French Revolution begins	A.D. 1827	First photograph taken
A.D. 1793	Louis XVI is executed	A.D. 1848	Karl Marx publishes *Communist Manifesto*
A.D. 1799	Napoleon overthrows the French government	A.D. 1861	Serfdom is abolished in Russia
		A.D. 1895	Lumière brothers invent the film projector
		A.D. 1895	Marconi invents radio

A.D. 1720	Yoruba kingdom of Oyo prospers	A.D. 1822	Liberia is founded as home for freed United States slaves
A.D. 1730	More than 50,000 Africans are shipped each year to the Americas as slaves, in the Triangular Trade	A.D. 1840	Zanzibar becomes a commercial center, exporting cloves and other spices
A.D. 1795	British seize Cape Colony from the Dutch	A.D. 1850	Slave trading is abolished in most countries
A.D. 1800	Benin City becomes a center for West African slave trade	A.D. 1853–1856	British explorer Dr. Livingstone crosses Africa
		A.D. 1867	Diamonds discovered in South Africa
		A.D. 1869	The Suez Canal is opened in Egypt
		A.D. 1872	Britain grants Cape Colony self-government

A.D. 1750	Japanese arts and commerce flourish under Tokugawa shogunate	A.D. 1823	The New South Wales Act allows the New South Wales colony in Australia to create a legislative body
A.D. 1750	Rice production in China increases greatly	A.D. 1842	After a war with Britain, China is forced to open its ports to Western traders
A.D. 1770	England's Captain Cook explores eastern coast of Australia	A.D. 1853	Matthew C. Perry enters Edo Bay
A.D. 1784	United States begins to trade with China	A.D. 1854	United States opens Japan to trade
A.D. 1788	The first fleet of ships carrying convicts from England arrives in Australia; the English colony of New South Wales is founded in Australia	A.D. 1868–1912	Meiji restoration in Japan brings industrialization; capital moves to Edo, present-day Tokyo
		A.D. 1894	Women win the right to vote in the Australian colony of South Australia

A.D. 1700	Sugar plantations flourish in Caribbean	A.D. 1804–1806	Louis and Clark explore Louisiana Territory
A.D. 1754–1763	French and Indian War is fought	A.D. 1821	Bolívar frees northern South America
A.D. 1775	American Revolution begins at Lexington	A.D. 1821	San Martín wins independence for Peru
A.D. 1776	Declaration of Independence signed	A.D. 1821	Mexico wins independence from Spain
A.D. 1781	British surrender to Americans at Yorktown	A.D. 1823	Monroe Doctrine opposes European interference in the Western Hemisphere
A.D. 1789	George Washington becomes first President of the United States	A.D. 1836	Texas gains independence from Mexico
A.D. 1791	Toussaint L'Ouverture leads revolt against French in Haiti	A.D. 1861–1865	United States Civil War is fought
		A.D. 1867	Canada's provinces unite
		A.D. 1869	Transcontinental Railroad completed
		A.D. 1876	Alexander Graham Bell invents telephone
		A.D. 1883	Thomas Edison invents lightbulb

WORLD HISTORY TIME LINE

	A.D. 1900–1925		A.D. 1925–1950
EUROPE	A.D. **1905** Einstein publishes his theory of relativity	A.D. **1926**	Scotland's John Logie Baird invents the television
	A.D. **1914** World War I begins	A.D. **1933**	Adolf Hitler rises to power in Germany
	A.D. **1917** Russian Revolution ends Tsarist rule and brings Communist Party to power	A.D. **1933–1945**	About 6 million European Jews are killed during the Holocaust
	A.D. **1919** Treaty of Versailles ends World War I	A.D. **1939**	Germany invades Poland; World War II begins
	A.D. **1920** League of Nations founded	A.D. **1944**	Allies land at Normandy, France on D-Day to free Europe from Hitler's advance
	A.D. **1924** Joseph Stalin becomes dictator of Soviet Union	A.D. **1945**	World War II ends
		A.D. **1945**	The United Nations is created
		A.D. **1949**	As Cold War intensifies, Western nations organize NATO

	A.D. 1900–1925		A.D. 1925–1950
AFRICA	A.D. **1912** The African National Congress is founded in the Union of South Africa	A.D. **1931**	South Africa gains independence from Britain
	A.D. **1914** European powers control nearly all of Africa	A.D. **1931**	First trans-African railway completed
	A.D. **1922** Howard Carter discovers King Tut's tomb	A.D. **1942**	Battle of El Alamein fought in Egypt during World War II
	A.D. **1923** Ethiopia joins League of Nations	A.D. **1948**	Apartheid system begins in South Africa

	A.D. 1900–1925		A.D. 1925–1950
ASIA AND AUSTRALIA	A.D. **1901** The Commonwealth of Australia comes into existence as a new nation	A.D. **1931**	Japanese occupy Chinese province of Manchuria
	A.D. **1910** Japan invades Korea	A.D. **1932**	Abd al-Aziz ibn Saud unifies a new kingdom called Saudi Arabia
	A.D. **1911–1912** Manchu dynasty ends in China; Sun Yat-Sen establishes a republic	A.D. **1934**	Mao Zedong leads Chinese Communists on the Long March
	A.D. **1913** Indian poet Rabindranath Tagore receives Nobel Prize for Literature	A.D. **1937–1945**	War breaks out between China and Japan
	A.D. **1920** Mohandas Gandhi begins nonviolent protest against British rule in India	A.D. **1945**	United States drops first atomic bombs on Hiroshima and Nagasaki
		A.D. **1947**	India and Pakistan gain independence from Britain
		A.D. **1948**	Israel gains independence
		A.D. **1949**	Mao Zedong establishes communist rule in China

	A.D. 1900–1925		A.D. 1925–1950
THE AMERICAS	A.D. **1903** Wright Brothers make first successful airplane flight	A.D. **1929**	Great Depression begins with the New York stock market crash
	A.D. **1908** Henry Ford produces first Model T car	A.D. **1933**	Franklin Roosevelt launches the New Deal to help end the Great Depression
	A.D. **1914** Panama Canal opens	A.D. **1941**	Japanese bomb Pearl Harbor; United States enters World War II
	A.D. **1918** President Wilson proposes "Fourteen Points" as a plan for lasting world peace	A.D. **1945**	United States scientists build first atomic bomb
	A.D. **1920** Women gain voting rights in the United States	A.D. **1948–1951**	The United States' Marshall Plan helps Europe recover from the war

A.D. 1950–1975		A.D. 1975–2000	
A.D. 1955	Communist countries sign the Warsaw Pact	A.D. 1979	Margaret Thatcher becomes first female prime minister of Britain
A.D. 1956	Eastern European countries revolt against communism	A.D. 1980	Lech Walesa leads a strike by Polish workers and starts the Solidarity movement
A.D. 1957	Russians launch *Sputnik* space mission	A.D. 1985	Soviet leader Mikhail Gorbachev introduces *glasnost*
A.D. 1961	Berlin Wall is built	A.D. 1989	Berlin Wall is torn down
		A.D. 1991	Cold War ends as the Soviet Union collapses
		A.D. 1991	Yugoslavia breaks up; civil war begins
		A.D. 1997	President Bill Clinton and Soviet leader Boris Yeltsin sign an agreement in Finland aimed at helping Russia join the global economy

A.D. 1952	Egypt gains independence from Britain	A.D. 1986	Severe droughts hit Africa, especially Ethiopia
A.D. 1956	Egypt takes control of the Suez Canal	A.D. 1986	Western nations put pressure on South Africa to abolish apartheid
A.D. 1957	Ghana gains independence from Britain	A.D. 1992	Foreign troops bring aid to Somalia
A.D. 1958	Sékou Touré used boycotts to help Guinea gain independence from France	A.D. 1993	Apartheid ends in South Africa
A.D. 1963–1990	Nelson Mandela imprisoned in South Africa	A.D. 1994	Nelson Mandela is elected president of South Africa
A.D. 1974	Nigeria becomes leading oil producer in Africa		

A.D. 1950–1953	Korean War is fought	A.D. 1978	Israel and Egypt hold peace-talks at Camp David in the United States
A.D. 1951	Australia forms an economic and political partnership with the United States	A.D. 1980	Iran-Iraq war begins
A.D. 1960	Arab nations form the Organization of Petroleum Exporting Countries, or OPEC	A.D. 1989	Chinese students protest for democracy in Beijing's Tiananmen Square
A.D. 1964	Palestinians found the Palestine Liberation Organization, or PLO	A.D. 1990–1991	Persian Gulf War is fought
A.D. 1966	Indira Gandhi becomes prime minister of India	A.D. 1993	Palestinian and Israeli leaders sign agreement in United States for Palestinian self-rule
A.D. 1965–1975	Vietnam War is fought	A.D. 1997	Jiang Zemin becomes the leader of China after the death of Deng Xiaoping
A.D. 1966–1969	Mao Zedong begins Cultural Revolution in China	A.D. 1997	Hong Kong becomes reunited with China after being a British colony since the 1800s
A.D. 1970	Japan becomes second-largest economic power in the world		

A.D. 1960–1965	Martin Luther King, Jr., leads civil rights movement in the United States	A.D. 1980–1992	Civil war breaks out in El Salvador
A.D. 1962	The United States faces down the Soviet Union in the Cuban Missile Crisis, a tense moment of the Cold War	A.D. 1987	Oscar Arias Sánchez is first Latin American to win Nobel Peace Prize
A.D. 1962	Jamaica gains independence from Britain	A.D. 1990–1991	United States leads fight against Iraq in Persian Gulf War
A.D. 1969	American Neil Armstrong becomes the first person on the moon	A.D. 1993	Floods in Mississippi River basin destroy homes and crops
		A.D. 1995	Canadians in Quebec narrowly vote to remain a part of Canada

Dictionary of GEOGRAPHIC TERMS

ARCHIPELAGO (är kə pel′ə gō) A group or chain of islands.

STRAIT (strāt) A narrow waterway that connects two larger bodies of water.

GULF (gulf) Part of an ocean that extends into the land; larger than a bay.

PLATEAU (pla tō′) An area of elevated flat land.

DAM (dam) A wall built across a river, creating a lake that stores water.

RESERVOIR (rez′ər vwär) A natural or artificial lake used to store water.

CANYON (kan′yən) A deep, narrow valley with steep sides.

MESA (mā′sə) A hill with a flat top; smaller than a plateau.

DUNE (dün) A mound, hill, or ridge of sand heaped up by the wind.

HILL (hil) A rounded, raised landform; not as high as a mountain.

BUTTE (būt) A small, flat-topped hill; smaller than a mesa or plateau.

OASIS (ō ā′sis) A fertile area in a desert that is watered by a spring.

VALLEY (val′ē) An area of low land between hills or mountains.

COAST (cōst) The land along an ocean.

DESERT (dez′ərt) A dry environment with few plants and animals.

BAY (bā) Part of an ocean or lake that extends deeply into the land.

ISTHMUS (is′məs) A narrow strip of land that connects two larger bodies of land.

ISLAND (ī′lənd) A body of land completely surrounded by water.

PENINSULA (pə nin′sə lə) A body of land nearly surrounded by water.

R46

VOLCANO (vol kā′nō) An opening in Earth's surface through which hot rock and ash are forced out.

MOUNTAIN (moun′tən) A high landform with steep sides; higher than a hill.

PEAK (pēk) The top of a mountain.

HARBOR (här′bər) A sheltered place along a coast where boats dock safely.

GLACIER (glā′shər) A huge sheet of ice that moves slowly across the land.

CANAL (kə nal′) A channel built to carry water for irrigation or navigation.

LAKE (lāk) A body of water completely surrounded by land.

PORT (pôrt) A place where ships load and unload their goods.

TRIBUTARY (trib′yə ter ē) A smaller river that flows into a larger river.

SOURCE (sôrs) The starting point of a river.

TIMBERLINE (tim′bər lin) A line beyond which trees do not grow.

RIVER BASIN (riv′ər bā′sin) All the land that is drained by a river and its tributaries.

WATERFALL (wô′tər fôl) A flow of water falling vertically.

MOUNTAIN RANGE (moun′tən rānj) A row or chain of mountains.

PLAIN (plān) A large area of nearly flat land.

RIVER (riv′ər) A stream of water that flows across the land and empties into another body of water.

BASIN (bā′sin) A bowl-shaped landform surrounded by higher land.

DELTA (del′tə) Land made of silt left behind as a river drains into a larger body of water.

MOUNTAIN PASS (moun′tən pas) A narrow gap through a mountain range.

MOUTH (mouth) The place where a river empties into a larger body of water.

FJORD (fyôrd) A deep, narrow inlet of an ocean between high, steep cliffs.

OCEAN (ō′shən) A large body of salt water; oceans cover much of Earth's surface.

Gazetteer

Gazetteer

This Gazetteer is a geographical dictionary that will help you to pronounce and locate the places discussed in this book. Latitude and longitude are given for cities and some other places. The page numbers tell you where each place appears on a map or in the text.

A

Aachen (ä′khən) Capital of Charlemagne's empire, c. 800; a city in present-day Germany; 51°N, 6°E. (m. 321, t. 321)

Accra (ə krä′) The capital and largest city of Ghana; 6°N, 0°. (m. 570, t. 568)

Acropolis (ə krop′ə lis) A hill in ancient Athens that became a religious center and meeting place; site of the Parthenon. (t. 205)

Africa (af′ri kə) The world's second-largest continent, lying south of Europe between the Atlantic and Indian oceans. (m. 607, t. 354)

Agra (ä′grə) A city in north-central India; capital of the Mogul empire around 1564–1658; 27°N, 78°E. (m. 393, t. 394)

Aksum (äk′süm) A powerful African kingdom and trading center, about 350–900, located in what is today Ethiopia. (m. 359, t. 359)

Alexandria (al ig zan′drē ə) A city in Egypt founded c. 332 B.C. by Alexander the Great; 31°N, 30°E. (m. 214, t. 214)

Alps (alps) Europe's highest mountains, extending in an arc from the Mediterranean coast to the Balkan peninsula. (m. 33, t. 33)

Anatolia (an ə tō′lē ə) Asia Minor; a peninsula in western Asia. (m. 390, t. 388)

Andes Mountains (an′dēz moun′tənz) The world's longest mountain chain, stretching along the west coast of South America. (m. 423, t. 422)

Angkor (ang′kôr) Ruined city in Cambodia; capital of the Khmer around 850–1430; 14°N, 104°E. (m. 399, t. 400)

Antarctica (ant ärk′ti kə) An ice-covered continent surrounding the South Pole. (m. G5)

Anyang (än′yäng) The ancient Chinese capital of the Shang dynasty; 36°N, 114°E. (m. 165, t. 165)

Apennine Mountains (ap′ə nīn moun′tənz) A mountain range on the Italian peninsula. (m. 225, t. 225)

Arabia (ə rā′bē ə) A large peninsula in southwestern Asia. (m. 263, t. 262)

Arabian Sea (ə rā′bē ən sē) A body of water that lies between Arabia and India; the northwestern part of the Indian Ocean. (m. 263, t. 263)

Arctic Ocean (ärk′tik ō′shən) The body of water north of the Arctic Circle and surrounding the North Pole. (m. G5)

Asia (ā′zhə) The largest continent, bounded on the west by Europe and Africa, on the south by the Indian Ocean, and on the east by the Pacific. (m. 616, t. 586)

Athens (ath′ənz) For many centuries the most powerful of all ancient Greek city-states; capital of present-day Greece; 38°N, 23°E. (m. 198, t. 197)

Atlantic Ocean (at lan′tik ō′shən) The body of water separating Europe and Africa from North and South America. (m. G5, t. 317)

Attica (at′i kə) A peninsula in east-central Greece on the Aegean Sea on which Athens was built. (m. 193, t. 193)

Australia (ôs trāl′yə) The world's smallest continent, bounded by the Indian and Pacific oceans; also a country. (m. 616, t. 478)

B

Babylonia (bab ə lō′nē ə) An ancient Mesopotamian empire that extended throughout the Fertile Crescent in the 1700s B.C. (m. 110, t. 112)

Baghdad (bag′dad) Capital and cultural center of the Muslim caliphate from A.D. 762 to 1100; present-day capital of Iraq; 33°N, 44°E. (m. 273, t. 272)

Balkan Peninsula (bôl′kən pə nin′sə lə) A peninsula in southern Europe, bounded by the Black, Aegean, and Adriatic seas. (m. 601, t. 600)

pronunciation key

a	at	ī	ice	u	up	th	thin
ā	ape	îr	pierce	ū	use	th	this
ä	far	o	hot	ü	rule	zh	measure
âr	care	ō	old	ù	pull	ə	about, taken,
e	end	ô	fork	ûr	turn		pencil, lemon,
ē	me	oi	oil	hw	white		circus
i	it	ou	out	ng	song		

Bangladesh (bän glə desh′) A nation established in 1971 on the Indian subcontinent, and mostly surrounded by India; formerly known as East Pakistan. (m. 583, t. 584)

Bastille (bas tēl′) A prison fortress in Paris that was attacked and destroyed on July 14, 1789, at the start of the French Revolution. (t. 488)

Beijing (bā′jing′) The capital of the People's Republic of China; first became China's capital during the reign of Kublai Khan in the 1200s; 40°N, 116°E. (m. 403, t. 403)

Beringia (bə rin′jē ə) A land bridge that connected North America and Asia during the Ice Age; located where the Bering Strait is today. (m. 285, t. 286)

Berlin (bər lin′) The capital of Germany, divided from 1945 to 1990 into West Berlin and East Berlin; 53°N, 13°E. (m. 601, t. 558)

Bethlehem (beth′lə hem) A small town south of Jerusalem where Jesus is said to have been born; 31°N, 35°E. (m. 247, t. 247)

Border Cave (bôr′dər kāv) A major archaeological site in Zululand, South Africa and home of Old Stone Age hunters and gatherers; 27°S, 32°E. (m. 47, t. 46)

Bowating (bō′ä ting) An Ojibwa village that was located on an island in the river connecting lakes Superior and Huron; 46°N, 83°W. (m. 441, t. 441)

Brazil (brə zil′) The largest nation in South America, on the northeastern part of the continent. (m. 623, t. 622)

Burma (bər′mə) A nation in Southeast Asia on the Bay of Bengal; now known as Myanmar. (m. 587, t. 586)

Byzantine empire (bi′zən tēn em′pīr) The name by which the eastern half of the Roman empire became known some time after A.D. 400. (m. 254, t. 255)

C

Cairo (kī′rō) The capital of modern Egypt and the largest city in Africa; 30°N, 31°E. (m. 570, t. 569)

Cambodia (kam bō′dē ə) A nation in Southeast Asia. (m. 587, t. 586)

Canada (kan′ə də) A country in North America bordering the United States. (m. 623, t. 622)

Canadian Shield (kə nā′dē ən shēld) A large rocky plain in northern Canada that was formed by glaciers during the Ice Age. (m. 423, t. 423)

Cape Town (kāp toun) Seaport city in South Africa, settled by the Dutch in the late 1600s; 34°S, 18°E. (m. 607, t. 606)

Caribbean Sea (kar ə bē′ən sē) A sea bounded on the north and east by the West Indies, and by Central and South America on the west and south. (m. 475, t. 474)

Carthage (kär′thij) An ancient city on the north coast of Africa; 37°N, 10°E. (m. 234, t. 234)

Central Plateau (sen′trəl pla tō′) A high plateau extending throughout central Mexico and bounded by high mountain ranges. (m. 287, t. 287)

Chartres (shärt) A city in northwestern France, noted for its cathedral; 48°N, 1°E. (m. 334, t. 332)

China (chī′nə) A nation in East Asia, and the most populous country in the world. (m. 616, t. 618)

Colosseum (kä lə sē′əm) A large stadium in ancient Rome where athletic events took place. (t. 241)

Constantinople (kon stan tə nō′pəl) A city established as the new eastern capital of the Roman empire by the emperor Constantine in A.D. 330, now called Istanbul; 41°N, 29°E. (m. 254, t. 254)

Copán (kō pän′) An ancient city of Middle America, in what is now Honduras, that was a center of classic Maya culture; 15°N, 89°W. (m. 299, t. 299)

Crete (krēt) A Greek island in the Mediterranean Sea, southeast of Greece. (m. 193, t. 193)

Cuzco (küs′kō) A city in southern Peru; capital of the Inca empire from the 1200s to the 1500s; 14°S, 72°W. (m. 435, t. 435)

D

Dolores (də lôr′əs) A city in central Mexico where Miguel Hidalgo began Mexico's independence movement in 1810; 29°N, 108°W. (m. 493, t. 494)

Dominican Republic (də min′i kən ri pub′lik) A Caribbean nation, on the eastern part of Hispaniola, that gained independence in 1844. (m. 623, t. 623)

E

Edo (ed′ō) The former name of Tokyo, Japan; became capital under the rule of the Tokugawa shoguns in the 1600s; 36°N, 140°E. (m. 411, t. 412)

Egypt (ē′jipt) A country in northeast Africa; birthplace of ancient Egyptian civilization. (m. 570, t. 569)

England (ing′glənd) Part of the United Kingdom, on the island of Great Britain. (m. 321, t. 326)

Ethiopia (ē thē ō′pē ə) A country in eastern Africa. (m. 607, t. 358)

Euphrates River (ū frā′tēz riv′ər) A river in southwestern Asia that flows through the southern part of the Fertile Crescent. (m. 105, t. 104)

Eurasia (yü rā′zhə) A large land mass that includes the continents of Europe and Asia. (t. 316)

Europe (yür′əp) The continent north of Africa between Asia and the Atlantic Ocean. (m. 601, t. 316)

F

Fertile Crescent (fûrt′əl kres′ənt) A fertile region in southwestern Asia that includes the region of Mesopotamia. (m. 105, t. 104)

Florence (flôr′əns) A city in present-day Italy; one of the great centers of Renaissance art; 44°N, 11°E. (m. 334, t. 337)

Forbidden City (fər bid′ən sit′ē) A walled area in Beijing built 1417–1420, during the Ming dynasty, that contained the palaces of the emperors. (t. 404)

Forum (for′əm) The city market and meeting place in the center of ancient Rome. (t. 233)

G

Gaul (gôl) An ancient region and Roman province that included most of present-day France. (m. 240, t. 237)

Gaza (gä′zə) A territory between Egypt and Israel on the southeastern coast of the Mediterranean Sea. Controlled by Israel from 1967 to 1994, after which it began to return to Palestinian control. (m. 578, t. 577)

Ghana (gä′nə) An empire, about 400–1235, located at the southwestern edge of the Sahara Desert; a present-day country in western Africa on the Gulf of Guinea. (m. 364, t. 363)

Gobi Desert (gō′bē dez′ərt) A large desert in east-central Asia. (m. 385, t. 386)

Golan Heights (gō′län hīts) Land occupied by Israel after the Six-Day War. 1967 (m. 578, t. 577)

Great Lakes (grāt lāks) A group of five large freshwater lakes on the border between the United States and Canada. (m. 423, t. 422

Great Rift Valley (grāt rift val′ē) A series of cliffs and canyons caused by powerful prehistoric earthquakes that extends from Mozambique in southeastern Africa north to the Red Sea. (m. 355, t. 355)

Great Wall of China (grāt wôl əv chi′nə) A long defensive wall extending 1,500 miles (2,415 km) through northern China; built between 1300 and 1600. (m. 172, t. 170)

Great Zimbabwe (grāt zim bäb′wā) A city in southern Africa that rose to power in the 1300s through gold mining and trading; 20°S, 30°E. (m. 377, t. 376)

H

Haiti (hā′tē) A Caribbean nation, on the western part of Hispaniola, that gained independence from France in 1804. (m. 623, t. 623

Harappa (hə ra′pə) A city of the ancient Harappan civilization, c. 2500–1600 B.C., located in the Indus Valley of South Asia; 31°N, 73°E. (m. 135, t. 135)

Himalayas (him ə lā′əz) The world's highest mountain range, forming the northern border of the Indian subcontinent. (m. 131, t. 131)

Hispaniola (his pən yō′lə) A Caribbean island settled by Spaniards in 1493; a present-day island that is divided into the Dominican Republic and Haiti. (m. 467, t. 467)

Hong Kong (häng käng) A large city and center of international trade developed as a British colony in mainland China; 22°N, 114°E. (m. 616, t. 619)

Huang River (hwäng riv′ər) [Yellow River] A river that flows from the Tibetan plateau, across northern China, and into the Yellow Sea. (m. 161, t. 160)

I

India (in′dē ə) The largest nation of the Indian subcontinent; became independent from British rule in 1947. (m. 583, t. 580)

Indian Ocean (in′dē ən ō′shən) The body of water south of Asia, between Africa and Australia. (m. G5, t. 372)

Indus Plain (in′dəs plān) A vast, dry region south of the Himalayas that is made fertile by deposits of silt from the Indus River; birthplace of the ancient Harappan civilization. (m. 131, t. 131)

Indus River (in′dəs riv′ər) A river that flows from Tibet, through the Himalayas and Hindu Kush into the Arabian Sea. (m. 131, t. 130)

Iraq (i rak′) A nation of western Asia that became independent in 1932. (m. 576, t. 576)

Israel (iz′rē əl) A country in western Asia, created in 1948 as a home for the Jews; ancient kingdom of Israelites. (m. 576, t. 577)

Istanbul (is tan bül′) Largest city in present-day Turkey; formerly the ancient city of Constantinople and later the capital of the Ottoman empire; 41°N, 29°E. (m. 390, t. 388)

J

Japan (jə pan′) An island nation off the eastern Asia mainland. (m. 616, t. 614)

Jerusalem (jə rü′sə ləm) An ancient city in western Asia; capital of present-day Israel; 31°N, 35°E. (m. 121, t. 124)

Johannesburg (jō han′əs bərg) The largest city in South Africa; 26°S, 28°E. (m. 607, t. 608)

Judea (jü dē′ə) The land in the eastern Mediterranean region populated by Jews at the time of the Roman empire. (m. 247, t. 246)

K

Kosala (kō sa′lə) An ancient kingdom in northern India where Siddhartha Gautama is said to have been born. (t. 151)

Kush (kush) An ancient kingdom in northeastern Africa, conquered by Egypt. It later regained independence and flourished through trade between c. 500 B.C. and A.D. 150. (m. 86, t. 86)

Kyoto (kyō′tō) A city in Japan; formerly the emperor's capital during the rule of the shoguns; 35°N, 136°E. (m. 411, t. 413)

L

La Venta (lə vent′ə) An ancient island town of Middle America on the east coast of what is now Mexico; center of Olmec culture in 1000 B.C.; 18°N, 94°W. (m. 293, t. 294)

Lake Texcoco (lāk tā skō′kō) A lake in what is now Central Mexico on which the Aztec built Tenochtitlán. (t. 427)

Laos (lä′ōs) A nation in Southeast Asia, between northern Thailand and northern Vietnam. (m. 587, t. 586)

Latium (lā′shē əm) A plain on the west coast of Italy on which the city of Rome was built. (m. 225, t. 225)

Lima (lē′mə) The capital of Peru, founded by Francisco Pizarro in 1535; 12°S, 77°W. (m. 467, t. 469)

Lower Egypt (lō′ər ē′jipt) The northern part of ancient Egypt. (m. 71, t. 71)

M

Macedonia (mas i dō′nē ə) An ancient kingdom ruled by Alexander the Great that conquered Greece and the Persian empire in the 300s B.C. (m. 214, t. 213)

Machu Picchu (mäch′ü pēk′chü) The site of a ruined Inca city on a mountain in the Andes northwest of Cuzco, Peru; 13°S, 72°W. (m. 435, t. 438)

Mali (mä′lē) African empire that flourished between the 1200s and 1400s; a present-day country in West Africa. (m. 364, t. 364)

Mecca (mek′ə) An Arabian oasis city believed to be the birthplace of Muhammad; 21°N, 40°E. (m. 267, t. 267)

Medina (mə dē′nə) An Arabian oasis town to which, according to Muslim writings, Muhammad migrated in A.D. 622; 24°N, 40°E. (m. 267, t. 268)

Mediterranean Sea (med i tə rā′nē ən sē) A large, almost landlocked arm of the Atlantic Ocean touching Europe, Asia, and Africa. (m. 193, t. 192)

Mekong River (mā′kong′ riv′ər) A river in Southeast Asia that flows from Tibet to the South China Sea. (m. 399, t. 398)

Memphis (mem′fis) Capital of Egypt's Old Kingdom, located on the Nile near present-day Cairo; 29°N, 31°E. (m. 76, t. 76)

Mesopotamia (mes ə pə tä′mē ə) The region between the Tigris and Euphrates rivers; birthplace of the Sumerian and Babylonian civilizations. (m. 105, t. 105)

Mexico (mek′si kō) A nation in North America, south of the United States. (m. 623, t. 624)

Mexico City (mek′si kō sit′ē) The capital and largest city of Mexico; formerly Tenochtitlán, it became the capital of New Spain after the Spanish conquered the Aztec in the 1500s; 19°N, 99°W. (m. 467, t. 469)

Middle America (mid′əl ə mer′i kə) An ancient region of North America that included southern Mexico and much of Central America. It was the birthplace of the ancient Olmec and Maya civilizations. (m. 287, t. 286)

Middle East (mid′əl ēst) A region of southwestern Asia that stretches from Turkey to Iran. (m. 576, t. 574)

Mogadishu (mōg ə dish′ü) A coastal city that dominated African gold trade between about 1000 and 1300; the present-day capital of Somalia; 2°N, 45°E. (m. 373, t. 374)

Mohenjo-Daro (mō hen′jō där′ō) A city of the ancient Harappan civilization, located in the Indus Valley; 27°N, 68°E. (m. 135, t. 135)

Mombasa (mom bä′sä) An important Swahili city-state and trading center between 1100 and 1500; the main port of Kenya on the Indian Ocean; 4°N, 40°E. (m. 373, t. 374)

Morocco (mə rok′ō) A country in northwestern Africa on the Atlantic Ocean and Mediterranean Sea. (m. 570, t. 367)

Moscow (mäs′kou) The capital and largest city of Russia; 56°N, 38°E. (m. 533, t. 536)

Mount Everest (mount ev′ər əst) The tallest mountain in the world, located in the Himalayas on the border between Nepal and Tibet; 28°N, 87°E. (m. 385, t. 385)

Mount Kilimanjaro (mount kil ə mən jär′ō) The tallest mountain in Africa, located in northeastern Tanzania; 3°S, 37°E. (m. 355, t. 355)

pronunciation key

a at; ā ape; ä far; âr care; e end; ē me; i it; ī ice; îr pierce; o hot; ō old; ô fork; oi oil; ou out; u up; ū use; ü rule; u̇ pull; ûr turn; hw white; ng song; th thin; th this; zh measure; ə about, taken, pencil, lemon, circus

Mount Olympus (mount ə lim′pəs) The highest mountain in Greece, where the ancient Greeks believed many of their gods and goddesses lived; 40°N, 22°E. (m. 198, t. 200)

N

Nazareth (na′ zə rəth) A small town in northern Judea where, according to the New Testament, Jesus grew up; 32°N, 35°E. (m. 247, t. 247)

New Delhi (nü del′ē) The capital of India and one of the most populous cities in the world; 29°N, 77°E. (m. 15, t. 15)

New South Wales (nü south wālz) English Colony founded on the East Coast of Australia in 1788; currently a state of Australia. (m. 479, t. 478)

New Spain (nü spān) Spanish colony in North America including Mexico, Central America, the southwest United States, and many of the Caribbean Islands from the 1500s to the 1800s. (m. 467, t. 469)

Niger River (nī′jər riv′ər) A river flowing from western Africa into the Gulf of Guinea. (m. 355, t. 355)

Nile River (nīl riv′ər) The world's longest river, which flows northward through East Africa into the Mediterranean Sea. (m. 71, t. 70)

Normandy (nôr′mən dē) A region in northwestern France on the English Channel. (m. 545, t. 326)

North America (nôrth ə mâr′i kə) The third-largest continent, located in the Western Hemisphere. (m. 623, t. 440)

North China Plain (nôrth chī′nə plān) A large, lowland region of eastern China that is watered by the Huang River; birthplace of Chinese civilization. (m. 161, t. 160)

North European Plain (nôrth yur ə pē′ən plān) A large, fertile area that extends from the Atlantic Ocean to the Ural Mountains. (m. 317, t. 318)

North Sea (nôrth sē) A large arm of the Atlantic Ocean, between Great Britain and continental Europe. (m. 317, t. 317)

Nubia (nü′bē ə) An ancient kingdom south of Egypt. (m. 86, t. 84)

Nunavut (nü′ nü vüt) A territory in Canada that is to be created for the Inuit in 1999. (t. 626)

P

Pacific Ocean (pə sif′ik ō′shən) The world's largest body of water, bounded by the Americas on the east and Asia and Australia on the west. (m. G5, t. 410)

Pakistan (pak′i stan) One of two independent nations formed in 1947 on the Indian subcontinent. (m. 583, t. 583)

Palestine (pal′ə stīn) Region in southwestern Asia that became the ancient home of the Jews; the ancient Roman name for Judea; in recent times, the British protectorate that became Israel in 1947. (m. 254, t. 253)

Pantheon (pan′thē on) A large, domed temple built in ancient Rome to honor many gods and goddesses. (t. 241)

Paris (par′is) Capital and largest city of France; 49°N, 2°E. (m. 601, t. 488)

Parthenon (pär′thə non) A temple to the goddess Athena, built 447–432 B.C. on the Acropolis in Athens. (t. 205)

Pearl Harbor (pûrl här′bər) A United States naval base in Hawaii that was bombed by the Japanese in 1941, causing the United States to enter World War II; 21°N, 158°W. (m. 544, t. 543)

Peloponnesus (pel ə pə nē′səs) A mountainous peninsula in southern Greece, between the Ionian and Aegean seas. (m. 193, t. 193)

Persian Gulf (pûr′zhən gulf) A body of water east of the Arabian peninsula that separates Arabia from Iran. (m. 263, t. 263)

Peru (pə rü′) Colonial lands held by Spain in South America from the 1500s to the 1800s; present-day country in western South America. (m. 467, t. 469)

Petra (pē′trə) The ancient Arabian capital of Nabataea, in what is today Jordan; 30°N, 35°E. (t. 264)

Phnom Penh (pə nom′ pen′) The capital of Cambodia; first became capital during the Khmer rule in the 1400s; 12°N, 105°E. (m. 399, t. 401)

Phoenicia (fə nē′shə) An ancient seafaring civilization located on the eastern shore of the Mediterranean Sea. (m. 193, t. 195)

Pompeii (pom pā′) An ancient city in southwestern Italy that was buried by the eruption of Mount Vesuvius in A.D. 79; 41°N, 14°E. (m. 240, t. 242)

Punt (punt) An ancient Egyptian name for an area of Africa south of Egypt. (m. 86, t. 87)

Q

Qin (chin) An ancient province in northern China that rose to power under Emperor Shihuangdi in 221 B.C. (m. 169, t. 168)

Qinling Mountains (chin′ling′ moun′tənz) A mountain range in north-central China. (m. 169, t. 169)

R

Red Sea (red sē) A narrow sea between Arabia and northeastern Africa. (m. 263, t. 263)

Rhodes (rōdz) A Greek island, lying east of Crete in the Aegean Sea. (m. 193, t. 193)

Rocky Mountains (rok′ē moun′tənz) A mountain range in North America that stretches from Alaska into Mexico. (m. 423, t. 422)

Rome (rōm) The former center of both the ancient Roman Republic and the Roman empire; capital of present-day Italy; 42°N, 12°E. (m. 225, t. 224)

Russia (rush′ə) A country in eastern Europe and northern Asia; the largest country in the world; a republic of the Soviet Union from 1922 to 1991. (m. 533, t. 532)

S

Sahara Desert (sə har′ə dez′ərt) The largest desert in the world, covering most of northern Africa. (m. 355, t. 355)

Sahel (sə həl′) The dry, grassy region south of the Sahara Desert, extending from Senegal to the Sudan. (m. 355, t. 355)

Santo Domingo (san′tō də ming′gō) A Spanish colony established on Hispaniola in 1496; the capital of the Dominican Republic; 19°N, 70°W. (m. 475, t. 475)

Sarajevo (sar ə yā′vō) The site of assassination that led to World War I; present-day capital of Bosnia; 44°N, 18°E. (m. 601, t. 527)

Seine River (sān riv′ər) A river that flows from eastern France northward into the English Channel. (m. 317, t. 319)

Serbia (sûr′bē ə) A country in eastern Europe. (m. 528, t. 527)

Sicily (sis′ə lē) An island in the Mediterranean Sea off the southwest tip of the Italian peninsula. (m. 225, t. 225)

Singapore (sing′ə pôr) A city and independent republic in Southeast Asia; 1°N, 104°E. (m. 616, t. 617)

Sofala (sō fäl′ə) A seaport village in eastern Mozambique; in the 1300s, an important trading center for the gold miners of Great Zimbabwe; 19°S, 35°E. (m. 377, t. 378)

Songhai (sông′hī) The most powerful empire in West Africa from about 1490 to 1590. (m. 364, t. 367)

South America (south ə mâr′i kə) The fourth-largest continent, located in the Western Hemisphere. (m. 623, t. 491)

South Korea (south kə rē′ə) A country in East Asia on the southern part of the Korean Peninsula; also a Pacific Rim nation. (m. 616, t. 617)

Southeast Asia (south ēst′ ā′zhə) A region of southern Asia bounded by the Indian and Pacific Oceans. (m. 587, t. 586)

Soviet Union (sō′vē et ūn′yən) The name commonly used for the Union of Soviet Socialist Republics, which was a country in eastern Europe and northern Asia; the largest country in the world from 1922–1991. (m. 544, t. 537)

Soweto (sə wē′tō) A black African township just outside Johannesburg, South Africa; 26°S, 28°E. (m. 607, t. 608)

Sparta (spär′tə) The largest ancient Greek city-state, located on the southern Peloponnesus; 37°N, 22°E. (m. 198, t. 198)

St. Petersburg (sānt pē′tərz bûrg) A Russian port city on the Baltic Sea; formerly the capital of Russia, it was called Leningrad when Russia was part of the Soviet Union; 60°N, 30°E. (m. 533, t. 534)

Strait of Magellan (strāt əv mə jel′ən) A narrow waterway at the southern tip of South America, linking the Atlantic and Pacific oceans. (m. 464, t. 465)

Suez Canal (sü ez′ kə nal′) A canal in northeastern Egypt connecting the Mediterranean and Red seas. (t. 569)

Sumer (sü′mər) A group of ancient city-states in southern Mesopotamia; the earliest civilization in Mesopotamia. (m. 110, t. 108)

T

Taj Mahal (täzh mə häl′) A grand tomb in Agra, India, built by Mogul emperor Shah Jahan to honor his wife. (t. 396)

Tenochtitlán (te noch tēt län′) The capital of the Aztec empire, founded around 1325 on the site of present-day Mexico City; 19°N, 99°W. (m. 427, t. 426)

Thailand (tī′land) A nation in Southeast Asia, formerly called Siam. (m. 587, t. 586)

Thebes (thēbz) An ancient city in Upper Egypt that became the capital of the New Kingdom; 26°N, 33°E. (m. 76, t. 81)

Tiananmen Square (tyen′än men skwâr) A square in Beijing, China where government troops killed hundreds of people who were demonstrating for democratic reform in 1989. (t. 619)

pronunciation key

a at; ā ape; ä far; âr care; e end; ē me; i it; ī ice; îr pierce; o hot; ō old; ô fork; oi oil; ou out; u up; ū use; ü rule, ù pull; ûr turn; hw white; ng song; th thin; th this; zh measure; ə about, taken, pencil, lemon, circus

Gazetteer

Tiber River (tī'bər riv'ər) A river flowing southward from north-central Italy across the Latium plain, and into the Tyrrhenian Sea. (m. 225, t. 225)

Tibetan Plateau (ti bet'ən pla tō') A high mountain plateau in Asia. (m. 385, t. 385)

Tigris River (tī'gris riv'ər) A river in southwestern Asia that flows through the eastern part of the Fertile Crescent. (m. 105, t. 104)

Timbuktu (tim buk tü') A trade and cultural center of the Songhai empire in the 1400s; a present-day town in the West African country of Mali; 16°N, 3°W. (m. 364, t. 364)

Tokyo (tō'kyō) The capital and largest city in Japan; formerly called Edo; 36°N, 140°W. (m. 411, t. 412)

Tonle Sap (tän lä' sap') A lake in western Cambodia. (m. 399, t. 399)

Turkey (tûr'kē) A nation established in 1923 in western Asia and southeastern Europe. (m. 576, t. 576)

U

United States (ū nī'tid stāts) A nation mainly in North America consisting of fifty states, the District of Columbia, and several territories. (m. 623, t. 622)

Upper Egypt (up'ər ē'jipt) The southern part of ancient Egypt. (m. 71, t. 71)

V

Valley of Mexico (val'ē əv mek'si kō) A fertile valley between two mountain chains in central Mexico. (t. 427)

Valley of the Kings (val'ē əv thə kingz) West of Thebes in ancient Egypt, the burial place of 30 New Kingdom pharaohs; 26°N, 33°E. (m. 93, t. 88)

Venezuela (ven ə zwā'lə) A country in northern South America on the Caribbean Sea. (m. 493, t. 496)

Versailles (vâr sī') A historic city in north-central France that contains the grand palace of Louis XIV; 49°N, 2°E. (t. 488)

Vietnam (vē et näm') A nation in Southeast Asia that was divided from 1954 until 1975 into North Vietnam and South Vietnam. (m. 581, t. 586)

W

West Bank (west bangk) An area in western Asia west of the Jordan River; controlled by Israel from 1967 to 1995, after which Palestinians gained partial control. (m. 578, t. 577)

West Indies (west in'dēz) An archipelago stretching from Florida to Venezuela, separating the Caribbean Sea from the Atlantic Ocean. (m. 475, t. 474)

X

Xianyang (shē än'yang) Capital city of the Qin dynasty during the rule of the emperor Shihuangdi; 34°N, 109°E. (m. 169, t. 169)

Y

Yalta (yôl'tə) A resort city in Ukraine; site of meeting between Franklin Roosevelt, Winston Churchill, and Joseph Stalin in 1945; 44°N, 34°E. (t. 557)

Yemen (yem'ən) A present-day country in the mountainous southwestern area of Arabia; location of the ancient Sabaean civilization. (m. R10, t. 264)

Yugoslavia (yū gō slä' vē ə) A nation that also included the republics of Bosnia and Herzegovina, Croatia, Macedonia, and Slovenia until 1991. (m. 601, t. 600)

Z

Zama (zä'mə) Site in northern Africa where the Roman army defeated the Carthaginian army in 202 B.C.; 36°N, 8°E. (m. 234, t. 235)

Zambezi River (zam bē'zē riv'ər) A river in southern Africa, flowing east through Zimbabwe and Mozambique into the Indian Ocean. (m. 355, t. 355)

Zanzibar (zan'zə bär) An important Swahili city-state and trading center between 1100 and 1500; an island port in Tanzania in the Indian Ocean; 6°S, 39°E. (m. 373, t. 374)

Biographical Dictionary

Biographical Dictionary

The Biographical Dictionary tells you about the people you have learned about in this book. The Pronunciation Key tells you how to say their names. The page numbers tell you where each person first appears in the text.

A

Abraham (ā′brə ham), 1700s B.C. Founder of Judaism who, according to the Bible, led his family from Ur to Canaan in obedience to God's command. (p. 121)

Ahmose (äm′ōs), d. 1546 B.C. New Kingdom pharaoh who drove the Hyksos out of the Nile Delta and reunited Egypt. (p. 85)

Akbar (ak′bär), A.D. 1542–1605 Ruler of the Mogul empire in India from A.D. 1556 to 1605. (p. 392)

Alexander II (al ig zan′dər), A.D. 1818–1881 Russian tsar who abolished serfdom in 1861. (p. 533)

Alexander the Great (al ig zan′dər), 356–323 B.C. King of Macedonia who conquered Greece, Persia, Egypt, and the Indus Valley; his conquests spread Greek culture throughout parts of three continents. (p. 212)

Amanishakhete (ä män ə shäk′hə tē), 100s B.C. Queen of Kush whose lavish tomb at Meroe reflects the richness of the Kingdom of Kush. (p. 359)

Arafat, Yasir (ar′ə fat), A.D. 1929– Leader of the Palestine Liberation Organization. (p. 577)

Aristide, Jean Bertrand (är′is tēd), A.D. 1953– Elected president of Haiti in 1990. (p. 625)

Aristotle (ar′ə stot əl), 384–322 B.C. Greek philosopher who was the private teacher of Alexander the Great. (p. 211)

Atahualpa (ä tə wäl′pə), A.D. 1502?–1533 The last Inca emperor, captured and killed by Francisco Pizarro. (p. 469)

Augustus (ô gus′təs), 63 B.C.–A.D. 14 First Roman emperor; won the civil war following Julius Caesar's assassination and went on to unify the empire and establish the Pax Romana. (p. 236)

Avicenna (av ə sen′ə), A.D. 980–1037 Persian philosopher and physician; wrote a medical encyclopedia that became a standard text in North Africa, western Asia, and Europe. (p. 274)

B

Ben-Gurion, David (ben gür′ē ən), A.D. 1886–1973 Israeli prime minister from 1949 to 1953 and from 1955 to 1963; he proclaimed Israel to be a new and independent country on May 14, 1948. (p. 577)

Benedict (ben′i dikt), A.D. 480?–547 Italian monk; founder of the Benedictine order. (p. 331)

Bolívar, Simón (bō lē′vär, sē mōn′), A.D. 1783–1830 Leader of the struggle for independence in South America; his armies freed Colombia, Venezuela, and Peru from Spanish rule. (p. 492)

C

Cabral, Pedro Álvarez (kə bräl′), A.D. 1467?–1520? Portuguese navigator who landed on the coast of Brazil in 1500 and claimed it for Portugal. (p. 467)

Caesar, Julius (sē′zər, jül′yəs), 100–44 B.C. Roman general who became the republic's dictator in 45 B.C. (p. 237)

Castro, Fidel (kas′trō), A.D. 1926– Cuban revolutionary leader; premier of Cuba since 1959. (p. 560)

Charlemagne (shär′lə mān), A.D. 742–814 King of the Franks from 768 to 814, and emperor of Rome from 800 to 814. (p. 321)

Chiang Kai-shek (chang′kī shek′), A.D. 1887–1975 Chinese Nationalist leader and president of Taiwan from 1950 to 1975. (p. 552)

Churchill, Winston (chûr′chil), A.D. 1874–1965 British prime minister from 1940 to 1945 and 1951 to 1955. He led Britain during World War II. (p. 543)

Cleopatra (klē ə pa′trə), 69–30 B.C. Ruler of the Egyptian government in Alexandria who backed Caesar in the civil war he waged from 49 to 45 B.C. (p. 237)

Columbus, Christopher (kə lum′ bəs), A.D. 1451?–1506 Italian explorer in the service of Spain who arrived in the Americas in 1492. (p. 464)

Confucius (kən fū′shəs), 551–479 B.C. Chinese philosopher who stressed the need to respect tradition; his teachings discussed the right and wrong uses of power. (p. 174)

Constantine (kon′stən tēn), A.D. 280–337 Roman emperor who founded Constantinople as the new eastern capital of the Roman empire. (p. 254)

pronunciation key

a	at	ī	ice	u	up	th	thin
ā	ape	îr	pierce	ū	use	th	this
ä	far	o	hot	ü	rule	zh	measure
âr	care	ō	old	ù	pull	ə	about, taken,
e	end	ô	fork	ûr	turn		pencil, lemon,
ē	me	oi	oil	hw	white		circus
i	it	ou	out	ng	song		

Cook, James (kŭk, jāmz), A.D. 1728–1779 A navigator and ship captain who explored and claimed land in Australia for England in 1770. (p. 479)

Copernicus, Nicolaus (kə pûr′ni kəs), A.D. 1473–1543 Polish astronomer; in 1514 he discovered that Earth and the other planets revolve around the sun. (p. 339)

Cortés, Hernando (kôr tes′, er nän′dō), A.D. 1485–1547 Spanish conquistador who defeated the Aztec in 1521. (p. 468)

D

Da Gama, Vasco (də gä′mə, väs′cō), A.D. 1460?–1524 Portuguese navigator who in 1498 sailed from Europe around Africa to Asia. (p. 464)

Da Vinci, Leonardo (də vin′chē, lē ə när′dō), A.D. 1452–1519 Italian Renaissance artist, inventor, and scientist. (p. 338)

De Klerk, F.W. (də klerk′), A.D. 1936– South African president from 1989 to 1994. He worked for a peaceful transition from the policy of apartheid to majority rule in South Africa. (p. 610)

Deng Xiaoping (dung′ shou′ping′), A.D. 1904–1997 Chairman of the Chinese Communist Party and of the People's Republic of China. (p. 618)

Dias, Bartholomeu (dē′ash, bâr tủ lủ mā′ủ), A.D. 1450?–1500 Portuguese ship captain whose voyage around the southern tip of Africa in 1487 led to the opening of a sea route between Europe and Asia. (p. 464)

Diocletian (dī ə klē′shən), A.D. 245–313 Roman emperor who divided the empire in two and oversaw the eastern part. (p. 253)

E

Elizabeth I (i liz′ə bəth), A.D. 1533–1603 Queen of England from 1558 to 1603; the English Renaissance flourished during her reign. (p. 346)

Equiano, Olaudah (i kwē ä′nō, ōl′ə dä), A.D. 1750–1797 Enslaved African writer. In 1789 he wrote an autobiography describing his life in slavery. (p. 476)

Erasmus (i raz′məs), A.D. 1466?–1536 Dutch writer and humanist; he favored reform of the Catholic Church but came to oppose the Protestant Reformation. (p. 343)

F

Francis of Assisi (fran′sis əv ə sē′zē), A.D. 1181–1226 Italian monk who founded the Franciscan order; he devoted his life to serving the poor and sick. (p. 332)

Frank, Anne (frangk), A.D. 1929–1945 Dutch-Jewish girl who, with other Jews, hid from the Nazis from 1942 to 1944; she was found and sent to a concentration camp where she died. (p. 546)

Franz Ferdinand (franz fur′də nand), A.D. 1863–1914 Archduke of Austria whose assassination led to the outbreak of World War I. (p. 527)

Fu Hao (fü′hou′), 1100s B.C. A Chinese king's wife who led troops to war. Her tomb contained records of her life and times. (p. 166)

G

Galilei, Galileo (gal ə lā′ē, gal ə lā′ō), A.D. 1564–1642 Italian astronomer, mathematician, and physicist. His telescopes proved the sun is the center of the solar system. (p. 456)

Gandhi, Indira (gän′dē), A.D. 1917–1984 Prime minister of India from 1966 to 1977 and from 1980 to 1984. (p. 17)

Gandhi, Mohandas (gän′dē), A.D. 1869–1948 Indian political and religious leader; he supported the use of nonviolent methods to bring about change. (p. 580)

Genghis Khan (geng′gəs kän′), A.D. 1162?–1227 Mongol conqueror. At its peak, his empire included China, western Asia, and parts of eastern Europe. (p. 403)

Gorbachev, Mikhail (gôr′bə chəf), A.D. 1931– Soviet secretary general of the Communist Party from 1985 to 1990, and last president of the Soviet Union, 1990–1991. (p. 597)

Gutenberg, Johannes (gü′tən bûrg), A.D. 1400?–1468 German printer; in 1448 he invented a printing press that used movable type. (p. 344)

H

Hammurabi (hä mủ rä′bē), 1800?–1750? B.C. King of the Babylonian empire; creator of the Code of Hammurabi, one of the world's oldest codes of law. (p. 112)

Han Gaozu (hän′gou′zü′), 200s B.C. A farmer-turned-general who, in 206 B.C., overthrew the Qin dynasty; he founded the Han dynasty. (p. 174)

Hannibal (han′ə bəl), 247?–183? B.C. General of Carthage who marched his army from Spain to Rome in the Second Punic War. (p. 234)

Hargreaves, James (här′grēvz), A.D. 1720–1778 English inventor of the spinning jenny. (p. 503)

Hatshepsut (hat shep′süt), 1520?–1482 B.C. One of the few women Egyptian pharaohs; organized a trade expedition to Egypt's southern neighbor, Punt. (p. 87)

Henry VIII (hen′rē), A.D. 1491–1547 King of England from 1509 to 1547 and founder of the Church of England; he broke with the Catholic Church because the pope would not grant him a divorce. (p. 345)

Henry, Prince (hen′rē), A.D. 1394–1460 Portuguese prince who directed the search for a sea route to the gold mines of western Africa. He also designed a fast, steerable ship known as a caravel. (p. 463)

Hidalgo, Miguel (ē däl′gō), A.D. 1753–1811 Mexican priest and revolutionary who led a revolt that started the Mexican war of independence. (p. 494)

Hitler, Adolf (hit′lər), A.D. 1889–1945 German dictator. He founded the National Socialist (Nazi) Party, which led Germany during World War II. (p. 540)

Ho Chi Minh (hō′chē′min′), A.D. 1890–1969 Communist leader in Vietnam who became head of the communist government in 1945. (p. 586)

Homer (hō′mûr), 700s B.C. Ancient Greek poet. (p. 200)

I

Iturbide, Agustin de (ē tür bē′de), A.D. 1783–1824 Mexican soldier and leader; he won Mexican independence from Spain and became ruler of Mexico from 1822 to 1823. (p. 495)

J

Jayavarman II (jä yä vär′män), A.D. 800s One of the first Khmer kings of Cambodia. (p. 399)

Jesus (jē′zəs), 4? B.C.–A.D. 29? Religious leader and founder of Christianity. (p. 247)

Jinnah, Mohammad Ali (jin′ə), A.D. 1876–1948 First president of Pakistan from 1947 to 1948. (p. 583)

John I (jon), A.D. 1167?–1216 King of England from A.D. 1199 to 1216; in 1215 he signed the Magna Carta, giving more rights to British nobles. (p. 326)

K

Kay, John (kā), A.D. 1704–1764 English watchmaker who invented the flying shuttle used in weaving. (p. 503)

Kennedy, John F. (ken′i dē), A.D. 1917–1963 The 35th President of the United States from 1961 to 1963. He successfully negotiated the removal of Soviet nuclear missiles from Cuba. (p. 560)

Khadija (ka dē′jä), d. A.D. 619 A wealthy merchant who became the first wife of Muhammad. (p. 267)

Khrushchev, Nikita (krüsh′chef), A.D. 1894–1971 Secretary general of the Soviet Communist Party from 1958 to 1964. (p. 560)

Khufu (kü fü′), 2650?–2600? B.C. Egyptian pharaoh who built the Great Pyramid. (p. 81)

Kublai Khan (kü′blə kän′), A.D. 1215–1294 Grandson of Genghis Khan, founder of China's Yuan Dynasty. (p. 403)

L

Lady Murasaki Shikibu (mür ä säk′ē shē kē′bū), A.D. 978?–1026? Japanese author who wrote *The Tale of Genji,* which is thought to be the world's first novel. (p. 414)

Lalibela (lä′lē be lä), b. A.D. 1100s Zagwe king who ruled Ethiopia from about A.D. 1185 to 1225. (p. 360)

Lenin, Vladimir Ilyich (len′in), A.D. 1870–1924 Bolshevik leader and founder of the Soviet Union. (p. 536)

Livy (liv′ē), 59 B.C.–A.D. 17 Historian of the Roman Republic who wrote about the struggle between plebeians and patricians of Rome. (p. 231)

Louis XVI (lü′ē), A.D. 1754–1793 King of France from 1774 to 1792; executed during the French Revolution. (p. 486)

Luther, Martin (lüth′ər), A.D. 1483–1546 German monk and leader of the Protestant Reformation. (p. 342)

M

Macquarie, Lachlan (mak wôr′ ē, läk län), A.D. 1761–1824 Governor of the English colony of New South Wales in Australia from 1810 to 1821. He supported the rights of the emancipees in New South Wales. (p. 481)

Magellan, Ferdinand (mə jel′ən), A.D. 1480?–1521 Portuguese explorer in the service of Spain; he set out to find a route to Asia by sailing around the southern tip of South America. (p. 462)

Mandela, Nelson (man del′ə), A.D. 1918– South African civil rights leader who became president of South Africa in 1994. (p. 606)

Mansa Musa (män′sä mü′sä), A.D. 1297?–1337? Emperor of Mali from 1312 to 1337, when the kingdom was at its peak of wealth and power. (p. 366)

Mao Zedong (mou′dze′dùng′), A.D. 1893–1976 Chinese communist leader and founder of the People's Republic of China. (p. 552)

Marie Antoinette (mə rē′ an twə net′), A.D. 1755–1793 Queen of France from 1774 to 1792, who was executed during the French Revolution. (p. 490)

pronunciation key

a at; ā ape; ä far; âr care; e end; ē me; i it; ī ice; îr pierce; o hot; ō old; ô fork; oi oil; ou out; u up; ū use; ü rule; ú pull; ûr turn; hw white; ng song; th thin; <u>th</u> this; zh measure; ə about, taken, pencil, lemon, circus

Biographical Dictionary

Marx, Karl (märks), A.D. 1818–1883 German philosopher and economist. His ideas, called Marxism, formed the basis of communism. (p. 505)

Medici, Lorenzo (med'i chē), A.D. 1449–1492 Ruler of Florence during the Renaissance and patron of artists such as Michelangelo. (p. 337)

Meiji (mā'jē'), A.D. 1852–1912 Japanese emperor from 1867 to 1912 who led Japan into a period of rapid modernization. (p. 510)

Menes (mē'nēz), 3100? B.C. King of Upper Egypt who united Upper and Lower Egypt. (p. 75)

Michelangelo (mī kəl an'jə lō), A.D. 1475–1564 Italian Renaissance sculptor, painter, architect, and poet. (p. 338)

Moctezuma (mäk tə zü'mə), A.D. 1468?–1520 Aztec emperor defeated and killed by the Spanish conquistador Hernando Cortés in 1520. (p. 468)

Morelos, José María (mō re'lōs), A.D. 1765–1815 Mexican priest and revolutionary who succeeded Miguel Hidalgo as rebel leader and issued a declaration of independence from Spain in 1813. He was captured and killed by Spanish soldiers in 1815. (p. 495)

Moses (mō'ziz), 1200s B.C. Prophet who led the Israelites out of slavery in Egypt. (p. 122)

Muhammad (mu ham'əd), A.D. 570?–632? Founder of Islam whose words are recorded in the Quran. (p. 267)

Mumtaz Mahal (mum täz' mä häl'), A.D. 1592–1631 Wife of Shah Jahan, emperor of India; the Taj Mahal in Agra, India, was built in her memory. (p. 396)

N

Napoleon Bonaparte (nə pō'lē ən bō'nə pärt), A.D. 1769–1821 French revolutionary general who became Emperor Napoleon I of France in 1804. (p. 491)

Nasser, Gamal Abdel (nas'ər), A.D. 1918–1970 First President of Egypt from 1956 to 1958, and of the United Arab Republic from 1958 to 1970. (p. 569)

Nehru, Jawaharlal (nā'rü), A.D. 1889–1964 Prime minister of India from 1947 to 1964 and father of Indira Gandhi; close associate of Mohandas Gandhi. (p. 583)

Newton, Isaac (nü'tən), A.D. 1642–1727 English scientist who studied gravity. (p. 459)

Nicholas II (nik'ə ləs), A.D. 1868–1918 Last Russian tsar from 1894 to 1917. Discontent with his policies led to the Russian Revolution of 1917. (p. 534)

Nkrumah, Kwame (en krü'mə), A.D. 1909–1972 Leader in the liberation of the Gold Coast from British rule and first president of Ghana from 1960 to 1966. (p. 567)

O

Osman (äs män'), A.D. 1258–1326? Founder of the Ottoman empire. (p. 389)

P

Pachakuti Inca (pä chä kü'tē), d. A.D. 1471 Inca emperor from 1438 to 1471; he greatly extended Inca borders in 1438 and became known as Sapa Inca, or Supreme Inca. (p. 435)

Paul (pôl), A.D. 11?–67? Follower of Jesus who helped spread Christianity throughout the Roman world. (p. 250)

Pericles (per'i klēz), 495?–429 B.C. Athenian general who led Athens during the war with Sparta; he made sure that poor as well as rich citizens could take part in government. (p. 206)

Perry, Matthew (per'ē), A.D. 1794–1858 U.S. naval officer who sailed to Japan in 1853 with a demand that Japanese ports be opened to U.S. trade. (p. 509)

Peter (pē'tər), A.D. 5?–67? One of the 12 apostles of Jesus; Roman Catholics consider him to be the first pope, or bishop of Rome. (p. 248)

Petrarch (pē'trärk), A.D. 1304–1374 Italian Renaissance poet and humanist. (p. 338)

Pizarro, Francisco (pē sär'rō), A.D. 1471?–1541 Spanish conquistador who in 1532 defeated the Inca emperor Atahualpa. (p. 468)

Plato (plā'tō), 428?–347? B.C. Greek philosopher and student of Socrates. (p. 201)

Polo, Marco (pō'lō), A.D. 1254–1324 Italian merchant who traveled to China, where he lived for 17 years, at times serving as diplomat for Kublai Khan. (p. 403)

Pope Urban II (ur'bən), A.D. 1042–1099 Pope who called for the First Crusade to reclaim Jerusalem from the Muslims. (p. 332)

R

Rabin, Yitzhak (rä bēn'), A.D. 1922–1995 Prime minister of Israel who negotiated a peace plan with Palestinians in the West Bank and Gaza. (p. 578)

Robespierre, Maximilien (rōbz'pē âr), A.D. 1758–1794 French revolutionary. He sent suspected traitors to the guillotine during the Reign of Terror from 1793 until his own death by guillotine in 1794. (p. 490)

Roosevelt, Franklin Delano (rō'zə velt), A.D. 1882–1945 The 32nd President of the United States. He led the nation against the Axis powers in World War II. (p. 543)

S

Sadat, Anwar (sə dat'), A.D. 1918–1981 Egyptian president who established peaceful relations with Israel in 1978. (p. 577)

San Martín, José de (sän mär tēn'), A.D. 1778–1850 Argentine soldier who led revolutions that freed Argentina and Chile from Spanish rule. (p. 496)

Sargon (sär′gon), died 2279? B.C. King of the city-state Kish; united the city-states of Sumer to create an empire. (p. 111)

Schliemann, Heinrich (shlē′män, hīn′rikh), A.D. 1822–1890 German archaeologist and discoverer of the remains of Troy. (p. 30)

Scipio (sip′ē ō), 234?–183? B.C. Roman general who defeated Hannibal in the Battle of Zama outside Carthage, North Africa, in 202 B.C. (p. 235)

Shah Jahan (shä jə hän′), A.D. 1592–1666 Mogul emperor of India; he built the Taj Mahal in Agra, India, in memory of his wife Mumtaz Mahal. (p. 396)

Shakespeare, William (shāk′spēr), A.D. 1564–1616 English dramatist and poet; considered one of the greatest writers in the English language. (p. 346)

Shihuangdi (shē′hwäng dē), 259?–210 B.C. Chinese emperor who founded the Qin dynasty and unified China with a standardized system of writing and money; his tomb contained the famous "clay army." (p. 168)

Siddhartha Gautama (sid där′tə gô′tə mə), 563?– 483? B.C. Ancient Indian religious leader known as the Buddha, or Enlightened One, who founded Buddhism. (p. 150)

Sinan (sə nän′), A.D. 1489–1588 Süleyman's chief architect; he designed more than 300 buildings, including the mosque in Istanbul. (p. 390)

Socrates (sok′rə tēz), 470?–399 B.C. Greek philosopher who discussed laws, customs, values, and religion with students; accused of urging young people to revolt, he was sentenced to death. (p. 206)

Spindler, Konrad (shpin′dlər), A.D. 1939– German archaeologist who analyzed the 5,000–year–old "Iceman" body found in the Alps in 1991. (p. 33)

Stalin, Josef (stä′lin), A.D. 1879–1953 Soviet revolutionary and dictator who ruled the Soviet Union from 1924 to 1953. (p. 537)

Süleyman (sü′lä män), A.D. 1495?–1566 Sultan of the Ottoman empire during its peak from 1520 to 1566. (p. 389)

Sun Yat-sen (sün′ yät sen′), A.D. 1866–1925 Leader of the Chinese Nationalists and founder of the Republic of China in 1912. (p. 550)

Sunjata (sän jä′tä), d. A.D. 1255 King of Mali who conquered all of Ghana. (p. 364)

Suryavarman II (sur yə vär′mən), A.D. 1100s Khmer king who filled his capital city of Angkor with magnificent Hindu temples. (p. 400)

T

Tokugawa Ieyasu (tō kü gä′wä ē yä′sü), A.D. 1543–1616 Shogun, or military commander, of the Tokugawa dynasty from 1603 to 1605; his family's shogunate kept Japan peaceful for more than 200 years. (p. 412)

Toussaint L'Ouverture (tü san′ lü vər tyür′), A.D. 1743?–1803 Haitian general; in 1802 he led a successful slave revolution, leading to the independence of Haiti in 1804. (p. 493)

Tutankhamun (tü täng kä′mən), 1371?–1352 B.C. Egyptian pharaoh who ruled from about the ages of 7 to 17; his tomb remained nearly untouched until its discovery in 1922. (p. 88)

V

Veale, Elizabeth (vēl, i liz′ ə bəth), A.D. 1767–1850 Early colonist of the English colony of New South Wales in Australia who helped establish the production of wool as an important Australian industry. (p. 480)

W

Walesa, Lech (wə len′sə), A.D. 1943– Polish labor leader who became the first president of democratic Poland in 1990. (p. 598)

Watt, James (wot), A.D. 1736–1819 Scottish engineer and inventor who developed a steam engine that burned coal in 1765. (p. 503)

William the Conqueror (wil′yəm), A.D. 1027–1087 Norman king; in 1066 he defeated Harold, the Anglo-Saxon king, to become the first Norman king of England. (p. 326)

Wudi (wü′dē), 100s B.C. Han emperor who ruled China from 140 B.C. to 87 B.C.; he set up a system of schools that prepared students for government jobs. (p. 176)

Y

Yeltsin, Boris (yel′tsin), A.D. 1931– Russian politician; in 1991 he became the first president of post-Soviet Russia. (p. 599)

Yoritomo (yōr ē tō′mō), A.D. 1147–1199 Japanese shogun, or military commander; in 1192 he attained supreme power from the emperor and ruled the country as a military dictator. (p. 411)

pronunciation key

a at; ā ape; ä far; âr care; e end; ē me; i it; ī ice; îr pierce; o hot; ō old; ô fork; oi oil; ou out; u up; ū use; ü rule, ù pull; ûr turn; hw white; ng song; th thin; th this; zh measure; ə about, taken, pencil, lemon, circus

Glossary

Glossary

This Glossary will help you to pronounce and understand the meanings of the vocabulary in this book. The page number at the end of the definition tells where the word first appears.

A

aborigine (ab′ ə rij′ ə nē) A person belonging to, or descending from, the group of people who first inhabited Australia. (p. 479)

absolute monarchy (ab′sə lüt mon′ər kē) A form of government headed by a ruler, or monarch, with unlimited power. *See* **divine right**. (p. 486)

accuracy (ak′yər ə sē) Being true or correct. (p. 604)

acropolis (ə krop′ə lis) A large hill in ancient Greece where city residents sought shelter and safety in times of war and met to discuss community affairs. (p. 197)

agora (ag′ər ə) A central area in Greek cities used both as a marketplace and as a meeting place. (p. 197)

agriculture (ag′ri kul chər) The raising of crops and animals for human use. (p. 52)

algebra (al′je brə) A type of mathematics to which Muslims made great contributions. (p. 275)

alliance (ə li′əns) An agreement between countries to work together in war or trade. (p. 527)

Allied Powers (al′id pou′ərz) In World War I, the nations allied against the Central Powers; included Serbia, Russia, France, Britain, and the United States. (p. 528)

Allies (al′īz) In World War II, the nations allied against the Axis powers, including Britain, France, the Soviet Union, the United States, and China. (p. 543)

anti-semitism (an tē sem′i tiz əm) Discrimination against and hatred of Jews. (p. 575)

apartheid (ə pär′tīd) The government policy of strict and unequal segregation of the races as practiced in South Africa from 1948 to the early 1990s. (p. 607)

apostle (ə pos′əl) One of the 12 closest followers of Jesus, chosen by him to help him teach. (p. 248)

aqueduct (ak′wə dukt) A high, arched structure built to carry water over long distances. (p. 238)

archaeology (är kē ol′ə jē) The study of the remains of past cultures. (p. 32)

archipelago (är kə pel′ə gō) A large group of islands. (p. 385)

architecture (är′ki tek chər) The science of planning and constructing buildings. (p. 257)

aristocracy (ar ə stok′rə sē) The class of a society made up of members of noble families, usually the most powerful group. (p. 487)

armada (är mä′də) A fleet of warships. (p. 346)

armistice (är′mə stis) An agreement to stop fighting; a truce. (p. 531)

artifact (är′tə fakt) An object made by someone in the past. (p. 25)

assembly (ə sem′blē) A lawmaking body of government made up of a group of citizens. (p. 206)

astrolabe (as′trə lāb) An instrument invented by Muslims that is used to determine direction by figuring out the position of the stars. (p. 275)

Axis (ak′sis) In World War II, the nations who fought the Allies, including Japan, Germany, and Italy. (p. 543)

B

bilingual (bī ling′gwəl) Able to speak two languages. (p. 626)

bishop (bish′ əp) A church official who leads a large group of Christians in a particular region. (p. 251)

boycott (boi′kot) A form of protest in which people join together to refuse to buy goods. (p. 568)

Buddhism (bůd′iz əm) A religion founded in India by Siddhartha Gautama which teaches that the most important thing in life is to reach peace by ending suffering. (p. 150)

bureaucracy (byů rok′rə sē) The large organization that runs the daily business of government. (p. 511)

pronunciation key

a	at	ī	ice	u	up	th	thin
ā	ape	îr	pierce	ū	use	th	this
ä	far	o	hot	ü	rule	zh	measure
âr	care	ō	old	ů	pull	ə	about, taken,
e	end	ô	fork	ûr	turn		pencil, lemon,
ē	me	oi	oil	hw	white		circus
i	it	ou	out	ng	song		

c

caliph (kā′lif) A Muslim leader who had both political and religious authority. (p. 273)

caravan (kar′ə van) A group of people and animals traveling together for safety, especially through a desert. (p. 264)

caravel (kar′ə vel) A sailing ship developed in Portugal in the 1400s that had greater directional control than earlier ships and could sail great distances more safely. (p. 463)

cardinal directions (kärd′ən əl di rek′shənz) The directions north, south, east, and west. (p. G6)

cartogram (kär′tə gram) A special kind of map that distorts the shapes and sizes of countries or other political regions to present economic or other kinds of data for comparison. (p. 506)

caste system (kast sis′təm) The social system in Hindu society in which a person's place is determined by the rank of the family into which he or she is born. (p. 144)

cathedral (kə thē′drəl) A large or important Christian church. (p. 332)

cause (kôz) Something that makes something else happen. *See* **effect.** (p. 118)

census (sen′səs) A periodic count of all the people living in a country, city, or other region. (p. 239)

Central Powers (sen′trəl pou′ərz) In World War I, the nations who fought against the Allied Powers, including Austria-Hungary and Germany. (p. 528)

chinampas (chin äm′paz) One of the floating islands made by the Aztec around Tenochtitlán for growing crops. (p. 427)

Christianity (kris chē an′i tē) A religion based on the teachings of Jesus, as recorded in the New Testament. (p. 246)

circa (sûr′kə) A Latin word, often abbreviated "c." that means "about" or "around." (p. 59)

citadel (sit′ə dəl) A walled fort that protects a city. (p. 135)

citizen (sit′ə zən) A person with certain rights and responsibilities in his or her country or community. (p. 197)

city-state (sit′ē stāt) A self-governing city, often with surrounding lands and villages. (p. 110)

civil disobedience (siv′əl dis ə bē′dēəns) A means of protest by refusing to obey a law that is considered to be unjust. (p. 582)

civil war (siv′əl wōr) An armed conflict between groups within one country. (p. 237)

civilization (siv ə lə zā′shən) A culture that has developed systems of specialization, religion, learning, and government. (p. 55)

Classic Period (klas′ik pêr′ē əd) A time of great cultural achievement for a civilization. (p. 299)

climate (klī′ mit) The weather pattern of an area over a long period of time. (p. 9)

climograph (klī′mə graf) A graph that shows the temperature and precipitation in a place over a period of months. (p. 290)

code of law (kōd uv lô) A written set of laws that apply to everyone under a government. (p. 113)

codex (kō′deks) A manuscript page such as the kind used by the Aztec to record historical, religious, governmental and scientific knowledge. (p. 430)

Cold War (kōld wôr) A term used for the battle of words and ideas that developed between the democratic nations of the West and the Soviet Union and Eastern Europe from about 1945 to 1990. (p. 556)

colony (kol′ ə nē) A territory or community that is under the control of another country. (p. 201)

commune (kom′ūn) A community in which resources, work, and living space are shared by all members of the group. (p. 554)

communism (kom′yə niz əm) A system in which the government owns all property and makes nearly all decisions for its citizens. (p. 537)

compass rose (kum′pəs rōz) A drawing on a map that shows directions. (p. G6)

concentration camp (kon sən trā′shən kamp) A place where people are imprisoned because of their heritage, religious beliefs, or political views. (p. 546)

conclusion (kən klü′zhən) A final statement or opinion reached by putting together information about a subject. (p. 210)

confederation (kən fed ə rā′shən) A group of states or provinces under a central government. (p. 497)

Confucianism (kən fū′shə niz əm) In China, a system of beliefs and behavior based on the teachings of Confucius, who said that people should lead good lives by studying ancient traditions; stressed the importance of respecting one's family and ancestors. (p. 175)

conquistador (kon kēs′tə dôr) A Spanish conqueror who came to the Americas to search for gold, land, and glory. (p. 468)

consul (kon′səl) One of two elected officials of the Roman Republic who commanded the army and were supreme judges. (p. 232)

continent (kon′tə nənt) One of Earth's seven large bodies of land. (p. G4)

convent (kon'vent) A religious community in which women, or nuns, live and pray. *See* **nun.** (p. 331)

convert (kən vūrt') To adopt or cause someone to adopt a new religion. (p. 470)

convict (kon' vikt) A person who has been found guilty by the government of committing a crime and receives a sentence of punishment. (p. 480)

credibility (kre də bi'lə tē) Believability. (p. 472)

Crusade (krü sād') Any of the journeys and battles undertaken by European Christians between 1095 and 1270, to win control of the Holy Land (Palestine) from the Muslims. (p. 332)

Cultural Revolution (kul'chər əl rev ə lü'shən) A campaign in China, 1966–1976, when the Communist Party under Mao Zedong called for the destruction of all noncommunist beliefs. (p. 554)

culture (kul' chər) The way of life of a group of people at a particular time, including their daily habits, beliefs, and arts. (p. 10)

cuneiform (kū nē' ə fōrm) A system of writing that used wedge-shaped symbols to represent sounds, ideas, and objects; developed in ancient Sumer. (p. 108)

custom (kus'təm) A way of living that people of the same culture practice regularly over time. (p. 14)

D

decision (di sizh'ən) a choice made from a number of alternatives. *See* **conclusion.** (p. 30)

Declaration of the Rights of Man and of the Citizen (dek lə rā'shən) A statement issued by the French National Assembly in August 1789 that all men were "born and remain free and equal in rights." (p. 488)

deforestation (dē for ə stā'shən) The process of clearing the land of forests, often to make space for farms and cities. (p. 318)

degree (di grē') In geography, a unit of measurement that indicates the distance between lines of latitude and longitude; a unit of measurement for temperature. (p. 12)

delta (del'tə) The flat, fan-shaped land made of silt deposited at the mouth of a river. (p. 71)

demand (di mand') In economics, people's desire for a particular item. *See* **supply.** (p. 363)

democracy (di mok'rə sē) A system of government in which citizens vote to make governmental decisions. (p. 199)

depression (di presh'ən) A severe slowdown in business characterized by high unemployment and falling prices. (p. 541)

dharma (där'me) In Hinduism, the laws and duties that guide the behavior of each caste member. (p. 145)

Diaspora (di as'pər ə) The scattering of Jews to many parts of the world. (p. 125)

dictator (dik'tā tər) A ruler who has absolute power. (p. 237)

distortion (di stôr'shən) In cartography, or map-making, the unavoidable inaccuracy caused by stretching or cutting parts of the globe to fit them onto a flat map. (p. 432)

distribution map (dis trə bū'shən map) A special purpose map that shows how a particular feature such as population density is spread over an area. (p. G11)

diversity (di vûr'si tê) Differences; variety. (p. 440)

divine right (di vīn' rīt) The belief that a monarch received authority to rule from God and therefore could not be questioned. *See* **absolute monarchy.** (p. 486)

domesticate (də mes'ti kāt) To train plants or animals to be useful to people. (p. 53)

drought (drout) A long period of dry weather. (p. 105)

dynasty (dī'nə stê) A line of rulers who belong to the same family. (p. 164)

E

Eastern Orthodox Christianity (ēs'tərn ôr'thə doks kris chē an'i tē) A branch of Christianity that developed in the Byzantine Empire and that did not recognize the pope as its supreme leader. (p. 255)

economy (i kon'ə mē) The way people manage money and resources for the production of goods and services. (p. 77)

effect (i fekt') Something that happens as a result of a cause. *See* **cause.** (p. 118)

Eightfold Path (āt'fōld path) In Buddhism, the basic rules of behavior and belief leading to an end of suffering. *See* **Four Noble Truths.** (p. 153)

elevation (el ə vā'shən) Height above sea level. (p. 228)

elevation map (el ə vā'shən map) A map that shows the height of land above sea level. (p. G10)

emancipee (i man' sə pē) A person who has been freed, or emancipated, from a sentence of punishment given to him or her by the government. (p. 481)

emperor (em'pər ər) The supreme ruler of an empire. (p. 168)

empire (em'pir) A group of lands and peoples ruled by one government. (p. 86)

equal-area projection (ē′kwəl ār′ē ə prə jek′shən) A map that is useful for comparing sizes of land masses, on which shapes at the center are fairly accurate but are very distorted at the edges of the map. (p. 432)

equator (i kwā′tər) An imaginary line circling Earth halfway between the North and South poles and dividing Earth into Northern and Southern Hemispheres. (p. G4)

erosion (i rō′zhən) The gradual wearing away of soil and rock by wind, glaciers, or water. (p. 162)

estates (e stāts′) The three social classes into which France was divided before the French Revolution, including the clergy, the aristocracy, and the common people. (p. 487)

ethnic group (eth′nik grüp) A people who share a heritage of common customs, values, and language. (p. 599)

European Union (EU) (yùr ə pē′ən ūn′yən) A group of European nations working to build a common economy and create cultural ties throughout Europe. (p. 601)

evaluate (i val′ū āt) To judge. (p. 31)

excavate (eks′ kə vāt′) To dig or to scoop out earth. (p. 32)

expedition (ek spi dish′ən) A group of people who go on a trip for a specific reason. (p. 87)

F

factory (fak′tə rē) A building in which machines used to manufacture goods are located. (p. 501)

famine (fam′in) A widespread lack of food resulting in hunger and starvation. (p. 162)

fascism (fash′iz əm) A totalitarian government that promotes a form of nationalism in which the goals of the nation are more important than those of the individual. (p. 540)

feudalism (fū′də liz əm) Starting in Europe around A.D. 800, a system for organizing and governing society, based on land and service. See **fief, lord, vassal.** (p. 322)

fief (fēf) In the Middle Ages, a property given to a vassal in exchange for his loyalty. (p. 322)

Five Pillars (fīv pil′ərz) The five basic duties of all Muslims. (p. 269)

Four Noble Truths (fôr nō′bəl trüthz) In Buddhism, the principles that rule life and promise an end to suffering. See **Eightfold Path.** (p. 153)

free enterprise (frē en′tər prīz) The economic system of private ownership of land and businesses that allows people to make their own economic decisions and profit from their own work. (p. 556)

G

generalization (jen ər ə lə zā′shən) A broad statement that points out a common feature shared by different kinds of examples. (p. 408)

geocentric (jē ō sen′trik) Based on the idea that Earth is the center of the universe and that the sun, stars, and planets revolve around Earth. (p. 456)

geography (jē og′rə fē) The study of Earth's environment and how it shapes people's lives and how Earth is shaped in turn by people's activities. (p. 8)

glacier (glā′shər) A great sheet of ice that moves slowly over a land surface. See **Ice Age.** (p. 286)

gladiator (glad′ē ā tər) A Roman athlete, usually a slave, criminal, or prisoner of war, who was forced to fight for the entertainment of the public. (p. 240)

global grid (glō′bəl grid) Pattern formed on a map or globe by the crossing of parallels and meridians. This pattern makes it possible to pinpoint exact locations. (p. 13)

glyph (glif) A writing symbol, often carved into stone, that stands for an object or a sound. See **stela.** (p. 302)

Grand Canal (grand kə nal′) A waterway in China connecting Beijing with cities to the south. (p. 403)

Grand School (grand skül) A school begun by Confucian scholars in China that trained students for government jobs. (p. 176)

grand mufti (grand muf′tē) A religious leader of the Ottoman empire responsible for interpreting the laws of Islam. (p. 389)

gravity (grav′i tē) The force that pulls objects toward Earth and that draws planets into orbits around the sun. (p. 459)

Green Revolution (grēn rev ə lü′shən) A campaign by the government of India in the 1950s to increase agricultural productivity. (p. 584)

griot (grē′ō) An oral historian and musician who became important in western Africa in the 1500s and still carries on oral traditions today. (p. 367)

gross domestic product (grōs də mes′tik prod′ukt) The total value of goods and services produced by a country during a year. (p. 506)

---

pronunciation key

a **at**; ā **ape**; ä **far**; âr **care**; e **end**; ē **me**; i **it**; ī **ice**; îr **pierce**; o **hot**; ō **old**; ô **fork**; oi **oil**; ou **out**; u **up**; ū **use**; ü **rule**; ù **pull**; ûr **turn**; hw **white**; ng **song**; th **thin**; <u>th</u> **this**; zh measure; ə **about, taken, pencil, lemon, circus**

guild (gild) In the Middle Ages, an organization of workers in a trade or craft that set standards and protected the interests of its members. (p. 324)

H

hacienda (hä sē en′də) A large agricultural estate owned by Spaniards or the church in Spain's American colonies. (p. 470)

harbor (här′bər) A sheltered place along a coast used to protect boats and ships. (p. 193)

heliocentric (hē lē ō sen′trik) Based on Copernicus's idea that the Earth and the other planets revolve around the sun. (p. 457)

hemisphere (hem′is fîr) One of the halves of Earth. (p. G4)

hieroglyphics (hī ər ə glif′iks) The ancient Egyptian system of writing that used symbols to stand for objects, ideas, or sounds. (p. 78)

hijra (hij′rə) The migration of Muhammad from Mecca to Medina in A.D. 622, marking the founding of Islam. (p. 268)

Hinduism (hin′dü iz əm) The religion of India that grew out of the beliefs of the ancient Aryan peoples; it stresses that one main force connects all of life. (p. 142)

historical map (hi stôr′i kəl map) A map that shows information about the past. (p. 280)

history (his′tə rē) The story or record of what has happened in the past. (p. 24)

Holocaust (hol′ə kôst) The deliberate killing of 6 million Jews solely because they were Jewish by the Nazis during World War II. (p. 546)

humanism (hū′mə niz əm) An idea important to the Renaissance that focused on human values and what people can achieve in this world. (p. 336)

hunter-gatherer (hun′tər gath′ər ər) A person of the Old Stone Age who met needs by hunting animals and gathering plants. (p. 46)

I

Ice Age (īs āj) Any of the periods of time in the past lasting for millions of years when glaciers spread to cover nearly half of Earth's land. (p. 286)

imperialism (im pîr′ē ə liz əm) The extension of a nation's power over other lands by military, political, or economic means. (p. 508)

indulgence (in dul′jəns) A pardon or forgiveness given by the Roman Catholic Church to people who act against Christian teachings. (p. 343)

Industrial Revolution (in dus′ trē əl rev ə lü′ shən) A time when great technological advances changed the way goods were made and the ways people lived; it began in England in the 1700s and then spread throughout Europe and the United States. (p. 500)

inflation (in flā′shən) A period of rising prices. (p. 541)

interaction (in tər ak′shən) The exchange of ideas and customs among cultures. (p. 16)

interdependent (in tər di pen′dənt) Depending upon one another to meet needs and wants. (p. 622)

intermediate directions (in tər mē′dē it di rek′shənz) The directions halfway between the cardinal directions; northeast, southeast, southwest, and northwest. (p. G6)

International Date Line (in tər nash′ə nəl dāt līn) An imaginary line in the Pacific Ocean marking the boundary between one day and the next. (p. 549)

Internet (in′ tər net) A constantly growing international group of interconnected computers. (p. 627)

Intifada (in tə fä′də) The Palestinian uprising against Israeli rule that began in 1987. (p. 578)

irrigation (ir i gā′shən) The watering of dry land by means of canals or pipes. (p. 72)

Islam (is läm′) The religion of Muslims based on the teachings of the prophet Muhammad in the A.D. 600s. (p. 266)

isthmus (is′məs) A narrow strip of land that connects two larger land masses. (p. 423)

J

Judaism (jü′dē iz əm) The religion of the Jewish people. (p. 120)

jury (jür′ē) A group of citizens chosen to hear evidence and make a decision in a court of law. (p. 206)

K

Kaaba (kä′bə) A religious temple in Mecca that became sacred to Muslims. (p. 267)

karma (kär′mə) In Hinduism and Buddhism, the end result of all of a person's good and bad acts, which determines his or her rebirth. (p. 152)

Korean War (kə rē′ən wôr) A war fought between communist North Korea, aided by China, and South Korea, aided by United Nations members, during 1950–1953. (p. 557)

L

landform (land′fôrm) A feature of Earth's surface, such as a mountain range, plain, or plateau. (p. 9)

large-scale map (lärj skāl map) A map that provides many details about a small area by measuring lesser distances in small units. (p. 92)

Latin America (lat′in ə mer′i kə) The cultural region including Mexico, the Caribbean, and South America that has been strongly influenced by Spain and Portugal. (p. 492)

latitude (lat'i tüd) Distance north or south of the equator, measured by a set of imaginary lines, or parallels, that run east and west around Earth. *See* **parallel.** (p. G4, 12)

League of Nations (lēg əv nā'shənz) An international council created in 1920 by the Allied Powers to try to prevent future wars. (p. 531)

levee (lev'ē) A wall built along a river bank to prevent flooding. (p. 162)

Line of Demarcation (līn əv dē mär kā'shən) An imaginary line drawn across North and South America in 1494 to divide the claims of Spain and Portugal. (p. 467)

locator (lō'kāt ər) A small map that shows where the subject area of a main map is located. (p. G8)

loess (les) A fine, yellow soil that is easily carried by wind and rain, found in China. (p. 161)

longitude (lon'ji tüd) Distance east or west of the prime meridian measured by a set of imaginary lines, or meridians, that run north and south from Earth's poles. *See* **meridian.** (p. G4)

lord (lôrd) In the Middle Ages, a noble who owned and controlled all activities on his manor. *See* **vassal.** (p. 322)

M

Magna Carta (mag'nə kär'tə) A legal document written by English lords in 1215 that stated certain rights and limited the power of the king. (p. 326)

maize (māz) Corn; a crop first grown in Middle America about 5,000 B.C. (p. 300)

Mandate of Heaven (man'dāt uv hev'ən) The belief that the Chinese emperor's right to rule came from the gods. (p. 175)

manor (man'ər) In the Middle Ages, a large self-sufficient estate granted to a lord and worked by serfs. (p. 320)

map key (map kē) A list of map symbols that tells what each symbol stands for. (p. G8)

Meiji Restoration (mā' jē' res tə rā' shən) The overthrow of Japan's shogun in 1868 and restoration of power to the emperor Meiji. (p. 510)

mercator projection (mər kā'tər prə jek'shən) A map that shows accurate shapes of land masses and correct straight-line directions, but which is distorted for areas near the poles. (p. 432)

meridian (mə rid'ē ən) Any line of longitude east or west of Earth's prime meridian. *See* **parallel.** (p. G4)

Messiah (mə sī'ə) A special leader the Jewish people believe will be sent by God to guide them and set up God's rule on Earth. Christians believe Jesus to be the Messiah. (p. 247)

mestizo (me stē'zō) A person of mixed Native American and Spanish ancestry. (p. 494)

Middle Ages (mid'əl āj'əz) A period in European history between A.D. 500 and about the 1500s. (p. 320)

Middle Passage (mid'əl pas'ij) The difficult voyage made by enslaved Africans across the Atlantic Ocean to the West Indies where they were sold. (p. 475)

Middle Way (mid'əl wā) In Buddhism, a way of life, neither too strict nor too easy, that results from following the Eightfold Path. (p. 153)

middle class (mid'əl klas) During the Industrial Revolution, the new class of business people. (p. 504)

migrate (mī'grāt) To move from one place to another to live, especially a large group of people. (p. 138)

missionary (mish'ə ner ē) A person who teaches his or her religion to people with different beliefs. (p. 470)

monarchy (mon'ər kē) A government ruled by a king or queen. (p. 197)

monastery (mon'ə ster ē) A community in which monks lead lives devoted to religion. *See* **convent.** (p. 331)

monk (mungk) A man who devotes his life to a religious group, often giving up all he owns. *See* **monastery.** (p. 151)

monotheism (mon'ə thê iz əm) A belief in one God. *See* **polytheism.** (p. 123)

monsoon (mon sün') A seasonal wind that blows across South Asia bringing dry weather in the winter and heavy rains in the summer. (p. 386)

mosque (mosk) A Muslim place of worship. (p. 273)

N

NAFTA (naf'tə) The North American Free Trade Agreement, which went into effect in 1993, allowing free trade for many goods traded between Canada, Mexico, and the United States. (p. 626)

nationalism (nash'ə nə liz əm) A strong loyalty to one's own country and culture. (p. 527)

---

pronunciation key

a at; ā ape; ä far; âr care; e end; ē me; i it; ī ice; îr pierce; o hot; ō old; ô fork; oi oil; ou out; u up; ū use; ü rule, ù pull; ûr turn; hw white; ng song; th thin; <u>th</u> this; zh measure; ə about, taken, pencil, lemon, circus

NATO (nā'tō) The North Atlantic Treaty Organization, a military alliance formed in 1949 by nations in western Europe and North America. (p. 557)

navigable (nav'i gə bəl) Able to be traveled by boats or ships. (p. 318)

New Stone Age (nü stōn āj) The period of human prehistory that lasted from 12,000 years ago to about 6,000 years ago, during which people still depended mainly on stone tools and began experimenting with agriculture. (p. 52)

New Testament (nü tes'tə mənt) The second part of the Christian Bible, containing descriptions of the life and teachings of Jesus and of his early followers. (p. 246)

noble (nō'bəl) A member of a ruling family or one of high rank. See **aristocracy.** (p. 165)

nuclear arms race (nü'klē ər ärmz rās) The Cold War competition between superpowers to develop more powerful and greater numbers of nuclear weapons. (p. 559)

nun (nun) A woman who devotes her life to religion, often living in a convent. See **convent.** (p. 331)

oasis (ō ā'sis) A well-watered area in a desert. (p. 263)

Old Stone Age (ōld stōn āj) The period of human prehistory that lasted until about 12,000 years ago, during which stone tools were the most common technology used by humans. (p. 45)

oligarchy (ol'i gär kē) A type of government in which a small group of citizens control decision-making. (p. 197)

oracle bone (ôr'ə kəl bōn) In ancient China, a cattle or sheep bone used to predict the future. (p. 167)

oral tradition (ôr'əl trə dish'ən) The passing on of history, beliefs, or customs by word of mouth. (p. 25)

P

Pacific Rim (pə sif'ik rim) The ring of countries surrounding the Pacific Ocean. (p. 616)

papyrus (pə pī'rəs) A kind of paper made from papyrus, a reed plant growing along the Nile, that the ancient Egyptians used for writing. (p. 79)

parable (par'ə bəl) A simple story that contains a message or truth. (p. 248)

parallel (par'ə lel) In geography, any line of latitude north or south of the equator; parallels never cross or meet. See **meridian.** (p. G4)

patrician (pə trish'ən) A member of the noble families who controlled all power in the early years of the Roman Republic. (p. 231)

patron (pā'trən) A supporter of the arts. (p. 337)

Pax Romana (paks rō mä'nə) A period of peace for the Roman Empire that began with the rule of Augustus in about 27 B.C. and lasted around 200 years. (p. 236)

peasant (pez'sənt) A small farm owner or farm worker. (p. 487)

Peloponnesian War (pel ə pə nē'zhən wôr) A war fought between Athens and Sparta in the 400s B.C., ending in a victory for Sparta. (p. 208)

peninsula (pə nin'sə lə) An area of land almost entirely surrounded by water. (p. 193)

per capita income (pūr kap'i tə in'kum) The amount of money each person would have if his or her country's total income were divided equally among its people. (p. 601)

pharaoh (fâ'rō) The title used by the rulers of ancient Egypt. (p. 75)

philosophy (fə los'ə fē) The study of or search for truth, wisdom, and the right way to live. (p. 206)

physical map (fiz'i kəl map) A map that primarily shows natural features of Earth, such as lakes, rivers, mountains, and deserts. (p. G10)

pilgrimage (pil'grə mij) A journey for religious purposes. (p. 269)

plague (plāg) A terrible disease that spreads quickly and kills many people. (p. 334)

plantation (plan tā'shən) A large farming estate where mainly a single crop is grown; until the mid-1800s slaves often worked on plantations. (p. 475)

plateau (pla tō') An area of flat land that rises above the surrounding land. (p. 105)

plebeian (pli bē'ən) A common farmer, trader, or craftworker in ancient Rome. (p. 231)

point of view (point əv vū) The position of someone toward the world or a subject, shaped by his or her thinking, attitudes, and feelings. (p. 328)

polar projection (pō'lər prə jek'shən) A map projection that shows the area around the North or South Pole. (p. 432)

polis (pō'lis) A city-state in ancient Greece. (p. 196)

political cartoon (pə lit'i kəl kär tün') A drawing that states an opinion about a political matter. (p. 572)

political map (pə lit'i kəl map) A map mainly showing political divisions, such as national or state boundaries, cities, and capitals. (p. G9)

polytheism (pol'ē thē iz əm) The belief in many gods and goddesses. See **monotheism.** (p. 111)

pope (pōp) The bishop, or church leader, of Rome and head of the Roman Catholic Church. (p. 251)

population density (pop yə lā'shən den'si tê) The number of people living in a given space. (p. 370)

prehistory (prē his'tə rē) The period before events were recorded in writing. (p. 33)

prime meridian (prīm mə rid'ē ən) The line of longitude marked 0° on the world map, from which longitude east and west are measured. (p. G4)

primary source (prī'mer ē sôrs) A first-hand account of an event or an artifact created during the period of history being studied. *See* **secondary source.** (p. 26)

profile (prō'fil) In geography, a map showing a cross-section of a land surface. (p. 228)

projection (prə jek'shən) A way of placing parts of Earth onto a flat map. (p. 432)

propaganda (prop ə gan'də) The spreading of persuasive ideas or attitudes that are often exaggerated or falsified in order to help or hurt a particular cause or group. (p. 541)

Protestantism (prot'ə stən tiz əm) The beliefs of Christians who opposed, or protested against, the Roman Catholic Church in the 1500s; the beliefs of people who follow a Protestant religion today. (p. 344)

province (prov'ins) A division of land within an empire or country. (p. 169)

Punic Wars (pū'nik wôrz) A series of conflicts between Rome and Carthage in the 200s B.C., ending in a victory for Rome. (p. 234)

Q

quipu (kē'pü) A knotted cord used for record-keeping by the Inca. (p. 437)

Quran (kü rän') The most holy book of Islam, believed to contain the teachings of Allah, or God, to Muhammad. (p. 266)

R

rain forest (rān fōr'ist) A warm, wet forest that receives more than 80 inches of rain per year. (p. 288)

Raj (räj) The period in India from the 1850s to 1947 when it was ruled by the British. (p. 581)

reform (ri fôrm') To change. (p. 343)

Reformation (ref ər mā'shən) A movement beginning in Europe in the 1500s, to bring reform to the Roman Catholic Church, and leading to Protestantism. (p. 344)

refugee (ref yù jē') A person who flees his or her country for safety. (p. 577)

region (rē'jən) An area with common features that set it apart from other areas. (p. 9)

Reign of Terror (rān əv ter'ər) The period 1793–1794 in revolutionary France when suspected traitors were beheaded in great numbers. (p. 490)

reincarnation (rē in kär na'shən) A Hindu belief that people move in a constant cycle of life, death, and rebirth. (p. 144)

relief map (ri lēf' map) A map that shows changes in elevation. (p. G10)

Renaissance (ren ə säns') A period of great cultural and artistic change that began in Italy around 1350 and spread throughout Europe. (p. 336)

representative (rep ri zen'tə tiv) A person who is elected by citizens to speak or act for them. *See* **Republic.** (p. 232)

republic (ri pub'lik) A form of government in which citizens elect representatives to speak or act for them. (p. 231)

revolution (rev ə lü'shən) The overthrow of an existing government and its replacement with another; any sudden or very great change. (p. 486)

Roman Catholicism (rō'mən kə thol'ə siz əm) A branch of Christianity that developed in the western Roman empire and that recognized the Pope as its supreme head. (p. 257)

Russian Revolution (rush'ən rev ə lü'shən) Beginning in 1917, the events leading up to the overthrow of tsarist rule and the eventual establishment of the Soviet government led by Vladimir Ilyich Lenin and the Bolsheviks. (p. 532)

S

Sabbath (sab'əth) A weekly day of rest, prayer, and study. (p. 124)

saint (sānt) A woman or man considered by a religious group to be especially holy. (p. 332)

samurai (sam'ù rī) A class of soldiers in fuedal Japan who were loyal only to their lords. (p. 411)

sanction (sangk'shən) A penalty placed against a nation to make it change its behavior, such as a refusal to buy its goods or sell it products. (p. 608)

savanna (sə van'ə) A broad, grassy, plain with few trees, found especially in large parts of Africa. (p. 356)

pronunciation key

a **at**; ā **ape**; ä **far**; âr **care**; e **end**; ē **me**; i **it**; ī **ice**; îr **pierce**; o **hot**; ō **old**; ô **fork**; oi **oil**; ou **out**; u **up**; ū **use**; ü **rule**; ù **pull**; ûr **turn**; hw **white**; ng **song**; th **thin**; <u>th</u> **this**; zh **measure**; ə **about**, tak**e**n, penc**i**l, lem**o**n, circ**u**s

scale (skāl) A unit of measure on a map, such as an inch, that is used to represent a distance on Earth. (p. G7)

scientific method (sī ən tif'ik meth'əd) A way of studying things through questioning and thorough testing. (p. 460)

scribe (skrīb) A professional writer who kept records and copied letters and official documents. (p. 78)

secondary source (sek'ən der ē sôrs) A record of the past, based on information from primary sources. (p. 27)

seismograph (sīz'mə graf) A scientific instrument that could detect earthquakes hundreds of miles away, invented during the Han dynasty. (p. 177)

Senate (sen'it) The lawmaking body and most powerful branch of government in ancient Rome's Republic. (p. 232)

serf (sûrf) In the Middle Ages, a person who was bound to work on a noble's manor. (p. 320)

Shinto (shin'tō) A Japanese religion marked by the belief in the spirits of nature. (p. 410)

shogun (shō'gən) The ruler of feudal Japan from the 1100s to the 1800s who, although appointed by the emperor, ruled the country as a military dictator. (p. 411)

silt (silt) A mixture of tiny bits of soil and rock carried and deposited by a river. (p. 71)

slash and burn (slash and bûrn) A farming method involving the cutting of trees, then the burning of them to provide ash-enriched soil for the planting of crops. (p. 293)

slavery (slā'və rē) The practice of one person owning another person. (p. 95)

small-scale map (smôl skāl map) A map that shows a big area in less detail by measuring its greater distance in large units. (p. 92)

social pyramid (sō'shəl pir'ə mid) A diagram illustrating the divisions within a culture; usually showing the most powerful person or group at the peak and the least powerful groups at the bottom. (p. 95)

socialism (sō'shə liz əm) An economic and political system based on collective or government ownership and control of all resources and industry; also a political philosophy based on the writings of Karl Marx. (p. 505)

specialization (spesh ə lə zā'shən) Training to do a particular kind of work. (p. 55)

stela (stē'lə) A tall, flat stone, often carved with writing, used to mark an important historical event. (p. 302)

steppe (step) A dry, grassy, treeless plain found in Asia and eastern Europe. (p. 163)

strait (strāt) A narrow channel, or body of water, connecting two larger bodies of water. (p. 464)

strike (strīk) A refusal to work as a protest against unfair treatment. (p. 534)

subcontinent (sub kon'tə nənt) A large landmass that is connected to the rest of a continent. (p. 131)

sugarcane (shủg'ər kān) A tall grass with a thick, woody stem containing a liquid that is a source of sugar. (p. 475)

sultan (sult' ən) Supreme ruler of the Ottoman empire. (p. 389)

summary (sum'ə rē) A brief statement of main ideas. (p. 172)

superpower (sü'pər pou ər) A term used for the world's strongest nations—the United States, China, and the Soviet Union—during the Cold War. (p. 556)

supply (sə plī') In economics, the available quantity of a good, product, or resource. See **demand.** (p. 363)

surplus (sûr'plus) An extra supply of something, such as crops that are not needed immediately for food. (p. 55)

symbol (sim'bəl) Anything that stands for something else. (p. G8)

T

technology (tek nol'ə jē) The use of skills and tools to meet practical human needs. (p. 45)

telescope (tel'ə skōp) An optical instrument for making distant objects, such as planets and stars, appear nearer and larger. (p. 457)

temperate (tem'pər it) Mild; moderate in temperature. (p. 317)

Ten Commandments (ten kə mand'mənts) According to the Hebrew Bible, the laws God gave to Moses on Mount Sinai. (p. 123)

terrace (ter'is) A level platform of earth built into a hillside, usually used for farming. (p. 437)

textile (teks'tīl) A cloth fabric that is either woven or knitted. (p. 501)

Three Fires Council (thrē firz koun'səl) A league or cooperative group formed by the Ojibwa and the neighboring Potawatomi and Ottawa to promote trade. (p. 441)

timberline (tim'bər līn) An imaginary line on high mountains or in the arctic; above or beyond it trees cannot grow. (p. 424)

time line (tīm līn) A diagram that shows when events took place during a given period of time. (p. 58)

time zone (tīm zōn) A geographic region where the same standard time is used. (p. 548)

topic sentence (top'ik sen'təns) A sentence that contains the main idea of a paragraph, often the first sentence in that paragraph. (p. 172)

Torah (tôr'ə) The first five books of the Hebrew Bible containing the laws and teachings of Judaism. (p. 123)

totalitarian (tō tal i târ'ē ən) A government in which a dictator or a small group of leaders control all aspects of people's lives. (p. 538)

township (toun'ship) A segregated area where blacks in South Africa were forced to live under apartheid. (p. 607)

trade (trād) The exchange of goods between peoples. (p. 56)

Treaty of Versailles (trē'tē əv vâr sī') The treaty that the Allied Powers forced Germany to sign at the end of World War I. (p. 531)

Triangular Trade (trī ang'gyə lər trād) From the 1500s to the mid-1800s, the triangular-shaped trade routes between the Americas, England, and Africa, which involved the buying and selling of captive Africans as well as guns, sugar, and iron goods. (p. 476)

tribune (trib'ūn) An elected leader of ancient Rome who represented the interests of the plebeians. (p. 232)

tribute (trib'ūt) A tax, often in the form of crops, paid by one ruler to another, usually to ensure peace or protection. (p. 428)

Triple Alliance (trip'əl ə lī'əns) The pact that the army of the Aztec made with the forces of Texcoco and Tlacopan in 1428 in order to gain control of the Valley of Mexico. (p. 428)

tropical (trop'i kəl) Of or relating to the area of Earth between the Tropic of Cancer (23.5°N) and the Tropic of Capricorn (23.5°S). (p. 287)

tsar (zär) In pre-revolution Russia, the emperor. (p. 533)

tundra (tun'drə) A vast, treeless plain in arctic or subarctic places such as Alaska and northern Canada. (p. 422)

Twelve Tables (twelv tā'belz) The earliest written collection of Roman laws, drawn up by patricians about 450 B.C., that became the foundation of Roman law. (p. 233)

U

unification (ū nə fi kā'shən) The joining of separate parts, such as kingdoms, into one. (p. 75)

United Nations (ū nī'tid nā'shənz) An organization founded in 1945 whose members include most of the world's nations. It works to preserve world peace, settle disputes, and aid international cooperation. (p. 557)

urbanization (ur bən ə zā'shən) The growth of cities. (p. 625)

V

values (val'ūz) Ideals or beliefs that guide the way people live. (p. 16)

vassal (vas'əl) In the Middle Ages, a noble who usually was given a fief by his lord in exchange for loyalty. (p. 322)

Vedas (vā'dəz) In Hinduism, the ancient books of sacred songs on which much of its religious beliefs are based. (p. 143)

Vietnam War (vē et näm' wôr) A civil war fought between South Vietnam, aided by the United States, and communist North Vietnam during 1954–1975. (p. 589)

W

warlord (wôr'lôrd) In China, 1912–1927, a strong local military leader who took advantage of political unrest to seize power in the area. (p. 551)

Warsaw Pact (wôr'sô pakt) A military alliance formed in 1955 by the Soviet Union and seven eastern European nations. (p. 557)

wigwam (wig'wom) A dome-shaped dwelling built by the Ojibwa and other Native Americans made of birch bark, cattail reeds, and wooden poles. (p. 443)

working class (wûrk'ing klas) People who work for wages, such as factory workers. (p. 504)

World War I (wûrld wôr) Called the "Great War" at the time, the war of 1914–1918 in which the Allied Powers defeated the Central Powers. (p. 531)

World War II (wûrld wôr) The war of 1939–1945 in which the Allies defeated the Axis powers. (p. 542)

Z

ziggurat (zig'ù rat) A large temple located in the centers of ancient Sumerian cities. (p. 111)

Zionism (zī'ə niz əm) A movement to create a national homeland for the Jewish people. (p. 575)

---

pronunciation key

a **at**; ā **ape**; ä **far**; âr **care**; e **end**; ē **me**; i **it**; ī **ice**; îr **pierce**; o **hot**; ō **old**; ô **fork**; oi **oil**; ou **out**; u **up**; ū **use**; ü **rule**; ù **pull**; ûr **turn**; hw **white**; ng **song**; th **thin**; <u>th</u> **this**; zh measure; ə **about**, taken, pencil, lemon, circus

index

index

This Index lists many topics that appear in the book, along with the pages on which they are found. Page numbers after an m refer you to a map. Page numbers after a p indicate photographs, artwork, or charts.

CREDITS

Cover: Giraudon/Art Resource

Maps: Geosystems

Charts and Graphs: Eliot Bergman: pp 57, 290, 291, 319, 387, 425; Hima Pamoedjo: pp 357, 487, 513, 625

Chapter Opener Globes: Greg Wakabayashi

Illustrations: Richard Cowdrey: pp. 48-49; John Edens: pp. 564-565; Joseph Forte: pp. 42-43, 102-103, 284-285, 352-353; George Gaadt: pp. 68-69, 222-223; Theodore Glazer: pp. 106; Adam Hook: pp. 80, 314-315; Patricia Isaza: pp. 602, 611, 620, 628; Hrano Janto: pp. 73, 95; David McCall Johnston: pp. 128-129, 158-159, 260-261, 442, 454-455; W.B. Johnston: pp. 109, 166; Dave Joly: pp. 17, 37, 55, 91, 107, 114, 163, 206, 275, 289, 333, 375, 391, 459, 511, 531, 568, 603, 621, 627; Robert Korta: pp. 420-421; Rudy Lazlo: pp. 216-217; Angus McBride: pp. 140-141, 484-485; Peg McGovern: pp. 36; Hima Pamoedjo: pp. 18-19, 51, 75, 365, 395, 406-407, 503, 628; Roger Payne: pp. 207; Oliver Rennert: pp. 54; Steven Stankiewicz: pp. 88-89; Robert Van Nutt: pp. 323, 405, 382-383, 524-525 Cover: i. Lee Bolton Picture Library

PHOTOGRAPHY CREDITS: All photographs are by the McGraw-Hill School Division (MMSD)except as noted below.

i: Giraudon/Art Resource. iii: m. The Picture Cube; b. Gerald Champlong/The Image Bank. iv: b. P. Aventu Rier/Gamma Liaison; t. The Granger Collection. v: b. Art Resource, Inc.; t. Lee Boltin; m. Daemmrich/The Image Works. vi: t.l. Scala Art Resource; m., b. Lee Boltin. vii: b. Lee Boltin Picture Library; t. Woodfin Camp Picture Agency; b. Phillips Collection. viii: t. Robert Harding Picture Agency; m.l. Corbis/Bettmann Archives; b. Phillip Makanna/Ghost. ix: EPA Scala. x: vautier/Woodfin Camp. G2: b. Patrick Ward; t. Michael Yamashita. G23: Elizabeth Wolf. G3: t. David Ryan/Photo 20-20; t. Nicholas DeVore III; b. Gerald S. Cubitt; m. Susan Griggs Agency. **Chapter 1** 2: t. Suraj N. Sharma/Dinodia Picture Agency; b. Gerald Champlong/The Image Bank; m. The Picture Cube. 3: b. David L. Brill. 4: b. Grisewood & Dempsey, Ltd. 45: Adam Woolfitt. 5: b.l. Grisewood & Dempsey, Ltd.; t. Hugh Sitton/Tony Stone Images. 6: Frank Labua/Gamma Liaison. 7: t. Wang Fuchun/China Stock; m. Freeman Patterson/Masterfile; m. Thomas Kanzler/Viesti Associates; b. Thomas Mangelson/Images of Nature. 8: t.l. Earth Imaging/Tony Stone Images. 10: b.l. Less Stone/Sygma; b.r. D. Donne Bryant; m.l. D. Donne Bryant. 14: t.l. Pablo Bartholomew. 15: t.l. Dinodia. 16-17: Pablo Bartholomew. 18: t.r. courtesy Brian Lawlor; t.l. courtesy Rachel Dennis; b.l. courtesy Anna Patricia DeMartinez; b.r. courtesy Olanike Olakunki. 19: rtesy Harry Tan. **Chapter 2** 22: b. Frank La Bua/Gamma Liaison. 23: b. Gordon Gohan/National Geographic Society; m. Tom Bean/Tony Stone Worldwide; t. R. Ian llyod/Westlight. 25: m. Comstock; b. Ken Vinocur/The Picture Cube. 26: r. UPI/Corbis- Bettmann. 27: Authentic old ads. 28: l. Corbis/Bettmann; t. Uniphoto Picture Agency. 30: b.l. Robert Freck/Woodfin Camp, Inc.; m. The Granger Collection; b.r. William Kennedy/The Image Bank. 32: t.r. Uniphoto Picture Agency. 34: t.l. Paul Hanny/Gamma Liaison; t.r. Sygma. 35: b.r. Hinterleitner/Gamma Liaison; m. Rex U.S.A, Ltd. 38: t.l. Comstock. 39: t. courtesy Gustavo Araoz; m. courtesy Nancy Marzulla; b. courtesy Brenda Pavlic. **Chapter 3** 44: t.l. Pierre Boulot/Woodfin Camp. 45: b.r. Chris Johns/Tony Stone Images; b.l. AnthroPhoto File. 46: t.l. Ira Block. 47: b.l. George Holton/Photo Researchers; b.r. Erwin and Peggy Bauer/Bruce Coleman, Inc. 48: t.l. Steve Elmore/The Stock Market; t.r. Reunions des Musees Nationaux, Paris; b. Dr. Peter Beaumont/McGregor Museum, South Africa. 49: t.r., Institute of Vertebrate and Paleonthology and Paleoanthropology, Beijing, China; b.r. Mark Newman/Photo Researchers. 5051: m. Gamma Liaison. 51: t.l. Boston Museum of Fine Arts/Explorer?; m. courtesy of The Trustees of the Victoria and Albert Museum; b.r. Image Bank. 52: t. Ed Malitsky/Liaison International. 53: b. Sonia Halliday Photography. 56: m., b. Dr. James Meelaart. 64: t.r. Israel Museum; t.l. The Granger Collection; m.r. The Metropolitan Museum of Art, Fletcher Fund, 1931 31.13.1; b. Gamma Liaison 65: m. Giraudon; b. Giraudon. 66: b.l. R. W. Nicholson. 66-67: Michael Yamashita, Woodfin Camp, Inc. 67: t.l. Brian Brake, Photo Researchers; m. Georg Gerster. **Chapter 4** 70: t.l. O.L. Mazzatesta/National Geographic Society. 72: b. Michael Holford/British Museum; m. Nino Mascardy/The Image Bank. 74: t.l. Superstock. 75: b. Wernher Krutein/Liaison International. 77: b. The Granger Collection; b. Louvre/Agence Photographique des Musees Nationale; l. source:Superstock/British Museum. 78: b.r. Lee Boltin; bkgnd. Brian Brake/Photo Researchers. 79: Bridgeman Art Library, British Museum/Art Resource. 82: m. Werner Forman Archive, The British Museum, London/Art Resource. 83: t.l. Giraudon; r. Paul Popper, Ltd.; b.l. Superstock. 84: t.r. Giraudon. 85: r. British Museum; t.l. Erich Lessing/PhotoEdit. 87: b. John G. Ross; t. Giraudon/Paris. 88: m. Kelvin Wilson. 89: b. Lee Boltin; t. Metropolitan Museum of Art. 90: t.l. Giraudon. 93: b. Mike Rothwell/FPG International. 94: t.r. The Granger Collection. 96: t.r. The Granger Collection. 97: b. Richard Steedman/The Stock Market. 98: l., r. The Granger Collection; m. Brian Brake/Photo Researchers. 99: b.l. Giraudon. **Chapter 5** 104: t.l. Nik Wheeler/Black Star. 108: t.l. Michael Holford/The British Museum. 111: m.r. Art Resource (Iraq Museum Baghdad); b. Nik Wheeler. 112: m.l. Baghdad Museum/Hirner Fotoarchive (Art Resource); b. Giraudon. 113: t.r. Musee du Louvre, Paris. 114-115:m. Comstock. 115: m. The Oriental Institute of Chicago. 116: m. Giraudon. 117: b.r. bicycles in Beijing, China; m. Bob Thomason/Tony Stone Images; t.r. Jerry & Sharon Austin/The Picture Cube. 118: b.l. Erich Lessing/Art Resource; b.r. British Museum. 120: t.l. The Bettmann Archive. 122: t. B.A. Stewart/National Geographic Society; b.m. Richard T. Nowitz. 123: b. The Jewish Museum. 124: t. Kay Chernush/The Image Bank; m. Zviki-Eshet/The Stock Market. 125: b. Miro Vintoniv/The Picture Cube. **Chapter 6** 130: t.l. Pramod Mistry/Dinodia. 131: b.l. Patrick Morrow. 132: t.r. Susan McCartney. 133: m.l. Ric Ergenbright; b. Charles Marden Fitch/Superstock. 135: b.r. Giraudon/Paris. 136: b. Harrison Forman; m. Jehangir Gazdar/Woodfin Camp, Inc. 137: t.r. Dilip Mehta/Contact Press. 138-139:b. George F. Mobley/National Geographic Society. 142: t.l. Lindsay Hebberd/Woodfin Camp, Inc. 142-143:b. Mike Yamashita. 144: t. Jeffrey Alford/Asia Access; m.r. Brian Vikander. 145: b. Robert Frerck/Odyssey Productions. 146: b. Arvind Garg/Gamma Liaison; m.l. Giraudon/New Dehli National Museum; m.r. Giraudon/Musee Guimet, Paris. 147: t.l. Galen Rowell. 148: m. EPA/Scala. 149: b. Ernt Jahn/Bruce Coleman, Inc.; t. Lindsay Hebberd/Woodfin Camp, Inc.; m. Scala/Art Resource, Inc. 151: t.r. The Granger Collection. 152: m.r. Hilarie Kavanagh/Tony Stone Worldwide; t. Everton/The Image Works. 153: b.r. Dinodia Picture Agency; b.l. Ric Ergenbright Photography. 154-155: Wolfgang Kaehler. 155: m. Pablo Bartholomew/Gamma Liaison. **Chapter 7** 160: t.l. Claus Meyer/Black Star. 161: (Background for Map) Wolfgang Kaehler. 162: m. Photographer Photos Co./Gamma Liaison; l. Forest Anderson/Gamma Liaison; r. Min Zhongjie/Sovphoto Eastphoto. 164: t.l. Smithsonian Institute. 165: b. James Burke/Life Magazine (c) 1961, Time Inc. 166: l. British Library/Werner Forman Archive/Art Resource, Inc. 167: t. ChinaStock Photo Library. 168: t.l. Wolfgang Kaehler. 169: b. Sovfoto/Eastfoto. 170: t.l. Xinhua News Agency; t.r. Gamma-Liaison. 171: m. Wolfgang Kaehler/Gamma-Liaison. 172-173:m. Rolan Lloyd/Westlight. 173: b.r. Wolfgang Kaehler. 174: t.l. Bibliotheque Nationale/Paris. 175: b. Bibliotheque Nationale/Superstock. 176: t.l. Anderson/Gamma Liaison. 177: b. Michael Holford. 178: b.l. Asian Art & Archaeology/Art Resource. 179: Wu Qing. 180: m. Bibliotheque Nationale/Giraudon; t.l. Xinxua/Gamma Liaison. 181: m.l. Sovfoto/Eastfoto; t. Minneapolis Institute of Arts; b.l. Sovfoto/Eastfoto. **Chapter 8** 185: b. Monica Stevenson for MMSD. 186: t.l. Werner Forman/Art Resource; t.r. Lee Boltin/Boltin Picture Library; b.l. Daemmrich/The Image Works. 186-187:b.r. Alan Beckey/The Image Bank. 187: r. Lauros-Giraudon/Art Resource. 188: b. James M. Gurney. 188-189: O. Louis Mazzatenta. 192: t.l. Rick Falco/Black Star. 194: t.l. Dimaggio/Kalish/The Stock Market; t.r. Calvin Larsen/Photo Researchers. 194-195:m. Art Resource, Inc. 195: b.r. Trireme Trust/Cambridge University, UK. 196: t.l. Robert Frerck/Woodfin Camp & Associates. 197: b. J. Pavlovsky/Sygma. 199: m.r. Michael Holford; b. Eric Lessing/Art Resource. 200: t.r. Art Resource. 201: b.l. FPG International. 202: t. Paul J. Sutton/Duomo. 202-203: Paul J. Sutton/Duomo. 203: t. Kathleen Kliskey/The Picture Cube; b. Al Tielemaus/Duomo. 204: t.l. Nimatallah/Art Resource. 205: t. David Lees; b. Harold Sund/The Image Bank. 209: t.l. Erich Lessing/Art Resource, Inc.; m. Art Resource. 210: Giraudon. 211: b. Culver Pictures. 212: t.l. Giraudon. 213: m.l. Art Resource; b.r. National Geographic Society. 215: m. Boltin Picture Library; t. Gilda Alberto Rossi/The Image Bank. 219: t.r., courtesy Robert Anderson; m. courtesy Martin Krause; b. courtesy Greek Tourist Board. **Chapter 9** 224: t.l. Mike Mazzaschi/Stock Boston. 226: Amanda Merullo/Stock Boston. 227: m.l. Michael Salas/The Image Bank. 230: t.l. Ronald Sheridan Photo Library. 231: b. John G. Ross/Art Resource. 233: b. Scala/Art Resource. 234-235: The Granger Collection. 236: t.r. Scala/Art Resource. 237: i. Ronald Sheridan/Ancient Art & Architecture Historical Museum of Vienna; r. Art Resource. 238-239:t. Randy Wells/Tony Stone Images. 239: m. Louis Goldman/Photo Researchers. 240-241: Elaine Harrington/The Stock Market. 240: m. Art Resource. 242: t.r. Scala/Art Resource; t.l. Erich Lessing/Art Resource; b.l. Alinari/Giraudon; b. D.L. Mazzatenta/National Geographic Society Image Collection. 243: t. Leonard Von Matt; b. Cauros/Giraudon. 244-245:m. Tone Stone Images. 245: m.r. Emory Kristof/National Geographic Society; b. David Ball/The Picture Cube; t. F.H.C. Birch/Sonia Halliday Photography. 246: t.l. Scala/Art Resource. (Sistine Chapel). 248: b. (Fra Angelico) Giraudon. 249: t. Superstock; b. Dean Conger/National Geographic Society. 250-251:b. UPI/Bettmann. 250: b. Jeff Greenberg/Photo Edit. 252: t.r. Erich Lessing/Art Resource. 253: b. Giraudon. 255: b. Giraudon; t. Allan Oddie/Photo Edit. 256: b. Marco Cristofori/The Stock Market. **Chapter 10** 262: b. The Stock Market; t.l. Robert Azzi/Woodfin Camp, Inc. 264-265:t. Superstock. 264: t. Tom Hollyman/Photo Researchers. 266: b. Eric Millette; t.l. Giraudon/Musee des Arts Africains et Doceanie, Paris. 268: t.r. Nabeel Turner/Tony Stone Images; t.l. Nicholas Devore/Tony Stone Images. 270: m. Superstock; t. Chip Hires/Gamma Liaison. 270-271:b. P. Manoukian/Sygma. 272: t.l. Michael Holford. 274: b.r. Michael Howell/Stock Boston, Inc.; l. Giraudon/Cairo National Library. 276: t.l. David Ball/The Stock Market; b. Art Resource, Inc. 276-277:m. Art Resource, Inc. 277: b. E.R. Degginger/Bruce Coleman, Inc.; t.r. Superstock. 278-279:m. The Granger Collection. 279: b. Tom Van Sant/Geosphere Project; t. Bibliotheque Nationale, Paris, France/Art Resource, Inc.; m. Giraudon. **Chapter 11** 286: t.r. Charles Hennechieu/Bruce Coleman, Inc. 288: t.l. Cindy Karp/National Geographic Society; t.r. Masterfile; b. Klaus Meyer/Black Star. 292: b. D. Donne Bryant Stock Photography; t.l. Rick Strange/The Picture Cube. 294: m. National Geographic Society. 294-295:m. National Geographic Society. 295: b. Kenneth Garrett/National Geographic Society. 296: t.l. Everton/The Image Works. 297: courtesy Nancy L. Hinchler Zuñiga. 298: t.l. Kathleen Campbell/Gamma Liaison; b. Hiro Matsumoto/Black Star. 300: b. Everton/The Image Works; m. Carolyn Schaefer/Gamma Liaison. 301: b.r. Kenneth Garrett/Woodfin Camp, Inc.; b.l. Kathleen Campbell/Gamma Liaison. 302: m. Vautier/Woodfin Camp, Inc. 303: t. Robert Freck/Woodfin Camp, Inc. 304: t. Markova/The Stock Market. 304-305:m. Ted Kaufman/The Stock Market. 305: t.r. Gamma-Liaison; m. Julian Baum/Photo Researchers. **Chapter 12** 309: b. Mager Photo for MMSD. 310: b.r. Christopher Liu/ChinaStock; t.r. Lee Boltin; t. Adam Woolfit/Woodfin Camp Inc.; b.l. Scala/Art Resource. 311: m.r. National Portrait Gallery, London/Superstock; b.r. Lee Boltin. 312-313: David Louis Olson. 312: l. Christopher A. Klein. 313: b. E. C. Erdis, Peabody Museum of Natural History; t. Robert S. Sacha. 316: t.l. Uniphoto 318: l. Bob Llewellyn/Superstock; b.r. Phyllis Greenberg/Comstock 320: t.l. Superstock 321: m. Superstock 322: m. Erich Lessing/Art Resource; b. Pascal Lebrun/Gamma Liaison 324: t.l. Zefo-Hans Adam/The Stock Market; r. Superstock 325: t. Jonathan Blair/Woodfin Camp and Assoc. 326: t.r. Michael Holford 326-327:b. Bridgeman/Giraudon 328-329:b. Giraudon 330: t.l. Evan Agostini/Gamma Liaison Int'l; m. Art Resource. 330-331:m. The Pierpont Morgan Library/Art Resource 331: b.r. Topham/The Image Works 332: l. Superstock 332-333:t. Adam Woolfit/Woodfin Camp 333: t.r. Adam Woolfitt/Woodfin Camp. 334: m. Howard Hughes/Superstock 335: t. The Granger Collection. 336: t.l. Evan Agostini/Gamma Liaison International. 337: b.l. Jim Zuckerman/Westlight; m. Scala/Art Resource, Inc. 338: b.r. Art Resource (Louvre) 339: m.r. Art Resource; t.l. Giraudon. 340: m.l. Time Museum, Rockford, Illinois; b.l. Metropolitan Museum of Art, H.O. Havemeyer Collection, bequest of Mrs. H.O. Havemeyer, 1929; m. The Granger Collection. 341: t.r. Kunstmuseum, Basel; b.r. Art Resource. 342: t.l. Photo Researchers. 343: m. Art Resource 344: b.l. Giraudon 346: t.l. Superstock. 346-347:t. Michael Holford. 348: m. The Granger Collection 349: t.l. The Kobal Collection; t.r. Martha Swope/Time Picture Syndication; b. The Granger Collection **Chapter 13** 354: t. Robert Caputo/Aurora. 356: l. Robert Caputo/Aurora; r. Alon Reininger/Contact Press Images. 358: l. Robert Caputo/Aurora; b.r. Georg Gerster/Comstock. 360: l. Wendy Stone/The Gamma Liaison Network; t.r. Robert Caputo/Aurora. 361: b. Kal Muller/Woodfin Camp & Associates. 362: t. Lee Boltin. 363: t.l. Volkmar Wentzel/National Geographic Society Image Collection; t.r. Aldo Tutino/Art Resource, Inc. 365: t.r. John Elk III/Bruce Coleman; m., m.l. The Granger Collection; b. Norman Myers/Bruce Coleman, Inc.; t. John Elk III/Bruce Coleman, Inc. 366: b.l. The Granger Collection. 367: t. Jeffrey Ploskonka/National Museum of African Art. 368: m. Marc and Evelyne Bernheim/Woodfin Camp 369: t.l., b.l. Jack Vartoogian; t.r. Jeffrey Salter. 370: l. Bruno De Hogues/Tony Stone Images. 371: m. Guido Alberto Rossi/The Image Bank. 372: t. Marc and Evelyne Bernheim/Woodfin Camp; b. Werner Forman Archive 374: b. Anne Martens/The Image Bank 376: t. Wendy Stone/ Gamma Liaison 378-379:t. James L. Stansfield/Nat'l Geographic Society. 378: b. Guido Alberto Rossi/The Image Bank. **Chapter 14** 384: t.l. Barbara Rowell. 386: l. Gamma Liaison; r. Galen Rowell 388: m. Giraudon 389: b. Superstock. 392: t.l. Superstock. 393: b.r. Superstock. 394: t.l. Christina Dameyer/Photo 20-20. 395: m. Courtesy of the Trustees of the Victoria and Albert Museum. 396: l. Air India Library; r. Dallas and John Heaton/Westlight. 397: m. Boltin Picture Library. 398: t.l. Kevin R. Morris/Tony Stone Images. 400: m. R.Ian LLoyd/Westlight. 400-401:m. Ernest Manewal/Photo 20-20. 402: m. Allan Seiden/The Image Bank. 406: b.l. SIPA Press/Art Resource; b.l. Giraudon. 407: b. Guido Alberto Ross/The Image Bank; t.r. The Granger Collection. 408: t.l. National Portrait Gallery,

London/Superstock; r. The Granger Collection 410: l. Ronald R. Johnson/Stockphotos, Inc 412: b.l. Boltin Picture Library 413: l. Fujifotos/The Image Works 414: l. Fukuhara, Inc./Westlight 414-415:m. Bridgeman/Art Resource 416: m. Superstock 417: r. Superstock **Chapter 15** 422: t.l. The Stock Market. 424: l. Aaron Strong/ Liaison International; r. Walter Leonardi/Gamma-Liaison. 426: t.l. Boltin Picture Library. 428: t. H. Tom Hall/ National Geographic Society. 428-429:t. Erich Lessing/Art Resource. 429: b. Boltin Picture Library. 430: b.l. Ned M. Seidler/National Geographic Society; t. Giraudon. 431: t. Art Resource, Inc. 434: t. Ric Ergenbright; b. Dallas Museum of Fine Art/Werner Forman Archive/Art Resource. 436: l. Ric Ergenbright; r. Nick Saunders/Barbara Heller/Art Resource. 437: t. Museum Fur Volkerkunde, Berlin/Werner Forman Archive/Art Resource; b. Wolfgang Kaehler. 438: t. Ric Ergenbright; b. Boltin Picture Library. 439: t.l. Bruce Coleman, Inc. 440: m. David Meunch 443: b. Greenlar/The Image Works 444: t.l. Peabody Museum/Harvard University, photo by Hille Burger; b.r. Lee Boltin; m.r. National Museum of the American Indian. 445: t.r. David Perdew/Stock South **Chapter 16** 449: b. Monica Stevenson for MMSD. 450: b. Superstock; t.r. Jonathan Blair/Woodfin Camp, Inc.; t.l. Lee Boltin; m. The Phillips Collection. 451: t.r. Eric Lessing/Art Resource; b.r. Michael Holford. 452-453: Gordon W. Gahan. 452: t. Don Kincaid. 453: t. National Maritime Museum, London; b.l. Jean-Leon Huens. 456: t.l. Museo Della Scienza, Scala/Art Resource. 457: l. Erich Lessing/Art Resource; r. The Granger Collection. 458: m.r. Erich Lessing/Art Resource; r. The Granger Collection. 460: b.l. Michael Holford. 461: b.r. European Space Agency. 462: t.l. Michael Holford. 463: m.r. The Granger Collection; b.r. Michael Holford. 465: t.l. Giraudon/Art Resource. 466: t.l. The Granger Collection. 468: l. Superstock; r. Giraudon. 469: t.r. Nick Saunders/Barbara Heller/Art Resource. 470: l. Nick Nicholson/The Image Bank; r. Alon Reininger/Woodfin Camp & Associates. 471: b.l. M. Timothy O'Keefe/Bruce Coleman, Inc. 472: b. The Granger Collection. 473: b.r. Roswell Museum and Art Center; Roswell Museum. 474: t.l. The Granger Collection. 476: t. Bridgeman/Giraudon. 478: t. Doug Armand/Tony Stone Images. 479: b. Image Works; t. Art Resource. 480: b. Image Works. 481: t. Image Works. **Chapter 17** 486: t.l. Superstock. 487: b. Giraudon. 489-492: Giraudon. 494: m. Giraudon. 495: m. Byron Augustin/DDB Stock Photo. 497: t. Super Stock. 498: m. Michael Evans/Sygma. 499: t. Gamma Liaison; m. Cindy Karp/Black Star; b. AP/Wide World Photos. 500: t.l. The Granger Collection. 501: t. Michael Holford; b. Victoria and albert Museum/Superstock. 502: t.l. Superstock 503: Josepa Szkoiddinski/The Image Bank. 504: l. Bridgeman/Giraudon; r. Granger Collection. 505: t. Superstock. 508: t.l. Robert Harding Picture Library. 509: m. The Granger Collection; b. National Portrait Gallery, Smithsonian Institution/Art Resource. 510: l. Jack Fields/Photo Researchers, Inc.; r. Lauros-Giraudon. 512: b. Wernher Krutein/Liaison International. 514: t.m. Robert Harding. 514-515: Robert Harding. **Chapter 18** 520: m. Gamma-Liaison International; b. Bettmann Archives.; t.l. c. Philip Makanna/Ghosts. 521: m. Robert Harding; The Bettmann Archives. 522: b. Sygma. 522-523: NASA. 526: t.l. Bettmann Archive. 527: b.r. Roger-Viollet. 529: Archive Photos. 530: m.r. Archive Photo; t.r. Roger-Viollet; b.l. Roger Viollet. 531: Bettmann Archive. 532: Art Resource, Inc. 534: l. PopperFoto/Archive Photos; r. Gamma-Liaison. 535: b. Roger-Viollet. 536: t.l. UPI/Bettmann. 537: l. Scala/Art Resource; r. Sovfoto/Eastfoto. 538: l. Archive Photos; b. Roger Viollet. 540: t.l. Hans Wild/Time Life 541: Roger-Viollet 542: l. Archive Photos; r. Roger-Viollet 545: m. Archive Photos 546-547: Gamma Liaison 549: m. Etienne De Malglaive/Liaison International 550: m. Sovfoto/Eastfoto 551-552: Roger-Viollet 553: m. Archive Photos 554: m. Sovfoto/Eastfoto 556-558: UPI/Bettman 559: t.l. Sygma 560: t.r. The Bettman Archive; t.l. Werner Wolff/Black Star 560-561:m. UPI/Bettman **Chapter 19** 567: t.l. Owen Franken/Stock Boston; t.l. Carrion/Sygma. 569: The Bettmann Archive. 571: t.r. Archive Photos. 574: Superstock. 575: b.r. The Bettmann Archive. 577: b.r. Sygma. 578: t.r. Allen Tannenbaum/Sygma. 579: m. Karen Wald Cohen/Interns for Peace 580: t.l. Tom Wagner/SABA; r. Ken Straiton/Stock Market. 581: b.r. Popperfoto. 584: l. Sygma. 584-585:m. J.Martin/Popperfoto. 586: t.l. Gamma Liaison/Wolfgang Kaehler. 588: b.r. Bettman; l. Charles Bonnay/Black Star. 589: t. Ray Cranbourne/Black Star 590: t.l. Bettman; m. Hain Edvard/Gamma Liaison International **Chapter 20** 595-596: P.Piel/Gamma-Liaison. 597: l. Peter Turnley/Black Star; r. Bouvet/Gamma Liaison. 598: m. Paul O'Driscoll/Gamma Liaison; l. Peter Turnley/Black Star. 600: Igmor Zamur/Gamma Liaison. 602: t.r. Vlastinir Shone/Gamma Liaison; r. Archive Photos. 605: courtesy Zlato Filipovic. 606: t.l. Peter Turnley/Black Star. 608: b.l. S. Balic/Sygma. 610: Reuters/Bettman. 611: t.r. Tibor Bognar/The Stock Market; b.r. Ed Lallo/Liaison International; m.r. Lawrence Hughes/The Image Bank. 612: t.l. Roy Franco/Panos. 613: courtesy Ashwell Zwane and Bernent Kekalakala. 614: t.l. Francis Li/Liaison International. 615: b.l. Tom Wagner/SABA; r. Ken Straiton/Stock Market. 617: t.r. Hirokuyi Matsumoto/Black Star. 618: m.r. P. Durand/Sygma; b.r. J. Langevin/Sygma; m.l. Bill Pierce/Sygma. 619: t.r. Liu Hueng Shing/Contact. 620: t.r. Mark Harris/Tony Stone Worlwide. 624: t.l. Richard Melloul/Sygma. 626: t.r. Jeff Titcomb/Liaison International; t.r. Stephen Derr/Image Bank. 628: t.r. Stephanie Maze/National Geographic Society. 631: t. courtesy Joanne Cheng; m. Georgey Kadar; b. Kassim Yahya. 635: b. Monica Stevenson for MMSD. Endpapers: Bridgeman/Art Library.

(continued from page ii)

Acknowledgments

Extract from **Children of the World** by E. Blauer, D.K. Wright, G. Holland, B.R. Rogers. Published by Gareth Stevens, Inc., Milwaukee, WI. Reprinted by permission.

From **The Sumerians: Their History, Culture and Character** by Samuel Noah Kramer. Copyright 1963 by The University of Chicago. Reprinted by permission of the publisher.

From **Pharaoh's People** by T.G.H. James. Copyright 1984 by T.G.H. James. Reprinted by permission of The University of Chicago Press.

From **God's Country: America in the Fifties** by J. Ronald Oakley. Copyright 1986 by J. Ronald Oakley. Red Dembner Enterprises Corp., New York.

From **Television** by Michael Winship. Copyright 1988 by Educational Broadcasting Corporation and Michael Winship. Random House, New York.

From **Monsoons**, edited by Jay S. Fein, Pamela L. Stephens. Copyright 1987 by John Wiley & Sons, Inc. A. Wiley-Interscience Publication, John Wiley & Sons, Inc.

From **The Ancient Civilization of Angkor** by Christopher Pym. Copyright 1968 by Christopher Pym. A Mentor Book published by The New American Library, N.Y. & Toronto.

From **Angkor Heart of an Asian Empire** by Bruno Dagens. English translation copyright 1995 by Harry N. Abrams, Inc., N.Y. and Thames and Hudson Ltd., London. Harry N. Abrams, Inc., Publishers.

From **The Travels of Marco Polo**, a modern translation by Teresa Waugh from the Italian by Maria Bellonci. Translation copyright 1984 by Sadgwick and Jackson Limited. Facts on File Publications, N.Y.

From **The Longest Walk: An Odyssey of the Human Spirit** by George Meegan. Copyright 1988 by George Meegan. Dodd, Mead & Company, N.Y.

From **The Way of the Earth: Encounters with Nature in Ancient and Contemporary Thought** by T.C. McLuhan. Copyright 1994 by T.C. McLuhan. Simon & Schuster, N.Y.

From "The land is everything." quote printed in **Native Peoples Magazine** Vol. 6, Number 3, Spring 1993, quote from Gerald Vizenor. Copyright 1993 by Media Concepts Group, Inc. Media Concepts Group, Inc., AZ.

From **Coming of Age in the Milky Way** by Timothy Ferris. Copyright 1988 by Timothy Ferris. An Anchor Book published by Doubleday, a division of Bantam Doubleday Dell Publishing Group, Inc., N.Y. The Anchor Books Edition was published by arrangement with William Morrow and Company.

From **The Diary of a Young Girl: The Definitive Edition** by Anne Frank. Otto H. Frank & Mirjam Pressler, Editors, translated by Susan Massotty. Translation copyright © 1995 by Doubleday, a division of Bantam Doubleday Dell Publishing Group, Inc. Used by permission of Doubleday, a division of Bantam Doubleday Dell Publishing Group, Inc.

From **Red Azalea** by Anchee Min. Copyright 1994 by Anchee Min. Pantheon Books, a division of Random House, N.Y.

From **China: The Long March** by Anthony Lawrence. Copyright 1986 by Intercontinental Publishing Corp., China National Publishing Industry Trading Corp. and China Photographic Publishing House. Merehurst Press, London.

From **Mme Sun Yat-sen** by Jung Chang with Jon Halliday. Copyright 1986 by Jung Chang and Jon Halliday. Penguin Books.

From **The Cold War** by Martin Walker. Copyright 1993 by Walker & Watson Ltd. A John Macrae Book, Henry Holt and Company, N.Y.

From **The Africans** by David Lamb. Copyright 1983 by David Lamb. Vintage Books, a division of Random House, N.Y.

From **Holy War: The Crusades and Their Impact on Today's World** by Karen Armstrong. Copyright 1988, 1991 by Karen Armstrong. Papermac, a division of Macmillan Publishers Limited, London.

From **Long Walk to Freedom: The Autobiography of Nelson Mandela** by Nelson Mandela. Copyright 1994 by Nelson Rolihlahla Mandela. Little, Brown and Company.

From **Zlata's Diary: A Child's Life in Sarajevo** translated with notes by Christina Pribichevich-Zoric. Translation Copyright by Fixot et editions Robert Laffont, 1994. Viking, published by the Penguin Group, Penguin Books USA Inc., N.Y.

From **Self-Made Man: Human Evolution from Eden to Extinction** by Jonathan Kingdon. Copyright 1993 by Jonathan Kingdon. John Wiley & Sons, Inc.

From **Mesopotamian Myths** by Henrietta McCall. Copyright by The Trustees of the British Museum. British Museum Publications, Ltd.

From **Legacy of the Indus: A Discovery of Pakistan** by Samina Quraeshi. Copyright 1974 by Samina Quraeshi. Poem on pg. 8 Copyright 1974 by Salman Tarik Kureshi. John Weatherhill, Inc.

From **The Vedic Experience Mantramanjari**, edited and translated with introductions and notes by Raimundo Panikkar. Copyright 1977 by Raimundo Panikkar. University of California Press.

From **Four-Dimensional Man: Meditations Through the Rg Veda** by Antonio T. de Nicolas. Copyright 1976 by Nicolas Hays, Ltd. Nicolas Hays Ltd.

From **The Wisdom of the Buddha**, by Jean Boisselier. Copyright 1993 by Gallimard. English translation Copyright 1994 Harry N. Abrams, Inc., N.Y. Harry N. Abrams, Inc., New York.

From **The Odyssey of Homer** a new verse translation by Allen Mandelbaum. Copyright 1990 by Allen Mandelbaum. University of California Press.

From **God's Bits of Wood**, Sembene Ousmane translated by Francis Price. Copyright 1962 Doubleday & Company Inc. Heinemann Educational Books Ltd.

From **Serowe Village of the Rain Wind** by Bessie Head. Copyright 1981 by Bessie Head. Heinemann Educational Books Ltd.

From **The Search for Africa**, by Basil Davidson. Copyright 1994 by Basil Davidson. Times Books/Random House.

From **Corpus of early Arabic sources for West African history**, translated by J.F.P. Hopkins, edited and annotated by N. Levtzion & J.F.P. Hopkins. Copyright 1981 by University of Ghana, International Academic Union, Cambridge University Press. Cambridge University Press.

From "China-the End of an Era" from *The Nation Magazine* by Orville Schell. The Nation Magazine, July 17/24, 1995.

TP1–TP8 **THE PRINCETON REVIEW HANDBOOK OF TEST-TAKING STRATEGIES**

Throughout the school year, students have been learning and practicing many new skills. These skills are often assessed in a standardized test format. This section offers helpful tips and strategies for you to familiarize students with standardized test-taking.

It is suggested that you periodically review these strategies with your students to prepare them for the standardized tests they will be taking. During this time tell students that by working hard and paying attention to what you say, they will be ready for success on these standardized tests. Also remind students that you will help them prepare for these tests so that they won't be nervous or anxious.

Ensuring success for all students is a major goal of McGraw-Hill's *Adventures in Time and Place.* We hope these strategies will make all your students more successful learners.

DEDUCTION AND OUTSIDE KNOWLEDGE

Most of the multiple-choice exams you take will include charts, graphs, maps, time lines, and political cartoons. For some questions, you will need to look at this data to find the answer. The process of looking at the information provided, finding the answer to the question, and choosing the correct answer from among the answer choices is called DEDUCTION.

Not all the answers to the questions will be in the data, however. Sometimes, multiple-choice tests ask you to remember a fact that you learned in social studies class. You won't be able to find the correct answer on a map, chart, graph, or drawing; the correct answer will be in your memory. We call these OUTSIDE KNOWLEDGE questions.

Look at the map below, and then answer questions 1 and 2.

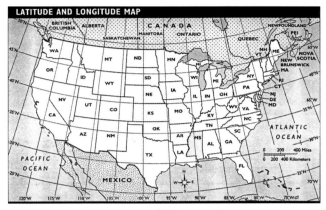

1 Which state is closest to 40°N latitude?

   A   Florida
   B   West Virginia
   C   Maine
   D   North Carolina

2 The weather in Texas is warmer than the weather in Wisconsin because Texas is

   F   closer to the equator
   G   a larger state
   H   closer to a body of water
   J   west of Wisconsin

Remember: Do not write in your textbook.

TP 1

The types of questions introduced on these pages are given as general guidelines, to help students become familiar with the questions they will see on standardized tests. Many questions, however, fall into more than one category.

DEDUCTION AND OUTSIDE KNOWLEDGE

OBJECTIVES:
* To familiarize students with two basic types of questions they are likely to see on nationally administered standardized tests.
* To alert students to the fact that some questions will require students to remember information they have learned in class.

Teaching suggestions: Read the first two paragraphs of the page aloud to students. Then have students answer the two sample questions on their own.

1. **B** This question can be answered with the map. Students should place one finger on the 40°N latitude line. They should then locate each of the four states included among the answer choices. They should notice that the line runs through the state of West Virginia, the correct answer.

2. **F** This question requires outside knowledge. Students' knowledge of the climatic characteristics of U.S. regions is frequently tested on national standardized tests at this grade level. Students should know that the U.S. climate is warmer in the south than in the north.

OBJECTIVES:
- To make students aware of valid alternate strategies to problem solving.
- To teach students to use process of elimination on multiple-choice tests when they are unsure of the correct answer.

Teaching suggestions: Read the first three paragraphs aloud to students. Then read the questions aloud and ask students to use process of elimination to eliminate answers that cannot be correct. Go through the answers, asking, **Is it possible the Pan American Highway could run from Mexico to Italy? Is it possible the Pan American Highway could run from Mexico to Cuba?** Encourage students to consider all answer choices, even when they believe they have found the correct answer before considering all choices. Say: **Let's look at the other answers to make sure that we have selected the best one.**

This skill will serve students well throughout their standardized test-taking careers.

1. **D** This question is a simple but effective illustration of how to use the process of elimination. Students probably do not know the southern destination of the Pan American Highway; however, they should be able to eliminate all of the incorrect answers based on their knowledge of world geography (and their understanding that highways cannot cross oceans). Go through the answers as indicated above.

2. **H** Students may not be able to eliminate ALL of the incorrect answers. They should remember from class that Christianity and Judaism originated in the Middle East. Students should be encouraged to eliminate as many as possible, and guess from among the remaining answers.

PROCESS OF ELIMINATION

When you take a multiple-choice test, you have an advantage that you don't have on other tests. On most tests, you must come up with the answers to the questions all on your own. For example, a test might ask "What is the capital of the United States?" You would then have to write the name "Washington D.C." on your answer sheet.

On a multiple-choice test, however, the correct answer is already written down for you; it is among the answer choices! All you have to do is figure out which of the answer choices is the correct one.

This is good news for you! It means that you can still answer a question correctly *even if you can't come up with the correct answer on your own*. That's because you can ELIMINATE choices that you know are *incorrect*. Eliminating answers this way will be especially helpful on OUTSIDE KNOWLEDGE questions. Sometimes you will be able to eliminate all of the choices except one. When that happens, it means that you have found the best answer by the PROCESS OF ELIMINATION.

Try using the process of elimination to answer this question:

1 The Pan American Highway extends from the northern tip of Mexico to the southern tip of—

A Italy
B Cuba
C Egypt
D Chile

Were you able to eliminate any *incorrect* answers? How many?

Now try using process of elimination To answer this question:

2 Which religion originated in India?

F Christianity
G Islam
H Buddhism
J Judaism

Sometimes process of elimination will help you eliminate ALL the incorrect answers. Sometimes it will only help you eliminate one or two. On a multiple-choice exam, it ALWAYS helps to use the process of elimination when you are unsure about which answer is correct, no matter what type of question you are working on.

Remember: Do not write in your textbook.

CRITICAL THINKING SKILLS

Some multiple-choice questions require you to use critical thinking skills to find the answer. These critical thinking skills may include:

- drawing conclusions
- evaluating information
- making generalizations

Read the quotation, then answer question 1.

"The good person is satisfied and calm; the mean person is always full of distress."
—Confucius, Chinese scholar and teacher, 500 B.C.

1 Confucius would probably have agreed with which of the following statements?

A	Justice is its own reward.	**C**	A little white lie never hurt anyone.
B	Might makes right.	**D**	There's a sucker born every minute.

Study the graph. Then answer question 2.

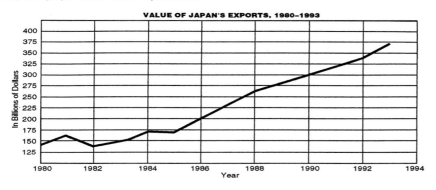

VALUE OF JAPAN'S EXPORTS, 1980–1993

2 Which of the following most likely caused the increase in the value of Japanese exports in 1987 and 1988?

F Japanese companies stopped advertising their products overseas in 1987.

G Japanese factories reduced production of goods in 1987.

H Prosperous nations like the United States increased the amount of Japanese goods they imported in 1987.

J Many Japanese factories closed in 1987.

Remember: Do not write in your textbook.

TP 3

Teaching suggestions: Read the first paragraph of the page aloud to the class. Discuss the skills listed. If necessary, review these skills with students to make sure they understand them. Point out that sometimes we use a combination of these or other critical thinking skills in order to answer questions.

Have students read the questions and choose the correct answers.

1. **A** Process of elimination should help students eliminate all the incorrect answers. The quote from Confucius states that "the good person is satisfied and calm." Confucius extols goodness. Each of the incorrect answers advocates unvirtuous behavior.

2. **H** The question asks for an explanation of the increase in value of Japanese exports. Again, students should be encouraged to use process of elimination, working through each answer. Each of the incorrect answers would best explain a decrease in value of Japanese exports. Had the Japanese stopped advertising products overseas, for example, one would expect sales of Japanese products to decrease, since fewer consumers would know about Japanese goods.

READING COMPREHENSION

OBJECTIVE:

- To familiarize students with one type of reading question that they are likely to see on nationally administered standardized tests.

Teaching suggestions: Often the questions on standardized tests that are text-heavy will require students to keep several short texts in mind, to compare or contrast people or things. Read the first paragraph aloud to students. Choose four students to read the four narratives accompanying the portraits of historical figures. Have students complete the two questions on their own.

1. **C** Golda Meir and Kublai Khan were government leaders; Pablo Neruda served as a diplomat. Of the four biographical sketches, only Peter Ilyich Tchaikovsky's makes no mention of political or governmental involvement.

2. **F** Neruda was a Nobel Prize winning poet; Tchaikovsky was a great composer. To answer correctly, students must understand that composers and poets work in the arts; therefore students should be able to infer that these people would be MOST interested in the arts.

READING COMPREHENSION

Some test questions specifically test your ability to read and understand what you have read. These questions may also require you to compare and contrast the people or things you read about.

Read about the four famous people. Then answer questions 1 and 2.

I was a great Chilean poet in the twentieth century. I won the Nobel Prize for Literature in 1971. I also served as a diplomat for my country.
Pablo Neruda

I was a great Russian composer of the nineteenth century. I wrote symphonies, concertos, and operas, but I am best known for my ballets *Swan Lake* and *The Nutcracker*.
Peter Ilyich Tchaikovsky

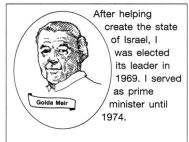
After helping create the state of Israel, I was elected its leader in 1969. I served as prime minister until 1974.
Golda Meir

I was the Mongol emperor who ruled Mongolia and China in the thirteenth century. I built the city of Beijing and greeted Marco Polo on his first visit to China.
Kublai Khan

1 Which of these people was probably LEAST involved in politics and government?

- **A** Pablo Neruda
- **B** Golda Meir
- **C** Peter Ilyich Tchaikovsky
- **D** Kublai Khan

2 Which two people were probably MOST interested in the arts?

- **F** Pablo Neruda and Peter Ilyich Tchaikovsky
- **G** Golda Meir and Pablo Neruda
- **H** Kublai Khan and Peter Ilyich Tchaikovsky
- **J** Peter Ilyich Tchaikovsky and Kublai Khan

Remember: Do not write in your textbook.

MAPS

The ability to read and understand maps is an important skill in social studies. Many of the multiple-choice tests you take will require you to read a map.

Look carefully at all the parts of a map. Maps contain a lot of information. Whenever you see a map, you should ask yourself questions like these:

- What do the titles of the maps tell you?
- Where are the map keys?
- What symbols are on the map keys? What do they stand for?
- Where is the compass rose on each map?
- Is there a map scale?

Study the two maps of Alberta, Canada. Then do questions 1 and 2.

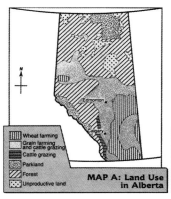 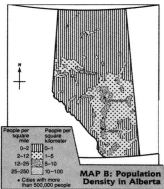

1   The land surrounding both of Alberta's major cities is primarily used as

   A   wheat farms
   B   grain farms and cattle ranches
   C   forests
   D   parkland

2   Which of the following best explains the population density of northern Alberta?

   F   The weather in northern Alberta is too cold to support a large population.
   G   Alberta's biggest cities are in its northern section.
   H   Wheat farming in northern Alberta attracts a large number of workers to the region.
   J   Most residents of Alberta prefer to live in the forest.

Remember: Do not write in your textbook.   **TP 5**

OBJECTIVES:
- To reinforce map skills learned in class.
- To familiarize students with one type of map-reading question that they are likely to see on nationally administered standardized tests.

Teaching suggestions: Read the first half of the page out loud. Call on students to read and answer each of the questions concerning the various features of the maps of Alberta.

1. **B** The phrase "land . . . is primarily used" should cue students to consult the "Land Use in Alberta" map. Instruct students to first locate Edmonton and Calgary on the map, then consult the key to determine the land use of the surrounding area. All the information needed to answer the question is in the map.

2. **F** This question directs students to consult the "Population Density in Alberta" map. It also requires students to draw an inference based on common sense, or use their knowledge of Canada's climate. Students can also use process of elimination on this question; answer **G** is clearly false, as both Edmonton and Calgary are in the southern half of Calgary; answer **H** is false since the population density is lower in the northern part of Alberta than in the southern part; **J** goes against common sense and is contradicted by the population density map, which shows the greatest population density in the south.

GRAPHS

Teaching suggestions: Read the first two paragraphs of the page aloud to the class. As you read paragraph one, ask students to think of examples of the different types of graphs discussed. Perhaps some are displayed in the classroom. You might also ask students to point out examples of the different types of graphs in their textbooks.

Have students read the questions and choose the correct answers.

1. **C** Some students might become confused by the fact the Belo Horizonte is not among the answer choices. Students should be reminded that, on a multiple-choice test, they must consider the answer choices before committing to an answer. Although the chart shows that Belo Horizonte has a population of nearly 4 million, Belo Horizonte cannot be the correct answer for the simple reason that it is not among the answer choices. Further consideration should lead students to the insight that the population of Rio de Janeiro is also very nearly 4,000,000.

2. **G** Services constitute 40 percent of Brazilian jobs in 1990.

3. **D** This question requires students to apply outside knowledge. Farmers (answer **B**) and cattle ranchers (answer **C**) fall under the category of agricultural workers; factory workers (answer **A**) fall under the category of industrial workers.

GRAPHS

Different types of graphs are used to present numerical information. A **line graph** shows how something changes over time. A line graph might be used to show how the population of the United States has grown over the years. A **bar graph** compares amounts. A **bar graph** might show the population of different United States cities. A **circle graph** shows how a whole is divided into smaller parts. For example, a circle graph might show how the government divides its budget to pay for roads, defense, education, and other services.

On some multiple-choice tests, you will see a set of questions accompanied by more than one graph. Each question will contain clues to tell you which graph you should read to find the answer. Take the extra time to make sure you are looking at the correct graph. This will help you avoid careless errors.

Use the graphs and your own knowledge to do questions 1 through 3.

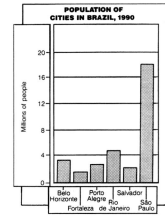
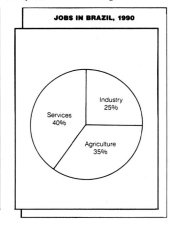

1 According to the graph, which city in Brazil had a population closest to 4,000,000 in 1990?

A Fortaleza	**C** Rio de Janiero
B Salvador	**D** Sao Paulo

2 In 1990, what part of the economy provided the greatest number of jobs to Brazilians?

F Industry	**H** Agriculture
G Services	**J** Arts and Entertainment

3 Which of the following jobs would fall under the category of "services"?

A Factory worker	**C** Cattle rancher
B Farmer	**D** Waitress

Remember: Do not write in your textbook.

POLITICAL CARTOONS

Some tests will ask you to look at and interpret a political cartoon. A political cartoon is an illustration or drawing that expresses a political point of view.

When you look at a political cartoon, ask yourself the following questions:

- What do the images in the cartoon represent? Are they *symbols* for something else? Uncle Sam is an example of a symbol. When he appears in a cartoon, he is being used as a symbol of the United States.
- What is the cartoonist's *point of view*? Is the cartoonist for or against the political issue that is the subject of the drawing? Look carefully at the details of the drawing. Do they provide hints about the artist's point of view?

Study the cartoon. Then do Numbers 1 through 3.

1 In the cartoon, the people under the umbrella represent

    A members of the United States Congress

    B citizens of the United States

    C Europeans who would like to move to the United States

    D foreign nations asking for financial assistance from the United States

2 The cartoonist would probably agree that the United States Constitution is

    F foolish   **H** important

    G difficult to understand   **J** outdated

3 Which of these would provide the most factual information about the United States Constitution?

    A a textbook about the United States government

    B a campaign poster for a Presidential candidate

    C a fictional movie about the American space program

    D an advertisement for a trip to Washington DC

Remember: Do not write in your textbook.   **TP 7**

OBJECTIVE:
- To familiarize students with one type of question that they are likely to see on nationally administered standardized tests.

Teaching suggestions: Read aloud all text preceding the political cartoon. Direct the bulleted questions to students and ask for their responses. If possible, present another political cartoon as an illustration, and use it to answer the bulleted questions. You might use a newspaper or news magazine cartoon. You might also select a political cartoon from the textbook.

Have students read the questions and choose the correct answers.

1. **B** The people under the umbrella are protected from 'injustice' and 'tyranny' which are symbolized by rain. The umbrella, which symbolizes the U.S. Constitution, protects citizens from injustice and tyranny.

2. **H** The cartoon clearly holds the Constitution in high regard. Each of the three incorrect answers indicate that the cartoonist's attitude toward the Constitution is a negative one.

3. **A** This is an outside knowledge question. It tests students' familiarity with reference sources, a commonly tested area on nationally administered standardized tests.

TIME LINES

Teaching suggestions: Have students practice locating information on a time line. Ask them what occurred in 45 B.C. (Julius Caesar became dictator of Rome).

1. **C** The Colosseum is completed in A.D. 80, which is halfway through the time line. Julius Caesar and Augustus only rule for portions of the time covered by the time line, as well. The Pax Romana covers almost all of the time represented on the time line, so that would be the best title.

2. **H** Students need only find "Augustus dies" on the time line.

TIME LINES

Historical information is sometimes presented in a time line. A time line shows events in the order in which they occurred. It should be read from left to right, like a sentence. Sometimes a time line is presented vertically, in which case it should be read from top to bottom.

Some questions may ask you to find information on a time line. They may also ask you to remember outside knowledge about the subject of the time line.

Look at the time line below. Then answer questions 1 and 2.

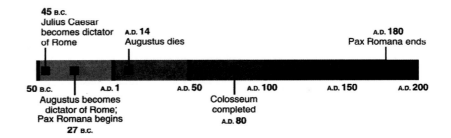

1 The best title for this time line would be:

- **A** The Building of the Colosseum
- **B** The Rule of Julius Caesar
- **C** The Pax Romana
- **D** The Rule of Augustus

2 In what year did Augustus die?

- **F** 45 B.C.
- **G** 27 B.C.
- **H** A.D. 14
- **J** A.D. 80

Remember: Do not write in your textbook.

USING A GLOBAL GRID

You can locate places on a map by using a grid of latitude and longitude lines. Use the global grid map below to complete the activities on this page. Write the letter of the answer on the line. For help, you can refer to pages G4–G11 in your textbook.

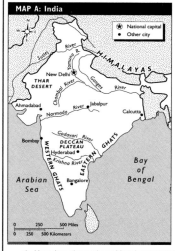

THE WORLD

___c___ 1. What are the lines that run north and south on the map called?

    a. latitude lines

    b. polar lines

    c. longitude lines

___a___ 2. Latitude lines measure distance in degrees north and south of this.

    a. equator

    b. prime meridian

    c. Western Hemisphere

___c___ 3. On the grid above, which longitude line is closest to Mexico City?

    a. 120°W

    b. 140°E

    c. 100°W

___c___ 4. What does the latitude line, or parallel, 60°S run through?

    a. three continents

    b. Antarctica

    c. three oceans

___b___ 5. Which city is nearest to 40°N, 120°E?

    a. Los Angeles

    b. Beijing

    c. Tokyo

___c___ 6. What is the approximate location of Nairobi?

    a. 40°N, 0°

    b. 0°, 40°W

    c. 0°, 40°E

USING MAPS OF DIFFERENT SCALES

The maps below show the same area using different scales. Use the maps to complete the activities that follow. For help, you can refer to pages G4–G11 in your textbook.

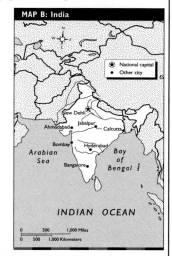

MAP A: India   **MAP B: India**

1. How does the scale on Map A compare with the scale on Map B?

    One inch stands for fewer miles on Map A than on Map B.

2. Which map shows a larger land area? Map B

3. Make a scale strip by placing the edge of a strip of paper under the scale lines on Map A. Then mark the distances in miles and kilometers.

    a. How many miles is Ahmadabad from New Delhi? about 500 miles

    b. Which city is about 300 miles northeast of Bangalore? Hyderabad

4. On Map B which city in southern India is about 1,000 miles from Calcutta?

    Bangalore

EXPLORING MEXICO'S RESOURCES

The map below shows some of Mexico's natural resources. Use the map to answer the questions that follow. For help, you can refer to pages G4–G11 in your textbook.

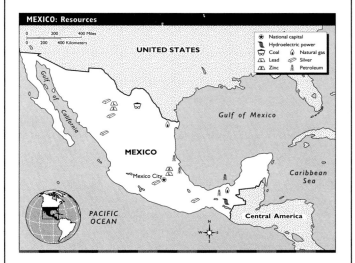

MEXICO: Resources

1. What does the locator map show?

    The locator map shows Mexico's location in the Western Hemisphere.

2. Why is the map key important to the map above?

    The map key tells what the symbols on the map mean.

3. What symbol is used for hydroelectric power? falling water

4. What resource is located along the Gulf of Mexico coast? petroleum

5. In what part of Mexico is coal mined? in the northern part of Mexico

---

READING AN ELEVATION MAP

The map below shows the elevation of China. Study the map and the map key. Then put an **X** next to each sentence that is correct. For help, you can refer to pages G4–G11 in your textbook.

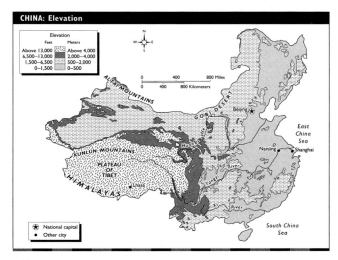

CHINA: Elevation

___X___ 1. The map of China is a physical map.

_____ 2. The elevation along the eastern coast of China is about 7,000 feet.

___X___ 3. The southwestern part of China is higher than 13,000 feet.

___X___ 4. The capital city of China has an elevation between 0 and 500 meters.

_____ 5. The city of Lhasa has a much lower elevation than Shanghai.

___X___ 6. Shanghai and Beijing have about the same elevation.

_____ 7. The elevation of most of China is less than 700 feet.

___X___ 8. The elevation of China increases as you travel west.

INDIAN EMPIRES

The map below shows the Indian empires that developed in the Americas. Use the information in the map to answer the questions that follow. If you need help, refer to pages G4–G11 in your textbook.

INDIAN EMPIRES

1. What type of map is this?

   It is an historical map.

2. What continents are shown on this map?

   North and South America

3. What three empires are shown on the map?

   Maya, Aztec, and Inca

   empires

4. By the year 1500 the city of Tenochtitlán was twice as large as London, England. What Indian group built this magnificent city?

   the Aztec

5. Today many tourists visit the ruins of Machu Picchu. Who built this city?

   the Inca

ONE COUNTRY'S REGIONS

Below is a profile of the physical, climate, and cultural regions found in one country. Use the information provided to answer the questions that follow. Then write the name of the country on the final line.

Location:	North America
Climate:	mostly temperate, but varies from tropical to arctic; arid to semiarid in west
Landforms:	vast central plain, mountains in west, hills and low mountains in east
Natural Borders:	Atlantic Ocean on the east, Gulf of Mexico to the south, Pacific Ocean on the west, Great Lakes to the north
Language:	predominately English; sizable Spanish-speaking minority
Ethnic Groups:	73% Caucasian, 12% African American, 10% Hispanic, 3% Asian, 1% Native American, 1% other
Major Religions:	93 mil. Protestant, 60 mil. Roman Catholic, 6 mil. Jewish, 4 mil. Mormon, 3 mil. Muslim, 3 mil. Eastern Orthodox
Government:	federal republic; strong democratic traditions; executive, legislative, and judicial branches
Administrative Divisions:	50 states and 1 district

Source: Information Please Almanac 1997

1. What physical regions make up the geography of this country?

   mountainous regions, plains, and hills

2. What climate regions are found in this country?

   temperate, tropical, arctic, arid, and semiarid climate regions

3. What political regions make up the country?

   50 states and 1 district

4. What are the majority of the people who live in this country like?

   The majority of the people are Caucasian, Protestant, and

   English-speaking.

   Name of Country: United States of America

USING LATITUDE AND LONGITUDE

Plan a trip in which you will visit each of the capital cities listed here. Use latitude and longitude to locate each city. Then label the city according to the letter on the right. For help, you can refer to pages 12–13 in your textbook.

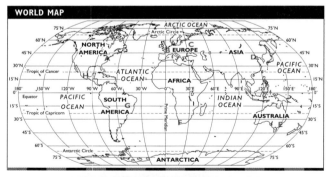

WORLD MAP

CITY	LOCATION	LABEL
Washington, D.C., U.S.A.	38°N, 77°W	A
Paris, France	48°N, 2°E	B
Moscow, Russia	55°N, 37°E	C
Beijing, China	40°N, 116°E	D
Canberra, Australia	35°S, 149°E	E
Cape Town, South Africa	34°S, 18°E	F
Brasília, Brazil	15°S, 47°W	G
Mexico City, Mexico	19°N, 99°W	H

A degree is a unit of measurement that describes the distance between lines of latitude and longitude. What is the approximate distance in degrees between the Tropic of Cancer and the Tropic of Capricorn?

about 47 degrees

FINDING CLUES TO INDIAN CULTURE

Details of everyday life can reveal a great deal about the culture in which people live. Use the pictures on the right to complete the activities on this page. For help, you can refer to pages 14–19 in your textbook.

1. Draw a line to the picture that shows a custom unique to the culture of India. What are other important parts of Indian culture?

   Hinduism, family temples, the

   mridanga, traditional foods such as

   uttapam

2. Draw a line to the picture that suggests the importance of language in Indian culture. What are four of the many languages spoken in India?

   English, Hindu, Sanskrit, Bengali

3. Draw a line to the picture that shows the interaction of Asian and European cultures. What are two examples of change in the Indian culture?

   style of chess, more freedom for

   women, Chinese and American foods

4. What are some similarities between Indian and American culture?

   Both countries are representative democracies, women have

   more rights than they did in the past, and families live together

   and share values and customs.

USING NEW WORDS

Use the words in the box to complete the puzzle below. For help, you can refer to the lessons in Chapter 1 in your textbook.

climate

geography

landform

culture

region

custom

interaction

values

Across

2. a Greek word meaning "Earth writing"

5. a natural feature, such as a mountain or a plain

6. the exchange of ideas and customs

8. the things people believe are most important in life

Down

1. an area with common features that set it apart from other areas

3. a way of life of a group of people, including daily habits, beliefs, and art

4. a way of living that people practice regularly over time

7. the weather pattern that an area has over a long period of time

---

LEARNING FROM A PRIMARY SOURCE

Below is a primary source from 1949. This advertisement called television a "miracle" that was "undreamed of 150 years ago." What can you learn about American culture in the 1940s from this ad?

Could *anything* be more exciting than television?

1. What does this ad tell you about Americans' attitude toward television in the 1940s?

   Possible answer: Americans viewed television as an exciting technological "miracle."

2. What does the ad suggest about families and family values in the 1940s?

   Possible answer: The average family consisted of a mother, father, and two children, and families enjoyed doing things together, such as watching television.

3. How might people in today's society view this ad?

   Possible answer: People might find the ad old-fashioned because it no longer represents American society and family life today.

4. Why is this ad considered a primary source?

   The ad was created during a specific period of time in American history, and it is not based on another source.

DECISION MAKING ABOUT ARTIFACTS

One of the most important tasks of historians is decision making. Below is a story about a scholar's decision that made headlines in May 1995. Answer the questions that follow the story. If you need help, refer to pages 30–31 in your textbook.

Dr. Kent Weeks is a scholar at the American University in Cairo, Egypt. His main goal is to find and preserve every possible artifact that exists in the Valley of the Kings. This valley, which is located on the west bank of the Nile River in Upper Egypt, is where most of the tombs of ancient Egyptian kings have been found.

In 1988 Dr. Weeks had a difficult decision to make. A site known as Tomb 5 had been identified as a good place to build a parking lot for tourists. When the site was first explored in 1820, a British scholar concluded that all the artifacts had been uncovered. Dr. Weeks, however, wasn't so sure. Should he explore the site one more time, or should he begin a new dig in a completely different part of the Valley of the Kings?

Dr. Weeks decided to explore Tomb 5 again. After seven years of slow, careful digging, he was finally able to pry open a stone door that had remained shut for thousands of years. There, before his eyes, was the discovery of a lifetime: a long corridor with ten doors on each side and at the end a statue of Osiris, the god of the afterlife. This and other artifacts led Dr. Weeks to conclude that he had found the last resting place of as many as 50 sons of Rameses II, the greatest of all the ancient Egyptian kings.

Michael D. Lemonick, "Secrets of the Lost Tomb," *Time*, May 29, 1995.

1. What was Dr. Weeks's goal?

   Dr. Weeks's goal was to find and preserve every possible artifact in the Valley of the Kings.

2. What alternatives did he consider?

   He considered reexploring Tomb 5 or digging in a different part of the Valley of the Kings.

3. What decision did he make? Why did he choose this alternative?

   Dr. Weeks chose to reexplore Tomb 5 because he realized that existing artifacts would be lost forever if a parking lot was built on the site.

WORKING AS AN ARCHAEOLOGIST

Suppose that you are an archaeologist like Konrad Spindler. You are studying the Iceman and his belongings that have been uncovered from a glacier in the Alps. Other archaeologists have decided to join you in your work. Summarize your findings for your colleagues by explaining what you think each of the artifacts reveals about the Iceman. If you need help, you can refer to pages 32–37 in your textbook.

An archaeologist at work

1. traces of grain in the melted snow and ice

   The Iceman had contact with farmers.

2. small net with wide spaces in the mesh

   The Iceman used the net to catch birds.

3. knife blades, rope, and hunting arrows

   When mountain climbing, the Iceman carried survival gear.

4. tiny crystals of sulfur and iron attached to black fungus

   The Iceman probably used the fungus to start fires.

5. two small beads of fungus on a leather strap

   This was probably the Iceman's medicine.

6. 2,000 grains of pollen from alder and pine trees

   The Iceman died in autumn.

7. amount of wear on the Iceman's teeth

   The Iceman was about 35 or 40 years old at death.

8. results of carbon dating of skin samples

   The Iceman lived between 5,000 and 5,300 years ago.

SOME WORDS ABOUT THE PAST

Answer each question in the space provided. For help, you can refer to the lessons in Chapter 2 in your textbook.

1. What is **history**?
   History is the story of the past.

2. How does an **oral tradition** help us remember our history?
   History is passed on from generation to generation by word of mouth.

3. Will the computer you are using today be an **artifact** in 50 years? Explain.
   Yes; any object made by a person or produced by a company in the past is an artifact.

4. What is the difference between **primary sources** and **secondary sources**?
   Primary sources are materials or texts created during a period of time under study, and secondary sources are based on studies of primary sources.

5. Is your social studies textbook a **primary source** or a **secondary source**?
   It is a secondary source.

6. What is the significant difference between **prehistory** and **history**?
   Prehistory produced no written records.

7. What major clues to the past are studied in the science of **archaeology**?
   Historical sites, artifacts, and human remains are clues to the past.

8. What does it mean to **excavate**?
   To excavate is to uncover by digging carefully.

EARLY DISCOVERIES

How did early people discover the uses of fire? Read the possible explanation below and then answer the questions that follow. If you need help, refer back to pages 44–49 in your textbook.

> They learned to carry it from the wilds, where it appeared when a volcano erupted, when lightning struck in the dry grass of the plains, or when some outcrop of coal or shale oil burst into flames by spontaneous combustion. Having captured fire, the first men learned to keep it going in their hearths. . . .
>
> Besides the protection it afforded, fire was a key to survival in other ways. Once Homo erectus discovered the art of cooking—perhaps by accident as a slab of meat fell onto a flaming hearth and was eaten—he seems to have cooked much of what he caught. . . .
>
> Besides cooking with fire, Homo erectus discovered other practical uses for it. It broadened his choice of tools and weapons. The observation that bone or antler grew hard in the heat of a campfire or that green wood did not always burn completely and instead hardened must have led him to employ fire in toolmaking.

Editors of Time-Life Books, *The First Men* (New York: Time-Life Books, 1973), pages 20–21.

1. How did hunter-gatherers discover possible uses for fire?
   First they learned how to keep fire going and then accidently learned how to use it to cook with and make weapons.

2. How did the technology of fire building change life in the Old Stone Age?
   Fire building made it possible for people to cook food, survive the cold, and improve their tools.

3. What other technology did hunter-gatherers use to meet their needs?
   They used sharp stone tools to kill animals and cut through their hides, and they used plants and seeds as medicine.

4. What do ancient rock paintings and carvings reveal about early people?
   They had found a way to express themselves through art, and they most probably valued beauty.

WRITING ABOUT AN EARLY COMMUNITY

You are an archaeologist who has uncovered the remains shown below during a dig. What conclusions can you draw from these remains about the community you have discovered and the people who lived there? Use the questions below to write a report on your findings.

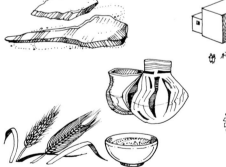

1. What kind of technology did the people use?
   They pounded stones to make sharp tools that they used for cutting animal hides and chopping wood, and they used fire to bake clay pottery.

2. What were their homes like?
   The brick homes had walls and several levels.

3. What kinds of food did they eat? How did they get this food?
   They ate wheat and barley, which had been planted.

4. Did the group practice specialization? How can you tell?
   Yes; in addition to farmers, there were craftsworkers who made pottery and jewelry.

USING A TIME LINE

The time line below shows important events in the development of sports and games. Use the time line to answer the questions. If you need help, look back at pages 58–59 in your textbook.

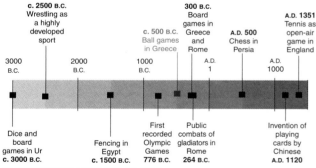

1. What period of time does the time line cover? Are most of the listed events B.C. or A.D.?
   The time line covers the period from 3000 B.C. to A.D. 1500; B.C.

2. When did the first recorded Olympic Games take place?
   776 B.C.

3. About how many years passed between the appearance of board games in Ur and board games in Greece and Rome?
   about 2,700 years

4. Which appeared earlier, gladiator combats in Rome or fencing in Egypt?
   fencing in Egypt

5. Which came later, the invention of playing cards or open-air tennis in England?
   open-air tennis in England

6. The Greeks began playing ball games about 500 B.C. Write this event in the correct place on the time line.

USING NEW WORDS

Choose a word from the box to complete each sentence. For help, you can refer to the lessons in Chapter 3 of your textbook.

civilization	agriculture	technology
New Stone Age	surplus	specialization
Old Stone Age	trade	domesticate

1. The earliest human beings lived during the **Old Stone Age**, which began over 2 million years ago.

2. They were hunters and gatherers who used simple **technology**, such as stone tools and fire building, to meet their needs.

3. About 12,000 years ago people began practicing **agriculture**, the raising of crops and animals for human use.

4. The world's first farmers learned to **domesticate** animals, such as wild goats, cattle, and sheep.

5. Early farmers, unlike their hunting-gathering ancestors, began to produce an oversupply, or **surplus**, of food.

6. Demands on farmers' time led to **specialization**, people training for specific tasks, such as turning wheat into bread flour.

7. During the **New Stone Age**, which ended about 6,000 years ago, towns and cities developed.

8. Complex changes in the way people lived and worked sparked the development of **civilization**, cultures with systems of religion, learning, and government.

9. People began to **trade**, or exchange goods, with people from faraway places.

THE NILE RIVER

You have been asked to write an entry about the Nile River for the *Geography Book of Records*. Use the outline map and the categories below to write your entry. For help, refer to pages 70–73 in your textbook.

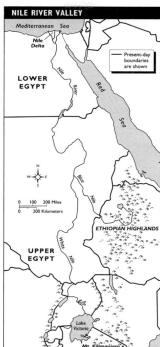

NILE RIVER VALLEY

LENGTH: The Nile is the world's longest river, flowing over 4,000 miles.

LOCATION: East Africa

DIRECTION IT FLOWS: It flows northward from the mountains of East Africa.

WHERE IT EMPTIES: Mediterranean Sea

FLOOD SEASON: The Nile floods its banks from July through October.

IMPORTANCE TO ANCIENT EGYPT: The Nile provided fertile soil, water for irrigation, and a means of transportation.

LANDSCAPE OF NILE REGION: To the north is a fertile delta. To the south, in Upper Egypt, the Nile flows through stone cliffs and desert sands.

THE ROLE OF THE PHARAOHS IN THE OLD KINGDOM

Complete the diagram below to explain how the pharaoh was the center of Egyptian civilization in the Old Kingdom. One entry has been done for you in each section. Then use the diagram to answer the question that follows. If you need help, refer to pages 74–81 in your textbook.

In Government

The pharaoh decided how Egypt's affairs should be run at all levels.
Area governors reported to the pharaoh.
The pharaoh depended on scribes to keep written records.

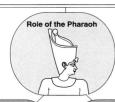

Role of the Pharaoh

In Religion

The pharaoh owned all the temples.
The pharaoh was worshiped as a child of the sun god. Massive pyramids were built as tombs to house the pharaoh in the afterlife.

In the Economy

All things belonged to the pharaoh.
The pharaoh collected taxes on everything produced in Egypt. Craftworkers and artists depended on the pharaoh for jobs.

Why did local leaders revolt against the pharaohs' government?
Massive government building projects strained the Egyptian economy and angered the people and their local government leaders.

EXPANSION AND TRADE IN ANCIENT EGYPT

You are a reporter for *Egypt Today*. Your job is to write a brief paragraph to go with each newspaper headline below. For help, refer to pages 84–91 in your textbook.

EGYPTIANS DEFEAT HYKSOS

Led by Pharaoh Ahmose, the Egyptians drove out the Hyksos and regained control of the Delta. This victory marks the beginning of the New Kingdom.

EGYPTIAN TRADERS BRING BACK AFRICAN RICHES

Caravans continue to bring back ebony, ivory, gold, precious stones, and other riches from the wealthy kingdoms of Africa. Trade routes between Egypt and these kingdoms opened up when Nubia became part of the Egyptian empire.

HATSHEPSUT SENDS GREAT EXPEDITION TO PUNT

Today Pharaoh Hatshepsut sent five ships and a caravan of scribes, soldiers, artists, and attendants on a journey south to open trade with the kingdom of Punt. This may be the pharaoh's biggest expedition yet.

TUTANKHAMUN IS BURIED IN SPLENDOR

Pharaoh Tutankhamun, who ruled from the age of 9 to 19, was buried today in a magnificent tomb with numerous objects from his household. They reveal much about Egyptian culture.

EGYPT GAINING FAME FOR NEW IDEAS AND SKILLS

Scribes are recording vast amounts of medical knowledge. Priest-scientists are busy writing down the mathematical rules that made possible the building of the pyramids and the study of the stars.

USING MAPS AT DIFFERENT SCALES

A map scale is a unit of measure, such as an inch, used to represent a distance on Earth. Use the maps below to answer the questions. If you need help, refer to pages 92–93 in your textbook.

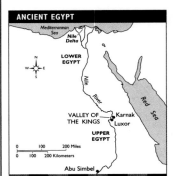

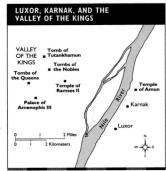

1. What does one inch represent on the map of ancient Egypt? 200 miles

   On the map of the Valley of the Kings? 2 miles

2. Compare the two maps. Which map is a small-scale map?

   map of ancient Egypt

3. Which map would you use to trace the route of the Nile River?

   map of ancient Egypt

4. Which map would you use to plan a walking tour of temples and royal tombs?

   map of Luxor, Karnak, and the Valley of the Kings

5. What is the distance from Abu Simbel to Luxor? about 225 miles

   Which map did you use to find the distance? map of ancient Egypt

6. Is the Tomb of Tutankhamun east or west of the Nile River? west
   Which map did you use to find the answer?

   map of Luxor, Karnak, and the Valley of the Kings

EGYPTIAN SOCIETY

Write a job description for the Egyptians in each picture below. If you need help, refer to pages 94–99 in your textbook.

1. Farmer

dig up fields for planting; dig canals and haul water for irrigation; grow and harvest crops

4. Homemaker

get water from local canal; bake and cook; go to market

2. Children

scatter seed during planting time; cut and carry at harvest time; perform chores

5. Woodcutter

build plows and make furniture

3. Scribe

measure crops and take away shares claimed by the pharaoh

6. Slave

assist farmers to dig canals and prepare land for planting; mine gold; work as house servant

---

RELATING WORDS TO ANCIENT EGYPT

Choose a word or phrase from the box to match each clue. For help, you can refer to the lessons in Chapter 4 in your textbook.

slavery	social pyramid	delta
pharaoh	irrigation	expedition
unification	papyrus	empire
economy	hieroglyphics	scribe
silt		

1. fertile, fan-shaped land created where Nile empties into Mediterranean Sea — delta

2. bits of soil and rock carried off by the Nile River — silt

3. technology used by Egyptian farmers to water their crops — irrigation

4. joining of Upper Egypt and Lower Egypt into one kingdom — unification

5. the way a country's people manage money and resources for the production of goods and services — economy

6. a writer who kept records in Egypt — scribe

7. name given to Egyptian rulers — pharaoh

8. system of writing made up of about 800 picture-signs — hieroglyphics

9. reed plant growing along the Nile used to make paper — papyrus

10. group of lands and peoples ruled by Egyptian government — empire

11. caravan of people sent to trade with Egypt's neighbors — expedition

12. practice of one person owning another person — slavery

13. how Egyptian society was shaped — social pyramid

TWO RIVERS: TIGRIS AND EUPHRATES

Use the map below to answer the questions. For help, refer to pages 104–107 in your textbook.

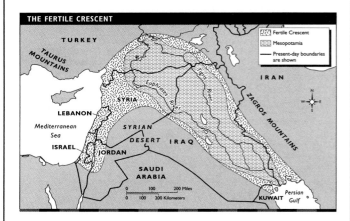

1. What two important rivers are shown on the map?

   Tigris and Euphrates rivers

2. Into what body of water do these rivers flow?

   into the Persian Gulf

3. In ancient times what civilization developed between the Tigris and Euphrates rivers?

   Mesopotamia

4. Parts of what countries make up the region once known as the Fertile Crescent?

   Iraq, Syria, Lebanon, Israel, Iran, Jordan, Kuwait, Turkey

5. How did ancient farmers in this region make their land productive?

   They used canal systems to control flooding and make the land fertile.

THE CODE OF HAMMURABI

The Code of Hammurabi contained over 200 laws. Read some of the laws listed below and answer the questions that follow. If you need help, refer to pages 108–115 in your textbook.

> If a citizen has stolen property of the temple or of the crown, that man shall die, and whosoever receives the stolen goods from his hand shall die.
>
> If a citizen steals the child of a citizen, he shall die.
>
> If a citizen has committed a robbery and is caught, that man shall die.
>
> If a son has struck his father, they shall cut off his hand.
>
> If a citizen has destroyed the eye of one of citizen status, they shall destroy his eye.
>
> If he has destroyed the eye of a vassal, he shall pay one mina (17.5 ounces) of silver.
>
> If he has destroyed the eye of a slave of a citizen, he shall pay half of his market value.

1. What kinds of behavior did the above laws punish?

robbery, kidnapping, causing physical injury

2. What punishment did the law require if a father complained that his son hit him during a quarrel?

The son's hand would be cut off.

3. Was everyone treated equally under Hammurabi's laws? Explain.

No; the punishment for blinding a slave was less severe than the punishment for blinding a citizen.

4. What are the advantages to society of having a written code?

Possible answer: All citizens know what the laws are and the penalties for breaking them.

IDENTIFYING CAUSE AND EFFECT

The passage below describes the fall of Sumer. As you read, look for cause and effect connections. A cause is something that makes something else happen. What happens as the result of a cause is an effect. If you need help, refer to pages 118–119 in your textbook.

> For over 1,000 years the city-states of Sumer were at war with each other. From 3000 B.C. to 2000 B.C., one city-state after another had its brief moment of glory and power. Constant rebellion weakened the vast Sumerian empire. City-states could no longer fight off attacks from their enemies, all of whom wanted the riches of the empire. Finally, nomadic warriors from the deserts and the hills surrounding Sumer scaled the walls of Ur and destroyed the city-state. Other city-states were similarly destroyed.
>
> The Sumerians never recovered from the attacks on their cities. Although the Sumerian empire was physically destroyed, its ideas lived on. Other empires developed in Mesopotamia, and the leaders of these empires adopted Sumerian ways. They built ziggurats, used cuneiform writing, and irrigated their fields.

1. What was the effect of constant warfare among the city-states of Sumer?

Constant warfare made the city-states too weak to fight off attacks from their enemies.

2. Why did nomadic warriors want to conquer the city-states of Sumer?

They wanted the riches of the empire.

3. What was the final cause of the fall of the Sumerian empire?

The empire never recovered from the attacks on its city-states.

4. How did Sumerian civilization affect other empires that developed in Mesopotamia?

These empires adopted Sumerian ideas, such as cuneiform writing and irrigation.

5. Why do historians study cause-effect connections?

They want to understand why events happened the way they did.

JUDAISM YESTERDAY AND TODAY

You have been asked to prepare a Question & Answer almanac entry on the Jewish religion. Below are the questions your editor has asked you to answer. Fill in the spaces with the answers. If you need help, refer to pages 120–125 in your textbook.

Q: What special agreement marked the beginning of Jewish history?

A: The covenant God made with Abraham in Canaan is considered to be the beginning of Jewish history.

Q: Who were the first Jews?

A: The descendants of Abraham, later called the Israelites, were the first Jews.

Q: What role did Moses play in Jewish history?

A: Moses, with the help of God, led the enslaved Israelites from Egypt.

Q: What laws were among those Moses received from God at Mount Sinai?

A: The Ten Commandments were among the laws Moses received at Mount Sinai.

Q: Why is the Torah so important to the Jewish people?

A: The Torah is the five books of laws and teachings God gave to Moses. It is the basis of life and faith for the Jewish people.

Q: What belief set the Israelites apart from other groups living in the Fertile Crescent?

A: The Israelites believed in only one God and practiced monotheism.

Q: Why is the city of Jerusalem so important to Jews today?

A: The city was once the capital of the kingdom of Israel and the site of a great temple built by Solomon. Today the city is a center of religious and political life.

USING NEW WORDS

Write the letter of the term that matches each definition. For help, refer to the lessons in Chapter 5 in your textbook.

a. city-state	**f.** Judaism	**j.** Sabbath
b. code of law	**g.** monotheism	**k.** drought
c. cuneiform	**h.** plateau	**l.** Torah
d. Diaspora	**i.** polytheism	**m.** ziggurat
e. Ten Commandments		

__l__ 1. first five books of the Hebrew Bible

__c__ 2. system of writing invented in Sumer

__d__ 3. scattering of Jews to many parts of the world

__g__ 4. belief in only one god

__h__ 5. area of flat, elevated land

__b__ 6. written set of laws that apply to everyone under a government

__k__ 7. long period of dry weather

__m__ 8. large building with a temple on its peak

__a__ 9. self-governing city and its surrounding villages

__i__ 10. belief in many gods and goddesses

__e__ 11. laws given by God to Moses at Mount Sinai

__f__ 12. religion of the Jewish people

__j__ 13. weekly day of rest, prayer, and study

Write a sentence about Sumer or Babylon. Use two words from the box in your sentence.

Possible answer: Sumerians practiced polytheism and worshiped their gods in a ziggurat.

Write a sentence about the beginnings of Judaism. Use two or more words from the box in your sentence.

Possible answer: Among the laws that God gave the Israelites, who believed in monotheism, were the Ten Commandments.

THE JOURNEY OF THE INDUS RIVER

Use the map to answer questions 1–4. If you need help, refer to pages 130–133 in your textbook.

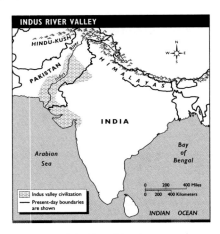

1. In what mountains does the Indus River originate?
   Himalayas

2. Into what body of water does the Indus River flow?
   Arabian Sea

3. Through what country does the Indus River mainly flow?
   Pakistan

4. In what ways does the Indus River resemble the Nile, Tigris, and Euphrates rivers?
   All carry silt and make farming possible in dry regions, and the valleys of all these rivers were centers of early civilizations.

INTERPRETING CLUES TO EARLY INDIAN CIVILIZATION

Archaeologists have pieced together a picture of India's ancient past from the artifacts that they have uncovered in the ruins of Harappa and Mohenjo-Daro. Descriptions of the ruins and some of the artifacts are listed in the box below. Write the letter of the description next to the information it revealed about life in ancient India. If you need help, refer to pages 134–139 in your textbook.

Ruins and Artifacts

a. jewelry made of lapis lazuli from Afghanistan
b. large warehouse used for storing grain
c. a sewer system and paved streets laid out in grid pattern
d. painted pottery, carved stone figures, bronze statues
e. stone seals with writing
f. massive fort with thick walls

Stone seal

Conclusions

__c__ 1. Cities were carefully planned and built.

__b__ 2. Farmers harvested crops and were able to set aside surplus grain.

__e__ 3. A system of marking belongings was used.

__a__ 4. Harappans traded with their neighbors.

__d__ 5. Craftworkers were highly skilled.

__f__ 6. The city was protected from enemy attacks and from floods.

COMPARING DIFFERENT KINDS OF MAPS

Comparing maps helps you to see relationships that you would not be able to see by looking at maps separately. Compare the maps below to answer the questions. If you need help, refer to pages 140–141 in your textbook.

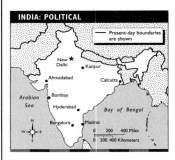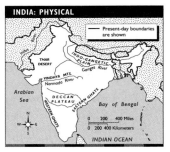

1. What are some physical features of India?
   Physical features include mountains, plateaus, plains, deserts, and rivers.

2. On what kinds of physical features are most cities located?
   They are located on plains and in valleys along rivers.

3. In what areas are the fewest cities (or no cities) located?
   mountain regions

4. What conclusions can you draw about the effect of physical features on the development of cities in India?
   Possible answer: Cities have developed in river valleys and on the plains and plateaus of India where the land is the most fertile and transportation is available.

HINDUISM YESTERDAY AND TODAY

Hinduism is one of the world's major religions, and 80 percent of the people in India are Hindus. The pictures below show some aspects of Hinduism. Use the pictures and pages 142–147 in your textbook to answer the questions.

1. What are the names of three gods and goddesses worshiped by different groups of Hindus today?
   Vishnu, Devi, Shiva

   Which one is considered the "Mother of Creation"?
   Devi

2. Where do Hindus worship their favorite gods?
   They worship at home, in temples, and at special festivals.

3. What are the Vedas and two important Hindu beliefs presented in them?
   The Vedas are the "Books of Knowledge" that tell Hindus how they should live. The Vedas introduced the ideas of reincarnation, castes, and dharma.

BUDDHISM YESTERDAY AND TODAY

Use the information below to complete the boxes of the diagram. One item has been completed in boxes 1–4. For help, you can refer to pages 150–155 in your textbook.

> Hindus believe in karma, a force caused by a person's good and bad acts.
>
> The Middle Way of life was meant to be neither too strict nor too easy.
>
> Suffering is caused by people's wants.
>
> Suffering can be ended if people stop wanting things.
>
> To stop wanting, people must follow eight basic laws.
>
> One ends suffering by following the Eightfold Path.

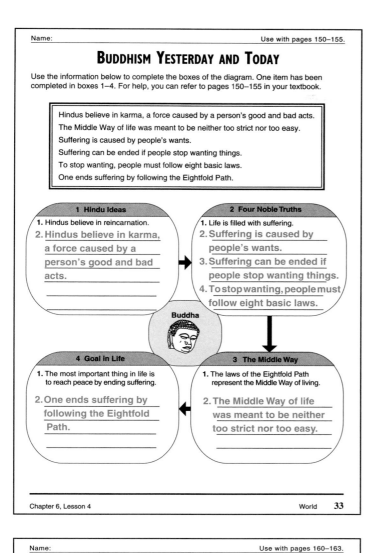

1 Hindu Ideas
1. Hindus believe in reincarnation.
2. Hindus believe in karma, a force caused by a person's good and bad acts.

2 Four Noble Truths
1. Life is filled with suffering.
2. Suffering is caused by people's wants.
3. Suffering can be ended if people stop wanting things.
4. To stop wanting, people must follow eight basic laws.

Buddha

4 Goal in Life
1. The most important thing in life is to reach peace by ending suffering.
2. One ends suffering by following the Eightfold Path.

3 The Middle Way
1. The laws of the Eightfold Path represent the Middle Way of living.
2. The Middle Way of life was meant to be neither too strict nor too easy.

USING NEW WORDS

Use the words in the box to complete the sentences below. For help, you can refer to the lessons in Chapter 6 in your textbook.

Buddhism	Four Noble Truths	migrate
caste system	Hinduism	monk
citadel	karma	reincarnation
dharma	Middle Way	subcontinent
Eightfold Path	Vedas	

1. At Mohenjo-Daro archaeologists have found the remains of a large fort or citadel.

2. Around 1500 B.C. the Aryans began to migrate to the Indian subcontinent, bringing their language, called Sanskrit.

3. The beginnings of the religion called Hinduism are found in the ancient Aryan songs called the "Books of Knowledge," or the Vedas.

4. In the caste system a person's place in society is set by the rank that he or she is born into.

5. The Vedas state that people move in a constant cycle of life, death, and rebirth, which is called reincarnation.

6. The Hindu religion includes hundreds of laws and duties called the dharma, outlined in the "Books of Knowledge."

7. Siddhartha Gautama, the founder of the religion called Buddhism, left his home and became a monk.

8. The Buddha believed in karma, a force caused by a person's good and bad acts that affects future lives.

9. The Buddha's ideas that suffering is central to life were expressed in Four Noble Truths.

10. The Buddha taught that the way to end suffering was to follow the Eightfold Path. These instructions outlined a way of living, neither too strict nor too easy, called the Middle Way.

A RIVER IN CHINA

Use the clues and the words in the box to complete the puzzle below. Write one letter of each word on a blank line. If you need help, refer back to pages 160–163 in your textbook.

Words

Ordos Desert
erosion
grapes
delta
famine
levees
plateau
loess
civilizations
North China Plain

Clues

1. major landform in China flooded by the Huang River
2. huge landform in Tibet where the Huang River begins
3. land feature created by deposits of silt
4. time of crop failure and starvation
5. crop harvested by Huang farmers
6. wearing away of soil by wind or water
7. what ancient farming communities developed into
8. earth walls farmers built to hold back the Huang
9. dusty, yellow soil deposited by wind
10. dry region around which the Huang curves

What is another name for the Yellow River? Huang River

1. NORTH CHINA PLAIN
2. PLATEAU
3. DELTA
4. FAMINE
5. GRAPES
6. EROSION
7. CIVILIZATIONS
8. LEVEES
9. LOESS
10. ORDOS DESERT

CHINESE WRITING: PAST AND PRESENT

The earliest Chinese writing had characters that were pictographs; they looked like pictures of objects. By the time of the Shang dynasty, the symbols in Chinese writing were simpler and could stand for objects or ideas. Answer the questions about Chinese writing below. If you need help, refer to pages 164–167 in your textbook.

1. Before the Shang dynasty, an early writing system had developed along which river?
   the Huang River

2. What objects with writing on them have been found from the Shang period? Circle the correct answers.
   (stones)   (bronze pots)   (oracle bones)

3. In the time of the Shang kings, how was writing on objects used to predict the future?
   Oracle bones with writing on them were heated until they cracked, and priests interpreted the cracks to find answers to questions.

Today there are different kinds of Chinese characters. Some are greatly simplified pictures. Others are formed by combining two or more pictographs. Each character stands for a word.

4. The Chinese character for the word *up* is on the left. Look at the one on the right. Can you guess its meaning? down

上 下

THE QIN EMPIRE

Some of Shihuangdi's ideas about how a government should be run are listed below. Explain how each idea helped him create a strong, unified empire. If you need help, refer to pages 168–171 in your textbook.

Shihuangdi's Idea	How It Helped Unify the Empire
He set up a single system of writing.	1. **helped local leaders communicate with the capital and helped the government to record and collect taxes**
He ordered farmers to build highways.	2. **linked the cities of the empire**
He collected taxes from farmers.	3. **made the empire rich**
He allowed farmers to own land.	4. **weakened the power of the nobles; ensured that there would be food for the empire**
He ordered farmers to strengthen walls along the northern border.	5. **kept people from the northern steppes from coming into the empire**

6. What geographical features helped Shihuangdi win control of the Qin region?
   the Huang River and the Quinling Mountains

7. Which of Shihuangdi's ideas would become lasting legacies?
   His centralized systems of writing, government, and money would live on for centuries.

WRITING A SUMMARY

A summary briefly states the main ideas contained in a piece of writing. As you read the selection below, look for the main idea in each paragraph. Then complete the activities that follow. For help, refer to pages 172–173 in your textbook.

The Han rulers wanted educated people for government jobs. Wudi was the first strong emperor of the Han dynasty. His rule lasted from 140 B.C. to 87 B.C. Wudi created schools to prepare students for government service. These schools were run by Confucian teachers.

Under Wudi's government, schools were set up in each province in China. The schools taught Chinese literature to students who would serve in local government. Very good students were sometimes sent to the best school in the empire. This was the Grand School.

More and more people were educated for government service. During Wudi's rule only 50 students were allowed to study at the Grand School. By A.D. 200 the school had more than 30,000 students. For one year students learned about ancient China's poetry, history, proper behavior, and folk songs. The teachers were China's most brilliant Confucian scholars. At the end of the year, students at the Grand School took a long test. If they passed, they earned jobs as government workers or as teachers in province schools. They also won great respect in society because they were so well educated.

1. Write the topic sentence of each of the paragraphs.
   The Han rulers wanted educated people for government jobs.
   Under Wudi's government, schools were set up in each province in China. More and more people were educated for government service.

2. Write a summary of the selection in three or four sentences.
   The Han emperors set up a system of schools to educate people for government service. In local schools and the Grand School, students studied Chinese literature. The education system grew, providing the empire with well-respected government officials and teachers.

THE TEACHINGS OF CONFUCIUS

Confucius was an important Chinese teacher and scholar. Some of his teachings, which his students wrote down in a book called *The Analects*, are listed below. Use his teachings and the information on pages 174–178 in your textbook to answer the questions.

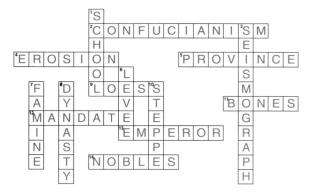

- Daily I examine myself on three points: Have I worked hard? Have I been loyal to my friends? Have I shared what I have learned?

- Do not worry about having an important job; worry about doing your job well.

- The good person is satisfied and calm; the mean person is always full of distress.

- When we see good and kind people, we should think of following their example; when we see criminal and greedy people, we should look at ourselves.

1. According to Confucius, what are the traits of a good person?
   A good person is satisfied, calm, hardworking, loyal to friends, and shares knowledge.

2. What are the traits of a good worker?
   A good worker works hard and is concerned about doing the job well rather than about the importance of the job.

3. What did Confucius mean when he advised people to think of themselves when they saw a criminal or a greedy person?
   Possible answer: People should look for their own negative traits and try to correct them.

4. How did Confucian ideas influence the Han dynasty?
   Confucian emphasis on education resulted in increased knowledge and remarkable inventions during the Han dynasty. The Han emperor Wudi started Confucian schools to educate government workers.

USING NEW WORDS

Use the words in the box to complete the crossword puzzle below. For help, you can refer to the lessons in Chapter 7 in your textbook.

Confucianism	dynasty	Mandate of Heaven
emperor	Grand School	levee
loess	famine	oracle bones
erosion	nobles	province
seismograph	steppe	

(Crossword puzzle)

Across:
2. CONFUCIANISM
4. EROSION
5. PROVINCE
9. LOESS
11. BONES
12. MANDATE
13. EMPEROR
14. NOBLES

Down:
1. SCHOOL
3. SEISMOGRAPH
6. LEVEE
7. FAMINE
8. DYNASTY
10. STEPPE

Across
2. teachings of Confucius
4. wearing away of soil
5. political division of land in the empire
9. dusty, yellow soil
11. used to predict future (1 of 2 words)
12. god-given right to rule (1 of 3 words)
13. supreme ruler of an empire
14. rich, powerful relatives of the king

Down
1. Grand _____, best place for Chinese to be educated
3. machine that detects earthquakes
6. wall that keeps a river within its banks
7. time when people starve
8. line of rulers from the same family
10. dry, treeless plain

THE GEOGRAPHY OF ANCIENT GREECE

Use the map to answer the questions below. For help, you may refer to pages 192–195 in your textbook.

ANCIENT GREECE

1. What seas border Greece?
   Aegean Sea, Mediterranean Sea, Ionian Sea

2. On what peninsula is Sparta located? **Peloponnesus**

3. On what peninsula is Athens located? **Attica**

4. What is the name of the biggest Greek island? **Crete**

5. Why has it always been difficult to travel by land in Greece?
   Nine out of every ten acres are hilly or mountainous.

COMPARING ATHENS AND SPARTA

The two Greek city-states of Athens and Sparta shared a common culture yet differed from each other in many ways. Read the sentences below carefully. If the sentence describes life in Athens, circle **A**. If the sentence describes life in Sparta, circle **S**. If the sentence describes both Athenian and Spartan life, circle **A** and **S**. If you need help, refer back to pages 196–201 in your textbook.

1. Only free men were citizens of their polis. ⒶⒶ Ⓢ
2. Athletes participated in the Olympic Games. Ⓐ Ⓢ
3. People honored Athena as their special protector and provider. Ⓐ S
4. People gathered at temples to worship Zeus, the most powerful Greek god. Ⓐ Ⓢ
5. Life revolved around an agora and an acropolis. Ⓐ Ⓢ
6. Boys spent a lot of time training to be soldiers. A Ⓢ
7. Girls practiced sports and were trained to be strong mothers of strong children. A Ⓢ
8. Girls stayed at home to help their mothers. Ⓐ S
9. Boys worked with their fathers in the fields or in craft shops. Ⓐ S
10. Women and slaves had few rights. Ⓐ Ⓢ
11. The government changed from an oligarchy to a democracy. Ⓐ S
12. Here people enjoyed hearing the stories of Homer. Ⓐ Ⓢ

THE GOLDEN AGE OF ATHENS

The pictures below show important people and places in Athenian life. Write a caption for each picture explaining how the person or place reflected the "Golden Age" of Greece. If you need help, refer back to pages 204–209 in your textbook.

Parthenon

Possible answer: The Parthenon lay at the center of the Acropolis, which was the largest in Greece and reflected the power and wealth of Athens.

Pericles

Possible answer: Pericles, an Athenian leader, arranged for citizens to be paid when they held an office or served on a jury.

Agora

Possible answer: People bought and traded goods in Athens' busy agora.

Plato

Possible answer: Plato, a famous philosopher, wrote down the teachings of Socrates.

MAKING CONCLUSIONS

Making a conclusion involves pulling together pieces of information so that they have meaning. Practice making a conclusion by reading the passage below and completing the activity that follows. If you need help, refer back to pages 210–211 in your textbook.

> The Athenian philosopher Socrates was tried and condemned to death for disturbing the public peace. Here is part of his speech to the jury after he received the death penalty, as reported by his student Plato.
> There is great reason to hope that death is a good, for one of two things: either death is a state of nothingness and utter unconsciousness, or . . . there is a change and migration of the soul from this world to another. Now if you suppose that there is no consciousness, but a sleep like the sleep of him who is undisturbed even by the sight of dreams, death will be an unspeakable gain. . . . Now if death is like this, I say that to die is gain; for eternity is then only a single night. But if death is the journey to another place, and there, as men say, all the dead are, what good, O my friends and judges, can be greater than this. . . . I . . . shall have a wonderful interest in a place where I can converse [talk] with Palamedes, and Ajax the son of Telamon, and the other heroes of old. . . . Above all, I shall be able to continue my search into true and false knowledge; as in this world, so also in that; I shall find out who is wise, and who pretends to be wise, and is not.

Mark **X** next to each statement that is a reasonable conclusion based on the information you have just read.

_____ 1. Socrates hoped that death would end his suffering.
__X__ 2. Socrates had no fear of death.
_____ 3. Socrates had difficulty sleeping.
__X__ 4. To Socrates, death could only be a good thing.
__X__ 5. Socrates believed that even in death he could continue his search for the truth.
_____ 6. When he slept, Socrates had disturbing dreams.
__X__ 7. In death Socrates hoped to be reunited with friends, judges, and heroes from the past.
_____ 8. Socrates believed that in the afterlife all people were wise.
_____ 9. Socrates was a popular teacher.
__X__ 10. Wisdom and knowledge were important to Socrates.

THE GREEK ALPHABET

The great library at Alexandria contained hundreds of thousands of books written in Greek. Suppose that you have found a piece of one of these books, a scroll written on a papyrus roll. To find the meaning of the words on the scroll, use the Greek alphabet as shown here. Below each Greek letter write its English equivalent.

Modern

A B C D E F H I K L M N O P Q R S T V X Z

Greek

Δ Β Γ Δ Ε F Θ S X Λ Μ Ν Ο Γ Φ Ρ Σ Τ Υ Χ Ι

1. ΓΟΛΣΣ
   polis

2. ΑΓΡΟΓΟΛΣΣ
   acropolis

3. ΣΟΓΡΑΤΕΣ
   Socrates

4. When Alexander the Great conquered the Persian empire, he spread Greek culture from Egypt to India. In addition to the Greek alphabet, what other Greek legacies did Alexander spread throughout his empire?

   The cities that Alexander built mirrored a Greek polis; they had an agora, a theater, temples, and a stadium. In these cities citizens took part in democratic assemblies. Alexander spread Greek achievements in math and science by building a library to house the scholarly work of Greek experts.

USING NEW WORDS

Choose a term from the box to answer each question. For help, you can refer to the lessons in Chapter 8 of your textbook.

acropolis	democracy	Peloponnesian War
agora	harbor	peninsula
assembly	jury	philosophy
citizen	monarchy	polis
colony	oligarchy	

1. What is the Greek word for a city-state? **polis**

2. Where did the ancient Greeks meet and conduct business? **agora**

3. What kind of government is headed by one ruler? **monarchy**

4. In what lawmaking body did people vote on issues that helped to shape the future of the city? **assembly**

5. What was the name of the conflict between Athens and Sparta and their allies? **Peloponnesian War**

6. Where do ships find a sheltered place along a coast? **harbor**

7. Who hears evidence and makes decisions in a court of law? **jury**

8. What is the name for the large hill around which Greek city-states were built? **acropolis**

9. What area of land is nearly surrounded by water? **peninsula**

10. What kind of government is run by a small group of people? **oligarchy**

11. Who has certain rights and responsibilities in his or her country or community? **citizen**

12. In what form of government do people vote to make decisions? **democracy**

13. If you wanted to search for wisdom and the right way to live, what would you study? **philosophy**

14. What is the name for a group of people who lived apart from Greece but kept economic ties with it? **colony**

THE GEOGRAPHY OF ANCIENT ITALY

Use the map to answer the questions. Refer to pages 224–227 in your textbook.

ANCIENT ITALY

1. What are two ways in which the geography of Italy is similar to that of Greece?
   Both are peninsulas in the Mediterranean Sea, and both are mountainous with fertile plains.

2. What mountain range separates Italy from the rest of Europe? **the Alps**

3. What mountain range runs down the center of Italy? **Apennine Mountains**

4. What large island is part of southern Italy? **Sicily**

5. What two geographic features made the location of Rome a favorable one?
   Possible answers: The hills helped to protect the city from attack; the plain of Latium had fertile soil; the Tiber River provided a means of transportation to the sea.

READING ELEVATION MAPS AND PROFILES

An elevation map shows the height of land above sea level. A profile map shows a cross section of a region. Use the maps below to answer the questions that follow. Refer back to pages 228–229 in your textbook.

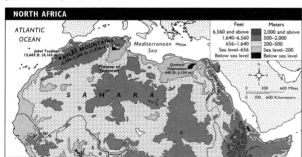

NORTH AFRICA

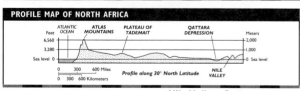

PROFILE MAP OF NORTH AFRICA

1. What land features are shown on both maps? **Nile Valley, Qattara Depression, Plateau of Tademait, Atlas Mountains**

2. On the profile map, what is the elevation of the Plateau of Tademait? **about 1,700 feet**

3. What is the highest peak in North Africa? **Jebel Toubkal**

4. On which map is it easier to see differences in elevation?
   Differences in elevation are easier to see on the profile map.

5. Which map would you use to show the relative location of landforms in the region?
   You would use the elevation map.

THE ROMANS AT WAR

In 390 B.C. an army of Gauls attacked Rome. The Roman historian Livy tells how the Gauls tried to surprise the Romans one night. Read the passage below and answer the questions that follow. For help, you may refer to pages 230–235 in your textbook.

> The Capitol of Rome was meantime in great danger; for the Gauls had [observed] the easy ascent [to it] by the rock at the Temple of Carmentis. On a moonlight night, after they had first sent ahead a man unarmed to test the way . . . they gained the summit all in silence. Not merely had they escaped the [sight] of the [guards], but even the dogs, sensitive as they are to noises at night, had not been alarmed. But they did not escape the notice of the geese; for these creatures were sacred to [the goddess] Juno, and had been accordingly spared despite the scarcity of food.
>
> Thus it befell that Marcus Manlius, who had been consul three years earlier, and who was a [respected] warrior, was awakened by their hissing and the flapping of their wings. He snatched his arms, and calling loudly to his fellows, ran to the spot. Here he [hit] with . . . a shield a Gaul who had already gained a foothold on the summit, and tumbled him headlong. . . . Manlius also slew certain others who in their alarm had cast aside their weapons and were clinging to the rocks. By this time the rest [of the Romans] had rushed together, and crushed the enemy with darts and stones, so that the whole band, dislodged from their foothold, were hurled down the precipice in general ruin.

1. Describe the Gauls' plan to attack the Romans.

They planned to surprise the Romans by silently climbing the rock at the Temple of Carmentis at night.

2. How did the Romans find out that the Gauls were attacking?

The Romans were awakened by the sound of geese hissing and flapping their wings.

3. What did Marcus Manlius do when he realized that the Gauls were attacking?

He alerted his fellow soldiers and led the Romans in fighting.

4. Rome's army defeated the Gauls. Later, Roman soldiers fought in the Punic Wars and in the Battle of Zama. What was the outcome of each of these conflicts for Rome?

Rome won both conflicts, gained control of Carthage's territory, and became the most powerful nation in the Mediterranean region.

PAX ROMANA

Explain how each of the following helped to keep the Roman empire together during the 200 years of the Pax Romana. For help, you may refer to pages 236–243 in your textbook.

1. Army

The Roman army defended the empire against bandits, built the empire's roads, and helped enforce laws.

3. Tax collectors

Tax collectors collected taxes from craftworkers and merchants to pay for the upkeep of the empire.

2. Roads

A network of roads helped to make communication, trade, and travel possible throughout the vast empire.

4. Laws

Roman governors, who also acted as judges, enforced Roman laws throughout the empire.

THE BEGINNINGS OF CHRISTIANITY

The first four books of the New Testament, known as the Gospels, give different kinds of information about Jesus. Read the excerpts below and answer the questions that follow. For help, you may refer to pages 246–251 in your textbook.

A. Jesus was born in the town of Bethlehem in Judea, during the time when Herod was king.

Matthew 2:1

B. They crossed the lake and came to land at Gennesaret, where the people recognized Jesus. So they sent for the sick people in all the surrounding country and brought them to Jesus. They begged him to let the sick at least touch the edge of his cloak; and all who touched it were made well.

Matthew 14:34–36

C. But I tell you who hear me: Love your enemies, do good to those who hate you, bless those who curse you, and pray for those who mistreat you.

Luke 6:27–28

D. What do you think a man does who has one hundred sheep and one of them gets lost? He will leave the other ninety-nine grazing on the hillside and go and look for the lost sheep. When he finds it, I tell you, he feels far happier over this one sheep than over the ninety-nine that did not get lost. In just the same way, your Father in heaven does not want any of these little ones to be lost.

Matthew 18:12–14

1. Which passage tells about Jesus as a historical person? A

2. Which passage tells about Jesus as a healer? B

3. Which passage shows Jesus teaching people the right way to live? C

4. Which passage presents a story that Jesus told? D

5. What is the name for the kind of story Jesus told? a parable

---

THE SHIFT FROM WEST TO EAST

Use the map to complete the activities below. Refer to pages 252–257 in your textbook.

THE ROMAN EMPIRE, A.D. 284

1. In A.D. 284 the emperor Diocletian divided the empire into two halves. Why?

The empire was too big to be ruled by one leader.

2. Circle the parts of the empire over which Diocletian ruled.

(Greece)   (Egypt)   Spain   Italy   (Palestine)   Britain

3. Locate and name the new capital city built by Constantine.

Constantinople

4. Give two reasons why Constantine located his capital on this site.

Constantinople was located on a major trade route, was easy to protect, and was far from Rome.

5. The western half of the Roman empire collapsed in the 400s, but the eastern half continued for another 1,000 years. What was the name of the eastern empire?

the Byzantine empire

6. What two forms of Christianity developed in the divided empire?

Roman Catholicism developed in the west, and Eastern Orthodox Christianity developed in the east.

SOME WORDS ABOUT ROME

Cross out the word in each group that does not belong. Then write a sentence telling how the remaining three words are related. If you need help, refer back to the lessons in Chapter 9 of your textbook.

1. Forum   patricians   ~~Messiah~~   Twelve Tables

   Possible answer: The patricians agreed to write Roman laws down on the Twelve Tables and post them in the city's Forum.

2. republic   ~~architecture~~   consuls   Senate

   Possible answer: The powerful Senate and the consuls were two branches of Rome's republic.

3. representatives   tribunes   plebeians   ~~Punic Wars~~

   Possible answer: Representatives in the assembly elected tribunes who worked to gain rights for Rome's plebeians.

4. ~~apostles~~   Pax Romana   aqueducts   census

   Possible answer: During the period known as Pax Romana, the emperor ordered the building of aqueducts and the taking of a census every five years.

5. Christianity   New Testament   parables   ~~gladiators~~

   Possible answer: The story of the birth of Christianity and the parables of Jesus can be found in the New Testament.

6. Eastern Orthodox Christianity   ~~dictator~~   Roman Catholicism   pope

   Possible answer: In the western half of the empire, Christianity became known as Roman Catholicism, and the pope was its leader; in the eastern half the religion became known as Eastern Orthodox Christianity.

7. Choose two of the words that you crossed out. Write two sentences explaining how each word relates to the history of ancient Rome.

   Possible answer: After defeating Carthage in the Punic Wars, Rome became the greatest power in the Mediterranean region. Julius Caesar was a dictator of Rome.

THE GEOGRAPHY OF ARABIA

Use the map to complete the activities below. Refer to pages 262–265 in your textbook.

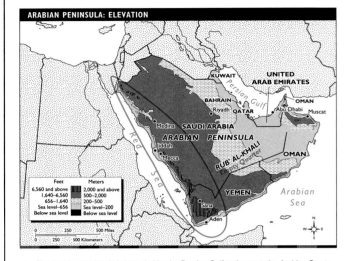

ARABIAN PENINSULA: ELEVATION

1. The Arabian peninsula is bounded by the Persian Gulf to the east, the Arabian Sea to the south, and the Red Sea to the west. Locate and label these waters on the map.

2. Which city on the map above has the highest elevation? Sana

3. Locate and circle the Jabal Al-Hijaz mountains of western Arabia.

4. In what areas of the Arabian peninsula did towns and cities develop?
   in fertile regions, at desert edges, and at oases

5. Name three modern nations that are located on the Arabian peninsula.
   Saudia Arabia, Yemen, Oman, United Arab Emirates, Kuwait, Qatar

---

THE RELIGION OF ISLAM

The pictures below show important parts of the Islamic religion. Use the pictures and the information on pages 266–271 in your textbook to answer the questions that follow.

1. What is the holy city of Islam?
   Mecca

2. Why is the year 622 important to Muslims?
   It is the starting point of the Islamic calendar.

3. What are the five basic duties of all Muslims?
   a. belief in one god, Allah
   b. prayer five times a day
   c. giving to those in need
   d. fasting during the month of Ramadan
   e. a religious pilgrimage to Mecca

4. What is the name of the sacred book containing these five duties?
   the Quran

5. What do Muslims believe is the origin of this sacred book?
   Muslims believe the Quran contains the holy teachings that Muhammad received from Allah.

A MUSLIM CALIPHATE

The caliphs of Baghdad built a huge library called the House of Wisdom. There Arab scholars translated and studied Greek, Roman, and Indian works. They also wrote books in the fields of medicine, math, science, and literature. Use each picture to answer the question that follows. For help, you may refer to pages 272–277 in your textbook.

A Persian doctor wrote a famous medical textbook. What was his name?
Ibn Sina or Avicenna

You use a system of numbers invented by Muslim mathematicians. What is the name for a type of mathematics these scholars developed?
algebra

People today still read a collection of folktales originally written in Arabic. What is the name of this book?
The Arabian Nights

Muslim scholars studied the stars and developed a calendar. What was the name of the instrument they used to figure out position from the stars?
astrolabe

READING HISTORICAL MAPS

Historical maps show places or events from the past. There are many of these maps in your textbook. Use the historical map below to complete the activities that follow. Refer to pages 280–281 in your textbook for help.

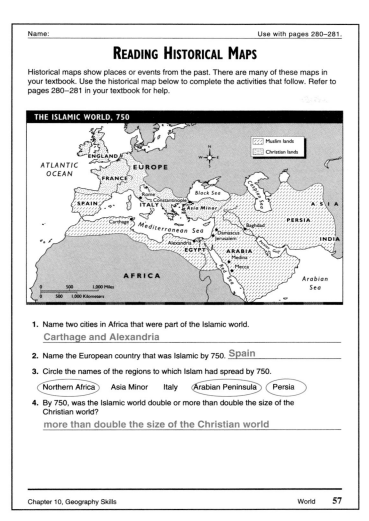

THE ISLAMIC WORLD, 750

1. Name two cities in Africa that were part of the Islamic world.
   Carthage and Alexandria

2. Name the European country that was Islamic by 750. Spain

3. Circle the names of the regions to which Islam had spread by 750.
   (Northern Africa) Asia Minor Italy (Arabian Peninsula) (Persia)

4. By 750, was the Islamic world double or more than double the size of the Christian world?
   more than double the size of the Christian world

USING NEW WORDS

Use the words in the box to complete the activity below. For help, you can refer to the lessons in Chapter 10 in your textbook.

algebra	Five Pillars	mosque
astrolabe	hijra	oasis
caliph	Islam	pilgrimage
caravan	Kaaba	Quran

Rearrange the letters to spell the word that fits the definition. Use capital letters where needed.

	Word	Definition
1.	pailch caliph	Muslim ruler
2.	quesom mosque	Muslim place of worship
3.	elbagar algebra	a type of mathematics
4.	blastearo astrolabe	instrument used to find position from stars
5.	soisa oasis	place with water in the desert
6.	ranavac caravan	group of people and animals traveling together
7.	mails Islam	Muslim religion
8.	narqu Quran	sacred book of Islam
9.	abaka Kaaba	temple in Mecca
10.	rajih hijra	Muhammad's move from Mecca to Medina
11.	veif sliplar Five Pillars	a Muslim's basic duties
12.	miggrapile pilgrimage	journey for religious purposes

CLIMATE REGIONS IN MIDDLE AMERICA

In Middle America there are three climate zones, each largely determined by elevation. Use the information in the diagram below to answer the questions that follow. If you need help, refer back to pages 286–289 in your textbook.

Climate Regions in Middle America

Elevation/Feet

Tierra Fría

—6,000—

Tierra Templada

—3,000—

Tierra Caliente

B = Bananas
BE = Beans
CA = Cacao
CF = Coffee
CO = Cotton
CR = Corn
P = Potatoes
S = Sugarcane
T = Tobacco
W = Wheat

1. a. What is the hottest region in Middle America called?
   tierra caliente

   b. What is the elevation of this region?
   sea level to 3,000 feet

   c. What crops grow in this region?
   bananas, tobacco, cotton,
   corn, sugarcane, cacao,
   coffee

2. a. In what region is the climate mild?
   tierra templada

   b. What is the elevation of this region?
   from 3,000 to 6,000 feet

   c. What crops grow in this region?
   bananas, tobacco, cotton,
   corn, sugarcane, cacao,
   coffee

3. a. In what region is the climate usually cold?
   tierra fría

   b. What is the elevation of this region?
   above 6,000 feet

   c. What crops grow in this region?
   wheat, corn, potatoes,
   beans

4. What do all the climate regions have in common?
   All the climate regions have
   a rainy season; they all
   grow corn.

COMPARING CLIMOGRAPHS

Study the climographs below. Then answer the questions. For help, you may refer to pages 290–291 in your textbook.

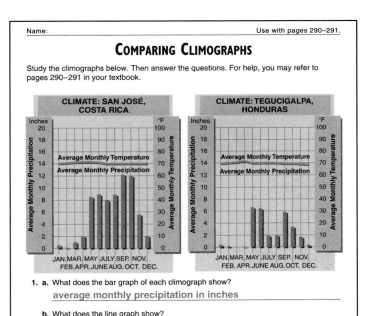

1. a. What does the bar graph of each climograph show?
   average monthly precipitation in inches

   b. What does the line graph show?
   average monthly temperature in degrees Fahrenheit

2. a. During which month does each city get the most precipitation?
   San José September   Tegucigalpa May

   b. What is the average temperature during this month?
   San José about 70°F   Tegucigalpa about 70°F

3. How are the climates of San José and Tegucigalpa similar?
   The temperatures are similar and do not vary much during the
   year, and both have a rainy season.

4. How does the climate of San José differ from that of Tegucigalpa?
   San José gets more precipitation than Tegucigalpa.

THE MYSTERIOUS OLMEC

Archaeologists have found the artifacts pictured below. In the space provided write the clues that each one reveals about the Olmec civilization. For help, you may refer to pages 292–296 in your textbook.

1. Carved head

Possible answer: The Olmec had specialized skills to carve out a large piece of sculpture. The large head may be a statue of an Olmec ruler.

2. Jaguar carving

Possible answer: The Olmec believed that certain animals had special powers and that the jaguar was the most powerful of all.

3. Rubber ball

Possible answer: The Olmec lived in an area where there were many rubber trees.

4. What do historians want to find out about the Olmec?

Historians want to learn what they called themselves and why their civilization declined.

THE WORLD OF THE MAYA

Read the descriptions and look at the pictures. Then complete the activity below. For help, you may refer to pages 298–303 in your textbook.

1. This is a pyramid temple at Copán.
   What other types of buildings have archaeologists found at Copán?
   a ball court, palaces

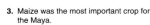

2. Maya writing is one source of information about the Maya.
   On what did the Maya write?
   stone buildings and stelae, books

3. Maize was the most important crop for the Maya.
   What other crops did farmers grow?
   beans, squash, peppers, cacaos, avocados, papayas

4. The Maya studied the stars and planets.
   What did the study of astronomy help them to do?
   develop an accurate calendar and record the exact dates of events

5. Why do we know more about the Maya civilization than about the Olmec civilization?
   We can read their writing, and descendants of the Maya speak a version of the ancient language and preserve many of the traditions.

SOME WORDS ABOUT MIDDLE AMERICA

Use the clues and the words in the box to complete the puzzle below. Write one letter of the word in each square. The mystery box in the puzzle spells out the name of a country in Middle America. For help, you may refer to the lessons in Chapter 11 in your textbook.

Words

Classic Period
Ice Age
slash and burn
glacier
maize
stela
glyph
rain forest
tropical

Clues

1. sheet of ice
2. farming method in which jungle is cleared and burned
3. important time of cultural achievement for a civilization
4. tall, flat stone
5. wooded area that receives more than 80 inches of rain per year
6. corn
7. period when ice covered nearly half of Earth's land mass
8. symbol used in Maya writing
9. located near the equator where the climate is usually warm

1. G L A C I E R
2. S L A S H   A N D   B U R N
3. C L A S S I C   P E R I O D
4. S T E L A
5. R A I N   F O R E S T
6. M A I Z E
7. I C E   A G E
8. G L Y P H
9. T R O P I C A L

THE GEOGRAPHY OF EUROPE

Use the map to answer the questions below. For help, you may refer to pages 316–319 in your textbook.

1. a. Name the largest peninsula in northern Europe.
   Scandinavian Peninsula

   b. Name the largest peninsula in southern Europe.
   Iberian Peninsula

2. a. What major river empties into the North Sea?
   Rhine River

   b. What river flows through central Europe to the Black Sea?
   Danube

3. a. What ocean lies to the north of Europe?
   Arctic Ocean

   b. What sea forms the southern boundary of Europe?
   Mediterranean Sea

4. a. What two mountain ranges separate the continent of Europe from Asia?
   Ural and Caucasus mountains

   b. What landform covers over 50 percent of Europe?
   North European Plain

LIFE IN THE MIDDLE AGES

Follow the directions and complete the activities below. For help, you may refer to pages 320–327 in your textbook.

1. Draw a line to the picture of a vassal.

What did a vassal do for his lord?
He served as a knight in the lord's army.

What did the lord give the vassal?
The lord gave each vassal a fief.

What word describes the relationship between lords and vassals?
feudalism

2. Draw a line to the picture of a serf.

Where did a medieval serf live?
A serf lived on a manor.

What did a serf have to do for his lord?
The serf worked on the lord's land and paid rent and taxes.

3. Draw a line to the picture of a craftworker.

Where did craftworkers live in the Middle Ages?
Craftworkers lived primarily in towns.

What was the name for a group of craftworkers?
a guild

DETERMINING POINT OF VIEW

As you read the following passages, try to determine the writer's point of view. For help, you may refer to pages 328–329 in your textbook.

> *Charlemagne fought many wars with neighboring peoples in order to establish the Frankish empire. The Saxons were one of these peoples. Charlemagne's secretary and close friend, Einhard, wrote a book in which he described Charlemagne's war with the Saxons:*
>
> No war ever undertaken by the Franks was waged with such persistence and bitterness, or cost so much labor, because the Saxons, like almost all Germans, were a ferocious folk, . . . hostile to our Faith, and they did not consider it dishonorable to transgress and violate all law—be it human or divine.
>
> William Stearns Davis, *Readings in Ancient History* (Boston: Allyn and Bacon, 1913), page 374.

1. How does Einhard view the Saxons?
He views them as ferocious, anti-Christian, and dishonorable.

2. What words or phrases reveal Einhard's feelings?
ferocious, hostile to our Faith

3. What helped to shape Einhard's point of view?
The Saxons and the Franks were enemies and had fought each other in a war.

> *Here is how Einhard describes Charlemagne:*
>
> The upper part of his head was round, his eyes very large and animated, nose a little long, hair fair, and face laughing and merry. Thus his appearance was always stately and dignified, whether he was standing or sitting; although his neck was thick and somewhat short, and his belly rather prominent; but the symmetry of the rest of his body concealed these defects.
>
> Einhard, *The Life of Charlemagne* (Ann Arbor, MI: Ann Arbor Paperbacks, The University of Michigan Press, 1960), page 50.

4. How does Einhard view Charlemagne? Do you think that he likes or dislikes him?
Einhard appears to admire and respect Charlemagne but recognizes some of his physical shortcomings.

5. What words or phrases reveal Einhard's feelings about Charlemagne?
animated, laughing and merry, stately and dignified

THE CALL FOR THE FIRST CRUSADE

Read the passage below and answer the questions. For help, you may refer to pages 330–335 in your textbook.

> *In 1095 the Byzantine emperor appealed for help against the Turks, who had captured Jerusalem and were threatening Constantinople. Pope Urban II called Christians to join a crusade against the Turks. Here is part of his speech:*
>
> For your brethren who live in the east are in urgent need of your help, and you must hasten to give them the aid which has often been promised them. For, as most of you have heard, the Turks and Arabs have attacked them. . . . They have killed and captured many, and have destroyed the churches and devastated the empire. If you permit them to continue . . . the faithful of God will be much more widely attacked by them. On this account I, or rather the Lord, beseech you as Christ's heralds to publish this everywhere and to persuade all people of whatever rank, footsoldiers and knights, poor and rich, to carry aid promptly to those Christians and to destroy that vile race from the lands of our friends. . . . Moreover, Christ commands it.
>
> Oliver J. Thatcher and Edgar H. McNeal, *A Source Book for Mediaeval History* (New York: Charles Scribner's Sons, 1905).

3. **a.** What armies did the Crusaders fight? What was their religion?
the Seljuk Turks, who were Muslim

b. Did the first Crusaders succeed in capturing Jerusalem?
yes

1. Whom did Pope Urban ask to go on the Crusade?
Christians of all ranks, both rich and poor

2. What did Urban say to persuade people to join the Crusade?
He said Christ commanded them.

4. During the Middle Ages how did people express their devotion to religion?
They worshiped in village churches, built cathedrals, made pilgrimages, and honored saints. Some people entered monasteries.

LEONARDO DA VINCI: A RENAISSANCE MAN

Leonardo da Vinci, who described himself as a "disciple of experiment," had many interests and talents. In a letter to the duke of Bari and Milan, he told what he could do for the duke. Read four parts of his letter and complete the activities that follow. For help, you may refer to pages 336–341 in your textbook.

> **A.** I have a sort of extremely light and strong bridges, adapted to be most easily carried, and with them you may pursue, and at any time flee from the enemy.
> **B.** I will make covered chariots, safe and unattackable, which, entering among the enemy with their artillery, there is no body of men so great but they would break them.
> **C.** In time of peace I believe I can give perfect satisfaction and to the equal of any other in architecture and the composition of buildings public and private.
> **D.** I can carry sculpture in marble, bronze, or clay, and also I can do in painting whatever may be done, as well as any other, be he who he may.
>
> Jean Paul Richter and Irma A. Richter, editors, *The Literary Works of Leonardo da Vinci* (London: Oxford University Press, 1936).

1. **a.** In which statement does Leonardo describe himself as an artist? **D**

b. Name the patron in Florence who invited Leonardo to set up a studio in his house.
Lorenzo Medici

2. **a.** In which statement does Leonardo describe himself as an inventor? **B**

b. Name three things that Leonardo planned or designed.
submarine, parachute, machine gun, flying machine

3. **a.** In which statement does Leonardo describe himself as an engineer? **A**

b. Why would the duke be interested in Leonardo's engineering ability?
Leonardo says he could help the duke be successful in war.

4. **a.** In which statement does Leonardo describe himself as an architect? **C**

b. Name another Renaissance artist who was an architect as well as a painter and sculptor.
Michelangelo

5. In what way was the Renaissance both a time of looking back and a time of looking forward?
The Renaissance looked back to the classical achievements of Greece and Rome and forward to future achievements and discoveries in art, literature, and science.

THE REFORMATION

Each pair of sentences below states a cause-effect relationship. Write **C** next to the sentence that states a cause and **E** next to the sentence that states an effect. If you need help, refer to pages 342–347 in your textbook.

C   **1.** Humanism gains popularity among Europe's scholars.

E   Some Christians begin to question the authority of the Pope.

E   **2.** Erasmus begins to criticize Church policy.

C   Priests grant indulgences, or pardons, to people who pay the Church to be forgiven.

E   **3.** The Reformation movement begins in Germany.

C   Martin Luther posts 95 Theses on a Wittenberg church door.

C   **4.** Johannes Gutenberg invents a printing press that uses movable type.

E   Luther's criticism of the Roman Church and a translation of the Bible into German spread quickly.

E   **5.** German leaders protect Martin Luther from the Church.

C   German leaders, loyal to their homeland, want to keep the taxes intended for Rome.

C   **6.** Catholic Church leaders meet in Trent.

E   The Catholic Church reforms some of its practices.

C   **7.** The Pope refuses to give King Henry VIII permission to divorce his queen.

E   Henry starts a new Protestant church, the Church of England.

Now it is your turn. Write a cause-effect sentence pair about the reign of Queen Elizabeth I. Tell which sentence states a cause and which sentence states an effect.

Possible answer: Cause—Spain hopes to return England to the Catholic faith. Effect—King Philip II sends a Spanish armada to attack England.

USING NEW WORDS

Write the letter of the correct word from the box next to its meaning. For help, you may refer to the lessons in Chapter 12 of your textbook.

a. armada	**h.** guild	**o.** monastery	**v.** Reformation
b. cathedral	**i.** humanism	**p.** navigable	**w.** Renaissance
c. convent	**j.** indulgence	**q.** nun	**x.** saint
d. Crusade	**k.** lord	**r.** patron	**y.** serf
e. deforestation	**l.** Magna Carta	**s.** plague	**z.** temperate
f. feudalism	**m.** manor	**t.** Protestantism	**aa.** vassal
g. fief	**n.** Middle Ages	**u.** reform	

p   **1.** deep enough for boat travel

i   **2.** concern with human interests and values

u   **3.** improve by making changes

g   **4.** manor given to a vassal by a lord

x   **5.** holy person

c   **6.** religious community of nuns

e   **7.** process of clearing forests

k   **8.** noble who owned a manor

l   **9.** English charter guaranteeing rights

z   **10.** mild climate

w   **11.** historical period of great creativity

aa   **12.** person who served a lord

t   **13.** branch of Christianity that broke away from Roman Catholicism

a   **14.** fleet of warships

s   **15.** terrible disease

v   **16.** movement that brought reform to the Church

j   **17.** pardon for sins

y   **18.** person who lived and worked on a manor

n   **19.** period between ancient Roman times and the 1400s

b   **20.** grand and beautiful church

q   **21.** woman who devotes her life to religion

m   **22.** large estate owned by a noble

f   **23.** way of organizing society based on land and military service

o   **24.** religious community of monks

r   **25.** person who supports the arts

d   **26.** first journey to gain control of Jerusalem

h   **27.** group of craftworkers

THE GEOGRAPHY OF AFRICA

You are planning a television documentary called "Amazing Africa." Use the map below to name the natural features you plan to film. For help, you may refer to pages 354–357 in your textbook.

1. The world's largest desert region:
Sahara

2. The world's longest river:
Nile River

3. The highest mountain in Africa:
Mt. Kilimanjaro

4. This river flows through southern Africa, emptying into the Indian Ocean:
Zambezi River

5. The narrow, dry grassland along the Sahara's southern edge:
Sahel

6. A gigantic valley, extending almost 3,000 miles:
Great Rift Valley

7. Two seas and two oceans that border Africa:
Mediterranean Sea, Red Sea, Atlantic Ocean, Indian Ocean

CIVILIZATIONS OF NORTHEASTERN AFRICA

Use the pictures below and the information on pages 358–361 in your textbook to answer the questions.

Kushite pyramid

Coins from Aksum

Church at Lalibela

1. a. What city was the capital of the kingdom of Kush?
Meroe

    b. How do we know that the Kushite kings were wealthy?
Remains of large palaces, temples, and pyramid-shaped tombs, and large amounts of gold in a royal tomb.

2. a. What do gold coins reveal about the kingdom of Aksum?
The cross shows the rulers were Christians, and gold shows the kingdom was wealthy.

    b. How did Aksum become a wealthy kingdom?
Aksum controlled major cities and trade routes.

3. a. In what modern country is this church located?
Ethiopia

    b. During whose rule were these stone churches built?
during the rule of Zagwe king Lalibela

WEST AFRICAN GOLD

Answer the questions on the lines provided. For help, you may refer to pages 362–367 in your textbook.

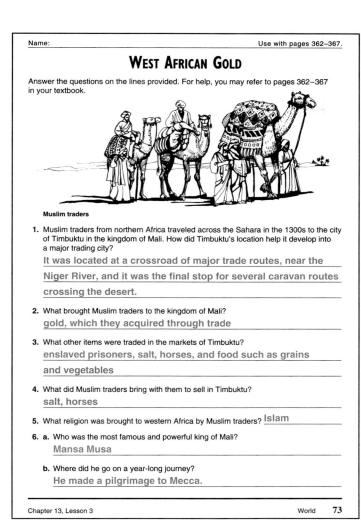

Muslim traders

1. Muslim traders from northern Africa traveled across the Sahara in the 1300s to the city of Timbuktu in the kingdom of Mali. How did Timbuktu's location help it develop into a major trading city?

   It was located at a crossroad of major trade routes, near the
   Niger River, and it was the final stop for several caravan routes
   crossing the desert.

2. What brought Muslim traders to the kingdom of Mali?

   gold, which they acquired through trade

3. What other items were traded in the markets of Timbuktu?

   enslaved prisoners, salt, horses, and food such as grains
   and vegetables

4. What did Muslim traders bring with them to sell in Timbuktu?

   salt, horses

5. What religion was brought to western Africa by Muslim traders? Islam

6. a. Who was the most famous and powerful king of Mali?

   Mansa Musa

   b. Where did he go on a year-long journey?

   He made a pilgrimage to Mecca.

READING A DISTRIBUTION MAP

A distribution map shows how one feature is spread over an area. The distribution map below shows the population density of northeastern Africa. Use the map to answer the questions. If you need help, refer to pages 370–371 in your textbook.

NORTHEASTERN AFRICA: POPULATION DENSITY

People per square mile	People per square kilometer
0–25	0–10
25–250	10–100
250–500	100–200
over 500	over 200

● Major city

1. Which country is more densely populated, Ethiopia or Somalia?

   Ethiopia

2. What is the population density of Cairo?

   over 500 people per square mile

3. What is the population density of most of Ethiopia?

   25–250 people per square mile

4. What is the most densely populated area in Sudan?

   area along the Nile River

5. Why is most of northern Africa uninhabited?

   The Sahara covers most of northern Africa.

THE SWAHILI CITIES

The English word *safari* comes from a Swahili word meaning "journey." In the early history of eastern Africa, many people journeyed to the Swahili cities along the coast. Traders from Asia and India came to the cities by ship. People from the inland areas of Africa came bearing products of the mines and forests. What goods and ideas were traded? Use the words in the box to fill in the chart below. If you need help, refer to pages 372–375 in your textbook.

cloth	leopard skins
fine pottery	metal tools
glass containers	rhinoceros horns
gold	tortoise shells
ivory	wheat
Islamic religion	Arabic words

What the traders brought from Asia	What the traders took away from eastern Africa
cloth	gold
fine pottery	ivory
glass containers	leopard skins
Islamic religion	rhinoceros horns
metal tools	tortoise shells
wheat	
Arabic words	

GREAT ZIMBABWE

In 1868 explorers found the ruins of Great Zimbabwe. Since that time, archaeologists have excavated the ruins, but there are still many mysteries about Great Zimbabwe. Read the following list. If the information listed is known about Great Zimbabwe, mark the item with a **K**. If the item remains a mystery, mark it with an **M**. For help, you may refer to pages 376–379 in your textbook.

K 1. type of stone used to build the walls

K 2. height of the stone walls

M 3. reason stone walls were built

M 4. lifestyle of the leaders of Great Zimbabwe

M 5. reason why one section of the city was called "the house of the great woman"

K 6. importance of gold as a source of wealth

K 7. trading partners of Great Zimbabwe

K 8. type of pottery made by the people of Great Zimbabwe

K 9. type of jewelry made by craftworkers

K 10. crops grown by Zimbabwe farmers

K 11. type of metal used by the people to make tools

M 12. reason why the city declined

M 13. reason why the city was abandoned

M 14. oral traditions of the people of Great Zimbabwe

K 15. size of the city's population during the early 1400s

Why do we know so little about Great Zimbabwe?

The people left no oral traditions or written records, only artifacts
that have been found and interpreted by archaeologists.

USING NEW WORDS

Write a word from the box next to its definition. Then locate and circle the words in the puzzle below. For help you may refer to the lessons in Chapter 13 in your textbook.

demand	supply
griot	savanna

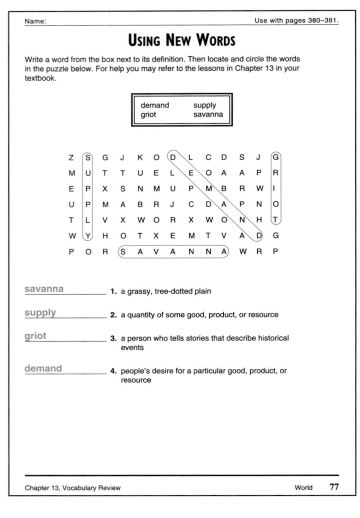

savanna   1. a grassy, tree-dotted plain

supply   2. a quantity of some good, product, or resource

griot   3. a person who tells stories that describe historical events

demand   4. people's desire for a particular good, product, or resource

---

GEOGRAPHY OF ASIA

Use the map to complete the activities below. Refer to pages 384–387 in your textbook.

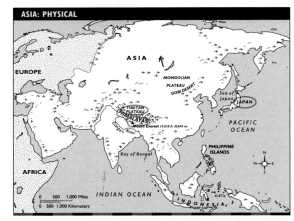

1. Locate and circle the Himalayas. Explain how they influence the climate of Asia. They block clouds that blow north from the Indian Ocean. As a result, there is a lot rain on the ocean-facing side of the mountains and very little rain on the northern side.

2. Locate and circle the large plateau on the northern border of the Himalayas.

   a. What is the name of this plateau? Tibetan Plateau

   b. What river begins in this plateau and flows through India into the Bay of Bengal? Ganges River

3. Locate and circle Japan, a country that is made up of 3,400 islands.

   a. What is the name for a group or chain of islands? archipelago

   b. Locate and name another group of islands in Asia. Philippine Islands, Indonesia

---

THE OTTOMAN EMPIRE

Read the following passage and answer the questions below. For help, you may refer to pages 388–391 in your textbook.

> In 1453 the Ottomans tried to capture the Byzantine city of Constantinople. The city had thick stone walls, with moats and ditches, and was surrounded on three sides by water. The Ottomans could not sail into the harbor because the Byzantines had blocked it with a heavy iron chain.
> The Ottoman leader, Muhammad II, had 70 light ships built and dragged on rollers overland to the Black Sea. The ships were then loaded with soldiers and guns. The Ottomans sailed the ships up to the city and attacked from the rear. They broke through the walls and captured the city. The last Byzantine emperor, Constantine, was killed.

1. Why was the city of Constantinople difficult to attack? It was surrounded on three sides by water and had thick stone walls, moats, and ditches; the Byzantines blocked the harbor with a chain.

2. How were the Ottomans able to capture the city? They attacked the city from boats that had been dragged on rollers overland to the Black Sea.

3. Why is the year 1453 considered a turning point in European history? The fall of Constantinople in 1453 ended the Byzantine empire and began a new era of Muslim rule in part of Europe.

4. Name two ways in which the Ottoman empire differed from the Byzantine empire. The Ottoman empire was Muslim, not Christian, and significantly larger and more prosperous than the Byzantine empire.

5. a. Under whose rule did the Ottoman empire reach its peak? under the rule of Sultan Süleyman

   b. How long did the Ottoman empire last? from 1453 to 1922

INDIA UNDER THE MOGULS

The following statements describe the Mogul emperor Akbar. On the lines provided write two facts that support each statement. For help, you may refer to pages 392–397 in your textbook.

Akbar

1. Akbar was a successful military leader. He almost never lost a battle. He expanded the Mogul empire.

2. Akbar helped the farmers and businesspeople living in his empire. He created a unified money system. He varied the amount of taxes farmers had to pay and had canals and wells built.

3. Akbar made changes to improve life for the Hindus in the empire. He included Hindus in his government and abolished the special tax on non-Muslims. He allowed Hindus to build new temples.

4. Akbar was interested in learning about other religions. He built a special building where religious leaders of different faiths could meet. He participated in the heated debates.

5. Although he couldn't read, Akbar was interested in learning. He had a big library with custom-made translations of classics. He had someone read to him every day.

6. Akbar was a patron of the arts. He brought Asia's best artists to his palace and visited their workshops. He worked with the craftworkers, discussed paintings, and played the drums.

ANGKOR WAT: A CAPITAL CITY

Read the passage below and answer the questions. Refer to pages 398–401 in your textbook for more information about Angkor Wat.

> In January 1860 a young Frenchman, Henri Mouhot, was traveling by canoe and on foot through thick forests in Southeast Asia. He saw in the distance a huge stone building with five towers: the temple of Angkor at Angkor Wat. Exploring the ruins, he found sculptures of lions and elephants, huge walls of stone, and collapsed towers. The deserted ruins were overgrown by large trees and vines. "The howling of wild animals, and the cries of a few birds, alone disturb the solitude," he wrote.
>
> Mouhot caught a tropical fever and died in the forest, without ever knowing that he had discovered the largest religious monument in the world. His notebook, with sketches of Angkor Wat, was recovered and published in Europe, leading others to explore the ruins and eventually restore some of them.
>
> Mouhot had many questions about his discovery. Now the answers to these questions are known. Can you answer them?

1. Who built Angkor Wat?
the king of the Khmer, Suryavarman II

2. Who discovered its remains in 1860?
Henri Mouhot

3. What was Angkor Wat?
a huge complex of temples, sculptures, and walls that expressed the Hindu religion

4. When and where was it built?
in the early 1100s, in Cambodia, near the "Great Lake," or Tonle Sap

5. How was Angkor Wat designed?
The temple was designed so that in spring the sun lit up the walls, which told stories about creation, and in winter the sun highlighted scenes describing death.

6. Why does Angkor Wat today contain both Buddhist and Hindu statues?
Over time, Khmer rulers, beginning with Jayavarman VII, honored Buddhist beliefs.

KUBLAI KHAN

Compare and contrast two great empires of China. Complete the chart below by writing each item from the box in the correct column. For help, refer to pages 402–407 in your textbook.

> - 1368: rebel Chinese forces drove out Mongols
> - 1209–1227: Mongols gained control of northern China
> - expansion of Grand Canal
> - Kublai Khan
> - first all-paper money system
> - Forbidden City
> - porcelain and silk products
> - emperors
> - extension of Great Wall
> - made Silk Road safe for travel

	YUAN DYNASTY	MING DYNASTY
ORIGIN	1209–1227: Mongols gained control of northern China	1368: rebel Chinese forces drove out Mongols
LEADERS	Kublai Khan	emperors
BUILDING PROJECTS	expansion of Grand Canal	Forbidden City; extension of Great Wall
ACHIEVEMENTS	first all-paper money system; made Silk Road safe for travel	porcelain and silk products

Kublai Khan

Ming vase

MAKING GENERALIZATIONS

Practice making generalizations by completing the activities below. For help, you may refer to pages 408–409 in your textbook.

A. Marco Polo wrote the following about Kublai Khan's capital city.

> - The city . . . is a center from which many roads radiate to many provinces.
> - In every suburb . . . there are many fine hostels which provide lodging for merchants coming from different parts [of the world].
> - It is a fact that every day more than 1,000 cart-loads of silk enter the city; for much cloth of gold and silk is woven here.
> - More precious and costly wares are imported into [the city] than into any other city in the world.
>
> Translated by Ronald Latham, *The Travels of Marco Polo* (New York: Penguin Books).

Put an X in front of each generalization that is supported by the above information.

_____ Kublai Khan's capital was the biggest city in the world.

___X___ Kublai Khan's capital had many roads connecting it to the provinces.

___X___ Kublai Khan's capital was an important center of trade.

B. Marco Polo described how the nobles behaved in Kublai Khan's presence.

> - All those who are within half a mile from the Great Khan . . . show their reverence for his majesty by conducting themselves . . . peaceably, and quietly.
> - Every . . . nobleman continually carries with him a little vessel of pleasing design into which he spits so long as he is in the hall, so that no one may make so bold as to spit on the floor.
> - They have handsome slippers of white leather, which they carry about with them. When they have come to court . . . they put on these white slippers . . . so as not to dirty the beautiful and elaborate carpets of silk.
>
> Translated by Ronald Latham, *The Travels of Marco Polo* (New York: Penguin Books).

Write one generalization that is supported by the above information.

Possible answers: There were strict rules for proper behavior at Kublai Khan's court; there were rules to keep Kublai Khan's court quiet and clean.

LIFE IN FEUDAL JAPAN

Below is a social pyramid of feudal Japan. Explain the role of each person or group in the life of feudal Japan. If you need help, refer back to pages 410–415 in your textbook.

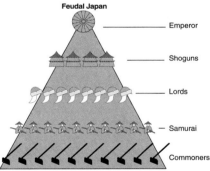

Feudal Japan

Emperor — ruled Japan in name only

Shoguns — ruled country as military dictators

Lords — controlled large pieces of land; served the shogun

Samurai — protected lords and their lands

Commoners — produced goods; showed respect to those above them

Culture flourished in feudal Japan. A popular form of poetry that was created at this time is called *haiku*. This is a short, unrhymed verse of three lines containing a total of 17 syllables in a 5, 7, and 5 pattern. Here is one example of haiku:

> In the morning light
> Purple rays of dawn creep down
> Covering the earth.

On your own, or with a partner, write your own haiku.

Answers will vary.

USING NEW WORDS

Write each word or term from the box in front of its definition. For help, you may refer to the lessons in Chapter 14 in your textbook.

| archipelago | grand mufti | samurai | shogun |
| Grand Canal | monsoon | Shinto | sultan |

1. <u>a r c h i p e l a g o</u> group or chain of islands

2. <u>m o n s o o n</u> seasonal wind that brings rain

3. <u>s u l t a n</u> supreme ruler of Ottoman empire

4. <u>g r a n d m u f t i</u> Muslim religious leader

5. <u>G r a n d C a n a l</u> link between Huang and Chang rivers

6. <u>S h i n t o</u> Japanese religion

7. <u>s h o g u n</u> Japanese military commander

8. <u>s a m u r a i</u> Japanese soldier

GEOGRAPHY OF THE AMERICAS

Use the places listed in the box to complete the passage below. For help, you may refer to pages 422–425 in your textbook.

| Amazon |
| Andes Mountains |
| Atlantic |
| Canadian Shield |
| Great Lakes |
| Isthmus of Panama |
| Pacific |
| Rocky Mountains |

THE AMERICAS

The <u>Isthmus of Panama</u> connects North and South America. The two continents are similar in important ways. Both are bordered by the <u>Atlantic</u> Ocean on the east and the <u>Pacific</u> Ocean on the west. Both have extensive seacoasts with many harbors. Along the western side of each continent is a range of mountains. In North America the mountains are called the <u>Rocky Mountains</u>. In South America the mountains are called the <u>Andes Mountains</u>.

There are also differences between the two continents. In South America the mountains are higher and steeper than those in North America, so travel in South America is more difficult. South America has the world's largest rain forest, along the <u>Amazon</u> River. In North America there is a large area of rocky land, not suitable for farming, called the <u>Canadian Shield</u>. There are also large lakes. The five <u>Great Lakes</u> were carved out by glaciers, centuries ago.

THE AZTEC CULTURE

The picture shows an Aztec man and woman preparing for a feast. Use the picture and pages 426–431 in your textbook to answer the questions.

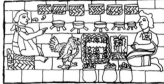

1. What kind of house did the people probably live in?
   a one-room stone or mud house

2. What kind of food might have been served at the feast?
   squash, tomatoes, chili peppers, and maize

3. Where did the people of the Aztec capital of Tenochtitlán grow their food?
   on chinampas, human-made islands, and along the shores of
   Lake Texcoco

4. What other source of food did the Aztec have?
   Conquered peoples were forced to send food as tribute.

5. The man and woman in the picture were probably members of the largest social group in Aztec society.
   a. What people were members of this group?
      farmers, merchants, craftworkers, and soldiers
   b. What groups had the lowest status in Aztec society?
      poor, landless farmers and slaves
   c. Who was at the top of Aztec society?
      the emperor

6. How important was religion to the Aztec?
   Religion played a central role in the lives of the Aztec. They
   built a Great Temple to honor their sun god and their rain god.

USING MAP PROJECTIONS

A projection is a way of placing parts of Earth on a flat map. Use the map below to answer the questions. For help, you may refer to pages 432–433 in your textbook.

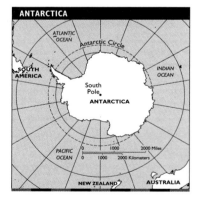

ANTARCTICA

1. a. Which continent is shown in the center of the map?
      Antarctica
   b. What other continents are shown on the map?
      Australia and South
      America

2. What three oceans are shown on the map?
   Atlantic, Pacific, Indian
   oceans

3. What is in the center of the map?
   the South Pole

4. a. What is this kind of map called?
      a polar projection map
   b. Who uses this type of map projection?
      navigators on airplanes
      that fly over the North or
      South Pole

5. What kind of map projection would you use to show the sizes of land masses?
   equal-area projection

THE INCA EMPIRE

Explain why each of the following items was important to the Inca. For help, you may refer to pages 434–439 in your textbook.

Cuzco

1. a. Why was Cuzco important?
It was the center of the Inca empire.

b. How did the Inca use their building skills to hold their empire together?
They built roads so people and news could travel quickly throughout the empire.

Quipu

2. a. What was the quipu used for?
keeping records

b. How did the quipu help the Inca rule their empire?
The quipu was a convenient and portable way to keep and transport records.

Mountain farming

3. a. How were the Inca able to grow food on hilly mountain slopes?
They constructed terraces, level platforms of earth that climbed each hill like a staircase.

b. What are some of the crops the Inca grew?
potatoes, maize, and peppers

Llamas

4. How did the Inca use the llama?
The llama was used as a pack animal to carry goods.

PEOPLES OF NORTH AMERICA: THE OJIBWA

The Ojibwa moved their villages to a different place each season of the year. Listed below are some of their other activities. Complete the calendar by matching each activity with the appropriate season. For help, you may refer to pages 440–445 in your textbook.

- collecting maple sap
- making maple syrup
- hunting deer, moose, bear, and fox
- fishing
- gathering nuts and berries
- harvesting wild rice
- smoking meat
- growing corn, beans, and squash
- making clothes out of animal skins

SPRING
collecting maple sap; making maple syrup

FALL
harvesting wild rice

SUMMER
fishing; gathering nuts and berries; growing corn, beans, and squash

WINTER
hunting deer, moose, bear, and fox; smoking meat; making clothes out of animal skins

---

USING NEW WORDS

Use the words in the box to answer the questions below. For help, you may refer to the lessons in Chapter 15 in your textbook.

chinampas	terraces	Triple Alliance
codex	Three Fires Council	tundra
diversity	timberline	wigwams
isthmus	tribute	quipus

1. What narrow strip of land connects North and South America? isthmus

2. What is the name of the treeless plain located in Alaska? tundra

3. Above what place on a mountain can trees not grow? timberline

4. Where did the Aztec grow food for the people who lived in Tenochtitlán?
chinampas

5. What did the Aztec force conquered people to pay them? tribute

6. The army of what group gained control of the entire Valley of Mexico?
Triple Alliance

7. What did the Aztec use to record information about their history, religion, and government? codex

8. What did the Inca build to help them grow crops on hilly slopes? terraces

9. What league was formed by the Ojibwa, the Potawatomi, and the Ottawa?
Three Fires Council

10. In what kind of homes did the Ojibwa live? wigwams

11. What word best describes the peoples who lived in North and South America before the arrival of the Europeans? diversity

12. What did the Inca use to keep records of trade throughout the empire?
quipus

EXPLORING THE UNIVERSE

Use the pictures below to answer the questions on this page. For help, you can refer to pages 456–460 in your textbook.

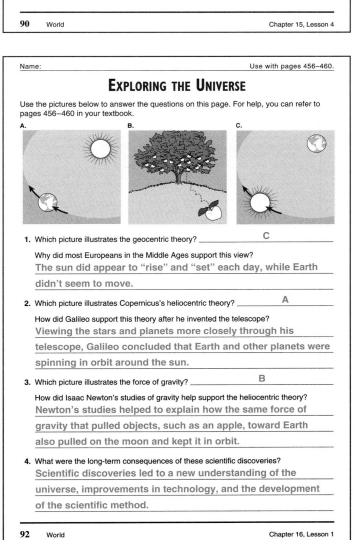

A.   **B.**   **C.**

1. Which picture illustrates the geocentric theory? C

Why did most Europeans in the Middle Ages support this view?
The sun did appear to "rise" and "set" each day, while Earth didn't seem to move.

2. Which picture illustrates Copernicus's heliocentric theory? A

How did Galileo support this theory after he invented the telescope?
Viewing the stars and planets more closely through his telescope, Galileo concluded that Earth and other planets were spinning in orbit around the sun.

3. Which picture illustrates the force of gravity? B

How did Isaac Newton's studies of gravity help support the heliocentric theory?
Newton's studies helped to explain how the same force of gravity that pulled objects, such as an apple, toward Earth also pulled on the moon and kept it in orbit.

4. What were the long-term consequences of these scientific discoveries?
Scientific discoveries led to a new understanding of the universe, improvements in technology, and the development of the scientific method.

VOYAGES OF EXPLORATION

Use the map below to complete the activities that follow. For help, you can refer to pages 462–465 in your textbook.

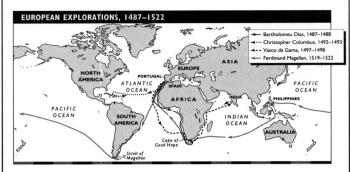

EUROPEAN EXPLORATIONS, 1487–1522

→ Bartholomeu Dias, 1487–1488
···▶ Christopher Columbus, 1492–1493
–·–▶ Vasco da Gama, 1497–1498
→ Ferdinand Magellan, 1519–1522

1. Write the name of the explorer next to the description of his voyage.

   a. Portugal to the southernmost tip of Africa **Bartholomeu Dias**

   b. Portugal around the Cape of Good Hope to India **Vasco da Gama**

   c. Spain through a strait at the tip of South America to the Pacific Ocean to the Philippines **Ferdinand Magellan**

   d. Spain to the Caribbean islands **Christopher Columbus**

2. How did the invention of the caravel help European explorers?

   The caravel enabled explorers to sail in almost any direction they wished.

3. Why were European explorers so eager to find an all-water route to Asia?

   Europeans wanted to find a trade route to Asia that was easier and faster than the land route along the Silk Road.

EXPLORING THE AMERICAS

Use the information in the box below to complete the chart. One entry has been filled in for you. Then answer the questions that follow. For help, you can refer to pages 466–471 in your textbook.

Pedro Álvarez Cabral	Francisco Pizarro	Hernando Cortés
present-day Mexico	near present-day Brazil	Christopher Columbus
conquest of Inca empire	conquest of Aztec empire	Hispaniola
beginning of Portuguese rule in Brazil	Andes Mountains	beginning of Spanish colonization in Americas

EXPLORER	LAND CLAIM	OUTCOME OF VOYAGE
Christopher Columbus	Hispaniola	beginning of Spanish colonization in Americas
Pedro Álvarez Cabral	**near present-day Brazil**	**beginning of Portuguese rule in Brazil**
Hernando Cortés	**present-day Mexico**	**conquest of Aztec empire**
Francisco Pizarro	**Andes Mountains**	**conquest of Inca empire**

1. What was the main goal of Spanish missionaries in the Americas?

   The missionaries wanted to convert the Indians to Catholicism.

2. What was life like for Indians who lived in the Spanish Americas?

   Many were forced to work on haciendas or in silver mines, and millions died of diseases brought over from Europe.

3. By the 1540s what two Spanish colonies dominated the Americas?

   New Spain and Peru

DETERMINING THE CREDIBILITY OF A SOURCE

Read the passages below. Then answer the questions to help determine the credibility of each source. Can the source be trusted for accuracy? For help, you can refer to pages 472–473 in your textbook.

A. Suppose that the following letter was written in the late 1500s by a Catholic priest asking to join a Spanish mission in the Americas.

I have heard from different sources that the Native Americans desire to serve our beloved Spain. The Indians, I have been told, are hungering for Christianity as well as Spanish culture. They are so anxious to become citizens of our honorable empire that they are begging for instruction. I pray that you will honor my request to join the mission and bless me in my great endeavor.

B. Suppose that the following letter was written in the late 1500s by a Catholic missionary in the Americas to a close friend in Spain.

We strive to bring the Native Americans into our villages to protect them from slave hunters and to teach them Christianity. Yet I am not so sure they understand what we are trying to do for them. I am not sure I understand myself. I always thought our goal was to save souls, but now I think the goal is to extend the realm of our empire.

1. Does the author have firsthand experience with the Native Americans? Explain.

   No, the author's information comes from other sources.

2. Does the author have a specific goal in mind? Explain.

   Yes, the author's goal is to convince the reader to let him join a mission.

3. Do you think the author's information about the Native Americans is credible? Explain.

   No, the author has never met the Native Americans and is portraying them in a certain way.

4. Does the author have firsthand experience with Native Americans? Explain.

   Yes, the author teaches them Christianity.

5. Does the author have a specific goal in mind? Explain.

   No, the author is confiding in a friend.

6. Do you think the author's information about the Native Americans is credible? Explain.

   Yes, the author is writing from firsthand experience and has no reason to give false or distorted information.

THE TRIANGULAR TRADE

The Triangular Trade was a network of trade routes. Use the map below to help you answer the questions that follow. Refer to pages 474–477 in your textbook.

TRIANGULAR TRADE ROUTES

1. What areas of the world were linked by the Triangular Trade routes?

   North America, West Indies, Europe, and West Africa

2. For what European goods did some West Indian plantation owners trade sugar?

   They traded sugar for fine furniture or cloth.

3. What part of the Triangular Trade route was the Middle Passage?

   the voyage from Africa's west coast across the Atlantic Ocean to the West Indies

4. What were conditions like for kidnapped slaves who traveled along the Middle Passage?

   They were chained up in overcrowded sections of the ship and fed spoiled food and unclean water. Many did not survive the journey.

5. Why were enslaved Africans important to colonies in the West Indies?

   Sugarcane plantations depended on slave labor to clear forests for planting, hoe the soil, harvest the sugarcane, and load barrels with sugar.

THE SUCCESS OF NEW SOUTH WALES

Answer the following questions about the colonization of New South Wales and discover how Australia became an important democracy in the Southern Hemisphere. Refer to pages 478–481 in your textbook.

1. Who was James Cook and what did he do?

James Cook was a respected English navigator who searched for Australia and claimed land for Great Britain there, naming it New South Wales.

2. Why were many people sent to New South Wales at first?

English jails were overcrowded and the government decided to send many of its prison convicts to work there.

3. What were some of the beliefs of the aborigines and how were these people affected by the arrival of the colonists?

The aborigines believed in the "dreamtime" and that land could not be owned by just one person. They were almost wiped out by the guns and diseases that the settlers brought with them from Europe.

4. Who were the emancipated people and who helped them win rights in the new colony?

The emancipated people were former convicts from England who had been freed from their sentences in Australia. Governor Lachlan Macquarie supported them in their efforts to win their rights.

5. What two events led to the development of democracy in Australia?

The creation of a legislative body with the New South Wales Act of 1823 and the right for free settlers and emancipated people to vote in 1842.

6. When and where did women win the right to vote in Australia?

The women of South Australia won the right to vote in 1894.

SOME WORDS ABOUT EUROPEAN EXPANSION

Answer each question on the lines provided. For help, you can refer to Chapter 16 in your textbook.

1. a. How do the **heliocentric** and **geocentric** views of the universe differ?

In the heliocentric view the sun is the center of the universe; in the geocentric view Earth is the center.

b. How did Galileo's **telescope** and Newton's studies of **gravity** help support the heliocentric view of the universe?

The telescope enabled scientists to study the movement of the stars and planets; gravity helped explain how a heliocentric universe works.

2. What is the **scientific method**?

The scientific method is a way of learning about nature by questioning, studying, and thoroughly testing an idea.

3. How did Prince Henry's **caravel** help explorers?

The caravel enabled explorers to sail in almost any direction.

4. What is a **strait**? A strait is a narrow channel between two larger bodies of water.

5. Who tried to **convert** the Native Americans—**conquistadors** or the **missionaries**?

the missionaries

6. What was the purpose of the **Line of Demarcation**?

to divide Spain's and Portugal's land claims in the Americas

7. Was **sugarcane** grown on **haciendas** or on **plantations**?

Sugarcane was grown on plantations in the West Indies.

8. What role did the **Middle Passage** play in the **Triangular Trade**?

The Middle Passage was the part of the Triangular Trade that carried enslaved Africans to the West Indies.

9. Was an **emancipee** formerly an **aborigine** or a **convict**?

a convict

THE EVENTS OF THE FRENCH REVOLUTION

Something that makes something else happen is a cause. What happens as the result of a cause is called an effect. Fill in the missing cause or effect in the sentence pairs below. If you need help, refer to pages 486–491 in your textbook.

1. Cause: The king has complete power to govern.

Effect: The three estates, or social classes, in France become dissatisfied with the king and his government.

2. Cause: The king wants to raise money by taxing the nobles.

Effect: The nobles refuse and demand a meeting of the Estates General.

3. Cause: People think the king is sending troops to break up the National Assembly.

Effect: The people storm the Bastille to get weapons to defend themselves.

4. Cause: The National Assembly issues the Declaration of the Rights of Man and of the Citizen.

Effect: The absolute monarchy is abolished, and France becomes a republic.

5. Cause: Catholic priests and others angered by the Assembly refuse to support the revolution.

Effect: Robespierre wages a Reign of Terror against his enemies.

6. Cause: The Reign of Terror leaves many people hoping for peace and stability.

Effect: The army gains power, and Napoleon takes control of the republic.

Write another cause and effect sentence pair about the French Revolution.

Possible answer: Cause—The ideas of "Liberty, Equality, Fraternity" spread throughout the world. Effect—National freedom movements begin in many countries.

REVOLUTIONS IN THE AMERICAS

Use the information in the box below to complete the chart. Then answer the questions that follow. For help, you can refer to pages 492–497 in your textbook.

Bolivia	Chile	Haiti
Mexico	Panama	Ecuador
Venezuela	Colombia	Argentina Peru
end slavery		
freedom from France		
freedom from Spain		

REVOLUTIONARY LEADER	COUNTRY OR COUNTRIES	REASON OR REASONS FOR REVOLUTION
Toussaint L'Ouverture	Haiti	end slavery freedom from France
Miguel Hidalgo	Mexico	end slavery freedom from Spain
José de San Martín	Argentina, Chile	freedom from Spain
Simón Bolívar	Venezuela, Colombia, Bolivia, Panama, Ecuador, Peru	freedom from Spain

1. What complaints against European nations did many Latin American colonies share?

The Europeans took their minerals and crops and gave little in return. The colonies also disliked paying taxes without having a say in the government.

2. What change occurred in Canada in 1867?

The Canadian provinces formed a confederation that was free to govern itself, although ultimate authority rested with the British crown.

Use with pages 500–505.

REVOLUTIONIZING INDUSTRY AND SOCIETY

Use the pictures on the left and the information on pages 500–505 in your textbook to complete the activities below.

1. Explain how textile machines helped revolutionize industry.

Machines made it possible for workers to produce textiles quickly and cheaply.

2. Give a reason why factories were built.

Factories were needed to house the new machines, which were too big to fit into a farmer's cottage.

3. Explain how the locomotive contributed to the spread of industry.

It increased trade because goods could be shipped greater distances in less time.

4. Describe the contributions of the middle and working classes to the British economy.

The middle class increased trade and manufacturing by running businesses and services; the working class helped manufacture goods.

Use with pages 506–507.

USING CARTOGRAMS

A cartogram is a special kind of map used to compare information about countries. On a cartogram the size of a country is related to the information that is being compared. Use the cartogram below to answer the questions. Refer to pages 506–507 in your textbook.

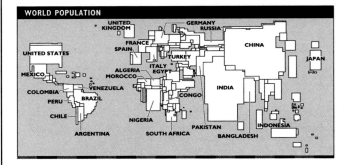

WORLD POPULATION

1. What information does the cartogram show?

populations of countries

2. How can you tell that India has a larger population than the United States?

India's size is larger than that of the United States.

3. Which country has the largest population in the world?

China

4. Which nation has more people, Argentina or Brazil?

Brazil

5. What additional information would you need to tell whether Russia is more crowded than Japan?

the area of both Russia and Japan in relation to their populations

6. Which African country has the largest population?

Nigeria

Use with pages 508–513.

A CHANGING JAPAN

Japan experienced rapid changes in its government, military, economy, and culture from the mid-1800s to the early 1900s. Complete the diagram by writing each activity from the box below in the appropriate category. Refer to pages 508–513 in your textbook.

Meiji Restoration	Feudal customs break down
Japan invades Korea	Charter Oath is issued
Diet is created	Japan attacks Chinese mainland
Railroads link major cities	Japan exports silk and tea
Japanese begin to wear suits or dresses	Japan enters into war against Russia
Western-style architecture becomes popular	Cotton mills are built

Government

Meiji Restoration

Charter Oath is issued

Diet is created

Military

Japan invades Korea

Japan attacks Chinese mainland

Japan enters into war against Russia

A Changing Japan

Economy

Railroads link major cities

Japan exports silk and tea

Cotton mills are built

Culture

Japanese begin to wear suits or dresses

Western-style architecture becomes popular

Feudal customs break down

Use with pages 516–517.

REVOLUTIONS AROUND THE WORLD

Write the letter of the term that is not related to the other three. Then write a sentence to show how the three remaining terms are related. For help, you can refer to the lessons in Chapter 17 of your textbook.

d **1. a.** divine right   **b.** revolution   **c.** absolute monarchy   **d.** socialism

Possible answer: The absolute monarchy in France and the king's belief in the divine right to rule led to revolution in France.

b **2. a.** peasants   **b.** Meiji Restoration   **c.** aristocracy   **d.** estates

Possible answer: The peasants and aristocracy belonged to different estates, or social classes, in France.

c **3. a.** Reign of Terror   **b.** Bastille   **c.** imperialism   **d.** Declaration of the Rights of Man and of the Citizen

Possible answer: Three important events of the French Revolution were the storming of the Bastille, the writing of the Declaration of the Rights of Man and of the Citizen, and the Reign of Terror.

d **4. a.** Latin America   **b.** mestizos   **c.** revolutions   **d.** bureaucracy

Possible answer: Many revolutions in Latin America were carried out by mestizos.

c **5. a.** textiles   **b.** factories   **c.** confederation   **d.** Industrial Revolution

Possible answer: During the Industrial Revolution the demand for textiles led to the building of factories.

c **6. a.** middle class   **b.** working class   **c.** aristocracy   **d.** Industrial Revolution

Possible answer: As a result of the Industrial Revolution, the middle class became more important and life for the working class became more difficult.

CAUSES AND EFFECTS OF WORLD WAR I

Each sentence pair below states a cause-effect relationship. Write **C** next to the sentence that states the cause and **E** next to the sentence that states the effect. For help, you can look back at pages 526–531 in your textbook.

1. __C__ **a.** Nationalism and tensions among European countries increased in the early 1900s.

   __E__ **b.** To prepare for the possibility of war, the countries of Europe trained armies and formed alliances.

2. __C__ **a.** A Serbian nationalist assassinated Archduke Franz Ferdinand, heir to the throne of Austria-Hungary.

   __E__ **b.** Austria-Hungary and its ally, Germany, declared war on Serbia.

3. __C__ **a.** German submarines sank the *Lusitania,* and German diplomats plotted an alliance with Mexico against the United States.

   __E__ **b.** The United States declared war on Germany and the other Central Powers.

4. __E__ **a.** Bloody battles were fought in trenches, at sea, and in the air.

   __C__ **b.** During World War I most warring nations had access to modern technology.

5. __E__ **a.** Germans were angry and felt alienated from the rest of Europe.

   __C__ **b.** The Treaty of Versailles blamed Germany for the war and forced the country to pay enormous fines.

Write a cause-effect sentence pair about life on the "home front" during World War I.

Possible answer: Daily life on the home front changed.

Governments controlled food supplies; people went hungry as a

result of high food prices; women went to work in the factories.

FROM RUSSIA TO THE SOVIET UNION

The sentences in the box describe conditions and changes in Russia before and after the Revolution of 1917. Write each sentence in the appropriate column. Then add a sentence of your own to each column. For help, refer to pages 532–539 in your textbook.

> • Wealthy nobles owned most of the farmland.
> • Private property, including farms, was outlawed.
> • Moscow was the capital.
> • St. Petersburg was the capital.
> • Collective farms were created.
> • Serfdom was abolished.
> • Communist leaders established a totalitarian society.
> • Tsars ruled as absolute monarchs.
> • Factory workers protested grim working conditions.
> • The nation became an industrial power.

Before the Russian Revolution	After the Russian Revolution
Wealthy nobles owned most of the farmland.	Private property, including farms, was outlawed.
St. Petersburg was the capital.	Moscow was the capital.
Serfdom was abolished.	Collective farms were created.
Tsars ruled as absolute monarchs.	Communist leaders established a totalitarian society.
Factory workers protested grim working conditions.	The nation became an industrial power.
Possible answer: Most Russians lived as they had in the Middle Ages.	Possible answer: Churches were closed and religious leaders arrested.

WORLD WAR II HEADLINES

The newspaper headlines below relate to events that occurred before, during, and after World War II. Answer the questions beneath each headline. For help, refer to pages 540–547 in your textbook.

> **Hitler and Nazis Gain Control of Germany**

a. In which year would this headline have been written? 1933

b. Which factors aided Hitler's rise to power?

Germany was economically depressed, and the Germans

longed to make their country great again.

> **German Tanks Roll into Poland! Britain and France Declare War on Germany!**

a. In what month and year would this headline have been written? September 1939

b. Who were the Allies and the Axis nations?

The Allies included Britain, France, the Soviet Union, China, and

the United States; the Axis included Japan, Germany, and Italy.

> **Japanese Bomb Pearl Harbor**

a. In which month and year would this headline have been written? December 1941

b. How did the United States react to this attack?

The United States entered World War II on the side of the Allies.

> **Concentration Camp Prisoners Freed**

a. In which two countries were concentration camps built during World War II?

Germany and Japan

b. To what does the term Holocaust refer?

The Holocaust refers to the deliberate destruction of human

life in Nazi concentration camps.

Write two newspaper headlines that might have been printed during World War II.

Possible answers: Allied Forces Invade Normandy; U.S. Bombs

Hiroshima; Japan Surrenders.

USING TIME ZONE MAPS

The world is divided into 24 time zones. Use the map to answer the questions on this page. For help, refer to pages 548–549 in your textbook.

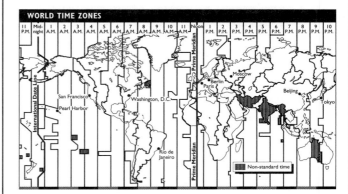

WORLD TIME ZONES

1. How many time zones east of Washington, D.C., is Berlin, Germany?
   six time zones

2. When German leaders surrendered in Berlin at 2:41 A.M. on May 7, 1945, what were the time and date in Washington, D.C.?
   8:41 P.M., May 6, 1945

3. When the Japanese bombed Pearl Harbor in Hawaii at about 8:00 A.M. on December 7, 1941, what were the time and date in Tokyo, Japan?
   3:00 A.M., December 8, 1941

4. Why would people traveling from Tokyo to Honolulu find that they were traveling "back in time"?
   When you travel east across the International Date Line, you
   subtract a day so that today becomes yesterday.

5. When it is 4:00 A.M. in San Francisco, what time is it in Washington, D.C.?
   In Paris, France? **7:00 A.M. in Washington; 1 P.M. in Paris**

THE BELIEFS OF MAO ZEDONG

The quotations below are from Mao Zedong, founder of Communist China. Read the quotations carefully. Then complete the activities that follow. For help, you can look back at pages 550–555 in your textbook.

> War is the highest form of struggle for resolving contradictions when they have developed to a certain state, between classes, nations, states, or political groups, and it has existed ever since the emergence of private property and of classes.
>
> We are advocates of the abolition of war; we do not want war, but war can only be abolished through war, and in order to get rid of the gun it is necessary to take up the gun. . . . When classes and states are eliminated there will be no more wars.
>
> George Seldes, "Quotations from Chairman Mao," *The Great Thoughts* (New York: Ballantine Books, 1985).

1. Put an **X** next to each sentence that describes Mao Zedong's beliefs about war.
   - __X__ **a.** The only way to end a war is to fight the war.
   - _____ **b.** War is the worst way to resolve problems.
   - __X__ **c.** Social classes and private property are responsible for causing wars.
   - __X__ **d.** Peace can be achieved by eliminating classes and states.

2. When and how did Mao and his Communist followers gain control of China?
   After years of civil war, Mao and the Communists drove the Nationalists from mainland China to the island of Taiwan.

3. How did Mao's "Great Leap Forward" affect life in China?
   Farmers and their families were forced to join communes and take on additional tasks such as steel production. The plan failed, and economic conditions worsened.

4. What were some effects of the Cultural Revolution?
   Many Chinese people were terrorized, and traditional religious and cultural beliefs were destroyed.

FANNING THE COLD WAR

Listed below are five problems that caused tension between the United States and the Soviet Union. How did the superpowers react in each Cold War situation? Complete each box below. For help, you can look back at pages 556–561 in your textbook.

1. **Problem:** Stalin forces Eastern European countries to accept communist government.
   United States Reaction: United States and European allies form NATO.

2. **Problem:** North Korea invades South Korea.
   United States Reaction: United States sends troops to help United Nations troops fight North Koreans.

3. **Problem:** Thousands of East Germans move to West Berlin.
   Soviet Reaction: East German police build a concrete wall between East and West Berlin.

4. **Problem:** Soviet leader Khrushchev sends nuclear missiles to Cuba.
   United States Reaction: President Kennedy orders Soviet ships to stay out of Cuban waters and places American forces on full alert.

WARS AND REVOLUTIONS

Write the letter of the term that is not related to the other three. Then write a sentence using the remaining three related terms. Refer to the lessons in Chapter 18.

__c__ 1. **a.** nuclear arms race   **b.** superpowers   **c.** free enterprise   **d.** Cold War
   During the Cold War the superpowers engaged in a nuclear arms race.

__a__ 2. **a.** warlord   **b.** NATO   **c.** Warsaw Pact   **d.** United Nations
   Despite growing tensions, the member nations of the Warsaw Pact and NATO remained members of the United Nations.

__b__ 3. **a.** Long March   **b.** alliance   **c.** communes   **d.** Cultural Revolution
   Mao Zedong led the Long March, created communes, and began the Cultural Revolution in China.

__a__ 4. **a.** tsar   **b.** inflation   **c.** depression   **d.** fascism
   High inflation and economic depression helped bring about the rise of fascism in post-World War I Europe.

__d__ 5. **a.** World War II   **b.** Axis   **c.** Allies   **d.** Korean War
   The Axis Powers fought the Allies during World War II.

__d__ 6. **a.** propaganda   **b.** nationalism   **c.** communism   **d.** strike
   Propaganda and nationalism helped advance communism.

__a__ 7. **a.** Russian Revolution   **b.** Central Powers   **c.** World War I   **d.** Allied Powers
   In World War I the Central Powers fought the Allied Powers.

__c__ 8. **a.** Treaty of Versailles   **b.** League of Nations   **c.** totalitarian   **d.** armistice
   After the armistice that ended World War I, the Treaty of Versailles was signed and the League of Nations was formed.

__b__ 9. **a.** Holocaust   **b.** alliance   **c.** concentration camps   **d.** World War II
   During World War II millions of Jews died in concentration camps in what became known as the Holocaust.

INDEPENDENCE IN AFRICA

Use the information in the box and the maps to complete the sections below. For help, you can look back at pages 566–571 in your textbook.

• Accra	• slave trade	• seizure of Suez Canal	• cacao
• Suez Canal	• military control of government	• Kwame Nkrumah	
• Cairo	• boycotts of British goods	• Gamal Abdel Nasser	
• cotton	• strikes against British companies	• gold	

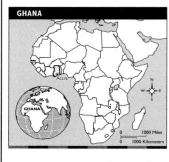
GHANA

EGYPT

Importance to Britain: slave trade, gold, cacao

Importance to Britain: cotton, Suez Canal

Leader of independence movement:
Kwame Nkrumah

Leader of independence movement:
Gamal Abdel Nasser

Methods used to gain independence:
boycotts of British goods, strikes against British companies

Methods used to gain independence:
military control of government, seizure of Suez Canal

Capital city: Accra

Capital city: Cairo

INTERPRETING POLITICAL CARTOONS

The political cartoon below was drawn by Thomas Nast, an artist who lived in the United States in the late 1800s. Look at the words and symbols in the cartoon. Then answer the questions that follow. For help, look at pages 572–573 in your textbook.

"Peaceful Neutrality: The Position of England and France on the Suez Canal"

1. You read about the Suez Canal in Lesson 1. Why was it so important to European countries?
   The Suez Canal connects the Red Sea and the Mediterranean
   Sea, thus providing a short route for ships sailing between
   Europe and Asia.

2. What are the two countries arguing about?
   control over the Suez Canal

3. The pyramid in the picture is used to represent Egypt. Why is the British leader standing on Egypt's side of the Suez Canal?
   Egypt was a British colony.

4. The caption to the cartoon reads "Peaceful Neutrality: The Position of England and France on the Suez Canal." Do you think the cartoonist felt that the countries were really at peace?
   Possible answer: No; Nast portrayed the countries as
   mistrustful and ready to fight to defend their claims.

HISTORY OF THE MIDDLE EAST

Use the information in the box to complete the chart below. Then answer the question at the bottom of the page. For help, you can look back at pages 574–578 in your textbook.

- Yasir Arafat and Yitzhak Rabin sign a peace agreement.
- The PLO begins its fight to regain land from Israel.
- The Republic of Turkey is established.
- Israel becomes an independent nation.
- Egypt and Israel sign the Camp David agreement.
- Israel gains Gaza, the Golan Heights, and the West Bank.
- Iraq becomes an independent nation.
- Palestinians in Gaza and the West Bank begin the Intifada.
- Yitzhak Rabin is assassinated.

CHANGES IN THE MIDDLE EAST	
YEAR	**EVENT**
1923	The Republic of Turkey is established.
1932	Iraq becomes an independent nation.
1948	Israel becomes an independent nation.
1967	Israel gains Gaza, the Golan Heights, and the West Bank.
1968	The PLO begins its fight to regain land from Israel.
1977	Egypt and Israel sign the Camp David agreement.
1987	Palestinians in Gaza and the West Bank begin the Intifada.
1993	Yasir Arafat and Yitzhak Rabin sign a peace agreement.
1995	Yitzhak Rabin is assassinated.

What is a primary cause of conflict between Palestinians and Jews over the area that is today Israel?
Both groups want to create a nation in the area that was once
their ancient homeland.

INDEPENDENCE IN INDIA

You have been asked to write an entry about independence in India for an almanac titled *The World Book of Facts*. The editor of the almanac has asked you to write answers to the following questions. For help, you can refer to pages 580–585 in your textbook.

The Great Mutiny

Q: In what year did the Great Mutiny spread across India?
A: 1857

Q: Prior to the Great Mutiny, who controlled most of India?
A: the East India Company, known as the Raj

Q: Why was India such a desirable colony?
A: India provided raw materials for British industries and a market for British goods.

Mohandas Gandhi

Q: When did Gandhi become an important leader in India?
A: 1915

Q: What were Gandhi's three goals for India?
A: independence from British rule, peace between Muslims and Hindus, and an end to mistreatment of the untouchables

Q: What are two examples of how Indians practiced civil disobedience?
A: The Indians boycotted British goods and refused to pay taxes.

Independence

Q: On what day did India and Pakistan gain independence?
A: August 15, 1947

Q: Why were two independent countries formed?
A: As a result of Hindu-Muslim conflicts, the Muslims were granted their own country—Pakistan.

Q: What changes took place in India after independence?
A: The Green Revolution boosted agriculture, the untouchable caste was abolished, and women gained new rights.

BEFORE AND AFTER THE VIETNAM WAR

Use the events in the box to complete the columns below. Then answer the questions that follow. For help, you can refer to pages 586–591 in your textbook.

- United States withdraws from Vietnam.
- Vietnam becomes French colony.
- Ho Chi Minh leads communist revolt.
- Communists seize control of South Vietnam.
- South Vietnamese flee communism.
- Vietnamese invade Cambodia.
- Vietnam is divided into North and South Vietnam.
- United States sends advisers to South Vietnam.

Before the Vietnam War	After the Vietnam War
Vietnam becomes French colony.	United States withdraws from Vietnam.
Ho Chi Minh leads communist revolt.	Communists seize control of South Vietnam.
Vietnam is divided into North and South Vietnam.	South Vietnamese flee communism.
United States sends advisers to South Vietnam.	Vietnamese invade Cambodia.

1. Why did the United States participate in the Vietnam War?
   The United States wanted to prevent the spread of
   communism.

2. How did the relationship between Vietnam and the United States change in the 1990s?
   In 1995 Vietnam and the United States began to trade and have
   diplomatic relations.

PUZZLING WORDS

Use the terms in the box and the clues to complete the crossword puzzle below. For help, you can refer to the lessons in Chapter 19 in your textbook.

Vietnam War	boycott	refugee
civil disobedience	Zionism	Raj
Green Revolution	anti-Semitism	Intifada

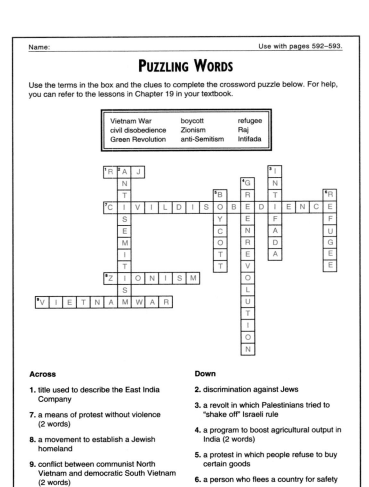

Across

1. title used to describe the East India Company

7. a means of protest without violence (2 words)

8. a movement to establish a Jewish homeland

9. conflict between communist North Vietnam and democratic South Vietnam (2 words)

Down

2. discrimination against Jews

3. a revolt in which Palestinians tried to "shake off" Israeli rule

4. a program to boost agricultural output in India (2 words)

5. a protest in which people refuse to buy certain goods

6. a person who flees a country for safety

THE FALL OF COMMUNISM IN EUROPE

Fill in the diagram below. Using the events in the box, explain what "miracle" happened in each of the countries in 1989, the "Year of Miracles." Then answer the question that follows. For help, you can refer back to pages 596–603 in your textbook.

Hungary

Soviet troops stand by as the country plans free elections in January.

In May people tear down an electric fence separating their country from democratic Austria.

Czechoslovakia

In November police beat students who were singing "We Shall Overcome."

By December citizens freely elect two new leaders who had been imprisoned.

1989: Year of Miracles

Poland

Workers' group, led by Lech Walesa, is recognized by government.

Solidarity party wins many seats in Parliament.

Germany

Erich Honecker steps down from office.

East Berlin opens its gates to West Berlin.

- In November police beat students who were singing "We Shall Overcome. "
- By December citizens freely elect two new leaders who had been imprisoned.
- Soviet troops stand by as the country plans free elections in January.
- In May people tear down an electric fence separating their country from democratic Austria.
- Workers' group, led by Lech Walesa, is recognized by government.
- Solidarity party wins many seats in Parliament.
- Erich Honecker steps down from office.
- East Berlin opens its gates to West Berlin.

Describe three changes that took place in Eastern Europe after the "Year of Miracles."

The Soviet republics declared their independence, ethnic conflicts broke out in Yugoslavia, and the European Union pledged to help its eastern neighbors build their economies.

EVALUATING INFORMATION FOR ACCURACY

The excerpt below is from a newspaper article written by reporter Mike O'Connor. The article discusses the progress of peace in Bosnia-Herzegovina since the Dayton peace accord ended the war there. Read the article. Then answer the questions that follow to evaluate the information for accuracy. For help, refer to pages 604–605 in your textbook.

> KRUSCICA, Bosnia-Herzegovina—Hundreds of Bosnian Muslims who had returned to homes they fled in the war have been driven out again, officials said Sunday.
> Over the last two weeks, the people of this village, who had been forced to leave by Bosnian Croats in 1993, have been coming back. . . . Sunday, though, the end of the short success story became clear. By the end of the day, the last of the Muslims had been forced to leave by groups of Croatian thugs.
> . . . U.N. officials said they were puzzled by both the sudden opening and the just-as-sudden end of cooperation. . . . "Croat politicians can help to implement the peace agreement or they can shut the whole thing down," said a U.N. official, speaking on condition of anonymity.
> Mike O'Connor, "Bosnian Muslims Driven Out of Homes a Second Time," *The New York Times*, August 4, 1997.

1. What is the reporter's purpose in writing this article?

   to describe the difficulties faced by these Bosnian Muslims and to show the problems of the peace agreement

2. How does the reporter view the situation of the Bosnian Muslims? How does he view the Bosnian Croats?

   He thinks the Muslims are being treated unfairly and that the Croats are being uncooperative and cruel to the Muslim refugees.

3. Which words in the article show the reporter's opinion of the Bosnian Croats?

   Croatian thugs

4. What are two facts that the reporter states in the article?

   Possible answers: Muslims had been forced to leave their homes in 1993; the Muslim refugees were forced to leave again on Sunday.

5. What other sources could you use to determine the accuracy of the article?

   Possible answer: articles written by other newspaper and magazine reporters as well as other observers of the war

---

DEMOCRACY IN SOUTH AFRICA

Write the events listed in the box in the correct place on the chart. Then answer the questions that follow. For help, you can refer back to pages 606–612 in your textbook.

- Black students lead protest in Soweto.
- The government bans the African National Congress (ANC).
- South Africa gains full independence from Britain.
- De Klerk abolishes most apartheid laws.
- World leaders begin to impose sanctions against South African government.
- South Africans elect Nelson Mandela president.
- President Frederik Willem de Klerk releases Nelson Mandela from prison.
- White leaders create system of apartheid.

CHANGES IN SOUTH AFRICA	
YEAR	EVENT
1948	White leaders create system of apartheid.
1960	The government bans the African National Congress (ANC).
1961	South Africa gains full independence from Britain.
1976	Black students lead protest in Soweto.
1980s	World leaders begin to impose sanctions against South African government.
1990	President Frederik Willem de Klerk releases Nelson Mandela from prison.
1991	De Klerk abolishes most apartheid laws.
1994	South Africans elect Nelson Mandela president.

1. How did the system of apartheid discriminate against blacks in South Africa?

   Blacks lost their land and were forced into townships; blacks could not attend white schools; black workers received poor wages.

2. What changes have occurred in South Africa since apartheid was ended?

   The government is building new homes for poor people; all-white schools have been opened to all races; all South African citizens can vote.

THE PACIFIC RIM NATIONS

The chart below describes the economic growth of some countries in the Pacific Rim.
Complete the chart by writing the name of the country next to the entries that tell about it.
Use the names on the map. If you need help, refer to pages 614–621 in your textbook.

PACIFIC RIM NATIONS

COUNTRY	FACTORS THAT AIDED THE ECONOMY	ECONOMY TODAY
Japan	demand for goods during Korean War; United States aid; good schools; government policies and investment	second highest GDP in world
South Korea	factories produced inexpensive clothes and shoes; complex technology	builds cars, electronics, and steel products
Singapore	tight government controls over society	giant in world trade; prosperous electronics industry
China	foreign companies set up businesses; farmers were given more control over their work	communist, but moving to free enterprise
Hong Kong	center for international trade as a former British colony	thriving, but future uncertain under Chinese control since 1997
Australia	ideal sheep grazing land; strong mineral exports; partnership with United States	large exports of computer parts; pioneer in solar research

---

WORKING TOGETHER IN THE AMERICAS

Listed below are challenges facing the
Americas in the second half of the 1900s.
Explain what the different countries in
the Americas have done, or are doing,
to meet each challenge. Refer to
pages 622–629 in your textbook.

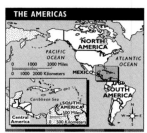

THE AMERICAS

1. **Challenge:** Many Latin countries were ruled by dictatorships.
   Action: In the 1980s democratic movements swept through the Americas, overthrowing the dictatorships.

2. **Challenge:** Much of Brazil's rain forest was destroyed by farming, logging, mining, and ranching.
   Action: Brazil's government is working with other nations to preserve the rain forests and to create jobs in the Amazon that are friendly to the environment.

3. **Challenge:** Crime organizations are involved in an illegal drug trade that brings little money to farmers who raise the coca plants used to make cocaine.
   Action: The United States and other nations are trying to stamp out the drug trade by destroying coca fields and helping farmers raise other crops.

4. **Challenge:** There is a need for closer ties and greater unity among the United States, Canada, and Mexico.
   Action: In 1993 NAFTA went into effect to increase trade by lowering taxes on goods traded among these countries.

What are some of the challenges the Americas face in the year 2000?
Possible answer: Latin American countries face the challenge of
improving life for its people, many of whom are poor, unemployed,
and living in overcrowded cities. Canada faces a challenge from
French Canadians who want Quebec to form a separate country.
The United States must define its role as a world power.

TERMS FROM THE MODERN WORLD

Match the terms with their meanings. Write the letter of the correct term next to its
definition. For help, you can refer to the lessons in Chapter 20 in your textbook.

a. ethnic group	**d.** apartheid	**g.** European Union	**j.** NAFTA
b. per capita income	**e.** township	**h.** Internet	**k.** Pacific Rim
c. interdependent	**f.** bilingual	**i.** urbanization	**l.** sanction
	m. gross domestic product (GDP)		

__b__ 1. the amount of money each person of a country would have if that country's total income were equally apportioned

__g__ 2. a group of Western European nations working to build a common economy

__l__ 3. a penalty placed against a nation to make it change its policies

__d__ 4. a system of laws that discriminated against black South Africans

__e__ 5. crowded areas in which South African blacks were forced to live

__k__ 6. the ring of countries surrounding the Pacific Ocean

__c__ 7. the dependence of countries on each other to meet the needs and wants of their peoples

__a__ 8. people who share a heritage of common customs, values, and language

__i__ 9. the growth of cities

__h__ 10. a group of interconnected computers around the world

__f__ 11. the ability to speak two languages

__j__ 12. agreement among the United States, Canada, and Mexico designed to increase trade

__m__ 13. goods and services produced in a country

CONTENT

Fill in the circle before the correct answer.

1. Culture is a people's _____.
- (a) way of life
- (b) technology
- (c) region
- (d) geography

2. A *climate region* is marked by similarities in _____.
- (a) customs
- (b) landforms
- (c) longitude
- (d) weather

3. What is one thing that helps make up a cultural region?
- (a) physical boundaries
- (c) weather
- (b) language
- (d) economy

4. Which fact about the boy Azeez shows what is meant by a *custom*?
- (a) He lives in a city.
- (c) He never eats meat.
- (b) He is Indian.
- (d) He has a brother.

5. Which is an example of cultural change in India?
- (a) Some Indian families now have temples in their homes.
- (b) Indian schoolchildren are learning to play musical instruments.
- (c) Indian women, especially in cities, have more freedom than before.
- (d) Many Indians speak Hindi.

Write the word or phrase from the box that best answers each question.

representative democracy	physical region	English
political region	cultural value	

6. What kind of region is the Mississippi River valley? physical region

7. In 1990, when East and West Germany joined to become the Federal Republic of Germany, what type of region was changed? political region

8. Most Hindus believe that all living things have souls. This is an example of a cultural value.

9. From what you learned in this chapter, what do many people in both Ireland and Canada speak? English

10. What kind of government does India have? representative democracy

---

SKILLS

Latitude and longitude are sometimes used to set boundaries between countries, states, and other areas. Use the map below to answer the questions. Write your answers on the lines.

LATITUDE AND LONGITUDE MAP

1. The southwestern corner of Tennessee is located at 35° N, 90° W.

2. 110°W marks the boundary between which two Canadian provinces?
Alberta and Saskatchewan

3. The point 40°N, 100°W lies on the boundary between what two states?
Kansas and Nebraska

4. The southernmost point in the continental United States shown on this map lies in what state and at about what latitude and longitude?
Florida; 25° N, 80° W

5. What three states meet at about 42°N, 120°W?
Oregon, California, and Nevada

WRITING

Write a short paragraph to answer each question. If you need more room, continue writing on the back of this page.

1. Use the map below to describe the continent of Australia in terms of climate regions.

CLIMATE REGIONS OF AUSTRALIA
- Tropical
- Semi-dry
- Desert
- Warm and rainy
- Warm and rainy with dry summer

See answer at right.

_____
_____
_____
_____
_____
_____

2. What is the difference between customs and culture? Give examples of each in your answer.

See answer at right.

_____
_____
_____
_____
_____
_____

WRITING ANSWERS

1. An adequate response will describe the five climate regions of Australia with some indication of their location. (Example: The northernmost parts of Australia have a tropical climate. The central part of Australia has desert and semi-dry climate regions. Two parts of the southern coast have a warm and rainy climate with a dry summer, and the eastern coast has a warm and rainy climate.) An excellent response will also describe the kinds of weather most likely to be found in these climate regions. (Examples: The tropical region is hot and humid. The desert and semi-dry regions are hot and dry.)

2. An adequate response will explain that culture is a people's way of life, while customs are things that people practice regularly. It will also give at least one example of each. For example, many of the peoples of Latin America share a common culture because they speak Spanish and share the same religion. Examples of customs might include types of food that people eat, how they dress, holidays they celebrate, and religious practices. An excellent response will further explain that culture is largely based on a people's beliefs, values, and ethnic heritage, and customs are daily or regular habits that reflect cultural values. Also, all cultures are made up of many different customs.

CONTENT

Fill in the circle before the correct answer.

1. Which is a *primary source* for learning about pioneer life?
   - (a) a history textbook
   - (b) an encyclopedia article
   - (c) a book based on pioneers' stories
   - (d) a letter by a pioneer woman

2. What is one problem faced by people who study ancient history?
   - (a) Many important sources have been destroyed or lost.
   - (b) There are no written records from ancient times.
   - (c) Most of the sources are primary sources.
   - (d) The original purpose of most artifacts is unknown.

3. What information about an archaeological sample can be obtained by carbon-14 testing?
   - (a) how old it is
   - (b) how quickly it decayed
   - (c) what it is made of
   - (d) what climate it is from

4. What made the "Iceman" discovery so interesting to archaeologists?
   - (a) The man had died in an accident.
   - (b) The man's clothing and possessions were preserved with him.
   - (c) The body was the first ever found in the Alps.
   - (d) The man's ax was made of copper and chipped stone.

5. How did archaeologists figure out what the Iceman's net was used for?
   - (a) They found prehistoric pictures of people using that kind of net.
   - (b) They studied the objects discovered near it.
   - (c) They compared it to a kind of net still in use in the region today.
   - (d) They tried fishing and catching birds with it.

Write the letter of the definition that best fits each term.

6. __d__ excavate
7. __c__ oral tradition
8. __b__ artifact
9. __e__ archaeology
10. __a__ prehistory

a. the time before writing was developed
b. an object made by someone in the past
c. the practice of passing on history from one person to another by word of mouth
d. to uncover by digging carefully
e. the study of the remains of past cultures

SKILLS

Read the following journal entry. It tells about a new site an archaeologist has come upon by accident. Then write your answer to each question.

> I was out for a hike when I came upon a large rock that had been moved by the recent heavy rains. Where the rock had been was the entrance to a cave. I looked in and could hardly believe my eyes! In a hollowed-out place in the back wall were a number of scrolls. One had fallen to the floor and was partly open, but I could not see clearly enough to identify the writing. I was very excited. What if the scrolls were made by the same people as those we had found earlier?
>
> I debated whether or not to enter. Entering could be dangerous, especially since erosion from the rains could have weakened the cave walls. On the other hand, if the cave collapsed or became flooded, the scrolls could be lost forever. If I went in, I could at least look at the writing and make some drawings. I did not have any equipment with me, not even my camera. To remove the scrolls without first mapping the site would break one of the first rules of archaeology.
>
> I finally decided to run back to the village and alert the rest of the team. They arranged for the needed equipment while I returned to the cave with my camera and began taking pictures from the entrance.

1. What was the archaeologist's goal after discovering the new site?
   to examine the scrolls, or to find out who made the scrolls

2. What decision did the archaeologist have to make?
   whether or not to enter the cave

3. What were two things that were considered in making the decision?
   the hazards of entering the cave, the risk of losing the scrolls if the cave
   collapsed or flooded, and whether or not to remove the scrolls

4. What did the archaeologist eventually decide to do?
   go for help, then return to the cave (with a camera)

5. Do you think the right decision was made? Tell why or why not.
   Answers will vary but should be supported by reasonable arguments and
   information from the journal entry.

WRITING

Read the selection. Then write a short paragraph to answer each question. If you need more room, continue writing on the back of this page.

> As a boy, Alex Haley heard many family stories about a long-ago ancestor named Kinte [kin-tay]. "The African" had been kidnapped while out cutting wood, shipped across the ocean, and sold into slavery in America. He never resigned himself to being a slave; when he later had a daughter, he told her about Africa and taught her his words for everyday things. The daughter told her children, and they told their children, and so on through the years.
>
> In 1965, Haley decided to find out if the stories were true. His main clues were the African words passed down through the family. This evidence led him to a village in Gambia, where he found an old man who could recite the history of the Kinte clan. Haley listened in amazement as the man told of a young man named Kunta Kinte, who in 1767 had gone out to cut wood and never been seen again. Haley had found his ancestor's people!
>
> Haley could not stop there. He kept hunting through historic documents such as ships' logs and plantation records. Eventually he learned the name of the ship that had brought Kinte to America. He even found the papers recording Kinte's sale to a new master! Haley's 1976 book *Roots* tells the story, from Kunta Kinte's boyhood through Haley's own birth in 1921. Haley combined the facts, the family stories, and details from his own imagination to come up with a powerful tale from American history.

1. Describe the sources Alex Haley used in learning about his family's history. Tell what kind of source each one was and how it helped him.
   See answer at right.

2. Suppose that 1,000 years from now, archaeologists discover a copy of *Roots*. Do you think it would be a good source of information about American history? Tell why or why not.
   See answer at right.

WRITING ANSWERS

1. An adequate response will mention at least one example of oral tradition and at least one primary source, and it will explain how these sources helped Haley. An excellent response will cite more examples of oral tradition and primary sources. Examples: (a) The family stories were oral tradition. They gave him basic information and the clues needed to start his research. (b) The African man who knew the clan history was also part of oral tradition. His information told Haley where his ancestor came from. (c) The historic documents (ships' logs, plantation records, sales record) were primary sources. They helped prove that the stories were true.

2. An adequate response will tell whether *Roots* would be a good source or not and give at least two supporting reasons. An excellent response will consider both sides of the argument, make a decision one way or another, and support the decision with several examples. Points in favor of *Roots* as a source include its basis in fact and the number of years of history it covers. Points against it include the facts that much of it is based on Haley's imagination and that it tells one family's story from one point of view.

CONTENT

Fill in the circle before the correct answer.

1. About how many years ago did the New Stone Age begin?
   (a) 12 thousand   (b) 40 thousand   (c) 600 thousand   (d) 2 million

2. Once people learned to build fires, they were able to _____.
   (a) hunt animals for food   (c) make their homes in caves
   (b) survive in cold climates   (d) make tools

3. Art from ancient times becomes especially important when _____.
   (a) there are no written records from those times
   (b) it shows what people looked like
   (c) it is in excellent condition
   (d) no one has seen it before

4. The surplus food produced by agriculture meant that _____.
   (a) less land was needed for farming use
   (b) farmers had more time for other activities
   (c) everyone had to become farmers
   (d) nonfarmers were free to develop other important skills

5. Stone Age people used technology when they _____.
   (a) saw lightning start a fire   (c) shaped stones to use in hunting
   (b) found shelter in caves   (d) gathered grass for bedding

Write the letter of the conclusion about Stone Age life that best fits each clue.

6. __e__ Animal bones were found together with Old Stone Age tools.

7. __a__ The Border Cave people made beads.

8. __c__ Many of Catal Huyuk's buildings were temples.

9. __d__ The people of Catal Huyuk produced woven wool cloth.

10. __b__ Obsidian products from Catal Huyuk were found in Syria, and Syrian pottery was found in Catal Huyuk.

a. The Border Cave people valued beautiful objects, not just useful ones.

b. The people of Catal Huyuk traded with the people of Syria.

c. Religion was an important part of daily life.

d. People had domesticated sheep or had learned to breed sheep for thicker wool.

e. People had learned how to hunt.

SKILLS

Use the time line to answer the questions.

EARLY BREAKTHROUGHS IN FARMING

10,000 B.C.   8000 B.C.   6000 B.C.   4000 B.C.

First crops planted **c. 9000 B.C.**   Cattle domesticated **c. 7000 B.C.**   Irrigation invented **c. 6000 B.C.**   Plow invented **c. 4000 B.C.**

1. About how many years does this time line cover?   6,000 years

2. About how many years passed between the first crops planted and the invention of irrigation?   3,000 years

3. What name do archaeologists use for the period covered by most of this time line?   New Stone Age

4. When was the plow invented?   4,000 B.C.

5. Put an X beside the conclusion you can draw from this time line.

_____ People did not use cattle for food after 7000 B.C.

_____ Cattle were domesticated between 10,000 B.C. and 7000 B.C.

__X__ Before 9000 B.C. people did not grow their own food.

_____ Before irrigation was invented, people did not plant crops.

WRITING

Write a short paragraph to answer each question. If you need more room, continue writing on the back of this page.

1. This drawing from a prehistoric rock carving in Arizona shows a group of people and some sheep. What do you think is happening in the picture? What conclusions can you draw from the picture?

Source: *Canyon de Chelly: Its People and Rock Art* by Campbell Grant, University of Arizona Press, 1978

See answer at right.

2. Imagine that you are a New Stone Age hunter-gatherer. You have never seen a city until, one day, you come upon Catal Huyuk. Describe what you see when you enter the city. What is most surprising or interesting to you? How do you feel about it?

See answer at right.

WRITING ANSWERS

1. An adequate response will note that the people seem to be herding sheep and therefore had begun to domesticate animals, and that they used tools (rocks and something like a whip). An excellent response will draw further conclusions. Examples: The people of that culture had learned to work together. Also, they liked to create art to depict such scenes.

2. An adequate response will mention the number or structure of the buildings and the existence of craftworkers. The response should include both literal details and subjective impressions. An excellent response will include more detail and show a greater awareness of the contrast between the nomadic hunter-gatherer life and early city life.

CONTENT AND SKILLS

Fill in the circle before the correct answer.

1. To understand Earth better, geographers divide it into different types of _____.
   - ⓐ landforms
   - ⓑ regions
   - ⓒ customs
   - ⓓ peoples

2. Contact between two cultures that often leads to cultural change is called _____.
   - ⓐ cultural interaction
   - ⓒ cultural region
   - ⓑ oral history
   - ⓓ values

3. A surplus is _____.
   - ⓐ an extra supply
   - ⓒ a group of farmers
   - ⓑ an early harvest
   - ⓓ an ancient settlement

4. The work of historians is similar to that of detectives because they both _____.
   - ⓐ display artifacts in museums
   - ⓒ use clues to solve mysteries
   - ⓑ create primary sources
   - ⓓ study ancient cultures

5. Archaeologists knew that people at Border Cave had made contact with people from the coast when they found _____.
   - ⓐ stone tools
   - ⓒ animal bones
   - ⓑ a seashell bead
   - ⓓ a painting of the ocean

6. Why did archaeologists working at the Iceman site melt the snow and filter the water?
   - ⓐ They wanted to see if the water was clean.
   - ⓑ They did not want to lose any evidence.
   - ⓒ They needed drinking water.
   - ⓓ They wanted to clean the Iceman.

7. Bits of sulfur and iron, which are used to make matches, were found in a piece of fungus carried by the Iceman. This suggests that the Iceman _____.
   - ⓐ was a miner
   - ⓒ traded with other people
   - ⓑ invented matches
   - ⓓ knew how to make fire

8. What important development began in the New Stone Age?
   - ⓐ agriculture
   - ⓑ cave painting
   - ⓒ stone tools
   - ⓓ fire

9. People training to do different kinds of work is an example of _____.
   - ⓐ archaeology
   - ⓑ specialization
   - ⓒ technology
   - ⓓ agriculture

10. Archaeologists learn about the people of the Stone Ages by studying _____.
    - ⓐ oral history
    - ⓑ maps
    - ⓒ diaries
    - ⓓ artifacts

CONTENT AND SKILLS

Suppose that you are studying the history of your community. Match the type of source to each example of information by writing the letter on the line.

11. __b__ primary source
12. __d__ secondary source
13. __a__ oral tradition
14. __c__ artifact

a. a story of long ago told by a resident of the area

b. a diary written by one of the founders of the community

c. an object from the past found at a construction site

d. a TV documentary about people who lived in the area

Use the map to answer questions 15–17.

SOUTH AMERICA

15. What type of region does this map illustrate?

   physical

16. What is the location (longitude and latitude) of Caracas?

   about 10° N, 70° W

17. What kind of landform would you find in Bogotá?

   mountains

Write the term that best fits each description on the left.

18. refers to the years since Jesus' birth __A.D.__   B.C.

19. refers to the years before Jesus' birth __B.C.__   A.D.

20. means "around" or "about" __circa__   circa

WRITING

Write a short paragraph to answer each question. If you need more room, continue writing on the back of this page.

1. Look at this sketch of a prehistoric archaeological site. What can you tell about the culture of the people who once lived in this settlement?

ARCHAEOLOGICAL SITE

TEMPLE — MEETING PLACE — GRAIN STORAGE

WALL
WELL
WORKSHOP
DWELLING
ANIMAL PENS
PURPOSE UNKNOWN

   See answer at right.
   _____
   _____
   _____
   _____

2. Suppose that you have to make a decision about whether or not to spend next summer working at an archaeological dig. Describe the steps you would take to make the decision.

   See answer at right.
   _____
   _____
   _____
   _____
   _____

WRITING ANSWERS

1. An adequate response should note that the people (a) raised grain and animals (indicated by the grain storage building and animal pens); (b) had developed a formal religion (indicated by the temple); and (c) had begun to develop specialization, or crafts (indicated by the workshops). An excellent response will connect these observations to other concepts and/or include more complex observations and speculations. Examples: The existence of agriculture and specialization indicates a New Stone Age (or later) site; the size of the temple complex indicates the importance of religion; the orderly arrangement of the public buildings suggests cooperation or planning in constructing that part of the settlement.

2. An adequate response will indicate that the student would set a goal, consider alternatives, and make a decision. An excellent response will apply these steps to the question of whether or not to work at an archaeological dig for the summer.

CONTENT

Fill in the circle before the correct answer.

1. Hieroglyphics helped Egyptian scribes keep records of _____.
   - (a) history
   - (b) speeches
   - (c) flooding
   - (d) taxes

2. Egyptian farmers used irrigation to _____.
   - (a) water their crops
   - (c) control flood waters
   - (b) make the soil more fertile
   - (d) travel among villages

3. In Egypt's Old Kingdom what did craftworkers and artists receive in return for the objects they made for the pharaohs?
   - (a) land
   - (c) money
   - (b) clothes and food
   - (d) golden bowls and stone statues

4. The Middle Kingdom is best described as a time when Egypt _____.
   - (a) first developed a written language
   - (b) began to use irrigation techniques
   - (c) increased contact with other cultures
   - (d) became a wealthy empire

5. In ancient Egypt most of the land and farms were owned by _____.
   - (a) hard-working farmers
   - (c) Nubians and Syrians
   - (b) skilled craftworkers
   - (d) government officials

Write the letter of the description that best fits each pharaoh.

6. __c__ Hatshepsut
7. __b__ Menes
8. __e__ Ahmose
9. __a__ Khufu
10. __d__ Tutankhamun

a. ordered the construction of the Great Pyramid

b. unified Egypt by overthrowing the king of Lower Egypt and became the first pharaoh

c. organized a two-year expedition to Punt, expanding trade beyond the Egyptian empire

d. ruled as a wealthy young pharaoh from about age 9 to 19

e. studied the Hyksos and used their weapons to drive them back out of Lower Egypt

SKILLS

Use the maps to answer the questions. Write your answers on the lines.

EGYPT: the Nile Valley

LUXOR

1. Approximately how far would a boat traveling from Cairo to Luxor go?

   about 400 miles

2. About how far is it from the Luxor museum to the Temple of Amun in Karnak?

   about 1 1/2 miles

3. Name a city that is in Upper Egypt.

   Luxor or Aswan

4. What is one advantage of a large-scale map over a small-scale map?

   It can show more detailed information.

5. Which map would you use to determine the direction you would travel to go from Luxor to Alexandria?

   the small-scale map

   (Egypt: the Nile Valley)

WRITING

Write a short paragraph to answer each question. If you need more room, continue writing on the back of this page.

1. How did the development of hieroglyphics affect ancient Egyptian culture? Tell what hieroglyphs were used for and how hieroglyphics changed Egyptian culture.

   See answer at right.

2. Look at the map of Egypt. Where would you expect to find the best farmland? Tell why.

   EGYPT

   See answer at right.

WRITING ANSWERS

1. An adequate response will explain that hieroglyphs were used for recording taxes and making calculations. These uses changed Egyptian culture by making complex accounting possible and by extending government control over its people. An excellent response will mention other uses of hieroglyphs (such as, writing letters and recording medical procedures and treatments). It will also explain other ways in which the use of hieroglyphs changed Egyptian culture. For example, it made possible the building of the pyramids, communicating over long distances, developing sophisticated medical knowledge, and inventing a calendar.

2. An adequate response will specify that the best farmland can be found along the Nile River, especially in the delta area of Lower Egypt, and will tell why. For example, the river brings down silt to fertilize the land and water for irrigating fields. An excellent response will also analyze the potential of other areas. For example, the land around Lake Nasser does not receive the benefits of flooding, but at least there is water. Much of the rest of Egypt is desert that offers neither good soil nor water.

CONTENT

Fill in the circle before the correct answer.

1. In ancient Sumer each city-state had a ziggurat where people went to _____.
   - ⓐ learn to write cuneiform
   - ⓑ worship a special god or goddess
   - ⓒ trade with people from other cities
   - ⓓ buy clothes and food

2. What factor made it especially difficult to farm in southern Mesopotamia?
   - ⓐ unskilled laborers
   - ⓒ not enough sunshine
   - ⓑ droughts and irregular floods
   - ⓓ rocky, infertile soil

3. The Code of Hammurabi was a _____.
   - ⓐ set of laws
   - ⓒ type of alphabet
   - ⓑ form of writing
   - ⓓ system of taxes

4. The Israelites left Canaan and went to Egypt in order to _____.
   - ⓐ escape slavery
   - ⓒ find food
   - ⓑ conquer Egypt
   - ⓓ own land

5. Nineveh was important because it became the _____.
   - ⓐ capital city of Babylonia
   - ⓒ birthplace of Judaism
   - ⓑ only city that defeated Egypt
   - ⓓ first city-state in Sumer

Read each sentence and write the name from the box of the person it describes.

Gilgamesh	Sargon	Hammurabi	Abraham	Moses

6. This king of Babylon dammed parts of the Euphrates River and attacked the Sumerians. **Hammurabi**

7. According to the Bible, this Hebrew prophet grew up in Egypt and traveled to Mount Sinai, where he was given the Torah. **Moses**

8. He was an important hero to the Sumerians. **Gilgamesh**

9. This king of Kish used cuneiform to expand his empire and unite the other city-states. **Sargon**

10. According to the Bible, the history of the Jewish people began when this man traveled to Canaan and made a covenant, or agreement, with God. **Abraham**

SKILLS

Read the passage. Then complete the chart below by writing in the missing causes and effects.

The Sumerians lived in an environment with limited resources. Southern Mesopotamia was very hot and dry, receiving hardly any rain each year. Trees cannot grow in such a place. Even rocks were hard to find. The Sumerians needed to find another material from which to build shelter. Fortunately, sunshine and clay were plentiful. As a result, the Sumerians packed moist clay into molds and left it to dry in the sun. Since the flat bricks could then be stacked, they were used to form the walls of buildings.

Because the Sumerians were not happy with the way the sun-dried bricks eventually crumbled, they found a better way to work with the clay. They found out that if they baked the bricks, they were harder and lasted longer. Using a natural material called asphalt to join the bricks, they could make a long-lasting wall. The Sumerians built massive and long-lasting ziggurats, parts of which have survived four thousand years. As a result, archaeologists can study these remains to learn about the Sumerians.

CAUSES	EFFECTS
1. They had plenty of materials for making clay, or they did not have any other materials for building.	1. The Sumerians made buildings out of clay.
2. The Sumerians made flat bricks that could be stacked.	2. They were used to form walls.
3. The sun-dried bricks eventually crumbled.	3. The Sumerians experimented with baked bricks.
4. The Sumerians used asphalt to join the bricks.	4. They made long-lasting walls.
5. Parts of the ziggurats they built have lasted four thousand years.	5. Archaeologists can study about the Sumerians from their remains.

WRITING

Write a short paragraph to answer each question. If you need more room, continue writing on the back of this page.

1. Describe the contributions of ancient Mesopotamian culture to our world today.

   See answer at right.

2. Much of Mesopotamia is now called Iraq. Today most of Iraq's people live in cities, some live in villages, and a few travel with their herds of animals (mostly sheep). Look at the map of Iraq. Based on what you have learned about farming and the development of cities, where would you expect most of the people of Iraq to live? Tell why.

   See answer at right.

WRITING ANSWERS

1. An adequate response will mention that the people of Mesopotamia developed a system of writing and a code of laws, and they invented both the wheel and irrigation. An excellent response will mention less obvious contributions, such as the development of schools, literature, and science.

2. An adequate response will indicate that most of the population lives in the lower plains along the major rivers and will give a logical reason. For example, towns and cities tend to prosper in areas where there is plenty of food, and farmers in Iraq are much more likely to succeed along the rivers than in other areas. An excellent response will provide more detail. For example, it might indicate that the population would be considerably smaller in the mountains where the soil is poor or in the desert where there is no water for crops. It might also refer to ancient Mesopotamia and the fact that it developed between the Tigris and Euphrates rivers, which still provide water and transportation.

CONTENT

Fill in the circle before the correct answer.

1. Archaeologists say that Mohenjo-Daro and Harappa might have been abandoned because of _____.

   (a) war   (b) drought   (c) invaders   (d) an earthquake

2. Much of the water that floods the Indus River comes from _____.

   (a) tides in the Arabian Sea   (c) rain falling on the Indus Plain

   (b) snow in the Himalayas   (d) streams in the Hindu Kush Mountains

3. What clue makes historians think that Mohenjo-Daro had a strong government?

   (a) sewer system design   (c) location of the city

   (b) weavers' use of cotton   (d) skill of the metalworkers

4. Why do historians know less about the Harappan civilization than they know about ancient Egyptian or Mesopotamian civilization?

   (a) People of the Harappan civilization did not trade with other cultures.

   (b) The written records have not been translated.

   (c) The Harappans did not construct large buildings.

   (d) No written records have survived the harsh climate.

5. Buddhism differs from Hinduism in that Buddhists believe _____.

   (a) all people go through a cycle of life, death, and rebirth

   (b) karma is a force based on people's behavior and affects their future lives

   (c) the most important goal is to reach peace by ending suffering

   (d) there is one powerful force that connects all life

Write the term that best completes each sentence: Vedas, caste, dharma, monk, Buddhism.

6. The laws and duties of members of each caste described in the Vedas are called _dharma_.

7. A special group within Hindu society is called a _caste_.

8. A _monk_ is a man who gives up his possessions and devotes his life to a religious group.

9. Ancient Aryan songs that became the beginnings of Hinduism were written down in the _Vedas_.

10. The teachings of Siddhartha Gautama became the basis of _Buddhism_.

SKILLS

Use the maps to answer the questions. Write your answers on the lines.

INDIA: PHYSICAL MAP

INDIA: AGRICULTURAL MAP

1. What is a primary use of the land along the Ganges River in northern India?

   farming

2. What is a primary use of land around Calcutta?

   farming

3. In which area of India is cotton the main crop?

   Deccan Plateau

4. What important crops are grown on the Northern Plains?

   cattle, barley, sugarcane

5. Where are the main areas of unused land in India located?

   in the northwest (Thar Desert) and far north (Himalayan Mountains)

WRITING

Write a short paragraph to answer each question. If you need more room, continue writing on the back of this page.

1. Look at the information about Pakistan's industries today. What similarities do you see between the economy of the ancient Indus Valley civilization and the economy of the country that exists in the same area today?

   CHIEF INDUSTRIES IN PAKISTAN TODAY

   - **Wheat**—the country's most important crop—is grown by farmers to feed their families

   - **Cotton-cloth manufacturing**—the country's second most important crop

   - **Food processing**—for example, milling grains, refining sugar, and producing vegetable oil

   - **Fertilizer production**

   - **Cigarettes**

   - **Carpets**

   - **Steel**

   See answer at right.

2. Describe the growth of agriculture in the ancient Indus Valley civilization.

   See answer at right.

WRITING ANSWERS

1. An adequate response should indicate the similarity between the importance of food and cotton production in ancient times and modern times. An excellent response will address each of the industries in the chart. Example: As in ancient times, Pakistani farmers grow food to feed their families. Cotton was and is a very important crop. Residents of the ancient cities were also involved with weaving cloth from cotton. The industries of fertilizer production, cigarette making, carpet making, and steel production were not a part of ancient life, although metalworkers did exist. Other craftworkers existed, just as part of the population in modern Pakistan works in manufacturing.

2. An adequate response will mention at least three features of life in the Indus Valley. Example: In the Indus Valley, farmers were usually able to use irrigation to grow two crops each year. Animals were domesticated and their use enabled farmers to plow larger fields. Cotton was grown and used to make cloth for the first time. An excellent response will detail other crops, such as rice, bananas, black pepper, mustard, and sesame. It will also note that farming began in the Indus Valley around 6000 B.C.

CONTENT

Fill in the circle before the correct answer.

1. In ancient China oracle bones were used by the Shang people to _____.
   - (a) record history
   - (b) cure illnesses
   - (c) win wars
   - (d) predict the future

2. During which time period did rulers first apply Confucian ideas about fairness and learning?
   - (a) Qin dynasty
   - (b) Shang dynasty
   - (c) Han dynasty
   - (d) Huang civilization

3. What was the main form of agriculture on the steppes north of the Huang Valley?
   - (a) herding sheep and cattle
   - (b) growing rice and other grains
   - (c) raising horses
   - (d) cultivating fruits

4. Loess created problems for Huang Valley farmers because it _____.
   - (a) poisoned the water
   - (b) clogged irrigation ditches
   - (c) left fine silt on the fields
   - (d) soaked up all the rainwater

5. The ancient huts uncovered by archaeologists at Anyang were once used for _____.
   - (a) workshops
   - (b) prisons
   - (c) storehouses
   - (d) temples

Read each sentence and write the name from the box of the person it describes.

Fu Hao	Shihuangdi	Han Gaozu	Confucius	Wudi

6. This emperor of the Han dynasty created schools to prepare people for government jobs.   **Wudi**

7. This teacher said that rulers must be wise and good, just as their subjects must be respectful.   **Confucius**

8. Archaeologists found the tomb of this woman, who was a leader of troops, a ruler of her town, and a king's wife.   **Fu Hao**

9. Although he was successful in creating a strong government, China's first emperor is remembered for his harsh rule.   **Shihuangdi**

10. This general was originally a farmer, before he led rebel armies to overthrow the Qin dynasty.   **Han Gaozu**

SKILLS

Read the passage below. Then answer the questions about writing a summary.

China is so large that many different forms of Chinese are spoken within its borders. People in one part of the country might not be able to understand people in another part. To help his people understand one another, an emperor named Shihuangdi set up a single system of writing that everyone in his empire could read. This form of writing, which is still used today, contains about 50,000 characters. It does not have an alphabet. In an alphabet each character stands for a sound. In Chinese each character stands for a thing or an idea, such as *house* or *down*. Using these characters, people in China could communicate with one another, even if they could not understand one another's spoken words. This standard form of writing helped Shihuangdi unite the people in such a vast region. It is one of the reasons the ancient nation of China has endured for so many centuries.

1. Which is the topic sentence of this passage?
   "To help his people understand one another, an emperor named Shihuangdi set up a single system of writing that everyone in his empire could read."

2. What supporting details tell you that the emperor's system of writing was important to China?
   It helped unite the people, and it has helped China endure for centuries.

3. Which sentence or sentences do not directly relate to the topic?
   "It does not have an alphabet. In an alphabet each character stands for a sound."

4. What is the purpose of the first sentence of this paragraph?
   It explains why people in China do not always understand one another.

5. Write one or two sentences to summarize this passage.
   Example: Shihuangdi developed a standard written form of Chinese so that people across his empire could communicate with one another.

WRITING

Write a short paragraph to answer each question. If you need more room, continue writing on the back of this page.

1. Explain how government was organized during the Han dynasty.
   See answer at right.

2. The three maps below make it clear that the growth of China was tied to control of the Huang and Chang rivers. Why was control of the rivers so important?

CHINA: Three Dynasties

See answer at right.

WRITING ANSWERS

1. An adequate response will describe how during the Han dynasty, emperors adopted some of the ideas of Confucianism, such as the view that a subject must respect the ruler, but the ruler must be wise and good. Han emperors also wanted to lessen the power of nobles and rule fairly. An excellent response will explain how the Han emperor Wudi created schools to prepare people for government service, so educated people—not just nobles—got government jobs.

2. An adequate response will explain that control of the rivers was important because the rivers made farming successful and served as protective geographic boundaries. An excellent response will explain these reasons in more detail. For example, the success of farming was important because it allowed for greater population and more farmers to help build and defend the growing empire. It may also mention that control of the rivers allowed rulers to control trade and transportation in and out of the empire.

CONTENT AND SKILLS

Fill in the circle before the correct answer.

1. The ancient Egyptians filled the tombs of their pharaohs with treasures to _____.
- ⓐ use the tombs as museums
- ⓒ keep the treasures safe from looters
- ⓑ take with them to the afterlife
- ⓓ show them respect

2. Menes was known as the pharaoh who _____.
- ⓐ unified Egypt
- ⓒ invented hieroglyphs
- ⓑ conquered Mesopotamia
- ⓓ destroyed Egyptian culture

3. In the ancient world of the Fertile Crescent, the Israelites' religion was different because they believed in _____.
- ⓐ an afterlife
- ⓒ only one God
- ⓑ many gods
- ⓓ reincarnation

4. Egypt's economy was based on _____.
- ⓐ religion
- ⓒ manufacturing
- ⓑ banking
- ⓓ farming

5. Farming in Mesopotamia was made possible by _____.
- ⓐ two rivers
- ⓒ many lakes
- ⓑ constant rain
- ⓓ a dry climate

6. Based on the layout of the city and its advanced engineering, historians believe that Mohenjo-Daro had _____.
- ⓐ good schools
- ⓒ frequent wars
- ⓑ strong local government
- ⓓ problems with earthquakes

7. The teachings of Siddhartha Gautama were the basis of _____.
- ⓐ Hinduism
- ⓑ Confucianism
- ⓒ Buddhism
- ⓓ Christianity

8. During the Shang dynasty in ancient China, land was owned by the _____.
- ⓐ nobles
- ⓑ farmers
- ⓒ monks
- ⓓ soldiers

9. Shihuangdi helped to unify China by setting up a single system of _____.
- ⓐ farming
- ⓑ irrigation
- ⓒ schools
- ⓓ writing

10. During the Han dynasty in China, great schools of learning were created by _____.
- ⓐ Shihuangdi
- ⓑ Han Gaozu
- ⓒ Wudi
- ⓓ Fu Hao

CONTENT AND SKILLS

For questions 11–16 choose the term from the box that best completes each sentence.

Moses	Rosetta Stone	Hammurabi	Aryans	Abraham	Vedas

11. The Bible describes how __Abraham__ traveled from Mesopotamia to Canaan and made a covenant with God.

12. __Hammurabi__ established a code of law in the Babylonian empire.

13. __Aryans__ migrated to India around 1500 B.C.

14. The __Rosetta Stone__ was the key that helped historians understand hieroglyphics.

15. According to the Bible, __Moses__ led the Israelites out of slavery in Egypt.

16. Among Hindus the __Vedas__ are the "Books of Knowledge."

For questions 17–20 write your answer to each question on the lines.

17. Name two religions based on a belief in reincarnation.

Hinduism and Buddhism

18. Write a summary of one or two sentences telling how the use of hieroglyphics and cuneiform changed the cultures of the ancient Egyptians and Sumerians.

Hieroglyphics and cuneiform enabled the Egyptians and Sumerians to keep

records of surpluses and taxes and communicate across long distances.

19. If you planned to walk around a city to visit its historic sites, what kind of map would give you the best level of detail?

large-scale map

20. Write a summary telling why loess was a blessing and a curse to Chinese farmers.

It made the soil very fertile, but it washed away easily; it also caused flooding

and blocked canals.

WRITING

Write a short paragraph to answer each question. If you need more room, continue writing on the back of this page.

1. Look at the physical map of river valley civilizations in parts of the ancient world. Explain why the Shang people in ancient China probably did not have contact with the people of other cultures, such as those on the Mediterranean Sea, the Red Sea, and the Indus River.

RIVER VALLEY CIVILIZATIONS

See answer at right.

2. In what ways did flooding affect agriculture in the ancient civilizations of Egypt, Mesopotamia, the Indus River valley, and China? What advantages did the floods offer? What were the disadvantages?

See answer at right.

WRITING ANSWERS

1. An adequate response should state that the distance and physical barriers made contact unlikely, and it will identify at least two barriers. An excellent response will also compare the travel routes among other civilizations to those of China. Example: The distance from the Huang River to the other rivers is very great. In addition, huge physical barriers including high mountains (Himalayas), large deserts, and vast bodies of water (Pacific and Indian oceans) made contact unlikely. The people of the Indus Valley, for example, could sail to the Arabian Sea and on to the Middle East, but the people of the Huang Valley could not use that route.

2. An adequate response should mention at least two advantages and two disadvantages of floods. Examples: Floods deposited silt, created fertile farmland, and provided plenty of water for irrigation. Floods also posed the dangers of drowning, of losing homes, and of losing crops. An excellent response will apply these advantages and disadvantages to specific civilizations. Example: The mineral-rich silt in Mesopotamia made the soil very fertile, enabling farmers to grow surplus crops. The Nile River generally flooded at a predictable time before crops were planted and softened the soil, which made it easier to start plants. Along the other rivers, however, flooding was more unpredictable. People sometimes lost their homes or lives during the floods. When floods along the Indus River came before the crops were harvested, they could destroy the crops, and people died during the famine that followed. Along the Huang River, uncontrolled floods easily eroded the loess, leaving unproductive land behind.

CONTENT

Fill in the circle before the correct answer.

1. The landscape of Greece is made up mostly of _____.
   - (a) mountains and hills
   - (c) large stretches of plains
   - (b) a wide river valley
   - (d) a gently rising plateau

2. An oligarchy is governed by _____.
   - (a) a single ruler or king
   - (c) a small group of wealthy, powerful men
   - (b) leaders elected by all the people
   - (d) a respected scholar or teacher

3. Which of these was a result of the Peloponnesian Wars?
   - (a) No single polis maintained control over Greece.
   - (b) Athens became the leading city-state.
   - (c) Greece was taken over by Persia.
   - (d) The Greek Golden Age began.

4. The city-state of Sparta was especially concerned with _____.
   - (a) strengthening its military
   - (c) acquiring more land for farming
   - (b) building democracy
   - (d) trading with other city-states

5. The Seven Wonders of the World were alike in that they were all _____.
   - (a) located in Greece
   - (c) made by people
   - (b) portraits of gods
   - (d) government buildings

Write the name from the box that best fits each description.

| Homer | Pericles | Alexander | Socrates | Herodotus |

6. an Athenian leader who worked to allow poor citizens to take part in government ___Pericles___

7. a philosopher who questioned Athenian laws, customs, and religion ___Socrates___

8. a poet whose works were part of the culture shared by all of Greece ___Homer___

9. an historian who wrote about ancient Greece and its culture ___Herodotus___

10. a Macedonian king who conquered Greece and made it part of his empire ___Alexander___

SKILLS

For each question circle the letter of the conclusion that can be made based on the information given.

1. Greek tragedies are part of the legacy we have inherited from ancient Greece. Although many Greek tragedies have been lost, works by Sophocles, Euripides, and Aeschylus have survived.
   - (a.) Tragedies written by ancient Greeks are still performed today.
   - b. The works of Sophocles are more entertaining than those of Euripides.

2. In *Oedipus Rex*, a Greek tragedy written by Sophocles, the main character is an admirable person who faces a difficult choice. As in most Greek tragedies, this character has a fault that eventually leads to his downfall.
   - a. Sophocles did not write many plays about admirable people.
   - (b.) The main character in most Greek tragedies has faults.

3. In ancient Greece only two or three actors performed in a tragedy, and they often had to play more than one character. The actors were always men, and they played both male and female roles.
   - (a.) Greek tragedies were performed in a way that is different from the way most plays are performed today.
   - b. The women of ancient Greece did not have any talent for acting.

4. Sophocles and Euripides wrote tragedies to help audiences feel better about their own lives. As they watched a tragedy, the audience felt pity for the main character's downfall or death.
   - a. Every play written by Sophocles or Euripides had a happy ending.
   - (b.) The purpose of a tragedy was to relieve the audience's feelings of fear or self-pity by showing them the suffering of the play's main character.

5. Plays in ancient Greece were performed in open-air theaters during religious festivals. Every theater had an altar to honor Dionysus or another god or goddess.
   - (a.) Plays in ancient Greece were produced to honor a god or goddess.
   - b. Performances were often canceled because of bad weather.

WRITING

Write a short paragraph to answer each question. If you need more room, continue writing on the back of this page.

1. In about 600 B.C. how were Athens and Sparta similar, and how were they different?

   See answer at right.

2. How might the geography of Greece have led to the development of many separate city-states rather than a single, united empire? Use the map below to help answer the question.

   ANCIENT GREECE: 450 B.C.

   See answer at right.

WRITING ANSWERS

1. An adequate response will explain that both Athens and Sparta were city-states. Life in both Athens and Sparta revolved around an agora and an acropolis, and the people in both places worshiped the same gods and goddesses. The major difference between them was that Athens emphasized farming and education, while Sparta emphasized military power. An excellent response will point out other similarities and other differences. For example, in both city-states leaders had to be citizens. Women and slaves were not considered citizens and had few rights. Sparta had many more slaves than Athens. In Sparta boys trained to be soldiers, and girls trained to be strong mothers of strong children. In Athens girls worked at home, while boys went to school and worked in farming or craftmaking. Also, in Athens the government began developing as a democracy.

2. An adequate response will describe at least one geographical feature (e.g., mountainous terrain, peninsulas, islands, lack of fertile valleys for farming) and explain how this feature made it difficult for ancient Greece to become a united empire. Example: Most of Greece is covered with mountains and hills. These features create natural boundaries, which must have made it difficult to travel from place to place. As a result, separate city-states grew up in these areas that were isolated from one another. An excellent response will give more than one feature and explain the results in more detail.

CONTENT

Fill in the circle before the correct answer.

1. Roman citizens included plebians and _____.
   ⓐ gladiators ⓑ patricians ⓒ slaves ⓓ Gauls

2. In the Roman republic the Senate was controlled by _____.
   ⓐ all men and women of Rome ⓒ members of Rome's noble families
   ⓑ workers and merchants ⓓ army commanders and soldiers

3. In the Punic Wars, Rome became the most powerful Mediterranean nation by defeating _____.
   ⓐ Greece ⓑ Carthage ⓒ Persia ⓓ Etruria

4. When Constantine became emperor, he made his capital in _____.
   ⓐ Rome ⓑ Gaul ⓒ Carthage ⓓ Constantinople

5. The Roman governors of Judea feared the growing popularity of Jesus because they thought he might _____.
   ⓐ punish the Jews ⓒ defeat the armies of Rome
   ⓑ criticize Roman gods ⓓ lead a revolt

Look at the time line and read the events below. Then write the correct letter next to each event to show when it happened.

History of the Roman Empire

a. 494 B.C.   b. 202 B.C.   c. 45 B.C.   d. A.D. 180   e. A.D. 284

500 B.C.   250 B.C.   A.D. 1   A.D. 250   A.D. 500

6. __c__ Julius Caesar becomes dictator of Rome
7. __a__ Roman plebians rebel, leading to the creation of the republic
8. __e__ Diocletian divides the Roman empire into two parts
9. __d__ Armies from northern Europe begin to invade the Roman empire
10. __b__ Rome defeats Carthage in the Battle of Zama

SKILLS

Use the elevation map of Italy to answer the questions.

ITALY: ELEVATION

1. In what part of Italy are the highest elevations? — in the Alps, or in the north
2. What is the elevation of Venice? — 0 ft. – 700 ft.
3. What is the elevation of the Apennines? — about 1,500 ft. – 7,000 ft.
4. How is this elevation map similar to a profile map?
   It shows differences in the height of land areas.
5. What could a profile map of Italy show better than this elevation map?
   It could show relative height better than an elevation map can.

WRITING

Write a short paragraph to answer each question. If you need more room, continue writing on the back of this page.

1. Read this version of a speech that Julius Caesar made to the Roman Senate in 63 B.C.

   Our ancestors were good at planning and full of courage in action. They also imitated whatever was worthwhile in the culture of other nations. For example, they copied the armor and weapons of the Samnites. Their official robes and symbols came from the Etruscans. In fact, they eagerly imitated any promising idea, whether it came from a friend or an enemy.

   Think of two "promising ideas" developed by the Romans that are imitated or used by people today. Describe each idea and explain why it is still useful and important to modern people.

   See answer at right.

2. In your opinion were most Romans better off during the years of the republic or during the Pax Romana? Give reasons to support your answer.

   See answer at right.

WRITING ANSWERS

1. An adequate response will mention two legacies or achievements of Roman civilization. Example: Romans developed the republican form of government, in which citizens elect government leaders to represent them. The Romans were also the first to make cement by mixing sand, lime, and stone. An excellent response will mention two or more legacies and explain why each is still important today. Examples: The republican form of government is widely used today, including in the United States. We still use concrete in the construction of modern buildings and roads. Other legacies include the Roman alphabet and Latin-based languages, aqueducts to bring water to cities, a mail system, the use of arches in buildings, a national census, and an advanced road system.

2. An adequate response will give persuasive reasons for stating that Romans were better off during the years of the republic or during the Pax Romana. Example: Romans were better off during the Pax Romana than during the years of the republic. Although citizens were no longer able to participate in government, their emperors helped to improve living conditions by building new roads, water systems, and public buildings. They also maintained strong armies for protection. An excellent response will explain in more detail why Romans were better off in one period than in the other.

CONTENT

Fill in the circle before the correct answer.

1. Much of the inner part of the Arabian peninsula is made up of _____.
   ⓐ mountains ⓑ valleys ⓒ deserts ⓓ forests

2. Why did the Nabatean civilization grow rich?
   ⓐ It had the largest area of fertile farmland in Arabia.
   ⓑ Its capital was an important place of worship for Muslims.
   ⓒ Its leaders conquered many colonies in the Mediterranean area.
   ⓓ Its capital was an important stop on a busy trade route.

3. The main activity of the Bedouin people was _____.
   ⓐ trading ⓑ farming ⓒ herding ⓓ hunting

4. The center of the Muslim world community is _____.
   ⓐ Mecca ⓑ Petra ⓒ Baghdad ⓓ Medina

5. In the early 1000s a Muslim named Avicenna made which of these contributions?
   ⓐ He described how diseases can spread through air and water.
   ⓑ He invented a tool for determining the position of the stars.
   ⓒ He developed the number system that we use today.
   ⓓ He designed and built important Muslim monuments.

Write the word or term from the box that best completes each sentence.

Quran	Mecca	Islam	Five Pillars	mosque

6. The religion of Muslim people is called _Islam_ .

7. According to Muslim belief, _Mecca_ is the city where Muhammad began teaching about Allah.

8. Muslims believe that the _Quran_ contains Allah's teachings to Muhammad.

9. The five basic duties of all Muslims are known as the _Five Pillars_ .

10. A _mosque_ is a place of worship where Muslims gather for prayer.

SKILLS

Look at the map. Beside each city listed below write the name of the leader or leaders who made it part of the caliphate: Muhammad, the first four caliphs, the Umayyad caliphs.

EXPANSION OF THE CALIPHATE: A.D. 622–750

1. Sana — Muhammad
2. Cordoba — Umayyad caliphs
3. Damascus — first four caliphs
4. Al-Fustat — first four caliphs
5. Ghazni — Umayyad caliphs

WRITING

Write a short paragraph to answer each question. If you need more room, continue writing on the back of this page.

1. Look at the map below. Find the route from Mecca to Damascus and the route from Mecca to Muscat. Which route do you think would be easier for a trader to travel? Support your answer using facts you have learned about the geography and climate of the Arabian peninsula.

ARABIAN TRADE ROUTES: 8TH CENTURY

See answer at right.

2. The Muslim caliphate thrived from the late 700s to the 1200s. What were some of the major achievements of the caliphate?

See answer at right.

WRITING ANSWERS

1. An adequate response will specify one of the two trade routes and explain why it would be easier to travel, mentioning facts about climate and geography. Example: It would be easier to travel from Mecca to Muscat. Even though most of this land is hot, dry desert, there are probably oases along the way. An excellent response will contrast the two routes in more detail. Example: This route does not have the mountainous terrain of the route between Mecca and Damascus, which makes traveling difficult.

2. An adequate response will describe several of the caliphs' achievements. For example, the caliphs gathered and preserved writings from many parts of the world in a library in Baghdad. Avicenna and other Muslim doctors developed medical textbooks and standard procedures in medicine. Muslim scholars in the caliphate developed Arabic numbers and made great advancements in algebra and other areas of mathematics. They made advancements in astronomy and mapmaking and improvements in the use of the astrolabe for navigation. They also made advancements in architecture in the process of building mosques. An excellent response will further explain some of the reasons for these developments. For example, the caliphs valued education and learning. The spread of Islam helped support the effort to seek and spread knowledge.

CONTENT

Fill in the circle before the correct answer.

1. Beringia is the name of the land bridge that connected North America to _____.
   - (a) Europe
   - (b) Asia
   - (c) Africa
   - (d) South America

2. The climate throughout Middle America is characterized by _____.
   - (a) hot summers and cold winters
   - (c) heavy precipitation all year long
   - (b) mild temperatures all year long
   - (d) a rainy season between May and October

3. What helped form the land bridge to Asia?
   - (a) glaciers
   - (b) volcanoes
   - (c) mud slides
   - (d) rain forest expansion

4. Which of these was an agricultural method used by the Olmec?
   - (a) rotating types of crops
   - (c) enriching the soil with ashes
   - (b) irrigating crops with canals
   - (d) using work animals to plow

5. The Maya were the first people of Middle America to _____.
   - (a) create a widely used written language
   - (b) invent practical uses for rubber
   - (c) carve stone statues of their rulers
   - (d) make and play musical instruments

Read each sentence and decide whether it tells about the Olmec, the Maya, or both groups. Write **Olmec**, **Maya**, or **both** on the line.

6. They planted crops including corn, beans, and squash. _____both_____

7. They developed an accurate calendar by studying the night sky. _____Maya_____

8. They made jewelry, which they traded with people from other parts of Middle America. _____Olmec_____

9. Yum Kax, the maize god, was an important part of their religion. _____Maya_____

10. Most of the people worked as farmers. _____both_____

SKILLS

Use the climographs to answer the questions. Write your answers on the lines.

Climograph A: San José, Costa Rica
Elevation: 3,759 feet/ 1,146 meters

Climograph B: New Orleans, Louisiana
Elevation: 4 feet/ 1.22 meters

Source: *Great International Atlas*

Source: *World Almanac and Book of Facts, 1995*

1. In which city does the amount of precipitation vary the most throughout the year? _____San José_____

2. Which city has temperatures below 60°F during some months? _____New Orleans_____

3. In which month does New Orleans have the least precipitation? _____October_____

4. Which city has temperatures above 80°F in July and August? _____New Orleans_____

5. In which month does San José have the least precipitation? _____February_____

WRITING

Write a short paragraph to answer each question. If you need more room, continue writing on the back of this page.

1. The map below shows the areas settled by the Olmec and the Maya. Compare and contrast the Olmec and Maya civilizations. How were they alike, and how were they different?

OLMEC AND MAYA CIVILIZATIONS

See answer at right.

_____
_____
_____
_____
_____
_____

2. Imagine that you are part of a group living in Middle America at the time of the Olmec civilization. Based on your knowledge of the area's climate and natural resources, describe the type of shelter you would need and the materials you would use to build it.

See answer at right.

_____
_____
_____
_____

WRITING ANSWERS

1. An adequate response will explain at least two similarities and two differences between the Olmec and the Maya. Similarities: Both civilizations centered on agriculture, both practiced polytheism, both developed products from rubber and played games with rubber balls, and both developed crafts, such as stone carving. Differences: The Olmec used the slash-and-burn method for farming, and they grew mainly corn, beans, and squash. The Maya developed many other crops, such as maize, peppers, and cacao. The Olmec believed that certain animals (especially the jaguar) had special powers; the Maya studied the stars and planets as part of their religion. The Olmec made huge stone carvings; the Maya built pyramids and palaces from stone blocks. An excellent response will explain other differences and similarities from an archaeological or historical perspective. For example, the Olmec flourished from 1200 to 400 B.C., while the Maya flourished from A.D. 250 to about 900. The Olmec left no written records of their civilization; the Maya developed a written language and left many records carved in stone. No one knows for sure why these two civilizations died out. The Olmec left artifacts behind; although the Maya civilization faded away, many people descended from the Maya still live in the region and practice Maya traditions.

2. An adequate response will describe a shelter that Middle Americans might have constructed with available materials and which is appropriate for the warm climate with dry and rainy seasons. Example: Since there are many trees and plants, it would be possible to build a shelter frame with branches and then cover the top with a roof of woven grasses and leaves. An excellent response will explain the advantages of such a shelter in more detail. For example, this shelter would give protection during the rainy season, but it would still let in breezes when the weather is hot.

CONTENT AND SKILLS

Fill in the circle before the correct answer.

1. In what ancient civilization did democracy have its beginnings?
   ⓐ Rome   ⓑ Greece   ⓒ Persia   ⓓ Phoenicia

2. The expansion of Alexander's empire led to the spread of _____.
   ⓐ democracy   ⓑ Islam   ⓒ Christianity   ⓓ Greek culture

3. In the Punic Wars, Rome defeated _____.
   ⓐ Carthage   ⓑ Sparta   ⓒ Persia   ⓓ Rome

4. Which type of map would best show how the boundaries of the Roman empire changed over several centuries?
   ⓐ elevation   ⓑ profile   ⓒ historical   ⓓ physical

5. Which type of visual would best show the average precipitation and average temperature in a certain area?
   ⓐ bar graph   ⓑ climograph   ⓒ time line   ⓓ profile map

6. The Roman governors of ancient Judea feared the growing popularity of _____.
   ⓐ Jesus   ⓑ Julius Caesar   ⓒ Hannibal   ⓓ Constantine

7. According to Muslim beliefs, what city is the center of Islam?
   ⓐ Baghdad   ⓑ Medina   ⓒ Petra   ⓓ Mecca

8. During the time of the caliphate, Avicenna made great advancements in the study and practice of _____.
   ⓐ Latin   ⓑ music   ⓒ medicine   ⓓ architecture

9. Which civilization developed the first system of writing in Middle America?
   ⓐ Olmec   ⓑ Aztec   ⓒ Maya   ⓓ Inca

10. The Olmec may have died out when their agriculture failed. The Olmec did not leave any written records. What conclusion can you make from these two statements?
    ⓐ No one knows how or why the Olmec civilization ended.
    ⓑ The Olmec were more successful farmers than the Maya.
    ⓒ Archaeologists have found books produced by the Olmec.
    ⓓ The Maya civilization faded as a result of many wars.

CONTENT AND SKILLS

Write the name from the box that best fits each description.

Sparta	Copán	Constantinople
Baghdad	Alexander	Muhammad
Socrates	Constantine	Augustus
Pompeii		

11. an important philosopher in the city-state of Athens   *Socrates*

12. a Roman city buried in the eruption of Mount Vesuvius in A.D. 79   *Pompeii*

13. an important center of Maya culture during the Classic Period   *Copán*

14. a ruler of the Roman empire during the Pax Romana   *Augustus*

15. the first leader of the religion of Islam   *Muhammad*

16. the capital of the Muslim caliphate, located on the Tigris River   *Baghdad*

17. the largest city-state and strongest military power in ancient Greece   *Sparta*

18. a ruler who granted freedom to Christians living in the Roman empire   *Constantine*

19. a ruler who conquered the Greek city-states and the empire of Persia   *Alexander*

20. the new capital of the Roman empire after the western empire collapsed   *Constantinople*

WRITING

Write a short paragraph to answer each question. If you need more room, continue writing on the back of this page.

1. Read the situations below. Tell which situation is an example of a democracy and which is an example of an oligarchy. Give reasons for your answers.

   Situation 1

   The Acme Company is considering a change in work hours. Some of the company's workers favor changing to a four-day work week of ten hours per day. Other workers want to work six days per week for only six hours per day. The three owners of the company announce that the new work week will be four ten-hour days. When some workers complain, the owners state, "The decision is final. We've made up our minds."

   Situation 2

   Mr. Yang's sixth-grade class is trying to decide whether they will take a field trip to the science museum or the art museum. "Let's take a vote," suggests Mr. Yang. After the students vote, Mr. Yang announces, "The science museum wins by a vote of 17 to 12."

   See answer at right.

2. Compare and contrast the achievements of the Muslim caliphate and the Maya civilization.

   See answer at right.

WRITING ANSWERS

1. An adequate response will state that Situation 1 illustrates an oligarchy and Situation 2 illustrates a democracy, and it will explain why. Example: Situation 1 is an oligarchy because the three owners of the company make the decisions. Situation 2 is a democracy because the students vote. An excellent response will explain the principles of each form of government and apply them to the situation. Example: Situation 1 is an oligarchy because the owners, who are the most powerful members of the group, make decisions for the entire group. Situation 2 is a democracy because all the members of the class take part in making a decision that affects them.

2. An adequate response will mention at least two important achievements of each civilization. An excellent response will present two or more achievements of each civilization as direct comparisons. Examples: The Muslims gathered, translated, and preserved many books in a library; the Maya developed a system of writing and a calendar. The Muslims made great advancements in medicine, created a system of Arabic numbers, and made advancements in mathematics, especially algebra. The Maya developed a system of glyphs to represent numbers, which they used to keep track of historical events and trade. The Muslims used astronomy and an improved version of the astrolabe for navigation, and they built mosques facing Mecca with great precision of measurement. The Maya used astronomy and mathematics to build pyramids and palaces that reflected changes in seasons with great precision.

CONTENT

Fill in the circle before the correct answer.

1. Most of Europe has a temperate climate because _____.
- (a) it is near the Arctic Circle
- (b) it has many powerful rivers
- (c) most of the land is at high elevations
- (d) warm winds blow in from the ocean

2. When the Magna Carta was written, it was important mainly because it _____.
- (a) freed slaves
- (b) limited the king's powers by law
- (c) gave lands to vassals
- (d) established the Christian Church

3. Under feudalism serfs were mainly responsible for _____.
- (a) working the fields
- (b) protecting the vassals
- (c) defending the manor
- (d) traveling with lords

4. During the later Middle Ages in Europe, Christian townspeople in many communities expressed their religious beliefs by _____.
- (a) becoming saints
- (b) building grand churches
- (c) becoming Protestants
- (d) making pilgrimages to Mecca

5. What was one reason the Renaissance began in Florence?
- (a) Artists and scholars found classical works in the city's museums.
- (b) Queen Elizabeth supported playwrights and poets.
- (c) The Medicis paid artists and scholars to pursue their work.
- (d) The Pope brought the Roman Church great wealth, which was spent on art.

Write the letter of the person best described by each sentence.

6. __e__ He urged Europeans to capture Jerusalem.

7. __c__ This monarch was one of the most powerful and popular ever to rule England.

8. __a__ This leader of the Franks was crowned emperor by Pope Leo III.

9. __b__ He designed a flying machine in Renaissance Italy.

10. __d__ He believed it was wrong to pay indulgences to gain forgiveness from the Church.

a. Charlemagne

b. Leonardo da Vinci

c. Queen Elizabeth I

d. Martin Luther

e. Pope Urban II

SKILLS

Read the passage below. Then answer the questions about determining point of view. Write your answers on the lines.

> I work most days in my lord's fields to grow his fancy herbs and vegetables. Come evening I drag my sore body home for a dish of porridge, rye bread, and buttermilk. Meanwhile, my lord enjoys a feast of foods I only dream of eating. The cooks say that his favorites are roast venison [deer], fresh trout from his pond fried in butter with almonds, roast peacock, and pears cooked with cinnamon, cloves, and honey.
>
> As much as I long to eat those fancy foods, I'll try to avoid the mistake my cousin made. Last winter, when food was running out, he couldn't resist helping himself to a deer. When my lord kills a deer, it's called hunting. If we kill one, it's poaching [stealing], and poor cousin paid the price with his life.
>
> All the same, I am luckier than some. We grow grains, onions, garlic, cabbage, and lettuce in our garden. Our cow keeps us well supplied with milk, cheese, and butter. Sometimes we have some bacon or pickled pork, although our faith forbids us from eating meat on Wednesdays, Fridays, and Saturdays. We can trade for salted or dried fish. We manage to get by, and as long as there isn't a drought, we are all right.

1. What is the subject of this passage?

life as a serf, life in the Middle Ages, or one man's life compared with that of his lord

2. From whose point of view is this passage written? a serf

3. What is the author's opinion of the lord?

He envies the lord; he also feels some contempt or scorn toward him.

4. Write one or two sentences from the passage that show how the author feels about his lord.

Examples: "Meanwhile, my lord enjoys a feast of foods I only dream of eating."

"When my lord kills a deer, it's called hunting. If we kill one, it's poaching."

5. Write two examples of words or phrases in the passage that show how the author feels about his own life.

Examples: drag my sore body, luckier than some, well supplied, manage to get by

---

WRITING

Write a short paragraph to answer each question. If you need more room, continue writing on the back of this page.

1. What were the Crusades, and how did they bring change to Europe? Use the map of the First Crusade below to help answer the question.

THE FIRST CRUSADE 1096–1099

See answer at right.

_____

_____

_____

_____

_____

_____

2. How did Gutenberg's invention of a printing press with movable type contribute to the Reformation?

See answer at right.

_____

_____

_____

_____

WRITING ANSWERS

1. An adequate response will explain that the Crusades were attempts by European Christians to capture Jerusalem from the Seljuk Turks. It would also state at least two changes brought about by the Crusades. For example, the Crusades passed through the Italian port cities of Genoa, Venice, and Rome, which brought trade and growth to those cities. When the Crusaders returned, they brought products and new knowledge from Asia and Africa. An excellent response will further explain that the Christians held Jerusalem for 100 years but eventually lost control of it. It will also describe how Crusaders, in their march across Europe, attacked many non-Christians, raiding Jewish communities in France and Germany.

2. An adequate response will explain that Gutenberg's press made printing cheaper and easier and that the use of the press helped to spread Martin Luther's criticism of the Roman Church and his translation of the Bible. An excellent response will further explain that before the invention of Gutenberg's press, almost everything was written in Latin. Luther wrote in German, and the wide distribution of his works in German, as well as a translation of the Bible into German, helped unite many German-speaking people on his side.

CONTENT

Fill in the circle before the correct answer.

1. About 4,000 years ago Africans began farming in the _____.
   - ⓐ Sahel
   - ⓑ rain forests
   - ● Sahara
   - ⓓ savannas

2. After the fall of Kush, important cities and trade routes in Ethiopia were controlled by the kingdom of _____.
   - ⓐ Meroe
   - ⓑ Aksum
   - ● Zagwe
   - ⓓ Punt

3. Both Ghana and Mali became very rich by controlling the _____.
   - ⓐ Red Sea
   - ⓑ Sahara Desert
   - ● gold trade
   - ⓓ ivory trade

4. For hundreds of years merchant-sailors from Asia traveled to the port cities of East Africa to buy _____.
   - ● ivory
   - ⓑ wheat
   - ⓒ salt
   - ⓓ metal tools

5. Why are historians uncertain what life was like in Great Zimbabwe?
   - ⓐ No ruins of the city were able to withstand the harsh environment.
   - ⓑ No artifacts remain because Great Zimbabwe was not wealthy.
   - ⓒ The people of Great Zimbabwe did not trade with people from other cultures.
   - ● There are no stories or written documents that have survived.

Write **true** or **false** next to each statement.

6. Lalibela was a Zagwe king who ruled Ethiopia from 1185 to 1225.   true

7. Mansa Musa was a Mali leader who conquered all of Ghana in the 1200s.   false

8. Songhai was a kingdom that replaced Mali as the most powerful kingdom in West Africa in about 1490.   true

9. Kush was a busy center of trade in the Mali empire.   false

10. Swahili was a civilization that developed in the coastal cities of East Africa.   true

---

SKILLS

Use the map of Africa to answer the questions. Write your answers on the lines.

MAJOR RELIGIONS IN AFRICA TODAY

1. How can you tell that this is a distribution map?
   It shows how one particular feature (religion) is distributed, or spread, over an area.

2. What religion dominates northern Africa? Islam

3. How would you describe the religions of Madagascar?
   The eastern coast has an area of Christianity, but most of the island has other religions.

4. Which city is located in an area that is primarily Christian? Cape Town

5. How would you describe the religions of central Africa?
   There is a mix of Christianity, Islam, and other religions.

WRITING

Write a short paragraph to answer each question. If you need more room, continue writing on the back of this page.

1. How did gold affect the rise of early kingdoms in West Africa?
   See answer at right.

2. How did the Swahili city-states become important international trade centers? Use the map below to help answer the question.

SWAHILI CITIES OF EAST AFRICA 1000–1500

See answer at right.

WRITING ANSWERS

1. An adequate response will explain that several early African kingdoms became wealthy because they controlled the gold trade. They became powerful by controlling trade routes to other parts of Africa, Europe, and Asia. Each fell to a greater power that wanted to control the valuable gold trade. An excellent response will give specific examples to support these ideas. Examples: Ghana controlled West Africa's supply of gold for over 500 years. It controlled the value of gold by keeping the supply scarce. In the 1300s gold became more valuable, and Mali also grew rich by controlling the gold trade. The empire of Songhai took over the gold trade in West Africa in about 1490, but it was later conquered by Morocco, whose leaders wanted to gain control of the gold.

2. An adequate response will explain that the Swahili city-states became trade centers because gold, ivory, and other goods produced in Zimbabwe were bought and sold in the Swahili port cities, which established trade routes to Asia. An excellent response will further explain that many Arab traders traveled to the Swahili ports to buy gold and ivory, and many of them settled there. Through these Arab settlers and other foreign merchants, the Swahili cities grew and established control over important international trade routes.

CONTENT

Fill in the circle before the correct answer.

1. Which of these separates India and Nepal from China?
   (a) Gobi Desert   (b) Himalayas   (c) Indian Ocean   (d) Mekong River

2. The Byzantine empire came to an end as a result of the _____.
   (a) fall of Constantinople   (c) birth of Süleyman
   (b) fall of Rome   (d) invasion by Moguls

3. Akbar ended the tax on all people in the Mogul empire who were _____.
   (a) Muslims   (b) enslaved   (c) non-Muslims   (d) Chinese

4. The rulers of the ancient Khmer people were considered to be _____.
   (a) priests   (b) emperors   (c) saints   (d) god-kings

5. Kublai Khan established control over all of China mainly by _____.
   (a) building canals to connect the Huang and Chang rivers
   (b) having Mongols oversee the government
   (c) creating jobs for people who had been farmers
   (d) protecting merchants on the Silk Road

Read each sentence below and write the name of the person from the box that it describes.

Shah Jahan	Genghis Khan	Kublai Khan	Süleyman	Yoritomo

6. This leader united the Mongols to conquer China.   **Genghis Khan**

7. Under this sultan the Ottoman empire reached its peak.   **Süleyman**

8. He built the Taj Mahal to honor his wife and Islamic beliefs.   **Shah Jahan**

9. This man was Japan's first shogun.   **Yoritomo**

10. This Mongol leader developed the world's first all-paper money system.   **Kublai Khan**

SKILLS

Read the facts below. Then answer the questions about making generalizations. Write your answers on the lines.

a. Rice is a principal agricultural product of India.

b. Rice is the most important food in the diet of the people of China.

c. The most important agricultural product in Japan is rice.

d. Rice fields require flooding by irrigation or periods of heavy rainfall, both of which are found in many parts of Asia.

1. What is a generalization?
   a broad statement of observation that can be applied to different kinds of examples

2. After you have selected examples, what is the next step in making a generalization?
   compare and contrast the examples

3. What topic is addressed by the facts listed above?
   the importance of rice in Asia

4. What generalization can you make from these facts?
   The countries of Asia depend mainly on rice, or rice is the most important agricultural product in Asia.

5. Which facts support your generalization?
   letters a, b, c

WRITING

Write a short paragraph to answer each question. If you need more room, continue writing on the back of this page.

1. What important changes did Akbar bring to the Mogul empire in India? Read the passage below to help answer the question.

   Akbar (1556–1605) was the most celebrated Mogul emperor. He greatly expanded the territories of the Mogul empire and established an efficient system of government. In an effort to put an end to the hatred between Hindus and Muslims, he tried to establish a new religion combining the religious beliefs of the two groups, but his efforts were unsuccessful.

   See answer at right.

   _____
   _____
   _____
   _____
   _____
   _____

2. How did Japan change under the rule of the Tokugawa shoguns?
   See answer at right.

   _____
   _____
   _____
   _____
   _____
   _____

WRITING ANSWERS

1. An adequate response will give three examples of changes that Akbar brought about. Examples: He included Hindus in his government, ended the tax on non-Muslims, and allowed Hindus to build temples. An excellent response will also conclude that under Akbar's rule, Hindus were treated more fairly, and the result of his changes was an era of harmony between the Hindu majority and the ruling Muslim minority.

2. An adequate response will state that Japan became unified and remained at peace for over 200 years under the Tokugawa shoguns. It also became isolated from other countries because foreign contact was forbidden. An excellent response will describe other ways in which Japan changed during this period. Examples: The Tokugawa shoguns established control over the country by forcing all of the lords to live in Edo (Tokyo). This brought about changes in Japan's feudal society; for example, samurais no longer fought wars, and many farmers moved to towns and cities. The development of Edo also brought about new traditions, such as Kabuki theater.

CONTENT

Fill in the circle before the correct answer.

1. The Great Lakes were formed by the movement of _____.
   - (a) glaciers
   - (b) volcanoes
   - (c) rivers
   - (d) storms

2. The Aztec took control of areas in the _____.
   - (a) Isthmus of Panama
   - (c) Canadian Shield
   - (b) Valley of Mexico
   - (d) Andes Mountains

3. The Aztec built chinampas to _____.
   - (a) perform religious rituals
   - (c) increase the land for building
   - (b) improve the drinking water
   - (d) create vegetable gardens

4. What was most important to keeping the Inca empire together?
   - (a) quipus
   - (c) farming on terraces
   - (b) a huge network of roads
   - (d) raising llamas

5. What was the main purpose of the Three Fires Council formed by Native Americans in the Great Lakes region?
   - (a) religion
   - (b) boat building
   - (c) trade
   - (d) cooperative farming

Write the letter of the name that best fits each description.

6. __c__ a mountaintop city built by the Inca

7. __d__ a trading center founded by the Ojibwa

8. __a__ a supreme ruler of the Inca in the 1400s

9. __b__ the capital city of the Aztec empire

10. __e__ the village in Peru in which the Inca empire began

a. Pachakuti
b. Tenochtitlán
c. Machu Picchu
d. Bowating
e. Cuzco

SKILLS

Look at the maps below. Then answer the questions about map projections.

MAP A: EQUAL-AREA PROJECTION	MAP B: MERCATOR PROJECTION	MAP C: POLAR PROJECTION

1. Why are maps of the world less accurate representations of Earth than a globe?
   A globe, like Earth, is a sphere, so cartographers must stretch and cut parts of it to make it fit onto flat paper.

2. Why do cartographers use projections to create complete maps of Earth?
   It is a way of showing parts of Earth on a flat map.

3. Which map projection distorts sizes the farther you move from the equator?
   Map B

4. Which map projection would be most useful for comparing the sizes of North America and South America? Map A

5. Which map shows about half the globe? Map C

WRITING

Write a short paragraph to answer each question. If you need more room, continue writing on the back of this page.

1. In what ways was the government of the Inca similar to the government of the Aztec?
   See answer at right.

2. The map below shows where the Ojibwa first settled. How did the Ojibwa use their natural environment?

OJIBWA LANDS: 1400–1500

Ojibwa lands
Present-day boundaries are shown.

Ojibwa
Lake Superior (Kitchigami)
Bowating   Ottawa
St. Lawrence River
Lake Michigan   Lake Huron   Lake Ontario
Potawatomi   Lake Erie
ATLANTIC OCEAN
0   500   1,000 Miles
0   500   1,000 Kilometers

See answer at right.

WRITING ANSWERS

1. An adequate response will explain at least two similarities between the Inca and Aztec systems of government. An excellent response will explain more than two similarities. Examples: Both were ruled by powerful emperors. Both had similar classes of people: nobles, craftworkers/merchants, and farmers. In both empires nobles were responsible for helping to run the empire.

2. An adequate response will give three or more examples of how the Ojibwa used their environment. Examples: They lived in wigwams built of wooden poles and birch bark. They lived near a lake during the summer. They fished and hunted, gathered nuts and berries, and grew vegetables. In the fall they moved to the marshes and gathered wild rice. In the winter they moved to areas where they could hunt. In spring they moved again to collect the sap of maple trees for making maple sugar. An excellent response will further explain that the Ojibwa depended to a great extent on the lakes and rivers in the region. They often traveled and traded by boat (canoes made from birch bark), and their most important villages were located on the shores of lakes or, like Bowating, on rivers that connected lakes.

CONTENT AND SKILLS

Fill in the circle before the correct answer.

1. Starting around A.D. 800 a system began in Europe that was called _____.
   - ⓐ monarchy
   - ⓑ feudalism
   - ⓒ Reformation
   - ⓓ Protestantism

2. The Middle Ages began after the _____.
   - ⓐ end of the western Roman empire
   - ⓒ First Crusade
   - ⓑ fall of the Ottoman empire
   - ⓓ Renaissance

3. Many of the early kingdoms of Africa became wealthy by _____.
   - ⓐ demanding tribute from serfs
   - ⓒ controlling the gold trade
   - ⓑ collecting taxes from merchants
   - ⓓ building large navies

4. Which kind of map shows how one particular feature is spread over an area?
   - ⓐ elevation
   - ⓑ physical
   - ⓒ distribution
   - ⓓ polar projection

5. A broad statement of observation applied to different kinds of examples is _____.
   - ⓐ an opinion
   - ⓑ a fact
   - ⓒ a point of view
   - ⓓ a generalization

6. The stretching and cutting that cartographers must do to make a flat map of a globe causes _____.
   - ⓐ distortion
   - ⓑ polarization
   - ⓒ generalization
   - ⓓ distribution

7. Which civilization was established in the land now called Cambodia?
   - ⓐ Songhai
   - ⓑ Kush
   - ⓒ Mogul
   - ⓓ Khmer

8. Which civilization settled in the Valley of Mexico?
   - ⓐ Inca
   - ⓑ Ojibwa
   - ⓒ Aztec
   - ⓓ Swahili

9. The Inca built their empire along the _____.
   - ⓐ Amazon River
   - ⓒ Isthmus of Panama
   - ⓑ Andes Mountains
   - ⓓ Gulf of Mexico

10. Which empire expanded over parts of three continents?
   - ⓐ Ottoman
   - ⓑ Inca
   - ⓒ Aztec
   - ⓓ Mogul

CONTENT AND SKILLS

Write the name from the box that best fits each description.

Copernicus	Lorenzo Medici	Charlemagne
Genghis Khan	Martin Luther	Johannes Gutenberg
Süleyman	Akbar	Tokugawa Ieyasu
Jayavarman II		

11. This astronomer discovered that Earth orbits the sun once each year.   _Copernicus_

12. This ruler of Florence paid artists and scholars to pursue their work.   _Lorenzo Medici_

13. The Ottoman empire reached its peak under this ruler.   _Süleyman_

14. This leader of the Franks conquered much of Europe in the 700s and 800s.   _Charlemagne_

15. This leader established the Mogul empire in India.   _Akbar_

16. This leader united the Mongols to conquer China.   _Genghis Khan_

17. He helped to unify Japan in the 1600s.   _Tokugawa Ieyasu_

18. His criticism of the Roman Church led to the Reformation.   _Martin Luther_

19. He invented a printing press with movable type.   _Johannes Gutenberg_

20. He was one of Cambodia's first kings.   _Jayavarman II_

WRITING

Write a short paragraph to answer each question. If you need more room, continue writing on the back of this page.

1. Use the map below to describe the Ottoman conquest of Constantinople. Why was this important to Europe and Asia?

THE OTTOMAN EMPIRE: 1500s

See answer at right.
_____
_____
_____
_____
_____
_____

2. Describe the feudal system that existed in Japan from the 1200s to the 1600s.

See answer at right.
_____
_____
_____
_____
_____
_____

WRITING ANSWERS

1. An adequate response will explain that Constantinople lay at the point that connected Europe and Asia. When a Turkish army conquered Constantinople in 1453 (eventually renaming it Istanbul), this event marked the fall of the Byzantine empire and the rise of the Ottoman empire as a power on three continents. An excellent response will further explain that Constantinople was built by the Roman emperor Constantine (in A.D. 330) and was a center of Christianity for more than 1,000 years. The fall of Constantinople signaled more than the fall of the Byzantine empire; it also marked the growth and expansion of Islam from the Middle East toward Europe.

2. An adequate response will describe at least two aspects of life under feudalism. Examples: In Japan lords controlled the land and served the emperor and shogun, while the samurai protected the lords. Below were the farmers, merchants, and craftworkers. An excellent response will note that in feudal Japan, the emperor was head of the country, but the shogun ruled as military dictator. It will also note that the Tokugawa shoguns changed feudal Japanese society by concentrating their power over the lords.

CONTENT

Fill in the circle before the correct answer.

1. Galileo's belief in the heliocentric view angered some people because it _____.
   - ⓐ stated that Earth was the center of the universe
   - ⓑ contradicted the teachings of the Catholic Church
   - ⓒ stated there was no God
   - ⓓ contradicted the teachings of Aristotle

2. The Line of Demarcation separated lands claimed by _____.
   - ⓐ Spain and Portugal
   - ⓒ England and France
   - ⓑ North America and South America
   - ⓓ the United States and Mexico

3. Which European conquered the empire of the Inca?
   - ⓐ Magellan
   - ⓑ Cortés
   - ⓒ da Gama
   - ⓓ Pizarro

4. In the triangular trade, ships sailed from West Africa to the West Indies with a cargo of _____.
   - ⓐ cloth
   - ⓑ guns
   - ⓒ gold
   - ⓓ enslaved people

5. Which country lost control over its colony in North America as a result of the French and Indian War?
   - ⓐ France
   - ⓑ Spain
   - ⓒ Portugal
   - ⓓ Great Britain

Write the name from the box that best fits each description.

James Cook	Galileo Galilei	Bartholomeu Dias
Isaac Newton	Pedro Álvarez Cabral	

6. He created a thermometer and a telescope.
   Galileo Galilei

7. He was the first European to sail around the Cape of Good Hope.
   Bartholomeu Dias

8. He was a navigator who claimed the east coast of Australia for England.
   James Cook

9. He conducted studies of gravity in the late 1600s.
   Isaac Newton

10. His voyage to South America began a period of Portuguese rule in Brazil.
    Pedro Álvarez Cabral

SKILLS

Read the passage below. Then answer the questions. Write your answers on the lines.

> In April of 1519, an Aztec traveler looked out over the Gulf of Mexico and saw a huge object in the sea. He was so shocked by the sight, he walked many miles to tell Emperor Moctezuma that he had seen a "small mountain floating in the midst [middle] of the water, and moving here and there without touching the shore."
>
> Moctezuma immediately sent his own messengers to the coast. When they returned, they reported: "in the middle of the water [was] a house from which appeared white men, their faces white and their hands likewise. They have long thick beards and their clothing is of all colors."
>
> On hearing this, the emperor sent back gifts of gold, featherwork, and beautiful stones and instructed the messengers to give them to the strange visitors.

Source for quotes: *The Mighty Aztecs* by Gene S. Stuart, National Geographic Society, Washington, D.C., 1981

1. Do you think the first messenger was a credible source? Tell why or why not.
   Example: He is not a credible source because he is an unknown traveler and has no reputation for accuracy.

2. Why did Moctezuma send his own men to the coast?
   to verify the report or check its accuracy

3. How can you determine whether the emperor's second source was credible?
   Example: Decide whether the source has expert knowledge of the subject, determine whether they have a reason to portray things in a certain way, or determine if they have a reputation for accuracy.

4. Do you think the first messenger had a reason to tell about what he had seen in a certain way? Explain why or why not.
   Examples: Yes, he wanted to make sure his story stirred interest; or no, he had no interest in lying about what he thought he saw.

5. How do you know that Moctezuma trusted the accuracy of his messengers' report?
   He responded to their report by sending gifts to the visitors.

WRITING

Write a short paragraph to answer each question. If you need more room, continue writing on the back of this page.

1. What were the major reasons for European explorations of the Americas in the 1400s and 1500s?
   See answer at right.

2. The map below shows the triangular trade route. Why did this route develop, and what did ships carry on each leg of the trip?

TRIANGULAR TRADE: 1600–1750

See answer at right.

WRITING ANSWERS

1. An adequate response will explain that the Europeans were searching for ways to reach Asia in order to increase trade or to gain wealth. Europeans sailed west across the Atlantic Ocean looking for a sailing route to Asia. Later they explored more of the Americas to gain lands, to find wealth (especially gold and furs), and to increase their own power. An excellent response will explain in more detail. For example, Europeans sought new routes to Asia because the current routes, such as the Silk Road, were long and expensive. They also sought faster routes because they knew they could make enormous profits with products from Asia, such as silk and pepper. Spaniards explored many parts of the Americas in search of wealth and the power they would gain from control of these areas. Another reason they explored the Americas was to bring Christianity to the native inhabitants. France and England explored the Americas to gain colonies and wealth, especially through the fur trade.

2. An adequate response will explain that triangular trade developed in order to transport sugar to European markets and bring enslaved Africans to North America and the West Indies. Ships from the West Indies carried sugar to Europe. Then they sailed from Europe to West Africa with guns, cloth, and other goods, which were traded for enslaved people. Ships sailed from West Africa to the West Indies with captives. An excellent response will further explain the reasons for triangular trade. For example, Europeans found that the West Indies was an ideal place to grow sugar, and they used Indians as forced labor. Because of disease and harsh working conditions, many Indians died. The triangular trade route developed as a way for plantation owners to bring more slaves to their plantations.

CONTENT

Fill in the circle before the correct answer.

1. Which was a major cause of the French Revolution?
   - ⓐ The Third Estate wanted equal rights.
   - ⓑ The people did not support Napoleon.
   - ⓒ The First Estate seized most of the land in France.
   - ⓓ Robespierre conducted a Reign of Terror.

2. Simón Bolívar fought mainly to free South Americans from _____.
   - ⓐ high taxes
   - ⓑ the Catholic Church
   - ⓒ colonial rule
   - ⓓ military obligations

3. Some of Karl Marx's ideas about what would happen to the world's economy became known as _____.
   - ⓐ absolute monarchy
   - ⓑ imperialism
   - ⓒ the Industrial Revolution
   - ⓓ socialism

4. In 1853 President Millard Fillmore sent four United States warships to Japan with a letter asking the Japanese to _____.
   - ⓐ buy Chinese products
   - ⓑ open its borders to trade
   - ⓒ allow whale hunting
   - ⓓ go to war

5. The Meiji Restoration was a revolution against _____.
   - ⓐ Commodore Perry
   - ⓑ the Diet
   - ⓒ the shoguns
   - ⓓ the bureaucracy

Write the name from the box that best completes each sentence.

Toussaint L'Ouverture	José de San Martín	James Hargreaves
Maximilien Robespierre	Miguel Hidalgo	

6. _Maximilien Robespierre_ executed suspected enemies of the revolution in France.

7. _James Hargreaves_ invented the spinning jenny.

8. _Toussaint L'Ouverture_ led a revolution against slavery in Saint Domingue.

9. _José de San Martín_ led revolutions in Argentina and Chile.

10. _Miguel Hidalgo_ tried to lead Mexico to independence from Spain.

SKILLS

Use the cartogram below to answer the questions.

World Population by Region: 1850

WORLD POPULATION BY REGION: 1850

Source: World Almanac, 1996.

1. What does this cartogram show?
   It shows the relative populations of world regions in 1850.

2. How is this different from a typical map of the world?
   The size of each continent is based on population, not physical size.

3. Which region had the largest population in 1850?
   Asia.

4. How did the population of North America compare with that of Europe?
   It was quite a bit smaller (about one tenth of the size).

5. What is one advantage of using a cartogram to show information?
   Examples: You can compare information about many countries; it can give a clear, quick picture of the information presented.

WRITING

Write a short paragraph to answer each question. If you need more room, continue writing on the back of this page.

1. How did the French Revolution and the American Revolution affect the desire for independence in Latin America? Use the time line below to help answer the question.

1760 — 1780 — 1800 — 1810 Call of Dolores — 1820 — 1840

American Revolution 1776
French Revolution 1789
Haiti gains independence 1804
Argentina wins independence 1816
Chile wins independence 1818
Mexico & Venezuela become independent 1821

See answer at right.
_____
_____
_____
_____

2. How did Japan change and expand during the Meiji era?
   See answer at right.
_____
_____
_____
_____

WRITING ANSWERS

1. An adequate response will explain that many Latin American countries were influenced by the United States Constitution. It will also explain that the French Revolution caused people in Latin America to think about gaining their own rights, and it will give some examples from the time line. The spirit of "Liberty, Equality, Fraternity" spread to Latin America and encouraged the people of several countries to fight for independence. Toussaint L'Ouverture led the struggle against slavery in Saint Domingue and eventually helped drive out the French to make Haiti an independent country. José de San Martín helped win independence for Argentina and Chile. Simón Bolívar helped gain independence for Venezuela and several other nations. Mexico, led by Hidalgo and Morelos, rebelled against Spain and finally won independence in 1821. An excellent response will explain the reasons for these revolutions in more detail. For example, the people in Latin America rebelled against colonial rule for many of the same reasons that the French people rebelled: they came to believe that their leaders should be accountable to the people, they wanted more of a say in their own governments, and they wanted equal rights. Many Latin American countries were able to gain their independence at that time because the wars with Napoleon kept their European rulers occupied.

2. An adequate response will describe three or more important changes that occurred during this era. For example, the new government put an end to feudalism, opened up the country to foreigners, gave its people a say in government, implemented advancements in technology and other subjects learned from foreign countries, and expanded its borders by invading Korea and attacking China and Russia. An excellent response will give more specific examples of these changes. For example, many Japanese adopted Western dress, customs, and styles of architecture, and the government built factories and expanded trade with other countries, especially in tea and silk. Japanese conquests in Asia led to the country's control of Korea, Taiwan, and land taken from Russia.

CONTENT AND SKILLS

Fill in the circle before the correct answer.

1. Who developed the telescope and helped prove the heliocentric theory?
   (a) Copernicus   (b) Newton   (c) Hargreaves   (d) Galileo

2. Which European conquered the Aztec?
   (a) Pizarro   (b) Cortés   (c) Cabral   (d) Dias

3. Which explorer led the first voyage around the world?
   (a) Magellan   (b) Dias   (c) da Gama   (d) Prince Henry

4. Many Europeans brought enslaved Africans to the West Indies to _____.
   (a) fight the Arawak   (c) work on sugar plantations
   (b) spread Christianity   (d) dig for gold and silver

5. Who was known as the "Liberator of South America"?
   (a) Simón Bolívar   (c) José María Morelos
   (b) Miguel Hidalgo   (d) Agustín de Iturbide

6. Before the French Revolution who held most of the political power in France?
   (a) the Church   (b) the army   (c) the king   (d) the Third Estate

7. The French Republic ended with the rise to power of _____.
   (a) Robespierre   (b) Napoleon   (c) King Louis XVI   (d) Marie Antoinette

8. What event brought about revolutionary changes in Japan?
   (a) the Meiji Restoration   (c) the invasion of Korea
   (b) the rise of the Tokugawa shogun   (d) the Chinese invasion of Japan

9. A written source of information is most likely to be credible if its author has _____.
   (a) a personal interest in the subject   (c) reason to portray things a certain way
   (b) expert knowledge in the subject   (d) knowledge of what the reader believes

10. What type of visual would be most useful for showing the relative sizes of populations among European countries?
   (a) time line   (b) line graph   (c) historical map   (d) cartogram

---

CONTENT AND SKILLS

Choose the term from the box that best fits each description. Write the term on the line.

Reign of Terror	Industrial Revolution	triangular trade
Charter Oath	Call of Dolores	Toussaint L'Ouverture
José de San Martín	Elizabeth Veale	Atahualpa
Lachlan Macquarie	James Watt	

11. an Inca emperor who was captured by Pizarro — Atahualpa

12. a governor of New South Wales who favored the rights of the freed convicts — Lachlan Macquarie

13. the inventor of the steam engine — James Watt

14. a statement by the government of Japan declaring that all Japanese would have a say in their government — Charter Oath

15. Maximilien Robespierre's war against enemies of the French Revolution — Reign of Terror

16. a period during which new inventions rapidly changed the world — Industrial Revolution

17. the leader of a revolution that led to the founding of Haiti as an independent nation — Toussaint L'Ouverture

18. a system in which sugar was transported to Europe and enslaved captives were transported to North America — triangular trade

19. the liberator of Argentina and Chile — José de San Martín

20. a statement by Miguel Hidalgo that stirred up revolution in Mexico — Call of Dolores

21. a manager of an estate who helped establish the production of wool as an important industry in Australia — Elizabeth Veale

---

WRITING

Write a short paragraph to answer each question. If you need more room, continue writing on the back of this page.

1. By 1770 which European countries controlled territories in the Americas, and why did they establish colonies in these areas?

TERRITORIES CONTROLLED BY EUROPEAN COUNTRIES: 1770

See answer at right.

_____
_____
_____
_____
_____
_____

2. Where did the Industrial Revolution begin, and what kinds of changes did it bring?

See answer at right.

_____
_____
_____
_____
_____
_____

WRITING ANSWERS

1. An adequate response will explain which European countries controlled what parts of the Americas and will give at least two reasons why these countries established colonies. Example: Spain controlled much of South America, except the region of Brazil. Spain also controlled all of Central America, southwestern North America, and Florida. Britain controlled most of eastern North America and some small areas in the Caribbean. France had only small colonies in the Caribbean, such as Haiti. All of these countries established colonies in the Americas to gain wealth and to expand their own trade and power. An excellent response will give more detailed reasons. For example, Spain established colonies to gain wealth, especially gold, and to spread Christianity. Britain established colonies to gain wealth from the fur trade and other natural resources in North America.

2. An adequate response will explain that the Industrial Revolution began in Britain and will give at least two examples of major changes it brought about. An excellent response will explain why it began in Britain and will mention three or more changes. Example: The Industrial Revolution began in Britain because British laws allowed people to start businesses, protect their property, and earn money. Britain also had a rich supply of coal and iron, and a stable government. The Industrial Revolution brought about many changes: the invention of machines made certain kinds of work much faster and cheaper, especially in the textile industry; advancements in production made more products available; inventions such as the steam engine made transportation much faster; the growth of factories over cottage industries brought about a change in jobs and population centers from rural farms to factories in the cities. The Industrial Revolution also increased the importance of the middle class and the size of the working class. Difficult working conditions eventually brought about demands for change, which led to the formation of unions and the development of new ideas, such as socialism.

CONTENT

Fill in the circle before the correct answer.

1. The United States entered World War I as a result of _____.
   - ⓐ the Treaty of Versailles
   - ⓒ the League of Nations
   - ⓑ German attacks on United States ships
   - ⓓ the assassination of Archduke Ferdinand

2. The Bolshevik Revolution of 1917 was led by _____.
   - ⓐ Tsar Alexander II
   - ⓒ Tsar Nicholas II
   - ⓑ Vladimir Lenin
   - ⓓ Joseph Stalin

3. What event marked the beginning of World War II in Europe?
   - ⓐ invasion of Poland
   - ⓒ invasion of the Soviet Union
   - ⓑ Battle of Britain
   - ⓓ occupation of Austria

4. At a meeting in Yalta in 1945, the Allied leaders agreed to _____.
   - ⓐ join the Warsaw Pact
   - ⓒ ban all nuclear weapons
   - ⓑ expand communism in Europe
   - ⓓ create the United Nations

5. In China the goal of the Cultural Revolution was to _____.
   - ⓐ make factories more productive
   - ⓒ destroy all noncommunist beliefs
   - ⓑ overthrow the Qing dynasty
   - ⓓ defeat the Nationalist army

Write the letter of the phrase that best describes each person.

6. __d__ Joseph Stalin
7. __c__ Nikita Khrushchev
8. __e__ Mao Zedong
9. __a__ Franz Ferdinand
10. __b__ Adolf Hitler

a. his murder led to the beginning of World War I

b. Nazi dictator who led Germany into World War II

c. reached an agreement with President John F. Kennedy that ended the Cuban missile crisis

d. leader of the Soviet Union during World War II

e. led the Communists to victory in China in 1949

SKILLS

Use the time zone map to answer the questions.

TIME ZONES

1. When the President arrives in his office in Washington, D.C., at 8:00 A.M. on Monday, what time and day is it in Moscow?

   4:00 P.M. on Monday

2. When it is 12:00 noon in London, what time is it in Moscow?

   3:00 P.M.

3. When it is 9:00 P.M. in Tokyo on Monday, what time and day is it in Los Angeles?

   4:00 A.M. on Sunday

4. If you are traveling from London to New York, what change should you make to your watch?

   set it back 5 hours

5. When you travel east across the International Date Line, what change should you make to the date indicator on your watch?

   subtract a day

WRITING

Write a short paragraph to answer each question. If you need more room, continue writing on the back of this page.

1. How did the rise of nationalism contribute to the outbreak of both world wars?

   See answer at right.

2. What was the Cuban missile crisis, and how was it resolved? Use the map below for reference.

CUBAN MISSILE CRISIS

   See answer at right.

WRITING ANSWERS

1. An adequate response will note that both world wars were started largely because of strong feelings of nationalism and the many alliances that European countries had established. An excellent response will give specific examples from both World War I and World War II. For example, in the early 1900s nationalism and tension between neighboring countries in Europe were on the rise. Countries formed alliances to help each other in case of war. When a Serbian nationalist killed Archduke Franz Ferdinand of Austria and his wife, Austria-Hungary and Germany (an ally) declared war on Serbia. Soon other allies of Serbia, including Russia, France, and Britain, entered the fighting, and World War I had begun. As for World War II, Hitler's extreme nationalism, called Nazism, was a major factor in his decision to occupy Austria and invade Poland, which led Great Britain and France to declare war on Germany. In Asia, Japan's nationalism led to invasions of China and Korea, which threatened United States interests in the region. To keep the United States from involvement in its expansionist plans, Japan attacked Pearl Harbor, which drew the United States into World War II.

2. An adequate response will explain that the Cuban missile crisis occurred when the United States discovered that Soviet missiles had been placed in Cuba and were just a short flight from the United States. President Kennedy blockaded Cuba. He threatened to attack the Soviet Union if any missiles were fired from Cuba. Khrushchev eventually removed the missiles. An excellent response will explain the event in historical context and provide more detail. Example: During the Cold War the Soviet Union and the United States were each concerned about the power that nuclear weapons gave the other and feared a nuclear attack. After the United States tried to end Castro's communist government in Cuba (the first communist government in the Americas), Khrushchev sent nuclear weapons to Cuba. This placed Soviet missiles very close to the United States and was thus very threatening. As part of the agreement that ended the crisis, the Soviet Union removed the missiles and the United States agreed to remove its missiles from Turkey.

CONTENT

Fill in the circle before the correct answer.

1. Britain wanted to maintain its power in Egypt in order to keep control of the _____.
- ⓐ ancient ruins   ⓑ gold mines   ⓒ Suez Canal   ⓓ Red Sea

2. Who was the first Arab leader to meet publicly with Israeli leaders to work toward peace?
- ⓐ Yasir Arafat   ⓑ Anwar Sadat   ⓒ Yitzhak Rabin   ⓓ David Ben Gurion

3. Which term refers to the Palestinian revolt to "shake off" Israeli rule?
- ⓐ anti-Semitism   ⓑ Zionism   ⓒ boycott   ⓓ Intifada

4. In India the goal of the Green Revolution was to _____.
- ⓐ make farms more productive
- ⓑ gain independence from Britain
- ⓒ define women's rights
- ⓓ abolish the caste system

5. Who led the communists during Vietnam's fight for independence after World War II?
- ⓐ Chiang Kai-shek
- ⓑ Mao Zedong
- ⓒ Ho Chi Minh
- ⓓ Pol Pot

Write the letter of the phrase that best describes each place.

6. __b__ Pakistan

7. __c__ Vietnam

8. __e__ Gold Coast

9. __a__ Palestine

10. __d__ Gaza

a. a land that was divided by the United Nations to form the independent nation of Israel

b. a country formed by Muslims who feared they would be treated poorly in a Hindu-led India

c. a former colony of France that became a battleground when the United States tried to stop the spread of communism

d. a part of the land that is to be used to establish a Palestinian homeland according to a 1993 agreement

e. the former name of Ghana, when it was the first colony south of the Sahara to gain independence

---

SKILLS

Study the political cartoon published earlier in this century. Use the cartoon to answer the questions below.

The Meaning of America

1. Who do you think the figure in the cartoon represents?

Uncle Sam, or the United States of America; the government of the United States.

2. What is the figure doing?

He is breaking the chains of tyranny for the world.

3. What is this cartoon about?

It is probably about the role the United States has played in defeating tyrannies or defending freedom in the world.

4. What specific events might the cartoon be referring to?

United States participation in World War I, World War II, and the Cold War

5. Write a sentence describing the cartoonist's point of view.

The cartoonist believes that the role of the United States is a defender of freedom.

WRITING

Write a short paragraph to answer each question. If you need more room, continue writing on the back of this page.

1. Why do you think it is difficult to resolve the conflict between the Jews in Israel and the Palestinians?

See answer at right.

2. How did India gain its independence from Britain? Use the time line below to help describe the major events and the results of India's struggle for independence.

| 1857 Great Mutiny | 1885 First Indian National Congress | 1915 Gandhi returns to India | 1947 India & Pakistan gain independence |

1850   1900   1950

See answer at right.

WRITING ANSWERS

1. An adequate response will note that both the Jews and the Palestinians have long considered the land in Israel to be their homeland. Both groups have strong feelings of nationalism, and when the Jews established the State of Israel, it created tension with the Palestinian Arabs who want their own independent nation in the same area. An excellent response will explain historical roots of the conflict. Example: The Jews were originally driven from Jerusalem when the Babylonians conquered the city and the Diaspora began. Later, the Romans took the city. Some Jews remained in the area. Those in exile never forgot their ancient homeland, and when anti-Semitism in Europe grew, many Jews became influenced by Zionism and moved to Palestine. This immigration increased after World War II, as many survivors from Nazi concentration camps arrived. Their return caused tension with Arabs who lived in Palestine because they feared their own dream for a nation would be lost. After war broke out in 1948 between Israel and its Arab neighbors, about 750,000 Palestinians left their home in Israel and became refugees.

2. An adequate response will describe the Great Mutiny, Gandhi's efforts to gain independence for India, and the birth of an independent India in 1947. An excellent response will describe other events, such as the First Indian National Congress, and the reason for the creation of Pakistan. Example: In 1857 Indian soldiers in the British army revolted against the Raj, but the revolt was put down. In 1885, at the first Indian National Congress, Indians demanded more involvement in the government. In 1905 the Congress began a boycott of British cloth. Beginning in 1915, Gandhi led the nonviolent effort to oust Britain, and in 1947 the British finally left. India became an independent nation. Because Muslims living in India were concerned about their fate in a nation under Hindu control, the separate nation of Pakistan was established at the same time.

CONTENT

Fill in the circle before the correct answer.

1. In the late 1980s the Soviet Union and many Eastern European countries moved toward _____.

   (a) democracy   (b) colonialism   (c) communism   (d) fascism

2. In the 1980s countries around the world set up sanctions against the government of South Africa in an effort to _____.

   (a) end the violent protests   (c) spur economic development
   (b) oppose the move to democracy   (d) end apartheid

3. South Korea is a Pacific Rim nation that has _____.

   (a) become poorer in recent years   (c) limited its trade
   (b) industrialized rapidly   (d) turned to communism

4. In Mexico during the 1970s, many new businesses and economic growth were financed by the discovery of _____.

   (a) coal   (b) diamonds   (c) oil   (d) gold

5. In the 1980s Brazil's government tried to help the economy by _____.

   (a) giving families tropical rain forest land to farm
   (b) outlawing mining and logging in the Amazon rain forest
   (c) encouraging families to move to other countries
   (d) helping farmers establish coca farms

Write the term from the box that best completes each sentence.

apartheid	European Union	NAFTA	Pacific Rim	per capita income

6. The _European Union_ is working to build a common economy throughout Europe.

7. The economic growth of countries such as Japan and Singapore has led to a shift in power toward the _Pacific Rim_.

8. The South African system of laws called _apartheid_ treated people of different races differently.

9. By signing _NAFTA_, the United States, Canada, and Mexico agreed to lower taxes on goods traded among them in an effort to increase trade.

10. The amount of money each person of a country would have if that country's total income were divided equally among its people is the _per capita income_.

SKILLS

In 1989 Solidarity won recognition from the government of Poland, and Lech Walesa became president of Poland in 1990. In 1995 Walesa ran for reelection. Read the articles about the results of the election. Then answer the questions below.

When a triumphant Lech Walesa became President of Poland in 1990, European communism appeared to be finished for good. . . . Now, barely five years later, ex-communists have returned to power across much of Eastern Europe, and last week the mighty Walesa himself fell victim to the comrades' comeback. Aleksander Kwasniewski, 41, a minister in the last communist Polish government, defeated the old Solidarity war-horse in a runoff presidential election. . . . The good news, however, is that nearly all those former communists, including Kwasniewski, appear to have abandoned their Marxist past. All reached power through free and democratic elections, they are pursuing policies of privatization and market economics, and they are clamoring [calling] for membership in both NATO and the European Union.
Source: *Time*, December 4, 1995

The confrontation politics that gripped Poland in the 1980s may be on the way back, a result of the narrow presidential victory that ex-Communist Alexander Kwasniewski scored last week over Lech Walesa. . . . Walesa vows to "strike back," but his capacity to stir trouble seems limited. Kwasniewski is committed to democracy, backs free-market reforms and favors membership in NATO and the European Union.
Source: *U.S. News & World Report*, December 4, 1995

1. Is the underlined sentence a statement of fact or opinion? Tell how you know.
   It is an opinion because it cannot be proven true.

2. How could you verify the information about Walesa in these articles?
   You could check the facts in other sources.

3. What is *Time*'s point of view about Kwasniewski?
   He is not really a communist anymore.

4. What reason might *Time* have to describe events from a certain point of view?
   Time might describe an event from a certain point of view because of the writer's
   American bias, to attract readers, or to express an opinion that might appeal to its
   readers. On the other hand, the article was written by a reporter whose job it is to
   tell people about world events.

5. Do you think the information in these articles is accurate? Tell why you think so.
   The information in these articles is probably accurate because it appeared in
   established newsmagazines, and both sources reported the same information.

WRITING

Write a short paragraph to answer each question. If you need more room, continue writing on the back of this page.

1. How did Japan develop into an economic power after World War II?
   See answer at right.

2. What happened in Eastern Europe during 1989, the "Year of Miracles," and why did it happen? Describe what happened in several of the countries identified in the map below.

EASTERN EUROPE: 1989

See answer at right.

WRITING ANSWERS

1. An adequate response will explain that Japan was rebuilt after the war with help from the United States, and it developed a strong economy by importing raw materials, turning them into expensive goods for export, and selling these goods to other nations. An excellent response will include other important factors. For example, Japan's economy began to grow rapidly during the Korean War, when United States troops were based in Japan and the Japanese provided them with many basic goods. Japan also helped develop its own economy by emphasizing business and technical skills in school to train young people for jobs in industry.

2. An adequate response will explain that all of these countries in Eastern Europe overthrew their communist governments and moved toward democracy and free enterprise. This movement began because when Gorbachev took power in the Soviet Union, he instituted the policies of glasnost and perestroika. These policies spread to other communist nations. An excellent response will give more detailed explanations of what happened in specific countries. For example, Hungary opened up its border with Austria, and many Eastern Europeans used this opening to escape to Western Europe. Solidarity won recognition from the government in Poland and then, in an election, won many seats in that nation's parliament. East Germany overthrew Erich Honecker and took down the Berlin Wall. Czechoslovakia overthrew its communist government and replaced it with elected leaders.

CONTENT AND SKILLS

Fill in the circle before the correct answer.

1. To understand Earth better, geographers divide it into different types of _____.
   - (a) landforms
   - (b) regions
   - (c) customs
   - (d) peoples

2. Contact between two cultures that often leads to cultural change is called _____.
   - (a) cultural interaction
   - (b) oral history
   - (c) cultural region
   - (d) values

3. A surplus is _____.
   - (a) an extra supply
   - (b) an early harvest
   - (c) a group of farmers
   - (d) an ancient settlement

4. The work of historians is similar to that of detectives because they both _____.
   - (a) display artifacts in museums
   - (b) create primary sources
   - (c) use clues to solve mysteries
   - (d) study ancient cultures

5. Archaeologists knew that people at Border Cave had made contact with people from the coast when they found _____.
   - (a) stone tools
   - (b) a seashell bead
   - (c) animal bones
   - (d) a painting of the ocean

6. Why did archaeologists working at the Iceman site melt the snow and filter the water?
   - (a) They wanted to see if the water was clean.
   - (b) They did not want to lose any evidence.
   - (c) They needed drinking water.
   - (d) They wanted to clean the Iceman.

7. Bits of sulfur and iron, which are used to make matches, were found in a piece of fungus carried by the Iceman. This suggests that the Iceman _____.
   - (a) was a miner
   - (b) invented matches
   - (c) traded with other people
   - (d) knew how to make fire

8. What important development began in the New Stone Age?
   - (a) agriculture
   - (b) cave painting
   - (c) stone tools
   - (d) fire

9. People training to do different kinds of work is an example of _____.
   - (a) archaeology
   - (b) specialization
   - (c) technology
   - (d) agriculture

10. Archaeologists learn about the people of the Stone Ages by studying _____.
   - (a) oral history
   - (b) maps
   - (c) diaries
   - (d) artifacts

CONTENT AND SKILLS

Write the name from the box that best completes each sentence.

Vladimir Lenin	Cultural Revolution
Yasir Arafat	Nelson Mandela
Jean-Bertrand Aristide	Gamal Abdel Nasser
Mohandas Gandhi	League of Nations
Cold War	Deng Xiaoping

11. In an attempt to prevent future wars, after World War I the Allied Powers established an international council called the _League of Nations_.

12. _Vladimir Lenin_ led the Bolshevik Revolution in Russia and founded the Union of Soviet Socialist Republics.

13. The _Cultural Revolution_ is the period in Chinese history when Mao called for the destruction of all noncommunist beliefs.

14. _Cold War_ refers to the struggle based on distrust between the United States and the Soviet Union.

15. _Yasir Arafat_ led the Palestine Liberation Organization in its struggle against Israel.

16. In 1952 _Gamal Abdel Nasser_ helped seize control of Egypt and led the country to independence.

17. _Mohandas Gandhi_ advocated the use of civil disobedience in India's fight for independence.

18. Because of his efforts to end apartheid, _Nelson Mandela_ was imprisoned for 27 years and was later elected the president of South Africa.

19. _Deng Xiaoping_ allowed more free enterprise in China than Mao had but crushed the protest for democracy in Tiananmen Square.

20. Military leaders overthrew _Jean-Bertrand Aristide_, the elected president of Haiti, in 1991, but the United States helped him regain his position in 1994.

WRITING

Write a short paragraph to answer each question. If you need more room, continue writing on the back of this page.

1. What was a major cause of World War II?

   See answer at right.

   _____
   _____
   _____
   _____
   _____
   _____

2. Study the political cartoon below. It was published in 1957. What do you think the cartoon is about, and what point of view does it convey?

   See answer at right.

   _____
   _____
   _____
   _____
   _____

WRITING ANSWERS

1. An adequate response will discuss at least one major cause of World War II. Example: A major cause of World War II was nationalism. Germany, Italy, and Japan all wanted to expand their borders and strengthen their own countries. An excellent response will describe specific events that caused the war. Example: Britain and France declared war on Germany when Hitler invaded Poland. When the Soviet Union was invaded by Germany, it also entered the war. The United States declared war on Japan after the bombing of Pearl Harbor and also joined the Allies when the Axis powers declared war on it.

2. An adequate response will note that the cartoon shows the United States public being protected from injustice and tyranny by the United States Constitution. An excellent response will note that the man holding the umbrella is Uncle Sam, often a symbol of the United States, and that the umbrella is a symbol for the protection that the Constitution offers. The point of view of the cartoon is pro-Constitution and suggests that the United States is a country where freedom is protected.